EMPLOYMENT LAW

Sweet & Maxwell's Textbook Series

Helen Desmond LL.B. LL.M.
*Lecturer in Law. International Centre for Management Law &
Industrial Relations, University of Leicester*

and

David Antill M.A.
*Academic Tutor. International Centre for Management Law &
Industrial Relations, University of Leicester*

LONDON
SWEET & MAXWELL
1998

Published in 1998 by
Sweet & Maxwell Limited of
100 Avenue Road, Swiss Cottage, London NW3 3PF
(http://www.smlawpub.co.uk)
Typeset by LBJ Typesetting Ltd of Kingsclere
Printed in Great Britain by
Clays Ltd, St Ives plc

No natural forests were destroyed to make this product;
only farmed timber was used and replanted

A CIP catalogue
record for this book
is available from
the British Library

ISBN 0–421–61980–5

©
Sweet & Maxwell
1998

PREFACE

This book in the Sweet & Maxwell's Textbook Series is designed for undergraduate students and for students undertaking professional examinations. Postgraduate students, particularly those who have not studied employment law at undergraduate level, or whose first degree is not in law will also find this text suitable. The text and design is based on our combined teaching experience and aims to provide a logical and progressive presentation, supported by diagrams and charts in line both with the policy of the series and our belief that presentation of complex data in diagrammatic form is a helpful aid to the learning process. In this connection we would like to thank Incomes Data Services for their kind permission to reproduce their IDS Brief Employment Law Card which sets out in summary form the compensation and time limits associated with the various employment law rights. This provides a useful quick reference checklist.

The return of a Labour Government following the Spring 1997 general election has led to a plethora of white papers, bills and draft orders, such as the National Minimum Wage and Human Rights Bills, and particularly for the purpose of implementing Directives, such as Working Time, Young Workers and Data Protection and those that now need implementing measures following re-ratification to extend to the United Kingdom Parental Leave, Part-time Workers and the Burden of Proof. The Working Time Regulations, which it is understood differ in certain respects from the draft proposals, were laid before Parliament on July 30 and are to be brought into force on October 1, 1998. The Data Protection Act 1998 received Royal Assent on July 16 and although originally expected to come into force by October 24, 1998, the Government has announced that it does not now expect it to be brought into force before January 1999. The National Minimum Wage Act 1998 received Royal Assent on July 31 and it is intended that it will come into force in April 1999 and Regulations are expected shortly. The new amending Directive 98/50 of June 29, 1998 on transfer of undertakings is briefly discussed in Chapter 9.

The law is as stated on April 1, 1998. However, the text has taken into account further developments up to July 1. In particular account has been taken of the *Fairness at Work* White Paper which, although it makes proposals for legislation, and in particular implementation of the Parental Leave Directive, there is no indication of a timetable for implementation of either this or the other proposals that are not to be the subject of consultation.

The first Order to be made under the Employment Rights (Dispute Resolution) Act 1998, which is discussed in Chapter 7, para. 7.5.4, brings into force on August 1, 1998 a number of provisions, amongst which is the renaming of industrial tribunals as employment tribunals. All references to "industrial tribunal" or "industrial tribunals", wherever they occur in any enactment are to be replaced by "employment tribunal" or "employment tribunals" and the Industrial Tribunals Act 1996 is now to be cited as the "Employment Tribunals Act 1996". The Order specifies other provisions to come into force on October 1, 1998 and the power of tribunals to reduce the unfair dismissal compensatory award where the employee fails to make use of an internal appeal procedure, and to make a supplementary award where the employer prevents the employee from making use of such a procedure, section 13 of the Act, will come into effect on January 1, 1999 and will apply in cases where the termination falls on or after that date. The Government has published *Guide to the Employment Rights (Dispute Resolution) Act 1998* which is available via the Internet at http://www.dti.gov.uk/erra.

The Public Interest Disclosure Act received Royal Assent on July 2, 1998 and is expected to come into force early in 1999. This inserts into the Employment Rights Act 1996 new provisions giving protection against dismissal and action short of dismissal in connection with a "protected disclosure". The Act, like the Regulations on Working Time and the National Minimum Wage Act, applies to all those who work for another person, thus moving away from the narrow definition of "employee" contained in the Employment Rights Act 1996 and the Government has invited views (*Fairness at Work*, para. 3.18) on whether some or all existing employment rights should be similarly extended.

The decision of the Advocate General in the *Seymour-Smith* case was delivered too late to be included, although reference has been made to the issues concerned in the proceedings. The two-year backdating rule contained in the Equal Pay Act 1970, s.2(5) was considered by the Advocate General in *Levez* and it is likely that the ECJ will hold it to be in breach of the principle of equivalence on the basis of comparison with rules governing other domestic actions for recovery of salary arrears. Section 2(5) is also to be considered by the ECJ, along with section 2(4) which precludes claims if the employee has not been employed in the employment "within the six months preceding the date of the reference", following a reference by the House of Lords in *Preston v. Wolverhampton Healthcare NHS Trust.*

We would like to thank all those who have helped during the preparation of this book, our colleagues at the International Centre at the University of Leicester who have shown patience throughout our many and most stressful moments and to Sue Thornton and Fiona Gelling whose skills where the www is concerned have saved us on many occasions. Particular thanks go to Professor Alan Neal and Colin Bourn for their support and for reading and commenting on drafts of various parts of the work and to Sue Smith in the Law Library at the University of Leicester without whose skills we would have been truly lost: we would like to thank her for her very expert help. Thanks must also go to our research assistants, students at the University at the time, Insar Hussein and Raza Mithani, who spent many hours in the library tracking down much useful information. We would like to congratulate Raza who graduated with a First and the 1998 Paul Heim Prize for best graduate of the year intending to qualify and practise as a barrister.

David would like to thank his former colleagues at NALGO and in UNISON who aroused and maintained his interest in employment law and Professor Keith Ewing for his helpful comments on aspects of the text. We would both like to thank our partners and families who have suffered that we might work, particularly David his partner Jonathan, for putting up with the domestic chaos that writing a text such as this creates and Helen her son Simon, without whom this work would have been finished considerably earlier!

Sweet & Maxwell staff have been wonderful to work with and have tolerated our lateness and dealt with our apprehensions and queries with patience and encouragement.

Needless to say we take full responsibility for any errors.

Helen Desmond
David Antill
August 1998

CONTENTS

Preface   v
Table of Cases   xiii
Table of Statutes   xxxix
Table of Statutory Instruments   li
Table of Abbreviations   lv

CHAPTER 1. FORMATION OF THE CONTRACT

1.1 The Underlying Basis of the Employment Relationship   1
1.2 Offer and Acceptance   3
1.3 Consideration   4
1.4 Capacity   7
1.5 Young People   8
1.6 Immigration and Free Movement of Workers   10
1.7 Asylum and Immigration Act 1996   14
1.8 Rehabilitation of Offenders and Criminal Records   16
1.9 Access to Personal Information   19
1.10 Trade Union Membership and Activities   23
1.11 Shop and Betting Shop Workers   24
1.12 Holidays and Working Time   26
1.13 Posted Workers   28
1.14 The Nature of the Relationship   30
1.15 Discrimination   42
1.16 Employment Incentives   46
1.17 Summary   48

CHAPTER 2. SOURCES OF TERMS OF THE CONTRACT

2.1 Precedent   51
2.2 Express Terms   52
2.3 Implied Terms   57
2.4 Collective Bargaining Agreements   60
2.5 Custom, Works Rules, Managerial Power and Policy Statements   69
2.6 Statute, Statutory Instruments and Codes of Practice   73
2.7 European Law   77

2.8   Statutory Statement of Terms   85
2.9   Summary   91

CHAPTER 3. THE DUTIES OF THE PARTIES

3.1   Duties Owed by the Employee   93
3.2   Mutual Duties   128
3.3   Duties Owed by the Employer   132

CHAPTER 4. ROLE OF PAY IN THE EMPLOYMENT RELATIONSHIP

4.1   Introduction   149
4.2   The Right to be Paid Whilst Working   149
4.3   The Right to be Paid When Absent From Work   154
4.4   Deductions from Pay   162
4.5   Regulation of Pay Rates   166
4.6   Summary   171

CHAPTER 5. VARIATION, TERMINATION AND DISCHARGE AT COMMON LAW

5.1   Introduction   173
5.2   Variation of the Contract of Employment   173
5.3   Termination   183
5.4   Notice   196
5.5   Discharge   200
5.6   Wrongful Dismissal Remedies   205
5.7   Summary   218

CHAPTER 6. DISCRIMINATION

6.1   The Legislative Framework   221
6.2   Equal Pay   230
6.3   Discrimination: Sex, Race and Disability   255
6.4   Statutory Commissions and Council   283
6.5   Reform and Summary   285

CHAPTER 7. UNFAIR DISMISSAL

7.1   Introduction   289
7.2   Qualifying Conditions and Exclusions   292
7.3   The Reasons for Dismissal   321
7.4   Automatically Unfair Reaons   336
7.5   Forum and Remedies   351
7.6   Summary   369

CHAPTER 8. ECONOMIC DISMISSALS

8.1   Introduction   371
8.2   Employee Protection During Economic Restructuring   371

8.3	Redundancy	373
8.4	Some Other Substantial Reason	406
8.5	Employer Insolvency	409
8.6	Summary	411

CHAPTER 9. TRANSFER OF UNDERTAKINGS

9.1	Introduction	413
9.2	Who Has To Be Consulted?	421
9.3	Is there a Transfer?	427
9.4	The Effects of a Relevant Transfer	436
9.5	Variation in Working Conditions	439
9.6	Collective Agreements and Trade Union Recognition	441
9.7	Pensions Not Transferred	443
9.8	Dismissal	444
9.9	Proposed Changes to the Transfer Regulations	447

CHAPTER 10. PREGNANCY AND CHILDBIRTH

10.1	Introduction	453
10.2	Time Off Work for Anti-natal Care	455
10.3	Dismissal on Grounds of Pregnancy	456
10.4	Right to Maternity leave and to Return to Work	467
10.5	Maternity Payments	492
10.6	Health and Safety and Suspension from Work	500
10.7	Parental and Paternity Leave	504
10.8	Reform and Summary	506

CHAPTER 11. COLLECTIVE ISSUES AND THE INDIVIDUAL EMPLOYMENT RELATIONSHIP

11.1	Collective Labour Law and the Individual Employment Relationship	511
11.2	Development of Collective Bargaining in the United Kingdom	513
11.3	Legal Framework for Collective Bargaining	515
11.4	Employees as Trade Union Members and Officials	519
11.5	The 1998 White Paper and Trade Union Recognition	521

APPENDIX 1.

| | IDS Brief Employment Law Fact Card | 528 |

| *Bibliography* | 531 |
| *Index* | 537 |

TABLE OF CASES

AB v. South West Water Services Ltd [1993] Q.B. 507; [1993] 2 W.L.R. 507; [1993] 1 All
    E.R. 609, CA 6.3.8
Abels v. Administrative Board of the Bedrijfsvereniging Voor de Metaal-Industrie en de
    Electrotechnische (135/83) CR 469, [1987] 2 C.M.L.R. 406, ECJ 9.9
Abernethy v. Mott, Hay and Anderson [1974] I.C.R. 323; 118 S.J. 294; I.R.L.R. 213, CA .. 7.3,
    7.3.2.1, 7.4.3
Abrahams v. Performing Right Society [1995] I.C.L.R. 1028; [1995] I.R.L.R. 486, CA .. 5.4.2
Adams v. G.K.N. Sankey Ltd [1980] I.R.L.R. 416, EAT 7.2.1.7
Adams v. Lancashire County Council, *sub nom.* Adams v. BET Catering Services [1997]
    I.C.R. 834; [1997] I.R.L.R. 436, CA; affirming [1996] All E.R. (E.C.) 473; [1996]
    I.R.L.R. 154, Ch D 9.7
Adamson v. B & L Cleaning Services Ltd [1995] I.R.L.R. 193, EAT 3.1.2.3
Addis v. Gramophone Co. Ltd [1909] A.C. 488 .... 5.6.1
Addison v. Denholm Ship Management (U.K.) Ltd [1997] I.R.L.R. 389, EAT 7.2.4
Adekeye v. The Post Office (No. 2) [1997] I.R.L.R. 105, CA...................... 10.4.2.6
Air Canada v. Lee [1978] I.C.R. 1202; [1978] 13 I.T.R. 574; [1978] I.R.L.R. 392, EAT ... 8.3.5.3
Airfix Footwear Ltd v. Cope [1978] I.C.R. 1210; [1978] I.R.L.R. 396, EAT 1.14.3
Albion Shipping Agency v. Arnold [1982] I.C.R. 22; [1981] I.R.L.R. 525, EAT 6.22, 6.2.6
Alboni v. Ind Coope Retail Ltd [1998] I.R.L.R. 131, CA 7.3
Alcan Extrusions v. Yates [1996] I.R.L.R. 327, EAT 5.3.3
Alcock v. Chief Constable of South Yorkshire Police; *sub nom.* Jones v. Wright [1992] 1
    A.C. 310; [1991] 3 W.L.R. 1057, HL 3.3.1.3
Aldridge v. British Telecommunications [1989] I.C.R. 790; [1990] I.R.L.R. 10, EAT ... 6.2.5
Alexander v. Home Office [1988] 1 W.L.R. 968; [1988] I.C.R. 685; [1988] I.R.L.R. 190,
    CA 6.3.8
—— v. Standard Telephones and Cables Ltd [1990] I.C.R. 291; [1990] I.R.L.R. 55, HC ... 5.6.3,
    9.6.1
—— v. —— (No. 2); Wall v. Standard Telephones and Cables (No. 2) [1991] I.R.L.R.
    286, HC 2.4, 2.4.2, 2.5.2
Ali v. Christian Salvesen Food Services Ltd; *sub nom.* Christian Salvesen Food Services
    Ltd v. Ali [1997] 1 All E.R. 721; [1997] I.R.L.R. 17, CA; reversing [1996] I.R.L.R.
    624, EAT 2.4.3
Allen v. Flood [1898] A.C. 1, HL 1.1
Alliance Paper Group plc v. Prestwick [1996] I.R.L.R. 25, Ch D 3.1.41, 3.1.4.3
American Cyanamid Co. v. Ethicon Ltd [1975] A.C. 396; [1975] 2 W.L.R., 316, HL... 3.1.2.6,
    3.1.4, 5.6.2
Amies v. Inner London Education Authority [1977] 2 All E.R. 100; [1977] I.C.R. 308,
    EAT 6.3.8
Anderson v. Pringle of Scotland Ltd [1998] I.R.L.R. 64, CS 5.63, 5.7, 8.3.4.1, 8.3.4.2
Annandale Engineering v. Samson [1994] I.R.L.R. 59, EAT 7.2.3
Aparau v. Iceland Frozen Foods plc [1996] I.R.L.R. 119, EAT 2.8.1, 2.8.4, 7.2.1.5
Archibald v. Rossleigh Commercials Ltd [1975] I.R.L.R. 231, IT 8.3.5.1

Armitage v. Johnson. See H.M. Prison Service v. Johnson
Arnold v. Beecham Group [1982] I.C.R. 744; [1982] I.R.L.R. 307, EAT 6.2.4
Aspden v. Webbs Poultry and Meat Group (Holdings) [1996] I.R.L.R. 521, QBD 4.3.1.1,
                                                                                                  7.3.2.1
Associated Newspapers v. Wilson; *sub nom.* Wilson v. Associated Newspapers; Associ-
    ated British Ports v. Palmer [1995] 2 A.C. 445; [1995] 2 W.L.R. 345; [1995] I.R.L.R.
    258, HL 1.10, 4.5.2, 7.4.2, 11.4.1, 11.5.3
Associated Picture Houses Ltd v. Wednesbury Corporation [1948] 1 K.B. 223 . . . .   5.6.4
Association of Pattern Makers and Allied Craftsmen v. Kirvin (1978) 13 I.T.R. 446;
    [1978] I.R.L.R. 318, EAT 8.3.3.5
Attorney-General v. Guardian Newspapers Ltd (No. 2) [1990] 1 A.C. 109, HL 3.1.3.1
Attwood v. Lamont [1920] 3 K.B. 577, CA 3.1.4.6

B. v. France (No. 57/1990/248/319) (1993) 16 E.H.R.R. 1; [1992] 2 F.L.R. 249,
    ECHR 6.3.4.2
Baker v. Kaye [1997] I.R.L.R. 219, QBD 1.2
Baldwin v. British Coal Corp. [1995] I.R.L.R. 139, QBD 5.4.2
Bank voor Handel en Scheepvaart N.V. v. Slatford [1953] 1 Q.B. 248; [1951] 2 T.L.R.
    755 . . . .   1.14
Banking Insurance and Finance Union v. Barclays Bank plc [1987] I.C.R. 495, EAT . . .   9.2.6
Banks v. Tesco Stores, IDS Brief 599/October 1997, p. 12 . . . . .10.5.2.1
Barber v. Guardian Royal Exchange Assurance Group (Case C–262/88) [1991] 1 Q.B.
    344; [1991] 2 W.L.R. 72; [1990] 2 All E.R. 660; [1990] I.R.L.R. 240, ECJ 6.1.1, 6.1.2,
                                                                                             6.2, 6.2,1, 6.2.1.1, 6.2.1.2, 6.2.8
—— v. Manchester Regional Hospital Board [1958] 1 W.L.R. 181; 122 J.P. 124 . . . .   5.6.3
—— v. Staffordshire CC [1996] I.C.R. 379; [1996] I.R.L.R. 209, CA 6.2.1.3
—— v. Thames Television [1992] I.C.R. 661; [1992] I.R.L.R. 410, CA 7.2.10
Barclays Bank v. James [1990] I.C.R. 333; [1990] I.R.L.R. 90, EAT 6.1.3
—— v. Kapur [1991] 2 A.C. 355; [1991] 2 W.L.R. 401; [1991] I.C.R. 208, HL 6.3.8
Barratt Developments (Bradford) v. Union of Construction Allied Trades and Techni-
    cians [1978] I.C.R. 319; (1977) 12 I.T.R. 478; [1977] I.R.L.R. 403, EAT 8.3.3.4
Barry v. Midland Bank plc [1998] I.R.L.R. 138, CA 6.2.6
Bass Leisure Ltd v. Thomas [1994] I.R.L.R. 104, EAT 5.3.3, 7.3.2.4, 8.3.5.4
Bass Taverns Ltd v. Burgess [1995] I.R.L.R. 596, CA 7.4.2, 7.4.4
Batchelor v. British Railways Board [1987] I.R.L.R. 136, CA 7.2.1.7
Baxter v. Harland & Wolff plc [1990] I.R.L.R. 516, NICA 3.3.1.3
Becker v. Finanzamt Münster Innenstadt (No. 8/81) [1982] E.C.R. 53; [1982] 1 C.M.L.R.
    499 . . . .   2.7.1
Bell v. Lever Bros [1931] 1 K.B. 557, CA; [1932] A.C. 161, HL 3.1.2
Benton v. Sanderson Kayser Ltd [1989] I.C.R. 136; (1988) 132 S.J. 1637; [1989] I.R.L.R.
    19, CA 8.3.4.2
Bents Brewery v. Hogan [1945] 2 All E.R. 570 . . . .   3.1.3
Benveniste v. University of Southampton [1989] I.C.R. 617; [1989] I.R.L.R. 122, CA . . .   6.2.6.1
Berg and Busschers v. Besselsen (Cases 144 and 145/87) [1988] E.C.R. 2559; [1990]
    I.C.R. 396; [1989] I.R.L.R. 447, ECJ 9.3.2
Berriman v. Delabole Slate Ltd [1985] I.C.R. 546; [1985] I.R.L.R. 305, CA 9.8.2
Bestuur van het Algemeen Burgerlijk Pensioenfonds v. Beune (Case C–7/93) [1995] All
    E.R. (E.C.) 19; [1995] I.R.L.R. 103, ECJ 6.1.1
BET Catering Services Ltd v. Ball, November 28, 1996, EAT 637/96 . . . .   9.6.1
Betts v. Brintel Helicopters Ltd (t/a British International Helicopters) [1997] 2 All E.R.
    840; [1997] I.R.L.R. 361, CA 9.3.6
Bhatt v. Chelsea and Westminster Health Care Trust (Unfair Dismissal) [1997] I.R.L.R.
    660; *The Times*, October 24, 1997, EAT 7.2.16

Bick v. Royal School for the Deaf (Case No. 11664/76) [1976] I.R.L.R. 326, IT 6.3

Biggs v. Somerset CC [1996] I.C.R. 364; [1996] I.R.L.R. 203, CA... 6.2.1.3, 6.2.2, 6.3.8, 7.2.2, 7.2.8

Bilka-Kaufhaus GmbH v. Karin Weber von Hartz (No. C–170/84) [1986] 2 C.M.L.R. 701; [1986] 5 E.C.R. 1607, ECJ 6.1.1, 6.1.2, 6.2.1.2, 6.2.6, 6.3.3.3

Birch and Humber v. University of Liverpool [1985] I.C.R. 470; (1985) 129 S.J. 245; [1985] I.R.L.R. 165, CA 5.3.1, 7.2.1.3, 8.3.4

Blackpool and The Fylde College v. National Association of Teachers in Further and Higher Education [1994] I.C.R. 648; [1984] I.R.L.R. 277, CA 11.5.3

Blackstone Franks Investment Management Ltd v. Robertson, *The Times*, May 4, 1998, CA 4.4.1

Blair v. Inverclyde Association for Mental Health, EAT 846/96 .... 10.4.1.6

Bonner v. H. Gilbert Ltd [1989] I.R.L.R. 475, EAT 8.3.7.4

Bork International A/S v. Foreningen of Arbejdsledere i Danmark [1989] I.R.L.R. 41, ECJ 9.3.2

Bossa v. Nordstress Ltd [1998] I.R.L.R. 284; *The Times*, March 13, 1998, EAT 2.7

Boston Deep Sea Fishing & Ice Co. v. Ansell (1888) 39 Ch. D. 339 .... 3.1.2, 7.3

Botzen v. Rolterdamsche Droogdok Maatschappij B.V. (No. 186/83) [1986] 2 C.M.L.R. 50, ECJ 9.4.2

Bouchaala v. Trust House Forte Hotels Ltd [1980] I.C.R. 721; [1980] I.R.L.R. 382, EAT 7.3.2.3

Bovey v. Board of Governors of the Hospital for Sick Children [1978] I.C.R. 934; (1978) 13 I.T.R. 416; [1978] I.R.L.R. 241, EAT 10.4.2.5

Boyd Line Ltd v. Pitts [1986] I.C.R. 244, EAT 1.14.4

Boyle v. E.O.C. (Case C–411/96) Employment Law Watch No. 5, Spring 1998 .... 10.5.6

Boyo v. Lambeth LBC [1994] I.C.R. 727; [1995] I.R.L.R. 50, CA 5.3.2.3, 5.6.2, 5.7

Boys and Girls Welfare Society v. McDonald [1996] I.R.L.R. 129, EAT 7.3.2.2

BP Chemicals Ltd v. Gillick [1995] I.R.L.R. 128, EAT 1.15

BP Oil Ltd v. Richards, EAT/768/82, April 12, 1983 .... 7.2.1.6

Bracebridge Engineering Ltd v. Darby [1990] I.R.L.R. 3, EAT 5.3.3, 6.3.4.1

Brasserie du Pêcheur S.A. v. Federal Republic of Germany; R. v. Secretary of State for Transport, ex p. Factortame (No. 3) (Cases C–46 & 48/93) [1996] I.R.L.R. 267; [1996] 1 E.C.R. 1029; [1996] 1 C.M.L.R. 889, ECJ 2.7.2

Bratko v. Beloit Walmsley Ltd [1995] I.R.L.R. 629, EAT 7.2.10

Breach v. Epsylon Industries Ltd [1976] I.C.R. 316; [1976] I.R.L.R. 180, EAT 1.3

Brearley v. Wm Morrisons Supermarkets COIT 3073/168B noted in *People Management*, September 12, 1996 .... 6.3.4.1

Brennan v. J.H. Dewhurst Ltd [1984] I.C.R. 52; [1983] I.R.L.R. 357, EAT 6.3.6

Briggs v. North Eastern Education and Library Board [1990] I.R.L.R. 181, NICA 6.3.3.1, 6.3.3.2, 6.3.3.3, 10.4.2.3

—— v. Oates [1991] 1 All E.R. 407; [1990] I.C.R. 473; [1990] I.R.L.R. 472, HC 3.1.4.5

Brindley (J.) v. Tayside Health Board [1976] I.R.L.R. 364, IT 1.15

Bristow v. City Petroleum Co. Ltd [1987] 1 W.L.R. 529; (1987) 131 S.J. 504; [1987] I.R.L.R. 340, HL 4.4

British Aerospace plc v. Green and Others [1995] I.C.R. 1006; [1995] I.R.L.R. 433, CA 8.3.4.1

British Aircraft Corp. v. Austin [1978] I.R.L.R. 332, EAT 3.21, 3.3.1.2

British Broadcasting Corp. v. Ioannou [1975] Q.B. 781; [1975] 2 All E.R. 999; [1975] I.C.R. 267, CA 1.14.2

—— v. Ioannou [1996] I.R.L.R. 508, EAT 7.2.1.6

—— v. Kelly-Phillip [1997] I.R.L.B. 578, EAT 7.2.16

British Coal v. Keeble [1997] I.R.L.R. 336, EAT 6.3.8

—— v. Smith [1996] 3 All E.R. 97; [1996] I.R.L.R. 399, HL 6.2.2

British Home Stores v. Burchell [1980] I.C.R. 303; *sub nom.* British Home Stores v. Birchell (1978) 131 I.T.R. 560; [1978] I.R.L.R. 379, EAT 7.3.2.2, 8.3.7.4

British Labour Pump Co. v. Byrne [1979] I.C.R. 347; [1979] I.R.L.R. 94, EAT 7.3.2.1, 7.3.2.2, 7.5.5.2

British Leyland (U.K.) v. Ashraf [1978] I.C.R. 979; (1978) 13 I.T.R. 500; [1978] I.R.L.R. 300, EAT 10.4.2.6

—— v. McQuilken [1978] I.R.L.R. 245, EAT 2.4

British Road Services Ltd v. Loughran [1997] I.R.L.R. 92, NICA 6.2.6

British Telecommunications Plc v. Roberts [1996] I.C.R. 625; [1996] I.R.L.R. 601, EAT 10.4.2.3

—— v. Ticehurst; *sub nom.* Ticehurst and Thompson v. British Telecommunications [1992] I.C.R. 383; (1992) 136 S.J.L.B. 96; [1992] I.R.L.R. 219, CA............ 3.1, 4.5.2

Broaders v. Kalkare Property Maintenance Ltd [1990] I.R.L.R. 421, EAT 7.2.3

Bromley v. Quick (H. & J.) [1988] I.C.R. 623; [1988] I.R.L.R. 249, C.A. 6.2.5

Brompton v. AOC International Ltd and UNUM Ltd [1997] I.R.L.R. 639, EAT 4.3.1.1

Brook v. London Borough of Haringey [1992] I.R.L.R. 478, EAT 8.3.4.2

Brooker v. Charrington Fuel Oils Ltd [1981] I.R.L.R. 147, CC..................... 4.4

Brooks v. British Telecommunications [1992] I.C.R. 414; [1992] I.R.L.R. 66, CA 7.2.10

Brown v. Chief Adjudication Officer [1997] I.R.L.R. 110; [1997] I.C.R. 266, CA....... 4.3.2

—— v. Rentokil [1992] I.R.L.R. 302, [1995] I.R.L.R. 211, CS 10.3

—— v. Stockton-on-Tees Borough Council [1988] 2 W.L.R. 935; [1988] I.C.R. 410; [1988] I.R.L.R. 263, HL 8.3.2.2

—— v. Stuart, Scott and Co. Ltd [1981] I.C.R. 166, EAT 5.2.4

Bruce and Others v. Wiggins Teape (Stationery) Ltd [1994] I.R.L.R. 536, EAT 4.2.2

Buchan v. Secretary of State for Employment, Ivey v. Secretary of State for Employment [1997] I.R.L.R. 80; [1997] B.C.C. 145, EAT 1.14

Buchanan-Smith v. Schleicher & Co. International Ltd [1996] I.C.R. 613; [1996] I.R.L.R. 547, EAT 9.4.2

Burdett-Coutts v. Hertfordshire County Council [1984] I.R.L.R. 91; (1984) 134 New L.J. 359, HC 5.2.3, 5.2.3.1, 5.3.3

Burrett v. West Birmingham Health Authority [1994] I.R.L.R. 7, EAT 6.3.4.3

Burroughs v. Timmoney [1977] I.R.L.R. 404, CS 2.4.3

Burton v. British Railways Board (No. 2) (No. 19/81) [1982] Q.B. 1080; [1982] 3 W.L.R. 387; [1982] I.R.L.R. 116, ECJ... 6.1.2, 6.2.8

Burton & Rhule v. De Vere Hotels [1996] I.R.L.R. 596, CA 6.3.4.1

Burton Group Ltd v. M. Smith [1977] I.R.L.R. 351, EAT 5.4.1

Bux v. Slough Metals [1973] 1 W.L.R. 1358; 117 S.J. 615; 1 All E.R. 262, CA......... 3.3.13

Byrne v. Birmingham City District Council [1987] I.C.R. 519; (1987) 85 L.G.R. 729, CA 7.2.8.1

—— v. Castrol (U.K.) Ltd EAT, 429/96, November 5, 1996 .... 8.3.4.1

C.P.S. Recruitment Ltd (t/a Blackwood Associates) v. Bowen and Secretary of State for Employment [1982] I.R.L.R. 54, EAT 8.3.7.2

Cabaj v. Westminster City Council [1996] I.C.R. 960, CA 7.3.1

Cadbury Ltd v. Doddington [1977] I.C.R. 982, EAT 7.5.5.2

Cain v. Leeds Western Health Authority [1990] I.C.R. 585; [1990] I.R.L.R. 168, EAT .... 7.3.2.2.

Caisse nationale d'assutance vieillesse des travailleurs salaries v. Thibault (Case C–136/95) ECJ, IDS Brief 583/February 1997 .... 10.3

Calder v. James Finaly Corporation [1989] I.C.R. 157; [1989] I.R.L.R. 55, CA 6.3.8

Caledonia Bureau Investment & Property v. Caffrey [1998] I.R.L.R. 110, EAT...... 10.4.1.6, 10.4.2.6

Caledonian Mining Co. v. Bassett [1987] I.C.R. 425; [1987] I.R.L.R. 165, EAT........ 7.2

Callo v. Brouncker (1831) 4 C. & P. 518 .... 5.3.4

Cambridge & District Co-operative Society Ltd v. Ruse [1993] I.R.L.R. 156, EAT..... 8.3.5.1

Camden Exhibition & Display v. Lynott [1966] 1 Q.B. 555; [1965] 3 W.L.R. 763, CA .. 2.4

Campbell v. Dunoon & Cowall Housing Association Ltd [1993] I.R.L.R. 496, CS 7.5.5.2

Capital Foods Retail Ltd v. Corrigan [1993] I.R.L.R. 430, EAT 7.2.2

Capper Pass Ltd v. Lawton [1977] 2 W.L.R. 26; 120 S.J. 768; [1976] I.R.L.R. 366, EAT 6.2.3

Carmichael and Leese v. National Power plc, *The Times*, April 2, 1998 .... 1.14.4

Caruana v. Manchester Airport plc [1996] I.R.L.R. 378, EAT 10.3

Cassidy v. Ministry of Health [1951] 2 K.B. 343; [1951] 1 T.L.R. 539; [1951] 1 All E.R.
574, CA 1.14
Casson Beckman & Partners v. Papi [1991] B.C.C. 68; [1991] B.C.L.C. 299, CA 3.1.2.1
Cast v. Croydon College [1997] I.R.L.R. 14, EAT 6.3.8
Catamaran Cruisers Ltd v. Williams and Others [1994] I.R.L.R. 386, EAT 8.4.1
Cayne v. Global Natural Resources plc [1984] 1 All E.R. 225, CA 3.1.4
Chadwick v. British Railways Board [1967] 1 W.L.R. 912; 111 S.J. 562; *sub nom.*
Chadwick v. British Transport Commission [1967] 2 All E.R. 945 .... 3.3.1.3
Chadwick v. Pioneer Private Telephone Ltd [1941] 1 All E.R. 522 .... 1.14
Chant v. Aquaboats [1978] 3 All E.R. 102; [1978] I.C.R. 643, EAT 7.4.2
Chapman v. Aberdeen Construction Group plc [1991] I.R.L.R. 505; 1993 S.L.T. 1205,
CS 2.2
—— v. Goonvean and Rostowrack China Cly Co. Ltd [1973] I.C.R. 310; [1973] 1 W.L.R.
678, CA 8.3.1.1
Chappell v. Times Newspapers Ltd [1975] 1 W.L.R. 482; [1975] I.C.R. 145, [1975]
I.R.L.R. 90, CA 5.6.3
Chattopadhyay v. Headmaster of Holloway School [1982] I.C.R. 132; [1981] I.R.L.R.
487, EAT 6.3.7
Chemidus Wavin Ltd v. Société par la Transformation et L'Exploitation des Resines
Industrielles S.A. [1978] 3 C.M.L.R. 514; [1977] 5 W.W.R. 155, CA 3.1.46
Chessington World of Adventures Ltd v. Reed [1997] I.R.L.R. 556, EAT 6.3.4.1, 6.3.4.2,
6.3.4.3
Chubb Fire Security Ltd v. Harper [1983] I.R.L.R. 311, EAT 8.4
Church v. West Lancashire NHS Trust [1998] I.R.L.R. 4, EAT 7.3.2.4, 8.3.1.3
Chuwen v. Debenhams Ltd, COIT/655/177 .... 1.8
Clark v. Novacold Ltd COIT Case No. 1801661/97 July 23, 1997, EOR Discrimination
Case Law Digest, No. 34 .... 6.3.2
—— v. Oxfordshire Health Authority [1998] I.R.L.R. 125, CA 1.14.4
—— v. Secretary of State for Employment [1997] I.C.R. 64, [1996] I.R.L.R. 578, CA;
reversing [1995] I.C.R. 673; [1995] I.R.L.R. 421, EAT 10.5.2.1
Clarke v. Eley (IMI) Kynoch Ltd [1983] I.C.R. 165; [1982] I.R.L.R. 482, EAT 6.3.3.1,
8.3.4.2, 10.4.23
Clarks of Hove Ltd v. Bakers Union [1978] 1 W.L.R. 1207; [1978] I.C.R. 1076, CA.... 8.3.3.5
Clarkson International Tools v. Short [1973] I.C.R. 191; 14 K.I.R. 400; [1973] I.R.L.R.
90, NIRC 2.6.1, 2.6.2
Clay v. A.J. Crump & Sons Ltd [1964] 1 Q.B. 533; [1963] 3 W.L.R. 866, CA 3.3.2
Clay Cross (Quarry Services) Ltd v. Fletcher [1978] 1 W.L.R. 1429; [1979] I.C.R. 1, CA 6.2.6
Clayton v. Vigers [1989] I.C.R. 713; [1990] I.R.L.R. 177, EAT 7.4.3
Clayton and Waller Ltd v. Oliver [1930] A.C. 209, HL 1.3
Clement-Clarke International v. Manley [1979] I.C.R. 74, EAT 7.5.5.2
Cleveland Ambulance NHS Trust v. Blane [1997] I.C.R. 851; [1997] I.R.L.R. 332,
EAT 7.5.5.2
Clymo v. Wandsworth London Borough Council [1989] I.C.R. 250; [1989] I.R.L.R. 241,
EAT 6.3.3.1, 10.4.23
Coco v. Clarke (A.N.) (Engineers) [1968] F.S.R. 415; [1969] R.P.C. 41 .... 3.1.3.1
Coleman v. Magnet Joinery [1975] I.C.R. 46; [1975] K.I.L.R. 139; [1974] I.R.L.R. 343,
CA 7.5.5.1
—— v. S. & W. Baldwin [1977] I.R.L.R. 342, EAT 5.3.2
Collier v. Sunday Referee Publishing Co. Ltd [1940] 2 K.B. 647, HC 1.3, 1.14.3
Collins v. Wilkins and Chapman P. Skidmore (1997) 26 I.L.J. 53 .... 6.3.4.2
Coloroll Pension Trustees v. Russell (Case C–200/91) [1995] All E.R. (E.C.) 23; [1995]
I.C.R. 179; [1994] I.R.L.R. 586; [1994] O.P.L.R. 179 .... 6.1.1, 6.2.11
Commission (E.C.) v. Belgium (No. 149/79) [1980] E.C.R. 3881; [1981] 2 C.M.L.R. 413,
ECJ 1.6
—— v. United Kingdom (No. 61/81) [1982] E.C.R. 2601; [1982] 3 C.M.L.R. 284,
ECJ 2.7.2, 6.25
—— v. —— (Case C–382/92) [1994] I.C.R. 664; [1994] I.R.L.R. 392, ECJ 2.6.1, 7.4.4,
8.3.3.1, 9.2.1, 9.3.4

Community Task Force v. Rimmer [1986] I.C.R. 491; [1986] I.R.L.R. 203, EAT 10.4.2.4

Comptoir Commercial Anversois and Power Son and Co., Re [1920] 1 K.B. 868 ...... 5.2.1.4

Construction Industry Training Board v. Labour Force Ltd (1970) 114 S.J. 704; [1970] 3
All E.R. 220, DC 1.14.5

—— v. Leighton [1978] 1 All E.R. 723; [1978] I.R.L.R. 577, EAT............... 2.8.2, 5.2.4

Cooper v. Plessey Semiconductors Ltd, *The Times*, August 11, 1983 .... 3.1.2

Coote v. Granada Hospitality Ltd (Case C–185/97), Employment Law Watch No. 5,
Spring 1998, ECJ 10.4.2.6

Coral Leisure Group v. Barnet (1981) 125 S.J. 374; [1981] I.C.R. 503, EAT 7.2.3

Corbett v. Corbett (No. 2) [1971] P. 110; [1970] 2 W.L.R. 1306, HC 6.3.4.2

Cossey v. U.K. (Case C–16/1989/176/232) [1991] 2 F.L.R. 492; [1993] 2 F.C.R. 97 (1990)
13 E.H.R.R. 622, ECHR 6.3.4.2

Costa v. ENEL (No. 14/64—Italian Ct) (No. 6/64–European Ct) [1964] C.M.L.R. 425;
[1964] E.C.R. 585, ECJ 2.7

Coulson v. Felixstowe Dock and Railway Co. [1975] I.R.L.R. 11, IT 4.3.1.1

Courtaulds Northern Spinning v. Sibson [1988] I.C.R. 451; [1988] I.R.L.R. 305, CA...... 2.3,
5.2.1.4

Courtaulds Northern Textiles v. Andrew [1979] I.R.L.R. 84, EAT 3.2.1

Cowen v. Haden Carrier [1983] I.C.R. 1; (1982) 126 S.J. 725, CA........... 8.3.1.1, 8.3.1.2

Cranleigh Precision Engineering Ltd v. Bryant [1965] 1 W.L.R. 1293; 109 S.J. 830; [1964]
3 All E.R. 289 .... 3.1.3.1

Crawford v. Swinton Insurance Brokers Ltd [1990] I.C.R. 8; [1990] I.R.L.R. 42,
EAT 9.8.2

Credit Suisse Asset Management Ltd v. Armstrong [1996] I.C.R. 882; [1996] I.R.L.R.
450, CA 2.5.2, 3.1.2.5, 3.1.2.6, 3.1.4

Crees v. Royal London Mutual Insurance Society Ltd [1997] I.R.L.R. 85, EAT...... 10.4.2.2,
10.4.2.4, 10.4.2.6, 10.8

Cresswell v. Board of Inland Revenue (1984) 128 S.J. 431; [1984] All E.R. 713; [1984]
I.R.L.R. 190, Ch D 3.1.1, 3.2.1, 5.2.1.4, 8.3.1.2

Crouch v. Kidsons Impey [1996] I.R.L.R. 79, EAT...................... 10.4.1.6, 10.4.2.6

Curling and Others v. Securicor Ltd [1992] I.R.L.R. 549, EAT...................... 8.3.5.4

Currie and Gray v. Pinnacle Meat Processors, September 6, 1996, Southampton IT
27788/96 & 27051/96, reported in I.R.L.B. 565, March 1997 .... 8.3.7

Cuthbertson v. AML Distributors [1975] I.R.L.R. 228, IT 5.2.4

Cutter v. Powell (1795) 6 Term Rep. 320 .... 4.2

D v. M [1996] I.R.L.R. 192, QBD 3.1.4, 3.1.4.5

D.M. Farr v. Hoveringham Gravels Ltd Nottingham [1972] I.R.L.R. 104, EAT........ 8.4.1

D.R. Ellis v. Brighton Co-Operative Society Ltd [1976] I.R.L.R. 419, EAT 8.4.1

D.R. Vaughan v. Weighpack Ltd [1974] I.C.R. 261; [1974] I.T.R. 226; [1974] I.R.L.R.
105, NIRC 7.5.5.2

Dalgleish v. Lothian and Borders Police Board, 1992 S.L.T. 721; [1991] I.R.L.R. 422,
CS 1.9.3, 3.1.3

Dattani v. Trio Supermarkets Ltd, *The Times*, February 20, 1998, CA............... 7.2.6

David (Lawrence) v. Ashton [1991] 1 All E.R. 385; [1989] I.R.L.R. 22, NICA......... 5.6.2

Davidson v. City Electrical Factors Ltd [1998] I.R.L.R. 108, EAT 7.2.8

Davies v. Girobank plc (Case C–197/97) E.O.R. No. 75 September/October 1997,
p. 43 .... 10.5.6

Dawney, Day & Co. Ltd v. de Braconier d'Alphen [1997] I.R.L.R. 442, CA.... 3.1.3.1, 3.1.4.3

Decro-Wall International S.A. v. Practitioners in Marketing; Same v. Same [1971] 1
W.L.R. 361; *sub nom.* Decro Wall International S.A. v. Practitioners in Marketing
(1970) 115 S.J. 171; [1971] 2 All E.R. 216, CA.......................... 5.3.2.2, 5.3.2.3

Dedman v. British Building and Engineering Appliances Ltd [1974] 1 W.L.R. 171; [1974]
I.C.R. 53; [1973] I.R.L.R. 379, CA 7.2.1.7

Defrenne v. Belgian State (No. 80/70) [1974] 1 C.M.L.R. 494; [1971] E.C.R. 455, ECJ 6.1.1
—— v. SABENA (No. 43/75) [1976] I.C.R. 547; [1976] 2 C.M.L.R. 98, ECJ 6.1, 6.1.1, 6.2.1.1, 6.2.2, 6.2.1.2, 7.2.2, 7.2.8, 10.5.2.1
Dekker v. Stichting Vormingscentrum Voor Jonge Volwassenen (VJV-Centrum) Plus (Case C–177/88) [1991] I.R.L.R. 27, ECJ 10.3, 10.4.2.3
Del Monte Foods Ltd v. Mundon [1980] I.C.R 694; [1980] I.R.L.R. 224, EAT 7.4.3
Delaney v. Staples (t/a De Montfort Recruitment) [1992] 1 A.C. 687; [1992] 2 W.L.R. 451; [1992] I.R.L.R. 191, HL 4.2, 4.2.2, 5.4.2, 7.5.1
Denco Ltd v. Joinson [1991] 1 W.L.R. 330; [1992] 1 All E.R. 463; [1991] I.R.L.R. 63, EAT 5.3.4
Denmark v. Boscobel [1969] 1 Q.B. 699; [1968] 3 W.L.R. 841, CA 5.3.2.2
Dennehy v. Sealink U.K. Ltd [1987] I.R.L.R. 120, EAT 6.2.5
Dentmaster (U.K.) Ltd v. Kent [1997] I.R.L.R. 636, CA .... 3.1.4.4.
Dentons Directories Ltd v. Hobbs, EAT 821/96 I.R.L.B. 577, September 1997, IDS Brief 1997/589, p. 6 .... 7.43, 10.3
Derwent Coachworks v. Kirby [1995] I.C.R. 48; [1994] I.R.L.R. 639, EAT 7.5.5.2
Devis (W.) & Sons v. Atkins [1997] A.C. 931; [1997] I.C.R. 662; [1997] I.R.L.R. 314, HL 7.3, 7.4.3, 7.5.5.2
Devonald v. Rosser & Sons [1906] 2 K.B. 728, CA 1.3
Dibro Ltd v. Hore [1990] I.C.R. 370; [1990] I.R.L.R. 129, EAT 6.2.5
Dietman v. London Borough of Brent [1988] I.C.R. 737; [1988] I.R.L.R. 299, CA 5.3.2.3
Dietz v. Stichting Thuiszorg Rotterdam (Case C–435/93) [1996] I.R.L.R. 692, ECJ 6.2.1.2
Digital Equipment Co. Ltd v. Clements (No. 2) [1997] I.C.R. 237; [1997] I.R.L.R. 140, EAT 6.38, 7.5.5.2, 8.3.7.3
DJM International Ltd v. Nicholas [1996] I.C.R. 214; [1996] I.R.L.R. 76, EAT 9.4.3
Dillenkofer v. Federal Republic of Germany (Cases C–46 & 48/93) [1997] I.R.L.R. 60, ECJ 2.7.2
Dines v. Initial and Pall Mall [1995] I.C.R. 11; [1994] I.R.L.R. 336, CA 9.2.5, 9.3.3
Diocese of Hallam Trustee v. Connaughton [1996] I.C.R. 860; [1996] I.R.L.R. 505, EAT 6.2.2
Discount Tobacco & Confectionery v. Armitage [1995] I.C.R. 431; [1990] I.R.L.R. 15, EAT 4.4.1, 7.4.2, 11.4.1
Distillers Co. (Bottling Services) Ltd v. Gardner [1982] I.R.L.R. 47, EAT 7.3.2.2
Dixon v. BBC [1979] I.C.R. 281; [1979] 2 W.L.R. 647, CA 1.14.2
Dooley v. Cammell Laird [1951] 1 Lloyd's Rep. 271, Assizes 3.3.1.3
Doughty v. Rolls-Royce plc [1992] I.C.R. 538; [1992] I.R.L.R. 126, CA 2.7.1, 6.1.2
Dowuona v. John Lewis [1987] I.C.R. 788; [1987] I.R.L.R. 310, CA 10.4.2.5
Dryden v. Greater Glasgow Health Board [1992] I.R.L.R. 469, EAT 2.5.2
Duffy v. Yeomans & Partners Ltd [1995] I.C.R. 1; [1994] I.R.L.R. 642, CA.... 7.3.2.2, 8.3.3.2
Dugdale v. Kraft Foods Ltd [1976] 1 W.L.R. 1288; (1976) S.J. 780; [1976] I.R.L.R. 368, EAT 6.2.3
Duke v. GEC Reliance [1988] A.C. 618; [1988] 2 W.L.R. 359; [1988] I.R.L.R. 118; [1988] 1 All E.R. 626, HL 2.7.1, 6.1.1, 6.1.2, 6.2.8, 10.3
Duncan Webb Offset (Maidstone Ltd v. Cooper [1995] I.R.L.R. 633, EAT 9.4.2
Dundon v. G.P.T. Ltd [1995] I.R.L.R. 403, EAT 8.3.2.3
Duratube Ltd v. Bhatti and Others, IRLB 585, January 1998 .... 9.8.1
Dulton v. Hawker Siddeley Aviation Ltd [1978] I.C.R. 1057; [1978] I.R.L.R. 390, EAT 8.3.6

Eagland v. British Telecommunications plc [1993] I.C.R. 644; [1992] I.R.L.R. 323, CA 2.8.2, 5.2.4
Earl v. Slater & Wheeler (Airlyre) Ltd [1973] 1 W.L.R. 51; [1972] I.C.R. 508; [1972] I.R.L.R. 115, NIRC 7.3
East Lindsey D.C. v. Daubrey [1977] I.C.R. 566; (1977) 12 I.T.R. 359; [1977] I.R.L.R. 181, EAT 7.3.2.1
East Sussex CC v. Walker [1972] 2 I.T.R. 280, NIRC 5.3.1, 7.2

Eaton Ltd v. King [1995] I.R.L.R. 75, EAT 8.3.4.1
—— v. Nuttall [1977] 1 W.L.R. 549; 121 S.J. 353; [1997] I.R.L.R. 71, EAT 6.2.3, 6.2.4
Egg Stores (Stamford Hill) v. Leibovici [1977] I.C.R. 269; [1976] I.R.L.R. 376, EAT .. 5.5.1.1,
                       5.7, 7.2.1.4
Electrolux Ltd v. Hutchinson [1977] I.C.R. 252; (1976) 12 I.T.R. 40, EAT 6.2.3
Emmott v. Minister for Social Welfare and Attorney-General (Case C–208/90) [1993]
 I.C.R. 8; [1991] I.R.L.R. 387, ECJ 6.2.1.3
Enderby v. Frenchay Health Authority and Health Secretary (Case C–127/92) [1994] 1
 All E.R. 495; I.R.L.R. 591, ECJ 6.2.6, 6.2.6.1
England v. Bromley L.B.C. [1978] I.C.R. 1, EAT 6.2.4
Esso Petroleum Co. Ltd v. Harper's Garage (Stourport) Ltd [1968] A.C. 269; [1967] 2
 W.L.R. 871; [1967] 1 All E.R. 699, HL 3.1.4.3
Etam plc v. Rowan [1989] I.R.L.R. 150, EAT 6.3.5
Eurobrokers Ltd v. Rabey [1995] I.R.L.R. 206, Ch D 3.1.2.5
Evans v. Sawley Packaging Co. Ltd, COIT 2916/185E, noted in *People Management*,
 September 12, 1996 .... 6.3.4.1
Evening Standard Co. Ltd v. Henderson [1987] I.C.R. 588; [1987] F.S.R. 165, CA 3.1.2.4,
                       3.1.2.5

F.C. Shepherd & Co. Ltd v. Jerrom [1986] I.R.L.R. 358, CA 5.5.1.2
F.D.R Ltd v. Holloway [1995] I.R.L.R. 400, EAT 8.3.4.1
F. Hernandes Vidal SA v. P Gomez Pérez (Case C–127/96) 9.3.6
F.W. Woolworth plc v. Smith [1990] I.C.R. 45; [1990] I.R.L.R. 39, EAT 10.4.2.1, 10.4.2.2,
                       10.4.2.4
Faccenda Chicken v. Fowler; Fowler v. Faccenda Chicken [1987] Ch. 117; [1986] 3
 W.L.R. 288; [1986] I.C.R. 297, CA 3.1.3, 3.1.3.1, 3.1.3.3
Factortame Ltd v. Secretary of State for Transport (No. 2) [1989] 2 W.L.R. 997; [1991] 1
 All E.R. 70, HL 2.7
Fairfield Ltd v. Skinner [1992] I.C.R. 836; [1993] I.R.L.R. 4, EAT 4.4.1, 4.4.2
Falkirk Council v. Whyte [1997] I.R.L.R. 560, EAT 6.3.3.1
Farrow v. Wilson (1869) L.R. 4 C.P. 744 .... 5.5.3
Ferguson v. John Dawson & Partners (Contractors) Ltd [1976] 3 All E.R. 817; (1976) 8
 Build. L.R. 38, CA 1.14
Fire Brigades Union v. Fraser [1997] I.R.L.R. 671, EAT 6.3.4.1
Fisscher v. Voor huis Hengelo B.V. [1994] I.R.L.R. 662; I.C.R. 635, ECJ 6.1.1, 6.2.1,
                       6.2.1.2
Fitzgerald v. Hall Russell Ltd [1970] A.C. 984; [1969] 3 W.L.R. 868, HL 7.2.8.1
Fitzpatrick v. British Railways Board [1992] I.C.R. 221; [1991] I.R.L.R. 376, CA 7.4.2
Flack v. Kodak Ltd [1986] I.C.R. 755; [1987] 1 W.L.R. 31, EAT 7.2.8.1
Fleming v. Secretary of State for Trade & Industry [1997] I.R.L.R. 682, CS 1.14
Focsa Services (U.K.) Ltd v. Birkett [1996] I.R.L.R. 325, EAT 5.3.2.3, 5.6.2
Ford v. Warwickshire County Council [1983] A.C. 71; [1983] I.C.R. 273, HL 7.2.8.1
Ford Motor Co. v. Amalgamated Union of Engineering & Foundry Workers [1969] 2
 Q.B. 303; [1969] 1 W.L.R. 339, CA 2.3, 2.4
Foreningen Af Arbejdsledere i Danmark v. Daddys Dance Hall (Case 324/86) [1988]
 I.R.L.R. 315; [1989] 2 C.M.L.R. 517, ECJ 9.3.2, 9.3.4, 9.3.6, 9.4, 9.4.1, 9.5
Foster v. British Gas (Case C–188/89) [1991] 2 A.C. 306; [1991] 2 W.L.R. 1075, HL;
 [1990] E.C.R. 1–3313, ECJ 2.7.1, 6.1.2, 6.2.8
—— v. National Power, *People Management*, August 28, 1997, p. 18 .... 3.3.1.3
Foster Wheeler (London) Ltd v. Jackson [1990] I.C.R. 757; [1990] I.R.L.R. 412,
 EAT 4.2.2
Francovich v. Italian Republic (Case C–6/90) [1995] I.C.R. 722; [1992] I.R.L.R. 84,
 ECJ 2.7.2
Frost v. Chief Constable of South Yorkshire Police [1998] Q.B. 255; [1997] 3 W.L.R.
 1194; [1997] 1 All E.R. 540, HL 3.3.1.3
Fyfe & McGrouther Ltd v. Byrne [1977] I.R.L.R. 26, EAT 3.2.1

G.F.I. Group Inc. v. Eaglestone [1994] I.R.L.R. 119; [1994] F.S.R. 535, HC 3.1.2.5

G.M.B. v. Rankin and Harrison [1992] I.R.L.R. 514, EAT 8.3.3.5
Gale v. Northern General Hospital NHS Trust; *sub nom.* Northern General Hospital
    NHS Trust v. Gale [1994] I.C.R. 426; [1994] I.R.L.R. 292, CA.................. 9.4.2
Galt v. British Railways Board [1983] 133 N.L.J. 870 .... 3.3.1.3
Gardner Ltd v. Beresford [1978] I.R.L.R. 63, EAT...................................... 5.3.3
Garland v. British Rail Engineering [1983] 2 A.C. 751; [1982] 2 W.L.R. 918, HL....... 6.1.1,
    6.1.3, 6.2.8
Garner v. Grange Furnishing Ltd [1977] I.R.L.R. 206, EAT.................... 5.3.2, 7.2.1.5
Gascol Conversions Ltd v. Mercer [1974] I.C.R. 420; 118 S.J. 219; [1974] I.R.L.R. 155,
    CA.. 2.2, 2.8.4, 5.2.2
General Billposting v. Atkinson [1909] A.C. 118, HL 3.1.4.5
General Cleaning Contractors Ltd v. Christmas [1953] A.C. 180; [1953] 2 W.L.R. 6;
    [1952] 2 All E.R. 1110, HL... 3.3.1.2, 3.3.1.3
General Rolling Stock Co., Re (Chapman's Case) (1866) L.R. 1 Eq. 346; (1872) L.R. 7
    Ch. 646 .... 5.5.3
General of the Salvation Army v. Dewsbury [1984] I.C.R. 498; [1984] I.R.L.R. 222,
    EAT.. 1.2, 7.2.8
George v. Beecham Group (Case No. 29 759/76) [1977] I.R.L.R. 43, IT............. 7.5.5.2
—— v. Davies [1911] 2 K.B. 445; [1911–13] All E.R. Rep. 914; 80 L.J.K.B. 924; 104 L.T.
    648; 27 T.L.R. 415, DC 5.5.2
Gerster v. Freistaat Bayern (Case C–1/95) [1998] I.C.R. 327; [1997] I.R.L.R. 699,
    ECJ... 6.3.3.3
Gibbons v. Associated British Ports [1985] I.R.L.R. 376, HC 2.4.3
Gilbert v. Kembridge Fibres Ltd [1984] I.C.R. 188; [1984] I.R.L.R. 52, EAT.......... 7.2.6
Gillespie v. Northern Health and Social Services Board (C–342/93) [1996] All E.R.
    (E.C.) 284; [1996] I.C.R. 498; [1996] I.R.L.R. 214, ECJ......... 10.3, 10.4.1.3, 10.5.2.1,
    10.5.5, 10.5.6
Gillies v. Richard Daniels and Co. Ltd [1979] I.R.L.R. 457, EAT 5.3.3
Gimber & Sons Ltd v. Spurrett [1976] 2 I.T.R. 308 .... 8.3.1.3
Glasgow City Council v. Zafar; *sub nom.* Strathclyde RC v. Zafar [1997] 1 W.L.R. 1659;
    [1998] I.R.L.R. 36, HL 6.3.7
Goodwin v. Cabletel U.K. Ltd [1998] I.C.R. 112; [1997] I.R.L.R. 665, EAT........... 7.4.4
Governing Body of Clifton Middle School v. Askew [1997] I.C.R. 808, EAT 9.3.7
Governing Body of the Northern Ireland Hotel and Catering College and North Eastern
    Education and Literary Board v. National Assoiacion of Teachers in Further and
    Higher Education [1995] I.R.L.R. 83, CA...................................... 9.2.2
Grant v. South West Trains Ltd (Case C–249/96) [1998] 1 F.C.R. 377; [1998] I.R.L.R.
    206, ECJ.. 2.5.2, 6.3.4.2
Graves v. Cohen (1929) 46 T.L.R. 21 .... 5.5.3
Gray v. Smith, COIT Case No. 03216–17/95, IDS Brief 584/March 1997.. 2.8.3, 3.3.3, 10.4.1.6
Greater Glasgow Health Board v. Carey [1987] I.R.L.R. 484, EAT 10.4.2.3
Greater Manchester Police Authority v. Lea [1990] I.R.L.R. 372, EAT............... 6.3.3.3
Green & Son (Castings) Ltd v. A.S.T.M.S. [1984] I.C.R. 352; [1984] I.R.L.R. 135,
    EAT.. 8.3.3.4
Gregory v. Tudsbury Ltd [1982] I.R.L.R. 267, IT 10.2
Griffin v. London Pension Fund Authority [1993] I.C.R. 564; [1993] I.R.L.R. 248,
    EAT.. 6.1.1
Griffin and Others v. South West Water Services Ltd [1995] I.R.L.R. 15, Ch D........ 2.7.1,
    8.3.3.1
Griggs v. Duke Power Co., 401 U.S. 424 (1971) 6.3.3.1
Grimaldi v. Fonds des Maladies Professionelles (Case C–322/88) [1990] I.R.L.R. 400;
    [1989] E.C.R. 4407, ECJ... 6.12, 6.3.4.1
Groener v. Minister for Education (Case C–379/87) [1989] E.C.R. 3967; 1 C.M.L.R. 401,
    ECJ 1.6
Grundy v. Sun Printing and Publishing Association (1916) 33 T.L.R. 77, CA.......... 5.4.1
Gunton v. Richmond-upon-Thames L.B.C. [1981] 1 W.L.R. 28; [1982] Ch. 448; [1980]
    I.R.L.R. 321, HL 5.3.2.2, 5.3.2.3, 5.6.2

Habermann-Beltermann v. Arbeiterwohlfahrt, Bezirksverband Ndb/OpfeV (Case C–421/92) [1994] I.R.L.R. 364, ECJ 10.3
Haden Ltd v. Cowen [1982] I.R.L.R. 314, CA 8.3.1.1, 8.3.1.3
Halford v. United Kingdom [1997] I.R.L.R. 471, ECHR 3.3.5
Halfpenny v. IGE Medical Systems Ltd [1997] I.C.R. 1007; [1998] I.R.L.R. 10, EAT 10.4.1.6, 10.4.2.6
Hall v. Woolston Hall Leisure Ltd, I.R.L.B. 591, April 1998, p. 14 .... 6.3.8
Hall (HM Inspector of Taxes) v. Lorimer [1994] 1 W.L.R. 209; [1994] 1 All E.R. 250; [1994] I.R.L.R. 171, CA 1.14
Hamlyn & Co. v. Wood & Co. [1891] 2 Q.B. 488, CA 2.3, 5.2.1.4
Hammersmith and Fulham L.B.C. v. Jesuthasan. *The Times*, March 5, 1998 .... 1.14.1
Hampson v. Department of Education and Science [1991] 2 A.C. 171; [1990] 3 W.L.R. 42; [1990] 2 All E.R. 25; [1990] I.R.L.R. 302, CA 6.3.3.3, 10.4.2.3
Handels- og Kontorfunktionaererernes Forbund i Danmark (acting for Pedersen and Others v. Faellesfoeningen for Danmaks Brugsforeninger (acting for Kvickly Skive and Others) (Case C–66/96), ECJ Employment Law Watch No. 5, Spring 1998 ... 10.5.6
Handels- og Kontorfunktionaererernes Forbund i Danmark v. Dansk Arbejdsgiverforening (acting for Danfoss) (Case C–109/88) [1989] I.R.L.R. 532; [1991] I.C.R. 74, ECJ 6.2, 6.3.7
—— v. —— (Case C–179/88) [1992] I.C.R. 332; [1991] I.R.L.R. 31, ECJ 10.3
—— v. —— (Case C–400/95) [1997] I.R.L.R. 643, ECJ 7.4.3, 10.3, 10.4.1.6, 10.8
Hannan v. TNT–IPEC (U.K.) Ltd [1986] I.R.L.R. 165, EAT 7.3
Hanover Insurance v. Schapiro [1994] I.R.L.R. 82, CA 3.1.4.3, 3.1.4.4
Hanson v. Fashion Industries (Hartlepool) Ltd [1981] I.C.R. 35; [1980] I.R.L.R. 393, EAT 7.2.8.2
Hardwick v. Leeds AHA [1975] I.R.L.R. 319, IT 7.3.2.1
Harman v. Flexible Lamps Ltd [1980] I.R.L.R. 418, EAT 5.3.1
Harmer v. Cornelius (1858) 5 C.B.(N.S.) 236 .... 3.1.5
Harris and Russell Ltd v. Slingsby [1973] 3 All E.R. 31; [1973] I.C.R. 454, NIRC 3.1.2.3, 5.4.2
Harrison v. Kent County Council [1995] I.C.R. 434, EAT 1.9.3
Harrods Ltd v. Remick [1998] 1 All E.R. 52; [1998] I.C.R. 156; [1997] I.R.L.R. 583, CA 1.15
Harvey v. Institute of the Motor Industry (No. 2) [1995] I.R.L.R. 416, EAT 7.2.8
Hassard v. McGrath and Northern Ireland Housing Executive (NIHE) unreported, December 6, 1996, NICA 9.4.2
Hay v. George Hanson (Building Contractors) Ltd [1996] I.R.L.R. 427, EAT 9.8.3
Hayes v. Malleable Working Men's Club and Institute [1985] I.C.R. 703; [1985] I.R.L.R. 367, EAT 10.3
Hayward v. Cammell Laird Shipbuilders (No. 2) [1988] A.C. 894; [1988] 2 W.L.R. 1134; [1988] 2 All E.R. 257; [1988] 2 C.M.L.R. 528, HL 6.2, 6.2.5
Heald v. NCB [1988] I.R.L.I.B, CA 7.3.2.2
Heath v. Longman (Meat Salesmen) Ltd [1973] 2 All E.R. 1228; [1973] I.C.R. 407, NIRC 7.2.5
Hedley Bryne & Co. Ltd v. Heller & Partners Ltd [1964] A.C. 465; [1963] 3 W.L.R. 100, HL 3.3.2, 3.3.2.1
Hellmut Marschall v. Land Nordrhein-Westfalen (Case C–409/95) [1997] All E.R. (E.C.) 865; [1998] I.R.L.R. 39, ECJ 1.15
Hellyer Brothers v. McLeod; Boston Deep Sea Fisheries v. Wilson [1987] 1 W.L.R. 728; [1987] I.C.R. 526; [1987[I.R.L.R. 232, CA 1.14.4
Hendry (P.M.) and Hendry (E.M.) v. Scottish Liberial Club Case No. 5/1290/76 [1977] I.R.L.R. 5, IT 1.8, 7.4.10
Henke v. Gemeincle Schierke and Verwaltungsgemeinschaft "Brocken" (Case C–298/94) [1996] I.R.L.R. 701, ECJ 9.3.7
Hereford & Worcester County Council v. Clayton I.R.L.B. 565, March 1997; *The Times*, October 8, 1996 .... 6.3.4.1
Hetton Victory Club v. Swainston [1983] I.C.R. 341; (1983) 127 S.J. 171; [1983] I.R.L.R. 164, CA 7.2.2

Heyman v. Darwins Ltd [1942] A.C. 356; [1942] 1 All E.R. 337 .... 3.1.4.5
Hickey v. Lucas Service U.K. Ltd, Case No. 1400979/96, Health and Safety Bulletin 260,
    August 1997 .... 10.6
High Table v. Horst [1997] I.R.L.R. 513, CA.................... 2.2, 5.2.1.4, 7.3.2.4, 8.3.1.3
Hill v. C.A. Parsons & Co. [1972] 1 Ch. 305; [1971] 3 W.L.R. 995, CA..... 5.3.2.2, 5.6.3, 5.6.4
Hill (R.F.) Ltd v. Mooney [1981] I.R.L.R. 258, EAT 5.3.3
Hilton International Hotels (U.K.) Ltd v. Kaissi [1994] I.C.R. 578; [1994] I.R.L.R. 270,
    EAT 10.4.1.6, 10.4.2.6
Hindes v. Supersine Ltd [1979] I.C.R. 517; [1979] I.R.L.R. 343, EAT 8.3.5.1
Hivac v. Park Royal Scientific Instruments Ltd [1946] Ch. 169; [1946] 1 All E.R. 350,
    CA 3.1.2.3
HM Prison Service v. Johnson; Armitage v. Johnson; Marsden v. Johnson; Johnson v.
    HM Prison Service [1997] I.C.R. 275; [1997] I.R.L.R. 162, EAT 6.3.8
Hofmann v. Barmer Ersatzkasse (No. 184/83) [1985] I.C.R. 731; [1986] 1 C.M.L.R. 242;
    [1984] E.C.R. 3047, ECJ 10.5.2.1
Hogg v. Dover College [1990] I.C.R. 39, EAT 5.3.3
Hollister v. National Farmers Union [1979] I.R.L.R. 238; [1979] I.C.R. 542, CA... 7.3.2.4, 8.4
Holman v. Johnson (1775) 1 Cowp. 341 .... 7.2.3
Home Office v. Holmes [1985] 1 W.L.R. 71; (1984) 128 S.J. [1984] I.C.R. 678, EAT... 6.3.3.1,
                                                          6.3.3.3, 10.4.2.3
——— v. Robinson [1981] I.R.L.R. 524, EAT 7.2.4
Hong Kong Fir Shipping v. Kawasaki Kisen Kaisha [1962] 2 Q.B. 26; [1962] 2 W.L.R.
    474, CA 5.3.2
Hooper v. British Railways Board [1988] I.R.L.R. 517, CA..................... 2.2, 7.3.2.2
Horsey v. Dyfed County Council [1982] I.C.R. 755; [1982] I.R.L.R. 395, EAT.... 6.3.1, 6.3.4.3
Hotston v. Wisbech Conservative Club [1984] I.C.R. 859; [1984] I.R.L.R. 422, EAT ... 7.3
Housing Services Agency v. Cragg [1997] I.C.R. 1050; [1997] I.R.L.R. 380, EAT...... 7.2.1.6,
                                                                   8.3.7.1
Howard v. Department for National Savings [1981] 1 W.L.R. 542; (1980) 125 S.J. 306;
    [1981] I.R.L.R. 40, CA 7.2.10
——— v. Pickford Tool Co. Ltd [1951] 1 K.B. 417; 95 S.J. 44, CA............. 3.1.2.3, 5.3.2.3
Howman & Son v. Blyth [1983] I.C.R. 416; [1983] I.R.L.R. 139, EAT............ 2.3, 4.3.1.1
Hughes v. D.H.S.S. [1985] A.C. 776; [1985] I.C.R. 419; [1985] I.R.L.R. 263, HL....... 7.2.10
——— v. Gwynedd Area Health Authority [1978] I.C.R. 161; [1977] I.R.L.R. 436,
    EAT 5.3.1
Hurley v. Mustoe [1981] I.C.R. 490; (1981) 125 S.J. 374; [1981] I.R.L.R. 208, EAT 6.3.1
Huvig v. France (1990) 12 E.H.R.R. 528, ECHR 3.3.5
Hyland v. J.H. Barker (North West) Ltd [1985] I.C.R. 861, EAT 7.2.3

Iceland Frozen Foods v. Jones [1983] I.C.R. 17; [1982] I.R.L.R. 439, EAT 7.3.3
Igbo v. Johnson Matthey Chemicals [1986] I.C.R. 505; (1986) 130 S.J. 524; [1986]
    I.R.L.R. 215, CA 5.3.2.3, 7.2.1.2, 7.2.6
Imperial Group Pension Trust v. Imperial Tobacco [1991] 1 W.L.R. 589; [1991] 2 All
    E.R. 597; [1991] I.C.R. 524; [1991] I.R.L.R. 66, HC...................... 2.2, 3.2.1
Industrial Rubber Products v. Gillon (1977) 13 I.T.R. 100; [1977] I.R.L.R. 389, EAT... 5.3.2,
                                                                   5.3.3
Ingram v. Foxon [1984] I.C.R. 685; [1985] I.R.L.R. 5, EAT 7.2.8.1
Initial Services Ltd v. Putterill [1968] 1 Q.B. 396; [1967] 3 W.L.R. 1032; [1967] 3 All E.R.
    145, CA 3.1.3.3, 3.1.3.4
Insitu Cleaning Co. Ltd v. Heads [1995] I.R.L.R. 4, EAT 6.3.4.1
Institute of the Motor Industry v. Harvey [1992] I.C.R. 470; [1992] I.R.L.R. 343,
    EAT 10.4.2.2, 10.4.2.6
International Computers Ltd v. Kennedy [1981] I.R.L.R. 28. EAT 5.4.1
International Sports Co. Ltd v. Thomson [1980] I.R.L.R. 340, EAT 7.3.2.1
Irani v. Southampton and Southwest Hampshire Health Authority [1985] I.C.R. 509;
    [1985] I.R.L.R. 203, HC 5.6.3
Ironmonger v. Movefield Ltd [1988] I.R.L.R. 461, EAT 1.14.5

Irving v. Post Office]1987] I.R.L.R. 289, CA 6.3.4.1
Iske v. P & O European Ferries (Dover) Ltd [1997] I.R.L.R. 401, EAT 10.5.2.1, 10.6

James v. Eastleigh Borough Council [1990] 2 A.C. 751; [1990] 3 W.L.R. 55; [1990]
    I.R.L.R. 288, HL 6.3.1, 6.3.4.3, 10.3
James W. Cook & Co. (Wivenhoe) Ltd v. Tipper [1990] I.C.R. 716; [1990] I.R.L.R. 386,
    CA 7.5.5.2, 8.4
Janciuk v. Winerite Ltd [1998] I.R.L.R. 63, EAT 5.3.2.3, 5.6.2, 7.3.1
Janes Solicitors v. Lamb-Simpson, 323/94, EAT 1.12
Janstorp International (U.K.) Ltd v. Allen [1990] I.C.R. 779; [1990] I.R.L.R. 417,
    EAT 4.2.2
Jenkins v. Kingsgate (Clothing Productions) Ltd (Case C–96/80) [1981] 1 W.L.R. 1485;
    (1981) 125 S.J. 587; [1981] I.C.R. 592; [1981] I.R.L.R. 228, ECJ   6.1.1, 6.1.3, 6.2.1.2, 6.2.6
Jepson and Dyas-Elliot v. The Labour Party [1996] I.R.L.R. 116, IT 1.15
J. H. Walker Ltd v. Hussain; *sub nom.* Hussain v. J. H. Walker Ltd; Azam v. J. H.
    Walker Ltd [1996] I.C.R. 291; [1996] I.R.L.R. 11, EAT 6.3.8
Joel v. Cammell Laird (Ship Repairers) Ltd [1969] I.T.R. 206, IT 2.4.2
—— v. Morrison (1834) 6 C. & P. 501, NP 6.3.4.1
John Brown Engineering Ltd v. Brown and Others [1997] I.R.L.R. 90, EAT 8.3.4.1
Johnson v. Chief Adjudication Officer (No. 2) [1995] 2 All E.R. (E.C.) 258; [1995] I.C.R.
    375; [1995] I.R.L.R. 157, ECJ 6.2.1.2
—— v. Nottingham Combined Police Authority [1974] 1 W.L.R. 358; [1974] I.C.R. 170,
    CA 8.3.2.1
—— v. Peabody Trust [1996] I.R.L.R. 387, EAT 5.2.1.4
Johnson-Croft v. Mezzo Ltd, Case No. 2202467/96, IRLB 586, February 1998, p. 11 ... 6.3.4.3
Johnstone v. Bloomsbury Health Authority [1992] Q.B. 333; [1991] 2 W.L.R. 1362;
    [1991] 2 All E.R. 293; [1991] I.R.L.R. 118, CA 2.2, 2.3, 3.3.1.2, 3.3.1.3
Jones v. Associated Tunnelling Ltd [1981] I.R.L.R. 477, EAT 2.3, 2.5.1, 2.8.4, 5.2.3.1,
    7.2.1.5
—— v. F. Sirl & Son (Furnishers) Ltd [1997] I.R.L.R. 493, EAT 5.3.2, 7.2.15
—— v. Gwent County Council [1992] I.R.L.R. 521, HC 5.6.4
—— v. Manchester Corporation [1952] 2 Q.B. 852; [1952] 1 T.L.R. 1589; [1952] 2 All
    E.R. 125; CA 3.1.5
—— v. Tower Boot Co. Ltd [1997] 2 All E.R. 406; [1997] I.C.R. 254; [1997] I.R.L.R.
    168, CA 6.3.4.1, 6.3.6
Jones, O'Brien v. Associated Fire Alarms [1968] 1 W.L.R. 1916; (1968) 112 S.J. 232,
    CA 2.5.1
Jules Dethier Equipment S.A. v. Dassy (Case C–319/94), *The Times*, March 18, 1998 .. 9.9

Kalanke v. Freie Hansestadt Bremen (Case C–450/93) [1995] I.R.L.R. 660, ECJ... 1.15, 2.7.3
Kampelmann v. Landschaftsverband Westfalen-Lippe; Stadtwerke Witten GmbH v.
    Schade; Haseley v. Stadtwerke Altena GmbH (Joined Cases C–253/96 to C–258/96)
    [1998] I.R.L.R. 333, ECJ 2.8
Katsikas v. Konstantinidis (Case C–132/91, 138/91, 139/91) December 16, 1992 [1993]
    I.R.L.R. 179, ECJ 9.8.3, 9.9
Kaufhaus GmbH v. Weber Von Hartz (Case C–170/84) [1986] I.R.L.R. 317, ECJ 6.1.1
Keane v. Clerical Medical Investment Group Ltd, Bristol, June 19, 1997 (IDS Brief 595),
    IT 9.2.6
Kelly v. Liverpool Maritime Terminal Ltd [1988] I.R.L.R. 310, CA 10.4.2.2, 10.4.2.6
Kenny v. South Manchester College [1993] I.C.R. 934; [1993] I.R.L.R. 265, HC 9.3.4
Kent County Council v. Gilham (No. 1) [1985] I.C.R. 227; [1985] I.R.L.R. 16, CA 7.2.9
Kent Management Services Ltd v. Butterfield [1992] I.C.R. 272; [1992] I.R.L.R. 394,
    EAT 4.4.1
Kerr v. The Sweater Shop (Scotland) Ltd; The Sweater Shop (Scotland) Ltd v. Park
    [1996] I.R.L.R. 424, EAT 4.4.1
Khanna v. Ministry of Defence [1981] I.C.R. 653; [1981] I.R.L.R. 331, EAT 6.3.7
Kidd v. D.R.G. (U.K.) Ltd [1986] I.C.R. 405; [1985] I.R.L.R. 190, EAT 6.3.3.2, 8.3.4.2
King v. The Great Britain-China Centre [1992] I.C.R. 516; [1991] I.R.L.R. 513, CA ... 6.3.7

Klass v. Germany [1979] 2 E.H.R.R. 214, ECHR 3.3.5
Kolfor Plant Ltd v. Wright [1982] I.R.L.R. 311, EAT..................... 10.4.2.5, 10.4.26
Kording v. Senator Fur Finanzen (Case C–100/95) [1997] I.R.L.R. 710, ECJ.......... 6.3.3.3
Kournavous v. J.R. Masterton & Sons (Demolition) [1990] I.C.R. 387; [1989] I.R.L.R.
    119, EAT 4.2.2
Kulatilake v. Nottingham Area Health Authority, October 17, 1980, CA 5.6.3
Kwik Save Stores Ltd v. Greaves [1997] I.C.R. 629; [1997] I.R.L.R. 268, EAT....... 10.4.1.6,
    10.4.2.2, 10.4.2.6, 10.8

Lagerwall v. Wilkinson Henderson & Clarke Ltd (1899) 80 L.T. 55 .... 1.3
Lancashire Fires Ltd v. SA Lyons & Company Ltd [1996] F.S.R. 629, [1997] I.R.L.R.
    113, CA 3.1.2, 3.1.2.3, 3.1.3.1
Landsorganisation i Danmark v. Ny Mølle Kro (Case C–287/86) [1989] I.R.L.R. 37,
    ECJ 9.3.1, 9.3.2, 9.3.4
Lane v. Shire Roofing Company (Oxford) Ltd [1995] I.R.L.R. 493; [1995] P.I.Q.R. P417,
    CA 1.14
Langston v. Amalgamated Union of Engineering Workers [1974] 1 W.L.R. 185; [1974] 1
    All E.R. 980; [1974] I.C.R. 180, CA.. 1.3
Lansing Linde Ltd v. Kerr [1991] W.L.R. 251; [1991] 1 All E.R. 418; [1991] I.C.R. 428,
    CA 3.1.2.6, 3.1.3.1, 3.1.4, 3.1.4.4
Lasertop Ltd v. Webster [1997] I.C.R. 828; [1997] I.R.L.R. 498, EAT............... 6.3.5
Lavery v. Plessey Telecommunications Ltd [1983] I.C.R. 534; [1983] I.R.L.R. 202, CA... 10.4,
    10.4.2.2, 10.4.2.5, 10.4.2.6
Laughton and Hawley v. BAPP Industrial Supplies [1986] I.C.R. 634; [1986] I.R.L.R.
    245, EAT 3.1.2.3
Laws v. London Chronicle (Indicator Newspapers) Ltd [1959] 1 W.L.R. 698; [1959] 2 All
    E.R. 285; 103 S.J. 470, CA....................................... 3.1, 5.3.4
Ledernes Hovedorganisation v. Dansk Arbejdsgiverforening (Case C–48/94) [1996]
    I.R.L.R. 51; [1996] I.C.R. 333; Rygaard [1996] I.R.L.R. 51, ECJ 9.3.6
Leicester University Students Union v. Mahomed [1995] I.C.R. 270; [1995] I.R.L.R. 292,
    EAT 8.4.1
Leighton v. Doyle (1982) 11 I.L.J. 185 .... 2.5.1
Leighton v. Michael [1995] I.C.R. 1091; [1996] I.R.L.R. 67, EAT........... 6.2.1, 6.3.8, 7.2.3
Lesney Products Ltd v. Nolan [1977] I.C.R. 235; (1976) 12 I.T.R. 6; [1977] I.R.L.R. 77,
    CA 8.3.1.2
Leverton v. Clwyd County Council [1989] 2 W.L.R. 47; (1989) 133 S.J. 45; [1989]
    I.R.L.R. 28, HL..................................... 6.2, 6.2.2, 6.2.4
Lewis v. Motorworld [1986] I.C.R. 157; [1985] I.R.L.R. 465, CA............... 3.2.1, 7.2.1.5
Lewis Woolf Griptight Ltd v. Corfield [1997] I.R.L.R. 432, EAT... 10.4.1.6, 10.4.2.2, 10.4.2.4,
    10.4.2.6
Lightfoot v. D & J Sporting Ltd [1996] I.R.L.R. 64, EAT 7.2.3
Lignacite Products Ltd v. Krollman [1979] I.R.L.R. 22, EAT 8.3.7.4
Links (A.) & Co. Ltd v. Rose, 1993 S.L.T. 209; [1991] I.R.L.R. 353, CS............. 7.3.2.1
Lister v. Romford Ice and Cold Storage Co. Ltd [1956] 2 Q.B. 180, CA; [1957] A.C. 555;
    [1957] 2 W.L.R. 258; 1 All E.R. 125, HL............................ 2.3, 3.1.5
Litster v. Forth Dy Dock & Engineering Co. Ltd [1990] 1 A.C. 546; [1989] 2 W.L.R. 634;
    [1989] 1 All E.R. 1134; [1989] I.C.R. 341, HL 9.8.1
Littlewoods Organisation v. Egenti [1976] I.C.R. 516; [1976] I.R.L.R. 334, EAT.. 7.3.1, 7.3.2.1
—— v. Harris [1977] 1 W.L.R. 1472; (1977) 121 S.J. 727, CA.................. 3.1.3.1, 5.6.2
Liverpool City Council v. Irwin [1977] A.C. 239; (1976) 238 E.G. 879, H.L....... 2.3, 5.2.1.4
Liversidge v. London Residuary Body [1989] I.C.R. 228, 87 L.G.R. 339, EAT......... 7.2.8
Living Design (Home Improvements) Ltd v. Davidson [1994] I.R.L.R. 67...... 3.1.4.5, 3.1.4.6
Lloyds Bank v. Secretary of State for Employment [1979] I.C.R. 258; [1979] 1 W.L.R.
    498, EAT 7.2.8.1
Lock v. Cardiff Railway Co. Ltd [1998] I.R.L.R. 358 .... 2.6.2
Logan Salton v. Durham CC [1989] I.R.L.R. 99, EAT.......................... 7.2, 7.2.6
London Transport Executive v. Clarke [1981] I.C.R. 355; (1981) 125 S.J., CA......... 5.3.2.2
London Underground v. Edwards (No. 2) [1997] I.R.L.R. 157, EAT..... 6.3.3.2, 6.3.3.3, 6.3.8

Lord Advocate v. Scotsman Publications [1990] 1 A.C. 815; [1989] 3 W.L.R. 358, HL;
   1988 S.L.T. 490, CS 1.9.3
Loughran and Kelly v. Northern Ireland Housing Executive [1998] I.R.L.R. 70,
   NICA 1.15
Lumley v. Wagner (1852) 1 De. G.M. & G. 604 .... 5.3.2.2

M v. Chief Constable of West Midlands Police (08964/96), *People Management*, April 3,
   1977 .... 6.3.4.2
M & S Drapers v. Reynolds [1957] 1 W.L.R. 9; 101 S.J. 44, CA 3.1.4.4
M.S.F. v. G.E.C. Ferranti (Defence Systems) Ltd (No. 2) [1994] I.R.L.R. 113, EAT ... 8.3.3.3
Macarthys v. Smith (No. 129/79) [1981] Q.B. 180; [1980] I.C.R. 672, ECJ........ 6.2.2, 6.2.6.
McLaren v. Home Office [1990] I.C.R. 824; (1990) 134 S.J. 908; [1990] I.R.L.R. 338,
   CA 5.6.4
McCree v. Tower Hamlets LBC 90 L.G.R. 137; [1992] I.C.R. 99; [1992] I.R.L.R. 56,
   EAT 4.4.1
McCulloch v. Moore [1968] 1 Q.B. 360; [1967] 2 W.L.R. 1366, DC 2.2
McDonald's Corp. and McDonald's Restaurants Ltd v. Steel and Morris, June 19, 1997,
   QBD 5.5.2
McFarlane v. E E Caledonia [1994] 2 All E.R. 1; [1994] 1 Lloyd's Rep. 16, CA 3.3.1.3
McGregor v. GMBATU [1987] I.C.R. 505; (1987) 84 L.S.Gaz. 497, EAT 6.2.6
McLaren v. National Coal Borad [1988] I.C.R. 370; [1988] I.R.L.R. 215, CA 7.3.1
Maclea v. Essex Line (1933) 45 LL. L. Rep. 254, DC 2.4.2
McClory v. Post Office [1993] 1 All E.R. 457; [1992] I.C.R. 758; [1993] I.R.L.R. 159,
   HC 2.2, 3.2.1
McMeechan v. Secretary of State for Employment [1997] I.C.R. 549; [1997] I.R.L.R. 353,
   CA 1.14.4, 1.14.5, 1.15
MacMillan v. Edinburgh Voluntary Organisations Council [1995] I.R.L.R. 536, EAT... 6.3.8
Macmillan Inc. v. Bishopgate Investment Trust (No. 2) [1993] I.C.R. 385, [1993] I.R.L.R.
   393, HC 3.1.2
McNee v. Charles Tennant & Co. Ltd [1989] I.C.R. 747, EAT 7.5.5.2
McNeill v. Messrs Charles Crimin (Electrical Contractors) Ltd [1984] I.R.L.R. 179,
   EAT 5.3.3
McPherson v. Dumpark House [1997] I.R.L.R. 277, EAT................ 10.4.1.6, 10.4.2.6
—— v. Rathgael Centre [1991] I.R.L.R. 206; [1990] N.I. 370, NICA 6.2.6
Magorrian and Cunningham v. Eastern Health and Social Services Board and Depart-
   ment of Health and Social Services (Case C–246/96) [1998] I.R.L.R. 86, ECJ 6.2.1.2
Mains v. M.D. Homes (Case No. 2200316/96) noted in EOR Discrimination Case Law
   Digest No. 34 .... 10.2
Malik v. Bank of Credit and Commerce International SA (in liquidation) [1998] A.C. 20;
   [1997] 3 W.L.R. 95; [1997] 3 All E.R. 1; [1997] I.R.L.R. 462, HL... 2.3, 3.2.1, 3.3.3, 5.6.1,
                                                           5.7, 9.5
Malloch v. Aberdeen Corp. [1971] 1 W.L.R. 1578; 115 S.J. 756, HL 5.6.4
Malone v. United Kingdom (1984) 7 E.H.R.R. 14, ECHR 3.3.5
Mandla v. Lee [1983] 2 A.C. 548; [1983] 2 W.L.R. 260; [1983] I.R.L.R. 209, HL 6.3.3.2
Maredelanto Compania Naviera S.A v. Bergbau-Handel GmbH Mihalis Angelos, The
   [1971] 1 Q.B. 164; [1970] 3 W.L.R. 601, CA 5.3.2
Market Investigations Ltd v. Minister of Social Security [1969] 2 Q.B. 173; [1969] 2
   W.L.R. 1, HC 1.14
Marks & Spencer plc v. Martins, *The Times*, January 15, 1998 .... 6.3.1
Marleasing SA v. La Comercial Internacional de Alimentación SA (Case C–106/89)
   [1990] E.C.R. I–4135; [1992] C.M.L.R. 305, ECJ..................... 2.7.1, 6.1, 6.3.4.2
Marley v. Forward Trust Group Ltd [1986] I.C.R. 891; [1986] I.R.L.R. 369, CA.... 2.4, 2.4.1,
                                                           5.6.3
Marley Tile Co. Ltd v. Shaw [1980] I.C.R. 72; (1979) 123 S.J. 803, CA; reversing [1978]
   I.R.L.R. 238, EAT 7.4.2
Marriott v. Oxford District Co-operative Society Ltd [1969] 3 All E.R. 1126 .... 5.3.1
Marrison v. Bell [1939] 2 K.B. 187; [1939] 1 All E.R. 745; CA 4.3.1.1

Marschall (Case C–409/95) [1998] I.R.L.R. 39, ECJ 1.15
Marshall v. English Electric Ltd [1945] 1 All E.R. 653; (1945) 61 T.L.R. 379 .... 2.5.1
—— v. Harland & Wolff [1972] 1 W.L.R. 899; 116 S.J. 484; [1972] I.C.R. 101; [1972] I.R.L.R. 90, NIRC 5.5.1.1, 7.2.1.4
—— v. Industrial Systems & Control Ltd [1992] I.R.L.R. 294, EAT 3.1.2.3
—— v. N.M. Financial Management Ltd [1995] 1 W.L.R. 1461; [1995] 4 All E.R. 785; [1996] I.R.L.R. 20, Ch D 3.1.4.6
—— v. Southampton and South West Hampshire Area Health Authority (Teaching) (No. 152/84) [1986] I.R.L.R. 141, ECJ 2.7, 2.7.1, 6.1.2, 6.2.8, 7.2.8, 7.2.10
—— v. —— (No. 2) (Case C–261/91) [1993] I.R.L.R. 441; [1994] Q.B. 126; [1993] W.L.R. 1054, ECJ 2.6.1, 6.3.8
Marshall (Cambridge) Ltd v. Hamblin [1994] I.C.R. 362; [1994] I.R.L.R. 260, EAT 5.4.2
Marshall (Thomas) (Exports) v. Guinle [1979] Ch. 227; [1978] 3 W.L.R. 116; (1978) 122 S.J. 295; [1978] 3 All E.R. 193; [1978] I.C.R. 905, HC 3.1.2.3, 3.1.3, 3.1.3.1, 5.3.2.2
Marriott v. Oxford District Co-operative Society Ltd [1969] 1 Q.B. 186; 3 W.L.R. 984; [1969] 2 All E.R. 1126, CA 7.2
Martin v. Glynwed Distribution Ltd [1983] I.C.R. 511; [1983] I.R.L.R. 198, CA ... 7.2, 7.2.1.3, 7.5.3
Mason v. Provident Clothing Co. [1913] A.C. 724, HL 3.1.4.6
Massey v. Crown Life Insurance Co. [1978] I.C.R. 590; [1978] 1 W.L.R. 676, CA 1.14
Mathewson v. R.B. Wilson Dental Laboratory [1989] I.R.L.R. 512, EAT 7.5.5.2
Matthews v. Kuwait Bechtel Corp. [1959] 2 Q.B. 57; [1959] 2 W.L.R. 702; [1959] 2 All E.R. 345, CA 3.3.1.3
Maund v. Penwith District Council [1984] I.C.R. 143; [1984] I.R.L.R. 24, CA 7.4.1, 8.3.2.1
Meade and Baxendale v. British Fuels Ltd [1996] I.R.L.R. 541, EAT 2.4.3, 9.5
Meade-Hill v. British Council [1996] 1 All E.R. 79; [1995] I.R.L.R. 478; [1995] I.C.R. 847, CA 5.2.3.2, 5.6.4, 6.3.3.2, 6.3.3.3, 6.3.3.4
Mears v. Safecar Security [1982] 3 W.L.R. 366; [1982] 2 All E.R. 865; [1982] I.C.R. 626; [1982] I.R.L.R. 183, CA 2.3, 2.5.1, 2.8.2, 4.3.1, 5.2.4
Meechan v. Secretary of State for Scotland, 1997 S.L.T. 936 .... 9.6.1
Meek v. Port of London Authority [1918] 2 Ch. 96; 87 L.J. Ch. 376; 119 L.T. 196; 82 J.P. 225; 34 T.L.R. 420; 16 L.G.R. 483, CA 2.5.1
Meer v. London Borough of Tower Hamlets [1988] I.R.L.R. 399, CA 6.3.3.1
Mennell v. Newell & Wright (Transport Contractors) Ltd [1997] I.C.R. 1039; [1997] I.R.L.R. 519, CA 4.4.1, 7.4.8
Merckx v. Ford Motors Co. Belgium S.A. (Case C–171/94) [1996] All E.R. (E.C.) 667; [1996] I.R.L.R. 467, ECJ 9.3.6, 9.5
Merton London Borough Council v. Gardiner [1981] Q.B. 269; [1981] 2 W.L.R. 232; [1981] I.C.R. 269, EAT 7.2.8
Methven v. Cow Industrial Polymers Ltd [1980] I.C.R. 463; (1980) 124 S.J. 374, CA ... 6.2.6.1
Midland Foot Comfort Centre v. M.J. Richmond Nee Hoppett and Secretary of State for Employment [1973] 2 All E.R. 294; [1973] I.T.R. 223; [1973] I.C.R. 219; [1973] I.R.L.R. 141, NIRC 8.3.1.4
Milligan v. Securicor Cleaning Ltd [1995] I.C.R. 865; [1995] I.R.L.R. 288, EAT 7.4.9
Ministry of Defence v. Cannock [1995] 2 All E.R. 449; [1994] I.C.R. 918; [1994] I.R.L.R. 509, EAT 6.3.8
—— v. Jeremiah [1980] Q.B. 87; [1979] 3 W.L.R. 857; [1979] I.R.L.R. 436, CA 6.3.1, 6.3.3.4, 6.3.4.1
—— v. Wheeler [1998] 1 W.L.R. 637; [1998] 1 All E.R. 790; [1998] I.C.R. 242; [1998] I.R.L.R. 23 .... 6.3.8
Mirror Group Newspapers Ltd v. Gunning [1986] 1 W.L.R. 546; [1986] I.C.R. 145; [1986] I.R.L.R. 27, CA 1.15
Missing Link Software v. Magee [1989] F.S.R. 361 .... 3.1.2.2
Monie v. Coral Racing [1980] I.C.R. 109; [1980] I.R.L.R. 96, CA 7.3.2.2
Mont (U.K.) Ltd v. Mills [1993] F.S.R. 577; [1993] I.R.L.R. 172, CA 3.1.3, 3.1.4, 3.1.4.4
Montreal v. Montreal Locomotive Works Ltd [1947] 1 D.L.R. 161 .... 1.14
Moon v. Homeworthy Furniture (Northern) Ltd [1977] I.C.R. 117; [1976] I.R.L.R. 298, EAT 8.4

Moorcock, The [1889] 14 P.D. 64, CA 2.3
Moore v. Duport Furniture Products Ltd (1982) 126 S.J. 98; [1982] I.C.R 84; [1982]
    I.R.L.R. 31, HL 7.2.6
Mooyart v. Sakura Finance International Ltd (Case C–23565/95) E.O.R. Discrimination
    Case Law Digest, No. 33, Autumn 1997 .... 6.4.1
Morgan v. Manser [1948] 1 K.B. 184; [1947] 2 All E.R. 666 .... 5.5.1
—— v. West Glamorgan County Council [1995] I.R.L.R. 68, EAT 4.2.2
Morganite Electrical Carbon v. Donne [1988] I.C.R. 18; [1987] I.R.L.R. 363, EAT 7.5.5.2
Morley v. Heritage [1993] I.R.L.R. 400, CA 1.12
Morris v. Ford Motor Co. Ltd [1973] 1 Q.B. 792; [1973] 2 W.L.R. 843, CA........... 3.1.5
—— v. Saxelby [1916] 1 A.C. 688, HL........................... 3.1.3, 3.1.4, 3.1.4.4
—— v. Walsh Western U.K. Ltd [1997] I.R.L.R. 562, EAT 7.2.8.1
Morton Sundour Fabrics Ltd v. Shaw (1967) 2 I.T.R. 84 .... 5.3.1, 5.4.1
MRS Environmental Services v. Dyke, *The Times*, March 25, 1997, EAT .... 9.4.1.
—— v. Marsh (1996) 93(29) L.S.G. 28; (1996) 140 S.J.L.B. 186, CA 7.4.9
Mugford v. Midland Bank [1997] I.C.R. 399; [1997] I.R.L.R. 208, EAT......... 8.3.3, 8.3.3.2,
                                                                    8.3.4.1, 8.4
Mughal v. Reuters (1993) 137 S.J.L.B. 275; [1993] I.R.L.R. 571, HC............. 3.3.1.3
Mulrine v. University of Ulster [1993] I.R.L.R. 545, NICA................... 5.5.2, 7.2.1.6
Murphy v. Birrell & Sons [1978] I.R.L.R. 458, EAT 7.2.8.1
—— v. Epsom College [1984] I.R.L.R. 271; [1985] I.C.R. 80, CA; affirming [1983] I.C.R.
    715, EAT 8.3.1.2, 8.3.2.1
Mustad v. Dosen [1964] 1 W.L.R. 109n; [1963] R.P.C. 41; *sub nom.* Mustad (O.) & Son
    v. Allcock (S.) & Co. and Dosen [1963] All E.R. 416, H.L.. .... 3.1.3.1

N. Rees v. Raken International Ltd [1975] I.R.L.R. 342, IT 5.4.1
N.W.L. v. Woods; N.W.L. v. Nelson [1979] 1 W.L.R. 1294; [1979] I.C.R. 867, HL.. 3.1.4, 5.6.2
Nagarajan v. Agnew; Nagarajan v. London Underground; Swiggs v. Nagarajan [1995]
    I.C.R. 520; [1994] I.R.L.R. 61, EAT.................................... 6.3.6, 10.4.2.6
National Association of Schoolmasters [1996] I.C.R. 1003; [1996] I.R.L.R. 438; [1996]
    C.O.D. 378, QBD 8.3.3.1, 9.1.2, 9.2.1
National Coal Board v. Galley [1958] 1 W.L.R. 16; [1958] 1 All E.R. 91; 102 S.J. 31,
    CA 2.4.1, 2.4.3
—— v. National Union of Mineworkers [1986] I.C.R. 736; [1986] I.R.L.R. 439, CA...... 2.4,
                                                                    2.4.2, 5.6.3
—— v. Ridgway [1987] 3 All E.R. 582; [1987] I.C.R. 641; [1987] I.R.L.R. 80, CA 11.4.1
—— v. Sherwin [1978] I.C.R. 700; [1978] I.R.L.R. 122, EAT 6.2.3
National Heart and Chest Hospitals Board of Governors v. Nambiar [1981] I.C.R. 441;
    sub nom. Board of Governors National Heart and Chest Hospitals v. Nambiar
    [1981] I.R.L.R. 196, EAT 7.3.3
National Vulcan Engineering Insurance Group Ltd v. Wade [1979] 1 Q.B. 132; [1978] 3
    W.L.R. 214, CA 6.2.6
Neale v. Hereford and Worcester County Council [1986] I.C.R. 471, [1986] I.R.L.R. 168,
    CA 7.3.3
Neath v. Hugh Steeper Ltd (Case C–152/91) [1994] 1 All E.R. 929; [1995] I.C.R. 158,
    ECJ 6.1.1, 6.2.1.1
Neil v. Ford Motor Co. Ltd [1984] I.R.L.R. 339, EAT 6.2.5
Nelson v. British Broadcasting Corp. [1977] I.C.R. 649; (1977) 12 I.T.R. 273; [1977]
    I.R.L.R. 148, CA 2.2, 8.3.1, 8.3.1.3, 8.3.2.1
—— v. —— (No. 2) [1980] I.C.R. 110;)1979) 123 S.J. 552; [1979] I.R.L.R. 346, CA ... 8.3.5.2
Nerva v. R.L. & G. Ltd (1996) 92(23) L.S.G. 35; [1996] I.R.L.R. 461, CA 4.2
Nethermere (St Neots) Ltd v. Gardiner [1984] I.C.R. 612; [1984] I.R.L.R. 240, CA.... 1.14.3,
                                                                    1.14.4
Newland v. Simons & Willer (Hairdressers) Ltd [1981] I.C.R. 521; [1981] I.R.L.R. 359,
    EAT 7.2.3
Newns v. British Airways plc [1992] I.R.L.R. 575, CA........................... 3.3.6, 9.1

Nicoll v. Falcon Airways Ltd [1962] 1 Lloyd's Rep. 245 .... 5.4.1
Nimz v. Freie and Hansestadt Hamburg (Case C–184/89) E.C.R. I–297 [1991] I.R.L.R. 222, ECJ 6.2.1.1, 6.2.7
Nokes v. Doncaster Amalgamated Collieries Ltd [1940] A.C. 1014; [1940] 3 All E.R. 549, HL 5.5.3, 7.2.8.3, 9.1
Nolte v. Landesversicherungsanstalt Hannover (Case C–317/93) [1996] I.R.L.R. 225; [1996] All E.R. (E.C.) 212, ECJ 6.3.3.3
Noone v. North West Thames Regional Health Authority (No. 2) [1988] I.R.L.R. 195, CA 6.3.8
Nordenfelt v. Maxim Nordenfelt Guns & Ammunition Co. [1894] A.C. 595 .... 3.1.4.7
North East Coast Shiprepairers Ltd v. Secretary of State for Employment [1978] I.C.R. 755; (1978) 122 S.J. 348; [1978] I.R.L.R. 149, EAT 1.14.6
Northern Joint Police Board v. Power [1998] I.R.L.R. 610, EAT 6.3.3
Norton Tool Co. v. Tewson [1973] 1 W.L.R. 45; [1972] I.C.R. 501; [1972] I.R.L.R. 86, NICR 7.5.5.2
Nothman v. Barnett L.B.C. [1979] 1 W.L.R. 67; [1979] I.C.R. 111, HL 7.2.10
Nova Plastics v. Froggatt [1982] I.R.L.R 146, EAT 3.1.2.3
Nu Swift International Ltd v. Mallinson [1979] I.C.R. 157; [1978] I.R.L.R. 537, EAT 10.4.1.1, 10.4.2.1

O'Brien v. Sim-Chem Ltd [1980] 1 W.L.R. 1011; [1980] I.C.R. 573, HL 6.2.4
O'Dea v. I.S.C. Chemicals Ltd [1996] I.C.R. 222; [1995] I.R.L.R. 605, CA 8.3.2.3
Office Angels v. Rainer Thomas [1991] I.R.L.R. 214, CA 3.1.4.1, 3.1.4.3
Ojutiku and Oburoni v. Manpower Services Commission [1982] I.C.R. 661; [1982] I.R.L.R. 418, CA 6.3.3.3, 10.3
O'Kelly v. Trusthouse Forte [1984] Q.B. 90; [1983] 3 W.L.R. 605; [1983] I.R.L.R. 369, CA 1.14.4
O'Laoire v. Jackel International Ltd [1990] I.C.R. 197; [1990] I.R.L.R. 70, CA.... 5.6.1, 7.5.1, 7.5.5.2
O'Neill v. Governors of St Thomas More R.C.V.A. Upper School [1996] I.R.L.R. 372, EAT 10.4.2.4
Open University v. Triesman [1978] I.C.R. 524; [1978] I.R.L.R. 114, EAT 7.2.1.6
Oriental Bank Corp. Ltd, Re (McDowall's Case) (1886) 32 Ch. D. 366 .... 5.5.3
Orlando v. Didcot Power Station Sports and Social Club [1996] I.R.L.R. 262, EAT.... 6.3.8
Osbourne v. Thomas Bolton & Sons Ltd, Case 794/248, EAT...................... 10.4.2.1
Ottoman Bank v. Chakarian [1930] A.C. 277, PC 3.1
Outlook Supplies Ltd v. Parry [1978] 2 All E.R. 707; [1978] I.C.R. 388; [1978] I.R.L.R. 12, EAT 6.2.6.1
Owusu v. London Fire and Civil Defence Authority [1995] I.R.L.R. 574, EAT 6.3.8

P v. S Cornwall CC (Case C–13/94); sub nom. P v. S (Sex Discrimination) [1996] All E.R. (E.C.) 397; [1996] I.C.R. 795; [1996] I.R.L.R. 347, ECJ 6.3.4.2
Paal Wilson and Co. v. Partenreederei [1983] 1 A.C. 854; [1982] 3 W.L.R. 1149, HL .. 5.5.1.2
Palmer and Saunders v. Southend-on-Sea Borough Council [1984] 1 W.L.R. 1129; [1984] I.C.R. 372; [1984[I.R.L.R. 119, CA 7.2.1.7, 7.2.2
Paris v. Stepney Borough Council [1951] A.C. 367; [1951] 1 All E.R. 42; [1951] 1 T.L.R. 25, HL 3.3.1.2
Parker & Farr v. Shelvey [1979] I.C.R. 896; [1979] I.R.L.R. 434, EAT 7.5.5.2
Parkes Classic Confectionary v. Ashcroft [1973] I.T.R. 43, DC 2.8.2
Parkinson v. March Consulting Ltd [1997] I.R.L.R. 308, CA.................... 7.3, 8.4.1
Parsons (C.A.) & Co. Ltd v. McLoughlin [1978] I.R.L.R. 65, EAT 7.3.2.2
Partington v. N.A.L.G.O. [1981] I.R.L.R. 537; 1981 S.L.T. 184, CS 2.4
Patel v. Nagesan [1995] I.C.R. 988; [1995] I.R.L.R. 370, CA 7.2.10
Peake v. Automotive Products [1978] Q.B. 233; [1977] I.C.R. 968, CA; reversing [1977] I.R.L.R. 105, EAT 6.1.3, 6.3.1
Peal Assurance plc v. MSF EAT 1162/96, February 26, 1997, EAT 8.3.4
Pename Ltd t/a Storage Lifting & Distribution Co. v. Paterson [1989] I.C.R. 12; [1989] I.R.L.R. 195, EAT 4.4.1

Pendragon plc v. Jackson [1998] I.R.L.R. 17; [1997] 12 C.L. 174, EAT 7.5.1
Pepper v. Webb [1969 1 W.L.R. 514; [1969] 2 All E.R. 216; (1969) 113 S.J. 186, CA . . .   5.3.4
Perera v. Civil Service Commission (No. 2) [1983] I.C.R. 428l [1973] I.R.L.R. 166,
    CA 1.15, 6.3.3.1, 6.3.3.2
Pertemps Group plc v. Nixon July 1, 1993, EAT 1.14.5
Pfaffinger v. City of Liverpool Community College; Muller v. Amersham & Wycombe
    College [1996] I.R.L.R. 508, EAT 7.2.1.6
Philip Hodges & Co. v. Kell [1994] I.C.R. 656; [1994] I.R.L.R. 568, EAT 10.4.2.4
Phillips Products Ltd v. Hyland [1987] 1 W.L.R. 659; (1985) 129 S.J. 47, CA. 2.2
Photo Production Ltd v. Securicor Transport Ltd [1980] 2 W.L.R. 283; [1980] 1 All E.R.
    556; [1980] A.C. 827, HL 3.1.4.5
Pickstone v. Freemans plc [1988] 3 W.L.R. 265; [1988] 2 All E.R. 803; [1988] I.C.R. 697,
    HL 6.1.1, 6.2.5
Piggott Bros & Co. Ltd v. Jackson [1992] I.C.R. 85; [1991] I.R.L.R. 309, CA . . . . 3.3.1.2.
Pink v. White [1985] I.R.L.R. 489, EAT 8.3.1.1
Pointon v. University of Sussex [1979] I.R.L.R. 110, CA 6.2
Polkey v. Dayton (A.E.) Services [1988] A.C. 344; [1987] 3 W.L.R. 1153 [1988] I.C.R.
    142; [1987] I.R.L.R. 503, HL 7.3.2.1, 7.3.2.2, 7.5.5.2, 8.3.3.2, 8.3.4.1, 8.3.7.3
Porcelli v. Strathclyde Regional Council [1986] I.C.R. 564; [1986] I.R.L.R. 134, CS 6.3.4.1
Porter and Nanayakkara v. Queen's Medical Centre (Nottingham University Hospital)
    [1993] I.R.L.R. 486, HC 9.3.4, 9.8.2
Post Office v. Fennell [1981] I.R.L.R. 221, CA 7.3.2.2
——— v. Lewis (1997) 94(18) L.S.G. 32, (1997) 141 S.J.L.B. 105; The Times, April 25,
    1997 . . . .   7.5.3
——— v. Marney [1990] I.R.L.R. 170, EAT 7.3.1
——— v. Roberts [1980] I.R.L.R. 347, EAT 5.6.1
——— v. Union of Post Office Workers [1974] I.C.R. 378; [1974] 1 W.L.R. 89; [1974]
    I.R.L.R. 22, HL 7.4.2
Post Office (Counters) Ltd v. Heavy [1990] I.C.R. 1; [1989] I.R.L.R. 513, EAT 7.3
Potter v. Hunt Contracts [1992] I.C.R. 337; [1992] I.R.L.R. 108, EAT 4.4.1
——— v. Secretary of State for Employment [1997] I.R.L.R. 21, CA 5.5.3
Potters-Ballotini v. Weston-Baker [1977] R.P.C. 202, CA 3.1.3.2
Powdrill and Atkinson v. Watson [1995] 2 A.C. 394; [1995] 2 W.L.R. 314; [1995] I.R.L.R.
    269, HL 8.5.1
Powell v. London Borough of Brent [1988] I.C.R. 176; [1987] I.R.L.R. 466, CA 5.6.3
Preston v. Wolverhampton Healthcare NHS Trust; Fletcher v. Midland Bank plc [1998]
    1 W.L.R. 280; [1998] I.R.L.R. 197, HL 6.1.1, 6.2.1.2
Prestwick Circuits Ltd v. McAndrew, 1990 S.L.T. 654; [1990] I.R.L.R. 191, CS 2.3
Price v. Civil Service Commission [1977] 1 W.L.R. 1417; [1978] I.C.R. 2; [1977] I.R.L.R.
    291, EAT 6.3.3.3
——— v. ——— (No. 2) [1978] I.R.L.R. 3, IT 1.15, 6.3.8
——— v. Smithfield and Zwanenberg Group Ltd [1978] I.C.R. 93; (1977) 12 I.T.R. 465;
    [1978] I.R.L.R. 80, EAT 8.3.7
Printers & Finishers Ltd v. Holloway [1964] (No. 2) 3 All E.R. 731; [1965] 1 W.L.R. 1;
    109 S.J. 47 . . . . 3.1.3, 3.1.3.1, 3.1.3.3, 5.6.2
Pritchard Ltd v. Boon and Milton [1919] I.R.L.R. 19, EAT 5.4.1
Property Guards Ltd v. Taylor and Kershaw [1982] I.R.L.R. 175, EAT 1.8
Provident Financial Group and Whitegates Estate Agency v. Hayward [1989] 3 All E.R
    298; [1989] I.C.R. 160; [1989] I.R.L.R. 84, CA 3.1.2.4, 3.1.2.5, 3.1.3.1
PSM International and McKechnie v. Whitehouse and Willenhall Automation [1992]
    I.R.L.R. 279; [1992] F.S.R. 489, CA 3.1.3.2
Pubblico Ministero v. Ratti (No. 148/78) [1979] E.C.R. 1629; [1980] 1 C.M.L.R. 96,
    ECJ 2.7.1
Putick v. Eastbourne Borough Council, COIT 3106/2, IDS Brief 590/June 1997 . . . . . . .10.4.2.3

Quinnen v. Hovells [1984] I.C.R. 525; (1984) 128 S.J. 431; [1984] I.R.L.R. 227, EAT . .   1.15

R.S. Components Ltd v. Irwin [1974] 1 All E.R. 41; [1973] I.C.R. 535, NIRC 7.3.2.4

R. v. Associated Octel Ltd [1996] 1 W.L.R. 1543; [1996] 4 All E.R. 846; [1996] I.C.R. 972; [1997] I.R.L.R. 123; [1997] Crim. L.R. 355, HL 3.3.1

—— v. Birmingham C.C., ex p. Equal Opportunities Commission [1989] A.C. 1155; [1989] 2 W.L.R. 520; [1989] I.R.L.R. 173, HL..................... 6.3.1, 6.3.4.3, 10.3

—— v. British Coal Corp. [1993] I.R.L.R. 103, HC 8.3.3.1

—— v. British Coal Corp., ex p. Vardy [1996] I.R.L.R. 438, DC 9.2.3

—— v. Brown (Gregory Michael) [1996] 1 A.C. 543; [1996] 2 W.L.R. 203; [1996] 1 All E.R. 545, HL 1.9.3

—— v. Civil Service Appeal Board, ex p. Bruce [1988] I.C.R. 649, CA.............. 1.4

—— v. Hertfordshire County Council, ex p. N.U.P.E. [1985] I.R.L.R. 258 .... 5.6.4

—— v. Industrial Disputes Tribunal, ex p. Portland Urban District Council [1955] 1 W.L.R. 949; 99 S.J. 539, CA 2.4

—— v. Lord Chancellor's Department, ex p. Nangle [1992] 1 All E.R. 897; [1991] I.C.R. 743; [1991] I.R.L.R. 343, DC.. 1.4

—— v. Ministry of Defence, ex p. Smith; R. v. Admiralty Board of the Defence Council, ex p. Lustig-Prean; R. v. Admiralty Board of the Defence Council, ex p. Beckett; R. v. Ministry of Defence, ex p. Grady [1996] Q.B. 517; [1996] 2 W.L.R. 305; [1996] I.R.L.R. 100, CA 6.3.4.2

—— v. National Heart and Chest Hospitals, ex p. Pardhanani, September 21, 1984, CA 5.6.3

—— v. Secretary of State for Defence, ex p. Perkins (Case C–168/97) [1997] I.R.L.R. 297, HC 6.3.4.2

—— v. Secretary of State for Employment, ex p. E.O.C. [1994] I.R.L.R. 176; [1995] 1 A.C. 1; [1994] 2 W.L.R. 409; [1994] I.C.R. 317, HL; affirming [1993] I.C.R. 251, CA 1.14.1, 2.7, 6.1.1, 6.2.1, 6.3.3.3, 6.3.8, 6.4.1, 7.2.2, 7.2.6, 7.2.8, 10.3

—— v. ——, ex p. Seymour-Smith and Perez [1997] 2 All E.R. 273; [1997] I.R.L.R. 315, HL 6.1.1, 6.3.3.3, 7.2.8, 10.3

—— v. Secretary of State for Health, ex p. Richardson [1995] All E.R. (E.C.) 865; *The Times*, October 27, 1995, QBD 6.2.8

—— v. Southampton Industrial Tribunal, ex p. INS News Group and Express Newspapers Ltd [1995] I.R.L.R. 247; *The Times*, April 22, 1995, QBD 7.5

Rae v. Glasgow City Council and Strathclyde Joint Police Board, 1998 S.L.T. 292; 1997 Rep. L.R. 79 .... 3.3.1.2

Rainey v. Greater Glasgow Health Board [1987] A.C. 224; [1986] 3 W.L.R. 1017; [1987] 1 All E.R. 65; [1987] I.C.R. 129; [1987] I.R.L.R. 26; [1987] 2 C.M.L.R. 11, HL..... 6.2.6, 6.3.3.3

Rank Zerox v. Churchill [1988] I.R.L.R. 280, EAT........................ 2.2, 2.3, 5.2.1.4

—— v. Stryczek [1995] I.R.L.R. 568, EAT 7.5.5.1

Rankin v. British Coal Corp. [1995] I.C.R. 744; [1993] I.R.L.R. 69, EAT 6.2.1.3

Rao v. Civil Aviation Authority [1992] I.C.R. 503; [1992] I.R.L.R. 203, EAT 7.5.5.2

Rask and Christensen v. ISS Kantineservice A/S (Case C–209/91) [1993] I.R.L.R. 133, ECJ 9.3.4

Ratcliffe v. North Yorkshire County Council, British Coal Corp. v. Smith [1995] 3 All E.R. 597; [1995] I.R.L.R. 439, HL 6.2.6

Ready Mixed Concrete (South East) v. Minister of Pensions and National Insurance [1968] 2 Q.B. 497; [1968] 2 W.L.R. 755........................... 1.14, 1.14.3

Reed Packaging Ltd v. Boozer [1988] I.C.R. 391; [1988] I.R.L.R. 333, EAT 6.2.5, 6.2.6

Rees v. Apollo Watch Repairs [1996] I.C.R. 466, EAT 10.4.2.4

—— v. United Kingdom (No. 2/1985/88/135) [1987] 2 F.L.R. 111; (1987) 17 Fam. Law 157, ECHR 6.3.4.2

Reid v. Camphill Engravers [1990] I.C.R. 435; [1990] I.R.L.R. 268, EAT.............. 5.3.3

Reigate v. Union Manufacturing Co. (Ramsbottom Ltd) [1918] 1 K.B. 592 .... 5.2.1.4

Reiss Engineering Co. Ltd v. Harris [1985] I.R.L.R. 232, HC...................... 3.1.2.2

Republic Bonifaci v. Italian Republic (Cases C–6/90 and C–9/90) [1992] I.R.L.R. 84; [1991] E.C.R.I 5357; [1993] 2 C.M.L.R. 66, ECJ 9.3.5

Retarded Children's Aid Society v. Day [1978] 1 W.L.R. 763; [1978] I.C.R. 437; [1978] I.R.L.R. 128, CA 7.5.3

Rewcastle v. Safeway, Case 22482/89, IT 6.3.4.3

Rewe-Zentralfinanz eG v. Landwirtschaftskammer für das Saarland (No. 33/86) [1976]
    E.C.R. 1989, ECJ 6.2.1.2
Richmond Gate Property Co., Re [1965] 1 W.L.R. 335; [1964] 3 All E.R. 936 .... 4.2
Ridge v. Baldwin [1964] A.C. 40; [1963] 2 W.L.R. 935, HL 5.6.3, 5.6.4
Rigby v. Ferodo [1988] I.C.R. 29; [1987] I.R.L.R. 516 ...... 3.3.1.2, 5.3.2.2, 5.3.2.3, 5.3.3, 5.6.3
Riley v. Tesco Stores Ltd [1970] I.R.L.R. 103, CA 7.2.2
Rinner Kühn v. F.W.W. Spezial-Gebäudereinigung GmbH & Co. K.G. (Case C–171/88)
    [1989] E.C.R. 2743; [1989] I.R.L.R. 493, ECJ 6.1.1, 6.3.3.3
Riordan v. War Office [1961] 1 W.L.R. 210; [1960] 3 All E.R. 774n., CA 5.4.1
Robb v. Green [1895] 2 Q.B. 315, CA 3.1.2.3, 3.1.3
Robert Cort & Sons Ltd v. Charman [1981] I.R.L.R. 437, EAT 7.2.1.7
Roberts v. Birds Eye Walls Ltd (Case C–132/92) [1994] I.R.L.R. 29; [1994] I.C.R. 338,
    ECJ 6.2.8
Roberts v. Tate & Lyle Industries Ltd (No. 151/84) [1986] 2 All E.R. 602; [1986] I.C.R.
    371; [1986] I.R.L.R. 150, ECJ 6.1.2, 6.2.8
Robertson v. British Gas Corp. [1983] I.C.R. 351; [1983] I.R.L.R. 302, CA... 2.2, 2.4.1, 2.4.3,
                                                               2.8.4, 5.2.2, 5.6.3, 9.6.1
—— v. Magnet Ltd (Retail Division) [1993] I.R.L.R. 512, EAT 7.3.2.2
Robertson and Rough v. Forth Road Bridge Joint Board [1995] I.R.L.R. 251, CS 3.3.1.3
Robinson v. Crompton Parkinson Ltd [1978] I.C.R. 401; [1978] I.R.L.R. 61, EAT 3.2.1
Rock Refrigeration v. Jones Seward Refrigeration [1997] 1 All E.R. 1; [1997] I.C.R. 938;
    [1996] I.R.L.R. 675, CA 3.1.4, 3.1.4.5
Rock-It-Cargo Ltd v. Green [1997] I.R.L.R. 581, EAT 7.2.6, 7.5.1
Rockfon A/S v. Specialiarbejderforbunet i Danmark, acting for Nielsen and Others
    (Case C–449/93) [1996] I.C.R. 673; [1996] I.R.L.R. 168, ECJ 8.3.3.4
Roe v. Minister of Health [1954] 2 All E.R. 131; [1954] 2 Q.B. 66; [1954] 2 W.L.R. 915,
    CA 3.3.1.3
Roger Bullivant Ltd v. Ellis [1989] I.C.R. 464, CA 3.1.3.2
Rotsart De Hertaing v. J. Benoidt Sa and Igc Housing Sevice SA (Case C–305/94) [1997]
    I.R.L.R. 127, ECJ 9.3.6, 9.4.1
Rovenska v. General Medical Council [1998] I.C.R. 85; [1997] I.R.L.R. 367, CA 6.3.8
Rubel Bronze and Metal Co. Ltd, Re [1918] 1 K.B. 315 .... 4.2, 5.3.2
Rummler v. Dato-Druck GmbH (No. 237/85) [1989] I.C.R. 774; [1987] I.R.L.R. 32,
    ECJ 6.2.4
Ryan v. Shipboard Maintenance [1980] I.C.R. 88; [1980] I.R.L.R. 16, EAT 1.14.2
Rybak v. Jean Sorelle Ltd [1991] I.C.R. 127; [1991] I.R.L.R. 153, EAT 7.2.2

Saavedra v. Aceground [1995] I.R.L.R. 198, EAT 4.2
Sadler v. Imperial Life Assurance Co. of Canada Ltd [1988] I.R.L.R. 388, HC 3.1.4.6
Safeway Stores v. Burrell [1997] I.C.R. 523; [1997] I.R.L.R. 200, EAT 7.3.2.4, 8.3.1.2,
                                                                              8.3.1.3
Sagar v. H. Ridehalgh & Son Ltd [1931] 1 Ch. 310, CA 2.5.1
St John of God (Care Services) Ltd v. Brooks and Others [1992] I.C.R. 715; [1992]
    I.R.L.R. 546, EAT 8.4.1
Sajil v. Carraro t/a Foubert's Bar, COIT 1890/34 .... 10.2
Saltman Engineering Co. Ltd v. Campbell Engineering Co. Ltd (1948) 65 R.P.C. 203,
    CA 3.1.3.1
Sanders v. Ernest A. Neale Ltd [1974] I.C.R. 565; [1974] 3 All E.R. 327; [1974] I.R.L.R.
    236, NIRC 5.3.2.2
—— v. Parry [1967] 1 W.L.R. 753; 111 S.J. 296 .... 3.1.4.7
Sarker v. South Tees Acute Hospitals NHS Trust [1997] I.C.R. 673; [1997] I.R.L.R. 328,
    EAT 1.2, 7.5.1
Savage v. Sainsbury (J.) [1981] I.C.R.I; [1980] I.R.L.R. 109, CA 7.2.1.7
Scally v. Southern Health and Social Services Board [1992] 1 A.C. 294; [1991] 3 W.L.R.
    778; [1991] 4 All E.R. 563; [1991] I.R.L.R. 522, HL 2.3, 2.8.3, 3.2.1, 3.3.3
Schmidt v. Austick's Bookshops Ltd [1978] I.C.R. 85; [1977] I.R.L.R. 360, EAT 6.3.4.3
—— v. Spar-und-Leihkasse der Früheren Ämter Bordesholm, Keil und Cronshapen
    (Case C–392/92) [1995] I.C.R. 237; [1994] I.R.L.R. 302, ECJ 9.3.6, 9.9

Schuler (L.) AG v. Wickman Machine Tool Sales [1974] A.C. 235; [1973] 2 W.L.R. 683,
  HL 2.2
Scott v. Coalite Fuels and Chemicals Ltd [1988] I.C.R. 355; [1988] I.R.L.R. 131,
  EAT 7.2.1.3
Scottish Daily Record & Sunday Mail (1986) Ltd v. Laird [1996] I.R.L.R. 665, IH..... 7.3.2.2
Scullard v. Knowles and Southern Regional Council for Education and Training [1996]
  I.C.R. 399; [1996] I.R.L.R. 344, EAT 6.2.2
Seager v. Copydex (No. 2) [1969] 1 W.L.R. 809; 113 S.J. 281; [1969] 2 All E.R. 718,
  CA 3.1.3.2
Sealey v. Avon Aluminium Co. Ltd [1978] I.R.L.R. 285, IT 7.2.5
Secretary of State for Employment v. ASLEF (No. 2) [1972] 2 Q.B. 455; [1972] 2 W.L.R.
  1370; [1972] I.C.R. 19, CA 2.5.2, 3.1, 3.2.1
—— v. Globe Elastic Threat Co. Ltd [1980] A.C. 506; [1979] 3 W.L.R. 143; [1979] I.C.R.
  706, HL 7.2.8
Secretary of State for Scotland v. Taylor [1997] I.R.L.R. 608, EAT.............. 2.5.2, 7.2.10
Secretary of State for Trade and Industry v. Bottrill [1998] I.R.L.R. 120, EAT 1.14
—— v. Cook [1997] I.R.L.R. 150, EAT 9.4.1
—— v. Forde [1997] I.C.R. 231; [1997] I.R.L.R. 397, EAT 8.5.2
Securior Guarding Ltd v. Fraser Security Services Ltd [1996] I.R.L.R. 552, EAT 9.4.2
Seldon v. The Kendall Co. (U.K.) Ltd, COIT 1669/22 .... 8.3.6
Selfridges Ltd v. Malik [1997] I.R.L.R. 577, EAT 7.5.5.2
Sellars v. Charrington Fuels Ltd [1989] I.R.L.R. 152, CA 7.2.8.1
Senior Heat Treatment v. Bell [1997] I.R.L.R. 614, EAT........................ 8.3.7, 9.8.3
Sheffield v. Oxford Controls Co. Ltd [1979] I.C.R. 396; [1979] I.R.L.R. 133, EAT... 5.3.1, 7.2
Shepherd (F.C.) & Co. v. Jerrom [1987] Q.B. 301; [1986] 3 W.L.R. 801; [1985] I.C.R.
  802, CA 5.5.1.2, 7.2.1.4
Shields v. Coomes (Holdings) Ltd [1978] I.C.R. 1159; [1978] 1 W.L.R. 1408,
  CA 6.1.3, 6.2.3
Shillito v. Van Leer (U.K.) Ltd [1997] I.R.L.R. 495, EAT 7.4.4
Shirlaw v. Southern Foundries (1926) Ltd [1939] 2 K.B. 206, CA 2.3
Short v. Henderson (1946) 115 L.J.P.C. 41; [1946] S.C. (H.L.) 24, HL 1.14
Showboat Entertainment Centre Ltd v. Owens [1984] 1 W.L.R. 384; (1989) 128 S.J. 152;
  [1984] I.R.L.R. 7, EAT... 6.3.1
Sillifant v. Powell Duffryn Timber Ltd [1983] I.R.L.R. 391, EAT............. 7.3.2.2, 7.5.5.2
Sim v, Rotherham Metropolitan Borough Council [1987] Ch. 216; [1986] 3 W.L.R. 851;
  [1986] I.R.L.R. 391, HC.. 2.5.2, 3.1
Simmonds v. Dowty Scals [1978] I.R.L.R. 211, EAT........................... 2.5.1, 2.8.4
Simmons v. Hoover Ltd [1976] 3 W.L.R. 901; 120 S.J. 540; [1976] I.R.L.R. 266,
  EAT 8.3.7.4
Simrad Ltd v. Scott [1997] I.R.L.R. 147, EAT 7.5.5.2
Sinclair v. Bowles (1829) 9 B. & C. 92 .... 4.2
Singh v. British Steel Corporation [1994] I.R.L.R. 131, IT 2.3
Skyrail Oceanic (Trading as Goodmos Tours) v. Coleman [1981] I.C.R. 864, [1981]
  I.R.L.R. 398, CA... 6.3.1, 6.3.4.3
Slater v. South West Marketing Ltd, COIT 3119/65 .... 4.2
Slaughter v. C. Brewer & Sons [1990] I.C.R. 730; [1990] I.R.L.R. 426, EAT 7.3.2.1
Smith v. Avdel Systems Ltd (Case C–408/92) [1995] All E.R. (E.C.) 132; [1995] I.C.R.
  596, ECJ 6.2.1.1
—— v. City of Glasgow District Council [1987] I.C.R. 796; [1987] I.R.L.R. 326, HL ... 7.3
—— v. Gardner Merchant Ltd [1996] I.R.L.R. 342, EAT 6.3.4.2
—— v. Safeway [1977] I.R.L.R. 360, EAT 6.3.4.3
Smiths Industries Aerospace and Defence Systems v. Rawlings [1996] I.R.L.R. 656,
  EAT 8.3.2.3
Snoxell v. Vauxhall Motors; Charles Early Ltd v. Smith [1978] Q.B. 11; [1977] 3 W.L.R.
  189; [1977] I.C.R. 700, EAT 6.2.6.1
Sorbie v. Trust Houses Forte Hotels Ltd [1977] Q.B. 931; [1976] 3 W.L.R. 918; [1977]
  I.C.R. 55, EAT.. 6.2, 6.2.3
Sothern v. Franks Charlesly & Co. [1981] I.R.L.R. 278, CA 7.2

South Durham Health Authority v. UNISON [1995] I.C.R. 495; [1995] I.R.L.R. 405,
  EAT 9.2.3
Sovereign Distribution Services Ltd v. Transport & General Workers Union [1990]
  I.C.R. 31; [1989] I.R.L.R. 334, EAT 8.3.3.5
Sovereign House Security Services Ltd v. Savage [1989] I.R.L.R. 115, CA 7.2
Spafax Ltd v. Harrison; Spafax v. Taylor [1980] I.R.L.R. 443, CA 5.2.1.4
Specialised Mouldings Ltd, Re, February 2, 1987, Ch D (I.R.L.B. April 1995) 8.5.1
Speciality Care plc v. Pachela [1996] I.C.R. 633; [1996] I.R.L.R. 633, EAT 7.4.2
Speed Seal Products v. Paddington [1986] 1 All E.R. 91; [1986] F.S.R. 309, CA 3.1.3.1
Spencer v. Paragon Wallpapers [1977] I.C.R. 301; (1976) 11 I.T.R. 294, EAT 7.3.2.1
Spijkers v. Gebroeders Benedik Abbatoir CV, (No. 24/85) [1986] 2 C.M.L.R. 296; [1986]
  3 E.C.R. 1119, ECJ 9.3.3, 9.3.6
Spillers-French (Holdings) Ltd v. U.S.D.A.W [1980] I.C.R. 31; (1979) 123 S.J. 654,
  EAT 8.3.3.3
Spring v. Guardian Assurance [1995] 2 A.C. 296; [1994] 3 W.L.R. 354; [1994] 3 All E.R.
  129, HL 3.2.1, 3.3.1.2, 3.3.2.1, 3.3.6
Stacey v. Bacock Power Ltd (Construction Division) [1986] Q.B. 308; [1986] 2 W.L.R.
  207; [1986] I.R.L.R. 3, EAT 7.3
Staffordshire County Council v. Black [1995] I.R.L.R. 234, EAT 6.3.3.2
Stapp v. The Shaftesbury Society [1982] I.R.L.R. 326, CA 7.2.1.7
Steel v. Union of Post Office Workers [1978] 1 W.L.R. 64; (1977) 121 S.J. 575; [1978]
  I.C.R. 181, EAT 6.3.3.3, 6.3.3.4
Steenhorst-Neerings v. Bestuur van de Bedrijfsvereniging voor Detailhandel Ambachfen
  en Huisvrouwen (Case C–338/91) [1994] I.R.L.R. 244, ECJ 6.2.1.2
Stenhouse Australia v. Phillips [1994] A.C. 391; [1974] 2 W.L.R. 134.......... 3.1.4, 3.1.4.3
Stephenson v. F.A. Wellworth & Co. Ltd, IDS Brief 594/1997, p. 12 .... 10.3
Stevenson v. Teesside Bridge and Engineering Ltd [1971] 1 All E.R. 296; (1970) 114 S.J.
  907, DC 7.3.2.4
Stevenson Jordan and Harrison Ltd v. McDonald and Evans [1952] 1 T.L.R. 101, CA;
  sub nom. Stephenson Jordan and Harrison v. MacDonald and Evans, 69 R.P.C. 10,
  CA 1.14
Stichting (Sophie Redmond) v. Bartol (Case C–29/91) [1992] I.R.L.R. 366, ECJ ... 9.3.2, 9.3.3,
                                                                                        9.3.6
Stoker v. Lancashire County Council [1991] I.R.L.R. 75, CA 7.3.1
Strathclyde Buses Ltd v. Leonard and Others; Ellum and Others v. Strathclyde Buses Ltd
  [1997], EAT 507 & 515/97 .... 8.3.1.2
Strathclyde Regional Council v. Wallace [1998] I.R.L.R. 146, HL.................. 6.2, 6.2.6
Stubbes v. Trower, Still & Keeling [1987] I.R.L.R. 321; (1987) 137 New L.J. 520, CA   2.2, 2.3
Stubbs v. Holywell Rly Co. (1867) L.R. 2 Exch. 311 .... 5.5.3
Sun Printers v. Westminster Press (1982) 126 S.J. 260; [1982] I.R.L.R. 292, CA 3.1.3.1
Sun Valley Poultry Ltd v. Mitchell and Others, EAT 164/96 (reported in IDS Brief 604/
  January 1998) 8.3.5.4
Sutcliffe & Eaton Ltd v. R. Pinney [1977] I.R.L.R. 349, EAT........................ 7.3.2.3
—— v. Hawker Siddeley Aviation Ltd [1973] I.C.R. 560; [1973] I.R.L.R. 304; [1974]
  I.T.R. 58, NIRC.. 2.2, 7.3.2.4
Sulton & Gates (Luton) Ltd v. Boxall [1979] I.C.R. 67; [1978] I.R.L.R. 486, EAT 7.3.2.1
Süzen v. Zehnacker Gebäudereinigung GmbH Krankenhausservice (Case C–13/95)
  [1997] I.R.L.R. 255; [1997] I.C.R. 662, ECJ.................................... 9.3.6, 9.9
Swain v. West (Butchers) Ltd [1936] 3 All E.R. 261, CA 3.1.2
Sybron Corp. v. Rochem Ltd [1985] Ch. 299; [1984] Ch. 112; [1983] I.C.R. 80, CA..... 3.1.2,
                                                                                3.1.2.1, 3.1.2.3
System Floors (U.K.) Ltd v. Daniel [1982] I.C.R. 54; [1981] I.R.L.R. 475, EAT..... 2.2, 2.8.4,
                                                                                        5.2.2
Systems Reliability Holdings plc v. Smith [1990] I.R.L.R. 377, HC .... 3.1.4.1.

Tai Hing Cotton Mill Ltd v. Lin Chong Hing Bank Ltd [1986] A.C. 80; [1985] 3 W.L.R.
  317, PC 3.3.1.3

Talke Fashions Ltd v. A.S.T.W.K.T. [1978] 1 W.L.R. 558; [1977] I.C.R. 833; [1977]
   I.R.L.R. 309, EAT 8.3.3.5
Taplin v. Shippam Ltd [1978] I.C.R. 1068; (1978) 13 I.T.R. 532; [1978] I.R.L.R. 450,
   EAT 7.5.5.2
Taylor v. Furness, Withy & Co. Ltd [1969] 1 Lloyd's L.R. 324; 6 K.I.R. 488 ....   1.2
—— v. Kent County Council [1969] I.T.R. 294; [1969] 2 Q.B. 560; [1969] 3 W.L.R. 156,
   DC 8.3.5.1
—— v. Parsons Peebles NEI Peebles Ltd [1981] I.R.L.R. 119, EAT 7.3.2.2
—— v. Triumph Motors British Leyland U.K. Ltd & Secretary of State for Employment
   [1975] I.R.L.R. 369, IT 7.2.8.1
Taylorplan Catering (Scotland) Ltd v. McInally [1980] I.R.L.R. 53, EAT 7.3.2.1
Tayside Regional Council v. McIntosh [1982] I.R.L.R. 272, EAT 2.2
Tele-Trading Ltd v. Jenkins [1990] I.R.L.R. 430, CA 7.5.5.2
Ten Oever v. Stichting Bedrijfspensioenfonds voor het Glazenwassers-en Schoonmaak-
   bedrijf (Case C–109/91) [1994] 1 All E.R. 9; [1993] I.R.L.R. 601, ECJ 6.1.1, 6.2.1.1,
                                                           6.2.8
Tennants Textile Colours Ltd v. Todd [1989] I.R.L.R. 3; [1988] 7 N.I.J.B. 88, NICA ...   6.2.5
Terrapin Ltd v. Builders' Supply Co. [1960] R.P.C. 128, CA 3.1.3.2
Therm-a-Stor Ltd v. Atkins (1982) 126 S.J. 856; [1983] I.R.L.R. 78, CA..............   7.4.2
Thomas v. Chief Adjudication Officer [1991] 2 Q.B. 164; [1991] 2 W.L.R. 886; [1990]
   I.R.L.R. 436, CA 6.2.8
—— v. National Coal Board [1987] I.C.R. 757; [1987] I.R.L.R. 451, EAT......... 6.2.2, 6.2.3
Thompson v. Walton Car Delivery and BRS Automotive Ltd [1997] I.R.L.R. 343,
   EAT 7.2.6
Tocher v. General Motors Scotland Ltd [1981] I.R.L.R. 55, EAT 8.3.5.4
Todd v. British Midland Airways Ltd [1978] I.C.R. 959; (1978) 122 S.J. 661; [1978]
   I.R.L.R. 370, CA 7.2.4
Tomlinson v. Dick Evans U Drive Ltd [1978] I.C.R. 639; [1978] I.R.L.R. 77, EAT.....   7.2.3
Torfaen Borough Council v. B & Q (Case C–145/88) [1990] 2 Q.B. 19; [1990] 2 W.L.R.
   1330, ECJ 1.11
Torr v. British Railways Board [1977] I.C.R. 785; [1977] I.R.L.R. 184, EAT 1.8
Tracey v. Zest Equipment [1982] I.C.R. 481; [1982] I.R.L.R. 268, EAT 7.2.1.2
TGWU v. Ledbury Preserves (1928) Ltd [1985] I.R.L.R. 412, EAT 8.3.3.5
—— v. Nationwide Haulage Ltd [1978] I.R.L.R. 143, IT 8.3.3.5
Trotter v. Forth Ports Authority [1991] I.R.L.R. 419, CA 5.4.2
Tsangacos v. Amalgamated Chemicals [1997] I.C.R. 154; [1997] I.R.L.R. 4, EAT 9.4.3
Tucker v. British Leyland Motor Corp. Ltd [1978] I.R.L.R. 493, EAT 1.12
Turley v. Allders Department Store Ltd [1980] I.C.R. 66; [1980] I.R.L.R. 4, EAT 10.3
Turner v. Labour Party and the Labour Party Superannuation Society [1987] I.R.L.R.
   101, CA 6.3.3.4
—— v. London Transport Executive [1977] I.C.R. 952; (1977) 121 S.J. 829; [1977]
   I.R.L.R. 441, CA 7.2.1.5
—— v. Sawdon & Co. [1901] 2 K.B. 653, CA 1.3
Turriff Construction Ltd v. Bryant (1967) 2 K.I.R. 659 DC; reversing *sub nom.* Chant v.
   Turriff Construction [1966] I.T.R. 380 .... 2.2, 2.8.4
Turvey v. Cheyney (C.W.) & Son [1979] I.C.R. 341; [1979] I.R.L.R. 105, EAT 8.3.5.3

U.B.A.F. Bank Ltd v. Davis [1978] I.R.L.R. 442, EAT 7.5.5.2
U.S.D.A.W. v. Leancut Bacon Ltd [1981] I.R.L.R. 295, EAT................ 8.3.3.1, 8.3.3.5
Union of Construction, Allied Trades and Technicians v. Brain [1981] I.C.R. 542; [1981]
   I.R.L.R. 224, CA 7.3
United Bank Ltd v. Akhtar [1989] I.R.L.R. 507, EAT............. 2.2, 2.3, 3.1, 3.2.1, 5.2.1.4,
                                                                 5.3.3, 5.6.4
United Kingdom v. Council of the European Union (Case C–84/94) [1997] I.R.L.R. 30,
   ECJ 1.12
United Kingdom Atomic Energy Authority v. E.F. Claydon [1974] I.C.R. 128; [1974]
   I.T.R. 185; [1974] I.R.L.R. 6, NIRC.....................................   2.2

University of Aston v. Malik [1984] I.C.R. 492; (1984) 81 L.S.Gaz. 1438; [1984] I.R.L.R. 492, EAT 7.2.8.1

Van Den Akker v. Stichting Shell Pensioenfonds (Case C–28/93) [1995] I.C.R. 596; [1995] All E.R. (E.C.) 156, ECJ 6.2.1.1
Van Der Heijden v. The Netherlands, No. 11002/84, 41 D.R. 264 (1985) 3.1.3.4
Van Duyn v. Home Office (No. 41/74) [1975] Ch. 358; [1974] E.C.R. 1337; [1975] 1 C.M.L.R. 1, ECJ 2.7, 2.7.1
Van Gend en Loos v. Nederlandse Belastingadministratie (No. 26/62) [1963] E.C.R. 1; [1963] C.M.L.R. 105, ECJ 2.7
Vaux and Associated Breweries v. Ward (1968) 112 S.J. 761; [1968] I.T.R. 385, DC ... 8.3.1.2
Vigers v. Cook [1919] 2 K.B. 475, CA 4.2
Vine v. National Dock Labour Board [1957] A.C. 488; [1957] 2 W.L.R. 106; [1956] 3 All E.R. 393, HL 5.3.2.2
Vogt v. Germany (1996) 21 E.H.R.R. 205; [1996] E.L.R. 232, ECHR 3.1.3.4
Von Colson and Kamann v. Land Nordrhein-Westfahlen (No. 14/83); Harz v. Deutsche Tradax GmbH (No. 79/83) [1984] E.C.R. 1891; [1986] 2 C.M.L.R. 430, ECJ... 2.7.1, 10.3
Vroege v. NCIV Instituut voor Volkshuisvesting BV (Case C–57/93); Fisscher v. Voorhuis Hengelo BV (Case C–128/93) [1995] All E.R. (E.C.) 193; [1994] I.R.L.R. 651, ECJ 6.1.1, 6.2.1, 6.2.1.2

W.A. Goold (Pearmak) Ltd v. McConnell [1995] I.R.L.R. 516, EAT................. 3.3.4
Waddington v. Leicester Council for Voluntary Service [1977] 1 W.L.R. 544; [1977] I.C.R. 266; [1977] I.R.L.R. 32, EAT 6.2.3
Waite v. Government Communications Headquarters 2 A.C. 714; [1983] 3 W.L.R. 389, [1983] I.C.R. 653, HL 7.2.10
Walker v. Northumberland County Council [1995] 1 All E.R. 737; [1995] I.C.R. 702; [1995] I.R.L.R. 35, QBD 3.3.1.2, 3.3.1.3, 3.1.3.3
Wallace v. CA Roofing Services Ltd [1996] I.R.L.R. 435, QBD 1.14.6
Wallace Bogan & Co. Ltd v. Cove [1997] I.R.L.R. 453, CA 3.1.4.3
Walls v. Sinnett (Inspector of Taxes) [1987] S.T.C. 236; (1986) 60 T.C. 150 .... 1.14
Waltons & Morse v. Dorrington (1997) I.R.L.R. 488, EAT 3.3.1.2, 3.3.4, 5.2.1.4, 7.2.1.5
Wandsworth LBC v. D'Silva [1998] I.R.L.R. 193, CA .... 2.5.2.
Ward and Lewarne v. Beresford & Hicks Furniture Ltd, December 16, 1996, EAT 860/95 IRLB 585 January 1998 .... 9.8.1
Warner v. Adnet Ltd, *The Times*, March 12, 1998, CA........................... 9.9
Warner Bros. v. Nelson [1937] 1 K.B. 209 .... 3.1.2.3, 5.3.2.2
Wass (W. & J.) v. Binns [1982] I.C.R. 486; (1982) 126 S.J. 608; [1982] I.R.L.R. 283, CA 7.3.2.2
Waters v. Commissioner of Police [1997] I.R.L.R. 589, CA.................... 3.3.1.3, 6.3.6
Watson v. Marylebone Optical Co. Ltd, COIT 2056/212, IDS Brief 591 .... 10.4.2.2
Weathersfield Ltd (t/a Van & Truck Rentals) v. Sargent [1998] I.C.R. 198; [1998] I.R.L.R. 14, EAT 6.3.1
Webb v. EMO Air Cargo (U.K.) (Case C–32/93) [1994] Q.B. 718; [1994] 4 All E.R. 115; [1994] I.C.R. 770; [1994] I.R.L.R. 482, ECJ; [1994] Q.B. 718; [1993] 1 W.L.R. 102; [1992] 4 All E.R. 929; [1993] I.C.R. 175; [1993] I.R.L.R. 27, HL; [1992] 2 All E.R. 43; [1992] I.C.R. 445; [1992] I.R.L.R. 116, CA..................... 6.3.3.3, 10.3, 10.4.2.3
—— v. —— (No. 2) [1995] 1 W.L.R. 1454; [1995] 4 All E.R. 577; [1995] I.C.R. 1021; [1995] I.R.L.R. 645, HL 10.5.5
Weddell (W.) & Co. Ltd v. Tepper [1980] I.C.R. 286; (1979) 124 S.J. 80; [1980] I.R.L.R. 96, CA 7.3.2.2
Weld-Blundell v. Stephens [1919] 1 K.B. 520; [1920] A.C. 956 .... 3.1.3.4
Wessex Dairies Ltd v. Smith [1935] 2 K.B. 80, CA 3.1.2.3
West Midlands Co-operative Society Ltd v. Tipton [1986] I.C.R. 192; [1986] A.C. 536; [1986] 2 W.L.R. 306, HL.................................... 7.2.1.7, 7.3, 7.3.1, 7.3.3
Western Excavating (E.C.C.) v. Sharp [1978] Q.B. 761; [1978] 2 W.L.R. 344, CA; reversing I.R.L.R. 27, EAT 2.2, 2.3, 5.2.1.4, 5.3.2, 5.3.3, 7.2.1.5, 8.3.7.4
Westminster City Council v. Cabaj [1996] I.C.R. 960; [1966] I.R.L.R. 399, CA..... 2.2, 7.2.1.5

Wheeler v. Patel and J. Golding Group of Companies [1987] I.R.L.R. 211; [1987] I.C.R. 631, EAT 9.8.2
Whent v. T. Cartledge Ltd [1997] I.R.L.R. 153, EAT................... 2.4.3, 9.6, 9.6.1, 9.6.2
Whitbread & Co. v. Thomas [1988] I.C.R. 776; [1988] I.R.L.R. 43, EAT........ 7.3.2.2, 7.3.3
White v. British Sugar Corp. (Case 37485/76) [1977] I.R.L.R. 121, IT................ 6.3.4.2
—— v. Reflecting Roadstuds [1991] I.C.R. 733; [1991] I.R.L.R. 331, EAT..... 2.2, 2.3, 3.2.1, 5.2.1.4, 5.3.2, 5.3.3
Wickers v. Champion Employment [1984] I.C.R. 365; (1984) 134 New L.J. 544, EAT 1.14.5
William Bogan & Co. v. Cove [1997] I.R.L.R. 453, CA.......................... 3.1.3.3
William Hill Organisation Ltd v. Tucker [1998] I.R.L.R. 313; The Times, April 8, 1998, CA... 1.3, 3.1.2.4, 3.1.4.7, 7.2
William Robinson and Co. Ltd v. Heuer [1898] 2 Ch. 451................... 3.1.2.3, 5.3.2.2
Williams v. Channel 5 Engineering Services Ltd, (Case No. 2302136/97), 105 Brief 609/ March 1998 .... 1.15
—— v. Compair Maxam Ltd [1982] I.C.R. 156; [1982] I.R.L.R. 83, EAT............. 8.3.4.1
Wilson v. Maynard Shipping Consultants AB [1978] Q.B. 665; [1978] 2 W.L.R. 466; [1977] I.R.L.R. 491, CA 7.2.4
—— v. Racher [1974] I.C.R. 428; (1974) 16 K.I.R. 212; [1974] I.R.L.R. 114, CA.... 2.1, 5.3.4
—— v. St Helens Borough Council [1996] I.C.R. 711; [1996] I.R.L.R. 320, EAT.... 2.4.3, 9.5
Wilsons & Clyde Coal Co. Ltd v. English [1938] A.C. 57; 101 S.J. 607.......... 3.3.1, 3.3.1.3
Wiltshire County Council v. National Association of Teachers in Further and Higher Education and Guy [1980] I.C.R. 455; (1980) 78 L.G.R. 455, CA; affirming [1978] I.R.L.R. 301, EAT 1.14.2
Wiluszynski v. London Borough of Tower Hamlets [1989] I.C.R. 493; [1989] I.R.L.R. 259, CA.. 4.5.2
Wishart v. National Association of Citizens Advice Bureaux Ltd [1990] I.C.R. 794; [1990] I.R.L.R. 393, CA 1.2, 5.6.3
Wood v. York City Council [1978] I.C.R. 840; [1978] I.R.L.R. 228, CA 7.2.8
Woods v. W.M. Car Services (Peterborough) Ltd [1982] I.C.R. 693; [1982] I.R.L.R. 413, EAT... 3.1, 3.2.1, 5.2.14, 5.3.3, 5.6
Worringham v. Lloyds Bank (No. 69/80) [1981] I.C.R. 558, ECJ 6.1.1
Wylie v. Dee & Co. (Menswear) [1978] I.R.L.R. 103, IT 6.3.5
Wynes v. Southrepps Hall Broiler Farm Ltd (1968) 3 I.T.R. 407, IT 8.2

Yemm and others v. British Steel plc [1994] I.R.L.R. 117, EAT..................... 4.2.2
Yewens v. Noakes (1880) 6 Q.B.D. 530; 50 L.J.Q.B. 132; 44 L.T. 128; 45 J.P. 8, 468; 28 W.R. 562; 1 T.C. 250, CA 1.14
Young v. Charles Church (Southern) Ltd (1998) 39 B.M.L.R. 146, CA................ 3.3.1.3
Young & Woods Ltd v. West [1980] I.R.L.R. 201, CA............................. 1.14
Young, James and Webster v. United Kingdom [1983] I.R.L.R. 35.............. 11.2.2, 11.3

X, Y and Z v. United Kingdom, The Times, April 23, 1997......................... 6.3.4.2

Zucker v. Astrid Jewels Ltd [1978] I.C.R. 1088; [1978] I.R.L.R. 385, EAT............ 7.4.2

TABLE OF STATUTES

References in the right-hand column are to paragraph numbers.

1726 Truck Act 4.4
1871 Trade Union Act (34 & 35 Vict.
     c. 31)—
     s.4(4) 2.4; 11.1.1
1875 Conspiracy and Protection of
     Property Act (38 & 39 Vict.
     c. 86) 11.1.1
1896 Truck Act (59 & 56 Vict. c. 44)—
     s.1 .... 4.4
1906 Trade Disputes Act (7 Edw. 7,
     c. 47) 11.1.1
     s.4(1) 11.1.1
     s.5(3) 11.2.1
1908 Port of London Act (8 Edw. 7,
     c. 68) 2.5.1
1913 Trade Union Act (2 & 3 Geo. 5,
     c. 30) 11.1.1
1933 Children and Young Persons Act
     (23 & 24 Geo. 5, c. 12) .. 1.4, 1.5
1936 Public Health Act (26 Geo. 5 & 1
     Edw. 8, c. 49)—
     s.205 .... 10.4.1.2, 10.4.2.4
1937 Children and Young Persons
     (Scotland) Act (1 Edw. 8 &
     1 Geo. 6, c. 37) 1.5
1940 Old Age and Widows Pension
     Act 6.1.2
1944 Disabled Persons (Employment)
     Act (7 & 8 Geo. 6, c. 10) .. 6.1.4,
                                 6.4.2
1945 Law Reform (Contributory Neg-
     ligence) Act (8 & 9 Geo. 6,
     c. 28) 3.3.1.3
1947 Statutory Instruments Act (10 &
     11 Geo. 6, c. 36) 2.6.1
1950 Shops Act (14 Geo. 6, c. 28) 1.10
     Pt. II 1.10
     s.47 .... 1.10
     Sched. 4 .... 1.10

1956 Restrictive Trade Practices Act
     (4 & 5 Eliz. 2, c. 68) 3.1.3.4
1958 Disabled Persons (Employment)
     Act (6 & 7 Eliz. 2, c. 33) ... 6.4.2
1960 Payment of Wages Act (8 & 9
     Eliz. 2, c. 37) 4.4
1963 Betting, Gaming and Lotteries
     Act (c. 2)—
     Sched. 5A 1.11; 7.4.5
     Children and Young Persons Act
     (c. 37) 1.5
     Offices, Shops and Railway
     Premises Act (c. 41) 3.3.1.2
     s.7 .... 3.3.1.2
     Contracts of Employment Act
     (c. 49) .. 2.0, 2.6, 2.8, 2.8.4; 5.2.2,
                5.4.1; 7.2.8, 7.2.11; 11.2
     s.4 .... 2.8.4
1964 Industrial Training Act (c. 64) 7.1
1965 Redundancy Payments Act
     (c. 62) 2.6; 7.2.8; 8.2, 8.3.3.5
1969 Family Law Reform Act
     (c. 46)—
     s.1, 9 .... 1.4
     Employers' Liability (Com-
     pulsory Insurance) Act
     (c. 57) 1.14
1970 Equal Pay Act (c. 41) 2.7; 6.1.3,
         6.1.4, 6.2, 6.2.1, 6.2.2, 6.2.8,
         6.3.6, 6.4.1; 7.2.3, 7.4.8;
         10.5.2.1, 10.6
     s.1 .... 6.1.3, 6.2
     (1) 1.1
     (2)(a) 6.2, 6.2.3, 6.2.5, 6.2.6
     (b) 6.2, 6.2.4, 6.2.5, 6.2.6
     (i) 6.2.4
     (c) 6.1.1, 6.2, 6.2.2, 6.2.5,
                           6.2.6
     (3) 6.1.3, 6.2, 6.2.4, 6.2.5, 6.2.6,
                6.2.6.1, 6.2.7, 6.3.3.3

1970 Equal Pay Act—*cont.*
          s.1(3)(b) 6.2.5, 6.2.6
          (4) 6.2.3
          (5) 6.2.4, 6.2.5
          (6) 6.2.2
              (a) 6.2.1
              (b) 6.2.6
          (8) 1.4
          s.2 .... 6.1.3, 6.2.1, 6.2.1.2
          (4), (5) 6.2.1, 6.2.1.2
          s.2A 6.2.5, 6.2.6
              (1) 6.2.5
                  (a) 6.2.5, 6.2.6
                  (b) 6.2.5
              (2) 6.2.5
          s.3 .... 6.2.7; 11.5.3.1
          s.6 .... 6.2.8
          (4) 6.2.8
          s.6A 6.2.1.2, 6.2.8
          s.6E(a) 6.2.8
1971 Attachment of Earnings Act
          (c. 32) 4.4.1
      Industrial Relations Act (c. 72) .. 2.4,
              2.6; 5.6.1, 5.6.3, 5.6.4; 7.2.8,
              7.5.1; 11.2, 11.2.1, 11.3.2
          ss.2–4 .... 8.2, 8.4
          ss.34, 35 .... 11.3.1
          ss.45, 46 .... 11.3.2
      Immigration Act (c. 77) 1.6, 1.7
1972 European Communities Act
          (c. 68) 2.6.1; 6.1.1
          s.1(2) 2.7
          s.2 .... 7.2.2
          (1) 2.7
          (2) 2.6.1, 2.7
          (3) 2.0
          s.3(1) 2.7
          Sched. 2 .... 2.6.1
1973 Employment Agencies Act
          (c. 35) 2.8
      Employment and Training Act
          (c. 50) 6.4.2
1974 Health and Safety at Work
          etc. Act (c. 37) 1.12, 1.14.3;
              2.6.1; 3.1.5, 3.3.1.1, 3.3.6;
              10.6, 10.8; 11.3.1
          s.2 .... 2.6.2; 3.3.1.1, 3.3.1.3
          (2) 3.3.1.1
              (a)–(e) 3.3.1.1
          (3) 3.3.1.1
          s.3 .... 2.6.2; 3.3.1.3
          (1) 3.3.1.1
          ss.4–6 .... 2.6.2; 3.3.1.3
          s.7 .... 2.6.2; 3.1.5, 3.3.1.3
          (a), (b) 3.1.5
          s.8 .... 3.1.5
          s.15 .... 2.6.1
          (1)–(9) 2.6.1

1974 Health and Safety at Work
          etc. Act—*cont.*
          s.16 .... 2.6.2; 10.6
          s.17(1), (2) 2.6.2
          s.38 .... 3.3.2.1
          s.47 .... 3.3.1.3
          (2) 3.3.1.3
          Sched. 3 .... 2.6.1
      Trade Union and Labour Rela-
          tions Act (c. 52) 7.1, 7.5.5.1;
                                        8.3.3.5
          s.18 .... 2.4
          Sched. 1,
          para. 5(2)(c) 5.2.1.1
      Rehabilitation of Offenders Act
          (c. 53) 1.8; 7.4.10, 7.4.12
          s.4(3) 1.8
              (b) 1.8; 7.4.10, 7.4.12
          (4) 1.8
1975 Social Security Act (c. 14) 6.2.8; 10.8
          s.27(1) 6.2.8
          s.53(1) 6.2.8
      Finance (No. 2) Act (c. 45)—
          s.38 .... 1.14.5
      Social Security and Pensions Act
          (c. 60) 6.2.8
      Sex Discrimination Act (c. 65) .. 1.15;
              6.1.3, 6.1.4, 6.2.2, 6.2.6,
              6.2.8, 6.3.1, 6.3.3, 6.3.3.1,
              6.3.3.2, 6.3.4.1, 6.3.5, 6.3.7,
              6.3.8; 7.2.8.4, 7.5.5.2; 10.1,
              10.3, 10.4.2.4, 10.6
          Pt I 6.1.3
          Pt. II 1.15; 6.1.3
          Pt. III 1.15
          s.1 .... 6.1.3
          (1) 10.3
              (a) 6.3.1, 6.3.4.1, 6.3.4.3,
                          6.3.7; 10.3, 10.6
              (b) 1.15; 5.2.3.2; 6.3.3,
                          6.3.3.1, 6.3.7; 10.4.2.3
              (i) 6.3.3
              (ii) 6.3.3, 6.3.3.3; 10.4.2.3
              (iii) 6.3.3; 10.4.2.3
          (3)(b)(i) 6.3.3
              (ii) 6.3.3.3
          s.2(1) 6.3
          s.3 .... 6.3
          (1)(b) 6.3.3
              (i) 6.3.3.2
              (ii), (iii) 6.3.3
          s.4 .... 6.3.6; 7.4.8
          (1)(a), (b) 6.3.6
              (d) 3.3.1.3
          s.5(3) 6.3.1, 6.3.3.2; 10.3
          s.6 .... 10.4.2.3, 10.4.2.6
          (1)(a) 1.15; 6.3.4.1, 6.3.5
              (b), (c) 6.3.1, 6.3.5

1975   Sex Discrimination Act—*cont.*
    s.6(2)(a) 6.3.1, 6.3.5; 10.6
      (b) 6.3.1, 6.3.4.1; 8.3.4.2;
                   10.4.2.3
      (c) 6.3.1
    s.7 .... 6.3.5
      (1)(a) 6.3.5
      (2) 6.3.5
        (a) 6.3.5
        (b) 6.3.5
          (ii) 6.3.5
        (ba) 6.3.5
        (c)–(h) 6.3.5
      (4) 6.3.5
    s.9 .... 1.15
    s.12(3) 6.3.4.1
    ss.13, 38 .... 1.15
    s.41 .... 6.3.4.1
      (1), (3) 6.3.4.1
    s.50(1) 10.6
    s.53 .... 6.4.1
      (1)(c) 6.5
    s.54 .... 6.4.1
    ss.56, 56A 6.4.1
    s.56A 2.6.2
      (10) 6.1.4, 6.4.1
    ss.57–60 .... 6.4.1
    s.65 .... 6.3.8
      (1) 6.3.8
        (b), (c) 6.3.8
      (1B) 6.3.8
      (2) 10.3
      (3) 6.3.8
    s.66(4) 6.3.8
    s.68(2)(a), (b) 10.6
    s.72 .... 1.15; 6.4.1
    s.74 .... 6.4.1
      (2)(b) 10.4.2.3
    s.75 .... 6.4.1
      (2)(e) 6.4.1
    s.76 .... 6.3.8
      (1), (5) 6.3.8
      (6) 6.3.8
        (b) 6.3.8
    s.77 .... 6.2.7
      (2) 5.2.2, 5.6.4
    s.82 .... 1.15; 10.4.2.6
      (1) 1.15
    ss.85, 85A, 85B 1.4
   Employment   Protection   Act
     (c. 71) 7.5.3, 7.5.5.1, 7.5.5.2;
                8.2; 10.1, 10.3; 11.3.2,
                       11.5.3.1
    s.11 .... 8.3.3.1; 9.6.1
    s.12 .... 8.3.3.1; 9.6.1
      (1) 11.3.2
    s.13 .... 8.3.3.1; 9.6.1

1975   Employment   Protection   Act—
    cont.
    s.14 .... 8.3.3.1; 9.6.1
      (1) 11.3.2
    ss.15, 16 .... 8.3.3.1; 9.6.1
    s.71 .... 5.6.1
    s.99 .... 8.3.3
      (3) 8.3.3.4
      (5) 8.3.3.3
    Schd. 11 .... 4.5.3
    Sched. 17 .... 8.2
    para. 4 .... 8.2, 8.4
1976   Congenital Disabilities (Civil Lia-
    bilities) Act (c. 28) 10.6
   Race Relations Act (c. 74) .. 1.7, 1.15;
         6.1.3, 6.3.3, 6.3.3.1, 6.3.4.3,
         6.3.8; 7.2.8.4, 7.4.8, 7.5.5.2
    s.1(1) 6.3.1
       (a) 6.3.1, 6.3.4.1, 6.3.7
       (b) .. 1.15; 6.3.1, 6.3.3, 6.3.4.3,
                  6.3.7, 6.3.8
         (i) 6.3.3, 6.3.3.2
         (ii) ... 6.3.3, 6.3.3.3, 6.3.4.3
         (iii) 6.3.3, 6.3.3.3
    s.2 .... 6.3.6
    s.3(1) 6.3.1, 6.3.3
      (4) 6.3.1, 6.3.3.2
    s.4(1)(a)–(c) 6.3.1, 6.3.5
      (b), (c) 6.3.1
      (2)(a) 6.3.1
        (c) 6.3.4.1; 8.3.4.2
    s.5 .... 6.3.5
      (1)(a), (b) 6.3.5
      (2) 6.3.5
        (a)–(d) 6.3.5
      (4) 6.3.5
    s.7 .... 1.15
    s.8 .... 2.7
    s.32 .... 6.3.4.1
      (1), (3) 6.3.4.1
    s.43 .... 6.4.1
    ss.44–46 .... 6.4.1
    s.47 .... 2.6.2; 6.4.1
      (10) 6.4.1
    ss.48–51 .... 6.4.1
    s.56 .... 6.3.8
      (1)(c) 6.3.8
    s.57(4) 6.3.8
    s.63 .... 6.4.1
    s.65 .... 6.4.1
      (2)(b) 6.3.7
    s.66 .... 6.4.1
      (2)(e) 6.4.1
      (3)–(4) 6.4.1
    s.68 .... 6.3.8
      (6), (7) 6.3.8
    ss.75, 75A, 75B 1.4
    s.78 .... 1.15

1976 Fair Employment (Northern Ireland) Act 1.15	1986 Insolvency Act—*cont.*
s.57 .... 1.15	s.44 .... 8.5.1
1977 Patents Act (c. 37) 3.1.2.2	(1)(b) 8.5.1
s.39 .... 3.1.2.2	Sched. 6 .... 5.5.3; 8.5.2
(1)(a) 3.1.2.2	Wages Act (c. 48) 4.2.2, 4.4
ss.40–42 .... 3.1.2.2	s.1 .... 9.5
Unfair Contract Terms Act (c. 50) 1.1; 2.3	s.7(1) 4.2.2
s.1(1) 2.2	s.8(3) 9.5
s.2 .... 2.2	s.12 .... 4.5.4
(1) 2.2; 3.3.1.2	Social Security Act (c. 50) .. 10.1, 10.5
(2) 3.3.1.2	Sex Discrimination Act (c. 59) .. 6.1.3,
s.3 .... 2.2	6.2.8
ss.5–7 .... 2.2	s.1(1)(b) 6.3.3.1
s.13 .... 2.2	(i)–(iii) 6.3.3.1
(1) 2.2	s.3(1) 6.2.8
Sched. 1, para. 4 .... 3.3.1.2	s.6 .... 6.2.7
1978 Theft Act (c. 31) 1.8	Public Order Act (c. 64)—
s.16(1) 1.8	s.4A 6.3.4.1
Employment Protection (Consolidation) Act (c. 44) 4.3.1.1; 6.2.1.3; 7.4.2, 7.4.3, 7.4.4; 10.3, 10.4	1987 Finance Act (c. 16) 4.5.2
	1988 Income and Corporation Taxes Act (c. 1)—
Pt. V 9.1.2	s.19(1) 4.3.2
s.23(1) 11.4.1	ss.169–184 .... 4.5.2
(a) 11.4.1	Sched. 8 .... 4.5.2
s.57(3) 8.3.2.3, 8.4.1	Employment Act (c. 19) 11.2.2
s.58 .... 8.3.2.3; 11.2.2	Access to Medical Reports Act (c. 28) 1.9, 1.9.1; 7.3.2.1
(3) 11.2.2	s.1 .... 1.9.1
s.59(1)(b) 5.6.3; 8.3.4	s.2(1) 1.9.1
s.60 .... 10.3	s.3 .... 1.9.1
s.66 .... 10.6	(2) 1.9.1
s.81(2) 8.3.1	ss.4, 5 .... 1.9.1
(b) 8.3.1.2, 8.3.1.2	Copyright, Designs and Patents Act (c. 48) 3.1.2.2
s.136 .... 7.5.1	s.11 .... 3.1.2.2
ss.141–149 .... 9.1.2	1989 Social Security Act (c. 24)—
s.153(1) 8.3.2.3	s.23 .... 6.1.2, 6.2.8
Sched. 13, para. 17 .... 9.1	Sched. 5 .... 6.1.2, 6.2.8
1980 Employment Act (c. 42) .. 7.1, 7.3.2.2; 10.1, 10.4.2.2; 11.3.2	Employment Act (c. 38) 1.5; 2.8
	s.16(1) 6.2.8
s.19(b) 8.3.3.1; 9.6.1	s.17 .... 8.2
s.98(4) 7.3	Fair Employment (Northern Ireland) Act 8.3.4.2
1982 Social Security and Housing Benefits Act (c. 24) 10.1	1990 Access to Health Records Act (c. 23) 1.9, 1.9.2
s.17(4) 4.3.2	Enterprise and New Towns (Scotland) Act (c. 35)—
Supply of Goods and Services Act (c. 29) 1.1	s.2(3) 6.4.2
1984 Data Protection Act (c. 35) 1.9, 1.9.2, 1.9.3	Employment Act (c. 38) .. 1.10, 11.2.2
	1992 Social Security Contributions and Benefits Act (c. 4) 10.5.2, 10.5.6, 10.8
1986 Insolvency Act (c. 45) 8.5.1, 8.5.2; 9.1.2	Pt. XI 10.1
	Pt. XIII 10.4.1.4
s.19 .... 8.5.1	s.151 .... 4.3.2
(4)–(6) 8.5.1	(1), (4) 4.3.2
(7)(a), (b) 8.5.1	s.152 .... 4.3.2
(8) 8.5.1	

1992 Social Security Contributions and
        Benefits Act—*cont.*
     s.153 .... 4.3.2
        (2)(a)–(d) 4.3.2
     s.154 .... 4.3.2
        (2), (3) 4.3.2
     s.155 .... 4.3.2
     s.156 .... 4.3.2
        (2)(a) 4.3.2
     ss.157–162 .... 4.3.2
     s.163 .... 4.3.2
        (1) 4.3.2
     s.164(4) 10.5.2.1
        (6) 10.5.6
     s.179 .... 9.1.2
     Sched. 11,
        para. 2(a)–(d) 4.3.2
        (e) 4.3.2
        (ii) 4.3.2
        (g), (h) 4.3.2
        para. 5 .... 4.3.2
     Sched. 12,
        para. 2 .... 4.3.2
     Local Government Act (c. 19) .. 9.3.4
     Trade Union and Labour Rela-
        tions (Consolidation) Act
        (c. 52) 7.4.3, 7.5.5.2
     s.4 .... 2.7
     s.12 .... 11.1
     s.28 .... 7.4.4
     s.29(1) 7.4.8
     s.47 .... 7.4.7
     s.58(1)(b) 7.4.2
     s.64 .... 11.2.2
     s.100(1)(a), (b) 7.4.11
     s.101 .... 7.4.12
     s.102(1) 7.4.11
     s.103 .... 7.4.7, 7.4.11
     s.105(6) 7.4.7
     s.137 .... 1.10; 7.4.2
        (1), (2), (5) 1.10
     s.145 .... 9.3.4
     s.146 ..... 1.10; 7.4.2, 7.4.12; 11.4.1
     s.152 .... 7.4.2, 7.4.4, 7.4.12, 7.5.5.2;
                                    8.3.2.3
        (1) 8.3.2
        (a)–(c) 7.4.2, 7.4.12
        (2) 7.4.2
        (a), (b) 7.4.2
        (3) 7.4.2
     s.153 .... 7.4.2, 7.4.12, 7.5.5.2; 8.3.2,
                                    8.3.2.3
        (a) 7.4.12
     s.154 .... 7.4.2, 7.4.12
     s.156 .... 7.4.12, 7.5.5.2
     s.157 .... 7.4.11, 7.4.12, 7.5.5.2
        (1) 7.5.5.2
     s.158(2)–(4) 7.5.5.2

1992 Trade Union and Labour Rela-
        tions (Consolidation) Act—
        cont.
     s.158(5)(a) 7.5.5.2
     s.160 .... 7.3
     s.161 .... 7.4.2, 7.4.12
        (1), (3) 7.5.5.2
     s.163(2) 7.5.5.2
     s.164(1) 7.5.5.2
     s.165(1) 7.5.5.2
     s.168 .... 4.3.5
     s.169 .... 4.3.5; 11.4
     s.170 .... 4.3.5; 11.3.1
        (1)(b) 11.4
        (2) 11.4
     ss.171, 172 .... 4.3.5
     s.178 .... 2.4; 11.3.1
        (1) 9.1.2
        (2) 11.3.1
        (3) 9.2.3
     s.179 .... 2.4, 2.4.3; 5.2.2; 9.6.1
        (1), (2) 11.3.1
     s.181 .... 11.3.1
        (2)(a), (b) 11.3.1
     s.182 .... 11.3.1
        (1)(a), (c), (e) 11.3.2
     s.188 .... 7.4.7, 7.4.12; 8.3.3, 8.3.3.1,
                       8.3.3.5; 9.1.2; 11.1, 11.3.1
        (1) 8.3.3, 8.3.3.1, 8.3.3.2,
                          8.3.3.4; 9.2.3, 9.2.4
        (1A)(a), (b) 8.3.3.1
        (1B) 8.3.3.1
        (a) 8.3.3, 8.3.4.1
        (b) 8.3.3
        (2), (5A) 8.3.3.1
        (7) 8.3.3.5
     s.189 .... 7.4.7, 7.4.12; 8.3.3, 8.3.3.5
        (1)(a)–(c) 8.3.3.5
        (2), (4) 8.3.3.5
        (6) 8.3.3.5
        (a) 8.3.3.5
     s.190 .... 7.4.7, 7.4.12; 8.3.3, 8.3.3.5
        (3) 8.3.3.5
     ss.191, 192 ..... 7.4.7, 7.4.12; 8.3.3,
                                    8.3.3.5
     s.193 .... 8.3.3
        (7) 8.3.3.5
     s.194 .... 8.3.3
        (1) 8.3.3
     s.195 .... 8.3.1.3
     s.199 .... 2.6.2
        (2)(a)–(c) 2.6.2
     s.200(1) 2.6.2
     s.201 .... 2.6.2; 7.3.1
     s.203 .... 2.6.2
     s.204(1) 2.6.2
     s.207 .... 2.6.2; 7.3.1
     s.218 .... 11.1.1, 11.2

1992 Trade Union and Labour Rela-
      tions (Consolidation) Act—
      cont.
      s.219 . . . . 11.2, 11.2.1
      s.226 . . . . 11.4, 11.5.3.1
      s.236 . . . . 3.1.2.4; 5.3.2.1
         (a), (b) 5.6.3
      s.237 . . . . 7.2.5; 9.1.2
         (2) 7.2.5
      s.238 . . . . 7.2.5; 9.1.2; 11.4
      s.245 . . . . 1.4
      s.295(1) 4.5.4; 9.1.2
      Sched. 2 . . . . 2.7
      Sched. 5 . . . . 7.4.4
1993 Trade Union Reform and
      Employment Rights Act
      (c. 19) 2.8; 7.2.9, 7.5.2, 7.5.4,
                    7.5.5.2; 10.3, 10.5
      s.13 . . . . 11.4.1, 11.5.3.2
      s.26 . . . . 2.8
      s.32 . . . . 6.2.7
      s.33 . . . . 9.3.4; 11.3.1
         (2) 9.3.4
         (3)(b) 9.3.4
      s.34 . . . . . . 8.3.3, 8.3.3.1, 8.4; 11.3.1
         (3), (4) 8.3.3.5
      s.35 . . . . 4.5.3
      s.49(1) 6.1.4
      Sched. 3 . . . . 10.1
      Sched. 4 . . . . 2.8
      Sched. 7,
         para. 15 . . . . 6.1.4
      Asylum and Immigration
      Appeals Act (c. 23) 1.7
      European   Communities
      (Amendment) Act (c. 32) 2.7
      Pension Schemes Act (c. 48) 9.7
1994 Statutory Sick Pay Act (c. 2) 4.3.2
      Insolvency Act (c. 7) 8.5.1
      s.1 . . . . 8.5.1
      s.5(2) 8.5.1
      Sched. 2 . . . . 8.5.1
      Race Relations (Remedies) Act
      (c. 10) 6.3.8
      Sunday Trading Act (c. 20) 1.10;
                                         7.4.5
      Sched. 4 . . . . 1.10
      Criminal Justice and Public
      Order Act (c. 33) 6.3.4.1
      s.125 . . . . 7.2.4
      Sale and Supply of Goods Act
      (c. 35) 1.1
      Deregulation and Contracting
      Out Act (c. 40) 1.11
      s.20(5) 1.11
      s.36 . . . . 8.3.4
         (1) 5.6.3
      Sched. 8 . . . . 1.11

1995 Pensions Act (c. 26) 6.2.8, 6.3.6;
                                         7.4.6
      s.16 . . . . 7.4.6
      s.62 . . . . . . 6.1.2, 6.1.3, 6.2.1.2, 6.2.8
         (1), (2) 6.1.3
      s.63 . . . . 6.1.3, 6.2.1.2, 6.2.8
      s.64 . . . . 6.1.3, 6.2.1.2, 6.2.8
         (2) 6.1.3
      ss.65, 66 . . . . 6.1.3, 6.2.1.2, 6.2.8
      s.126 . . . . 6.1.3, 6.2.8
      Sched. 4 . . . . 6.2.8
      Pt. I 6.1.3
      Disability Discrimination Act
      (c. 50) . . . 1.15; 6.1.4, 6.3.6, 6.3.8;
                                         7.2.8.4
      Pt. II 6.1.4, 6.4.2
      Pt. VI 6.4.1
      s.1 . . . . 6.3.1
         (1) 1.15; 6.3.2
      s.2 . . . . 7.4.8
      s.3 . . . . 2.6.2; 6.3.1
         (3) 2.6.2; 6.3.1
      s.4(1)(a)–(c) 6.3.1
         (2) 6.3.1
         (d) 6.3.1, 6.3.4.1; 8.3.4.2
      s.5(1) 6.3.2, 6.3.7
         (a) 6.3.4.1
         (b) 6.3.1
         (2) 6.3.1
         (b) 6.3.1
         (3) 6.3.2
      s.6 . . . . 6.3.1
         (1) 1.15
         (a) 6.3.1
         (2) 6.3.2
         (3) 1.15
         (4) 6.3.2
         (a)–(e) 6.3.1
      s.7(1) 6.3.1
      s.8(2) 6.3.8
         (c) 6.3.8
         (4) 6.3.8
      s.50 . . . . 6.4.2
         (4) 6.4.2
         (9)(a), (b) 6.4.2
      s.53 . . . . 6.4.2
         (1)(a) 2.6.2
         (4) 2.6.2
      s.54 . . . . 6.4.2
      s.55 . . . . 6.4.2; 7.4.8
      s.56 . . . . 6.4.2
      s.58 . . . . 6.3.4.1
         (5) 6.3.4.1
      s.61 . . . . 6.4.2
      s.64 . . . . 1.4
      s.68 . . . . 1.15

1995	Disability Discrimination Act—*cont.*	
	Sched. 1	6.3.1
	para. 2(1)	6.3.2
	para. 4(1)	6.3.2
	Sched. 3	6.4.1
	Sched. 5	6.4.2
1996	Industrial Tribunals Act (c. 17)	7.5.4
	Pt. I	7.5
	Pt. II	7.5, 7.5.3
	s.3	1.2; 7.5.1
	(2)	7.5.1
	s.4(1)–(3)	7.5
	s.9	7.5.2
	s.10	7.5.3
	s.18	7.2.6, 7.2.8.4
	(2), (3)	7.2.6
	s.21	7.5.1, 7.5.3
	(1)	7.5
	s.28(2), (4)	7.5
	s.29(2)	7.5.3
	Employment Rights Act (c. 18)	1.2, 1.14.1, 1.14.2; 3.3.1.1, 3.3.1.2; 4.4; 7.1, 7.2.8, 7.5.4, 7.5.5.2; 8.2; 10.1, 10.5.2.1, 10.6, 10.8
	Pt. I	2.2, 2.4.1, 2.5.1, 2.8, 2.8.3, 2.8.4
	Pt. II	7.2.4, 7.5.1
	Pt. IV	1.10, 1.11; 7.4.5
	Pt. VI	4.3.4; 7.2.4
	Pt. VII	7.2.4
	Pt. VIII	7.2.4; 10.1, 10.3, 10.8
	Pt. X	1.8; 7.2.4, 7.4.9; 8.3.2; 9.1.2
	Pt. XI	8.2, 8.3.7
	Pt. XII	8.5.2
	Pt. XIV, Ch. 1	7.2.8
	s.1	1.12; 2.4, 2.5.2, 2.8, 2.8.2, 2.8.4; 3.3.4; 5.2.2, 5.2.4, 5.7; 7.2.4
	(1)(a)	4.4.1
	(3)(a)–(c)	2.8
	(4)	1.12; 2.8; 4.3.2
	(a)–(c)	2.8
	(d)(i)	1.12; 2.8; 4.3.2
	(ii)	2.8; 4.3.1.1
	(iii)	2.8
	(e)–(g)	2.8
	(j)	2.4.1, 2.8
	(k)(i)–(iv)	2.8
	(5)	2.8
	s.2	2.5.2; 7.2.4
	(1)	3.3.1.2; 4.3.1.1, 4.3.3
	(2)	3.3.1.2
	(4)	1.12; 4.3.3
	(6)	2.8

1996	Employment Rights Act—*cont.*	
	s.3	2.5.2; 3.3.4; 7.2.4
	(1)(a)	7.3.1
	(b)(ii)	3.3.4
	(3)	2.8; 7.3.1
	s.4	2.8.1; 5.2.2; 7.2.4
	s.4(1)	5.2.4
	(4), (5)	5.2.2
	(7)	2.8.1
	s.5	7.2.4
	s.6	2.8; 7.2.4
	s.7	7.2.4
	s.8	4.2.3, 4.5.4; 7.2.4
	(1)	4.2.4
	(2)(a)–(d)	4.2.4
	(4)	4.2.2
	s.9	4.2.3, 4.2.4; 7.2.4
	s.10	4.2.3; 7.2.4
	s.11	2.3, 2.4.3, 2.8.2; 5.2.4
	(1)	4.2.4; 5.2.4
	(3)(b)	4.2.4
	s.12	5.2.4
	(1)	5.2.4
	(4)	4.2.4
	s.13	4.2.2, 4.2.4, 4.4, 4.4.1, 4.5.4; 5.4.2; 7.2.4, 7.4.8; 9.5
	(1)	4.4.1
	(a), (b)	4.4.1
	(2)(a), (b)	4.4.1
	(3)	4.2.2, 4.4.1
	(4)	4.2.2
	s.14	4.4, 4.4.2; 7.2.4
	(1) (a), (b)	4.4.2
	(2)–(4)	4.4.2
	(5)	4.4.2, 4.4.3
	(6)	4.4.2
	s.15	4.4; 7.2.4
	s.16	4.4; 7.2.4
	s.17, 18	4.4, 4.4.1; 7.2.4
	s.19	1.4; 4.4, 4.4.1; 7.2.4
	ss.20, 21	4.4, 4.4.1; 7.2.4
	s.22	4.4; 7.2.4
	s.23	2.4.3; 4.4; 7.2.4
	(1)(a)	7.4.8
	ss.24–26	4.4; 7.2.4
	s.27	4.2.2, 4.4; 7.2.4
	(1)	4.2.2
	(a)–(j)	4.2.2
	(2)	4.2.2
	(a)–(e)	4.2.2
	s.28	7.2.4; 8.5.2
	ss.29–35	7.2.4
	s.36(2)	7.4.5
	(a)–(c)	1.11
	(3)	7.4.5
	(a), (b)	1.11
	(5), (6)	1.11

1996   Employment Rights Act—*cont.*
    s.37(1), (2) 1.11
    s.38(2) 1.11
    s.39 .... 1.11
    s.40 .... 1.11; 2.8; 7.4.5
    s.41 .... 7.4.5
      (1)(a)–(c) 1.11
      (d), (e) 3.3.2.1
      (2), (3) 1.11
    s.42 .... 1.11
      (1) 2.8
      (4) 1.11
      (5) 1.11; 2.8
    s.43 .... 1.11
    s.44 ..... 3.3.1.2; 7.2.4, 7.4.4, 7.4.12
      (1) 3.3.1.2
    s.45 .... 7.2.4, 7.4.5
    s.46 .... 7.2.4, 7.4.8, 7.4.12
    s.47 .... 7.2.4, 7.4.12; 9.2.6
    ss.48, 49 .... 7.2.4
    s.50 .... 4.3.4, 4.3.6; 7.2.4
      (2), (4) 4.3.6
    s.51 .... 4.3.4, 4.3.6; 7.2.4
    s.52 .... 4.3.4; 7.2.4; 8.3.6, 8.5.2
      (1) 4.3.4; 8.3.6
    s.53 .... 4.3.4; 7.2.4
      (1) 8.3.6
      (2) 8.3.7
      (5) 4.3.4; 8.3.6
    s.54 .... 4.3.4; 7.2.4
      (3) 4.3.4
    s.55 ...... 4.3.4; 7.2.4, 7.4.12; 8.5.2;
                10.1, 10.2
      (1)(b) 10.2
    s.56 ... 4.3.4; 7.2.4, 7.4.12; 10.1, 10.2
    s.57 .. 4.3.4. 4.3.5; 7.2.4, 7.4.12; 10.1
    ss.58, 59 ... 4.3.4. 4.3.5; 7.2.4, 7.4.6,
                     7.4.12
    s.60 .... 4.3.4. 4.3.5; 7.2.4, 7.4.6
    s.61 .... 4.3.4. 4.3.5; 7.2.4, 7.4.12
    ss.62, 63 .... 7.4.12
    s.64 .... 7.2.4; 8.5.2; 10.6
      (1) 10.6
    s.66 .... 7.2.4, 7.4.2; 8.5.2; 10.1, 10.6
      (2) 7.4.3; 10.3
    s.67 .... 7.4.2; 10.6
      (2)(a), (b) 10.6
    s.68 .... 7.4.2, 7.4.8; 10.6
    s.70 .... 7.4.2; 10.6
    s.71 .... 7.2.4; 10.1, 10.4.1, 10.4.1.6,
          10.4.2, 10.4.2.4, 10.4.2.6
      (1), (2) 10.4.1.3, 10.4.1.4
    s.72 .... 7.2.4; 10.4.1, 10.6
      (1) 10.4.2.4
    s.73 ..... 7.24; 10.4.1, 10.4.2.4, 10.8
    s.74 .... 7.2.4; 10.4.1, 10.4.1.1,
         10.4.1.6, 10.4.2.1, 10.4.2.2,
            10.4.2.4, 10.4.2.6

1996   Employment Rights Act—*cont.*
    s.74(1) 10.4.2.2
      (2) 10.4.2.4
      (3)(a) 10.4.1.2
      (b) 10.4.2.1
    s.75 .... 7.2.4; 10.4.1, 10.4.1.1,
        10.4.1.6, 10.4.2.2, 10.4.2.4,
                   10.4.2.6
      (1), (2) 10.4.2.1, 10.4.2.2,
                   10.4.2.4
    s.76 .... 10.4.1.1, 10.4.2.4
      (1) 10.4.1.6, 10.4.2.4
      (2), (3) 10.4.1.6
    s.77 ...... 7.2.4, 7.4.3, 7.4.12; 10.3,
              10.4.1, 10.4.1.7
      (2) 10.4.1.7
    s.78 .... 7.2.4, 10.4.1, 10.4.1.2
    s.79 ..... 7.2.4; 10.1; 10.4, 10.4.1.2,
        10.4.2, 10.4.2.1, 10.4.2.2,
        10.4.2.3, 10.4.2.4, 10.4.2.5
      (1) 10.4.2, 10.4.2.4, 10.8
      (b) 10.8
      (2) 10.4.2.3, 10.4.2.4
      (a)–(c) 10.4.2.4
    s.80 .... 7.2.4, 10.4.2.4
      (1) 10.4.2.1, 10.4.2.6
      (2) ... 10.4.2.2, 10.4.2.4, 10.4.2.6
    s.81 .... 7.2.4; 10.4.2.3, 10.4.2.4,
                   10.4.2.5
      (2) 8.3.5.4
      (3)(a), (b) 10.4.2.4
    s.82 .... 10.4.2.4, 10.4.2.5
      (1)–(5) 10.4.2.2, 10.4.2.4,
                 10.4.2.6
    ss.83, 84 .... 10.4.2.5
    s.85 .... 10.4.2.5
      (1), (2) 10.4.2.5
    s.86 ..... 5.4.1; 7.2.1.7, 7.2.4, 7.2.11,
          7.4.8; 8.3.7.2; 11.2
      (1) 5.4.2, 5.7; 7.2.11
      (a)–(c) 5.4.2
      (2) 5.4.2
      (3) 5.4.2; 7.2.11
      (4) 4.3.2
      (6) 5.4.2
    s.87 .... 5.4.1; 7.2.4
    s.88 .... 7.2.4
    s.89 .... 7.2.1, 7.2.4
    ss.90, 91 .... 7.2.4
    s.92 ... 7.2.1, 7.2.4, 7.2.9, 7.3, 7.4.12;
              10.4.2.6
      (4) 7.2.9; 10.3
      (5) 7.2.9
    s.93 .... 7.2.4; 10.3
    s.94 .... 1.11; 5.3.4; 7.2, 7.2.1, 7.2.8;
          10.4.2.6; 11.2
      (1) 5.5, 5.6; 9.1.2

1996 Employment Rights Act—*cont.*
s.95 . . . . 5.3.2.3; 7.2.1; 10.4.2.6
  (1)(a) 5.3.3; 10.4.2.2
    (b) 1.14.2; 5.5.2; 7.2.1.6
    (c) 2.2; 3.2.1, 3.3.1.2;
          5.2.1.1, 5.3.2.3, 5.3.3,
          5.4.2; 7.2.1.5; 8.4
s.96 . . . . 1.15; 7.2.1, 7.2.4; 10.3,
        10.4.1.6, 10.4.2.5, 10.4.2.6
  (1) 7.2.1; 10.4.2.2, 10.4.2.4,
          10.4.2.5
    (a) 10.4.2.6
    (b) 10.4.2.5, 10.4.2.6
  (2), (3) 10.4.2.3, 10.4.2.4
  (4) 10.4.2.4
    (a), (b) 10.4.2.4
  (5) 10.4.2.4
s.97 . . . . 7.2.1
  (1)(a) 7.2.1.7
s.98 . . . . 7.2.1, 7.3, 7.3.2.2; 8.4;
        10.4.2.6
  (1) 5.3.2.3, 5.6; 7.3
    (b) . . 7.3, 7.3.1, 7.3.2.4, 7.4.9,
        7.4.12; 8.4; 9.1.2; 10.3;
        11.5.3.2
    (c) 8.3.1.4
  (2) 7.3.2.3; 8.4
    (a), (b) 7.3, 7.3.1, 7.3.2.1,
        7.3.2.2
    (c) 7.3, 7.3.1, 7.3.2.2,
        7.3.2.4; 8.3.4, 8.4
    (d) 7.3, 7.3.1, 7.3.2.3
  (3)(a) 7.3.2.1
  (4) 3.2.1; 7.3, 7.3.2.2, 7.3.3,
        7.4.3, 7.4.12; 8.3.1.4,
        8.3.2.3, 8.3.3.2, 8.3.4, 8.4,
        8.5; 9.8.2; 10.3; 11.5.3.2
    (a) 2.3; 7.4.9
    (b) 2.3; 7.3.2.2, 7.4.9
s.99 . . . . 7.2.1, 7.4.3; 10.1, 10.3
  (1) 7.4.12; 10.4.1.6
    (a) 7.4.3; 10.3, 10.4.1.6
    (b) 7.4.3; 10.3, 10.4.1.6,
        10.4.1.6
    (c) 7.4.3; 10.3
    (d) 7.4.3; 10.3, 10.4.1.6
    (e) 7.4.3; 10.4.1.7
  (3) 7.4.3, 7.4.12; 10.4.1.5,
        10.4.1.6
    (b) 7.4.3
  (4) 10.4.2.4
s.100 . . . 7.2.1, 7.4.2, 7.4.4; 10.1, 10.6
  (1)(a), (b) 7.4.12, 7.5.5.2
s.101 . . . . 7.2.1, 7.2.1.6, 7.4.5, 7.4.12
  (2), (3) 7.4.5
s.102 . . . . 7.2.1, 7.4.6, 7.4.12
  (1) 7.5.5.2

1996 Employment Rights Act—*cont.*
s.103 . . . . 7.2.1, 7.4.7, 7.4.12, 7.5.5.2
  (4)(b) 7.5.5.2
s.104 . . . . 7.2.1, 7.4.8, 7.4.12
  (1)(a)–(c) 7.4.8
  (2)(a), (b) 7.4.8
s.105 . . . . 7.2.1; 8.3.1.4; 10.1
  (1) 8.3.2
    (a) 7.4.4
    (b) 8.3.4
    (c) 7.4.4; 8.3.2
    (d), (e) 7.4.4
  (2) 7.4.3, 7.4.12; 8.3.2; 10.3
  (3) 7.4.4; 8.3.2
  (4) 8.3.2
    (a), (b) 7.4.5, 7.4.12
  (5) 7.4.6, 7.4.12; 8.3.2
  (6) 7.4.7, 7.4.12; 8.3.2
  (7) 7.4.8, 7.4.12; 8.3.2
s.106 . . . . 10.3.1
s.107 . . . . 7.3
s.108 . . . . 7.2.8, 7.4, 7.4.9; 10.3
  (1) . . . 7.2.1, 7.2.3, 7.4.3, 7.4.12
  (3)(b) 7.4.2, 7.4.3, 7.4.12;
        10.3
    (c)–(g) 7.4.12
s.109 . . . . 6.2.8; 7.4
  (1) 7.2.1, 7.2.10, 7.4.3
    (a) 7.2.10
      (i), (ii) 7.4.12
  (2) 7.2.10
    (b) 7.4.3, 7.4.12
    (c), (e)–(g) 7.4.12
s.110 . . . . 7.2.1, 7.2.7, 7.2.8.4
s.111 . . . . 6.2.1.3, 6.3.8; 7.2.2
  (2) 7.2.1, 7.2.1.7, 7.2.2
    (b) 7.2.1, 7.2.2
s.112 . . . . 7.5.5.1
  (4) 5.3.3; 7.5.5.2
s.113 . . . . 7.5.5.1, 7.5.5.2
  (a), (b) 5.3.3
s.114(1) 7.5.5.1
  (2)(a) 7.5.5.1, 7.5.5.2
    (b), (c) 7.5.5.1
  (3) 5.6.1
s.115(2)(a)–(f) 7.5.5.1
s.116 . . . . 7.5.5.1
  (1) 7.5.5.1
    (a)–(c) 7.5.5.1
  (2) 7.5.5.1
  (3)(a)–(c) 7.5.5.1
  (5) 7.5.5.1
s.117(2) 7.5.5.2
  (3) 7.5.5.2
    (b) 7.5.5.2
  (5)(a), (b) 7.5.5.2
s.118 . . . . 1.8; 7.5.5.2
  (3) 7.4.12, 7.5.5.2

1996 Employment Rights Act—*cont.*
   s.119 .... 7.5.5.2
       (2), (4), (5) 7.5.5.2
   s.120 .... 7.5.5.2
       (1) 7.4.12, 7.5.5.2
   s.121 .... 7.5.5.2
   s.122 .... 7.5.5.2
       (1)–(4) 7.5.5.2
   s.123 .... 7.5.5.2
       (1) 5.6.1; 7.5.5.2
       (4), (6), (7) 7.5.5.2
   s.124 .... 5.6.1; 7.5.5.2
       (1), (3), (4) 7.5.5.2
   s.125 .... 7.5.5.2
       (1)–(4) 7.5.5.2
       (5) 7.5.5.2
         (a), (b) 7.5.5.2
   s.126 .... 5.6.1; 7.5.5.2
   s.127 .... 7.5.5.2
   s.128 .... 7.5.5.2
       (1) 7.4.12
   s.129(2), (3) 7.5.5.2
   s.130 .... 7.5.5.2
       (1) 7.5.5.2
   s.131 .... 7.5.5.2
   s.135 .... 5.3.1; 9.1
       (1) 8.3.1.4
         (a) 5.3.1; 8.3.6
         (b) 8.3.6
   s.136 .... 7.2.1, 7.2.1.2
       (1)(a) 7.2.1.2
         (b) 5.5.2; 7.2.1.6
       (3) 8.3.7.2
         (b) 8.3.7.2
       (5)(b) 5.5.3; 8.3.7
   s.138 .... 8.3.5.2
       (1) 8.3.5
       (2) 8.3.5
         (a) 8.3.5
       (3) 8.3.5
         (a) 8.3.5
         (b) 8.3.5
           (ii) 8.3.5
       (4), (6) 8.3.5
   s.139 .... 8.3.1.3, 8.6
       (1) .. 2.2; 7.3.2.4; 8.3.1, 8.3.5.4,
                          8.3.7
         (a) 8.3.1
           (i) .. 8.3.1, 8.3.1.1, 8.3.1.2
           (ii) 8.3.1, 8.3.5.4
         (b) ... 7.2.1.6; 8.3.1, 8.3.1.2,
                         8.3.1.3
           (i), (ii) 8.3.1
       (4)(a) 8.3.7
       (6) 7.2.1.6
   s.140 .... 8.3.7.4
       (1) 8.3.7.4
         (a)–(c) 8.3.7.4

1996 Employment Rights Act—*cont.*
   s.141(2) 8.3.5
       (3)(a) 8.3.5
         (b) 8.3.5, 8.3.5.1
         (d) 8.3.5
   s.142(2)(a) 8.3.7.2
   s.143 .... 8.3.7.4; 11.4
       (2), (3), (5) 8.3.7.4
   s.155 .... 7.2.8; 8.3.7
   s.156 .... 8.3.7.2
       (1) 7.2.10
   s.158(1) 8.3.7.2
   ss.160, 161 .... 8.3.7.2
   s.163(2) 8.3.1.3
   s.164 .... 8.3.7
       (1)(b) 8.3.7
       (2), (3) 8.3.7
   s.165 .... 8.3.7
       (2)–(4) 8.3.7
   ss.168, 169 .... 7.4.8
   s.170 .... 7.4.8
       (2) 7.3.2.4
   s.182 .... 1.14.5; 8.5.2
   s.183 .... 8.5.2
   s.184 .... 1.14; 8.5.2
       (1)(a)–(d) 8.5.2
   s.185 .... 8.5.2
   ss.186, 187 .... 8.5.2
   s.188(4) 8.3.3.3
         (a)–(f) 8.3.3.3
       (7) 8.3.3.3
   s.189 .... 8.5.2
   ss.193–195 .... 1.4
   s.196 .... 7.2.1, 7.2.4; 9.1.2
       (1) 7.2.4
   s.197 .... 1.14.2; 5.5.2; 7.2.1, 7.2.1.6,
                     7.2.4; 9.1.2
       (1) 7.2.1.6
       (3) 7.2.1.6; 8.3.7
       (4) 7.2.1.6
       (5) 7.2.1.6; 8.3.7.1
   s.198 .... 7.2.1, 7.2.4; 9.1.2
   s.199 .... 7.2.1, 7.2.4; 9.1.2
       (1), (2) 7.2.4
   s.200 .... 7.2.1, 7.2.4; 9.1.2
   s.201 .... 7.2.4; 9.1.2
   s.203 .... 5.3.2.3; 7.2.6, 7.5.1, 8.3.5.4
       (1) 7.2.1.2, 7.2.1.6, 7.2.6,
                   8.3.5.4; 10.4.2.6
       (2)(c), (e) 7.2.6
         (f) 7.2.1, 7.2.1.6, 7.2.6
       (3), (6) 7.2.6
   s.206 .... 5.5.3
   s.210 .... 7.2.8
       (4) 7.2.8
   s.211 .... 7.2.8
       (1)(a) 1.2; 7.2.8
   s.212 .... 7.2.8, 7.2.8.1

1996 Employment Rights Act—*cont.*
  s.212(2) .. 7.2.8.1; 10.4.2.2, 10.4.2.4,
                  10.4.2.6
    (3) 7.2.8.1
      (a), (b) 7.2.8.1
      (c) 7.2.1.6, 7.2.8.1
      (d) 7.2.8.1
  ss.213, 214 .... 7.2.8
  s.215 .... 7.2.8, 7.2.8.2
  s.216 .... 7.2.8
    (1)–(3) 7.2.8.2
  s.217 .... 7.2.8
  s.218 .... 5.5.3; 6.1.2; 7.2.8; 9.1
    (1)–(3) 7.2.8.3
    (4) 5.5.3; 7.2.8.3
    (5) 5.5.3; 6.1.2; 7.2.8.3
    (6)–(8) 7.2.8.3
  ss.220–229 .... 4.2.3
  s.230 .... 1.2, 1.14, 1.14.4; 7.2
    (1) 1.14, 1.14.6
    (2) 1.14
    (3) 4.4.1, 4.5.4
  s.232(1) 1.11
  s.235 .... 10.4.2.3
  s.236 .... 5.6.3

1996 Employment Rights Act—*cont.*
  ss.237, 238 .... 7.2.1
  Sched. 2,
    para. 14(1) 7.2.8
  Asylum and Immigration Act
    (c. 49) 1.6, 1.7, 1.16
  s.8 .... 1.7
    (2), (5), (8) 1.7
  Statutory Instruments (Produc-
    tion and Sale) Act (c. 54) .. 2.6.1
1997 Protection from Harassment Act
    (c. 40) 6.3.4.1
  Police Act (c. 50) 1.8
  Pt. V 1.8; 2.6.2
  s.112 .... 1.8
    (3) 1.8
  s.113 .... 1.8
    (5) 1.8
  s.114 .... 1.8
  s.115 .... 1.8
    (4), (5), (8) 1.8
  ss.116, 117 .... 1.8
  s.122 .... 1.8; 2.6.2
    (3) 1.8
  s.124 .... 1.8

TABLE OF STATUTORY INSTRUMENTS

References in the right-hand column are to paragraph numbers.

1962 Non-ferrous Metals (Melting and Founding) Regulations 1962 (S.I. 1962 No. 1667)—
reg. 13(1), (4) 3.3.1.3

1975 Rehabilitation of Offenders Act 1974 (Exemptions) Order 1975 (S.I. 1975 No. 1023) 1.8
Sex Discrimination (Questions and Replies) Order 1975 (S.I. 1975 No. 2048) 6.3.7

1976 Occupational Pensions Schemes (Equal Access to Membership) Regulations 1976 (S.I. 1976 No. 142) 6.2.8
reg. 12 .... 6.2.1.2
Conduct of Employment Agencies and Employment Businesses Regulations 1976 (S.I. 1976 No. 715)—
reg. 9(6)(a)–(c) 2.8
Employment Protection (Offshore Employment) Order 1976 (S.I. 1976 No. 766) ... 7.2.4
Sex Discrimination (Northern Ireland) Order 1976—
art. 3(1)(b)(ii) 6.3.3.3

1977 Employment Protection (Offshore Employment) (Amendment) Order 1977 (S.I. 1977 No. 588) 7.2.4
Employment Protection Code of Practice (Disciplinary Practice and Procedures) Order 1977 (S.I. 1977 No. 867) ... 5.3.4, 5.5.1.1

1980 Control of Lead at Work Regulations 1980 (S.I. 1980 No. 1248)—
reg. 16 .... 10.6

1981 Employment Protection (Offshore Employment) (Amendment) Order 1981 (S.I. 1981 No. 208) 7.2.4
Transfer of Undertakings (Protection of Employment) Regulations 1981 (S.I. 1981 No. 1794) 2.6.1, 2.7; 5.5.3; 6.1.2; 7.2.8.3, 7.4.9; 9.1, 9.1.2, 9.3.4; 11.3.1
reg. 2 .... 9.1.2
   (1) 9.1.2, 9.3.4
   (2), (3) 9.1.2
reg. 3 .... 9.1.2, 9.3.1
   (1), (4) 9.1.2, 9.3.1
reg. 4 .... 9.1.2, 9.4.1
   (1) 9.1.2, 9.9
   (a), (b) 9.1.2
reg. 5 .... 2.4.3; 9.1.2, 9.4, 9.5
   (1) ... 5.5.3; 6.1.2; 9.1.2, 9.4.1, 9.5, 9.8.2
   (2) 7.2.6, 9.8.2
   (3) 7.2.6, 9.8.2
   (a) 9.1.2, 9.4.1, 9.4.3
   (b) 9.1.2, 9.4.3
   (3) 9.1.2, 9.8.1
   (4A)   5.5.3; 6.1.2; 9.1.2, 9.8.2, 9.8.3, 9.9.1
   (4B) .. 5.5.3; 6.1.2; 9.1.2, 9.8.3, 9.9.1
   (5) 9.1.2, 9.5, 9.6, 9.8
reg. 6 .... 9.1.2, 9.6
   (a) 9.1.2
reg. 7 .... 9.1.2, 9.7
reg. 8 .... 9.1.2, 9.5, 9.8, 9.8.1
   (1) .. 2.4.3; 7.4.9, 7.4.12; 9.1.2, 9.5, 9.8
   (2) 2.4.3; 7.4.9, 7.4.12; 9.1.2, 9.5, 9.8.1, 9.8.2, 9.9
   (b) 9.5

1981 Transfer of Undertakings (Pro-
      tection of Employment)
      Regulations 1981—cont.
      reg. 9 .... 9.1.2
          (1) 9.1.2, 9.6.1
          (2)(a) 9.1.2, 9.6.1
      reg. 10 ..... 7.4.7, 7.4.12; 9.1.2, 9.2,
                    9.2.2, 9.2.6, 11.1
          (1) 9.1.2, 9.2.2
          (2) ... 9.1.2, 9.2.2, 9.2.4, 9.2.6
          (a) 9.1.2, 9.2.4
          (b), (d) 9.2.5
          (2A) 9.2.2, 9.2.7
          (3) 9.1.2
          (4) 9.1.2, 9.2.4
          (5) 9.1.2, 9.2.5
          (6) 9.1.2
          (a), (b) 9.2.5
          (6A) 9.1.2
          (7) 9.1.2, 9.2.5
          (8) 9.1.2, 9.2.4
          (b) 9.2.3
      reg. 11 ...... 7.4.7, 7.4.12; 9.1.2, 9.2
          (1) 9.2.6
          (a)–(c) 9.2.6
          (3) 9.1.2
          (4) 9.2.6
          (8) 9.2.3
          (a), (b) 9.2.6
          (11) 9.2.6
      reg. 11A 9.1.2
      reg. 12 .... 2.4.3; 9.1.2, 9.5
1982 Statutory Sick Pay (General)
      Regulations 1982 (S.I. 1982
      No. 894) 4.3.2; 10.1
      reg. 3(1), (2) 4.3.2
      reg. 5 .... 4.3.2
      reg. 10–13 .... 4.3.2
      Statutory Sick Pay (Mariners,
      Airman and Persons
      Abroad) Regulations 1982
      (S.I. 1982 No. 1349) 4.3.2
      reg. 10 .... 4.3.2
1983 Race Relations Code of Practice
      Order 1983 (S.I. 1983 No.
      1081) 2.6.2
      Equal Pay (Amendment) Regu-
      lations 1983 (S.I. 1983 No.
      1794) 2.7.2; 6.2.6
      reg. 2(1) 6.2.5
1984 Occupational Pension Schemes
      (Contracting Out) Regu-
      lations 1984 (S.I. 1984 No.
      380) 11.3.1

1984 Occupational Pension Schemes
      (Contracting Out) Regu-
      lations Amendment Regu-
      lations 1984 (S.I. 1984 No.
      1104) 11.3.1
1985 Redundancy Payments (Varia-
      tion of Rebates) Order 1985
      (S.I. 1985 No. 259) 8.2
      Sex Discrimination Code of Prac-
      tice Order 1985 (S.I. 1985
      No. 387) 2.6.2
      Unfair Dismissal (Variation of
      Qualifying Period) Order
      1985 (S.I. 1985 No. 782) 10.3
      Ionising Radiations Regulations
      1985 (S.I. 1985 No. 1333)—
      reg. 16 .... 10.6
1988 Control of Substances Hazardous
      to Health Regulations 1988
      (S.I. 1988 No. 1657)—
      reg. 11 .... 10.6
1989 Health and Safety (Enforcing
      Authority) Regulations 1989
      (S.I. 1989 No. 1903) 3.3.2.1
1990 Industrial Tribunals (Interest)
      Order 1990 (S.I. 1990 No.
      479) 6.3.8
1991 Employment Codes of Practice
      (Revocation) Order 1991
      (S.I. 1991 No. 1264) 8.2, 8.4
1992 Employment Code of Practice
      (Picketing) Order 1992 (S.I.
      1992 No. 476) 2.6.2
      Management of Health and
      Safety at Work Regulations
      1992 (S.I. 1992 No. 2051) .. 2.6.1,
             2.6.2; 3.3.1.1, 3.3.1.3; 7.4.4;
                                      10.6
      reg. 3 .... 3.3.1.3; 10.6
      reg. 12 .... 3.1.5
      reg. 13A 3.3.1.1; 10.6
          (2), (3) 10.6
      reg. 13B 3.3.1.1; 10.6
      reg. 13C 3.3.1.1
      Health and Safety (Display
      Screen Equipment) Regu-
      lations 1992 (S.I. 1992 No.
      2792) 1.14.3; 3.3.1.1
      Manual Handling Operations
      Regulations 1992 (S.I. 1992
      No. 2793) 3.1.5, 3.3.1.1
      Provisions and Use of Work
      Equipment Regulations
      1992 (S.I. 1992 No. 2932) 3.3.1.1
      Personal Protective Equipment
      at Work Regulations 1992
      (S.I. 1992 No. 2966) 3.3.1.1
      reg. 10, 11 .... 3.1.5

1992 Workplace (Health, Safety and
       Welfare) Regulations 1992
       (S.I. 1992 No. 3004) 3.3.1.1
       reg. 6 .... 3.3.1.2
1993 Access to Health Records (Con-
       trol of Access) Regulations
       1993 (S.I. 1993 No. 746) ... 1.9.2
       Trade Union Reform and
       Employment Rights Act
       1993 (Commencement No. 1
       and Transitional Provisions)
       Order 1993 (S.I. 1993 No.
       1908) 6.1.4
       Employment Protection (Con-
       tinuity of Employment)
       Regulations 1993 (S.I. 1993
       No. 2165) 7.5.5.1
       Industrial Tribunals (Constitution
       and Rules of Procedure)
       Regulations 1993 (S.I. 1993
       No. 2687) 6.2.5, 6.2.6; 7.5,
                              7.5.3, 7.5.4
       Sched. 1 .... 7.5
       r. 7 .... 7.5.3
         (1), (8) 7.5.3
       r. 8 .... 7.5
       r. 9(1) 7.5
       r. 13(6) 7.5
       r. 14 .... 7.5
         (1) 7.5
       Sched. 2 .... 6.2.6
       Sex Discrimination and Equal
       Pay (Remedies) Regulations
       1993 (S.I. 1993 No. 2798) .. 2.6.1;
                           6.3.8; 7.2.8; 10.3
       Employment Appeal Tribunal
       Rules 1993 (S.I. 1993 No.
       2854) 7.5
       r. 23(2), (3) 7.5.3
       r. 30 .... 7.5.3
1994 Industrial Tribunals (Constitu-
       tions and Rules of Pro-
       cedure)   (Amendment)
       Regulations 1994 (S.I. 1994
       No. 536) 6.2.6; 7.5
       reg. 8 .... 7.5.1
       Industrial Tribunals Extension of
       Jurisdiction (England and
       Wales) Order 1994 (S.I.
       1994 No. 1623)   4.2.2; 5.4.1; 7.5.1
       art. 3 .... 1.2; 7.2.6, 7.5.1
         (2) 7.5.1
           (c) 1.2
       art. 7(a) 7.5.1
       Industrial Tribunals Extension of
       Jurisdiction   (Scotland)
       Order 1994 (S.I. 1994 No.
       1624) 1.2; 5.4.1

1994 Social Security Act 1989 (Com-
       mencement No. 5) Order
       1994 (S.I. 1994 No. 1661) .. 6.1.2
       Race Relations (Interest on
       Awards) Regulations 1994
       (S.I. 1994 No. 1748) 6.3.8
       Sunday Trading Act 1994
       Appointed Day Order 1994
       (S.I. 1994 No. 1841) 1.11
       Statutory Maternity Pay (Com-
       pensation of Employers) and
       Miscellaneous Amendment
       Regulations 1994 (S.I. 1994
       No. 1882) 10.5.1, 10.5.2.1
       reg. 2(1) 10.5.4
       reg. 3 .... 10.5.4
       reg. 4 .... 10.5, 10.5.4
       Maternity (Compulsory Leave)
       Regulations 1994 (S.I. 1994
       No. 2479) 10.4.2.4
       reg. 2 .... 10.4.1.2
       Health and Safety at Work
       (Amendment) Regulations
       1994 (S.I. 1994 No.
       2865) 3.3.1.1; 10.6
       Suspension from Work (on
       Maternity Grounds) Order
       1994 (S.I. 1994 No. 2930) ... 10.6
1995 Employment   Protection
       (Part-time   Employees)
       Regulations 1995 (S.I. 1995
       No. 31) .. 1.14.1; 2.7; 6.1.1; 7.2.2,
                              7.2.8; 10.3
       Statutory Sick Pay Percentage
       Threshold Order 1995 (S.I.
       1995 No. 512) 4.3.2
       Employment   Protection
       (Increase of Limits) Order
       1995 (S.I. 1995 No. 1953) .. 7.5.1
       Collective Redundancies and
       Transfer of Undertakings
       (Protection of Employment)
       (Amendment) Regulations
       1995 (S.I. 1995 No. 2587) .. 2.6.1;
                 7.4.5, 7.4.7, 7.4.9, 7.4.12;
                              9.1.2, 9.2.1
       reg. 3 .... 8.3.3.1, 8.3.3.2
       Employment Code of Practice
       (Industrial Action Ballots
       and Notice to Employers)
       Order 1995 (S.I. 1995 No.
       2729) 2.6.2
       Occupational Pension Schemes
       (Equal Treatment) Regu-
       lations 1995 (S.I. 1995 No.
       3183) ... 6.1.2, 6.1.3, 6.2.1.2, 6.2.8
       reg. 5 .... 6.2.1.2
       reg. 13 .... 6.2.8

1995 Occupational Pension Schemes (Equal Treatment) Regulations 1995—*cont.*
reg. 15 .... 6.2.8
 (2)(c) 6.1.1
1996 Sex Discrimination and Equal Pay (Miscellaneous Amendments) Regulations 1996 (S.I. 1996 No. 438) ... 6.2.5, 6.3.8
reg. 8A 6.2.5
 (12) 6.2.5
reg. 9(2B), (2C) 6.2.5
 (2E) 6.2.5, 6.2.6
Statutory Maternity Pay (Compensation of Employers) Amendment Regulations 1996 (S.I. 1996 No. 668) .. 10.5.1
reg. 2 .... 10.5.4
Statutory Maternity Pay (General) Amendment Regulations 1996 (S.I. 1996 No. 1335) 10.5.5
Disability Discrimination (Meaning of Disability) Regulations 1996 (S.I. 1996 No. 1455) 6.3.1
Health and Safety (Consultations with Employees) Regulations 1996 (S.I. 1996 No. 1513) 7.4.4
reg. 8 .... 7.4.4
Industrial Tribunals (Constitution and Rules of Procedure) (Amendment) Regulations 1996 (S.I. 1996 No. 1757) 6.2.5; 7.5
reg. 10 .... 7.5.3
Disability Discrimination (Guidance and Code of Practice) (Appointed Day) Order 1996 (S.I. 1996 No. 1996) .. 2.6.2

1996 Employment Protection (Recoupment of Jobseeker's Allowance and Income Support) Regulations 1996 (S.I. 1996 No. 2349) 7.5.5.2
Statutory Sick Pay (General) Amendment Regulations 1996 (S.I. 1996 No. 3042) .. 4.3.2
Employment Protection (Continuity of Employment) Regulations 1996 (S.I. 1996 No. 3147) 7.2.8.4
Immigration (Restrictions on Employment) Order 1996 (S.I. 1996 No. 3225) 1.7
1997 Health and Safety (Young Persons) Regulations 1997 (S.I. 1997 No. 135) .. 1.5, 1.16; 3.3.1.1
1998 Employment Protection Code of Practice (Disciplinary Practice and Procedures) Order 1998 (S.I. 1998 No. 44) 2.6.2; 7.3.1
Employment Protection Code of Practice (Disclosure of Information) Order 1998 (S.I. 1998 No. 45) 2.6.2
Employment Protection Code of Practice (Time Off) Order 1998 (S.I. 1998 No. 46) 2.6.2
Children (Protection at Work) Regulations 1998 (S.I. 1998 No. 276) 1.5, 1.16
Statutory Maternity Pay (Compensation of Employers) Amendment Regulations 1998 (S.I. 1998 No. 522) 10.5.2.1

TABLE OF ABBREVIATIONS

ACAS	Advisory, Conciliation and Arbitration Service
ARD	Acquired Rights Directive (Council Directive 77/187)
CAC	Central Arbitration Committee
CBI	Confederation of British Industries
CCO	continuation of contract order
CRD	Collective Redundancies Directive (Council Directive 75/129)
CRE	Commission for Racial Equality
CS	Court of Session
DDA 1995	Disability Discrimination Act 1995
DfEE	Department for Education and Employment
DTI	Department of Trade and Industry
EA 1989	Employment Act 1989
EA 1990	Employment Act 1990
EAT	Employment Appeal Tribunal
ECA 1972	European Communities Act 1972
ECHR	European Court of Human Rights
ECJ	European Court of Justice
EEA	European Economic Area
EEPTU	Electrical Electronic Telecommunications and Plumbing Union
EFTA	European Free Trade Association
EOC	Equal Opportunities Commission
EPA 1975	Employment Protection Act 1975
EPCA 1978	Employment Protection (Consolidation) Act 1978
EqPA 1970	Equal Pay Act 1970
ERA 1996	Employment Rights Act 1996
ETO	economic, technical or organisational
GOC	Genuine Occupational Qualification
EWC	expected week of childbirth
HSWA 1974	Health and Safety at Work etc. Act 1974
IA 1986	Insolvency Act 1986
ICTA 1988	Income and Corporation Taxes Act 1988
ILJ	Industrial Law Journal
ILO	International Labour Organisation
IRA 1971	Industrial Relations Act 1971
IT	industrial tribunal
ITA 1996	Industrial Tribunals Act 1996

JES	job evaluation scheme
LEL	lower earnings limit
LIFO	last in, first out
MA	maternity allowance
MAP	maternity allowance period
MLP	maternity leave period
MPP	maternity pay period
MSLA	Minimum School Leaving Age
NDR	notified date of return
NI	National Insurance
NICA	Northern Ireland Court of Appeal
NICs	National Insurance contributions
NIRC	National Industrial Relations Court
NMW	National Minimum Wage
NRA	normal retiring age
OLS	Overseas Labour Section
PA 1997	Police Act 1997
PHR	pre-hearing review
QW	qualifying week
ROA 1974	Rehabilitation of Offenders Act 1974
RRA 1976	Race Relations Act 1976
SDA 1975	Sex Discrimination Act 1975
SDA 1986	Sex Discrimination Act 1986
SMP	statutory maternity pay
SOSR	some other substantial reason
SSCBA 1992	Social Security Contributions and Benefits Act 1992
SSHBA 1982	Social Security and Housing Benefits Act 1982
SSP	statutory sick pay
TUC	Trades Union Congress
TULRCA 1992	Trade Union and Labour Relations (Consolidation) Act 1992
TUPE	Transfer of Undertakings (Protection of Employment) Regulations 1981
TURERA 1993	Trade Union Reform and Employment Rights Act 1993
UCTA 1977	Unfair Contract Terms Act 1977

Chapter 1

FORMATION OF THE CONTRACT

Chapter one examines the formation of the contract of employment, particularly in the light of the increasing number of statutory provisions that are relevant in this area. Although the common law leaves an employer free to contract with whoever he chooses and for whatever reason, statute has increasingly imposed restrictions upon his freedom in the selection and recruitment process, breach of some of the provisions attracting criminal sanctions.

1.1 THE UNDERLYING BASIS OF THE EMPLOYMENT RELATIONSHIP

The legal frame within which the employment relationship is said to exist today is that of contract. It is necessary for the creation of the relationship that there be offer, acceptance and consideration and an intention to create legal relations, thus in formulation the relationship resembles contract. Likewise in termination, contractual principles are evident in that the contract may be frustrated, there may be consensual termination or in the event of a breach the other party can choose to accept the breach and continue with the contract, or choose to treat the contract as repudiated and sue for damages. Contractual principles are also evident in operation in that implied terms form an important part of the working of the relationship and the tests for implying a term into the contract did not initially distinguish the contract of employment from contracts generally. Indeed legislation assumes the underlying basis of contract and works from the contract as a "starting point". This is most evident in the Equal Pay Act 1970, section 1(1) of which states that "if the terms of a contract under which a woman is employed . . . do not include . . . an equality clause they shall be deemed to include one."

That contract should form the basis of the relationship of employer and worker was said by Maine[1] to be the mark of a civilised society. It is, as Wedderburn (1986)[2] said, "the fundamental institution to which one is forced to return again and again" and as Kahn Freund (1954)[3] said, the contract of employment is "the cornerstone of the edifice" of labour law in that it distinguishes the relationship as one of an exchange of

---

[1] *Ancient Law* (1861), p. 182.
[2] *The Worker and The Law*, p. 106.
[3] *Legal Framework* (1954), p. 45.

1

promises, a promise to work or to be available for work in exchange for payment, from older forms of relationship based on status.

The relationship of master/servant was, however, categorised in *Blackstone's Commentaries on the Laws of England*[4] as akin to that of husband and wife, parent and child, and guardian and ward as one of the great relations in private life. However, Kahn Freund (1977)[5] argued that Blackstone's concept of employment was "a portrait of a society which had long ceased to exist", being based on the status associated with servants and agricultural labour, of compulsory employment under the Poor Laws, the fixing of wages and the inability to terminate the relationship at will, to the exclusion of skilled craftsmen and those employed in shipping and in the expanding industries such as mining, shipping and steel. That the relationship is regarded as within the law of contractual relationships presupposes an element to freedom of choice to enter into or terminate the relationship and this is incompatible with compulsory labour.

Rideout (1966)[6] has, however, argued that the concept of individual contract is irrelevant and totally unsuited to the modern employment situation because "the fundamentals of contract are basically alien to the entire relationship"[7]. It expresses a notion of equality which is not present.

A recognition of the unequal nature of the relationship led to protective legislation to protect the weaker party and today this is manifested in the web of health and safety legislation. Statute has, however, increasingly encroached not just upon the terms of the contract, but upon the formation stage. This is perhaps not dissimilar from the law of contract itself, where such statutes as the Unfair Contract Terms Act 1977, Supply of Goods and Services Act 1982 and Sale and Supply of Goods Act 1994, affect the terms of the contract and the conduct of the parties to the contract. It is only perhaps in employment contracts that policy has intervened so extensively, restricting with whom one may contract even to the extent of providing financial incentives to contract with particular people, the terms of the contract and the conduct and termination of the contract, that it becomes arguable that the degree of intervention is such that it has the effect of removing the relationship from that of contract to which it was elevated, back to one of a special protective relationship of a kind previously called status.

For example, freedom of contract means that it is permissible to enter into a contract of employment, as with any other contract, with whoever one wishes, subject only to capacity, and that:

> "An employer . . . may refuse to employ (a workman) from the most mistaken, capricious, malicious, or morally reprehensible motives that can be conceived, but the workman has no right of action against him." *per* Lord Davey.

Allen v. Flood [1898] A.C. 1 at 172, HL.

This chapter demonstrates that statute has intervened extensively in that this is no longer so, yet in an inherent contradiction the restrictions and protections afforded are based around a pre-existing contractual model of the employment relationship.

---

[4] 1765.
[5] *"Blackstone's neglected child: the contract of employment"* (1977) 93 L.Q.R. 508–528.
[6] *"The contract of employment"* (1966) 19 C.L.P. 111–127.
[7] p. 113.

1.2 OFFER AND ACCEPTANCE

Being based upon contractual principles, an unconditional offer, with the presence of an intention to create legal relations and consideration, once accepted, albeit just by turning up for work, forms a contract. Thereafter any change of mind by either party amounts to a breach of contract giving rise to a claim in damages. It is therefore important to identify the point at which contractual relations are formed. In *Taylor v. Furness, Withy & Co. Ltd*[8] it was held that it was the exchange of an allocation letter and a letter from the firm welcoming the employee:

"At the moment when the plaintiff handed in his notice (of allocation) he presented himself for employment with the defendants. They, in circumstances which in reality could properly be described as contemporaneously, took the plaintiff into their employment, provided him with the letter which said so, and gave him the identity card which would only be given to those who were taken into the defendant's employ." *per* Brabin J.

Taylor v. Furness, Withy & Co. Ltd [1969] 1 Lloyd's Rep. 324 at 331.

Consequently, when the employer subsequently discovered that the workman did not have appropriate union membership, as a result of which other employees would not work with him, returning him to the pool from which he had come under a statutory allocation scheme amounted to a breach of contract.

In the event of a conditional offer, where the condition is not fulfilled, the offer will lapse. The condition may be either objective, such as passing a particular examination, or the holding of a driving licence, or subjective, such as receipt of a "satisfactory" health check[9] or reference, in which case the only requirement is that the discretion must be exercised in good faith. In *Wishart v. National Association of Citizens Advice Bureaux Ltd*[10] an offer of employment was made "subject to receipt of satisfactory written references". The defendant's claimed they made an offer which never become unconditional and hence never became capable of acceptance unless and until satisfactory references were furnished, and that meant satisfactory to them, a subjective approach, which Mustill L.J. said he had "a strong inclination" to follow.

In *Sarker v. South Tees Acute Hospital NHS Trust*[11] an offer of employment was withdrawn before Ms Sarker had started work, as a result of which she brought a claim for breach of contract, utilising the industrial tribunal (IT) under jurisdiction conferred by Industrial Tribunals Extension of Jurisdiction (England and Wales) Order 1994,[12] Art. 3 of which provides that:

"Proceedings may be brought before an industrial tribunal in respect of a claim of an employee for the recovery of damages or any other sum (other than a claim for damages, or for a sum due, in respect of personal injuries) if—

(a) the claim is one to which [s.3 ITA 1996] applies and which a court in England and Wales would under the law for the time being in force have jurisdiction to hear and determine;

[8] [1969] 1 Lloyd's Rep. 324.
[9] *Baker v. Kaye* [1997] I.R.L.R. 219, HC.
[10] [1990] I.R.L.R. 393, CA.
[11] [1997] I.R.L.R. 328, EAT.
[12] S.I. 1994 No. 1623 (Scotland: S.I. 1994 No. 1624).

> (b) the claim is not one to which article 5 applies; and
> the claim arises or is outstanding on the termination of the employee's employment."

Because the contract had been brought to an end before work had been started the issue arose as to whether the claim was one for damages for breach of a "contract of employment", and whether the claim "arises or is outstanding on the termination of the employee's employment". The Employment Appeal Tribunal (EAT) held that the "mere fact that the duties would only be performed on a date subsequent to this contract having been entered into cannot take it outside the concept of a contract of employment". Having decided that there was a contract of employment, the EAT turned to consider article 3(c) of the 1994 Order, namely whether this was a claim which "arises or is outstanding on the termination of the employee's employment". It was accepted that having decided that there was a contract of employment, the applicant was "an employee" since Employment Rights Act 1996 (ERA 1996), s.230 defines "employee" as "an individual who has entered into or works under . . . a contract of employment". However, by section 211(1)(a) an employee's period of continuous employment begins "on the day on which the employee starts work . . ." and since the employee here had not started work it was argued that there could be no "employment" to terminate.

Taking a purposive construction of the 1994 Order,[13] and note of *General of the Salvation Army v. Dewsbury*[14] that "starts work" is not intended to refer to the undertaking of the full-time duties of the employment, the EAT held that:

> ". . . it is enough that the individual has entered into a contract of employment— he or she is then an employee, even if he or she has not actually started performing the appropriate duties under the contract of employment." *per* Keene J.

> *Sarker v. South Tees Acute Hospitals NHS Trust* [1997] I.R.L.R. 328 at p. 331, EAT.

This interpretation of article 3(c) of the 1994 Order enables an employee, where work has not been started, to have access to an IT to peruse a contractual claim.

1.3 CONSIDERATION

At common law the formation of a contract of employment is not seen as differing from the making of any other contract, there must therefore be consideration. Generally, this is the mutual exchange of promises: the employer to pay wages in exchange for the employee being ready and willing to work, meaning that provided that the employer pays the contractually agreed wage, the employee has no complaint if work is not provided. There are occasions, however, where consideration can be the provision of work itself, resulting in a failure to provide work amounting to a breach of contract, even where the contractually agreed wage is paid.

---

[13] S.I. 1994 No. 1623 (Scotland: S.I. 1994 No. 1624).
[14] [1984] I.R.L.R. 222, EAT.

Although Article 23(i) of the Universal Declaration Human Rights, 1948 provides that everyone has the right to work, that has been held to be merely aspirational. In *Langston v. AUEW*,[15] a case concerning the now repealed provisions of the Industrial Relations Act 1971 (IRA 1971), a car welder who earned a basic wage plus premium payments for night shifts and overtime, resigned from the union over a prolonged dispute concerning the post-entry closed shop. In response to union pressure the employer suspended Langston on full pay, as a result of which he claimed that by inducing his employers to suspend him, the union had induced a breach of contract, and were therefore guilty of an unfair industrial practice under the IRA 1971. In response to the employer's claim that there had been no breach of contract, because Langston had been paid full pay, Lord Denning M.R. referred to *Collier v. Sunday Referee Publishing Co. Ltd*[16] where Asquith J. said:

"It is true that a contract of employment does not necessarily, or perhaps normally, oblige the master to provide the servant with work. Provided I pay my cook her wages regularly she cannot complain if I choose to take any or all of my meals out. In some exceptional cases there is an obligation to provide work. For instance, where the servant is remunerated by commission, or where (as in the case of an actor or singer) the servant bargains, amongst other thing, for publicity, and the master, by withholding work, also withholds the stipulated publicity": *per* Asquith J.

Collier v. Sunday Referee Publishing Co. Ltd [1940] 2 K.B. 647 at 650, HC.

Asquith J. based his judgment on two old authorities, *Turner v. Sawdon & Co.*[17] and *Lagerwall v. Wilkinson, Henderson & Clarke Ltd*[18] where it was held that a commercial traveller, and a salesman respectively, retained for a fixed period and paid a salary, were held to have no legal complaint so long as salary continued to be paid, notwithstanding that they were left by their employer with nothing to do. The employers were not bound to supply work to enable their employee to "keep his hand in" or to "avoid the reproach of idleness". Lord Denning said of those judgments:

"That was said 33 years ago. Things have altered much since then . . . In these days an employer, when employing a skilled man, is bound to provide him with work. By which I mean that the man should be given the opportunity of doing his work when it is available and he is ready and willing to do it. A skilled man takes a pride in his work. He does not do it merely to earn money. He does it so as to make his contributions to the well-being of all. He does it so as to keep himself busy, and not idle. To use his skill, and to improve it. To have the satisfaction which comes of a task well done." *per* Lord Denning M.R.

Langston v. Amalgamated Union of Engineering Workers [1974] I.C.R. 180 at 190, CA.

This finding of a general right to work, through consideration for the contract, was said to be contrary to all earlier authority, and unworkable. When *Langston* returned to the

[15] [1974] 1 All E.R. 980, CA.
[16] [1940] 2 K.B. 647, HC.
[17] [1901] 2 K.B. 653, HC.
[18] (1899) 80 L.T. 55.

National Industrial Relations Court (NIRC),[19] however, Sir John Donaldson said that despite increasing acceptance of the proposition that everyone had a right to work, in the same sense that he has a right to eat and a right to be housed, this is a general right, not a right to work for any particular employer or in any particular place, and that the right is based upon public policy rather than contract, and that for the present purposes the court was concerned only with contractual rights. He identified the crucial question as being: what is the consideration moving from the employers under the contract of employment?

The NIRC looked at authorities which represented exceptions to the principle that consideration was the promise to pay. For example, in *Herbert Clayton and Jack Waller Ltd v. Oliver*[20] the opportunity to perform was held, for an actor, to be part of the consideration, and *Devonald v. Rosser & Sons*[21] where commission or piece work was the express obligation to pay an agreed rate for work done, plus the implied obligation to provide a reasonable amount of work to give an opportunity to earn piece rates. It was held that Langston's contract, comprising of a mixture of night shifts and overtime, each with advantages and disadvantages, placed a duty on management to allocate days, nights, overtime working and place of work in such a way as to give a fair opportunity to enjoy the rough as well as the smooth and, in particular, of earning premium payments. Once the employers suspended Langston, they deprived him of his opportunity of earning premium payments, and that was a breach of his contract of employment. Under these circumstances even if the employer pays an additional sum to represent that which would have been earned, such payments are regarded as damages for breach of contract.

The basic contractual position is as stated by Smith M.R. in *Turner v. Sawdon & Co.*[22] that there is no duty on the employer to provide his salesman with the opportunity to "keep his hand in", but his duty is to pay him in exchange for him being ready and willing to work. Instances where there is a particular interest in the performance of the contract itself, are exceptions to that rule, and this is demonstrated in *Herbert Clayton and Jack Waller Ltd v. Oliver*[23] where an actor who, having been given a leading role in a play, was then allocated a lesser role. The House of Lords held that on the particular facts, the specific job offered was an intregal part of the consideration—the work was as important as the pay, and availability to work was not sufficient consideration.

There is another set of cases where the provision of work itself in terms of a particular job in a particular place has been held to be the consideration: in *Herbert Collier v. Sunday Referee Publishing Co. Ltd*[24] it was held that the sale of a newspaper for which the plaintiff held the office of chief sub-editor, had destroyed the office and breached the contract:

> "The plaintiff was not employed to perform certain functions at large. He was not engaged to do the kind of work commonly done by any chief sub-editor, but was employed to be the chief sub-editor of a specific Sunday newspaper, and the defendants made it impossible for him to remain so by discontinuing publication

---

[19] *Langston v. Amalgamated Union of Engineering Workers (No. 2)* [1974] I.C.R. 510, NIRC.
[20] [1930] A.C. 209, HL.
[21] [1906] 2 K.B. 728, CA.
[22] [1901] 2 K.B. 653, CA.
[23] [1930] A.C. 209, HL.
[24] [1940] K.B. 234, HC.

of that newspaper. By so doing they destroyed the office to which they appointed him." *per* Asquith J.

Herbert Collier v. Sunday Referee Publishing Co. Ltd [1940] 4 K.B. 234 at 236, HC.

It should be noted, however, that this was not a contract of indefinite duration, but for a fixed term of 12 months. However, in the more recent case of *Breach v. Epsylon Industries Ltd*[25] Phillips J. in the EAT said that the underlying thought in *Turner v. Sawdon* "is somewhat out of date and old fashioned now".

1.4 CAPACITY

The ERA 1996, s.19, extends specific statutory provisions contained in the Act to Crown employees, although by section 193 statutory employment rights may be withdrawn on the grounds of national security.[26] In addition, the Equal Pay Act 1970, s.1(8) (EqPA); Sex Discrimination Act 1975, s.85 (SDA); Race Relations Act 1976, s.75 (RRA) and Disability Discrimination Act 1995, s.64 (DDA), provide that these statutes extend to Crown employees. The ERA 1996, ss.194–195 extends specific provisions to House of Lords and House of Commons staff respectively, as does the SDA 1975, ss.85A–85B and RRA 1976, ss.75A–75B.

Civil servants hold office to which they are appointed by the Crown, their service being regulated and run using common law powers and through the royal prerogative exercised by Orders in Council and by the Civil Service Order in Council 1995, and may be dismissed at will. The Minister for the Civil Service is authorised to make regulations regarding employment and these are contained in a *Civil Service Management Code*.[27] In *R. v. Civil Service Appeal Board ex parte Bruce*[28] it was held that there is no contract between a civil servant and the Crown, because although the contractual elements of offer, acceptance and consideration were all present, there was no intention to create legal relations: this had the result that the applicant could pursue an employment grievance by judicial review. However, in *R. v. Lord Chancellor's Department ex parte Nangle*[29] it was held that an intention to create legal relations in this context means "an intention to enter into a contract legally enforceable in the courts" and that the onus, which was a heavy one, is on the party asserting a lack of intention. The internal disciplinary proceedings of the Lord Chancellor's Department were held to be similar to those that might be used by any large employer, and in general the documentation:

> "laid down with great clarity rights, obligations and entitlements, dealing with such matters as pay, hours of attendance, holidays, sick leave, discipline and many other similar matters which are the stock in trade of a contract of employment." Stuart-Smith L.J. *R. v. Lord Chancellor's Department ex parte Nangle* [1991] I.R.L.R. 343 at 346.

---

[25] [1976] I.C.R. 316 at 320, EAT. Note now *William Hill Organisation Ltd v. Tucker* [1998] I.R.L.R. 313, CA.
[26] Bradley and Ewing (1997).
[27] *ibid.* p. 308.
[28] [1988] I.C.R. 649, CA.
[29] [1991] I.R.L.R. 343, HC.

The result being, that despite a paragraph in the *Code* describing the relationship as one regulated by the prerogative and based on personal appointment, the court held that the "relationship of employer and employee, master and servant, which plainly exists here must of its very nature be one that involves an intention to create legal relations".

In any event, any person holding an office or employment under the Crown who does not have a contact of employment is deemed to do so by the Trade Union and Labour Relations (Consolidation) Act 1992 (TULRCA 1992), s.245 for purposes to industrial action.

In addition, to be enforceable the contract must be one the individual concerned is capable in law of entering. The contractual capacity of minors,[30] is governed by common law and the general rule is that contracts are enforceable as against a minor only insofar as they are either necessary or beneficial to them. In *Bromley v. Smith*[31] it was held that the contract should be looked at as a whole and if it only contains those terms on which a minor could reasonably expect to get employment then it would be for his benefit, any stipulation which is repugnant and is severable, may be severed, leaving the remainder of the contract which is for the minor's benefit to bind him.

1.5 YOUNG PEOPLE

Responsibility for the law governing the employment of young people is split between a number of government departments, the Health and Safety Commission and local authorities and present laws can be found in statutes and regulations and by-laws made by local authorities passed under powers contained in the Children and Young Persons Act 1933.

Council Directive 94/33 on the Protection of Young People at Work was agreed by the Council of Ministers in June 1994. Adopted under Article 118a the Directive is applicable to all Member States, and by Article 17 is to be implemented by June 22, 1996, although the United Kingdom secured a four year opt-out from some provisions.[32] Article 1 sets out the purpose of the Directive, namely:

> "1. Member States shall take the necessary measures to prohibit work by children. They shall ensure, under the conditions laid down by this Directive, that the minimum working or employment age is not lower than the minimum age at which compulsory full-time schooling as imposed by national law ends or 15 years in any event.
> 2. Member States ensure that work by adolescents is strictly regulated and protected under the conditions laid down in this Directive.
> 3. Member States shall ensure in general that employers guarantee that young people have working conditions which suit their age.
>
> They shall ensure that young people are protected against economic exploitation and against any work likely to harm their safety, health or physical, mental, moral or social development or to jeopardise their education."

Council Directive 94/33, Art. 1.

[30] Aged 18, Family Law Reform Act 1969, ss.1 and 9.
[31] [1909] 2 K.B. 235, HC.
[32] By Art. 17(1)(b) the U.K. has an extended implementation date of June 22, 2000 for specified provisions, when the Council is to decide if this provision is to be extended further.

The Directive applies to three categories defined as follows:

- "young person", which relates to everyone below the age of 18;

- "child", which relates to anyone less than 15 years old or still subject to compulsory full-time schooling under national law;

- "adolescent", which relates to anyone at least 15 years old but less than 18 years old who is no longer subject to compulsory full-time education,

and prohibits working by children, requiring measures to be introduced to protect the position of young people who are at work under exceptions which are contained in Article 4, paragraph 2(a)–(c), namely

(a) children pursuing cultural, artistic, sports or advertising actives who are covered by Article 5;

(b) children at least 14 years old working under a combined work/training scheme or in-plant work-experience scheme; or

(c) children at least 14 years old performing light work, other than cultural or similar work, which may also be undertaken by children 13 years old for a limited number of hours a week in certain categories of work, in which case, for children who are subject to compulsory full-time schooling, a period free of any work must be provided for, as far as possible, in the school holidays.

Where categories of young people are in employment under the exceptions to the general principle of prohibiting working by children, the subsequent Articles of the Directive set down a regulatory system for Member States to adopt for the protection of young people.

A number of amendments to domestic law are necessary, much of the protective legislation governing the 16 to 18-year-old age group in the labour market having been removed by provisions contained in the Employment Act 1989 (EA 1989) as part of the United Kingdom Government's commitment to deregulation. The split of responsibility for young people between different authorities resulted in the publication of four sets of consultation documents containing proposals for implementation of the Directive.[33] The H&SC's consultation document resulted in the Health and Safety (Young Persons) Regulations 1997,[34] which implement the requirements of Articles 6 and 7 of the Directive and provide that:

- employers are prohibited from employing a young person (under 18) unless they have first made or reviewed a risk assessment taking particular account of specified risks to the health and safety of young people (previous legislation required employers to carry out regular risk assessments, but not before any particular individual started work);

---

[33] A consultation document, *Employment of Children*, Department of Health, October 1995; *DTI, A consultation document on measures to implement provisions to the E.C. Directive on the protection of young people at work*, URN 97/508, February 1997; *The Health and Safety (Young persons) Regulations 1996: Proposals to implement the health and safety provisions of the E.C. Directive on the protection of young people at work*, Health and Safety Commission, CD106 C50, March 1996.

[34] S.I. 1997 No. 135.

- before employing a person under compulsory school age, the employer must also inform their parents (or those with parental responsibility or rights for them) of the outcome of the assessment and the controls that have been introduced;

- prohibit the employment of young people for certain kinds of work, unless they are over compulsory school age and the work is necessary for their training, or they will be supervised by a competent person, or any risk will be reduced to the lowest level that is reasonably practicable;

with the aim of protecting young people from economic exploitation and any work which may cause them physical or mental harm.

However, the Department of Trade and Industry (DTI) consultation paper, along with that of the Department of Health, were withdrawn by the incoming government following the general election in Spring 1997. New proposals were slow in coming forward and were not made until February 1998, when the Health Minister announced that implementing measures would be brought forward[35] and Regulations have been laid[36] to amend and extend Children and Young Persons Acts 1933 and 1963 and the Children and Young Persons (Scotland) Act 1937, which will come into force on August 4, 1998.

Implementation of the requirements in the Directive affecting young workers (those above minimum school leaving age but under 18) remain outstanding and these are now expected to be implemented by October 1, 1998, in conjunction with the implementation of the Working Time Directive 93/204.[37]

During the second reading of the Employment of Children Bill[38] the Under-Secretary of State for Health, Paul Boateng, in addition to announcing the new Regulations, confirmed the announcement already made,[39] to the effect that the Government "envisaged a larger programme of work" and intended to set up a joint review of all child employment protection legislation reporting to Ministers by the end of 1998. In addition, to fulfilling minimum E.C. standards it was announced that the Government "fully and unequivocally support the principles behind ILO Convention 138" and that it was determined to ratify the convention.[40] As a result, the Employment of Children Bill was withdrawn.

1.6   IMMIGRATION AND FREE MOVEMENT OF WORKERS

The size of the labour pool is controlled by the numbers who have a right to work in the United Kingdom. The Immigration Act 1971 (as amended) gives "British citizens" the right to both live and work in the United Kingdom without permission by making them immune from immigration controls. There are six classes of British citizenship and it is only those that have the status of "British citizen" that have the right of abode in the United Kingdom (that carries with it the right to work); British overseas citizens,

---

[35] *Hansard*, H.C. cols 726–727, February 13, 1998.
[36] The Children (Protection at Work) Regulations 1998 (S.I. 1998 No. 276).
[37] *Hansard*, H.C. col. 1222, February 3, 1998.
[38] A private member's bill sponsored by Chris Pond, M.P.
[39] Department of Health Press Release, December 11, 1997.
[40] *Hansard*, H.C. cols 727–730, February 13, 1998 (Convention Concerning Minimum Age for Admission to Employment which came into force June 19, 1976).

British dependent territories citizens, British nationals (overseas), British protected persons and British subjects, do not have the right of abode and are therefore not free to live and work without immigration clearance.

The other two main categories of foreign nationals not subject to immigration control are Commonwealth citizens with the right of abode and EEA[41] nationals who are exercising free movement rights under Community law, and members of their family. In addition to which there is exemption from immigration controls for members of diplomatic missions in the United Kingdom for so long as they remain part of their mission's diplomatic staff, and family members who form part of their household; members of a visiting force serving or posted for service in the United Kingdom; and the crew members of ships or planes arriving in the United Kingdom until their outgoing flight departs.

European Union law, Articles 48–52 E.C. Treaty, provides for freedom of movement for E.U. nationals between the various Member States, as an adjunct to the single market, to take up an offer of employment and to move freely within the territory of Member States for this purpose. A broader approach towards free movement was taken in the Treaty on European Union, which introduced the concept of "Union citizenship", whereby every person holding the nationality of a Member State shall be a citizen of the Union.[42] Article 8a(1) provides that:

> "Every citizen of the Union shall have the right to move and reside freely within the territory of the Member States, subject to the limitations and conditions laid down in this Treaty and by the measures adopted to give it effect."

By the Agreement on the European Economic Area 1992, with effect from January 1994, the benefits of the internal market were extended to nationals of the seven EFTA (European Free Trade Association) countries. Article 28 establishes the right of free movement for workers among E.C. Member States and EFTA States, which entails the abolition of any discrimination based on nationality between workers of E.C. Member States and EFTA States as regards employment, remuneration and other conditions of work and employment.[43] EEA nationals who are migrant workers have rights established in Article 48 of the E.C. Treaty to accept offers of employment actually made; move freely within the Member States and EFTA States for this purpose; stay in an E.C. Member State or EFTA State for the purpose of employment in accordance with the rules governing the employment of United Kingdom nationals; remain in the territory of an E.C. Member State or an EFTA State after having been employed there, subject to certain conditions; and Article 49 provides for the making of secondary legislation by the Council to bring about the freedoms set out in Article 48.

By Article 48(4) the right to take up employment does not extend to employment in the public service. It was held in *Commission v. Belgium*[44] that this exception:

> ". . . removes from the ambit of Article 48(1) to (3) a series of posts which involve direct or indirect participation in the exercise of power conferred by public law and duties designed to safeguard the general interests of the State or of other

[41] European Economic Area.
[42] E.C. Art. 8.
[43] Art. 28(2) Agreement on the European Economic Area.
[44] Case 149/79 [1980] E.C.R. 3881, ECJ.

public authorities. Such posts in fact presume on the part of those occupying them the existence of a special relationship of allegiance to the State and reciprocity of rights and duties which form the foundation of the bond of nationality."

Case 149/79 *Commission v. Belgium* [1980] E.C.R. 3881, ECJ.

In *Commission v. Belgium*[45] it was recognised that there were "special difficulties" in the case of public bodies where they have assumed "responsibilities of an economic and social nature or are involved in activities which are not identifiable with the functions which are typical of the public service yet which by their nature still come under the sphere of application of the Treaty." In such cases it was said that whether such activities come within the exception "depends on whether or not the posts in question are typical of the specific activities of the public service in so far as the exercise of powers conferred by public law and responsibility for safeguarding the general interests of the State are vested in it."

Accordingly, it is thought that only rarely will the exception extend to cover posts in public bodies responsible for administering "commercial services", such as the supply of water, electricity and gas, post and telecommunications, television and radio, public transport, airlines and shipping lines, while the exception does not cover similar bodies in the private sector, for example, in the United Kingdom, the privatised utilities.[46]

The creation of European citizenship, the public service exception in Article 48(4) and the guidance provided by the Commission, clearly leads to some tension, and this is identified in the following extract:

"There is an inherent conflict between Article 48(4) and the creation of the internal market and increased European integration on the other. The public service exception is geared to a conception of the State performing certain essential activities related to its function as the State, where the legitimate interests of the State can best be served and protected by the recruitment of the State's own nationals to perform certain tasks on its behalf.

However, this view of the public service exception is founded on a conception of nationality which may face increasing strain. It is based on a very traditional notion of loyalty to the State and finds its parallel in the denial to foreigners of political rights . . .

It is clear that these provisions [of the Treaty on European Union on citizenship] will alter the perceptions of Member States concerning nationals of other Member States. They blur the distinction between the State's own nationals and nationals of other Member States in several ways which go to the heart of the concept of nationality. Previously, Community law, and in particular the case-law of the Court of Justice, had concentrated on the economic and social integration of Community migrants (viewed as economic actors by the Treaty) in order to create a Community citizenship. As Community nationals are now to enjoy political rights deriving from Community law, it will become progressively more difficult to justify a different treatment of them as regards employment in the public service, which is founded upon political considerations."

D. O'Keeffe, *Judicial Interpretation of the Public Service Exception to the Free Movement of Workers* in Hartley (1994).[47]

[45] *ibid.*
[46] I.R.L.B. 568, May 1997, p. 3.
[47] Quoted in Craig *et al.* (1997) p. 681.

The right to free movement is supported by a number of Regulations and Directives which ensure that migrant workers enjoy non-discriminatory treatment in relation to access to employment and provision of employment-related benefits. In *Scholz*[48] the ECJ said that Articles 1 and 3 of Regulation 1612/68[49] "merely clarify and give effect to the rights already conferred by Art. 48 of the Treaty". The Regulation provides, in Article 1, that any national of a Member State has "the right to take up an activity as an employed person, and to pursue such activity, within the territory of another Member State" with the same priority as nationals. Article 2 provides that the worker may "conclude and perform contracts of employment" in accordance with the laws of the host State. Any provisions which discriminate against foreign nationals or which are designed to hinder foreign nationals from obtaining work are not permissible, with the exception of "conditions relating to linguistic knowledge required by reason of the nature of the post to be filled". Successful use of this exception is demonstrated in *Groener v. Minister for Education*[50] where refusal of a post because of an inability to comply with the requirement to speak Gaelic was upheld, even though it was not necessary to use Gaelic at work, but it was a clear policy of national law to maintain and promote the use of the Irish language as a means of expressing national culture and identity.[51]

Regulation 1612/68 also gives the right for an EEA migrant worker's spouse and their descendants who are under 21 years old or dependants, and dependent relatives in the ascending line of the worker and his spouse, regardless of nationality, to "install themselves" with a migrant worker who is a national of one Member State and who is employed in another Member State.[52] Directive 68/360 facilitates the exercise of the worker's right of free movement and applies also to his family. Nationals and members of their families may leave the Member State on the production of a valid identity card or passport, specifying the person's nationality, which the Member State is obliged to issue or renew (Art. 2(1)), and by Article 3(1) Member States must allow workers and their families to enter the territory on the production of an identity card or passport and only in the case of family members who are not EEA nationals may entry clearance (EEA family permit) be required. They also have the same rights of residence as the worker, on production of the required documents, and to take up employment, other than in the public service.[53]

Outside the categories discussed, and where the principle of free movement does not apply, those intending to work in the United Kingdom must obtain immigration permission, entry clearance, applications for which are made to British embassies, consulates or High Commissions abroad. The Home Office governs policy for overseas nationals already in this country and for British missions overseas which issue the variety of entry clearances. The other type of clearance is the work and training and work experience permit schemes (TWES) which are administered by the *Df*EE, all of which are governed by Immigration Rules 1994,[54] although conditions for the award of work permits are governed, not by the Rules, but by internal departmental rules of policy.

---

[48] Case 419/92 [1994] E.C.R. I–505, ECJ.
[49] On Freedom of Movement for Workers within the Community.
[50] Case 379/87 [1989] E.C.R. 3967, ECJ.
[51] See C. Barnard, *E.C. Employment Law* (Wiley & Sons, 1995).
[52] Art. 10.
[53] See P. Craig and G. De Burca, (1997), Chap. 15.
[54] *Statement of Changes in Immigration Rules*, May 23, 1994, HMSO.

Applications for work permits must be made by the United Kingdom organisation which is proposing to employ a named worker for a specific post and can be made for any period of time up to a maximum of four years.[55] Permits are only issued for those with degree level or professional qualifications or who have specialist skills, who have at least two years' work experience relevant to their application and must have an adequate command of English. The employer must satisfy the overseas labour section (OLS) of the *DfEE* that there are no other employees in the United Kingdom or the rest of the EEA capable of doing the particular job and may require evidence that the post has been advertised and that no suitable applications were forthcoming from people in these two categories. To allow an overseas national to start work in the United Kingdom before a work permit has been obtained, is now a criminal offence under the Asylum and Immigration Act 1996.

1.7 ASYLUM AND IMMIGRATION ACT 1996

The Asylum and Immigration Act 1996, which came into effect in January 1997, amends and supplements the Immigration Act 1971 and the Asylum and Immigration Appeals Act 1993. The Act has three objectives, the third of which is "to reduce economic incentives which attract people to come to this country in breach of our immigration laws"[56] and to this end section 8 is intended to make it harder for people to work illegally in the United Kingdom by placing on employers a responsibility to consider applicants' eligibility to work, ensuring that only those legally entitled to live and work in the United Kingdom are offered employment. Under the Act it is an offence for employers to employ[57] a person aged 16 or over who is subject to immigration control, "employ" meaning employed under a contract of service or apprenticeship regardless of hours worked or whether their status is permanent or casual.[58] The common law test of "employee" is imported into the Act,[59] but for the sake of clarity the Home Office guidance[60] points out that an employer is not liable for:

- the employees of a contractor undertaking work on his behalf, such as workers provided by an independent gangmaster to pick crops;

- self employed people or freelance workers;

- employees obtained from an employment agency who remain employees of the agency.

The offence is committed by "the employer" but by section 8(5) it is possible for an individual to be liable, in addition to a body corporate, where the offence is committed with the "consent or connivance" or as a result of neglect of an individual officer or employee.

[55] Applications are made on form WP1.
[56] *Hansard*, col. 699, December 11, 1995.
[57] On or after January 27, 1997.
[58] *ibid*. p. 13.
[59] s.8(8), on which see 1.14 below.
[60] *Asylum and Immigration Act 1996—Section 8, Prevention of illegal working: Guidance for employers*, Immigration and Nationality Directorate, Home Office, December 1996.

Section 8(2) of the Act provides a defence, for which two conditions must be satisfied. Firstly, before the employment began, an original document was produced for this purpose which appeared to relate to the employee (the employer is not expected to validate the document) and was one of the following[61]:

- a document issued by a previous employer, the Inland Revenue, the Benefits Agency, the Contributions Agency or the Employment Service (or their Northern Ireland equivalents) which states the national insurance number of the person named in it (including a P45, a pay slip, a P60, and a NINO card or letter issued by one of those government bodies, but *not* a document showing a "temporary" national insurance number which is made up of the letters TN, the employee's date of birth and the letter F or M indicating the employee's sex);

- a passport which describes the holder as a British citizen or as having the right of abode in, or an entitlement to readmission to, the United Kingdom (but *not* an old British visitor's passport);

- a passport which contains a "certificate of entitlement to the right of abode" issued by or on behalf of the Government;

- a certificate of registration or naturalisation as a British citizen;

- a birth certificate issued in the United Kingdom, the Channel Islands, the Isle of Man or the Republic of Ireland, of both the short and standard type;

- a passport or national identity card, issued by a State which is a party to the EEA Agreement, which describes the holder as a national of that State;

- a passport or travel document which is endorsed to show that the holder is exempt from immigration control, has indefinite leave to enter or remain, or has no time limit on his or her stay in the United Kingdom (or a letter issued by the Home Office which contains that information);

- a passport or travel document which is endorsed to show that the holder has current leave to enter or remain and is not precluded from taking the employment in question (or a letter issued by the Home office which contains that information);

- a United Kingdom residence permit issued by the Home Office to a national of another State party to the EEA Agreement;

- a passport or travel document which is endorsed to show that the holder has a current right of residence in the United Kingdom as the family member of a named national of another State party to the EEA Agreement who is resident in the United Kingdom;

- a letter issued by the Immigration and Nationality Directorate of the Home Office which indicates that the person named in it is a British citizen or has permission to take employment;

- a work permit or other approval to take employment issued by the Department for Education and Employment or the Training and Employment Agency (Northern Ireland);

[61] Immigration (Restrictions on Employment) Order 1996 (S.I. 1996 No. 3225).

- a passport which describes the holder as a British Dependent Territories citizen and indicates that that status derives from a connection with Gibraltar.

The second condition is that the employer retain a copy of that document while the person concerned is employed and for at least six months after he has left. An offence is committed, however, even though a relevant document was seen and copied, if it can be shown that the employer knew that to employ that person was an offence under section 8 or an employer continues to employ a person after he knows that the employee is not entitled to work. Mere suspicion that the employment might constitute an offence would not be sufficient to make the employer liable. A fine of up to £5,000 can be made for each offence under the act and fines are cumulative. Employers are therefore required to check the status of those they intend to employ before they take them on. There is, however, no requirement to carry out retrospective checks on those employed before the effective date.

The Home Office guidance reminds employers of their duty under the Race Relations Act 1976 not to discriminate on grounds of race and advises that:

> "If you refuse to consider anyone who looks or sounds foreign, this is likely to be unlawful discrimination under the Race Relations Act. . . . The best way to ensure that you do not discriminate is to treat all applicants in the same way at each stage of the recruitment process. You may ask for a document at any stage—but if you ask for a document from one applicant make sure you ask for a document from all applicants being considered at that stage. . . . If you carry out checks only on potential employees who by their appearance or accent seem to . . . be other than British this too may constitute unlawful racial discrimination. . . ."

> *Asylum and Immigration Act 1996—Section 8, Prevention of illegal working: Guidance for employers,* Home Office, December 1996, p. 3.

The Commission for Racial Equality has pointed out that the duties of employers under the Race Relations Act 1976 have not been affected by the new Act and has published guidance for employers on compliance with the 1976 Act when complying with the Asylum and Immigration Act.[62]

1.8   REHABILITATION OF OFFENDERS AND CRIMINAL RECORDS

The Rehabilitation of Offenders Act 1974 (ROA 1974), which is intended to rehabilitate offenders who have not been reconvicted of a serious offence for a given period, makes it unlawful to exclude, or to dismiss, a rehabilitated offender for the reason that he has a spent conviction.[63] Once a conviction is spent, the general effect of the Act is to treat it as if it had not taken place and section 4(3) relieves a job applicant of the duty to disclose a spent conviction. The length of time it takes for a conviction to become spent under the act varies depending on the length of the sentence in question.

The Act has severe limitations in that not only is the length of prison sentence that is capable of becoming spent very short, but there are a large number of jobs and

---

[62] *The Asylum and Immigration Act 1996 Implications for Racial Equality*: Provisional guidance for employers on compliance with the Race Relations Act 1976.
[63] s.4(3)(b).

professions that are excluded from the Act. It was announced recently that these exemptions[64] are to be rationalised.[65]

It has been held that if an occupation is not within the exemptions detailed in the relevant order made under section 4(4) of the Act, it cannot be treated as exempt: there is no ability to "opt-out" of the Act. In *Property Guards Ltd v. Taylor*[66] employees signed a statement to the effect that neither they nor any member of their family had been convicted of a criminal or civil offence, when in fact they had both been convicted of minor offences of dishonesty. The EAT upheld a finding of unfair dismissal and further upheld the IT decision not to reduce compensation for contribution because the applicants were under no obligation to disclose spent convictions. The Act does not, however, relieve job applicants from disclosing unspent convictions when asked about them. In *G. E. Torr v. British Railways Board*[67] an employee answered "no" on a job application form to a question asking "Have you at any time been found guilty by a Court . . . of any offence . . .?". When the employer discovered, as a result of a reference, that the employee had a conviction and sentence of three years' imprisonment, the company suspended him and brought a prosecution alleging that he dishonestly obtained for himself a pecuniary advantage—his job as a guard—contrary to section 16(1) of the Theft Act. The employee pleaded guilty, was given a conditional discharge and then summarily dismissed. In dismissing his appeal against a finding that his dismissal was not unfair, it was said:

> ". . . there is no rule of law that employers must follow and extend the social philosophy which found expression in the Rehabilitation of Offenders Act, and to assert such a principle of public policy would only lead to confusion." *per* Cumming-Bruce L.J.

G. E. Torr v. British Railways Board [1977] I.R.L.R. 184 at 186, EAT.

A major limitation in the operation of the Act is that there are no specific enforcement provisions and dismissal for failure to disclose a spent conviction is not included under Part X of the ERA 1996 as an automatically unfair reason for dismissal, although it appears that an application for unfair dismissal is the method of enforcement as demonstrated in *Property Guards Ltd v. Taylor and Kershaw*[68] and *Hendry & Hendry v. Scottish Liberal Club*.[69] In *Chuwen v. Debenhams Ltd*[70] an employee stated on his application form that he was working in America at a time when he had in fact been in prison serving a sentence that had since become spent. The employer dismissed him when he discovered the false information, giving that as the reason for dismissal. On an application for unfair dismissal the IT found that if the employer had found out that the employee had simply been elsewhere during that period they would not have dismissed: the real reason for dismissal was the spent conviction, and the dismissal was held to be unfair. This route is, however, subject to the qualifying service requirements in ERA 1996, s.108. It is, as a result, not open to someone who has been refused employment on the basis of a spent conviction, and

---

[64] Contained in Rehabilitation of Offenders Act 1974 (Exemptions) Order 1975 (S.I. 1975 No. 1023).
[65] *Hansard*, H.C. cols 468–469, July 9, 1997.
[66] [1982] I.R.L.R. 175, EAT.
[67] [1977] I.R.L.R. 184, EAT.
[68] [1982] I.R.L.R. 175, EAT.
[69] [1977] I.R.L.R. 5, IT (Case No: S/1290/76).
[70] COIT/655/177.

there is no means of compelling an employer to engage a person with a spent conviction.

In June 1996, building on responses to an earlier Green Paper,[71] the Government published a White Paper proposing new arrangements in England and Wales for disclosure from criminal records for employment-related purposes. It proposed setting up a criminal records agency to undertake criminal record checks from centralised computer facilities and liaison with local police forces to replace the system whereby local forces conduct, free of charge, checks on criminal records for prospective employers in a limited range of occupations. The white paper[72] proposed that because of the large requirement for such checks from a variety of diverse sources, involving the police in time consuming exercises, the progressive introduction of a new national computerised criminal justice record service, Phoenix, would provide the opportunity for a "one-stop criminal record check" system.

The paper proposed that employers or licensing bodies working in areas requiring pre-employment access to criminal records be required to register with the Criminal Records Agency,[73] and that a code of practice regulating the use of criminal record information be prepared. These proposals were enacted as Part V of the Police Act 1997 (PA 1977), and the Agency will have direct access to Phoenix, for the purposes of undertaking criminal record checks of which there are three types:

- *Criminal conviction certificates* (CCC): PA 1997, s.112 provides for a new certificate to be available to individuals only, on payment of a flat rate fee, which is intended to meet the demand from employers in a range of businesses where exceptions to the provisions of the ROA 1974 do not apply. Although not available to employers direct, it is intended that the CCC will provide those employers who request such a record from prospective employees, such as taxi and minicab drivers, applicants for consumer credit licences, sex establishment and entertainment licences, and applicants for and holders of licences such as heavy goods vehicle and passenger service vehicle operators, with a statement which will record details of every conviction of the applicant held in the central records, or state that there are no convictions. By section 112(3) the CCC will not include cautions or convictions that are spent under the ROA 1974.

- *Criminal record certificates* (CRC): by PA 1997, s.113 a CRC will be available to employers of all those groups who are exceptions to the provisions of the ROA 1974, a list of which is contained in Annex A to the White Paper,[74] and includes employers in the private and voluntary sectors. A joint application will be made by an individual and the organisation which is seeking the check and the certificate will provide information about "every relevant matter relating to the applicant which is recorded in central records or will state that there is no such matter". A "relevant matter" is defined in section 113(5) as a conviction within the meaning of the ROA 1974, including spent convictions and, more controversially, cautions and bind-overs.

- *Enhanced criminal record certificate* (ECRC): PA 1997, s.115 provides for an enhanced criminal record certificate for particularly sensitive areas of work or

---

[71] *Disclosure from Criminal Records for Employment Vetting Purposes*, Home Office, 1993, Cm. 2319.
[72] *On the Record, The Government's proposals for access to criminal records for employment and related purposes in England and Wales*, Home Office, 1996, Cm. 3308.
[73] A Next Steps Agency, as part of the Home Office.
[74] See Rehabilitation of Offenders Act 1974 (Exceptions) Order 1975 (S.I. 1975 No. 1023).

licensing where vetting already takes place: prospective employees, trainees and volunteers who have regular, unsupervised, contact with children and young people under 18 and those applying for gaming, betting and lottery licences, details of which are listed in section 115(4)–(5). In addition to the information contained in the criminal record certificate, this certificate will include additional details from police records, including non-conviction information. Application for the ECRC will be made by the individual and countersigned by the registered person and the ECRC will be sent to the individual and registered person, except that the certificate sent to the registered person may contain additional relevant information which, in the opinion of the chief officer providing it ought not to be included in the certificate "in the interests of the prevention or detection of crime; and can, without harming those interests, be disclosed to the registered person", section 115(8).

Section 122 puts an obligation on the Secretary of State to publish, and from time to time revise, a code of practice and those who register under the Act have to agree to abide by the Code, but no monitoring system is established, other than by section 122(3) whereby the Secretary of State may refuse to issue a certificate under sections 113 or 115 if he believes there has been a failure to comply with the Code.

Around 35 per cent of men and eight per cent of women under age 35 in the United Kingdom have a criminal record and amongst those working with ex-offenders it is feared that these provisions will make it more difficult for them to make a new start. In addition, there is concern about the amount of discretion allowed to the police which is "so broad as to be virtually untrammeled" and the lack of effective remedy for disclosure of inaccurate information. Section 117 provides for an application for a new certificate issued under sections 112–116 where the applicant believes the certificate to be inaccurate, but there is no provision for damages for injury caused by the issuing of wrong information, and more fundamentally, no ability under the Act to get inaccurately recorded information corrected. It is, however, by section 124 an offence to make an unauthorised disclosure of information provided for the purposes of either criminal record certificates or enhanced criminal record certificates. Disclosure of information about unspent convictions which are revealed by a criminal conviction certificate is not, however, an offence.[75]

1.9 ACCESS TO PERSONAL INFORMATION

At common law there is no right of access to personal information which is held by an employer on either his employees or prospective employees and from time to time this situation has led to concern about abuse of such information.[76] There are currently three statutes that are appropriate to the employment relationship: Access to Medical Reports Act 1988 and Access to Health Records Act 1990, which cover manual data, and the Data Protection Act 1984 which covers electronically held data. Directive 95/46 on the protection of individuals with regard to the processing of personal data and on the free movement of such data, establishes common rules for data protection

[75] See S. Uglow and V. Telford, (1997).
[76] See R. Norton Taylor, (1988) *Blacklist: the inside story of political vetting* noted in Birkinshaw (1996), p. 248.

among Member States and facilitates the free flow of personal data within the E.U. in the interests of improving the operation of the single market. This was adopted in July 1995 and requires all Member States to implement its provisions by October 24, 1998. There are a number of significant differences between the 1994 Act and the Directive and following consultation on implementation of the Directive, the Data Protection Bill,[77] which repeals the 1994 Act, was introduced in the House of Lords on January 15, 1998.

1.9.1   Access to Medical Reports Act 1988

Section 1 provides a right of access to any medical report relating to the individual which is to be, or has been, supplied by a medical practitioner for employment or insurance purposes. By section 3 an employer or insurance company cannot seek a medical report on an individual for employment or insurance purposes without that patient's knowledge and consent. The patient has the right to see the medical report before it is passed to the employer or insurance company by the medical practitioner commissioned to prepare the report, and also the right to request that corrections be made to any part of the report he considers incorrect or misleading, and to refuse permission for the report to be passed on (s.5).

The employer is required, by section 3(2), to inform the employee of these rights when seeking consent and where an individual has requested access to a report he must contact the medical practitioner to arrange access within 21 days of the employer's application, otherwise by section 4 the practitioner is nevertheless entitled to supply the report to the employer.

Section 2(1) defines "employment purposes" sufficiently widely to cover present, past and prospective employees or the self employed, and "medical report" as "a report relating to the physical or mental health of the individual prepared by a medical practitioner who is or has been responsible for the clinical care of the individual." The Act therefore applies to applications to a person's medical practitioner (who has been responsible for his clinical care) for reports for both pre-employment purposes and during employment, and by the definition of "care" the Act extends to company nominated medical practitioners. The Act does not apply to any report prepared before the statute came into force.[78]

1.9.2   Access to Health Records Act 1990

Access to manually maintained records is not covered by the Data Protection Act 1984. However, the Access to Health Records Act 1990 implemented by regulations[79] provides for access to manually held health records which relate to the physical or mental health of a patient that have been made by a health professional, whether practising in the public or private sector, in connection with either care or treatment of the patient. "Health professional" is widely defined and includes not only a registered medical practitioner, whether in general or hospital practice, but also nurse, midwife, dentist, optician, health visitor, clinical psychologist, pharmacist, chiropodist, dietician, physiotherapist, occupational therapist, speech therapist, art or music therapist and others.

---

[77] House of Lords Bill 61.
[78] January 1, 1989.
[79] Access to Health Records (Control of Access) Regulations 1993 (S.I. 1993 No. 746).

Access may be applied for by the subject of the record or any person authorised in writing by the subject. If an employee is authorising an employer in this respect, there is no ability within the Act for the employee to have prior access, other than by making an application for access himself before giving authority to the employer to gain access. The Act applies to health records made by a health professional after the Act came into effect,[80] except insofar as it is necessary to render intelligible information to which the subject is entitled.[81]

1.9.3 Data protection

The Data Protection Act 1984, which was passed primarily to incorporate the European Convention on Data Protection 1981, applies only to electronically held data, and prohibits the holding of personal data by a data user on a data subject unless the data user registers with the Data Protection Registrar, supplying detailed information about the type and source of data and the purposes for which it is held. He must agree to comply with the eight data protection principles contained in the Act, which are taken from the Articles of the Council of Europe's Convention for the Protection of Individuals with regard to Automatic Processing of Personal Data, to which the United Kingdom is a signatory.[82] The Act makes it a criminal offence to fail to register and creates rights for data subjects to request and obtain copies of information held on them, and a right to request rectification and erasure where data is inaccurate.[83]

There are a number of significant differences between the 1984 Act and the Data Protection Directive 95/46, in that the Directive:

- defines certain key concepts differently;
- extends data protection controls to certain manual records;
- sets detailed conditions for processing personal data;
- sets tighter conditions for processing sensitive date;
- requires certain exemptions for the media;
- strengthens individuals' rights;
- strengthens the powers of the supervisory authority;
- sets new rules for the transfer of personal data outside the E.U.; and
- allows the existing registration scheme to be simplified.[84]

A Bill[85] has been published to implement the Directive which will repeal the 1984 Act, and establish a single overall data protection framework which will accommodate the differences between domestic law and the Directive, rather than a dual system which was strongly opposed in the consultation exercise undertaken in March 1996 by the

---

[80] November 1, 1991.
[81] See generally IDS Brief 588/May 1997.
[82] No. 108 of January 18, 1981.
[83] P. Birkinshaw, (1996).
[84] *Data Protection: The Government's Proposals*, July 28, 1997, p. 1. (http://www.homeoffice.gov.uk/datap1.htm).
[85] Data Protection Bill, House of Lords Bill 61.

previous Government. The Bill covers the rights of data subjects in Part II, the notification requirements by data controllers in Part III, Part IV deals with exemptions, and enforcement is dealt with in Part V.

The Directive requires data "controllers" to register with a Data Protection Commissioner, with wider enforcement powers than the Registrar, and a duty of promoting good practice. It is the duty of the "data controller" to comply with the eight data protection principles in relation to all personal data with respect to which he is the data controller, subject to that which is exempt, as detailed in Part IV. The principles are detailed in Schedule 1, Part I to the Bill, and Part II of that Schedule provides interpretation for those principles.

The Bill defines "data" in sufficiently broad terms to extend to non-automated data but only insofar as it is "recorded as part of a relevant filing system" or with the intention that it should do so. A "relevant filing system" is defined as any set of information relating to individuals to the extent that it is "structured, either by reference to individuals or by reference to the criteria relating to individuals, in such a way that particular information relating to a particular individual is readily accessible".

"Processing" is defined in the bill in clause 1, and means obtaining, recording or holding the data or carrying out any operation or set of operations on the data, including organisation, adaptation or alteration of the data, retrieval, consultation or use of the data, disclosure by transmission, dissemination or otherwise making available or erasure or destruction of the data. This would seem to fill the void created by the House of Lords decision in *R. v. Brown*[86] in which it was held that reading information from a screen but taking no further action was not "using" data: it would, however, be "processing".

The Directive provides rights for data subjects: the right to consent to the processing of personal data, unless the processing of data is necessary for a limited range of reasons and the right to object, on request and free of charge, to the processing of personal data for direct marketing purposes. Data subjects are given the right not to have a decision made about them which produces legal effects concerning them or significantly affects them and which is based solely on automated processing of data intended to evaluate certain personal aspects relating to them, such as their performance at work, creditworthiness, reliability or conduct. These rights are given effect in the Bill in Part II, clauses 7–10 and Schedule 2.

The Directive prohibits the processing of personal data revealing racial or ethnic origin, political opinions, religious or philosophical beliefs or trade union membership and the processing of personal data concerning health or sex life except where the data subject has given his "explicit consent" to such processing and national law does not prevent him from doing so. In the Bill "sensitive personal data" is defined in clause 2 and the processing of such data is subject to Schedule 3.

The Directive provides that the rights of data subjects may be restricted under certain circumstances, such as the necessity to safeguard national security, or for defence or reasons of public security and the prevention, investigation, detection and prosecution of criminal offences or breaches of ethics for regulated professions, and the Bill reflects these exemptions in Part IV. Clause 36 introduces Schedule 7 which contains miscellaneous exemptions, amongst which is included references given for the purposes of education or employment or prospective education or employment, examination marks and examination scripts.

---

[86] [1996] 1 All E.R. 545, HL.

The Bill gives power to the Commissioner to issue an enforcement notice if satisfied that the data controller has contravened the data protection principles. By clause 52, it is an offence for a person knowingly or recklessly to obtain, disclose or procure personal data without the consent of the data controller and an individual has a right to seek compensation for damage or distress caused by a data controller's failure to comply with the requirements of the Bill: the court has power to order rectification, blocking, erasure or destruction of inaccurate personal data.

Although the Directive must be implemented in all Member States within three years, by October 1998, Member States may provide that they have until October 24, 2007 to bring processing of data held in manual filing systems on the implementation date into conformity with the Directive's general principles and its provisions relating to the processing of sensitive data. In this respect, although the Bill provides for the relevant sections regarding the Commissioner to come into force on the day on which the Act is passed, it makes provision, clause 64(3), for the remaining provisions to be implemented by order.

Personal manual data held by an employer on an employee may, in the absence of any protection to be offered following implementation of the Directive, be protected from unauthorised disclosure under the common law on confidentiality. In *Dalgleish v. Lothian and Borders Police Board*[87] the Court of Session held, *obiter*, that staff records, including the names and addresses of employees, were, prima facie, confidential information, supplied for the purpose of the relationship of employer and employee, and as such was protected from disclosure to a third party. In reaching this conclusion Lord Cameron quoted from what was then the most recent *Spycatcher* case:

> "What is confidential information is a matter of the precise circumstance of the case, but generally, something which is already widely known is not confidential: and what becomes widely known (otherwise than through the agency of the person against whom the duty of the confidence is to be enforced) ceases to be confidential . . .
>
> What is a confidential relationship is likewise not precisely defined. It is clear that employment is one such relationship . . .
>
> The duty to preserve a confidence arises from the application of equity, and does not depend on express or implied contract . . ." *per* Lord Coulsfield.
>
> *Lord Advocate v. Scotsman Publications Ltd* [1988] S.L.T. 490 at 494, CS.

In addition, the right to privacy and to access to information will be affected by the Government's proposals for a freedom of information Act[88] and enactment of the Human Rights Bill.[89]

1.10 TRADE UNION MEMBERSHIP AND ACTIVITIES

It is unlawful to discriminate against job applicants on the grounds of their trade union membership status by refusing to employ them or making an offer subject to a condition regarding membership or non-membership of a trade union, or to indicate in

---

[87] [1991] I.R.L.R. 422, Court of Session.
[88] *Your right to know: freedom of information*, December 1997, Cm. 3818.
[89] House of Lords Bill 38, October 23, 1997.

advertisements that a vacancy is only open to a person who is or is not a member of a trade union or that any such requirement will be imposed. The relevant statutory provisions are contained in TULRCA 1992, s.137(1) which was introduced by the Employment Act 1990. Section 137(2) provides that a person unlawfully refused employment has a right of complaint to an industrial tribunal, and a person is taken to have been refused employment if:

". . . he seeks employment of any description with a person and that person—

(a) refuses or deliberately omits to entertain and process his application or enquiry, or

(b) causes him to withdraw or cease to pursue his application or enquiry, or

(c) refuses or deliberately omits to offer him employment of that description, or

(d) makes him an offer of such employment the terms of which are such as no reasonable employer who wished to fill the post would offer and which is not accepted, or

(e) makes him an offer of such employment but withdraws it or causes him not to accept it."

Trade Union and Labour Relations (Consolidation) Act 1992, s.137(5).

If an offer is made on conditions contrary to section 137(1), which is not accepted because the condition is not satisfied, or the applicant is unwilling to fulfil them, then the applicant is treated as having been refused employment for that reason. The provisions refer to a "person" as opposed to an "employee" and it is therefore argued that the protection offered by section 137 extends to the self-employed or those working under a contract for services, and in that respect is akin in its application to discrimination legislation generally as opposed to that applicable to employment protection.

These provisions were aimed at preventing the pre-entry closed shop. However, in *Harrison v. Kent County Council*,[90] on a complaint that the reason for refusal to offer a job related to trade union activities, Mummery J., construing the provisions of section 137 for the first time, held that trade union membership and activities overlap and to divorce the fact of membership and the incidents of membership is illusory. However, following the restrictive interpretation given to section 146 of the 1992 Act by the House of Lords in *Associated Newspapers v. Wilson; Associated British Ports v. Palmer*,[91] as pointed out by Deakin & Morris (1995) "the scope for arguing that (membership) extends to activities . . . seems negligible if not non-existent".

1.11   SHOP AND BETTING SHOP WORKERS

Although the liberalisation of Sunday trading formed part of the Thatcher Government's deregulation initiative, it has a somewhat longer history, with an equally long campaign opposed to reform. Between 1961 and the publication of the Auld Report in 1982[92] there were some 18 attempts to amend the Shops Act 1950: by section 47 of

---

[90] [1995] I.C.R. 434, EAT.
[91] [1995] I.R.L.R. 258, HL.
[92] *The Shops Acts: Late-night and Sunday Opening*, Report of the Committee of Inquiry into the Proposals to Amend the Shops Acts (Auld Committee), November 1984 (Cmnd. 9376).

which there was a general prohibition on Sunday trading in England and Wales, but not in Scotland, except for hairdressers and barbers, and the large number of exceptions contained in Schedule 4. Part II of the Act provided for a statutory weekly half-day holiday and for meal breaks for shop assistants, with a restriction on the number of Sundays in the month that could be worked, and for time off in lieu of Sunday working. It also contained special provisions governing the hours of employment of young persons.[93]

Following the Auld Report, that recommended "the abolition ... of all legal restrictions on the hours for which shops may be open to serve customers", the Government brought forward the 1985 Shops Bill which was defeated by a campaign by USDDAW and the Keep Sunday Special Campaign. In 1993 a White Paper was produced,[94] by which time, not only had public opinion changed, but some stores were openly defying the Sunday trading laws and it could be argued that the driving force behind what became the Sunday Trading Act 1994, was the widespread defiance of the restrictive trading laws laid down in the Shops Act 1950 by a number of DIY stores, as demonstrated for example in *Torfaen Borough Council v. B. & Q. plc.*[95]

Provisions regarding Sunday working for shop and betting workers are now contained in the ERA 1996, Part IV: for shop workers these provisions derive from the Sunday Trading Act 1994, Schedule 4, which came into effect August 26, 1994[96] and for betting shop workers from Betting, Gaming and Lotteries Act 1993, Schedule 5A, which was inserted into the Act by the Deregulation and Contracting Out Act 1994.[97]

In a series of horrifyingly complex provisions the concept of "protected" shop and betting worker, and "opted-out" shop and betting worker, is created, and to which certain rights attach. A "shop worker" is defined by section 232(1) as meaning an employee who, under his contract of employment, is or may be required to do shop work, and not very helpfully "shop work" is defined in the same section as work in or about a shop.

A "protected" worker for these purposes is someone who was employed as a shop worker on August 25, 1994, or as a betting worker on January 2, 1995, the day before the provisions of the appropriate Acts came into effect, has been continuously employed as such until the act complained of and throughout the period his relations with his employer were governed by a contract of employment (s.36(2)(a)–(c)). Even if the shop or betting worker was not employed on the date the relevant provisions came into effect, he still has the status of a "protected" worker if his contract of employment is such that under it he could not be required to work on Sunday regardless of the provisions of Part IV of the 1996 Act (s.36(3)(a) and (b)). A "protected" shop or betting worker loses his status as "protected" if he gives his employer an opting-in notice: which by section 36(6) must be in writing, signed and dated by the employee, in which the worker expressly states that he wishes to work on Sundays or that he does not object to working on Sundays, and after giving notice he has expressly agreed with his employer to do shop work, or betting work, on Sunday or even on a particular Sunday, (s.36(5)).

An "opted-out" shop or betting worker is someone who under his contract of employment is or may be required to work on Sunday, but is not employed to work

[93] *id.* p. viii.
[94] *Reforming the Law on Sunday Trading: A Guide to the Options for Reform* (Cmnd. 2300).
[95] [1990] 2 Q.B. 19.
[96] S.I. 1994 No. 1841.
[97] s.20(5), Sched. 8.

only on Sunday (s.40), and who has given his employer an opting-out notice stating that he objects to working on Sunday, has been continuously employed from the date of giving the notice until the date of the act complained of and remained a shop or betting worker during that time, (s.41(1)(a)–(c)). An "opted-out" shop or betting worker loses his status as "opted-out" if, in accordance with section 41(2), after giving his employer an "opting-out notice", he gives an "opting-in notice" and after giving the "opting-in notice" he expressly agrees with his employer to do shop or betting work on Sunday or on a particular Sunday.

Section 37(1) and (2) ERA 1996 provides that any contract of employment for a protected shop or betting worker is unenforceable to the extent that it requires them to do shop or betting work on a Sunday; or requires the employer to provide such work on Sunday; and by section 43 similar provisions apply to opted-out shop or betting workers after the expiry of the three-month notice period, providing in both cases the person has not lost his status as a protected or opted-out worker.

Where a contract of employment requires an employer of a protected shop or betting worker to provide guaranteed hours, and some of those hours were or might have been on a Sunday, section 38(2) provides that the employer does not have to provide increased working hours on weekdays to compensate for the loss of the hours on Sunday, and by section 39 the employer may reduce the pay of the protected worker by the "relevant proportion". These two provisions apply only to protected shop or betting workers and do not apply to those who are categorised as opted-out workers.[98]

Where a person becomes a shop or betting worker the employer must, by section 42, within two months, provide the worker with a written statement in the form contained in section 42(4). If the employer fails to comply with this, or the shop or betting worker becomes an opted-out worker, the notice period for the coming into effect of the opting-out notice becomes one month instead of the three months provided for in section 41(3). Section 42(4) and (5) contain the prescribed form for the notice for section 42 purposes for shop workers and betting workers respectively.

1.12   HOLIDAYS AND WORKING TIME

At common law there is no general restriction on the number of working hours, or consequential premium payments for overtime hours, and no general right to holidays or rest periods, except insofar as there is a common law duty to ensure a safe working environment, to ensure that fellow employees are adequately trained and the working environment does not present a hazard. In addition, under the Health and Safety at Work etc. Act 1974 there is a general statutory duty on employers to consider the health, safety and welfare of employees, to provide a safe system of work and a safe working environment[99] and specific E.C. Regulations provide for specific limits on the working hours and rest periods of certain workers.[1]

In general, however, unlike the employment regime in other European countries,[2] working hours, break periods and entitlement to holidays are currently matters

---

[98] See generally IDS Brief 591/June 1997.
[99] s.2.
[1] Council Regulation 3820/85 of December 20, 1985 and 3821/85 of December 20, 1985 govern driving time, break and rest periods for road transport.
[2] *DTI Consultation Document on measures to implement provisions of the E.C. Directive on the organisation of working time*. URN: 96/1126, Annex D.

governed by the contract and are the subject of either domestic or sector or national collective agreement. Where there is an entitlement to holiday, whether and at what rate it is to be paid, and whether upon termination there is an entitlement to accrued holiday pay, is also a question of contractual terms, express or implied, or collective agreement. The contractual nature of holiday arrangements is demonstrated in *Tucker v. British Leyland Motor Corp. Ltd*[3] and the ERA 1996, s.1(4) requires the employer to specify in the statement issued under section 1, not only the remuneration but any terms and conditions relating to hours of work and entitlement to holidays, including public holidays, and holiday pay (s.1(4)(d)(i)). Details of entitlement to holidays is one of the particulars required by section 2(4) (see para. 2.8) to be included in a single document, and the particulars should be sufficient to enable the employee's entitlement, including any entitlement to accrued holiday pay upon termination, to be precisely calculated. The necessity to inform employees of the applicable arrangements is highlighted in *Janes Solicitors v. Lamb-Simpson*.[4] The EAT distinguished *Morley v Heritage*,[5] and the conclusion cannot be avoided that the employer in *Janes Solicitors* was being "penalised" for his failure to have issued a statutory statement of terms as required by the ERA 1996, s.1.

It was this general lack of a right in the area of holidays and reliance on contract that led to objections by the United Kingdom to the ratification of ILO Convention No. 132,[6] Article 3 of which requires a minimum of three weeks' annual holiday with normal average earnings for all "employed persons", subject to a minimum service qualification. In addition, the Community Charter of the Fundamental Social Rights of Workers 1989, which was adopted by all Member States except the United Kingdom, stipulates, in Article 8, that every worker shall have a right to annual paid leave. However, Directive 93/104 concerning certain aspects of the organisation of working time was adopted in November 1993, and gives a general right to "workers" to paid holidays, places restrictions on working hours, provides entitlements to break periods and lays down standards with regard to nightwork and unsocial hours working. The Directive has an implementation date of November 23, 1996, but does not apply to the emergency services or to workers in air, rail, sea, inland waterway or lake transport, sea fishing, other work at sea and doctors in training, or to certain specific activities of bodies such as the armed forces and the police. Having been adopted as a health and safety measure under Article 118a, the Directive is applicable to the United Kingdom.

The Government of the day, along with employers' organisations, condemned the Directive as creating a burden on business at a time when the philosophy was one of deregulation, whilst the TUC hailed the Directive as a threshold, claiming that the United Kingdom has the longest working hours in Europe, and that the Directive will set some standards which good employers already enforce, but will make bad employers better.

The British Government challenged the Directive under Article 173 for an annulment on the basis that it had wrongly been adopted under the Article 118a procedure, which requires only qualified majority voting, rather than under Articles 100 or 235, which require unanimity within the Council, on the basis that Article 118a only permits the adoption of directives which have a genuine and objective link to the health and safety of workers, and measures concerning working time, leave and rest

[3] [1978] I.R.L.R. 493, CC.
[4] 323/94, EAT.
[5] [1993] I.R.L.R. 400, CA.
[6] Convention concerning Annual Holidays with Pay (Revised), 1970.

periods had too tenuous a link with health and safety, being essentially a social policy measure. Alternatively they sought an annulment of Article 4 of the directive, the requirement for a rest break where the working day is longer than six hours; the first and second sentences of Article 5, minimum uninterrupted rest period of 24 hours per each seven-day period; Article 6(2), maximum average working time for each seven-day period of 48 hours; and Article 7, the requirement for annual paid leave of at least four weeks. However, the ECJ held[7] that the directive had been correctly adopted on the basis of Article 118a, and was not inconsistent with the principle of subsidiarity. The Court allowed the application to the extent of annulling the second sentence of Article 5 in that the minimum rest period of 24 hours does not have to be on a Sunday.

Following the European Court's decision on the validity of the Directive the Government of the day published a consultation document,[8] on the issues and options relating to implementation in the United Kingdom. Following a change of Government in the 1997 general election the consultation proposals were withdrawn. New proposals have not been forthcoming, but it has been announced that it is intended to have Regulations in force to implement the Directive by October 1998[9] and will also incorporate working-time restrictions on adolescents contained in the Young Workers Directive, 94/33.[10]

In its work programme for 1996[11] the Commission announced that it would publish a White Paper on the sectors excluded from the scope of the E.C. Working Time Directive, and in July 1997 a White Paper concluded that action should be taken at European Union level to protect the health and safety of those workers excluded from Directive 93/104. The Commission has invited comments on its conclusion[12].

1.13   POSTED WORKERS

The Directive on the temporary posting of workers to another E.U. State, Directive 97/71, was adopted by the Council of Ministers in September 1996. Originally a "social dumping" measure, the aims of the Directive are four-fold:

- it abolishes obstacles to the free movement of labour and to the freedom to provide services;

- it clarifies which employment rules apply to posted workers especially where they are subcontracted;

- it removes the threat of unfair competition posed by cheap migrant labour; and

- it establishes a core of mandatory rules for the minimum protection of posted workers.[13]

---

[7] Case C–84/94, *United Kingdom v. Council of the European Union* [1997] I.R.L.R. 30, ECJ.
[8] *A consultation document on measures to implement provisions of the E.C. Directive on the Organisation of Working Time*, URN 96/1126.
[9] *Hansard*, H.C. February 5, 1998, col. 1222.
[10] I.R.L.B. 588, p. 14. See Summary, 1.17 for details and draft regulations.
[11] COM(95) 512, November 10, 1995.
[12] IDS brief 595/August 1997.
[13] IDS Employment Europe, "*Posted workers: too muddled, too late?*", Issue 425, May 1997.

A "posted worker" is defined in Article 2 as a worker who, for a limited period, carries out his work in the territory of a Member State other than the State in which he normally works, with the definition of "worker" being that which applies in the law of the Member State to whose territory the worker is posted, but does not extend to a crew member of a seagoing merchant vessel. Article 1 sets out the scope of the Directive in that it applies to three posting situations:

- when an undertaking seconds an employee (*i.e.* a person with whom it has an employment relationship) from one of its establishments to another in a second Member State;

- when one company subcontracts one of its employees to another undertaking in a second Member State in order to carry out a contract for providing services;

- when a "temporary employment agency" or "placement agency" hires out a worker (with whom it has an employment relationship for the duration of the posting) to a "user undertaking" established or operating in a second member state.

Whatever the law applicable to the employment relationship, undertakings must guarantee workers posted to their territory the basic terms and conditions of employment, as provided for in Article 3, laid down, whether by law, regulation or administrative provision, in the "host" Member State where the work is carried out:

- maximum work and minimum rest periods;

- minimum paid annual holidays;

- minimum rates of pay, including overtime rates as defined by national law of the Member State in whose territory the worker is posted (this does not apply to supplementary occupational retirement pension schemes);

- conditions for hiring-out workers, in particular the supply of workers by temporary employment undertakings;

- health and safety and hygiene at work;

- protective measures with regard to the terms and conditions of pregnant women or women who have recently given birth, of children and of young people; and

- equal treatment between men and women, and other provisions on non-discrimination.

Although in the original version only postings lasting more than three months were subject to regulated terms, the directive covers all postings irrespective of length, though there are limited exemptions on minimum pay and holidays. The length of the posting is calculated from the beginning of the posting period taking into account any previous periods for which the post has been filled by the posted worker.

All Member States, including the United Kingdom, are required to implement these provisions by September 16, 1999.[14]

---

[14] Directive on the posting of workers, EIRR 278, March 1997, pp. 31–33.

1.14   THE NATURE OF THE RELATIONSHIP

For the purposes of the application of many statutory protections it is necessary to establish that the relationship between the person giving work and the person doing it is that of employer and employee, as opposed to that of an independent contract, or some other form of relationship. The ERA 1996, s.230 contains a definition of "employee":

> s.230(1) "an individual who has entered into or works under (or, where the employment has ceased, worked under) a contract of employment" and
>
> s.230(2) "contract of employment" means "a contract of service or apprenticeship, whether express or implied, and (if it is express) whether oral or in writing."

This is a restrictive definition, particularly in the light of the changed and changing nature of the employment relationship. A report by the Institute of Employment Rights (1996) considers that little and insufficient attention has been given to the implications of the changing nature of the employment relationship and the extent of the spread to "non-standard" forms of contracts, from part-time or casual working, through to job share or fixed term contracts is indicated by survey results.[15]

Nevertheless, for statutory purposes the law is concerned to find a "contract of service", as distinguished from a contract for services, or self-employment. To this end a number of tests have been developed over time, from the "control test" propounded by Bramwell L.J. in *Yewens v. Noakes*[16]: based on the notion that "A servant is a person subject to the command of his master as to the manner in which he shall do his work". Although this test expresses an employment relationship that is set in its day, what Kahn Freund[17] called a pre-industrial age, whereby the employer was both manager and technical expert and superior to the employee in skill and knowledge, it was still in use as late as 1941 in *Chadwick v. Pioneer Private Telephone Ltd*.[18]

That test gave way to consideration of a number of factors, an early example of which is demonstrated in the judgment of Lord Thankerton in *Short v. J. and W. Henderson Ltd.*[19] In *Stevenson Jordan and Harrison Ltd v. McDonald and Evans*[20] Denning L.J. identified the distinguishing feature between an employee and an independent contractor as being whether an employee was integrated into the organisation, and in doing so attempted to overcame the problem of skilled and technical staff over whom the employer exercises little control. The use of this test is demonstrated in *Cassidy v. Ministry of Health*[21] where it was held that a hospital doctor was an employee.

A more flexible multiple or mixed test was propounded by McKenna J. in *Ready Mixed Concrete (South East) Ltd v. Minister of Pensions and National Insurance*[22] in which, in addition to considering the degree of control exercised over what was to be

---

[15] Only 16 per cent of the survey sample said that the entire workforce was employed on a permanent full-time basis, IRS Employment Trends 570.
[16] (1880) 6 Q.B.D. 530, CA.
[17] (1951) 14 M.L.R. at 505–8 quoted in Davies & Freedland (1984).
[18] [1941] 1 All E.R. 522.
[19] [1946] S.C. H.L. 24, HL.
[20] [1952] 1 T.L.R. 101, CA.
[21] [1951] 1 All E.R. 574, CA.
[22] [1968] 1 All E.R. 433, DC.

done and how and by what method it was to be done, the court also looked at the method of consideration, in that whereas a servant is obliged to supply his own labour, freedom to get others to perform the work was held to be inconsistent with a contract of employment, as was the chance of profit and risk of loss. Taking all this together it was held that the contract was not one of service, but that the factors indicated that the worker was an entrepreneur rather than an employee.

In *Market Investigations v. Minister of Social Security*,[23] Cooke J., drawing upon earlier judgments of Denning L.J.[24] and Lord Wright,[25] said:

"... the fundamental test to be applied is this 'Is the person who has engaged himself to perform these services performing them as a person in business on his own account?' If the answer to that question is 'yes,' then the contract is a contract for services."

A test which he recognised may be easier to apply in the case of an established business, but said that the test was not decisive and proceeded to ask two questions:

"First, whether the extent and degree of the control exercised by the company, if no other factors were taken into account, be consistent with her being employed under a contract of service. Second, whether when the contract is looked at as a whole, its nature and provisions are consistent or inconsistent with its being a contract of service, bearing in mind the general test I have adumbrated" *per* Cooke J.

Market Investigations v. Minister of Social Security [1969] 2 Q.B. 173 at 185.

The label placed on the relationship by the parties is not conclusive as to the nature of the relationship. This is demonstrated in a number of cases which usually arise as a result of the label of self employment for the taxation advantages available, which is called into question when some event requires a different label to be attached to the relationship. This occurred in *Ferguson v. John Dawson & Partners (Contractors) Ltd*[26] in which the Court of Appeal, Lawton L.J. dissenting, held that although the parties' expressed intention might be a relevant factor in deciding the true nature of the contract, regard should be had to the arrangement as a whole and the reality of the situation, which the Court held was a contract of employment. Lawton L.J. in his dissenting judgment expressed the view that a man should be able to offer his services on whatever basis he wished, and that as the parties had entered an agreement that their relationship would be that of self employment, the courts should uphold that. He was concerned at the application of policy in the face of the intention of the parties:

"Maybe the law should try to save workmen from their folly; but it should not encourage them to change a status which they have freely chosen when it suits them to do so. . . . it would be contrary to public policy to allow a man to say he was self-employed for the purpose of avoiding the incidence of taxation but a servant for the purpose of claiming compensation." *per* Lawton L.J. (dissenting).

Ferguson v. John Dawson & Partners (Contractors) Ltd [1976] 3 All E.R. 817 at 829, CA.

---

[23] [1969] 2 Q.B. 173, HC.
[24] *Bank voor Handel en Scheepvaart N.V. v. Slatford* [1953] 1 Q.B. 248.
[25] *Montreal v. Montreal Locomotive Works Ltd* [1947] 1 D.L.R. 161.
[26] [1976] 3 All E.R. 817, CA.

Nevertheless in *Young & Woods Ltd v. West*[27] the Court of Appeal held that, notwithstanding that a choice had been offered upon starting work as to the basis of the working relationship, the courts should look beneath the label to discover the reality of the situation. In doing so it was held that the true legal relationship was not self-employment, since the workman was not carrying out the services provided as a person in business on his own account. The policy implications of so deciding were discussed by Stephenson L.J.:

> "I am satisfied that the parties can resile from the position which they have deliberately and openly chosen to take up and that to reach any other conclusion would be, in effect, to permit the parties to contract out of the Act and to deprive, in particular, a person who works as an employee within the definition of the Act under a contract of service of the benefits which this statute confers upon him. If I consider the policy of the Act I can see the dangers . . . of employers anxious to escape from their statutory liabilities under this legislation or the Factories Acts offering this choice to persons whom they intend to employ, as Mr West was employed, as employees within the definition of the Act and pressing them to take that employment—it may be even insisting upon their taking that employment—on the terms that it shall not be called that employment at all, but shall be called a contract for services with a self-employed person . . ." *per* Stephenson L.J.

Young & Woods Ltd v. West [1980] I.R.L.R. 201 at 207, CA.

The court distinguished *Massey v. Crown Life Insurance Co.*[28] where the Court of Appeal, although accepting that the parties could not alter the true nature of their relationship by putting a different label on it, a change of label during the course of the relationship was held to be a true reflection of the nature of that relationship. It was held in *Massey* that if the parties' relationship is ambiguous it is open to the parties by agreement to stipulate what the legal situation between them is to be, the agreement then becoming the best material from which together the true legal relationship may be judged. Lawton L.J. in *Massey* said that it was the written contract, with its detailed terms which distinguished *Massey* from *Ferguson* and made it "entirely different" with a genuine intention, initiated by *Massey,* to change the status. In both *Ferguson v. John Dawson & Partners (Contractors) Ltd*[29] and *Young & Woods Ltd v. West*[30] the label had been decided at the outset of the relationship, although in *Young & Woods Ltd v. West* the case note does make it clear that West was offered an alternative when he chose to be treated as self-employed.

In *Lane v. Shire Roofing Company (Oxford) Ltd*[31] the Court of Appeal had to consider the situation in relation to a health and safety issue when a workman fell from a ladder. Henry L.J. held that:

> "When it comes to the question of safety at work, there is a real public interest in recognising the employer/employee relationship when it exists, because of the

[27] [1980] I.R.L.R. 201, CA.
[28] [1978] I.C.R. 590, CA.
[29] [1976] 3 All E.R. 817, CA.
[30] [1980] I.R.L.R. 201, CA.
[31] [1995] I.R.L.R. 493, CA.

responsibilities that the common law and statutes such as the Employers' Liability (Compulsory Insurance) Act 1969 places on the employer" *per* Henry L.J.

Lane v. Shire Roofing Company (Oxford) Ltd [1995] I.R.L.R. 493 at 495, CA.

Reviewing the authorities, Henry L.J. said that the element of control, in terms of who lays down what is to be done, the way in which it is to be done, the means by which it is to be done, and the time when it is done is important, as is who provides the material, plant and machinery and tools used. But that where there was discretion as to how the job is done the test should be broadened to ask, "whose business was it?" Despite being treated as self-employed it was held that the answer to the question "Whose business was it?" in relation to the particular job, "could only be answered by saying that it was the respondent's business and not the appellant's". As a result the respondent owed the duties of employer to his employee.

The various tests that have been developed appear confusing and designed, not to give a formula to be applied with a view to answering the question in a particular case, but rather as a means of justifying the answer already found from a general overall appearance of the facts of a particular case. In *Hall (HM Inspector of Taxes) v. Lorimer*[32] in a unanimous judgment, Nolan L.J. in the CA said: "I agree with the views expressed by Mummery J. in the present case at p. 944D of the report where he says:

"In order to decide whether a person carries on business on his own account it is necessary to consider many different aspects of that person's work activity. This is not a mechanical exercise of running through items on a check list to see whether they are present in, or absent from, a given situation. The object of the exercise is to paint a picture from the accumulation of detail. The overall effect can only be appreciated by standing back from the detailed picture which has been painted, by viewing it from a distance and by making an informed, considered, qualitative appreciation of the whole. It is a matter of evaluation of the overall effect of the detail, which is not necessarily the same as the sum total of the individual details. Not all details are of equal weight or importance in any given situation. The details may also vary in importance from one situation to another.

The process involves painting a picture in each individual case. As Vinelott J. said in *Walls v. Sinnett* [1986] 60 T.C. 150 p. 164:

'It is, in my judgment, quite impossible in a field where a very large number of factors have to be weighed, to gain any real assistance by looking at the facts of another case and comparing them one by one to see what facts are common, what are different and what particular weight is given by another Tribunal to the common facts. The facts as a whole must be looked at, and what may be compelling in one case in the light of all the facts may not be compelling in the context of another case.' "

Hall (HM Inspector of Taxes) v. Lorimer [1994] I.R.L.R. 171 at 174, CA, quoting from Mummery J. [1992] 1 W.L.R. 939 at 944, EAT.

In *Lorimer* there was no investment in equipment or stock, no monetary contribution and no chance of profit or risk of loss in the sense outlined by Cooke J. in *Market*

[32] [1994] I.R.L.R. 171, CA.

Investigations Ltd v. Minister of Social Security.[33] Nevertheless, it was held that the provision of labour alone to a large number of clients, the risk being in finding sufficient clients and work, and of ensuring payment, was sufficient to bring Lorimer within Schedule D for taxation purposes, and consequently enabled him to offset his legitimate business expenses against his earnings, action not open to an employee.

There has been some doubt about whether a person with a controlling interest in a company, but who works for the company and is paid a salary, can be an "employee" within the ERA 1996, s.230, in order to be able to make claim under section 182, in the event of the company's insolvency, for debts covered by section 184. In *Secretary of State for Trade and Industry v. Bottrill*[34] it was held by the EAT that there was no rule of law that prevented a controlling shareholder from being an "employee" for statutory purposes. Mr Bottrill had a contract of employment with the company but when the company went into voluntary liquidation his claim for a redundancy payment and other debts owed by the company was rejected by the Secretary of State because of Mr Bottrill's controlling interest in the company. In the earlier decision of *Buchan and Ivey v. Secretary of State for Employment*[35] a person with a controlling interest was held not to be an employee despite contractual arrangements to the contrary. The reasoning in *Buchan and Ivey* was summed up by Morison J. (President) in *Secretary of State for Trade and Industry v. Bottrill*[36]:

> "because it seemed to them that in the context of employment legislation it would be impossible to conceive of circumstances in which events giving rise to a claim for compensation could not have occurred without the individual claimant's concurrence. How could it be thought that Parliament conferred on an individual a right to bring proceedings to claim compensation for an act which could not have happened without his consent?" *per* Morison J.

Secretary of State for Trade and Industry v. Bottrill [1998] I.R.L.R. 120 at 123, EAT.

But in *Bottrill* it was held that an "industrial tribunal is not required to assess fault". The EAT in *Bottrill* distinguished *Buchan and Ivey* and relied on the later Court of Session (CS) case of *Fleming v. Secretary of State for Trade & Industry*[37] where it was held that whether a person is an "employee" is a question of fact and that although being a majority shareholder is a relevant factor, the significance of that factor will depend on the circumstances, but that it was not the case that he could never be an employee.

1.14.1 Part-time workers

Although there is no definition in the ERA 1996 of "part-time", prior to regulations passed following the House of Lords decision in *R. v. Secretary of State for Employment ex parte EOC*[38] employees' eligibility for a range of statutory benefits depended not only on a qualifying period of employment, but also on the number of hours worked.

---

[33] [1969] 2 Q.B. 173, HC.
[34] [1998] I.R.L.R. 120, EAT.
[35] [1997] I.R.L.R. 80, EAT.
[36] [1998] I.R.L.R. 120, EAT.
[37] [1997] I.R.L.R. 682, CS.
[38] [1993] I.C.R. 251, CA.

Employees with a contract for eight hours a week or more, but less than 16, had a longer qualifying period of five years, whilst those with a contract for less than eight hours a week, were not eligible for statutory benefits regardless of the length of time worked. In *R. v. Secretary of State for Employment ex parte EOC* the House of Lords issued a declaration that these statutory provisions were discriminatory. As a result employment protection legislation with qualifying hours thresholds was amended.[39]

In *London Borough of Hammersmith & Fulham v. Jesuthasan*[40] the facts arose before implementation of the amending regulations. Being a part-time worker Jesuthasan did not qualify to bring a claim for unfair dismissal and redundancy pay. However, the Court of Appeal held that it was not necessary for him to bring a claim for indirect discrimination under the Sex Discrimination Act and to demonstrate that the hours provisions had a disparate impact on him: he was entitled to proceed under the ERA 1996. It was held that the council was not entitled to rely on provisions of domestic law, that had been judicially declared to be incompatible with E.U. law, in order to defeat a claim that the applicant had been entitled to make at the time of his dismissal. The hours thresholds had been displaced by E.U. law, and the fact that they were displaced because they indirectly discriminated against women was irrelevant.

In June 1997 the European-level social partners[41] concluded a framework Agreement on Part-time Work,[42] and this has subsequently been incorporated into a Directive, (97/81). The purpose of the Agreement is to provide for the removal of discrimination against part-time workers, to improve the quality of part-time work and "to facilitate the development of part-time work on a voluntary basis and to contribute to the flexible organisation of working time in a manner which takes into account the needs of employers and workers".[43]

Clause 4 provides that in respect of employment conditions, part-time workers shall not be treated in a less favourable manner than comparable full-time workers solely because they work part-time unless different treatment is justified on objective grounds. A "part-time worker" is defined as an employee whose normal hours of work, calculated on a weekly basis or on average over a period of employment of up to one year, are less than the normal hours of work of a comparable full-time worker.

The Agreement was concluded under the social policy Agreement annexed to the Maastricht Treaty on European Union, and is therefore not applicable to the United Kingdom because of the United Kingdom "opt-out", neither is it included in the extension Directives, extending the Works Council and Parental Leave Directives to the United Kingdom (see para. 10.7).

The Equal Opportunities Commission (EOC) has welcomed the Directive[44-45] as a significant development which will considerably improve the situation of part-time workers, 83 per cent of whom are women, by ensuring parity of treatment between full-time and part-time employees, but has questioned whether the scope of legislation should be widened to embrace part-time workers who are self-employed or on temporary contracts. They also express concern that Member States have the discretion to exclude casual part-time workers and to limit access to conditions of service by making these subject to a period of service or earnings qualification[46] that

---

[39] Employment Protection (Part-time Employees) Regulations 1995 (S.I. 1995 No. 31).
[40] Court of Appeal, February 26, 1998. IDS Brief 609/March 1998.
[41] ETUC, UNICE, CEEP.
[42] EIRR 285, October 1997, p. 31.
[43] Clause 1.
[44-45] EOC, *Education and Employment Committee, Submission from the EOC— Part-Time Work,* October 1997.
[46] Clause 4.4.

consideration will also need to be given to the effect of the national insurance threshold on the hours of work, earnings and benefit entitlements of part-time workers.

The report highlights that Britain has the third highest density of part-time working in Europe, the highest being in the Netherlands at 37.4 per cent, and Sweden at 26.4 per cent, followed by the United Kingdom with 24.5 per cent, but that whereas in Britain part-time work is concentrated in lower level service jobs, in other E.C. countries it is found more extensively in professional occupations. In the United Kingdom a high proportion, 44.3 per cent, of the female workforce work on a part-time basis. This is higher than the E.U. average of 31.3 per cent, the only other country having a higher proportion being the Netherlands, with 67.3 per cent of women working part-time.

1.14.2 Fixed term contracts

Although not defined, the ERA 1996 contains specific provisions relating to fixed term contracts. In *Dixon v. BBC*[44] it was held that notwithstanding that the contract for a given period contains a notice provision for either party, this does not prevent the contract being a fixed term contract within the relevant provisions. This reversed the earlier decision of the Court of Appeal in *BBC v. Ioannou*[48] which gave the employer the opportunity to evade the provision that non-renewal amounts to a dismissal for statutory purposes merely by inserting a notice clause. That would clearly have permitted widespread evasion of the protection offered.

In order to be a fixed term contract for these purposes expiry must be on a definable date. However, there has been some controversy as to whether task contracts are capable of being fixed term contracts for these purposes. In *Wiltshire County Council v. NATFHE and Guy*[49] Phillips J. in the EAT said that a contract of employment which came to an end on the happening of an uncertain future event would be a contract for a "fixed term" and that a contract "for the duration of the present government" or "during the life of the present sovereign" or "for some other period capable of being determined by reference to a prescribed test" would be a contract for a fixed term. However, in *Ryan v. Shipboard Maintenance*[50] this approach was doubted: ". . . we do not think that a contract for the duration of the job can be 'fixed term' because it is indeterminate as to termination . . ." *per* Kilner Brown J., and in the CA in *Wiltshire County Council v. NATFHE and Guy* Lord Denning M.R. disapproved of Phillips' J. statement:

> "Mr. Justice Phillips mentioned contracts which are terminable on a completely uncertain event such as the duration of the government or the life of the sovereign, or something like that. It seems to me that such a contract is not employment for a fixed term at all. It does not come within the provision. It is not the subject of 'dismissal' . . ." *per* Lord Denning M.R.

Wiltshire County Council v. NATFHE and Guy [1980] I.R.L.R. 198 at 200, CA.

---

[47] [1979] I.C.R. 281, CA.
[48] [1975] 2 All E.R. 999, CA.
[49] [1978] I.R.L.R. 301, EAT.
[50] [1980] I.R.L.R. 16, EAT.

The Court of Appeal, in the *Wiltshire CC* case, approving the decision of the EAT in *Ryan v. Shipboard Maintenance*, held that the contract being for a session, contemplated a clear ending which could be identified at the outset of the contract, and was therefore a fixed term contract within the meaning of the section. The wide interpretation given to the term by Phillips J. in the EAT was disapproved of: therefore, a task contract is not a fixed term contract, unless the completion of that task or event can be dated with reasonable certainty at the start of the contract.

Although non-renewal of a fixed term contract is, by the ERA 1996, s.95(1)(b), dismissal, section 197 enables an employer to exclude certain rights (see para. 7.2.1.6).

1.14.3 Homeworkers

Between 1981 and 1984 the incidence of homeworking tripled.[51] Although women make up 45 per cent of the employed workforce, they account for 82 per cent of all homeworkers, and homeworkers tend to be older than other employees, and more likely to work beyond retirement age. With the development of technology, making homeworking across a range of technical and skilled jobs increasingly possible, the nature of homeworking has undergone a change from being associated with the characteristics of low skill to that known as "telework", or "telecommuting".

Classifying such workers as employees for employment protection purposes presents difficulties when based upon the traditional tests that have developed for these purposes. There is usually little control exercised over the activities of homeworkers and often there is little reciprocity, in that the worker is free to choose to work and the employer is not bound to give work or provide the opportunity to earn. However, in *Airfix Footwear Ltd v. Cope*[52] the EAT held that a female "outworker" assembling shoe parts from home, was an employee because a contract of employment had grown up. She had worked over a seven year period, during which time she generally worked five days a week, and the employer retained control when such control was necessary. However, the EAT recognised that where the work was sporadic and the company was under no obligation to provide work, such a relationship may well not amount to a contract of employment, but rather each occasion would amount to a separate contract, as was held in *Market Investigations Ltd v. Minister of Social Security.*[53]

In *Nethermere (St Neots) Ltd v. Gardiner*[54] the company, who manufactured boys' trousers, employed both factory based workers and homeworkers, the applicants being part-time homeworkers who sewed trouser flaps and pockets using machines provided by the company. They arranged their own hours of work to suit their circumstances, and likewise the amount of work they accepted, the employer not being obliged to give them work. For the employer it was argued that this lack of a continuing obligation to provide work and pay, and a continuing obligation on the employee to do the work provided was fatal to establishing a contract of employment.

The Court of Appeal, looking at the authorities and applying *Collier v. Sunday Referee Publishing Co. Ltd*[55] held that "the normal rule is that a contract of employment does not oblige the master to provide the servant with work in addition to wages." The Court relied on MacKenna J. in *Ready Mixed Concrete (South East) Ltd v. Minister of Pensions and National Insurance*[56]:

---

[51] A Felstead, *et al.* (1996).
[52] [1978] I.C.R. 1210, EAT.
[53] [1969] 2 Q.B. 173, HC.
[54] [1984] I.C.R. 612, CA.
[55] [1940] 2 K.B. 647, HC.
[56] [1968] 2 Q.B. 497, DC.

"A contract of service exists if these three conditions are fulfilled. (i) The servant agrees that, in consideration of a wage or other remuneration, he will provide his own work and skill in the performance of some service for his master. (ii) He agrees, expressly or impliedly, that in the performance of that service he will be subject to the other's control in a sufficient degree to make that other master. (iii) The other provisions of the contract are consistent with its being a contract of service." *per* MacKenna J.

Ready Mixed Concrete (South East) Ltd v. Minister of Pensions and National Insurance [1968] 2 Q.B. 497 at 515, DC.

In a majority judgment, Kerr L.J. dissenting, Stephenson L.J. doubted whether even that irreducible minimum identified by MacKenna J. could be discerned on the facts, but nevertheless refused to interfere with the findings of the EAT that, "On the evidence there was just enough material to make a contract of service a reasonably possible inference in favour of the applicants."

A finding that a homeworker is an employee has far-reaching consequences for an employer, beyond that of becoming liable to deduct PAYE and to pay national insurance contributions. He must also comply with employment protection legislation that extends to employees and, in addition, comply with Health and Safety at Work etc. Act 1974 and Regulations. This means that companies who employ more than five people must have a written policy, carry out a risk assessment and set up processes by which notification of accidents can take place. In the case of homeworkers, this means distribution and training initiatives which reach the entire workforce. In the case of teleworkers the Display Screen Equipment Regulations 1992[57] apply (see para. 3.3.1).

1.14.4 Temporary or casual workers

Even though a job carried out on a casual basis may continue for some years, the lack of mutuality associated with casual work has proved fatal to efforts to establish a relationship of employer and employee: the very nature of the work is that the employer is not bound to offer work and the employee is not bound to accept it when it is offered. In *O'Kelly v. Trusthouse Forte*[58] the question arose as to whether "regular" casuals were employees in circumstances where the applicants worked virtually every week for hours varying from as little as three, up to 57, but that over the previous year had worked an average of 31 hours a week. They were placed on the "regular" list as a result of their reliability and given preference over other casuals for functions, although they were not guaranteed work. It was confirmed that the correct approach is to consider all features of the relationship, giving each such weight as seems appropriate "to determine whether the person was carrying out business on his own account."

The workers concerned were paid weekly in arrears, from which income tax and national insurance was deducted, but did not get paid sick pay and did not participate in the company pension scheme, or enjoy any of the other fringe benefits. Holiday pay entitlement was based on the number of full weeks worked during the preceding year, although the payment arrangements were different from those applicable to permanent staff. There was a recognised formal grievance procedure applicable to casuals, and they

---

[57] Health and Safety (Display Screen Equipment) Regulations 1992 (S.I. 1992 No. 2792).
[58] [1983] I.R.L.R. 369, CA.

were supplied with uniforms, as were permanent staff. It was however noted that it was not the intention of the parties that their arrangement would lead to employee status, and that custom in the industry was that such casuals were not employees.

The Court of Appeal held that lack of mutuality prevented such a relationship being that of employer and employee: there was no obligation on the employer to offer work, and no obligation on the applicants to accept work if it was offered. In view of this it was held that the applicants were in business on their own account as independent contractors supplying services and that the argument put forward of a "global contract" did not assist since if there was a "global contract" it was made up of individual contracts whereby the applicants were in business on their own account.

The Court of Appeal in *Clark v. Oxfordshire Health Authority*,[59] in allowing the employer's appeal against an EAT decision that there was a global contract in the case of a "bank nurse" who worked on a series of individual contracts between which she was not paid, did so on the basis of lack of mutuality. In a decision of the court, Sir Christopher Slade noted the decisions in *Nethermere (St Neots) Ltd v. Gardiner*[60] and *McLeod v. Hellyer Bros Ltd*[61] and said that:

> ". . . the (health) authority was at no relevant time under any obligation to offer the applicant work nor was she under any obligation to accept it. I would, for my part, accept that the mutual obligations required to found a global contract of employment need not necessarily and in every case consist of obligations to provide and perform work. To take one obvious example, an obligation by the one party to accept and do work if offered and an obligation on the other party to pay a retainer during such periods as work was not offered would in my opinion, be likely to suffice. In my judgment, however, as I have already indicated, the authorities require us to hold that *some* mutuality of obligation is required to found a global contract of employment." *per* Sir Christopher Slade.

Clark v. Oxfordshire Health Authority [1998] I.R.L.R. 125 at 130, CA.

No mutuality was found to exist during non-work periods but in the light of the Court of Appeal decision in *McMeechan v. Secretary of State for Employment*,[62] the case was referred back to the industrial tribunal to consider whether there was a dismissal, if so when that occurred and if at the relevant time there was a specific engagement which amounted to a contract of service which could provide the basis for an unfair dismissal claim.

In the light of the decision in *Clark* and the CA decision in *McLeod*[63] which also rejected the concept of a global contract to span intervening periods between working, the decision in *Boyd Line Ltd v. Pitts*,[64] cannot be sustained. In *Boyd Line* a skipper who worked for the same firm for over 30 years, but was stood down between voyages, was held to be an employee employed under a global contract which governed the whole period of employment. Although the EAT noted that the facts in *McLeod* were "superficially different", they also said that: "We feel it probable . . . that we would have decided the matter differently from the majority of the industrial tribunal", but

[59] [1998] I.R.L.R. 125, CA.
[60] [1984] I.R.L.R. 240, CA.
[61] [1987] I.R.L.R. 232, CA.
[62] [1997] I.R.L.R. 353, CA.
[63] [1987] I.R.L.R. 232, CA.
[64] [1986] I.C.R. 244, EAT.

felt themselves constrained by the dicta of Sir John Donaldson M.R. in *O'Kelly v. Trusthouse Forte plc*[65] as to the role of the EAT when dealing with findings of fact by an industrial tribunal.

In *McLeod*,[66] the Court of Appeal explored whether:

". . . a contract of employment (within the ERA 1996, s.230) (whether it be given the extra-statutory name 'global' or 'umbrella' or any other name) can exist in the absence of mutual obligations subsisting over the entire duration of the relevant period. Any doubts as to this point were laid to rest by the decision of this court in *Nethermere (St Neots) Ltd v. Gardner* [1984] I.R.L.R. 240 where there was full analysis and discussion of the *Airfix* case. Though Kerr L.J., in his final conclusion, dissented from the majority on a narrow ground . . ., all three members of this court were agreed that there must be mutual legally binding obligations on each side to create a contract of service." *per* Slade L.J.

McLeod v. Hellyer Brothers Ltd; Wilson v. Boston Deep Sea Fisheries Ltd [1987] I.R.L.R. 232 at 239, CA.

In the light of these decisions, and working within the statutory definitions, it appears that the only way that a temporary worker with no mutuality of obligation can establish a contract of employment is to be able to bring themselves within the principle of the Court of Appeal decisions in *McMeechan* and *Clark*—by having a single contract which is capable of establishing the status of employee. Most periods of work on a casual basis would, however, not extend to the qualifying period necessary to be eligible to bring a claim for redundancy or unfair dismissal, even if there is sufficient mutuality to establish an employment relationship. Note should, however, be taken of the decision in *Carmichael and Leese v. National Power plc*[66] in which Chadwick L.J., in the Court of Appeal, said that the women, who were on standby to act as guides at Blyth power stations, had entered into contracts of employment by signing and returning letters accepting the jobs. The words "on a casual basis" in the letters did not negate the women's rights: to do so would result in them being independent contractors, which would be "wholly artificial". It must be right that to label part-time workers as self-employed is artificial and in an area which is heavily policy orientated, policy should be directed to including rather than excluding workers who clearly are not "in business on their own account".

1.14.5   Agency workers

Workers who operate via an employment agency have represented a hybrid form of worker, not easily being cast in either category of "employee" or "self-employed", no matter how long they remain on the books of a particular agency, or how long they are assigned to work for a particular client. This is because there is usually no mutuality of obligation as between the agency and the worker or between the worker and the company to which they are assigned: no obligation by the agency or worker to offer work and accept work and no "control" over the worker, but likewise no evidence that the agency worker is "in business on his own account". Agencies are obliged to deduct

[65] [1983] I.C.R. 728 at 761, CA.
[66] [1987] I.R.L.R. 232, CA.
[67] *Daily Telegraph*, March 28, 1998.

PAYE and national insurance from worker's wages,[68] but this does not make the agency an employer for these purposes and this was confirmed in *Wickens v. Champion Employment*.[69] The EAT held that although there was no evidence that workers were carrying on business on their own account, neither were they employees of the agency because there was no obligation to accept or provide work. This was confirmed in *Ironmonger v. Movefield Ltd*,[70] even though the worker had worked for a particular company through the same agency for five years: the EAT there relied on *Construction Industry Training Board v. Labour Force Ltd*,[71] namely:

"The sole question before the Tribunal on this part of the case was, as I have said, whether the contracts were contracts of service. These contracts were contracts whereby the workman contracted with the respondents to do work for a third party, the contractor. It was not a question of the respondents lending the services of one of their own employees to the contractor, because the workman never contracted to render services to the respondents at all. I think that there is much to be said for the view that, where A contracts with B to render services exclusively to C, the contract is not a contract of services, but a contract sui generis, a different type of contract from either of the familiar two . . ." *per* Cooke J.

Construction Industry Training Board v. Labour Force Ltd [1970] 3 All E.R. 220 at 225, HC.

In *McMeechan v. Secretary of State for Employment*[72] the question arose as to whether the applicant had been an employee of the agency for whom he worked, which he needed to establish in order to successfully claim against the Secretary of State under the ERA 1996, s.182 when the agency became insolvent. The Court of Appeal held that a temporary worker can have the status of employee of the employment agency in respect of each assignment actually worked, notwithstanding that the same worker may not be entitled to employee status under his general terms of engagement, and:

"In so far as *Pertemps Group plc v. Nixon* purported to lay down any principle contrary to those propositions it should not, in my judgment, be followed. The holding that there was no authority to support the competence of an industrial tribunal to spell a contract of service out of a single engagement cannot be maintained in the face of *O'Kelly* and *Nethermere*. Nor is any support to be found for it in the authorities on which the judgment in *Pertemps* purported to rely. *Wickens*, being a decision on a general engagement, had no application. The obiter dicta of Cooke J. in *Construction Industry Training Board v. Labour Force Ltd* [1970] I.R.L.R. 461 that, on the special facts there considered, the unusual concept of a contract sui generis that was neither of service nor for services had been called into play. They provide no justification at all, however, for holding that an industrial tribunal in entirely different circumstances was excluded, as a matter of law, from finding that a single engagement had given rise to a contract of employment." *per* Waite L.J.

McMeechan v. Secretary of State for Employment [1997] I.R.L.R. 353 at 360, C.A.

---

[68] Finance (No. 2) Act 1975, s.38.
[69] [1984] I.C.R. 365, EAT.
[70] [1988] I.R.L.R. 461, EAT.
[71] [1970] 3 All E.R. 220, HC.
[72] [1997] I.R.L.R. 353, CA.

The Court distinguished *Wickens*[73] since in that case the judgment related, not to one particular individual, but was a "general engagement case" where the applicant was seeking to establish that all the agency personnel were "employees" in order to bring the numbers employed above the minimum limit of 20 so as to found her claim for unfair dismissal, and "surprisingly" had not had their attention drawn to *O'Kelly* and *Nethermere*.

The Court of Appeal confirmed that whether the contract is one of employment is a question of law to be determined on interpretation of the particular documents "in its factual matrix". In this particular case, after noting the degree of control and power to dismiss that the agency reserved to themselves in the contract, it was held that on the totality of the conditions of service there had, in fact, been created an employment relationship between the applicant and the agency, despite the agency's terms which labelled him as "self-employed", and the lack of mutuality. Having the status of employee McMeechan qualified under the ERA 1996, s.182 to claim payments from the Secretary of State in respect of the one contract.

1.14.6   Contract of apprenticeship

A contract of apprenticeship, being a contract whose primary purpose is training rather than work, although assimilated into employment protection legislation, coming within the definition in the ERA 1996, s.230(2), remains a distinct entity at common law. It is a contract for a fixed period on terms contained in the contract, as demonstrated in *North East Coast Shiprepairers Ltd v. Secretary of State for Employment*[74] and cannot be terminated for redundancy. In *Wallace v. CA Roofing Services Ltd*[75] Sedley J. held that the rules associated with apprenticeship extended to a training contract, where although there was no written contract of apprenticeship, the written statement of terms and conditions stated that the job title was "apprentice sheet metal worker". Other terms were consistent with such an arrangement which had been orally agreed, and the rate of pay and daily work were typical of an apprenticeship. Therefore, when the four year contract was terminated after 19 months it held to be a breach of contract.

1.15   DISCRIMINATION

It is unlawful for an employer to discriminate on grounds of race, sex or disability in the arrangements he makes for the purpose of determining who should be offered employment, in the terms on which employment is offered, or in refusing or deliberately omitting to offer employment. Sex, race and disability discrimination legislation covers a wider range of workers than does employment protection legislation, and is not restricted in application solely to those working under a contract of service. The Sex Discrimination Act 1975 (SDA 1975), s.82, and the Race Relations Act 1976 (RRA 1976), s.78, defines "employment" as "employment under a contract of service or of apprenticeship or a contract personally to execute any work or labour . . ." and the Disability Discrimination Act 1995 (DDA 1995), s.68, slightly differently

---

[73] [1984] I.C.R. 365, EAT.
[74] [1978] I.R.L.R. 149, EAT.
[75] [1996] I.R.L.R. 435, HC.

as ". . . or a contract personally to do any work". The purpose of this wording was said by Lord Coulsfield in *BP Chemicals Ltd v. Gillick*[76] to be to bring within the definition cases which might otherwise have been considered to be cases of contracts for services rather than contracts of service. In *Quinnen v. Hovells*[77] the EAT held that the definition provided in the SDA 1975, s.82(1), was intended to cover all categories of self-employed people supplying personal services and covered, in that instance, self-employed workers paid on a commission basis.

In *Mirror Group Newspapers Ltd v. Gunning*[78] the Court of Appeal held that to come within the definition there must be some obligation by one contracting party personally to execute any work or labour, and that must be the dominant purpose of the contract, but that "any" did not refer to quantity. Therefore, a contract, the purpose of which was the regular and efficient distribution of newspapers, did not fall within the definition, because even though it was anticipated that the applicant would be personally involved there was no contractual obligation on the part of the distributor to be personally involved in the day-to-day performance of the contract.

The same definition of employment as is contained in the SDA 1975, RRA 1976 and DDA 1995 is also contained in the Fair Employment (Northern Ireland) Act 1976, s.57, and "employer" is defined under section 57 of that Act as "the person entitled to the benefit of that contract". In *Loughran and Kelly v. Northern Ireland Housing Executive*[79] the Northern Ireland Court of Appeal held that the concept of "employment" is intended to be a wide and flexible one and as such the appointment of a solicitor to a panel maintained by the Housing Executive was capable of coming within the definition, although, following *Mirror Group Newspapers Ltd v. Gunning*,[80] the personal service must be by the contracting party. Therefore, a solicitor who was a sole principal and proprietor who was seeking to have himself appointed to the panel fell within the definition of "employment." This was not, however, the case with a solicitor who, was one of several partners in a firm.

The RRA 1976, s.7 extends the definition of "employment" to contract workers in that it prohibits discrimination by "principals" against contract workers employed by a contractor where the work is "for" the principal. In *Harrods Ltd v. Remick*,[81] the applicants were employed by various companies with concessionaires counters in Harrods. The employers' agreements with Harrods required the employees to be "approved" by Harrods before they could work there. Harrods did not approve of these particular employees, who were, as a result, dismissed. The EAT held that "for" in the RRA 1976, s.7 is not limited to cases where those doing work are under the managerial power or control of the principal, but it had to be given a construction which was both consistent with the statutory language, and in keeping with the statutory purpose of providing a remedy to victims of discrimination. Accordingly, "for" meant "for the benefit of", and there was no requirement that the supply of workers should be the dominant purpose for the contract between the principal and the employer. In this case it was held that the work was "for" Harrods.

The same provisions are mirrored in the SDA 1975, s.9, and in *BP Chemicals Ltd v. Gillick*[82] a project account assistant who was paid by an agency who supplied her to BP,

---

[76] [1995] I.R.L.R. 128, EAT.
[77] [1984] I.R.L.R. 227, EAT.
[78] [1986] I.R.L.R. 27, CA.
[79] [1998] I.R.L.R. 70, NICA.
[80] [1986] I.R.L.R. 27, CA.
[81] [1997] I.R.L.R. 583, CA.
[82] [1995] I.R.L.R. 128, EAT.

on return after having given birth was offered alternative work by BP at a lower rate of pay. She did not accept, was not offered further work by the agency, and received her P45. She claimed she had been discriminated against on grounds of sex and sought to proceed against BP. The EAT held that section 9 "was clearly applicable" and was not, as claimed by the defendant, restricted to prohibiting discrimination against a contract worker who is actually working. The purpose of section 9, they said, is to prohibit discrimination in the selection by the principal from among workers supplied under an agency arrangement. In addition, as Ms Gillick had worked for BP in excess of two years, following the Court of Appeal decision in *McMeechan v. Secretary of State for Employment*[83] it would be open to her to seek to establish employment under a contract of employment between herself and BP in order to claim unfair dismissal under the ERA 1996, s.94, dismissal being under section 96 in the failure to permit a return to work.

In *Jepson and Dyas-Elliott v. The Labour Party*[84] a successful challenge was made against the refusal to consider two applicants for selection as Labour Party parliamentary candidates because the constituencies to which they applied were required to have all-women shortlists. It was held that such a refusal was contrary to the SDA 1975, s.13, which is not restricted to discrimination in employment, but is widely drafted to cover all kinds of professions, vocations, occupations and trades, whether paid or unpaid and whether or not they are "employment" as defined in section 82: it was therefore held to extend to those holding public office. In reaching its decision the industrial tribunal found authority in the ECJ decision in *Kalanke v. Freie Hansestadt Bremen*[85]:

> "National rules which guarantee women absolute and unconditional priority for appointment or promotion go beyond promoting equal opportunities and overstep the limits of the exception in Article 2(4) of the Directive (76/207).
>
> Furthermore, in so far as it seeks to achieve equal representation of men and women in all grades and levels within a department, such a system substitutes for equality of opportunity as envisaged in Article 2(4) the result which is only to be arrived at by providing such equality of opportunity."
>
> Case C–450/93 *Kalanke v. Freie Hansestadt Bremen* [1995] I.R.L.R. 660 at 667, ECJ.

Article 2(4) provides an exception to the general principle in Article 2(1) of the Equal Treatment Directive in respect of measures intended "to promote equal opportunity for men and women, in particular by removing existing inequalities which affect women's opportunities".

However, in *Hellmut Marschall v. Land Nordrhein-Westfalen*,[86] the ECJ, relying on *Kalanke,* upheld a rule which was similar, except that there was a proviso or saving clause. The Advocate General held that such a proviso could only make the rule compatible with the Directive if the proviso itself was unobjectionable, which he did not consider to be the case, because it appeared to be based on so-called "traditional secondary criteria". Nevertheless, the Court said that:

> "even where male and female candidates are equally qualified, male candidates tend to be promoted in preference to female candidates particularly because of

[83] [1997] I.R.L.R. 353, CA.
[84] [1996] I.R.L.R. 116, IT.
[85] Case C–450/93 [1995] I.R.L.R. 660, ECJ.
[86] Case C–409/95 [1998] I.R.L.R. 39, ECJ.

prejudices and stereotypes concerning the role and capacities of women in working life and the fear, for example, that women will interrupt their careers more frequently, that owing to household and family duties they will be less flexible in their working hours, or that the will be absent from work more frequently because of pregnancy, childbirth and breastfeeding.

For these reasons, the mere fact that a male candidate and a female candidate are equally qualified does not mean that they have the same chances.

It follows that a national rule in terms of which, subject to the application of the saving clause, female candidates for promotion (and the same could apply to appointment) who are equally as qualified as the male candidate are to be treated preferentially in sectors where they are under-represented may fall within the scope of Article 2(4) if such a rule may counteract the prejudicial effects on female candidates of the attitudes and behaviour described above and thus reduce actual instances of inequality which may exist in the real world."

Case C–409/95 *Hellmut Marschall v. Land Nordrhein-Westfalen* [1998] I.R.L.R. 39 at 47, ECJ.[87]

The precise meaning of this form of words is a little unclear, but it seems that the proviso provided the opportunity for the ECJ to meet the criticism that greeted the decision in *Kalanke*. In any event, the amended Article 119 (141), following the Treaty of Amsterdam, when ratified and implemented, will provide that the principle of equal treatment will not prevent any Member State from maintaining or adopting measures providing for specific advantages in order to make it easier for the under-represented sex to pursue a vocational activity or to prevent or compensate for disadvantages in professional careers.

By the SDA 1975, s.38 it is unlawful to publish or cause to be published an advertisement which indicates, or might reasonably be understood as indicating, an intention by a person to do any act which is or might be unlawful by virtue of Part II or III of the Act. "Advertisement" carries a wide definition which is contained in section 82, and by section 72 only the EOC may bring proceedings in such a situation. However, in *J. Brindley v. Tayside Health Board*[88] it was held that a job advertisement is an "arrangement" for determining who should be offered employment and as such fell within section 6(1)(a) of the Act: it was open to any person to complain of discrimination, notwithstanding the provisions of section 72 of the Act.

The Disability Discrimination Act 1995, s.1(1) provides that it is unlawful to discriminate against disabled applicants and by section 6(1) where (a) any arrangements made by or on behalf of the employer, or (b) any physical features of premises occupied by the employer, place the disabled person concerned at a substantial disadvantage in comparison with persons who are not disabled, the employer is placed under a duty to take reasonable steps, depending on all the surrounding circumstances of the case, to prevent the arrangements or feature having that effect (s.6(3)). The Code of Practice issued under the 1995 Act,[89] para. 5.19 says that an employer is not required to make changes in anticipation of applications from disabled people generally. It is only if the employer knows or could reasonably be expected to know

---

[87] *Marschall* (Case C–409/95) [1998] I.R.L.R. 39, ECJ.
[88] [1976] I.R.L.R. 364, IT.
[89] *Code of Practice for the elimination of discrimination in the field of employment against disabled persons or persons who have had a disability.*

that a particular disabled person is, or may be, applying and is likely to be substantially disadvantaged by the employer's premises or arrangements that the employer may have to make changes. In *Williams v. Channel 5 Engineering Services Ltd*[90] the tribunal stressed that "the whole tenor of the Act read with the Code of Practice" is that employers should avoid discrimination by considering the needs of future disabled employees. In order to do so good employment practice would, perhaps, dictate that a question about disability is included in the job application form so that an employer is in a position to cater for the needs of future disabled applicants.

Unlike the United States of America[91] and some other European countries there are no laws within the United Kingdom making it unlawful to discriminate on the basis of age in the selection and appointment of job applicants. Nevertheless, age discrimination in the recruitment process, which is thought to be widespread, may be unlawful under either the SDA 1975, s.1(1)(b) or the RRA 1976, s.1(1)(b), as demonstrated in the cases of *Price v. Civil Service Commission*[92] and *Perera v. Civil Service Commission*,[93] where it can be shown that such a requirement has a disparate impact upon one sex or marital or racial group. There is a growing reluctance amongst some professional journals to accept advertisements which specify an age criteria and amongst recruitment consultants to accept a brief with such criteria, and the Employment Service also operates a scheme to query age specifications in notified vacancies, but back bench attempts, via private members' bills, to prohibit discrimination in job advertisements have been unsuccessful.

Apart from age it is possible for other criteria, such as a requirement for a formal qualification, to amount to indirect discrimination, particularly against older people who are less likely to have gained a degree or formal qualifications of any kind, but also against younger people, and specifying a given period of experience may have the same effect, but this is not in itself unlawful.

In the White Paper *Fairness at Work*[93a] the government has stated that following the pattern set in the National Minimum Wage Bill, which is applicable to all those who work for another person, as opposed solely to employees, they intend to consult on the idea similarly extending "some or all existing employment rights by regulation". Such an extension may render irrelevant the complex web of case law on the definition of "employees".

1.16   EMPLOYMENT INCENTIVES

Increasing concerns at the level of unemployment, and particularly long-term unemployment, have led to a succession of incentives and programmes of subsidies to encourage employers to take on long-term unemployed people. There has, however, been a degree of scepticism about such "job schemes" since many of the participants return to the unemployment register when the employment subsidy is discontinued. Such schemes are regarded as displacement schemes in that they encourage the reallocation of jobs to take advantage of the subsidy, rather than a growth in jobs. Research into the Australian Working Nation Programme, involving a Job Compact

---

[90] Case No. 2302136/97, IDS Brief 609/March 1998.
[91] The Age Discrimination in Employment Act 1967.
[92] [1978] I.R.L.R. 3, IT.
[93] [1982] I.C.R. 350, EAT.
[93a] Cm. 3968, http://www.dti.gov.uk/IR/fairness, para. 3.1.8.

and a Jobstart scheme, showed that "with up to 70 per cent of the participants returning to the 'dole queue', the programme quickly became open to the charge of 'churning'—recycling long-term unemployed people through short-term schemes".[94]

The Labour Government that took power as a result of the election in Spring 1997, came to office committed to introduce a scheme to encourage the long term unemployed into the labour market and particularly to address the issue of the young unemployed. As part of an overall Welfare-to-Work initiative they introduced a New Deal, which it is intended will run alongside the other initiatives, although other initiatives are intended to be integrated into Welfare-to-Work, which includes measures to reform benefits, provide childcare for young mothers and which will eventually incorporate plans for school-leaver education and training.

The New Deal is co-ordinated by the Employment Service and funded with £3.5 billion from a "windfall tax" on the privatised utilities. The scheme is designed to move 250,000 18 to 24-year-olds, who have been out of work for more than six months, off benefits via four options, all of which include an element of training:

- a job with a private sector employer which will be subsidised for six months: employers who take on 18 to 24-year-olds who have been out of work for more than six months receive a subsidy of £60 a week for those employed for at least 30 hours a week and £40 for those employed for 24 to 29 hours, and a training grant of up to £750; the decision to open the scheme to include part-time workers was welcomed by the retail sector in particular, where new jobs being created are generally part-time;

- a job for six months with a government environmental task force;

- six months' work with a voluntary-sector employer; or

- a year's full-time education or training for people who do not hold an NVQ level 2 or equivalent.[95]

The programme covering 18 to 24-year-olds started on a nation wide basis in April 1998, after being piloted in selected Pathfinder areas from January 1998. The initiative has been set up with the involvement of many large employers and other interested parties, but has still attracted the criticism that it will not create jobs, but displace those already in work. There are, however, a number of new elements present in the New Deal:

- a prolonged "gateway" of up to four months involving extensive counselling before presentation to an employer;

- an Employment Service case-worker for each individual;

- someone from the community or a local company, but independent of the scheme's organisers, to act as a "mentor" and who can represent the interests to those running the scheme[96];

with the aim of avoiding criticism attached to other schemes that people are pushed forward into unsuitable positions they do not want to accept, with the result that the

---

[94] *People Management*, February 5, 1998, pp. 39–40.
[95] *Design of the New Deal for 18–24 year olds*.
[96] See generally *People Management*, August 28, 1997, pp. 33–35.

placement is unsuccessful and the employer terminates the arrangement as soon as the subsidy ceases. The target is said to be to have approximately half the opportunities under the New Deal with private sector involvement, and to recruit up to 50,000 "mentors". Because the scheme is concentrated on the young long-term unemployed and is a supply-side initiative—persuading the long-term unemployed to take up work, with the public and voluntary sectors acting as a "back-stop" where no private sector work is available—it is said that the scheme will only move existing jobs around, causing companies to take on younger people instead of retaining existing, higher paid workers, and in particular, older workers, replicating the effects of the Job Release Scheme, which had at its core the replacement of older workers.[97]

Following criticisms, plans were announced to extend the scheme to those over 25 years old who have been unemployed for more than two years. Employers will receive a subsidy of £75 a week for up to 26 weeks, and additional funding of £250m has been committed to this. Alternatively, a person in this age group could take up full-time study for up to 12 months on a course designed to reach an accredited qualification. Previously somebody receiving Jobseeker's Allowance could not study for more than 16 hours a week without affecting their allowance. The scheme is to be extended further to cover lone parents.

1.17 SUMMARY

This analysis of the areas of law affecting the formation of the employment contract demonstrates the wide range of laws, many of which are recent in origin, involved at formation stage. There are a number of contentious areas, most particularly in the means of classification by which employment rights are extended to "employees". The common law tests have, as demonstrated, led to a wholly artificial classification of some workers, and although this appears now to have been recognised by the Court of Appeal, with increasing emphasis on atypical forms of work it is an area that stands out as one in need of reform. See now *Fairness at Work*, White Paper, para. 3.18.

The incoming Government was expected to re-look at the employment provisions of the Asylum and Immigration Act 1996 and at the ability for fixed term contracts to contain an "opt out". In so far as implementation of Directive 94/33 on the Protection of Young People at Work is concerned the Health and Safety (Young Persons) Regulations 1997 introduced changes to health and safety Regulations so as to implement Articles 6 and 7. The Children (Protection at Work) Regulations 1998[98] implement the provisions relating to children working and the consultation paper on implementation of the Working Time Directive[99] contains the proposals for implementation by regulation of provisions creating entitlement to minimum rest and break periods, and to health and capacities assessment if assigned to night work in relation to adolescent workers: those above minimum school leaving age but below age 18. The final element of the Directive, relating to work on ships at sea, comes under the Department of Environment, Transport and the Regions and is likewise to be implemented by Regulation to be announced.[1] The draft Regulations are annexed below.

---

[97] P. Makeham & P. Morgan, *Evaluation of the Job Release Scheme* (July, 1980), Department of Employment Research Paper No. 13.
[98] S.I. 1998 No. 276 to come into force August 4, 1998.
[99] URN: 98/645.
[1] para. 6 above.

DRAFT WORKING TIME REGULATIONS—CONSULTATION PAPER SUMMARY

Purpose of the Regulations

The Regulations will implement the EC Working Time Directive (93/104/EC) and the EC Young Workers Directive (94/33/EC) as far as it relates to adolescents.

Coverage

The regulations apply to workers over the minimum school leaving age.

The definition of worker covers those with a contract of employment plus a wider group who undertake work under other forms of contract (*e.g.* agency and temporary workers, freelancers, etc.) but does not cover the self-employed. The regulations exclude from scope workers involved in the following activities or sectors of activity: transport; sea fishing, other work at sea; and doctors in training. It also excludes certain activities of the armed forces, police and the civil protection services.

There are some special provisions which relate to adolescent workers, these are workers who are over the minimum school leaving age but under 18.

Weekly working hours limits

The regulations will set a working time limit of an average of 48 hours per week. The standard averaging period is 17 weeks, but can be extended to 26 weeks if the workers are covered by one of the "exceptions" or up to 52 weeks by an agreement between employers and workers.

Individuals can voluntarily agree to disapply the weekly working hours limits. Where workers choose to do this, employers are required to maintain records of the hours they have worked.

Measures relating to night time working

Night workers are subject to a working time limit of an average of 8 hours in each 24 hour period. The standard averaging period is again 4 months but can be extended by one of the "exceptions" or by an agreement between employers and workers.

Night workers whose work involves special hazards or heavy physical or mental strain are subject to an 8 hour limit for each 24 hour period.

Adult night workers are entitled to a health assessment (an adolescent worker to a health and capacities assessment) before being required to perform night work and periodically thereafter.

Rest breaks and periods

Adult workers will be entitled to one day off each week. Adolescent workers are entitled to two days off. Adult workers will be entitled to 11 hours consecutive rest per day. Adolescent workers are entitled to 12 hours consecutive rest per day. Adult workers will be entitled to a minimum 20 minute rest break if their working day is longer than 6 hours. Adolescent workers are entitled to a minimum 30 minute rest break if they work for longer than 4 hours.

These provisions are subject to "exceptions" which provide flexibility in certain circumstances.

Paid annual leave

Workers will be entitled to three weeks paid annual leave (rising to 4 weeks in November 1999). For workers who have just started work with an employer, their entitlement does not arise until a 3 month qualifying period has been completed.

Exceptions

- **Unmeasured working time**—Covers workers whose working time is not measured and/or predetermined or can be determined themselves. Examples in the Working Time Directive include managing executives and family workers. Effectively these workers will only be subject to the paid annual leave provisions.

- **Specified circumstances**—Flexibility is on the basis that workers receive compensatory rest. The specified circumstances include security and surveillance activities, activities involving the need for continuity of service of production (such as dock work, hospital services, the provision of utilities, civil protection services, agriculture, etc.) and where there is a foreseeable surge of activity such as in tourism.

- **Force Majeure**—Unexpected and unpredictable occurrences beyond an employer's control.

- **Employer/Worker agreements**—Collective agreements can be made with an independent trade union. "Workforce" agreements can be made with workers where there is no recognised trade union. The workforce can either individually sign the agreement (which is more practical for small firms) or the workforce can elect representatives to negotiate on their behalf. The Regulations provide for a mechanism for representatives to be chosen.

Enforcement

The limits (*e.g.* the weekly working time and night work limits) in the Regulations will be enforced by the health and safety enforcing authorities, *e.g.* the Health and Safety Executive and Local Authorities.

The entitlements (*e.g.* the rest periods and breaks and the paid annual leave) will be enforced by Industrial Tribunals.

Source: Summary at http://www.dti.gov.uk/ir/worktime.htm, April 21, 1998.

Chapter 2

SOURCES OF TERMS OF THE CONTRACT

Although the employment relationship is, as discussed above based upon contract, the sources from which the terms emanate are somewhat diverse. This chapter deals with the principal sources from which the terms of the contract are derived and in doing so examines the range of sources from which terms may be incorporated into the individual contract of employment.

It is probable that in a large number of cases, upon engagement only a few of the pertinent terms of employment will be discussed, and these will probably be of a limited nature, perhaps covering salary, job title and content, holidays and place of work: the details of all the terms of employment emerging during employment and may in practice never be specifically agreed upon by the employee. It is therefore important to consider the sources recognised by the law as having the ability to contain terms which can be incorporated into the contract and the terms that the common law implies into all contracts of employment in the absence of agreement to the contrary.

At common law the employer has the freedom to contract on whatever terms he chooses and agrees with or imposes on the job applicant, and the resulting contract is enforceable providing that it does not breach the common law, for example, by being for an illegal or immoral purpose or in restraint of trade.

In seeking to discuss the rules governing the relationship, there are a number of established sources upon which one can draw, such as custom, express and implied terms, collective agreements and codes of practice, as well as the statutory policy statements issued by the employer. Over the last 50 years or so, and perhaps dating from the Contracts of Employment Act 1963, statute has played an increasingly important role as a source of terms, providing a separate code from which an employer cannot derogate. The interpretation of statutory provisions has been influenced by European law, by the principle of direct applicability, and also direct effect and the requirements of the European Communities Act 1972, s.2(3) and guidance from the European Court in such cases as *Marleasing SA v. La Commercial internacional de Alimentacion SA*.[1] In addition, the jurisprudence of the European Court of Human Rights will become increasingly important when the Human Rights Bill comes into operation (HL Bill 38, Session 1997–98).

2.1 PRECEDENT

The common law develops by the use of precedent and cases provide a wealth of information and guidance upon which to draw as a source of law in areas not governed

---

[1] Case C–106/89 [1990] E.C.R. I–4135, ECJ.

by legislation, such as the identification of a contract of service or the rules relating to illegality, or as an aid to interpretation of statutory provisions. However, in *Wilson v. Racher*[2] Edmund Davies L.J. warned against the use of precedent in the area of employment relationships:

> "Reported decisions provide useful but only general guides, each case turning upon its own facts. . . . [older cases] may be wholly out of accord with current social conditions. What would today be regarded as almost an attitude of Czar-serf, which is to be found in some of the older cases where a dismissed employee failed to recover damages, would I venture to think, be decided differently today."
> *per* Edmund Davies L.J.

Wilson v. Racher [1974] I.R.L.R. 114 at 115, NIRC.

Kahn-Freund (1965) said that as a source of rules the courts have played a share, but only a minor share. Case law, he said, could only deal with "pathological situations", whereas the rules needed in labour law must work *ex ante*—must direct people what to do before, not after they have acted. Case law, operating *ex post facto* although establishing rules, does not do so until some given situation has gone wrong and needs deciding upon. The normal function of the court is to "lock the stable door after the horse has bolted" so as to keep the others in, but normally it is only statute which can protect the first horse, the courts being mainly about the unforeseen and the exceptional.

2.2 EXPRESS TERMS

Although there is an extensive and growing list of exceptions to the freedom to contract, not only with whoever an employer wishes, but also upon whatever terms he wishes, terms of the contract, clearly and unambiguously stated, have been upheld by the courts. In *Rank Zerox v. Churchill*[3] the EAT, in allowing the employer's appeal, held that the contractual words were clear and therefore enforceable and could not be subject to an implied term. Any suggestion that the courts should set aside or interpret contractual terms by reference to implied terms has given the courts some conceptual difficulties in view of the dedication of the common law to the contract and the freedom of the parties to contract on whatever terms they choose and be bound by their bargain. In *Nelson v. BBC*[4] when considering whether a flexibility clause was binding on the corporation so as to prevent a redundancy arising when the particular service in which Nelson was working closed down, Roskill L.J. said that it was a basic principle of contract law that if a contract makes express provision in unrestricted language, it is impossible in the same breath to imply into that contract a restriction on that.

Appeal decisions which have relied on contractual tests for the interpretation of statutory provisions, of which *Western Excavating (ECC) Ltd v. Sharp*[5] is perhaps the most prominent, have tended to enforce this contractual approach to employment law. In deciding the test to be adopted for the purpose of what is now ERA 1996,

---

[2] [1974] I.R.L.R. 114, NIRC.
[3] [1988] I.R.L.R. 280, EAT.
[4] [1977] I.R.L.R. 148, CA.
[5] [1978] I.R.L.R. 27, CA.

s.95(1)(c), whether an employee has been dismissed where he has terminated his own employment in circumstances where he is entitled to do so because of the employer's conduct what is known as constructive dismissal. Lord Denning, in a test that is still applicable today, said, "In my opinion the contract test is the right test", and that in applying the statutory test of "unreasonable conduct", it was held that the EAT had gone wrong in law.

In the later case of *White v. Reflecting Roadstuds Ltd*[6] the EAT held that it was unnecessary to imply terms into a contract as to how an express term regarding job flexibility was to be exercised:

"... it does not seem to us as a matter of law that it is necessary to imply either terms suggested by this Industrial Tribunal in order to give these clear contractual terms business efficacy." *per* Wood J. (President).

White v. Reflecting Roadstuds Ltd [1991] I.R.L.R. 331 at 335, EAT.

Therefore, when the applicant resigned because of implementation by the employer of a flexibility clause, he was held not to have been constructively dismissed because the employer was merely exercising a contractual right, which did not have to be exercised subject to what the Industrial Tribunal had held were two fundamental implied terms: in a reasonable manner and that there would be no unilateral reduction in the employee's pay as a result of the exercise of the term.

This contractual approach is also demonstrated in the search for an interpretation of ERA 1996, s.139(1)—deciding where a person was "employed" for the purposes of deciding whether a redundancy has occurred. In *Sutcliffe v. Hawker Siddeley Aviation Ltd*[7] Sir John Donaldson said:

"The words 'where he was so employed' ... do not mean 'where he in fact worked'. They mean 'where under his contract of employment he could be required to work'." *per* Sir John Donaldson.

Sutcliffe v. Hawker Siddeley Aviation Ltd [1973] I.R.L.R. 304, NIRC.

This same interpretation was applied in *United Kingdom Atomic Energy Authority v. E.F. Claydon*,[8] and this was followed by the EAT in *Rank Xerox v. Churchill*.[9] However, this strict adherence to contractual principles was not followed in the later case of *High Table Ltd v. Horst*[10] where Peter Gibson L.J. in the Court of Appeal, approving the earlier Divisional Court decision in *McCulloch v. Moore*,[11] held that in answering the question "where was the employee employed", it is not the terms of the contract that are of primary importance, rather:

"... [it] is one to be answered primarily by a consideration of the factual circumstances which obtained until the dismissal ... [and is one] that can safely be left to the good sense of the industrial tribunal." *per* Peter Gibson L.J.

High Table Ltd v. Horst [1997] I.R.L.R. 513 at 518, CA.

[6] [1991] I.R.L.R. 331, EAT.
[7] [1973] I.R.L.R. 304, NIRC.
[8] [1974] I.R.L.R. 6, NIRC.
[9] [1988] I.R.L.R. 280, EAT.
[10] [1997] I.R.L.R. 513, CA.
[11] [1968] 1 Q.B. 360, DC.

Likewise in connection with disciplinary, grievance or appeals procedures which have contractual status, having been incorporated, by whatever method, into the contract of employment. In *Westminster City Council .v Cabaj*,[12] in reviewing the authorities as to whether a breach for that reason amounted to unfair dismissal for statutory purposes, Morritt L.J. said employers ought to follow agreed disciplinary procedures. He held, nevertheless, that although failure to follow a contractual appeals procedure was not just a procedural error, but a significant contractual failure, but that did not inevitably require a finding of unfair dismissal.

Statutory provisions represent a minimum level of protection and the parties are free to contract on more favourable terms. By its nature as a contract of personal service there is rarely a "contract", in the sense of a single written document, which sets down all the terms relating to the employment relationship. Rather, there will commonly be a variety of documents and sources. To be enforceable, a term does not have to be in writing or in a particular form. There are, however, certain matters that are required by the ERA 1996, Part I, to be in writing, and any changes to those matters to likewise be notified in writing, on which see para. 2.8 below. Although it was held in *System Floors (U.K.) Ltd v. Daniel*[13] that a statutory statement issued under Part I of the 1996 Act is evidence of the contractual terms, rather than the contract itself, it appears from the decision of the Court of Appeal in *Gascol Conversions Ltd v. Mercer*[14] that if the statement is signed by the employee, the statement may be elevated to the status of the contract itself, with the result that contractual principles apply, and oral evidence cannot be introduced to rebut the terms contained in the statement. In *Gascol Conversions Ltd v. Mercer*[15] Lord Denning pronounced the statutory statement, to be "clearly a binding contract" when it was signed, "I confirm receipt of a new contract of employment . . .", although in *Robertson v. British Gas*[16] Lord Ackner in the Court of Appeal accepted the dicta in cases following *Mercer,* particularly that of Lord Parker in *Turriff Construction Ltd v. Bryant*[17] that:

> "It is, of course, quite clear that the statement . . . is not the contract; it is not even conclusive evidence of the terms of a contract." *per* Lord Parker C.J.
>
> *Turriff Construction Ltd v. Bryant* (1967) 2 K.I.R. 659 at 662, DC.

In *Tayside Regional Council v. McIntosh*[18] Lord McDonald in the EAT in Glasgow, having been referred to broad principles of contract law to the general effect that it is not competent to contradict, modify or explain writings by parole or other extrinsic evidence, observed that there were many exceptions to these general principles and that a strictly contractual approach "is somewhat esoteric and inappropriate to the interpretation of the terms upon which a vehicle mechanic is employed in the water services department of a local authority."

The conflict between the implementation in a tribunal setting of contractual rules and the need for a more pragmatic approach to traditional contractual principles was, however, viewed rather differently by the Court of Appeal in *Hooper v. British Railways*

---

[12] [1996] I.R.L.R. 399, CA.
[13] [1981] I.R.L.R. 475, EAT.
[14] [1974] I.C.R. 155, CA.
[15] *ibid*.
[16] [1983] I.R.L.R. 302, CA.
[17] (1967) 2 K.I.R. 659, DC.
[18] [1982] I.R.L.R. 272, EAT.

Board,[19] where the Court not only confirmed that the rule in *Wickman Machine Tool Sales Ltd v. L. Schuler AG*[20]—that an agreement cannot be construed in the light of the subsequent actions of the parties—as being appropriate in an industrial tribunal, but also that industrial tribunals are not free to apply principles of law in any sense different from those applicable in ordinary courts in determining the terms of the contract of employment of the applicant in proceedings before them. The contention that it is not appropriate to apply strict canons of legal construction in an industrial context and that the industrial tribunal should in principle be entitled to receive and to act upon evidence as to how agreements between employers and employees are implemented in practice was said not to be acceptable.

The courts have, if somewhat hesitatingly, come to accept, along with the development of the duty of mutual trust and confidence, that an express term that bears harshly upon the employee must be exercised subject to an appropriate implied term, and there are now a number examples of this. See, *e.g. Johnstone v. Bloomsbury*[21] and particularly the judgment of Stuart-Smith L.J. who found no difficulty in reaching the conclusion that the power to require the employee to work up to 88 hours per week had to be exercised in the light of the other contractual terms and in particular the employer's duty to take care for their employee's safety.

In *Imperial Group Pension Trust Ltd v. Imperial Tobacco Ltd*[22] it was held by the High Court that the express term in the pension fund rules giving a power to give or withhold consent to increases in pension benefits had to be exercised in accordance with an implied obligation of good faith.

In *United Bank v. Akhtar*[23] the EAT upheld a decision that in exercising a contractual mobility clause the employer was under a duty to give reasonable notice of the requirement to relocate and that they were under an implied obligation not to exercise their contractual right to require relocation in such a way as to render it impossible for an employee to comply with his contractual obligation to move. This was taken one step further in *McClory v. Post Office*,[24] where, whilst refusing to imply rules of natural justice into the employment relationship, it was held that there was, however, an implied term that the employer cannot exercise his power under a contractual provision on unreasonable grounds, even though there is no general duty on an employer to behave reasonably. So an employer's right to suspend could not be exercised on unreasonable grounds.

Although the courts have, as demonstrated, been prepared to move away from a strictly contractual approach to permit an interpretation that favours the employee, they demonstrated a reluctance in *Stubbes v. Trower, Still & Keeling*[25] to accept that the respondents were entitled to repair an omission in their contract with an articled clerk by calling for the implication of an implied term. In *Stubbes*[26] the respondents had made an offer of employment as an articled clerk, which was accepted, but the offer failed to specify that it was subject to passing examinations. When Stubbes failed his

---

[19] [1988] I.R.L.R. 517, CA.
[20] [1974] A.C. 55, HL.
[21] The applicant was still in employment when he commenced the action, although he left the employment of the Health Authority during the action, as a result of which he successfully sought to amend his claim, striking out his application for a declaration as this was no longer applicable.
[22] [1991] I.R.L.R. 66, HC.
[23] [1989] I.R.L.R. 507, EAT.
[24] [1993] I.R.L.R. 159, HC.
[25] [1987] I.R.L.R. 321, CA.
[26] *ibid.*

examinations and decided not to resit, the firm refused to employ him, as a result of which Stubbes claimed damages for breach of contract. Mustill L.J. said that the respondents could have included an express condition consistant with regulation 48 of the Law Society's Qualifying Regulations, but had chosen not to do so, they were therefore bound by their contractual arrangement.

In addition to being subject to an implied term, a contract of employment may be subject to statutory provisions contained in the Unfair Contract Terms Act 1977 (UCTA 1977), s.2(1) of which provides:

> "A person cannot by reference to any contract term or to a notice given to persons generally or to particular persons exclude or restrict his liability for death or personal injury resulting from negligence."
>
> Unfair Contract Terms Act 1977, s.2(1)

In her article, however, Watson (1995)[27] states that the most wide-ranging protection that the UCTA 1977 can offer to employees is only available if it can be established that employment contracts fall within section 3. This requires one of the contracting parties to be "dealing as a consumer or on the other's written standard terms of business." The question then arises as to whether the employee deals as a consumer or whether he is contracting on the employer's written standard terms of business. Watson points out that whilst in *Chapman v. Aberdeen Construction Group plc*[28] it seems to have been accepted that the employment contract in that case could be a consumer contract for these purposes, employment contracts "should *always* be treated as a consumer contract". If these hurdles are overcome, the UCTA 1977 offers a valuable source of protection to employees in that an employer could not, when he is in breach, exclude or restrict his liability or claim to be entitled to render a contractual performance substantially different from that which was reasonably expected of him, or render no performance at all unless the term satisfied the test of reasonableness. The words "exclude" and "restrict" in section 3 are given a broad meaning by section 13 in that:

> "To the extent that this Part of this Act prevents the exclusion or restriction of any liability it also prevents—
> (a) making the liability or its enforcement subject to restrictive or onerous conditions;
> (b) excluding or restricting any right or remedy in respect of the liability, or subjecting a person to any prejudice in consequence of his pursuing any such right or remedy;
> (c) . . .
> and (to that extent) sections 2 and 5 to 7 also prevent excluding or restricting liability by reference to terms and notices which exclude or restrict the relevant obligation or duty."
>
> Unfair Contract Terms Act 1977, s.13(1) (Varieties of exemption clause).

Slade J. in *Phillips Products Ltd v. Hyland*[29] said that in considering "exclusion" or "restriction" it was not the form, but the effect of the term that was relevant. Stuart-

---

[27] *"Employees and the Unfair Contract Terms Act"* (1995) 24 I.L.J. 323.
[28] [1991] I.R.L.R. 505, CS.
[29] [1987] 1 W.L.R. 659, CA.

Smith L.J. in the Court of Appeal in *Johnstone v. Bloomsbury Health Authority*[30] expressed the view that if the defendant employer in that case was entitled to succeed in his application to strike out the claim that he could not lawfully require the employee to work so many hours in excess of his standard working week as would foreseeably injure his health, it was arguable that he could only do so because the effect of the contractual term, which required a working week of up to 88 hours, must be construed as an express assumption of risk by the plaintiff. If that was a correct analysis, then the substance and effect, though not the form, of the term would fall within section 1(1) of the UCTA 1977.

2.3 IMPLIED TERMS

The contract of employment, being a contract for personal services, is, of its very nature, something that needs to be flexible to reflect the changing nature of the personal relationship: a set of pre-agreed comprehensive rules is generally not found and is inappropriate. However, in the absence of express agreement on specific topics the common law will fill the gaps in the contract by implying terms. Although in *Singh v. British Steel Corporation*,[31] it was said that: "The function of judicial implication is to repair an obvious oversight", it can be seen from recent cases that the courts have become inventive and are increasingly willing to shape the duties of the parties to an employment contract regardless of intention, instead of seeking to discover the unexpressed intentions of the parties as expressed in the "Oh, of course!" test: if the parties had been asked at the time of the contract they would have said, "Of course," it's so obvious it goes without saying.[32] It has, however, been pointed out that such implied terms operate as "default rules"[33] in that the parties are free to express rules to the contrary.

The "business efficacy" test—that the law is raising an implication from the presumed intention of the parties, with the object of giving to the transaction such efficacy as both parties must have intended that at all events it should have. This test, as stated by Bowden L J. in *The Moorcock*[34] is often quoted as the traditional test for the implication of terms. However, in *Lister v. Romford Ice and Cold Storage Co. Ltd*[35] Viscount Simonds drew a distinction between the search for a term to give business efficacy to the particular contract, a test stated as being more appropriate to a relationship between "both parties who are business men", and to ask instead: "whether in the world in which we live today it is a necessary condition of the relation of master and man . . ."[36]

In approving a test based on general considerations Viscount Simonds disapproved of the test enunciated by Lord Denning in the Court of Appeal,[37] when he said that a term should be implied wherever the court consider that it is reasonable to do so in all the circumstances. This disapproval of the test of reasonableness was made clear in the old case of Hamlyn & Co. v. Wood & Co.[38]:

---

[30] [1991] I.R.L.R. 118, CA.
[31] [1974] I.R.L.R. 131, IT.
[32] As developed in *Shirlaw v. Southern Foundries (1926) Ltd* [1939] 2 K.B. 206 at 227, CA *per* McKinnon L.J.: the officious bystander test.
[33] *Malik v. BCCI* [1997] I.R.L.R. 462 at 468, HL, *per* Lord Steyn.
[34] (1889) P.D. 64, CA.
[35] [1957] A.C. 555, HL.
[36] [1957] A.C. 555 at 576, HL.
[37] [1956] 2 Q.B. 180, CA.
[38] [1891] 2 Q.B. 488, CA.

"I have for a long time understood that . . . the Court has no right to imply . . . such stipulation, unless, on considering the terms of the contract in a reasonable and business manner, an implication necessarily arises that the parties must have intended that the suggested stipulation should exist. It is not enough to say that it would be a reasonable thing to make such an implication. It must be a necessary implication in the sense that I have mentioned." *per* Lord Esher M.R.

Hamlyn & Co. v. Wood & Co. [1891] 2 Q.B. 488 at 491, CA.

In *Liverpool City Council v. Irwin*[39] it was held by the House of Lords that terms should be read into the contract such as the nature of the contract itself implicitly required: a test of necessity, and confirmed that the courts do not have power to introduce into contracts terms on the basis of what they think is reasonable.

"The touchstone is always *necessity* and not merely *reasonableness.*" *per* Lord Edmund-Davies.

Liverpool City Council v. Irwin [1977] A.C. 239 at 266, HL.

However in *Howman & Son v. Blyth*[40] the EAT, following the earlier Court of Appeal decision in *Mears v. Safecar Security Ltd*,[41] in ascertaining the length of paid sick leave, held that they should imply that which was reasonable: that which industrial relations and common sense demands. In *Mears* Stephenson L. J. in the Court of Appeal held that:

". . . an industrial tribunal . . . [is] not tied to the requirements of the test propounded by Scrutton and MacKinnon L.J., a test for commercial contracts which goes back to *The Moorcock* . . . but can and should consider all the facts and circumstances of the relationship between the employer and employee concerned, including the way in which they had worked the particular contract of employment since it was made, in order to imply and determine the missing term which ought to have been particularised by the employer and so to complete the contract." *per* Stephenson L.J.

Mears v. Safecar Security Ltd [1982] I.R.L.R. 183 at 189, CA.

Both *Mears* and *Howman* were, however, concerned with applications under what is now the ERA 1996, s.11.[42]

The contractual approach, and the honouring of the express agreement reached between the parties, without the implication of a term that the employer's right be exercised reasonably, was upheld in *Rank Zerox v. Churchill*[43]:

"In our judgment the implication of the test of reasonableness and the attempt by the majority to introduce that test into the construction of a straightforward express term of the contract was an error in law". *per* Wood J. (President).

Rank Zerox v. Churchill [1988] I.R.L.R. 280 at 282, EAT.

[39] [1977] A.C. 239 at 254, HL.
[40] [1983] I.C.R. 416, EAT.
[41] [1982] I.R.L.R. 183, CA.
[42] See Leighton and Doyle (1982) 11 I.L.J. 185–188.
[43] [1988] I.R.L.R. 280, EAT.

In *White v. Reflecting Roadstuds Ltd*[44] the EAT held that to imply such a term would ". . .introduce the reasonableness test by the back door".

In *Johnstone v. Bloomsbury Health Authority*[45] the contract provided for a standard working week of 40 hours, with a power to require a further 48 hours a week "on average". In response to a claim that this express contractual requirement to work an average of 88 hours a week, which on occasion extended in excess of 100 hours, causing fatigue, depression exhaustion and stress, was in breach of the implied obligation to safeguard the employee's health, it was held in the Court of Appeal, Leggatt L.J. dissenting, that the employer was bound to exercise the optional express rights subject to the implied obligation.

Sir Nicholas Browne-Wilkinson V.C. said that express and implied terms of the contract have to be capable of co-existence without conflict and reconciled the terms here by saying that the employers' right to call for overtime under the express terms of the contract was not an absolute right: the employers had a discretion as to the number of hours of overtime that the employee could be called upon to work—therefore there was no incompatibility between the express and implied term: therefore there was no reason why the employer's discretion to call for overtime should not be exercised in conformity with the normal implied duty to take reasonable care not to injure their employee's health.

In his dissenting judgment, however, Leggatt L.J. held that as a matter of law reliance on an express term cannot involve breach of an implied term. Employers could not, therefore, by the mere fact of requiring the plaintiff to work no more than his contracted 88 hours, be in breach of contract.

To succeed in a claim that unambiguous express terms should be subject to an implied term, it was stated by the Court of Appeal in *Stubbes v. Trower, Still & Keeling*[46] that it had to be shown that the implication of such a term was necessary, that the contract would have made no sense without it, and that the term was omitted from the written and oral negotiation because it was so obvious that there was no need to make it explicit. The appeal was allowed because "there was no compelling reason why the contract should be regarded as making better sense with the proposed term included than without it".[47]

However, where the task is to imply a term in the absence of an express term the courts are willing to look at the way the parties have conducted the contract and imply a term which in all the circumstances the parties, if reasonable, would probably have agreed if they had directed their minds to the problem.[48] There has, nevertheless, been a softening of the approach by the courts. In *Scally v. Southern Health and Social Services Board*, Lord Bridge, giving the judgment of the House, said that although the implication of a term requiring the employer to inform employees of the opportunity to buy added years of pension entitlement could not be justified as necessary to give business efficacy to the contract as a whole, such a term was nevertheless implied because it was necessary to imply such an obligation to make the right a meaningful one in a situation where terms of employment are negotiated with a representative body, or otherwise incorporated, and the employee could not reasonably be expected to be aware of the term unless it was drawn to his attention. This rather likens the

---

[44] [1991] I.R.L.R. 331, EAT.
[45] [1991] I.R.L.R. 118, CA.
[46] [1987] I.R.L.R. 321, CA.
[47] *per* Mustill L.J. at 324.
[48] *Jones v. Associated Tunnelling Co. Ltd* [1981] I.R.L.R. 477, EAT.

contract of employment to a consumer contract under the Unfair Contract Terms Act 1977, as discussed above.

Mobility has been a particularly fertile area for the invention and operation of the requirement that express terms be exercised reasonably. In *United Bank Ltd v. Akhtar*[49] the EAT held that in exercising their discretion under the contractual mobility clause, the employer was required, by necessary implication, to give the employee reasonable notice. It was held to be necessary to imply such a term in order not to render it impossible, or frustrate the employee's efforts to comply with his contractual obligations. The employer had an implied duty not to conduct themselves in a manner calculated or likely to destroy or seriously damage the relationship of confidence and trust between him and the employee, and this required the giving of reasonable notice in the exercise of their power to require mobility of his employees.

Where there is no express term in the contract the courts have, however, reverted to the more traditional tests framed so as to seek the intention of the parties. This is evidenced in *Courtaulds Northern Spinning Ltd v. Sibon*[50] where, in the absence of an express term as to mobility, the Court of Appeal held that as it was not possible for there to be no place of work, to give the contract business efficacy it is essential to imply into the contract a term which the parties if reasonable would probably have agreed if they had directed their minds to the problem.

It is this proactive approach of the courts in creating incidents of employment without regard, or even the pretence of a search for what the parties intended, that has led these terms to be referred to as "overriding terms".[51] The confusion has its origins in the duality of principle sources of employment law, that whilst the superior courts are concerned to impose contractual tests on the employment relationship, treating the dispute before them as they would any other contract, a view that is perhaps best demonstrated by the approach of the Court of Appeal in *Western Excavating v. Sharp*,[52] the tribunals are concerned principally with the application of statutory provisions which require consideration of, *inter alia*, the reasonableness of the employer's actions and equity and the substantial merits of the case.[53] Nevertheless, as pointed out by Napier:

> ". . . whatever the formula employed, the important point is that, in practice, the implication of terms is one of the main ways in which effect is given to what judges think ought to be the duties and rights of employees."
>
> B. Napier (1977) *"Judicial Attitudes to the Employment Relationship"* (1977) 6 I.L.J. 6–11.

2.4   COLLECTIVE BARGAINING AGREEMENTS

The Trade Union and Labour Relations (Consolidation) Act 1992, s.178 defines collective agreements. Such agreements have traditionally been regarded not as legally binding contracts but as "industrial peace treaties", with the result that they were unenforceable.[54]

---

[49] [1989] I.R.L.R. 507, EAT. See also *Prestwick Circuits Ltd v. McAndrew* [1990] I.R.L.R. 191, CS.
[50] [1988] I.R.L.R. 305, CA.
[51] T.I. Smith and G.H. Thomas (1996), p. 97.
[52] [1978] I.R.L.R. 27, CA.
[53] ERA 1996, s.98(4)(a) and (b).
[54] For a background, see R. Lewis *"Collective agreements: the Kahn-Freud legacy"* (1979) 42 M.L.R. 613–622.

Before the Industrial Relations Act 1971, there was nothing in law to explain why such agreements were generally not contracts and therefore not legally enforceable as between employer and the union[55] and in 1968 the Donovan Report[56] by a majority, reported that although they were not in principle opposed to the use of legal sanctions for the enforcement of agreed procedures they rejected the proposal to make collective agreements, whether substantive or procedural, legally enforceable. Lord Robens and Sir George Pollock dissented from that view, saying that the only way to make agreements effective, was to make them enforceable.

Nevertheless, in the first case ever to come before the courts to decide this issue, *Ford Motor Co. v. Amalgamated Union of Engineering & Foundry Workers*,[57] Kahn-Freund's analysis as to enforceability had a decisive impact upon the reasoning of the Court. The case came before Geoffrey Lane J. on an application by the company to renew injunctions issued *ex parte* to stop a strike, in breach of collective agreements, over a dispute regarding variation of conditions of employment. He discharged the injunctions on the basis that the company had not demonstrated that the agreements were contracts. He found that the wording was aspirational and vague, demonstrating that the parties had no intention that the agreements should be binding contracts, but that they were by their nature undertakings binding in honour only:

> "If one applies the subjective test and asks what the intentions of the various parties were, the answer is that so far as they had any express intentions they were certainly not to make the agreement enforceable at law. If one applies an objective test and asks what intention must be imputed from all the circumstances of the case the result is the same." *per* Geoffrey Lane J.

Ford Motor Co. v. Amalgamated Union of Engineering & Foundry Workers [1969] 2 Q.B. 303 at 330, CA.

The common law position, as stated in the *Ford* case, namely that there is a presumption that collective agreements are not intended to be legally enforceable contracts, was reversed in the Industrial Relations Act 1971, s.34 which enacted a conclusive presumption that, in the absence of an agreed opt-out clause, the parties to such an agreement intended to create legal relations. In fact, most agreements contained a "Tinalea" (this is not a legally enforceable agreement) clause. This position was reversed, and the common law position re-established, with the passing of the Trade Union and Labour Relations Act 1974, s.18 whereby there is a conclusive presumption that the parties to a collective agreement did not intend a legally enforceable contract, unless they agreed in writing that they intended to do so. These provisions are now contained in the Trade Union and Labour Relations (Consolidation) Act 1992 (TULRCA), s.179.

The issue of the status of collective agreements was revisited in the Green Papers of 1981 and 1991,[58] but no action has taken place on proposals to reverse the existing presumption against enforceability.

---

[55] Trade Union Act 1871, s.4(4) prevented enforcement or recovery of damages for the breach of agreements between one trade union and another. See Donovan Report, para. 470.

[56] *Royal Commission on Trade Unions & Employers' Associations 1965–1968*, Cmnd. 3623.

[57] [1969] 2 Q.B. 303, CA.

[58] Green Paper, *Trade Union Immunities*, Cmnd. 8128 (1981), para. 243; Green Paper, *Industrial Relations in the 1990s: Proposals and further reform of industrial relations and trade union law*, Cm. 1602 (1991), Chap. 8.

It is uncommon for a clause complying with section 179 to be included in a collective agreement.[59] However, a similar effect was achieved in *Partington v. NALGO*[60] where a collective agreement permitted an employer to require certain employees in particular situations to return to work during a strike called by the union in order to provide safety cover. The Court of Session was willing to find that such a term, being incorporated into the individual contract of employment, became enforceable and denied the union the power to expel the union member because he returned to work during the strike, thereby giving effect to the collective agreement without the need to find that the collective agreement itself was legally enforceable and in the absence of a term complying with the TULRCA 1992, s.179, enforceability can be achieved by means of incorporating terms of the collective agreement into the individual contract.

However, it is necessary to draw a distinction between so called "normative" and "contractual" terms of a collective agreement: between those that have individual characteristics, which the courts are willing to incorporate into the individual contract, and those laying down obligations for the collective parties, which tend to raise policy issues, and which the courts are unwilling to enforce by the mechanism of incorporation. This distinction is demonstrated in *National Coal Board v. National Union of Mineworkers*[61] which involved a 1946 agreement between the National Coal Board (NCB) and the National Union of Mineworkers (NUM) granting exclusive recognition to the NUM and setting up a scheme for dealing with disputes. In addition, it contained a clause that the parties agreed "to adopt the scheme . . . and to be bound thereby accordingly".

The dispute arose out of the year long strike in the coalmining industry between March 1984 and 1985, during which a breakaway union, the Union of Democratic Mineworkers (UDM), was formed. The NCB, recognising that the UDM represented a substantial proportion of mineworkers, negotiated with them, and gave notice to terminate the 1946 agreement. In view of the NUM response, the NCB issued an originating summons against them seeking declarations that the 1946 agreement and the scheme it set up was not legally enforceable.

Scott J. looked at the judgment of Geoffrey Lane J. in *Ford Motor Co. v. AUEW*[62] and the Donovan Report. He said that to be legally enforceable the agreement must contain a provision stating that it was the intention to be so and that "bound" was insufficient to fulfil the criteria: it must contain a written statement that the parties intended the agreement to be legally enforceable. The NCB was therefore granted the declaration it sought: that the 1946 agreement was not legally enforceable. As the agreement was not enforceable, the scheme set up by the agreement could not survive the termination of the agreement itself.

In counterclaims individual miners sought declarations and injunctions as to the extent that the provisions of the 1946 agreement and scheme had become incorporated into their individual contracts, and therefore enforceable by individual mineworkers whose contracts contained the following: "I declare that my wages and conditions of service shall be regulated by and subject to such national, district and pit agreements as are for the time being in force."

---

[59] Note that the new collective agreement concluded between Government Communications Headquarters and the Government Communications Staff Federation and the Civil Service Unions is declared to be legally enforceable. Foreign Office Press Release, September 3, 1997, I.R.L.B. 578, p. 16.

[60] [1981] I.R.L.R. 537, CS.

[61] [1986] I.C.R. 736, Ch.D.

[62] [1969] 2 All E.R. 481, CA.

Relying on Lord Denning in *R. v. Industrial Disputes Tribunal ex parte Portland Urban District Council*[63] and quoting from the *Encyclopaedia for Labour Relations Law*:

> "It has become increasingly acknowledged that it is easier to imply the substantive terms of collective employment than procedural provisions with a collective flavour. The T.U.C. has expressed the view that—'The procedure agreement is not part of the contract of employment' (see Employment Grievances and Disputes Procedures in Britain, Wedderburn & Davies, p. 51)."

Encyclopaedia for Labour Relations Law, Vol. 1, para. 2–1270.

Scott J. held that the procedural provisions of the 1946 agreement, containing as it did machinery for collective bargaining and for resolving industrial disputes, whilst of great importance, were not apt for contractual enforcement by individual employees. An indication was that within the procedures established no part was played by any individual mineworker: "It simply does not lend itself at all to enforceability at the suit of an individual mineworker". He held that references in the individual mineworkers' contracts were to those national agreements which contained substantive provisions regarding wages or conditions of service.

The purpose of the collective agreement was explained by Lord McDonald in *British Leyland U.K. Ltd v. McQuilken*[64]:

> "The terms of a collective agreement between employers and unions may or may not fall to be regarded as incorporated within the individual contract of employment. . . . In our opinion in the present case the terms of the agreement between the appellants and the unions did not alter the respondent"s individual contract of employment. That agreement was a long-term plan, dealing with policy rather than the rights of individual employees under their contracts of employment." *per* Lord McDonald.

British Leyland U.K. Ltd v. McQuilken: [1978] I.R.L.R. 245 at 246, EAT.

In both cases because the terms of the collective agreement were not apt for incorporation into the individual contract they could not be enforced by individual employees, and because the agreement was not a binding contract it could not be enforced by the union concerned.

Where a term is expressly incorporated by general words into the individual contract, it was held in *Alexander v. Standard Telephones & Cables Ltd (No. 2); Wall v. Standard Telephones & Cables Ltd (No. 2)*[65] that it is still necessary to consider whether any particular part is apt to be a term of the individual contract. In the absence of express incorporation, and where it is necessary to infer contractual intent, in addition to considering the aptness of the term for incorporation, it is also necessary to consider the character of the document and the relevant part of it.

In *Alexander & Wall* statutory statements, issued under what is now ERA 1996, s.1, provided that basic terms and conditions of employment were in accordance with and subject to the provisions of the collective agreements negotiated at plant level with the

[63] [1955] 1 W.L.R. 949, CA.
[64] [1978] I.R.L.R. 245, EAT.
[65] [1991] I.R.L.R. 286, HC.

appropriate union, which agreements contained provisions that any compulsory redundancy would be on the basis of service.[66] The High Court held that although redundancy terms were capable of being incorporated, the wording of the statutory statements was insufficient to effect an express incorporation, since although, relying of *Marley v. Forward Trust Group Ltd*,[67] redundancy terms were capable of being incorporated into the individual contract, it was not amongst the headings of the numbered paragraphs in the individual statutory statements. In the absence of express incorporation the court went on to look at whether contractual intent could be inferred, and held that where none of the other clauses in the collective agreement were apt for incorporation it would require some cogent indication that the redundancy clauses had a different character, and decided that the clauses were not sufficiently cogently worded to support an inference of incorporation.

The Court in *Alexander & Wall* adopted a strict contractual approach to the question of incorporation. It is difficult to see the objection to incorporation, since the redundancy terms contained in the collective agreement, although procedural in so far as they laid down the procedure to be followed in the event of a compulsory redundancy, were substantive in that they had an effect on the individual in so far as dismissal was concerned. The decision can, however, be distinguished on its facts from the earlier Court of Appeal decision in *Marley v. Forward Trust Group Ltd*,[68] and not just because of the vehicle for incorporation, the statutory statement, but also because of the somewhat uncertain state of the company's paperwork, and the remedy being sought: firstly, an interlocutory injunction restraining the employees' dismissal for redundancy,[69] which was refused, and at the trial, damages for breach of the terms regarding redundancy and for losses resulting from that breach, which it was claimed would have continued until retirement.

The court appears to have been influenced by the fact that the documents in question (the statutory statement and the collective agreement) were not themselves enforceable contracts. The Court of Appeal had earlier, in *Marley v. Forward Trust Group Ltd*,[70] established the orthodoxy that although the collective agreement is not itself legally enforceable, parts of it can be incorporated into the individual contract and thus become enforceable, and in *Camden Exhibition & Display v. Lynott*[71] Lord Denning adopted a forthright approach. The terms of the collective agreement are, he said, incorporated into the contract of each man "in so far as they are applicable to his situation". This approach provides for incorporation of appropriate individual terms rather than procedural terms.

A conceptual problem arises with the acceptance of the principle of incorporation, in that no benefit or detriment can flow from an agreement to which the individual is not a party: where there is no privity. It therefore becomes necessary to find a vehicle by which the individual employee can benefit from the terms of a collective agreement to which they are not a party. This is in sharp contrast to the situation in other countries, such as France, Germany, United States and Sweden where the collective agreement is recognised as setting a general minimum basic level—a floor of rights, which can be improved upon, but which cannot be derogated from.

---

[66] Otherwise known as LIFO: last in, first out.
[67] [1986] I.R.L.R. 369, CA.
[68] *ibid.*
[69] [1990] I.R.L.R. 55, HC.
[70] [1986] I.R.L.R. 369, CA.
[71] [1966] 1 Q.B. 555, CA.

2.4.1 Incorporation

Terms of a collective agreement may be incorporated into the individual contract expressly, impliedly or by the mechanism of agency.

Where an individual contract of employment contains an express provision bringing into the contract terms from a collective agreement, the effect is to make the contract subject to those terms, either at the date of the individual contract, or subject to amendment as the collective agreement is re-negotiated. In *National Coal Board v. Galley*[72] Pearce L.J. in the Court of Appeal accepted this method of incorporation from a written contract providing that wages should be regulated "by such national agreement . . . for the time being in force".

In *Robertson v. British Gas*[73] Ackner, L.J. in the Court of Appeal held that the contract was to be found in the letter of appointment which contained the words, "Incentive bonus scheme conditions will apply . . .". This gave rise to a contractual obligation that there be an incentive bonus for the job, the terms of which were to be found in the collective agreement in force at the time of the commencement of employment—thus importing expressly into the contract an obligation to pay that bonus.

In *Marley v. Forward Trust Group Ltd*[74] the employee's contractual terms were contained in three documents. A letter referred to a statutory statement, which contained the wording: "The personnel manual contains further information on the matters covered by this notice and other items of interest to staff and is available for perusal within your office". The personnel manual provided "Redundancies will be handled in accordance with the procedure outlined in section A25 of the personnel manual." Section A25 was a collective agreement which was applicable to Mr Marley. Lawton L.J. had no hesitation in finding that the terms relating to a redundancy situation (in the collective agreement) were incorporated into the employee's contract, and, applying *Robertson*, were enforceable at the suit of the employee.

Part I of the ERA 1996, s.1(4)(j), provides for the statutory statement to contain particulars of "any collective agreements which directly affect the terms and conditions of the employment including, where the employer is not a party, the persons by whom they were made . . .". Although the statutory statement is not the contract, it is strong evidence of the contract (see para. 2.8.3 below).

2.4.2 Implied incorporation

In the absence of express incorporation, the courts arc willing to imply terms from a collective agreement into the individual contract of employment where it is the custom in the particular industry to do so. In *Maclea v. Essex Line Ltd*[75] despite it not being part of his individual contract, the plaintiff claimed that he was entitled to wages in lieu of leave for each complete year of his service. The rule was contained in a collective agreement, and although they were not referred to in his contract he claimed that they were impliedly incorporated. Acton J. noted the evidence that in the shipping industry when people were engaged by being told to join a ship without more, it was

---

[72] [1958] 1 All E.R. 91, CA.
[73] [1983] I.R.L.R. 302, CA.
[74] [1986] I.R.L.R. 369, CA.
[75] (1933) 45 LL.L. Rep. 254, DC.

assumed by both sides that engagement was upon the terms and conditions of the National Maritime Board as varied from time to time, and concluded that by custom these terms formed part of the individual contract.

In *Joel v. Cammell Laird (Ship Repairers) Ltd*[76] it was held that when deciding whether it was customary for terms of a collective agreement to govern individual contacts the burden was on the respondent to show specific knowledge of the agreement by the person alleged to be bound and conduct on the part of that person from which it is clear that he accepted the agreement and worked under it. These elements were satisfied here such as to incorporate the requirement to move. The company was therefore entitled to dismiss employees for failure to do so and no redundancy payment was therefore due. The court did note, however, that careful scrutiny should be exercised over implying changes in the contract of service, especially where this is done by a method in which the employee is not a direct party.

Despite reference in the statutory statement that "basic terms and conditions" were governed by a collective agreement, in *Alexander v. Standard Telephones & Cables Ltd (No. 2); Wall v. Standard Telephones & Cables Ltd (No. 2)*[77] the applicants' claim for damages for breach of the negotiated redundancy selection procedure was rejected. The court held that as this was insufficient to expressly incorporate the terms of the agreement, one was dealing with implied incorporation and the mere existence of a collective agreement was not itself sufficient; it must be demonstrated that there was a contractual intent to incorporate the term in question, and referring to the *NCB v. NUM*[78] case regarding the necessity for the term to be apt and appropriate for incorporation, Hobhouse J. said that that was easier to find for everyday terms such as pay, than for procedural terms. In rejecting the case, he held that the terms relating to selection procedure for redundancy were not apt for incorporation.

2.4.3   Problems of incorporation

When an employer concludes a collective agreement through an employers association, the question as to what happens when the employer withdraws from the association arose in *Burroughs v. Timmoney*.[79] The employer was a member of the Engineering Employers Federation (EEF). A national agreement contained a guaranteed-week agreement, with provision for it to be suspended when production in another federated establishment was disrupted due to industrial action. When the employer resigned from the EEF, he withdrew the guaranteed week and on a challenge by the employees it was held that they had acquired a vested right to a guaranteed week, but likewise the employer had acquired a right to the proviso to suspend it in the event of disruption in supplies due to a strike in a federated establishment.

It was confirmed by the Court of Appeal in both *National Coal Board v. Galley*[80] and *Robertson v. British Gas Corp.*[81] that once terms from a collective agreement are incorporated into an individual contract those terms continue to bind both parties, despite the discontinuance of the collective agreement. In *Robertson* Mr Robertson's offer of employment stated that "Incentive bonus scheme conditions will apply". The

---

[76] [1969] I.T.R. 206, IT.
[77] [1991] I.R.L.R. 286, HC.
[78] *National Coal Board v. National Union of Mineworkers* [1986] I.C.R. 736, Ch.D.
[79] [1977] I.R.L.R. 404, CS.
[80] [1958] 1 W.L.R. 18, CA.
[81] [1983] I.R.L.R. 302, CA.

terms and conditions of the incentive bonus scheme were to be found in the national agreement which existed at the time the offer of employment was made, although the tariff was varied from time to time. When the employer gave notice to terminate the collective agreement and ceased payment, Robertson brought an action in the County Court to recover arrears of wages due to non payment of the bonus. The Court of Appeal held that the letter of appointment contained a contractual entitlement to a bonus scheme, the terms of which were to be found in the collective agreement, and having been incorporated into the individual contract the rate of bonus at the time of termination of the agreement had survived the termination of the collective agreement itself. There was therefore an obligation to pay bonus at that rate and the employee was entitled to arrears of pay.

> "The collective agreement could, as occurred in this case, be determined; but that did not determine the tariff which had been imported into the agreement, first when the agreement was originally made, and then altered as time went by by the consensual agreement between the trade union and the employer, it being an importation to the contract that that variation should bind the parties to this contract of employment . . . it follows that that tariff could not be affected by the unilateral determination of the collective agreement." *per* Ackner L.J.

Robertson v. British Gas Corp. [1983] I.R.L.R. 302 at 304, CA.

Two issues arise as a result of the decision in *Robertson*: firstly, if the bonus rate contained in the collective agreement had been reduced to a nominal sum prior to termination, it would presumably have been that nominal rate that would have been incorporated into the individual contract and therefore have survived termination. Alternatively, had the letter of appointment merely stated that entitlement to bonus would be in accordance with the collective agreement for the time being in force, when the agreement was terminated, entitlement would no longer exist.

In *Gibbons v. Associated British Ports*[82] a test case was brought in which a declaration was sought as to the effect of a termination by the union of a collective agreement, and whether a basic weekly minimum wage in the agreement could still be enforced. It was held that even though the collective agreement was conclusively presumed not to have been legally enforceable, the terms regarding wages had been incorporated into the individual contracts and therefore survived termination of the agreement, with the result that the individual contracts could only be varied with the agreement of individual employees.

The EAT in *Whent v. T. Cartledge Ltd*[83] had to consider the position of employees who, by virtue of regulation 5 of the Transfer of Undertakings (Protection of Employment) Regulations 1981 (TUPE)[84] transferred to the transferee on the same terms and conditions following the contracting-out of a council contract. Shortly after the transfer, Cartledge, the new employer, gave notice to the GMB, withdrawing recognition and stating that any collective agreements affecting transferred employees would no longer have effect. In response to the employer's assertions that employee's pay was frozen at the level last fixed before the employers withdrew from the NJC agreement, the employees sought a declaration under the ERA 1996, s.11 as to the

[82] [1985] I.R.L.R. 376, HC.
[83] [1997] I.R.L.R. 153, EAT.
[84] S.I. 1981 No. 1794.

particulars that should have been included in their statutory statements, and a declaration[85] that the employers had made unauthorised deductions. The employees believed that, despite derecognition of the union their pay and pay increases remained fixed by reference to those established by the NJC. The employees' contracts provided that:

> "During your employment with the authority, your rate of remuneration, overtime and premium payments, standard hours of work, entitlement to holidays and holiday period, holiday pay (including the basis for calculation of accrued holiday pay) sick leave and sick pay, and the periods of notice required to terminate your employment will be in accordance with the agreement made by the National Joint Council for Local Authorities Administrative, Professional, Technical and Clerical Services and set out in the scheme of Conditions of Service, as supplemented by the authority's rules and wages records, and as amended from time to time . . ."

The EAT applied *Robertson v. British Gas Corp.*[86] and held that the terms of the NJC agreement, in so far as they were incorporated into the individual contracts of employment, survived the employer's withdrawal from the collective agreement, and employees continued to benefit from new terms as negotiated under the agreement. The EAT did however say, *obiter*, that the employer was not bound *ad infinitum* since it could negotiate variations of contract with individual employees or terminate their contracts and offer new ones. In connection with these suggestions, the earlier cases of *Wilson v. St Helens Borough Council*[87] and *Meade and Baxendale v. British Fuels Ltd*[88] appears to have been overlooked: in *Wilson* the EAT held, *obiter*, that as a matter of public policy the employer was precluded from varying employee's contracts if the reason for doing so was the transfer. In connection with the suggestion that the employees' contracts could be terminated and employees re-engaged on new terms; in *Meade* the EAT held that a dismissal, albeit here carried out by the transferor, although effective to terminate employment, was unfair. These cases have now been heard by the Court of Appeal[89] which held that, in the *Meade* case, allowing the appeal, the termination by the transferor was ineffective to terminate the contract because the reason for doing so was the transfer, and further that if dismissal and re-engagement on less favourable terms occurs for a reason connected with the transfer then it is ineffective under TUPE, reg. 12, as an attempt to limit the effect of regulations 5 and 8. However, in *Wilson,* because of the finding that the variation was not due to the transfer, but for an economic or organisational reason, it was held to have been lawful, as was the dismissal, the principal reason for which was redundancy, not transfer.

Although the courts are willing to imply incorporation into the individual contract, they are not willing to imply a term into the collective agreement itself. In *Ali v. Christian Salvesen Food Services Ltd*[90] the Court of Appeal considered an annualised hours agreement which provided for 1,824 hours to be worked during a 12-month period, but in which no provision was made for the eventuality that an employee might cease work before the 12-month period was completed and the 1,824 hours worked.

---

[85] Under ERA 1996, s.23.
[86] [1983] I.R.L.R. 302, CA.
[87] [1996] I.R.L.R. 320, EAT.
[88] [1996] I.R.L.R. 541, EAT.
[89] [1997] I.R.L.R. 505, CA.
[90] [1997] 1 All E.R. 721, CA.

Mr Ali left employment having worked for only 22 of the 52 week cycle, and claimed to be entitled to be paid for the hours worked in excess of the "norm" of working hours by reference to which his standard wage had been calculated.

Waite L.J. said that the importation of an implied term depended upon the "intention of the parties as collected from the words of the agreement and the surrounding circumstances", which he said was a carefully negotiated compromise between two potentially conflicting objectives and for a substantial labour force. If a term was omitted, the inference was that it was intentional as being too controversial or complicated. It was "an agreement which, by its very nature, would require it to be applied to many eventualities that it did not, and could not realistically, cover specifically".

Summary

By TULRCA 1992, s.179, a collective agreement is conclusively presumed not to have been intended to be a legally enforceable contract, unless the agreement is in writing and contains a statement that the parties intend it should be a legally enforceable contract: it is unusual to find a "tinalea" clause.

Despite it not being enforceable as an agreement individual terms that have a personal impact upon individual employment conditions may become binding by incorporation into the individual contract. Once this process has been achieved the incorporated term has the same contractual effect as all other terms of the contract of employment: they become binding on both parties and cannot be unilaterally varied. If the employee is able to demonstrate that his contract has incorporated within it a term from the collective agreement he may stand on his rights and enforce the contract with the incorporated term whilst remaining in employment.

2.5 CUSTOM, WORKS RULES, MANAGERIAL POWER AND POLICY STATEMENTS

The employment relationship operates within a framework of day to day decision making and the exercise of power relations whereby management may make and change operational rules and groups of workers may develop working practices, either in relation to the operation of work itself, or in relation to other aspects of working life. Such rules may, over a period of time, and subject to certain rules, become recognised as part of the contract of employment.

2.5.1 Custom

It is possible for actions that have their source purely in custom and practice to become part of the contract: custom and practice "meaning informal rules, conventional arrangements, or merely behaviour which had become tolerated over time—in order to justify their own claims or resist those of management" (Brown, 1972).

In *Sagar v. H. Ridehalgh & Son Ltd*[91] it was held that in order for a custom, in this case the deduction from wages, to become an enforceable source of rules it must be shown to be reasonable, in the sense of fair, certain, in the sense of precise, and

---

[91] [1931] 1 Ch. 310, CA.

notorious, in the sense of well known, within either the particular trade or area. There is no requirement for actual knowledge, and in *Sagar* it was said of a custom that had operated "for upwards of thirty years" that it was hard to believe that the employee did not know of the practice, but that since it had been operated continuously to all weavers it was "immaterial whether they knew it or not". The mere operation of a practice—suspension as a disciplinary measure—was, according to de Parcq L.J. dissenting in *Marshall v. English Electric Ltd*,[92] insufficient to establish a custom to incorporate as a contractual term.

In *Meek v. Port of London Authority*[93] it was held that the long established practice, whereby the London & India Docks Company (LIDC) had paid all income tax for employees, could not be a term of employee's contracts, and as a consequence transferred to the Port of London Authority (PLA) under the Port of London Act 1908, s.60, whereby the Port Authority was to take on employees on the same terms and conditions. Astbury J. held that the practice was not binding on the LIDC, and therefore on the PLA because it was not known by employees at the time of entering employment. This case can, however, be distinguished in that the Court held that they were not here dealing with a trade practice, but with a method adopted, albeit universally, for the purpose of assisting and benefiting its servants. It was held that "it would require a very strong case indeed to turn a practice of bounty into a usage of obligation".

Custom cannot be used to overcome an express term of the contract and in view of the requirement, contained in ERA 1996, Pt I, of a statutory statement detailing the main terms of employment, the reliance on custom as a source of contractual terms is diminished. However, in *Jones v. Associated Tunnelling Co. Ltd*[94] evidence derived from the practice of employment was admitted to show the employee's obligation as to mobility. This was taken further in *Mears v. Safecar Security Ltd*[95] where Stephenson L.J. confirmed the ability of the tribunal to examine the subsequent conduct of the parties to determine what was agreed between them. The difference here being that unlike earlier cases, for example *O'Brien v. Associated Fire Alarms*[96] (job location), *Simmonds v. Dowty Seals Ltd*[97] (hours of work), *Mears* applies this principle to static terms of the contract.[98] It therefore appears that with the extensive powers assumed by the courts to imply terms into the contract, the practice of the parties becomes, today, evidence of the intention of the parties as to the terms of the contract.

2.5.2   Managerial power, works rules and policy statements

An employer's prerogative, by his relative power, is sufficiently broad as to allow a wide range of workplace practices to be governed by unilaterally prepared rules and policy statements. Although such rules and statements are not, in themselves, contractual, they may be incorporated into the contract of employment by acquiescence and practice, depending upon the nature of the document and the extent of the steps taken to bring the rules to the notice of the workers concerned.

[92] [1945] 1 All E.R. 653.
[93] [1918] 1 Ch. 415, Ch.D.
[94] [1981] I.R.L.R. 477, EAT.
[95] [1982] I.R.L.R. 183, CA.
[96] [1968] 1 W.L.R. 1916, CA.
[97] [1978] I.R.L.R. 211, EAT.
[98] See *Leighton v. Doyle* (1982) 11 I.L.J. 185.

Perhaps the most often sighted case demonstrating the status of works rules is *Secretary of State for Employment v. ASLEF (No. 2)*.[99] This involved a work-to-rule whereby the railway workforce, as a form of industrial action, meticulously observed all the rules in British Rail's operating rule book, but with the intention of causing the maximum disruption of services. In response to the granting of an order by the National Industrial Relations Court (NIRC) for a ballot of the workforce, the unions appealed on the grounds, *inter alia*, that the Secretary of State was mistaken in believing that the work-to-rule involved breaches of contract. In the Court of Appeal Lord Denning said that the rule book, which had 280 pages and 239 rules, and many sub-rules, was entirely different from the collective agreements which provided the main content of the workers' contracts of employment. He said that although each man had signed a form saying that he would abide by the rules:

> ". . . these rules are in no way terms of the contract of employment. They are only instructions to a man as to how he is to do his work." *per* Lord Denning.

Secretary of State for Employment v. ASLEF (No. 2) [1972] I.C.R. 19, CA.

The point is made that such rules are normally very detailed and generally out of date, and as such are to be construed reasonably. In *Sim v. Rotherham Metropolitan Borough Council*,[1] although what Scott J. said was colloquially known as "the Burgundy Book", which contained "detailed and comprehensive" agreements between teachers' organisations and local education authorities, was silent as to the duty to cover for absent colleagues, it was held that there was a duty to provide cover, because by the nature of their profession the provisions did not attempt to detail the obligations imposed on teachers. It is possible, however, for such rules to become incorporated into the individual contract, and today if they cover any of the matters referred to in ERA 1996, ss.1–3, there is a requirement that they be in writing, where they become, not contractual, but evidence of the contract.

The introduction of a rule regarding a non-smoking working environment came in for scrutiny in *Dryden v. Greater Glasgow Health Board*,[2] in which it was confirmed that a rule, so long as it does not contradict any express or implied term of the contract, is within the discretion of the employer, even though it is detrimental to some employees, in this instance smokers:

> "There can, in our view, be no doubt that an employer is entitled to make rules for the conduct of employees in their place of work, and he is entitled to give lawful orders, within the scope of the contract; nor can there be any doubt, in our view, that once it has been held that there is no implied term in the contract which entitled the employee to facilities for smoking, a rule against smoking is, in itself, a lawful rule. . . . Where the rule is introduced for a legitimate purpose, the fact that it bears hardly on a particular employee does not, in our view, in itself justify an inference that the employer has acted in such a way as to repudiate the contract with that employee" *per* Lord Coulsfield.

Dryden v Greater Glasgow Health Board [1992] I.R.L.R. 469 at 471, EAT.

It is therefore the case that works rules being merely rules of operation addressed to the workforce at large, are not contractual and may be varied by the employer without

---

[99] [1972] 2 Q.B. 455, CA.
[1] [1986] I.R.L.R. 391, HC.
[2] [1992] I.R.L.R. 469, EAT.

entitling the employee to claim a breach of contract. They are not, however, entirely without legal effect in that the employee is under a duty to obey all lawful orders and to co-operate with his employer.

Staff handbooks on the other hand, may be contractual. In *Credit Suisse Ltd v. Armstrong*[3] the Court of Appeal had to consider whether the terms of a staff handbook, introduced by being sent to all employees with a covering memorandum and a form to be signed to acknowledge receipt, formed part of the employees' contracts where they had been acknowledged. Employees argued that this was an attempt by the employer to unilaterally vary their terms of employment. The staff handbook, referred to by Neill L.J. as "a substantial publication", had a note at the foot describing the contents as "contractual unless otherwise described", but the covering memorandum did not point out or draw attention to substantial and important changes in the terms of employment. Nevertheless, it was held, albeit in interlocutory proceedings, that it was likely that the employer would succeed in establishing that the defendants' contracts contained the amended terms. In reaching this finding the court was influenced by the fact that the employees concerned were "men of experience and sophistication who are used to looking at complex documents".

In upholding an industrial tribunal finding that an equal opportunities policy was incorporated into and formed part of the contract of employment, the EAT in *Secretary of State for Scotland v. Taylor*[4] rejected the employer's contention that as a mere "mission statement" a less strict form of construction should apply.

It therefore appears that staff handbooks and policy statements, containing as they do matters affecting the individual in his relationship with his employer, may be contractual, whilst works rules which address the conduct of the workforce as a whole, are for guidance only, and in this respect a parallel may be drawn with the incorporation of terms from collective agreements. This view is supported by the decision in *Wandsworth LBC v. D'Silva*[5] where the Court of Appeal held that whether a code of practice, in this case on staff sickness, is contractually binding depends upon whether it should properly be regarded as conferring a right on the employee or whether it is merely setting out good practice which managers were intended to follow:

> ". . . the code is doing no more than providing guidance for both the supervisors and the employees as to what is expected to happen. The code does not set out what is contractually required to happen. The whole process in the initial stages is sensibly designed to be flexible and informal in a way which is inconsistent with contractual rights being created." *per* Lord Woolf M.R.

Wandsworth LBC v. D'Silva [1998] I.R.L.R. 193 at 197, CA.

This approach to incorporation was also applied in *Grant v. South West Trains*[6] to the equal opportunities policy, which was held to be "in very general, even idealistic, terms" and in applying *Alexander v. Standard Telephone & Cables Ltd (No. 2)*,[7] it was held that the policy displayed no evidence of a contractual intention.

---

[3] [1996] I.C.R. 883, CA.
[4] [1997] I.R.L.R. 608, EAT.
[5] [1998] I.R.L.R. 193, CA.
[6] [1998] I.R.L.R. 188, HC.
[7] [1991] I.R.L.R. 286, HC.

2.6 STATUTE, STATUTORY INSTRUMENTS AND CODES OF PRACTICE

Dating from the Contract of Employment Act 1963 and the Redundancy Payments Act 1965, and particularly from the Industrial Relations Act 1971, there has been a veritable deluge of legislation, both primary and secondary, governing the employment relationship. At the time of writing there are, as has become usual in this area of the law, a number of statutes at various stages of the legislative process. As the date approaches for the publication of this book the Employment Rights (Dispute Resolution) Bill will complete its passage through Parliament,[8] and a number of either primary or secondary measures have either been announced, *e.g.* the Data Protection Bill,[9] working time regulations[10] and regulations to implement the remaining parts of the Young Workers Directive[11] or are awaited, *e.g.* on parental leave and part-time workers.[12]

2.6.1 Statutory instruments

Power to make regulations is to be found in primary legislation and in the employment context secondary legislation is widely used to implement detailed rules. The two principle sources from which a huge volume of secondary legislation has emanated are the Health and Safety at Work etc. Act 1974 and the European Communities Act 1972.

Section 15 of the Health and Safety at Work etc. Act 1974 (HSWA 1974) provides:

"(1) . . . the Secretary of State, the Minister of Agriculture, Fisheries and Food or the Secretary of State and that Minister acting jointly shall have power to make regulations under this section for any of the general purposes of this Part . . .

(2) . . . health and safety regulations may for any of the general purposes of this Part make provision for any of the purposes mentioned in Schedule 3 . . ."

Subsections (3) to (9) go on to provide the purposes for which regulations may be made. An example of the use of this enabling power was the implementation of the Framework Directive 89/391 on the Introduction of Measures to Encourage Improvements in the Safety and Health of Workers at Work, which was put into operation by the Management of Health and Safety at Work Regulations 1992 under which six major sets of regulations (and their accompanying codes of practice) came into effect. Section 2(2) of the ECA 1972 provides that:

"Subject to Schedule 2 to this Act, at any time after its passing Her Majesty may by Order in Council, and any designated Minister or department may by regulations, make provision—

(a) for the purposes of implementing any Community obligation of the United Kingdom, or enabling any such obligation to be implemented, or of enabling

---

[8] The Bill received Royal Assent on April 8, 1998.
[9] HL Bill 61 to implement Directive 95/46.
[10] To implement Directive 93/104.
[11] 94/33.
[12] To implement Directives 96/34 and 97/81 respectively.

any rights enjoyed or to be enjoyed by the United Kingdom under or by virtue of the treaties to be exercised;

(b) for the purpose of dealing with matters arising out of or related to any such obligation or rights or the coming into force, or the operation from time to time, of subsection (1) above;

and in the exercise of any statutory power or duty, including any power to give directions or to legislate by means or orders, rules, regulations or other subordinate instrument, the person entrusted with the power or duty may have regard to the objects of the Communities and to any such obligation or rights as aforesaid."

Section 2(2) has been utilised for the implementation of many regulations to implement European legislation. Just by way of example: the Transfer of Undertakings (Protection of Employment) Regulations 1981[13] were intended to implement Council Directive 77/187, and were themselves subsequently amended by the Collective Redundancies and Transfer of Undertakings (Protection of Employment) (Amendment) Regulations 1995[14] (which followed successful infraction proceedings by the European Commission in *E.C. Commission v. U.K.*).[15] Likewise, following the European Court decision in *Marshall v. Southampton and South West Hampshire Area Health Authority (No. 2)*[16] the Sex Discrimination and Equal Pay (Remedies) Regulations 1993[17] were introduced to implement the decision of the ECJ.

The procedure for the passing of regulations is laid down in the enabling statute. There are two types of statutory instrument:

(1) legislative powers conferred on a minister of the Crown and stated to be exercisable by statutory instrument, as with HSWA 1974, s.15; and

(2) legislative powers conferred on the Queen in Council and stated in the parent Act to be exercisable by Order in Council, as with powers under ECA 1972, s.2(2).

One reason for the different procedure is that some powers may need to be exercised by any department of the government in which case the procedure of an Order in Council may be more appropriate, whereas other regulations may concern only one department. Also the greater formality of an Order in Council is thought appropriate to some classes of legislation. There are a variety of procedures for making regulations, some of which are positive, in that they require an affirmative resolution of each House before coming into force, or negative, by which the instrument, once made, comes into force unless it is annulled by resolution of either House. The Statutory Instruments Act 1946 introduced some general provisions to promote uniformity of procedure but unlike primary legislation, regulations are not subject to parliamentary debate and there is no opportunity for amendments to be made, although all statutory instruments come before the Joint Committee on Statutory Instruments for scrutiny.[18] Nevertheless, the negative procedure and resulting lack of Parliamentary debate has

---

[13] S.I. 1981 No. 1794.
[14] S.I. 1995 No. 2587.
[15] Case C–382/92, 383/92 [1994] I.R.L.R. 392, ECJ.
[16] Case C–261/91 [1993] I.R.L.R. 441, HL.
[17] S.I. 1993 No. 2798.
[18] See generally Bradley and Ewing (1997), Chap. 27.

resulted in criticism of the use of secondary, as opposed to primary legislation, for the implementation of some contentious measures.[19]

2.6.2 Codes of practice

Power for various bodies to make codes of practice are contained in various statutes and the purpose is to provide detailed guidance on the relevant legislation. In particular powers for the Advisory, Conciliation and Arbitration Service (ACAS) to issue and revise codes of practice is contained in TULRCA 1992, ss.199, 201, and the matters to which this power extends are listed in section 199(2)(a)–(c). To date ACAS has issued three codes and these have recently been updated to take account of the consolidation Acts, TULRCA 1992 and ERA 1996:

- Disciplinary Practice and Procedures in Employment[20]

- Disclosure of Information to Trade Unions for Collective Bargaining Purposes[21] and

- Time off for Trade Union Duties and Activities[22]

Under TULRCA 1992, s.203, codes of practice may also be issued by the Secretary of State containing practical guidance for the purpose of promoting the improvement of industrial relations, or promoting what appears to him to be desirable practices in relation to the conduct by trade unions of ballots and elections.

The codes issued to date under this section are:

- Picketing (1992)[23] and

- Industrial Action Ballots and Notice to Employers (1995)[24]

Codes issued by the Secretary of State have proved contentious and it has been argued that unlike those issued by ACAS, they do not represent a consensus view of industrial relations practice and should therefore be the subject of legislation rather than codes of practice. However, by TULRCA 1992, ss.200(1) and 204(1) ACAS and the Secretary of State respectively, are required to publish a draft of the code and to consider any representations made on it.

In addition several other bodies have powers to issue codes: the Health & Safety Commission has powers under the Health and Safety at Work, etc., Act 1974, s.16, to issue codes of practice to provide practical guidance in connection with the requirements of any of the provisions contained in sections 2 to 7 of the 1974 Act or health and safety regulations and codes are frequently issued as part of health and safety regulations, for example, Management of Health and Safety at Work Regulations 1992[25] which are accompanied by an approved code of practice.[26]

---

[19] As with the draft Working Time Regulations, to implement Directive 93/104, Annex D in the Green Paper 4RN: 98/645.

[20] The Employment Protection Code of Practice (Disciplinary Practice and Procedures) Order 1998 (S.I. 1998 No. 44).

[21] The Employment Protection Code of Practice (Disclosure of Information) Order 1998 (S.I. 1998 No. 45).

[22] The Employment Protection Code of Practice (Time Off) Order 1998 (S.I. 1998 No. 46).

[23] S.I. 1992 No. 476.

[24] S.I. 1995 No. 2729.

[25] S.I. 1992 No. 2051.

[26] Health and Safety Commission Code of Practice: Management of health and safety at work.

The Commission for Racial Equality, under powers contained in the Race Relations Act 1976, s.47 has issued a *Code of Practice for the Elimination of Racial Discrimination and the Promotion of Equality of Opportunity in Employment* (1983),[27] and the Equal Opportunities Commission, under powers contained in the Sex Discrimination Act 1975, s.56A, has issued a code, the *Code of Practice for the Elimination of Discrimination on the Grounds Sex and Marriage and the Promotion of Equality of Opportunity in Employment* (1985).[28]

Under the Disability Discrimination Act 1995, s.53(1) the Secretary of State for Education and Employment has powers to issue, and revise, codes of practice containing such practical guidance as he considers appropriate with a view to eliminating discrimination in the field of employment against disabled persons and persons who have had a disability; or encouraging good practice in relation to the employment of disabled persons and persons who have had a disability. Under this power a code of practice has been issued, *Code of Practice for the Elimination of Discrimination in the Field of Employment Against Disabled Persons or Persons Who Have Had a Disability* (1996)[29] and guidance has also been issued under DDA 1995, s.3.[30]

In connection with new powers to issue criminal conviction certificates: a code of practice for organisations seeking access to criminal record information on employees or prospective employees was contained in the White Paper[31] and the Police Act 1997, s.122 places a duty on the Secretary of State for the Home Department to publish a code of practice in connection with Part V of the Act.

Failure to observe the provisions of a statutory code of practice does not of itself render a person liable to legal proceedings. A code is, nevertheless, admissible in evidence in proceedings before an industrial tribunal, and in the case of the Health and Safety Commission in criminal proceedings. The statutory provisions governing this are contained in TULRCA 1992, s.207; SDA 1975, s.56A; RRA 1976, s.47; and DDA 1995, s.53(4), respectively. Likewise, DDA 1995, s.3(3) requires an industrial tribunal or a court which, in determining for any purposes of the Act whether a person's impairment has a substantial and long term adverse effect on his or her ability to carry out normal day to day actives, must take into account any of the guidance which appear to it to be relevant.

The status of codes of practice was referred to in *Clarkson International Tools v. L.J.N. Short*[32] in connection with the ACAS code on disciplinary practice and procedure:

"... The code itself sets general standards, underlines general objectives and points the way to achievement. But it does not set out to provide the answer to every problem and requires to be applied with wisdom in varying situations ... These recommendations will usually be applicable but circumstances can arise in which it is impossible or inappropriate to apply them, although the onus is on those who seek to assert the exceptional situation will be a heavy one. ... those

[27] See Race Relations Code of Practice Order 1983 (S.I. 1983 No. 1081).
[28] Sex Discrimination Code of Practice Order 1985 (S.I. 1985 No. 387).
[29] S.I. 1996 No. 1986.
[30] *Guidance on matters to be taken into account in determining questions relating to the definition of disability.*
[31] *On The Record, The Government's Proposals for Access to Criminal Records for Employment and Related Purposes in England and Wales,* Cm. 3308, App. C.
[32] [1973] I.R.L.R. 90, NIRC and in *Lock v. Cardiff Railway Co. Ltd* [1998] I.R.L.R. 358 Morison J. said tribunals should always have it to hand as a guide to themselves as to what is good sound industrial practice.

who seek to allege exceptional circumstances justifying a departure from the principles and practice set out in the code must satisfy the court or tribunal that the situation was truly exceptional." *per* Sir John Donaldson.

Clarkson International Tools v. Short [1973] I.R.L.R. 90 at 91, NIRC.

The Health and Safety at Work etc. Act, s.17(1) provides that where in any criminal proceedings for an alleged breach of any health and safety legislation, the situation is governed by a code of practice, then section 17(2) applies, namely:

"Any provision of the code of practice which appears to the court to be relevant to the requirement or prohibition alleged to have been contravened shall be admissible in evidence in the proceedings; and if it is proved that there was at any material time a failure to observe any provision of the code which appears to the court to be relevant to any matter which it is necessary for the prosecution to prove in order to establish a contravention of that requirement or prohibition, that matter shall be taken as proved unless the court is satisfied that the requirement or prohibition was in respect of that matter complied with otherwise than by way of observance of that provision of the code."

Health and Safety at Work etc. Act 1974, s.17(2).

The Health and Safety Executive issues guidance on how to comply with regulations. These regulations do not have the same status as codes of practice but confusion has arisen as between codes and guidance, principally emanating from the practice of printing some regulations with accompanying code of practice, *e.g.* (*Management of Health and Safety at Work Regulations 1992*), whilst other regulations may be accompanied only by guidance, *e.g.* (*Provision and Use of Work Equipment Regulations 1992*.[33] This situation has been commented upon by the Health and Safety Commission (HSC) in its Review of Health and Safety Regulation as a situation that is in need of clarification.[34]

2.7 EUROPEAN LAW

The Treaty of Rome 1957 (EEC Treaty) was signed by the founding members of the European Economic Community and the United Kingdom acceded to the Treaty in 1972 since when the aims and role of the Community have been broadened through and are contained in the Single European Act of 1986, which created a single market, and the Treaty on European Union (the Maastricht Treaty) of 1992, which *inter alia* changed the name of the European Economic Community to the European Community and envisages a common citizenship.

The Treaties are given effect in domestic law by the European Communities Act 1972, s.2(1) of which provides that Treaty provisions and obligations "are without further enactment to be given legal effect" in the United Kingdom, creating enforceable Community rights. Section 2(2) provides that E.C. obligations and matters arising out of or related to obligations may be implemented by delegated legislation

[33] B. Barrett and R. Howells (1995), p. 237.
[34] p. 1, para. 40.

and as demonstrated at 2.6.1 above, regulations, as opposed to primary legislation, are commonly used to implement Directives and obligations, *e.g.* Transfer of Undertakings (Protection of Employment) Regulations 1981[35] implementing Directive 77/187 and the Employment Protection (Part-Time Employees) Regulations 1995,[36] implementing the House of Lords' decision in *R. v. Secretary of State for Employment ex parte EOC*.[33] Section 4 of the 1992 Act requires that, subject to Schedule 2, "any enactment passed or to be passed, . . ., shall be construed and have effect subject to the foregoing provisions of this section", placing on the courts a duty to interpret previous as well as future enactments in accordance with Treaty obligations.

The Treaty on European Union was given effect by the passing of the European Communities (Amendment) Act 1993 by which Titles II, III and IV, and the protocols of the Union Treaty are deemed to be treaties under which sections 1(2) and 2(1) of the European Communities Act 1972 have legal effect in the United Kingdom.

Despite the fact that the E.C. Treaties contain no provision establishing the legal status of the Treaties themselves in the national law of the Member States the European Court has used several concepts to give effect to Community law in Member States, the conceptual basis for these being rooted in Articles 5 and 189 of the E.C. Treaty. Article 5 provides that:

> "Member States shall take all appropriate measures, whether general or particular, to ensure fulfilment of the obligations arising out of this Treaty or resulting from action taken by the institutions of the Community. They shall facilitate the achievement of the Community's tasks.
>
> They shall abstain from any measure which could jeopardise the attainment of the objectives of this Treaty."

> Article 5 E.C. Treaty.

Whilst Article 198 sets out the effect of various instruments of the Community it does not refer to Articles of the Treaty:

> "In order to carry out their task, the Council and the Commission shall, in accordance with the provisions of this Treaty, make regulations, issue directives, take decisions, make recommendations or deliver opinions. A regulation shall have general application. It shall be binding in its entirety and directly applicable in all Member States.
>
> A directive shall be binding, as to the result to be achieved, upon each Member State to which it is addressed, but shall leave into the national authorities the choice of form and methods.
>
> A decision shall be binding in its entirety upon those to whom it is addressed.
>
> Recommendations and opinions shall have no binding force."

> Article 189 E.C. Treaty.

Nevertheless in *Van Gend en Loos v. Nederlands Administratie der Balastingen*[38] the Court of Justice said:

[35] S.I. 1981 No. 1794.
[36] S.I. 1995 No. 31.
[37] [1994] I.R.L.R. 176, HL.
[38] Case C–26/62 [1963] E.C.R. 1, ECJ.

". . . the Community constitutes a new legal order of international law for the benefit of which the states have limited their sovereign rights, albeit within limited fields, and the subjects of which comprise not only Members States but also their nationals. Independently of the legislation of Member States, Community law therefore not only imposes obligations on individuals but is also intended to confer upon them rights which become part of their legal heritage. These rights arise not only where they are expressly granted by the Treaty, but also by reason of obligations which the Treaty imposes in a clearly defined way upon individuals as well as upon the Member States and upon the institutions of the Community . . ."

Case C–26/62 *Van Gend en Loos v. Nederlands Administratie der Balastingen* [1963] E.C.R. 1 at 12, ECJ.

The effect of the Treaty was expanded upon in Costa v. ENEL[39];

"By contrast with ordinary international treaties, the EEC Treaty has created its own legal system which, on the entry into force of the Treaty, became an integral part of the legal systems of the Member States and which their courts are bound to apply.

By creating a Community of unlimited duration, having its own institutions, its own personality, its own legal capacity and capacity of representation on the international plane and, more particularly, real powers stemming from a limitation of sovereignty or a transfer of powers from the States to the Community, the Member States have limited their sovereign rights, albeit within limited fields, and have thus created a body of law which binds both their nationals and themselves.

The integration into the laws of each Member State of provisions which derive from the Community, and more generally the terms and the spirit of the Treaty, make it impossible for the States, as a corollary, to accord precedence to a unilateral and subsequent measure over a legal system accepted by them on a basis of reciprocity. Such a measure cannot therefore be inconsistent with that legal system. The executive force of Community law cannot vary from one State to another in deference to subsequent domestic laws, without jeopardising the attainment of the objectives of the Treaty set out in Article 5(2) and giving rise to the discrimination prohibited by Article 7.

. . .

The precedence of Community law is confirmed by Article 189, whereby a regulation 'shall be binding' and 'directly applicable in all Member States'. This provision, which is subject to no reservation, would be quite meaningless if a State could unilaterally nullify its effects by means of a legislative measure which could prevail over Community law.

It follows from all these observations that the law stemming from the Treaty, an independent source of law, could not, because of its special and original nature, be overridden by domestic legal provisions, however framed, without being deprived of its character as Community law and without the legal basis of the Community itself being called into question.

The transfer by the States from their domestic legal system to the Community legal system of the rights and obligations arising under the Treaty carries with it a

[39] Case C–6/64 [1964] E.C.R. 585, ECJ.

permanent limitation of their sovereign rights, against which a subsequent unilateral act incompatible with the concept of the Community cannot prevail . . ."

Case C–6/64 *Costa v. ENEL* [1964] E.C.R. 585 at 593, ECJ.

The effect of this can be seen operating in the United Kingdom context in *Factortame Ltd v. Secretary of State for Transport (No. 2)*[40] in which, in a response to the ECJ ruling that where the only obstacle to the granting of interim relief was a rule of national law, then that national law should be set aside by the national court. Lord Bridge said:

"Under the terms of the 1972 Act it has always been clear that it was the duty of a United Kingdom court, when delivering final judgment, to override any rule of national law found to be in conflict with any directly enforceable rule of Community law" *per* Lord Bridge.

Factortame Ltd v. Secretary of State for Transport (No. 2) [1991] 1 All E.R. 70 at 108, HL.

In *Bossa v. Nordstress Ltd*[41] it was held that the Race Relations Act 1976, s.8, which precludes from the Act those working wholly or mainly outside Great Britain, was in conflict with the provisions of Article 48 of the E.C. Treaty which requires Member States to ensure that freedom of movement for workers shall be secured within the Community. The EAT considered the ECJ decision in *Van Duyn v. Home Office*,[42] which held that Article 48 is directly applicable in Member States, and concluded that it is "the duty of the industrial tribunal to override any provision in the Race Discrimination legislation which is in conflict with it",[43] thus enabling the industrial tribunal to consider the complaint in the normal way, notwithstanding RRA 1976, s.8.

Under Article 177 the Court of Justice has jurisdiction to give preliminary rulings concerning the interpretation of the Treaty.

"Where such a question is raised before any court or tribunal of a Member State, that court or tribunal may, if it considers that a decision on the question is necessary to enable it to give judgment, request the Court of Justice to give a ruling thereon.

Where any such question is raised in a case pending before a court or tribunal of a Member State, against whose decisions there is no judicial remedy under national law, that court or tribunal shall bring the matter before the court of Justice."

Article 177 E.C. Treaty.

This is given domestic effect in ECA 1972, s.3(1) and an example of a reference to the ECJ under this procedure is *Marshall v. Southampton and South West Hampshire Area Health Authority (Teaching)*[44] the result of which was the Sex Discrimination Act 1986.

---

[40] [1991] 1 All E.R. 70, HL.
[41] [1998] I.R.L.R. 284, EAT.
[42] Case C–41/74 [1974] E.C.R. 1337, ECJ.
[43] p. 287 at 27.
[44] Case C–152/84 [1986] I.R.L.R. 141, ECJ.

2.7.1 Effect of Directives

Although by Article 189 Directives are not directly applicable in that each Member State needs to take domestic action to bring a particular directive into operation, the Court of Justice has developed the concept of direct effect whereby in some circumstances Directives are capable of creating enforceable community rights. In *Van Duyn v. Home Office*,[45] the Court explained the reason for this development:

> "In particular, where the Community authorities have, by directive, imposed on Member States the obligation to pursue a particular course of conduct, the useful effect of such an act would be weakened if individuals were prevented from relying on it before their national courts and if the latter were prevented from taking it into consideration as an element of Community law."

Case C–41/74 *Van Duyn v. Home Office* [1974] E.C.R. 1337 at 1337, ECJ.

In order to be directly effective a Directive must fulfil the following criteria:

- the date for implementation set out in the directive must have passed: *Pubblico Ministero v. Ratti*[46];
- it must create individual rights;
- it must be clear and unambiguous; and
- it must be relied upon against an emanation of the state.

In *Marshall v. Southampton and South West Hampshire Health Authority (Teaching)*[47] the ECJ relied on the earlier authority of *Becker v. Finanzamt Munster-Innenstadt*,[48] namely wherever the provisions of a Directive appear, as far as their subject matter is concerned, to be unconditional and sufficiently precise, those provisions may be relied upon by an individual against the State where that State fails to implement or implement correctly the Directive in national law by the end of the period prescribed. In *Marshall* it was held that whilst a Directive may not of itself impose obligations on an individual, that Article 5(1) of Directive 76/207 could be relied upon directly against the respondents as a public employer. This was held to be "necessary to prevent the State from taking advantage of its own failure to comply with Community law".

The meaning of state body for these purposes was explained in *Foster v. British Gas plc*.[49] British Gas Corporation was an emanation of the State in that it was set up under statute, financed by the Treasury, was subject to guidance by the appropriate Minister, and had a privileged position in the market which was protected by statute. As such it was held to be an "organ of the state". When the case returned to the House of Lords it was held that as the employer was part of the public sector the applicant could succeed by a direct application of Directive 76/207, the Equal Treatment Directive.

In *Griffin v. South West Water Services Ltd*[50] it was held that a privatised water company is a state authority against which E.C. Directives are capable of direct

---

[45] Case C–41/74 [1974] E.C.R. 1337, ECJ.
[46] Case C–148/78 [1979] E.C.R. 1629, ECJ.
[47] [1986] I.R.L.R. 140, HL.
[48] Case C–8/81 [1982] E.C.R. 53, ECJ.
[49] Case C–188/89 [1990] E.C.R. I–3313, ECJ.
[50] [1995] I.R.L.R. 15, HC.

enforcement. Blackburne J. held that the conditions laid down by the ECJ in *Foster v. British Gas plc* were fulfilled and that the question was not whether the body in question is under the control of the State, but whether the public service in question is under the control of the State: the legal form of the body is irrelevant is the fact that it is a commercial concern.

As was demonstrated in *Duke v. GEC Reliance*[51] a Directive cannot have direct effect against a non-state body. However, where a Directive is not of direct effect the ECJ held in *Marleasing SA v. La Commercial Internacional de Alimentacion SA*,[52] relying on the decision in *Von Colson and Kamann v. Land Nordrhein- Westfalen*,[53] that national courts have a duty under Article 5 to take all appropriate measures, whether general or particular, to fulfil their obligations and that:

> ". . . in applying national law, whether the provisions in question were adopted before or after the directive, the national court called upon to interpret it is required to do so, as far as possible, in the light of the wording and the purpose of the directive in order to achieve the result pursued by the latter and thereby comply with the third paragraph of **Article 189** of the Treaty."

> Case C–106/89 *Marleasing SA v. La Commercial Internacional de Alimentacion SA* [1990] E.C.R. I–4135 at 4135, ECJ.

Despite giving domestic legislation the "purposive" construction called for in *Marleasing*, the requirement that a directive can only have direct effect as against an emanation of the state can mean, in the event of non- or improper implementation, that employees working in non-state bodies do not have the benefit of the provisions of directives until they are enacted domestically: see, for example *Doughty v. Rolls Royce plc*.[53a]

2.7.2 Failure to implement community obligations

The Commission has a power under Article 169 to bring proceedings against a Member State if it considers that they have failed to fulfil an obligation under the Treaty. In *Commission v. United Kingdom*[54] the Commission made an application for a declaration that the United Kingdom had failed to implement Directive 75/117 in that the Equal Pay Act provisions meant that the right to seek a remedy was dependent upon a job evaluation study having been carried out, and that was at the discretion of the employer. It was held that, amounted to a denial of the right in circumstances where no job evaluation had been made. The Equal Pay (Amendment) Regulations 1983[55] amended the Equal Pay Act 1970 to reflect the ECJ decision. In addition, Article 170 provides that a Member State which considers another Member State has failed to fulfil an obligation under the Treaty may bring the matter before the Court of Justice.

In *Francovich v. Italian Republic*[56] the ECJ held that the principle of liability in damages for breach of Community law by a Member State is inherent in the scheme of

[51] [1988] I.R.L.R. 118, HL.
[52] Case C–106/89 [1990] ECR I–4135, ECJ.
[53] Case C–14/83 [1984] E.C.R. 1891, ECJ.
[53a] [1992] I.R.L.R. 126, CA.
[54] Case C–61/81 [1982] I.C.R. 578, ECJ.
[55] S.I. 1983 No. 1794.
[56] Case C–6/90 [1992] I.R.L.R. 84, ECJ.

the Treaty and the ECJ held in *Dillenkofer v. Federal Republic of Germany*[57] that a failure to take any measure to transpose a Directive in order to achieve the result prescribed within the period laid down for that purpose, constituted *per se* a serious breach of Community law and consequently gave rise to a right of reparation for individuals suffering injury, if the result prescribed by the Directive entailed the grant to individuals of rights whose content was identifiable and a casual link existed between the breach of the State's obligation and the loss and damage suffered.

The issues raised as to the exercise of this right were addressed in *Brasserie du Pecheur SA v. Federal Republic of Germany* and *R. v. SS for Transport, ex p. Factortame (No. 3)*[58] where the ECJ held that the principle that Member States are obliged to make good damage caused to individuals by breaches of Community law applied where the national legislature was responsible for the breach and:

- the rule of Community law breached is intended to confer individual rights;

- the breach is sufficiently serious—the test for which is whether the Member State manifestly and gravely disregarded the limits on its discretion;

- there is a direct causal link between the breach and the damage sustained by individuals;

and the principle applies even where the provisions concerned are directly effective.[59]

2.7.3   Social policy background

Member States, with the exception of the United Kingdom, adopted the Community Charter of the Fundamental Social Rights of Workers (the Social Charter) in 1989 which, although it lacked any direct legal status, authorises the Commission to prepare a programme of measures to implement its objectives. The charter set out 12 "fundament social rights of workers":

- the right to freedom of movement;

- right to be free to choose and engage in an occupation according to the regulations governing each occupation;

- the right to improvement of living and working conditions, including a right to a weekly rest period and to annual paid leave;

- the right to adequate social protection and to an adequate level of social security benefits;

- the right of association in order to constitute professional organisations or trade unions of their choice for the defence of their economic and social interests;

- the right of access to vocational training;

- the right of equal treatment for men and women, and a commitment to the development of equal opportunities;

---

[57] Joined Cases (178, 188–190/94 [1997] I.R.L.R. 60, ECJ.
[58] Joined Cases C46 & 48/93 [1996] I.R.L.R. 267, ECJ.
[59] See further T. Hervey and Rostant, "After Francovich: State Liability and British Employment Law" (1996) 25 I.L.J. 259.

- a right to information, consultation and participation for workers;

- a right to enjoy satisfactory health and safety conditions in the working environment;

- a commitment to a minimum employment age not lower than the minimum school-leaving age and to introduce protection for young people who are in employment;

- a right for every worker at the time of retirement to resources affording him a decent standard of living; and

- a right for all disabled persons to additional concrete measures aimed at improving their social and professional integration.

As a result a Social Action programme was introduced under which 17 Directives were proposed. Because of problems of achieving unanimous support use has been made of Article 118A, which was introduced into the Treaty of Rome, Title III, by the Single European Act 1986 which extended the use of qualified majority voting to health and safety matters. Directive 93/104, the Working Time Directive was introduced using this procedure, see para. 1.12 above.

The Treaty on European Union 1992 (the Maastricht Treaty) made significant amendments to the Treaty of Rome, but was not included in the main body of the Treaty because of United Kingdom opposition. Instead, the amendments formed a separate protocol on social policy by which all Member States except the United Kingdom adopted an agreement on social policy which is annexed to the protocol, which is annexed to the Treaty of Rome, and is known as the "Social Chapter". The result has been to create a twin-track system whereby a social policy measure could be adopted either under the Treaty of Rome, in which case it is binding on all Member States, or under the Social Chapter, in which case it binds all states except the United Kingdom.

Following a change of government in the United Kingdom in 1997, a commitment by the incoming Labour Government to adopt the "Social Chapter" was achieved at the Intergovernmental Conference in Amsterdam, which resulted in the Treaty of Amsterdam. This amends the Treaty on European Union, the Treaties establishing the European Communities and certain related Acts and the "Social Chapter" is to be incorporated into the main body of the Treaty of Rome, thus becoming binding on all Member States. As the Amsterdam Treaty does not take effect until ratified by all Member States, Ministers have adopted texts on the basis of Article 100 of the E.C. Treaty, extending the two Directives already agreed under the Social Chapter procedure, on European works councils[60] and parental leave,[61] to the United Kingdom.

When the Amsterdam Treaty is ratified the United Kingdom will be subject to the social policy agreement negotiated at Maastricht, under which two further Directives were adopted during the second half of 1997, a Directive on the burden of proof in sex discrimination cases (O.J. L176/88) and Directive 97/81 giving effect to the social partners' framework agreement on part-time work. The Treaty also covers the following:

- In the Amsterdam Treaty Article 119 specifically refers to work of equal value:

[60] Directive 94/45 of September 22, 1994.
[61] Directive 96/34C of June 3, 1996.

"Each Member State shall ensure that the principle of equal pay for male and female workers for equal work or work of equal value is applied."

- The wording of the provisions on positive action contained in the social policy Agreement has been altered to reflect the ECJ's decision in *Kalanke v. Freie Hansestadt Bremen*,[62] the relevant part of Article 119 now stating:

    "With a view to ensuring full equality in practice between men and women in working life, the principle of equal treatment shall not prevent a Member State from maintaining or adopting measures providing for specific advantages in order to make it easier for the under-represented sex to pursue a vocational activity or to prevent or compensate for disadvantages in professional careers."

- A new Article, 6a, is inserted into the Treaty and provides:

    "Without prejudice to the other provisions of this Treaty and within the limits of the powers conferred by it upon the Community, the Council, acting unanimously on a proposal from the Commission and after consulting the European parliament, may take appropriate action to combat discrimination based on sex, racial or ethnic origin, religion or belief, disability, age or sexual orientation."

However, any measure must be adopted unanimously, rather than by the qualified majority voting procedure.

- Article 2 states that a task of the Community, *inter alia*, is to promote throughout the Community a harmonious, balanced and sustainable development of economic activities, a high level of employment and of social protection, equality between men and women, sustainable and non-inflationary growth, a high degree of competitiveness and convergence of economic performance, a high level of protection and improvement of the quality of the environment, the raising of the standard of living and quality of life, and economic and social cohesion and solidarity among Member States.

- Article 3 adds the following paragraph:

    "2. In all activities referred to in this Article, the Community shall aim to eliminate inequalities, and to promote equality, between men and women."[63]

2.8   STATUTORY STATEMENT OF TERMS

The Employment Rights Act 1996, Pt I, requires employers to supply employees with a written statement of specified terms of their employment, and amendments to those terms. The provisions, which were originally contained in the Contracts of Employment Act 1963, have been amended on a number of occasions, most recently by the

[62] Case C–450/93 [1995] I.R.L.R. 660, ECJ.
[63] See EOR No. 75 September/October 1997, p. 30.

Trade Union Reform and Employment Rights Act 1993[64] which implemented amendments necessary to comply with Directive 91/533 on an employer's obligation to inform employees of the conditions applicable to the contract of employment relationship.

The requirement is that not later than two months after the beginning of employment, the employer must give every employee whose employment is to last more than one month, regardless of the hours worked, a written statement setting out certain details relating to their employment. If the employee leaves before the end of the two-month period, section 2(6) provides that it is still necessary to provide a statement. By section 1(4) the following information is required to be given in a single document:

- the name of the employer and the employee (s.1(3)(a));

- the date employment began, (s.1(3)(b)), and continuous employment began if there is previous employment which counts towards continuity (s.1(3)(c));

- the scale or rate of remuneration or method of calculating remuneration (s.1(4)(a));

- the interval at which remuneration is paid (s.1(4)(b));

- any terms and conditions relating to hours of work (s.1(4)(c));

- any terms and conditions relating to holiday entitlement (which must be sufficiently specific to allow the employee's holiday entitlement to be precisely calculated), including public holidays and holiday pay (s.1(4)(d)(i));

- the title of the job which the employee is employed to do or a brief description of the work for which he is employed (s.1(4)(f). Following the decision of the ECJ in *Kampelmann v. Landschaftsverband Westfalen-Lippe; Stadtwerke Witten GmbH v. Schade; Haseley v. Stadtwerke Altena GmbH*, Joined Cases C–253/96 to C–258/96 [1998] I.R.L.R. 333 doubt has been cast on whether s.1(4)(f) has correctly transposed the requirements of Article 2(2)(c)(ii) of Directive 91/533.); and

- either the place of work or, where the employee is required or permitted to work at various places, an indication of that and of the address of the employer (s.1(4)(h)).

In addition, the following information must be supplied within two months after the beginning of employment, but may be supplied by instalments:

- any terms and conditions relating to incapacity or work as a result of sickness or injury, including sick pay provisions (s.1(4)(d)(ii)), if any. Notification of these details may be done by referring an employee to some other reasonably accessible document, which by section 6 the employee has a reasonable opportunity of reading in the course of employment;

- pensions and pension schemes (s.1(4)(d)(iii)). As with terms relating to sickness, above, notification may be by referring an employee to some other reasonably accessible document. However, if the pension scheme is established by statute and provisions require new employees to be given information about employees' pension rights or the determination of questions

---

[64] s.26, Sched. 4, as from November 30, 1993.

affecting those rights by section 1(5) there is no requirement under section 1(4)(d)(iii);

- the length of notice the employee is obliged to give and entitled to receive to terminate his contract (s.1(4)(e));

- where the employment is not intended to be permanent, the period for which it is expected to continue or, if it is for a fixed term, the date it is intended to end (s.1(4)(g)); and

- any collective bargaining agreements which directly affect the terms and conditions of employment including, where the employer is not a party, the persons by whom they were made (s.1(4)(j)).

Where the employee is required to work outside the United Kingdom for more than one month there is a requirement for additional information to be given:

- the period the person is to work outside the United Kingdom (s.1(4)(k)(i));

- the currency in which remuneration is to be paid in that period (s.1(4)(k)(ii));

- details of additional remuneration or benefits connected with working outside the United Kingdom (s.1(4)(k)(iii)); and

- repatriation arrangements (s.1(4)(k)(iv)).

If an employee is to begin working outside the United Kingdom for more than one month within two months of starting employment the statement provided for in section 1 must be provided before he leaves the United Kingdom to begin that work (s.1(5)).

Under the ERA 1996, s.42(1), where a person becomes a shop or betting worker to whom section 40 applies, the employer must, within two months give the employee a written statement in a prescribed form, as contained in section 42(4), detailing rights to "opt out" of Sunday working by the giving of three months' notice to do so. If the employer fails to provide this statement a shop worker or betting worker need only give one months' notice of opting out. This right applies to new and existing shop and betting workers but does not apply to those employed only to work on Sunday.

In addition, the employer is required by section 3 to include in the statement a note of any disciplinary and grievance rules that are applicable to the employee, specifying a person to whom an employee may apply in any disciplinary matter and the person with whom any grievance should be taken up and the procedure for doing so. If there are further steps involved those steps need to be explained. Alternatively, the employee may be referred to a reasonably accessible document explaining the steps. By section 3(2) the provisions contained in section 3 do not apply to rules, disciplinary decisions, grievances or procedures relating to health and safety at work.

Under provisions introduced by the Employment Act (EA) 1989, and now contained in the ERA 1996, s.3(3), an employer with less than 20 employees is not required to comply with the requirement to provide disciplinary rules or the details of the person with whom to discuss any disciplinary decision and the procedure for doing so.

There is no requirement for information to be supplied to those falling outside the category of "employee". However, by Regulations made under the Employment Agencies Act 1973 a contractor is required, on entering a contract with a worker who is to be supplied to a hirer, to give the worker a written statement containing full details of the terms and conditions of employment.[65]

2.8.1 Changes in information contained in a statement

Any changes to the conditions required to be contained in the statutory statement must be notified to the employee at the earliest opportunity, or within one month of coming into effect, and in the same manner as the original statement (s.4). This does not give authority to the employer to vary the terms of employment without consent as under normal contractual principles an unaccepted unilateral variation represents a breach of contract and may provide grounds for a claim for constructive dismissal. Thus in *Aparau v. Iceland Frozen Foods*,[66] when the employee refused to move under the terms of a mobility clause unilaterally inserted into a new statutory statement the EAT held that the employee had been constructively dismissed because although this occurred a year after the amendment was issued, the employee had refused to sign the amended statement. The EAT expressed the view that caution should be exercised when deciding whether an employee had implicitly agreed to a unilateral change by the employer. Failure to give written notification of changes, as required by section 4, does not, however, make the changes ineffective.[67]

Where the employer's name or identity changes in circumstances where continuity of employment is not broken, providing no other particulars change this may be treated as a change under section 4, rather than requiring the issue of a new statement (s.4(7)).

2.8.2 Application to an industrial tribunal

Where an employer fails to issue a statement under sections 1 or 4, or the statement issued does not comply with what is required, an employee may, by section 11, make a reference to an industrial tribunal which has power to determine what *ought* to have been included or referred to in order to comply with sections 1 or 4. Once the tribunal has decided that issue, those terms are then treated as if given by the employer. Problems have, however, arisen in connection with the powers of tribunals in this respect and whether the tribunal has the power under section 11 to insert terms or to interpret terms in a statutory statement.

In *Construction Industry Training Board v. Leighton*[68] Kilner Brown J. in the EAT took a restrictive view of the tribunal's powers saying that a tribunal could not "re-write or amend a binding contract which has one small area of misunderstanding between the parties". The position was clarified by Stephenson L.J. in *Mears v. Safecar Security Ltd*[69] in which he said:

> "S[ection] 11 would seem to impose on the Tribunal the statutory duty to find the specified terms, and in the last resort invent them for the purpose of literally

---

[65] Conduct of Employment Agencies and Employment Businesses Regulations 1976 (S.I. 1976 No. 715), reg. 9(6)(a)–(c).
[66] [1996] I.R.L.R. 119, EAT.
[67] *Parkes Classic Confectionery v. Ashcroft* [1973] I.T.R. 43.
[68] [1978] I.R.L.R. 60, EAT.
[69] [1982] 2 All E.R. 865, CA.

writing them into the contract. In discharging that duty, the Tribunal can and must go into all the facts and circumstances of the case and, when those fail to provide a basis for implying a specified term, to justice, and the implication of a reasonable term. If the Tribunal have not enough material in the facts and circumstance to determine what *would* have been agreed, they must determine what *should* have been agreed, bearing in mind that it is the employer"s breach of *his* statutory duty which has made the employee's application for a reference necessary and that in consequence they would generally be right to resolve any doubt about what particulars ought to be included in favour of the employee." per *Stephenson L.J.*

Mears v. Safecar Security Ltd [1982] I.R.L.R. 183 at 191, CA.

As a result of this, proposed amendments to the Employment Bill 1982, aimed at clarifying the tribunal's powers in this respect, were withdrawn. It must be noted, however, that the comments by Stephenson L.J. in *Mears* were *obiter* on this issue. In the subsequent case of *Eagland v. British Telecommunications plc*[70] this view was rejected by the Court of Appeal. Parker L.J. said that the guidance in *Mears* could not be agreed with and that it was undesirable that such guidance should remain in the authorities. Leggatt L.J. agreed with that view and stated:

". . . I too am unable to envisage circumstances in which it might become appropriate for an Industrial Tribunal to invent a term. I use the word "invent" as it was used by Lord Justice Stephenson in *Mears v. Safecar Security Ltd* [1982] I.R.L.R. 183 at p. 191, 54 in the sense of determining either what term should have been agreed or what term would have been reasonable. If an essential term, such as a written statement must contain, has not been agreed, there will be no agreement. If it has, it is the duty of the Industrial Tribunal, where necessary, to identify the term as having been agreed, whether expressly, by necessary implication, or by inference from all the circumstances, including in particular the conduct of the parties, without recourse to invention." per Leggatt L.J.

Eagland v. British Telecommunications plc [1992] I.R.L.R. 323 at 327, CA.

The matter remains largely unresolved and clearly this does not accord with the wishes of Parliament that the amendment to the 1982 Bill was only dropped because it appeared that the courts had resolved the issue. Painter (1996)[71] asks whether there is likely to be a difference in outcome depending on whether the approach is "identification" or "invention" of the missing term?

2.8.3 Enforcement

Although between 1963 and 1965 the requirements for a statutory statement were enforced by a fine, there is today no sanction to enforce these provisions. However, there is authority, as demonstrated by the House of Lords decision in *Scally v. Southern Health and Social Service Board*[72] and the subsequent industrial tribunal case of *Gray v.*

[70] [1992] I.R.L.R. 323, CA.
[71] Painter, Holmes & Migdal (1996), p. 100.
[72] [1991] I.C.R. 771, HL.

Smith[73] that employers not only have a duty to inform employees of employment terms, and any changes as set out in Part I of the 1996 Act, but an implied duty to keep employees informed of collectively agreed benefits necessitating action by the employee of which he would otherwise be unaware. In *Gray v. Smith*[74] a Belfast Industrial Tribunal held, in circumstances where the employer had failed to supply any written terms, that the employer had forfeit his right to rely on the strict statutory provisions relating to the right to return to work after maternity leave. The employee was held to have been discriminated against on grounds of sex and unfairly dismissed even though she had failed to comply with the relevant statutory requirements.

2.8.4   Status of the statutory statement

The statutory statement issued under Part I of the 1996 Act is not the contract of employment and the terms contained in the statement are only evidence of the terms of the contract. Despite the early case of *Gascol Conversions Ltd v. Mercer*[75] where Lord Denning said: "this was clearly a binding contract" when referring to the statement, the law is generally thought to be found in *System Floors (U.K.) Ltd v. Daniel*[76] where Browne-Wilkinson J. examined *Gascol Conversions* and stated:

> "It seems to us, therefore, that in general the status of the statutory statement is this. It provides very strong prima facie evidence of what were the terms of the contract between the parties. Nor are the statements of the terms finally conclusive: at most, they place a heavy burden on the employer to show that the actual terms of contract are different from those which he has set out in the statutory statement." *per* Browne-Wilkinson J.

> *System Floors (U.K.) Ltd v. Daniel* [1982] I.C.R. 54 at 58, EAT.

The importance of this is that although the common law rule is that written contractual terms cannot be ousted by oral evidence to the contrary, the parole evidence rule, here oral evidence may be introduced to show that the statement is inaccurate, and in *Simmonds v. Dowty Seals* the employee successfully demonstrated that the hours in the original statement had been informally orally varied.[77]

In *Robertson & Jackson v. British Gas Corp.*[78] a case where the employees disputed their statutory statements on the basis that it did not accurately reflect the bonus terms that were agreed during the interview and contained in their letter of appointment, the Court of Appeal approved the statement by Browne-Wilkinson J. in *System Floors v. Daniel*, Ackner L.J. noting that Browne-Wilkinson J. "distinguished, and in our view properly distinguished" *Gascol Conversions*.[79] It is therefore the case that through *System Floors* and *Robertson* the position is achieved which was stated by Lord Parker C.J. in *Turriff Construction Ltd v. Bryant*,[80] a case brought soon after the original Contracts of Employment Act 1963 became operative:

---

[73] IDS Brief 584/March 1997, p. 14.
[74] *ibid.*
[75] [1974] I.C.R. 420, CA.
[76] [1982] I.C.R. 54, EAT.
[77] [1978] I.R.L.R. 211, EAT.
[78] [1981] I.C.R. 302, CA.
[79] At 303.
[80] (1967) 2 I.T.R. 292.

"It is of course, quite clear that the statement made pursuant to s.4 of 1963 Act (s.1 of 1996 Act) is not the contract; it is not even conclusive evidence of the terms of a contract." *per* Lord Parker C.J.

Turriff Construction Ltd v. Bryant [1967] 2 K.I.R. 659 at 662, DC.

In *Robertson & Jackson v. British Gas Corp.*[81] the employer asserted that the statement contained the terms of employment. However, the Court of Appeal held that the contract itself overrides any inconsistency that there may be between the contract and the statutory statement, holding that the statutory statement could not be used as an aid to interpretation of the letter of appointment which contained entitlement to the contractual bonus scheme.

A failure to object to terms in a statutory statement is not to be taken as acceptance where the terms do not have an immediate impact. This is demonstrated in both *Jones v. Associated Tunnelling Ltd*[82] and *Aparau v. Iceland Frozen Foods*[83] both of which involved an attempt by the employer to implement a flexibility clause which had been unilaterally inserted into an amended statutory statement. The employees, who refused to move, resigned and were held to have been constructively dismissed. In *Jones* Browne-Wilkinson J. said that the appeal tribunal were not inclined to imply assent to a variation by mere failure of the employee to object to a unilateral variation by the employer of terms of employment contained in the statutory statement, which were not themselves contractual. However, the longer a statement is in the possession of the employee, where the term concerned is of immediate and not future application, the more difficult it will become for the employee to successfully dispute the new terms on the basis that with the passage of time the employee will be deemed to have acquiesced to the amended term.

2.9 SUMMARY

Although the employment relationship is referred to in terms of "the contract of employment" the sources of the terms of that relationship are varied and diverse, many of which do not depend upon agreement between the parties.

Express agreement between the parties may, and often does, make up a very small part of the overall terms, with the main terms, such as hours of work, holiday entitlement, bonus arrangements and pay, together with provisions for pay review, being either settled by collective agreement, or derived from standard terms. Rules of behaviour, such as smoking, style of dress, etc., are drawn up by management acting under their prerogative and contained in a handbook and in works rules.

Relying on the contract as the underlying basis of employment, such rules may be binding, but a distinction has to be made between those rules which have an effect on the individual and are therefore capable of incorporation into the individual contract and those which do not have contractual status and may therefore be unilaterally altered by the employer.

European law is an important source of employment law, not just by the direct applicability of articles, but also by directives which not only have direct effect as

---

[81] [1981] I.C.R. 302, CA.
[82] [1981] I.R.L.R. 477, EAT.
[83] [1996] I.R.L.R. 119, EAT.

against an emanation of the state, but may do so indirectly when used as an aid to interpretation of domestic law.

It should be noted that the Directive giving effect to the Social Partner's Agreement on part-time work, Directive 97/81, has, in fact, been extended to the United Kingdom by means of a separate "mini Directive" adopted under Article 100 of the Treaty of Rome and the United Kingdom, along with other Member States, is required to transpose the provisions into national legislation by December 15, 1999: that is two years from the date of adoption of the substantive Directive, rather than from the date of the mini extension Directive.

Chapter 3

The Duties of the Parties

As has been seen from Chapter 2, the terms of the employment contract can derive from a range of sources. At common law there are a number of duties, which in the absence of express terms to the contrary apply to the parties to the employment relationship. The arrangement of this chapter is to examine the duties owed by employees towards the employer, and on occasion towards fellow employees, then the mutual duty of trust and confidence, which is said to arise from the duty of co-operation and obedience owed by the employee and finally to examine those duties owed by the employer. The interrelationship between the sources of terms and the main terms of the contract is set out in the diagram on page 148 to give an overview of the text.

3.1 Duties Owed by the Employee

3.1.1 Duty of co-operation and obedience

The duties imposed upon the employee are a reflection of the historic subservient nature of the relationship of master and servant, with a duty to serve as directed and to obey reasonable and lawful orders. The importance of obedience was emphasised by Lord Evershed M.R. in *Laws v. London Chronicle (Indicator Newspapers) Ltd*[1]:

> ". . . wilful disobedience of a lawful and reasonable order shows a disregard . . . of a condition essential to the contract of service, namely the condition that the servant must obey the proper orders of the master, and that unless he does so the relationship is, so to speak, struck at fundamentally." *per* Lord Evershed M.R.

> *Laws v. London Chronicle (Indicator Newspapers) Ltd* [1959] 1 W.L.R. 698, CA.

This extends to a duty to co-operate and not to frustrate the employer's commercial objectives. In *Secretary of State for Employment v. ASLEF (No. 2)*[2] the Secretary of State applied to NIRC for an order for a ballot of a group of train drivers involved in a work-to-rule. The question arose as to whether the work-to-rule, during which the employees meticulously observed all the rules in British Rail's operating rule book was,

[1] [1959] 1 W.L.R. 689, CA.
[2] [1972] 2 Q.B. 455, CA.

as the union claimed, merely fulfilling the contract even though they were obeying the rules with the intention of causing the maximum disruption of service. Buckley L.J., reasoned that a wilful act of one party, which although not departing from the literal letter of the agreement, nevertheless defeats the commercial intention of the parties in entering into the contract, constitutes a breach of an implied term to perform the contract in such a way as not to frustrate that commercial objective. As a result, wilful obstruction constitutes a breach of contract because goodwill is an essential element of the employment relationship. Roskill L.J. said that there was an implied term that each employee, in obeying lawful orders will not obey them in a wholly unreasonable way. Thus, it emerged that there is a duty on the employee not to be deliberately non co-operative and not to act so as to obstruct the employer's operations: he must be flexible and adaptable.

The duty not to be deliberately unco-operative and not to act in such a way so as to obstruct and frustrate the employer's operations is implicit in a contract of employment with a person in a supervisory or professional capacity. This is demonstrated in *Ticehurst v. British Telecommunications plc*[3] where on an application for unpaid wages following industrial action the Court of Appeal held that the implied term to serve the employer faithfully must apply to a manager who is necessarily charged with the supervision of staff and in exercising discretions, which must be exercised faithfully and in the interests of the employers. As there was a breach of this implied term of their contracts, BT was entitled to refuse to accept part-performance and therefore to suspend payment. Likewise, in *Sim v. Rotherham Metropolitan Borough Council*[4] Scott J. held that teachers who withdrew their co-operation in supplying absence cover had breached their contracts because as professionals they had a duty to fulfil their professional obligations to care for their students, despite the fact that their contracts were silent on the issue of cover.

In *Cresswell v. Board of Inland Revenue*,[5] although not going so far as supporting the defendants' argument that it is one of the managerial prerogatives to be able to change the nature of the job in the interests of the organisation as a whole, Walton J. said that although the duty to co-operate did not give management a "free-reign" to make changes in employment, they did have a discretion to change the way in which the job was done and the employee is expected to adapt to new methods and techniques in performing his duties. So where the employer was introducing computerisation, the employee is expected to co-operate provided that the employer arranged for him to receive the necessary training.

The duty to co-operate in the face of the exercise of managerial prerogatives was demonstrated in the earlier case of *Woods v. W.M. Car Services (Peterborough) Ltd*[6] where, although the case has developed some notoriety as a result of the *obiter* remarks of Lord Denning, nevertheless the Court of Appeal upheld the decision regarding the behaviour of the employee who had a duty to co-operate with her employer's attempts:

> "understandably, to reorganise the business he now controlled to conform with his own ideas as to how it should run. . . . Misunderstandings between the employers and employee had in the last analysis produced a state of affairs which would have

---

[3] [1992] I.R.L.R. 219, CA.
[4] [1986] I.R.L.R. 391, HC.
[5] [1984] I.R.L.R. 190, Ch D.
[6] [1982] I.C.R. 693, CA.

prevented the employers from exercising properly their discretion if not their right to reorganise their business. The obdurate refusal of the employee to accept conditions very properly and sensibly being sought to be imposed upon her was unreasonable. Employers must not, in my opinion, be put in a position where, through the wrongful refusal of their employees to accept change, they are prevented from introducing improved business methods in furtherance of seeking success for their enterprise." *per* Watkins L.J.

Woods v. W.M. Car Services (Peterborough) Ltd [1982] I.C.R. 693 at 702, CA.

The employee's duty to obey orders is limited to those orders which are lawful. Authority for this can be found in *Ottoman Bank v. Chakarian*,[7] and *United Bank Ltd v. Akhtar*[8] also demonstrates this point since it was held that the employee's failure to report to a new location in the face of instructions to do so amounted to constructive dismissal in circumstances where the instructions were in breach of an implied duty that they be exercised by the giving of reasonable notice.

3.1.2 Duty of fidelity

An employee owes not only his contractual employer but also an employer to whom he is seconded, a duty of fidelity, which encompasses faithful service and confidentiality and loyalty. Certain aspects of this duty have been encompassed by the growth of the overriding duty of trust and confidence as between the parties, which is discussed at para. 3.2 below. However, the duty of fidelity involves not just a duty of faithful service whilst in employment, but of confidentiality which, whilst existing during employment, continues to bind the employee after employment in so far as confidential information amounting to a trade secret is concerned. These points are demonstrated in *Lancashire Fires Ltd v. SA Lyons & Co. Ltd*[9] which involved both aspects to the duty.

That the contract of employment is not a contract *uberrimae fidei*, of utmost good faith, is demonstrated in *Bell v. Lever Bros*[10] where the House of Lords refused to imply a duty that an employee is obliged to disclose his own breaches of contract. Lord Atkin said that the servant owes a duty not to steal, but having stolen, there is not a "superadded duty" to confess that he has stolen. To imply such a duty, he said, would be a departure from the "well-established usage of mankind" and would be to create obligations entirely outside the normal contemplation of the parties. Neither is an employee, other than a company director, in a fiduciary position. This means that there is no general rule that an employee is obliged to inform his employer of any matter which relates to the employer's business affairs and which would be of interest to the employer. Confirmation of this position, first stated in *Boston Deep Sea Fishing & Ice Co. v. Ansell*[11] was given more recently in *Macmillan Inc. v. Bishopsgate Investment Trust plc*[12] where it was said that it was not enough for the information to be of value to the employer.

However, the duty of fidelity may oblige employees in a managerial or supervisory position to disclose the misconduct of fellow employees. In *Sybron Corp. v. Rochem*

[7] [1930] A.C. 277, PC.
[8] [1989] I.R.L.R. 507, EAT.
[9] [1997] I.R.L.R. 113, CA.
[10] [1932] A.C. 161, HL.
[11] (1888) 39 Ch. 399, CA.
[12] [1993] I.R.L.R. 393, HC.

Ltd[13] the Court of Appeal held that the employer of a Director where during his period of employment the Director had, with his main subordinates, conspired in an operation described as a "massive commercial fraud", could reclaim pension payments and policies from which the Director had benefited upon retirement. Stephenson L.J. referred to the judgment of Scrutton L.J. in the Court of Appeal and Lord Atkin in the House of Lords in *Bell v. Lever Bros.*,[14] both of whom referred to a duty to disclose the misconduct of fellow servants, and said that in *Swain v. West (Butchers) Ltd*[15] the Court of Appeal held that it was the plaintiff's duty, as part of his contract of service, to report to the board any acts which were not in the interests of the company.

The Court in *Sybron*[16] went on to find that there is no general duty to report a fellow servant's misconduct or breach of contract; whether there is such a duty depends on the contract and on the terms of employment of the particular servant. He may be so placed in the hierarchy as to have a duty to report either the misconduct of his superior, as in *Swain's* case[17], or the misconduct of his inferiors, as in *Sybron*,[18] regardless of whether in doing so it has the effect of disclosing his own involvement in the wrongdoing. This duty can extend to fairly humble levels, such as foreman, because: "When a man is a foreman he becomes part of management . . . in a position of trust (and ought to) have come to management at the earliest time to say this sort of thing was going on and sought guidance how to deal with it."[19]

3.1.2.1 *Secret profits and the duty to account*

The employee's duty of fidelity, involving faithful service and the duty not to injure the employer's interests, also involves the duty not to make secret profits, for which, as in *Sybron*,[20] the employee can be accountable. In *Sybron*,[21] the employee owed a fiduciary duty, but the duty to account extends to those other than Directors, as demonstrated in *Casson Beckman & Partners v. Papi*[22] where, in the Court of Appeal, Lloyd L.J. said that the duty to account was implied into the contract of employment. However, both Balcombe L.J. and Sir Denys Buckley referred to the duty to account as being equitable rather than contractual.

The principle that emerges is that where employees personally benefit as a result of their position as an employee, they will usually have to give up at least some of their profit to their employer. Whether the legal device by which this is determined is a term implied into the contract or by reason of a fiduciary duty placed upon them in view of the position held or a duty to account in equity makes no difference to the end result.

3.1.2.2 *Copyright and inventions*

As with profits, the employee is under a duty to account to his employer for any inventions in the course of employment. In the case of literary musical or artistic work the Copyright Designs and Patents Act 1988 provides that the employer is the first owner of any copyright in the work (s.11). If the work is not carried out in the course

13 [1983] I.C.R. 801, CA.
14 [1931] 1 K.B. 557, CA at 586–587 and [1932] A.C. 161, HL at 228.
15 [1936] 3 All E.R. 261, CA.
16 [1983] I.C.R. 801, CA.
17 [1936] 3 All E.R. 261, CA.
18 [1983] I.C.R. 801, CA.
19 *Cooper v. Plessey Semiconductors Ltd*, *The Times*, August 11, 1983 and quoted in Davies & Freedland (1984), p. 313.
20 [1983] I.C.R. 801, CA.
21 *ibid.*
22 [1991] B.C.C. 68, CA.

of employment but in the employee's spare time the position is less clear, and may depend on the connection between the literary work and the employee's normal work. For example, a computer programme written by a software development manager, albeit in his own time, was the subject of a successful injunction.[23] Claims by the employee that the programme had actually been written for a rival firm did not further his argument, since the court was reluctant to permit an employee to benefit from lack of faithfulness during employment.

Since the Patents Act 1977 rights as between employer and employee with regard to inventions by an employee made after June 1, 1978 are governed solely by section 39 of the Act. Under section 39(1)(a) an employee's invention is taken to belong to the employer if it was made in the course of the normal duties of the employee or in the course of duties falling outside his normal duties but specifically assigned to him, and the circumstances in either case were such that an invention might reasonably be expected to result from the carrying out of the employee's normal duties. In *Reiss Engineering Co. Ltd v. Harris*[24] the High Court held that a fitter, who subsequently became responsible for servicing and then selling pumps, who whilst under notice of redundancy developed a valve, did not do so "in the course of his normal duties" within section 39(1)(a), which was held to mean those duties which he was actually employed to do. The court rejected the employer's argument that the normal duties of the employee include those duties implied by the duty of fidelity. Falconer J. said that the duty of fidelity is to carry out faithfully the work the employee is employed to do to the best of his ability, but that it does not assist in the formulation of the actual duties which the employee is employed to do.

However, by sections 40 to 41 the employee is entitled to remuneration for an invention if it belongs to the employer under section 39 and it can be shown that it has been of outstanding benefit to the employer or if it belonged to the employee and he assigned or leased it to the employer but received inadequate benefit from that arrangement in relation to the benefits derived by the employer. By section 42 any agreement seeking to diminish the employee's rights is void.

3.1.2.3 *Entering into competition with the employer*

The courts will not prevent an employee setting up his own business in competition with his ex-employer, nor enforce an agreement not to do so where this would operate in restraint of trade. However, whilst in employment the employee's duty towards his employer will prevent him using his position to aid that process in that it is a breach of the duty of faithful service for an employee to enter into competition with his employer, or work for another employer at the same time where, in view of either the nature of the work or the position held, it is likely to lead to a conflict, he is in a fiduciary position, or has entered an agreement not to do so.

In *Robb v. Green*[25] an employee tradesman left his employer and set up a similar business. Before leaving he copied out lists of the plaintiff's customers and then tried to persuade them to transfer their custom to him. Lord Esher M.R., said that in a contract of service the court must imply a stipulation that the servant will act in good faith towards his master, because it is a thing which must necessarily have been in the view of both parties when they entered into the contract. It is impossible to suppose that a master would have put a servant into a confidential position of this kind, unless

---

[23] *Missing Link Software v. Magee* [1989] F.S.R. 361.
[24] [1985] I.R.L.R. 232, HC.
[25] [1895] 2 Q.B. 315, CA.

he thought that the servant would be bound to use good faith towards him; or that the servant would not know, when he entered into that position, that the master would rely on his observance of good faith in the confidential relation between them. In view of this the Court issued an injunction to restrain the use of the list gained in breach of the implied duty. In *Wessex Dairies Ltd v. Smith*,[26] whilst still in employment Smith solicited the company's customers to transfer their custom to him when he ceased to be employed by the company. Maugham L.J. looked at the judgment in *Robb v. Green*[27] and said he preferred Smith L.J.'s more general implication, namely: "I think that it is a necessary implication which must be engrafted on such a contract that the servant undertakes to serve his master with good faith and fidelity". An employee has an implied duty to look after his master's interests and not his own, hence soliciting custom and the deliberate canvassing at a time when he was under an obligation to serve his employer was to act in such a way as to damage the employer's interests.

It appeared at one time that the courts were prepared to differentiate between actions which were merely preparatory, and therefore acceptable, and those which went beyond preparation and therefore amounted to a breach of fidelity. In *Adamson v. B & L Cleaning Services Ltd*[28] the EAT held that in seeking to tender for work currently being done by his employers, by placing his name on the tender list, Adamson was in breach of his implied contractual duty of fidelity and was not unfairly dismissed. Adamson sought to establish that an employee is entitled to take steps to look for alternative employment without failing in his duty to his employer, and that that is indistinguishable from taking preparatory steps to set up in competition. This was based on two earlier authorities: firstly, in *Harris & Russell Ltd v. Slingsby*[29] it was said:

"This Court . . . would regard it as wholly insufficient reason to dismiss a man, that he was merely seeking employment with a competitor, unless it could be shown that there were reasonably solid grounds for supposing that he was doing so in order to abuse his confidential position and information with his present employers. In the nature of things, when a man changes employment, it is more likely he will be seeking fresh employment with someone in the same line of business and, therefore, a competitor of his present employers." *per* Sir Hugh Griffiths.

Harris & Russell Ltd v. P.S.G. Slingsby [1973] I.R.L.R. 221 at 222, NIRC.

Secondly, in *Laughton and Hawley v. Bapp Industrial Supplies Ltd*[30] the EAT held that employees of a company that supplied nuts and bolts were entitled to write to their employer's suppliers informing them that they intended to start up in business trading in nuts and bolts and asking for details of their products.

The court in *Adamson* accepted that tendering for the future business of an employer's customers in competition with the employer was factually different from an employee soliciting his employer's customers (whilst in employment) to transfer their custom after he had left employment. However, placing ones name on a tender list was held to amount to more than indicating an intention to set up in competition: it was actually competing whilst still in employment.

[26] [1935] 2 K.B. 80, CA.
[27] [1895] 2 Q.B. 315, CA.
[28] [1995] I.R.L.R. 193, EAT.
[29] [1973] I.R.L.R. 221, NIRC.
[30] [1986] I.R.L.R. 245, EAT.

Laughton and Hawley v. Bapp Industrial Supplies Ltd[31] was considered in *Lancashire Fires Ltd v. SA Lyons & Co. Ltd*[32] where it was held that arranging a finance agreement, an exclusive sales agreement, the purchasing of relevant pieces of equipment, renting and renovating premises and working on establishing a manufacturing process in his spare time amounted to more than taking "preliminary steps". He was:

> ". . . not simply seeking employment with a competitor or taking preliminary steps to set up his own business. His activities . . . , 'placed him well on the wrong side of the line.' Indeed, any employee with technical knowledge and experience can expect to have his spare-time activities in the field in which his employers operate carefully scrutinised in this context." *per* Sir Thomas Bingham M.R.

Lancashire Fires Ltd v. SA Lyons & Co. Ltd [1997] I.R.L.R. 113 at 122, CA.

These cases demonstrate the efforts by the courts to seek to satisfy the conflicting notion that whilst in employment an employee owes a duty of fidelity to his employer with the rule that the law will not permit a restraint of trade, and thus the ability for an employee to compete with his ex-employer. It can be argued that *Laughton and Hawley v. Bapp Industrial Supplies Ltd*[33] can be confined to its facts, in that it involved employees, who were intending to set up in competition and to that end contacted suppliers rather than customers. It is difficult to see, when dealing with customer contact, what actions would be "merely preparatory", and therefore not a breach of the duty of faithful service. In *Marshall v. Industrial Systems & Control Ltd*[34] it was argued by the applicant that the facts were analogous with *Laughton*,[35] in that the contact was with a supplier rather than with customers of the employer. The EAT, however, distinguished *Laughton*[36] on the basis that:

> "It is one thing, as was decided in *Laughton and Hawley* . . ., to form an intention to set up in competition, and another, . . . to form a plan or an arrangement with another important manager to try and persuade another to join them in order to deprive the company, of which he was managing director, of their best client. There was no doubt, . . . that it was not merely a plan but concrete arrangements had been made to obtain the business . . ." *per* Lord Mayfield.

Marshall v. Industrial Systems & Control Ltd [1992] I.R.L.R. 294 at 296, EAT.

This decision could equally well have been based on the principle laid down in *Sybron Corp. v. Rochem Ltd.*[37] That enforcement of the duty depends not just on the degree of the actions taken, but on the status of the individual concerned is demonstrated by *Thomas Marshall (Exports) Ltd v. Quinle*[38] where although the agreement between the parties was deficient in that it did not prevent Marshall, a Managing Director, "using" confidential information, when he defrauded his employers by using confidential

---

[31] *ibid.*
[32] [1997] I.R.L.R. 113, CA.
[33] [1986] I.R.L.R. 245, EAT.
[34] [1992] I.R.L.R. 294, EAT.
[35] [1986] I.R.L.R. 245, EAT.
[36] *ibid.*
[37] [1983] I.C.R. 801, CA.
[38] [1979] 1 Ch. 227.

information it was held that this was a breach of good faith and the court granted an interim injunction to restrain that use.

A claim that employees are expected, under the implied duty of loyalty, to work exclusively for an employer and that any work for a competitor or in competition is to be regarded as being a breach of trust or a failure to give loyal service, depends on the nature of the job. So in *Nova Plastics Ltd v. Froggatt*[39] the spare time working for a rival company by an odd job man did not amount to a breach of loyal service, but in *Hivac v. Park Royal Scientific Instruments Ltd*,[40] where the nature of the work being undertaken by five manual workers for a direct competitor of their day-time employer, was such that it led to the implication that it was likely to damage the interests of the employer and thereby breach their duty of fidelity. Although an injunction was granted in *Hivac*, a case involving "mere manual workers", it was stated that the law would be reluctant to impose restrictions preventing efforts to use spare time to increase earnings because whilst an employee is paid for five-and-half days a week, the rest of his time is his own to use what is probably his only skill to earn his living.

So, it appears that there is no breach of the duty of fidelity by employees, unless under an express contractual duty to the contrary, if they carry out casual work for another employer in their own time, providing there is no conflict between the two jobs. A plumber who does odd jobs as a plumber in his spare time, either on his own account or for another employer, taking work from his full-time employer, would therefore be in breach of his duty of fidelity, but not if he worked, for example, as a mini-cab driver.

In *Thomas Marshall*[41] it was argued by the employee that contractual restrictions not to be directly or indirectly engaged, concerned or interested in any other business save for that of the company, were not enforceable because the contract automatically came to an end upon the repudiatory breach by the employee. Authorities as to whether a repudiatory breach automatically terminates the contract of employment, therefore placing employment contracts on a different basis from contracts generally where a repudiatory breach entitles the other party to elect whether to carry on with the contract, whilst seeking damages for the breach, are, as Sir Robert Megarry observed ". . . in a far from satisfactory state".[42] Suffice to say here that the High Court in *Marshall v. Guinle*,[43] relying on what Sir Robert Megarry called "the *Lumley v. Wagner* line of cases"[44] held that even though a repudiatory breach would normally destroy the essential relationship of trust and confidence, the contract of employment is no different from contracts generally and did not automatically bring the contract, and therefore the restrictions within it, to an end.

3.1.2.4 *Limitation on contractual restrictions*

The basic position was stated by Dillon L.J. in *Provident Financial Group plc and Whitegates Estate Agency Ltd v. Hayward*,[45] that in a contract for personal service the courts will not normally make an order as between an employer and employee if the effect would be to compel the employee to go back to work for his previous employer.

---

[39] [1982] I.R.L.R. 146, EAT.
[40] [1946] 1 All E.R. 350, CA.
[41] [1979] 1 Ch. 227.
[42] *ibid.* at p. 239 at D: see para. 5.3.2.1 below.
[43] *ibid.*
[44] *William Robinson & Co. Ltd v. Heuer* [1898] 2 Ch. 451 ,*Warner Brothers Pictures Incorp. v. Nelson* [1937] 1 K.B. 209, *Howard v. Pickfod Tool Co. Ltd* [1951] 1 K.B. 417.
[45] [1989] I.R.L.R. 84, CA.

This position, which is described as tantamount to slavery, is confirmed by the Trade Union and Labour Relations (Consolidation) Act 1992, s.236 and in *Evening Standard Co. Ltd v. Henderson*[46] it was said that it is trite law that:

". . . you cannot get an injunction against an employee under a contract of service to enforce a negative covenant if the consequences of that injunction would be to put the employee in the position that he would either have to go on working for his former employers or starve or be idle." *per* Lawton L.J.

Evening Standard Co. Ltd v. Henderson [1987] I.R.L.R. 64 at 66, CA.

However, if consideration for the contract is not just pay, but the provision of work itself, the employer will himself be in breach by failing to provide work, and in *Hayward*[47] Dillon L.J. recognised that this category may extend beyond artists to "skilled workmen and even chartered accountants".

3.1.2.5 *Garden leave*

This ability to enforce the contractual notice period, but without requiring the employee to work throughout part or all of that period, has become known as "garden leave" and so long as the employer has not accepted short (or no notice) from the employee, and keeps his part of the contract, in that he continues to provide the employee with all his contractual benefits, he can enforce the contract, including the duty of fidelity or the contractual restrictions where these are more comprehensive.

The means of enforcement is by application to the High Court for an interlocutory injunction. Since the opportunity for an individual to maintain and exercise his skills is a matter of general concern, terms which operate in restraint of trade raise questions of public policy, consequently the court may restrict the period for which the restriction is to operate. However, it was observed in *Credit Suisse Ltd v. Armstrong*[48] by Neill L.J. that: "The court's reaction to these clauses has been more flexible than in the case of restrictive covenants" where an injunction prevents an ex-employee from working at their skill, yet no longer being paid by their employer, and for this reason the court not only has power to grant an injunction, but to "narrow the scope of the contractual embargo".

The issues for consideration by the court are demonstrated in *Provident Financial Group plc and Whitegates Estate Agency Ltd v. Hayward*.[49] Hayward was financial director of an estate agency whose contract specified that he would not undertake any other business or profession or become an employee or agent of any other person during the contract. There was also a provision that the employer was not under a duty to provide work and that the notice period was six months. The employee gave notice, but cut short the notice period, writing to the employer informing him of his intention to take up work for a supermarket chain as financial controller of their chain of estate agents' offices. As a result, the employer sought an interlocutory injunction to enforce the contract and thereby restrain the employee from working for anyone else until after the expiry of the notice period. Dillon L.J. emphasised that the grant of an injunction was a matter of discretion and that the Court ought to exercise caution:

[46] [1987] I.R.L.R. 64, CA.
[47] n. 45 above. See now *William Hill Organisation Ltd v. Tucker* [1998] I.R.L.R. 313, CA.
[48] [1996] I.C.R. 882, CA.
[49] n. 45 above.

"The practice of long periods of 'garden leave' is obviously capable of abuse. It is a weapon in the hands of the employers to ensure that an ambitious and able executive will not give notice if he is going to be unable to work at all for anyone for a long period of notice." *per* Dillon L.J.

Provident Financial Group plc and Whitegates Estate Agency Ltd v. Hayward [1989] I.R.L.R. 84 at 86, CA.

He distinguished the earlier case of *Evening Standard Co. Ltd. v. Henderson*[50] on its facts because in *Henderson*[51] the employer was prepared to allow the employee to work during the notice period, whereas in *Hayward*,[52] because the employer's concerns were for the security of "confidential information" to which Hayward had been privy, they were seeking an order which would involve the employee being idle. Dillon L.J. was unimpressed at the "confidential" tag placed by the company on the information in question, observing that, "it is very common for employers to have somewhat exaggerated views of what will or may affect their businesses". Even, as in this case, where consideration was merely pay as opposed to the provision of work itself, and despite an express contractual provision that the company was not under an obligation to provide work, Dillon L.J. said that it is not enough just that the employee has contracted in certain terms and will not starve if the terms are enforced against him while the employer continues to pay him in full. The employee has a concern to work and a concern to exercise his skills. In considering the detriment the employer would suffer if the clause were not enforced by injunction, the court held that there was no real prospect of serious or significant damage and that the company could sue in damages for the employee's breach of contract.

In the earlier case of *Evening Standard Co. Ltd v. Henderson*[53] Lawton L.J. took a rather more robust view of the agreement between the parties, saying that the defendant ought not to be allowed to do the very thing his contract was intended to stop him doing, namely working for somebody else during the notice period, but that this had to be balanced against the law that the employee cannot be forced by injunction to work for the plaintiffs and must not be reduced to a position of starvation or idleness. However, the position was resolved because the employer had made an offer to allow the employee to go back to work and the court observed that if he chose not to accept that option he could merely continue to receive his salary for his notice period: any resulting "idleness" would be of his own choosing. Lawton L.J. said that it seemed to him that it was unsatisfactory if employees, having entered into contracts and enjoyed the benefits, could then break them to move to other better paying jobs, and that the law would stand by as they could "snap their fingers" at their old employer in the knowledge that their employer could not get an injunction.

This emphasis on the benefits gained by the employee during the contract and the contractual position the employee had willingly agreed to when it suited him to do so, is demonstrated in *Eurobrokers Ltd v. Rabey*[54] where Rabey, a money broker, resigned with immediate effect where his contract obliged him to give six months' notice. The contract also contained a clause providing that if inadequate or short notice was given the company could hold him to the terms for up to six months in circumstances where

[50] [1987] I.R.L.R. 64, CA.
[51] *ibid.*
[52] [1989] I.R.L.R. 84, CA.
[53] n. 50 above.
[54] [1995] I.R.L.R. 206, HC.

it would be reasonable to believe that he was proposing to join a competitor. The company refused to accept Rabey's repudiation and when he refused to take six months' "garden leave" sought an interlocutory injunction to prevent him from undertaking work or rendering services to any business likely to be in competition.

Having concluded that there was a serious issue to be tried, the court considered whether damages would suffice. In deciding to issue an injunction for the full six months the court was influenced by the extent of the customer contacts that had been built up at the company's expense, and which the company was entitled to protect, whereas there was no evidence that the employee would suffer any loss as a result of an injunction or that his skill would be adversely affected. This more employer centred approach was not in evidence in the earlier case of *GFI Group Inc. v. Eaglestone*[55] where the employer of a Foreign Exchange Options Broker sought to enforce a 20-week notice provision in circumstances where the broker's success depended upon his personal relationship with traders, a relationship fostered by an annual expense account of some £59,000, in addition to a salary of £100,000, plus a bonus. When the company learnt that during his notice period, despite a contract term prohibiting the undertaking of work for anyone else, the employee intended to work for a company which was setting up in competition, the employer sought an injunction to enforce the 20-week notice period. In granting the injunction the court reduced the period to 13 weeks as being that "absolutely necessary" to protect the employer. This decision, which recognised that if the defendant moved directly to the other firm it would enable them to have some substantial benefit from Eaglestone's customer connection built up through GFI's investment in him, was influenced by the fact that two other members of the team, whose contracts only provided for four weeks' notice, had already joined the competitor firm, and therefore any damage had, to a certain extent, already been done.

In *Credit Suisse Asset Management Ltd v. Armstrong*[56] the contracts in question contained a clause providing for a six month "garden leave" period, which was to be followed by a period of six months covered by a restrictive covenant. In a challenge to the restrictive covenant the employees argued that the time specified in the covenant should be set off against the period of garden leave. The Court of Appeal held, however, that although the court could exercise its discretion as to the length of garden leave, if the restrictive covenant is valid the court was entitled to enforce it. Restrictive covenants are discussed further at para. 3.1.4 below.

3.1.2.6 *Summary*

Considerations for the court when considering whether to grant an interlocutory injunction to enforce a "garden leave" provision are:

- An injunction is only available when damages are an inadequate or insufficient remedy;

- being equitable relief the equitable maxims apply, and in this context the employer must come with clean hands—he must not himself be in breach of contract;

- the period of notice/restraint must not be for an unreasonable or excessive period;

---

[55] [1994] I.R.L.R. 119, HC.
[56] [1996] I.C.R. 882, CA.

- consideration for the contract must not be the provision of work itself, or affect a trade or profession where the employee has a concern to work and to exercise his skills;

- the employer must be able to demonstrate that there is a real prospect of serious or significant damage to them if the clause is not enforced by injunction and establish a present and future intention to continue to fulfil his contractual obligations—including pay and other contractual benefits;

- whether to grant an injunction is discretionary and decided on the balance of convenience test—*American Cyanamid Co. v. Ethicon Ltd* [1975] A.C. 396, HL, except in circumstances where it is probable that any injunction granted will expire before the case could come on for trial—*Lansing Linde Ltd v. Kerr* [1991] I.C.R. 428, CA, confirmed in *Credit Suisse Ltd v. Armstrong* [1996] I.C.R. 882, CA.

3.1.3 Duty not to disclose confidential information

The implied duty of fidelity and good faith that operates during employment encompasses a duty of confidentiality: an employee must not misuse or disclose confidential information or trade secrets acquired in the course of employment. Whilst in employment this duty will extend to information and trade processes that may be confidential or secret in the wider sense: that which amounts to a trade secret as well as that which falls short of being so. This is demonstrated in *Bents Brewery v. Hogan*[57] where the court held that, apart from any contractual term an individual pub manager could disclose his own terms and conditions, what he could not do was to disclose salaries of others because that was information acquired as a result of opportunities afforded by his service.

The mutuality of the duty of confidentiality in the employment relationship is demonstrated in *Dalgeish v. Lothian and Borders Police Board*[58] where the Court of Session held, *obiter*, that, prima facie, confidential information held by the employer *qua* employer was likewise protected from disclosure. The names and addresses of employees, information in the hands of the employer as employer and for the purposes of the employment relationship could not lawfully be disclosed to Lothian Regional Council in response to their request made for the purposes of establishing the identity of persons who were in arrears in respect of community charge payments.

Although the duty of fidelity ends when employment is terminated, there is a narrower ongoing duty that extends only to trade secrets:

> "The duty of good faith, . . . , arises out of the obligation of loyalty inevitably owed by an employee to his employer. Once the employment relationship ceases, there is no continuing occasion for loyalty. All that is left is a residual duty of confidentiality in respect of the employer's trade secrets." *per* Simon Brown L.J.

> *J.A. Mont (U.K.) Ltd v. Mills* [1993] I.R.L.R. 172 at 177, CA.

There is therefore a different status accorded to different types of information at various stages of the employment relationship. Those stages and the appropriate

---

[57] [1945] 2 All E.R. 570, HC.
[58] [1991] I.R.L.R. 422, CS.

content of the duty was categorised in *Faccenda Chicken Ltd v. Fowler*[59]; the plaintiff's sales manager left the company and set up in competition and eight of the plaintiff's employees subsequently left to join him in the new venture. Between them they knew not only the names and addresses of the plaintiff's customers in their sphere of activity but had a knowledge of the detailed routes taken by refrigerated delivery vehicles; customers' requirements; times of deliveries; and individual pricing information, termed at first instance by Goulding J. as "the sales information". In the Court of Appeal Neill L.J. summarised the rules and conditions applicable at the various stages:

"(1) Where the parties are, or have been, linked by a contract of employment, the obligations of the employee are to be determined by the contract between him and his employer . . .

(2) In the absence of any express term, the obligations of the employee in respect of the use and disclosure of information are the subject of implied terms.

(3) While the employee remains in the employment of the employer the obligations are included in the implied terms which imposes a duty of good faith or fidelity on the employee. . . . (a) the extent of the duty of good faith will vary according to the nature of the contract . . . (b) that the duty of good faith will be broken if an employee makes or copies a list of the customers of the employer for use after his employment ends or deliberately memorises such a list, even though, except in special circumstances, there is no general restriction on an ex-employee canvassing or doing business with customers of his former employer . . .

(4) The implied term which imposes an obligation on the employee as to his conduct after the determination of the employment is more restricted in its scope than that which imposes a general duty of good faith. It is clear that the obligation not to use or disclose information may cover secret processes of manufacture such as chemical formulae . . . or designs or special methods of constructions and other information which is of a sufficiently high degree of confidentiality as to amount to a trade secret.

. . . the obligation does not extend, however, to cover all information which is given to or acquired by the employee while in his employment, and in particular may not cover information which is only "confidential" in the sense that an unauthorised disclosure of such information to a third party while the employment subsisted would be a clear breach of the duty of good faith. . . ." *per* Neill L.J.

Faccenda Chicken Ltd v. Fowler [1986] I.C.R. 297 at 308–309, CA.

To determine whether any particular item of information falls within the implied term so as to prevent its use or disclosure by an employee after his employment has ceased, it is necessary, he said, to consider all the circumstances of the case, and cited a number of matters to which attention must be paid:

(a) The nature of the employment involved: employment where "confidential" material is habitually handled may impose a high obligation of confidentiality because the employee could be expected to realise its sensitive nature to a

[59] [1986] I.C.R. 297, CA.

greater extent than if he were employed in a capacity where such material reaches him only occasionally or incidentally;

(b) The nature of the information itself: information will only be protected if it can properly be classed as a trade secret or as material which, while not properly described as a trade secret is in all the circumstances of such a highly confidential nature as to require the same protection as a trade secret eo nomine;

(c) Whether the employer impressed on the employee the confidentiality of the information, so that the attitude of the employer towards the information would provide evidence which may assist in determining whether or not the information can properly be regarded as a trade secret; and

(d) Whether the relevant information can be easily isolated from other information which the employee is free to use or disclose: this is not to be regarded as conclusive, but the fact that the alleged "confidential" information is part of a package of information and that the remainder of the package is not confidential is likely to "throw light" on whether the information in question is really a trade secret. *per* Neill L.J. in *Faccenda Chicken Ltd v. Fowler* [1986] I.C.R. 297 at 310–311, CA.

The Court of Appeal went on to decide that although there are some circumstances where price information may be confidential in the sense of being a trade secret, for example the price put forward in a tender document, on the facts neither the information about prices, nor the sales information as a whole had the degree of confidentiality necessary to support the case for the employer: it did not amount to a trade secret. The reasoning was:

"(1) The sales information contained some material which the plaintiffs conceded was not confidential if looked at in isolation.

(2) The information about the prices was not clearly severable from the rest of the sales information.

(3) Neither the sales information in general, nor the information about the prices in particular, though of some value to a competitor, could reasonably be regarded as plainly secret or sensitive.

(4) The sales information, including the information about prices, was necessarily acquired by the defendants in order that they could do their work. . . . each salesman could quickly commit the whole of the sales information relating to his own area to memory.

(5) The sales information was generally known among the van drivers who were employees, as were the secretaries, at quite junior level. This was not a case where the relevant information was restricted to senior management or to confidential staff.

(6) There was no evidence that the plaintiffs had ever given any express instructions that the sales information or the information about prices was to be treated as confidential." *per* Neill L.J.

Faccenda Chicken Ltd v. Fowler [1986] I.C.R. 297 at 313, CA.

In the course of employment an employee acquires and builds up a body of knowledge as a result of exposure to situations that arise and developments made, and in *Herbert Morris Ltd v. Saxelby*[60] Lord Parker distinguished this obtaining of skill and knowledge gained by reason of employment and training from personal knowledge of, and acquaintance with, the employer's trade secrets. Likewise in *Faccenda Chicken Ltd v. Fowler* the Court of Appeal sought to draw a distinction between that information which is memorised by exposure and can be utilised by an ex-employee for his or his new employer's benefit, and information which has been written down or copied[61] and secreted away and confidential information amounting to a trade secret, which the court is willing to protect from disclosure or use.

In seeking to distinguish the difference between an employees "stock of knowledge" and confidential information the Court in *Faccenda Chicken* relied on the judgment of Cross J. in *Printers & Finishers Ltd v. Holloway*[62] in which the court refused to grant an injunction to restrain a manager from using information acquired while working for his ex-employer on the basis that it would put the manager in an impossible position in that any restraint imposed by the court would effectively prevent him from practising his trade:

"... one must bear in mind that not all information which is given to a servant in confidence and which it could be a breach of his duty for him to disclose to another person during his employment is a trade secret which he can be prevented from using for his own advantage after the employment is over, even though he has entered into no express covenant with regard to the matter in hand. For example, the printing instructions were handed to Holloway to be used by him during his employment exclusively for the plaintiffs' benefit. It would have been a breach of duty on his part to divulge any of the contents to a stranger while he was employed, but many of these instructions are not really 'trade secrets' at all. Holloway was not, indeed, entitled to take a copy of the instructions away with him; but in so far as the instructions cannot be called 'trade secrets' and he carried them in his head, he is entitled to use them for his own benefit or the benefit of any future employer." *per* Cross J.

Printers & Finishers Ltd v. Holloway [1965] R.P.C. 239 at 253, Ch D.

Here, the court said the information in question was part of the stock of knowledge of the employee and could not be protected after the contract had come to an end in the absence of a restrictive covenant, and in *Thomas Marshall (Exports) Ltd v. Guinle*[63] Sir Robert Megarry V.-C. pointed out that Cross J. in *Holloway* distinguished between the recall of information or skills and the fund of knowledge and experience which the employee might well not realise that it was improper to use and the memorising of a formula or a list of customers, or what was said in confidence at a particular meeting.

So, whilst the courts will not protect post employment information which is part of the acquisition of skill, experience and knowledge built up as part of doing a job, it will do so during employment because such information comes within the duty of fidelity which continues throughout employment. In *Faccenda Chicken* Neill L.J. said of the information in question that: "... it is quite plain that this knowledge was nevertheless 'confidential' in the sense that it would have been a breach of the duty of good faith for

---

[60] [1916] 1 A.C. 688, HL.
[61] *Robb v. Green* [1895] 2 Q.B. 315, CA.
[62] [1964] 3 All E.R. 371, Ch D.
[63] [1979] 1 Ch. 227.

the employee, while the employment subsisted, to have used it for his own purpose or to have disclosed it to a competitor of his employer", nevertheless, it was not confidential in terms of amounting to a trade secret, and therefore could not be protected by the courts, short of a restrictive covenant.

3.1.3.1 *Confidential information as distinguished from trade secret*

There is some debate as to whether information which is merely confidential in that it falls short of being a trade secret, although not protected under the rules regarding confidentiality, can be protected by contractual arrangements between the parties—by a restrictive covenant. In any event, as different rules apply to information which is confidential in the sense that it amounts to a trade secret, as aptly put by Staughton L.J. in *Lansing Linde Ltd v. Kerr*[64] "It appears to me that the problem is one of definition: what are trade secrets, and how do the differ (if at all) from confidential information?" He there accepted the suggestion put forward by counsel for the defendant that "a trade secret is information which, if disclosed to a competitor, would be liable to cause real or significant harm to the owner of the secret". He added, however, that, "It must be information used in a trade or business, and secondly that the owner must limit the dissemination of it or at least not encourage or permit widespread publication." He said that a trade secret "can thus include not only secret formulae for the manufacture of products but also, in an appropriate case, the names of customers and the goods which they buy. . . ."

This is contrary to the Court of Appeal decision in *Faccenda Chicken Ltd v. Fowler*[65] where it was held that names and addresses of customers; routes for deliveries; individual customer's requirements; days of week and times deliveries were made and pricing structures were not the sort of information that fell within the class of confidential information which the employee was obliged not to use or disclose after employment had come to an end. Although the court did go on to say that in certain circumstances information about prices could be invested with a sufficient degree of confidentiality to render it a trade secret, the Court found in *Faccenda* that in any event the information was widely known at a relatively junior level and express instructions as to confidentiality had never been given.

Whilst recognising that "It is far from easy to state in general terms what is confidential information or a trade secret", Sir Robert Megarry V.-C. in *Marshall*,[66] *per curiam*, said of information or secrets in an industrial or trade setting:

> "First, I think that the information must be information the release of which the owner believes would be injurious to him or of advantage to his rivals or others. Second, . . . the owner must believe that the information is confidential or secret, i.e., that it is not already in the public domain. It may be that some or all of his rivals already have the information: but as long as the owner believes it to be confidential I think he is entitled to try and protect it. Third, . . . the owner's belief under the two previous heads must be reasonable. Fourth, I think that the information must be judged in the light of the usage and practices of the particular industry or trade concerned. It may be that information which does not satisfy all these requirements may be entitled to protection as confidential information or trade secrets: but I think that any information which does satisfy

---

[64] [1991] I.C.R. 428, CA.
[65] 1986] I.C.R. 297, CA.
[66] [1979] 1 Ch. 227, HC.

them must be of a type which is entitled to protection." *per* Sir Robert Megarry V.-C.

Thomas Marshall (Exports) Ltd v. Guinle [1979] 1 Ch. 227 at 248, HC.

In *Printers & Finishers Ltd v. Holloway*[67] Cross J. said that it was clearly impossible to define a trade secret and it should perhaps be noted that the courts today take a rather more sceptical view of the employer's judgement of what amounts to confidential information. In *Provident Financial Group plc and Whitegates Estate Agency Ltd v. Hayward*,[68] after noting Lord Denning in *Littlewoods Organisation Ltd v. Harris*[69] that, ". . . it is so difficult to draw the line between information which is confidential and information which is not: and it is very difficult to prove a breach when the information is of such a character that a servant can carry it away in his head", Dillon L.J. said: "But it is very common for employers to have somewhat exaggerated views of what will or may affect their business". However, in *Dawnay, Day & Co. Ltd v. De Braconier d'Alphen*[70] Evans L.J. was prepared to accept, without further comment, the employer's case, which was upheld at first instance, that "rates of differential discounts (as opposed to standard discounts) and the identities of favoured clients who were allowed to have them . . . business plans (in particular, for the new desks or screen systems); and remuneration of individual team leaders and other brokers" was confidential information capable of protection by means, in that case of a restrictive covenant.

The Law Commission in its report on *Breach of Confidence*[71] agreed with Lord Greene in *Saltman Engineering Co. Ltd v. Campbell Engineering Co. Ltd*[72] that "information must have the necessary quality of confidence about it, but also the recipient must have reason to be aware that the information is communicated to him in confidence . . .".

In *Lancashire Fires Ltd v. S A Lyons & Co. Ltd*[73] Sir Thomas Bingham, in a judgment of the Court, held that it is not incumbent upon the employer to point out to his employee the precise limits of that which he seeks to protect as confidential, particularly where it is an integral part of the process and the limits are not easy to draw, even with the assistance of an expert witness. Given his position in the company the test was objective: he must have known that the production process included aspects which were a trade secret. In *Attorney-General v. Guardian Newspapers Ltd (No. 2)*[74] Lord Goff said that although it was necessary for the defendant to have had notice that the information is confidential:

> "I have used the word 'notice' advisedly, in order to avoid the . . . question of the extent to which actual knowledge is necessary; though I of course understand knowledge to include circumstances where the confidant has deliberately closed his eyes to the obvious." *per* Lord Goff.

Attorney-General v. Guardian Newspapers Ltd (No. 2) [1990] 1 A.C. 109 at 281, HL.

[67] [1964] 3 All E.R. 731, HC.
[68] [1989] I.R.L.R. 84, CA.
[69] [1977] 1 W.L.R. 1472, CA.
[70] [1997] I.R.L.R. 442, CA.
[71] Law Commission, 1981.
[72] (1948) 65 R.P.C. 203, CA.
[73] [1997] I.R.L.R. 113, CA.
[74] [1990] 1 A.C. 109, HL.

So that information that initially is confidential can spread to a point whereby the recipient does not know, nor has any reason to believe that it is confidential, although in *Sun Printers v. Westminster Press*[75] it was said that the fact that there were others that knew did not necessarily deprive the information of its confidential character. Nevertheless, there comes a point in the dissemination of information when it can no longer be regarded as confidential and is deemed to be in the public domain. In *Coco v. A. N. Clark (Engineers) Ltd*[76] Megarry J. said, referring to Lord Greene in *Saltman*[77] that,

> "'something which is public property and public knowledge' cannot *per se* provide any foundation for proceedings for breach of confidence. However confidential the circumstances of the communication, there can be no breach of confidence in revealing to others something which is already common knowledge. But this must not be taken too far. Something that has been constructed solely from materials in the public domain may possess the necessary quality of confidentiality: . . ." *per* Megarry J.

Coco v. A. N. Clark (Engineers) Ltd [1969] R.P.C. 41 at 47, HC.

Confidential information may be published by a number of parties but it is only where the publication is by or with the consent of the person to whom the duty is owed that the person who owes the duty of confidentiality is released from that duty. In *Speed Seal Products v. Paddington*,[78] following the filing of an application by the defendant ex-employee for a European patent and publication in their marketing brochures, they sought to have a claim by the employer for injunctive relief struck out on the ground that it was inappropriate because the information was, by that route, already public knowledge. Fox L.J., relying on *O. Mustad & Son v. S. Allcock & Co. Ltd*,[79] confirmed that where publication had been made by or with the consent of the owner of the confidential information, the person owing the duty of confidentiality was released from that duty. However, relying on *Cranleigh Precision Engineering Ltd v. Bryant*[80] and the judgment of Roskill J., Fox L.J. said that the fact that a third party had published the information did not necessarily release the person owing the duty from that duty and the court would act to prevent the person owing the duty from abusing his position, notwithstanding the publication by a third party. Where publication, as here, took place by or with the consent of the person owing the duty, it was held that such a person should be in no better position than if publication had been by a stranger: the court would protect the confidentiality by injunction if restraining further publication would afford the plaintiff real protection and should be slow to conclude that injunctive relief was inappropriate.

3.1.3.2 *The springboard doctrine*

The courts have developed an exception to the principles set out in *Faccenda Chicken* whereby equity will protect, post employment, the use of information by ex-employees which falls short of a trade secret in circumstances where information, such as price

[75] [1982] I.R.L.R. 292, CA.
[76] [1969] R.P.C. 41, HC.
[77] (1948) 65 R.P.C. 203 at 215, CA.
[78] [1986] 1 All E.R. 91, CA.
[79] [1963] 3 All E.R. 416, HL.
[80] [1964] 3 All E.R. 289, HC.

and customer lists has been gained or removed during employment, so that they do not, by the use of that information gain a "head-start" over others entering the market. However, because in doing so the power exists to interfere with the contractual rights of third parties, Lloyd L.J. said in *PSM International plc v. Whitehouse*[81] that "the courts should be chary" of exercising such a power.

This area of the law was explained by Roxburgh J. in *Terrapin Ltd v. Builders' Supply Co.*[82] as follows, which was approved by Roskill J. in *Cranleigh*:

> ". . . the essence of this branch of the law, whatever the origin of it may be, is that a person who has obtained information in confidence is not allowed to use it as a springboard for activities detrimental to the person who made the confidential communication, and springboard it remains even when all the features have been published or can be ascertained by actual inspection by any member of the public . . . the possessor of such communication must be placed under a special disability in the field of compensation in order to ensure that he does not get an unfair start . . ." *per* Roxburgh J.

Terrapin Ltd v. Builders' Supply Co. [1960] R.P.C. 128 at 130, CA.

As pointed out by Lord Denning in *Seager v. Copydex Ltd. (No. 2)*,[83] the law in this area does not depend on any implied contract, it depends on the broad principle of equity that "he who has received information in confidence shall not take unfair advantage of it. He must not make use of it to the prejudice of him who gave it without gaining consent". He should not get a start over others by using such information, or at least without paying for it.

In both *Seager*[84] and *Terrapin*[85] it was held that the information used by the defendant was the springboard which enabled them to devise the particular product. In *Terrapin* this was held to be so even though the plaintiff had published literature and sold equipment incorporating the information, since by using the confidential information the defendant had saved considerable time and expense and had achieved a significant head start over competitors. However, in *Lancashire Fires Ltd v. S A Lyons & Co. Ltd*[85a] the Court of Appeal rejected the finding at first instance that the matter was a "springboard case" giving the ex-employee a head start of a month or two. The court accepted that the information was not public or available from any other source. Therefore it was held that had the ex-employee not acted in breach of his duty of confidentiality he would not have been setting up his rival works at all.

In *Roger Bullivant Ltd v. Ellis*,[86] in allowing the defendants appeal against the granting of an injunction without limit of time, the Court of Appeal confirmed that the purpose of granting relief was to protect the innocent, not to punish the guilty. Accordingly, and relying on Lord Denning in *Potters-Ballotini v. Weston-Baker*[86a] that "a springboard does not last forever", the court placed a limit on the duration of the order preventing an ex-employee from entering into or fulfilling contracts with any

---

[81] [1992] I.R.L.R. 279, CA.
[82] [1960] R.P.C. 128.
[83] [1969] 2 All E.R. 718, CA.
[84] *ibid.*
[85] [1960] R.P.C. 128.
[85a] [1997] I.R.L.R. 113, CA.
[86] [1989] I.C.R. 464, CA.
[86a] [1977] R.P.C. 202, CA.

person whose name and address appeared on the card index system belonging to the plaintiff that the defendant had taken with him when he left employment. In considering how long the advantage derived from what the court termed the "vast quantity of information" that was taken, the court was guided, not only by how long it would have taken to build up the information from scratch, but also by the contract of employment which contained a clause limiting the transacting of any business with any person or company with whom business had been conducted within the previous 12 months. That, said Nourse L.J., provided a clear indication of the period which the plaintiffs themselves regarded as reasonable for the purposes of protecting their business interests.

3.1.3.3   *Protection post-employment of information falling short of a trade secret*

The cases cited throughout this section arise from what Cross J. in *Printers & Finishers Ltd v. Holloway*,[87] identified as a failure by the employer to protect himself by exacting from the employee a restrictive covenant and then seeking to extend the law regarding the protection of confidential information beyond its limits of trade secrets.

This is typically demonstrated in the case of *William Bogan & Co. v. Cove*[88] where the Court of Appeal held that solicitors fall into no special category, and therefore because there was no improper use of information amounting to a trade secret, in the absence of a covenant employees could not be constrained from using their knowledge of the firm and its clients to contact them and seek instructions to further their new business set-up in competition:

> "In my judgment, therefore, the respondent firm has failed to establish the point of law without which its action cannot succeed. In the absence of an express covenant there was no contractual restraint against canvassing or soliciting clients of the respondent firm, and equity does not supply the shortcoming." *per* Leggatt L.J.

William Bogan & Co. v. Cove [1997] I.R.L.R. 453 at 455, CA.

The ex-employees had not stolen lists of names, nor made approaches during their employment and therefore the information, which fell short of a trade secret, as did names and addresses of customers in *Faccenda Chicken*,[89] was not capable of protection in the absence of a restrictive covenant.

3.1.3.4   *Disclosure of information in the public interest*

It is not a breach of duty for an employee to disclose to an appropriate authority any information received in confidence where the disclosure is justified in the public interest—that is in the case of crime or fraud. It would, however, be rare for the information to be of such a nature so as to justify disclosure to the press. In *Initial Services Ltd v. Putteril*[90] it was held that disclosure to a newspaper by an ex-sales-manager of breaches of the Restrictive Trade Practices Act 1956 in the supply of goods by his ex-employer to the public sector, was justifiable even though disclosure was to a newspaper:

---

[87] *op. cit.* n. 67.
[88] [1997] I.R.L.R. 453, CA.
[89] [1986] I.C.R. 297, CA.
[90] [1967] 3 All E.R. 145, CA.

"Weld-Blundell v. Stephens Banks, L.J., rather suggested that the exception was limited to the proposed or contemplated commission of a crime or a civil wrong; but I should have thought that that was too limited. The exception should extend to crimes, frauds and misdeeds, both those actually committed as well as those in contemplation, provided always—and this is essential—that the disclosure is justified in the public interest. The reason is because ([1919] 1 K.B. 520 at 527) 'no private obligations can dispense with that universal one which lies on every member of the society to discover every design which may be formed, contrary to the laws of the society, to destroy the public welfare.' . . . The disclosure must, I should think, be to one who has a proper interest to receive the information. Thus it would be proper to disclose a crime to the police; or a breach of the Restrictive Trade Practices Act, 1956, to the registrar. There may be cases where the misdeed is of such a character that the public interest may demand, or at least excuse, publication on a broader field, even to the press." *per* Lord Denning M.R.

Initial Services Ltd v. Putterill [1967] 3 All E.R. 145 at 148, CA.

In the face of increasing concern, particularly amongst health service and other public sector staff, that speaking out about malpractice or fraud in the workplace leaves them vulnerable to victimisation, there have been several back bench attempts to bring forward legislation to provide protection for employees who disclose information in the public interest. In addition, in both the first and second reports, the Committee on Standards in Public Life[91] recommended the introduction of whistleblowing procedures for employees in various public bodies, including the NHS and education and a private member's Bill, the Public Interest Disclosure Bill, sponsored by Conservative M.P. Richard Shepherd, was introduced in the House of Commons in June 1997, and with Government support appears to be destined to become law.[92]

The enactment of the Human Rights Bill, Schedule 1 of which contains Article 10 on the freedom of expression, will provide judicial access to the jurisprudence of the European Court of Human Rights when considering such matters in domestic courts. Vickers (1997)[93] points out that in 1985 in *Van der Heijden v. The Netherlands*[94] the Commission acknowledged that dismissal for exercising the right to free speech involves restricting and penalising that freedom, and can deter speech as much as total prohibition, but that the Court has been slow to take that view in relation to dismissal. However in 1995 in *Vogt v. Germany*,[95] albeit by 10 votes to nine, it was held that dismissal for expressing freedom of speech was a breach of the Convention right to freedom of speech for a public sector worker.

3.1.3.5 *Summary*

- Whilst in employment the employee owes his employer a duty of fidelity which encompasses a duty of faithful service and confidentiality covering information which includes, but is not limited to, trade secrets;

---

[91] *First Report of the Committee on Standards in Public Life,* Cm. 2850 (1995), Recommendation 53; *Second Report of the Committee on Standards in Public Life: Local Public Spending Bodies,* Cm. 3270 (1996), Recommendation 2.
[92] The Public Interest Disclosure Act 1998 received Royal Assent on July 2, 1998 and is likely to come into effect in early 1999.
[93] pp. 594–602.
[94] No. 11002/84, 41 D.R. 264 (1985).
[95] (1996) 21 E.H.R.R. 205, ECHR.

- Post employment the law will continue to provide protection against the misuse of confidential information gained during employment, but only in so far as it amounts to a trade secret;

- The court will issue an injunction preventing the ex-employee gaining a springboard advantage over others by the use of information gained in breach of their duty. The aim is to protect the employer and therefore is limited in time;

- It is necessary to distinguish trade secrets which the court will protect from stock of knowledge which cannot be protected;

- Information which is merely confidential in general terms—falling short of a trade secret—may only be protected by the courts post employment where the employer has entered into a restrictive covenant with the employee during employment, and then only subject to certain conditions;

- There is no general restriction on an ex-employee canvassing and doing business with the customers of his former employer, or making use of information acquired during employment for his own or for his new employer's benefit.

3.1.4 Restrictive covenants

The method of extending protection of information falling short of a trade secret, or for preventing the employee joining or setting up in competition after employment has ended is by way of a restrictive covenant, entered into either during employment, or upon termination.

In the absence of a restrictive covenant the duty imposed during employment cannot be extended merely by making a lump sum payment of salary. In *J A Mont (U.K.) Ltd v. Mills*[96] it was held that a severance agreement that provided for a year's salary with a condition not to join another company in the same industry within one year of leaving employment was too wide and therefore void. The Court of Appeal rejected the alternative argument that as the employee had received a year's salary he owed a duty of fidelity during that year and could therefore be prevented from working for a competitor in breach of that duty. The Court held that the year could not be equated with "garden leave" because the employee was no longer employed: the duty of fidelity ceased when the contract of employment came to an end.

The principles governing the grant or refusal of an injunction in interlocutory proceedings are those set out by Lord Diplock in *American Cyanamid Co. v. Ethicon Ltd.*[97] In *D v. M*[98] Law J. summarised these:

"The usual rule is that the court should consider whether there is a serious issue to be tried, that is, whether the claim is not frivolous or vexatious . . .; it is not to enter upon the question whether the plaintiff has shown that he will probably succeed, or demonstrated a prima facie case. If there is a serious question to be tried, then the injunction is to be granted or refused according to the court's

[96] [1993] I.R.L.R. 172, CA.
[97] [1975] A.C. 396, HL.
[98] [1996] I.R.L.R. 192, HC.

perception of the balance of convenience. As to that, the order will be refused if it is shown that the plaintiff would be adequately compensated by award of damages; . . . Otherwise the court must balance the need to protect the plaintiff against the injury he may suffer if the order is withheld and yet he succeeds at trial, against the need to protect the defendant from the injury which would be inflicted upon him by grant off the injunction in the event that he defeats the claim at trial." *per* Law J.

D v. M [1996] I.R.L.R. 192 at 195, HC.

This is subject to the exception that the court may properly consider the prospect of the plaintiff succeeding in the action if the grant or refusal of an injunction at the interlocutory stage would in effect dispose of the action.[99] This is demonstrated in *Lansing Linde Ltd v. Kerr*[1] where the Court of Appeal upheld the refusal of an injunction in interlocutory proceedings on the basis that the judge had properly taken into account the prospects of the plaintiff's success in the substantive trial, having regard to the fact that it would not be possible to hold a trial before expiry, or substantial expiry, of the period for which protection was being sought, in this case a year. In doing so the court relied on the judgment of Lord Diplock in *N.W.L. Ltd v. Woods*[2] when he said that a judge ought to "give full weight to all the practical realities of the situation to which the injunction will apply" and that the *American Cyanamid* decision:

> "was not dealing with a case in which the grant or refusal of an injunction at that stage would, in effect, dispose of the action finally in favour of whichever party was successful in the application, because there would be nothing left on which it was in the unsuccessful party's interest to proceed to trial. . . . Cases of this kind are exceptional, but when they do occur they bring into the balance of convenience an important additional element." *per* Lord Diplock.

N.W.L. Ltd v. Woods [1979] I.C.R. 867 at 880, HL.

The general policy of the law towards such clauses was restated in *Credit Suisse Asset Management Ltd v. Armstrong*[3]: that they raise issues of public policy because "The opportunity for an individual to maintain and exercise his skills is a matter of general concern" *per* Neill L.J. The courts have consequently imposed stringent limits on what restraints on competition will be enforced and a restrictive covenant in a contract of employment will be void *ab initio* unless the restraints imposed are reasonable having regard to the interests of the parties and in the public interest.[4] The employer cannot protect himself simply on the ground that competition by an ex-employee will harm his business. Any claim for protection ". . . must be based upon the identification of some advantage or asset inherent in the business which can properly be regarded as, in a general sense, his property, and which it would be unjust to allow the employee to appropriate for his own purposes . . ."[5] and the plaintiff has to satisfy the court that the

---

[99] *Cayne v. Global Natural Resources plc.* [1984] 1 All E.R. 225, CA.
[1] [1991] I.C.R. 428, CA.
[2] [1979] I.C.R. 867, HL.
[3] [1996] I.R.L.R. 450 at 454, CA.
[4] *per* Phillips L.J., *Rock Refrigeration v. Jones* [1997] 1 All E.R. 1, CA.
[5] *per* Lord Wilberforce, *Stenhouse Australia Ltd v. Phillips* [1974] A.C. 391 at 400, PC.

restrictions are "no more than adequate protection to the benefit of the party in whose favour it is imposed".[6] The restraint must therefore be no wider nor greater in duration than is necessary to protect the employer's legitimate proprietary rights.

3.1.4.1   *As between vendors and purchasers*

In considering restrictive covenants as between vendors and purchasers the courts have been more liberal, taking the view that a purchaser is entitled to have the full benefit of what he buys. This is demonstrated in *Alliance Paper Group plc v. Prestwich*[7] where the plaintiff had purchased 75 per cent of the company in which Prestwich was managing director and a major shareholder. As part of the £11.8 million sale Prestwich entered into a non-competition, non-poaching non-soliciting restrictive covenant which the company successfully applied to enforce when Prestwich set up in competition and senior sales people started to defect. The more liberal rules relating to vendors and purchaser can also be seen operating in much more modest situations: in *Systems Reliability Holdings plc v. Smith*[8] there was a restrictive covenant in a share sale agreement for 1.6 per cent share holding owned by Smith, which yielded £247,000. The agreement, which covered a period of 18 months and was on a world-wide basis, was held by the court to be "entirely reasonable" on the basis that this fell to be considered under the rules applicable to vendors despite the small shareholding.

3.1.4.2   *As between employer and employee*

In covenants between master and servant in seeking to ascertain the reasonableness of the restraint the courts will consider the nature of interest sought to be protected— there must be a legitimate interest which must be capable of protection and the area of restraint and the period of restraint must afford no more than adequate protection to the benefit of the party in whose favour it is imposed.

In *Office Angels v. Rainer-Thomas*[9] the legality of a detailed restraint clause was considered where it provided that for six months immediately following termination the employee would not solicit custom or deal with or supply any person or firm who was a client of the company at any time during which the employee was employed by the company, or work for another firm or on his own account in the business of employment agency within a 3,000 metre radius of any branch at which the employee had worked for four weeks or more during the six months before leaving. The company sought an injunction when the ex-employee began work with another agency in circumstances that fell foul of the restraint clause. The Court of Appeal confirmed the position that non-competition clauses are not upheld by the courts unless there is some advantage or asset which can properly be regarded as the employer's property and from which it would be unjust to allow the employee to benefit. It was held that the employer had not shown that the restriction was no wider than was necessary for the protection of their legitimate interests. Whilst the covenant covered some 6,000—7,000 clients and 34 branches, no more than 100 were known to the employee since the vast number of contacts were made and maintained by telephone, which made the clause "irredeemably too wide". The court said of the geographical restriction that "its fire is missing the target" since the majority of client contact was carried out by telephone and therefore the location of the office was of little or no relevance. The

---

[6] *per* Lord Parker, *Herbert Morris Ltd v. Saxelby* [1916] A.C. 688, HL.
[7] [1996] I.R.L.R. 25, HC.
[8] [1990] I.R.L.R. 377, HC.
[9] [1991] I.R.L.R. 214, CA.

Court said that to be acceptable the covenant would have covered those areas which had been allocated to the employee.

3.1.4.3 *Legitimate interest capable of protection*

To be upheld the employer must demonstrate that there is a legitimate interest to protect, and in *Office Angels v. Rainer-Thomas*[10] it was held that the agency's connection with client firms and its pool of temporary labour were a legitimate subject for protection. Likewise, in *Wallace Bogan & Co. Ltd v. Cove*[11] Leggatt L.J. said that both clients and customers form part of an employer's goodwill which the employer is entitled to protect by an express covenant in reasonable restraint of trade.

The question arose in *Dawnay, Day & Co. Ltd v. de Braconier d'Alphen*[12] whether a joint venturer had sufficient interest to be permitted to enforce anti-competition and anti-solicitation covenants against his fellow joint venturer. Evans L.J. surveyed the authorities, including *Esso Petroleum Co. Ltd v. Harper's Garage (Stourport) Ltd*,[13] where Lord Wilberforce said that: "the doctrine of restraint of trade is one to be applied to factual situations with a broad and flexible rule of reason"[14] and concluded that:

> ". . . far from confining the circumstance in which covenants in restraint of trade may be enforced to certain categories of case, and defining those categories strictly, the courts have moved in the opposite direction. The established categories are not rigid, and they are not exclusive. Rather, the covenant may be enforced when the covenantee has a legitimate interest, of whatever kind, to protect, and when the covenant is no wider than is necessary to protect that interest." *per* Evans L.J.

Dawnay, Davy & Co. Ltd v. de Braconier d'Alphen [1997] I.R.L.R. 442 at 446 CA.

So in that case the fact that the plaintiff was neither the purchaser of a business from the defendants, nor their employer, did not mean that the covenants could not be enforced. Their undertaking to contribute the capital for the development of the joint business, and the contribution after it was made, amounting to some £1,165,000, gave them a clear commercial interest in safeguarding themselves against competition from the defendants, and they were entitled to claim protection for that interest. Evans L.J. found persuasive authority in the judgment of Lord Wilberforce in *Stenhouse Ltd v. Phillips*[15]:

> ". . . the employer's claim for protection must be based upon the identification of some advantage or asset inherent in the business which can properly be regarded as, in a general sense, his property, and which it would be unjust to allow the employee to appropriate for his own purposes, even though he, the employee, may have contributed to its creation." *per* Lord Wilberforce.

Stenhouse Australia Ltd v. Phillips [1974] A.C. 391 at 400, PC.

[10] [1991] I.R.L.R. 214, CA.
[11] [1997] I.R.L.R. 453, CA.
[12] [1997] I.R.L.R. 442, CA.
[13] [1968] A.C. 269, HL.
[14] p. 331.
[15] [1974] A.C. 391 at 400, PC.

As to whether an employer has an interest in maintaining a stable, trained workforce and a right to protect it via a non-poaching clause, is something upon which the authorities have varied. In *Ingham v. ABC Contract Services*[16] the Court of Appeal held that a company had "a legitimate interest in maintaining a stable, trained workforce" in what was a highly competitive business. However, in *Hanover Insurance v. Schapiro*[17] an earlier Court of Appeal decision, it was held that although the goodwill of a business may depend on its staff, that does not make the staff an asset of the company "like apples or pears or other stock in trade" and thereby entitle the employer to impose a covenant against competition—a restriction to prohibit a defendant poaching any employee would be invalid as a covenant against competition. Faced with these conflicting authorities, neither of which, as interlocutory judgments, were binding, the Court in *Dawnay*,[18] agreed with the Court in *Ingham* that "an employer's interest in maintaining a stable, trained workforce is one which he can properly protect within the limits of reasonableness by an undertaking of this sort". In the earlier case of *Alliance Paper Group plc v. Prestwich*[19] the High Court likewise followed in decision in *Ingham* and upheld a non-poaching clause covering "staff in a senior capacity" which the court held was not too uncertain since the court could, if required, identify those who fell into the prohibited group.

The plaintiffs in these cases have been concerned to protect themselves from competition, via non-poaching clauses, by senior employees in the highly competitive financial services and insurance sector, and whether such a provision is valid will depend on the facts of each case. This was alluded to in *Dawnay*, by Evans L.J. who said he had: "some reservations as to whether the validity or otherwise of a non-solicitation covenant of this kind should properly be regarded as a question of law".[20] Part of the challenge in that case was that the non-competition clause, drafted as it was to include not only the kind of business being carried on at the time of leaving, but also including other kinds of business which were in an advanced state of preparation, was for that reason wider than necessary to protect the business of the plaintiff and therefore an unlawful restraint of trade. The Court in *Dawnay*,[21] upheld the clause on the basis that new business plans took a considerable time to develop and the defendants were privy to those plans.

3.1.4.4   *Reasonableness of the restraint*

For a restraint clause of whatever type to be considered reasonable and not therefore in restraint of trade, it must afford no more than adequate protection to the party in whose favour it is imposed.[22] An over ambitious restraint, in terms of the subject matter it seeks to protect, the geographical area, the time period, or the interest sought to be protected, will be void and unenforceable as an unreasonable restraint of trade.

In *J.A. Mont (U.K.) Ltd v. Mills*[23] the covenant sought to prevent a member of the senior management team from joining another company in the paper tissue industry for a year. In the Court of Appeal it was held that the restraint was "altogether too

---

[16] (1997) I.R.L.B. 577, September, p. 7, CA.
[17] [1994] I.R.L.R. 82, CA.
[18] [1997] I.R.L.R. 442, CA.
[19] [1996] I.R.L.R. 25, HC.
[20] n. 18 above at 448.
[21] [1997] I.R.L.R. 442, CA.
[22] *Herbert Morris Ltd v. Saxelby* [1916] 1 A.C. 688, HL *per* Lord Parker.
[23] [1993] I.R.L.R. 172, CA.

wide" in that it made no attempt to focus upon the restraint necessary to guard against misuse of confidential information, which was the cause of the employer's concern. It was therefore held to be void as an unlawful restraint of trade. The fact that the employee had received a severance payment covering the 12 months of the restraint period was held to be nothing to the point since "If this were so, such restraints could always be purchased outright" but public policy "clearly has regard . . . to the public interest in competition and in the proper use of an employee's skills".[24]

A longer period of restraint is more likely to be valid with senior employees, or those in possession of long-term plans. For example, in *Lansing Linde Ltd v. Kerr*[25] a restriction sought to prevent the employee working for a competitor for 12 months after he left service. When he left and joined a United Kingdom competitor Lansing Linde applied for an interlocutory injunction to prevent breach of the restrictive covenant. The Court of Appeal held that as a member of the senior management team with access to business and product development plans for the future a restraint for a 12 month period was reasonable, but because Kerr's role was limited to the United Kingdom and Europe a world-wide ban was an unreasonable restraint, and therefore the refusal of an injunction was upheld.

In *Hanover Insurance Brokers Ltd v. Schapiro*[26] the Court of Appeal upheld a restraint preventing senior employees, including those who had held the position of chairman and managing director during the 12 months after the termination of employment, from soliciting customers or clients who were customers or clients during the 12 months immediately preceding the termination of employment. This was interpreted by the Court to be customers of the insurance broking side of the business in which the employees concerned were engaged, as opposed to the other activities of the company. Dillon L.J. distinguished the case from *M & S Drapers v. Reynolds*[27] which concerned a collector-salesman on the basis that:

> "The managing director is not regarded in the same light as the traveller or canvasser. A managing director can look after himself whereas a traveller is not so well placed to do so. The law must protect him." *per* Lord Denning.
>
> *M & S Drapers v. Reynolds* [1957] 1 W.L.R. 9 at 19, CA.

Nevertheless, a wide non-competing restraint against a technician to vehicle dealers and car rental companies who carried out his job after only a six-week training period was upheld in a somewhat surprising decision by the Court of Appeal in *Dentmaster (U.K.) Ltd v. Kent*.[28] A non-competing restraint restricted to the employee's particular area of operation and a non-solicitation covenant which operated throughout England, prohibited the canvassing of business from anyone who was a customer of the plaintiffs during the previous 12 months and also to anyone with whom the defendant had done business at any stage during the entire course of his employment. Counsel for the defendant argued unsuccessfully that in a nation-wide restriction, where the employee is exercising a relatively minor skill that could be readily acquired by others, and a non-solicitation clause without limit in time as to when business contact occurred could not be justified.

---

[24] *per* Simon Brown L.J. at 169.
[25] [1991] I.C.R. 428, CA.
[26] [1994] I.R.L.R. 82, CA.
[27] [1957] 1 W.L.R. 9, CA.
[28] [1997] I.R.L.R. 636, CA.

3.1.4.5   *Validity in the event of employer's breach of contract*

Injunctive relief is an equitable remedy and as such is discretionary and subject to the equitable maxims, and in this situation to successfully enforce a restrictive covenant the employer must not himself be in breach of contract: he must come with clean hands. Therefore, if the employer is himself in breach—for example by giving no notice or less notice than required by the contract—he will not be able to enforce the restrictive covenant.

In a line of cases restrictive covenants expressed to be effective even in the event of the employer's breach, have been held to be unreasonable and therefore unenforceable for that reason. In *Rock Refrigeration v. Jones Seward Refrigeration*[29] on promotion to the position of sales director the employee entered into a contract containing a restrictive covenant expressed to come into effect after the termination of the contract "howsoever arising" or "howsoever occasioned". The plaintiff issued proceedings for damages and injunctive relief when, after giving notice and leaving, the employee went to work for a competitor in breach of the covenant.

In *Briggs v. Oates*[30] the question arose as to whether a solicitor employed under a contract for five years, which contained non-solicitation and non-competition clauses expressed to apply in the event of termination "for whatever reason" was bound by the restraint clause in a situation where the partnership was dissolved before the five year term had expired. Scott J. found that the termination of the partnership arrangement was a repudiation of the contract, that being so, the defendant was entitled to consider himself as constructively dismissed, and consequently the outstanding contractual obligations of the injured party were discharged as a matter of law, the result, said Scott J. did not depend on a construction of the contract. He then went on to say that: "A contract under which an employee could be immediately and wrongfully dismissed, but would nevertheless remain subject to an anti-competitive restraint, seems to me to be grossly unreasonable. I would not be prepared to enforce restraint in such a contract."

In the subsequent Court of Session decision in *Living Design (Home Improvements) Ltd v. Davidson*,[31] in reliance upon the comments of Scott J. in *Briggs v. Oates*,[32] Lord Coulsfield when considering covenants which were to run for six months after the termination of the employee's employment "however that comes about and whether lawful or not" said:

> "In my view, a restrictive covenant which is phrased so as to operate on the termination of the employment of an employee, however that comes about, and whether lawfully or not, is manifestly wholly unreasonable. In that respect, I agree with the observations in *Briggs v. Oates*, . . . Those observations may have been obiter but they seem to me to be clearly correct." *per* Lord Coulsfield.

Living Design (Home Improvements) Ltd v. Davidson [1994] I.R.L.R. 69 at 71, CS.

The result of this decision was that the restraint was, *per se* unenforceable against the employee, regardless of whether the contract was terminated in circumstances where the employer was himself in breach.

---

[29] [1997] 1 All E.R. 1, CA.
[30] [1990] I.R.L.R. 472, HC.
[31] [1994] I.R.L.R. 69, CS.
[32] [1990] I.R.L.R. 472, HC.

In *D v. M*,[33] a non-soliciting and non-competition clauses in a restrictive covenant were expressed to apply in circumstances of a termination "for any reason whatsoever" and "irrespective of the cause or manner" of termination. Relying on the House of Lords decision in *General Bill Posting Co. v. Atkinson*,[34] and after referring to *Living Design*[35] and *Briggs v. Oates*,[36] neither of which Laws J. said were binding upon him, he said:

> ". . . in my judgment the principle enunciated in those decisions is clearly right. A restrictive covenant, having effect after the termination of a contract of service or for services, which on its face applies to the employer's benefit even where the termination has been induced by his own breach is necessarily unreasonable. Such a provision, if given effect, would constitute an evasion to the rule in *General Billposting* [1909] A.C. 118. Indeed, so far as I can see, the only purpose of inserting the material words ('for whatever reason' or 'whether lawful or unlawful' or however otherwise industrial tribunal might be expressed) would be to secure coercive rights to the employer which would survive his own contractual misconduct. I cannot think that that would be reasonable." *per* Laws J.

D v. M [1996] I.R.L.R. 192 at 198, HC.

In the case of *PR Consultants Scotland Ltd v. Mann*,[37] decided before *D v. M* but not cited to Laws J. in that case, the Court of Session, in refusing to grant an injunction, distinguished *Living Design*[38] on the basis that the wording under consideration, "howsoever caused", was not apt to cover unlawful terminations. However, Lord Caplan said: ". . . a provision which provided for the operation of a covenant on a termination of employment however caused, be it lawfully or unlawfully on the part of the employer, would be objectionable".

The Court of Appeal in *Rock Refrigeration*,[39] having reviewed the authorities, held that a restrictive covenant that contained a clause expressing itself valid after termination of the contract "howsoever caused", or other wording which purported to give effect to the restrictive covenant even where the employer was in breach of the contract, was not for that reason invalid and unenforceable, and in doing so overruled *D v. M*[40] as being founded on a misconception of the decision of Scott J. in *Briggs v. Oates*.[41]

The court confirmed the rule set out in *General Billposting*,[42] that as a matter of law, and regardless of the terms of any restrictive covenant, an employee who accepted an employer's repudiation of the contract of employment was not thereafter bound by the restrictions on his activities because as Morritt L.J. said: "covenants, however expressed, cannot achieve the legally impossible". He noted that covenants expressed to apply after termination howsoever termination occurred had only recently been found to be invalid on grounds only of their inclusion and pointed out that there were 12 reported cases between 1964 and 1991, nine of which were decisions of the Court of

[33] [1996] I.R.L.R. 192, HC.
[34] [1909] A.C. 118, HL.
[35] [1994] I.R.L.R. 69, CS.
[36] [1990] I.R.L.R. 472, HC.
[37] [1996] I.R.L.R. 188, CS.
[38] [1994] I.R.L.R. 69, CS.
[39] [1997] 1 All E.R. 1, CA.
[40] [1996] I.R.L.R. 192, HC.
[41] [1990] I.R.L.R. 472, HC.
[42] [1909] A.C. 118, HL.

Appeal, in which "covenants in similar terms were not alleged or found to be invalid on this ground". He pointed out, however, that a restrictive covenant is not invalidated by every breach of contract: the breach must be repudiatory. In this connection Simon Brown L.J. pointed out that any wrongful termination of the contract by the employers will necessarily involve a repudiatory breach.

In *Rock Refrigeration*[43] Simon Brown L.J. said that it was not until "this recent run of cases, erected upon the slender foundation if Scott J.'s *obiter dictum* in *Briggs v. Oates*" that it had been thought that such phrases rendered the covenant unenforceable. The Court held that the decision in *Briggs* was based on the rule in *General Billposting* and it was only on the basis that he was wrong in this conclusion that Scott J. indicated that he would hold void a clause which would otherwise have the effect of imposing restraints after wrongful termination of the defendant's employment. Phillips L.J. said that "This expression of view was thus both hypothetical and *obiter*" and therefore an erroneous basis for the decisions in *Living Design v. Davidson*[44] and *D v. M*.[45]

Although *Rock Refrigeration*[46] clarifies the issue regarding that status of clauses which express themselves to apply regardless of whether the termination is lawful or not: it leaves outstanding one area of uncertainty. This is alluded to in the judgment of Simon Brown L.J. and discussed in the judgment of Phillips L.J.[47] Simon Brown L.J., in overruling *D v. M*, expressed the view that:

> "All this, I should perhaps add, assumes (a) that all restrictive covenants necessarily become unenforceable upon the employee's acceptance of the employer's repudiatory breach—i.e. that the *General Billposting* principle remains wholly unaffected by the *Photo Production Ltd v. Securicor Transport Ltd* [1980] 1 All E.R. 556, [1980] A.C. 827 line of authority." *per* Simon Brown L.J.

Rock Refrigeration Ltd v. Jones [1997] 1 All E.R. 1 at 9, CA.

However, Phillips L.J. expressed his hesitation about basing a general rule on the decision in *General Billposting*. He noted that in *Heyman v. Darwins Ltd*[48] Lord Porter expressed reservations that upon acceptance of the renunciation of a contract, the contract is rescinded. Phillips L.J. said that:

> "The theory that the contract was abrogated upon acceptance of a repudiation, or a fundamental breach, was finally laid to rest by the decision of the House of Lords in *Photo Production Ltd v. Securicor Transport Ltd* where Lord Diplock summarised the effect of accepting a repudiation as follows:
>
> '(a) there is substituted by implication of law for the primary obligations of the party in default which remain unperformed a secondary obligation to pay money compensation to the other party for the loss sustained by him in consequence of their non-performance in the future and (b) the unperformed obligations of the other party are discharged.'" *per* Phillips L.J.

Rock Refrigeration Ltd v. Jones [1997] 1 All E.R. 1 at 19, CA.

[43] [1997] 1 All E.R. 1, CA.
[44] [1994] I.R.L.R. 69, CS.
[45] [1996] I.R.L.R. 192, HC.
[46] [1997] 1 All E.R. 1, CA.
[47] see C. Hill (1997) N.L.J. Practitioner, May 2.
[48] [1942] 1 All ER 337, HL.

Whilst acknowledging that there is no difficulty applying those words to reciprocal positive obligations that arise under a contract of employment, Phillips L.J. said: ". . . there are real difficulties in applying those words to the negative obligations that are placed on an employee by a restrictive covenant in relation to the period after his employment has ceased." In view of this he expressed the view that an application of the principle in *General Billposting*[49] could lead to absurd decisions and that: "I think it at least arguable that, having regard to the subsequent development of this area of the law, not every restrictive covenant will be discharged upon a repudiatory termination of the employment".[50]

3.1.4.6 *Severance*

Restrictive covenants are not as flexible as garden leave clauses in that the courts will not modify the terms and hold the clause valid. A restrictive covenant is held to be reasonable and therefore enforceable, or otherwise unenforceable. However, as Lord Coulsfield observed in *Living Design*[51] ". . . the Court can sever the unreasonable part of a restriction, where that can be done simply b(y) deletion of the offending part, without in consequence rewriting the contract or altering its scope; . . . the Court should not strike out words where to do so would alter the scope and intention to the agreement". He also approved to the observations of Lord Moulton in *Mason v. Provident Clothing Co.*[52] that in the case of a covenant by an employee, there should be severance only if the enforceable part is clearly severable, and even so only where it is of trivial importance or technical and not part of the main import and substance of the clause.

In *Attwood v. Lamont*[53] Lord Sterndale M.R. said: ". . . a contract can be severed if the severed parts are independent of one another and can be severed without the severance affecting the meaning of the part remaining. . . . This is sometimes expressed . . . by saying that the severance can be effected when the part severed can be removed by running a blue pencil through it".[54]

In *Living Design*[55] the contract contained a clause, "the restrictions . . . are considered reasonable by the employee but in the event that any such restriction shall be found to be void but would be valid if some part thereof would be deleted or the period or area of application reduced, such restriction shall apply with such modification as may be necessary to make it valid and effective." The court said that as they had power to sever the unreasonable part of a restriction it was doubtful whether a clause such as this enabled the court to do anything more than it could do in any event. However, it was held that it was "very doubtful whether the offending part of the clause could be said not to be part of its main import and substances, and it is certainly not trivial." Therefore, despite the elaborate contractual provisions designed to cover all eventualities, the court refused to grant the injunction sought.

Sumption Q.C. sitting as a deputy High Court Judge in *Marshall v. N. M. Financial Management Ltd*[56] held that to determine whether a clause in unlawful restraint of

---

[49] [1909] A.C. 118, HL.
[50] See further M. Jefferson (1997) *"Restraint of trade: dismissal and drafting"*, I.L.J. (1997) 26 62–68 at 66.
[51] [1994] I.R.L.R. 69 at 71, CS.
[52] [1913] A.C. 724, HL.
[53] [1920] 3 K.B. 571, CA.
[54] *ibid.* 577.
[55] [1994] I.R.L.R. 69, CS.
[56] [1996] I.R.L.R. 20, HC.

trade could be severed and the remainder of the clause enforced, he would adopt the three conditions of severance set out in *Sadler v. Imperial Life Assurance Co. of Canada Ltd*[57] namely:

(1) The unenforceable provision is capable of being removed without the necessity of adding to or modifying the wording of what remains—the "blue pencil test";

(2) The remaining terms continue to be supported by adequate consideration;

(3) The removal of the unenforceable provision does not so change the character of the contract that it becomes "not the sort of contract that the parties entered into at all".

The second and third test, he said, had their principle modern authority in *Chemidu Wavin Ltd v. Societe por la Transformation et L'Exploitation des Resines Industrielles SA*,[58] and he said that he would add a fourth condition:

(4) That the severance must be consistent with the public policy underlying the avoidance of the offending part.

3.1.4.7 *Summary*

This section has explained the implied duties on the employee both during employment and that continue to flow after termination in so far as confidential information is concerned and the chart on pp. 126–127 summarises these in the categories during and post-employment. Post termination the continuing duty, which derives from the duty of fidelity, extends only in so far as trade secrets are concerned.

An employer can, however, seek to protect a wider range of information and processes and prevent competition by entering into a "garden leave" clause or a restrictive covenant: a restrictive covenant is an unlawful restraint of trade unless it can be shown that:

- there is an interest that needs protection;
- the person seeking the injunction has an interest to protect; and
- the means chosen to do so is reasonable.

The courts may sever an offending part of a covenant utilising the "blue-pencil test" leaving the remainder of the covenant enforceable providing it does not thereby become a different sort of contract and does not offend against public policy.

Where the contract is repudiated in circumstances where the innocent party accepts the repudiation, the restrictive covenant may not be enforceable against him. That the covenant contains a clause to the contrary does not render the restraint void for that reason.

---

[57] [1988] I.R.L.R. 388, HC.
[58] [1978] 3 C.M.L.R. 514, CA.

3.1.5 Health and safety

At common law there is an implied term that an employee owes his employer a duty to use reasonable care in relation to the carrying out of his job.[59] In the event of damage being caused to a third party whilst acting in the course of his employment, the employer may be vicariously liable for any liability that results. In the much criticised case of *Lister v. Romford Ice and Cold Storage Co. Ltd*[60] the House of Lords held that the employer's insurers were entitled to an indemnity against the employee as a result of the employer becoming vicariously liable for damages resulting from the employee's negligence. An inter-departmental committee was set up to investigate the position and recommended that trade unions might, by collective bargaining, seek insurance cover for their members, but this does not appear to have happened to any significant extent. In *Jones v. Manchester Corporation*[61] it was held that an employer cannot have a right of indemnity if he himself has contributed to the damage or bears some responsibility. In addition, in *Morris v. Ford Motor Co. Ltd*[62] the Court of Appeal held that, in an industrial setting subrogation was unacceptable and unrealistic and that there was an implied term that this right was excluded.

The Health and Safety at Work etc. Act 1974 and regulations now imposes a whole range of duties both on the employee and the employer and there is a duty on employees to act safely while at work and to inform their employer of unsafe situations at their workplace. These may be summarised:

- The Health and Safety at Work etc. Act 1974, s.7(a) and (b) places a duty on employees while at work to take reasonable care for his own health and safety and for that of others who may be affected by his acts or omissions at work and to co-operate with his employer in so far as the exercise of any duties or requirements placed on him under any relevant statutory provisions is concerned.

- By section 8, a general duty is imposed in that no person shall intentionally or recklessly interfere with or misuse anything provided in the interests of health, safety or welfare.

- By the Management of Health and Safety at Work Regulations 1992[63], reg. 12, a duty is imposed on every employee to use anything provided by his employers (under their statutory duties) in accordance with training and instructions and to inform the employers of any work situation representing a serious and imminent danger to health and safety, and of any shortcomings in the employer's protection arrangements.

- By the Personal Protective Equipment at Work Regulations 1992,[64] regs 10 and 11, a duty is imposed to use personal protective equipment provided, in accordance with training and instructions, to take all reasonable steps to return it, and to report forthwith any loss of or obvious defect in it.

[59] *Harmer v. Cornelius* (1858) 5 C.B.N.S. 236 at 346, *per* Willes J.
[60] [1957] 1 All E.R. 125, HL.
[61] [1952] 2 All E.R. 125, CA.
[62] [1973] Q.B. 792, CA.
[63] S.I. 1992 No. 2051.
[64] S.I. 1992 No. 2966.

Summary - Duties relating to Confidential Information

During Employment	Post Employment	
Duty of Fidelity	Ongoing Duties	Agreement Between Parties
During employment employee owes employer an implied duty of fidelity which includes: • good faith • confidentiality and any duty of express confidentiality agreed between parties DUTY OF FIDELITY Includes duty of loyal service and confidentiality in the general sense. Senior employees may be obliged to disclose misconduct of fellow employees: • *Sybron Corp. v. Rochem Ltd* • *Swain v. West (Butchers) Ltd* Encompasses duty of loyalty and good faith: • *Ticehurst v. British Telecommunications* Must not enter into competition: • *Robb v. Green* • *Sanders v. Parry* • *Wessex Dairies Ltd v. Smith* • *Adamson v. B&L Cleaning Services* • *Marshall v. Industrial Systems & Control* but see • *Laughton and Hawley v. Bapp Industrial Supplies Ltd* Spare time working may be a breach of duty of fidelity or of express term • *Thomas Marshall v. Quinle* • *Hivac v. Park Royal Scientific Instruments Ltd* but • *Nova Plastics Ltd v. Froggett*	Confidential Information amounting to trade secret protected as ongoing incident of the contract even after the contract comes to an end. ONGOING DUTIES Mere confidential information cannot be protected after employment relationship, and therefore duty of fidelity comes to and end. • *Faccenda Chicken Ltd v. Fowler* • *Wallace Bogan & Co. Ltd v. Cove* Information must have the quality of a trade secret in order to attract protection post employment • *Lansing Linde Ltd v. Kerr* Trade secret must be distinguished from stock of knowledge which employee is entitled to use for his own or new employer's benefit • *Printers & Finshers v. Holloway* • *Herbert Morris Ltd v. Saxleby* Information must have necessary quality of confidentiality about it, but not for the employer to point out precise limits of that which he seeks to protect as confidential • *Lancashire Fires Ltd v. SA Lyons* Information in the public domain cannot be confidential • *Coco v. AN Clark (Engineers) Ltd*	By means of a restrictive covenant agreed during employment ermployer may protect himself post employment. Restriction may be: • non-dealing restraint • non-solicitation restraint • non-competition clause or a combination of these. AGREEMENT BETWEEN THE PARTIES restrictive covenant will only be upheld as a matter of public policy, if no wider nor greater in duration than is necessary to protect the employer's legitimate proprietary rights. • *Nordenfelt v. Maxim Nordenfelt Guns & Ammunition Co. Per Lord MacNaghten.* Otherwise unlawful restraint of trade and void *ab initio.* Must be legitimate interest capable of protection Clients and customers • *Wallace Brogan & Co. Ltd v. Cove* Joint venture • *Dawnay Day & Co. Ltd v. de Braconier d'Alphen* Stable trained workforce • *Ingham v. ABC Contract Services* • *Alliance Paper Group plc v. Prestwich*

Summary - Duties relating to Confidential Information—continued

During Employment	Post Employment	Agreement Between Parties
Duty of Fidelity	*Ongoing Duties*	*Agreement Between Parties*
Garden Leave • *Evening Standard Co. Ltd v. Henderson* • *Provident Group plc v. Hayward* • *GFI Group Inc v. Eaglestone* • *Eurobrokers Ltd v. Rabey* • *Credit Suisse Asset management v. Armstrong* But note • *William Hill Organisation Ltd v. Tucker, per Morritt L.J. (obiter)* Confidentiality • *Bents Brewery v. Hogan* Confidential Information held by employer qua employer likewise subject to rule • *Dalgleish v. Lothian & Borders Police* Once employment comes to an end so does duty of loyalty and confidentiality • *J A Mont (U.K.) Ltd v. Mills* All that remains, short of contractual protection via restrictive covenant, is residual duty of confidentiality in respect of trade secrets • *Wallace Bogan & Co. Ltd v. Cove*	But the fact that disclosure made by third party or defendant himself does not release person owing the duty from that duty • *Cranleigh Precision Engineering Ltd v. Bryant* • *Speed Seal Products v. Paddington* Spring Board Doctrine • *Terrapin Ltd v. Builders' Supply Co.* • *Seager v. Copydex Ltd (No2)* Limited in Time • *Roger Bullivant Ltd v. Ellis*	Unreasonably wide restraint void • *Office Angels Ltd v. Rainer-Thomas* Whilst 12 month restriction reasonable for senior manager, world wide ban not justified as activities limited to U.K. • *Lansing Linde v. Kerr* but in light of increasing international natue of business that not limited to U.K., may not render restriction unresonable. Any part of the U.K. unreasonable when activities limited to South of England and Midlands • *Greer v. Sketchley* In the event of employers breach of contract • *General Billposting Co. Ltd v. Atkinson* • *Briggs v. Oates* now see • *Rock Refrigeration v. Jones* As between vendor and purchaser • *Alliance Paper Group plc v. Prestwich* • *Systems Reliability Holdings plc v. Smith*

- By the Manual Handling Operations Regulations 1992,[65] reg. 5, to make full and proper use of any system for manual handling provided by the employers.[66]

3.2   MUTUAL DUTIES

3.2.1   Duty to maintain the trust and confidence

The duty of trust and confidence includes a duty on the parties to treat each other with respect and civility and not to behave in an unreasonable way. This appears to be unremarkable except that it has to be reconciled with the history of the employment relationship as being categorised as one of subordination expressed in terms of master/servant, of a duty of obedience and fidelity and with a duty not to frustrate the employer's commercial objectives, as demonstrated in *Secretary of State for Employment v. ASLEF (No. 2)*,[67] *Cresswell v. Board of Inland Revenue*[68] and in *Woods v. W.M. Car Services (Peterborough) Ltd*,[69] where the tension is demonstrated: Watkins L.J. giving one of the reasons for dismissing the employee's appeal said:

> "The obdurate refusal of the employee to accept conditions very properly and sensibly being sought to be imposed upon her was unreasonable. Employers must not, in my opinion, be put in a position where, through the wrongful refusal of their employees to accept change, they are prevented from introducing improved business methods in furtherance of seeking success for their enterprise." *per* Watkins L.J.

Woods v. W.M. Car Services (Peterborough) Ltd [1982] I.R.L.R. 413 at 416, CA.

Lord Denning, in likewise dismissing the appeal, nevertheless, said that the modern approach was:

> "It is the duty of the employer to be good and considerate to his servants. Sometimes it is formulated as an implied term not to do anything likely to destroy the relationship of confidence between them: see *Courtaulds Northern Textiles Ltd v. Andrew* [1979] I.R.L.R. 84. But I prefer to look at it this way: the employer must be good and considerate to his servants. Just as a servant must be good and faithful, so an employer must be good and considerate. Just as in the old days an employee could be guilty of misconduct justifying his dismissal, so in modern times an employer can be guilty of misconduct justifying the employee in leaving at once without notice." *per* Lord Denning M.R.

Woods v. W.M. Car Services (Peterborough) Ltd [1982] I.R.L.R. 413 at 415, CA.

Recent emphasis, through a series of House of Lords cases, *Scally v. Southern Health and Social Services Board*,[70] *Imperial Group Pension Trust Ltd v. Imperial Tobacco*

---

[65] S.I. 1992 No. 2793.
[66] See generally Smith and Wood (1996), pp. 652–669.
[67] [1972] 2 Q.B. 455, CA.
[68] [1984] I.R.L.R. 190, CA.
[69] [1982] I.R.L.R. 413, CA.
[70] [1991] 4 All E.R. 563, HL.

Ltd,[71] *Spring v. Guardian Assurance*[72] and *Malik v. BCCI SA plc*[73] have given prominence to this implied and mutual duty of trust and confidence. In *Malik v. BCCI SA*[74] Lord Steyn said of the duty:

"It is expressed to impose an obligation that the employer shall not 'without reasonable and proper cause, conduct itself in a manner calculated and likely to destroy or seriously damage the relationship of confidence and trust between employer and employee.' . . . The evolution of the term is a comparatively recent development. The obligation probably has its origins in the general duty of co-operation between the contracting parties. . . . The reason for this development is part of the history of the development of employment law in this century. The notion of a 'master and servant' relationship became obsolete. . . . It was the change in legal culture which made possible the evolution of the implied term of trust and confidence. . . . It is true that the implied term adds little to the employee's implied obligations to serve his employer loyally and not to act contrary to his employer's interests. . . ." *per* Lord Steyn.

Malik v. BCCI SA [1997] 3 All E.R. 1 at 15, HL.

The evolution of the implied terms and responsibilities of the parties to the employment contract have, as noted by Lord Slynn in *Spring*, involved the imposition of far greater duties being imposed on the employer, and the cases stress the importance of the impact of the employer's behaviour on an incident by incident basis where these are brought within the rubric of trust and confidence.

In *BAC v. Austin*[75] Phillips J. said of a failure to respond to repeated requests for safety equipment, that it amounted to unreasonable behaviour and lack of co-operation by the employer which was a breach of the implied duty to maintain trust and confidence. The behaviour in question was a conversation in which "there was a certain amount of provocative observation on both sides" amounting to unjustified criticism which was held to be a form of abuse. The effect of unjustified criticism upon the contractual relationship was explained by Arnold J. in *Courtaulds v. Andrews*[76]:

"Here is a man, a sensible man, with a long record of satisfactory work in a supervisory capacity whose immediate superior in the management ladder thinks that he is a good workman and thinks he can do the job properly. Nevertheless, . . . that manager says to him 'You can't do the bloody job'. Now it seems to us that, in those particular circumstances, that is conduct which is likely to destroy the trust relationship which, in the circumstances, is a necessary element in the relationship between this supervisory employee and his employers." *per* Arnold J.

Courtaulds v. Andrews [1979] I.R.L.R. 84 at 86, EAT.

Being a fundamental term of the contract it is possible that in the event of a breach an employee may terminate his own contract and claim to have been constructively

---

[71] [1991] 2 All E.R. 597, HL.
[72] [1994] 3 All E.R. 129, HL.
[73] [1997] 3 All E.R. 1, HL.
[74] *ibid.*
[75] [1978] I.R.L.R. 332, EAT.
[76] [1979] I.R.L.R. 84, EAT.

dismissed within ERA 1996, s.95(1)(c). This was explained by Kilner Brown J. in *Robinson v. Crompton Parkinson Ltd*[77] where it was held that an employer had breached his duty by acting hastily and unfairly in accusing an employee of theft and calling in the police in a situation where insufficient evidence existed. As no apology was forthcoming his fellow workmates assumed that he was guilty:

"In a contract of employment, and in conditions of employment, there has to be mutual trust and confidence between master and servant. Although most of the reported cases deal with the master seeking (a) remedy against a servant or former servant for acting in breach of confidence or in breach of trust, that action can only be upon the basis that trust and confidence is mutual. Consequently where a man says of his employer, 'I claim that you have broken your contract because you have clearly shown you have no confidence in me, and you have behaved in a way which is contrary to that mutual trust which ought to exist between master and servant,' is entitled in those circumstances, it seems to us, to say that there is conduct which amounts to a repudiation of the contract." *per* Kilner Brown J.

Robinson v. Crompton Parkinson Ltd [1978] I.R.L.R. 61 at 62, EAT.

In *Robinson* the EAT relied on an earlier decision of *Fyfe & McGrouther Ltd v. Byrne*[78] where Lord McDonald said:

". . . the Industrial Tribunal were justified in deciding that the respondent had terminated his contract of employment and that the circumstances were such that he was entitled to terminate it without notice by reason of the appellant's conduct. They had indicated in the clearest terms that they no longer had any confidence in him or his honesty and it is not unreasonable that he should consider that by adopting this attitude in a situation for which he was not responsible they had destroyed any basis of confidence that could ever exist between them and him in the future. This therefore is, in our view, a proper case of constructive dismissal. . ." *per* Lord McDonald

Fyfe & McGrouther Ltd v. Byrne [1977] I.R.L.R. 26 at 30, EAT.

In *Lewis v. Motorworld*[79] the Court of Appeal held that in assessing whether the employer's behaviour amounted to a breach of the implied term of mutual trust and confidence, incidents other than the final one should be taken into consideration, even if the employee had failed to treat that earlier behaviour as repudiatory. The Court also confirmed that the behaviour had to be viewed objectively: the employer's intention not being relevant.

Brodie (1996) calls attention to the fact that the major importance of the implied duty of trust and confidence lies in its impact on the obligations of the employer: it is apt to cover the great diversity of situations in which a balance has to be struck between an employer's interest in managing his business as he sees fit and the employee's interest in not being unfairly and improperly exploited. This can be demonstrated by the diversity of situations which the House of Lords has held can

---

[77] [1978] I.R.L.R. 61, EAT.
[78] [1977] I.R.L.R. 26, EAT.
[79] [1985] I.R.L.R. 465, CA.

amount to a breach of trust and confidence. In the *Imperial Group Pension Trust* case[80] it was held that an employer's right under the pension fund rules to give or withhold its consent to increases in pension benefits was subject to the obligation of good faith—that the employer would not, without reasonable and proper cause, conduct themselves in a manner calculated or likely to destroy or seriously damage the relationship of confidence and trust between the parties.

In *Malik*[81] the employer's business collapsed as a result of a massive fraud which was perpetrated by those controlling the bank. The applicants were made redundant by the liquidators and found difficulty in getting further employment in the banking field because of the stigma emanating from their association with the collapsed bank, even though they were unaware of and had no part in the fraud. On their application for stigma compensation the House of Lords held that the employer owed a duty that he would not, without reasonable and proper cause destroy or seriously damage the relationship of confidence and trust between employer and employee.

Although there is no general duty on employers to exercise their contractual powers reasonably or in accordance with the rules of natural justice, as confirmed in *McLory v. Post Office*,[82] the High Court also held that the employer could only exercise his contractual right of suspension on reasonable grounds and could only continue the suspension for as long as there were reasonable grounds for doing so. However, in *White v. Reflecting Roadstuds*[83] Wood J., in discussing *United Bank Ltd v. Akhtar*,[84] said that:

> "This case must be examined with care. It is too broad an understanding of the words of Mr. Justice Knox (in *Akhtar*) to say that the implied term was that the employer should act reasonably. We do not so understand him and indeed, so to find would fly in the face of authority of *Western Excavating* ([1978] I.R.L.R. 27) . . . itself. It would be to reintroduce the reasonableness test by the back door. The term found to be implied by Mr. Justice Knox and those sitting with him was that the employer when dealing with a mobility clause in a contract of employment should not exercise his discretion in such a way as to prevent his employee from being able to carry out his part of the contract. This is a very different consideration." *per* Wood J. (President).

White v. Reflecting Roadstuds [1991] I.R.L.R. 331 at 335, EAT.

It should be noted that in *Spring v. Guardian Assurance plc*[85] it was held by the House of Lords that an employer who undertakes to give a reference is under a duty not to act unreasonably or carelessly in providing it. Although this case was decided as a duty of care in tort, Lord Goff said that: "Where the relationship between the parties is that of employer and employee, the duty of care could be expressed as arising from an implied term of the contract of employment".

It could be argued that for the employer to behave in an unreasonable way, without reasonable and proper cause, is to destroy or seriously damage the relationship of confidence and trust between employer and employee as explained in *Malik,* and that

---

[80] [1991] 2 All E.R. 597, HL.
[81] [1997] 3 All E.R. 1, HL.
[82] [1993] I.C.R. 758, HC.
[83] [1991] I.R.L.R. 331, EAT.
[84] [1989] I.R.L.R. 507, EAT.
[85] [1994] 3 All E.R. 129, HL

therefore an expansion of the duty of trust and confidence has introduced the obligation on the employer to behave reasonably and thereby brings common law terms into line with the test applied under ERA 1996, s.98(4): the test for deciding whether the dismissal was fair or unfair, and in this respect Brodie (1996) argues that: "a doctrine of mutual trust and confidence informed by procedural standards does not impinge on 'good" employers at all". Hepple (1981)[86] has observed that:

> "The need to base decisions relating to 'constructive' dismissal on the breach of a fundamental term by the employer, has led the tribunals to imply terms of this kind in situations where the employer's conduct might otherwise have been described as 'unreasonable,' although the E.A.T. has been careful to stress that there is not an implied term that an employee will be treated in a reasonable manner, only a term that the employer will not act in a way that, judged reasonably and sensibly, destroys mutual trust and confidence."

3.3   DUTIES OWED BY THE EMPLOYER

3.3.1   Welfare and health and safety

It is implied into every contract of employment, extending beyond the mutual duty of trust and confidence, that the employer will take all reasonable care of the welfare and health and safety of his employees. The employer's duties were stated by Lord Wright to be threefold:

> ". . . the provision of a competent staff of men, adequate material and a proper system and effective supervision . . ." *per* Lord Wright.

Wilsons & Clyde Coal Co. Ltd v. English [1938] A.C. 57 at 78.

Lord Wright was here relying on authorities going back to the nineteenth century. Today, both by case law development and by primary and secondary legislation an employer's duties towards his workers with regard to welfare and health and safety have considerably increased.

This increase can perhaps be traced to the report of the Robens Committee[87] which was set up in 1970 to review the whole area of occupational health and safety. Its report, published in 1972,[88] identified that health and safety legislation was badly structured, too complex and was fragmented, with responsibility being split between a number of government departments with little or no co-ordination. The key proposal was for a major new statute setting out general principles, with individual and detailed dangers being dealt with by delegated legislation.

3.3.1.1   *Health and Safety at Work etc. Act 1974*

The Health and Safety at Work etc. Act 1974, which resulted from the recommendations of the Robens Committee, creates enabling powers and sets up an administrative system through the Health and Safety Commission and Executive which have power to

---

[86] Hepple (1981), para. 292, p. 135.
[87] Cmnd. 5034.
[88] *Report of the Committee on Safety and Health at Work*, Cmnd. 5034 (1972).

do anything which is calculated to facilitate, or is conducive or incidental to the performance of any of the functions of either body.

Section 2 of the Act provides that the employer has a duty to ensure, so far as is reasonably practicable, the health, safety and welfare at work of all his employees:

". . . the matters to which that duty extends include in particular—

(a) the provision and maintenance of plant and systems of work that are, so far as is reasonably practicable, safe and without risks to health;

(b) arrangements for ensuring, so far as is reasonably practicable, safety and absence of risks to health in connection with the use, handling, storage and transport of articles and substances;

(c) the provision of such information, instruction, training and supervision as is necessary to ensure, so far as is reasonably practicable, the health and safety at work of his employees;

(d) so far as is reasonably practicable as regards any place of work under the employer's control, the maintenance of it in a condition that is safe and without risks to health and the provision and maintenance of means of access to and egress from it that are safe and without such risks;

(e) the provision and maintenance of a working environment for his employees that is, so far as is reasonably practicable, safe, without risks to health, and adequate as regards facilities and arrangements for their welfare at work."

Health and Safety at Work etc. Act 1974, s.2(2).

By section 2(3) the employer has a duty to prepare, and revise as often as may be appropriate, a written statement of his general policy with respect to the health and safety at work of his employees and the organisation and arrangements for carrying out that policy, and to bring the statement and any revision of it to the notice of all his employees.

The Health and Safety at Work etc. Act 1974, s.3(1), imposes duties on an employer in connection with persons other than their employees: an employer is required to conduct his undertaking in such a way as to ensure, so far as is reasonably practicable, that persons not in his employment who may be affected are not exposed to risks to their health and safety. In *R. v. Associated Octel Ltd*[89] it was held that the employer was liable under section 3(1) for injuries suffered by the employee of an independent contractor during maintenance and repair work being carried out to a chlorine tank at the appellants' chemical plant. Whilst the contractor's employee was inside the tank a light bulb broke and the electric current caused the acetone vapour to ignite, causing a flash fire and explosion in which he was badly injured. The question arose as to whether the activity in question amounted to the employer's *conduct of his undertaking* within section 3(1). The House of Lords held that anything which constitutes the running of a plant is part of the conduct of the employer's undertaking and ancillary activities carried out by independent contractors may form part of the employer's undertaking but will not always do so. Here the activity was integrated with the general conduct of the business, and as such was held to be part of the employer's undertaking.

Directive 89/391 on the introduction of measures to encourage improvements in the safety and health of workers at work, the Framework Directive, contains general

[89] [1997] I.R.L.R. 123, HL.

principles concerning the prevention of occupational risks, the protection of safety and health, the elimination of risk and accident factors, the informing, consultation, balanced participation and training of workers and their representatives. Article 16 of the Directive provides that individual Directives shall be adopted by the Council in the areas listed in the Annex. This was one of the first of six Directives to be adopted under the Article 118a procedure which resulted in the "British Six Pack", made in 1992, all of which came into effect on January 1, 1993: all six sets of regulations have in common that they apply to most workplaces and they impose upon employers the duty to assess and respond to risks. They also stress the need to train and inform workers.

(i) The Management of Health and Safety at Work Regulations 1992[90] were made to implement the framework Directive 89/391 on the *introduction of measures to encourage improvements in the safety and health of workers at work*. Regulations 13A, 13B and 13C were introduced by the Health and Safety at Work (Amendment) Regulations 1994[91] in order to implement provisions of Directive 92/85 on the *introduction of measures to encourage improvements in the safety and health of pregnant workers and workers who have recently given birth or are breastfeeding*, other parts of which are now contained in ERA 1996.

(ii) The Workplace (Health, Safety and Welfare) Regulations 1992[92] which specifically cover offices, require employers to conform to minimum standards of structural safety, hygiene and welfare within the workplace, requiring employers to ensure that workplaces, equipment and devices are maintained in efficient working order and in a good state of repair. Employers should ensure that it is possible to carry out work safely and comfortably at workstations, and that frequently used equipment is within easy reach. Access to workstations and seating should be adapted for disabled workers if necessary. Made to implement Directive 89/654 *concerning the minimum safety and health requirements for the workplace* which was the first Directive to be made under the Framework Directive.

(iii) The Provision and Use of Work Equipment Regulations 1992[93] made to implement Directive 89/655 *concerning the minimum safety and health requirements for the use of work equipment by workers at work*, the second individual Directive within the meaning of Article 16(1) of Directive 89/391, which requires employers to take the measures necessary to ensure that the work equipment made available to workers is suitable for the work to be carried out or properly adapted for that purpose and may be used by workers without impairment to their safety or health.

(iv) The Personal Protective Equipment at Work Regulations 1992[94] made to implement Directive 89/656 on the *minimum health and safety requirements for the use by workers of personal protective equipment at the workplace*, the third individual Directive.

[90] S.I. 1992 No. 2051.
[91] S.I. 1994 No. 2865.
[92] S.I. 1992 No. 3004.
[93] S.I. 1992 No. 2932.
[94] S.I. 1992 No. 2966.

(v) The Manual Handling Operations Regulations 1992[95] made to implement Directive 90/269 on the *minimum health and safety requirements for the manual handling of loads where there is a risk particularly of back injury to workers*, the fourth individual Directive within the meaning of Article 16(1) of Directive 89/391, which requires employers to take appropriate organisational measures, or use appropriate means, in particular mechanical equipment, in order to avoid the need for the manual handling of loads by workers, or to use appropriate means to reduce the risk involved in the manual handling of such loads where the need for manual handling cannot be avoided.

(vi) The Health and Safety (Display Screen Equipment) Regulations 1992[96] made to implement Directive 90/270 on the *minimum safety and health requirements for work with display screen equipment*, the fifth individual Directive within the meaning of Article 16(1) of Directive 89/391. The regulation lays down minimum safety and health requirements for work with display screen equipment and places an obligation on employers to assess and review health and safety risks to persons using VDU workstations.

In addition, the Health and Safety (Young Persons) Regulations 1997[97] (discussed in para. 1.5 above) places particular responsibility on employers with regard to young workers, 16- and 17–year-olds.

In the event of a breach of duty under the Health and Safety at Work etc. Act 1974, criminal proceedings may be brought by inspectors, with the consent of the Director of Public Prosecutions, under powers contained in the 1974 Act,[98] or by the Procurator Fiscal in Scotland, or enforced by local authorities under regulations.[99] Inspectors appointed under the 1974 Act have wide powers to enter premises and to carry out examinations and inspections and to issue improvement and prohibition notices, failure to comply with which is a criminal offence.

3.3.1.2 *Implied terms under the contract of employment*

It is implied into every contract of employment that the employer will exercise all due skill and take reasonable care for the welfare of his employees. This covers physical and mental health, machinery and equipment as well as working environment and it was noted by Lord Slynn in *Spring v. Guardian Royal Exchange*,[1] that changes in the burden on the employer in so far as his duties to his employees are concerned, now involve duties to care not only for the physical health of his employees, but also for their financial and even psychological welfare.[2]

In *Waltons & Morse v. Dorrington*[3] it was held that there is an implied term in contracts of employment that the employer will provide and monitor for employees, so far as is reasonably practical, a working environment which is reasonably suitable for the performance by them of their contractual duties. The employee had a right not to be required to sit in a smoke-filled atmosphere, even though such an environment

---

[95] S.I. 1992 No. 2793.
[96] S.I. 1992 No. 2792.
[97] S.I. 1997 No. 135.
[98] s.38.
[99] Health and Safety (Enforcing Authority) Regulations 1989 (S.I. 1989 No. 1903).
[1] [1994] 3 All E.R. 129, HL.
[2] *ibid.* at 161.
[3] [1997] I.R.L.R. 488, EAT.

could not, it was held, be proved to be a risk to health. Although the employer had taken some steps to deal with the smoky atmosphere these had been ineffective and the EAT upheld the finding by the industrial tribunal that it was reasonably practicable for them to have provided the applicant with a working environment which was suitable for the performance of her contractual duties.

A claim for damage suffered as a result of working in a smoky environment, known as passive smoking, was dismissed by the Court of Session in *Rae v. Glasgow City Council and Strathclyde Joint Police Board*.[4] The applicant's claim was that having worked for the respondent for 15 years in an office shared with heavy smokers, as a result of which she suffered respiratory illness, her employer was in breach of both the employer's duty to take reasonable care for her health and safety, and his statutory duty under the Offices, Shops and Railway Premises Act 1963[5] to provide "effective and suitable provision" for adequate ventilation of her office. Although the court dismissed the common law claim because of lack of evidence of a breach of duty, they accepted that section 7 of the 1963 Act, which concerned foul air in the workplace, was capable of including cigarette smoke.

An employer has a duty to take employee's complaints about matters concerning health and safety seriously and to deal with them promptly. In *B.A.C v. Austin*[6] the EAT held that this forms part of the employer's duty to take reasonable care for the safety of their employees:

> "There is no doubt, and it has been the law for more than 100 years now, that employers are under a duty to take reasonable care for the safety of their employees. . . . employers, as part and parcel of that general obligation, are also under an obligation under the terms of the contract of employment to act reasonably in dealing with matters of safety, or complaints of lack of safety, which are drawn to their attention by employees, unless the matter . . . is obviously not bona fide or is frivolous . . ." *per* Phillips J.

B.A.C v. Austin [1978] I.R.L.R. 332 at 335, EAT.

This duty must be exercised on a subjective basis: considering the limitations of the individual employee. For example, in *Paris v. Stepney Borough Council*[7] it was held that the employer had to exercise greater care of a one-eyed man in so far as risk of injury to his sight was concerned, in view of his increased vulnerability.

In certain circumstances an employee may be entitled to stop or to refuse to work in a dangerous area or with dangerous machinery or products. In *Piggott Bros & Co. Ltd v. Jackson*[8] the applicants refused to work with PVC-coated material that gave off unusual fumes affecting those working on the factory floor. They did so after returning from sick leave, having been advised by the Employment Medical Adviser from the Health and Safety Executive to seek medical advice when they became concerned about the fumes. The Court of Appeal held that although the employer took some steps, he failed to take reasonable steps to deal with the problem created by the materials concerned, and was therefore in breach of contract. Today the position is

[4] I.R.L.B. 581, November 1997, p. 11, CS.
[5] Duty to make "effective and suitable provision" for adequate ventilation, s.7. Now see Workplace (Health, Safety and Welfare) Regulations 1992, Reg. 6.
[6] [1978] I.R.L.R. 332, EAT.
[7] [1951] 1 All E.R. 42, HL.
[8] [1991] I.R.L.R. 309, CA.

governed by the ERA 1996 whereby an employee working in a place of work where there is no safety representative or safety committee is, by ERA 1996, ss.44 and 100 protected from suffering a detriment or being dismissed (s.44(1) and s.100(1)(c) and (d) respectively):

> "(d) in circumstances of danger which the employee reasonably believed to be serious and imminent and which he could not reasonably have been expected to avert, he left (or proposed to leave) or (while the danger persisted) refused to return to his place of work or any dangerous part of his place of work, or
>
> (e) in circumstances of danger which the employee reasonably believed to be serious and imminent, he took (or proposed to take) appropriate steps to protect himself or other persons from the danger,"

ERA 1996, s.4(1)(d) and (e) (and s.100(1)(c) and (d)).

These provisions also apply in circumstances where there is a safety committee or representative but it was not reasonably practical for the employee to raise the matter by those means.

In *Walker v. Northumberland County Council*[9] it was held that an employer owes a duty to his employees not to cause them psychiatric damage by the volume or character of the work which they were required to perform and that this duty existed both as an implied term and in tort:

> "It is clear law that an employer has a duty to provide his employee with a reasonably safe system of work and to take reasonable steps to protect him from risks which are reasonably foreseeable. Whereas the law on the extent of this duty has developed almost exclusively in cases involving physical injury to the employee as distinct from injury to his mental health, there is no logical reason why risk of psychiatric damage should be excluded from the scope of an employer's duty of care or from the co-extensive implied term in the contract." *per* Coleman J.

Walker v. Northumberland County Council [1995] I.R.L.R. 35 at 41, HC.

In addition to the duty to take employees' complaints about matters concerning health and safety seriously and to deal with them promptly there is also a duty for employers to ensure that they employ people who are adequately trained, qualified and experienced so as to be able to discharge their duties competently and safely and to deal with foreseeable events, and this includes a general duty to adequately supervise and direct employees. In *General Cleaning Contractors Ltd v. Christmas*[10] a window cleaner, following the practice of window cleaners generally, stood on the sill of a window to clean the outside. While holding on to one sash for support the other fell down on his fingers causing him to let go, fall to the ground and suffer injury. The House of Lords held that the employers were negligent in that not only had they failed to provide a safe system of work, they ought to have instructed their employees how to avoid accidents:

> ". . . it is the duty of an employer to give such general safety instructions as a reasonably careful employer who has considered the problem presented by the

---

[9] [1995] I.R.L.R. 35, HC.
[10] [1952] 2 All E.R. 1110, HL.

work would give to his workman. . . . workpeople are very frequently, if not habitually, careless about the risks which their work may involve. It is, in my opinion, for that very reason that the common law demands that employers should take reasonable care to lay down a reasonably safe system of work." *per* Lord Oaksey

General Cleaning Contractors Ltd v. Christmas [1952] 2 All E.R. 1110 at 1114, HL.

A breach of an implied duty of care will, as demonstrated in *Piggott Bros & Co. Ltd v. Jackson*,[11] amount to a repudiatory breach, and in *Rigby v. Ferodo*[12] the House of Lords confirmed that the contract of employment is not automatically brought to an end by a repudiatory breach committed by the employer. As with contracts generally, the employee has the option whether to accept the breach and terminate his own employment, being entitled, under the ERA 1996, s.95(1)(c), to then claim to have been constructively dismissed, or to continue with the contract and sue for damages arising from the breach. See para. 5.3.2 below on repudiation and termination at common law.

In *Johnstone v. Bloomsbury Health Authority*[13] one of the claims made was that the employers were under a duty to take all reasonable care for the safety and well-being of the plaintiff senior house officer and that being required some weeks to work in excess of 100 hours, with inadequate periods of sleep, as a result of which he suffered from stress, depression, lethargy, diminished appetite and inability to sleep, exhaustion and had suicidal feelings, was a breach of that implied duty.[14] The Court of Appeal, Leggatt L.J. dissenting, held that the express term giving the employer discretion to require up to 48 hours overtime, in addition to the standard 40 hours, had to be exercised subject to the employer's implied obligation to safeguard his employees' health.[15] In addition, the Unfair Contract Terms Act 1977 (UCTA 1977), s.2(1) provides that in certain circumstances "a person cannot by reference to any contract term . . . exclude or restrict his liability for death or personal injury resulting from negligence". The Court of Appeal held that the employee had an arguable case in connection with his claim as to the applicability of the UCTA 1977. By Schedule 1, para. 4, sections 2(1) and 2(2) do not extend to a contract of employment except in favour of the employee, but in *Johnstone v. Bloomsbury*[16] Stuart-Smith L.J. said that he took this to mean that if there is in a contract of employment a term excluding or restricting the liability of the employer to the employee, the latter can rely on the provisions of section 2(1) and (2).

3.3.1.3 *Duty of care in tort*

The employer owes a duty of care in tort to his employees and to others where there is a relationship of proximity such that it is reasonably foreseeable that negligence on his behalf will result in foreseeable damage to that person.[17] The employer is not, however,

---

[11] [1991] I.R.L.R. 309, CA.
[12] [1987] I.R.L.R. 516, HL.
[13] [1991] I.R.L.R. 118, CA.
[14] The applicant was still in employment when he commenced the action, although he left the employment of the Health Authority during the action, as a result of which he successfully sought to amend his claim, striking out the application for a declaration as this was no longer applicable.
[15] Dr Johnstone accepted £5,000 plus costs in settlement of his claim without the case being tried on the facts.
[16] [1991] I.R.L.R. 118, CA.
[17] *General Cleaning Contractors Ltd v. Christmas* [1952] 2 All E.R. 1110, HL.

required to ensure that employees are absolutely safe. He only breaches his duty of care to employees if he fails to take reasonable steps to avoid a foreseeable risk of injury. What is reasonable depends upon the likelihood of injury occurring and the likely seriousness of that injury (the magnitude of the risk). The position is summed up in *Walker v. Nothumberland County Council*[18]:

> "It is reasonably clear from the authorities that once a duty of care has been established the standard of care required for the performance of that duty must be measured against the yardstick of reasonable conduct on the part of a person in the position of that person who owes the duty. The law does not impose upon him the duty of an insurer against all injury or damage caused by him, however unlikely or unexpected and whatever the practical difficulties of guarding against it. It calls for no more than a reasonable response, what is reasonable being measured by the nature of the neighbourhood relationship, the magnitude of the risk of injury which was reasonably foreseeable, the seriousness of the conse-quence for the person to whom the duty is owed of the risk eventuating and the cost and practicality of preventing the risk." *per* Coleman J.

Walker v. Northumberland County Council [1995] I.R.L.R. 35 at 41–42, HC.

In *Roe v. Minister of Health*[19] Denning L.J. stressed that a defendant cannot be held liable for that which is unknown: "we must not look at the 1947 accident with 1954 spectacles". In 1963 the Ministry of Labour, recognising the risks of industrial noise to hearing, published guidelines regarding levels of noise at work. In *Baxter v. Harland & Wolff plc*[20] the employer argued that he could not be liable for hearing loss which occurred prior to publication of the report. The Northern Ireland Court of Appeal held the employer liable for injuries caused between the 1950s and 1962 because he knew that noise created in the shipyard was causing deafness to some employees, but took the existence of the problem for granted and through apathy and neglect did nothing about it. Had he applied his mind to it there was sufficient medical, scientific and legal knowledge available on the problem prior to 1963 and the employer had a duty to keep abreast of contemporary knowledge.

It has been held that a claim may be made for both breach of an implied term of the contract and in negligence,[21] and this was stated in *Wilsons & Clyde Coal Co. Ltd v. English*[22]:

> "It appears clear, then, that, when the workman contracts to do the work, he is not to be held as having agreed to hold the master immune from the latter's liability for want of due care in the provision of a reasonably safe system of working." *per* Lord Thankerton.

Wilsons & Clyde Coal Co. Ltd v. English [1938] A.C. 57 at 67, HL.

However, more recently, in *Johnstone v. Bloomsbury Health Authority*,[23] based on the authority of *Tai Hing Cotton Mill Ltd v. Lin Chong Hing Bank Ltd*,[24] a different view

[18] [1995] I.R.L.R. 35, HC.
[19] [1954] 2 All E.R. 131, CA.
[20] [1990] I.R.L.R. 516, CA.
[21] *Matthews v. Kuwait Bechtel Corp.* [1959] 2 Q.B. 57, CA.
[22] [1938] A.C. 57, HL.
[23] [1991] I.R.L.R. 118, CA.
[24] [1986] A.C. 80, PC.

has been expressed by the Court of Appeal. Sir Nicholas Brown-Wilkinson V.-C. in *Johnstone*[25] said:

">. . . where there is a contractual relationship between the parties their respective rights and duties have to be analysed wholly in contractual terms and not as a mixture of duties in tort and contract. It necessarily follows that the scope of the duties owed by one party to the other will be defined by the terms of the contract between them." *per* Nicholas Brown-Wilkinson V.C.

Johnstone v. Bloomsbury Health Authority [1991] I.R.L.R. 118 at 124, CA.

Nevertheless, compliance with the employer's statutory responsibilities does not necessarily absolve him from liability to his employee at common law and a claim may be made for both a breach of statutory duty and negligence. In *Waters v. Commissioner of Police of the Metropolis*[26] a female police constable complained about an act of victimisation in breach of the SDA 1975, s.4(1)(d) and negligence. Although a failure to comply with any duties imposed by the HSWA 1974, ss.2–7, by section 47 does not confer a right of action in civil proceedings, section 47(2) provides that damage resulting from a breach of a duty imposed by health and safety regulations may do so, except in so far as regulations provide otherwise. In *Bux v. Slough Metals Ltd*[27] although the employer fulfilled his obligations under the Non-Ferrous Metals (Melting and Founding) Regulations[28] to provide goggles, the Court of Appeal held that they had not fulfilled their common law duty of reasonable care for the safety of their workmen, which was not abrogated by the introduction of the regulations. More was called for and a prudent employer would, in the light of the dangerous work being undertaken and the knowledge that workmen consistently failed to wear them, have given instructions regarding the wearing of the goggles and such instructions should have been followed up by supervision. The applicant's breach of regulation 13(4), which imposed a duty to make full and proper use of the goggles, resulted in a finding of contributory negligence and in accordance with the Law Reform (Contributory Negligence) Act 1945, s.1, damages were reduced by 40 per cent.

It is now recognised that employees performing physical repetitive actions, not just keyboard, but other industrial and office tasks, are liable to suffer repetitive strain injury (RSI), resulting in long-term physical injury. Early cases of RSI, such as *Mughal v. Reuters*,[29] were dismissed on the basis that the condition was psychosomatic rather than physical and that sufferers were people with "eggshell personalities who needed to get a grip on themselves" and that all that was necessary was that British Standard equipment is either provided or available; there was little more that an employer could do. However, following the successful case of *Foster v. National Power*[30] employers need to take positive steps on complaints by employees, to assess and where necessary to redesign tasks. Foster regularly spent up to seven hours a day counting and collating papers in the run-up to National Power's privatisation and when she complained of severe pains in her wrists and fingers the employer failed to take any action for over a year.

[25] [1991] I.R.L.R. 118, CA.
[26] [1997] I.R.L.R. 589, CA.
[27] [1974] 1 All E.R. 262, CA.
[28] S.I. 1962 No. 1667, reg. 13(1).
[29] [1993] I.R.L.R. 571, HC.
[30] See *People Management*, August 28, 1997, p. 18.

Liability for stress suffered as a result of pressures in the workplace has been an increasingly important development in recent years. Whilst in *Johnstone v. Bloomsbury Health Authority*[31] the Court of Appeal, by a majority, held that the contractual power to require staff to work overtime had to be exercised in the light of the implied obligation to safeguard the employee's health, in the later case of *Walker v. Northumberland County Council*[32] Coleman J. in the High Court held that the employer was in breach of his duty of care in relation to a second breakdown resulting from overwork. There was no liability for the first breakdown because it was held that it was not reasonably foreseeable that the workload to which the plaintiff was exposed gave rise to a material risk of injury. However, when he returned to work and was exposed to the same work pressures it was reasonably foreseeable that without the provision of additional assistance there was a foreseeable risk of a further breakdown and a reasonable employer would have provided additional assistance.[33]

Although there are no specific provisions which require measures to be taken to prevent stress at work the Management of Health and Safety at Work Regulations 1992,[34] Reg. 3, requires the employer to assess the nature and scale of risk to occupational health in order to identify the measures he needs to take.

The Health and Safety Executive has published a guide for employers on work-related stress which outlines the main causes of occupational stress and sets out steps employers can take to prevent harmful levels of stress and *The Code of Practice, Management of Health and Safety at Work*, issued in conjunction with the 1992 Regulations[35] by the Health and Safety Commission (HSC) provides that:

> "When allocating work to employees, employers should ensure that the demands of the job do not exceed the employees' ability to carry out the work without risk to themselves or others. Employers should take account of the employees' capabilities and the level of their training, knowledge and experience. If additional training is required, it should be provided."

> *The Code of Practice, Management of Health and Safety at Work*, para. 70, Health and Safety Commission.

The position is well established that damages are recoverable in negligence for psychiatric injury brought on by the fear of reasonably foreseeable personal injury to oneself, or from seeing or hearing reasonably foreseeable injury suffered by a person with whom one has a close tie of love and affection: in these circumstances a duty of care is owed.[36] The courts have been reluctant to extend the class of potential plaintiff where the injury suffered is not physical and although there are cases concerning psychiatric injury suffered by employees where they have been successful in recovering damages against a negligent employer, in *Alcock v. Chief Constable of South Yorkshire*[37] these were categorised by Lord Oliver as being a special class of cases where the shock, which amounted to psychiatric injury, was suffered as a result of a negligent act of the defendant which put the plaintiff in the position of being, or thinking that he was

---

[31] [1991] 2 All E.R. 293, CA.
[32] [1995] I.C.R. 789, HC.
[33] See K. Manji *"Occupational Stress"* (1996) N.L.J. March 8, pp. 330–331 and October 18, p. 1516.
[34] S.I. 1992 No. 2051.
[35] *ibid.*
[36] *Alcock v. Chief Constable of South Yorkshire* [1992] 1 A.C. 310, HL.
[37] *ibid.*

about to be or had been, the involuntary cause of another's injury.[38] For example, in *Dooley v. Cammell Laird*[39] a crane driver working in a shipyard succeeded in recovering damages as a result of shock suffered when a sling fell from his crane causing the load of timber to fall into the ship's hold where the driver knew his fellow work mates were working; and in *Galt v. British Railways Board*[40] a train driver thought he had killed two fellow workmen when he came across them as his train rounded a corner and it was impossible to stop his train.

In addition, in *Chadwick v. British Transport Commission*[41] an employer was held liable to a third party who suffered psychiatric injury caused to a man who acted as a rescuer in circumstances where the defendant had negligently operated his train in such a way that it was foreseeable that a crash would occur and that people would go to assist. If they did so it was held that it was foreseeable that they would suffer trauma as a result of the horrors experienced in the course of carrying out the rescue.

Beyond these classes of case the courts have been reluctant to extend the duty of care owed by the employer where the injury suffered is psychiatric, and this can be seen in *McFarlane v. EE Caledonia*[42] which resulted from the catastrophe on the oil platform *Piper Alpha* in which 164 people died and many more were seriously injured. The plaintiff, an off duty painter on an oil rig in the North Sea, was lying on his bunk on one of the vessels, the *Tharos*, which went to the scene to attempt to fight the fire and render assistance. From the *Tharos*, which was never closer than 100 metres to the platform, McFarlane witnessed a rescue boat being engulfed in a fireball killing its occupants and also saw men jumping from the platform to their death. The *Tharos* was undamaged, apart from some blistering paint, and no one on board was injured and Mr McFarlane's claim for damages for psychological injury suffered as a result of what he saw was unsuccessful, he was not a primary victim nor a rescuer and failed to bring himself within the recognised categories for secondary victims laid down by the House of Lords in *Alcock*.[43]

In *Robertson and Rough v. Forth Road Bridge Joint Board*[44] it was held that the general duty of care owed by an employer to an employee does not extend to psychiatric injuries brought about by seeing a fellow employee injured or killed, and that an employee who merely witnessed an accident was in no different position than any other bystander or witness at the scene of the accident. It was therefore confirmed that in order for the employer to be liable to the employee in such a situation it is necessary that the restraints laid down in *Alcock*[45] be complied with. The Court confirmed that these restraints did not apply where the witness was a rescuer, where the accident was so horrific as to cause a person of ordinary disposition to sustain psychiatric injury, or in the case of workmen, where he himself was the involuntary cause of the death or injury, or believed himself to be.

In *Frost v. Chief Constable of South Yorkshire Police*,[46] which was joined on appeal in the House of Lords with *Duncan v. British Coal Corporation*, the issue arose again as to the circumstances in which an employee could recover damages for post-traumatic

---

[38] *per* Lord Oliver, *Alcock v. Chief Constable of South Yorkshire* [1992] 1 A.C. 310 at 408, HL.
[39] [1951] 1 Lloyd's Rep. 271, Assizes.
[40] [1983] 133 N.L.J. 870, HC.
[41] [1967] 2 All E.R. 945, HC.
[42] [1994] 2 All E.R. 1, CA.
[43] [1992] 1 A.C. 310, HL.
[44] [1995] I.R.L.R. 251, CS.
[45] [1992] 1 A.C. 310, HL.
[46] [1997] 1 All E.R. 540, CA.

stress disorder suffered as a result of tending victims of his employer's negligence. The case arose from the Hillsborough disaster, which resulted in what were described by Taylor L.J. in his report[47] as "truly gruesome" scenes when 95 spectators were crushed to death and over 400 were injured. The scenes were witnessed by onlookers who in *Alcock*[48] all failed to recover damages for psychiatric injury suffered as a result of seeing the events. None of the plaintiffs succeeded because those with the necessary relationship were not present at the scene and those who were present were held not to have the necessary relationship. *Frost*, however, involved the question of whether police officers on duty on the day of the tragedy could recover damages from their employer for the psychiatric injury suffered as a result of the "horrific scene of carnage" they witnessed at the football stadium. *Duncan* involved a pit deputy who developed a psychiatric illness as a result of the harrowing experience of attempting to revive a colleague crushed to death as a result of his employer's negligence. A majority of the Court of Appeal, held, in relation to those police officers who had been at the scene of the tragedy and Duncan, that the employer owed them a duty of care not to cause them psychiatric injury. In connection with the duty owed by the employer where the injury suffered is psychiatric, as opposed to physical, it was held:

> ". . . whereas in cases outwith the master and servant relationship the courts have found it necessary, in identifying those to whom a duty of care is owed, to draw a distinction between primary and secondary victims and to impose limiting criteria to determine those within the second category who can recover, in the master and servant context a duty of care exists by reason of that relationship. . . . A rescurer, whether a policeman or layman, may recover against a tortfeasor for physical or psychiatric injury sustained during a rescue. An employee may, depending on the circumstances, recover against his employer for physical or psychiatric injury caused in the course of his employment by the employer's negligence. . . ." *per* Rose L.J.

Frost v. Chief Constable of South Yorkshire Police [1997] 1 All E.R. 540 at 550, CA.

So, in connection with claims for psychiatric injuries, the restrictive criteria laid down in *Alcock*[49] do not apply to employees where the psychiatric injury is suffered as a result of the antecedent negligence of the employer.

The decision in *Frost and Duncan*[50] was applied in *Young v. Charles Church (Southern) Ltd*[51] where a majority of the Court of Appeal held that the plaintiff, who was a scaffolder's labourer, was a primary victim to whom the employer owed a duty of care with regard to psychiatric injury even though he had not at the time feared injury, but was clearly at risk. He was self-employed for tax and national insurance purposes, but it was held that he was under the directions of the defendants and treated as an employee in all other respects. He suffered post traumatic stress disorder as a result of witnessing the electrocution of a colleague after a scaffold pole that the plaintiff had just handed him touched an overhead 33,000 volt power line. Young witnessed the victim on fire and another colleague was burnt as a result of the arcing effect.

[47] Cm. 765, p. 15, para. 8.3.
[48] [1992] 1 A.C. 310, HL.
[49] *ibid.*
[50] [1997] 1 All E.R. 540, CA.
[51] *Health and Safety Bulletin* 262, October 1997, p. 14; 39 B.M.L.R. 146, CA.

3.3.2 Liability for statements

In *Clay v. A.J. Crump & Sons Ltd*[52] an architect negligently orally advised a demolition contractor regarding the demolition of a wall, as a result of which the wall collapsed, killing an employee of the demolition contractor. The demolition contractor was contractually liable and the question arose as to whether the architect could be liable in tort. In an extension to the law of negligence, the House of Lords in an earlier judgment in *Hedley Byrne & Co. Ltd v. Heller & Partners Ltd*[53] accepted that there could be liability for negligently given statements, and Upjohn L.J. in *Clay* said that he could see no reason why that decision should not apply and upheld a finding of liability by the architect, as well as the demolition contractor and building contractor.

3.3.2.1 *References*

The employer is not under a duty to provide a reference for employees. However, the House of Lords in *Spring v. Guardian Assurance plc*[54] held, by a majority, applying the principles of *Hedley Byrne & Co. Ltd v. Heller & Partners Ltd*[55] that if an employer does give a reference to a prospective employer he is under a duty of care: he is required to use reasonable care and skill in ensuring the accuracy of any facts which are communicated to the recipient of the reference from which he might form an adverse opinion of the employee. In addition, it was held that, in so far as employees are concerned an employer's duty to take reasonable care in preparing a reference could, in appropriate circumstances, be expressed as arising from an implied term of the contract. The existence of a duty of care in negligence was held, by a majority, to be different and distinguishable from any general duty in regard to reputation, namely defamation and injurious and malicious falsehood.

3.3.3 Duty to keep employees informed

In what was described by Lord Steyn in *Malik v. BCCI SA*[56] as a change in legal culture, it was held by the House of Lords in *Scally v. Southern Health and Social Service Board*[57] that the employer was under an implied obligation to inform employees of the existence of a valuable right which had been incorporated into employees' contracts of employment. Lord Bridge, in a judgment of the House, stated that such a duty arose out of the contract of employment, not in the tort of negligence. This applied where the term, which was a right to purchase "added years" of pension entitlement in a superannuation fund which the employees were obliged to join, was known to the employer, but not the employees, and the only way employees could have become aware of it was by having it brought to their attention by the employer. Lord Bridge said that this was a novel situation, in that terms of the contract, in a classical contractual situation, having been agreed between the parties are, ex-hypothesi, known to both parties. He, however, distinguished contracts of employment:

> "It is increasingly common for individuals to enter into contracts, particularly contracts of employment, on complex terms which have been settled in the course

[52] [1964] 1 Q.B. 533, CA.
[53] [1964] A.C. 465, HL.
[54] [1994] 3 All E.R. 129, HL.
[55] See n. 53.
[56] [1997] 3 All E.R. 1, HL.
[57] [1991] I.R.L.R. 522, HL.

of negotiations between representative bodies or organisations and many details of which the individual employee cannot be expected to know unless they are drawn to his attention." *per* Lord Bridge

Scally v. Southern Health and Social Service Board [1991] I.R.L.R. 522 at 524, HL.

In order to prevent the duty from being too wide, it applies in circumstances where the relationship is one of employer and employee and the following circumstances apply:

"(1) the terms of the contract of employment have not been negotiated with the individual employee but result from negotiation with a representative body or are otherwise incorporated by reference; (2) a particular term of the contract makes available to the employee a valuable right contingent upon action being taken by him to avail himself of its benefit; (3) the employee cannot, in all the circumstances, reasonably be expected to be aware of the term unless it is drawn to his attention." *per* Lord Bridge

Scally v. Southern Health and Social Service Board [1991] I.R.L.R. 522 at 525, HL.

This duty to inform the employee of contractual benefits affecting him was extended in *Gray v. Smith*[58] when an Industrial Tribunal held that an employer had "demonstrated a reckless disregard for his duties in relation to his employee's employment rights . . ." by failing to provide her with a contract of employment or statutory statement, and having failed to provide guidance concerning statutory maternity rights was held to have waived his right to rely on strict adherence with the statutory maternity provisions. The result was that the employee, who had failed to comply with the notice provisions entitling her to return to work after the birth of her baby, was held to have been discriminated against and to have been unfairly dismissed.

The decision in *Gray v. Smith* appears to take something of a blind leap from the decision in *Scally v. Southern Health and Social Service Board*.[59] Whilst it would be a logical application off *Scally*[60] to argue that an employer has a duty, in these circumstances, to bring to the attention of an employee details of contractual maternity provisions contained in a collective agreement, it is difficult to see that it can be used to find that an employer owes a duty to inform employees of legislative provisions that may affect them.[61]

3.3.4 Duty to provide an opportunity to obtain redress of any grievance

In *W. A. Goold (Pearmak) Ltd v. McConnell*[62] the employer had not established a procedure for dealing with grievances and had never given employees a written statement of their terms and conditions. The ERA 1996, s.1 provides for employees to be given a statement of the principle terms of employment, and by section 3(1)(b)(ii) this should include a note of the person to whom the employee can apply to seek redress of any grievance, and how an application is to be made. When a grievance

---

[58] COIT Case Nos. 03216–17/95, IDS Brief 584, March 1977, p. 14.
[59] [1991] I.R.L.R. 522, HL.
[60] *ibid.*
[61] See IDS Brief 584, March 1977, p. 14.
[62] [1995] I.R.L.R. 516, EAT.

arose in connection with a substantial reduction in take-home pay, which resulted from a change in sales methods, the employees were "fobbed off" and constantly frustrated in their efforts to raise the issue. The EAT held that Parliament, as evidenced by the ERA 1996, s.3, clearly "considered that good industrial relations practice requires employers to provide their employees with a method of dealing with grievances in a proper and timeous fashion" and as a result it is an implied term of the contract of employment that employers will reasonably and promptly afford a reasonable opportunity to their employees to obtain redress of any grievance they may have. A failure to do so is a breach of the implied term and to allow grievances to fester in an atmosphere of prevarication and indecision is sufficiently serious to entitle the employee to terminate his employment and to claim constructive dismissal. The point is made that this case could equally well have been dealt with by a finding that the employer was in breach of the obligation of mutual trust and confidence.[63]

In connection with a complaint about smoking in the workplace and the resulting smoky working environment, in *Waltons & Morse v. Dorrington*[64] the EAT held that employers efforts to deal with complaints amounted to tinkering with the problem and culminated with a response that, "There is no more to be done, accept it or leave," was, in addition to a breach of the implied duty to provide a reasonably tolerable working environment, also a breach of the requirement to properly address the concerns raised by an employee.

3.3.5 Duty to respect employees' privacy

In *Halford v. United Kingdom*[65] the European Court of Human Rights (ECHR) held that it was a violation of Article 8 of the European Convention on Human Rights, which provides for the right to respect for private and family life, home and correspondence, for an employer to intercept calls made on office telephones without warning that they would be liable to interception, because without such warning there is a reasonable expectation that calls will be private. It was also held that such interference could not fall within Article 8.2, and therefore be lawful, since such bugging was not "in accordance with the law" as domestic law does not provide any regulation of interception of calls made on telecommunications systems outside the public network.

Alison Halford launched industrial tribunal proceedings for sex discrimination following a protracted and hostile disagreement involving eight rejected applications for promotion to the position of Deputy Chief Constable. She claimed that her work and home telephones had been interfered with for the purpose of interception of calls with "the primary objective of gathering material to assist in the defence of the sex discrimination proceedings". That Article 8 applies to telephone calls was decided in *Malone v. United Kingdom*[66] when the ECHR decided that telephone calls made from home were capable of being covered by the notions of "private life" and "correspondence" within the meaning of Article 8.1.[67]

Employers proposing to monitor employees' communications should therefore inform employees that this is the practice.[68] The same principle is capable of applying

---

[63] D. Brodie (1996), p. 121.
[64] [1997] I.R.L.R. 488, EAT.
[65] [1997] I.R.L.R. 471, ECHR.
[66] (1984) 7 E.H.R.R. 14, ECHR.
[67] See also *Klass v. Germany* (1978) 2 E.H.R.R. 214, ECHR, *Huvig v. France* (1990) 12 E.H.R.R. 528, ECHR.
[68] But note Directive 97/66 concerning the processing of personal data and the protection of privacy in the telecommunications sector.

to electronic mail and facsimile messages and incorporation of the ECHR via the Human Rights Bill, will reinforce the right of privacy for employees via Article 8, which Liberty has called "a 'catch all' law for protecting privacy", and which is included in Schedule 1 to the Bill. Any breach of the duty to respect employees' privacy may also be sufficient to amount to a breach of mutual trust and confidence. In fact, a breach of any of the implied terms of the contract of employment is capable of giving rise to a breach of the duty of mutual trust and confidence.

3.3.6 Summary

The chart on p. 148 sets out in diagrammatic form and cross-referenced to the relevant paragraphs in both this and Chapter 2 the relationship between the main sources of terms of the contract, discussed in Chapter 2, and the main terms of the contract, discussed above. Today, as noted by Lord Slynn in *Spring v. Guardian Assurance plc*[69] the changes which have taken place in the employer/employee relationship whether by statute or by judicial decision have imposed greater duties on the employer. Much of this can be reduced to the duty of trust and confidence which is capable of encompassing a whole range of behaviour. Note should also be taken of *Newns v. British Airways plc*[70] in which Steyn L.J. said that there is an implied term in a contract of employment imposing on an employer a duty of good faith towards the employee and that this means that the employer must observe a duty of good faith in performance of the contract: good faith conveying the notice of fair dealing.[71] Scott L.J., on the other hand, expressed the view that this was a mutual duty[72] which could, in appropriate circumstances, be enforced by injunction.

Duties within the employment relationship, although traditionally emanating from implied and express terms are increasingly sourced by statute, and the Health and Safety at Work etc. Act 1974 is an example, which, fuelled by Directives, has imposed a whole range of responsibilities and duties on the employer. Enactment of the Human Rights Bill, the Public Interest Disclosure Bill (which has now become the Public Interest Disclosure Act 1998) and proposals by the Law Commission for trade secrets[73] will take this process further.

---

[69] [1994] 3 All E.R. 129 at 161, HL.
[70] [1992] I.R.L.R. 575, CA.
[71] *ibid.* at 578.
[72] *ibid.* at 577.
[73] *Misuse of Trade Secrets*, Law Commission Consultation Paper No. 150.

Sources and Terms of the Contract of Employment

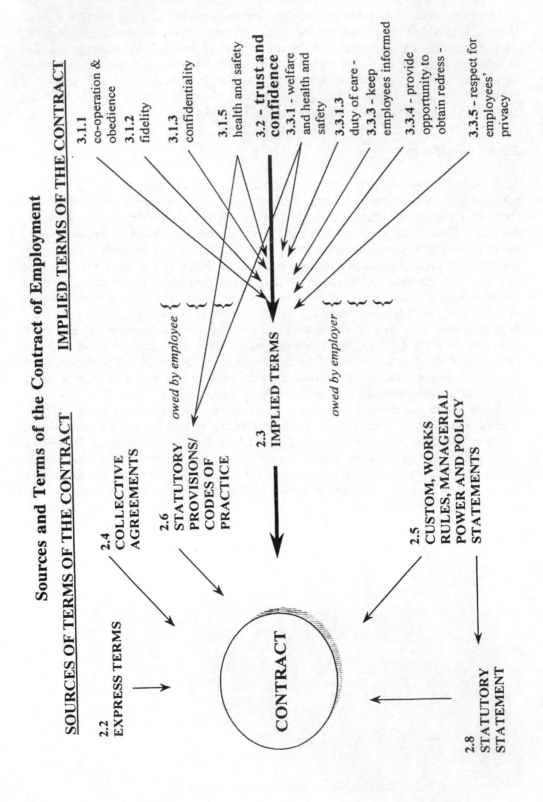

SOURCES OF TERMS OF THE CONTRACT

IMPLIED TERMS OF THE CONTRACT

3.1.1 co-operation & obedience

3.1.2 fidelity

3.1.3 confidentiality

3.1.5 health and safety

3.2 – trust and confidence

3.3.1 – welfare and health and safety

3.3.1.3 duty of care –

3.3.3 – keep employees informed

3.3.4 – provide opportunity to obtain redress –

3.3.5 – respect for employees' privacy

owed by employee

owed by employer

2.3 IMPLIED TERMS

2.4 COLLECTIVE AGREEMENTS

2.6 STATUTORY PROVISIONS/ CODES OF PRACTICE

2.5 CUSTOM, WORKS RULES, MANAGERIAL POWER AND POLICY STATEMENTS

2.2 EXPRESS TERMS

CONTRACT

2.8 STATUTORY STATEMENT

Chapter 4

ROLE OF PAY IN THE EMPLOYMENT RELATIONSHIP

4.1 INTRODUCTION

This chapter considers the common law and statutory regulation of pay in the employment relationship. The main employee protection provisions are introduced and explained.

4.2 THE RIGHT TO BE PAID WHILST WORKING

Under the common law, entitlement to wages is dependant upon work being done:

> ". . .the essential characteristic of wages is that they are consideration for work done or to be done under a contract of employment. If a payment is not referable to an obligation on the employee under a subsisting contract of employment to render his services it does not in my judgment fall within the ordinary meaning of the word 'wages'." *per* Browne-Wilkinson L.J.

> *Delaney v. Staples (t/a De Montfort Recruitment)* [1992] I.R.L.R. 191, HL.

The individual contract of employment primarily determines whether and how wages are paid, if at all,[1] to the employee. There is no prescriptive legal form in which wages have to be paid. It depends on the contractual agreement reached between the parties. The consideration supplied by the employer for the work done, can be provided in the form of commission,[2] fees, in tips proffered by customers[3] and so on. In *Saavedra v.*

---

[1] *Re Richmond Gate Property Co. Ltd* [1964] 3 All E.R. 936; [1965] 1 W.L.R. 335. Here a managing director of a company in liquidation had not had his pay determined in the company's articles and it was found that contractually he was not entitled to recover any payment for his work.

[2] Courts often have to construe the agreement relating to how the commission is to be paid. In *Slater v. South West Marketing Ltd*, COIT 3119/65 the employee's commission was paid per month "against calculated sales". When he resigned he claimed that the company's failure to pay his final commission was an unauthorised deduction from his wages. The tribunal found alternatively that this commission was merely wages paid in advance and that the employer was entitled to claw-back commission which had not been earned.

[3] *Pauley v. Kenaldo Ltd* [1953] 1 All E.R. 226; [1953] 1 W.L.R. 187.

Aceground Ltd T/A Terrazza Est[4] it was held that "What is 'properly payable' to those who give service is that which is paid for service. The employers cannot lawfully allocate part of the service charge to themselves, notwithstanding that distribution of the sum collected is a matter for their discretion." In *Nerva and others v. R. L. & G. Ltd*[5] however, the Court of Appeal reaffirmed a High Court decision that a distinction could be made between tips given to waiters in the form of cheque or credit card payments, which were contractually redistributed to the employees by the employer, and cash tips given directly to the staff. The former was held to be "remuneration" and as such counted against sums due the employee under the (then in force) minimum wage provisions; whilst the latter did not count as remuneration for such purposes. Whatever the niceties of the legal arguments ventilated in the Court, centring on issues as to whether the employer acted as the agent of the customer in disbursing the tips, this decision would seem to be against public policy on wage regulation. This view is expressed strongly in the dissenting judgment of Aldous L.J.:

> "Cheque and credit card tips are not given by the customer to increase the bank account of the employers or to discharge any liability of the employers to pay a minimum wage. The intention of the customer is the same when paying a tip by credit card or cheque as when paying cash." *per* Aldous L.J.

> *Nerva and others v. R. L. & G. Ltd.* [1996] I.R.L.R. 461 at 461, CA.

Employees engaged on an hourly or piece work basis would not be guaranteed a set wage or salary although there may be a contractual obligation by the employer to offer a reasonable amount of work.[6]

In theory, at common law, no remuneration may be payable if the entire contract of employment is not performed. This is based on the eighteenth century case of *Cutter v. Powell*[7] where the widow of a dead sailor, who died at sea was found not to be entitled to any of the wages originally agreed. But as has been pointed out,[8] such a situation is unlikely today as most employment contracts consist of set periods of performance linked to frequency of payment by the employer. Generally however, the common law principle of "no work no pay" will usually apply. This is why pay is not due if an employee takes part in any form of industrial action which results in none or partial performance of the contract (see 4.4.3 below).

4.2.1 What is pay?

Historically, pay has not always been commonly transmitted in currency (see para. 4.4 below) but in whatever form it is given, the exchange of labour or work for money, (the wage-work bargain) is at the heart of the individual employment relationship. The rate and form of pay has traditionally been governed by common law principles of contract but this area of law is now heavily overlain with statute, whose purpose is variously, to regulate how and in what form wages are paid and to sometimes set their rate. (see para. 4.5 below). The text opens with consideration of the statutory definition of wages.

---

[4] [1995] I.R.L.R. 198, EAT.
[5] [1996] I.R.L.R. 461, CA.
[6] *Re Rubel Bronze & Metal Co. Ltd and Vos* [1918] 1 K.B. 315.
[7] (1795) 6 Term Rep. 320, followed in Sinclair v. Bowles (1829) 9 B. & C.92 and *Vigers v. Cook* [1919] 2 K.B. 475, CA.
[8] I.T. Smith and G. Thomas *Industrial Law* (6th ed., Butterworths, London, 1996), p. 156.

4.2.2 Meaning of wages: ERA 1996, s.27

The statutory definition of wages is now found in the ERA 1996, s.27(1). Generally "wages" include any sums payable to the worker in connection with his or her employment. This can include:

- any fee, bonus, commission, holiday pay or other emolument[9];
- statutory sick pay[10];
- statutory maternity pay[11];
- guarantee payment[12];
- payment for time-off for carrying out trade union duties[13];
- remuneration for suspension on medical or maternity grounds[14]
- sums due from a reinstatement or re-engagement order[15];
- wages arising from a continuation of contract order by an industrial tribunal[16];
- sums due from a protective award against an employer for infringement of the collective redundancy consultation provisions.[17]

Section 27(2) specifically excludes certain categories of payment from the statutory definition however. These include:

- loans or advances on wages[18];
- expenses incurred by the worker related to the employment[19];
- any payments connected with the retirement or compensation for loss of office, *i.e.* a pension, allowance or gratuity[20];
- any redundancy payment[21];
- any payment which is not to do with the worker's "capacity as a worker".[22]

These statutory definitions are important because it is only wages as statutorily defined which are protected from unlawful deductions by the employer under the ERA 1996, s.13 (see para. 4.4.1 below).

If an employer makes an "error of computation" that is, simply miscalculates the wages contractually due to an individual, this is not an unauthorised deduction[23] under

---

[9] ERA 1996, s.27(1)(a).
[10] ERA 1996, s.27(1)(b).
[11] ERA 1996, s.27(1)(c).
[12] ERA 1996, s.27(1)(d).
[13] ERA 1996, s.27(1)(e).
[14] ERA 1996, s.27(1)(f).
[15] ERA 1996, s.27(1)(g).
[16] ERA 1996, s.27(1)(h).
[17] ERA 1996, s.27(1)(j).
[18] ERA 1996, s.27(2)(a).
[19] ERA 1996, s.27(2)(b).
[20] ERA 1996, s.27(2)(c).
[21] ERA 1996, s.27(2)(d).
[22] ERA 1996, s.27(2)(e).
[23] ERA 1996, s.13(4).

the Act. It is a non-payment which under common law was recoverable as damages for a breach of contract action in the County Court (see *Delaney* below). A deliberate attempt by an employer to change a system of payment, even if the employer believes that he is entitled to vary the contract is not an error of computation as statutorily defined. In *Yemm and others v. British Steel plc*[24] the employer unilaterally changed the shift pattern of workers which reduced their pay levels. The Employment Appeal Tribunal held that "An employer who makes a conscious decision not to make a payment because he believes that the contract entitles him to take that course is not making an 'error of computation', however wide the meaning given to those words in s.8(4). He may be making an error in the sense that he may be mistaken about the terms and effect of the contract but such an error cannot be characterised as an error of computation."[25] The effect of this decision is to prevent employers unilaterally varying contracts and then using the defence of error of computation to oust the jurisdiction of an industrial tribunal. In *Bruce and others v. Wiggins Teape (Stationery) Ltd*,[26] a similar case where an employer unilaterally withdrew an enhanced shift rate, the agrieved employees got short shrift, so to speak, when they claimed that this was an unauthorised deduction. The industrial tribunal found that "the Wages Act nowhere provides that any employer may not reduce the rate of pay which he pays to his employees without their agreement. . . . It deals with deductions and not reductions." This argument was robustly overturned by the Employment Appeal Tribunal who could find no such distinction in the Act or any authority which would permit such an unauthorised deduction.

Is "payment in lieu" wages?

One of the common problems which the courts had to deal with in the early period following the enactment of the Wages Act 1986 was whether "payment in lieu" counted as wages as statutorily defined. Different divisions of the Employment Appeal Tribunal came to different conclusions after examination of the statutory wording.[27]

The argument over the definition of pay in lieu was largely settled[28] in *Delaney v. Staples (t/a De Montfort Recruitment)*:

"A payment in lieu of notice is not 'wages' within the meaning of the Wages Act [ERA 1996, s.27(1)] where it relates to a period after the termination of the employment. Wages are payments in respect of the rendering of services during the employment, so that all payments in respect of the termination of the contract are excluded save to the extent that they are expressly included under s.7(1). [s.27(1).] Thus, payments in respect of 'garden leave' are 'wages' within the meaning of the Act since they are advance payments of wages falling due under a subsisting contract of employment. But all other payments in lieu, whether or not contractually payable, are not wages since they are payments relating to the termination of the employment and not to the provision of services under the employment. Accordingly, payments in lieu are not wages." *per* Lord Bridge of Harwich.

Delaney v. Staples (t/a De Montfort Recruitment) [1992] I.R.L.R. 191 at 191, HL.

[24] [1994] I.R.L.R. 117, EAT.
[25] See also: *Morgan v. West Glamorgan County Council* [1995] I.R.L.R. 68.
[26] [1994] I.R.L.R. 536, EAT.
[27] See: *Kournavous v. JR Masterton & Sons (Demolition)* [1989] I.R.L.R. 119, EAT, and *Janstorp International (U.K.) Ltd v. Allen* [1990] I.R.L.R. 417, EAT where pay in lieu was regarded as wages, and also: *Foster Wheeler (London) Ltd v. Jackson* [1990] I.R.L.R. 412, EAT where it was decided in the opposite.
[28] I.T. Smith and G. Thomas (1996), p. 182.

The employee in *Delaney* was summarily dismissed and claimed under the Wages Act that she was owed £55.50 commission and holiday pay and £82 in lieu of notice. The Court of Appeal held that under the ERA 1996, s. 13(3) she could recover the commission as it was a deduction which had not been agreed, but the question of whether "payment in lieu" was "wages" as statutorily defined, went to the House of Lords. It decided, after a broad review of the nature of payments in lieu that it was not. Lord Browne-Wilkinson identified four categories of payment in lieu[29]:

1. Where an employer gives proper notice of termination to the employee and informs him or her that they do not need not to work out the contract to the termination date, but gives them wages for the notice period in a lump sum, this is known as "garden leave," and there is no breach of contract by the employer. The lump sum represents advance payment of wages.

2. Where the contract of employment expressly provides for termination either with notice, or summarily without notice on the payment of a sum in lieu of notice, there is no breach of contract and the payment is not wages for work done.

3. Where at the end of the employment, the employer and the employee agree that the employment is to finish on payment of a sum in lieu of notice, there is no breach and again the payment is not wages for work done.

4. The commonest type of lieu is where without the agreement of the employee, the employer summarily dismisses the employee and offers a payment in lieu of contractual notice. Because effectively the employment relationship is ended the payment in lieu cannot be wages for work done.

The practical effect of this decision at the time was that the non-payment of "wages" could be the subject of an ERA 1996, s.13 claim for unauthorised deductions whereas the recovery of non-payment of "wages in lieu" had to be taken as a common law claim for recovery of damages in a county court. This difficulty was removed by the Industrial Tribunals Extension of Jurisdiction Order 1994[30] which now allows industrial tribunals to deal with such cases.

4.2.3   How is pay calculated?

For the purposes of applying the statutory employee protection provisions which require industrial tribunals to make awards based on the calculation of a weeks' pay the ERA 1996, ss.220 to 229 provide that there are four alternative methods of calculation. Three are based on where the individual works normal hours but receives different rates of pay within those hours and the fourth is based on where an individual does not work regular hours.

4.2.4   Right to an itemised pay statement: ERA 1996, ss.8–10

The ERA 1996, s.8 directs that an employer should give a written itemised pay statement to the employee on, or before the day on which he or she is paid.[31] This

---

[29] Delaney v. Staples (t/a De Montfort Recruitment) [1992] I.R.L.R. 193, HL, para. 12.
[30] S.I. 1994 No. 1623.
[31] ERA 1996, s.8(1).

statement must include details of the gross amount received,[32] any fixed and variable deductions,[33] the net amount received,[34] and if the net amount is paid in different ways,[35] this should be indicated.

Separate details of all standing fixed deductions must be given in writing every 12 months to the employee.[36] These provisions are not concerned "solely [with] the accuracy of an amount stated in any such provisions".[37] That is largely the provenance of ERA 1996, s.13 (right not to suffer unauthorised deductions). The remedy for failure to comply with these provisions is a declaration by an industrial tribunal of "what particulars ought to have been included or referred to in a statement."[38]

If a tribunal finds that "any unnotified deductions have been made" in the 13 weeks preceding the application to the tribunal, it can order the employer to make up these deductions to the employee.[39] The Employment Appeal Tribunal in *Cambiero v. Aldo Zilli & Sheenwalk Ltd t/a Signor Zilli's Bar*[40] considered these provisions to be penal, so that if on the facts these deductions have been made without notification, albeit that they are lawful deductions for PAYE, income tax and national insurance, the employer would still be liable to pay twice for the full 13 week period.

4.3 THE RIGHT TO BE PAID WHEN ABSENT FROM WORK

4.3.1 Contractual regulation of pay

Under normal principles of common law, the right to be paid when absent from work would entirely depend upon contractual entitlement. The general assumption would be that in a situation where no work is done, no wages are due to be paid, unless the contract of employment directs otherwise. Statutory employee protection measures of the last 30 years or so decree that in certain specifically prescribed circumstances, employees will have a statutory entitlement to be paid when absent from work. The text introduces the main circumstances when this arises.

4.3.1.1 *Contractual sick pay*

The statutory statement of employment particulars directs[41] that an employer must include in that statement details of any terms and conditions relating to "incapacity for work due to sickness or injury, including any provision for sick pay. . .". Details of sick pay have to be given in writing to the employee as an express term in the written statement of particulars of employment,[42] but the employer is not statutorily obliged to pay sick pay. In the absence of express terms the court may have to decide if there is an implied term.

---

[32] ERA 1996, s.8(2)(a).
[33] ERA 1996, s.8(2)(b).
[34] ERA 1996, s.8(2)(c).
[35] ERA 1996, s.8(2)(d).
[36] ERA 1996, s.9.
[37] ERA 1996, s.11(3)(b).
[38] ERA 1996, s.11(1).
[39] ERA 1996, s.12(4).
[40] July 9, 1997, EAT 273/96 (reported in I.R.L.B. 586, February 1998).
[41] ERA 1996, s.1(4)(d)(ii), formerly: EPCA 1978, s.1(3)(d)(ii).
[42] ERA 1996, s.2(1).

"In older cases it was held that, in the absence of an express term, there was an implied term that sick pay should be paid."[43] This presumption is now largely reversed by the Court of Appeal decision in *Mears v. Safecar Security*[44] which determined that a court would have to examine all the facts of the case before any such implication could be made:

"In the present case, therefore, if there had been no factors pointing either way, nothing for or against sick pay, then the statutory duty to determine particulars of a term or condition to comply with [ERA 1996, s.1(4)(d)(ii)] could have been discharged only by resorting to the presumption that the wage is to be paid until the employment ended. However, every one of the factors in the present case pointed in the direction of no work, no wages having been agreed. It was the practice of the company not to pay wages to employees absent sick, and the practice was well known to the company's employees. The company would not have made an exception in the appellant's favour. He did not ask for sick pay before taking on the job and if he had asked and been told what the practice was, he would most probably have taken the job. He took leave without sick pay for nearly seven months and never asked for sick pay. Even after the end of his employment, it was some time before he thought of asking for sick pay. He plainly never expected to get sick pay and he never got it." *per* Stephenson L.G.

Mears v. Safecar Security Ltd [1982] I.R.L.R. 183 at 184, CA.

Further guidance on the rules regarding contractual sick pay were given by the Employment Appeal Tribunal in *Howman & Son v. Blyth*,[45] First they decided that "It could not be accepted, as argued on behalf of the respondent, that the Court of Appeal's decision in *Marrison v. Bel*[46] and *Mears v. Safecar Security Ltd* were binding authority that, if there is an obligation to pay sick pay at all, then in the absence of an express term to the contrary, sick pay is payable so long as the employment continues". Secondly, they determined that in today's circumstance an employer could not continue to pay sick pay indefinitely, they need only pay what was usual in a particular industry. To meet the costs of the long term sickness of their employees, many employers take out insurance policies, the terms of which impact upon the contractual entitlement to sick pay.

Employer's permanent health insurance

Some employers seek to defray the costs of the long-term sickness of their employees, by taking out insurance cover which permits the sick employee to continue in employment providing that the insurance company continues to cover the costs of the sickness pay. This is quite an expensive benefit to maintain when employees are ill for long periods or when the benefit is payable until retiring age or death. It is perhaps no surprise therefore, that the case law arising from such contractual entitlements has arisen in situations where the employer is trying to avoid paying all or some of these entitlements. An early case decided that such provisions were not indeed entitlements but only "financial provision" which did not indicate "the amount of absence to which

[43] Pitt (1997), p. 167.
[44] [1982] I.C.R. 626; [1982] I.R.L.R. 183.
[45] [1983] I.R.L.R. 139, EAT.
[46] [1939] 2 K.B. 187; [1939] 1 All E.R. 745, CA.

an employee is entitled if he is sick".[47] In this particular case, the employee's written terms and conditions of employment provided that "In the event of your being absent from work through sickness or injury you will be paid your full salary subject to such deductions mentioned below, for a period of six calendar months calculated from the end of the first month in which such absence commenced and half salary for a further six months."[48] On the facts of this case, where the employee had been sick for 49 out of 104 weeks, and had been offered redeployment albeit at a lower grade, it is perhaps hard not to agree with the industrial tribunal's finding that it was a fair dismissal because:

> "there comes a time when the employer cannot continue to employ someone who is not performing his part of the contract. Such absence is detrimental to the business and when a Tribunal is considering the question of fairness, it has to consider not only fairness to the employee but fairness to the business as well."

Incidentally, this decision in *J. Coulson v. Felixstowe Dock and Railway Co.*[49] established that the application of a disciplinary process against a genuinely sick employee was not appropriate,[50] advice which was later reiterated by ACAS to employers when handling sick absence.[51]

The question of whether an employer can dismiss for incapability when this has the effect of depriving the employee of entitlement under a permanent health scheme was considered by the High Court in *Aspden v. Webbs Poultry and Meat Group (Holdings).*[52] Here a manager was contractually entitled to a particularly generous scheme, which, in the event of total incapacity from sickness or injury, provided for payment of three-quarters of the annual salary until "the employee's death, retirement date, or the date on which he ceased to be an eligible employee, which included dismissal on any ground." Unfortunately the written contract of employment, because it had been modelled on that for a previous manager, also contained an express term that ". . . if he shall be unable (because of accident or illness) to discharge his duties hereunder for a total of 183 days (whether working or not) in any 12 consecutive calendar months, the company may by notice in writing terminate this agreement forthwith or on such date as may be specified in such notice." The High Court noted the discrepancy between this term and the provisions of the health insurance scheme and found that:

> "Notwithstanding that the written contract of employment contained an express provision allowing the employers to terminate by reason of prolonged incapacity alone, a term would be implied in order to give effect to the undoubted mutual intention of the parties when the contract was signed that the provisions for dismissal in that contract would not be operated so as to remove the employee's entitlement to benefit under the permanent health insurance scheme already in force." *per* Sedley J.

> *Aspden v. Webbs Poultry and Meat Group (Holdings) Ltd* [1996] I.R.L.R. 521 at 522, HC.

In another health insurance case, where an employee was receiving full benefit entitlement under his employer's scheme, after he was deemed incapable of work by

---

[47] *Coulson v. Felixstowe Dock and Railway Co.* [1975] I.R.L.R. 11, IT.
[48] *Coulson v. Felixstowe Dock and Railway Co.* [1975] I.R.L.R. 13 para. 22, IT.
[49] [1975] I.R.L.R. 11, IT.
[50] [1975] I.R.L.R. 13, para. 21, I.T.
[51] ACAS Discipline at Work (1987), The ACAS advisory handbook.
[52] [1996] I.R.L.R. 521, HC.

sickness, the High Court found that the employer had repudiated the contract by stopping payment of these benefits when it was discovered that the employee was undertaking part-time work elsewhere. In *Brompton v. AOC International Ltd and UNUM Ltd*[53] the High Court held further, that because the employee had accepted the repudiation by taking other work on a fixed term contract, he was no longer entitled to the insurance benefits. Not so, said the Court of Appeal, this was not an ordinary situation of repudiation of the employment contract. The contract only really existed in name. It had been replaced by a contract under which the employee would be paid half his salary until retirement age, but no work would be expected in return. The Court also considered that there was a good deal to be said for Seddon J.'s decision in *Aspden* that because the whole purpose of a health insurance scheme would be defeated if the employers could just dismiss for incapacity, then there must be an implied term, which by reason of business efficacy prevented the employer from doing this.[54]

4.3.2 Sick pay and statutory sick pay: Social Security Contributions and Benefits Act 1992, ss.151–163; Statutory Sick Pay Act 1994

Statutory entitlement to sick pay guarantees that any employee who falls sick and is consequently unable to work for up to 28 weeks in a period of three years, receives a minimum payment (currently: £57.70 April 1998) from his or her employer. Many employees however, receive considerably in excess of this figure dependant on their contractual entitlement (see para. 4.3.2.2 below). The statutory provisions are, however, a safety net for many employees who would probably not receive any payment if it was not for the state scheme, which supplements other parts of the social security system. Employers themselves disburse the statutory sick pay (SSP) to their employees and in return receive a rebate from the Government. The rebate is only recoverable, when the employer's disbursements of SSP in any one month exceed 13 per cent of their own liability for national insurance contributions in that same period.[55] The original scheme was introduced in 1982,[56] coming into effect the following year.[57] It was amended by the Social Security Act 1985 and the current law is consolidated into the Social Security Contributions and Benefits Act 1992 (SSCBA), ss.151–163. This Act was amended in 1994[58] only to the extent that it modified the above mentioned rebate system in which small employers had been able to claim up to 100 per cent reimbursement of SSP. The main regulations which apply in this area are the Statutory Sick Pay (General) Regulations 1982 (S.I. 1982 No. 894). The legislation is largely enabling and the regulations complex, permitting it is alleged, "the DSS [civil servants] to make up the rules as they go along by precise, but rarely intelligible, regulations."[59] The text for this section is indebted to the analysis of these regulations found in Harvey.[60]

Main points about SSP

- Many, if not most employees, have a contractual right to sickness pay and are part of the employer's sick pay scheme, where a typical arrangement is for the

---

[53] [1997] I.R.L.R. 639, CA.
[54] *Brompton v. AOC International Ltd and Unum Ltd* [1997] I.R.L.R. 643 para. 32, EAT.
[55] Statutory Sick Pay Percentage Threshold Order 1995 (S.I. 1995 No. 512).
[56] Social Security and Housing Benefits Act 1982 (SSHBA 1982).
[57] April 6, 1983.
[58] Statutory Sick Pay Act 1994.
[59] *Harvey on Industrial Relations and Employment Law* (Butterworths, London, 1997), p. H/1.
[60] *op. cit.*

employer to make up the difference between the SSP payment and the employee's wages for a given period. Entry to these schemes is often based on an individual employee's length of service with the employer. Such a scheme, may, after five years service provide for up to six months sick pay at the normal rate of remuneration followed by another six months at half pay.[61] Private schemes do not effect the state scheme although an employee cannot claim twice.[62]

- If an employee is part of a company sick pay scheme this should be specified in the written statement of particulars of employment–ERA 1996, s.1(4).

- SSCBA s.151 provides that an employer must pay SSP, at the current statutory rate, when an employee is away sick, for up to the equivalent of 28 weeks.[63] Payment cannot be made for the first three days of sickness however. These "waiting days" as they are known, being a particular cause of hardship for those employees who are totally reliant on the state scheme.

- SSP is only payable to "employees" as statutorily defined.[64] These are individuals over 16 working under a contract of service or in an office and who are liable to pay Schedule E income tax.[65] Clarification is given by the Sick Pay Regulations[66] which say that even if an employee does not pay tax under Schedule E he or she can be an "employed earner" for SSP purposes. This category of workers includes: office cleaners, some temporary agency workers, a spouse's employee, some teachers and lecturers and ministers of religion.

- The Act excludes certain categories of individual from claiming SSP. These include: pensioners[67]; men over 65 and women over 60[68]; employees on contracts of less than three months[69]; employees who do not earn enough to attract national insurance contributions[70]; people already on state invalidity pension or severe disablement allowance[71] or state sickness allowance[72] or state maternity allowance[73]; pregnant employees[74]; prisoners[75]; employees who are outside the EEC when sick[76] and employees who are on strike.[77] Some of these individuals are expected to subsist on the state benefits which are available.

---

[61] National Joint Council For Local Authorities' Administrative, Professional, Technical And Clerical Services, *Scheme of Conditions of Service,* January, 1994, para. 50(1).
[62] SSCBA 1982, Sched. 12, para. 2.
[63] SSCBA 1992, s.155.
[64] SSCBA 1992, s.163.
[65] Tax payable under Schedule E is usually paid by individuals working under a contract of employment, and is deducted at source by the employer under the pay as you earn (PAYE) system under ICTA 1988, s.19(1).
[66] Sick Pay (General) Regulations 1982 S.I. 1982 No. 894).
[67] SSCBA 1982, Sched. 11, para. 2(a).
[68] SSCBA 1982, Sched. 11 para. 2(a), s.163(1).
[69] SSCBA 1982, Sched. 11 para. 2(b).
[70] SSCBA 1982, Sched. 11 para. 2(c).
[71] SSCBA 1982, Sched. 11 paras 2(d) and 5.
[72] SSCBA 1992, Sched. 11 para. 2(e).
[73] SSCBA 1982, Sched. 11 para. 2(e)(ii).
[74] SSCBA 1982, Sched. 11 para. 2(h).
[75] reg. 3(2).
[76] SSP (Mariners, Airman and Persons Abroad) Regulations 1982 (S.I. 1982 No. 1349), reg. 10.
[77] SSCBA 1992, Sched. 11 para. 2(g).

- To claim SSP the individual must be an employee at the time of sickness under a contract of service. This was a problem in *Brown v. Chief Adjudication Officer*[78] where an employee was engaged on a series of one day contracts so that the "period of entitlement" always ended with the contract on the day before the illness. The Social Security Commissioner concluded that the effect of the SSCBA 1992, s.153 was that the employee was not entitled to SSP because her contract of service always ended with the last day worked. The Court of Appeal found that what is now ERA 1996, s.86(4) applied in this situation, because it provides that an employee who has been continuously employed for three months under a contract certain of one month or less, is deemed to be employed under a contract of indefinite length.

- To be paid SSP the employee must be suffering from "some specific disease or (physical or mental) disablement[79] which prevents him or her from doing the work they are contracted to do during a "period of incapacity".

- Illnesses of three days or less cannot be claimed for[80] during a period of incapacity from work. The "period of entitlement" to SSP determines when the employee is entitled to SSP. This is calculated according to "qualifying days". The first "qualifying day" is normally the fourth day of illness, but SSP is only paid for those days which are qualifying days as agreed between employee and employer.[81] Many employers agree that all five days of a normal week of Monday to Friday are qualifying days but the full seven calendar days can also be agreed. There must be at least one qualifying day *per* week.[82] The qualifying days can vary from week to week with only one day being designated in a holiday week. If agreement cannot be reached on qualifying days then these are determined by the Regulations.[83]

- An employee claiming sick pay has to wait for three "qualifying days" before entitlement to SSP begins. Therefore an employee going sick for a week starting on a Thursday, where Saturday and Sunday are not agreed as "qualifying days" would not be entitled to receive any SSP until the following Tuesday.

- The level of SSP due is based on the normal weekly earnings of the employee. For employees earning less than the "lower earnings limit" for national insurance contributions there is a single rate applicable (£57.70 April 1998[84]). The maximum entitlement payable is the equivalent of 28 weeks' sick pay,[85] that is £1,615.60 at current rates.

- The Act permits the employer, within limits, to regulate how the SSP is claimed and what evidence the employee must give about the sickness leave. The employee or their representative must inform the employer that they are unfit for work. If they do not do so the employer may at his discretion

---

[78] [1997] I.R.L.R. 110, CA.
[79] SSCBA 1992, s.151(4).
[80] SSCBA 1992, s.151(1).
[81] SSCBA 1992, s.154(2).
[82] SSCBA 1992, s.154(3).
[83] Sick Pay (General) Regulations, reg. 5.
[84] DSS, April 1998, *Supplement to the Statutory Sick Pay Manual for Employers* (Leaflet CA29).
[85] SSCBA 1992, s.151(4).

withhold payment.[86] The employer must also keep a record of when he did and did not pay SSP for every employee.[87] Research shows that in the NHS, some employers are also compiling very accurate statistics on sickness absence. Of 51 NHS and independent healthcare organisations surveyed, two-thirds recorded sickness absence for all staff; one quarter said their absence statistics were very accurate, two-thirds said such data was accurate and about 6 per cent said it was very accurate.[88]

- Payment of SSP ceases when the "period of entitlement" comes to an end because the employee:

  — recovers[89];
  — has received the maximum entitlement[90] or has received SSP in a linked period, that is within 56 calendar days of a previous period of incapacity;
  — has his or her contract terminated[91];
  — reaches the eleventh week before her expected confinement[92];
  — is imprisoned[93];
  — is sick outside the EEC.[94]

Statutory Sick Pay (General) Amendment Regulations 1996[95]

From April 6, 1997, the 1996 Amendment Regulations have enabled employers to "opt-out" of the state scheme providing it equals or exceeds the current rate of SSP. The employer does not need to inform the Inland Revenue or the Contributions Agency of their decision to "opt-out". He will comply with the regulations providing that they provide a contractual payment, for a day of sickness which equals or exceeds the SSP level. The intention of the amending legislation was to simplify record keeping so that employers do not need to keep two sets of records, one for their occupational sick pay scheme and another for SSP.

4.3.3   Holiday pay

ERA 1996, s.1(4)(d)(i) provides that the statutory statement of initial employment particulars issued to employees should include details of entitlement to holidays, including public holidays. This written statement should also include details of any entitlement to holiday pay and precisely how accrued holiday pay is to be calculated in the event of the contract being terminated. If there are no particulars to record on holiday entitlement, this should be stated[96] and all these particulars should be contained in one document which states the main terms of the contract.[97]

---

[86] SSCBA 1992, s.156(2)(a).
[87] SSHBA 1992, s.17(4); reg. 13.
[88] Pay and Workforce Research, Managing sickness absence: preliminary results of PWR's pilot study, 1997.
[89] SSCBA 1992, s.153(2)(a).
[90] SSCBA 1992, s.153(2)(b).
[91] SSCBA 1992, s.153(2)(c).
[92] SSCBA 1992, s.153(2)(d).
[93] Sick Pay (General) Regulations 1982, reg. 3(1).
[94] regs. 10 to 13.
[95] S.I. 1996 No. 3042.
[96] ERA 1996, s.2(1).
[97] ERA 1996, s.2(4).

At the time of writing, there is no statutory obligation on employers to grant paid holiday leave to any employee, but the Government has announced that it is committed to implementing the European Working Time Directive 93/104.[98] Article 7(1) of the Directive requires that Member States enact legislation which ensures that every *worker* is given an entitlement of at least four weeks paid annual leave. Further, Article 7(2) also directs that such leave can not be replaced with an allowance in lieu unless the employment relationship is terminated.

4.3.4 Payment whilst looking for work or retraining: ERA 1996, ss.52–54

ERA 1996, Part VI, ss.50—63 are the main statutory provisions which permit an employee to take paid and unpaid leave either to do very specific things which are in the public or collective interest, or are to help the individual in a particular situation. An employee who is under notice of redundancy is permitted to take reasonable time off during working hours to look for a new job or to arrange for training for a new job.[99] The amount of remuneration to be paid is to be paid at the appropriate hourly rate.[1] There is a cap on the amount of reasonable time off to be paid in that it must not exceed 40 per cent of a week's pay for the total of the notice period.[2] (See Chapter 8, para. 8.3.6). The remedy for failure to comply with these provisions is that an industrial tribunal will make a declaration that the complaint is well founded and will order the employer to pay an appropriate sum.[3]

4.3.5 Payment whilst on employee representative duties: ERA 1996, ss.61–63; TULRCA 1992, ss.168–172

Employee representatives who are elected, or are in the process of being elected to represent employees undergoing redundancy or transfer are entitle to reasonable paid time off to undertake their duties.[4] (See Chapters 8 and 9). Similar rights to a declaration and orders to pay remuneration apply as with the other time-off entitlements.

4.3.6 Payment whilst on public duties: ERA 1996, ss.50–51

Employees who serve as a justice of the peace, or who serve on a local authority, a statutory tribunal, a police authority, a board of prison visitors, an NHS trust, a governing body of a school or on environment agency are all permitted to take paid time off for undertaking such duties.[5] The amount of time they can take off however is subject to how much time they may already take off on trade union business and on the circumstances of the employer's business and the effect the absence of the employee has on the business.[6]

---

[98] Cm. 3968, *Fairness At Work*, DTI May 1998, para. 5.6.
[99] ERA 1996, s.52(1).
[1] ERA 1996, s.53.
[2] ERA 1996, s.53(5).
[3] ERA 1996, s.54(3).
[4] ERA 1996, s.61.
[5] ERA 1996, s.50(2).
[6] ERA 1996, s.50(4).

4.4   Deductions from Pay

Historically, the state has legislated to both regulate the level of and the form of pay received by some workers. In the eighteenth and nineteenth centuries it was common for manufacturers and mine owners to pay their factory workers in kind or in truck[7] rather than in coin of the realm. Workers exchanged vouchers to buy goods at inflated prices at the employer owned tommy-shop situated at the factory gate or pit-head. "By this practice the Coal and Iron masters compel their workmen to accept two-thirds of their wages in goods, such as Sugar, Soap, Candles, Meat, Bacon, Flour, etc. instead of money, at an unreasonable large profitt."[8] From as early as 1726[9] there was a Truck Act[10] on the statute book requiring that employers in the woollen industry pay their workers in money. Many masters just ignored these provisions however and the magistrates rarely enforced them.[11] From 1831 to 1940 a new series of Tuck Acts[12] were enforced which gave rights to manual workers[13] and shop assistants to be paid in "current coin of the realm" and which placed restrictions on the deductions which employers could make for bad workmanship. As recently as 1987, the judicial House of Lords ruled in *Bristow v. City Petroleum Co. Ltd*[14] that an employer who regularly deducted up to 17 per cent of a petrol station attendant's wages to make up for loss of cash and stock, irrespective of whether it was the employee's fault, was in breach of the Truck Act 1896, s.1.

Concern by the government to allow for modern and secure systems of payment of wages led to the passing of the Payment of Wages Act 1960 which permitted cashless pay, for example by credit transfer or by cheque. Such an arrangement was conditional upon agreement with the employee, and the traditional method of facilitating this was for the employer to offer a one-off payment to the employee to transfer to cashless pay. Manual workers could however, still insist on cash payment and the Wages Act 1986 was enacted to repeal the Truck Acts and introduce new protections for *all* workers. These protections have been criticised for being more concerned with the process of making deductions rather than with their fairness.[15] The Wages Act 1986 was consolidated into ERA 1996 and the provisions on deductions are now found in ERA 1996, ss.13–27. These provisions are based on the principle that the employer is not allowed to make any deductions from a worker's pay unless authorised to do so, either by law, or by the agreement of the individual worker.

4.4.1   Right not to suffer unauthorised deductions: ERA 1996, s.13

Section 13(1) provides that an employer may not make unauthorised deductions from wages *unless*:

[7] "**Truck**—1553 . . . The payment of wages other-wise than in money; the system or practice of such payment, the *t. system*; occas., goods supplied in lieu of wages 1743."—Shorter Oxford English Dictionary 3rd ed., rev., OUP, Oxford, 1975).
[8] 19th century Home Office Report: H. O., 40. 17. cited in J.L. Hammond, and Barbara (1920) *The Town Labourer 1760–1832* (Labour Research Department & Longmans, London, 1920), p. 68.
[9] "The old Truck enactments were very numerous and date from about the year 1464." *per* Lord Justice Bridge of Harwich, *Bristow v. City Petroleum Co. Ltd* [1987] I.R.L.R. 340, HL., para. 10. This case gives a close review of the 19th century Truck Acts.
[10] 12 George I. c. 34.
[11] J.L. Hammond & Barbara, p. 67.
[12] See I.T. Smith and J. Wood, *Industrial Law* (3rd ed., 1986), for details of these Truck Acts.
[13] *Brooker v. Charrington Fuel Oils Ltd* [1981] I.R.L.R. 147, CC.
[14] [1987] I.R.L.R. 340, HL.
[15] I.T. Smith and G. Thomas (1996), p. 180.

- they are authorised by statute or by a "relevant provision" of the employment contract[16]; or

- the individual worker has agreed the deductions in writing.[17]

A "relevant provision" is defined as a written term of the contract given to the worker before the deduction has been made[18] or a term which can be implied from the contract overall.[19]

An unauthorised deduction is statutorily and simply defined as the wages paid on any occasion where their sum "is less than the total amount of the wages properly payable" to that worker after the authorised deductions have been subtracted.[20] "Worker" is broadly defined as including: anyone working under a contract of service, or apprenticeship or who undertakes personal services, but excludes the situation where the receivers of such service are clients or customers of the individual who is carrying out a trade or business.[21]

Examples of statutory deductions which are commonly made under the Attachment of Earnings Act 1971 include court orders to recover debt, to enforce a maintenance order, to administer insolvency proceedings and to recover fines for criminal offences. These are all lawful deductions from wages. There has to be an actual deduction not a proposed or threatened deduction before a complaint can be made by a worker.[22]

Between 1986 and 1994 there was a lot of case law on the interpretation to be given to the statutory meaning accorded: "deduction" and "wages." This was because employees claiming unfair dismissal often also made claims in the county courts for recovery of unlawful deductions (such as notice money) under the Wages Act. With the extension of jurisdiction to industrial tribunals to deal with contractual claims in 1994 these issues can now be considered under the one jurisdiction.

In *Pename Ltd t/a Storage Lifting & Distribution Co v. Paterson*[23] the employee was told at an interview that he would loose one week's pay if he left without giving notice and a letter was afterwards sent confirming this term as part of his conditions of employment. The employee did leave without giving the contractual notice and this was held to be an unlawful deduction under the ERA 1996, s.13(2)(a), (b), because the employee had not signalled his agreement to it in writing. In *Kerr v. The Sweater Shop (Scotland) Ltd* a differently constituted Employment Appeal Tribunal said the signing of the agreement was not vital, but that the correct approach in deciding whether a deduction is lawful is to ascertain whether agreement has beeen given:

"The effect of those provisions is that for a contractual term authorising a deduction to be valid, the employee need not have assented to it in writing but must nevertheless be held to have agreed to it, whether expressly or impliedly, in the sense of continuing to work once the term had been validly brought to his attention. The decision in *Pename Ltd v. Paterson*, which suggested that

---

[16] ERA 1996, s.13(1)(a).
[17] ERA 1996, s.13(1)(b).
[18] ERA 1996, s.13(2)(a).
[19] ERA 1996, s.13(2)(b).
[20] ERA 1996, s.13(3).
[21] ERA 1996, s.230(3).
[22] *Mennell v. Newell & Wright (Transport Contractors) Ltd* [1997] I.R.L.R. 519, CA.
[23] [1989] I.R.L.R. 195, EAT.

agreement of the employee in writing is essential to the validity of a deduction from wages, could not be agreed with." *per* Johnston L.J.

Kerr v. The Sweater Shop (Scotland) Ltd; The Sweater Shop (Scotland) Ltd v. Park [1996] I.R.L.R. 424 at 424, EAT.

In *Kerr*, the employer had only notified the workers by means of a factory notice, that the company rules incorporated into their individual contracts of employment would be varied to the extent that in the event of dismissal for misconduct, employees would lose their accrued holiday pay. This was held not to comply with section 13(1)(b) which requires individual notification of such deductions so thereby giving the worker an opportunity to accept or reject the variation.

A clear and unambiguous agreement in writing that the deduction is to be made from the individual worker's wages is also necessary said the EAT in *Potter v. Hunt Contracts Ltd.*[24] Here, a lorry driver was dismissed with an outstanding loan for an HGV drivers course unpaid, some of which the employers recovered from his last wages. The Employment Appeal Tribunal found that this was an unlawful deduction because there was not a written document stipulating that the loan would be paid from the employee's wages and no indication that the individual had agreed to this.

It also seems that although the legislative provisions are primarily concerned with the correct procedure for making deductions after they have been agreed, there may be occasions when industrial tribunals have to examine the fairness of the decision by the employer to make a deduction.

> "Where there is a dispute as to the justification of a deduction, s.1(1)(a) contemplates that the Industrial Tribunal must embark upon a resolution of that dispute. It requires the Tribunal to ask whether the deduction that was made was authorised to be made by virtue of any relevant provision of the worker's contract." *per* Hutchison J.

Fairfield Ltd v. Skinner [1993] I.R.L.R. 4 at 4, EAT.

In *Fairfield*, a summarily dismissed van driver had his final wages reduced by a sum representing a "provisional deduction for van telephone calls and private mileage in excess of free allowance". Because there was no evidence advanced that these expenses actually amounted to the sum deducted (£150) this was declared an unlawful deduction.

Employers can not make deductions which relate to actions or to the conduct of a worker before written consent is given by that worker. This is to prevent any pressure being put on the employee to agree the deduction.[25] Workers in the retail industry also have the added protection afforded by the ERA 1996, ss.17 to 21 which provide that in the event of a contractual term permitting deductions from wages because of cash shortages in the till or stock deficiencies, an employer is not permitted to deduct a sum equivalent to more than 10 per cent from the gross wages paid.

The abolition of a pay supplement which an employee was contractually entitled to receive, after he was statutorily transferred from one London authority to another was held to be in contravention of what is now ERA 1996, s.13(1)(a). The employee had been employed by the Greater London Council (GLC) and after its abolition was

---

[24] [1992] I.R.L.R. 108, EAT.
[25] *Discount Tobacco and Confectionery Ltd v. Williamson* [1993] I.R.L.R. 327, EAT.

transferred to the London Borough of Tower Hamlets, ". . . he had been granted a London supplement of £6 a week in return for agreeing to be paid by credit transfer instead of in cash. This 'non-cash' supplement was subject to future increases according to a set formula and was to continue throughout the employee's working life."[26]

Lastly, whether an employer has a right to deduct unearned commission on the termination of employment has proved quite a vexatious issue for the courts. In *Kent Management Services Ltd v. Butterfield*[27] because the contract expressly said that commission and bonuses would normally be paid, the Employment Appeal Tribunal found that it fell into the statutory definition of wages because it was "within the reasonable contemplation of both parties that in ordinary circumstances it will be payable." The position was more complicated in *Robertson v. Blackstone Franks Investment Management Ltd*[28] where a self-employed investment consultant received an advance against future commissions of £10,500 which it was agreed was to be repaid over two years. Eight months after the contract started, the employee was dismissed with none of the commission repaid. At the Court of Appeal it was found that the employers were entitled to recover the advance commission as it was payment made in respect of future wages which could be offset at termination against wages already earned.

4.4.2 Excepted deductions: ERA 1996, s.14

An employer is allowed to make a deduction from pay if there has been an overpayment of wages[29] or of expenses[30]; or where deductions have been made as a consequence of statutory disciplinary procedures[31]; or because of a statutory requirement[32]; or where the worker has agreed to the deduction to a third party (*e.g.* union dues)[33]; or where the worker has been on strike or taken industrial action[34]; or where the worker has agreed for a court or tribunal order to be made for payments to his employer.[35]

To make any of these deductions the industrial tribunal relies on evidence that the statutory situation exists as defined. For example in *Fairfield v. Skinner*[36] (see above) the employer summarily dismissed a van driver for poor attendance and deducted a nominal sum of £150 from his final wages for the expenses of private telephone calls and private mileage. The Employment Appeal Tribunal supported the industrial tribunal's view that the contract supported such deductions if the evidence had shown that the employer was factually entitled to implement them.

4.4.3 When taking industrial action: common law doctrine of entire performance

The common law principle of "no work no pay" is reflected in the statutory provisions which allow employers to make a deduction from wages "where the worker has taken

---

[26] *Mccree (Appellant) v. London Borough Of Tower Hamlets* [1992] I.R.L.R. 56, EAT.
[27] [1992] I.R.L.R. 394.
[28] April 7, 1998, CA, reported in IDS Brief 613 May 1998.
[29] ERA 1996, s.14(1)(a).
[30] ERA 1996, s.14(1)(b).
[31] ERA 1996, s.14(2).
[32] ERA 1996, s.14(3).
[33] ERA 1996, s.14(4).
[34] ERA 1996, s.14(5).
[35] ERA 1996, s.14(6).
[36] [1993] I.R.L.R. 4.

part in a strike or other industrial action and the deduction is made by the employer on account of the worker's having taken part in that strike or other action.'[37] Not performing the contract can put the employee in a vulnerable position regarding entitlement to pay, especially if the employer indicates that unless the contract is performed in full, no remuneration will be forthcoming.[38]

4.5   REGULATION OF PAY RATES

4.5.1   State regulation of pay rates as a tool of economic policy

The text has so far considered the determination of pay by the contract of employment, as well as examining how statute has intervened to regularise this condition of the contract and to imply entitlement to pay in certain situations such as sickness and maternity. Brief consideration is now given to why and how the state plays a role in setting the actual pay levels of some workers, and the legal instruments it chooses to exercise this role.

4.5.2   Performance and profit related pay

One of the central objectives of industrial relations policy promulgated by the Conservative Governments of 1979 to 1997 was to try and detach pay bargaining and the negotiating of annual wages from the collective sphere of trade union and employer negotiating to the personal sphere of individual bargaining. This was part of the Hayekian economic philosophy[39] which strongly informed government policy in this period. Part of this belief was that trade unions were both democratically and economically injurious towards the state and the individual.

Hayek considered that:

> "the individual employment contract has no special character; it is but one contract among many, to be governed by common principles of 'freedom of contract' and the general law. The employed person has chosen by his contract to have 'the regular income for which he sells his labour'; he must therefore do 'the bidding of others,' in contrast to the 'independent' entrepreneur. The employee's freedom depends on choice between 'a great number and variety of employers,' and that can be achieved only in a competitive market. The pressures of organised groups such as trade unions on that market create distortions and must therefore be ended."[40]

So, at the same time that the government was strongly regulating the activities of trade unions (see Chapter 11) it was encouraging new schemes of pay bargaining:

---

[37] ERA 1996, s.14(5).
[38] See: *Wiluszynski v. London Borough of Tower Hamlets* [1989] I.R.L.R. 259, CA; and *British Telecommunications plc v. Ticehurst* [1992] I.R.L.R. 219, CA.
[39] Friedrich August von Hayek (b. 1899), Austrian free market economist who believed that money supply had to be strictly regulated in order to control inflation even if this leads to very high levels of unemployment.
[40] Lord Wedderburn (1989) "Freedom of Association and Philosophies of Labour Law" (1989) 18 I.L.J. 9, p. 9. (John Hendy has described this article as "a brilliant analysis" of how the legal changes to employment rights under Mrs Thatcher's administrations were derived from the thinking of this economist—J. Hendy, *A Law Unto Themselves. Conservative Employment Laws: A National and International Assessment*, (3rd ed., 1993), Institute of Employment Rights.

"More and more companies are seeking to base pay on individual skills and performance. As their membership has declined, some trade unions have found it harder to secure and retain recognition by employers. Many companies have developed new arrangements for consulting and informing their employees directly—rather than through trade union officials—about the performance of their business and their plans for the future. Some have developed new ways of involving their employees directly in the prosperity of their firms through schemes for share ownership and profit-related pay."[41]

There was therefore government encouragement to devise employment remuneration packages which were not collectively bargained and not linked to an automatic annual review. The Finance Act 1987 provided 100 per cent tax relief on profit-related pay providing it was attached to an Inland Revenue Approved Scheme.[42] These schemes had to apply to 80 per cent of the employees and the PRP element of the pay was not to exceed 20 per cent of total net pay. The government's intention was to directly link employees' pay with the profitability of an enterprise but this was abandoned as it was found that some employers used PRP schemes to cut wage bills through tax relief.[43] The potential insecurity of such schemes for many employees compared with the golden handshakes given to the chairmen of newly privatised enterprises was widely criticised even by proponents of personal bargaining: "while performance-related pay may be desirable in theory, in the context of generally excessive British pay settlements it is often far too loosely operated, especially for senior executives."[44] Tax relief on PRP is now being phased out and is due to end in 2000.

Pay schemes linked to the profitability of the enterprise, for example employee share ownership (ESOPS) and to the performance of the individual employee were however increasingly introduced by employers in this period. It has been pointed out that the legal effect of the introduction of pay dependant upon variables, can reduce the level of wages guaranteed by the contract[45]; although there is nothing to prevent the contracting parties agreeing such variables. "Agree" is the key word however. Agreement should be secured on both the criteria and on how they are applied.[46] Performance Related Pay (PRP) is often expressed as commission often linked to financial targets, volume of sales, or completed projects. As has been seen above (see para. 4.4.1) commission may not always come within the statutory definition of "wages". Leighton and ODonnell advise that "when pay contains an enhanced element such as commission it is vital to express the intention unambiguously" and to state clearly whether commission is related to gross or net sales, if it is to be paid in arrears or in advance and what happens if the sales levels are not maintained.[47] Many employers link such schemes with personal appraisal schemes which may become contractual providing that there is clear incorporation into the contract.

Lastly, it was because of employer intention in the dockyards and in the newspaper industry to break trade union involvement in pay negotiations, which led them to offer

[41] *Industrial Relations in the 1990s, Proposals for further reform of industrial relations and trade union law* Cm. 1602 (1991), Department of Employment.
[42] ICTA 1988, ss.169–184 and Sched. 8.
[43] S. Deakin and G.S. Morris (1995), p. 272.
[44] C.G. Hanson, *Taming the Trade Unions, A Guide To The Thatcher Government's Employment Reforms, 1980–90* (Macmillan/Adam Smith Institute, London, 1991).
[45] S. Deakin and G.S. Morris (1995), p. 271.
[46] P. Leighton and A. ODonnell *The New Employment Contract* (Brealey, London 1995), p. 164.
[47] *ibid.*, p. 165.

dockyard workers and journalists personally negotiated contracts and individually agreed pay rates in exchange for their individual trade union membership and collectively agreed contracts. This was deemed by the House of Lords not to amount to victimisation on grounds of trade union membership[48] (see Chapter 11, para. 11.4.1) although the 1998 White Paper has announced that such action will be made unlawful.[49-50]

4.5.3   Wages councils, purpose, history and abolition

Although there was a relative lack of legal controls on collective bargaining from the 1890s to 1979 "it was public policy to support the extension of joint regulation of pay and conditions."[51] The object of government policy was to both maintain industrial peace and to protect the low paid. This object was to be achieved through sectoral bargaining in joint Whitley Councils (see Chapter 11, para. 11.2) and this process of collective bargaining between employer's and trade union representatives became well established in both private and public sector employment, reaching its peak in the 1960s and 1970s. Such structured bargaining was not possible in industries where trade union membership was low and collective organisation weak. Government intervention to protect individual employees and to sometimes encourage union organisation was manifested in such instruments as the Fair Wages Resolutions of the House of Commons in 1892, 1896 and 1946 which provided that government contractors had to observe minimum conditions and terms of employment. Individuals covered by such Orders had their wages set at a minimum level appropriate to their sector or grade. Later, Schedule 11 of EPA 1975 enabled such sector level agreements to be applied, by neutral arbitration to non-unionised employers. Wages councils were originally set up in 1909 as trade boards in sectors where low pay was prevalent and trade unions weak. Later legislation encouraged their setting up so that by the 1950s there were 65 councils, covering two-and-a-half million workers plus farm workers, amounting to about 12 per cent of the workforce.[52] These councils set a minimum rate for a particular trade or industry, and also set higher rates for particular occupations. Overtime rates and holiday entitlements were also set.

One of the criticisms of the wages councils was that they tended to follow rather than set the going rate in any particular sector.[53] They did however provide some protection for individual workers who could take civil action against the employer to enforce payment. In addition, employers who failed to observe the order committed a criminal offence. Perceived by some trade unionists as a very unsatisfactory substitute for genuine full-bodied collective bargaining and regarded as impeding free competition by Conservative Governments in the 1980s and 1990s, the wage councils' powers were reduced in 1986[54] and finally abolished in 1993.[55] Four years later, a newly

---

[48] *Associated Newspapers Ltd v. Wilson; Associated British Ports v. Palmer and Others* [1995] I.R.L.R. 258, HL.

[49-50] *Fairness At Work*, Cm. 3968 DTI., May 1998., para. 4.25.

[51] S. Deakin, J. Michie and F. Wilkinson *Inflation, Employment, Wage-bargaining and the Law*, (Institute of Employment Rights, London, 1992), p. 11.

[52] P. Davies and M. Freedland, *Labour Legislation and Public Policy* (Clarendon Press, Oxford, 1993 p. 30. (Alternative figures given are around 20% in 1945-F.J. Bayliss, *British Wage Councils* (Blackwell, Oxford, 1962).

[53] P. Davies and M. Freedland, *op. cit.* p. 30.

[54] Wages Act 1986, s.12.

[55] Trade Union Reform and Employment Rights Act 1993 (TURERA 1993), s.35.

restored Labour Government was set to tackle the problem of low pay by the introduction of a national minimum wage.

4.5.4 National minimum wage

The newly elected Labour Government established a Low Pay Commission (LPC) in 1997 chaired by Professor George Bain which was "charged with examining the economic, employment and social justice considerations of a legally enforceable national minimum wage." The National Minimum Wage (NMW) Bill had its first reading in the House of Commons on November 26, 1997. In line with its overall policy of getting people from welfare back into work, the Government's aim was to establish a fair minimum wage for workers over compulsory school-leaving age. The level of the minimum rate per hour had been the subject of some controversy between trade unions and employer's bodies. The Bill itself was nearing the end of the committee stage by late Spring 1998 and its main proposals are summarised below. Implementation of these measures is at present anticipated for Spring 1999.[56]

Perhaps the most surprising part of the Bill is the proposed width of its application and the thoroughness of its enforcement instruments. It will be applied not just to "employees" as narrowly defined in the TULRCA 1992, s.295(1)[57] but to all workers over 16 years of age who work under a contract of employment or any other contract.[58] This is the same definition of worker to be found in the ERA 1996, s.230(3). The Bill also proposes extending fair wage protection to agency workers,[59] and to home workers.[60] Crown employment and service in the armed forces[61] will also be covered. The Secretary of State will also have the power to extend the Regulations to other categories of workers.

The Secretary of State will have the legal power to set the minimum wage[62] (NMW), which will consist of one single rate which will be applied irrespective of different areas or sectors of employment; of different sized businesses, or of different ages and types of occupation. Clause 3 of the Bill will permit the Secretary of State to exclude those under the age of 26 from receiving NMW—a proposal not welcomed by many at the time.

The Low Pay Commission itself will advise the Secretary of State on the rate of NMW, its application and any excluded categories of worker.[63] In pursuing these obligations, the LPC will have a statutory obligation to consult workers' and employers' organisations and to have regard to the effect of the recommended rate on the economy and its effectiveness.

The statute will place the burden of keeping accurate records[64] on the employer who will be required to produce them for inspection by the employee concerned,[65] by an industrial tribunal and by enforcement officers. Workers will have the right to

---

[56] IRLB 585, January 1998.
[57] "employee means an individual who has entered into or works under (or, where the employment has cased, worked under) a contract of employment".
[58] cl. 51(3).
[59] cl. 31.
[60] cl. 32.
[61] An amendment was tabled in Parliament by the DTI on the April 3, 1998, to exclude Army, Navy and Royal Air Force uniformed personnel, although civilian staff will be covered by the legislation (*The Times*, April 4, 1998).
[62] cl. 2.
[63] cll. 5 to 8.
[64] cl. 9.
[65] cl. 10.

complain to an industrial tribunal if these records are not produced.[66] They will also have a right under the ERA 1996, s.13, or under a breach of contract action, to claim for an unlawful deduction if the NMW is not paid.[67] Workers who are not "employees" will have the right to receive a written statement giving details of the NMW, in the same way as employees presently have the right under the ERA 1996, s.8 to receive an itemised pay statement.[68] Such workers will also be deemed to have the same enforcement rights as employees.[69] All workers will have a statutory right not to suffer a detriment or to be dismissed for bringing an NMW claim.[70] It will be an automatically unfair dismissal if an employee is sacked because they brought a complaint against the employer. These complaints will be subject to conciliation by ACAS officers.[71]

The first level of enforcement thus mirrors that for other statutory entitlements such as the right not to be unfairly dismissed. The belt and braces approach to NMW enforcement however, is illustrated by the second and third levels of the process. At the second level it is proposed to have a system of officials[72] who will take a proactive role in being able to enter employers' premises and demand appropriate records. These officers will have the power to serve an enforcement notice on an employer to pay the NMW.[73] In the event of the employer not complying with this notice the officer may complain to an industrial tribunal on behalf of one or more workers to recover the difference between the wage paid and the NMW[74] or the officer may serve a financial penalty at twice the rate of the NMW for each day that the employer is not in compliance.[75] Such fines will be paid to the Secretary of State. The final and most draconian penalty against a recalcitrant employer will be police action against them for committing the criminal offence of refusing to pay the NMW, or failure to keep the required records, or knowingly to produce false records or intentionally obstructing an official trying to obtain such information.[76] There will be a maximum fine of up to level 5 (currently £5,000) for anyone found guilty of these offences. Some employers' organisations particularly criticised this aspect of the legalisation as being "entirely inappropriate to our voluntarist tradition of employee relations."[77]

Not surprisingly, the most controversial aspect of the legislation was the setting of the actual level of the minimum wage and the enforcement mechanism proposed. There was much debate about the level of the appropriate rate, how it was to be calculated[78] and the mechanism to be adopted for its updating. The TUC announced its preference of "£4.00 per hour plus" without specifying an exact rate whilst the largest public sector trade union UNISON wanted a figure based on half the male median earnings, which based on the 1997 New Earnings Survey was: £4.61 per hour.

---

[66] cl. 11.
[67] cl. 15.
[68] cl. 12.
[69] cl. 16.
[70] cll. 21 to 24.
[71] cl. 27.
[72] cl. 13.
[73] cl. 17.
[74] cl. 18.
[75] cl. 19.
[76] cl. 28.
[77] Mark Childs, Chairman of CBI employee resourcing panel, "Does minimum wage need court backing?" *Personnel Today* December 11, 1997.
[78] For example: whether it should be based on total earnings per hour and all taxable benefits such as bonuses, profit sharing payments, occupational pensions, travel costs and tips, or on the basic rate received per hour. "Bonus decision dogs minimum wage talks," People Management, October 23, 1997.

Employers' organisations were predicting dire consequences for jobs if the figure was much more than £3.00 per hour.[79]

First, it was estimated that if set at a level of "half male median earnings" (at £4.42 per hour) some four-and-a-half million workers would benefit.[80] Secondly, it was claimed that the implementation of a NMW will have even more dramatic effects for women. This is because out of some six-and-a-half million workers earning less than £4.50 an hour, 4.2 million are women workers.[81] In addition, some two million women and half-a-million men earn less than the level at which national insurance contributions become payable—£62 per week in 1996.[82] Thirdly, there have been different views expressed on the effect a NMW would have on bargaining and on the economy. The CBI claimed that the NMW would lead to a demand for restoring differentials between higher and lower paid workers which would impact adversely upon the economy; whereas the TGWU claimed that it would have a positive impact on labour intensive sectors such as retail, hotels and restaurants.[83] The Minister[84] responsible for implementing the new legislation, who, because of his background in the low paid and low trade union organised catering industry, was committed to introducing the NMW, also saw benefits for employers. These were that the NMW would stop crude under-cutting by competitors who paid wages as low as £1.20 per hour and the fact that the NMW should stem high turnover of staff thus saving companies high recruitment and training costs. On June 18, 1998, the Low Pay Commission published its recommendation of £3.60 per hour before deductions with a proposed initial Development Rate of £3.20 per hour for 18 to 20 year olds.[85] The government decided that a NMW of £3.60 per hour should be introduced from April 1999 with the Development Rate starting at £3.00 per hour in April 1999 rising to £3.20 per hour in June 2000.[86] Whatever the practical implications of the new measures, the legal significance appears to be that there will be an implied term of minimum remuneration inserted into workers' contracts.

4.6 SUMMARY

The level of pay received and the hours of labour which have to be exchanged for this remuneration are probably the key components of the employment relationship. This Chapter has endeavoured to demonstrate how the law intervenes in this exchange. It can be seen that the first level of intervention is at contract formulation, where agreement is made freely by the principal parties to the contract. The second level of intervention, now firmly established by statute, prescribes that those elements of the contract relating to pay have to be recorded in writing, and are protected from unlawful deductions as well as being protected upon termination of the contract. The third and last level of intervention is where terms relating to a statutory level of payment may be implied into the contract.

[79] Labour Research Bargaining Report 178, December 1997.
[80] Figures cited from Office for National Statistics (ONS) in Labour Research Bargaining Report 175, September 1997.
[81] "EOC: minimum wage will boost pay equity," *People Management*, December 4, 1997.
[82] Autumn 1996 Labour Force Survey/EOC/Centre for Economic Performance.
[83] Labour Research Bargaining Report 178, December 1997.
[84] Ian McCartney M.P., Minister of State, DTI.
[85] *The National Minimum Wage—First Report of the Low Pay Commission*, HMSO, 18/6/98, ISBN 0–10–1397623.
[86] IDS Brief 616, July 1998.

Chapter 5

Variation, Termination and Discharge at Common Law

5.1 Introduction

This Chapter reviews the common law concepts of variation, termination and discharge of the employment contract.

- A contractual "variation" is defined. It is shown how such a variation may be expressly or impliedly inserted into the contract of employment and how it may be resisted or rejected by the other party. The effect of statutory regulation is explored.

- The common law position of dismissal at will or with notice is explored. Also discussed, is the situation when the contract of employment is repudiated. The conflicting doctrines developed by the courts to resolve this breakdown in the employment relationship are explained.

- Termination of the contract caused by the employer's behaviour: "constructive dismissal" is contrasted with those dismissals which are prompted by the employee's conduct: "summary dismissal".

- The common law position on the giving of notice based largely on older notions of employee status is contrasted with modern statutory regulation aimed at injecting a degree of social equity into the employment relationship.

- Where a contract of employment is interrupted through sickness or imprisonment, the contract may be discharged at law with no dismissal occurring. These cases are explained.

- Other examples of discharge are explored with reference to fixed term contracts, death, dissolution and the transfer of engagements.

- The three main remedies for wrongful dismissal: damages, injunctive relief and judicial review, are explained and contrasted.

5.2 Variation of the Contract of Employment

At common law, the terms and conditions of employment can only be varied by the direct parties to the employment contract, usually the employer and the employee.

Third parties such as trade unions and employers' associations may also have an interest in incorporating terms into the employment contract, but these situations are subject to the principles of privity and agency and are considered in Chapter 2, para. 2.4. For the moment consideration is given to the legal theory that it is the direct contracting parties, who, after giving consideration, enter voluntarily into a legally binding agreement. In reality, the strict contractual approach to construing the contract of employment is not always successful. The employment relationship is dynamic. It is often quite difficult for the contracting parties, even in good faith, to anticipate all the changing circumstances which may, with the passage of time, impact upon it. For example, an employer's competitiveness may be reduced by national economic circumstances, or an employee's performance may be affected by illness. In such circumstances, the parties to the employment contract may have no choice but to vary the original terms of the employment contract. If this can be achieved through mutual agreement there is a lawful variation but where agreement cannot be reached, any variation by one party amounts to a breach of contract. The interests of parties to an employment contract differ and being a contract for personal service it is not a relationship which lends itself to the application of contractual principles not based on the changing needs of the parties.

The search for remedies for breach or variation of the employment contract starts with the construction of the contract itself and an analysis of the terms of the contract, both express and implied. Any changes subsequently introduced by the parties may amount to a variation but not necessarily to a breach of the fundamental terms of the contract. In this section consideration is given to:

- What is a variation of the contract of employment?
- Express and implied variation.
- Acceptance or rejection of the variation.
- Variation with agreement.

5.2.1   What is a variation of the contract of employment?

Under the law of contract, variation of the original terms of a legally enforceable agreement can only occur with the agreement of the contracting parties and supported by consideration. In the employment field, the consideration is normally the promise of the exchange of labour for wages. A variation is a change which effects the terms of what has been called the "wage-work" bargain. Examples include the employer changing the working hours, or rates of pay, altering job responsibilities or moving the place of work of the employee. Alternatively, the employee could vary the original contract through irregular or partial performance of his or her duties or through persistent attendance at hours not specified in the contract. Such situations, can, depending upon how the original contract is formulated, amount to a breach or to a repudiation of the contract itself. If this occurs, the injured party may then turn to the law to restore their contractual rights.

5.2.1.1   *Variation through flexibility or through mobility*

The most common types of variation of the employment contract instituted by the employer is where an employee is asked or told to work differently or where his or her place of work is changed. Two questions can be considered in such situations. First, does the contract itself permit such changes? For example, in *Johnson v. Peabody Trust*[1] an employee who was engaged as a skilled roofer had a written clause in his contract: "15 . . . Where possible, tradespersons will be expected to carry out multi-trade operations." This clause, it was held by the EAT, permitted the employers, when the demand for roof repairs diminished, to switch the employee to other work such as plastering. Here, an express term operated to imply that the employee was required to work flexibly, but the courts have differentiated between the employer asking an employee to do a new job, which the contract does nor provide for and changing the method of doing the same job. In *Creswell and others v. Board of Inland Revenue*,[2] clerical staff and tax officers found that they could not rely on customary working practices to resist new working methods arising from the introduction of computerisation into the work place:

> "An employee is expected to adapt himself to new methods and techniques introduced in the course of his employment. On his side, the employer must provide any training or retraining. It is a question of fact in each particular case whether the retraining involved the acquisition of such esoteric skills that it would not be reasonable to expect the employee to acquire them." *per* Walton J.

Creswell and others v. Board of Inland Revenue [1984] I.R.L.R. 190 at 191, HC.

In looking very carefully at how the individual jobs had allegedly changed with the introduction of computers, the High Court judge, Walton J. concluded: "Although doubtless, all of us, being conservative (with a small 'c') by nature desire nothing better than to be left to deepen out accustomed ruts, and hate change, a T[ax] O[fficer] has no right to remain in perpetuity doing one defined type of tax work in one particular way." Here the court itself is implying a term that the employee is required to work with a reasonable degree of flexibility in a situation where the nature of the job had not changed, but the method of performing it had.

The second question to be asked when a flexibility or mobility variation occurs is: does it amount to a repudiatory breach of the contract itself? In *White v. Reflecting Roadstuds Ltd*[3]; the employee, like *Johnson* had an express flexibility clause incorporated into his written contract: "The company reserves the right, when determined by requirements of operational efficiency, to transfer employees to alternative work and it is a condition of employment that they are willing to do so when requested." Mr White was transferred to another department where the level of pay was less than he had been earning. He considered that this variation amounted to a fundamental repudiation of his contract, resigned and claimed constructive unfair dismissal at an industrial tribuanl. The tribunal found that he had been unfairly dismissed because the employer's express right to transfer an employee to alternative work was subject to two fundamental implied terms: that the right would be exercised in a reasonable manner and that there would be no unilateral reduction in the employee's pay. These would appear, at face value, to be quite sensible implications to make. Also, they would seem to conform to sound contractual principles. First, that the contractual terms themselves are applied reasonably and secondly, that any breach in fundamental terms, such as a

---

[1] [1996] I.R.L.R. 387, EAT.
[2] [1984] I.R.L.R. 190; [1984] I.C.R., 508, HC.
[3] [1991] I.R.L.R. 331; [1991] I.C.R. 733, EAT.

reduction in pay, could lead to a repudiatory breach of the contract for which the employee could seek a remedy.

However the EAT, after considering the authorities, put a more sophisticated gloss on these principles and overturned this decision. In reviewing the leading cases on mobility and flexibility Wood J. held:

- The express flexibility term was not subject to these particular implied terms "in order to give the contract business efficacy";

- To imply that a mobility clause "should be handled reasonably" would "reintroduce the reasonableness test into constructive dismissal cases by the back door and would fly in the face of authority of *Western Excavating (EEC) Ltd v. Sharp.*[4]"

- *Akhtar*[5] was only authority for the proposition that in applying a mobility clause "an employer should not exercise his discretion in such a way as to prevent the employee from being able to carry out his part of the contract".

- ". . . there is an overriding contractual term as to the relationship of confidence and trust between employer and employee."[6]

- ". . . where an employer acts within the contract of employment, the fact that thereby there is caused a loss of income to the employee does not render the employer's act a breach of contract."

The judgment in this case, can perhaps be seen as a return to the hegemony of contractual principle over the notion of "reasonableness" in the employment relationship. To illustrate this, the five main elements in the EAT's decision in *White* may be considered.

First, the finding that the express flexibility term itself was *not* subject to implied terms "that the right would be exercised in a reasonable way and that there would be no unilateral reduction in the employee's pay," was based on an examination of the authorities[7] which go back to 1891. To recap, what emerges is that three factors were required when implying terms into a written contract:

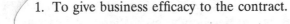

1. To give business efficacy to the contract.

2. To give effect to the obvious intentions of the contracting parties.

3. To complete the contractual arrangements.

In *White*, the EAT reiterates the dictum of Lord Esher in *Hamlyn*[8] that judicial construction of a written contract is governed by contractual intent: "The touchstone is always necessity and not merely reasonableness. . ." The "necessity" being the necessity to give legal force to the terms of the written contract.

[4] [1978] I.R.L.R. 27, CA.
[5] *United Bank Ltd v. Akhtar* [1989] I.R.L.R. 507, EAT.
[6] *Woods v. WM Car Services (Peterborough) Ltd* [1982] I.R.L.R. 413, CA.
[7] *ibid.; Courtaulds Ltd v. Sibson* [1981] I.R.L.R. 305; *United Bank Ltd v. Akhtar* [1989] I.R.L.R. 507; *Liverpool City Council v. Irwin* [1977] A.C. 239; *Hamlyn and Co. v. Wood and Co.* [1891] 2 Q.B. 488; *Reigate v. Union Manufacturing Co. (Ramsbottom) Ltd* [1918] 1 K.B. 592 at 605; *Re Comptoir Commercial Anversois v. Power, Son and Co.* [1920] 1 K.B. 868 at 899; *Western Excavating (EEC) Ltd v. Sharp* [1978] I.R.L.R. 27, CA.
[8] *Hamlyn and Co. v. Wood and Co.* [1891] 2 Q.B. 488.

Secondly, the EAT cited the binding authority of *Western Excavating* where the Court of Appeal had looked at the statutory definition of unfair constructive dismissal[9] (see Chapter 9) and compared the so called "contract" and "unreasonableness" tests for this statutory remedy. In short, it settled for the former remedy because the statutory wording of the obligation on the employer not to unfairly dismiss was too broad.[10] The long established contractual test was to be applied. If an employer's conduct was such as to vary or repudiate a fundamental term of the contract the employee was entitled to regard the contract as being discharged from further performance.

Thirdly, the contract test was also applicable to a mobility clause. The decision in *Akhtar*, which concerned a bank clerk who was given one week's notice to move from Leeds to Birmingham, was not about whether a mobility term in itself was applied reasonably, but whether it was applied in a way authorised by the contract. The EAT drew attention to the words of Knox J. made in the tribunal's previous decision in *Akhtar* that:

"... there is a clear distinction between implying a term which negates a provision which is expressly stated in the contract and implying a term which controls the exercise of a discretion which is expressly conferred in a contract." *per* Knox J.

United Bank Ltd v. Akhtar [1989] I.R.L.R. 507 at 508, EAT.

Provided that a contractual discretion is not exercised in a capricious way, the employer in applying a variation does not have his prerogative to manage challenged by having to be reasonable in exercising that prerogative. In this case, the bank clearly had the contractual right to move their employee's work base, but by giving insufficient notice of the change had prevented the employee from performing his contract. This was not permissible.

Fourthly, the EAT considered that, on the authorities, there was an overriding implied term of mutual trust and confidence in the employment contract. Brodie[11] is extremely critical of the contradictory judgments of the courts where they have assessed what appear to be conflicting terms arising from mutual trust and confidence. He contrasts *Rank Xerox v. Churchill*[12] where the EAT preferred to rely on the letter of the contract which contained an express term that required transfer to another location if required by the company, to the original industrial tribunal ruling, that such a term was subject to the implication that "this had to be within reasonable daily travelling distance"; with *Akhtar* where the management prerogative is not challenged.[13]

In *White* it was clear that mutual trust and confidence was absent. The reason given for the transfer, and which was not contested, was the employee's absence from work and the problems this caused his workmates who were paid a team bonus. The employer was not getting the performance he expected and the employee, after the transfer, was not getting the level of pay that he claimed he was contractually entitled to receive. There was some dispute about exactly how much the employee lost as a result of the transfer but the industrial tribunal found that it was probably much less than was claimed. In any event, the fifth important finding of relevance to variation in

---

[9] TULRA 1974, Sched. 1, para. 5(2)(c), now ERA 1996, s.95(1)(c).
[10] *Western Excavating (EEC) Ltd v. Sharp* [1978] I.R.L.R. 27, CA, at para. 21.
[11] *"The Heart of the Matter: Mutual Trust and Confidence"* (1966) 25 I.L.J. 2 at 129.
[12] [1988] I.R.L.R. 280.
[13] [1989] I.R.L.R. 507.

employment contracts was the EAT's reference to binding authority in the case of *Spafax Ltd v. Harrison*[14] that "a loss of income does not render the employer's act a breach of contract." In *Spafax*, a case about restrictive covenants in employment contracts, the Court of Appeal found that the action of the employer in imposing a new method of working, which reduced the income of its employee, was not a repudiatory breach of the contract. The employee was paid on a commission basis however, where it could be anticipated that income might go up or down depending on the volume of sales. So the contract, in effect, anticipated such changes. Similarly in *White,* the employees were paid on a bonus system dependent on the volume of work performed. In a contractual situation where the rate of income was fixed, an employer's variation which reduced the amount of income might well be a contractual breach (see para. 5.3.2).

In summary, the question of when a variation to an employment contract, whether instigated by the employer or by the employee, amounts to a repudiation, or to a fundamental breach of the contract itself, will often depend upon the construction of the particular contract. In more recent cases however, the appellate courts have indicated that it is the reasonableness of the variation which will be considered. For example in *Waltons & Morse v. Dorrington*[15] the EAT found that the employers were in breach of an implied term in requiring an employee to work "in an environment which was affected by the smoking habits of fellow employees." The implied term being the provision of "a working environment which is reasonably suitable for the performance by them of their contractual duties." Common sense as opposed to reliance on strict contract construction, is called in aid in *High Table Ltd v. Horst*.[16] Here, the Court of Appeal held that "If an employee has worked in only one location under his contract of employment for the purposes of the employer's business, it defies common sense to widen the extent of the place where he was so employed, merely because of the existence of a mobility clause." The primary factual test of where an employee works therefore takes precedence over the contractual test.

An examination of how terms which are incorporated into the employment contract may be varied, is made in the next section.

5.2.2 Express and implied variation

As described in Chapter 2, para. 2.3, terms of the employment contract may, at common law, be expressly or impliedly incorporated into the contract. The contract itself can be reduced to a written document or series of documents, or may be formed orally, or indeed can be a combination of both. Variation of contractual terms can therefore occur within all these formats. Since 1963 there has also been a statutory obligation on employers to issue the employee with a written statement of his or her terms and conditions of employment.[17] This obligation is now found in the Employment Rights Act 1996, s.1 which, as we have seen, in the above mentioned Chapter, places a statutory obligation on employers to issue a written statement of initial employment particulars to most employees. ERA 1996, s.4 also requires an employer to notify the employee of changes to his or her employment particulars. This

---

[14] [1980] I.R.L.R. 443, CA.
[15] [1997] I.R.L.R. 488, EAT.
[16] [1997] I.R.L.R. 513, CA.
[17] Contracts of Employment Act 1963.

requirement does not mean however, that the employer is legally entitled to unilaterally change the terms of the employment contract. The written statement is only prima facie evidence of the contractual terms.[18] The agreement of the employee still has to be secured. Such agreement may be given expressly by the individual employee who may be asked personally to agree the new changes in writing[19] or by implication through incorporation from collective agreements.[20]

Robertson and Jackson[21] illustrates the interaction between the common law requirement for any contractual variations to be agreed and the statutory requirement[22] on the employer to notify agreed contractual changes to their employees. Robertson and Jackson were meter readers/collectors employed by British Gas. They both received letters stating that their terms and conditions of employment included entitlement to payment under an incentive bonus scheme. They also received, some years later, a statutory statement of employment particulars which also referred to the bonus scheme payable under the Whitley Council Agreement.[23] The bonus term had been expressly incorporated into the contract through their letter of engagement and also impliedly incorporated into their contract through an agreement negotiated with the trade unions.

To reduce labour costs the employers terminated their agreement with the trade union on the bonus payment scheme and stopped paying the bonuses. Because collective agreements are not legally enforceable contracts[24] the trade unions had no legal remedy, but the two meter readers took an action in the county court claiming arrears of wages. They were successful both in the county and in the appeal courts. The Court of Appeal ruled:

> "The terms and conditions of that incentive bonus were to be found in the collective agreement which existed at the date of the letter of appointment and the terms of the collective agreement were incorporated into the individual contracts of employment. Although from time to time the collective agreement modified the bonus which was payable, and that variation became incorporated in the employees" contracts, the argument on behalf of the employers that if a bonus scheme was not in force under the collective agreement, no bonus was payable could not be accepted. There was an obligation to pay the incentive bonus imported expressly into the contracts of employment and that could not be affected by unilateral determination of the collective agreement." *per* Ackner LJ.

Robertson and Jackson v. British Gas Corp. [1983] I.R.L.R. 302 at 302, CA.

In considering the legality of this contractual variation, the Court of Appeal had to evaluate the authority of the original letters of appointment, which stated "Incentive bonus scheme conditions will apply to meter reading and collection work," against a subsequently issued statutory statement of terms which purported to vary these terms,

---

[18] *System Floors (U.K.) Ltd v. Daniel* [1981] I.R.L.R. 475; [1982] I.C.R. 54, EAT.
[19] *Gascol Conversions Ltd v. Mercer* [1974] I.R.L.R. 155, CA.
[20] *Robertson and Jackson v. British Gas Corp.* [1983] I.C.R. 351, CA.
[21] *ibid.*
[22] ERA 1996, s.4.
[23] A generic term for an employer/ employee joint negotiating body, originally named after John H. Whitley, the Liberal M.P. and Speaker of the House of Commons, who chaired (1917–18) a government committee on relations between employers and employees. In *Robertson* this body was the National Joint Council for Gas Staffs and Senior Officers.
[24] TULRCA 1992, s.179.

by saying that they were subject to the collective agreements then in force. But Ackner L.J. clearly indicated that employers could not use the statutory statement to unilaterally vary contractual terms:

". . . I know of no principle that permits an employer's statement years after the contract was made of his understanding of what the contract means, albeit provided pursuant to a statutory obligation, as being admissible evidence for the interpretation of the contract itself."

Robertson and Jackson v. British Gas Corp. [1983] I.R.L.R. 302 at 304, CA.

The original letter of appointment clearly stated that a bonus would be paid. This was an unqualified express term of the contract, until varied in agreement with the individual or through his or her trade union.

In addition to there being a common law breach if a contractual term is altered unilaterally, there is, as mentioned above, a statutory requirement on employers to notify employees in writing of changes which have been agreed. Employees may however, be referred to a reasonably accessible collective agreement for changes to notice entitlement,[25] and to other reasonably accessible documents for changes to sick pay, to pension entitlements and to disciplinary provisions.[26]

5.2.3   Acceptance or rejection of the variation

A variation may become binding by acceptance, and acceptance may be express or implied, either by conduct or the passage of time.

In *Burdett-Coutts and others v. Hertfordshire County Council*[27] the local authority varied the contract of service of school meals supervisors by reducing their wages and hours of work. The education authority issued a written unilateral variation to their employees, who subsequently made it clear through their trade union, that they did not accept the changes. A declaration was secured against the authority in the High Court that they were not entitled in law to vary the contracts of employment. The "dinner-ladies" were awarded arrears of wages which should have been paid to them under the original contract.

In defence of their action, the employers argued that by continuing working and accepting the reduced wages, the employees had impliedly accepted new terms of employment. In view of the strong protests made by the employees' trade union, the High Court judge robustly disposed of this argument, and in so doing supported the elective theory (see para. 5.3.2) of repudiation:

"Faced with the choice which every innocent party to a contract has, the plaintiffs had not accepted the repudiation but were standing on the original contract and claiming recovery, as they were entitled to do, of the total wages which should have been paid under the original contract." *per* Kenneth Jones J.

Burdett-Coutts and others v. Hertfordshire County Council [1984] I.R.L.R. 91 at 92, HC.

---

[25] ERA 1996, s.4(5).
[26] ERA 1996, s.4(4).
[27] [1984] I.R.L.R. 91, HC.

5.2.3.1 *Continuing to work*

When one party varies a contract, the other party to the contract has a choice of either accepting, or rejecting (as in *Burdett-Coutts*) or maybe trying to modify the variation which has occurred. Doing nothing at all and continuing to work without protest may imply agreement to the change in terms. In *Jones v. Associated Tunnelling Co. Ltd*[28] the employers changed the place of work of their employee who subsequently resigned. It became necessary to decide whether the change was one the employer was contractually able to make. The EAT held that the employers had not breached the contract, because, there was an implied term that the employee would be required to work within a reasonable daily travelling distance from home. But the tribunal also distinguished those variations which may have an immediate impact on the employment relationship, such as reducing the rate of pay. Continuing to work in such a situation without protest, may infer acceptance, whereas continuing to work in the face of a variation such as a mobility clause, which had no immediate effect, would not necessarily indicate assent to the variation. Choosing to reject the term and leave, taking the behaviour to be a breach of contract may be premature because an attempted variation may be within the contractual terms and not something the employee can reject without himself being in breach of contract.

5.2.3.2 *Discriminatory variations*

A contractual variation which has an unlawful discriminatory effect cannot be relied upon by the employer. In *Meade-Hill and National Union of Civil and Public Servants v. British Council*[29] the British Council announced that they were moving their head office from London to Manchester and were concerned that they were not securing enough voluntary agreements to move from its middle managers. Mrs Meade-Hill upon promotion, had accepted a variation in her terms of service that she was subject to a mobility clause. The employers indicated that managers refusing to move might be treated as being in breach of contract. They were therefore indicating in advance, that they would in those circumstances, be accepting their employees' repudiation of the employment contract.

The employee and her union sought a declaration in the county court that the mobility clause was unenforceable on the grounds that it was discriminatory,[30] "because a greater proportion of women than men from the relevant pool were secondary earners, and thereby less able or willing to move house." The application was dismissed by the court holding that it was impossible to say if the mobility clause was discriminatory "in the absence of a concrete situation." In a majority judgment allowing the appeal and remitting it back to the county court, the Court of Appeal considered the effect of the SDA 1975, s.1(1)(b) on the contract of employment. This is the section which makes it unlawful to apply a condition where the number of women who can comply with it is "considerably smaller" than the proportion of men who comply with it. It was found that the impact of such a term "is to be judged when the impugned term becomes incorporated into the contract between the parties, rather than the point at which it becomes reasonably foreseeable that the term is one with which the applicant will be unable to comply, or the stage at which it is sought by the employer to enforce the term against an individual in any particular set of circumstances." In short, if the discriminatory contractual mobility term is not invoked by the employer it is still unlawful at the time it was incorporated into the contract.

[28] [1981] I.R.L.R. 477.
[29] [1995] I.R.L.R. 478, CA.
[30] SDA 1975, s.77(2).

5.2.4 Variation and the statutory statement of employment particulars

Providing that there is no pressure applied to them, the parties to a contract of employment can, of course, voluntarily agree to vary the original terms. The problem is an evidential one. As has been seen in para. 5.2.2 above, evidence of the varied terms might be found in a statutory written notice of changed terms.[31] But what if there is a dispute about what exactly was agreed?

In a dispute over the level of wages for example, the employee could pursue an action in the county court seeking a determination on the correct construction of that term. Alternatively, under the ERA 1996, s.11 a claim could be pursued in an industrial tribunal for a determination of the terms which should have been included in the statutory statement of particulars.[32] In reviewing the early case law[33] on section 12 of the ERA 1996, where an industrial tribunal may so determine that an employer has been deemed to have given the employee a specific statement of terms, Smith and Wood[34] considered that there were two main problems. First, that an industrial tribunal could only declare what terms were agreed between the parties and should therefore be included in the written statement. Secondly, although a tribunal had the jurisdiction to make this declaration where an employer had neglected to give all the information on contractual terms required by statute[35] it did not have the authority to do so where the employee disputed their accuracy. This rather narrow interpretation of legislation originally purporting to inject some consistency and equity into the employment relationship, is criticised by these commentators who also point out that the situation has now been ameliorated somewhat by the Court of Appeal decision in *Mears v. Safecar Security Ltd*.[36]

In *Mears* the Court of Appeal ruled that a complaint about the statement of employment particulars under what is now section 11 of the ERA 1996 does include the situation where the employee is claiming that the terms agreed were not included or accurately represented in the statement. Here, the job of the tribunal is to determine what was expressly or impliedly agreed and insert the correct terms into the employer's statement of terms. In applying this statutory remedy, the tribunal is not constrained by strict common law notions of contract construction:

> "In order to imply and determine the missing term which ought to have been particularised by the employer and so to complete the contract, the Tribunal can and should consider all the facts and circumstances of the relationship between the employer and employee concerned, including the way in which they had worked the particular contract of employment since it was made." *per* Slynn J.(P.)
>
> *Mears v. Safecar Security Ltd* [1982] I.R.L.R. 183 at 184, CA.

The industrial tribunal is therefore directed not just to examining the contract at the moment of formulation but also to imply terms from the working relationship existing

---

[31] ERA 1996, s.4(1).
[32] ERA 1996, s.11(1).
[33] *Cuthbertson v. AML Distributors* [1975] I.R.L.R. 228 IT, *Construction Industry Training Board v. Leighton* [1978] I.R.L.R. 60, *Brown v. Stuart, Scott and Co. Ltd* [1981] I.C.R. 166.
[34] I.T. Smith and J. Wood, (1996), p. 75.
[35] ERA 1996, s.12(1).
[36] [1982] 2 All E.R. 865; [1982] I.R.L.R. 183, CA.

during the two month period in which the employer is permitted to draw up the statutory statement of terms. The Court of Appeal also went further and ruled obiter that if one or more terms, specified under section 1 of the ERA 1996 had not been agreed between employer and employee, the tribunal would "in the last resort invent them for the purpose of literally writing them into the contract." This appeared to be stretching the theory of contract construction too far and a reversion to the previous position that an industrial tribunal's jurisdiction was only declaratory, and that they could not invent terms that were not agreed[37] was subsequently signalled by the Court of Appeal in *Eagland v. British Telecommunications plc.*[38]

5.3   TERMINATION

In this section, an examination is made of the different legal positions which arise when a contract is terminated with and without the agreement of the contracting parties. This is a controversial and much developed area of employment law, where there is both close interaction and friction between the long established principles of contract law, arising from the common law cases on termination of the contract of employment, and the more recent statutory principles of "equity" and "fairness" which regulate how dismissals can be made.

Consideration is given to:

- Termination with agreement.

- Repudiation of the contract of employment.

- Constructive dismissal.

5.3.1   Termination with agreement

If both employer and employee voluntarily agree to end the employment contract, it is discharged at law without any further performance required by the parties, other than that anticipated by the contract, for example a restrictive covenant to restrict an employee's choice of employer, place of work or industry for a limited period post-termination. A problem can arise however, where the employee claims that there was not a genuine discharge of the contract because the dismissal was not truly consensual. This situation arose in *Harman v. Flexible Lamps Ltd*[39] where the employer's claim that the contract had been discharged through mutual agreement at an interview, was, on evidential grounds not accepted by the EAT: the employer had said that it was "in their mutual interests to part company". Because of the amount of sickness absence however, the dismissal was still found to be fair, but the tribunal also found that the contract was not discharged at law. The employee had been dismissed by the employer.

In considering whether there has been an agreed termination, the courts will look for strict evidence of a purported resignation: "Notice of termination by an employee (as with notice of dismissal by an employer—*Morton Sundour Fabrics Ltd v. Shaw*[40]),

---

[37] With the possible exception of notice, where common law implies a reasonable period of notice into all contracts of employment.
[38] [1993] I.C.R. 644; [1992] I.R.L.R. 323, CA.
[39] [1980] I.R.L.R. 418, EAT.
[40] (1967) 2 I.T.R. 84; (1967) 2 K.I.R. 1.

must be specific; it must specify the date when it is to take effect or, if it does not specify the date, at least make it possible for the date to be deduced with certainty from what is said".[41]

In *Marriott v. Oxford District Co-operative Society Ltd*[42] Lord Denning stressed the true consensual nature of an agreed termination, when he said that the agreement must be voluntary and without undue pressure on the employee. It must be, he said, a genuine bilateral termination and one of the criteria is to ask whether it was the employer or the employee who took the initiative. So, where the employer invites the employee to retire, the resignation will usually be treated as a dismissal—just as the "resign or else" situation has been treated as dismissal. In *East Sussex County Council v. Walker*[43] Sir John Brightman said that if an employee is told that she is no longer required in her employment and is expressly invited to resign, as a matter of common sense she was dismissed, even though it was the employee who took the first and more respectable alternative by signing a letter of resignation, rather than being in receipt of a letter of dismissal. This was confirmed in *Sheffield v. Oxford Controls Co. Ltd*[44] where the EAT said where an employee resigns rather than being dismissed that was still dismissal because the employee had no choice whether to stay or go. The sole question came down to how one went.

Redundancy is a typical situation where employees can be under considerable pressure to resign and therefore be said to have voluntarily terminated their contracts. By so resigning they may gain access to benefits not otherwise available. It is also an area where there are statutory rights such as compensatory redundancy payments.[45] In *Birch and Humber*[46] the Court of Appeal took a strictly contractual perspective on the question of whether an employee's acceptance of an invitation to accept voluntary early retirement provisions meant that a dismissal had occurred, or whether the termination had been voluntary. If the termination was voluntary there was no entitlement to redundancy pay, which is dependent upon a dismissal having occurred.

Bowers and Honeyball[47] draw attention to Freedland's view[48] "that this decision betrays the CA's adherence more to *laissez-faire* ideals in the common law rather than to issues such as the policy behind the legislation." The reasoning of the court would seem to bear this out. First, they ruled that even though the University was making savings by cutting some 300 jobs, there was no evidence that the appellants were going to be the subject of compulsory retirement before their normal retirement age. Secondly, the employer had never encouraged applicants to think that they would be entitled to redundancy payments if they volunteered for early retirement. Indeed they had specifically stated that it was not a redundancy scheme and that "any retirement under (the scheme) is subject to the agreement of *both* the University and the member of staff concerned." To secure a redundancy payment under the ERA 1996, s.135(1)(a) the employee has to be dismissed "by reason of redundancy". In *Birch* the Court of Appeal found that there had not been a "dismissal" but that the contract had been "terminated by mutual agreement".

---

[41] *F. Hughes v. Gwynedd Area Health Authority* [1977] I.R.L.R. 436, EAT.
[42] [1969] 3 All E.R. 1126.
[43] [1972] I.T.R. 280.
[44] [1979] I.R.L.R. 133, EAT.
[45] ERA 1996, s.135.
[46] [1985] I.R.L.R. 165, CA.
[47] J. Bowers, and S. Honeyball (1996), p. 78.
[48] S. Freedland (1985) 14 I.L.J. 243.

5.3.2   Repudiation of the contract of employment

Under common law, a repudiation or breach of any contract can take different forms. First, one party may expressly refuse to perform the obligations attached to their side of the bargain. If this is done in advance of the contract's performance date this is called an *anticipatory breach*. Secondly, an implied repudiation can be incurred by a party if they take some action which prevents them from fulfilling the obligations of the contract. Lastly, a party may be unable to perform all or some of the conditions of the contract. If a major part of the contract is not performed this may constitute a *breach of condition*; but if only a small part is unperformed, this is likely to lead to a *breach of warranty*. The injured party in such circumstances is entitled to recover damages and also has the option of bringing the contract to an end, providing that a serious breach, *i.e.* a breach of condition has taken place. A breach of condition, sometimes referred to as a fundamental breach, entitles the injured party to elect to continue with the contract, or to avoid the original agreement altogether and thereby be discharged from performing any of the contractual obligations. The first alternative gives the injured party an opportunity to accept the defective contract, or to seek full performance and perhaps damages for any losses sustained. The second alternative ends the contract completely and leaves the injured party with only an action for damages. These general principles relating to contractual breach form the background to one of the most controversial and developing areas of employment law. The controversy is focused on what remedies are available when there is a breach of the employment contract. Two conflicting theories: the "automatic" and "elective" models of repudiation have emerged which give different remedies. Before considering these, an examination is made of some typical situations where the employment contract is fundamentally breached.

Such a breach, whether committed by the employer or by the employee, alters the contract so that it is substantially different from that which was originally intended by the contracting parties. For example, if an employer completely changes the job duties or unilaterally reduces the rate of pay of an employee this can amount to a repudiatory breach of the contract. In *Coleman*[49] the EAT found that a unilateral change in the job duties of a long-serving acting manager, one of whose main duties was the buying of greengrocery, constituted a repudiation of the contract:

> "Not only were the buying duties the most interesting and enjoyable ones, and ones to which the appellant attached considerable importance both in terms of job satisfaction and prestige, they were also very important from a trading point of view. After 36 years' employment with well defined duties, the appellant had been left with residual duties which were of a very humdrum character. Such a change, mounting to a requirement for the appellant to do something fundamentally different, was not something which without his consent the respondents were entitled to demand." *per* Philips J.

> *Coleman v. S. & W. Baldwin* [1977] I.R.L.R. 342 at 342, EAT.

In *Industrial Rubber Products v. Gillon*[50] the employers, in seeking to comply with a statutory pay freeze, unilaterally reduced the pay of employees. The EAT found that

---

[49] *Coleman v. S. & W. Baldwin* [1977] I.R.L.R. 342, EAT.
[50] [1977] I.R.L.R. 389, EAT.

"A unilateral reduction in the basic rate of pay, even for good reasons and to a relatively small extent, is a material breach of a fundamental element in the contract of employment." This situation however, is different from where an employer causes a reduction in wages but is still acting within the terms of the contract, as in *White v. Reflecting Roadstuds Ltd.*[51] In *White* the employer transferred an employee, whose work was poor, to a lower paid department. Because the contract contained an express mobility clause, and the employers were found to be exercising this responsibly, the loss in pay did not constitute a repudiatory breach.

There is no single all embracing definition of a fundamental contractual breach. A court has to look at the contract as a whole and the type and number of wrongful acts committed[52] but characteristics of a repudiatory breach can include:

- Deprivation of what the other party originally contracted for.[53]
- Where a vital part of the contract is breached.[54]
- An indication that a party is not willing to be bound by an essential term of the contract. In *Western Excavating*[55] an employee who was fined for misconduct at work was left in financial difficulties and sought an advance on his pay. After this was refused, he resigned and collected holiday pay due to him. He subsequently claimed unfair constructive dismissal (see para. 5.3.3). The Court of Appeal found that the employee's resignation was not caused by a repudiatory breach on the part of the employer, who was under no obligation to advance loans to their employees. By resigning, the employee had shown that he was no longer willing to be bound by the contract.
- A series of breaches having a cumulative effect. In *Jones v. F Sirl and Son*[56] an employee who had worked for nearly 30 years for the same company and was now the manageress, had her petrol allowance reduced, her non-contributory pension scheme terminated, her job duties changed and a new manager appointed alongside her. Taken cumulatively, the EAT decided that these actions amounted to "very serious and fundamental breaches of her contract" by the employers.
- A final breach after a series of small breaches. In *Garner v. Grange Furnishing Ltd*[57] an employee with 26 years service walked out after he was "treated like an office-boy." Although this incident was minor in itself, the employer was found to have committed a repudiatory breach because this was the latest in a series of incidents, between the employee and his manager who had tried to withhold pay increases.

At common law, such a situation discharges the contract of employment. It is simply brought to an end. Consideration will now be given to the principles which the courts have followed in identifying a repudiatory breach of the employment contract.

5.3.2.1 *Automatic and elective theories of repudiation*

As mentioned earlier, two opposing theories have occupied the thinking of the judiciary seeking to define a repudiatory breach of the employment contract. An

---

[51] [1991] I.R.L.R. 332, EAT.
[52] Re *Rubel Bronxe and Metal Co. Ltd* [1918] 1 K.B. 315.
[53] *Hong Kong Fir Shipping v. Kawasaki Kisen Kaisha* [1962] 2 Q.B. 26.
[54] *The Mihalis Angelos* [1971] 1 Q.B. 164.
[55] *Western Excavating (ECC) Ltd v. Sharp* [1978] I.R.L.R. 27, CA.
[56]]1997] I.R.L.R. 493, EAT.
[57] *Garner v. Grange Furnishing Ltd* [1977] I.R.L.R. 206, EAT.

examination of the theories is required to understand the different legal remedies available to employers and to employees who suffer a repudiatory breach. A breach of contract under generally applicable contract law, usually gives the wronged party a remedy in damages. This, it can be argued, may not be a sufficient remedy for an employee who has lost his job as the result of a repudiatory breach by the employer. But courts are reluctant and usually unable to force employers to retain employees, or to take back former workers that they do not want in their employment. This is because such a situation would be in breach of the implied term of mutual trust and confidence which resides in all employment contracts (see para. 5.6) In addition, the enforcement of personal service would amount to a contract for slavery. The nineteenth century Master and Servant Acts came close to upholding such contracts.[58] Today however, an employer who is the subject of a repudiatory action by the employee cannot secure specific performance because statutory provisions prohibit a court from compelling an employee to work.[59] It can be seen that contracts of employment present special problems when a repudiatory breach occurs. An examination of the case law illustrates how some of these have been dealt with.

5.3.2.2 *Does the innocent party have to accept the breach?*

The conflicting theories can be reduced to one all important question. Is the innocent party required to accept the breach for the contract to come to an end, or without acceptance, can the contract of employment, like other contracts survive an unaccepted repudiation? In *Vine v. National Dock Labour Board*[60] Viscount Kilmuir L.C. affirmed the decision of Jenkins L.J. in the Court of Appeal that in an ordinary master and servant repudiation, the contract is brought to an end and a claim for damages only arises. The reasoning being, as indicated above, that a contract of employment is an exception to the normal rule of contracts, in that it is a contract of personal service dependent upon the mutual goodwill and trust between the parties. Once this has broken down, it is pointless to continue with the relationship. Nearly 20 years later this view was still influential in *Sanders v. Ernest A. Neale Ltd.*[61] Here, the National Industrial Relations Court had to decide whether seven employees who had taken industrial action, and had been asked to work normally, but had refused to do so, were dismissed because the employer had accepted the repudiatory actions of its employees; or whether the contract was repudiated by the employer who had not given contractual notice of dismissal. The NIRC held:

> "The general rule concerning contracts of employment is that they are terminated by notice whether or not the notice is given in breach of contract or whether or not the employee accepts the notice as having that effect. Unlike repudiations of other kinds of contracts, repudiations of contracts of employment do not give the innocent party the right to elect to treat the contract as discharged by the breach or to treat it as a continuing subject to his right to damages." *per* Donaldson J.

Sanders v. Ernest A. Neale Ltd [1974] I.R.L.R. 236, NIRC.

A number of cases in the 1970s cast doubt on the validity of the non-enforcement rule as a matter of law rather than as a matter of fact. For although undoubtedly in

---

[58] S. Deakin and G.S. Morris (1995), p. 23.
[59] TULRCA 1992, s.236.
[60] [1957] A.C. 488; [1956] 3 All E.R. 939 at 944, HL.
[61] [1974] I.R.L.R. 236; [1974] I.C.R. 565, NIRC.

many cases the mutual trust and confidence will not exist after a serious repudiation, this will not always be the case. One such example is *Hill v. C.A. Parsons and Co. Ltd.*[62] Here, the employer, under pressure from a trade union, issued a dismissal notice to an employee who had refused to join a trade union closed shop. The individual employer and employee relationship had not broken down and the Court of Appeal granted an injunction restraining the employer from dismissing the employee. In reviewing this case and others where the automatic principle was criticised, Donaldson J. in *Sanders*, distinguished *Hill* as one of those rare cases where, because trust and confidence still resided between the parties, it was still practical to continue the employment contract after the repudiation. He invited further guidance from the Court of Appeal and House of Lords on *Hill.*

Sir John Donaldson P. in the same case, compares *Denmark v. Boscobel*[63] with *Decro-Wall International SA v. Practitioners in Marketing Ltd.*[64] In *Denmark* the classical theory of automatic termination is spelt out:

> "It has long been well settled that, if a man employed under a contract of personal service is wrongfully dismissed, he has no claim for remuneration due under the contract after the repudiation. His only money claim is for damages for having been prevented from earning his remuneration." *per* Salmon L.J.

> *Denmark v. Boscobel* [1969] 1 Q.B. 699 at 726, CA.

Donaldson P. compares this with Salmon L.J.'s extended *dicta* in *Decro-Wall* which acknowledges that although in strict law, the contract cannot be terminated without the acceptance of the wronged party, in practice, a remedy can only be obtained by the innocent party accepting the breach and acknowledging that the contract is at an end:

> "I doubt whether a wrongful dismissal brings a contract of service to an end in law, although no doubt in practice it does. Under such a contract a servant has a right to remuneration . . . in return for services. If the master, in breach of contract, refuses to employ the servant, it is trite law that the contract will not be specifically enforced. As I hope I made plain in the *Denmark Productions* case, the only result is that the servant, albeit he has been prevented from rendering services by the master's breach, cannot recover remuneration under the contract because he has not earned it. He has not rendered the services for which the remuneration is payable. His only money claim is for damages for being wrongfully prevented from earning his remuneration. And like anyone else claiming damages for breach of contract, he is under a duty to take reasonable steps to minimise the loss he has suffered through the breach. . . I doubt whether in law a contract of service can be unilaterally determined by the master's breach. Perhaps a servant could sit still whilst the contract ran its course with the knowledge that the contract was, in law, still alive. But, in practice, this knowledge could be of little real comfort to him because he would be failing to take reasonable steps to minimise his loss—and since a claim for damages is his only money remedy, he would be prejudicing that claim by doing nothing. Accordingly

[62] [1972] 1 Ch. 305; [1971] 3 All E.R. 1345, CA, *per* Lord Denning M.R. and Sachs L.J.
[63] [1969] 1 Q.B. 699, CA.
[64] [1971] 2 All E.R. 216, [1971] 1 W.L.R. 361, CA.

he would, as a rule, be far better off to treat his contract as it were at an end, and this is usually what happens." *per* Salmon and Sachs L.JJ.

Decro-Wall International SA v. Practitioners in Marketing Ltd [1971] 2 All E.R. 216 at 223, CA.

In criticising the majority judgements in these two cases, Sir John Donaldson P. asks "Why should not the servant sue for wages if it is the act of the employer which has prevented his performing the condition precedent of rendering services?" A question to which he does not have to answer in *Sanders*, because there it was found that it was the employees who had repudiated their employment contract by taking industrial action.

A series of cases in the following decade, from *Thomas Marshall (Exports) Ltd v. Guinle*[65] to *Rigby v. Ferodo Ltd*,[66] appear to bear out the general proposition that a contract of employment is not different from other contracts. Where there has been a repudiatory breach, the innocent party may elect to accept or to reject that breach.

In *Thomas Marshall (Exports) Ltd v. Guinle*[67] a managing director working under a fixed term contract containing restrictive clauses on competition and confidential information, used inside information to solicit his employer's customers. He resigned with four years of the contract to run. His former employers sought an injunction to prevent him from soliciting their customers, but the employee claimed that he was no longer bound by the restrictive covenants in the contract because the contract itself had terminated with his repudiation. Megarry V.C. robustly rejected the automatic argument and citing some early cases[68] concluded that it could not be right that a wrongdoer could benefit by his own fundamental breach of the contract. He granted an injunction to the employer restraining the employee from acting outwith the contract.

In *Gunton v. Richmond-upon-Thames LBC*[69] the Court of Appeal, in holding that a college registrar had been wrongfully dismissed because his employers had not complied with the contractual disciplinary procedures found that a wrongful dismissal:

"... does not terminate the contract of employment until the employee has accepted the employer's repudiation of the contract. The argument on behalf of the employers that an unequivocal dismissal of itself terminates the contract of employment could not be upheld. The general doctrine that a repudiation by one party does not terminate the contract applies to contracts of employment as it applies to the generality of contracts." *per* Buckley L.J.

Gunton v. Richmond-upon-Thames LBC [1980] I.R.L.R. 321 at 322, CA.

Although the relationship of employer and employee had clearly broken down in this situation, the contract was not deemed to be terminated until the employee had received the contractual obligation of a dismissal process carried out in accordance with the contractual disciplinary procedures (see para. 5.6).

That the seriousness of the breach is a factor in determining what effect it has on the contract is illustrated in *London Transport Executive v. Clarke*.[70] A London Transport

---

[65] [1978] 3 All E.R. 193; [1978] I.C.R. 905.
[66] [1987] I.R.L.R. 516; [1988] I.C.R. 29, HL.
[67] [1978] 3 All ER 193; [1978] I.C.R. 905.
[68] *Lumley v. Wagner* (1852) 1 De. G.M. & G. 604; *Wlliam Robinson and Co. Ltd v. Heuer* [1898] 2 Ch. 451; *Warner Bros v. Nelson* [1937] 1 K.B. 209.
[69] [1980] I.R.L.R. 321, CA.
[70] [1981] I.C.R. 355, CA.

employee went on holiday without permission and the question to be answered was: did the employee repudiate the contract through his own misconduct or did his employer repudiate the contract by dismissing him? In a dissenting judgment Lord Denning M.R. adhered to the automatic approach by indicating that, when dealing with misconduct terminations, there are two possibilities. If the employee shows an intention to bring the contract to an end, for example, by getting another job or by thieving from the employer, the employee in effect dismisses himself without the need for the employer to accept his repudiation. But, if on the other hand, the employee's conduct is such as to not entirely disrupt the contract, but could, under common law, be grounds for dismissal, for example: by refusing to obey a lawful order from the employer, it is then up to the employer whether to accept the employee's repudiation. In summary, if there is not a fundamental breach of the contract the employer may elect not to accept a misconduct repudiation, but "if the employer does elect to dismiss, it is the employer who 'terminates' the contract". [1981] I.R.L.R. 166 at 167, CA.

5.3.2.3   *The problem of "self-dismissal"*

There are two problems associated with the principle of self-dismissal and some commentators firmly disavow the principle itself.[71] The first problem is the calculation of the actual date of termination itself. Is it when the repudiatory act occurs or is it when the employer knows about the breach and accepts it? Secondly, such a concept was used by employers to evade legislative provisions[72] which were designed to prevent them from contracting out of their statutory obligations. This situation is illustrated in a number of cases where employees who went on long holidays to visit relatives abroad, did not return on the originally agreed dates and were subsequently dismissed. They had been asked before going on leave, to sign or agree to a contractual variation that their contracts would automatically terminate on a certain date if they had not returned to work by that date. In *Igbo v. Johnson Matthey Chemicals Ltd*[73] the Court of Appeal decided that this type of contractual variation was unlawful because it converted the statutory right not to be unfairly dismissed[74] into a conditional right not to be unfairly dismissed.

Returning to *Clarke* and the common law however, Templeman L.J. in giving the majority decision in the Court of Appeal, considered that the difference between the two theories was of no practical importance because "self-dismissal would determine the contract when the worker walked out or otherwise committed a repudiatory breach of the contract whereas accepted repudiation determines the contract when the employer expressly or impliedly gives notice to the worker that the employer accepts the repudiation and does not wish to affirm the contract." He concludes that self-dismissal and its acceptance by the employer often occur impliedly and simultaneously but that the difficulty with the self-dismissal theory occurs where an employee is seeking to establish that he was constructively unfairly dismissed. The statutory concept of constructive dismissal[75] permits an employee to terminate the contract without notice "by reason of the employer's conduct", whereas the common law concept as defined by Denning L.J. suggest that it is the employee's conduct which can

[71] K.D. Ewing and A. McColgan (1995) *Law at Work*, (2nd ed., Unison Open College, 1995), p. 254.
[72] ERA 1996, s.203.
[73] [1986] I.R.L.R. 215; [1986] I.C.R. 505, CA.
[74] ERA 1996, s.95.
[75] ERA 1996, s.95(1)(c).

amount to self-dismissal. Ewing is clear that: "There is no concept of self-dismissal in English or Scots law. If an employee is guilty of misconduct, the contract can only be ended by the employee subsequently resigning or by the employer dismissing. The employee's conduct does not itself terminate the contract."[76] (See para. 5.3.3.)

The elective principle was also upheld in *Dietman v. London Borough of Brent*[77]— where the Court of Appeal considered that a social worker who had been summarily dismissed for professional negligence in a child abuse case, had, by accepting another job, elected to accept the council's summary dismissal of her. The Court of Appeal agreed with the High Court's finding that her admitted "gross negligence" did not amount to "gross misconduct" as contractually defined and that her summary dismissal was therefore unfair as statutorily defined.[78] (see Chapter 7). As a result, her remedy, because of her acceptance of the repudiation, was confined to damages only. If she had not accepted the repudiation, she would have been entitled to a contractual disciplinary hearing. This was because under the elective principle, she would have been affirming her obligations under the contract. By accepting termination of it she was confined to damages which were the wages she would have earned in the period taken to convene a disciplinary hearing plus contractual notice.

In *Rigby v. Ferodo Ltd*[79] an employee had his wages unilaterally reduced by 5 per cent but he continued to work and sued for the loss. In the House of Lords the employer's counsel drew attention to the dissenting judgments in *Gunton* and *Clarke* which supported the automatic theory of repudiation. He argued that these cases were wrongly decided, and suggested that:

1. Where there is a breach of an essential term; *and*

2. A wish by the repudiator to discontinue or to change the contract; and

3. Where the innocent party has no practical option other than to accept;

the contract is terminated.

If this argument had been accepted by the House of Lords, the only remedy obtainable would have been damages amounting to the notice period for the unilateral termination of the old contract. Lord Oliver did not accept this argument:

> "I entirely fail to see how the continuance of the primary contractual obligation can be made to depend upon the subjective desire of the contract-breaker and I do not understand what is meant by the injured party having no alternative but to accept the breach." *per* Oliver L.J.
>
> *Rigby v. Ferodo Ltd* [1987] I.R.L.R. 516 at 518, HL.

He relied on Asquith L.J.'s classical dictum that "an unaccepted repudiation is a thing writ in water and of no value to anybody".[80] Because the wage reduction had expressly not been agreed by the employee, the elective theory directed that it was an unlawful variation and that the remedy was restoration of the contractual pay level plus recovery of the 5 per cent deduction.

---

[76] *op. cit.*
[77] [1988] I.R.L.R. 299; [1988] I.C.R. 842, CA.
[78] ERA 1996, s.98(1).
[79] [1988] I.C.R. 29, HL.
[80] *Howard v. Pickford Tool Co. Ltd* [1951] 1 K.B. 417 at 421.

5.3.2.4   *Automatic theory still relevant but not dominant?*

Despite strong judicial support for the elective principle of repudiation, the particular problems associated with construction of the contract of employment still give rise to cases such as *Boyo v. London Borough of Lambeth*[81] where although the Court of Appeal was bound by the decision in *Gunton* it felt that the automatic principle had merit in this case. An accountant accused of fraud in connection with housing benefit was suspended on full pay. Whilst awaiting trial, the council sent him a letter saying his actions had frustrated his contract of employment and that his salary would cease after the contractual notice period had been effected. The criminal charges were dismissed at trial and Mr Boyo commenced an action against Lambeth asserting that he was and had been available for work, and was therefore owed arrears of salary. The employers resisted this action claiming:

1. The contract had been determined by law or frustrated by the employee; or

2. The employee had been dismissed for gross misconduct.

In the county court it was held, in accordance with the principles established in *Gunton v. Richmond-upon-Thames LBC*[82] that the employee had accepted the employer's repudiation by starting appeal proceedings against the council. The council amended their plea in the Court of Appeal accepting that they had wrongfully dismissed Mr Boyo but contesting the level of damages. The question at issue was now the actual date of the repudiation itself. Upon this question rested the level of damages payable to the employee.

In a judgment which looked carefully at the case law on the automatic and elective theories of repudiation, the Court of Appeal felt bound by its own decision in *Gunton* that "a unilateral repudiation of the contract by the employers does not terminate the contract of employment until accepted by the employee." Although there was dispute about exactly when the employee had accepted the repudiation, the Court of Appeal upheld the county court ruling that there was not a contractual obligation on the employers to delay terminating the contract until after the completion of criminal proceedings against the employee. In addition, it also upheld the county court who ruled that the damages for wrongful dismissal should be based on a reasonable period for carrying out the contractual disciplinary procedures.[83] So Mr Boyo failed to obtain an increase in the damages awarded to him. In surveying the authorities on the principles of repudiation, the Court of Appeal criticised the remedies as applied in *Gunton* referring to the reasoning of Sachs LJ and Salmon L.J. in *Decro-Wall*[84] "(i) Why should not the servant sue for wages if it is the act of the employer which has prevented his performing the condition precedent [*i.e.* working] of rendering services?" Never the less they felt themselves bound by *Gunton* to uphold the award of damages subject to a duty to mitigate loss by the employee.

5.3.3   Constructive dismissal

The statutory concept of constructive dismissal[85] permits an employee to terminate "the contract under which he is employed (with or without notice) in circumstances in

---

[81] [1995] I.R.L.R. 50, CA.
[82] [1980] I.R.L.R. 321, CA.
[83] See also: *Focsa Services (U.K.) Ltd v. Birkett* [1996] I.R.L.R. 325, EAT, and *Janciuk v. Winerite Ltd* [1998] I.R.L.R. 63, EAT.
[84] [1971] 1 W.L.R. 361.
[85] ERA, 1996, s.95(1)(c).

which he is entitled to terminate it without notice by reason of the employer's conduct." This formulation, which is discussed in detail in Chapter 7, para. 7.2.1.5., derives from the common law position that in response to an employer's repudiatory behaviour, the employee may be entitled to resign and claim damages for breach of contract. Applying the elective theory of repudiation, this permits the wronged party to decide whether to accept or waive the breach, and if he takes the former course, to pursue a legal remedy. The statutory remedies for being constructively unfairly dismissed permit the payment of compensation[86] or reinstatement and re-engagement.[87] The case law arising from these provisions is now considerable[88] and is heavily concerned with two questions. First, what level and type of behaviour by the employer "entitles" an employee to leave and to submit an unfair constructive dismissal claim? Secondly, should the courts apply a strictly contractual meaning to "entitlement" or a broader test of employer "reasonableness"?

There is no specific test of reasonableness or type of employer conduct which automatically entitles an employee to terminate the contract and make an application to an employment tribunal for constructive unfair dismissal. Ewing and McColgan[89] conveniently list some examples of breaches giving rise to constructive dismissal. These include: failure to deal with a complaint of sexual or racial harassment[90]; unilateral reduction of wages[91]; a demand to perform work outside an employee's contractual obligations[92]; behaviour by the employer which destroys the implied term of mutual trust and confidence[93]; an instruction to move the employee's place of work which is outwith the contract[94]; and lastly where an express mobility or flexibility clause is operated in such a way that the employee can not comply with it.[95]

Some of these cases have been considered in para. 5.2 above. In particular, the difficulties caused by the judicial approach to the statutory wording have already been discussed in *Western Excavating (ECC) Ltd v. Sharp* above. It should be noted that the statutory concept of constructive dismissal mirrors the common law position in that the breach should be serious enough to be repudiatory of the contract. Although the Court of Appeal in *Western Excavating* determined that such a breach should be strictly construed according to the rules of contract, Smith and Thomas point out, that, increasingly, the EAT has "shown itself ready to read into contracts of employment a new implied term obliging the employer to treat the employee with trust and respect."[96] This has broadened the concept of constructive dismissal and led to the considerable development of the case law mentioned above.

To secure compensation for any unfair dismissal, including constructive unfair dismissal, it was thought that a *de facto* dismissal was necessary. *Alcan Extrusions v. Yates*[97] appears to have changed the situation. Here, the employers tried to impose a

---

[86] ERA 1996, s.112(4).
[87] ERA 1996, s.113(a)(b).
[88] For example, M. Rubenstein and Y. Frost (1997) cite some 80 leading judgments.
[89] K.D. Ewing and A. McColgan (1995), p. 47.
[90] *Bracebridge Engineering Ltd v. Darby* [1990] I.R.L.R. 3, EAT.
[91] *Industrial Rubber Products v. Gillon* [1977] I.R.L.R. 389, EAT; *White v. Reflecting Roadstuds Ltd* [1991] I.R.L.R. 331, EAT; *R.F. Hill Ltd v. Mooney* [1981] I.R.L.R. 258, EAT; *Reid v. Camphill Engravers* [1990] I.R.L.R. 268, EAT; *Gillies v. Richard Daniels and Co. Ltd* [1979] I.R.L.R. 457, EAT; *F.C. Gardner Ltd. v. Beresford* [1978] I.R.L.R. 63, EAT.
[92] *McNeilll v. Messrs Charles Crimin (Electrical Contractors) Ltd* [1984] I.R.L.R. 179, EAT.
[93] *Woods v. W.M. Car Services (Peterborough) Ltd* [1981] I.R.L.R. 347, EAT.
[94] *Bass Leisure Ltd v. Thomas* [1994] I.R.L.R. 104, EAT.
[95] *United Bank Ltd v. Akhtar* [1989] I.R.L.R. 507, EAT.
[96] I.T. Smith and G.H. Thomas, G.H. (1996), p. 379.
[97] *Alcan Extrusions v. Yates* [1996] I.R.L.R. 327, EAT.

radically different shift system on employees involving longer and more unsociable hours, reduced pay rates and restricted holidays. The men continued to work under protest but claimed that the changes amounted to a fundamental breach of their contracts of employment and applied for unfair dismissal compensation. The Employment Appeal Tribunal upheld the industrial tribunal's finding of a dismissal under what is now ERA 1996, s.95(1)(a) and that it was unfair as statutorily defined. Both courts based their decision on the authority of *Hogg v. Dover College*[98] which was a similar situation where the employer was held to have committed a fundamental breach:

> "In reaching that decision, the tribunal chairman concluded that the case was analogous to *Hogg v. Dover College*. That case involved a teacher who received a letter from his employers telling him that he would no longer be head of department, that he would be employed only part time, and that his salary would be halved. In those circumstances, the EAT concluded that, 'both as a matter of law and common sense, he was being told that his former contract was from that moment gone. There was no question of any continued performance of it. It is suggested, on behalf of the employers, that there was a variation, but again, it seems to us quite elementary that you cannot hold a pistol to somebody's head and say "henceforth you are to be employed on wholly different terms which are in fact less than 50% of your previous contract." We come unhesitatingly to the conclusion that there was a dismissal; the applicant's previous contract having been wholly withdrawn from him.'"

> Industrial tribunal decision in *Hogg* cited in *Alcan Extrusions v. Yates and others* [1996] I.R.L.R. 327 at 327, EAT.

In *Alcan* the EAT could not accept the employer's argument that a similar fundamental breach of terms was only a potential repudiatory breach giving the employee the option to continue working or to resign and claim constructive dismissal. It found that "Very substantial departures from an original contract of employment can amount to termination of that contract and its replacement by the offer of a different and inferior contract." The EAT decision in *Alcan* has been criticised as "contrary to authority and . . . likely to be difficult to apply in practice" as well as being "bad in principle". White[99] contrasts *Rigby* and *Burdett-Coutts* with *Alcan* and *Hogg*. In the former cases the employers tried to effect unilateral variations by claiming that there had been a termination of the old contract and an offer to re-employ on new terms. This argument was rejected by the courts, whereas in *Hogg* and *Alcan* the test applied by the courts "was not whether the employer intended to bring the contract to an end but whether the variation effectively amounted to the existing contract being withdrawn so that no further peformance of it was possible." On a matter of principle and practicality White considers that it is unsatisfactory if an employee can claim, in a common law action that the contract is still continuing whilst mounting a separate statutory action which depends upon the same contract being terminated by the employer.

5.3.4 Summary dismissal

The common law concept of summary dismissal, it could be argued, is the obverse of the principle of constructive dismissal, in that it is the repudiatory behaviour of the

---

[98] [1990] I.C.R. 39, EAT.
[99] R. White (1997) "Repudiatory Breach and the Definition of Dismissal" (1997) 26 I.L.J. 252.

employee which permits the employer to accept the repudiation and dismiss the employee. Dismissal of an employee without notice will be wrongful however unless the employer can prove that it is justified by the employee's breach.

In the older nineteenth century cases, dismissal without notice reflected the master and servant notion of the employment relationship. Employees could be dismissed for moral misconduct, wilful disobedience and habitual neglect.[1] The modern test is much more based on whether the employee has breached an essential element of the contract.[2] Implied terms in the employment contract, such as a willingness to work honestly and to obey lawful orders, may if seriously breached, justify summary dismissal by the employer. Theft or damage to an employer's property and violence at work would therefore normally invite summary dismissal. Such behaviour would probably be viewed as gross misconduct by the employee.

A more "indirect" form of gross misconduct is illustrated by *Denco Ltd v. Joinson*.[3] Here, an AEU[4] shop steward and chairman of the union joint representative committee used an unauthorised password to gain access to the confidential computer files of another subsidiary company. This company had only recently recognised the AEU. The EAT held that:

> "Unauthorised use of, or tampering with, computers is an extremely serious industrial offence. If an employee uses an unauthorised password in order to attempt to enter a computer known to contain information to which he is not entitled, that of itself is gross misconduct which prima facie will attract summary dismissal. The employee's motive is immaterial. It is a question of 'absolutes' and should be compared with dishonesty." *per* Wood J.

Denco Ltd. v. Joinson [1991] I.R.L.R. 63 at 63, EAT.

Despite the introduction of a statutory "model" of procedural and substantive fairness[5] into the dismissal process, *Denco* is important because it illustrates the enduring influence of implied common law terms in the maintenance of the employment relationship (see Chapter 3). Here, it was argued that the employee, as a senior union official, had a special relationship of trust and confidence with his employer. In breaching that trust, the employer elected to accept his repudiation and summarily dismissed him despite 20 twenty years service and previous clean record.

This may seem somewhat harsh given that the employer's security measures were also criticised by the industrial tribunal. In highlighting this, the EAT emphasised "that management should make it abundantly clear to the workforce that interfering with computers will carry severe penalties. Rules concerning access to and use of computers should be reduced to writing and left near the computers for reference." In other words, the nature of such repudiatory conduct is to be made clear to the workforce. It is also argued that a less harsh decision may have been arrived at if "the motive behind the unauthorised access [had] been shown to be just simple curiosity or experimentation."[6]

Refusal to obey a single order from the employer is not in itself behaviour necessarily justifying summary dismissal. A single outburst of bad temper by a

[1] *Callo v. Brouncker* (1831) 4 C. & P. 518.
[2] *Laws v. London Chronicle (Indicator Newspapers) Ltd* [1959] 1 W.L.R. 698; [1959] 2 All E.R. 285.
[3] [1991] I..R.L.R. [1991] 63; [1991] I.C.R. 172, EAT.
[4] Associated Engineering Union.
[5] ERA 1996, s.94—right not to be unfairly dismissed.
[6] B. Napier (1992) "Computerization and Employment Rights" (1992) 21 I.L.J. 1.

gardener towards his employer, without any background of unwillingness to properly perform the contract[7] was distinguished from a similar case[8] where the Court of Appeal found that the refusal to obey an order was part of a pattern of unco-operative repudiatory behaviour by the employee.

Most of the case law concerning dismissal for gross misconduct now arises from the statutory unfair dismissal provisions[9] which stress the importance of a fair procedure for dismissal.[10] Summary dismissal is still a remedy which is available to employers in the face of serious repudiatory action by the employee. It can be seen that ACAS advice to employers on what constitutes gross misconduct is based on common law principles:

> "Gross misconduct is generally seen as misconduct serious enough to destroy the employment contract between the employer and the employee and make any further working relationship and trust impossible. It is normally restricted to very serious offences—for example physical violence, theft or fraud—but may be determined by the nature of the business or other circumstances."

Discipline at Work, The ACAS advisory handbook (ACAS, 1987), p. 29.

ACAS also advises that employers should "give all employees a clear indication of the type of misconduct which, in the light of the requirements of the employer's business, will warrant dismissal without the normal period of notice or pay in lieu of notice."[11]

5.4   NOTICE

5.4.1   Common law notice

The modern common law position is that an employee is employed under a contract of indeterminate length subject to a reasonable period of notice. If not expressly stated, a reasonable period of notice may be implied from a variety of factors including the frequency of payment, for example weekly or monthly, or from the status of the employee. An airline pilot[12] was found to be entitled to three months' notice whereas a newspaper editor was subject to a year's notice.[13] Some half a century after the latter case however, it was maintained in *N. Rees v. Raken International Ltd*[14] that "The common law standard as to what constitutes 'reasonable' notice varies according to job rank rather than the length of service." Even so, the introduction of statutory minima periods of notice based on length of service[15] has probably reduced the significance of employee status. Under common law, the legal remedy for a breach of the contractual notice period is a claim for damages to recover pay for the notice not given, that is, further pay in lieu of notice. It should also be noted, that the question of what is a

---

[7] *Wilson v. Racher* [1974] I.R.L.R. 114, CA.
[8] *Pepper v. Webb* [1969] 2 All E.R. 216, CA.
[9] ERA 1996, s.94.
[10] S.I. 1977 No. 867, *ACAS Code of Practice 1 for Disciplinary Practice and Procedures in Employment*.
[11] *Discipline at Work, The ACAS advisory handbook* (ACAS, 1987), p. 29.
[12] *Nicoll v. Falcon Airways Ltd* [1962] 1 Lloyd's Rep. 245.
[13] *Grundy v. Sun Printing and Publishing Association* (1916) 33 T.L.R. 77.
[14] [1975] I.R.L.R. 342, IT.
[15] CEA 1963, now ERA 1996, ss.86 and 87.

reasonable period of notice, can now be raised in industrial tribunals as a common law action arising from termination of employment.[16]

A notice of termination must be clearly given[17] and include the date of termination or allow it to be inferred:

> "As a matter of law an employer cannot dismiss his employee by saying 'I intend to dispense with your services at some time in the coming months.' In order to terminate the contract of employment the notice must either specify the date or contain material from which that date is positively ascertainable."

> *Morton Sundour Fabrics Ltd. v. Shaw* (1967) 2 I.T.R. 84 at 85.

The above case is one of a number,[18] where an employee had anticipated being made redundant and had resigned before formal and precise notice of dismissal for redundancy had been received. In such a situation, the employee may lose entitlement to statutory redundancy rights including compensation payments.

Once explicitly given, notice of termination can not be withdrawn without the agreement of the other party.[19]

The common law power of the employer to be able to dismiss with notice, irrespective of the reason for the dismissal, put the employee in a very weak position. The introduction of statutory regulation governing how such notice must be given, allied with legislation on the procedures to be followed when dismissing employees has perhaps diminished that power somewhat. The next section considers how the giving of contractual notice is regulated by statute.

5.4.2 Statutory notice

As has been seen above, one of the defects in the common law position was that it made no allowance for length of service. Long-serving employees on weekly contracts would still only be entitled to one week's notice. The ERA 1996, s.86(1) now directs that the employer gives a minimum period of notice to the employee based on his length of continuous service:

> "86.—(1) The notice required to be given by an employer to terminate the contract of employment of a person who has been continuously employed for one month or more—

> (a) is not less than one week's notice if his period of continuous employment is less than two years,
> (b) is not less than one week's notice for each year of continuous employment if his period of continuous employment is two years or more but less than twelve years, and
> (c) is not less than twelve weeks' notice if his period of continuous employment is twelve years or more."

> ERA 1996, s.86(1).

---

[16] S.I. 1994 No. 1623/4.
[17] *Pritchard Ltd v. Boon and Milton* [1919] I.R.L.R. 19, EAT.
[18] *International Computers Ltd v. Kennedy* [1981] I.R.L.R. 28, EAT; *Burton Group Ltd v. M. Smith* [1977] I.R.L.R. 351, EAT; *Morton Sundour Fabrics Ltd v. Shaw* (1967) 2 I.T.R. 84.
[19] *Riordan v. War Office* [1961] 1 W.L.R. 210; *Harris and Russell Ltd v. Slingsby* [1973] I.C.R. 454.

The ERA 1996, s.86(2) also directs that an employee who has been continuously employed for one month or more, is required to give not less than one week's notice to his employer. This section permits either party to waive their right to notice or to accept a payment in lieu of notice.[20] Lastly, section 86(6) allows either party to terminate the contract without notice "by reason of the conduct of the other party". This provision thus facilitates summary dismissal by an employer for misconduct and constructive termination by the employee on the grounds of the employer's conduct.[21]

An employee who waives his right to notice loses his right to a payment in lieu.[22] This is because such payments are regarded as damages for contractual breach rather than wages: "Payment in lieu of notice is not a consensual payment due under a contract. Termination of a contract of employment without notice is a breach of contract sounding in damages. If the right to notice is waived, termination of the contract without notice is not a breach and no damages are due."[23] The distinction between the two is important, because under common law, there is a duty on a party claiming a breach of contract to mitigate losses arising from that breach. Within the context of a contract of employment, this normally means looking for another job. This obligation does not arise in a damages claim.[24]

Giving wages in lieu is a common practice where an employer wishes to dispense with an employee's services immediately, to avoid perhaps, the effects of low motivation on the part of the worker under notice. It is not unlawful if both parties agree to it. But what is the position of an employee who is offered wages in lieu but would prefer to work out his notice? In *Marshall (Cambridge) Ltd v. Hamblin*[25] a car salesman gave three months' contractual notice to his employer. His wages comprised a basic wage plus commission. The commission comprising some 75 per cent of his earnings. The employers wanted the employee to leave immediately and offered payment in lieu at the basic rate. The EAT, in a majority judgment, overturned an industrial tribunal decision that he had been unfairly dismissed and found:

> "Where the contract of employment gives the employer the option of making a payment in lieu of notice, the employer is not in breach of contract by cutting short the period of notice already given by an employee, provided that he makes a payment in lieu. The employee has no right to work out his notice. Until such time as that notice expires, the contract of employment continues and the employer is entitled to utilise a term of that contract to bring the employment to an end at an earlier date than that on which the employee's notice expires." *per* Hargrove J.

Marshall (Cambridge) Ltd v. Hamblin [1994] I.R.L.R. 260 at 260, EAT.

The tribunal found that the employee's remedy for his lost commission was in a county court claim. In a strong dissenting judgment it was pointed out that this put the employee in a very weak position when he gave notice and could not have been intended by the original contracting parties:

---

[20] ERA 1996, s.86(3).
[21] ERA 1996, s.95(1)(c).
[22] *Trotter v. Forth Ports Authority* [1991] I.R.L.R. 419, CA.
[23] *Trotter v. Forth Ports Authority* [1991] I.R.L.R. 419, CS.
[24] *Abrahams v. Performing Right Society* [1995] I.C.R. 1028; [1995] I.R.L.R. 486, CA. (But note that: I.T. Smith, and G.H. Thomas (1996) at p. 304 consider this case to contain 'some extremely dubious dicta . . . and is best tactfully forgotten.")
[25] [1994] I.R.L.R. 260, EAT.

"Assuming at the start of the contract both the employer and employee, in this case, had been asked whether that payment meant that the employer could, as soon as an employee gave notice of termination, bring his working period at the firm to an end by payment of wages and thereby prevent him from earning or being in a position to earn his commission, both parties without hesitating would have replied that such a situation was wrong. They would have agreed that there was an implied term, that such a payment in lieu only applied if the employer was giving notice and that any other shortening of the employee's period of work must be by agreement." *per* D.O. Gladwin dissenting.

Marshall (Cambridge) Ltd v. Hamblin [1994] I.R.L.R. 260 at 262, EAT.

That there is still a degree of uncertainty about this issue is indicated by the unanimous decision of the EAT in *Marshall* to allow an appeal to the Court of Appeal.

In *Delaney v. Staples*[26] the leading case on deductions from wages, and referred to in *Marshall*,[27] Lord Browne-Wilkinson proposes a rough classification of "payments in lieu" under four heads as:

1. *Wages in advance*—Where the employer gives proper notice of termination but informs the employee that he need not work (but can take "garden-leave") until the termination date and gives a lump sum to cover this period. The employment contract continues until the expiry of notice. Although no work is done the employee is simply given "advance wages".

2. *Contractual notice or summary dismissal*—Where the contract expressly provides that it may be terminated by notice *or* by payment in lieu of notice, summarily. The employer does not breach the contract providing payment is made in lieu but this payment is not wages "in the ordinary sense" because it is not payment for work to be done. The contract ends with the issuing of the notice or on the date of the payment in lieu.

3. *Voluntary termination on payment of a sum in lieu*—Where both parties agree to terminate the contract for payment in lieu, the outcome is the same as above—the payment is not strictly wages.

4. *Summary dismissal by the employer without the agreement of the employee, who is offered payment in lieu of notice*—The commonest form of such payment, where the employment relationship is ended, no work is undertaken and the lieu payment cannot be wages. As there is no agreed variation, this is a wrongful dismissal and the payment made is for damages not wages.

In summary, category (1) appears to be wages in advance, whilst category (4) is damages, whereas categories (2) and (3) are not strictly wages. It would appear that the employer who seeks to avoid a challenge from an employee wishing to work his notice, would be best advised to incorporate an express term into the original contract of employment permitting dismissal with wages in lieu.[28] McColgan[29] also considers that all four categories should be considered as payment in lieu of wages for purposes of the statutory right not to suffer unauthorised deductions of wages.[30]

---

[26] [1992] I.C.R. 483; [1992] I.R.L.R. 191, HL.
[27] [1994] I.R.L.R. 260 at 262, EAT.
[28] I.T. Smith and G.H. Thomas (1996), p. 304.
[29] A. McColgan (1992) 21 I.L.J. p. 219.
[30] ERA 1996, s.13.

An example of the category (3) position described above, is found in *Baldwin v. British Coal Corporation*[31] Here, a coal mine deputy's contract was terminated, without the statutory 12 weeks' notice to which he was contractually entitled, after he had agreed to a voluntary redundancy package. The question was whether by voluntarily agreeing a redundancy payment, the employee had also impliedly or expressly waived his right to notice and to payment associated with notice? The High Court held that "Termination of the plaintiff coal mine deputy's contract of employment without due notice so as to enable him to qualify for a special redundancy payment, was not a breach of contract giving rise to damages in circumstances in which the plaintiff had either agreed to the termination or waived his right to notice." On evidential grounds Garland J. found that the employee had accepted short notice in order to be dismissed for redundancy and approving Coulsfield L.J. in *Trotter v. Forth Ports Authority*[32] concluded "If the right to notice was waived, termination of the contract without the required notice was not a breach and no damages were due."[33]

5.5   DISCHARGE

At common law a contract may be discharged or ended in four main ways: first, through none or inadequate performance of the contract. Secondly, through a repudiatory breach of the original contract. Thirdly, through the agreement of the contracting parties and fourthly, through some extraneous event external to the contract. When any one of these four situations occur the contract is discharged at law, it simply ceases to exist. Within the context of the employment relationship, discharge of an employment contract will mean that it has come to an end without the necessity of either a dismissal by the employer or a resignation by the employee. In such an event, the employee may lose entitlement to common law and to statutory rights, such as a claim for unfair dismissal.[34] In this section, discharge of the employment contract through frustration and through agreement is considered.

5.5.1   Frustration of the contract

A contract is frustrated in law when it is brought to an end by some outside event or extraneous change of situation, not foreseen or provided for by the parties at the time of contracting, which makes it impossible for the contract to be performed at all, or at least renders its performance something radically different from what the parties contemplated when they entered into it.[35] The outside event or extraneous change of situation concerned, and the consequences of either in relation to the performance of the contract, must have occurred *without the fault or the default of either party* to the contract.

5.5.1.1   *Frustration through sickness*

Egg Stores (Stamford Hill) Ltd v. L. Leibovici[36] supplies a clear legal definition of frustration which is particularly important in wrongful dismissal: ". . . in a case of

---

[31] [1995] I.R.L.R. 139, HCQB.
[32] [1991] I.R.L.R. 419, CS.
[33] [1995] I.R.L.R. 139 at 142, HCQB.
[34] ERA 1996, s.94(1).
[35] *Morgan v. Manser* [1948] 1 K.B. 184; [1947] 2 All E.R. 666.
[36] [1976] I.R.L.R. 376, EAT.

frustration it is not necessary that the employer should have taken steps to end the contract. The whole point of frustration is that it operates automatically to discharge the contract as a result of the event bringing it about."

Whether to formally dismiss an employee, or to take the view that the contract of employment has been discharged through frustration, is an important decision for an employer. A dismissal may attract a wrongful or unfair dismissal action from the employee, whereas following a lawful discharge the employer has no further contractual obligations. The timing of the employer's action may be crucial. In *Egg Stores* the EAT held that "whilst it is not necessary for the employer to have taken steps to end the employment for frustration to have taken place, that the employer had not thought it right to dismiss the absent employee will often be extremely relevant."

The relevance of this action is related to the concept of *fairness*. The EAT judgment refers specifically to how fair the situation is on the employer in the context of "has the time arrived when the employer can no longer be expected to keep the absent employee's post open for him?" In suggesting how employers can answer this question, the court also suggests a wide number of factors to be taken into account such as:

> "1. the length of the previous employment;
>
> 2. how long it had been expected that the employment would continue;
>
> 3. the nature of the job;
>
> 4. the nature, length and effect of the illness or disabling event;
>
> 5. the need of the employer for the work to be done, and the need for a replacement to do it;
>
> 6. the risk to the employer of acquiring obligations in respect of redundancy payments or compensation for unfair dismissal to the replacement employee;
>
> 7. whether wages have continued to be paid;
>
> 8. the acts and the statements of the employer in relation to the employment, including the dismissal of, or failure to dismiss, the employee; and
>
> 9. whether in all the circumstances a reasonable employer could have expected to wait any longer."[36a]

A somewhat comprehensive list, extending earlier dicta by Sir John Donaldson in *R.A. Marshall v. Harland Wolf Ltd and Secretary of State For Employment*[37] which suggests, that in the context of frustration of the employment contract through sickness, the EAT's concept of fairness embraces both employers and employees. It should be borne in mind however, that these are only suggested factors which an employer may consider before regarding a contract as having been frustrated. They are very broad and not necessarily to be relied upon by an employee claiming wrongful or unfair dismissal. ACAS has sought to inject some consistency in this situation by issuing a handbook, supplementary to the code of practice: *Disciplinary Practice and Procedures in Employment,*[38] which gives advice to employers on the handling of longer-term absence through ill-health, and how to deal with employees who have special health

[36a] n. 36 above, at 378.
[37] [1972] I.R.L.R. 90, NIRC.
[38] S.I. 1977 No. 867.

problems such as alcohol or drug abuse.[39] The handbook does not have the legal status of a Code of Practice but has been influential in this area.

The EAT's advice in *Egg Stores* was directed at giving advice to industrial tribunals particularly in cases where the contract of employment can be determined at short notice, which is perhaps in the majority of employment contracts. It distinguished between two kinds of events which may frustrate a contract. The first being the dramatic or sudden event such as an accident, the effects of which are quickly realised and the second being an accident or illness, the outcome of which is uncertain. The list of matters enumerated in their judgment was designed to assist tribunals in assessing when a frustration of the contract has occurred. This specific case was remitted to a hearing by another industrial tribunal because the EAT ruled that it had misdirected itself when it had held that the contract was not frustrated because the employers had not yet taken steps to terminate it. The first instance tribunal had confused the legal requirements upon frustration and dismissal cases when it had ruled that the onus of proof was on the employer to prove that frustration had taken place.

5.5.1.2 *Frustration through imprisonment*

In *F.C. Shepherd and Co. Ltd v. Jerrom*[40] an apprentice plumber who got involved in gang violence outside work as a result of which he was arrested and sentenced to Borstal training for six months to two years. His employers terminated his training service agreement. Upon release from Borstal, the employee asked for his job back, was refused and claimed unfair dismissal. The industrial tribunal found that the employers had repudiated his contract of employment by not complying with the procedures in the relevant collective agreement for terminating the contracts of apprentices. The industrial tribunal held that the employee had accepted the repudiation by bringing an unfair dismissal action and was awarded compensation of £7,000 for the breach without any reduction for compensatory fault. The decision and award were upheld by the EAT.

This ruling was comprehensively overturned on appeal by the Court of Appeal who found:

1. The contract had been brought about by frustration when the employee was sentenced to a period of Borstal training. The serious misconduct rules which the industrial tribunal held had been breached by the employer, applied only to conduct at work.

2. A contract could be ended through frustration according to the principles laid down in *Paal Wilson*:

". . . two essential factors must be present. First there must be some event capable of rendering performance of the contract impossible or something radically different from what the parties contemplated when they entered into it. Secondly, that event must occur without the fault or default of either party." *per* Lawton L.J.

F.C. Shepherd & Co. Ltd v. Jerrom [1986] I.R.L.R. 358 at 358, CA.

In *Shepherd* the Court of Appeal ruled that "Correctly understood, the principle that the frustrating event must have occurred without the fault or default of either party to

---

[39] ACAS, *Discipline at Work, The ACAS advisory handbook* (1987).
[40] [1986] I.R.L.R. 358, CA.

the contract means that a party who was at fault cannot rely on frustration due to his own act." Although the employee argued that he had not imprisoned himself and therefore was not at fault, the Court found that it was his action in committing a crime which led to the sentence of imprisonment. This frustrating event had inserted a substantial break in the employee's period of training and would have led to him being a lesser trained employee, a situation which would have affected the employer's plans for him to take over the skilled job of a retiring worker. By claiming that the employers had constructively dismissed him when terminating the apprenticeship agreement, the apprentice was initially able to secure the full compensatory award through taking an action for constructive unfair dismissal. When the Court ruled that his contract had been frustrated through his own misconduct, the employer was discharged of any further contractual obligations. The contract was terminated through operation of law without any action needed by the employer and because there was no "dismissal" there could be no claim for unfair dismissal.

5.5.2   Fixed term contracts

Historically, a general hiring was presumed to be for a year to guarantee seasonal employment for agricultural labourers.[41] This has no validity now and all hirings under a contract of employment are, unless specified otherwise, presumed to be for an indefinite duration and subject to termination upon reasonable notice. As has been seen in para. 5.4.1 above, reasonable notice, if not expressly provided for in the contract or implied through custom and practice or trade usage[42] will be construed by a court or employment tribunal, from the terms of the contract itself.

An increasingly significant feature of modern employment however, is, what some might consider a return to the historical insecurity of hiring found formerly in both agriculture and in industry (for example in the dockyards) where employees were hired for limited or fixed terms of employment which were sometimes as short as one day. Such short term hirings are not uncommon in the fast-food business today where temporary staff may be engaged on zero-hour contracts.[43] In 1994, some 1,396,000 employees were reported as being in temporary work.[44] The term of employment is usually to complete a specific task or cycle of work.[45] At common law, if a contract of employment is for a fixed period, the contract is itself discharged upon the contractual termination date. This area is now heavily regulated by statute so that non renewal of a fixed term contract,[46] or termination of a fixed term contract unreasonably, may constitute an unfair dismissal or redundancy dismissal.[47] The legislative provisions do, however, permit employees on fixed term contracts to opt out of their unfair dismissal and redundancy rights.[48] Such provisions being originally formulated to allow employers flexibility when recruiting staff for a foreseeable short duration. See Chapter 7, para. 7.2.1.6. for the case law arising from these provisions.

---

[41] I.T. Smith and G.H. Thomas (1996), p. 297.
[42] *George v. Davies* [1911] 2 K.B. 445.
[43] *McDonald's Corp. and McDonald's Restaurants Ltd v. Steel and Morris*, June 19, 1997, HC QBD, No. 1990–M–NO. 5724.
[44] *Employment Gazette* (1995) Department of Employment, February 1995.
[45] *Mulrine v. University of Ulster* [1993] I.R.L.R. 545, NICA.
[46] ERA 1996, s.95(1)(b).
[47] ERA 1996, s.136(1)(b).
[48] ERA 1996, s.197.

5.5.3   Death, dissolution, transfer and insolvency

The common law position whereby an employment contract may be subject to the death, dissolution, transfer of assets and insolvency of the employer has been much qualified by statutory developments. These are briefly reviewed below.

Because at common law an implied condition of a contract is the continued existence of the parties to it, where there is the death of an employee[49] or of an employer[50] the contract of employment is discharged and thereby brought to an end. Statute now intervenes to ensure that where an employer dies and the business is discontinued, the employee is entitled to a redundancy payment[51] but if it is carried on by the deceased's personal representatives, the employee's continuity of employment for statutory purposes is maintained.[52] An employee who dies whilst instituting tribunal proceedings against an employer may have these proceedings continued by a personal representative.[53]

When a business is transferred or sold by one employer to another, the common law concept of mutuality of agreement operates to terminate the contract of employment. This is because the contract of employment is personal to the employee and cannot be disposed of like other business assets. Common law doctrine does not permit a contract of personal service to be enforced by the courts. In theory, therefore, the employee who is faced with a transfer situation can choose voluntarily not to work for the new employer.[54] In practice however, most employees in such a situation are probably more concerned with preserving their employment status and conditions. The continuity of employment status and terms in such a situation was introduced by statute through the TUPE Regulations 1981.[55] These provide that "a relevant transfer shall not operate so as to terminate the contract of employment of any person employed by the transferor in the undertaking or part transferred but any such contract which would otherwise have been terminated by the transfer shall have effect after the transfer as if originally made between the person so employed and the transferee".[56] The common law position on the voluntary nature of such a transfer is now preserved in the TUPE Regulations 1981.[57] An extensive case law has now developed around the statutory transfer provisions which were introduced into domestic law to implement E.C. Directive 77/187—the "Acquired Rights Directive." This is dealt with in Chapter 9. Lastly, continuity of employment may also be protected by the ERA 1996, s.218 which provides that the contract is not broken where the business or undertaking is transferred as a going concern, or where there is change in the status of the employer, for example "a change in the partners, personal representatives or trustees".[58]

In an insolvency situation, the situation as to whether the contract of employment is discharged or the employee is dismissed is not straightforward.[59] This appears to depend upon whether there is an immediate cessation of business and a compulsory

[49] *Stubbs v. Holywell Rly Co.* (1867) L.R. 2 Exch. 311; *Graves v. Cohen* (1929) 46 T.L.R. 21.
[50] *Farrow v. Wilson* (1869) L.R. 4 C.P. 744.
[51] ERA 1996, s.136(5)(b).
[52] ERA 1996, s.218(4).
[53] ERA 1996, s.206.
[54] *Nokes v. Doncaster Amalgamated Collieries Ltd* [1940] A.C. 1015.
[55] Transfer of Undertakings (Protection of Employment) Regulations 1981 (S.I. 1981 No. 1794).
[56] TUPE, reg. 5(1).
[57] TUPE, reg. 5(4A).
[58] ERA 1996, s.218(5).
[59] I.T. Smith and G.H. Thomas (1996), p. 291.

winding up. In such a situation there would be a notice of dismissal.[60] The appointment of a receiver may also terminate contracts of employment.[61] Lastly, when an employer becomes insolvent certain debts have priority, such as wages,[62] accrued holiday pay, contractual and statutory sick pay. Employee claims for damages arising from the employer's insolvency may, since *Potter v. Secretary of State for Employment*[63] have to be pursued in the High Court.

5.6 WRONGFUL DISMISSAL REMEDIES

A useful definition of what could be termed the classical or "old" concept of wrongful dismissal is given by Lord Denning M.R.:

> "Often a servant was dismissed by his employer at a moment's notice. He was given 'the sack' (old parlance) meaning the bag in which he kept his tools. He brought an action for wrongful dismissal. The master pleaded in defence simply that 'the plaintiff misconducted himself in the said service', giving particulars of the misconduct, see *Bullen and Leake*, 3rd edition (1868) page 650. His plea was based on the simple proposition that it was the duty of the servant to give good and faithful service: and that he had been guilty of misconduct of so serious a kind that it justified his dismissal. In modern terminology, he had been guilty of a repudiatory breach. The judges refused to lay down any general rule as to what causes would justify the dismissal of a servant. They left it to the jury. . .". *per* Denning M.R.

Woods v. W. M. Car Services (Peterborough) Ltd [1982] I.R.L.R. 413 at 414, CA.

This cameo description encapsulates the nature of the employment relationship in the middle of the nineteenth century, that it was based on status and not on contract and that remedies for breach were sought by the employer in the criminal courts.[64] Today remedies are sought in the civil jurisdiction only. If an employee is the subject of a repudiatory breach of his employment contract, that is, the "innocent party," he has two main remedies: to pursue a wrongful dismissal claim in the High Court or county court, or to submit an application to an employment tribunal claiming unfair dismissal. The remedies are not mutually exclusive, claims may be submitted to both jurisdictions at the same time. The much older common law route of wrongful dismissal provides remedies based on contractual entitlement, usually for damages only, whereas the more recent[65] statutory remedy can provide compensation and re-engagement if the tribunal finds that the contractual breach constituted an unfair dismissal as statutorily defined.[66] If the employer is the subject of the breach, at common law there may also be a remedy in damages or in injunctive relief, but the more usual remedy is for the employee to be dismissed.

---

[60] Re *General Rolling Stock Co. (Chapman's Case)* (1866) L.R. 1 Eq. 346; Re *Oriental Bank Corp. Ltd (McDowall's Case)* (1886) 32 Ch.D. 366.
[61] *ibid.* n. 147.
[62] Insolvency Act 1986, Sched. 6.
[63] [1997] I.R.L.R. 21, CA.
[64] See: S. Deakin, and G. Morris (1995), p. 23.
[65] ERA 1996, s.94(1).
[66] ERA 1996, s.98(1).

In addition to damages and injunctive relief, the third common law remedy for wrongful dismissal is an application for judicial review when an issue of administrative justice is involved, such as the dismissal of a public office holder. This section considers wrongful dismissal remedies within the context of:

- Damages
- Injunctive relief
- Judicial review

5.6.1 Damages

In *O'Laoire v. Jackel International Ltd*[67] a dismissed manager pursued wrongful dismissal and unfair dismissal actions simultaneously. At the industrial tribunal, it was found that he was unfairly dismissed because of the employer's breach of his contractual entitlement to be appointed as the managing director upon the retirement of the recumbent post-holder. Reinstatement was ordered. Compensation was assessed at £100,700 but reduced to the then statutory maximum of £8,000. In the separate action for wrongful dismissal the employee also claimed damages for loss of salary for breach of the contractual notice provisions; for loss of benefits, for loss of employment opportunities and for distress and injury to feelings.

The decision in the High Court (QBD) was that there was no contractual obligation on the employer to appoint Mr O'Laire as managing director and that the only damages he was lawfully entitled to was for the notice period, minus the £8,000 awarded by the industrial tribunal. These were assessed at £9,495.44. At the Court of Appeal however, the employee's damages were increased because it was ruled that it could not be shown that there was "double recovery" in this case. This was because the industrial tribunal did not allocate the £8,000 maximum award to any one element of the calculated total loss of £100,700.

The question of the amount of damages that the dismissed employee was entitled to was very much at the heart of this appeal which illustrates the difference in remedies available through common law and by statute in the industrial tribunal. At common law, damages are restricted to losses directly arising from the contractual breach. Usually this will only amount to the recouping of wages for the notice period. It is argued by Davies and Freedland, that the original statutory drafting relating to compensation for an unfair dismissal,[68] was based on the notion that "unfair dismissal was a species of statutory tort and that the appropriate way of measuring compensation was not by reference to past service but by reference to the loss flowing from the employer's wrongful act."[69] So although the current statutory provisions extend financial compensation to *future* contractual entitlements:

> "If the complainant would have benefited from a improvement in his terms and conditions of employment had he not been dismissed, an order for reinstatement shall require him to be treated as if he had benefited from that improvement from the date on which he would have done so but for being dismissed."

Employment Rights Act 1996, s.114(3).

---

[67] [1991] I.R.L.R. 170, CA.
[68] Introduced in IRA 1971.
[69] P. Davies, and M. Freedland (1993), p. 208.

It is noticeable that the formula adopted in the IRA 1971 and now found in the ERA 1996, s.123(1) is based on the contractual notion of damages arising from a repudiatory breach of the contract:

> "**123.**—(1) Subject to the provisions of this section and sections 124 and 126, the amount of compensatory award shall be such amount as the tribunal considers just and equitable in all the circumstances having regard to the loss sustained by the complainant in consequence of the dismissal in so far as that loss is attributable to action taken by the employer."

> Employment Rights Act 1996, s.123(1).

Davies and Freedland[70] also point out that in these circumstances it was not surprising that a duty to mitigate loss was also built into the statutory formula alongside the more revolutionary ideas of re-engagement and re-instatement.[71] Arguments in the early 1970s revolved around whether reinstatement should be a mandatory remedy but "the 1970 Bill, 1971 Act and 1975 reforms all protected the freedom of the employer to buy its way out of an award of reinstatement upon payment of a relatively modest lump sum."[72] In *O'Laoire* the employers refused to comply with the tribunal's reinstatement order and the matter went back to the tribunal for assessment of compensation as reported above, the amount of which was subject to statutory maxima. This was why the employee was seeking wrongful dismissal damages in the High Court.

The issue of whether the employee was contractually entitled to be appointed managing director and whether he was entitled to all the terms and conditions that went with the post was a matter of fact which the Court of Appeal doubted. "At best the contractual entitlement would have been that, at the date of contract, the defendants had a bona fide intention to make the plaintiff managing director on the retirement of the incumbent." In allowing the plaintiff employee's appeal in part the Court of Appeal agreed with the High Court judge that his entitlement to stock options was not a contractual right. This was because they were only exerciseable with the consent of the board of directors which would not be given. All that he had lost was the chance of obtaining and exercising such options. So his final damages were only increased slightly to reflect those months of notice not given for when the industrial tribunal originally determined he should have been appointed managing director. He also retained the £8,000 awarded by the tribunal, for the reason that these were not awarded under a specific head for which he was also claiming in his wrongful dismissal action.

The Court of Appeal sympathised with his claim for damages for loss of reputation and injury to feelings but said their hands were tied by the House of Lords' decision *Addis v. Gramophone Co. Ltd* [1909] A.C. 488 which laid down that a servant dismissed by his master could not claim damages arising from the manner of that dismissal. Six years later, the House of Lords decision in *Malik and another v. Bank of Credit and Commerce International SA* [1997] I.R.L.R. 462, HL overturned this long established principle and laid down another head of damages: "Damages for loss of reputation

---

[70] *ibid.*
[71] EPA 1975, s.71.
[72] P. Davies and M. Freedland (1993), p. 210.

caused by breach of contract may be awarded, provided that a relevant breach of contract can be established and the requirements of causation, remoteness and mitigation can be satisfied."

In *Malik* the judicial House of Lords determined that the employee was entitled to damages for loss of reputation caused by the corrupt way in which his former employers had operated. By operating in such a way the employers had broken the implied common law term of mutual trust and confidence. The law report[73] appears to show that Steyn L.J. was much influenced by Brodie's[74] argument that "The major importance of the implied duty of trust and confidence lies in its impact on the obligations of the employer." The nub of Brodie's argument is that there are two conflicting approaches to mutual trust and confidence. The "traditional usage" which considers whether as a matter of fact there is trust and confidence between the parties and the implied term which imposes such behaviour on the parties. The first approach he labels descriptive and the second he describes as prescriptive. His argument is that the descriptive approach is now outdated and that because there is now a duty on employers to "treat their employees in a manner consonant with mutual trust and confidence" the law should, unless there is evidence to the contrary, ignore the absence of such trust and confidence.

It was argued in *Malik* that for an employer to breach the implied term of trust and confidence, the employee had to be aware of the employer's conduct which caused the breach; without knowledge of the employer's wrongdoing the employee's confidence and trust would not be broken. Brodie argues that such a principle can only favour the employer and cites *Post Office v. Roberts*[75] where an employer gave an unjustifiably bad appraisal report. He asks if the employer in this case should benefit by concealing such action until after termination of the contract?

5.6.2   Injunctive relief and restrictive covenants

As has been seen, under the common law, an employee who is wrongfully dismissed will normally only have a legal remedy in damages arising from the repudiatory breach of the employer. Such damages will, in a summary dismissal situation, only amount to the recovery of "wages" (see para. 5.4.2) due for the contractual notice not given.[76] Damages will not necessarily be a sufficient remedy however, if a former employee is subject to a restrictive covenant after termination of his employment. In *Lawrence David Ltd v. Ashton*[77] a sales director of a company manufacturing side-loading vehicles was subject to a restrictive covenant in his contract of employment which forbade him for working for any of his employer's competitors for two years after the termination of his employment. The High Court refused to grant an interlocutory

---

[73] *Malik and another v. BCCI* [1997] I.R.L.R. 462 at 468, HL at para. 55.
[74] D. Brodie "The Heart of the Matter: Mutual Trust and Confidence" (1996) 25 I.L.J. 2 at 129.
[75] [1980] I.R.L.R. 347.
[76] In *Janciuk v. Winerite Ltd* [1998] I.R.L.R. 63, EAT, a summarily dismissed employee tried to claim for the loss of a chance, that had the disciplinary process been operated, he might not have been dismissed. On the authority of *Gunton, Boyo,* and Focsa, the EAT reaffirmed that he was only entitled to compensation for the period that it would have taken to carry out the disciplinary procedure. The court also found that "it must be assumed that had the contract been performed lawfully, the employer would have dismissed the employee at the first available moment, namely after the procedure had been exhausted." This approach assumes that the finding would go against the employee. There are no damages payable in such a wrongful dismissal and there is no system of compensation with reduction for contributory fault to mirror the *Polkey* deductions (see Chapter 8, para. 8.3.7.3) made in unfair dismissal cases.
[77] [1989] I.R.L.R. 22, NICA.

injunction to the employer to enforce the covenants after they had dismissed their employee. At the Court of Appeal however, the interlocutory injunction was granted subject to an early trial so that the employer, if proved right at trial would have an adequate remedy, and that the employee would have an adequate remedy in damages if he was proved right at trial.

The issues

American Cyanamid v. Ethicon Ltd [1975] A.C. 396, which was not applied in the High Court should have been applied said the Court of Appeal:

> "The *American Cyanamid* principles governing the granting of interlocutory injunctions where either there is an unresolved dispute on the affidavit evidence before the court or a question of law to be decided, apply in cases of interlocutory injunctions in restraint of trade just as in other cases." *per* Fox L.J.

Lawrence David Ltd v. Ashton [1989] I.R.L.R. 22 at 23, NICA.

The High Court had not erred in refusing to grant an injunction in this case because the employers had not clearly defined the confidential information or trade secrets which they sought to protect:

> "It is a cardinal rule that any injunction must be capable of being framed with sufficient precision so as to enable the person injuncted to know what it is he is prevented from doing." *per* Fox L.J.

Lawrence David Ltd v. Ashton [1989] I.R.L.R. 22 at 23, NICA.

Obiter dicta per Balcombe L.J.

> "Cases in which an employer seeks to enforce a restrictive covenant in a contract of employment are singularly appropriate for a speedy trial and the courts will be able to make time available if it is not taken up by argument at the interlocutory stage where the application of *American Cyanamid* indicates the desirability of an interlocutory injunction.
>
> . . . the longer the period of the interlocutory injunction, the more likely it is that the plaintiff may suffer damage if the injunction is wrongly granted which is uncompensatable by the plaintiffs on their cross-undertaking and, therefore it becomes necessary to consider the relative strength of each party's case as revealed by the affidavit evidence, under the last stage of the *American Cyanamid* process and *NWL Ltd v. Woods*."

Lawrence David Ltd v. Ashton [1989] I.R.L.R. 22 at 23, NICA.

In reviewing the authorities Balcombe L.J. reaffirmed the principles laid down in *Littlewoods Organisation Ltd v. Harris*[78] when Lord Denning M.R. summed up the difficulties associated with restrictive covenants:

> ". . . experience has shown that it is not satisfactory to have simply a covenant against disclosing confidential information. The reason is because it is so difficult

---

[78] [1977] 1 W.L.R. 1472 at 1479A.

to draw the line between information which is confidential and information which is not; and it is very difficult to prove a breach when the information is of such a character that a servant can carry it away in his head." *per* Denning M.R.

Littlewoods Organisation Ltd v. Harris [1977] 1 W.L.R. 1472 at 1479A cited in *Lawrence David Ltd v. Ashton* [1989] I.R.L.R. 22 at 26, NICA.

He goes on to discuss the "only practicable solution" found in *Printers and Finishers Ltd v. Holloway*[79] that the law will only enforce a covenant "reasonably necessary to protect trade secrets. . ."

Conclusion

In applying *American Cyanamid* in the *Lawrence David* case, the Court of Appeal had to decide whether there was a serious issue to be tried and whether damages would be an adequate remedy when the case came to trial. It concluded that there were serious issues to be tried:

1. Was there a repudiatory breach accepted by the defendant? *Issues of fact*:
   - What was the manner of dismissal?
   - Has he been paid his contractual entitlements?

2. Was this a repudiatory breach ? *Issues of law*:
   - Not every contractual breach is repudiatory.

In considering the remedies, the court was concerned that long-term damage may ensue to the employee if the issue was not brought to a speedy trial. The injunction was thus granted, but limited to a specific part of the covenant and to a specific date for a hearing.

5.6.3 Injunctive relief and specific performance

It has been seen previously, that under the common law, a contract of personal service cannot be enforced at law. In addition, an employer who is the subject of a repudiatory action by the employee cannot secure specific performance because statutory provisions prohibit a court from compelling an employee to work:

"**236.** No court shall, whether by way of—

(a) an order for specific performance or specific implement of a contract of employment, or
(b) an injunction or interdict restraining a breach or threatened breach of such a contract,

compel an employee to do any work or attend at any place for the doing of any work."

Trade Union and Labour Relations (Consolidation) Act 1992, s.236.

A court cannot therefore compel an employee to work, but what is the situation where the employee wants to work but the employer does not want his labour? Four cases are

---

[79] [1965] 1 W.L.R. at 6.

now reviewed where the employee was seeking, in effect, to compel the employer to employ him:

1. In *Irani v. Southampton and South-West Hampshire Health Authority*[80] the employee was seeking an interlocutory injunction to prevent the employer from dismissing him until contractual disciplinary procedures had been carried out.

2. In *Alexander and others v. Standard Telephones and Cables Ltd*[81] the employees were also seeking an interlocutory injunction restraining the employer from dismissing them, but this was for the purposes of ensuring, that the employers did not do so, before they had complied with contractual redundancy procedures.

3. In *Wishart v. National Association of Citizens Advice Bureaux Ltd*[82] the plaintiff was seeking an interlocutory injunction requiring that he be provided with the employment he was offered at an interview.

4. Lastly, in *Powell v. London Borough of Brent*[83] a local authority employee who had been promoted within her department and then had the job offer withdrawn after another applicant took out a grievance, sought an interlocutory injunction restraining the employer from readvertising the post and to require them to treat her as properly appointed to the post.

In *Irani v. Southampton and South-West Hampshire Health Authority* the plaintiff was a part-time opthamologist who "fell out" with his consultant. His employers, after an informal enquiry, concluded that there was an irreconcilable personality conflict between their two employees and dismissed Mr Irani with six weeks' notice. The dismissed employee sought an injunction in the High Court to restrain the employer from dismissing him until the contractual discipline procedures had been carried out. The employer resisted the action arguing that the normal rule against specific performance precluded the court from granting such an injunction.

Warner J. granted an interlocutory judgment restraining the employer from dismissing their employee until it had carried out the contractual disputes procedure as laid down in the Whitley machinery. It is the route which led to this decision which is important. The High Court judge reviewed the leading cases on wrongful dismissal and in particular those cases which dealt with the issue of specific performance.

The employer's counsel argued that even if the "acceptance" theory was correct: that the contract of employment is not terminated without the acceptance of the wronged party, the courts still had to apply the long established rule that they would not require specific performance of a contract of employment. He further sought to distinguish *Hill v. C. A. Parsons and Co. Ltd* [1972] Ch. 305, where an employer had been restrained by an interlocutory injunction, from dismissing an employee who had refused to join a closed shop, on the exceptional facts of the case. In *Hill* there was still mutual trust and confidence residing in the parties and the law was about to be changed[84] which would then permit the employer to continue employing the employee even though he was not a member of the trade union closed shop.

---

[80] [1985] I.R.L.R. 203, HC.
[81] [1990] I.R.L.R. 55, HC.
[82] [1990] I.R.L.R. 393, CA.
[83] [1987] I.R.L.R. 466, CA.
[84] IRA 1971.

In *Irani* Warner J. reviewed the authorities on specific performance, quoting:

> "Very rarely indeed will a court enforce, either by specific performance or by injunction, a contract for services, either at the behest of the employers or of the employee. The reason for this is obvious: if one party has no faith in the honesty or integrity or the loyalty of the other, to force him to serve or to employ that other is a plain recipe for disaster," *per* Geoffrey Lane L.J.

> *Chappell v. Times Newspapers Ltd* [1975] I.R.L.R. 90 at 95 cited in *Irani v. Southampton and South West Hampshire Health Authority* [1985] I.R.L.R. 203 at 207, HC.

and remarked, that in Mr Irani's case, it was common ground that the honesty, integrity and loyalty of the employee was not in doubt.

He next considered the oldest authority to which he had been directed *Barber v. Manchester Regional Hospital Board*[85] where it was held that the employer was not obliged to prolong the notice period given to an employee to enable him to exercise his contractual rights of appeal. The employee's only remedy lay in damages. In that case the plaintiff employee was not only seeking injunctive relief to be able to obtain his contractual obligations under the Whitley agreement, he was also claiming wages for the rest of his working life. *Barber* was therefore dismissed as of little assistance in the instant case. Warner J. also considered that its authority was weakened because it had been decided according to the automatic theory before any of the case law on the elective theory had been developed. More assistance was found in *Ridge*, a case involving dismissal of a chief constable. In this case is found the famous dictum of Lord Reid:

> "The law regarding master and servant is not in doubt. There cannot be specific performance of a contract of service, and the master can terminate the contract with his servant at any time and for any reason or for none. But if he does so in a manner not warranted by the contract he must pay damages for breach of contract. So the question in a pure case of master and servant does not all depend on whether the master has heard the servant in his own defence: it depends on whether the facts emerging at the trial prove breach of contract." *per* Lord Reid.

> *Ridge v. Baldwin* [1964] A.C. 40 at 65.

Despite the emphasis on contractual obligations and the dismissal of any obligations arising out of the application of due process, Warner J. did find some assistance in Lord Reid's dictum in *Ridge*[86] when his Lordship opined that ". . . this kind of case can resemble dismissal from office where the body employing the man is under some statutory or other restriction as to the kind of contract which it can make with its servants or the grounds on which it can dismiss them". The defendant health authority in *Irani* was statutorily obliged to incorporate terms from Whitley agreements into individual employment contracts and was constrained by these agreements in the manner in which its employees could be dismissed.

Warner J. then goes on to consider other cases where an injunction to enforce specific performance was at issue such as *Kulatilake v. The Nottingham Area Health*

---

[85] [1958] 1 W.L.R. 181.
[86] *op. cit.*

Authority[87] where the Court of Appeal "did not regard it as a foregone conclusion that such a person could not obtain an injunction requiring the health authority concerned to go through the requisite procedure." He also considered a similar case *R. v. National Heart and Chest Hospitals, ex parte Pardhanani*[88] where a key employee, the hospital treasurer, was suspended for 18 months. Here the Court of Appeal discharged the injunction at the employer's suit, on the balance of convenience test, that the employer might have to wait an inordinate amount of time before trial of the issue.

In reviewing the authorities Warner J. was therefore establishing that remedies in a wrongful dismissal case were not necessarily limited to damages arising out of a breach of contractual obligations.

The judgment

In granting an interlocutory judgment restraining the employers from dismissing Mr Irani until the Whitley dispute procedures had been carried out, Warner J. examined the arguments put forward by counsel for the employer who sought to distinguish *Hill v. C. A. Parsons & Co. Ltd* on the grounds that it was exceptional:

1. There was still confidence and trust between employer and employee;

2. The IRA 1971 was about to come in force and change the law on "opting-out" from closed shops;

3. Damages would not be an adequate remedy.

Warner J. then compared *Parsons* with *Irani*:

1. He agreed that it was similar to *Parsons* in that the employer had no criticism of the employee but felt that for other reasons, that it was impossible to retain him.

2. In *Parsons* the employee was seeking the protection of incoming legislation[89]; whereas in *Irani* the employee was seeking the protection of contractual procedures for dismissal.

3. Like *Parsons* the argument for damages as an adequate remedy was not convincing. In both cases the employees stood to loose their jobs if the injunctions were discharged.

4. Further, Warner J. considered the decision in *Barber* that damages were the only remedy for a failure to give notice was now outdated. He continued, "that damages at common law for dismissal are not generous" and that if *Barber* was followed it meant that a health authority could ignore part of its contractual disputes procedure.

In *Alexander and others v. Standard Telephones and Cables Ltd*[90] The specific issue was whether the employees' contracts included a term that they would not be made redundant without LIFO being applied. LIFO was a traditional redundancy model in

---

[87] October 17, 1980, CA, LEXIS.
[88] September 21, 1984, CA.
[89] An issue which itself is controversial in that normally the courts can only act on legislation in force.
[90] [1990] I.R.L.R. 55; [1990] I.C.R. 291, HC.

industry whereby those employees who had served an employer for some time were given preference over recently recruited staff. It is perhaps not so dominant now. It could fall foul of the sex discrimination legislation because, for example, longer serving staff are more likely to be men. Employers will often argue that in a redundancy situation, they will need to maintain their prerogative to select the most effective mix of staff to run their business. It is also probable that the importance of such agreements is much diminished since the EPCA provisions (Employment Protection Consolidation Act 1978, s.59(1)(b)) regarding redundancy selection in breach of agreed procedures were repealed by the Deregulation and Contracting Out Act 1994, s.36(1). It is now not unlawful to select for redundancy in breach of such an agreement.

The company insisted on retaining certain workers whose skills and flexibility they required and negotiations broke down between themselves and the trade union. The plaintiff employees sought an *ex parte* injunction to restrain the company from implementing dismissal notices until LIFO had been fully complied with. In effect they were claiming that the employer had repudiated their contracts by issuing the dismissal notices, maintaining that this was contrary to an agreed term that they could not be dismissed for redundancy unless this was done on the basis of LIFO.

The High Court ruled that there was a serious issue to be tried and reviewed the cases on the incorporation of terms from collective agreements into individual employment contracts.[91] Aldous J. declined to answer this question fully on an interlocutory motion and concentrated his focus on remedies. He started by noting that the courts have, as a matter of principle, refused to grant injunctions which would compel employers to re-employ or continue to employ workers in whom they had lost confidence. Under common law the position of such workers seeking a remedy would usually be a right to damages, but only for any unserved notice period for which they were entitled, under their contract. In seeking an appropriate remedy in *Alexander* the judge examined the case authorities in *Rigby v. Ferodo Ltd*[92] to ascertain the remedies available, where the innocent party in a repudiation of the contract, for example the redundant workers in *Alexander*, did not accept the repudiation. He decided that which ever theory of repudiation was correct the remedy for the wrongful repudiation of the contract lay in damages and not in an injunction to enforce specific performance. It was on this principle that the application for injunctive relief was dismissed. Any loss caused by the redundancy would be covered by the redundancy payments already made and would cover loss of wages until the issue came to trial. This reaffirmation of the common law rule on specific performance is much criticised by Brodie.[93]

The question of whether a redundancy selection procedure was incorporated into a contract of employment was answered in the affirmative by the Scottish Court of Sessions in *Anderson v. Pringle of Scotland Ltd*[94] which granted interim suspension and interdict against the employer prohibiting the selection of employees for redundancy other than by the process of LIFO (see Chapter 8, para. 8.3.4.1). In reviewing the authorities, but not *Alexander*, the Court acknowledged that generally, the courts will not enforce specific performance on employers who do not wish to take back employees, but added that "In the contemporary world, intervention before dismissal must be seen as a matter of discretion, rather than impossibility." In the instant case

---

[91] *Robertson v. British Gas Corp.* [1983] I.R.L.R. 302, CA; *Marley v. Forward Trust Group Ltd* [1986] I.R.L.R. 369, CA; *National Coal Board v. National Union of Mineworkers* [1986] I.R.L.R. 439, CA.
[92] [1987] I.R.L.R. 516.
[93] D. Brodie "The Heart of the Matter: Mutual Trust and Confidence" (1996) 25 I.L.J. 2 at 129.
[94] [1998] I.R.L.R. 64, CS.

there was no lack of trust and confidence in the employee and the employers should therefore be true to the bargain made with the trade union over 10 years ago. One distinguished commentator considers that the logic of this case "is so compelling that it seems certain to herald further actions by employees attempting to secure court orders restraining threatened wrongful dismissal or other fundamental breaches of contract by the employer."[95]

In *Wishart v. National Association of Citizens Advice Bureaux Ltd*[96] the plaintiff had been offered a job subject to satisfactory medical enquiries. Subsequent to this offer, the employer discovered a poor attendance record for which the plaintiff could not give a full explanation. In the light of this, the job offer was withdrawn. In the High Court an interlocutory injunction was granted restraining the employers from appointing someone else until the issue came to trial. Cox J. considered that this was a case similar to *Powell v. London Borough of Brent*[97] where a local council employee had been offered promotion which was subsequently withdrawn. In the Court of Appeal Mustill J. allowed the appeal and discharged the injunction, on the grounds that even if a strong contract of employment had been entered into, *Wishart* was not to be compared with *Powell* as a case which is an exception to the rule against specific performance. In *Powell* the employers had some confidence in their employee whereas in *Wishart* there had never been an employment relationship and it would be wrong to grant mandatory relief to force "the defendants to accept as an employee a person they did not wish to employ and had rejected on grounds of suitability."

In contrast to Mr Wishart, whose appointment was subject to "satisfactory references" which the Court of Appeal defined *obiter dicta*, as references satisfactory to the employer, Mrs Powell had the benefit of a writ being served on her employers, to the effect that for one month they would treat her as being promoted to that post. It seems that in the four month period before the Court of Appeal appeal, she managed to convince her employers that she was competent to do the job. The criteria for granting an injunction for specific performance are clearly laid down by the Court in *Powell* and appear to be based mainly on the employer's confidence in an employee to be able to perform the contract:

> "The court will not by injunction require an employer to let a servant continue in his employment, when the employer has sought to terminate that employment and to prevent the servant carrying out his work under the contract, unless it is clear on the evidence, not only that it is otherwise just to make such a requirement but also that there exists sufficient confidence on the part of the employer in the servant's ability and other necessary attributes for it to be reasonable to make the order. It is unlikely that a plaintiff will be able to satisfy the court that, despite strenuous opposition by her employers to her continuing the job, nevertheless there subsist the necessary confidence to justify the making of an injunction. Sufficiency of confidence must be judged by reference to the circumstances of the case, including the nature of the work, the people with whom the work must be done and the likely effect upon the employer and the employer's operations if the employer is required by injunction to suffer the plaintiff to continue in the work."
> *per* Gibson L.J.

Powell v. London Borough of Brent [1987] I.R.L.R. 466 at 467, CA.

[95] M. Rubenstein, IRLR *Highlights*, Vol. 27, No. 2, February 1998.
[96] [1990] I.R.L.R. 393, CA.
[97] [1987] I.R.L.R. 466, CA.

5.6.4 Judicial review and declaration

A judicial declaration states what the rights of the parties are without a coercive order, although parties seeking such a remedy, usually also seek a prohibitory injunction to enforce an action.[98] Damages are the more usual remedy for an employee wrongfully dismissed, but where mutual trust and confidence is retained this remedy may be applicable, as it was in *Hill v. C.A. Parsons*[99] where an employer was prohibited from dismissing an employee until the IRA 1971 had come into force and made dismissal for non-membership of a trade union unlawful. In *Jones v. Gwent County Council*[1] however, the relationship of trust and confidence between a college lecturer and her governing body had clearly broken down after the employers had issued her with a dismissal letter, following the holding of two disciplinary hearings at which she had been cleared of misconduct. A declaration was granted by Chadwick J. that the dismissal was invalid because it did not comply with the contractual disciplinary terms of her contract. Further, an interlocutory injunction was granted restraining her employers from dismissing her until "proper grounds exist and after carrying out a proper procedure in accordance with her contract of employment."

In contrast to the above "disciplinary" case, there was no animosity as such in *Meade-Hill and National Union of Civil and Public Servants v. British Council*[2] where the remedy for a wrongful variation of the employment contract was sought as a declaration of invalidity in the county court. Damages were obviously of no use to the employee who was unwilling to move her place of work as requested by the employer. It was claimed that a contractual mobility clause indirectly discriminated against women employees, because they were often the second earners in the family and had to move with their husband's job. But the employee was still bound by her mobility clause. Other cases on the application of such clauses have determined that such clauses should be applied reasonably[3] but in *Meade-Hill* it was the statutory right to not have discriminatory terms inserted into a contract[4] which was the basis for her action in the county court. As seen in para. 5.2.3 above, a declaration that the mobility clause was indirectly discriminatory was granted on appeal in the Court of Appeal.

The remedy of declaration may be of value to the employee who enjoys a special status such as an office holder[5] and to whom by virtue of this status or his contractual terms, cannot be dismissed before the rules of natural justice, or the requirements of a statutory or contractual procedure, have been complied with. Some public employees may be able to avail themselves of this right, but judicial review is a public law remedy not applicable to private contractual matters and the courts have devised a series of sometimes conflicting tests.[6]

To reduce expenditure to conform with central government policy, two local authorities[7] terminated, *with notice* the contracts of its school meals service employees and offered to re-employ them on terms and conditions of service which were inferior

---

[98] R. Upex (1994), p. 356.
[99] [1972] Ch. 305 at 314, 319.
[1] [1992] I.R.L.R. 521, HC.
[2] [1995] I.R.L.R. 478, CA.
[3] *United Bank v. Akhtar* [1989] I.R.L.R. 507, EAT.
[4] SDA 1975, s.77(2).
[5] *Ridge v. Baldwin* [1964] A.C. 40; *Malloch v. Aberdeen Corp.* [1971] 1 W.L.R. 1578.
[6] S. Deakin and G. Morris (1995), p. 374.
[7] *(1) R. v. Hertfordshire County Council, ex parte NUPE and others, (2) R. v. East Sussex County Council, ex parte NUPE and others* [1985] I.R.L.R. 258, CA.

to those that had been negotiated in the national agreement. The applicants assisted by their trade union, sought a judicial review. They argued in the Divisional Court that the councils could have sought other ways to reduce expenditure such as reducing the wages of all Education Department staff. Their appeal was dismissed. In upholding this dismissal on appeal, the Court of Appeal ruled:

> "That the decision of the employers to give notice terminating contracts of employment was not unreasonable because it followed the principles set out in: *Associated Picture Houses Ltd v. Wednesbury Corporation* [1948] 1 K.B. 223—'that, in all the circumstances, no reasonable authority could have adopted the course of action which was in fact adopted, if it had taken account of all relevant considerations and had left out of account all irrelevant collateral matters." *per* Donaldson M.R.

> (1) *R. v. Hertfordshire County Council, ex parte NUPE and others;* (2) *R. v. East Sussex County Council, ex parte NUPE and others* [1985] I.R.L.R. 258 at 258, CA.

They also ruled, *obiter dicta* Sir John Donaldson, that the remedy of judicial review was not applicable because there was not a breach of a public law right; "it is at least arguable that no employee of a local authority can properly be described as an 'officer' unless he fills an office which has an existence independent of the person who for the time being fills it." In this case the public authority was determined to have not abused its statutory powers by acting unreasonably and in addition, "dinner ladies" were not independent office holders so were not entitled to the public law remedy of judicial review.

The "dinner ladies" as public employees can be compared with the special position of crown servants. In *McLaren v. Home Office*[8] Mr McLaren was a prison officer whose letter of appointment said "You will understand that, in consequence of the constitutional position of the Crown, the Crown has the right to change its employees' conditions of service at any time, and the Crown's employees hold their appointments at the pleasure of the Crown".

A national agreement on shift-time working was agreed between the Prison Officers' Association and the Home Office which was implemented in practice through local agreements. A dispute occurred at Wandsworth Prison with the prison officers refusing to work the new shifts. They were sent home and not paid for the days they had not worked. The employees sought a declaration in the High Court that the national and local agreements were incorporated into their contracts of employment or their conditions of service and that the employer had breached these agreements. They also sought repayment of wages withheld. This claim was struck out on the basis that because there was no contract of employment between the parties, the remedy was a matter of public law and any claims in this matter had to be by way of judicial review.

At the Court of Appeal this judgment was overturned: "The question whether a public body, having power to enter into a contract of service with a particular individual, has or has not done so in a particular case must necessarily be a question of private, and not of public law." It also ruled "That someone can be dismissed at pleasure because he holds an office or is employed by the Crown does not mean that there do not exist other terms as to his service which are contractually enforceable and in respect of which he can have a private law remedy."

[8] [1990] I.R.L.R. 338, CA.

Obiter dicta—in determining whether a public servant can bring proceedings by way of judicial review:

1. Any employee of a public body, can bring proceedings "for damages, a declaration or an injunction (except in relation to the Crown)."

2. Where there is a statutory disciplinary or disputes machinery a public servant may have a remedy of judicial review.

3. Employer decisions of general application may, if the employer is a public body be challenged by judicial review.

4. Judicial review is not available "where disciplinary procedures are of a purely domestic nature. . .".

5.7   SUMMARY

This chapter has reviewed the common law concepts of wrongful variation, termination and discharge of the employment contract. The individual sections dealt with the following subjects:

Variation of the contract of employment (para. 5.2)

- A variation can only be made with consent.

- Agreement to a variation may be express or implied.

- The contract may or may not permit a variation.

- Common examples of variations are where an employee is asked to work flexibly or to move their place of work.

- A variation may constitute a repudiatory breach of the contract if it breaches a fundamental term of the contract.

- Employers have a statutory obligation to notify employees of changes to a contract of employment which have been agreed.—ERA 1996, s.1.

Termination (para. 5.3)

- If a termination is truly consensual there is no dismissal, only a discharge of the contract itself.

- A fundamental breach of the employment contract may lead to it's termination.

- A fundamental breach of the employment contract is one which substantially alters the contract from its originally agreed form, for example a change in job duties or rates of pay.

- There is no single definition of a fundamental contractual breach in an employment context, it will depend upon the facts of the case.

- A fundamental breach of the contract constitutes repudiatory action which permits the injured party to seek a legal remedy.

- The remedy available for a repudiatory breach depends upon whether the court accepts that the injured party can elect to accept the repudiation (the elective theory), or, whether the contract is terminated by the repudiatory action itself (the automatic theory).

- If the elective theory is dominant, an injured party may elect to continue the employment relationship whilst seeking a remedy for the breach, for example, injunctive action to maintain the contract.

- If the automatic theory is dominant, an injured party may only have recourse to damages and may have no access to the statutory remedy of unfair constructive dismissal.

- Although the elective theory has increasingly found favour in the appellate courts, there may still be situations where the automatic theory is appropriate—*Boyo v. London Borough of Lambeth* [1995] I.R.L.R. 50, CA.

- Repudiatory behaviour by an employee can, under the common law, entitle the employer to summarily dismiss the employee without notice.

Notice (para. 5.4)

- Under common law, an employee is presumed to be hired under a contract of indeterminate length terminable only by reasonable notice.

- Reasonable notice can be implied from a variety of factors including status and frequency of payment.

- Statutory provisions—ERA 1996, s.86(1) now regulate how much notice should be given.

Discharge (para. 5.5)

- An employment contract may be ended or discharged through performance; by agreement; through repudiation; or because of the effect of some event, extraneous to, but impacting upon the contract. The latter event is said to "frustrate" the operation of the contract.

- A frustrating condition is one which was unforeseen by the contracting parties and which either makes performance impossible or radically different from that contemplated upon formation of the contract.

- The case law advises that employee sickness and imprisonment may be determined as events which frustrate and thereby discharge the contract without the need for any further action by the employer; but employers are still expected to reach such a decision fairly after evaluating the effect of the employee's absence—*Egg Stores v. Lebovici* [1976] I.R.L.R. 376, EAT.

Wrongful dismissal remedies (para. 5.6)

- The modern remedy for a wrongful dismissal is through two routes which are not mutually exclusive: a damages claim in the High Court or County Court and a claim for compensation or re-engagement/re-instatement in an employment tribunal.

- At common law, damages are usually restricted to losses arising from the contractual breach—usually the recovery of wages for the contractual notice period.

- Claimants for wrongful dismissal damages also have an obligation to mitigate any losses arising from the breach, by for example, seeking alternative employment.

- Damages for loss of reputation and injury to feelings were not recoverable until the House of Lords decision in *Malik and another v. Bank of Credit and Commerce International SA* [1997] I.R.L.R. 462, HL overturned this long established principle.

- The granting of an injunctive remedy may be secured by a claimant where the award of damages would not be appropriate, for example, where an employer is seeking to enforce a restrictive covenant, or where an employee is seeking to prevent dismissal until contractual dismissal procedures have been undertaken, or even where an employee is seeking the application of a contractual redundancy selection procedure.[9]

- A judicial declaration, usually linked to a prohibitory order to enforce an action may be the appropriate remedy where an individual holds office, subject to the requirements of a statutory or contractual dismissal procedure. The remedy of judicial review is not open to all public servants however.

Finally, the academic writing on contractual variation in the employment context is extensive. The following brief and highly selective list of journal articles will give some of the flavour of the debate:

- D. Brodie, "Specific Performance and Employment Contracts" (1998) 27 I.L.J. 37.

- H. Carty "Dismissed Employees: The Search for a More Effective Range of Remedies" (1989) 52 M.L.R. 449.

- K.D. Ewing "Remedies for Breach of the Contract Of Employment" (1993) 52 C.L.J. 405.

- D. Lewis "Whistleblowers and Job Security" (1995) 58 M.L.R. 209.

- G. Pitt " Dismissal At Common Law: The Relevance In Britain Of American Developments" (1989) 52 M.L.R. 23.

- S. Sedley (1994), "Public Law And Contractual Employment" (1994) 23 I.L.J. 201.

---

[9] *Anderson v. Pringle of Scotland Ltd* [1998] I.R.L.R. 64, CS.

Chapter 6

DISCRIMINATION

6.1 THE LEGISLATIVE FRAMEWORK

The law covering discrimination on grounds of sex is heavily influenced and overlaid by a number of European instruments, which may, on occasion, supplant domestic law where the principle of direct applicability applies, or in so far as emanations of the state are concerned where a Directive is of direct effect. In addition, the ECJ has held, in *Marleasing SA v. La Commercial Internacional de Alimentacion SA,*[1] that even where a Directive is not of direct effect and the issue falls to be decided under domestic statutory provisions, the courts have a duty to interpret national laws in such a way as to peruse the objective of the Directive. The nature of the right to equality was stated by the ECJ in the third *Defrenne* case,[2] when the court said:

> "The Court has repeatedly stated that respect for fundamental personal rights is one of the general principles of Community law, the observance of which it has a duty to ensure. There can be no doubt that the elimination of discrimination based on sex forms part of those fundamental human rights. Moreover, the same concepts are recognised by the European Social Charter of 18th November 1961 and by Convention No. 111 of the International Labour Organisation of 25th June 1958 concerning discrimination in respect of employment and occupation." (para. 26).

Case C–149/77 *Defrenne v. SABENA* [1978] 3 C.M.L.R. 312 at 329, ECJ.

The acceptance of the elimination of discrimination based on sex as being a fundamental human right, brings European law to the heart of the law on discrimination and an understanding of the European instruments in question is therefore a necessary prerequisite to a study of this area of the law.

6.1.1 The equal pay principle

The equal pay principle is enshrined in Article 119 of Title VIII of the Treaty and as explained by the Court in *Defrenne v. SABENA*:

[1] Case C–106/89 [1990] E.C.R. I–4135, ECJ.
[2] Case C–149/77 [1978] 3 C.M.L.R. 312, ECJ.

"Article 119 pursues a double aim. First, in the light of the different stages of development of social legislation in the member states, the aim of article 119 is to avoid a situation in which undertakings established in states which have actually implemented the principle of equal pay suffer a competitive disadvantage in intra-community competition as compared with undertakings established in states which have not yet eliminated discrimination against women workers as regards pay.

Secondly, this provision forms part of the social objectives of the community, which is not merely an economic union, but is at the same time intended, by common action, to ensure social progress and seek the constant improvement of the living and working conditions of their peoples, as is emphasised by the preamble to the Treaty.

This aim is accentuated by the insertion of article 119 into the body of a chapter devoted to social policy . . .

This double aim, which is at once economic and social, shows that the principle of equal pay forms part of the foundations of the community."

Case C–43/74 *Defrenne v. SABENA* [1976] I.C.R. 547 at 565–66, paras 9–12.

Article 119 provides that:

"Each Member State shall during the first stage ensure and subsequently maintain the application of the principle that men and women should receive equal pay for equal work.

For the purpose of this Article 'pay' means the ordinary basic or minimum wage or salary and any other consideration, whether in cash or in kind, which the worker receives, directly or indirectly, in respect of his employment from his employer.

Equal pay without discrimination based on sex means:

(a) that pay for the same work at piece rates shall be calculated on the basis of the same unit of measurement;

(b) that pay for work at time rates shall be the same for the same job."

In addition, Article 1 of Directive 75/117[3] is wider than the Directive and covers not only equal pay for equal work but also the provisions of ILO Convention No. 100 in terms of the concept of work of equal value, and provides that:

"The principle of equal pay for men and women outlined in Article 119 of the Treaty, . . ., means for the same work or for work to which equal value is attributed, the elimination of all discrimination on grounds of sex with regard to all aspects and conditions of remuneration.

In particular, where a job classification system is used for determining pay, it must be based on the same criteria for both men and women and so drawn up as to exclude any discrimination on grounds of sex."

Directive 75/117, Art. 1.

In *Jenkins v. Kingsgate (Clothing Productions) Ltd*[4] the ECJ held Directive 76/117 to be designed to facilitate the practical application of Article 119, and not to have

---

[3] February 10, 1975.
[4] Case C–96/80 [1981] I.C.R. 593, ECJ.

altered the content or scope of Article 119, which means that it is directly applicable because it works through Article 119 and does not stand alone. By Article 2 Member States are required to introduce into their national legal systems measures to allow disputes concerning the principle of equal pay to be adjudicated upon to ensure that the principle is applied. The Treaty of Amsterdam amended Article 119 to include the concept of equal value within the wording of the Article itself.

It was held by the ECJ in *Defrenne v. SABENA*[5] that Article 119 is directly applicable in the event of direct and overt discrimination and gives rise to individual rights which the national courts must protect. The direct applicability was held to be dated from January 1962 in original Member States, and 1973[6] in new Member States, but the ECJ ruled that because "the parties concerned had been led to continue with practices contrary to the principle of article 119" it was taking an "exceptional course" in holding that Article 119 could not be relied upon to support claims concerning equality of pay during periods prior to the date of the present judgment.[7] The direct applicability is vertical and horizontal: it is not limited in its application to state bodies, as demonstrated in *Worringham v. Lloyds Bank Ltd*[8] and was initially somewhat reluctantly accepted by the House of Lords, as displayed in *Garland v. British Rail Engineering*[9]:

> ". . . it is a principle of construction of United Kingdom statutes, now too well established to call for citation of authority, that the words of a statute passed after the Treaty has been signed and dealing with the subject matter of the international obligation of the United Kingdom, are to be construed, if they are reasonably capable of bearing such a meaning, as intended to carry out the obligation and not to be inconsistent with it. A *fortiori* is this the case where the Treaty obligation arises under one of the Community treaties to which section 2 of the European Communities Act 1972 applies." *per* Lord Diplock.

Garland v. British Rail Engineering [1982] 2 W.L.R. 918 at 934–35, HL.

Sometimes quite elaborate statutory interpretations were given in order to prevent the court from holding that in view of the incompatibility, Article 119 would be directly applicable. An example of this is the interpretation given by the House of Lords to the Equal Pay Act 1970, s.1(2)(c) in *Pickstone v. Freemans plc*.[10] This approach has been overtaken by an embracing of the concept of supremacy:

> ". . . Community law is part of English law just as an Act of Parliament or a Statutory Instrument or the common law are parts of English law. . . . Where there is a conflict between Community law and domestic law, Community law prevails. . . . The rule as to what prevails in the event of a conflict between domestic law and Community law is a rule of Community law which, by virtue of the European Communities Act, has become a rule of English law. The legal technique which is used for resolving such a conflict between domestic and

---

[5] Case C–43/74 [1976] I.C.R. 547, ECJ.
[6] January 1, 1973, the date the Accession Treaty came into force.
[7] April 8, 1976.
[8] Case C–69/80 [1981] I.C.R. 558, ECJ.
[9] [1982] 2 W.L.R. 918, HL.
[10] [1988] I.C.R. 697, HL. Note too *Duke v. GEC Reliance* [1988] I.R.L.R. 118, HL *per* Lord Templeman.

Community law is for the court to disapply that part of domestic law which conflicts with Community law." *per* Schiemann L.J.

Preston v. Wolverhampton Healthcare NHS Trust [1997] I.R.L.R. 233 at 235, CA.

In *R. v. S.S. for Employment, ex parte EOC*,[11] the House of Lords granted a declaration that different hours thresholds as a qualifying condition for eligibility for redundancy payment and the right to bring unfair dismissal proceedings were incompatible with Article 119. Because more women than men work part-time hours a requirement for those working part-time hours to work for longer in order to qualify for the same benefits had a disparate impact on women and to that extent discriminated against women. This case resulted in the subsequent abandonment of different eligibility criteria in domestic law for all employment protection rights.[12]

"Pay" in Article 119 is broadly defined and in *Worringham v. Lloyds Bank Ltd*[13] the ECJ held that occupational retirement schemes, where contributions are determined by scheme rules are "clearly covered" by the concept of "pay" since rights under such schemes are earned as part of the reward for services and are therefore consideration received in respect of employment.[14] This thus distinguishes occupational schemes from social security schemes which the court held in *Defrenne v. Belgian State*[15] did not fall within Article 119 since they were directly governed by legislation and held to be determined more by social policy than by the employment relationship. In *Bilka-Kaufhaus GmbH v. Weber von Hartz*[16] the ECJ clarified the position in that although the occupational pension scheme in question was adopted in accordance with provisions laid down by legislation, it was based on agreement between employers and staff and had the effect of supplementing benefits paid under national legislation and financed by the employer. This was, as a result, held to be part of the consideration received by the worker from the employer in respect of his employment and therefore within Article 119.

The Court returned to this distinction in *Bestuur van het Algemeen Burgerlijk Pensioenfonds v. Beune*[17] and confirmed that:

"... although consideration in the nature of social security benefits is not in principle alien to the concept of pay, that concept, as defined in article 119, cannot embrace social security schemes or benefits such as, for example, retirement pensions, directly governed by statute to the exclusion of any element of negotiation within the undertaking or occupational sector concerned, which are obligatorily applicable to general categories of employees. Such schemes give employees the benefit of a statutory scheme, to whose financing the contributions of workers, employers and possibly the public authorities are determined not so much by the employment relationship between the employer and the worker as by considerations of social policy."

Case C–7/93 *Bestuur van het Algemeen Burgerlijk Pensioenfonds v. Beune* [1995] I.R.L.R. 103 at 116, ECJ.

---

[11] [1994] I.R.L.R. 176, HL.
[12] The Employment Protection (Part-time Employees) Regulations 1995 (S.I. 1995 No. 31).
[13] Case C–262/88 [1981] I.C.R. 558, ECJ.
[14] p. 573.
[15] Case C–80/70 [1971] E.C.R. 455, ECJ (*Defrenne No. 1*).
[16] Case C–170/84 [1986] I.R.L.R. 317, ECJ.
[17] Case C–7/93 [1995] I.R.L.R. 103, ECJ.

But nevertheless went on to hold that the "only possible criterion is whether the pension is paid to the worker by reason of the employment relationship between him and his former employer, that is to say the criterion of employment based on the wording of Article 119 itself" so that a general statutory pension scheme for civil servants formed part of "pay" and within Article 119. This renders the EAT decision in *Griffin v. London Pension Fund Authority*[18] doubtful in that it was there held that Article 119 does not apply to pensions paid under the Local Government Superannuation Scheme.[19]

In *Barber v. Guardian Royal Exchange Assurance Group*[20] the ECJ held that pensions paid under a contracted-out occupational pension scheme were "pay" within Article 119, and in *Coloroll Pension Trustees Ltd v. Russell*[21] the ECJ held that Article 119 extended to both contracted-out and non contracted-out occupational pension schemes. Whilst in *Ten Oever v. Stichting Bedrijfspensioenfonds voor het Glazenwassers-en Schoonmaakbedrijf*[22] it was held that a survivor's pension, under a scheme funded by the industry's employees and employers, to the exclusion of any financial contribution from the public purse, fell within the concept of pay, notwithstanding that consideration derives from the survivor's spouse's membership of the scheme. However in *Neath v. Hugh Steeper Ltd*[23] the Court held that the use of actuarial factors differing according to sex in funded fixed-benefit occupational pension schemes did not fall within the scope of Article 119, and this was confirmed in the *Coloroll Pension Trustees* case, but this leaves open whether it is permissible to use sex-based actuarial factors in money purchase schemes.[24] Although the right of access to an occupational pension scheme was held in *Bilka-Kaufhaus GmbH v. Weber von Hartz*[25] to come within Article 119 this appears to have taken a low profile and did not re-emerge as an issue until confirmed by the ECJ in *Vroege v. NCIV Instituut Voor Volkshuisvesting BV*[26] and *Fisscher v. Voorhuis Hengelo BV*[27] (see para. 6.2.1.2 further on this regarding the ECJ's ruling as to the temporal limitation in *Barber* in so far as access is concerned).

In *Barber*[28] the ECJ held that benefits paid in connection with redundancy, whether paid under a contract of employment, by virtue of legislative provisions or on a voluntary basis, and pensions paid under a contracted-out occupational scheme, come within the definition of "pay" and therefore fall within Article 119. This brings within Article 119 eligibility for statutory redundancy payment. The position regarding compensation for unfair dismissal is, however, less certain and in the reference to the ECJ in *R. v. Secretary of State for Employment ex parte Seymour-Smith and Perez*,[29] the House of Lords has asked whether compensation for unfair dismissal falls within "pay" and therefore within Article 119.

Article 119 extends to fringe benefits, whether or not they are contractual and in *Garland v. British Rail Engineering Ltd*[30] it was held that special non-contractual

---

[18] [1993] I.R.L.R. 248, EAT.
[19] See M. Tether (1995) 24 I.L.J. 194–203.
[20] Case C–262/88 [1990] I.R.L.R. 240, ECJ.
[21] Case C–200/91 [1995] All E.R. (E.C.) 23, ECJ.
[22] Case C–109/91 [1993] I.R.L.R. 601, ECJ.
[23] Case C–152/91 [1994] 1 All E.R. 9, ECJ.
[24] Occupational Pension Schemes (Equal Treatment) Regulations 1995 (S.I. 1995 No. 3183), reg. 15(2)(c) now covers this position in so far as domestic law is concerned.
[25] Case C–170/84 [1986] I.R.L.R. 317, ECJ.
[26] Case C–57/93 [1994] I.R.L.R. 651, ECJ.
[27] Case C–128/93 [1994] I.R.L.R. 662, ECJ.
[28] Case C–262/88 [1990] I.R.L.R. 240, ECJ.
[29] [1997] I.R.L.R. 315, HL.
[30] Case C–12/81 [1982] 2 W.L.R. 918, ECJ.

concessionary travel arrangements provided during employment and which continued after retirement, fell with the second paragraph of Article 119. Also in *Rinner-Kuhn v. FWW Spezial-Gebaudereinigung*[31] the ECJ held that sick pay was "pay" within Article 119 so that national legislation that provided for sick pay on the basis of differential qualifying hours was precluded by Article 119 where that differential could not be justified on objective grounds unrelated to sex.

6.1.2   The principle of equal treatment

Article 1 of Directive 76/207[32] provides for the principle of equal treatment as regards access to employment, including promotion, and to vocational training and as regards working conditions. Article 2 states that the principle of equal treatment means that there shall be no discrimination whatsoever on grounds of sex either directly or indirectly by reference in particular to marital or family status including selection criteria,[33] for access to all jobs or posts[34] access to vocational guidance and training and retraining[35] and working conditions.[36]

Whilst by Article 189, Directives have no general legal effect, in *Marshall v. Southampton & SW Hants Health Authority (Teaching)*[37] the ECJ held that Article 5(1) of Directive 76/207 was sufficiently precise and unconditional to be relied upon directly against the respondent Health Authority as an emanation of the State because it is necessary to prevent the State from taking advantage of its own failure to comply with Community law. This was followed in *Foster v. British Gas plc*,[38] in relation to a public corporation because despite day-to-day autonomy it was, by statute controlled by the State who retained its surplus and whose monopoly was protected by statute. However, in *Duke v. GEC Reliance*[39] it was confirmed that Directive 76/207 has no horizontal direct effect: it is not directly effective against a non-state body in the absence of domestic implementing legislation, even, as in *Doughty v. Rolls-Royce plc*[40] where the State is a one hundred per cent shareholder.

Directive 79/7[41] on the progressive implementation of the principle of equal treatment for men and women in matters of social security covers such things as unemployment, disability allowances, and attendance allowances for carers and is of interest for employment law purposes for its interface with Directive 76/207, in that Article 7(1) of Directive 79/7 permits national governments to maintain differential ages for men and women for the purposes of eligibility for "old-age and retirement pensions and the possible consequences thereof for other benefits". It was the interpretation of this provision that led to the continuation of differential compulsory retirement ages in companies, and consequential differential rules in occupational pension schemes, mirrored on the different ages for eligibility for a state pension which has stood at 60 for women and 65 for men since the Old Age and Widows' Pension Act 1940.

---

[31] Case C–171/88 [1989] I.R.L.R. 493, ECJ.
[32] Adopted February 11, 1976, implementation date August 9, 1978.
[33] Art. 2.
[34] Art. 3.
[35] Art. 4.
[36] Art. 5.
[37] Case C–152/84 [1986] I.R.L.R. 140, ECJ.
[38] Case C–188/89 [1990] I.R.L.R. 353, ECJ.
[39] [1988] I.R.L.R. 188, HL.
[40] [1992] I.R.L.R. 126, CA.
[41] Adopted December 19, 1978, implementation date December 19, 1984.

Early decisions by the ECJ were to the effect that company severance schemes with different ages for eligibility fell within Directive 76/207, and in any event within the "consequences thereof for other benefits" exception in Directive 79/7, so that in *Burton v. British Railways Board*[42] an early retirement scheme available five years before normal retirement was held not to be discriminatory where normal retirement was based on different ages mirroring those for state pension. However, in *Roberts v. Tate & Lyle Industries Ltd*,[43] it was said that the exception to the prohibition of discrimination on grounds of sex provided for in Article 7(1) of Directive 79/7 applies only to the determination of pensionable age for the purposes of granting old-age and retirement pensions and to the consequences thereof *for other social security benefits*.[44] Subsequently, it was held in *Bilka-Kaufhaus GmbH v. Weber von Hartz*[45] that benefits under occupational social security schemes come within the definition of "pay" and thus under Article 119, and that rules governing access, being an integral part of the scheme, also fall to be considered under Article 119, thus removing the influence of Directive 79/7 from the employment field. Note should be taken however, that the exception in Article 7(1) of Directive 79/7 was replicated in Article 9 of Directive 86/378, and this arose for discussion in *Barber*.

Directive 86/378[46] applies the principle of equal treatment to occupational social security schemes which supplement or replace statutory social security schemes and which are not governed by Directive 79/7. This applies to occupational schemes which provide protection against risks for sickness; invalidity; old age, including retirement; industrial accidents and occupational diseases and unemployment. The provisions of the Directive were to have been implemented by Social Security Act 1989, s.23 and Sched. 5, however, only the unfair maternity and parental leave provisions were brought into force.[47] The Directive as regards the equal treatment rules relating to occupational pension schemes was overtaken by the rapidly developing case law in this area, with the result that Directive 96/97 was adopted in December 1996 which amends the 1986 Directive to bring it into line with the ECJ's judgments in *Barber* and subsequent cases. The equal treatment principle was introduced domestically into occupational pension schemes in Pensions Act 1995, ss.62–66 and Regulations[48] from January 1996.

Commission Recommendation 91/131,[49] on the protection of the dignity of women and women at work is accompanied by a code of practice which provides practical guidance and encourages the implementation of the recommendations in a way appropriate to the size and structure of the appropriate organisation. Its aim is to ensure that sexual harassment does not occur, and that adequate procedures are available to deal with the problem and prevent its reoccurrence in the event that it does arise.

Recommendations have no binding force, although in *Grimaldi v. Fonds des Maladies Professionelles*[50] the ECJ said that Commission Recommendations could not be considered as lacking in legal effect. National courts are bound to take them into

[42] Case C–19/81 [1982] I.R.L.R. 116, ECJ.
[43] Case C–151/84 [1986] I.R.L.R. 150, ECJ.
[44] para. 35.
[45] Case C–170/84 [1986] I.R.L.R. 317, ECJ.
[46] Adopted July 24, 1986, implementation date January 1, 1993.
[47] S.I. 1994 No. 1661 from June 23, 1994.
[48] Occupational Pension Schemes (Equal Treatment) Regulations 1995 (S.I. 1995 No. 3183).
[49] Adopted November 27, 1991.
[50] Case C–322/88 [1990] I.R.L.R. 400, ECJ.

consideration in order to decide disputes submitted to them, in particular where they clarify the interpretation of national provisions adopted in order to implement them or where they are designed to supplement binding Community measures.

In July 1996 the Labour and Social Affairs Council adopted a Resolution concerning the European Year Against Racism,[51] 1997, with the objective of highlighting the threat posed by racism, xenophobia and anti-Semitism, to respect for fundamental rights and to the economic and social cohesion of the Community and on the measures necessary to encourage reflection and discussion on these issues.

6.1.3   Domestic framework

The Equal Pay Act 1970 (EqPA 1970), which only applies to contractual terms and conditions, was first passed in 1970, but did not come into force until December 29, 1975, at the same time as the Sex Discrimination Act 1975. The discrepancy between the pay of males and females was such, as a result of widespread stereotypical assumptions about women's work, resulting in low pay for women doing the same work as men and widespread work segregation with low pay being attached to women's work, that it was felt necessary for this "lead-in" time in order to permit employers to adjust to the changes that would be necessary. In fact, as a result of "persistent undervaluing of women's skills and the gender stereotyping of jobs which restrict women's earnings both in the short term and over their lifetime" despite over 20 years of legislation the gender pay gap has remained stubborn. Having stood at 35 per cent in 1976, women employees working full time earn on average only 80 per cent of the average hourly earnings of men full-time employees: a gender pay gap of 20 per cent.[52] However, the gender pay gap is wider, at 72 per cent, when compared on the basis of average weekly earnings because men tend to work longer hours (42 hours on average) than women (38 hours). Also, men are more likely to receive overtime and other additional payments: on average men receive £48 per week from such payments and women only £17.[53] In younger age groups the gap is less than for that in older groups: in her early twenties a woman earns 91 per cent of a man's hourly pay. In her early thirties this falls to 87 per cent, in her early forties to 75 per cent whilst in her fifties to a low of 72 per cent.

Current legislation making discrimination on grounds of sex or marriage unlawful in so far as non contractual benefits are concerned, is to be found in Sex Discrimination Act 1975 (SDA 1975), which covers discrimination, direct and indirect (although these are not terms used in the statutes) and by way of victimisation. Drafted on the same model, the Race Relations Act 1976 (RRA 1976) makes discrimination on racial grounds and victimisation unlawful.

The demarcation between the EqPA 1970 and SDA 1975, Parts I and II, can be troublesome: early decisions, *e.g. F.B. Peake v. Automotive Products Ltd*,[54] stressed that the two Acts were mutually exclusive and lead to different remedies. However, the courts subsequently stressed that so far as possible the two Acts should be construed together so as to produce a harmonious result:

> "In the sphere of employment the provisions of the Sex Discrimination Act 1975 and the Equal Pay Act 1970 aimed at eliminating discrimination on the ground of

---

[51] [1996] O.J. C237.
[52] *New Earnings Survey 1996*, Office for National Statistics.
[53] *Briefings on Women and Men in Britain: Pay*, December 1996, Equal Opportunities Commission.
[54] [1977] I.R.L.R. 105, EAT *per* Phillips J. at 107.

sex are closely interlocking and provide in effect a single comprehensive code. The particular provisions designed to prevent overlapping between the two statutes are complex, and it may often be difficult to determine whether a particular matter of complaint falls to be redressed under one Act or the other. But what is abundantly clear is that both Acts should be construed and applied as a harmonious whole and in such a way that the broad principles which underlie the whole scheme of legislation are not frustrated by a narrow interpretation or restrictive application of particular provisions." *per* Bridge L.J.

Shields v. Coomes (Holdings) Ltd [1978] I.C.R. 1159 at 1178.

Subsequently in *Jenkins v. Kingsgate (Clothing Productions) Ltd (No. 2)*[55] Browne-Wilkinson J. said that the EqPA 1970 was "an integral part of one code against sex discrimination", although the differences between the two Acts and the complexities involved are demonstrated in *Barclays Bank plc v. James*[56] where the employer sought to argue that the employee, in alleging that differential retirement ages were discriminatory and unlawful under SDA 1975 (as amended by the SDA 1986) was really arguing for an equality clause under EqPA 1970, since by going via the EqPA 1970 the employer could seek to establish a genuine material factor defence under the EqPA 1970, s.1(3), whereas under the SDA 1975 there is no defence available for direct discrimination. In *North Yorks CC v. Ratcliffe* Lord Slynn, giving the judgment of the House disapproved of the reasoning of the Court of Appeal in which they had imported into the EqPA 1970, s.1 the concepts of direct and indirect discrimination from the SDA 1975, s.1.

The situation is further confused by the overlay of European law in that Article 119, although concerned with pay, is not confined to the terms of the EqPA 1970 and as demonstrated above, is not limited to contractual matters, therefore many of the cases which in domestic law would fall to be considered under the SDA 1975, come within the ambit of Article 119, *e.g.* in *Garland v. British Rail Engineering Ltd*[57] although the travel concession was held to be "pay" within Article 119, the case was brought under the SDA 1975 because the concession was non-contractual.

The Pensions Act 1995, ss.62–66 and Regulations[58] implement Directive 86/378. The provisions are modelled on the EqPA 1970 and contain the equal treatment rule regarding pension schemes in that an occupational pension scheme which does not contain an equal treatment rule is regarded as doing so, section 62(1). The rule is described in section 62(2) as one which relates to the terms on which a person becomes a member of the scheme and the terms on which members of the scheme are treated. The Act, by section 126, gives effect to Schedule 4, Part I of which provides for equalisation for men and women of the age of eligibility for state pensions. This is achieved by equalising at age 65 progressively over a period of 10 years beginning on April 6, 2010, meaning that by March 2020 the state pension age will have risen to 65 for all women. However, section 64(2) preserves sex discrimination under the state scheme in that the equal treatment rule does not operate to prevent any state scheme variation between men and women.

[55] [1981] I.R.L.R. 388, EAT.
[56] [1990] I.R.L.R. 90, EAT.
[57] Case C–12/81 [1982] 2 W.L.R. 918, ECJ.
[58] Occupational Pension Schemes (Equal Treatment) Regulations 1995 (S.I. 1995 No. 3183), which amend EqPA 1970, s.2.

6.1.4 Codes of practice

In the context of the Fourth Community Action Programme on equal opportunities for men and women (1996–2000)[59] the commission has published a code of practice[60] to serve as a working tool for those involved in, or likely to be in a position to further the principle of equal pay for men and women for work of equal value. The code highlights the lack of progress towards equal pay and identifies some of the causes and gives practical guidance as to the areas to examine in order to deal with the problems involved.

Following consultations between the Equal Opportunities Commission and representatives of employers and employees, the Commission has issued a code of practice, *Code of Practice on Equal Pay*,[61] to provide practical guidance and good practice recommendations for employers, explaining the law and the cause of pay inequality. It also provides a step-by-step process for detecting and addressing pay discrepancies. By SDA 1975, s.56A(10) whilst a failure to observe any provisions of the code does not of itself render a person liable to any proceedings, in any proceedings before an industrial tribunal under the EqPA 1970[62] or the SDA 1975 the code is admissible as evidence and taken into account.

The Disability Discrimination Act 1995 received Royal Assent on November 8, 1995 and has been brought into force by a succession of commencement Orders, Part II of the Act, relating to employment, being brought into force from December 2, 1996. Prior to this the law was needs, as opposed to rights, based, and worked through a quota system under the Disabled Persons (Employment) Act 1944 which was generally accepted as being ineffective and rarely enforced. Although a number of voluntary initiatives were introduced which promoted good practice, there was no redress at law for disabled people discriminated against for reasons relating to their disability. The campaign for reform, manifested by a private member's Bill, the Civil Rights (Disabled Persons) Bill in the 1993–94 parliamentary session, was motivated by and grew from the Americans with Disabilities Act 1990 which acted as motivation for reform. The Bill was, however, defeated at Report stage by Conservative backbench M.P.s, and widespread condemnation of this led the Government to undertake to bring forward their own proposals. A Green Paper followed proposing limited reform,[63] and this was followed by a White Paper[64] and the Disability Discrimination Bill to implement what Doyle (1996) refers to as "many (but not all) of the proposals contained in the White Paper". The Act makes it unlawful to discriminate against disabled persons in connection with employment, and also extends to the provision of goods and services and facilities.

6.2 Equal Pay

The stated aim of the Equal Pay Act 1970 (as amended) is to prevent discrimination between men and women, as regards terms and conditions of employment and it

---

[59] Adopted by Council Decision 95/593/EEC [1995] O.J. L335/37.
[60] *A Code of Practice on the Implementation of Equal Pay for Work of Equal Value for Women and Men,* Brussels July 17, 1996, COM(96) 336 final.
[61] EOC January 1997.
[62] Inserted by TURERA 1993, s.49(1), Sched. 7, para. 15, as from August 30, 1993 (S.I. 1993 No. 1908).
[63] *A Consultation on Government Measures to Tackle Discrimination Against Disabled People,* Department of Social Security, 1994.
[64] *Ending Discrimination Against Disabled People,* Cm. 2729 (1995).

operates by implying an equality clause into all contracts of employment. This is not, however, a general right in that in order to be entitled to an equality clause the applicant must bring herself, or himself, within one of the three tests contained in section 1, namely:

- section 1(2)(a)—the applicant must be employed on like-work with the comparator in the same employment;

- section 1(2)(b)—the applicant must be employed on work rated as equivalent with that of the applicant in the same employment;

- section 1(2)(c)—the applicant is employed on work of equal value to that of a man in the same employment.

The burden is on the employee to show that the selected comparator is doing the same or broadly similar work, that the work has been rated as equivalent in a job evaluation scheme (JES) or that the work is of equal value, and that the comparator's contract contains more favourable terms. The comparison required, it was held by the House of Lords in *Hayward v. Cammell Laird Shipbuilders Ltd*,[65] is on a term by term basis irrespective of whether the woman is as favourably treated when comparing the whole of both contracts and this approach was adopted by the ECJ in *Barber v. Guardian Royal Exchange Assurance Group*[66] where the court held that the application of the principle of equal pay must be ensured in respect of each element of remuneration and not only on the basis of an overall assessment of the remuneration package. The court reasoned that if national courts were under an obligation to make an assessment and a comparison of all the various components of remuneration, judicial review would be difficult and the effectiveness of Article 119 would be thus diminished. The principle is for genuine transparency permitting effective review (*Handels-og Kontorfunktionaerernes Forbund i Danmark v. Dansk Arbejdsgiverforening, acting for Danfoss*)[67] which the Court said is only assured if the principle of equal pay is applied to each of the elements of remuneration. However, in *Leverton v. Clwyd County Council*[68] it was held that in a claim for equal pay, where there are differing hours and holidays it was appropriate to translate these to a notional hourly rate for comparison purposes.

By section 1(3) an equality clause does not operate in relation to a variation between the woman's contract and the man's contract if the employer is able to discharge the burden of showing that the difference is "genuinely due to a material factor which is not the difference of sex". The concept of objective justification has been introduced by ECJ when dealing with indirect discrimination, which can be defended by showing that the behaviour in question corresponds to a business need unrelated to sex, and is both appropriate and necessary to achieving that end. The Equal Opportunities Commission (EOC) point out[69] that both the material factor defence and objective justification are "essentially explanations for how the difference in pay arises and are closely related". However, case law has developed to the point where in *Strathclyde Regional Council v. Wallace*[70] the House of Lords confirmed that in a case under the

---

[65] [1988] I.R.L.R. 257, HL.
[66] Case C–262/88 [1990] I.R.L.R. 240, ECJ.
[67] Case C–109/88 [1989] I.R.L.R. 532, ECJ.
[68] [1989] I.R.L.R. 28, HL.
[69] *Code of Practice on Equal Pay*, EOC, 1997, para. 18.
[70] [1998] I.R.L.R. 146, HL.

1970 Act, in a defence under section 1(3) there is not incorporated a test to objectively justify the difference in pay except where the difference is as a result of indirect discrimination.

It was stressed by Lord Browne-Wilkinson in *Wallace*[71] that the purpose of section 1 of the Act is to eliminate sex discrimination in pay not to achieve fair wages, so that the 1970 Act is not available where the woman is being paid more than the man (or vice versa—see s.1(13)), but not as much more as she feels she deserves. In *Pointon v. University of Sussex*[72] it was said that as the man and the woman were on the same grade there was no term of the woman's contract which was less favourable, and therefore where the JES was untainted by sex she could not use the 1970 Act to argue that she should have been on a higher grade.

Once an equality clause is implied into an individual's contract, it was held in *Sorbie v. Trust Houses Forte Hotels Ltd*[73] that it remains there until some other event occurs, but it does not disappear just because the comparator leaves, moves or gets promoted.

6.2.1 Application

Unlike employment protection legislation, the EqPA 1970 does not apply only to employees, but has a wider application and applies to those "employed at an establishment in Great Britain"[74] and "employed" is defined in section 1(6)(a) as "employed under a contract of service or of apprenticeship or a contract personally to execute any work or labour . . .". The case law on this provision is discussed at para. 1.15.[75]

As the equality clause operates on the contract the common law rules as to illegality or immorality apply (on which see para. 7.2.3), the decision in *Leighton v. Michael and Charalambous*,[76] being confined to sex, and probably race discrimination, since the SDA 1975 and RRA 1976 do not operate through the contract of employment.

By section 2 a complaint is to an industrial tribunal and by section 2(4) the applicant must have been employed by the defendant within the six months preceding the date of the reference. There is a power for the tribunal to issue an order declaring the rights of the parties on the application of the employer and to award arrears of remuneration, but by section 2(5) arrears of remuneration or damages are limited and may be backdated for a maximum of two years from the date on which proceedings were instituted. Case law developments on the interpretation of section 2(4)–(5) have been rapid and detailed and has revolved around four cases: *Barber v. Guardian Royal Exchange Assurance Group*,[77] *Vroege v. NCIV Instituut voor Volkshuisvesting BV*,[78] *Fisscher v. Voorhuis Hengelo BV*[79] and *R. v. Secretary of State for Employment ex parte Equal Opportunities Commission*.[80]

---

[71] [1998] I.R.L.R. 146, HL.
[72] [1979] I.R.L.R. 110, CA.
[73] [1977] I.C.R. 55, EAT.
[74] The Act does not extend to Northern Ireland.
[75] See *Quinnen v. Hovells* [1984] I.C.R. 525 *per* Waite J. at 530 F.
[76] [1996] I.R.L.R. 67, EAT.
[77] Case C–262/88 [1990] I.R.L.R. 240, ECJ.
[78] Case C–57/93 [1994] I.R.L.R. 651, ECJ.
[79] Case C–128/93 [1994] I.R.L.R. 662, ECJ.
[80] [1994] I.R.L.R. 176, HL.

6.2.1.1   *Consequences of the ECJ decision in Barber*

When the ECJ held in *Barber v. Guardian Royal Exchange Assurance Group*[81] that benefits paid to a worker in connection with redundancy, whether contractual or not, and in particular covered occupational contracted-out pension schemes, were within Article 119, the Court noted, as prompted to do so by the U.K. Government, that the potential cost implications of such a finding would be high because of the high incidence of derogation from the principle of equality between men and women in such schemes. The Court noted that the derogation from the principle of equality in matters of social security in so far as the granting of old-age pensions is concerned, contained in Directive 79/7, Art. 7(1), had been incorporated into Directive 86/378, Art. 9, and that by this Member States were permitted to defer the compulsory application of the principle of equal treatment with regard to the determination of pensionable age for the purpose of granting old-age or retirement pensions until either the date equality is achieved in statutory schemes or until equality is required by a Directive:

> "In the light of those provisions, the Member States and the parties concerned were reasonably entitled to consider that Article 119 did not apply to pensions paid under contracted-out schemes and that derogations from the principle of equality between men and women were still permitted in that sphere." para. 43

It was therefore held that:

> "the direct effect of Article 119 of the Treaty may not be relied upon in order to claim entitlement to a pension with effect from a date prior to that of this judgment [May 17, 1990], except in the case of workers or those claiming under them who have before that date initiated legal proceedings or raised an equivalent claim under the applicable national law." para. 45.

> Case C–262/88 *Barber v. Guardian Royal Exchange Assurance Group* [1990] 2 All E.R. 660 at 703–704, ECJ.

There was some uncertainty as to the precise interpretation of this temporal limitation with a number of variations available. It was unclear whether the limitation applied only to pensions paid before May 17, 1990 or whether it extended to all pensions earned as a result of service prior to that date. It was also uncertain whether the limitation encompassed all forms of discrimination in occupational pensions or whether it was limited to certain forms of discrimination.

Following extensive lobbying by employers and organisations representing employers, accompanied by suggestions as to the cost of implementing various options, the preferred and least expensive interpretation was embodied in a Protocol to the Treaty of European Union[82] following the Intergovernmental Conference at Maastricht. The Protocol provides:

> "For the purposes of Article 119 of the Treaty establishing the European Community, benefits under occupational social security schemes shall not be

---

[81] Case C–262/88 [1990] I.R.L.R. 240, ECJ.
[82] February 7, 1992.

considered as remuneration if and in so far as they are attributable to periods of service prior to 17 May 1990, except in the case of workers or those claiming under them who have before that date initiated legal proceedings or introduced an equivalent claim under the applicable national law."

The precise scope of the application of the *Barber* judgment in relation to the temporal limitation was amongst the questions framed by the High Court in the reference to the European Court in *Coloroll Pension Trustees v. Russell*.[83] However, the judgment of the court in *Ten Oever v. Stichting Bedrijfspensioenfonds voor het Glazenwassers-en Schoon-maakbedrijf*[84] was delivered first, in which the ECJ held that equality of treatment in the matter of occupational social security could be claimed only in relation to benefits payable in respect of periods of employment subsequent to the date of the *Barber* judgment, May 17, 1990, except where claims had already been made prior to that date, thus giving the same interpretation as contained in the *Barber* Protocol. In *Ten Oever* this meant that although survivor's benefits were held to be "pay" within Article 119, there was no entitlement on the facts since the employee's wife had died in 1988 and equality only applied to contributions from May 17, 1990. In *Neath v. Hugh Steeper Ltd*[85] the Court confirmed this limitation and its application to transfer benefits and lump-sum options.

Even after clarification of the effect of the temporal limitation in *Barber* it remained unclear what steps needed to be taken in order to achieve equalisation, and in a number of cases the court has sought to clarify these. In *Smith v. Avdel Systems Ltd*[86] the pension scheme rules were changed by increasing the pension age for women from age 60 to 65, thus providing a common age of 65, but by removing the favourable age previously enjoyed by women, and doing so based on both past and future benefits, a woman retiring before age 65 would have her benefits reduced by four per cent for each year preceding her sixty-fifth birthday, and 20 per cent if retiring at age 60. The question for the court was whether in complying with equality requirements, it was permissible to take away from the favoured class and to do so for both past and future benefits.

The ECJ noted that in their earlier judgments in *Defrenne v. Sabena*[87] they ruled that compliance with Article 119 could be achieved otherwise than by raising the lowest salaries and that a national court must set aside any discriminatory provision in national law without having to request or await prior removal, such as by collective bargaining or legislation, *Nimz v. Freie und Hansestadt Hamburg*.[88] The court held that it follows that the only proper way of complying with Article 119 is to grant to the persons in the disadvantaged class the same advantages as those enjoyed by the persons in the favoured class. In the context of the temporal limitation in the *Barber* judgment this meant considering the position in three time periods:

- Periods of service before May 17, 1990, the date of the *Barber* judgment: since the principle of equality does not apply to this period employers and trustees are not required to ensure equality of benefits. Therefore Community

---

[83] Case C–200/91 [1995] All E.R. (E.C.) 23, ECJ.
[84] Case C–109/91 [1993] I.R.L.R. 601, ECJ.
[85] Case C–152/91 [1994] 1 All E.R. 9, ECJ.
[86] Case C–408/92 [1995] I.C.R. 596, ECJ.
[87] Case C–43/75 [1976] I.C.R. 547 at 566, para. 15.
[88] Case C–184/89 [1991] E.C.R. I–297, 320–321, paras 18–20.

law imposed no obligation which would justify retroactive reduction of the advantages which women enjoyed.

- Periods between the date of the *Barber* judgment and the date the scheme adopted equality measures, July 1, 1991: benefits and conditions for the disadvantaged group had to be the same as those for the advantaged group during this period, so that the pension rights for men had to be calculated on the basis of the same retirement age as that for women.

- Periods after the entry into force of rules designed to eliminate discrimination (July 1, 1991): Article 119 does not preclude measures which aimed to achieve equality by reducing the advantageous benefits enjoyed by one sex— by increasing the retirement age for women.

At the same time the court delivered judgment in *Van Den Akker v. Stichting Shell Pensioenfonds*[89] to the same effect.

6.2.1.2   *Consequences of the ECJ decision in Vroege and Fisscher*

It was unclear from the ECJ judgment in *Barber* whether the decision extended to all forms of discrimination. In *Vroege v. NCIV Instituut voor Volkshuisvesting BV*[90] the applicant was excluded from the pension scheme under a rule which set the working of at least 80 per cent of full-time hours as the threshold. The scheme rules were amended to avoid the disparate impact of such a rule, however, the benefits were not backdated and the applicant claimed backdating to the commencement of her employment. Likewise, in *Fisscher v. Voorhuis Hengelo BV*[91] the applicant was excluded from the pension scheme by scheme rules because she was a married woman. When she was admitted to the scheme she was given three years additional service but claimed that her pension rights should be backdated to the beginning of her employment.

The ECJ pointed out that in *Bilka-Kaufhaus GmbH v. Hartz*[92] it was held that benefits paid under an occupational pension scheme, where that scheme is based on agreement with the employees and their representatives and is not funded by the State (so that it constitutes a social security scheme), constitute "pay" for the purposes of Article 119. It was noted from the judgment in *Jenkins v. Kingsgate (Clothing Productions) Ltd,*[93] that a pay policy with a lower hourly rate for part-time work than for full-time work may entail discrimination between men and women and that:

> ". . . the same applies where part-time workers are refused a company pension. Since such a pension falls within the concept of 'pay', within the meaning of the second paragraph of Article 119, it follows that, hour for hour, the total remuneration paid by the employer to full-time workers is higher than that paid to part-time workers. It follows that an occupational pension scheme which excludes married women from membership entails discrimination directly based on sex, contrary to Article 119." paras 13–14

> Case C–128/93 *Fisscher v. Voorhuis Hengelo BV* [1994] I.R.L.R. 662 at 664, ECJ.

---

[89] Case C–28/93 [1995] I.C.R. 596, ECJ.
[90] Case C–57/93 [1994] I.R.L.R. 651, ECJ.
[91] Case C–128/93 [1994] I.R.L.R. 662, ECJ.
[92] Case 170/84 [1986] I.R.L.R. 317, ECJ.
[93] Case C–96/80 [1981] I.R.L.R. 228, ECJ.

Based on like reasoning it was held in *Vroege* that an occupational pension scheme which excludes part-time workers from membership involves discrimination directly based on sex, contrary to Article 119. Having so decided the court considered whether the temporal limitation in *Barber* applied. The Court said that the limitation in *Barber* concerned only those kinds of discrimination which employers and pension schemes could reasonably have considered to be permissible as a result of the derogation contained in Directive 86/379, and that as it had been clear since the decision in *Bilka*, decided in 1985, that a breach of the rule of equal treatment through rules of access had been "caught by Article 119". As the judgment in *Bilka* contained no limitation similar to that in *Barber* the direct effect of Article 119 in relation to the right to join an occupational scheme dated from April 8, 1976, the date of the ECJ judgment in *Defrenne* (where the ECJ first held that Article 119 was directly applicable), and that Protocol No. 2 annexed to the Treaty on European Union, being concerned solely with benefits paid under an occupational scheme, did not apply to the right to belong to such a scheme, which is governed entirely by the decision in *Bilka*. However, a worker claiming retroactively to join an occupational pension scheme must be placed in the same and not a more favourable position, and must therefore pay contributions in the same way as those not excluded from membership.

In so far as national rules containing time limits for bringing actions under national laws are concerned, the ECJ reiterated that:

> "in the absence of Community rules on the matter, the national rules relating to time limits for bringing actions are also applicable to actions based on Community law, provided that they are no less favourable for such actions than for similar actions of a domestic nature and that they do not render the exercise of rights conferred by Community law impossible in practice." para. 39.

> Case C–128/93 *Fisscher v. Voorhuis Hengelo BV* [1994] I.R.L.R. 635 at 666, ECJ.

These points were confirmed by the ECJ in *Dietz v. Stichting Thuiszorg Rotterdam*.[94]

Taken that the average funding rate for an occupational pensions scheme is of the order of 20 per cent and that an employee would expect to contribute between four–eight per cent of pensionable salary, an employer's contribution, at between 12–16 per cent, represents a considerable part of a remuneration package and backdating of membership provides a very valuable asset, a much greater benefit being for those denied access to a non-contributory scheme, where the employer pays the entire contribution, and pursuing a backdating claim incurs no cost to the employee. So widespread was the practice of denying access to pension schemes on sex based grounds that some 60,000 claims were lodged with tribunals following the ECJ decision in *Vroege* and *Fisscher*,[95] as a result of which 22 TUC-co-ordinated test cases representing a variety of industries and the public sector were prepared all representing periods prior to the implementation of the equal treatment provisions contained in the Pensions Act 1995, ss.62–66.

In *Preston v. Wolverhampton Healthcare NHS Trust; Fletcher v. Midland Bank plc*,[96] the applicants claimed to have been unlawfully excluded from occupational pension schemes because membership was dependent upon working a minimum number of hours per week. The Court of Appeal held that the EqPA 1970, s.2(4) applied so that

---

[94] Case C–435/93 [1996] I.R.L.R. 692, ECJ.
[95] Case C–57/93 & C–128/93 [1995] I.C.R. 635, ECJ.
[96] [1998] I.R.L.R. 197, HL.

claims were out of time unless they had been brought during the employee's employment, or within six months of termination, or from the end of the particular contract of employment, and that in accordance with section 2(5) a successful applicant would be entitled to no more than two years' backdated membership of the pension scheme in question, which would mean from the date proceedings commenced in the industrial tribunal.

On appeal the House of Lords made a reference to the ECJ on the question of the validity of the time limitations contained in EqPA 1970, ss.2(4) and (5).[97] It also referred to the ECJ the question of when there are a series of contracts, such as in the case of teachers, "employed in the employment" in section 2(4), as held by the Court of Appeal to mean employment in the particular contract, so that contracts could not be aggregated, and therefore the claim for equality had to be brought within six months of the ending of each contract, was incompatible with Article 119 as rendering it "impossible in practice" to enforce full pension rights. The applicants relied on the fact that if proceeding under the Race Relations or Sex Discrimination Act, or for a breach of contract, no such limitation would apply and that national procedural rules relating to a claim under Article 119 are less favourable and fall outside the rule in *Rewe-Zentralfinanz eG v. Landwirtschaftskammer fur das Saarland*[98]: that time limits under national law must not bc lcss favourable for that type of action than for similar actions of a domestic nature and must not render the exercise of rights conferred by Community law impossible in practice. The House of Lords noted the reference already made to the ECJ in *Levez v. T.H. Jennings (Harlow Pools) Ltd*[99] in which the limitation contained in section 2(5) was being challenged in circumstances where the applicant's arrears of pay were awarded for some 31 months because she did not discover that there were common terms for managers, from which she was excluded, until after she left employment. The ECJ was there being asked whether the backdating rule contained in EqPA 1970, s.2(5) was compatible with Community law and the interpretation to be given to "similar domestic actions".[1]

The House of Lords in *Preston* and *Fletcher*[2] also noted the decision of the ECJ in *Magorrian and Cunningham v. Eastern Health and Social Services Board and Department of Health and Social Services*[3] in which the Court held that where part-time workers are indirectly discriminated against on grounds of sex as regards access to an occupational pension scheme periods of service dating from April 8, 1976, the date of the decision in *Defrenne No. 2*,[4] must be taken into account and that in such a claim based on Article 119, Community law precludes the application of national rules that limit entitlement to commencement of proceedings. The ECJ distinguished its earlier decisions in *Steenhorst-Neerings v. Bestuur van de Bedrijfsvereniging voor Setailhandel*[5]

---

[97] The Occupational Pension Schemes (Equal Access to Membership) Regulations 1976 (S.I. 1976 No. 142), reg. 12 provides that where the equality clause relates to access to membership the right to be admitted (the deemed entry date) may not be earlier than April 6, 1978 (the date the regulations came into force) or two years before the institution of proceedings, whichever is the later. These regulations have been replaced by Occupational Pension Schemes (Equal Treatment) Regulations 1995 (S.I. 1995 No. 3183) following implementation of the Pensions Act 1995 and reg. 5 inserts into EqPA a new s.6A to the same effect as reg. 12 of the 1976 Regulations.

[98] Case C–33/76 [1976] E.C.R. 1989, ECJ.

[99] Case C–326/96 [1996] I.R.L.R. 499, EAT.

[1] *ECJ Employment Law Watch* No. 6, Spring/Summer 1998.

[2] [1998] I.R.L.R. 197, HL.

[3] Case C–246/96 [1998] I.R.L.R. 86, ECJ.

[4] Case C–43/75 [1976] E.C.R. 455, ECJ.

[5] Case C–338/91 [1994] I.R.L.R. 244, ECJ.

and *Johnson v. Chief Adjudication Officer (No. 2)*[6] on backdating because it was held that in a claim for access to an occupational pension scheme what is being sought is not just the retroactive award of certain additional benefits, but recognition of entitlement to full membership of the occupational pension scheme. To permit a restriction on this recognition would, it was held, limit in time the direct applicability of Article 119 where no such limitation had been laid down by the Court. It would appear from the judgment in the Court in *Magorrian* that Community law does not preclude the application of section 2(5) to claims relying on Article 119 for the retroactive award of benefits, but only where that entitlement is not linked to the right to join an occupational pension scheme.[7]

6.2.1.3 *Consequences of the House of Lords decision in ex parte EOC*

In *Biggs v. Somerset County Council*[8] the Court of Appeal held that the applicant was out of time for bringing a case based on the *EOC* decision, because that case was held to be declaratory of the law and time therefore ran from the effective date of termination on the normal principles contained in the ERA 1996, s.111. The court went on, however, to hold that the principle laid down in *Emmott v. Minister for Social Welfare and Attorney-General*,[9] that a domestic time limitation cannot begin to run against an applicant until such time as Community law had been properly transposed by a defaulting Member State, did not apply because "the validity of Article 119 in U.K. law does not depend on any implementation by the U.K. Parliament; it is part of U.K. law".[10] There is nothing remarkable in this, but it was also held that whilst Article 119 may be relied upon in domestic law to circumvent domestic law barriers which are incompatible with Community law, Article 119 does not create rights of action which have an existence apart from domestic law, and this was confirmed by the Court in *Barber v. Staffordshire County Council*.[11]

The *EOC* case gave rise to a large backlog of cases from women who, because of the hours thresholds,[12] were ineligible to bring proceedings for unfair dismissal or a redundancy payment, many of which, like *Biggs*,[13] relate to events which occurred some years previously. Whilst the argument in domestic law for denying the right for these to proceed is neat, if not logical, the additional hurdle of Article 119 is not quite so easily surmounted. The debate here is whether Article 119 gives rise to "a free standing claim": a right to proceed in domestic courts using Article 119 irrespective of domestic law, or whether Article 119 operates to disapply any domestic provision that is incompatible with it. There is authority for both these arguments, for example for the former view see *Rankin v. British Coal Corp.*,[14] and *Biggs* and *Barber* are examples of the latter. Some of these cases go back a considerable period of time, as does *Biggs* itself but policy considerations for disallowing these cases have taken priority.

---

[6] Case C–410/92 [1995] I.R.L.R. 157, ECJ.
[7] I.R.L.B. 584, p. 9.
[8] [1996] I.R.L.R. 203, CA.
[9] Case C–208/90 [1991] I.R.L.R. 387, ECJ.
[10] *ibid. per* Neill L.J.
[11] [1996] I.R.L.R. 209, CA (heard on the same day by the CA composed by the same judges as in *Biggs*: Neill, Auld, L.JJ. and Sir Iain Glidewell.
[12] Contained in the Employment Protection (Consolidation) Act 1978.
[13] [1996] I.R.L.R. 203, CA.
[14] [1993] I.R.L.R. 69, EAT.

6.2.2 Need for a comparator

Unlike the Sex Discrimination Act, for an applicant proceeding under the Equal Pay Act there is a need, whether claiming like work, work rated as equivalent or work of equal value, for an actual, as opposed to a theoretical, comparator. The choice of comparator is for the applicant who may choose as many comparators as they wish, although in *Leverton v. Clwyd County Council*[15] Lord Bridge, *obiter*, cautioned against "applicants who cast their net over too wide a spread of comparators". The comparator must, however, be "in the same employment". Section 1(6) defines this:

> "men shall be treated as in the same employment with a woman if they are men employed by her employer or any associated employer at the same establishment . . . which include that one and at which common terms and conditions of employment are observed either generally or for employees of the relevant class."

The ECJ held in *Macarthys Ltd v. Smith*[16] that Article 119 was not confined to situations in which men and women were contemporaneously employed, but that a woman could compare herself with a man who held the post before she took up employment. On return to the Court of Appeal it was accepted that in the event of an inconsistency Article 119 took priority over the inconsistent domestic legislation, in view of which Ms Smith was awarded an equality clause with that of her predecessor. The position is a little unclear as to whether, in view of the basis of comparison under Article 119, which is not limited to contemporaneous employment, the EqPA must be interpreted to give effect to this, or whether the EqPA requires contemporaneous employment, so a case concerning non contemporaneous employment has to be brought under Article 119, which raises a difficulty in view of the decision in *Biggs v. Somerset County Council*[17] that Article 119 provides no free standing right. In *Albion Shipping Agency v. Arnold*,[18] Browne-Wilkinson J. said that this "throws up very difficult questions as to the interaction between a provision of the EEC Treaty which has direct application in the United Kingdom . . . and a United Kingdom statute . . . dealing with the same subject matter but conferring different rights". The position appears unresolved and in *Diocese of Hallam Trustee v. Connaughton*[19] the question arose as to whether a comparison could be made with a successor. Following her resignation, Ms Connaughton's job was advertised at some £2,300 more than her own final salary, and an appointment was made at nearly £9,000 in excess of it. Based on the decision in *Macarthys* the EAT held that as Article 119 is not limited to comparisons of men and women in contemporaneous employment, it extends to a comparison with a successor as well as a predecessor.

To be employed "in the same employment" the comparator must be employed at the same establishment or if at different establishments they must be covered by common terms and conditions. In *Leverton v. Clwyd County Council*[20] the applicant made a claim under section 1(2)(c) comparing herself with male colleagues employed by the same local authority but spread over 11 establishments, employed on terms and

---

[15] [1989] I.R.L.R. 28, HL.
[16] Case C–129/79 [1980] I.C.R. 672, ECJ.
[17] [1996] I.R.L.R. 203, CA.
[18] [1982] I.C.R. 22, EAT.
[19] [1996] I.R.L.R. 505, EAT.
[20] [1989] I.R.L.R. 28, HL.

conditions governed by the same collective agreement. Ms Leverton had different
working hours and different holidays, but the House of Lords, taking a practical
approach, held that the concept in section 1(6) of common terms and conditions
observed generally at different establishments contemplated that they would be
applicable to a wide range of employees whose individual terms may well vary as
between each other, but that if governed by the same collective agreement they fell
within the concept of "common" for the purposes of section 1(6). In *Thomas v.
National Coal Board*[21] the issue of "in the same employment" arose in connection with
a claim by 1500 canteen assistants employed throughout the United Kingdom. They
were comparing their work with that of one man employed as a canteen assistant, but
on permanent nights and paid more because of recruitment difficulties. It was held that
they were employed "in the same employment" because although incentive bonus
payments and concessionary entitlements were negotiated locally, they were all
covered by the same national agreement which itself made provision for these benefits,
although not for the degree of entitlement, which was for local bargaining. This
reasoning was followed by the House of Lords in *British Coal Corporation v. Smith*[22]
which involved a comparison between canteen workers and cleaners with surface
mineworkers and clerical workers. Lord Slynn, in agreeing with Lord Bridge in
Leverton,[23] said that common terms and conditions means terms and conditions that
are substantially comparable on a broad common-sense basis, rather than the same
terms subject only to *de minimis* differences, the legislative purpose being to enable a
fair comparison to be made.

In *Scullard v. Knowles and Southern Regional Council for Education and Training*[24]
the applicant was attempting to compare her job as manager of a unit of a voluntary
association with managers of 11 other such bodies throughout the United Kingdom,
each of which were attached to a different regional council. At first instance it was held
that the advisory councils were not companies and not therefore "associated
employers" for the purposes of section 1(6). The EAT held that in excluding
employees of different employers which, though not companies, were all under the
control, either direct or indirect, of a third party, who had common terms and
conditions, section 1(6) was more restrictive than Article 119, as interpreted in
Defrenne (No. 2).[25] It was there held that Article 119 applied to cases in which "men
and women receive unequal pay for equal work which is carried out in the same
establishment or service, whether public or private" and was not confined to
undertakings with a particular form. In this respect section 1(6) was incompatible with
Article 119 which took precedence.

6.2.3 Like work—section 1(2)(a)

It is not necessary for the applicant to establish that she is employed on the same work
as her comparator: the requirement is that she is employed on "like work" which is
defined by section 1(4):

> "A woman is to be regarded as employed on like work with men if, . . ., her work
> and theirs is of the same or a broadly similar nature, and the differences (if any)

[21] [1987] I.R.L.R. 451, EAT.
[22] [1996] I.R.L.R. 404, HL.
[23] [1989] I.R.L.R. 28, HL.
[24] [1996] I.R.L.R. 344, EAT.
[25] Case C–43/74 [1976] I.C.R. 547, ECJ.

between the things she does and the things they do are not of practical importance in relation to terms and conditions of employment; and accordingly in comparing her work with theirs regard shall be had to the frequency or otherwise with which any such differences occur in practice as well as to the nature and extent of the differences."

This involves proving that her work and his were the same or broadly similar in nature to that of the comparator. If there are any differences between the things she does and the things he does, having regard to the frequency, nature and extent of those differences, they must not be of practical importance in relation to the terms and conditions of employment. In *Sorbie v. Trust Houses Forte Hotels Ltd*[26] Phillips J. held that "employed on like work" meant with reference to the contract of employment, so that waitresses engaged on the same contract to do the same work were doing "like work" and the actual work carried out by the comparator was not relevant. Conversely, in *Electrolux Ltd v. Hutchinson*[27] Phillips J. said that contractual differences requiring men, but not women to accept transfer to a different job, to work compulsory overtime and to work Sunday and night shifts were insufficient to show that the differences in the work done by the applicant and that done by the men were of practical importance so as to prevent the applicants being engaged on like work with the men. The relevant consideration was the frequency with which those contractual differences were operated, thus preventing employers from by-passing the Act merely by having special contractual tasks for men. This was confirmed by the Court of Appeal in *Shields v. Coomes (Holdings) Ltd*[28] where the man's contractual obligations were held to be irrelevant unless they resulted in "actual and not infrequent differences in practice".

Early decisions in this area took a broad view of "broadly similar in nature" and in *Capper Pass Ltd v. J.B. Lawton*[29] it was said that this could be answered by a general consideration of the type of work involved and of the skill and knowledge required to do it, making a broad judgment without minute consideration of the differences, insubstantial differences being disregarded. If the work is broadly similar, in asking whether any differences that exist are of practical importance, any "trivial differences, or differences not likely in the real world to be reflected in the terms and conditions . . . ought to be disregarded". Phillips J. said that the intention of the Act is clearly that the industrial tribunal "should not be required to undertake too minute an examination or be constrained to find that work is not like work merely because of insubstantial differences".

Where the difference is the hours at which the job is performed, disagreement has occurred as to whether this is a difference that prevents the work, which is otherwise the same, from being broadly similar. In *Dugdale v. Kraft Foods Ltd*[30] it was held that the mere time at which the work is performed should be disregarded for the purposes of considering differences under section 1(4) and this was confirmed in *National Coal Board v. Sherwin*[31] where it was said that a shift premium can be paid to reflect unsocial hours working, but that it must not be set at such a level as to attract a charge of indirectly introducing sex based discrimination. However, in *Thomas v. NCB*[32] it was

[26] [1977] I.C.R. 55, EAT.
[27] [1977] I.C.R. 252, EAT.
[28] [1978] I.C.R. 1159, CA.
[29] [1976] I.R.L.R. 366, EAT.
[30] [1976] I.R.L.R. 368, EAT.
[31] [1978] I.R.L.R. 122, EAT.
[32] [1987] I.R.L.R. 451, EAT.

held that permanent night work amounted to more than a difference of mere time at which the work was performed, which could be recognised by a shift premium for unsocial hours: there was a difference in personal risk and responsibility which formed part of the conditions of the job which was a difference of practical importance.

In analysing the function undertaken by the man and the woman, it was held in *Eaton Ltd v. Nuttall*[33] that the circumstances in which the job was done and the degree of responsibility involved were to be considered, so that the fact that an error by the woman would involve less serious consequences than an error made by the man could amount to a difference in the job he did and the job she did. The court noted the earlier authority of *Waddington v. Leicester Council for Voluntary Service*[34] where it was held that the obligation to supervise, to take responsibility or to control, if actually carried out, was a sufficient difference.

6.2.4   Work rated as equivalent—section 1(2)(b)

Where a woman is employed on work which has been rated as equivalent with that of a man in the same employment she must bring her claim for an equality clause under section 1(2)(b). Section 1(5) provides that work is regarded as rated as equivalent with that of a man if their jobs have been given equal value under a job evaluation scheme (JES) which has considered the demands made on all or any of the employees in an undertaking, or a group of undertakings, under headings such as effort, skill and decision. The burden of showing that the JES complies with these requirements, and that therefore she is entitled to an equality clause, rests on the applicant, but once a valid evaluation has been carried out which has rated the work as equivalent, the applicant is entitled to an equality clause. In *Ratcliffe v. North Yorkshire County Council*[35] 1,300 dinner ladies whose jobs had been rated as equivalent in an evaluation study applied for an equality clause after their employer had reduced their salaries in order to compete with outside contractors:

> "It is plain that [an] evaluation was made and the women were found to be engaged on work rated as equivalent to work done by men. That is sufficient for the women to be entitled to a declaration by the Industrial Tribunal in their favour unless s.1(3) of the Act . . . is satisfied." *per* Lord Slynn.

Ratcliffe v. North Yorkshire County Council [1995] I.C.R. 833 at 840, HL.

There are a variety of methods of evaluating jobs and the Act does not specify the method of evaluation that needs to be adopted. In *Eaton Ltd v. Nuttall*[36] the EAT added an appendix to its judgment describing the principle methods of evaluation and giving a brief description against each heading and said:

> "It seems to us that s.1(5) can only apply to what may be called a valid evaluation study. By that, we mean a study satisfying the test of being thorough in analysis and capable of impartial application. It should be possible by applying the study to arrive at the position of a particular employee at a particular point in a particular

---

[33] [1977] 3 All E.R. 1131, EAT.
[34] [1977] I.R.L.R. 32, EAT.
[35] [1995] I.R.L.R. 833, HL.
[36] [1977] I.R.L.R. 71, EAT.

salary grade without taking other matters into account except those unconnected with the nature of the work. It will be in order to take into account such matters as merit or seniority etc, but any matters concerning the work (*e.g.* responsibility) one would expect to find taken care of in the evaluation study. One which does not satisfy that test, and requires the management to make a subjective judgment concerning the nature of the work before the employee can be fitted into the appropriate place in the appropriate salary grade, would seem to us not to be a valid study for the purpose of s.1(5)." *per* Phillips J.

Eaton Ltd. v. Nuttall [1977] I.R.L.R. 71 at 74, EAT.

In that case although there had been an evaluation there were three rates for the job in question, the one that applied to the individual employee was at the discretion of the management, and this degree of subjectivity meant that the scheme failed to comply with section 1(5). That an evaluation scheme must be objective to be valid was confirmed by the ECJ in *Rummler v. Data Druck GmbH*[37] and where criteria are used which favour one sex, such as muscular strength, there must be a balancing criteria, such as manual dexterity.

It was held in *England v. Bromley LBC*[38] that an employee cannot bring himself within section 1(5) by demonstrating that a particular scheme should have been adopted under which the jobs in question would have been rated as equivalent, nor could he argue that on the scheme adopted he should have been rated as equivalent. It is not the role of the industrial tribunal to decide on the most appropriate scheme or where the applicant should have been rated, merely to decide whether there was a scheme which rated the jobs of equal value and whether it complied with the requirements of section 1(5). So where Bromley had decided not to accept the "London Scheme" which would have rated the jobs as of equal value, but adopted instead a modified scheme which did not, the applicant failed. However, it was held in *O'Brien v. Sim-Chem Ltd*[39] that it was sufficient that the scheme had rated the jobs as of equal value even though it had not been introduced. The distinguishing factor between these two cases is that in *O'Brien* the company had accepted the evaluation study and had written to all those concerned advising them of their grading and appropriate salary range, but had not implemented it because of a Government voluntary pay policy, whereas in *England v. Bromley LBC* the scheme had been rejected by the employer in favour of another scheme, and it is at the employer's discretion as to which scheme is adopted. Lord Diplock in *O'Brien* held that once an evaluation had been completed it fulfilled the requirement for "determined" in section 1(2)(b)(i) and it was at that stage that a comparison became possible.

In the later case of *Arnold v. Beecham Group*[40] a job evaluation exercise was carried out but not implemented. In holding that it was a valid exercise the EAT said that section 1(5) is fulfilled only if there was a complete study, and a study was complete when accepted or adopted by the employers and employees as a valid study. Since the parties had done that by holding a meeting in which grades had been fixed and an appeals process set up, even though it had not been implemented the jobs in question had been graded as equivalent and that was sufficient for a declaration that the terms of the woman's contract were to be modified.

[37] [1987] I.R.L.R. 32, ECJ.
[38] [1978] I.C.R. 1, EAT.
[39] [1980] I.C.R. 573, HL.
[40] [1982] I.C.R. 744, EAT.

6.2.5 Equal value—section 1(2)(c)

The provision enabling a claim for equal pay for different work in the absence of a job evaluation scheme was introduced into the EqPA 1970 by the Equal Pay (Amendment) Regulations 1983[41] after the ECJ, in *Commission v. United Kingdom*,[42] held that making the right to equal pay for work of equal value dependent on the existence of a job evaluation scheme, as did EqPA 1970, s.1(2)(b) which could only be carried out with the consent and co-operation of the employer, was effectively denying the right to bring an equal value claim where no study had been carried out. The ECJ therefore held that the United Kingdom had failed to fulfil its Treaty obligations under Article 119. The 1983 Regulations amended the EqPA 1970 in three ways: They

- introduced section 1(2)(c) to enable a woman employed on work to which section 1(2)(a) or (b) did not apply, to make an application for equal value with that of a man in the same employment on the basis of the demands made on her under such headings as effort, skill and decision;

- introduced a separate defence for claims arising under section 1(2))(c)—to be found in section 1(3)(b);

- introduced a new section 2A to provide a separate procedure for dealing with cases arising under section 1(2)(c).

In addition, special tribunal rules for dealing with claims under section 1(2)(c) were introduced and these are now contained in the Industrial Tribunals (Constitution and Rules of Procedure) Regulations 1993.[43]

The regime created by the rules of procedure has been variously criticised as being lengthy, time consuming and expensive, to the point of amounting to a denial of justice to those seeking to bring an equal value claim. In this respect in 1993/94 a complaint was made by both the EOCs in Britain and Northern Ireland to the European Commission that the costs and delays were such that the United Kingdom was failing to meet its Treaty obligations in that Directive 76/207, Art. 6 requires Member States to introduce such measures as are necessary "to enable all persons who consider themselves wronged by failure to apply to them the principle of equal treatment within the meaning of Articles 3, 4 and 5 to pursue their claims by judicial process after possible recourse to other competent authorities". However, the Commission responded in late 1996 that it did not intend to take action. Judicial comment on the procedure has been frequent:

> "The present case is typical of many and there is no doubt that a number of aspects of this jurisdiction merit urgent review. We are concerned here with procedural matters. The present restrictions on procedure imposed by the Rules give rise to delays which are properly described as scandalous and to amount to a denial of justice to women seeking [a] remedy through the judicial process. During these delays women could be subject to working in a most uncomfortable

---

[41] S.I. 1983 No. 1794, reg. 2(1).

[42] Case C–61/81 [1982] I.C.R. 578, ECJ.

[43] S.I. 1993 No. 2687 (Schedule 2). Following enactment of the Employment Rights (Dispute Resolution) Act 1998 and the commencement order (S.I. 1998 No. 1658) from August 1, 1998 Industrial Tribunals become Employment Tribunals and the title of the 1993 Regulations is accordingly amended.

environment and with an unresolved grievance. To reverse the coin, there seems to be no limit on the number of successive applications which can be made with one or more different comparators, and the present procedures give scope for tactical use by applicants which amongst other things may involve substantial expenditure." *per* Wood J. (President).

Aldridge v. British Telecommunications plc [1990] I.R.L.R. 10 at 14–15, EAT.

In *Hayward v. Cammell Laird Shipbuilders Ltd*[44] the industrial tribunal observed that:

"The procedure to be followed in cases brought under s.1(2)(c) of the Act is to be found in the Regulations which are, one is bound to comment, both lengthy and complex. The amending regulations are, of course, designed specifically to deal with this type of case, and create a procedure which differs markedly from that which obtains in other types of case which come before the Tribunals."

Section 1(2)(c) is only available where the work is not like work within section 1(2)(a) or work rated as equivalent within section 1(2)(b). In *Pickstone v. Freemans plc*[45] the issue arose as to whether section 1(2)(c) could be used where female warehouse operatives were comparing themselves with male warehouse operatives who were paid more, even though there was one male warehouse operative who was paid the same as the women. The Court of Appeal held that the wording of section 1(2)(c) was clear and unambiguous and that since the women were doing "likework" and therefore could pursue a claim under section 1(2)(a) if the comparator was being paid more, there was no right to proceed using section 1(2)(c), but that since work of equal value was covered by Article 119, which was directly applicable, there was a right to proceed using Article 119. The House of Lords, however, referred to the fact that the 1983 Regulations were presented to Parliament as giving full effect to the decision in *Commission v. United Kingdom* and as such it was "entirely legitimate" to take this into account for the purpose of ascertaining the intention of Parliament. There were, the court said, two interpretations to the exclusionary wording in section 1(2)(c) and bearing in mind the purpose of the regulations the House held that they were intended to have effect only where the particular man with whom the applicant sought comparison is employed on like work. Any other interpretation, they held:

"would leave a large gap in the equal work provision, enabling an employer to evade it by employing one token man on the same work as a group of potential women claimants who were deliberately paid less than a group of men employed on work of equal value with that of the women. This would mean that the United Kingdom had failed yet again fully to implement its obligations under article 119 of the Treaty and the Equal Pay Directive, and had not given full effect to the decision of the European Court in *Commission of the European Communities v. United Kingdom* .... It is plain that Parliament cannot possibly have intended such a failure." *per* Lord Keith.

Pickstone v. Freemans plc [1988] I.C.R. 697 at 711, HL.

It was therefore held that the exclusion did not operate to prevent an equal value claim whenever the employer could identify a man doing like work or work rated as equivalent, within section 1(2)(a) and (b) with that of the applicant.

[44] [1984] I.R.L.R. 463 at 464, IT.
[45] [1988] I.C.R. 697, HL (note [1987] 3 All E.R. 757, CA).

Under section 2A(1)(a) there is a preliminary stage in that if the industrial tribunal is satisfied that there is no reasonable grounds for deciding that the work is of equal value the tribunal must dismiss the case. If it is not satisfied then it may appoint an independent expert from a panel maintained by the Advisory, Conciliation and Arbitration Service (ACAS) to prepare a JES and stay the proceedings until that report is received. The tribunal has a discretion as to whether to commission a report by an independent expert following amendments made in 1996.[46] Under rule 9(2E) of Schedule 2 to the 1993 Regulations it is open to the tribunal to allow the employer to argue his defence under section 1(3)(b) at this stage, and it was held in *Reed Packaging Ltd v. Boozer*[47] that the object of considering the defence at a preliminary hearing is to decide whether or not the claim should be allowed to proceed. In view of this if the defence under section 1(3) is made out, then the tribunal must dismiss the complaint and not go on to appoint an independent expert.

Section 2A(2) of the 1970 Act provides that there are "no reasonable grounds" under section 2A(1) if there has been a JES which complies with the requirements of section 1(5) under which the work of the man has been given different values and there are no reasonable grounds for believing that the evaluation study is tainted with discrimination. In *Neil v. Ford Motor Co. Ltd*,[48] one of the first cases to come before the tribunals under this procedure, it was held that there is no presumption that an existing JES discriminates on grounds of sex but the burden is on the applicant and whilst the tribunal should not be reluctant to draw inferences, where there are reasonable grounds for drawing them "we should not lightly set in train a new evaluation unless we are tolerably certain that there are reasonable grounds for believing the previous job evaluation study to have been distorted by discrimination".

However, it was held in *Bromley v. H. & J. Quick Ltd*[49] that where an existing JES exists but has not been prepared by an analytical and objective method sufficient to fulfil the requirements of section 1(5), that is not sufficient to prevent the tribunal appointing an independent expert. If the employer has undertaken an evaluation study since the complaint was made it was held in *Dibro Ltd v. Hore*[50] that it is admissible at this stage in order for the tribunal to decide whether it complies with section 1(5). In order to assist the tribunal in determining the question under section 2A(1) and of "looking at matters in the round" it was held in *Dennehy v. Sealink U.K. Ltd*[51] that it is open to the applicant to produce expert evidence at this stage in order to demonstrate that the existing JES does not comply with section 1(5).

If the tribunal appoints an independent expert under section 2A(1)(b), although he is free as to the method of evaluation adopted, the procedure relating to the expert's report is contained in the Rules.[52] The expert's role has been surrounded in controversy, principally over the delays that have occurred[53] and amendments to the procedure were made in an attempt to meet these criticisms. The report is not conclusive on the question of comparison—when it is received the hearing is resumed at which it is for the tribunal to decide whether to admit the report in evidence,

---

[46] S.I. 1996 No. 438 from July 31, 1996.
[47] [1988] I.R.L.R. 333, EAT.
[48] [1984] I.R.L.R. 3, IT.
[49] [1988] I.C.R. 623, CA.
[50] [1989] I.R.L.R. 129, EAT.
[51] [1987] I.R.L.R. 120, EAT.
[52] r.8A of Sched. 2 to the 1993 Regulations introduced by the Industrial Tribunals (Constitution and Rules of Procedure) (Amendment) Regulations 1996 (S.I. 1996 No. 1757), as from July 31, 1996.
[53] ACAS estimates an average period of 11 months to complete a report, *Bargaining Report*, July 1997.

although there is a presumption that it will be admitted.[54] At the resumed hearing the parties have a right to cross-examine the expert, and either party may call their own expert evidence, but this is limited to one expert each and is subject to prior notice being given.[55] However, no evidence may be adduced on any matter of fact upon which the report's conclusion is based, nor can witnesses be questioned on such matters.[56] In *Haywood v. Cammell Laird Shipbuilders Ltd*[57] the tribunal refused to allow the employer to challenge the expert's report once it had been admitted in evidence, suggesting that such a report could be challenged by submitting their own expert report before the independent expert's report had been admitted in evidence. However, in *Tennants Textile Colours Ltd v. Todd*[58] it was held that although the rules restrict the rights of the parties, it does not mean that the findings of fact in the independent expert's report are binding on the parties once it is admitted in evidence. It is also open to the employer to raise a defence under section 1(3)(b) if he did not do so at the preliminary hearing and it is then for the tribunal to reach a conclusion as to the question of equal value based on the whole of the evidence.

6.2.6 Defence

If a woman has shown that she is employed on like work, work rated as equivalent or work of equal value with her comparator, and that there is a difference in a contractual term then she has, prima facie, made out a case whereby the difference is attributed to a difference in sex. However, if the difference is genuinely due to a material factor which is not the difference of sex then there is no unlawful discrimination: the presumption of discrimination has been rebutted. In *National Vulcan Engineering Insurance Group Ltd v. Wade*[59] Lord Denning said that the burden of proof on the employer under section 1(3) is not a very heavy one, it is on the balance of probabilities.

This section was amended, along with the introduction of equal value in section 1(2)(c)[60] by the introduction of a separate test under section 1(3)(b) in that for a case falling within section 1(2)(a) or (b) the material factor which is not a difference in sex, must be a material difference between the woman's case and the man's. Whereas for a case which falls to be considered under section 1(2)(c), an equal value case, section 1(3)(b) applies in that the material factor which is not a difference of sex may be such a material difference. This was intended to introduce the market forces defence to a claim under section 1(2)(c), which the courts had refused to allow as a defence to a claim of like work and work rated as equivalent under section 1(2)(a)–(b). Before the introduction of section 1(2)(c) case law had developed whereby the test was one of a personal equation and in *Clay Cross (Quarry Services) Ltd v. Fletcher*[61] Lord Denning said that:

> "the tribunal is not to have regard to any extrinsic forces which have led to the man being paid more. An employer cannot avoid his obligations under the Act by

[54] S.I. 1993 No. 2687, Sched. 2, r.8A(12).
[55] *ibid.* r.9(2B).
[56] r.9(2C).
[57] [1985] I.C.R. 71, IT.
[58] [1989] I.R.L.R. 3, NICA.
[59] [1979] 1 Q.B. 132, CA.
[60] Equal Pay (Amendment Regulations) 1983 (S.I. 1983 No. 1794).
[61] [1979] I.C.R. 1, CA.

saying: 'I paid him more because he asked for more," or 'I paid her less because she was willing to come for less.' If any such excuse were permitted, the Act would be a dead letter. Those are the very reasons why there was unequal pay before the statute." *per* Lord Denning.

Clay Cross (Quarry Services) Ltd v. Fletcher [1979] I.C.R. 1 at 5, CA.

The personal equation involved a consideration of such factors as longer service, qualifications, greater output or productivity or some other factor personal to his doing the job, and the general bargaining factor by which he came to be employed was not part of that equation. However, in *Albion Shipping Agency v. Arnold*[62] it was held, relying on the ECJ decision in *Jenkins v. Kingsgate (Clothing Productions) Ltd*,[63] that in deciding whether or not the principle of equal pay for equal work under Article 119 has been infringed it is legitimate to consider whether economic or other circumstances account for the differences, and the EAT also found evidence for this in the ECJ judgment in *Macarthys v. Smith*.[64] The EAT concluded that the 1970 Act had to be read "to enable economic circumstances to be relied upon as constituting a 'material difference'". The statutory provisions were then overtaken by case law in the decision in *Rainey v. Greater Glasgow Health Board*,[65] in which the House of Lords, in not applying the decision in *Clay Cross (Quarry Services) Ltd v. Fletcher*,[66] held that "material" meant "significant and relevant," all the relevant circumstances had to be considered, and that these might go beyond the personal equation, and provided there was no intention to discriminate it was possible for section 1(3) to include economic reasons.

The court arrived at this decision by examining the ECJ decision in *Jenkins v. Kingsgate (Clothing) Ltd*[67] and that of Browne-Wilkinson J.[68] who, in the EAT upon return from the ECJ, concluded that the differentials in pay could be justified by showing that it was reasonably necessary for the employer to achieve economic advantages. In addition, in *Bilka-Kaufhaus GmbH v. Weber von Hartz*[69] the ECJ held that in a defence under Article 119 it is sufficient for the employer to show economically justified grounds and for the national court to decide whether the measures chosen corresponded to a real need on the part of the undertaking. This demonstrated, said Lord Keith in the House of Lords in *Rainey* that the defences under Article 119 and section 1(3) are the same and on the facts in *Rainey* the court held that there had been sound administrative reasons for the difference in pay— different negotiating machinery—which had, in fact, resulted not in the appellant being paid less, since she and all new entrants, men and women, were paid on Whitley Council rates, but those who had transferred in from the private sector being paid more because of the need to attract outside specialists The reasoning of Lord Keith in *Rainey* regarding section 1(3) was accepted by the House of Lords in *Leverton v. Clwyd CC*, a case brought under section 1(2)(c). This appeared to leave the way open for employers to successfully argue that the man is paid more because he would not work for less—the very sort of situation that has led to pay inequalities in the past.

[62] [1982] I.C.R. 22, EAT .
[63] Case C–96/80 [1981] I.C.R. 592, ECJ.
[64] Case C–129/79 [1980] I.C.R. 672, ECJ.
[65] [1987] I.C.R. 129, HL.
[66] [1979] I.C.R. 1, CA.
[67] Case C–96/80 [1981] I.C.R. 715, ECJ.
[68] [1981] I.C.R. 715, EAT.
[69] Case C–170/84 [1987] I.C.R. 110, ECJ.

However, in *Enderby v. Frenchay Health Authority*[70] an equal value case involving a speech therapist, a profession dominated by women, where comparison was sought with higher paid clinical psychologist and pharmacist, professions dominated by men, the ECJ made several findings which have subsequently led to some confusion. The ECJ held that where significant statistics disclose an appreciable difference in pay between two jobs of equal value, one of which is carried out almost exclusively by women and the other predominately by men, there is a prima facie case of discrimination and the onus is on the employer to show that that difference is based on objectively justified factors unrelated to any discrimination on grounds of sex. The difference in pay cannot be defended by using the criteria of objective justification merely by the fact that the different respective rates of pay for two jobs of equal value were arrived at by collective bargaining processes, which although carried out by the same parties, are distinct, and taken separately, have in themselves no discriminatory effect. The court reasoned that to do so would allow employers to circumvent the principle of equal pay merely by having separate bargaining structures for the different groups. The Court confirmed that a difference could be objectively justified by the need to increase the pay of a particular job to attract candidates, but that it is for national courts to determine to what extent and what proportion is objectively justified by market forces, if necessary by applying the principle of proportionality. This raises the issue that whilst part of the difference may be justified, the remainder may not: market forces cannot therefore be a "blanket" to cover past inherent discrimination.

In *British Road Services Ltd v. Loughran*[71] a majority of the Northern Ireland Court of Appeal held that for the presumption of discrimination to arise it was sufficient that a "significant number", as opposed to "almost exclusively" in *Enderby*, of the claimant group are women, so that where 75 per cent of the claimant group were women and all the group with which they were comparing themselves were men, that was sufficient to raise the presumption.

In *Ratcliffe v. North Yorkshire County Council*[72] the work of the women dinner ladies had been rated as equivalent under a job evaluation scheme with other posts within the various grades. Following the introduction of compulsory competitive tendering (CCT) the council set up a direct service organisation (DSO) to compete with private contractors. To make themselves more competitive in bidding for school meals contracts it was decided that catering staff would have their pay reduced. This led to the equal pay claim, the female catering assistants comparing themselves with male local authority employees with whom their work had already been rated as equivalent. The Court of Appeal held that the terms were "genuinely due to" the operation of market forces: the need to compete was therefore a successful defence under section 1(3). The House of Lords, however, disagreed and restored the decision of the industrial tribunal which had held that the perceived need to reduce the pay of dinner ladies to be able to compete on the open market was a material factor, but because the labour market for dinner ladies was almost exclusively female, it was a factor due to sex. Lord Slynn, in a judgment of the House, said that the categories under the EqPA 1970, s.1(2)(a)–(c) must not be confused with direct and indirect tests in the SDA 1975: the EqPA 1970 must be interpreted without bringing in the distinction between "so-called 'direct' and 'indirect' discrimination". The relevant question under the EqPA 1970 is whether treatment has been accorded for men and women employed on

---

[70] Case C–127/92 [1994] 1 All E.R. 495, ECJ.
[71] [1997] I.R.L.R. 92, NICA.
[72] [1995] I.R.L.R. 439, HL.

like work or work rated as equivalent—the jobs here had been rated as equivalent on a
JES and the House of Lords said that it was impossible to argue that the industrial
tribunal had been wrong in finding that the council had not discharged the burden on
them under section 1(3).

Unlike under the SDA and Article 119, in a defence under EqPA 1970 it was held in
Tyldesley v. TML Plastics Ltd[73] that it was unnecessary for an employer to prove that
the difference in pay was objectively justified as well as proving that the variation was
genuinely due to a material factor which was not the difference in sex. Mummery J.
said that the test of objective justification as laid down in *Enderby* only applies where
the factor relied upon to explain the differential is itself tainted by gender, because it is
indirectly discriminatory or because it adversely impacted on women as a group in the
sense indicated by ECJ in *Enderby*. The comments in the House of Lords in *Rainey*
that, in order to establish a defence under section 1(3) objective justification must be
shown, apply only in cases where the factor to be relied upon is one which affects a
considerably higher proportion of women than of men, so as to be indirectly
discriminatory unless justified: *Jenkins v. Kingsgate* and *Enderby* both fall into this
category and are not authority for the situation, as in the present case, where there is
no indirect discrimination. Mummery J. said that in an EqPA claim a difference in pay
explained by a factor not itself a factor of sex or tainted by sex discrimination should,
in principle, constitute a valid defence, and even if the differential was explained by a
careless mistake, which could not possibly be objectively justified, that would amount
to a defence provided that the tribunal is satisfied the mistake was of sufficient
influence to be significant or relevant. The EAT said that the questions that arise for
decision where a defence is raised under section 1(3) are:

- What variation (if any) is there between the woman's contract and the man's
  contract?
- To what factor is that variation genuinely due?

  In answering that the employer must:

  - identify *the factor* (which must *not* be the difference of sex);
  - satisfy the tribunal that it is a *material* factor;
  - satisfy the tribunal that the factor is a material *difference* between the
    woman's case and the man's case.

The EAT allowed the employer's appeal because the industrial tribunal had placed an
additional burden on the employer of showing objective justification for the discrimination, that the company were pursuing measures to correspond to a real need and
that they were appropriate and necessary to meet that need: that was, it was held,
unnecessary in the absence of indirect discrimination where section 1(3) applied. This
reasoning was applied in *Barry v. Midland Bank plc*[74] where the Court of Appeal
dismissed the appeal because there was no evidence of indirect discrimination in the
severance scheme: the burden of proving indirect discrimination is on the employee,
who had failed to produce statistical evidence of the composition of the relevant
groups.

The judgment of Mummery J. in *Tyldesley*[75] was approved by the House of Lords in
Strathclyde Regional Council v. Wallace.[76] In a judgment of the House, Lord Browne-

---

[73] [1996] I.R.L.R. 395, EAT.
[74] [1998] I.R.L.R. 138, CA.
[75] [1996] I.R.L.R. 395, EAT.
[76] [1998] I.R.L.R. 146, HL.

Wilkinson said that there is a valid defence under section 1(3) if the difference in pay is explained by genuine factors not tainted by sex discrimination. In this connection:

> "The requirement of genuineness would be satisfied if the industrial tribunal came to the conclusion that the reason put forward was not a sham or a pretence. For the matters relied upon by the employer to constitute 'material factors' it would have to be shown that the matters relied upon were in fact causally relevant to the difference in pay, ie that they were significant factors. Finally, the employer had to show that the difference of sex was not a factor relied upon." *per* (for the House) Lord Browne-Wilkinson.

Strathclyde Regional Council v. Wallace [1998] I.R.L.R. 146 at 148, HL.

There is only an additional burden on the employer to objectively justify the factors giving rise to the difference in pay where the employer is relying on a factor which is "gender discriminatory", and Lord Browne-Wilkinson expressed the view that *McPherson v. Rathgael Centre*,[77] where there was no element of gender discrimination, but the court required the employer to objectively justify the disparity, had been wrongly decided. Here the employers relied on five factors which were held to be genuine reasons for the difference in pay, and being significant and causally relevant factors leading to the disparity, the employer was not required to objectively justify them.

Under section 1(3)(b), which provides a defence to an equal value claim under section 1(2)(c), the employer is permitted to provide evidence not only of a genuine material difference between her case and his case, but may also show that the difference is due to some other material factor apart from sex. The wording of this subsection is unfortunate and confusing, but was implemented following the ECJ decision that the United Kingdom had failed to properly implement Article 119 by failing to provide for an equal value claim in the absence of an existing JES,[78] along with the equal value ground under section 1(2)(c), the section 2A procedure and tribunal rules of procedure[79] which set up a special, and extremely complex, regime for equal value claims. In *McGregor v. GMBATU*[80] Wood J. considered the difference between the wording in section 1(3) before the implementation of section 1(3)(b). He said that there was no longer the limitation of comparing his case and her case, which meant that authorities predating the amendment were not of assistance.

Under the rules[81] the section 1(3)(b) defence may be heard at the initial hearing, and if successful at that stage under section 2A(1)(a) the tribunal must dismiss the case. In *Reed Packaging Ltd v. Boozet*[82] the EAT said that the object of considering the defence at this preliminary hearing is to decide whether or not the claim should be allowed to proceed, but that if the defence is successful the tribunal would be failing in its duty if it did not dismiss the applicant's claim. It used to be the case that the employer had two bites of the cherry in that if his defence failed at the preliminary hearing he had an additional opportunity of raising it at the full hearing. This was, however, amended so that rules preclude the industrial tribunal from considering the

---

[77] [1991] I.R.L.R. 206, NICA.
[78] *Commission v. United Kingdom* [1982] I.C.R. 578, ECJ.
[79] Industrial Tribunals (Rules of Procedure) (Equal Value Amendment) Regulations 1983 now Industrial Tribunals (Constitution and Rules of Procedure) Regulations 1993 (S.I. 1993 No. 2687), Sched. 2.
[80] [1987] I.C.R. 505, EAT.
[81] r.9(2E).
[82] [1988] I.R.L.R. 333, EAT.

defence at the full hearing, other than in exceptional circumstances, where it has been considered at the preliminary hearing.[83]

6.2.6.1   Red circling and section 1(3)

Where either an employee or a group of employees have had their wages protected for a reason unconnected with sex, such as, for example, a reorganisation, and employees outside that group are treated alike, the employer is able to claim that the difference between those in the group and those outside it is genuinely due to a material difference within section 1(3). In *Snoxell v. Vauxhall Motors and Charles Early Ltd v. Smith*[84] Phillips J. held that the employer's reason for a difference had to be "genuine, clear and convincing" and provided the reason they had not been red-circled was that they were women, that the red-circling did not itself result from previous discrimination and that it did not continue for longer than was necessary, this could be a successful defence. However, in *Snoxell* it was held that the reason the women applicants were not within the red circle anomaly was because they had not been permitted to enter the all male grade and to allow the red circling would merely perpetuate the earlier discrimination. In *Outlook Supplies Ltd v. Parry*[85] it was successfully argued that a long service employee who worked as an assistant accountant, but who returned to work after illness as an accounts supervisor fell into this category when on humane grounds his employers agreed to continue to pay him at his old rate. A female accounts supervisor who was being paid less was therefore unsuccessful in seeking an equality clause when comparing herself with him because he fell into a "protected category".

To demonstrate that a person or group with which the applicant is comparing herself is protected as being within a "red circle" is doing no more than discharging the burden in section 1(3) of showing that the difference is genuinely due to a material difference other than sex and in *Methven v. Cow Industrial Polymers Ltd*[86] Dunn L.J. said that "to speak of a particular factual situation as a 'promotion case' or a 'red circle case' depends upon what the speaker means by 'promotion' or 'red circling', and leads to such phrases being construed as if they appeared in the statute, which they do not."

When special factors, like economic constraints, which at the time justify a lower salary, come to an end it was held in *Benveniste v. University of Southampton*[88] that there is no longer a material difference to justify the difference in pay.

6.2.7   Collective agreements

In *Commission v. United Kingdom*,[88] the ECJ held, in infraction proceedings, that the United Kingdom had failed to properly implement Directive 76/207 in that Art. 4(b) requires that Member States are required to take all necessary steps to ensure that any provisions contrary to the principle of equal treatment which are included in collective agreements and employer's internal rules may be declared void or amended. The Court held that the power to refer collective agreements to the Central Arbitration Committee (CAC) for amendment was insufficient implementation of the requirements laid down in the Directive.

---

[83] S.I. 1996 No. 438.
[84] [1977] I.C.R. 700, EAT.
[85] [1978] I.R.L.R. 12, EAT.
[86] [1980] I.C.R. 463, CA.
[87] [1989] I.R.L.R. 122, CA.
[88] Case C–165/82 [1984] I.C.R. 192, ECJ.

As a result of this decision section 77 of the SDA 1975 was amended by section 6 of the SDA 1986 to provide that any discriminatory provision in a collective agreement is deemed to be void, and the repeal of the EqPA 1970, s.3 which provided amendment powers for CAC. A further amendment was made by the TURERA 1993, s.32 to vest power in an industrial tribunal for complaints to be made on the validity of terms of a collective agreement that may affect the applicant that may breach the principle of equal treatment and complaints may be made under SDA provisions. In *Nimz v. Freie und Hansestadt Hamburg*[89] the ECJ held that a national court faced with a provision in a collective agreement that is found to be in breach of Article 119 should disapply that provision and in *Enderby* the ECJ confirmed that a discriminatory collective agreement could not provide a defence under EqPA 1970, s.1(3).

6.2.8 Death or retirement

Although the Social Security Act 1975[90] provided for equal access to occupational pension schemes for men and women, domestic law did little to encourage or facilitate equal opportunity of membership and benefits. It has already been noted that Directive 79/7 provided for differential state pension ages to continue[91] and that this was mirrored in Directive 86/378, Art. 9, all of which has been built around the historic differential age for eligibility for state pension which was widely mirrored in company policy for retirement age, eligibility for occupational pensions and redundancy and severance packages. This discrimination could not be challenged as the EqPA 1970, s.6 contained an exclusion in that an equality clause did not operate in relation to terms related to death or retirement "or to any provision made in connection with death or retirement" and an equivalent provision operated in relation to the SDA.[92] Nevertheless, a number of decisions by the ECJ have brought about a succession of changes in this area, with legislative amendments lagging somewhat behind case law developments.

The ECJ decision in *Garland v. British Rail Engineering*[93] highlighted the incompatibility between domestic law and Article 119 in that it was held that special travel concessions available during employment, and continued on into retirement, were "pay" and therefore within Article 119, whilst in domestic law proceedings, which were brought under the SDA because the concession was non-contractual, were barred by section 6(4). On return from the ECJ the House of Lords adopted the EAT reasoning that "the words of the exception created by subsection (4) ought not to be construed so widely as to include a privilege that existed during employment and is allowed by the employer to continue after retirement. But it was the successful challenge to differential occupational retirement ages in *Marshall v. Southampton & SW Hants Health Authority (Teaching)*[94] that led to consequential statutory amendments.

Ms Marshall was dismissed because she had passed age 60, the compulsory retirement age for women, whereas men did not have to retire until 65. Her claim for unlawful discrimination under the SDA was dismissed because it was excluded by section 6(4). However, her claim under Directive 76/207, which was referred to the

[89] Case C–184/89 [1991] I.R.L.R. 222, ECJ.
[90] s.53(1) and Occupational Pensions Schemes (Equal Access to Membership) Regulations 1976.
[91] Contained in the Social Security Act 1975, s.27(1), 60 for women, 65 for men.
[92] s.6(4).
[93] Case C–12/81 [1982] I.C.R. 420, ECJ.
[94] Case C–152/84 [1986] I.R.L.R. 140, ECJ.

ECJ by the Court of Appeal, was successful in that the ECJ held that such a policy was contrary to Article 5(1) which provides for equal treatment as regards working conditions, including conditions governing dismissal, and it did not fall within the derogation in Directive 79/7, Art. 7(1) which has been progressively restricted. In *Roberts v. Tate & Lyle Industries Ltd*[95] Article 7(1) was held to apply only to the determination of pensionable age for the purposes of granting old-age and retirement pensions and to the consequences thereof for other social security benefits and this has subsequently been confirmed in a succession of cases on a variety of social security benefits.[96] Because Ms Marshall's employer was an emanation of the state the Directive was held to be directly effective, with the result that her enforced retirement was unlawful as a breach of Directive 76/207, a right which could thereafter be enforced by those whose employer fell within the definition of "emanation of the state", as demonstrated in *Foster v. British Gas plc*,[97] but not by those whose employer fell outside that definition, on which see *Duke v. GEC Reliance*.[98] The result of this unsatisfactory split between the rights of public sector as opposed to private sector employees was that the blanket prohibition of matters of death and retirement was amended by the passing of the SDA 1986,[99] which introduced an amendment into the SDA 1975 with a corresponding amendment to the EqPA 1970 so that, albeit by rather confusing wording, it became unlawful to discriminate against a woman in provisions relating to death or retirement, in relation to access to opportunities for promotion, transfer or training or dismissal or demotion: this makes it unlawful to have different retirement ages for men and women.

This did not deal with the implementation of the equality requirements in occupational social security schemes contained in Directive 86/378 which were originally to be implemented by the Social Security Act 1989, s.23 and Sched. 5, but were not introduced because of rapidly developing case law and the resulting uncertainty, most notably arising from the ECJ decision in *Barber v. Guardian Royal Exchange Assurance Group*.[1] Mr Barber complained under the SDA when a severance package built around the differential normal retiring age of 62/57, modelled on the state pension age differential of five years, provided for him to receive a deferred pension and a lump sum, whereas a woman, at the age of 52 was entitled to a more advantageous package which included an early retirement package. Barber's application was rejected by the EAT as excluded by the SDA 1975, s.6(4) since it involved a provision in relation to retirement. In addition, applying *Burton v. British Railways Board*[2] it was held that this was a claim for access which fell within Directive 76/207, which is not directly effective, as opposed to being "pay" within Article 119. On a reference to the ECJ by the Court of Appeal on whether such a situation fell within Directive 76/207 or whether benefits under the severance scheme were "pay" and therefore within Article 119, the ECJ, in a landmark ruling, held that benefits paid by

[95] Case C–151/84 [1986] I.R.L.R. 150, ECJ.
[96] *Thomas v. Chief Adjudication Officer* [1990] I.R.L.R. 436, CA (severe disablement allowance or invalid care allowance); *R. v. Secretary of State for Health ex parte Richardson*, *The Times*, October 27, 1995 (prescription charges).
[97] Case C–188/89 [1990] I.R.L.R. 353, ECJ.
[98] [1988] I.R.L.R. 188, HL.
[99] SDA 1986, s.3(1) amended what is now ERA 1996, s.109 to provide that in the absence of a NRA or a sexually neutral NRA, the upper age limit for unfair dismissal is 65. Sexually neutral upper age limit for eligibility for redundancy payment, provided for in ERA 1996, s.156 was not introduced until EA 1989, s.16(1).
[1] Case C–262/88 [1990] I.R.L.R. 240, ECJ.
[2] Case C–19/81 [1982] I.R.L.R. 116, EAT.

an employer in a compulsory redundancy come within the definition of "pay" and therefore fall within Article 119, as do pensions paid under a contracted-out occupational pension scheme:

> "If a woman is entitled to an immediate retirement pension when she is made compulsorily redundant, but a man of the same age is entitled in similar circumstances only to a deferred pension, then the result is unequal pay as between those two categories of workers which the national court can itself establish by considering the components of the remuneration in question and the criteria laid down in A119." para. 38.

This decision rendered Directive 86/378, which required the implementation of equal treatment in occupational social security schemes by January 1, 1993, somewhat redundant: it was subsequently amended by Directive 96/97. Following a consultation process on the age of eligibility for state pension,[3] the government rejected a lowering of the age of eligibility for state pension for men from 65 to 60 and also the concept of a decade of retirement which reflects the fact that an increasing number of people are leaving the labour market before their state pension age, and opted to standardise, largely for cost reasons, at age 65. The Pensions Act 1995 deals, *inter alia*, with:

Eligibility for state pension—

- section 126 and Schedule 4 introduces a common age of 65 by 2020: women born before April 5, 1950 retain the age of 60, those born after that date progressively moving to 65, so that those born after April 6, 1955 attaining pensionable age when 65; and

- sections 62–66 and the Occupational Pension Schemes (Equal Treatment) Regulations 1995 introduces into pension schemes the equal treatment rule which is modelled on the EqPA 1970, but only does so in relation to service after May 17, 1990,[4] importing the *Barber* temporal limitation. At the same time the limits contained in the EqPA 1970 apply in that only those who are still employed in the relevant employment or who have made a claim within six months of leaving the employment are eligible to seek a remedy and a successful applicant is not entitled to an award in respect of arrears going back more than two years before proceedings were instituted.[5] The regulations contain exemptions from the principle of equal treatment in the area of bridging pensions and actuarial factors,[6] thus confirming the case law in *Roberts v. Birds Eye Walls Ltd*[7] and *Ten Oever v. Stichting Bedrijfspensioenfonds voor het Glazenwassers-en Schoonmaakbedrijf*[8] respectively.

6.3 DISCRIMINATION: SEX, RACE AND DISABILITY

There is no qualifying period of employment required to bring a case of discrimination, neither is there an upper age limit. The Sex Discrimination Act refers to women,

---

[3] Options for Equality in State Pension Age, Cm. 1723 (1991).
[4] EqPA 1970, s.6E(a) inserted by the 1995 Regulations.
[5] EqPA 1970, s.6A inserted by the 1995 Regulations.
[6] regs 13 and 15 respectively.
[7] Case C–132/92 [1994] I.R.L.R. 29, ECJ.
[8] Case C–109/91) [1993] I.R.L.R. 601, ECJ.

but by section 2(1) has equal application to men and covers discrimination on marital grounds in that by section 3 it is unlawful to discriminate, either directly or indirectly against married persons of either sex on the ground of their marital status. This provision provides protection for married as against single people, but does not provide protection for single people as demonstrated in *B.C. Bick v. Royal West of England School for the Deaf*[9] where the applicant's claim following dismissal the day before she intended to marry was excluded because at the time of dismissal she was not married. It is argued that this restriction is in breach of Directive 76/207 which provides that "there shall be no discrimination whatsoever on grounds of sex, either directly or indirectly in particular by reference to marital or family status".

6.3.1   Direct discrimination

The Sex Discrimination Act 1975, s.1(1)(a), Race Relations Act 1976, s.1(1)(a) and Disability Discrimination Act 1995, s.5(1) provide that it is unlawful to treat a person less favourably on grounds of sex, racial grounds or for reasons which relate to that person's disability. Racial grounds is defined in the RRA 1976, by section 3(1) as colour, race, nationality or ethnic or national origins, and is to be distinguished from racial group, which is applicable to indirect discrimination under the RRA 1976, s.1(1)(b) which is discussed below. The correct approach to the two-stage test under the RRA 1976, s.1(1) is, it was held in *Marks & Spencer plc v. Martins*,[10] to ask first if there was less favourable treatment, then ask whether the reason for it was racial.

For purposes of the DDA 1995, by section 1 a person has a disability if he has a physical or mental impairment which has a substantial and long-term adverse effect on his ability to carry out normal day-to-day activities, and this is fleshed out by Schedule 1, Regulations[11] and by statutory guidance[12] issued by the Secretary of State under section 3, which does not impose any legal obligation but a tribunal is required by section 3(3) to take account of the guidance, where relevant, when determining certain questions arising from the statutory definition.

It is also discrimination under the DDA 1995, s.5(2) if an employer fails to make reasonable adjustments as required by section 6. The duty arises where, any arrangements made by or on behalf of an employer, or any physical feature of premises occupied by the employer, place the disabled person at a substantial disadvantage as compared with persons who are not disabled and consists of a duty to take such steps as it is reasonable, in all the circumstances of the case, for him to take in order to prevent the arrangements or features having that effect (s.6(1)), (a) applying only in relation to arrangements for determining to whom employment should be offered. In determining what is "reasonable" regard is to be had to section 6(4)(a)–(e) of that subsection and the Code of Practice,[13] and by section 6(4)(c) regard may be had to the financial or other costs which could be incurred by the employer and the extent to which it would disrupt his activities. Doyle (1996) points out that support for a variety of initiatives may be available under the Government's Access to Work Scheme.

---

[9] Case 11664/76 [1976] I.R.L.R. 326, IT.
[10] IDS Brief/February 1998.
[11] Disability Discrimination (Meaning of Disability) Regulations 1996 (S.I. 1996 No. 1455).
[12] *Guidance on matters to be taken into account in determining questions relating to the definition of disability* (HMSO, London, 1996).
[13] *Code of Practice for the elimination of discrimination in the field of employment against disabled persons or persons who have had a disability*, paras 4.12–4.34.

In the employment context the employee may complain if he is discriminated against, in terms of being treated less favourably as described in the SDA 1975 and the RRA 1976, s.1(1)(a) or the DDA 1995, s.5(1) in any of the following areas relating to recruitment, as discussed at para. 1.15, except that by the DDA 1995, s.7(1) the employment provisions of the Act do not apply to employers with fewer than 20 employees:

- in the arrangements the employer makes for the purpose of determining who should be offered employment, SDA s.6(1)(a), RRA s.4(1)(a), DDA s.4(1)(a); or

- in the terms on which the employer offers employment, SDA s.6(1)(b), RRA s.4(1)(b), DDA s.4(1)(b); or

- by refusing or deliberately omitting to offer employment, SDA s.6(1)(c), RRA s.4(1)(c), DDA s.4(1)(c),

and during the employment relationship:

- in the terms of employment which the employer affords the employee, RRA s.4(2)(a), DDA s.4(2)(a);

- in the way the employer affords the employee access to opportunities for promotion, transfer or training, or to any other benefits, facilities or services, or by refusing or deliberately omitting to afford the employee access to them, SDA s.6(2)(a), RRA s.4(2)(b), DDA s.4(2)(b)–(c); or

- by dismissing the employee, or subjecting the employee to any other detriment, SDA s.6(2)(b), RRA s.4(2)(c), DDA s.4(2)(b).

For the purposes of showing less favourable treatment the comparison, unlike the EqPA 1970, is hypothetical, but it is required that "the relevant circumstances in the one case are the same, or not materially different", SDA s.5(3), RRA s.3(4). In *Weathersfield Ltd t/a Van & Truck Rentals v. Sargent*[14] the employee had been given instructions to discriminate on racial grounds as a result of which she resigned because of the "intolerable position" in which she had been placed. The resignation was held to be a constructive dismissal, and therefore fell within the RRA 1976, s.4(2)(c). In connection with the comparator the EAT referred to *Showboat Entertainment Centre Ltd v. Owens*[15] where the EAT rejected the suggestion that a comparison should be made with the way that the employer would have treated another manager who refused to carry out racialist instructions. Morison J. said: "Without being over-complicated about it . . . the actual or hypothetical comparator to be used under s.1 was somebody who was prepared to go along with the employer's unlawful instruction".

An employer's motives are irrelevant in deciding whether he has discriminated. In *James v. Eastleigh Borough Council* the Court of Appeal[16] accepted the Council's argument that the less favourable treatment was not on grounds of sex since the aim of the differential pricing policy at the local swimming pool was to "aid the needy" rather

---

[14] [1998] I.R.L.R. 14, EAT.
[15] [1984] I.R.L.R. 7, EAT.
[16] [1989] I.R.L.R. 318, CA ([1990] I.R.L.R. 288, HL).

than give preference to one sex over the other, any discrimination was indirect, and therefore capable of being justified. The House of Lords, however, relying on their earlier decision in *R. v. Birmingham City Council ex parte Equal Opportunities Commission*,[17] applied an objective approach, and held that the purity of the discriminator's subjective motive, intention or reason for discriminating cannot save the criterion applied from the objective taint of discrimination on grounds of sex" (*per* Lord Bridge).

The making of generalised stereotypical assumptions falls within "less favourable treatment" and in *Horsey v. Dyfed County Council*,[18] applying the Court of Appeal judgment in *Skyrail Oceanic Ltd v. Coleman*,[19] it was held that the refusal to second a woman to a location on the basis that she would be unlikely to return because her husband had a permanent job in that location was held to be discrimination on marital grounds since it was based on the assumption that married women gave up their employment to join their husbands: the council had treated a married woman differently from the way it would have treated a married man. Similarly, in *Hurley v. Mustoe*[20] it was held that the refusal of employment because she had young children was directly discriminatory within section 1(1)(a) where there was no evidence that the respondent's policy applied to men.

In *Jeremiah v. Ministry of Defence*[21] that only men, and not women, had to work in a shop turning out colour bursting shells which was dusty and dirty work involving wearing heavy overalls with the need to shower afterwards was held to be unlawful, and the Court of Appeal distinguished the comments of Lord Denning in *Peake v. Automotive Products Ltd*[22] that it "is not discriminatory for mankind to treat womankind with the courtesy and chivalry which we have been taught to believe is right conduct in our society".

Direct discrimination cannot be justified, except that the DDA 1995, s.5(1)(b) provides a defence of justification for the less favourable treatment, and in this respect differs from both other domestic statutes and European law. Likewise, a defence of justification is provided for in the duty to make adjustments (s.5(2)(b)), but only if the reason for the failure is both material to the circumstances of the particular case and substantial.

6.3.2 Disability discrimination

The industrial tribunal case of *Clark v. Novacold Ltd*[23] offers an insight into the interpretation of the various provisions of the DDA 1995. Following a back injury received at work C was unable to walk even short distances properly and could not lift heavy loads and was unable to work. A doctor's report indicated that it was extremely difficult to anticipate C's return to work in the near future, as a result of which the employer obtained a report from the consultant who stated that C had a soft tissue injury which "should improve over a period of up to 12 months from the time of the injury", but he was unable to give an exact time when it would be possible for C to

---

[17] [1989] I.R.L.R. 173, HL.
[18] [1982] I.R.L.R. 755, EAT.
[19] [1981] I.C.R. 864, CA.
[20] [1981] I.R.L.R. 208, EAT.
[21] [1979] I.R.L.R. 436, CA.
[22] [1977] I.R.L.R. 365, CA.
[23] COIT Case No. 1801661/97 July 23, 1997, EOR Discrimination Case Law Digest, No. 34.

return to work. As a result C's employment was terminated in response to which C claimed that he had been discriminated against for a reason related to his disability.

(1) The first issue was whether C was "disabled" within section 1(1). The industrial tribunal were satisfied that of the day-to-day activities that are listed in paragraph 4(1) of Schedule 1, C's mobility, manual dexterity, physical co-ordination and ability to lift, carry or otherwise move everyday objects were substantially and adversely affected by his physical impairment.

(2) The second issue was whether the effects on C's ability to carry out normal day-to-day activities were long-term. Schedule 1, para. 2(1) stipulates that the effect of an impairment is long-term if it has lasted for 12 months or is likely to last for at least 12 months. The tribunal held that the appropriate time for determining whether C's disability was likely to last 12 months was at the date on which the alleged act of discrimination occurred. This was the date of dismissal. The tribunal referred to *DfEE Guidance* which states that it is likely that an event will happen if it is "more probable than not" that it will happen. The tribunal noted that at the time of dismissal C had been ill for five months and was showing no signs of improvement. They concluded that the medical evidence indicated that the condition was likely to continue beyond 12 months and C's impairment was therefore long-term.

(3) The third question was whether the reason for C's dismissal related to his disability: The tribunal rejected the employer's argument that the reason was either C's continued absence or the fact that he was no longer capable of performing the main functions of his job and that these were reasons which did not relate to C's disability. They held that the reason that C could no longer do his job was related to his disability.

(4) The fourth question was whether the employers had treated C less favourably than they treated or would treat others to whom the reason did not apply—section 5(1). The employer argued that the comparison should be made with people who had continuing and long-term absences. C argued that the comparison should be with non-disabled people. The industrial tribunal held that the comparison in section 5(1) must be confined to somebody who was off work for the same length of time as the applicant and the treatment to be examined was the treatment (actual or hypothetical) which would be given to such a person. As the tribunal were of the view that such a person would have been treated no differently from C, they concluded that the employers had not discriminated against C.

Notwithstanding their rejection of C's claim at this stage, the tribunal went on to consider issues relating to justification and noted that for less favourable treatment to be justified the reason for it has to be both material to the circumstances of the particular case and substantial (s.5(3)). They said that had they had to decide this point they would have held that the employers were not justified in treating C as they did as there would have been no organisational or economic consequences of keeping him on their books once they stopped paying him sick pay.

It is pointed out[24] that the choice of comparator has the effect of emasculating the protection offered to disabled people and that the comparison should be with a person to whom the disability-related reason—the absence from work or inability to do the job—did not apply. This means that the comparator is a person who is at work or who is able to carry out his job and on this basis there is here a prima facie case of less favourable treatment.

---

[24] IDS Brief 598/October 1997.

Based on section 6(2), which limits the application of the duty to make adjustments to "any term, condition or arrangements on which employment, promotion, a transfer, training or any other benefit is offered or afforded", the industrial tribunal held that the provisions relating to reasonable adjustments do not apply to dismissals. The question is whether section 6(4), the "arrangements on which employment . . . is . . . afforded" includes the time up to dismissal. That this is so is supported by para. 6.21 of the Code of Practice which says that "dismissal . . . of a disabled person for a reason relating to the disability would need to be justified and the reason for it would have to be one which could not be removed by any reasonable adjustment"[25] and Boyle (1996) takes this view.[26]

6.3.3 Indirect discrimination

Indirect discrimination is the application of a rule or policy which is the same regardless of sex, racial group or marital status but which has a disparate or adverse impact on a person on the grounds of their sex, racial group or marital status. The provisions of the SDA 1975 and the RRA 1976 are found in identical terms in section 1(1)(b) of the relevant Act and those concerning marital status in the SDA 1975, s.3(1)(b) and provide that a person discriminates where they apply:

- a requirement or condition which would apply equally to someone not of the same sex/racial group/to an unmarried person of the same sex—SDA, RRA s.1(1)(b), SDA s.3(1)(b);

- the proportion of persons of the applicant's sex/racial group/marital status who can comply with it is considerably smaller than the proportion of persons of the opposite sex/different racial group/unmarried people of the same sex who can comply—SDA, RRA s.1(1)(b)(i), SDA s.1(3)(b)(i), and

- that the respondent cannot show to be justified irrespective of sex—SDA, RRA s.1(1)(b)(ii), SDA s.3(1)(b)(ii), and

- the requirement or condition is to the applicant's detriment because they cannot comply with it—SDA, RRA s.1(1)(b)(iii), SDA s.3(1)(b)(iii).

This necessity to comply with the detailed requirements of the Sex DiscriminationAct in order to be successful contrasts with Directive 76/207, Art. 2 which provides that the principle of equal treatment means that "there shall be no discrimination whatsoever on grounds of sex either directly or indirectly by reference in particular to marital or family status".

For the purposes of the RRA 1976, s.1(1)(b), racial group is defined in section 3(1) as a group of persons defined by reference to colour, race, nationality or ethnic or national origins. In *Mandla v. Lee*[27] Lord Fraser said that for a group to be an ethnic group it must regard itself and be regarded by others, as a distinct community by virtue

---

[25] n. 13 above.
[26] para. 338, p. 48. The EAT ([1998] I.R.L.R. 420) has upheld the IT reasoning on the fourth question—the comparator: "The true comparator . . . was a person who was unable to fulfil all the requirements of his job but whose inability was not related to disability . . .". The EAT held that the IT had erred and that the duty to make reasonable adjustments, DDA 1995, s.6, extends to dismissals.
[27] [1983] I.R.L.R. 209, HL.

of certain characteristics: it is essential that there is a long shared history, of which the group is conscious as distinguishing it from others and a memory of which it keeps alive; a cultural tradition of its own, including family and social customs and manners, often but not necessarily associated with religious observance. In addition, he said, the following characteristics are relevant: either a common geographical origin, or descent from a small number of common ancestors; a common language; a common literature peculiar to the group; a common religion different from that of neighbouring groups or from the general community surrounding it; being a minority or being an oppressed or a dominant group within a larger community, and a person can fall into a racial group by birth or by adherence.[28] In *Northern Joint Police Board v. Power*[29] it was held that both the Scots and the English are separate "racial groups" within section 3(1) as defined by reference to "national origins", which is a necessary precondition to a claim under the RRA 1976, s.1(1)(b).

6.3.3.1 *Requirement or condition*

In *Home Office v. Holmes*[30] the EAT said that: "It appears to us that words like 'requirement' and 'condition' are plain, clear words of wide import fully capable of including any obligation of service whether for full or part time, and we see no basis for giving them a restrictive interpretation in the light of the policy underlying the Act, or in the light of public policy . . ."[31]

This statement was agreed with by the NICA in *Briggs v. North Eastern Education and Library Board*.[32] In choosing not to follow the more restrictive interpretation in *Clymo v. Wandsworth London Borough Council*[33] Hutton, L.C.J. in *Briggs* agreed with Waite J. in *Holmes* and with the following:

> "In our view it is not right to give these words (*requirement or condition*) a narrow construction. The purpose of the legislature in introducing the concept of indirect discrimination into the 1975 Act and the Race Relations Act 1976 was to seek to eliminate those practices which had a disproportionate impact on women or ethnic minorities and were not justifiable for other reasons. The concept was derived from that developed in the law of the United States which held to be unlawful practices which had a disproportionate impact on black workers as opposed to white workers: see *Griggs v. Duke Power Co* [1971] 401 US 424. If the elimination of such practices is the policy lying behind the Act, although such policy cannot be used to give the words any wider meaning than they naturally bear it is in our view a powerful argument against giving the words a narrower meaning thereby excluding cases which fall within the mischief which the Act was meant to deal with." *per* Browne-Wilkinson J.
>
> *Clarke v. Eley (IMI) Kynoch* [1982] I.R.L.R. 482 at 485, EAT.

Although being required to work full-time is a "requirement or condition" for the purposes of the SDA 1986, s.1(1)(b), implementation of the Social Partners' Framework Agreement on Part-time Work, adopted by Directive 97/81, may require

[28] *ibid*. at 211–212.
[29] [1998] I.R.L.R. 610, EAT.
[30] [1984] I.R.L.R. 299, EAT.
[31] *per* Waite J. at 301.
[32] [1990] I.R.L.R. 181, NICA.
[33] [1989] I.R.L.R. 241, EAT.

consideration of the adequacy of the section 1(1)(b) tests under section 1(1)(b)(i), (ii) and (iii) as a means of implementation. As this Directive was adopted under the Social Chapter an extension Directive, similar to those adopted in the case of works councils and parental leave will need to be adopted (see para. 2.9).

The restrictive interpretation given to "requirement or condition" by the Court of Appeal in *Perera v. Civil Service Commission*[34] has, however, meant that many acts of discrimination have been beyond challenge because they have been described as preferences rather than an absolute "must". In *Perera*[35] it was held that where there were a number of factors taken into account by an interview panel, such as lack of British nationality, command of English, experience in the United Kingdom and age, except where the combined lack of a number of those factors constituted an absolute bar to selection, a "requirement or condition" for these purposes could not be demonstrated. This case has repeatedly been followed, although on occasions with judicial reluctance, see for example *Meer v. London Borough of Tower Hamlets*[36] *per* Balcombe L.J. However, in *Falkirk Council v. Whyte*,[37] it was held that a preference for "management training and supervisory experience" was a requirement or condition within the SDA 1975, s.1(1)(b). This was held to be so even though it was not an absolute bar, and in so holding the EAT was "not inclined to follow the race discrimination cases and, in particular, that of *Perera.*"

6.3.3.2 *Can comply*

By the SDA 1975 and RRA 1976, s.1(1)(b)(i) and the SDA 1975, s.3(1)(b)(i) the "requirement or condition" must be one which is such that a considerably smaller proportion of women than men, or persons not of that racial group, or unmarried persons of the same sex, can comply with it. "Can comply" was held in *Price v. Civil Service Commission*[38] to mean that the claimant only had to show that she could not comply "in practice". This interpretation was accepted and reinforced by the House of Lords in *Mandla v. Lee*,[39] Lord Fraser saying that it must have been intended by Parliament, not to mean "can theoretically", but "can in practice", so that although it was physically possible was for the Sikh boy in question to comply with the "no turban" rule, since he could only do so by giving up his "distinctive customs and cultural rules", it was held not to be a rule with which he could comply in practice or "consistently with the customs and cultural conditions of the racial group".

Considerably smaller proportion

In considering whether there is a considerably smaller proportion some comparison needs to be made. The question that arises is what is the pool for comparison purposes to seek to establish the disproportionate impact. Section 5(3) of the SDA 1975 (and the RRA 1976, s.3(4)) provides that a comparison must be such that the relevant circumstances in the one case are the same or not materially different, in the other. It has been held that the choice of pool is a question of fact and one which it was held in *Kidd v. D.R.G. (U.K.) Ltd*[40] was "entrusted by Parliament to the good sense of the tribunals, whose selection will be influenced by the need to fit it as closely as possible to the varying circumstances of each case." *per* Waite J.

[34] [1983] I.R.L.R. 166, CA.
[35] *ibid.*
[36] [1988] I.R.L.R. 399, CA.
[37] [1997] I.R.L.R. 560, EAT.
[38] [1977] I.R.L.R. 291, EAT.
[39] [1983] I.R.L.R. 209, HL.
[40] [1985] I.C.R. 405, EAT.

In *Briggs v. North Eastern Education and Library Board*[41] *Price v. Civil Service Board*[42] and the Court of Appeal in *Meade-Hill v. British Council*[43] were prepared to accept that the relevant "requirement or condition" had a disproportionate impact on the applicant and that the industrial tribunal could take into account its own knowledge and experience in deciding the issue. However, in other cases quite sophisticated statistical evidence has been considered: for example in *R. v. SS for Employment ex parte Seymour Smith*[44] although it was held that under Community law there had to be a "considerable difference" in the number or percentage of one group over the other, the weight to be attached to the word "considerable" must not be exaggerated. In *Perera v. Civil Service Commission*[45] the EAT stressed that it would be "most undesirable" if elaborate statistics were needed to prove a case.

In *Staffordshire County Council v. Black*[46] it was held that "considerably smaller" are ordinary words in common usage and where the proportion of women teachers over 50 who could comply with the requirement to be full-time (89 per cent), as compared with the proportion of male teachers over age 50 who were full-time (97 per cent) a difference of 7.5 per cent, it was not a considerably smaller proportion. Nevertheless in *London Underground v. Edwards (No. 2)* it was held that:

> "The industrial tribunal is entitled to have regard to the possibility that, where the number of women as against the number of men, is in percentage terms, very slight, some kind of generalised assumption may exist at the workplace that the particular type of work is 'men's' and not 'women's' work . . . and to their common knowledge about the proportionately larger number of women than men in employment who have childcare responsibilities." *per* Morison J. (President).

London Underground v. Edwards (No. 2) [1997] I.R.L.R. 157 at 160, EAT.

This means that in a segregated labour force previous discriminatory practices cannot thereby exclude a sex discrimination claim by a lone or small number of women.

6.3.3.3 *Can the discriminator justify the requirement or condition?*

A defence is provided for indirect discrimination in that by the SDA 1975, s.1(1)(b)(ii) and s.1(3)(b)(ii) and the RRA 1976, s.1(1)(b)(ii) the employer can bring evidence to show that the requirement or condition is justifiable irrespective of the sex or racial group or marital status of the applicant, but a note of caution was sounded by Waite J.:

> "The scheme of the anti-discrimination legislation involves casting a wide net throwing upon employers the onus of justifying the relevant requirement or condition in particular instances. One must be careful, however, not to fall into the error of assuming that because the net is wide, the catch will necessarily be large." *per* Waite J.

Home Office v. Holmes [1984] I.C.R. 678 at 684, EAT.

In *London Underground Ltd. v. Edwards*[47] the defence failed because it was held to be feasible for the employer to introduce a scheme that would cater for single parents or

[41] [1990] I.R.L.R. 181, NICA.
[42] [1977] I.R.L.R. 291, EAT.
[43] [1986] 1 All E.R. 79, CA.
[44] [1995] I.C.R. 889, DC, *per* McCullough J. at 915, *per* Neill L.J. at 950–952 and CA.
[45] [1982] I.R.L.R. 147, EAT.
[46] [1995] I.R.L.R. 234, EAT.
[47] [1995] I.R.L.R. 355, EAT.

those with primary responsibility for children without significant detriment to the objectives of the new rosters. In doing so the EAT held that it was necessary to have regard to the test stated by Balcombe L.J. in the Court of Appeal in *Hampson v. Department of Education and Science*,[48] which was approved by the House of Lords in *Webb v. E.M.O. Air Cargo (U.K.) Ltd*,[49] that the tribunal must balance the discriminatory effect of the requirement against the reasonable needs of the employer and that only if the discriminatory effect can be objectively justified by those needs can the requirement be justifiable.

The test as stated by Balcombe L.J. in *Hampson* is based on the test set out by Stephenson L.J. in *Ojutiku v. Manpower Services Commission*,[50] which was approved by House of Lords in *Rainey v. Greater Glasgow Health Board*[51] and is the test which was stated in *Steel v. Union of Post Office Workers*.[52] In *Steel* following aboliton of the practice that postwomen could not achieve permanent full-time status, seniority and consequently promotion prospects were affected because full-time status was counted from the date of aboltion of the rule, as opposed to commencement of employment. In holding this to be discriminatory the case was referred back to the industrial tribunal to decide whether the lack of backdating could be justified within section 1(1)(b)(ii). In his judgment Phillips J. in the EAT likened the test to be carried out to that under the EqPA 1970, s. 1(3) in that it is insufficient merely to consider the needs of the enterprise in relation to the purpose for which the requirement or condition has been imposed, but that it is necessary to weigh up those needs against the discriminatory effect of the requirement or condition:

> ". . . it is right to distinguish between a requirement or condition which is necessary and one which is merely convenient, and for this purpose is relevant to consider whether the employer can find some other and non-discriminatory method of achieving his object." *per* Phillips J.

Steel v. Union of Post Office Workers [1997] I.R.L.R. 288 at 290–291, EAT.

In applying the same test the EAT in *Greater Manchester Police Authority v. Lea*[53] held that the Police Authority had not justified the condition that those in receipt of an occupational pension should not be considered for appointment since there was no relevant need for the conditon which was applied to take account of the needs of the unemployed. The EAT held that it was not enough for it to be shown that the condition was imposed "in pursuance of an intrinsically entirely laudable and otherwise reasonable policy of helping the unemployed". However, in *Briggs v. North Eastern Education and Library Board* the Northern Ireland Court of Appeal, applying the *Hampson* test, held that the reasonable needs of the employer, that badminton practice should be conducted in the interest of the school and for the benefit of the girls, clearly necessitated that badminton practice should be carried out in the afternoon after school and not in the lunch break. It was therefore held that the discriminatory effect of the requirement to hold badminton practice after school was objectively justified within the relevant Northern Ireland Order which mirrors that contained in the SDA 1975, s.1(1)(b)(ii).[54]

[48] [1989] I.R.L.R. 69, CA.
[49] [1993] I.R.L.R. 218, HL.
[50] [1982] I.C.R. 661, CA.
[51] [1987] I.R.L.R. 26, H.L.
[52] [1978] I.C.R. 181, EAT.
[53] [1990] I.R.L.R. 372, EAT.
[54] Sex Discrimination (Northern Ireland) Order 1976, Art. 3(1)(b)(ii).

The *Hampson* test was approved by the House of Lords in *R. v. Secretary of State for Employment ex parte EOC*[55] in which the House applied the objective standard of justification set out by the ECJ in the equal pay case of *Bilka-Kaufhaus GmbH v. Weber von Hartz*,[56] namely:

"It is for the national court, which has sole jurisdiction to make findings of fact, to determine whether and to what extent the grounds put forward by the employer to explain the adoption of a pay practice which applies independently of a worker's sex but in fact affect more women than men may be regarded as objectively justified [on] economic grounds. If the national court finds that the measures chosen by *Bilka* correspond to a real need on the part of the undertaking, are appropriate with a view to achieving the objectives pursued and are necessary to that end, the fact that the measures affect a far greater number of women than men is not sufficient to show that they constitute an infringement of Article 119."

Case C–170/84 *Bilka-Kaufhaus GmbH v. Weber von Hartz* [1986] I.R.L.R. 317 at 320, ECJ.

and as applied to the issue of leglislative policy in *Rinner Kuhn v. F.W.W. Spezial-Gebaudereinigung GmbH & Co. K.G.*, namely:

"if the State can show that the means chosen meet a necessary aim of its social policy and that they are suitable and requisite for attaining that aim, the mere fact that the provision affects a much greater number of female workers than male workers cannot be regarded as constituting an infringement of article 119.

It is for the national court . . . to assess the facts and interpret the national legislation, to determine whether and to what extent a legislative provision, which, though applying independently of the sex of the worker, actually affects a greater number of women than men, is justified by reasons which are objective and unrelated to any discrimination on grounds of sex."

Case C–171/88 *Rinner Kuhn v. F.W.W. Spezial-Gebaudereinigung GmbH & Co. K.G.* [1989] E.C.R. 2743 at 2760, ECJ.

That the application of *Bilka* and *Rinner-Kuhn* is appropriate in cases of discrimination arising under Directive 76/207 as well as Article 119 was confirmed by the ECJ in *Gerster v. Freistaat Bayern*[57] and *Kording v. Senator Fur Finanzen*.[58]

In the *EOC* case Lord Keith said these criteria oblige the Member State to show that the means chosen:

- meet a necessary aim of its social policy;

- are suitable for attaining that aim; and

- are requisite for attaining that aim.

The House held that the regulations setting down differential qualifying thresholds for the right to bring proceedings for unfair dismissal and redundancy compensation which

[55] [1994] I.R.L.R. 176, HL.
[56] Case C–170/84 [1996] E.C.R. 1607, ECJ.
[57] Case C–1/95 [1997] I.R.L.R. 699, ECJ.
[58] Case C–100/95 [1997] I.R.L.R. 710, ECJ.

discriminated against women, although aimed at a social policy of increasing the availability of part-time work, were not necessary for that purpose: the defence of justification was, therefore, not successful.

Likewise, relying on the guidance given by Lord Keith in the *EOC* case it was held by the Court of Appeal in *R. v. SS for Employment ex parte Seymour Smith*,[59] in a challenge to the two year qualifying period for unfair dismissal and redundancy payment, that although maximising employment opportunities is a necessary aim of social policy, the means chosen for doing so was "neither suitable nor requisite for attaining the aim of increased employment" and was therefore not justified. However, in *Nolte v. Landesversicherungsanstalt Hannover*[60] the ECJ held that the social and employment policy aim of excluding persons in "minor" or "marginal" part-time employment from a range of statutory benefits, and therefore contributions, with the aim of fostering demand for such employment, was objectively unrelated to any discrimination on grounds of sex and that the national legislature was reasonably entitled to consider that the legislation was necessary to achieve that aim.

The House of Lords has referred *R. v. SS for Employment ex parte Seymour Smith*[61] to the ECJ and if the court holds that the conditions are discriminatory, whether in breach of Article 119 or Directive 76/207, they will have to decide the issue of the appropriate test for justification and whether the imposition of a two year qualifying period is "suitable and requisite" for attaining the social policy aim of increasing the availability of part-time work, bearing in mind that notwithstanding the decision in *Nolte*, the ECJ in *Rinner-Kuhn* rejected reliance on generalised statements concerning categories of workers as objective criteria unrelated to any discrimination on grounds of sex.

In the White Paper *Fairness at Work*[62] the Government announed a range of proposals aimed at the policy of increasing competitiveness through flexible working arrangements. One of the proposals as part of the package of measures for individuals is a reduction of the qualifying period for unfair dismissal from the two year period being challenged in *R. v. SS for Employment ex parte Seymour Smith* to one year, with no proposals to differentiate in so far as small employers are concerned.[63]

6.3.3.5 *Detriment*

In *Jermiah v. Ministry of Defence*[64] it was held that detriment "does not mean anything more than 'putting under a disadvantage'" (*per* Brandon J.) and that a detriment exists if a reasonable worker would or might take the view that the duty was in all the circumstances to his detriment (*per* Brightman L.J.). In *Steel v. Union of Post Office Workers*[65] it was held that the detriment had to be suffered at the time that the applicant had to comply with the requirement or condition and this was followed by a majority in *Turner v. Labour Party and the Labour Party Superannuation Society*.[66] However, in *Mead-Hill v. The British Council*[67] it was held by a majority (Stewart-Smith L.J. dissenting) that discrimination occurred when a mobility clause was included in

[59] [1995] I.C.R. 889, HC and CA.
[60] Case C–317/93 [1996] I.R.L.R. 225, ECJ.
[61] [1997] I.R.L.R. 315, HL.
[62] Cm. 3968 (1998), http://www.dti.gov.uk/IR/fairness/.
[63] para. 3.9
[64] [1979] I.R.L.R. 436, CA.
[65] [1978] I.C.R. 181, EAT.
[66] [1987] I.R.L.R. 101, CA.
[67] [1995] I.R.L.R. 485, CA.

the contract, albeit that it had not been operated upon, nor was there any evidence that the employer intended to operate it in the foreseeable future.

6.3.4 Particular situations

6.3.4.1 *Harassment*

Harassment, in terms of unwanted behaviour which is unwelcome and unpleasant can take a number of forms, be for a variety of reasons and can affect men as well as women.[68] Behaviour capable of constituting harassment and a detriment could be obvious, such as violence and bullying or less obvious forms such as verbal intimidation or ignoring someone and what has been called "mobbing".[69]

Commission Recommendation 91/131, on the protection of the dignity of women and men at work states that "unwanted conduct of a sexual nature, or other conduct based on sex affecting the dignity of women and men at work, including the conduct of superiors and colleagues, is unacceptable and may in certain circumstances, be contrary to the principle of equal treatment within the meaning of Articles 3, 4 and 5 of Directive 76/207/EEC". Following the ECJ decision in *Grimaldi v. Fonds des Maladies Professionelles*[70] domestic courts are bound to take Recommendations into consideration in order to decide disputes submitted to them, in particular where they are capable of clarifying the interpretation of provisions of national or Community law.

Although not referred to specifically in discrimination statutes, harassment can constitute direct discrimination in that a person is treated less favourably within the SDA 1975 and RRA 1976, s.1(1)(a), and the DDA 1995, s.5(1)(a) and subjected to "any other detriment" within the SDA 1975, s.6(2)(b), RRA 1976 s.4(2)(c), and DDA 1975, s.4(2)(d), "detriment" for these purposes having been held in *Ministry of Defence v. Jeremiah*[71] to mean no more than disadvantage.

In *Strathclyde Regional Council v. Porcelli*[72] the court identified the issues under section 1(1)(a) not as being whether there was sexual harassment, but whether the complainant was subjected to treatment on the ground of her sex (because she was a woman) and if so, whether she was treated less favourably by her male colleagues than the man with whom she falls to be compared. It was contented that Mrs Porcelli's workmates would have been equally unpleasant to another colleague they disliked and that the treatment metered out to her was not done because of her sex. In response to this argument Lord Emslie said that section 1(1)(a) was concerned with "treatment" and not with motive, therefore it did not follow that because the campaign pursued against Mrs Porcelli as a whole had no sex related motive or objective, the treatment of her, which was of the nature of sexual harassment, is not to be regarded as having been "on the ground of her sex". In his opinion the particular campaign was adopted against Mrs Porcelli because she was a woman, and would not have been used against an equally disliked man.

---

[68] IPD Key Facts, *Harassment at Work,* Institute of Personnel and Development, May 1997 suggests that as well as sexual grounds, intimidating behaviour can occur on grounds of race, ethnic origin, gender or sexual orientation, disabilities, sensory impairments or learning difficulties, status as an ex-offender, age, AIDS/HIV and physical characteristics or personal beliefs.

[69] Described by R. Ramge, "Mobbing in the workplace" (1996) N.L.J., October 25, as including the harmful treatment of or the putting of harmful pressure on an employee, often with the intention and effect of inducing him to leave.

[70] Case C–322/88 [1990] I.R.L.R. 400 ECJ.

[71] [1980] I.C.R. 13, CA.

[72] [1986] I.R.L.R. 134 CS.

It is generally the persistent nature of unwanted attention that converts attention into harassment once it has been made clear that it is regarded by the recipient as offensive. In *Porcelli* oral insults formed part of a campaign of action that also involved "vindictive and unpleasant treatment which took various forms". However, it was held in *Bracebridge Engineering Ltd v. Darby*[73] that a single act of sexual harassment may constitute detriment for the purpose of the SDA 1975, s.6(2)(b), provided that it was sufficiently serious and in *Insitu Cleaning Co. Ltd v. Heads*[74] the EAT found oral remarks alone made on a single occasion sufficient when made by the bosses' son to a female employee nearly twice his age and which the recipient found to be "very embarrassing and distressing". This, it was held, was a form of bullying and not acceptable in the workplace in any circumstances. Whether one act is capable of constituting a detriment within section 6(2)(b) is a question of fact and degree for the tribunal, the EAT held.

In *Hereford & Worcester County Council v. Clayton*[75] the EAT upheld a decision that a female fire fighter was less favourably treated than male fire-fighters who were not subjected to the same "harsh and unfriendly regime". Although subjected to what was described as "appalling discrimination" involving verbal aggression, intimidation and humiliation inflicted upon her by male colleagues in particular, the EAT held that a remark by a fire brigade officer to his watch that "the bad news" was that the new member of the watch was going to be a woman, was capable of amounting to a detriment for the purposes of the SDA 1975, s.6(2)(a). Even though the remark had not been made to Ms Clayton directly, that did not prevent it from having detrimental consequences for her.

Bullying and humiliating conduct by a manager can lead to breach of the implied duty of mutual trust and confidence, as in *Brearley v. Wm Morrisons Supermarkets*,[76] where the manager subjected a subordinate to humiliating oral attacks in the presence of others, referring to him as being "brain dead" and "illiterate". In addition, where bullying involves physical actions that cause injury or an unsafe working environment the employer could be in breach of the duty to provide a safe working environment. This occurred in *Evans v. Sawley Packaging Co. Ltd*,[77] where the employee needed hospital treatment following attacks and where his car was interfered with. A failure by an employer to take action to prevent attacks may itself amount to a breach of trust and confidence.

A failure to act may also amount to direct discrimination under the SDA 1975, s.12(3) as demonstrated in *Fire Brigades Union v. Fraser*[78] in that the union denied a man, against whom allegations of sexual harassment had been made, representation and financial assistance with legal fees in respect of the resulting disciplinary hearing. No action was ultimately taken against the accused, but the union had supplied a high level of support to the woman and in contrast in order "to send the right message" had assumed the guilt of the man.

Under the discrimination statutes[79] the employer may be liable for wrongful acts done by an employee acting in the course of his employment. The interpretation given to "in the course of employment" has caused difficulty in that at common law the

[73] [1990] I.R.L.R. 3, EAT.
[74] [1995] I.R.L.R. 4, EAT.
[75] I.R.L.B. 565, March 1997.
[76] COIT 3073/168B, noted in *People Management*, September 12, 1996.
[77] COIT 2916/185E, noted *ibid.*
[78] [1997] I.R.L.R. 671, EAT.
[79] SDA 1975, s.41, RRA 1976, s.32 and DDA 1995, s.58.

employer is not liable when the employee goes outside his employment and is negligent whilst on "a frolic of his own".[80] The question that has arisen is whether this common law doctrine should be imported into the discrimination statutes, the consequence of which is that the more heinous the behaviour, the less likely is the employer to be vicariously liable. In *Irving v. The Post Office*,[81] importing the common law doctrine, it was held that the employer was not liable for racially abusive remarks written by a postman on envelopes he delivered because it was misconduct that did not form part of his duties.

In *Jones v. Tower Boot Co. Ltd*,[82] where a youth of mixed ethnic origin was repeatedly subjected by two fellow employees to severe verbal and physical racial abuse, a complaint alleged that the conduct amounted to racial discrimination within the RRA 1976, ss.1(1)(a) and 4(2)(c) for which the employers were responsible by virtue of section 32(1). In a robust judgment the Court of Appeal held that in interpreting section 32(1) regard had to be had to the purpose of 1976 Act and that the words "in the course of employment" had to be given their natural everyday meaning and were not to be construed restrictively by reference to the principles governing an employer's vicarious liability at common law.

The Court of Appeal held that it would be particularly wrong to allow racial harassment on the scale that was suffered to "slip through the net of employer responsibility" by applying an unnatural meaning: that would seriously undermine the statutory scheme of the Discrimination Acts and flout the purposes which they were passed to achieve.

This followed the decision in *Burton & Rhule v. De Vere Hotels*[83] where it was held that an employer may, apart from the acts of employees, also be liable for unlawful acts of harassment carried out by visitors to the premises. It was held that an employer "subjects" an employee to the "detriment" of racial harassment for purposes of the RRA 1976, s.4(2)(c) if he causes or permits harassment serious enough to amount to a "detriment", and an employer "subjects" for these purposes if he causes or allows the harassment to happen in circumstances which were sufficiently under his control that he could, by the application of good employment practice, have prevented or reduced. The Court of Appeal decision in *Burton v. De Vere Hotels Ltd*[84] was applied to an employer/employee relationship in *Chessington World of Adventures Ltd v. Reed*.[85] The employer was aware of the campaign of harassment and took no steps to prevent it, although it was clearly something over which they could have exercised control. This application of the test developed in *Burton* to the employer/employee relationship obviates the necessity of using the statutory vicarious liability test under which it is a defence for the employer "to prove that he took such steps as were reasonably practicable to prevent the employee from doing that act".[86] Following the decision in *Jones v. Tower Boot Co. Ltd*,[87] the outcome is likely to be the same, indeed in *Chessington World of Adventures Ltd v. Reed*[88] the EAT said: "if the tribunal was wrong in its finding as to direct liability, we would affirm the result on the ground that the

[80] *Joel v. Morrison* (1834) Car. & P. 502, *per* Parke B.
[81] [1987] I.R.L.R. 289, CA.
[82] [1997] 2 All E.R. 406, CA.
[83] [1996] I.R.L.R. 596, CA.
[84] *ibid.*
[85] [1997] I.R.L.R. 556, EAT.
[86] SDA 1975, s.41(3), RRA 1976, s.32(3), DDA 1995, s.58(5).
[87] [1997] 2 All E.R. 406, CA.
[88] [1997] I.R.L.R. 556, EAT.

appellant was vicariously liable for the acts of harassment of its employees under s.41(1) of the [SDA]". Nevertheless, it is difficult to see what purpose those provisions serve if direct liability applies in an employer/employee relationship.

In any event, in order to have a statutory or a direct defence, and to be able to demonstrate compliance with the statutory codes, it is necessary for the employer to have a procedure for dealing with complaints of harassment which is known to all employees and through which complainants are able to have their complaints taken seriously and investigated swiftly and confidentially, whilst ensuring the rights of all are protected. In *Insitu Cleaning Co. Ltd v. Heads*[89] the EAT said that the employer should adopt a separate procedure to deal exclusively with complaints of sexual harassment and that it should contain an informal first step which would enable complaints to be dealt with sympathetically before matters get out of hand and that any complaint should be dealt with "from the perception of the person aggrieved" making sure that the procedure is known and that an accessible counselling service is available.

The European Commission describes sexual harassment as "an affront to the dignity of the individual and is one of the most offensive and demeaning experiences an employee can be subjected to".[90] In this connection following Recommendation 92/131 and the Code of Practice which was annexed thereto[91] the European Commission has launched a consultation with the social partners at European level on a "Framework Agreement" on sexual harassment, indicating that if the social partners are unable to agree on a collective agreement it will consider the possibility of a Directive.[92]

Although not passed specifically for dealing with workplace harassment, both the Public Order Act 1986, s.4A,[93] which created a criminal offence of intentional harassment and the Protection from Harassment Act 1997, intended primarily to deal with the problem of stalkers by prohibiting a person from pursing a course of conduct which he knows or ought to know amounts to harassment of another, are capable of extending to the workplace.

6.3.4.2   *Gender reassignment and sexual orientation*

Discrimination on grounds of sexual orientation is not specifically dealt with in domestic or E.C. legislation although the Code of Practice accompanying Commission Recommendation 91/131 on the protection of the dignity of women and men at work, refers, *inter alia*, to lesbians and gay men as being particularly vulnerable to harassment. The courts, however, have traditionally taken an orthodox approach towards the application of discrimination legislation in cases of gender as opposed to sex discrimination.

Gender reassignment

In *Rees v. United Kingdom*[94] it was said that "the term 'transsexual' is usually applied to those who while belonging physically to one sex, feel convinced that they belong to the other; they often seek to achieve a more integrated, unambiguous identity by undergoing medical treatment and surgical operations to adapt their physical characteristics to their psychological nature. . . ."

---

[89] [1995] I.R.L.R. 4, EAT.
[90] Consultation of Management and Labour on the Prevention of Sexual Harassment at Work, COM (96) 373 final.
[91] See M. Rubenstein "Sexual Harassment, European Commission Recommendation and Code of Practice", (1991) 21 I.L.J. 70–74.
[92] EOR No. 75, September/October 1997.
[93] Introduced by the Criminal Justice and Public Order Act 1994.
[94] (1987) 9 E.H.R.R. 56, ECHR: 36, 355.

In interpreting discrimination legislation in such circumstances the courts have taken the traditional view expressed in *Corbett v. Corbett*,[95] that a person's sex is fixed at birth and cannot be changed. This manifested itself in the decision in *Collins v. Wilkins & Chapman*[96] where an equal pay case failed because the chosen male comparator had been born a woman. However, changing attitudes are reflected in decisions of the European Court of Human Rights (ECHR) and the ECJ. In *B. v. France*[97] the ECHR, distinguishing its earlier judgments in *Rees*[98] and *Cossey*[99] found a violation of Article 8 of the Convention in that an applicant, who had undergone surgery to become a woman could not adopt a feminine name or change her status. Although more recently in *X, Y and Z v. United Kingdom*[1] the Court has adopted a more traditional approach.

In *P v. S and Cornwall County Council*[2] a general manager taken on as a male employee, notified her employer that she intended to undergo gender reassignment. During sick leave for initial surgical treatment she was given notice and not permitted to return from sick leave during which the final surgical stage of an assignment process took place. On a complaint for discrimination the industrial tribunal, following earlier authority in *E. A. White v. British Sugar Corp. Ltd*,[3] where it was held that the basis of comparison under the SDA was to be considered against a female to male transsexual. The tribunal in *P v. S* therefore held that the dismissal could not amount to sex discrimination under the SDA since that Act only applies to cases in which a man is treated differently from a woman and, under English law, ones sex is determined at birth: the applicant was therefore a man. However, the tribunal made a reference to the ECJ as to the interpretation of Directive 76/207[4], namely:

> "does the dismissal of a transsexual for a reason related to a gender reassignment constitute a breach of the Directive?" and "whether Article 3 of the Directive which refers to discrimination on grounds of sex prohibit(s) treatment of an employee on the grounds of the employee's transsexual state?"

Advocate General Tesauro in his opinion said that: ". . . I regard as obsolete the idea that the law should take into consideration, and protect, a woman who has suffered discrimination in comparison with a man, or vice versa, but denies that protection to those who are also *discriminated against*, again by reason of sex, merely because they fall outside the traditional man/woman classification . . . Articles 2(1) and 5(1) of Council Directive 76/207/EEC must be interpreted as precluding the dismissal of a transsexual on account of a change of sex".[5]

Following this, the ECJ held that the Equal Treatment Directive could not be confined simply to discrimination based on the fact that a person is one or other sex. They said that the Directive is the expression of the principle of equality, which is one of the fundamental principles of Community law. In view of its purpose and the fundamental nature of the rights which it seeks to safeguard, the scope of the Directive

---

[95] [1970] 2 W.L.R. 1306, HC.
[96] P. Skidmore (1997) 26 I.L.J. 53.
[97] (1993) 16 E.H.R.R. 1.
[98] n. 94 above.
[99] *Cossey v. U.K.* (1991) 13 E.H.R.R. 622: 801.
[1] *The Times*, April 23, 1997 (refusal to register post-operative transsexual as father of child born to female partner by artificial insemination by donor).
[2] C–1399/94 [1996] I.R.L.R. 347, ECJ.
[3] Case 37485/76 [1977] I.R.L.R. 121, IT.
[4] The applicant was employed in an educational establishment accepted to be an emanation of the State.
[5] p. 351.

also applies to discrimination based essentially, if not exclusively, on the sex of the person concerned. The person was to be treated as belonging to the sex to which they belonged before the reassignment. To tolerate such discrimination would be tantamount to a failure to respect the dignity and freedom to which he or she is entitled. Therefore, dismissal of a transsexual for a reason related to a gender reassignment must be regarded as contrary to Article 5(1) of Directive 76/207.

Following the decision in *P v. S*[6] it has been accepted that the Equal Treatment Directive, being directly effective as against an emanation of the State, applies against a Police Authority,[7] but pending amendment of domestic law the position of those in the private sector is dependent upon interpretation of the SDA.

In *Chessington World of Adventures Ltd v. Reed*,[8] following the giving of notice to her employer of an intention to undergo a change of identity from male to female, Ms Reed was subjected to a three year period of serious harassment resulting in a period of sick leave and her dismissal. On a complaint of discrimination the employer argued that the Directive was not directly effective and the SDA required a comparison to be made between persons of different biological sexes and could not, therefore, apply to discrimination on grounds of gender reassignment. The EAT, however, on the authority of *Marleasing SA v. La Comercial Internacional de Alimentacion SA*[9] and the House of Lords judgment in *Webb No. 2*,[10] said that the SDA should be interpreted consistently with Directive 76/207 and that it was discrimination on the grounds of sex to dismiss an employee on grounds of pregnancy in circumstances where no direct comparison could be made with a male employee. It followed, the EAT said, that not every act of discrimination under the Act was necessarily based on a comparison between a man and a woman and that the SDA could therefore be interpreted in line with the ruling in *P v. S*.[11] The court, therefore concluded that treating someone less favourably on the grounds of a declared intention to undergo gender reassignment was a sex-based act and that there was no requirement for a male/female comparison to be made.

The *DfEE* subsequently issued a consultation paper on proposals to legislate[12] to prohibit discrimination in employment on grounds of transsexualism.[13]

Sexual orientation

The EAT in *Smith v. Gardner Merchant Ltd*[14] held that there is no jurisdiction under the SDA to entertain a complaint of discrimination by reason of sexual orientation, which, it was held, is not discrimination on grounds of sex. In so deciding the Court noted the Court of Appeal judgment in *R. v. Ministry of Defence ex parte Smith and Grady; R. v. Admiralty Board of the Defence Council ex parte Lustig-Prean and Beckett*[15] in which it was held that to dismiss a man or to subject him to any other detriment on grounds of his homosexuality cannot be regarded as contrary to the Equal Treatment Directive.

[6] C–1399/94 [1996] I.R.L.R. 347, ECJ.
[7] *M v. Chief Constable of West Midlands Police* (08964/96), *People Management*, April 3, 1997.
[8] [1997] I.R.L.R. 556, EAT.
[9] (Case C–106/89) [1990] E.C.R. I–4135, ECJ.
[10] [1995] I.R.L.R. 645, HL.
[11] C–1399/94 [1996] I.R.L.R. 347, ECJ.
[12] By Regulations made under the ECA 1972 to amend the SDA 1975.
[13] *Consultation Paper: legislation regarding discrimination on ground of transsexualism in employment,* January 1998.
[14] [1996] I.R.L.R. 342 , EAT.
[15] [1996] I.R.L.R. 100, CA.

In *Smith and Grady; Lustig-Prean and Beckett*[16] a judicial review challenge was made against the Ministry of Defence policy of dismissing from the armed services anyone of homosexual orientation—anyone sexually attracted to a member of their own sex—irrespective of whether they were engaged in homosexual conduct or remained celibate. In the Court of Appeal Sir Thomas Bingham M.R. said:

> "I find nothing whatever in the Treaty of Rome or in the Equal Treatment Directive which suggests that the draftsmen of those instruments were addressing their minds in any way whatever to problems of discrimination on grounds of sexual orientation. Had it been intended to regulate discrimination on that ground it could easily have been done, but to my mind it plainly was not. It is true that the Commission's code of practice, drawn up many years after the Treaty and the Directive, makes reference to sexual orientation, but it seems to me quite plain that this code is directed to banning unacceptable behaviour in the workplace and not to regulating employment policy in relation to sexual orientation." *per* Sir Thomas Bingham M.R.

> *R. v. Ministry of Defence ex parte Smith and Grady; R. v. Admiralty Board of the Defence Council ex parte Lustig-Prean and Beckett* [1996] I.R.L.R. 100 at 105, CA.

The Ministry of Defence maintains that the ban is necessary because homosexuality is "incompatible with military service" and that if it were lifted it would "damage morale and unit effectiveness". Nevertheless, a further challenge to the ban is being perused in *R. v. Secretary of State for Defence ex parte Perkins*.[17] Encouraged by the Opinion of the Advocate-General and the judgment of the ECJ in *P v. S*, Lightman J. referred to the ECJ the question:

> "Must the requirement in A.2(1) of Council Directive 76/207 . . . that there shall be 'no discrimination on the grounds of sex either directly or indirectly by reference in particular to marital or family status' be interpreted as including discrimination based on a person's sexual orientation."

Lightman J. expressed the view that

> "After the decision in the *Cornwall case*, it is scarcely possible to limit the application of the Directive to gender discrimination as was held in the *Smith* case, and there must be a real prospect that the European Court will take the further courageous step to extend protection to those of homosexual orientation . . . .".

> *R. v. Secretary of State for Defence ex parte Perkins* (Case C–168/97) [1997] I.R.L.R. 297 at 303, HC.

The outcome of the reference in *Perkins*, although factually different, is less certain following the decision of the ECJ in *Grant v. South West Trains Ltd*[18] where travel concessions granted to spouses and opposite sex partners were not available to same sex partners. Following a reference to the ECJ the Advocate General delivered an

---

[16] *ibid.*
[17] Case C–168/97 [1997] I.R.L.R. 297, HC.
[18] Case C–249/96 [1998] I.R.L.R. 206, ECJ.

opinion that the travel concession, being "pay" fell within Article 119 and that following the decision in *P v. S*, Article 119 should likewise preclude discrimination based on gender. The ECJ, however, whilst confirming that travel concessions were "pay" and therefore the issue fell for consideration under Article 119, distinguished *P v. S* and held that a condition which applies in the same way to female and male workers cannot be regarded as discrimination based on sex within Article 119. The Court said that Community law does not cover discrimination based on sexual orientation, although it observed that the Treaty of Amsterdam provides for the insertion in the E.C. Treaty of an Article 6a which will allow action to be taken to prohibit discrimination based, *inter alia*, on sexual orientation.

6.3.4.3   *Employer dress codes*

The question arises as to whether, in applying a conventional dress code which reflects stereotypical assumptions of appearance an employer is either directly discriminating, in terms of less favourable treatment, or is indirectly discriminating in applying a requirement or condition.

In *Schmidt v. Austicks Bookshops Ltd*[19] the applicant was dismissed for refusing to obey the employer's dress code in that she wore a skirt, and not trousers, and an overall. She complained that the requirement to wear a skirt and not trousers constituted discrimination under the SDA 1975, s.1(1)(a). Phillips J. said that it was necessary to take a broad view: there were restrictions for men too, albeit more limited ones, and because men and women were different, the rules in the two cases were not the same.

The matter came before the Court of Appeal in *Smith v. Safeway plc*[20] where the employer had a dress code which required that for male staff their hair should be tidy and not below shirt collar length with no unconventional hairstyles or colouring, with a rule for female staff that hair should be tidy, with shoulder-length hair clipped back and no unconventional styles or colouring. The applicant, a male delicatessen assistant who was dismissed because his ponytail grew too long to go under his hat, complained that he had been discriminated against. The EAT, Pill J dissenting, distinguished *Schmidt*[21] drawing a distinction between rules governing the wearing of jewellery and dress which are of a transient nature and those governing hair length which extend beyond the workplace. The Court of Appeal, however, dismissed this argument, and in allowing the appeal adopted the reasoning of Phillips J. in *Schmidt*. Whilst acknowledging that the sexes had been treated differently it was held that this did not amount to less favourable treatment because the code applied and was enforced equally as between male and female staff, albeit that the rules were different as between the sexes. Phillips L.J. said that there is an important distinction between discrimination between the sexes and discrimination against one or other of the sexes and that it is the latter which is unlawful. Adopting the "package approach" what mattered was that rules applied to both sexes, and they did not fall to be considered on a "garment by garment" basis.

The same approach was adopted by the EAT in *Burrett v. West Birmingham Health Authority*[22] in which it was held that a female nurse was not "treated less favourably" by being required to wear a cap when her male colleague was not required to do so, since

---

[19] [1977] I.R.L.R. 360, EAT.
[20] [1996] I.R.L.R. 456, CA.
[21] [1977] I.R.L.R. 360, EAT.
[22] [1994] I.R.L.R. 7, EAT.

the requirement to wear a uniform applied equally to male and female nurses: albeit that the uniform differed.

As the claim here is one of direct discrimination there is no defence of justification: the burden is on the employer to show that the treatment is not less favourable. In doing so Peter Gibson L.J. in *Smith* accepted reliance on the wish of the employer "to present a conventional image for the sound commercial reason that that is what its customers wanted". As pointed out by Skidmore (1997)[23] this reliance on the employer's motive "should have had no place in this judgment" in view of the House of Lords' decisions in both *R. v. Birmingham CC ex parte Equal Opportunities Commission*[24] and *James v. Eastleigh BC*,[25] that the motive of the discriminator has no place in deciding whether discrimination occurred.

If the dress rule is interpreted as a "requirement or condition" for the purpose of the SDA 1975/RRA 1976, s.1(1)(b) so as to be indirect discrimination, the same result is achieved in that, as demonstrated in *Johnson-Croft v. Mezzo Ltd*,[26] the fact that it is strictly enforced for all staff and is imposed to maintain a specific image is capable of amounting to objective justification for the purposes of section 1(1)(b)(ii).

It is perhaps difficult to reconcile the acceptance of rules which reinforce conventional standards of appearance, with both the consequences of the ECJ decision in *P v. S* and the subsequent interpretation of the SDA in *Chessington World of Adventures Ltd v. Reed*,[27] and the line of cases which demonstrates the refusal of the courts to accept behaviour which reinforces conventional attitudes towards the role in society of one sex or the other, as demonstrated in *Horsey v. Dyfed CC*[28] and confirmed by the Court of Appeal in *Skyrail Oceanic Ltd v. Coleman*.[29] In this respect the attention of the court in *Smith v. Safeway plc* was drawn to the decision in *Rewcastle v. Safeway*[30] where the industrial tribunal said:

> ". . . we question whether a policy which is designed to mirror 'conventional' differences between the sexes can be reconciled with the underlying rationale of the sex discrimination which is to challenge traditional assumptions about sexes, not only as to their roles in society and the tasks they perform, but also as to their appearance and dress."

To which Phillips L.J. merely said:

> "I am unaware of any justification for those last few words. I can accept that one of the objects of the prohibition of sex discrimination was to relieve the sexes from unequal treatment resulting from conventional attitudes, but I do not believe that this renders discriminatory an appearance code which applies a standard of what is conventional."[31]

6.3.5 Genuine occupational qualifications

Both the SDA 1975, s.7 and the RRA 1976, s.5 provide that discriminatory acts are not unlawful where there is a genuine occupational qualification (GOQ). An employer is

[23] P. Skidmore "Sex, gender and comparators in employment discrimination" (1997) 26 I.L.J. 51–61.
[24] [1989] I.R.L.R. 173, HL.
[25] [1990] I.R.L.R. 288, HL.
[26] Case No. 2202467/96, I.R.L.B. 586, February 1998, p. 11.
[27] [1997] I.R.L.R. 556, EAT.
[28] [1982] I.C.R. 755, EAT.
[29] [1981] I.R.L.R. 398, CA.
[30] Case 22482/89, IT.
[31] p. 459.

therefore permitted to discriminate on sexual or racial grounds only in the following areas:

- by SDA s.7(1)(a), RRA s.5(1)(a)—in the arrangements the employer makes for the purpose of determining who should be offered employment, s.6(1)(a)/ s.4(1)(a);

- by SDA s.7(1)(a), RRA s.5(1)(a)—by refusing or deliberately omitting to offer the job, s.6(1)(c)/s.4(1)(c);

- by SDA s.7(1)(b), RRA s.5(1)(b)—in the way the employer affords the employee access to opportunities for promotion, transfer or training, or to any other benefits, facilities or services, or by refusing or deliberately omitting to offer such opportunities, s.6(2)(a)/s.4(2)(b)

and then only for the reasons listed in the SDA 1975, s.7(2)(a)–(h) and the RRA 1976, s.5(2)(a)–(d), even where only some of the contractual duties fall within those reasons. The reasons contained in the SDA 1975 were amended by the SDA 1986 following successful proceedings brought by the Commission[32] to remove the blanket exemption of working in a private household, which was replaced with a more selective private household exemption now contained in section 7(2)(ba). The burden is on the employee to show that discrimination has occurred, it is then for the employer to show that being a particular sex or racial group is a genuine occupational qualification for the job.

By the SDA 1975, s.7(4), the majority of the reasons in section 7(2), and in the RRA 1976 by section 5(4) all the reasons in section 5(2), do not apply in relation to the filling of a vacancy at a time when the employer already has male employees; who are capable of carrying out the duties and whom it would be reasonable to employ on those duties and whose numbers are sufficient to meet the employer's likely requirements without undue inconvenience. In *Lasertop Ltd v. Webster*[33] when a man responded to an advertisement and was told that the posts involved were for women only it was claimed that as the position was in a women-only health club being a woman was a genuine occupational qualification within section 7(2)(b)(ii)—that the job needs to be held by a woman to preserve decency or privacy because she is likely to do work in circumstances where women might reasonably object to the presence of a man because they are in a state of undress or are using sanitary facilities, and that section 7(4) did not apply because at the time of recruiting the club had not opened. Expressing the view that they were conscious that their construction of these provisions "may lead to an apparent lacuna in the protection against discrimination afforded to job applicants where a business is being set up" the EAT allowed the employer's appeal on the bases that *"already"* in section 7(2)(b)(ii) involved a factual, not hypothetical question, and at the time of recruiting the employer had no employees at the particular club for which he was recruiting.

On the other hand in *Etam plc v. Rowan*[34] the defence was rejected where the man, as a sales assistant, would be required to visit women in the fitting rooms and on occasion to take measurements because these aspects of the job could have been carried out by one of the 16 other members of staff. A similar reasoning prevailed in

[32] Case C–165/82 [1984] I.C.R. 192, ECJ.
[33] [1997] I.R.L.R. 498, EAT.
[34] [1989] I.R.L.R. 150, EAT.

Wylie v. Dee[35] to the requirement to take inside leg measurements: it did not have to be done by a man in order to preserve decency and privacy, and in any event if an objection were raised there were other assistants who could be called upon.

The GOQ defence cannot be invoked in a claim for marital discrimination or victimisation.

6.3.6 Victimisation

The SDA 1975, s.4, RRA 1976, s.2 and DDA 1995, s.55 contain provisions in similar terms in that it is unlawful discrimination to victimise a person by treating them less favourably for doing a protected act, provided for in (a)–(d) and covering the bringing of proceedings, giving evidence or information in connection with proceedings under any of the Acts. The SDA 1975 extends these provisions to the EqPA 1970.

These provisions are narrowly interpreted as demonstrated in *Nagarajan and Swiggs v. London Regional Transport.*[36] The applicant claimed that he had suffered discrimination under the RRA 1976, s.4(1)(a)—in the "arrangements" made for determining who should be offered employment and was victimised contrary to section 2(1)(a) because he had previously brought complaints alleging discrimination. The CA held that in order for a victimisation claim under section 4(1)(a) to succeed it must be shown that the person alleged to have carried out the victimisation was also the person who had made the "arrangements" for determining who should be offered employment. The Court of Appeal distinguished *Brennan v. J.H. Dewhurst Ltd,*[37] which was a case on similar facts, but brought as one of direct discrimination where this restrictive interpretation did not apply. This means that an employer may escape liability if one person makes the "arrangements" for recruitment, whilst another, in carrying out those "arrangements", carries out the act of victimisation.

Continuing with this restrictive approach, this time in connection with the SDA 1975, in *Waters v. Commissioner of Police*[38] a female police officer had made a complaint of harassment against a fellow officer as a result of which she alleged that her name had been removed from a list of officers trained for special duties, an act she claimed was victimisation under section 4(1)(d). In rejecting the complaint under section 4(1)(d) the Court of Appeal said that it was necessary to construe the words literally and in doing so said that the alleged act of discrimination had not been done by the Commissioner and was not one for which he could be vicariously liable under section 41 because the alleged perpetrator was not acting in the course of his employment. The industrial tribunal had not applied the test in *Jones v. Tower Boot Co. Ltd,*[39] nevertheless, the Court of Appeal held that: "it is inconceivable, . . ., that any tribunal applying the *Tower Boot* test could find that the alleged assault was committed in the course of T's employment".

6.3.7 Proving discrimination

With the burden of proof lying on the applicant, he has to show either direct discrimination within the SDA 1975 or RRA 1976, s.1(1)(a), DDA 1995, s.5(1),

---

[35] [1978] I.R.L.R. 103, IT.
[36] [1998] I.R.L.R. 73, CA/IDS Brief 606/February 1998, pp. 6–8.
[37] [1984] I.C.R. 52 EAT.
[38] [1997] I.R.L.R. 589, CA.
[39] [1997] I.R.L.R. 168, CA.

indirect within the SDA 1975 or RRA 1976, s.1(1)(b) s.3(1)(b) or victimisation. This is not an easy burden to discharge but there are statutory procedures in place to assist the applicant to elicit information from the employer in the form of a "question and answer" procedure[40] and the applicant may apply for an order of discovery. In addition, in cases brought under the RRA 1976 it was held in *King v. Great Britain-China Centre*[41] that in certain circumstances tribunals may draw inferences of discrimination. In *Zafar v. Glasgow City Council*[42] Lord Browne-Wilkinson approved the guidance given by Neill L.J. in the *King* case and said that these should apply both to cases of sex and race discrimination:

"(1) It is for the applicant who complains of racial discrimination to make out his or her case. Thus, if the applicant does not prove the case on the balance of probabilities, he or she will fail.

(2) It is important to bear in mind that it is unusual to find direct evidence of racial discrimination. Few employers would be prepared to admit such discrimination even to themselves. In some cases the discrimination will not be ill-intentioned but merely based on an assumption [that] 'he or she would not have fitted in.'

(3) The outcome of the case will therefore usually depend on what inferences it is proper to draw from the primary facts found by the tribunal. These inferences can include, in appropriate case, any inferences that it is just and equitable to draw in accordance with s.65(2)(b) of the Act of 1976 from an evasive or equivocal reply to a questionnaire.

(4) Though there will be some cases where, for example, the non-selection of the applicant for a post or for promotion is clearly not on racial grounds, a finding of discrimination and a finding of a difference in race will often point to the possibility of racial discrimination. In such circumstances, the tribunal will look to the employer for an explanation. If no explanation is then put forward, or if the tribunal considers the explanation to be inadequate or unsatisfactory, it will be legitimate for the tribunal to infer that the discrimination was on racial grounds. This is not a matter of law but, as May L.J. put it in *Noone,* 'almost common sense'.

(5) It is unnecessary and unhelpful to introduce the concept of a shifting evidential burden of proof. At the conclusion of all the evidence, the tribunal should make findings as to the primary fact and draw such inferences as they consider proper from those fact. They should then reach a conclusion on the balance of probabilities, bearing in mind the difficulties which face a person who complains of unlawful discrimination and the fact that it is for the complainant to prove his or her case." *per* Neill L.J.

King v. Great Britain-China Centre [1991] I.R.L.R. 513 at 518 CA.

Lord Browne-Wilkinson said that remarks in *Khanna v. Ministry of Defence*[43] and *Chattopadhyay v. Headmaster of Holloway School*[44] that inferences "should" be drawn was "putting the matter too high" and should not be followed.

---

[40] Sex Discrimination (Questions and Replies) Order 1975 (S.I. 1975 No. 2048).
[41] [1991] I.R.L.R. 513, CA.
[42] [1998] I.R.L.R. 36, HL.
[43] [1981] I.R.L.R. 331, EAT.
[44] [1981] I.R.L.R. 487, EAT.

In so far as European law is concerned it appears from *Handels og Kantorfnktionaererne Forbund I Danmark v. Dansk Arbejdegiverforening (acting for Danfoss)*,[45] an equal pay case, that in the absence of transparency the burden of proof will lie on the employer to show that his pay practice is not discriminatory. Directive 97/80 on the burden of proof in cases of sex discrimination has been adopted to "ensure effective enforcement of the principles of equal treatment". It proposes that Member States should take measures to ensure that the burden of proof transfers to the employer where the complainant establishes a "fact from which it may be presumed that there has been direct or indirect discrimination". It will then be for the employer "to prove that there has been no breach of the principle of equal treatment". Adopted under the Agreement on Social Policy annexed to the Maastricht Treaty on European Union, and is therefore not applicable to the United Kingdom because of the United Kingdom "opt-out", neither is it included in the extension directives, extending the works council and parental leave Directives to the United Kingdom. However, it is proposed to extend the burden of proof Directive, along with the Directive on part-time workers by a separate extension Directive, which will then mean implementation by January 1, 2001. It is arguable the practice adopted by tribunals through the decision in *King* already conforms with the Directive, but that an amending instrument will be necessary in so far as direct discrimination is concerned.[46]

6.3.8 Enforcement, remedies and procedure

Unlike the EqPA 1970, discrimination legislation does not operate on the contract, thus in *Leighton v. Michael*[47] the EAT said that there was nothing in the statute or in public policy to prevent an applicant proceeding with a claim of sexual harassment and victimisation when the contract was tainted with illegality. However, in *Hall v. Woolston Hall Leisure Ltd*[48] although the EAT confirmed an award of injury to feelings, it declined to make an award for loss of earnings in such a situation since this claim was based on a contract of employment performed illegally to the knowledge of the claimant and would offend a basic principle of the administration of justice.

A complaint under the SDA 1975 and RRA 1976 must be made to an industrial tribunal "before the end of the period of three months beginning when the act complained of was done"[49] and unlike proceedings for unfair dismissal there is no requirement for a minimum service qualification. Provision is made, the SDA 1975, s.76(6) and the RRA 1976, s.68(7), whereby any continuing act of discrimination extending over a period shall be treated as done at the end of the period, and an omission as done when the person in question decides upon it.[50] In *Owusu v. London Fire and Civil Defence Authority*[51] the EAT held that an act extends over a period if it "takes the form of some policy, rule or practice, in accordance with which decisions are taken from time to time" as distinguished from the doing of an act with continuing consequences. So that in *Calder v. James Finlay Corp. Ltd*[52] a "men only" rule

[45] Case C–109/88 [1989] I.R.L.R. 532, ECJ.
[46] EOR, No. 76, November/December 1997 pp. 37–39. See para. 2.9 re extension of part-time workers directive and 1.12 re working time directive.
[47] [1996] I.R.L.R. 67, EAT.
[48] I.R.L.B. 591, April 1998, p. 14.
[49] SDA 1975, s.76, RRA 1976, s.68.
[50] SDA 1975, s.76(6), RRA 1976, s.68(7).
[51] [1995] I.R.L.R. 574, EAT.
[52] [1989] I.R.L.R. 55, CA.

excluding women from a subsidised mortgage was held to be a continuing discriminatory policy which extended throughout employment and therefore fell to be treated under the SDA 1975, s.76(6)(b) as if done at the end of the period of employment. Likewise in *Barclays Bank Ltd v. Kapur*[53] exclusion of overseas service for pension purposes for ethnic minority, but not expatriate workers was upheld by the House of Lords to be continuing discrimination in terms of access to benefits.

There is a fine line between a policy, rule or practice and the doing of an act with continuing consequences: for example, in *Rovenska v. General Medical Council*[54] a Czech doctor who was repeatedly refused registration as a medical practitioner was held not to be out of time in presenting his case since time ran from the refusal of each application. Whereas in *Cast v. Croydon College*[55] a request to job-share or to work part-time which was refused, but which was repeated on a number of occasions, was held for the purposes of section 76(1) to be done on the first refusal since, in a circular argument the EAT said that section 76(1) specifies that the three months begins "when the act complained of was done": Ms Cast's argument was, of course, that it was "done" on the occasion of the last refusal.[56] An occasion of a single act with continuing consequences is more clearly demonstrated in *Amies v. ILEA*[57] where there was a refusal to promote.

The tribunal has a discretion to hear a case out of time and *British Coal v. Keeble*,[58] a case on similar facts to those in *Biggs v. Somerset County Council*,[59] the EAT considered the wording of the SDA 1975, s.76(5),[60] which permits out of time cases where it is "just and equitable" to do so as compared with that of the ERA 1996, s.111 applicable in the *Biggs* case. It was held that it was open to the tribunal to find that it was "just and equitable" to permit the case out of time following the decision in *R. v. SS for Employment ex parte EOC*[61] notwithstanding that the reason was the applicant's mistake as to their legal position.

Where a complaint is upheld the tribunal has power to make one (or more) of the following orders such as it considers it "just and equitable"[62]:

- A declaration;

- Compensation; calculation of compensation for unlawful discrimination can cover past and future losses and loss of pension rights. When calculating future loss the EAT in *Ministry of Defence v. Cannock*[63] stressed that speculation as to what would have happened should be assessed in "a broad and sensible manner" and not as matters of fact to be decided on the balance of probabilities.

In *Marshall v. Southampton and South-West Hampshire Area Health Authority (No. 2)*[64] the ECJ held that it is contrary to Article 6 of Directive 76/207 for national

[53] [1991] I.C.R. 208, HL.
[54] [1997] I.R.L.R. 367, CA.
[55] [1997] I.R.L.R. 14, EAT.
[56] This decision was reversed on appeal. [1998] I.R.L.R. 318, CA.
[57] [1977] I.C.R. 308, EAT.
[58] [1997] I.R.L.R. 336, EAT.
[59] [1996] I.R.L.R. 203, CA.
[60] Corresponding provisions in identical terms are contained in the RRA 1976, s.68(6).
[61] [1994] I.R.L.R. 176, HL.
[62] SDA 1975, s.65, RRA 1976, s.56, DDA 1995, s.8(2).
[63] [1994] I.R.L.R. 509, EAT.
[64] Case C–271/91 [1993] I.R.L.R. 445, ECJ.

provisions to lay down an upper limit on the amount of compensation recoverable by a victim of discrimination which must have a real and dissuasive effect on the employer, and that an award of interest is an essential component of compensation. As a result the Sex Discrimination and Equal Pay (Remedies) Regulations 1993[65] removed the statutory maximum on awards of compensation and enabled tribunals to award interest. This was mirrored for cases coming within the RRA 1976 in the Race Relations (Remedies) Act 1994 and Race Relations (Interest on Awards) Regulations 1994[66] which enables interest to be awarded from the date of the decision. In addition, the Industrial Tribunals (Interest) Order 1990 makes interest payable on awards from the day after the day of decision unless paid within 14 days. The DDA 1995 does not provide for a maximum limit on compensation awards.

Under both the SDA 1975 and RRA 1976 acts of unintentional indirect discrimination did not attract an award for compensation, as demonstrated in *MacMillan v. Edinburgh Voluntary Organisations Council*[67]—the DDA 1995 does not extend to acts of indirect discrimination. However, following *Marshall (No. 2)*[68] which demonstrated that the Directive contained no such limitation, the position was changed by the Sex Discrimination and Equal Pay (Miscellaneous Amendments) Regulations 1996[69] with regard to sex discrimination, which inserted into the SDA 1975, s.65(1)(1B).[70] This enables a tribunal to make an award in a case of indirect unintentional discrimination where the respondent proves that the requirement or condition was not applied with the intention of treating the complainant unfavourably and it would not be just and equitable only to grant another remedy. The case law on the meaning of "intention" is still therefore relevant and in *J.H. Walker v. Hussain*[71] a policy, in a company with a large Muslim workforce, that no holidays would be taken over a period covered by the Islamic festival of Eid, was held to be indirectly discriminatory under the RRA 1976, s.1(1)(b). As to whether this was intentional, Mummery J. said that intention signifies the state of mind of the person who, when he does the relevant act, *wants* to bring about the unfavourable treatment and *knows* that the prohibited result will follow. Since the company knew that the rule would adversely affect Muslim employees but went ahead anyway it was held that the tribunal were entitled to infer that they wanted to bring about the unfavourable treatment.

A broad view was adopted in *London Underground Ltd v. Edwards*[72] where a change in working patterns was held to be indirectly discriminatory to the applicant, a single parent. The tribunal was entitled to draw inferences from the fact that the new arrangements were introduced with the knowledge that they would adversely affect the applicant, a single parent. As Bourn (1996) points out, if an employer goes ahead with applying a requirement having had the adverse impact drawn to his attention and without holding a different view, liability to pay compensation will arise where the requirement is subsequently found to be unlawful.

Unlike compensation for unfair dismissal, for sex, race and disability discrimination, compensation may include a sum for injury and hurt to feelings arising directly from

---

[65] S.I. 1993 No. 2798. Applies to all awards of compensation from November 22, 1993 (date of commencement).
[66] S.I. 1994 No. 1748.
[67] [1995] I.R.L.R. 536, EAT.
[68] Case C–271/91 [1993] I.R.L.R. 445, ECJ.
[69] S.I. 1996 No. 438.
[70] Effective March 25, 1996.
[71] [1996] I.R.L.R. 11, EAT.
[72] [1995] I.R.L.R. 355, EAT.

the act of discrimination whether or not compensation is awarded under any other head.[73] In *Alexander v. Home Office*[74] the Court of Appeal said that damages should not be minimal, because that would trivialise or diminish respect for the public policy to which the Act gives effect, but awards should be restrained. Following the lifting of the statutory maximum it has been unclear as to whether cases decided before then, such as *Noone v. North West Thames Regional Health Authority*,[75] where it was said that £3,000[76] for injury to feelings was at the "top end of the bracket", are still authoritative guidance, although in *Orlando v. Didcot Power Station Sports & Social Club*[77] it was said that the abolition of the compensation limit in discrimination cases does not mean that awards for injury to feelings must necessarily be higher than before the limit was removed. In *Armitage and H.M. Prison Service v. Johnson*,[78] which involved "a campaign of appalling treatment", the EAT approved an award of £20,000 for injury to feelings and distinguished *Noone* both because the facts were different and because "We think the award . . . might well have been higher had there been no statutory limit". Nevertheless, despite the severity of the incidents and the campaign of harassment Smith J. said: "Suffice it to say that although we think that the award is on the high side, we do not think it so high that we should interfere".[79]

Aggravated damages, which are compensatory, are a recognised head of damages in cases of race and sex discrimination and are appropriate when the sense of injury to the employee is justifiably heightened by the manner in which or motive with which the employer acted: where the defendant "may have behaved in a high-handed, malicious, insulting or aggressive manner".[80] In *Armitage*,[81] confirming that aggravated damages are available for the statutory torts, £7,500 was held not to be "so high as to be outside the bracket of reasonable awards" taken that the employer's investigation added to the injury suffered instead of offering the remedy it should have and the greatest mitigation, an apology, was never offered.

Despite the Court of Appeal judgment in *Alexander v. Home Office*[82] to the contrary, in *AB v. South West Water Services Ltd*,[83] a public nuisance case, the Court of Appeal held that, exemplary damages, which punish the wrongdoer, are only available in respect of torts which existed prior to 1964. They are, therefore, not available in discrimination cases. However, the Law Commission has recommended that people who suffer "deliberate and outrageous" breaches of their rights under discrimination legislation should be entitled to exemplary damages.[84]

Although discrimination cases are not subject to the Recoupment Regulations (see 7.5.5.2 below) the common law principle of mitigation applies and the method of calculation adopted by the Court of Appeal in *Ministry of Defence v. Wheeler*[85] in connection with discrimination cases was approved in *Digital Equipment Co. Ltd v. Clements (No. 2)*.[86] The tribunal has powers, when a complaint is well founded, to

---

[73] SDA 1975, s.66(4), RRA 1976, s.57(4), DDA 1995, s.8(4).
[74] [1988] I.R.L.R. 190, CA.
[75] [1988] I.R.L.R. 195, CA.
[76] In *Armitage v. Johnson* it was pointed out that this would be £4,250 "at today's values".
[77] [1996] I.R.L.R. 262, EAT.
[78] [1997] I.R.L.R. 162, EAT.
[79] at 166.
[80] *Alexander v. Home Office* [1988] I.R.L.R. 190, CA *per* May L.J. at 193.
[81] [1997] I.R.L.R. 162, EAT.
[82] [1988] I.R.L.R. 190, CA.
[83] [1993] 1 All E.R. 609, CA.
[84] *Aggravated, Exemplary and Restitutionary Damages*, Law Commission Report No. 247, December 15, 1997.
[85] [1998] I.R.L.R. 23, CA.
[86] [1998] I.R.L.R. 134, CA.

make a recommendation "that the respondent take within a specified period action appearing to the tribunal to be practicable for the purposes of obviating or reducing the adverse effect on the complainant of any act of discrimination to which the complaint relates".[87] However, the DDA 1995 requires the action to be "reasonable" as opposed to "practicable".

As an example, in *Price v. Civil Service Commission (No. 2)*[88] a recommendation was made namely:

> "That both respondents [Civil Service Commission and Whitley Council] use their best endeavours to agree in time for implementation in the competition year of 1980 what upper age limit if any, other than that which presently exists, ought to be applied by the first respondent to candidates for direct entry to Executive Officer posts in the Civil Service."

If an employer fails to comply with a recommendation "without reasonable justification", by section 65(3) the tribunal has a discretion, where a compensation order was made under s.65(1)(b), to increase the amount of compensation such as "they think it just and equitable to do so", or to make a compensation order if one was not made.

6.4   STATUTORY COMMISSIONS AND COUNCIL

6.4.1   The Equal Opportunities Commission (EOC) and Commission for Racial Equality (CRE)

The EOC and CRE are statutory bodies set up under the SDA 1975, s.53 and RRA 1976, s.43 with the duty to:

- work towards the elimination of discrimination;

- whilst the EOC has a duty to promote equality of opportunity between men and women generally; the CRE has a duty to promote equality of opportunity and good relations between persons of different racial groups; and

- to keep under review the working of the relevant Act, the remit of the EOC encompassing the EqPA 1970 and health and safety legislation, in so far as provisions that require men and women to be treated differently (s.55), and submit to the Secretary of State proposals for amendment.

The rules governing the composition of the EOC are contained in Schedule 3, and its duties are contained in Part VI of the 1995 Act. The powers and duties of the CRE are similar and are contained in Part VII of the 1976 Act.

There is a duty to publish an annual report to include a general survey of developments of matters within the scope of the Commissions' duties[89] and a power to undertake or assist, either financially or otherwise, research and educational activities in pursuit of the relevant duties generally.[90] By section 44 of the 1976 Act, the CRE

---

[87] SDA 1975, s.65(1)(c), RRA 1976, s.56(1)(c), DDA 1995, s.8(2)(c).
[88] [1978] I.R.L.R. 3, IT.
[89] SDA 1975, s.56, RRA 1976, s.46.
[90] SDA 1975, s.54, RRA 1976, s.45.

has a power, not mirrored in the SDA 1975 for the EOC, to give financial or other assistance to any organisation concerned with the promotion of equality of opportunity and good relations between persons of different racial groups.

Both Commissions have a power[91] to issue codes of practice at their discretion, containing practical guidance for the purpose of the elimination of discrimination and/or the promotion of equality of opportunity in employment. The procedure to be followed is set down and it is provided that any code issued under the relevant section is admissible in evidence in any proceedings before an industrial tribunal and any provision that is relevant may be taken into consideration.[92] Under this power the EOC has published *Code of Practice for the Elimination of Discrimination on the Grounds of Sex and Marriage and the Promotion of Equality of Opportunity in Employment* (1985) and *Code of Practice on Equal Pay* (1997). The CRE has published *Code of Practice for the Elimination of Racial Discrimination and the Promotion of Equality of Opportunity in Employment* (1983). In *Mooyart v. Sakura Finance International Ltd*[93] the tribunal said: "It is . . . reprehensible that no attention whatsoever has been given by the respondents to the provisions of the Code of Practice on race equality".

Both Commissions have a power, either on their own volition, or at the request of the Secretary of State, to conduct, under the terms set out in the Acts, formal investigations for purposes connected with their duties, with a power to obtain information for this purpose, and to make recommendations.[94] Likewise, both Commissions have a power to help and assist aggrieved persons.[95] The Commissions have a discretion as to whether to offer assistance, they are bound to consider applications for assistance (by s.66(3)–(4) the CRE must respond to a request for assistance), and may grant it if the case raises a question of principle or it is unreasonable to expect the claimant to deal with the case unaided because of either the complexity of the case, the applicant's position in relation to the respondent, or any other matter, and that assistance may range from advice to "any other form of assistance which the Commission may consider appropriate"[96]

It is unlawful to publish or cause to be published any advertisement which indicates an intention to discriminate, and the EOC and CRE have sole jurisdiction to bring proceedings under this section,[97] as well as in cases of instructions and pressure to discriminate.

In pursuing its statutory function the Commissions have *locus standi* to bring judicial review proceedings and the EOC has successfully resorted to this, most notably in *R. v. SS for Employment ex parte EOC*[98] in successfully challenging the hours thresholds in unfair dismissal and redundancy payment legislation.

6.4.2 National Disability Council (NDC)

The DDA 1995, s.50 lays down a duty for the setting up of a National Disability Council and Schedule 5 deals with membership, terms of office and remuneration of

---

[91] SDA 1975, s.56A, RRA 1976, s.47.
[92] SDA 1975, s.56A(10), RRA 1976, s.47(10).
[93] Case No. 23565/95 EOR Discrimination Case Law Digest, No.33, Autumn 1997.
[94] SDA 1975, ss.57–60, RRA 1976, ss.48–51.
[95] SDA 1975, ss.74–75, RRA 1976, ss.65–66.
[96] SDA 1975, s.75(2)(e), RRA 1976, s.66(2)(e).
[97] SDA 1975, s.72, RRA 1976, s.63.
[98] [1994] I.R.L.R. 176, HL.

Council members. The duty of the Council is to advise the Secretary of State either on its own initiative, or when asked to do so by the Secretary of State, on:

- the elimination of discrimination against disabled persons and persons who have had a disability;

- measures which are likely to reduce or eliminate such discrimination; and

- matters related to the operation of the Act or provisions made under the Act.

This distinguishes the Council from the EOC and CRE in that there is no power, and section 50(4) specifically excludes a power to investigate any complaint which is the subject of any proceedings under the Act. By section 51 the Council has power to issue codes of practice, but this power varies from the corresponding provisions for the EOC and CRE in that the Council has no discretion, but must merely respond to a request from the Secretary of State and by section 53 the Secretary of State has a power himself to issue codes of practice. A code issued under either procedure being admissible in evidence in any proceedings under the Act.

In provisions which again distinguish the Council and severely limit its power, by section 50(9)(a)–(b) it is not empowered to give advice on its own initiative on the operation of any provision or of arrangements made under: the Disabled Persons (Employment) Acts 1944–58; Employment and Training Act 1973; Employment Rights Act 1996, section 2(3) of the Enterprise and New Towns (Scotland) Act 1990 or on matters related to the operation of the 1995 Act (or of any provisions made under it) in so far as they arise under Part II of the Act, the employment provisions, under sections 53 to 54, codes of practice prepared by the Secretary of State, under section 56, statutory discrimination questionnaire in employment cases, or under section 61, arrangements for the provision of supported employment.

The Council is therefore purely an advisory body with none of the powers of the Commissions to provide assistance or advice to complainants, to conduct formal investigations into suspected acts or patterns of discrimination or to bring proceedings on behalf of complainants or on its own initiative or to review and monitor the operation of the legislation[99] In its first annual report[1] the NDC called on the Government to set up a Disability Rights Commission with statutory powers to help disabled people enforce their rights, following which the Minister of Equal Opportunities announced the setting up of a Disability Task Force to examine achieving full civil rights for disabled people with the establishment of a Disability Rights Commission with a role analogous to that of the EOC and CRE.[2] In addition, the small firm exemption contained in section 7 of the Act is the subject of a review[3] by the Task Force.

6.5 REFORM AND SUMMARY

In their report *Equal Pay for Men and Women, Strengthening the Acts* the EOC highlighted an "urgent need to establish a legal framework and procedures which

---

[99] Doyle (1996), para. 9.1.16.
[1] NDC Annual Report, April 1996–March 1997 and EOR No.75, September/October 1997, p. 12.
[2] *People Management* December 4, 1997, p. 10.
[3] *The Employment Provisions and Small Employers—A Review*, EOR No. 78, March/April 1998, p. 8.

facilitate rather than impede an individual's access to judicial determination", and repeated a recommendation made in their 1988 report[4] for an Equal Treatment Act "which would consolidate all the legislation contained in the Sex Discrimination and Equal Pay Acts, take into account the requirements of European Community law, and thereby create one accessible single comprehensive statute".[5] Although piecemeal amendments have been made to the legislation, the addition of separate, and different legislation in connection with disability and the possibility of further European instruments in the field of discrimination following the Treaty of Amsterdam, which introduces a new Article 6a (renumbered Article 13 in consolidated version of the Treaty) that: "the Council, acting unanimously on a proposal from the Commission and after consulting the European Parliament, may take appropriate action to combat discrimination based on sex, racial or ethnic origin, religion or belief, disability, age or sexual orientation", there is a need for a single Act capable of extension by the addition of different grounds, and a single Commission to enforce it. Of the options put forward by Hepple *et al.* (1997) some would lead to this result and in his article Wintemute (1977)[6] supports this model based on the Irish Employment Equality legislation.

In accordance with its duty under the SDA 1975, s.53(1)(c) to keep the workings of the SDA and EqPA under review, the EOC has issued a consultation document, *Equality in The 21st Century' A New Approach*[7] in which they seek views on proposals for a "fundamental restructuring to bring clarity, coherence, accessibility and effectiveness into an improved legislative framework" in the light of the "complexity and confusion" of the present laws which "impede rather than facilitate" progress.[8]

The EOC's main proposal is to replace the current laws by a single statute based on the principle of a fundamental right to equal treatment between men and women. It would encompass the SDA and EqPA, incorporate European Community law and guarantee freedom from discrimination on grounds of sex, pregnancy, marital or family status, gender reassignment and sexual orientation, although the EOC stress that this is not exhaustive. In addition, the EOC proposes a fundamental shift in emphasis from individual to collective remedies and a simplified and enhanced framework of rights and benefits for pregnant workers.[9]

In the light of the impending implementation of the Directive on Part-time Work and Parental Leave, proposals to accommodate discrimination on grounds of gender orientation, enactment of the Human Rights Bill and an announcement by the Commission of its intention to make early use of the new Article 6a of the Treaty of Rome once the Treaty of Amsterdam has been ratified,[10] the recommendation of the EOC for reform which establishes a single statute gains increased emphasis.

The White Paper *Fairness at Work*[11] contains a Chapter on family-friendly policies which deals with implementation of the Parental Leave Directive and changes to maternity leave[12] "to ensure that it is easier for parents to balance work and family

[4] *Equal Treatment for Men and Women,* EOC, March 1988.
[5] EOC, November 1990, para. (xii), p. 2.
[6] pp. 259–262.
[7] *A consultation on proposed legislative amendments to the Sex Discrimination and Equal Pay Acts*, EOC, 1998. See also *The Sex Discrimination Legislation: Recommendations for Change*, EOC for N. Ireland, 1997.
[8] The consultation period was to the end of April 1998. A revised set of proposals is to be published on the basis of the consultation process.
[9] See I.R.L.B. 587, February 1998, p. 16.
[10] I.R.L.B 593, May 1998, p. 19.
[11] Cm. 3968, (1998), http://www.dti.gov.uk/IR/fairness/fore.htm, May 21, 1998.
[12] See summary, Chap. 10.

life".[13] The proposal is to achieve "a coherent package of rights" for parents and to integrate the implementation of the Directive with existing employment rights for pregnant women which it is pointed out "have developed piecemeal and their complexity and potential for abuse have been criticised by employers, employees, the judiciary and the House of Commons Employment Committee.[14] It is therefore intended to "review existing maternity provisions alongside the new rights in order to achieve a coherent package that is easier to understand and operate" with legislation creating a framework of basic rights, supported by regulations on the details. The Government is therefore seeking views on particular aspects of maternity leave, proposing to reduce the qualifying period for long maternity leave to one year, and to align eligibility for parental leave with this, which is the maximum qualifying period permitted by the Directive, with similar rights to return and protection against dismissal or other action if an employee exercises a right to parental leave or takes time off for urgent family reasons.

The Government has announced the intention to set up a "fully fledged" Disability Rights Commission and recommendations by the Disability Rights Task Force (DRTF), envisage functions for a Commission along the lines of those currently undertaken by the EOC and CRE, with a general duty to work towards the elimination of discrimination against disabled people and to promote equalisation of opportunities; a power to review existing codes of practice and issue best practice guidance and a power to assist individuals to enforce their rights under the Disability Discrimination Act and European Convention on Human Rights, Art. 14, to bring representative actions and to be able to investigate whether public authorities are infringing rights once the Human Rights Act comes into force in cases where a breach of Article 14 is an issue.[15]

---

[13] para. 5.11.
[14] para. 5.13.
[15] 23.4.98 *Hansard*, H.C., col. 685, April 23, 1998, http://www.disability.gov.uk.

Chapter 7

UNFAIR DISMISSAL

7.1 INTRODUCTION

The right not to be unfairly dismissed is explained in six stages:

7.1 introduction;

7.2 qualifying conditions and exclusions;

7.3 potentially fair reasons for dismissal;

7.4 automatically unfair reasons for dismissal;

7.5 procedural fairness; and

7.6 forum and remedies.

It is a useful introduction to a study of the complex rules involved in the law relating to the statutory remedy of unfair dismissal, to briefly survey the circumstances that led to legislation.

In 1965 the Donovan Committee was set up "to consider relations between managements and employees and the role of trade unions and employers' associations in promoting the interests of their members and in accelerating the social and economic advance of the nation, with particular reference to the Law affecting the activities of these bodies; and to report."

At that time statutory intervention into the contractual employment relationship consisted of minimum notice periods, introduced by the Contracts of Employment Act 1963 and the right to a redundancy payment, introduced by the Redundancy Payments Act 1965. Both rights being based on length of service as to eligibility for the right itself and the value of the right in terms of length of notice and amount of redundancy payment.

In 1964 the United Kingdom ratified the International Labour Organisation (ILO) Recommendation 119 On Termination of Employment, which provided that termination of employment should not take place "unless there is a valid reason for such termination connected with the capacity or conduct of the worker, or based on the operational requirements of the undertaking. . ." Some reasons not being regarded as valid reasons for dismissal namely:

- union membership or participation in union activities outside working hours or within working hours with the consent of the employer;

- seeking office as, or acting as, workers' representative;
- the filing, in good faith, of a complaint against an employer alleging violation of laws or regulations;
- race, colour, sex, marital status, religion, political opinion, national extraction or social origin;

and it contained:

- a requirement for provision of appeals against termination;
- the provision of a period of notice of termination or for compensation to be paid in lieu of notice;
- a requirement for a criteria for determining the selection of employees affected by redundancy and the re-engagement of workers;

The recommendation was adopted by the United Kingdom on the basis that its aspirations already operated in the United Kingdom via collectively negotiated agreements. However, in 1967 it was reported[1] that whilst in unionised firms and nationalised industries formal procedures were good and operated as part of collective bargaining arrangements, in non unionised firms "well below twenty per cent of firms had any formal procedures". In addition, smaller firms, categorised as firms with less than 2,000 employees, were unlikely to have any form of internal procedure, with the exception of those in the public sector. However, following the tradition of voluntarism, the Committee recommended that there should be no employment protection legislation, but that encouragement be given for voluntary agreed procedures in both unionised and smaller non-unionised firms; that the minister should keep under review the possible need for a statutory machinery to supplement these voluntary arrangements, and that even then any statutory machinery should only apply where no collectively negotiated procedures existed.

The criticism of this report was that in excess of 80 per cent of the working population were not covered by any form of collective agreement, and of the remaining 20 per cent they were mostly confined to larger firms. Even so, the introduction of a dismissal and grievance procedure offered no employment protection since at common law on dismissal an employer was only liable to pay for the notice period, unless the dismissal was in breach of agreed procedure which had become incorporated into the individual contract. Even then the only protection available was via a delayed dismissal or compensation in lieu of notice, and then still subject to mitigation for losses suffered as a result of a breach of contract.

Recommendation 119 was up rated to a Convention in 1982, Termination of Employment Convention 1982,[2] and maternity was added to the list of invalid reasons for dismissal. The United Kingdom refused to ratify the Convention on the basis that it would impose a burden on business which it was the stated aim to alleviate and that support for procedural matters was by voluntary arrangements. Nevertheless Donovan observed that although:

"In the eye of the law employer and employee are free and equal parties to the contract of employment. . . .An employee has protection at common law against

---

[1] *Dismissal Procedures*, Minister of Labour's National Joint Advisory Council Committee on Dismissal Procedures, 1967, HMSO (para. 121) noted Donovan Report, para. 525.
[2] Convention concerning termination of employment at the initiation of the employer: Convention 158.

'wrongful' dismissal, but this protection is strictly limited; . . . In practice many employees enjoy much greater security against dismissal than is implied in the law. . . There is nevertheless a very general feeling, shared by employers as well as trade unions, that the present situation is unsatisfactory, and it was reflected in the submissions of many who gave evidence to us. . . . We share in full the belief that the present situation is unsatisfactory. In practice there is usually no comparison between the consequences for an employer if an employee terminates the contract of employment and those which will ensue for an employee if he is dismissed. In reality people build much of their lives around their jobs. . . .

From the point of view of industrial peace, it is plain also that the present situation leaves much to be desired. In the period 1964–1966 some 276 unofficial strikes took place each year on average as a result of disputes about whether individuals should or should not be employed, suspended or dismissed. The committee on dismissals analysed stoppages—whether official or unofficial—arising out of dismissals *other than redundancies* over this period and found that there were on average 203 a year. It can be argued that the right to secure a speedy and impartial decision on the justification for a dismissal might have averted many of these stoppages, though some cases would no doubt still have occurred where workers were taking spontaneous action to try to prevent a dismissal being given effect."

Royal Commission on Trade Unions and Employers' Associations 1965–68, Chapter IX, pp. 141–143.[3]

Donovan identified an urgent need for better protection and recommended early legislation on the concept of dismissal for a valid reason, with the employer being obliged to explain the grounds for dismissal following a complaint by the employee.[4] They recommended that the forum for these complaints be the industrial tribunals[5] which were originally set up under the Industrial Training Act 1964 and which had had their jurisdiction expanded for the purposes of the Redundancy Payments Act 1965, and that these be reconstituted as labour tribunals.

Where the employer was found to have dismissed in breach of an agreed procedure the Commission would ideally have liked to see the remedy as being reinstatement.[6] However, they noted that this may have been unacceptable as the only remedy and therefore envisaged that an order for reinstatement could be the primary relief, but that at the option of either employer or employee compensation should be granted instead,[7] but to accord with what they felt was reality they recommended that an order for compensation be the primary relief, with reinstatement being available where both parties chose to accept this within a "brief period of time". The Commission emphasised that in lodging a complaint against dismissal, speed should be of the essence, hence the recommendation that the employee be obliged to do so within five working days of dismissal,[8] but reflecting on the qualifying period of two years' for eligibility for a redundancy payment under Redundancy Payments Act, the Commission said:

---

[3] Cmnd. 3623 (1968).
[4] *ibid.*, para. 529 and 544.
[5] *ibid.*, para. 548.
[6] *ibid.*, para. 551.
[7] *ibid.*, para. 552.
[8] *ibid.*, para. 546.

"We see no justification . . . for limiting protection from unfair dismissal to those with at least two years' service. We see no justification for setting any upper age limit. Nor in our view should there be a lower age limit since an unfair dismissal may be a blow to a young person's self-respect or injure his career in a way which means he is hit particularly hard."

Donovan Commission Report (1968), para. 555.

Following publication of the Report, the incoming government enacted the Industrial Relations Act 1971 which ignored many of the recommendations of the Donovan Commission, and as a result of the reactions by trade unions proved to be virtually unenforceable. This resulted in repeal in the Trade Union and Labour Relations Act 1974 (TULRA), which re-enacted the unfair dismissal provisions of the 1971 Act, with amendments:

- the burden of proving the fairness of the dismissal was placed on the employer (this was restored in the Employment Act 1980 (EA 1980) to status quo);
- the qualifying period from two years to 26 weeks (in 1985 it was increased again to two years); and
- constructive dismissal was added.

By this route was born the statutory unfair dismissal provisions, which today are consolidated in the Employment Rights Act 1996, (ERA 1996) not as part of a labour code, but superimposed on the contractual relationship, along with other subsequently introduced statutory rights, all with their own detailed qualifying conditions, leading to a complex web of provisions and regulations all of which assumes an underlying base of the common law.[9]

7.2 QUALIFYING CONDITIONS AND EXCLUSIONS

ERA 1996, s.94 provides that an employee has the right not to be unfairly dismissed by his employer. This right is, however, subject to a number of qualifying conditions and exclusions, not least is that it is only applicable to "employees", those working under a contract of employment, section 230. This issue is discussed at para. 2.4 above. A worker who falls outside the common law definition of employee, or an employee who comes within one of the exclusions or exemptions, or fails to fulfil one of the statutory requirements is unable to pursue a statutory remedy for unfair dismissal, being left merely with a remedy for wrongful dismissal.

The flow chart at p. 294 gives an overview of the qualifications and exclusions and the various qualifications and exclusions are numbered to correspond with the following text.

7.2.1 Dismissal

For statutory purposes dismissal is defined in the ERA 1996, s.95 for unfair dismissal purposes and section 136 for redundancy purposes in the same terms. In addition,

[9] See Ewing (1996), p. 42.

dismissal is deemed by section 96(1), to have occurred where an employer fails to permit a woman to return from maternity leave where she has a right to do so under section 79. This is dealt with at para. 10.4.2.4.

As dismissal is a jurisdictional matter, it is for the applicant to prove (as with the other qualifying conditions). Once given, notice cannot be unilaterally withdrawn, and there is no right to work the notice period, except where consideration for the contract is the provision of work itself.[10]

7.2.1.1 *Dismissal as opposed to resignation*

Where the contract comes to an end by mutual consent there can be no dismissal. Lord Denning in *Marriott v. Oxford District Co-operative Society Ltd*[11] stressed the necessity for the agreement to be voluntary and without undue pressure on the employee. It must, he said, be a genuine bilateral termination and one of the criteria is to ask "who took the initiative?" Where the employer "invites" the employee to resign, the resignation will usually be treated as a dismissal. The practical approach adopted by the courts is demonstrated in the early case of *East Sussex CC v. Walker*[12] where Sir John Brightman said that if an employee is told that she is no longer required and is expressly invited to resign, as a matter of common sense she was dismissed even though the employee takes the first and more respectable alternative of resigning rather than being dismissed. Likewise, if the resignation is procured by fraud or pressure then it is treated as dismissal. In *Caledonian Mining Co. Ltd v. Bassett*,[13] it was held that where employees had been falsely inveigled to resign with the express purpose of avoiding paying redundancy payment, they had, in reality, been dismissed.

However, in some circumstances a resignation under threat may amount to a consensual termination. In *Martin v. MBS Fastenings (Glynwed) Distribution Ltd*[14] the Court of Appeal upheld a decision that an employee who had chosen to resign rather than face a disciplinary hearing was not dismissed, but had in fact resigned: he had the option of remaining in employment and taking a chance with the outcome of the disciplinary hearing.

A resignation in exchange for a financial inducement is unlikely to be dismissal, even where the employee is invited to resign. In *Logan Salton v. Durham County Council*,[15] having received advance notice of a disciplinary hearing the applicant entered into an agreement to resign, which involved a payment. The EAT held that the agreement had been entered into willingly and without duress after proper advice and for good consideration: termination was therefore consensual. The EAT confirmed, in *Sheffield v. Oxford Controls Co. Ltd*,[16] that where a person resigns rather than being dismissed that was still dismissal because the employee has no choice whether to stay or go, the sole question coming down to how he goes, but, where it is the money that induces termination, that is not dismissal.

In a heat of the moment resignation what might otherwise appear to be a clear resignation, should not be construed as such. In *Sovereign House Security Services Ltd v. Savage*,[17] following the judgment of Fox L.J. in *Sothern v. Franks Charlesly & Co.*,[18]

---

[10] *William Hill Organisation Ltd v. Tucker* [1998] I.R.L.R. 313, CA.
[11] [1969] 3 All E.R. 1126, CA.
[12] [1972] 7 I.T.R. 280, NIRC.
[13] [1987] I.R.L.R. 165, EAT.
[14] [1983] I.R.L.R. 198, CA.
[15] [1989] I.R.L.R. 99, EAT.
[16] [1979] I.R.L.R. 133, EAT.
[17] [1989] I.R.L.R. 115, CA.
[18] [1981] I.R.L.R. 278, CA.

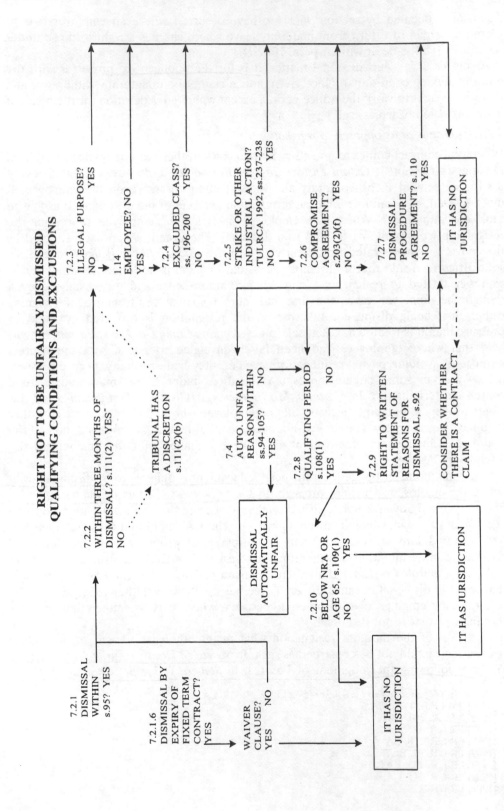

RIGHT NOT TO BE UNFAIRLY DISMISSED
QUALIFYING CONDITIONS AND EXCLUSIONS

there was found to be evidence upon which the industrial tribunal could conclude that when a security officer responded to being told of his suspension pending a police investigation into missing money by saying, "I am not having any of that, you can stuff it, I am not taking the rap for that" and telephoning his immediate supervisor to tell him he was "jacking the job in", he was not resigning.

7.2.1.2 *Self dismissal*

Problems have surrounded the area of self dismissal, most typically in relation to consent for an extended holiday conditional upon agreement that failure to return on time would result in the contract ending automatically. In *Tracey v. Zest Equipment*[19] the EAT held such an agreement did not amount to termination by mutual agreement: there is a presumption that the employee would not readily give up acquired statutory rights. This was confirmed by the CA in *Igbo v. Johnson Matthey Chemicals*[20] where it was held that such an agreement was void under the ERA 1996, s.203(1).

7.2.1.3 *Voluntary early retirement*

Voluntary early retirement normally arises in circumstances of workforce reduction where, as part of a redundancy strategy the employer calls for volunteers as a means of preventing compulsory redundancy, providing inducements by way of enhanced pension rights. If the retirement is considered a consensual termination the retiree forfeits any eligibility to a redundancy payment because there is no dismissal under section 136.

In *Birch v. University of Liverpool*,[21] having volunteered and been accepted for such a scheme Mr Birch found he was denied a redundancy payment because his termination did not amount to dismissal:

> "In my opinion (s.136(1)(a)) on its true construction, is directed to the case where, on a proper analysis of the facts, the contract of employment is terminated by the employer alone. It is not apt to cover the case where, on such an analysis, the contract of employment has been terminated by the employee, or by the mutual, freely given, consents of the employer and the employee. In a case where it has been terminated by such mutual agreement, it may properly be said that the contract has been terminated by both the employer and the employee jointly, but it cannot, in my view, be said that it has been terminated by the employer alone.
>
> The authorities, I think, require one to look at the realities of the facts, rather than the form of the relevant transaction, in deciding whether the contract has been 'terminated by the employer' within the meaning of the subsection. As Sir John Donaldson M.R. in *Martin v. Glynwed Distribution Ltd* [1983] I.R.L.R. 198 at p.201: 'Whatever the respective actions of the employer and the employee at the time when the contract of employment is terminated, at the end of the day the question always remains the same, "Who *really* terminated the contract of employment?" '
>
> . . . On the facts of the present case it seems to me that, . . ., there can be only one answer: that is that the contract of employment . . . was terminated not by the

---

[19] [1982] I.C.R. 481, EAT.
[20] [1986] I.C.R. 505, CA.
[21] [1985] I.R.L.R. 165, CA.

employer but by the freely given mutual consent of the employer and employee."
per Slade L.J.

Birch v. University of Liverpool [1985] I.R.L.R. 165 at 171, CA.

This was held to be a case of financial inducement as opposed to pressurisation, and as a result consensual. This view was supported in *Scott v. Coalite Fuels and Chemicals Ltd*[22] even though notice of dismissal had already been served when a subsequent offer to voluntarily early retire was accepted.

7.2.1.4 *Long term absences*

Where long term absence is concerned the concept of frustration has, somewhat controversially, been introduced to argue that the contract has come to the end by the operation of law and not of the parties, as a result of which there is no dismissal. The general principle is that a contract is frustrated if it becomes impossible to perform or performance of which would result in a radically different outcome from that intended by the parties at the time the contract was made.

It was accepted by Sir John Donaldon in *Marshall v. Harland & Woolf*[23] that the doctrine is capable of applying to contracts of employment, notwithstanding that such contracts can be terminated by short notice, although observing that the shorter the notice period required, the less likely is the doctrine to be applicable. It has been applied both in relation to long-term sickness, *Egg Stores (Stamford Hill) Ltd v. Leibovici*,[24] and absence caused by imprisonment, *F.C. Shepherd & Co. Ltd v. Jerrom*,[25] notwithstanding that the non-availability results, albeit indirectly, from the fault of the employee.

It is argued that the industrial tribunal should not be considering technical and esoteric rules of contract, the result of which is to deny them jurisdiction, instead of assessing the fairness of the dismissal on general principles.

Frustration is discussed at para. 5.5.1.

7.2.1.5 *Constructive dismissal*

The employee is only entitled to claim that his resignation amounts to a dismissal within section 95(1)(c) where the employer's behaviour amounts to a repudiatory breach of contract. In *Western Excavating v. Sharp*[26] Lord Denning disapproved of earlier authorities which held that such a right existed where the employer's behaviour was merely unreasonable[27]: he condemned the unreasonableness test as leading to "whimsical decisions". The contract test has subsequently prevailed, as a result of which the case law revolves around whether the employer's conduct amounted to a repudiatory breach of an express or implied term of the contract. Whether conduct is repudiatory will depend on the terms of the contract, including implied terms, but conduct cannot be repudiatory if the contract expressly or impliedly permits it, nor is it every breach of contract that amounts to repudiatory conduct. In *Lewis v. Motorworld Garages Ltd*[28] the Court of Appeal held that conduct is repudiatory if, viewed objectively, it evinced an intention by one party no longer to be bound by the contract.

[22] [1988] I.R.L.R. 131, EAT.
[23] [1972] I.C.R. 101, NIRC.
[24] 1977] I.C.R. 260, EAT.
[25] [1985] I.C.R. 802, CA.
[26] [1978] I.R.L.R. 27, CA.
[27] *Turner v. London Transport Executive* [1977] I.R.L.R. 441, CA.
[28] [1985] I.R.L.R. 465, CA.

It is not just a single breach that is capable of amounting to a repudiation. In *Garner v. Grange Furnishing Ltd*[29] it was held that a series of small incidents over a period of time, if it makes it impossible for the employee to go on working, is also capable of amounting to a repudiation, so long as cumulatively the incidents demonstrate an intention by the employer no longer to be bound by the contract.

If an employee does not leave promptly following repudiatory conduct but waits until he has found alternative work, the question arises as to the operating cause of the resignation and whether the delayed resignation amounts to constructive dismissal, or is a mere resignation. In *Jones v. F. Sirl & Son (Furnishers) Ltd*[30] the employer made a number of changes to Mrs Jones's terms and conditions, cutting her petrol allowance and terminating her membership of a non-contributory pension scheme. The final event was a demotion as a result of someone being appointed to take over a large part of her duties and three weeks after this, having received an offer of employment from another firm, she gave notice and subsequently claimed to have been constructively dismissed. The industrial tribunal, whilst holding the employer's conduct amounted to a series of breaches of contract, rejected the claim on the basis that the offer of alternative employment was the motivating factor, as opposed to the employer's conduct. The EAT, however, allowed the appeal:

". . . It is clear from the case law . . ., that in order to decide whether an employee has left in consequence of fundamental breach, the industrial tribunal must look to see whether the employer's repudiatory breach was the *effective* cause of the resignation. It is important, in our judgment, to appreciate that in such a situation of potentially constructive dismissal, particularly in today's labour market, there may well be concurrent causes operating on the mind of an employee whose employer has committed fundamental breaches of his contract of employment entitling him to put an end to it. Thus an employee may leave both because of the fundamental and repudiatory breaches, and also because of the fact that he has found another job. In such a situation, which will not be uncommon, the industrial tribunal must find out what the effective cause of the resignation was, depending on the individual circumstances of any given case." *per* J. Smith Q.C.

Jones v. F. Sirl & Son (Furnishers) Ltd [1997] I.R.L.R. 493 at 494, EAT.

The question of a delayed response was also considered in *Waltons & Morse v. Dorrington*.[31] Morison, J. in the EAT referred to *Harvey on Employment Law*, viz.:

"There is no fixed time limit within which the employee must make up his mind. It depends upon all the circumstances including the employee's length of service, the nature of the breach and whether the employee has protested at the change. Mere protest will not, however, prevent an inference that the employee has waived the breach, although exceptionally a clear reservation of a right might do so. Where the employee is faced with giving up his job and being unemployed or waiving the breach, it is not surprising that the courts are sometimes reluctant to conclude that he has lost his right to treat himself as discharged by the employer merely by working at the job for a few months." *Harvey on Employment Law*.

[29] [1977] I.R.L.R. 206, EAT.
[30] [1997] I.R.L.R. 493, EAT.
[31] [1997] I.R.L.R. 488 at 492, EAT.

and concluded that the Industrial Tribunal had been right to decide that because Mrs Dorrington needed the money from her job because of family commitments, a delay in handing in her notice, in the light of her length of service did not amount to acceptance of the breach of contract.

Where the employer's conduct is repudiatory, but not of immediate practical effect, the courts have stressed that caution should be exercised before implying consent to the variation by continuing to work without objecting to the variation. The EAT in *Aparau v. Iceland Frozen Foods plc*[32] accepted that the law had been correctly stated in *Jones v. Associated Tunnelling Co. Ltd,*[33] *obiter*, so although Mrs Aparau had continued to work after her terms of employment had been unilaterally varied it was held that she had not accepted the variation so that when she resigned some 12 months later over being instructed to relocate in line with the new term, she was held to have been constructively dismissed.

Although a breach of contract may be repudiatory and entitle the employee to terminate their employment and claim constructive dismissal under section 95(1)(c), it was held in *Westminster City Council v. Cabaj*[34] that a breach of contract does not necessarily involve an unfair dismissal.

7.2.1.6 *Expiry of a fixed term contract*

At common law where a contract for a fixed period expires without being renewed, no liability arises: the contract is discharged. However, by the ERA 1996, ss.95(1)(b) and 136(1)(b), expiry of a fixed term contract without it being renewed is deemed to be a dismissal.

This is capable of having far-reaching consequences as demonstrated in *Pfaffinger v. City of Liverpool Community College* and *Muller v. Amersham & Wycombe College*[35] where it was held that the combined effect of the ERA 1996, ss.136(1)(b) and 139(1)(b) is that when a college lecturer's contract expired at the end of the academic year without being renewed, because the colleges' need for employees to carry out the function of lecturing ceases or diminishes from the beginning of the vacation until the start of the new term: "there is no teaching during that period and therefore no need for teachers. That is a redundancy situation." By section 212(3)(c) the employment is deemed to be continuous where there is a temporary cessation of work, but it was held that that did not prevent a redundancy occurring since "cease" in section 139(1)(b), by section 139(6), is defined as ceasing "permanently or temporarily". The combined effect was held to be that:

> . . . where there is a succession of fixed-term contracts which expire, there may be a dismissal for redundancy on the expiration of each contract. So, for example, where a part-time lecturer has three fixed-term contracts, one for each term during the academic year, he may be dismissed three times during that year for redundancy. This may sound surprising to some but, on the present state of the authorities and the legislation, that is the position." *per* Mummery J. (President)
>
> *Pfaffinger v. City of Liverpool Community College and Muller v. Amersham & Wycombe College* [1996] I.R.L.R. 508 at 512.

[32] [1996] I.R.L.R. 119, EAT.
[33] [1981] I.R.L.R. 477, EAT.
[34] [1996] I.R.L.R. 399, CA.
[35] [1996] I.R.L.R. 508, EAT.

However, by sections 197(1) and 197(3), the right to bring unfair dismissal proceedings and the right to a redundancy payment do not apply where in a contract for a fixed term of one year or more (two years for redundancy) if the dismissal consists only of the expiry of the fixed term without its being renewed and before the term expires the employee has agreed in writing to exclude any claim to unfair dismissal or redundancy rights, except that the parties cannot agree to oust the unfair dismissal provisions in relation to section 101, a protected shop or betting shop worker who refuses to work on Sunday. The agreement may be either in the contract itself or in a separate agreement and by section 203(2)(f), is an exception to section 203(1) which makes void any agreement to exclude or limit the operation of any provision of the ERA 1996.

Where the original fixed term contract has been renewed or extended difficulties have arisen where the final contract or extension period is less than one year for unfair dismissal, or two years for redundancy situations. In *British Broadcasting Corporation v. Ioannou*[36] Lord Denning, in the Court of Appeal, dissenting on the point, said that where there is a succession of fixed-term contracts, the waiver clause will only be valid, to avoid an unfair dismissal or redundancy claim, if the final extension is for at least a year, or two years respectively. However, in *Mulrine v. University of Ulster*[37] the Northern Ireland Court of Appeal disagreed with this, holding that as long as the last contract was merely an extension or renewal of the previous contract, which was for one or two years respectively, as opposed to a re-engagement under a new contract, the waiver would be valid to oust jurisdiction of the industrial tribunal no matter what the length of the extension.

In *Housing Services Agency v. Cragg*,[38] a redundancy payments case, the EAT noted the conflicting authorities and subjected the statutory waiver provisions to scrutiny. They concluded that "the final contract test" propounded by Lord Denning in *BBC v. Ioannou* and followed in *BP Oil Ltd v. Richards*[39] was correct insofar as it related to an unfair dismissal waiver. It was held that section 197(1) required the waiver to appear in the final contract which must be for a period of one year or more in order to be effective. However, insofar as the redundancy payment waiver is concerned the EAT concluded that *Ioannou* was wrongly applied in *Open University v. Triesman*[40] because the ERA, ss.197(3)–(5) required that there must be a waiver agreement both in relation to the original fixed-term contract and during the currency of each extension of the fixed term, there is no requirement for each extension to be for a period of two years, since it is the first contract that is in question:

"... we accept the final contract test propounded by Lord Denning and followed in *BP* in so far as it relates to unfair dismissal waiver. Questions of renewal and re-engagement are not too difficult; they are simply irrelevant when considering unfair dismissal waiver." And later

"It may be said that by drawing, we think for the first time, a clear distinction between the unfair dismissal and redundancy payment waiver provisions, that will create an anomaly. Hitherto, employers have proceeded on the basis that there is

[36] [1975] I.R.L.R. 184, CA.
[37] [1993] I.R.L.R. 545, NICA.
[38] [1997] I.R.L.R. 380, EAT.
[39] EAT/768/82 April 12, 1983.
[40] [1978] I.R.L.R. 114, EAT.

no material distinction (save for the one-and two-year terms) between the two. So be it . . . " *per* Peter Clark J.

Housing Services Agency v. Cragg [1997] I.R.L.R. 380 at 386, EAT.

This final contract test was confirmed as appropriate to unfair dismissal also in *BBC v. Kelly-Phillips*[41] where the purported unfair dismissal waiver was held to be invalid because the last in a series of fixed-term contracts under which an employee worked was not "for a year or more" as required by the ERA 1996, s.197(1). Lyndsay J. rejected the argument put forward that the contract of employment from which Ms Kelly-Phillips had been dismissed was, by a succession of renewals, one for a fixed term which had begun with the start of the first contract and which, by renewal or extension, expired when the relationship came to an end.

In so deciding, the EAT preferred the "final contract" test enunciated by Lord Denning in *British Broadcasting v. Ioannou*[42] rather than that of *Mulrine v. University of Ulster*[43] where the Northern Ireland Court of Appeal said that the crucial question was whether a second or subsequent contract was an extension, or "part and parcel", of a first or preceding contract, as opposed to a re-engagement under a new contract.

This "final contract" test was, however, thrown into doubt in *Bhatt v. Chelsea and Westminster Health Care Trust*[44] when Kirkwood J. rejected it in relation to an unfair dismissal claim on the basis that a fixed term contract of a year or more could be renewed or extended under the same contract, in which case the old contract continued, along with the waiver clause. In such a case, he reasoned that the point of focus for the purposes of section 197(1) is not the final extension, but the term of the extended contract. Section 95(1)(b), he said, envisaged that the term could be renewed without a new contract being made, but with the old contract continuing. It was therefore necessary to distinguish whether there is a renewal of the term under the old contract, an extension, or whether the renewal was under a new contract. Where the only change was an extension of the fixed term, that was an extension under the same contract with no dismissal, dismissal occurring when the final extension was not renewed. If the extended contract was for a fixed term of one year or more then the contract fell within section 197. Therefore, although Mr Bhatt's final period of employment was for three months, the waiver in this case was effective and the applicant was unable to claim unfair dismissal.

The reasoning of the EAT in *Bhatt* was subsequently approved by the Court of Appeal in *Kelly-Phillips* which approved of the reasoning of the majority of the Court of Appeal in *Ioannou* and that of the Northern Ireland Court of Appeal in *Mulrine*. The position is now that where a contract is extended for a period of less than a year, it can still be a contract for a year or more for the purposes of section 197(1) since it is the whole period of the contract which is to be considered: any extended term being part of the original contract. In so deciding the Court recognised that this may give rise to abuse, but was not persuaded that that justified giving the statutory wording a " 'gloss' which otherwise it could not bear."

Fixed-term contracts have become widespread, both in the public and private sectors,[45] and the labour government was committed to abolishing the ability to opt out

[41] [1991] I.R.L.R. 571, EAT.
[42] [1975] I.R.L.R. 184, CA.
[43] [1993] I.R.L.R. 545, NICA.
[44] [1998] I.R.L.R. 660, EAT.
[45] The BBC is reported to employ a quarter of their 20,000 workforce on fixed-term contracts.

of the protections afforded by the ERA 1996 upon dismissal by non-renewal. Government proposals are awaited, but it appears that there may have been a weakening of resolve in this area.[46] However, following on from the agreement and directive on part-time working, the preamble of which states that "it is the intention of the parties to consider the need for similar agreements relating to other forms of flexible work", the three European-level social partner organisations have indicated that they are willing to enter into talks with the aim of reaching agreement on fixed-term contracts. Talks would take place within the context of the Commission's consultation exercise on atypical work, which began in 1995.[47]

7.2.1.7 *Effective date of termination*

This is the starting point for calculating the time for presenting a case to the Tribunal, see para. 7.5 below, and the point at which the continuous period of employment is calculated in order to establish the qualifying service requirements for various employment rights: *e.g.* unfair dismissal, written statement of reasons for dismissal, minimum notice and redundancy payment; and for the calculation of the basic award which is service based.

Section 97 provides that the effective date is

- where notice is served by the employee, the date of expiry of the notice;

- where notice is served by the employer, the date of expiry of the notice, except that where the employee is eligible to receive minimum notice under section 86, it is the date when the minimum period of notice would have expired if that is later than the expiry of the notice actually given;

- where no notice is given it is the date on which the termination takes effect;

- where a fixed term contract expires without being renewed, it is the date on which the term expires.

Where the employer does not require the notice period to be served, but makes a payment representing the salary for the remainder of the notice period the issue arises as to whether the effective date of termination is the date upon which the employee actually leaves or the date upon which he would have left had he worked through his notice period. Which one of these dates applies depends on the construction placed upon the letter of dismissal. In *Adams v. GKN Sankey Ltd*[48] it was held that where the employee is given notice, but not permitted to work, being paid salary in lieu of working out the notice period, the effective date of termination is the date when the notice would have expired and the fact that a person is not required to work during the period of notice does not mean that the employment terminated earlier than the date upon which it would have expired if permitted to work. This is to be distinguished from a situation where no notice is given but a payment is made in lieu of salary. In *Dedman v. British Building and Engineering Appliances Ltd.*[49] Lord Denning said that the salary paid in such a situation should be regarded as compensation for immediate dismissal and not by way of continuation of the employee's employment, so that the

---

[46] *Personnel Today*, January 15, 1998. See, however, *Fairness at Work*, para. 3.13. The Government is seeking views on the proposal to prohibit the use of waivers for unfair dismissal but allowing them for redundancy.
[47] I.R.L.B. 588, March 1998, p. 14.
[48] [1980] I.R.L.R. 416, EAT.
[49] [1973] I.R.L.R. 379, CA.

effective date of termination is the date on which the immediate dismissal took place. Where the immediate, or summary, dismissal is in breach of contract for whatever reason, it was held in *Stapp v. The Shaftesbury Society*[50] that that will give rise to a remedy for breach of contract at common law, but does not affect the termination date. Likewise, when summary dismissal takes place in breach of a procedure agreement it was held in *Batchelor v. British Railways Board*[51] that the breach of procedure may give rise to an action for wrongful dismissal, but that cannot affect the termination date. This is difficult to reconcile with the acceptance theory: that a repudiatory breach of contract does not automatically terminate the contract, but that as with contracts in general needs to be accepted by the employee. In *Robert Cort & Sons Ltd v. Charman*[52] the EAT confirmed that in this context the automatic theory of termination applies, because it is implicit in section 97(1)(a) and so that the ordinary employee is able to understand the position: the effective date of termination will not therefore depend on subtle legalities of the law of repudiation and acceptance of repudiation.[53]

Where there is an appeal against dismissal, once the appeals procedure has been exhausted, the question arises as to whether the effective date of termination is the date of dismissal or the date the appeals procedure was exhausted. In *J. Sainsbury Ltd v. Savage*[54] the employer's procedure agreement provided that a summarily dismissed employee would be suspended without pay pending the outcome of any appeal against dismissal. The Court of Appeal held that:

> ". . . the contract of employment is saved if the appeal succeeds, because the employee is reinstated with full back pay. But if the appeal fails, then the inevitable result is that the employee is not only deprived of his right to work as from (the date of suspension) but also of his right to remuneration from that date. If he has had no right to work . . . and no right to be paid. . ., the contract of employment must have been determined as from (the date of dismissal)." *per* Brightman L.J.

> *J. Sainsbury Ltd v. Savage* [1981] I.C.R. 1 at 7, CA.

In *West Midlands Co-operative Society Ltd v. Tipton*[55] the House of Lords agreed with the reasoning in *Sainsbury*, unless the contract of employment expressly provides to the contrary. It was held in *Palmer and Saunders v. Southend-on-Sea Borough Council*[56] that the mere fact that there is an appeal against dismissal does not stop time running for the purposes of section 111(2) or fulfil the requirement of "not reasonably practicable" such as to justify the industrial tribunal in exercising it's discretion to permit a case to be heard out of time.

7.2.2 Time restriction

By section 111(2) a complaint of unfair dismissal, and the majority of other employment rights enforceable before the industrial tribunal, must be presented before

---

[50] [1982] I.R.L.R. 326, CA.
[51] [1987] I.R.L.R. 136, CA.
[52] [1981] I.R.L.R. 437, EAT.
[53] See J. McMullen "A synthesis of the mode of termination of contracts of employment" (1982) 41 C.L.J. 110–141.
[54] [1981] I.C.R. 1, CA.
[55] [1986] I.R.L.R. 112, HL.
[56] [1984] I.R.L.R. 119, CA.

the end of the period of three months beginning with the effective date of termination. In *Swainston v. Hetton Victory Club*[57] it was held that the normal rule is that the three month time limit expires at midnight on the last day of that period, even where that is a non-working day if the application can be placed through a letter box or dealt with in some other way held out by the Regional Office as a means by which it will receive communications because "presentation" does not require any action on the part of the body to whom the presentation is made.

Section 111(2)(b) contains a discretion for the industrial tribunal to hear cases outside the three month time limit and "within such further period as the tribunal considers reasonable in a case where it is satisfied that it was not reasonably practicable for the complaint to be presented before the end of that period of three months." In deciding the meaning of "reasonably practicable" it was held in *Palmer v. Southend-on-Sea*[58] that the statutory words should be read as meaning "reasonably feasible" to present the complaint to the IT within three months. Poor advice, whether from the Citizens' Advice Bureau—*Riley v. Tesco Stores Ltd.*[59]—from a solicitor—*Capital Foods Retail Ltd v. Corrigan*[60]—or trade union official is not a sufficient reason to allow the tribunal to exercise its discretion. However, in *Rybak v. Jean Sorelle Ltd,*[61] Knox J. reviewed the authorities concerning erroneous advice causing late presentation and decided that EAT could treat advice from an industrial tribunal employee differently from that of a solicitor or Citizens Advice Bureau Office, and allowed the late claim under section 111(2)(b). As it appears from *Palmer*[62] that time continues to run during the domestic appeals process, a claim must be presented pending the outcome of the appeals process in order to preserve the employee's position.

Controversially, in *Biggs v. Somerset County Council*[63] the Court of Appeal held that the three month time limit ran from the date of dismissal, and not from the date of a House of Lords' decision in *R. v. Secretary of State for Employment ex p. EOC,*[64] nor did time run from the date of the regulations[65] implementing a change in the law to comply with the House of Lords' decision. In considering whether it was reasonably practicable for the complaint to be presented within the three months limit, Neill L.J., supporting the view expressed by Mummery J. in the EAT, said that it was reasonably practicable for the claim to have been presented within the time prescribed:

"Her mistake as to what her rights were was, as has now been made clear, a mistake of law. It was not a mistake of fact. The decision in the EOC case . . . was declaratory of what the law has always been ever since the primacy of Community law was established by s.2 of the European Communities Act 1972 . . . Accordingly, since 1 January 1973, and certainly since the decision of the ECJ in *Defrenne v. Sabena*, . . ., there was no legal impediment preventing someone who claimed that he had been unfairly dismissed from presenting a claim and arguing that the restriction on claims by part-time workers was indirectly discriminatory. It seems to me that in the context of (s.111) the words 'reasonably practicable" are directed

[57] [1983] I.R.L.R. 164, CA.
[58] [1984] I.R.L.R. 119, CA.
[59] [1970] I.R.L.R. 103, CA.
[60] [1993] I.R.L.R. 430, EAT.
[61] [1991] I.C.R. 127, EAT.
[62] [1984] I.R.L.R. 119, CA.
[63] [1996] I.R.L.R. 203, CA.
[64] [1994] I.R.L.R. 176, HL.
[65] S.I. 1995 No. 31.

to difficulties faced by an individual claimant. Illness provides an obvious example. In the case of illness the claimant may well be able successfully to assert that it was not 'reasonably practicable' to present a claim within three months. But the words 'reasonably practicable', when read in conjunction with a 'reasonable' period thereafter, point to some temporary impediment or hindrance." *per* Neill L.J.

Biggs v. Somerset County Council [1996] I.R.L.R. 203 at 207, CA.

Although this decision makes sense on the facts, since the dismissal took place some 20 years beforehand, the reasoning regarding the decision in the *EOC* case seems bizarre because a claim made before the House of Lords' decision in the *EOC* case by somebody without the required service and hours qualification would have been rejected as not complying with the relevant legislation.

7.2.3   Illegality

A contract that is tainted with illegality or immorality is void *ab initio*: the courts will not enforce such a contract or allow any statutory rights in respect of it. The situation most commonly encountered in the employment relationship is that of attempts to avoid the payment of PAYE and national insurance contributions by paying and receiving payment or part payment of wages in cash, and the employer subsequently raises the illegality to prevent the application for a statutory remedy resulting from dismissal being heard by an industrial tribunal.

"The reason why rights and obligations which arise from a contract which is illegal will not be enforced in the Courts was expressed by Lord Mansfield as long ago as 1775 in *Holman v. Johnson* [1775] 1 Cowp. 341 to be founded on general principles of public policy. 'The principle of public policy is this, *ex dolo malo nonoritur actio*'. A distinguished judge using the idiom of 1977 and borrowing from A P Herbert has expressed it in language more apt to be used amongst those concerned with this branch of the law as "the dirty dog gets no dinner here". We take it to be clear law that someone who tried to assert in the Courts a right contained in an illegal contract will not succeed." *per* Bristow J.

Tomlinson v. Dick Evans U Drive Ltd [1978] I.R.L.R. 77 at 78, EAT.

Early decisions tended to adopt the blanket approach that all contracts tainted with illegality were void, regardless of whether the employee knew of the illegality, since ignorance of the law is no excuse. However, case law has developed to the position that such contracts may be valid in certain situations, thus enabling an employee to seek a statutory remedy, but the rules have developed on a case by case basis. In *Leighton v. Michael*[66] the EAT held that an industrial tribunal's jurisdiction to consider a complaint of alleged sex discrimination is not dependent upon the existence of an enforceable contract of employment. The majority held that such a claim is not founded upon the contract of employment and does not seek to enforce contractual obligations. The right not to be discriminated against on the ground of sex is conferred by statute on persons who are employed, and it was held that there is nothing in the

[66] [1996] I.R.L.R. 67, EAT.

statute, or in public policy, to disqualify a person, who is in fact employed, from protection by reason of illegality in the contract of employment if the claim is not founded upon, or seeking to enforce, contractual obligations. Support for this was gained from Directive 76/207, Art. 5(1), the expression "working conditions" emphasises the objective conditions of working rather than the legally enforceable nature of the contract under which work is done. Whilst equal pay is enforced by the EqPA 1970 whereby, a contract of employment that does not contain an equality clause, is deemed to do so, there is, in fact, no corresponding provision in the SDA relating to equal treatment.

Likewise, if was confirmed in *Annandale Engineering v. Samson*[67] that illegality that is merely incidental to the contract, as opposed to arising under the contract, does not operate to prevent the enforcement of statutory rights that operate on the contract. The EAT held that payments given to kennel hands by owners when their dogs won a race were not part of the contractual remuneration, either expressly or by implication from its performance. They were not on a par with, for example, tips given to waiters which are then regularly shared out by the employer. Thus, any illegality did not arise under the contract so that contract remained valid, enabling the employee to bring his claim.

Where payments are associated with the contract:

"... a distinction has to be drawn between (a) cases in which there is a contractual obligation to do an act which is unlawful, and (b) cases where the contractual obligations are capable of being performed lawfully and were initially intended so to be performed, but which have in fact been performed by unlawful means. As to category (a), the answer to the question depends on what is often called the rules of severance, *i.e.* how far is it possible to separate the tainted contractual obligations from the untainted. As to category (b), the question is whether the doing of an unlawful act by a party to a contract precludes his further enforcement of that contract." *per* Browne-Wilkinson J., Vice-Chancellor

Coral Leisure Group Ltd. v. Barnett [1981] I.C.R. 503 at 508, EAT.

In *Barnett*[68] the employee procured and paid prostitutes in the course of carrying out his legitimate duties, but this was held not to prevent him from claiming a remedy for unfair dismissal since he did not enter the employment with the intention of procuring prostitutes. The illegal or immoral act in this case was done in the course of performing an otherwise lawful contract, and it was held that the applicant knew nothing of the prostitutes until after he had entered the employment. It therefore never became a term of his contract that he should employ prostitutes, it was merely a method of carrying out his general duty of preserving Coral's goodwill.

Where a contract is being performed illegally the question of whether the employee knew of the illegality but continued working arose in *Newland v. Simons & Willer (Hairdressers) Ltd*[69] where the EAT held that if the employee continued working knowing of the illegal mode of performance by his employer, which involved part payment in cash, then the employee is affected by that and excluded from claiming his statutory rights, knowledge to be judged subjectively: the mere fact that the employee ought to have known, but did not know being insufficient.

[67] [1994] I.R.L.R. 59, EAT.
[68] [1981] I.C.R. 503, EAT.
[69] [1981] I.R.L.R. 359, EAT.

The illegality doctrine has been applied, even where the result seems to be that the applicant suffers a severe penalty or disability as a result, and even if only a small sum of money is involved. This is demonstrated in *Hyland v. J.H. Barker (North West) Ltd*[70] where the applicant had been employed by the same employer for 16 years, between 1967 and 1983. For two months in 1982 he received a tax free lodging allowance, in addition to wages, while working away from home even though he in fact returned home each night: the payment was therefore not a reimbursement but extra wages upon which tax should have been paid. After he was dismissed he claimed unfair dismissal and redundancy and the illegality was raised to deny the industrial tribunal jurisdiction. However, instead of finding that the illegality rendered the contract void, the EAT held that in the four weeks in which the lodging allowance was paid, the contract of employment was illegal, but that that did not mean that before or after that period it was illegal. However, because "continuously employed" (in the ERA 1996, s.108(1)) means continuously employed under a legal contract of employment, that period during which the illegality occurred broke continuity, with the result that there was insufficient service post the illegal period to qualify to claim unfair dismissal. This rather strange interpretation means that statutory rights could have been perused despite the illegality, had there been sufficient service past the illegal act and appears to be in conflict with the idea that a contract tainted with illegality is void *ab initio*.

Tax evasion, which is illegal, has to be distinguished from tax avoidance, which is not. In *Lightfoot v. D & J Sporting Ltd*[71] it was held that a salary paid in two parts with the aim of avoiding tax liability was not unlawful when the second part was paid to the applicant's wife:

> "Was it a proper method of reducing tax, open and above board, which either had been disclosed to the Revenue or would be disclosed to the Revenue? . . . I think every married barrister and solicitor and surveyor and probably every married person who pays tax under Schedule D, is advised by his accountant to arrange to pay a reasonable sum to his wife for her services if she gives them in the profession and the sum is modest." *per* Judge Hull Q.C.

> *Lightfoot v. D & J Sporting Ltd* [1996] I.R.L.R. 64 at 66, EAT.

Likewise, it was held in *Broaders v. Kalkare Property Maintenance Ltd*[72] that a fraud on the employer, as opposed to the Revenue, in an otherwise legal contract, is not to be treated in the same way, in that such acts do not taint the contract with illegality, although dishonesty will be relevant to the question of whether the dismissal is fair or unfair.

7.2.4 Excluded classes of employment

The Employment Rights Act 1996, ss.196–200 provides that certain categories are excluded from specific employment rights:

Employment outside Great Britain

Section 196(1) provides that an employee who is engaged in work wholly or mainly outside Great Britain is not entitled to a statement of employment particulars under

---

[70] [1985] I.C.R. 861, EAT.
[71] [1996] I.R.L.R. 64, EAT.
[72] [1990] I.R.L.R. 421, EAT.

sections 1–7 or to a minimum period of notice and to be paid during the notice period, sections 86–91, unless the work outside Great Britain is for the same employer or the law which governs his contract of employment is the law of England and Wales or Scotland.

Likewise an employee who under his contract of employment ordinarily works outside Great Britain, is excluded from the following rights:

- sections 8–10—itemised pay statement;

- protection of wages provisions in Part II of the 1996 Act, ss.13–27;

- guarantee pay provisions in Part III, ss.28–35;

- protection from suffering a detriment in employment, Part VI, ss.44–49;

- time off work ss.50–63, except from ss.58–60, the right to time off for a pension scheme trustee;

- the suspension provisions provided for in Part VII, ss.64–70;

- the maternity rights contained in Part VIII, ss.71–85;

- Sections 92 and 93, the right to a written statement of reasons for dismissal;

- Part X, unfair dismissal, which applies only if:
  - the employee is dismissed at or after the end of the maternity leave period, section 84, or
  - dismissal occurs as a result of a failure to permit return after childbirth, section 96.

Interpretation of "ordinarily works outside Great Britain" has varied, ranging from an analysis of the practice: where the employee spent the majority of his working hours, to the contractual base test: where the contract states the employee's base is. In *Wilson v. Maynard Shipbuilding Consultants AB*[73] the Court of Appeal said that the issue could not be decided merely by looking at what actually happened, it was necessary to look at the express or implied terms of the contract to see where the employee's base was and in the absence of special factors leading to a contrary conclusion, it is likely to be the country where the employee's base is to be for the purpose of his work. This decision was followed in *Todd v. British Midland Airways Ltd*[74] where an airline pilot who spent fifty three per cent of his time overseas, but who was based in Britain, was held not to ordinarily work outside Great Britain.

ERA 1986, s.201 contains a power to extend employment legislation to offshore employment and this has been achieved by the Employment Protection (Offshore) Employment Orders 1976.[75] In *Addison v. Denholm Ship Management (UK) Ltd*,[76] it was held that Article 2(1)(b) of the Regulations, which extends employment protection rights to activities "connected with" the exploitation of the natural resources in any designated area, covers crews manning vessels providing the workers for the installation as they are sufficiently "connected with" the running of the installation itself. Such workers are therefore entitled to bring industrial tribunal proceedings.

[73] [1977] I.R.L.R. 491, CA.
[74] [1978] I.R.L.R. 370, CA.
[75] S.I. 1976 No. 766 as amended by S.I. 1977 No. 588 and S.I. 1981 No. 208.
[76] [1997] I.R.L.R. 389, EAT.

Mariners and share fishermen

ERA 1996, s.199(1) excludes from various sections and parts of the ERA "persons employed as a seaman in a ship registered in the United Kingdom under a crew agreement the provisions and form of which are of a kind approved by the Secretary of State, and section 199(2) excludes share fishermen: master and crew of a fishing vessel who are remunerated solely by a share in the profits or gross earnings of the vessel."

Police Officers

ERA 1996, s.200 provides that specified provisions do not apply to employment in the police service. In *Home Office v. Robinson*[77] this section was held to cover prison officers, and Criminal Justice and Public Order Act 1994, s.125 clarifies the position and provides that prison staff are not to be regarded as the police service.

7.2.5   Strike or other industrial action

To protect the neutrality of tribunals they were deprived of jurisdiction to hear a claim of unfair dismissal where, at the date of dismissal, the employee was taking part in a strike or other industrial action, or the employer was conducting or instituting a lock-out, unless the employer had selected only some for dismissal or re-engagement. The intention was not only to preserve neutrality, but as explained in *Heath v. J.F. Longman (Meat Salesmen) Ltd*[78]:

> ". . . the manifest overall purpose of [the section] is to give a measure of protection to an employer if his business is faced with ruin by a strike. It enables him in those circumstances, if he cannot carry on business without a labour force, to dismiss the labour force on strike; to take on another labour force without the stigma of its being an unfair dismissal." *per* Sir Hugh Griffiths

> *W. Heath v. J.F. Longman (Meat Salesmen) Ltd* [1973] I.R.L.R. 214 at 215, NIRC.

If an employer selectively dismissed or re-engaged, as demonstrated in *Sealey v. Avon Aluminium Co. Ltd*,[79] those employees selected for dismissal or not re-engaged could pursue an unfair dismissal remedy.

The position today is governed by the TULRCA 1992, s.237 in so far as unofficial industrial action is concerned, which is defined in section 237(2), in the event of which there is no right to complain of unfair dismissal. Where the industrial action is official, the position is covered by the TULRCA 1992, s.238, in that the industrial tribunal has no jurisdiction where at the date of dismissal the employer was conducting or instituting a lockout, or the complainant was taking part in a strike or other industrial action, except that this protection is lost in two situations: where

(a) one or more relevant employees have not been dismissed; or

(b) a relevant employee has, before the expiry of three months beginning with the date of dismissal been offered re-engagement and the complainant has not been offered re-engagement.

[77] [1981] I.R.L.R. 524, EAT.
[78] [1973] I.R.L.R. 214, NIRC.
[79] [1978] I.R.L.R. 285, IT.

7.2.6 Restrictions on contracting out and compromise agreements

By the ERA 1996, s.203(1) any agreement is void in so far as it purports to exclude or limit the operation of any provisions of the 1996 Act or to preclude a person from bringing any proceedings under the Act before a tribunal. However, in *Logan Salton v. Durham CC*[80] the EAT, in distinguishing *Igbo v. Johnson Matthey Chemicals*,[81] held that an agreement reached between the parties which was a contract separate from the contract of employment and was entered into willingly, without duress, after proper advice and for good consideration did not fall foul of section 203(1).

There are a number of statutory exceptions to section 203(1) provided for in section 203(2)(a)–(f).

By section 203(2)(e) a tribunal has no jurisdiction where an agreement has been reached and where a conciliation officer has acted under the Industrial Tribunals Act 1996, s.18. Conciliation Officers receive copies of all originating applications, and are under a statutory duty, ITA 1996, s.18(2), to attempt to conciliate between the parties, either at the request of either party or on his own initiative, where he considers that there is a reasonable prospect of success. Section 18(3) provides that it is only where the employee does not wish reinstatement or re-engagement or that reinstatement or re-engagement is not practicable that an agreement can be promoted on the basis of compensation to be paid by the employer. Any information disclosed to the Conciliation Officer in connection with performing his functions under section 18 is not admissible in evidence, but once agreement has been brokered in this way, the ERA 1996, s.203(2)(e) provides that such an agreement is binding to oust the jurisdiction of the Industrial Tribunal. The agreement may be submitted to the tribunal for promulgation as a formal decision or recorded on Form COT 3, but it was held in *Gilbert v. Kembridge Fibres Ltd*[82] that it is not, in fact, necessary for the agreement, once recorded by the Conciliation Officer on a "COT 3", to be signed by the parties in order to be binding, since the Conciliation Officer has performed his functions under section 203, and that is sufficient to make it an exception to the rule in section 203.

It became common practice in industry for firms to agree a settlement with the applicant and then call in an ACAS officer to draw up a formal agreement and witness the signatures of the parties, thus bringing the agreement within the provisions of section 203(2)(e). In *Moore v. Duport Furniture Products Ltd*[83] the House of Lords upheld an agreement reached in that way and held that where the parties had already reached an agreement as to compensation the Conciliation Officer is not required to promote reinstatement or re-engagement nor to investigate the fairness of the settlement reached or to explain the law to the parties.

Following the growth in such practices and the excessive workload involved, ACAS issued guidelines to tighten this system in that officers would not act in such cases (non industrial tribunal cases) where the qualifying period is not satisfied, where employment ended voluntarily or in any case unless the officer had acted already to conciliate between the parties. As a result of this policy change the number of conciliated cases declined substantially.[84]

By section 203(2)(f) a tribunal has no jurisdiction where a compromise agreement has been made which conforms with the criteria set out in section 203(3). The agreement:

[80] [1989] I.R.L.R. 99, EAT.
[81] [1986] I.R.L.R. 215, CA.
[82] [1984] I.R.L.R. 52, EAT.
[83] [1982] I.R.L.R. 31, HL.
[84] ACAS Annual Report 1991.

- must be in writing;
- must relate to a particular complaint, one agreement cannot with a broad brush, dispose of all statutory complaints;
- the employee (or worker) must have received independent legal advice from a qualified lawyer (in England this means a barrister (in Scotland an advocate) whether in practice as such or employed to give legal advice, or a solicitor who holds a practising certificate, as to the terms and effect of the proposed agreement and, in particular, its effect on his ability to pursue his rights before an industrial tribunal. Independent legal advice means that the lawyer concerned is not acting for the employer or an associated employer, section 203(6);
- there must be in force, when the adviser gives the advice, a policy of insurance covering the risk of a claim by the employee or worker in respect of loss arising in consequence of the advice;
- the agreement must identify the adviser and
- the agreement must state that the conditions regulating compromise agreements under the ERA are satisfied.

In *Rock-It-Cargo Ltd v. Green*[85] the EAT held that failure to pay money due under a compromise agreement made in accordance with the ERA 1996, s.203, the matter could be brought before the industrial tribunal. It was held that a compromise agreement is an agreement as to the terms of which the employee's employment was to be brought to an end, and "is quite plainly connected with that contract of employment" and therefore falls within Regulation 3 of the 1994 Regulations extending the jurisdiction of Industrial Tribunals to hear contract claims.[86]

However, in *Thompson v. Walton Car Delivery and BRS Automotive Ltd.*[87] a contract was lost by BRS to Waltons, who made it clear that they did not want to take over the staff, as a result of which BRS dismissed the staff and negotiated a compromise agreement. It was argued by Waltons that they could rely on the compromise agreement between BRS and the employees, such that they were not liable for the dismissals. The EAT held that the transfer was a relevant transfer within the TUPE Regulations,[88] but as the compromise agreement had not been completed until after the transfer had taken place it could not aid the transferee who was not a party to it. The transferee inhered liability for the dismissals, which were automatically unfair, under regulation 5(2) of the TUPE Regulations—on which see para 9.1.2. below. For detailed discussion on the TUPE Regulations, see Chapter 10.

Even though a claim for unfair dismissal may be settled by a compromise agreement, it was held by the Court of Appeal in *Dattani v. Trio Supermarkets Ltd*[89] that that did not preclude the applicant from commencing county court proceedings for unpaid wages, even though the wages claim could have been made at the same time as the unfair dismissal claim and pursued through the industrial tribunal: the applicant was not estopped by the doctrine of *res judicata* from pursuing his contractual remedy which was not incorporated within his Industrial Tribunal claim, nor did it form part of the compromise agreement.

---

[85] [1997] I.R.L.R. 581, EAT.
[86] Industrial Tribunals Extension of Jurisdiction (England and Wales) Order 1994, S.I. 1994 No. 1623.
[87] [1997] I.R.L.R. 343, EAT.
[88] S.I. 1981 No. 1794.
[89] *The Times*, February 2, 1998.

Reference should be made to para. 7.5.4 below with regard to changes to be implemented on the question of compromise agreements through the Employment Rights (Disputes Resolution) Bill 1998.

7.2.7 Dismissal procedure agreements

Where the parties have jointly successfully applied to the Secretary of State under the ERA 1996, s.110 for the agreement between them to be approved, approval means that those covered by the agreement forego their statutory dismissal rights in favour of those contained in the agreement, except that dismissal and selection for redundancy for specified reasons continues to be governed by the relevant sections of the ERA 1996. The only approved order to date is that between the Electrical Contractors' Association and the Electrical Electronic Telecommunication and Plumbing Union (EEPTU).

7.2.8 Qualifying period of employment and continuity

Eligibility for the right not to be unfairly dismissed and the right to a redundancy payment, along with the range of the other rights contained in the ERA 1996, require a period of continuous employment. A statutory concept for eligibility for statutory rights, continuity was first introduced in the Contracts of Employment Act 1963 in connection with eligibility for the newly created right to a minimum period of notice, and when a right to redundancy pay was introduced in the Redundancy Payments Act 1965 the right was only available for those employees with the required period of continuous employment. That pattern was followed when the right not to be unfairly dismissed was introduced by the Industrial Relations Act 1971, and the required period of continuous employment for unfair dismissal purposes is today contained in the ERA 1996, s.108. This provides that section 94 does not apply to the dismissal of an employee unless he has been continuously employed for a period of not less than two years ending with the effective date of termination. Section 155 contains a corresponding provision for eligibility for a redundancy payment. Prior to January 1983 periods of continuous employment were counted in "weeks". However, from January 2, 1983 the unit of calculation was changed to months and years.

Until February 6, 1995 qualifying service was built up depending upon the contractual hours in any one week. So that for unfair dismissal and redundancy pay purposes the qualifying period was two years where the employee worked under a contract for sixteen hours a week or more; five or more years where the contract normally involved eight or more hours but less than 16, and where the contract involved less than eight hours a week there was no right, regardless of the length of employment involved. The EOC[90] challenged these differential thresholds on the basis that they were indirectly discriminatory in that they had a disparate impact on women since it was recognised that more men than women worked for more than 16 hours a week, and as such was incompatible with Article 119 and Directive 76/207.

The House of Lords was not persuaded by the Government's social policy arguments put forward as justification for the discrimination and issued declarations that the differential thresholds were incompatible with Article 119 and Directive 75/117 in

[90] *R. v. Secretary of State for Employment, ex p. Equal Opportunities Commission* [1994] I.R.L.R. 176, HL.

relation to redundancy payments and Directive 76/207 in relation to the right to claim unfair dismissal. Subsequent regulations[91] removed from domestic law all provisions based on continuous employment which incorporated a working hours threshold. As the Regulations contain no transitional provisions the question arises as to whether part-time service prior to the coming into force of the Regulations counts towards continuous service. The ERA 1996, Sched. 2, para. 14(1) provides that "Chapter 1 of Part XIV applies to periods before this Act comes into force as it applies to later periods". In *Harvey v. Institute of the Motor Industry (No. 2)*[92] the EAT held that the courts should be slow to construe a legislative provision in a way which perpetuates a breach of European Law for longer than is necessary. Although there the court was discussing Sex Discrimination and Equal Pay (Remedies) Regulations 1993,[93] which removed the upper limit on compensation for sex discrimination cases following the ECJ decision in *Marshall v. Southampton and South West Hampshire Health Authority (Teaching) (No. 2)*,[94] those comments could equally be applied to the application of the 1995 Regulations. In addition, in *Biggs v. Somerset County Council*,[95] the Court of Appeal held that applications presented on the basis of the EOC Case[96] were out of time which ran from the effective date of termination, rather than the date of judgment, since the decision in the EOC Case[97] was merely declaratory of the law since at least 1 June 1976, the date of the ECJ decision in *Defrenne v. SABENA (No. 2)*,[98] in which it was held that Article 119 was directly applicable. If the EOC judgment was indeed declaratory of the law, service consisting of part-time hours prior to the introduction of the 1995 Regulations must be included when calculating continuity. There is, however, now no need to go back further than 1976 since the maximum period for the calculation of the basic award or for redundancy payment is 20 years.

The challenge by the EOC did not extend to the unfair dismissal/redundancy pay two year qualifying period itself. However, in *R. v. Secretary of State for Employment ex p. Seymour-Smith*, the House of Lords discharged the declaration issued by the CA to the effect that the two year limitation was incompatible with the equal treatment directive. Lord Hoffman, giving the judgment of the court, held that the directive was not directly effective as between individuals, only as against the state or emanations of the state, and was therefore not capable of affecting the private rights of the parties. As to whether the Regulations were compatible with Article 119, it was held that although the applicants had no *locus standi* the appeal would be heard and the following questions be referred to the ECJ:

"1. Does an award of compensation for breach of the right not to be unfairly dismissed under national legislation such as the (Employment Rights Act 1996) constitute 'pay' within the meaning of Article 119 of the E.C. Treaty?

2. If the answer to question 1 is 'Yes', do the conditions determining whether a worker has the right not to be unfairly dismissed fall within the scope of Article 119 or that of Directive 76/207?

[91] Employment Protection (Part-time Employees) Regulations, 1995 (S.I. 1995 No. 31), effective February 6, 1995.
[92] [1995] I.R.L.R. 416, EAT.
[93] S.I. 1993 No. 2798.
[94] Case C–271/91 [1993] I.R.L.R. 445, ECJ.
[95] [1996] I.R.L.R. 203, CA.
[96] [1994] I.R.L.R. 176, HL.
[97] *ibid*.
[98] Case 43/74 [1976] I.C.R. 547, ECJ.

3. What is the legal test for establishing whether a measure adopted by a member state has such a degree of disparate effect as between men and women as to amount to indirect discrimination for the purposes of Article 119 of the E.C. Treaty unless shown to be based upon objectively justified factors other than sex?

4. When must this legal test be applied to a measure adopted by a member state? In particular at which of the following points in time, or at what other point in time, must it be applied to the measure: (a) when the measure is adopted; (b) when the measure is brought into force; or (c) when the employee is dismissed?

5. What are the legal conditions for establishing the objective justification, for the purposes of indirect discrimination under Article 119, of a measure adopted by a member state in pursuance of its social policy? In particular, what material need the member state adduce in support of its grounds for justification?"

Pending the outcome of this case, the EAT in *Davidson v. City Electrical Factors Ltd*[99] ruled that "in any case where the qualifying period for employment is admitted to be between one and two years in relation to a claim for unfair dismissal, such *must* be "sisted" pending the outcome of the *Seymour-Smith* case and[1] Morison J. confirmed that this decision is binding on all tribunals.[2]

The provisions relating to the calculation of continuous employment are contained in the ERA 1996, Part XIV, Chapter 1, ss.210–219, and apply to statutory, as opposed to contractual rights, and by section 210(4) there is a presumption of continuity, so it is for the employer to prove that there is insufficient continuity to qualify for the right being sought. In *Wood v. York City Council*[3] it was held that a man may change his job, his place of work or the terms of his employment, he may even enter a new contract of employment, but provided he is employed by the same employer this change in the contractual terms will not affect his period of continuous employment. A period with the same employer is to be treated as continuous unless it comes within one of the specified exceptions.

Any week during the whole or part of which an employee's relations with his employer are governed by a contract of employment counts in computing the period of employment, section 212 and the statutory provisions regarding the calculation of continuity cannot be varied by agreement between the parties. In *Merton LBC v. Gardiner*[4] despite agreement that service was continuous as between different local authorities over a 12 year period it was held that it was not open to the parties to agree statutory continuity, which was limited to service with the final employer. Likewise, in *Liversidge v. London Residuary Body*[5] it was held that in the absence of statutory provisions to cover the situation continuity was broken when responsibility for water was transferred from the local authority to the water authority, and then again when transferred back to the local authority, so that despite doing the same job for twenty

---

[99] [1998] I.R.L.R. 108, EAT.
[1] p. 110.
[2] IDS Brief 612/May 1998.
[3] [1978] I.R.L.R. 228, CA.
[4] [1981] I.C.R. 269, EAT.
[5] [1989] I.C.R. 228, EAT.

years, continuity dated only from the date of transfer back to the local authority. The House of Lords in *Secretary of State for Employment v. Globe Elastic Threat Co. Ltd*[6] confirmed that continuous employment relates only to employment with one employer, apart from the statutory exceptions. Although agreement as to continuity may give a contractual right, it cannot not give rise to statutory rights.

The period of continuous employment, by section 211(1)(a) begins with the day on which the employee starts work, except that for the purposes of eligibility for redundancy payment, and calculation of the amount of that payment, continuity does not begin until the employee's eighteenth birthday. In *The General of the Salvation Army v. Dewsbury*[7] it was held that "starts work" means the beginning of the employee's contract, and not the date upon which he commences his duties. So where the contract was stated to commence on Saturday, May 1, but the applicant did not start work until Tuesday, May 4, because of a Bank Holiday, the period of continuous employment was held to commence on Saturday, May 1.

7.2.8.1   *Periods of absence which do not break continuity and count towards continuity*

A week which does not count towards continuity, breaks continuity except that section 212(2) and (3) contain exceptions where a period of absence which is not governed by a contract not only does not break continuity but counts towards the period of continuous employment:

- By section 212(2) any week the employee is absent for reasons of pregnancy or childbirth, following which she returns to work under the right given in section 79, counts towards continuity.

- section 212(3) provides that any week not covered by a contract of employment during the whole or part of which an employee is covered by paragraphs (a)–(d) counts towards continuity:

  - incapable of work because of sickness or injury, but for not more than 26 weeks, section 212(3)(a);
  - absent on account of a temporary cessation of work, section 212(3)(b). In *Fitzgerald v. Hall Russell Ltd*[8] the House of Lords, by a majority, held that the court had to focus on the position of the individual employee and consider whether there was work available for him to do. So where the employer had work, but not work for the applicant, there was a cessation within section 212(3)(b). A redistribution of the same amount of work was held in *Byrne v. Birmingham City District Council*[9] not to amount to a cessation, even though as a result of being placed in a "pool" the applicant was not offered work for about a month.

    A succession of fixed-term contracts that expired every year at the start of the summer holidays was held in *Ford v. Warwickshire County Council*[10] to be a temporary cessation within section 212(3)(a), the House of Lords holding that it does not matter that the absences from work are regular, predictable and agreed in advance between the employer and

---

[6] [1979] I.C.R. 706, HL.
[7] [1984] I.R.L.R. 222, EAT.
[8] [1970] A.C. 984, HL.
[9] [1987] I.C.R. 519, CA.
[10] [1983] I.C.R. 273, HL.

employee. All that is relevant is that there should be no contract of employment during the period and that there is no work for the employee to do. In *University of Aston v. Malik*[11] the employer's argument that there was work to do, just no money to pay for it was referred to by Balcombe, J. as "intellectual genesis". Work, he said, meant paid work. It was held that if there was no paid work available then the employee is out of work whether the non-availability is because of lack of orders or lack of money.

As to whether that cessation is temporary, in *Fitzgerald v. Hall Russell Ltd*[12] Lord Upjohn, *obiter*, advocated a "broad brush approach" looking back afterwards to consider all the circumstances. He said that it is necessary to look at the original dismissal with hindsight, that is to say with the knowledge of all that has happened since the original dismissal until the second dismissal, and then decide whether in all the circumstances of the case the original dismissal can properly be described as due to a temporary cessation of work.

In *Flack v. Kodak Ltd*[13] the Court of Appeal rejected the mathematical approach of Lord Diplock in *Ford v. Warwickshire County Council*,[14] holding that the proper approach is to take into account all the relevant circumstances and in particular to consider the length of the period of absence in the context of the period of employment as a whole, in accordance with the test laid down in *Fitzgerald v. Hall Russell Ltd.*[15] Even though there was a gap of 86 days with periods of employment on either side of 17 and 12 days respectively, taken over the whole period it was held that the case fell within section 212(3)(b), as being a temporary cessation. However, in *Sellars v. Charrington Fuels Ltd*[16] the stricter "mathematical approach" was applied where over a fifteen year period the applicant had spent approximately half of each year in and half out of employment. The Court of Appeal held that the test in *Ford*[17] applied equally to cases involving a regular pattern of absences.

- absent in circumstances such that, by arrangement or custom, he is regarded as continuing in the employment of his employer for any purpose, section 212(3)(c). In *Lloyds Bank v. Secretary of State for Employment*[18] an arrangement of 35 hours per week on alternate weeks was considered as to whether each week off broke continuity, or whether the "arrangement" could be brought within sub paragraph (3). Talbot J., in an imaginative judgment, relying on the speech of Lord Morris in *Fitzgerald v. Hall Russell Ltd*[19] held that the whole of section 212 was designed in the interests of employees to enable those with *de facto* breaks still to bring themselves within employment protection legislation. By this route he reached the conclusion that the weeks during which the

[11] [1984] I.C.R. 492, EAT.
[12] [1970] A.C. 984, HL.
[13] [1986] I.C.R. 775, EAT.
[14] [1983] I.C.R. 273, HL.
[15] [1970] A.C. 984, HL.
[16] [1989] I.R.L.R. 152, CA.
[17] [1983] I.C.R. 273, HL.
[18] [1979] I.C.R. 258, EAT.
[19] [1970] A.C. 984, HL.

applicant did not work and was not required to work were periods not governed by a contract, rather than periods governed by a contract requiring her not to work: her contract was held to terminate at the end of each weeks' work and begin again when she re-started work.

In *Morris v. Walsh Western United Kingdom Ltd*[20] it was held that section 212(3)(c) envisages that the "arrangement" is in place when the employee is absent from work, and an "arrangement" made after return to work was not within the provision. In doing so the EAT distinguished *Ingram v. Foxon*[21] and followed that in *Murphy v. A. Birrell & Sons*[22]

An "arrangement" for the continuation of employment can arise as the result of a collective agreement, so that in *Taylor v. Triumph Motors British Leyland U.K. Ltd & Secretary of State for Employment*[23] a union management agreement that employment would be considered to be continuous if broken by a break of less than six months was sufficient to constitute an "arrangement" for the purposes of section 212(3)(c).

- absent from work wholly or party because of pregnancy or childbirth, section 212(3)(d).

7.2.8.2 *Periods of absence which do not break continuity but do not count towards continuity*

By section 215 for the purposes of qualifying for both unfair dismissal and calculating the amount of redundancy payment, if the employee was employed outside Great Britain during the whole or any part of the week and was an employed earner for the purposes of Class 1 NICs that week does not count towards continuity, but does not break continuity.

Likewise, by section 216(1) a week does not count towards continuity if during any part of it the employee takes part in a strike but by section 216(2) and (3) continuity is not broken. In *Hanson v. Fashion Industries (Hartlepool) Ltd*[24] the employee was dismissed while participating in a strike, but re-engaged after a break of nine weeks, under a contract which stated that her continuous employment began afresh when she started work again. When she subsequently went on maternity leave and claimed maternity pay the question arose as to when her period of continuous employment started.The EAT held that the provisions relating to continuity provide "a statutory code and it is to that statutory code that one has to look when considering the length and continuity of service". It was not open to the parties to agree that continuity was broken when the statute quite clearly stated that was not so.

7.2.8.3 *Change of employer*

At common law when there is a change of employer the contract of employment automatically terminates, thus breaking continuity and one employer cannot assign to another the benefit of a contract of employment. In *Nokes v. Doncaster Amalgamated Collieries Ltd*[25] Lord Atkin said that this was simply to provide protection for the individual employee otherwise the master could change and the employee would have

---

[20] [1997] I.R.L.R. 562, EAT.
[21] [1985] I.R.L.R. 5, EAT.
[22] [1978] I.R.L.R. 458, EAT.
[23] [1975] I.R.L.R. 369, IT.
[24] [1981] I.C.R. 35, EAT.
[25] [1940] 3 All E.R. 549, HL.

no say, and may even have no knowledge, rendering employees "serfs and not servants". However, by section 218(1)–(8) there are a number of situations in which, when the employer changes, for statutory, but not for contractual purposes, continuity of employment is not broken. The Transfer of Undertakings (Protection) of Employment Regulations 1981,[26] which implement Directive 77/187, the Acquired Rights Directive, provides that where there is a "relevant transfer" it does not operate to terminate the contract of employment of any person employed by the transferor, but any such contract which would otherwise have been terminated by the transfer shall have effect after the transfer as if originally made between the employee and the transferee, except where the employee objects to this. All the transferor's rights, powers, duties and liabilities under or in connection with any such contract are transferred to the transferee. The law surrounding the Transfer Regulations which have been interpreted to cover both statutory and contractual matters is explained in Chapter 9.

7.2.8.4 *Re-employment after unfair dismissal*

The Employment Protection (Continuity of Employment) Regulations 1996[27] provide for preservation of continuity of employment where reinstatement or re-engagement takes place as a result of:

- a claim made under section 110—dismissal procedure agreement;
- the presentation of a complaint of dismissal arising under ERA 1996, SDA 1975, RRA 1976 or DDA 1995;
- action taken by an ACAS conciliation officer under ITA 1996, s.18;
- the making of a compromise agreement for the purposes of ERA 1996, SDA 1975, RRA 1976 or DDA 1995 or made in relation to industrial tribunal claims for breach of contract.

7.2.9 Right to written statement of reasons for dismissals

ERA 1996, s.92 provides that an employee is entitled to a written statement giving particulars of the reasons for dismissal if:

- he is given notice of dismissal;
- his contract is terminated without notice; or
- his fixed-term contract expires without being renewed.

The right to a statement under this section is confined to employees with not less than two years" continuous employment on the effective date of termination and is available only if the employee requests it. The employer must provide the statement within 14 days of the request. If the employee is dismissed at any time while pregnant or after childbirth in circumstances in which her maternity leave period ends by reason of the dismissal: by section 92(4) there is then no requirement for two years continuous

---

[26] S.I. 1981 No. 1794.
[27] S.I. 1996 No. 3147, effective 13 January 1997.

employment and the statement is available as of right. There is no right to a statement in the event of a constructive dismissal.

The statement is, by section 92(5), admissible in evidence in any proceedings and there is a right to make a complaint to an industrial tribunal if the employer unreasonably fails to provide a statement or the particulars of reasons given in purported compliance with section 92 are inadequate or untrue. The TURERA 1993 introduced the wording "unreasonably fails" replacing the previous ground for complaint, of if the employer "refused" to give a statement. In *Kent County Council v. Gilham*[28] it was held by the Court of Appeal that a covering letter which refers unambiguously to an earlier letter sent to the employee giving the reasons for dismissal, is sufficient compliance with section 92 provided a copy of the earlier letter is attached. In addition, the sending of the statement to the employee's duly authorised agent, for example a legal representative, is sufficient.

7.2.10   Upper age limit

ERA 1996, ss.109(1) and 156(1) provides that the right not to be unfairly dismissed or to receive a redundancy payment, does not apply to an employee where if on or before the effective date of termination:

- in the undertaking in which the employee was employed there was a normal retiring age (NRA) for an employee holding the position held by the employee and—the age was the same whether the employee holding that position was a man or a woman, that normal retiring age, and

- in other cases, the age of 65.

These provisions were amended to be sexually neutral following the ECJ decision in *Marshall v. Southampton & South-West Hampshire Area HA (Teaching)*.[29]

The principle is that where there is a NRA for that position in the undertaking concerned and it is a common age and not discriminatory, that is the age beyond which there will be no eligibility for either unfair dismissal or redundancy payment, regardless of the age at which that is set. If there is no NRA, or the NRA that has been set is discriminatory as between men and women, then the age beyond which there will be no eligibility will be 65. That the section creates two separate hurdles, as opposed to one test with two hurdles, was confirmed by the House of Lords in *Nothman v. Barnett LBC*.[30]

The first step is therefore to discover whether there is a NRA and if so what that age is. In *Waite v. Government Communications Headquarters*,[31] Waite was dismissed when $60^{1}/_{2}$ and the question arose as to whether there was a NRA, and if so, what that age was.

Lord Fraser, giving the judgment of the House, reviewed the law and said that:

> "I . . . reject the view that the contractual retiring age conclusively fixes the normal retiring age. I accept that where there is a contractual retiring age,

---

[28] [1985] I.R.L.R. 16, CA.
[29] Case C–152/84 [1986] I.R.L.R. 141 ECJ, SDA 1986.
[30] 1979] I.C.R. 11, HL.
[31] [1983] I.C.R. 653, HL.

applicable to all, or nearly all the employees holding the position which the appellant employee held, there is a presumption that the contractual retiring age is the normal retiring age for the group. But it is a presumption which, in my opinion, can be rebutted by evidence that there is in practice some higher age at which employees holding the position are regularly retired, and which they have reasonably come to regard as their normal retiring age. . . . 'Normal' in this context is not a mere synonym for 'usual'. The word 'usual' suggests a purely statistical approach by ascertaining the age at which the majority of employees actually retire, without regard to whether some of them may have been retained in office until a higher age for special reasons—such as a temporary shortage of employees with a particular skill, or a temporary glut of work, or personal consideration for an employee who has not sufficient reckonable service to qualify for a full pension. The proper test is in my view not merely statistical. It is to ascertain what would be the reasonable expectation or understanding of the employees holding that position at the relevant time. The contractual retiring age will *prima facie* be the normal, but it may be displaced by evidence that it is regularly departed from in practice. The evidence may show that the contractual retirement age has been superseded by some definite higher age, and, if so, that will have become the normal retiring age. Or the evidence may show merely that the contractual retiring age has been abandoned and that employees retire at a variety of higher ages. In that case there will be no normal retiring age and the statutory alternative (of 65) will apply." *per* Lord Fraser

Waite v. Government Communications Headquarters [1983] I.R.L.R. 341 at 344, HL.

Applying these principles it was held that the NRA was 60, that there was insufficient evidence of a practice permitting relevant employees to retain their office after attaining NRA. That a code governing conditions provided that those with less than twenty years' reckonable service "should" be allowed to continue in service was held not to mean "must", and following *Howard v. The Department for National Savings*[32] *per* Lord Denning M.R., was held to mean "should normally be allowed".

These principles were applied to similar facts in Hughes v. DHSS[33] where the contractual retiring age was 60, but a practice allowed employees to stay until age 65. Hughes, having worked past 60 was dismissed following a change of policy to implement retirement at 60. The House of Lords held that a policy to allow employees to stay on after NRA could only be relied upon so long as it remains in force. Although the reasonable expectation may initially have been to work to age 65 there had been a change in policy and at the date of dismissal (which is the date at which the NRA is to be judged) the expectation had changed to 60, which had become the NRA.

Whilst both *Waite* and *Hughes* were concerned with the employer's right to change his policy of allowing employees to remain beyond NRA, in *Bratko v. Beloit Walmsley Ltd*[34] the situation arose where the employer sought to change the NRA itself. All employees had a contractual and NRA of 65. Following failed attempts to negotiate a reduction in that age the employer, after giving notice of his intention to unilaterally reduce the age to 64, followed this with individual notices of that change. When

---

[32] [1981] I.R.L.R. 40, CA.
[33] [1985] I.R.L.R. 263, HL.
[34] [1995] I.R.L.R. 629, EAT.

dismissed the question arose as to whether *Waite v. GCHQ* applied in that, having been notified of the new NRA, the reasonable expectation at the time of dismissal was that employment would be terminated at 64 instead of 65.

The EAT distinguished *Waite* and *Hughes* as being confined to a challenge that the NRA had been varied to some higher age. The employee relied on the CA in *Brooks v. British Telecommunications plc*.[35] where it was held that the NRA is an aspect of an employer's employment policy and that by a change in administrative policy, an employer can introduce a new specific age which thereafter becomes the new NRA for the purposes of section 109(1)(a), so long as no breach of the employees' rights under their contracts of employment is involved. The employer, on the other hand, relied on *Barber v. Thames Television plc*.[36] which involved a phased unilateral reduction in the NRA from 65 to 60 which resulted in Barber being compulsorily retired at 64.

In *Bratko* Judge Hicks Q.C. said:

> ". . . it would be surprising in principle if the employer could change the normal retiring age to the disadvantage of the employee without taking the steps necessary to obtain a change in the contractual retirement age, typically by either a consensual variation by terminating the contracts by lawful notice and offering fresh ones. Secondly, we do not believe it to be coincidental or unadvised that Lord Fraser (in *Waite*) four times uses the word 'higher' . . . it is true that in *Waite* it was an increase which was in question, but Lord Fraser, in our understanding, is not dealing merely with the facts of *Waite*, but with the policy of the Act. In our view, that informs the way in which he expresses the possibility of a departure from the contractual retirement age." *per* Judge Hicks Q.C.

Bratko v. Beloit Walmsley Ltd [1995] I.R.L.R. 629 at 632, EAT.

The EAT in *Bratko*, concluded that "the reasoning in *Brooks* is to be preferred" and that the employer's action in reducing the age at which employees had to retire without reducing the contractual retiring age by agreement or any other lawful or effective way, did not establish a new normal retiring age. The EAT in *Bratko v. Beloit Walmsley Ltd* did not consider the CA decision in *Patel v. Nagesan*[37] which confirmed that a unilateral variation did not create a NRA where none existed before.

In the absence of law which prohibits discrimination on the basis of age, the reasoning in the *Brakto* and *Patel* decisions makes sense on normal contractual principles. However, in *Secretary of State for Scotland v. Taylor*[38] the EAT had to consider whether dismissal at 55 as part of a policy to lose 1,000 staff was a breach of contract where there was an equal opportunities policy which specifically referred to age and which was held to be incorporated into the contract of employment. Lord Johnston held that although the equal opportunities policy was contractual it was not envisaged that it would apply once employment had been brought to an end by retirement and that retirement in itself was not discriminatory since employment after the age of 55 was entirely at the employer's discretion. The case appears not to have been argued on the basis of the reasoning in *Brakto* and *Patel*—that there was no NRA of 55 since the unilateral variation did not take effect.

---

[35] [1992] I.R.L.R. 66, CA.
[36] [1992] I.R.L.R. 410, CA.
[37] [1995] I.R.L.R. 370, CA.
[38] [1997] I.R.L.R. 608, EAT.

Perhaps it is premature, but should age be added to the grounds upon which it is unlawful to discriminate not only would this provide a remedy in *Taylor* and similar cases but section 109(1) might then be *ultra vires*.

7.2.11 Minimum notice periods

The right to minimum periods of notice was first introduced by the Contracts of Employment Act 1963, and is now contained in the ERA 1996, s.86 and applies to a person, as opposed to an employee, with continuous employment of one month or more.

Section 86(1) provides for notice by the employer of not less than one week where the period of continuous employment is less than two years, not less than one week's notice for each year of continuous employment between two and 12 years and not less than 12 weeks' notice if the period of continuous employment is 12 years or more. The employee, on the other hand, is obliged to give not less than one weeks' notice where he has been continuously employed for one month or more. Section 86(3) provides that any shorter contractual notice period is void, but the statutory notice period may be waived or payment in lieu may be accepted.

7.3 THE REASONS FOR DISMISSAL

By ERA 1996, s.98, in order to determine whether the dismissal is fair or unfair, it is for the employer to show the reason for dismissal and that it is a potentially fair reason: that means that it falls within the prima facie fair reasons contained in section 98(2)(a)–(d) or is for some other substantial reason of a kind such as to justify dismissal, section 98(1)(b). Then, by the ERA 1996, s.98(4):

> "Where the employer has fulfilled the requirements of subsection (1), the determination of the question whether the dismissal is fair or unfair (having regard to the reason shown by the employer)—
>
> (a) depends on whether in the circumstances (including the size and administrative resources of the employer's undertaking) the employer acted reasonably or unreasonably in treating it as a sufficient reason for dismissing the employee, and
> (b) shall be determined in accordance with equity and the substantial merits of the case."

In *Union of Construction, Allied Trades and Technicians v. Brain*[39] Lord Donaldson outlined the stages in the process:

> "The section operates in three stages. First, the employer has to show why in fact he dismissed the employee. I say 'why in fact' because the Act does not concern itself with possible justifications which occur to the employer later or which did not move him at the time. This is no great burden upon the employer. He must, after all, know why he dismissed the employee.

---

[39] [1981] I.R.L.R. 224, CA.

Next the employer has to show that this reason falls into one of the four categories of reasons set out in subsection (2) of the section or that it was 'some other substantial reason of a kind such as to justify the dismissal of an employee holding the position which that employee held'; see subsection (1)(b). This is not an exercise in elaborate legal classification. All that is required is that the Tribunal shall consider whether, looking at the matter broadly and giving the words their ordinary meaning, the reason for the dismissal falls within one or other of these five descriptions.

The third stage consists of the Tribunal asking itself the question, 'Has the employer satisfied us that in the circumstances (having regard to equity and the substantial merits of the case) he acted reasonably in treating this conduct as a sufficient reason for dismissing the employee': see subsection (4). Whether someone acted reasonably is always a pure question of fact, so long as the Tribunal deciding the issue correctly directs itself on the matters which should and should not be taken into account. But where Parliament has directed a Tribunal to have regard to equity—and that, of course, means common fairness and not a particular branch of the law—and to the substantial merits of the case, the Tribunal's duty is really very plain. It has to look at the question in the round and without regard to a lawyer's technicalities. It has to look at it in an employment and industrial relations context and not in the context of the Temple and Chancery Lane. It should, therefore, be very rare for any decision of an Industrial Tribunal under this section to give rise to any question of law. And this is quite plainly what Parliament intended." *per* Lord Donaldson

Union of Construction, Allied Trades and Technicians v. Brain [1981] I.R.L.R. 224 at 227, CA.

In *Post Office (Counters) Ltd v. Heavy*[40] the EAT stressed that the question of reasonableness falls for consideration after the employer has established the reason, also that, following amendments in the EA 1980, s.98(4) lays no burden of proof on either party: the question being one for the industrial tribunal to decide in the light of section 98(4) itself, but clearly, on the evidence put forward by the parties.

Unlike an action for wrongful dismissal,[41] it was established in *Earl v. Slater & Wheeler (Airlyne) Ltd*[42] that in seeking to establish the reason for dismissal in unfair dismissal proceedings, the employer may only rely on what he knew or ought to have known when he dismissed the employee. This, and the Court of Appeal judgment in *Abernethy v. Mott, Hay and Anderson,*[43] that it must be a reason in existence at the time when the employee is given notice,[44] was approved by the House of Lords in *W. Devis & Sons Ltd. v. R.A. Atkins,*[45] so that where an employee was dismissed for refusing to obey instructions, the company were prevented from introducing evidence of misconduct which would have justified dismissal, but which was not known about when the dismissal took place. A reason which comes to the attention of the employer after dismissal but which would nevertheless have justified dismissal, goes to damages and not to the reason for dismissal.

[40] [1990] I.C.R. 1, EAT.
[41] *Boston Deep Sea Fishing & Ice Co. v. Ansell* (1888) 39 ChD 339.
[42] [1972] I.R.L.R. 115, NIRC.
[43] [1974] I.R.L.R. 213, CA.
[44] *per* Lord Denning MR.
[45] [1977] I.R.L.R. 314, HL.

In *Parkinson v. March Consulting Ltd*[46] the Court of Appeal distinguished *W. Devis & Sons Ltd v. R.A. Atkins*[47] as a case of summary dismissal and relying on *Stacey v. Babcock Power Ltd (Construction Division)*,[48] held that when dismissal is by notice the reason has to be determined both by reference to the reason for giving the notice and the reason when the dismissal occurs, which involves considering the reasons throughout the notice period. Sir Iain Glidewell said that the date of dismissal being the date the contract terminates, the tribunal is entitled to take into account the reason given in the notice, in a response to a request under section 92, and any other relevant facts or correspondence before the date of termination. The Court of Appeal confirmed in *Alboni v. Ind Coope Retail Ltd*[49] that an industrial tribunal is bound to have regard to events between notice of dismissal and the date that dismissal took effect, both for the purposes of determining the reason for dismissal and whether the employer acted reasonably in treating that reason as sufficient reason for dismissal. The House of Lords' decisions in *W. Devis & Sons Ltd. v. R.A. Atkins*[50] and *West Midlands Co-operative Society v. Tipton*[51] were confined by the Court of Appeal to cases involving summary dismissal and subsequent appeal whereby a reason that emerges at the appeal, that is after termination has occurred, cannot retrospectively be used to justify a dismissal which was, in fact, based on an insufficient reason.

However, if the employer puts the wrong label on his reason for dismissal it may not necessarily be fatal to his case. In *Hannan v. TNT-IPEC (U.K.) Ltd*[52] the EAT held that the tribunal was not entitled to find a dismissal fair on a ground not pleaded or argued where the difference in grounds goes to facts and substance and there would or might have been some substantial or significant difference in the way the case was conducted, so that the employee was thereby prejudiced. But where the different grounds are really different labels, the late introduction is not a ground for interference on appeal. *Hotson v. Wisbech Conservative Club*[53] is an example of a change of reason which went to substance rather than label. Inefficiency was given as the reason for dismissal, although the real reason was suspected dishonesty. The EAT held that although the employer is not tied to the label, where the original reason given for dismissal is lack of capability, the substitution or addition of suspected dishonesty as a reason, even though precisely the same facts may be relied upon by the employer, goes beyond a mere change of label: it is too serious and too significant to be given such an innocuous character.

The House of Lords in *Smith v. City of Glasgow District Council*[54] stressed that the search under section 98(1) is for the principal reason for dismissal, which is important in relation to section 98(4) because it had to be decided that the employer acted reasonably in treating *it* as a sufficient reason for dismissing the employee, *it* referring back to the reason or principal reason under section 98(1). So where multiple reasons were put forward and one of these was held not to have been made out, when the industrial tribunal failed to go on to establish whether one of the other reasons was the principle reason for dismissal, as a matter of law the employer had failed to establish

---

[46] [1997] I.R.L.R. 308, CA.
[47] [1977] I.R.L.R. 314, HL.
[48] [1986] I.R.L.R. 3, EAT.
[49] [1998] I.R.L.R. 131, CA.
[50] [1977] I.R.L.R. 314, HL.
[51] [1986] I.R.L.R. 112, HL.
[52] [1986] I.R.L.R. 165, EAT.
[53] [1984] I.R.L.R. 422, EAT.
[54] [1987] I.R.L.R. 326, HL.

the reason for dismissal, making the dismissal unfair. This is a warning against the "scatter approach" to the giving of reasons, in that if an employer is unsuccessful in persuading the industrial tribunal that reason A is the principle reason for dismissal, to then argue against itself that reason B was the principle reason may, where the difference goes to substance, result in the tribunal finding that there was, in fact, no reason for these purposes.

In establishing the reason for dismissal, by the ERA 1996, s.107 provides that "no account shall be taken of any pressure which by calling, organising, procuring or financing a strike or other industrial action, or threatening to do so . . ." In addition, the TULRCA 1992, s.160 provides that where the employer was induced to dismiss by pressure of a strike and that the pressure was exercised because the complainant was not a member of a trade union, a particular trade union, or one of a number of trade unions, at the initiative of either the employer or applicant, providing the request is made before the hearing, the court will join that person and may make an order that compensation be paid by that person.

7.3.1 Code of practice and disciplinary procedures

The ACAS Code of Practice,[55] sets out the need to let employees know via a disciplinary rules and procedures, the standard of conduct expected and the ERA 1996, s.3(1)(a) requires a statement under section 1 to include any disciplinary rules applicable to the employee or referring the employee to a document specifying such rules, except that by an amendment introduced by the EA 1989, this does not apply if on the day employment began the number of employees was less than 20, section 3(3). Such codes should be designed to emphasise and encourage improvements in individual conduct, as opposed to being viewed primarily as a means of imposing sanctions, but employees should be made aware of the likely consequences of breaking rules. In particular, employees should be given a clear indication of the type of conduct which may warrant summary dismissal: that is dismissal without notice.[56]

Paragraph 10 of the Code provides that "Disciplinary procedures should;

(a) Be in writing.

(b) Specify to whom they apply.

(c) Provide for matters to be dealt with quickly.

(d) indicate the disciplinary actions which may be taken.

(e) Specify the levels of management which have the authority to take the various forms of disciplinary action, ensuring that immediate superiors do not normally have the power to dismiss without reference to senior management.

(f) provide for individuals to be informed of the complaints against them and to be given an opportunity to state their case before decisions are reached.

(g) Give individuals the right to be accompanied by a trade union representative or by a fellow employee of their choice.

---

[55] ACAS Code of Practice 1—disciplinary practice and procedures in employment. The Employment Protection Code of Practice (Disciplinary Practice & Procedures) Order 1998 (S.I. 1998 No. 44) issued under powers contained in the TULRCA 1992, s.201.
[56] *ibid.*, para. 8.

(h) Ensure that, except for gross misconduct, no employees are dismissed for a first breach of discipline.

(i) Ensure that disciplinary action is not taken until the case has been carefully investigated.

(j) Ensure that individuals are given an explanation for any penalty imposed.

(k) Provide a right of appeal and specify the procedure to be followed."

In practice this translates to a procedure that typically will involve a series of warnings before considering disciplinary action. Where a first or minor offences is concerned an informal or oral warning issued by the immediate supervisor may be appropriate in order to improve conduct. Where the conduct calls for a more formal approach the code recommend that:

(a) a formal oral warning or, if the issue is more serious, there should be a written warning setting out the nature of the offence and the likely consequences of further offences.

(b) Further misconduct might warrant a final written warning which should contain a statement that any recurrence would lead to suspension or dismissal or some other penalty.

(c) The final step might be disciplinary transfer, or disciplinary suspension without pay (but only if these are allowed for by an express or implied condition of the contract of employment), or dismissal, according to the nature of the misconduct. Special consideration should be given before imposing disciplinary suspension without pay and it should not normally be for a prolonged period.[57]

In operation the ACAS Code recommends that the facts are established promptly; that the individual is interviewed before any decision is taken; that he is given an opportunity to state his case and have someone with him if he wishes,[58] all of which appears to be an application of the duty to act fairly, and in *McLaren v. National Coal Board*[59] Sir John Donaldson M.R. said: that "standards of fairness are immutable" and that no amount of industrial warfare could justify failing to give an employee an opportunity of giving an explanation of the alleged conduct.

The Code is admissible in evidence in proceedings before an industrial tribunal, but failure to observe any provision does not of itself render that person liable to proceedings.[60] Nevertheless, the importance of procedure has been stressed repeatedly and the ACAS Code "has become so much a part and parcel of good industrial relations that everybody . . . should give very considerable weight to the sort of procedures laid down in the Code of Practice",[61] so that a potentially fair reason for dismissal may be found to be unfair where the dismissal was not carried out in a fair way.

---

[57] *ibid.*, para. 12.
[58] *ibid.*, para. 11.
[59] [1988] I.R.L.R. 215, CA. Note in the *Fairness at Work* White Paper Cm. 3968 1998, para. 4.29 it is proposed to create a legal right for employees to be accompanied by a fellow employee or trade union representative of their choice during grievance and disciplinary procedures.
[60] TULRCA 1992, s.207.
[61] *Littlewoods Organisation v. Egenti* [1976] I.C.R. 516, EAT, *per* Kilner-Brown J.

Although a statutory statement is not contractual, it is evidence of the contractual terms and in this way a disciplinary procedure could become binding. Alternatively, disciplinary procedures may be contractual by being incorporated via collectively negotiated agreements or other documentation, and the question arises as to whether a breach of a contractual procedure agreement affects the fairness of the dismissal:

> "So far we have been approaching the industrial tribunal's reason that the denial of Mr. Marney's contractual right of appeal resulted in the dismissal being unfair. In our judgment that, by itself, is an over simplification. It is not every denial of a contractual right that has that result. It is, in our judgment, only when the circumstances warrant that conclusion, and in this type of case of a defective appellate stage there has to be a circumstance that renders the appellate stage defective in the sense that it should or could have found and demonstrated a flaw in the decision at first instance in the internal procedures of the employer." *per* Knox J.

Post Office v. Marney [1990] I.R.L.R. 170 at 174, EAT.

This was approved by the Court of Appeal in *Cabaj v. Westminster City Council*,[62] when Morritt L.J., in a case concerning a defective appeal panel, surveyed the authorities and concluded that a dismissal in breach of a contractual disciplinary code had relevance to the statutory test of fairness only insofar as it had denied the applicant the opportunity of demonstrating that the real reason for dismissal was insufficient. However, although internal disciplinary procedures ought to be followed, a failure to do so was held not to be so fundamental that it will lead, as a matter of course, to a finding of unfair dismissal. This decision is based on an earlier judgment of the Court of Appeal in *Stoker v. Lancashire County Council*[63] and the decision of the House of Lords in *West Midlands Co-operative Society Ltd. v. Tipton*[64]:

> "A dismissal is unfair if the employer unreasonably treats his real reason as a sufficient reason to dismiss the employee, either when he makes his original decision to dismiss or when he maintains that decision at the conclusion of an internal appeal. By the same token, a dismissal may be held to be unfair when the employer has refused to entertain an appeal to which the employee was contractually entitled and thereby denied to the employee the opportunity of showing that, in all the circumstances, the employer's real reason for dismissing him could not reasonably be treated as sufficient. . . ." *per* Lord Bridge

West Midlands Co-operative Society Ltd v. Tipton [1986] I.C.R. 192 at 204, HL.

In the event of a contract claim for failure to follow contractual procedure, the measure of damages was held in *Jancik v. Winerite Ltd*[65] to be based upon an assessment of the time for which, had the procedure been followed, the employee's employment would have continued, not upon the chances that if the procedure had been followed the employee might never have been dismissed: the tribunal not being concerned with whether correct use of procedure would have caused the employer to

[62] [1996] I.C.R. 960, CA.
[63] [1992] I.R.L.R. 75, CA.
[64] [1986] I.C.R. 192, HL.
[65] [1998] I.R.L.R. 68, EAT.

change his mind, but only how long it would have taken him to dismiss if he had followed the procedure. This relegates the contractual right to a procedure as a mere delay of the inevitable, and ignores the principle of contractual damages; to place the party in the position he would have been in if the breach had not occurred.

7.3.2 Potentially fair reasons for dismissal

In accordance with ILO Recommendation 116 there are a limited number of reasons for dismissal upon which the employer can rely and these are contained in section 98(2)(a)–(d) and section 98(1)(b):

7.3.2.1 *Capability or qualifications*

Capability is defined in section 98(3)(a) and means capability assessed by reference to skill, aptitude, health or any other practical or mental quality. In *Sutton & Gates (Luton) Ltd v. Boxall*[66] it was said that section 98(2)(a) is to be construed relatively narrowly—to cases where the employee is incapable of satisfactory work, and cases where a person has not come up to standard through his own carelessness, negligence or maybe idleness are more appropriately dealt with as cases of misconduct. However, in *Abernethy v. Mott, Hay & Anderson*[67] it was held that inflexibility and lack of adaptability come within aptitude and mental qualities. In *Littlewoods Organisation Ltd v. Egenti*[68] the EAT stressed the importance of the different labels in that the requirement of various steps of procedure which exist in cases of dismissal for misconduct, which it is a disciplinary measure, is different when the complaint is lack of competence or capability, when the question of sanction is irrelevant. Warnings are important in that they can be considered constructively in letting the employee know what is expected and then for checking attainment and giving guidance and advice on achievement, with the possibility of training to improve performance. On the other hand, the level of incompetence may be so great that no amount of warning or help would result in an improvement in work.

By the definition of capability, sickness absence also falls to be considered under this head, however, consideration of sickness absence under section 98(2)(a) does not extend to extremely severe or excessively prolonged absences since it can be there argued that the contract is frustrated (see para. 5.5.1 above). In addition, it was held in *International Sports Co. Ltd v. Thomson*[69] that an unacceptable level of intermittent absences due to minor ailments may be attributed to misconduct under section 98(2)(b), and subject to disciplinary procedure and warnings with a view to improvement or dismissal, since in such a case the absences are not outside the individual employee's control. When absence is due to ill health under section 98(2)(a) it was held in *East Lindsey D.C. v. Daubney*,[70] unless there were wholly exceptional circumstances, before an employee is dismissed steps should be taken, which are sensible in all the circumstances, to consult the employee to inform themselves of the true medical position, simply because if the employee is not consulted injustice may occur. In so deciding, Phillips J. relied on his own earlier judgment in *Spencer v. Paragon Wallpapers*[71] where he said that before dismissal the position had to be

---

[66] [1978] I.R.L.R. 486, EAT.
[67] [1974] I.C.R. 323, CA.
[68] [1976] I.C.R. 516, EAT.
[69] [1980] I.R.L.R. 340, EAT.
[70] [1977] I.R.L.R. 181, EAT.
[71] [1977] I.C.R. 301, EAT.

weighed up, balancing the employer's need for work to be done, against the needs of the employee for time to recover, so that where it was established that the employee was going to be absent for a further four to six weeks, having already been absent for two months, when the employer needed labour to fulfil orders, it was held that the dismissal was not unfair. The question in every case said Phillips J. is: whether, in all the circumstances the employer can be expected to wait any longer, and if so how much longer? In a company of sufficient size and resources, even where it is no longer reasonable for the employer to wait, it may be appropriate for him to offer less onerous work. It was held in *Hardwick v. Leeds AHA*[72] that what the employer must not do is to have a policy and apply it regardless of circumstances, and in the event of an employee being a member of his employer's permanent health insurance, despite an express clause allowing the employer to dismiss in the event of prolonged absence, it was held in *Aspden v. Webbs Poultry and Meat Group (Holdings)*[73] that in order to give effect to the mutual intention of the parties, the court would imply a term that save for summary dismissal, the employer would not terminate the contract while the employee was incapable of work so as to defeat the terms of the scheme.

There may be special factors rendering consultation unnecessary, so that in *Taylorplan Catering (Scotland) Ltd v. McInally*[74] dismissal as a result of a depressive illness due to the stress of living and working in an isolated and lonely environment in Shetland, when the employer's need was for someone of robust health able to withstand the stress of isolation, was not unfair, despite the absence of consultation: the employer's need was plain and it was equally plain the employee could fulfil that need. It should be noted that this decision was partly based on the view that consultation would have made no difference to the decision to dismiss: the *British Labour Pump v. Byrne*[75] principle, which was overruled in *Polkey v. A.E. Dayton Services Ltd*,[76] but in *A. Links & Co. Ltd v. Rose*[77] the Court of Session said that the law in relation to the duty on the employer in the event of dismissal as a result of ill health was correctly stated in *East Lindsey District Council v. Daubney*[78] and *Taylorplan Catering (Scotland) Ltd. v. McInally.*[79]

An employee's consent is needed before approaching his general practitioner for medical information and, in the absence of a contractual term, there is no implied right to require an employee to undergo a medical examination, and in either event under provisions of the Access to Medical Reports Act 1988 the employee has a right to indicate that he wishes to see a report before it is disclosed. Under the Act the employee has a right to object to a report and to request that it be amended. The doctor does not have to accept the amendments and if he does not do so it must be made clear that the employee does not agree with the report or he can then refuse to consent to disclosure. In *Slaughter v. C. Brewer & Sons*[80] it was held, *obiter*, that a blatant and persistent refusal to obtain an appropriate medical report or attend a medical examination may amount to contributory conduct.

[72] [1975] I.R.L.R. 319, IT.
[73] [1996] I.R.L.R. 521, HC.
[74] [1980] I.R.L.R. 53, EAT.
[75] [1979] I.C.R. 347, CA.
[76] [1987] I.R.L.R. 503, HL.
[77] [1991] I.R.L.R. 353, CS.
[78] [1977] I.R.L.R. 181, EAT.
[79] [1980] I.R.L.R. 53, EAT.
[80] [1990] I.R.L.R. 426, EAT.

7.3.2.2 Conduct

By contrast with cases falling within section 98(2)(a), the use of warnings, rather than guidance and advice, is appropriate to cases of misconduct falling within section 58(2)(b), and in certain severe cases of misconduct summary dismissal may be justified. It is difficult in this area to attempt a classification of the type of conduct which is likely to justify dismissal, because an employer's response must be reasonable, and this requires a need for an investigation and for the behaviour in question to be considered in relation to all the circumstances of the case, including the need for consistency in the treatment by each employer of his employees. In *The Post Office v. Fennell*[81] an employee complained of unfair dismissal after being dismissed for an assault on a colleague, alleging that dismissal had not been the penalty imposed on others for the same conduct. The Court of Appeal, in confirming that the dismissal was unfair, said that the need to have regard to equity and the substantial merits of the case, section 98(4)(b), comprehends the concept that employees who behave in much the same way will have metered out to them much the same punishment. However, in *Heald v. NCB*,[82] in considering differing treatment metered out to five men convicted of unlawful assembly during the miners strike, it was found that there was no unfair dismissal when only three were dismissed. The Court of Appeal said that although the facts were comparable, fairness had to be determined at the time of dismissal and since the more lenient treatment had been metered out to the second group of men, the first group could not compare themselves with them. In *Cain v. Leeds Western Health Authority*,[83] whilst agreeing that there should not be inconsistent treatment between cases, the EAT also pointed out that facts are seldom exactly comparable and mitigating circumstances might well make a difference.

In cases of suspected dishonesty, the employer is not required to prove the employee's guilt. In *British Home Stores Ltd v. Burchell*,[84] in a test subsequently approved by the Court of Appeal in *W. Weddell & Co. Ltd v. Tepper*,[85] Arnold J. held that in cases where an employer dismisses because he suspects or believes that the employee has committed an act of misconduct, in determining whether the dismissal is fair or unfair the tribunal has to decide whether the employer entertained a reasonable suspicion amounting to a belief in the guilt of the employee:

> "That is really stating shortly and compendiously what is in fact more than one element. First of all, there must be established by the employer the fact of that belief; that the employer did believe it. Secondly, that the employer had in his mind reasonable grounds upon which to sustain that belief. And thirdly, we think, that the employer, at the stage at which he formed that belief on those grounds, at any rate at the final stage at which he formed that belief on those grounds, had carried out as much investigation into the matter as was reasonable in all the circumstances of the case. It is the employer who manages to discharge the onus of demonstrating those three matters, we think, who must not be examined further. It is not relevant, as we think, that the Tribunal would itself have shared that view in those circumstances. It is not relevant, as we think, for the Tribunal to examine the quality of the material which the employer had before him, for

[81] [1981] I.R.L.R. 221, CA.
[82] [1988] I.R.L.I.B. 359, CA.
[83] [1990] I.R.L.R. 168, EAT.
[84] [1978] I.R.L.R. 379, EAT.
[85] [1980] I.R.L.R. 96, CA.

instance to see whether it was the sort of material, objectively considered, which would lead to a certain conclusion on the balance of probabilities, or whether it was the sort of material which would lead to the same conclusion only upon the basis of being 'sure' as it is now said more normally in a criminal context, or, to use the more old-fashioned term, such as to put the matter 'beyond reasonable doubt'. The test, and the test all the way through, is reasonableness; and certainly, as it seems to us, a conclusion on the balance of probabilities will in any surmisable circumstance be a reasonable conclusion." *per* Arnold J.

British Home Stores Ltd v. Burchell [1978] I.R.L.R. 379 at 380, EAT.

This test was subsequently extended by the EAT in *Distillers Co. (Bottling Services) Ltd v. Gardner*[86] to misconduct other than dishonesty. However, in *Boys And Girls Welfare Society v. McDonald*[87] the EAT warned against a simplistic application of the *Burchell* test as it was decided before the EA 1980 amendment establishing a neutral burden of proof. In any event, the EAT said, the three fold test may not be appropriate where there is no real conflict on the facts. Nevertheless, in *Scottish Daily Record & Sunday Mail (1986) Ltd v. Laird*[88] the Court of Session held that although the burden of proof is no longer on the employer, in considering whether the employer acted reasonably in dismissing the employee, the employer, in an appropriate case, is required to lead some evidence to show that the requirements described at each of the three stages of the *Burchell* test were satisfied. However, the *Burchell* guidelines may be inappropriate where the employer reasonably suspects one or more employees to be guilty of misconduct, but cannot identify which particular employee. In *Monie v. Coral Racing*[89] the Court of Appeal held that where there is a reasonable suspicion that one of two or possibly both employees must have acted dishonestly, it is not necessary for the employer to believe that either of them acted dishonestly: the *Burchell* test that a reasonable suspicion of misconduct is not enough and that an actual belief in the employee's guilt is necessary, was not intended to be of universal application.

In *Whitbread & Co. v. Thomas*[90] it was held that the principle in *Monie* is capable of applying to capability or conduct not involving dishonesty in that an employer may be acting fairly in dismissing all members of the group, even where it is possible that not all were guilty, if three conditions were satisfied: the act would justify dismissal if committed by an identifiable individual; the industrial tribunal must be satisfied the act was committed by one or more of the dismissed group all of whom have been shown to be individually capable of having committed the act in question; the industrial tribunal must be satisfied that the employer has carried out a proper investigation to identify the person or persons responsible.

In so far as criminal offences outside employment are concerned, the ACAS Code, para. 15(c), provides that these should not be treated as automatic reasons for dismissal regardless of a nexus between the offence and the duties. "The main considerations should be whether the offence is one that makes the individual unsuitable for his or her type of work or unacceptable to other employees. Employees should not be dismissed solely because a charge against them is pending or because they are absent through having been remanded in custody."

---

[86] [1982] I.R.L.R. 47, EAT.
[87] [1996] I.R.L.R. 129, EAT.
[88] [1996] I.R.L.R. 665, CS.
[89] [1980] I.R.L.R. 96, CA.
[90] [1988] I.R.L.R. 43, EAT.

In connection with fighting in the workplace: in *C.A. Parsons & Co. Ltd v. McLoughlin*[91] the EAT said that the dangers associated with fighting at the workplace are sufficiently widely accepted for an employer to be able to rely on them as justifiable grounds for dismissal without the need to specify it as such. Even where there is a rule to this effect, that will not make a dismissal for that reason fair, since, as emphasised in *Taylor v. Parsons Peebles NEI Peebles Ltd*[92] it is not the reasonableness of the policy, but the reasonableness of employer's reaction that is the question. In deciding to apply a rigid sanction of automatic dismissal without considering the employee's length of service was unfair: the employee had 20 years of good conduct.

In *British Labour Pump v. Byrne*,[93] a case involving theft from the employer, the dismissal was held to be unfair because the employer had failed to follow a fair procedure in investigating the incident, a decision upheld on appeal. However the EAT added that where the employer had not followed the correct procedure the industrial tribunal should ask whether the employers had shown on the balance of probabilities that they would have taken the same decision had they held an inquiry, and had they received the same information which that inquiry would have produced. In addition, have the employers shown that in the light of the information which they would have had, had they gone through the proper procedure, they would have been behaving reasonably in still deciding to dismiss? This became known as the "inevitability rule" and was applied by the EAT in *W. & J. Wass Ltd v. Binns*, and upheld by the Court of Appeal,[94] so that a failure to give the employee an opportunity to state his case was held not to amount to unfair dismissal because had the employer done so he would have reached the same conclusion.

However, in *Sillifant v. Powell Duffryn Timber Ltd*[95] Browne-Wilkinson J., said:

> ". . . the *British Labour Pump* principle appears to have become established in practice without it being appreciated that it represented a fundamental departure from both principle and the earlier decisions. If we felt able to do so we would hold that it is wrong in principle and undesirable in its practical effect. It introduces just that confusion which *Devis v. Atkins* was concerned to avoid between the fairness of the dismissal (which depends solely upon the reasonableness of the employer's conduct) and the compensation payable to the employee (which takes into account the conduct of the employee whether known to the employer or not)." . . . *per* Browne-Wilkinson J. (President)

Sillifant v. Powell Duffryn Timber Ltd [1983] I.R.L.R. 91 at 97, EAT.

Nevertheless, the EAT felt bound by authority and unable to depart from the principle. In the subsequent case of *Polkey v. A.E. Dayton Services*,[96] in a decision of the House it was said:

> ". . . the *British Labour Pump* principle (involves) an impermissible reliance upon matters not known to employers before the dismissal and a confusion between unreasonable conduct in reaching the conclusion to dismiss, which is a necessary

---

[91] [1978] I.R.L.R. 65, EAT.
[92] [1981] I.R.L.R. 119, EAT.
[93] [1979] I.R.L.R. 94, EAT.
[94] [1982] I.R.L.R. 486, CA.
[95] [1983] I.R.L.R. 391, EAT.
[96] 1987] I.R.L.R. 503, HL.

ingredient of an unfair dismissal, and injustice to the employee which is not a necessary ingredient of an unfair dismissal, although its absence will be important in relation to a compensatory award.

It follows that . . . the *British Labour Pump* principle and all decisions supporting it are inconsistent with the relevant statutory provision and should be overruled and, in particular, the decision of the Court of Appeal in *W & J Wass Ltd v. Binns* . . . should be overruled." *per* Lord Mackay V.C.

Polkey v. A.E. Dayton Services [1987] I.R.L.R. 503 at 507–08, HL.

The reasoning of Browne-Wilkinson in *Sillifant v. Powell Duffryn Timber Ltd*[97] at page 97, was adopted by Lord Mackay and although *Polkey* is a case concerning redundancy, the affirmation of the importance of procedural fairness is seen as of general application. It was stressed, however, by both Lords Mackay and Bridge, that an industrial tribunal is not bound to hold that any procedural failure by the employer renders the dismissal unfair: it is one of the factors to be weighed in deciding whether or not the dismissal was within section 98. Lord Mackay in setting out the exception said:

"If the employer could reasonably have concluded in the light of the circumstances known to him at the time of dismissal that consultation or warning would be utterly useless he might well act reasonably even if he did not observe the provisions of the code".[98]

On the other hand, Lord Bridge said:

"If the employer has failed to take the appropriate procedural steps . . . the one question the industrial tribunal is *not* permitted to ask in applying the test of reasonableness posed by (s.98(4)) is the hypothetical question whether it would have made any difference to the outcome if the appropriate procedural steps had been taken. . . . It is quite a different matter if the tribunal is able to conclude that the employer himself, at the time of dismissal, acted reasonably in taking the view that, in the exceptional circumstances of the particular case, the procedural steps normally appropriate would have been futile, could not have altered the decision to dismiss and therefore could be dispensed with. In such a case the test of reasonableness under (s.98(4)) may be satisfied".[99]

There appears to be a difference in view as to the exception to the principle, Lord Mackay adopting an objective approach, whilst Lord Bridge adopts a subjective approach. Whether the employer must actually address his mind to whether or not to dispense with the correct procedure was the subject of the appeal in *Duffy v. Yeomans & Partners Ltd*.[1] Balcombe L.J.[2] referred to *Hooper v. British Railways Board*[3]:

"I do not consider that there is any distinction in substance between the principle formulated by Lord Mackay and that discernible in the speech of Lord Bridge. If

---

[97] [1983] I.R.L.R. 391, EAT.
[98] [1987] I.R.L.R. 503, HL p. 504.
[99] *ibid.*, p. 508.
[1] [1994] I.R.L.R. 642, CA.
[2] With whom Saville L.J. and Sir Roger Parker agreed.
[3] [1988] I.R.L.R. 517, CA.

there was any such distinction, we would have to give effect to that stated by Lord Mackay with which their lordships all agreed. It is, I think, clear that Lord Bridge did not take the view that he was stating any different test. He was, in my judgment, emphasising one aspect of the principle stated by Lord Mackay, namely that the reasonableness of the action taken by the employers is to be judged by reference to the facts and factors known to the employer at the time of making the decision." *per* Ralph Gibson L.J.

Hooper v. British Railways Board [1988] I.R.L.R. 517 at 528, CA.

and to *Robertson v. Magnet Ltd (Retail Division)*[4] in which the suggestion found favour. In *Duffy v. Yeomans & Partners Ltd*[5] Balcombe L.J. said that:

". . . there is no warrant for the proposition that there *must* be a deliberate decision by the employers that consultation would be useless, with the corollary that in the absence of evidence that such a decision was made, a finding by an industrial tribunal that a dismissal for redundancy was reasonable is necessarily wrong *in law*. There is nothing in the wording of (s.98(4)), or in its exposition by Lord Mackay, to lead to such a result; if and in so far as that is the effect of Lord Bridge's speech, then I agree with the judgment of Ralph Gibson LJ, cited above, that we must give effect to the principles formulated by Lord Mackay, with which all the other Law Lords agreed.

It is what the employer (as a reasonable employer) could have done which is required to be tested; so the tribunal must ask whether an employer, acting reasonably, could have failed to consult in the given circumstances. . . . I fear that there was a grave danger that this area of the law is becoming over-sophisticated, and that there is an attempt to lay down as rules of law matters which are no more than factors which an industrial tribunal should take into account in reaching its decision whether the employer acted reasonably in the circumstances of the particular case." *per* Balcombe L.J.

Duffy v. Yeomans & Partners Ltd [1994] I.R.L.R. 642 at 645, CA.

7.3.2.3 *Contravention or statutory duty of restriction*

In applying this reason, it was held in *Bouchaala v. Trust House Forte Hotels Ltd*[6] that the wording of section 98(2)(d) does not make it permissible for an employer to act on a mistaken belief: it must actually be the case that it would be unlawful for the employee to continue to work. However, it was held in *Sutcliffe & Eaton Ltd v. R. Pinney*[7] that just because continuing to work would be a breach of a particular law, does not thereby render the dismissal fair: as with the other reasons for dismissal in section 98(2) it is a prima facie fair reason.

7.3.2.4 *Economically motivated dismissals*

There are two reasons under which dismissals for a reason unconnected with the employee themselves may be categorised and thereby prima facie fair:

[4] [1993] I.R.L.R. 512, EAT.
[5] [1994] I.R.L.R. 642, CA.
[6] [1980] I.R.L.R. 382, EAT.
[7] [1977] I.R.L.R. 349, EAT.

Redundancy

By ERA 1996, s.98(2)(c) redundancy, which is defined in section 139(1), is prima facie a fair reason for dismissal. It is for the employer to establish that the employee was dismissed as a result of redundancy, since the statutory presumption for redundancy pay purposes provided for in section 170(2), does not extend to unfair dismissal. In doing so the employer must show a cessation or diminution of work in the place of employment in which "the employee was employed". This has been variously interpreted as between the contract test, as demonstrated in *Sutcliffe v. Hawker Siddeley Aviation Ltd*,[8] where Sir John Donaldson said that those words meant "where under his contract of employment he could be required to work", meaning that any express, or indeed implied mobility term could mean that despite a diminution of work in one location, there is no redundancy where work is available at another location falling within the range of the mobility clause, as demonstrated in *Stevenson v. Teesside Bridge and Engineering Ltd*.[9] However, in *Bass Leisure Ltd v. Thomas*[10] the court rejected this approach as raising "substantial difficulties", instead interpreting the statute as requiring "a factual enquiry, taking into account the employee's fixed or changing place or places of work and any contractual terms which go to evidence or define the place of employment and its extent, but not those (if any) which make provision for the employee to be transferred to another".[11] Peter Gibson L.J, in a judgment of the court, in *High Table v. Horst*[12] found "broad agreement with this interpretation of the statutory language".[13]

In order for a redundancy to exist section 139(1) requires that there is a diminution in the requirements of the business "for employees to carry out work of a particular kind". In this connection there is a conflict of authority as to whether "bumping" amounts to redundancy: this is a process whereby employees compete for a reduced number of jobs, the least well qualified being declared redundant, although his job remains, albeit filled by another employee who otherwise would have been dismissed. In *Church v. West Lancashire NHS Trust*,[14] Morison J. in disagreeing with the EAT in *Safeway Stores v. Burrell*,[15] held that there can be no redundancy in such a situation. He reasoned that the redundancy must occur at the time of dismissal, but in a "bumping" situation the employee's post is treated as vacant at the time that he and others are invited to apply for it, he must have been dismissed at some stage earlier than the redundancy: a "bumped" employee was not therefore, as a result of this decision, redundant.

A residual category for a prima facie fair dismissal, section 98(1)(b), some other substantial reason justifying dismissal, it has been held is not to be interpreted *ejusdem generis* with the previous categories.[16] As such it is capable of use in what Bowers and Clarke (1981) called "quasi redundancies" or business reorganisation, *e.g Hollister v. NFU*.[17] Dismissal for economic reasons is discussed in Chapter 8.

---

[8] [1973] I.R.L.R. 304, NIRC.
[9] [1971] 1 All E.R. 296, DC.
[10] [1994] I.R.L.R. 104, EAT.
[11] *ibid.*, pp. 112–113.
[12] [1997] I.R.L.R. 513, CA.
[13] *ibid.*, p. 518.
[14] [1998] I.R.L.R. 4, EAT.
[15] [1997] I.R.L.R. 200, EAT.
[16] *RS Components Ltd v. Irwin* [1973] I.C.R. 535, *per* Brightman J., pp. 540–41.
[17] [1979] I.R.L.R. 238, CA.

7.3.3 Whether dismissal is an appropriate response to the behaviour in question

During the 1970s and 1980s the cases expressed confusion over the question of whether it was fair (not to dismiss in the way that occurred, which is dealt with above) but whether it was fair to dismiss at all for that reason—rather than to impose some other penalty. Under section 98(4) the tribunal must ask themselves how a reasonable employer would have acted, but must not ask themselves what they would have done. In *Iceland Frozen Foods Ltd. v. Jones*[18] Browne-Wilkinson J., in a judgment approved by the House of Lords in *Polkey*[19] held that:

> "Since the present state of the law can only be found by going through a number of different authorities, it may be convenient if we should seek to summarise the present law. We consider that the authorities establish that in law the correct approach for the Industrial Tribunal to adopt in answering the question posed by (s.98(4)) of the (1996) Act is as follows.
>
> (1) the starting point should always be the words of s.98(4) themselves;
> (2) in applying the section the Industrial Tribunal must consider the reasonableness of the employer's conduct, not simply whether they (the Industrial Tribunal) consider the dismissal to be fair;
> (3) in judging the reasonableness of the employer's conduct an Industrial Tribunal must not substitute its decision as to what was the right course to adopt for that of the employer;
> (4) in many (though not all) cases there is a band of reasonable responses to the employee's conduct within which one employer might reasonably take one view, another quite reasonably take another;
> (5) the function of the Industrial Tribunal, as an industrial jury, is to determine whether in the particular circumstances of each case the decision to dismiss the employee fell within the band of reasonable responses which a reasonable employer might have adopted. If the dismissal falls within the band the dismissal is fair: if the dismissal falls outside the band it is unfair." *per* Browne-Wilkinson J;

Iceland Frozen Foods Ltd v. Jones [1982] I.R.L.R. 439 at 442, EAT.

This analysis was approved by the Court of Appeal in *The County Council of Hereford and Worcester v. Neale*,[20] when, in allowing the appeal, it held that the EAT had substituted its own view for that of the industrial tribunal. May L.J. *obiter* said that the EAT should avoid "fixing the parameters of reasonable response to a given set of circumstances".[21]

This necessity for an employer to satisfy himself whether the reason is not only the proper reason but that dismissal is the fair response was emphasised in *Whitbread & Co. v. Mills*[22] where the EAT held that where the internal procedure consists of a disciplinary hearing and an appeal against that decision by way of review, as opposed to rehearing, both must be fair and the review cannot rectify the failures of the first. If

---

[18] [1982] I.R.L.R. 439, EAT.
[19] [1994] I.R.L.R. 642, CA.
[20] [1986] I.R.L.R. 168, CA.
[21] *ibid.*, p. 173.
[22] [1988] I.R.L.R. 501, EAT.

there is a rehearing *de novo* the omission may be corrected. The dismissal held to be unfair because the employer had not conducted an investigation sufficient to satisfy himself that the reasons put forward for dismissal were reasonable grounds and that a reasonable employer would have conducted an investigation of the allegations before deciding to dismiss. The House of Lords in *West Midlands Co-operative Society Ltd v. Tipton*,[23] approving *National Heart and Chest Hospitals Board of Governors v. Nambiar*,[24] stressed that matters that come to light during the appeal process may be taken into account in considering the overall equity and substantial merits of the case.

7.4 AUTOMATICALLY UNFAIR REASONS

There are some reasons that are automatically unfair reasons for dismissal in that once it is shown that the reason for dismissal falls under one of these heads, the dismissal is unfair for that reason alone. In connection with the ERA 1996, s.108, the requirement for two years continuous service and the ERA 1996, s.109, the requirement for the applicant to be below the NRA or age 65, in order to be eligible to make an application for unfair dismissal or redundancy, do not apply in these circumstances.

7.4.1 Burden of proof

The burden of proof for identifying the reason for dismissal falls on the employer and in *Maund v. Penwith District Council*[25] it was held by the Court of Appeal that this remains so where the reason is automatically unfair. Where the employer relies on a reason which is challenged, Griffiths L.J. said that the burden then passes to the employee to show that there is a real issue as to whether that was the true reason, but the burden is lighter than that placed upon the employer: he merely has to produce sufficient evidence to raise some doubt about the reason for the dismissal. Once this evidential burden is discharged, the onus remains on the employer to prove the reason for the dismissal. However, where the reason for dismissal has to be established to confer jurisdiction on the tribunal, the onus is on the employee to establish the reason for dismissal.[26]

7.4.2 Trade union reasons

By the TULRC 1992, s.152 it is automatically unfair if the reason, or principal reason for dismissal is that the employee (as opposed to worker):

(a) was, or proposed to become, a member of an independent trade union, or

(b) had taken part, or proposed to take part, in the activities of an independent trade union at an appropriate time, or

(c) was not a member of any trade union, or of a particular trade union, or of one of a number of trade unions, or had refused, or proposed to refuse, to become or remain a member;

---

[23] 1986] I.C.R. 192, HL.
[24] [1981] I.C.R. 441, EAT.
[25] [1984] I.R.L.R. 24, CA.
[26] Harvey, para. 810–820.

and includes a refusal of a non union member to make payments in lieu of union dues or his objection or proposed objection to such payments, section 152(3). By the TULRCA 1992, s.154 the reasons listed in section 152(1)(a)–(c) are inadmissible reasons.

It is also automatically unfair to dismiss for redundancy on grounds related to union membership or activities where the circumstances constituting the redundancy applied equally to one or more other employees who have not been dismissed by the employer and the reason why he was selected was an inadmissible reason, TULRCA 1992, s.153.

In order to come within the protection offered by sections 152–3, the employee must have been taking part in "activities of an independent trade union". The courts initially gave a restrictive interpretation to these requirements as demonstrated in *Therm-a-Stor Ltd v. Atkins*[27] where following a claim for recognition the management dismissed 20 employees. Even though all those dismissed were union members it was held by the Court of Appeal that the dismissals fell outside the section because they were in response to the union's claim for recognition, and there was no evidence that selection was because of their union membership. Following the decision of the House of Lords in *Associated Newspapers Ltd v. Wilson* and *Associated British Ports v. Palmer*,[28] there is some uncertainty as to whether protection under the section extends beyond the mere status of union membership and applies to dismissal for making use of essential services offered by the union, as was held in *Discount Tobacco & Confectionery v. Armitage*,[29] The principal in *Armitage* was supported by the EAT in *Speciality Care plc v. Pachlea*[30] where Judge Clark reviewed the House of Lords' decisions in *Associated Newspapers Ltd v. Wilson* and *Associated British Ports v. Palmer*, in order to consider whether *Armitage* had received the "judicial kiss of death"[31] and concluded that:

". . . we regard it as important that we provide clear guidance to industrial tribunals as to the correct approach to be taken . . .

(1) *Armitage* was and remains unquestionably correct on its facts. . . . *Armitage* remains undisturbed on its facts in our judgement.
(2) That means . . . that where a complaint of dismissal by reason of union membership is made, as in this case, it will be for the tribunal to find as a fact whether or not the reason or principal reason for dismissal related to the applicant's trade union membership not only by reference to whether he or she had simply joined a union, but also by reference to whether the introduction of union representation into the employment relationship had led the employer to dismiss the employee. Tribunals should answer that question robustly, based on their findings as to what really caused the dismissal in the mind of the employer."
per Judge Clark

Speciality Care plc v. Pachlea [1996] I.R.L.R. 248 at 252, EAT.

It has been held that personal activities of a union member are not trade union activities within section 152(1)(b). In *Chant v. Aquaboats Ltd*[32] an employee, who was a

---

[27] [1983] I.R.L.R. 78, CA.
[28] [1995] I.R.L.R. 258, HL.
[29] [1990] I.R.L.R. 15, CA.
[30] [1996] I.R.L.R. 248, EAT.
[31] *Harvey on Industrial Relations and Employment Law,* para. Q.652.
[32] [1978] 1 All E.R. 102, EAT.

union member, but not a union official, organised a petition complaining about safety standards. It was held that his dismissal was not unfair because he was not organising the petition on behalf of the union and therefore was not carrying out union activities: the mere fact that those involved are trade unionists does not make the activity a trade union activity. Today Mr Chant may be able to bring his case under the ERA 1996, s.100 and possibly subsection (c). In an interpretation more in keeping with the purpose of the section, the Court of Appeal in *Fitzpatrick v. British Railways Board*[33] held that although the trade union activities referred to in section 58(1)(b) were confined to activities in the employment from which the employee alleged that she had been unfairly dismissed, what happened in the employee's previous employment may form the reason for dismissal in subsequent employment:

"If an employer, having learnt of an employee's previous trade union activities, decides that he wishes to dismiss that employee, that is likely to be a situation where almost inevitably the employer is dismissing the employee because he feels that the employee will indulge in industrial activities of a trade union nature in his current employment. There is no reason for a rational and reasonable employer to object to the previous activities of an employee except in so far as they will impinge upon the employee's current employment." *per* Woolf L.J.

Fitzpatrick v. British Railways Board [1991] I.R.L.R. 376 at 379, CA.

Although the employee had not taken part in union activities in her present employment at the date of dismissal it was held that a dismissal which took place following discovery of a previous history, which was omitted from the job application, but which was that of a prominent union activist with links with "ultra-left Trotskyite groups", was motivated by a fear of involvement in union activities, and therefore fell within the words of section 152(1)(b)—"activities which the employee . . . proposed to take part in". Had the employer known about her union activities earlier and as a result refused to recruit her she would have had no remedy since the TULRCA 1992, s.137 provides protection only as against a refusal of employment because of a requirement to join or not to join a trade union.

In addition, it is necessary for the purposes of section 152, that the union activity take place at an "appropriate time", defined in section 152(2) as meaning (a) a time outside the employer's working hours, or (b) a time within his working hours at which, in accordance with arrangements agreed with or consent given by his employer, it is permissible for him to take part in the activities of a trade union. In *The Marley Tile Co. Ltd v. Shaw*[34] it was held that "appropriate time" is not restricted to cases where an express arrangement has been agreed or express consent given for union activities to take place during an employee's normal working hours. Such consent may be implied from the general relationship between management and unions. So, raising an individual member's grievance by the respondent shop steward was a trade union activity and it was carried out at an appropriate time because it was held, this is usually accepted in industrial relations even if the management has not specifically given permission for it: it is implied by the basic willingness of the management to work together with the union. Although it was also held that the employer's consent could not be implied from his silence when an announcement was made that the activity was going to take place.

[33] [1991] I.R.L.R. 376, CA.
[34] [1978] I.R.L.R. 238, EAT.

In *Zucker v. Astrid Jewels Ltd*[35] it was said that the House of Lords" decision in *Post Office v. Union of Post Office Workers*[36] makes it clear that an employee is entitled to take part in union activities whilst he is on the employer's premises but not actually working. Merely because an employee is on the premises during a time in respect of which he is being paid does not mean that the employee is necessarily required to be at work. So a paid meal break was held to be an appropriate time and not a time within working hours so as to require the employer's consent to take part in trade union activities.

In *Bass Taverns Ltd v. Burgess*[37] a shop steward, who was a manager of licensed premises, made disparaging remarks about the company during an induction presentation. This led to his demotion which he took to be a constructive dismissal. On the question of whether the incident fell within section 152 of the 1992 Act the Court of Appeal said that having been given a consent to recruit, that must include a consent to underline the services which the union can provide and that may reasonably involve a submission to prospective members that in some respects the union will provide a service which the company does not. A consent to recruit was not subject to an implied limitation that the recruiter should say nothing to criticise or undermine the company. Although the respondent had admitted that he had "gone over the top" it was held that this did not provide a basis for finding that during his speech he was not taking part in trade union activities at an appropriate time. In relation to what was said:

". . .I find nothing beyond the rhetoric and hyperbole which might be expected at a recruiting meeting for a trade union or, for that matter, some other organisation or cause. Neither dishonesty nor bad faith are suggested. While harmonious relations between a company and a union are highly desirable, a union recruiting meeting cannot realistically be limited to that object. A consent which at the same time prevents the recruiter from saying anything adverse about the employer is no real consent. Given that there was consent to use the meeting as a forum for recruitment, it cannot be regarded as an 'abuse of privilege" to make remarks to employees which are critical of the company." *per* Pill, L.J. (with whom Sir Ralph Gibson and Balcombe L.J. agreed)

Bass Taverns Ltd v. Burgess [1995] I.R.L.R. 596 at 598, CA

By the TULRCA 1992, s.161 an employee presenting a complaint under section 152 may apply, within seven days of the effective date of termination, for interim relief pending the outcome of the tribunal hearing. The application must be supported by a certificate signed by an authorised union official stating that on the date of dismissal the employee was or proposed to become a member of the union and that there appear to be reasonable grounds for supposing that the grounds for dismissal were those alleged. If the tribunal finds that the claim is "likely" to be successful at a full hearing it will, if the employer is willing, make an order for reinstatement or re-engagement in another job on terms and conditions not less favourable than those that would have applied had he not been dismissed. If the employer is unwilling to offer either reinstatement or re-engagement or fails to attend the tribunal will make an order for the employee's contract of employment to continue both for purposes of pay and continuity.

[35] [1978] I.R.L.R. 385, EAT.
[36] [1974] I.R.L.R. 22, HL.
[37] [1995] I.R.L.R. 596, CA.

In addition, the unfair dismissal provisions are supported by a right for an employee not to have action short of dismissal taken against him by his employer for those reasons set out in the TULRCA 1992, s.146. Following the interpretation given to these provisions by the House of Lords in *Associated Newspapers Ltd v. Wilson* and *Associated British Ports v. Palmer*,[38] as Painter et al. (1996) points out, it is difficult to conceive of an action short of dismissal which will be covered by this interpretation of these provisions.

Where an award for compensation is made for an inadmissible reason under the TULRCA 1992, s.152, or redundancy falling within section 153, by the TULRCA 1992, s.157 providing that an order of reinstatement or re-engagement is requested, the tribunal is directed to make a special award. Details concerning the special award can be found at para. 7.5.5.2, below.

7.4.3   Pregnancy and childbirth

The relevant provisions, contained in the EPCA 1978, were amended and substituted by the TURERA 1993, in order to comply with the requirements of Directive 92/85 on the introduction of measures to encourage improvements in the safety and health of pregnant workers and workers who have recently given birth or are breastfeeding. The provisions are now contained in the ERA 1996, s.99, and an employee who is dismissed is regarded as unfairly dismissed if any one of the incidences listed in section 99(1)(a)–(e) is the reason, or the principal reason for dismissal:

(a) the reason (or . . . principal reason) for the dismissal is that she is pregnant or any other reason connected with her pregnancy,

(b) her maternity leave period is ended by the dismissal and the reason (or . . . principal reason) for the dismissal is that she has given birth . . . or any other reason connected with her having given birth to a child,

(c) her contract of employment is terminated after the end of her maternity leave period and the reason (or . . . principal reason) for the dismissal is that she took, or availed herself of, the benefits of, maternity leave,

(d) the reason (or . . . principal reason) for the dismissal is a relevant requirement, or a relevant recommendation, as defined by s.66(2), (the health and safety grounds, which supports ss.66 and 68, the duty to suspend on maternity grounds and the duty to pay during suspension;

(e) her maternity leave period is ended by the dismissal, and the reason (or . . . principal reason) for the dismissal is that she is redundant and s.77 has not been complied with. (entitlement to be offered suitable alternative employment)

In addition, by section 99(3) it is automatically unfair dismissal, in the case of a woman who has the right to return to work, if before the end of the MLP she submits a medical certificate stating that because of ill health she would be incapable of returning to work and her contract was terminated within four weeks of the end of the MLP where the absence continued to be covered by a medical certificate, if the reason,

---

[38] [1995] I.R.L.R. 258, HL.

or principal reason, is that the woman has given birth or any other reason connected with giving birth. Controversy has surrounded whether the special protection afforded to pregnant women extends beyond the four weeks provided for in section 99(3)(b) in circumstances where continued absence is due to a pregnancy related reason. In *Handels-og Kontorfunktionaerernes Forbund I Danmark v. Dansk Handel & Service*[39] (the *Larsson* case) the ECJ held that the special protected period provided for under Directive 92/85 did not extend to the situation where a woman is dismissed after her maternity leave has ended because of absence due to a pregnancy-related illness, even where the illness first appeared during pregnancy itself.

Prior to amendment, protection against dismissal for reasons connected with pregnancy and maternity leave, was only available where the woman concerned had two years' continuous employment. However, the ERA 1996, s.108(3)(b) provides that the requirements for two years' continuous employment, contained in the ERA 1996, s.108(1), does not apply to dismissals falling within section 99. Rather oddly, and in a provision I suggest is not destined to be heavily utilised, section 109(2)(b) provides that the requirement in section 109(1) for the woman to be below the NRA or 65 does not apply to dismissals falling within section 99!

In *Brown v. Stockton-on-Tees Borough Council*[40] although there was a genuine redundancy situation when funding for her position was withdrawn by the Manpower Services Commission, Mrs Brown was not selected for a new position because of her pregnancy. Although both the EAT and Court of Appeal held that the reason for dismissal was redundancy and as such subject to the test of fairness now contained in the ERA 1996, section 98(4), the House of Lords, in a purposive judgment, allowed the appeal, holding that the dismissal fell under section 99. Lord Griffiths said of this section:

> "(it) must be seen as part of social legislation passed for the specific protection of women and to put them on an equal footing with men. I have no doubt that it is often a considerable inconvenience to an employer to have to make the necessary arrangements to keep a woman's job open for her whilst she is absent from work in order to have a baby, but this is a price that has to be paid as a part of the social and legal recognition of the equal status of women in the workplace. If an employer dismisses a woman because she is pregnant and he is not prepared to make the arrangements to cover her temporary absence from work he is deemed to have dismissed her unfairly. I can see no reason why the same principle should not apply if in a redundancy situation an employer selects the pregnant woman as the victim of redundancy in order to avoid the inconvenience of covering her absence from work in the new employment he is able to offer others who are threatened with redundancy. It surely cannot have been intended that an employer should be entitled to take advantage of a redundancy situation to weed out his pregnant employees." *per* Lord Griffiths

> *Brown v. Stockton-on-Tees Borough Council* [1988] I.R.L.R. 263 at 266, HL.

Statute now covers this situation in that redundancy for any of the reasons contained in section 99(1)(a)–(d) is, by section 105(2) automatically unfair.

The EAT in *Clayton v. Vigers*,[41] following the decision in *Brown*,[42] held that the words "any other reason connected with her pregnancy" in section 99(1)(a) ought to

[39] Case C–400/95 [1997] I.R.L.R. 643, ECJ.
[40] [1988] I.R.L.R. 263, HL.
[41] [1990] I.R.L.R. 177, EAT.
[42] [1987] I.R.L.R. 230, CA.

be read widely so as to give full effect to the mischief at which the statute was aimed. Therefore, when a woman was told by her employer, after her baby was born, that her employer had been unable to employ a temporary and had had to take on a permanent replacement, it was held that she had been dismissed for a "reason connected with her pregnancy".

In order to have unfairly dismissed an employee for pregnancy, or a reason connected with her pregnancy, it was held in *Del Monte Foods Ltd. v. Mundon*[43] that at the time of dismissal the employer had to know or believe that the employee was pregnant. In *Mundon* the EAT held that the industrial tribunal had been wrong to hold that although the employer had formed an intention to dismiss before knowing that the employee was pregnant, they were to be taken to have fallen foul of ERA 1996, s.99, merely because they implemented that decision after being told of the pregnancy:

> "What the Tribunal appear to have done is to have said that although the company decided to dismiss initially for some other reason, yet, merely because they knew of the pregnancy, they are to be taken to have dismissed because of the pregnancy. It does not seem to us that the mere fact that they subsequently knew that this woman was pregnant, yet went ahead with an earlier decision to dismiss because of gastro-enteritis, can possibly be sufficient to show that she had been dismissed by reason of the pregnancy." *per* Slynn J.

Del Monte Foods Ltd. v. Mundon [1980] I.R.L.R. 224 at 226, EAT.

The *Del Monte* decision was approved and followed in *Dentons Directories Ltd v. Hobbs*.[44] Hobbs was dismissed for "numerous absences" from work after taking two weeks off sick, being certified absent for "depression". She alleged that her dismissal was for a reason connected with her pregnancy within section 99(1)(a), which she knew about at the time of the first absence for depression, and which she claimed had caused the depression. Her employer, however, claimed not to have known of the pregnancy at the time of dismissal. The EAT, following *Abernethy v. Mott, Hay and Anderson*[45] and *W. Devis & Sons Ltd v. Atkins*,[46] held that the employer's reason for dismissing someone is a subjective question: the tribunal must ask what factors were operating on the employer's mind when the decision to dismiss was taken:

> ". . . to disregard entirely the presence or absence of any knowledge or belief on the part of the employer and simply to see whether in fact the reason for dismissal was one which could subsequently be seen to have been connected with pregnancy would put an employer in a very difficult position. If he were held to have dismissed an employee with automatic unfairness, when he dismissed for pro-longed absenteeism, even when he does not know or believe that she is pregnant, it would mean that any employer who was dismissing *bona fide* for absenteeism would always be at risk of it being subsequently shown that those periods of absence were connected with her pregnancy. That seems to us to run counter to the many decisions which stress the importance of the subjective element in the identified reason for dismissal." *per* Keene J.

Dentons Directories Ltd v. Hobbs IRLB 577, September 1997, pp. 9–10.

[43] [1980] I.R.L.R. 224, EAT.
[44] EAT 821/96, I.R.L.B. 577, September 1997, pp. 9–10.
[45] [1974] I.R.L.R. 213, CA.
[46] [1977] I.C.R. 662, HL.

By section 92(4) an employee dismissed at any time while pregnant or where maternity leave ends by dismissal is entitled to a written statement of the reasons for dismissal, without the requirement of the two-year qualifying period and without having to make a request. These are discussed further in Chapter 10.

7.4.4 Health and safety

The provisions contained in the ERA 1996, s.100 were inserted into the EPCA 1978 by the TURERA 1993, s.28 and Schedule 5, from August 30, 1998 in order to comply with the framework Directive on the introduction of measures to encourage improvements in the safety and health of workers at work, Directive 89/391, most of the requirements of which were put into effect by the Management of Health and Safety at Work Regulations 1992.[47] By section 100 it is automatically unfair dismissal, and by section 105(3) redundancy, where the reason, or principal reason is that the employee:

- was appointed by the employer to be responsible for health and safety matters, (s.100(1)(a));

- being a worker representative on health and safety matters or a member of a safety committee representative, performing or proposing to perform any functions in connection with these appointments, (s.100(1)(b));

- took part, or proposed to take part, in consultations with the employer, or an election of representatives, under the Health and Safety (Consultations with Employees) Regulations 1996.[48] This amendment was inserted by regulation 8 of the 1996 Regulations[49] following the ECJ decision in *Commission v. United Kingdom*[50] and amendments issued to redundancy consultation requirements[51] to require them to be extended beyond recognised trade unions, (s.100(1)(ba));

- where there is no Health and Safety representative or committee or there was, but it was not practicable to utilise the, the employee raised with the employer circumstances he reasonably believed were harmful or potentially so, (s.100(1)(c));

- in circumstances of danger he reasonably believed to be imminent he left or proposed to leave or refused to return to the scene of the danger, (s.100(1)(d));

- in circumstances applicable to (d) he took or proposed to take action to protect himself or others. There is a defence under this head in that any dismissal for this reason is not automatically unfair if the employer can show that the steps the employee took or proposed to take were so negligent that a reasonable employer might have dismissed in the circumstances (s.100(1)(e)).

---

[47] S.I. 1992 No. 2051.
[48] S.I. 1996 No. 1513.
[49] *ibid*.
[50] Case C–382/92 [1994] I.C.R. 664, ECJ.
[51] The Collective Redundancies and Transfer of Undertakings (Protection of Employment) (Amendment) Regulations 1995 (S.I. 1995 No. 2587).

The automatic unfair dismissal provisions are supported by a parallel right not to suffer a detriment short of dismissal, ERA 1996, s.44. In *Shillito v. Van Leer (U.K.) Ltd*[52] Peter Clark J. pointed out that the protection afforded under section 44 is analogous to that afforded to shop stewards under the TULRCA 1992, s.152 as demonstrated in *Bass Taverns v. Burgess.*[53] In *Goodwin v. Cabletel U.K. Ltd*[54] whilst it was confirmed that the protection afforded to a designated employee carrying out health and safety duties must not be diluted, not every act, however malicious and irrelevant, must necessarily be treated as a protected act.

Health and safety is discussed at paras 3.1.5 and 3.3.1.1. above.

7.4.5   Protected or opted-out shop or betting shop worker

ERA 1996, Pt. IV contains provisions formerly in the Sunday Trading Act 1994 and the Betting, Gaming and Lotteries Act 1963. By sections 101 and 105(4)(a)–(b) it is automatically unfair to dismiss or select for redundancy a protected shop worker or an opted-out shop worker or protected or opted-out betting worker if the reason, or principal reason for the dismissal is that he refused or proposed to refuse to work on Sundays or on a particular Sunday or by section 101(3) had served or proposed to serve an opting-out notice.

A worker is a "protected" shop or betting shop worker if he fulfils the requirements of sections 36(2) and (3): he was not contracted to work on Sundays and has not given his employer an opting-in notice. An "opted-out" worker is one who is, or may be required to work on Sundays and who has given written notice to his employer that he objects to working on Sunday, sections 40–41. By section 101(2) it is not automatically unfair to dismiss an opted-out shop or betting worker where the reason is that he refused or proposed to refuse to work on Sunday(s) before the end of the notice period. It is, however, unfair to dismiss a shop or betting worker who has given or proposed to give an opting-out notice, section 101(3). In addition, by section 45 there is a right for a protected or opted-out shop or betting worker not to suffer a detriment short of dismissal in the same situations as apply to automatic unfair dismissal.

7.4.6   Trustee of occupational pension scheme

Following the "Maxwell affair", in which £600 million of pension fund assets disappeared, the House of Commons Social Security Committee made a strong recommendation that a Government enquiry should be set up to review the law.[55] As a result The Pension Law Review Committee (the Goode Committee) was set up in June 1992 to review the framework of law and regulation within which occupational pension schemes operate, taking into account the rights and interests of the interested parties. Many of the proposals, and the principles underpinning the Committee's report[56] were enshrined in the Pensions Act 1995.

One of the principle recommendations of the Committee, with significant modifications, became the Pensions Act 1995, s.16 which requires the appointment, under rules

[52] [1997] I.R.L.R. 496, EAT.
[53] [1995] I.R.L.R. 596, CA.
[54] [1997] I.R.L.R. 665, EAT.
[55] Social Security Committee Session 1991–2, *The Operation of Pension Funds*, 2nd report, HC, 61–ii, para. 10.
[56] Pension Law Reform: *The Report of the Pension Law Review Committee* (Goode Report) Cm. 2342 September 1993, HMSO.

approved under a statutory consultation procedure, of member-nominated trustees and once appointed such trustees may only be removed with the agreement of all the trustees. Any scheme member can be nominated and the employer is bound to accept the nomination so long as the nominated person is a scheme member. The ERA 1996, s.102 supports this in that it is automatically unfair to dismiss or, by section 105(5) to select for redundancy such a trustee, where the reason, or principal reason is that the employee, being a trustee of a relevant occupational pension scheme, was performing or proposing to perform any functions as a trustee.

The protection afforded to member-nominated trustees under section 102 is supported by a right not to suffer a detriment short of dismissal, section 46, and a right to time off for performing any duties as a trustee or undergoing training relevant to the performance of those duties, sections 58–60.

7.4.7 Employee representative

By the ERA 1996, s.103 an employee is unfairly dismissed if the reason or principal reason for dismissal, or by section 105(6) selection for redundancy, is that the employee was a employee representative for the purposes of redundancy consultation under the provisions laid down in the TULRCA 1992, ss.188–192 or under TUPE, regs. 10 and 11 or is a candidate in an election for an employee representative and that he was performing or proposing to perform any functions or activities as an employee representative or a candidate.

These provisions were introduced by the Transfer Regulations by Collective Redundancies and Transfer of Undertakings (Protection of Employment) (Amendment) Regulations 1995[57] to support the employee representative provisions introduced for redundancy consultation purposes as a result of the decision of the ECJ[58] that domestic law, requiring consultation only with representatives of recognised trade unions, did not comply with Directive 75/129 on the implementation of the laws of the Member States relating to collective redundancies and Directive 77/187 on the approximation of the laws of the Member States relating to the safeguarding of employees" rights in the event of transfers of undertakings, businesses or parts of businesses.

The rights contained in sections 103 and 105(6) are supported by a right not to suffer a detriment short of dismissal, section 47.

7.4.8 Assertion of a statutory right

The ERA 1996, s.104 provides that a dismissal, or by section 105(7) selection for redundancy, is automatically unfair where the reason, or principal reason, for the dismissal is victimisation in that the employee brought proceedings against the employer to enforce a relevant statutory right, section 104(1)(a) or alleged that the employer had infringed a right which is a relevant statutory right, section 104(1)(b). It is immaterial whether the employee actually has the right or that the right has been infringed (s.104(2)(a) and (b)), so long as the claim is made in good faith. This section was inserted into the 1978 Act by the TURERA 1993, s.29(1) from August 30, 1993.

---

[57] S.I. 1995 No. 2587.
[58] Case C–383/92 [1994] I.C.R. 664, ECJ.

The relevant statutory rights covered are detailed in section 104(4)(a)—(c): any right conferred under ERA 1996 so long as the remedy is by way of complaint to an Industrial Tribunal; the right to minimum notice under ERA 1996, s.86; and rights conferred under the TULRCA 1992, namely

- right not to suffer deductions of unauthorised or excessive subscriptions, section 68;

- certificate of exemption or objection to contributing to political fund, section 86;

- action short of dismissal on grounds related to union membership or activities, section 146;

- time off for carrying out trade union duties, section 168;

- payment for time off for carrying out trade union duties, section 169 and

- time off for trade union activities, section 170.

Similar protection already exists for those covered by discrimination legislation[59] and is also contained in the DDA 1995, s.55.

In *Mennell v. Newell & Wright (Transport Contractors) Ltd*[60] the employer attempted to introduce a new contract providing for a deduction from final salary or other payment to recover certain training costs. Mr Mennell refused to sign, and when dismissed later the same year sought to claim under the ERA 1996, s.104, in that his refusal to sign was because he disagreed with the recoupment and that in doing so he was asserting a statutory right not to suffer an unlawful deduction from wages, contrary to ERA 1996, s.13. The Court of Appeal held that there is no right in respect of a threatened deduction of wages, section 23(1)(a) providing for a complaint only where the employer "has made a deduction". Nevertheless, that did not prohibit a claim since section 104(2)(a) and (b) provides that it is immaterial whether or not the employee has the right, or whether the right has actually been infringed: it is sufficient that the employee has alleged that the employer had infringed the statutory right and that the making of the allegation was the reason, or principal reason for dismissal.

7.4.9 Transfer of undertaking

By regulation 8(1) of Transfer of Undertakings (Protection of Employment) Regulations, 1981[61] which implemented Directive 77/187, where either before or after a relevant transfer, an employee of either the transferor or transferee is dismissed, that employee is treated as unfairly dismissed if the transfer or a reason connected with it is the reason or principal reason for the dismissal. However, by regulation 8(2) if the reason or principal reason for dismissal is an economic, technical or organisational reason entailing changes in the workforce of either the transferor or transferee, either before or after the transfer, then the dismissal is to be treated as a potentially fair one falling within ERA 1996, s.98(1)(b)—some other substantial reason. In which case

---

[59] RRA 1976; DDA 1995, s.2; SDA, 1975, s.4, which also provides protection for those making a complaint under Equal Pay Act, 1970.
[60] [1997] I.R.L.R. 519, CA.
[61] S.I. 1981 No. 1794.

whether the dismissal is fair or unfair will fall to be considered under section 98(4)(a) and (b).

The issues that arise in order to bring a claim within this regulation are discussed in Chapter 9.

In *Milligan v. Securicor Cleaning Ltd*,[62] the EAT held that the wording in regulation 8(1) "that the employee shall be treated for the purposes of Part X of the 1996 Act . . . as unfairly dismissed" did not have the effect of importing into the Transfer Regulations the need for two years' continuous employment provided for in ERA 1996, s.108. The effect of this decision was reversed by an amendment introduced into the Collective Redundancies and Transfer of Undertakings (Protection of Employment) (Amendment) Regulations 1995[63] and *Milligan* was subsequently overruled by the Court of Appeal in *MRS Environmental Services Ltd v. Marsh*.[64] It is therefore necessary to have two years' continuous employment in order to qualify for this right.

7.4.10 Spent conviction

Although not recorded specifically as automatically unfair dismissal, the Rehabilitation of Offenders Act 1974 provides protection for those with "spent" convictions in that section 4(3)(b) provides that once a criminal conviction has become "spent" under the Act, a failure to disclose it is not a proper ground for dismissing or excluding a person from any office, profession, occupation or employment, or prejudicing him in any way in any occupation or employment. In *P.M. & E.M. Hendry v. Scottish Liberal Club*[65] it was held that as dismissal for a spent conviction was not within the potentially fair reasons for dismissal contained in the ERA 1996, s.98(2), the dismissal was unfair.

7.4.11 Special award and interim relief

Interim relief may be applied for where dismissal is for any of the reasons for which a special award is available. A tribunal must make a special award, in addition to a basic and compensatory award, where the dismissal, or selection for redundancy, was for an inadmissible reason, TULRCA 1992, s.157, a health and safety reason within section 100(1)(a) and (b), carrying out duties as a trustee as provided for by section 102(1), and an employee representative or candidate in an election under section 103, where reinstatement or re-engagement is requested. These remedies are discussed further at para. 7.5.5.2, below.

7.4.12 Summary

This part of Chapter 7 has discussed the reasons, dismissal or selection for redundancy for which amount to automatically unfair dismissal, together with the supporting statutory provisions and these are summarised in the following chart.

---

[62] [1995] I.R.L.R. 288, EAT.
[63] S.I. 1995 No. 2587.
[64] IDS Brief 571/1996.
[65] Case No. S/1290/76 [1977] I.R.L.R. 5, IT.

Automatically Unfair Reasons for Dismissal		
STATUTORY PROVISIONS	REASON OR PRINCIPAL REASON FOR DISMISSAL	CONDITIONS
para. 7.5.2 **Trade Union Reasons—Trade Union and Labour Relations (Consolidation) Act 1992**		
s.52 (1)(a)	was or proposed to become a member of independent TU, or	s.152 & 153 are by TULRCA 1992, known as "inadmissable reasons". By TULRCA 1992, s.154 an inadmissable reason is not subject to the qualifying period contained in ERA 1996, s.108(1) nor the upper age limit contained in ERA 1996, s.109(1)(a)(i) and (ii).
s.152(1)(b)	had taken part, or proposed to do so, in activities of an independent trade union at an appropriate time, or	TULRCA 1992, s.161 employee presenting complaint under s.152 may apply, within 7 days of dismissal for interim relief.
s.152(1) (c)	was not, or proposed to refuse to become, or remain member of independent trade union or a particular trade union or number of particular trade unions	TULRCA 1992, s.156 minimum basic award applicable.
		TULRCA 1992, s.157 right to special award where reinstatement/re-engagement sought.
		Above provisions supported by TULRCA 1992, s.146: right not to have action short of dismissal taken against him for the purpose of preventing or deterring him from:
s.153(a)	redundancy where circumstances applied equally to other employees in the same undertaking who held similar positions and were not dismissed and reason was trade union reason contained in TULRCA 1992, s.152.	<ul><li>becoming or remaining a member of an independent trade union, or for penalising him for doing so;</li><li>taking part in the activities of an independent trade union at an appropriate time or penalising him for doing so; or</li><li>compelling him to be or become a member</li></ul>

Dismissal or Redundancy for any of the following reasons—Employment Rights Act 1996		
para. 7.5.3 ss.99(1)&(3)— dismissal s.105(2)— redundancy	Reasons of pregnancy and childbirth, or the ending of MLP because she gave birth; dismissed after taking MLP; ending of MLP because of redundancy and failure to offer suitable alternative work to comply with s.77.	s.108(3)(b) no requirement for qualifying service; s.109(2)(b) upper age limit provisions do not apply. Provisions supported by: right to time-off for anti-natal care, ERA ss.55-57; right to a written statement giving particulars of reasons for dismissal under s.92 without having to request it and in the absence of 2 years' qualifying service if dismissal occurs at any time while pregnant or after childbirth in circumstances in which MLP ends by reason of the dismissal, s.92(4)
para. 7.5.4 s.100 -dismissal s.105(3) - redundancy	Employee/health & safety representative for health & safety matters/taking part in elections or employee where no health & safety representative/withdrawal of labour for health & safety reason.	ERA 1996, s.108(3)(c) no requirement for qualifying service; s.109(2)(c) upper age limit provisions do not apply; s.118(3) right to special award where reinstatement or re-engagement requested; s.100(1)(a) designated by employer to carry out health & safety activities; s.100(1)(b) employee representative on health & safety matters or members of safety committee s.120(1) entitled to minimum basic award. Supported by right not to suffer detriment short of dismissal (s.44) and may apply for interim relief, s.128(1).
para. 7.5.5 s.101—dismissal s.105(4)(a)&(b) —redundancy	Protected or opted-out shop or betting-shop workers or such worker who has given or proposed to give opting-out notice for refusing to work on Sunday(s).	s.108(3)(d) no requirement for qualifying service; s.109(2)(d) upper age limit provisions do not apply.
para. 7.5.6 s.102—dismissal s.105(5)— redundancy	Trustee of occupational pension scheme for performing or proposing to perform any function as a trustee.	s.108(3)(e) no requirement for qualifying service; s.109(2)(e) upper age limit provisions do not apply. s.120(1) minimum basic award; s.118(3) right to a special award where reinstatement or re-engagement requested. May apply for interim relief, s.128(1). Supported by right not to suffer detriment short of dismissal ERA 1996, s.46. NB—right to paid time-off for performing duties or relevant training, ss.58-59.

Dismissal or Redundancy for the following reasons—Employment Rights Act 1996, continued		
para. 7.5.7 s.103- dismissal s.105(6)— redundancy	Employee representative, or candidate in election, for purposes of redundancy consultation under TULRCA 1992, ss.188-192 or TUPE, regs. 10 & 11.	s.108(3)(f) no requirement for qualifying service; s.109(2)(f) upper age limit provisions do not apply. s.120(1) minimum basic award; s.118(3) right to a special award where reinstatement or re-engagement requested, may apply for interim relief, s.128(1). Supported by right not to suffer detriment short of dismissal, s.47. Right to paid time-off, to perform functions, ss.61-63.
para. 7.5.8 s.104—dismissal s.105(7) — redundancy	Assertion of statutory right.	s.108(3)(g) no requirement for qualifying service; s.109(2)(g) upper age limits do not apply.

Change of Employer—Transfer of Undertakings (Protection of Employment) Regulations 1981		
para. 7.5.9 Reg. 8 dismissal	Immediately before or after a relevant transfer except where reason is economic, technical or organisational reason entailing changes in the workforce then dismissal falls within ERA 1996, s.98(1)(b) and falls to be considered under s.98(4).	Following the *Milligan v. Securicor Cleaning*, Reg 8 of the TUPE Regulations 1981 was amended by Collective Redundancies and Transfer of Undertakings (Protection of Employment) (Amendment) Regulations 1995. *Milligan* overruled by Court of Appeal in *MRS Environmental Services Ltd v. Marsh*. Two years' continuous service therefore required.

Rehabilitation of Offenders Act 1974		
para. 7.5.10 s.4(3)(b)	Dismissal for failure to disclose a spent conviction where not in a category that is exempt under regulations.	

7.5 FORUM AND REMEDIES

In seeking a remedy for unfair dismissal the forum is before the industrial tribunals, with an appeal under ITA 1996, s.21(1) on a point of law only, to the Employment Appeal Tribunal, and thereafter to the Court of Appeal and finally the House of Lords. The powers and procedure of industrial tribunals is governed by Part I of the 1996 Act and regulations[66] and those of EAT by Part II and regulations.[67] The composition of both the industrial tribunals and the EAT is, by ITA 1996, s.4(1) and s.28(2) tripartite in that a legally qualified chairman, or judge in the case of the EAT, sits with two lay members, representatives of employers and workers. Section 4(2) provides for those cases listed in section 4(3) to be heard by a chairman sitting alone, any resulting appeal being heard by a judge alone, section 28(4).

The tribunal is not bound by rules relating to the admissibility of evidence and has a discretion to "conduct the hearing in such manner as it considers most appropriate for the clarification of the issues before it and generally to the handling of the proceedings".[68] By Rule 8(2) of the Rules of Procedure, hearings are held in public. There is, however, a power in cases of national security for a Minister of the Crown to direct that an industrial tribunal sit in private, ITA 1996, s.10 and a discretion, ITA 1996, ss.11–12,[69] in cases involving allegations of sexual offences, or sexual misconduct and in proceedings on a complaint under DDA 1995, s.8, for the industrial tribunal to make a restricted reporting order,[70] but even where the order is sought by both parties, it should not be made automatically: the tribunal should still go on to decide whether such an order would be in the public interest. There is also a power,[71] in cases involving allegations of sexual offences, to delete or omit from any decision, document or record of proceedings available to the public "any identifying matter" which may lead to identification of any person either affected by or making an allegation.

In *R. v. Southampton Industrial Tribunal, ex p. INS News Group Ltd*[72] two newspapers challenged an order excluding members of the public, apart from witnesses, from the hearing, made under Rule 9(1) of the Rules of Procedure. In granting certiorari to quash the order the High Court held that the powers of the tribunal to sit in private were limited to those contained in rule 8, and no power existed within that rule to make an order to exclude the public. The Court said that the tribunal should look to rule 14 and the power contained therein to issue a restricted reporting order to prohibit the publication of evidence since that was the means by which parliament had "struck the balance between the needs of the press and the needs of tribunals to do justice in circumstances where witnesses feared that their evidence might be published in an unattractive and inappropriate manner".

7.5.1 Industrial tribunals

Since the Donovan Commission recommended in 1968 that industrial tribunals be reconstituted as labour tribunals and empowered to hear a variety of labour disputes,

---

[66] Industrial Tribunals (Constitution and Rules of Procedure) Regulations 1993 (S.I. 1993 No. 2687) as amended by S.I. 1994 No. 536 and S.I. 1996 No. 1757. Also Industrial Tribunals Practice Direction No. 1, Nov. 1994.
[67] Employment Appeal Tribunal Rules 1993 (S.I. 1993 No. 2854). Also Employment Appeal Tribunal Practice Direction March 1996.
[68] S.I. 1993 No. 2687, Sched. 1, Rules of Procedure, rule 9(1).
[69] *ibid.*, rule 14.
[70] Held in *X v. Y*, *The Times*, April 18, 1997 CA, to be a broad discretionary power unlikely to be overturned on appeal.
[71] S.I. 1993 No. 2687, Sched. 1; Rules of Procedure, r. 13(6).
[72] I.R.L.B. 519 April 1995.

including the recommended statutory unfair dismissal jurisdiction, providing a single unified forum for the hearing of employment grievances, industrial tribunals have had their jurisdiction increased on a number of occasions as a result of new employment rights.[73] The expansion in jurisdiction, together with other factors, resulted in registered applications increasing between 1984–85 and 1993–94, from 39,191 to 71,661,[74] with further increases in jurisdictions expected to lead to some 88,000 applications in 1998 to 99.[75] Most recently, and 26 years after Donovan recommended removal of the multiplicity of jurisdictions with the concentration in one tribunal all cases arising from the contract of employment[76] jurisdiction was extended by Industrial Tribunals Extension of Jurisdiction (England and Wales) Order 1994,[77] under powers contained in the ITA 1996, s.3 to enable certain contract claims arising or outstanding on termination of employment to be heard by industrial tribunals. In 1995 to 6 industrial tribunals disposed of 3,495 cases under this jurisdiction, almost the same as the number of sex discrimination cases.

In *Sarker v. South Tees Acute Hospitals NHS Trust*[78] the purpose of the regulations was described a being:

> "In a narrow sense, the purpose is to prevent an employee bringing a (ITA 1996, s.3) claim in a tribunal during the continuation of his or her employment. Why should that be an objective of the legislature? The answer to that takes one to the purpose of the 1994 Order itself. . . . (it is) intended to avoid the situation where an employee (or for that matter an employer) is forced to use both a tribunal and a court of law to have all his or her claims determined. In simple terms, the purpose of the extension of jurisdiction was to enable an industrial tribunal to deal with both a claim for unfair dismissal (which we take as an obvious example) and a claim for damages for breach of the same contract of employment. Two sets of proceedings are thus avoided." *per* Keene J.

Sarker v. South Tees Acute Hospitals NHS Trust [1997] I.R.L.R. 328 at 331, EAT.

The impetus for the implementation of contract jurisdiction, powers for which were first contained in IRA 1971, arose from cases such as *O'Laoire v. Jackel International Ltd*[79] where Lord Donaldson *obiter*, said that having a duplication of proceedings could not be in the interests of justice and considerable hardship could arise for someone both unfairly and wrongfully dismissed having to pursue different remedies in different courts. In *Delaney v. Staples*[80] the House of Lords held that whilst the claim for unpaid commission and accrued holiday pay fell within the definition of "wages" and was therefore enforceable in the industrial tribunal under ERA 1996, Pt. II, a claim for payment in lieu of notice, being damages for breach of contract, was instead enforceable in the County Court. This, Lord Browne-Wilkinson said, *obiter*:

---

[73] Jurisdiction at December 1994 is contained in Appendix A, *Resolving Employment Rights Disputes: Options For Reform,* Cm. 2707.
[74] Cm. 2707, para. 3.2.
[75] *ibid.*, para. 3.9. In the year to December 1996 the total number of cases received was 81,676, but after withdrawn and settled cases, the number decided was 25,092 (Annual Report of the Council on Tribunals for 1996/7).
[76] *Royal Commission on Trade Unions and Employers' Association* 1965–1968 Cmnd. 3623, para. 573.
[77] S.I. 1994 No. 1623.
[78] [1997] I.R.L.R. 328, EAT.
[79] [1990] I.R.L.R. 70, CA.
[80] [1992] I.R.L.R. 191, HL.

". . . produces an untidy and unsatisfactory result. On any dismissal, the summary procedure of the Industrial Tribunal under the act will be exercisable in relation to unpaid wages (in the ordinary sense), holiday pay, commission, maternity leave etc., but claims relating to the failure to give proper notice will continue to have to be brought in the County Court. The employee is therefore forced either to bring two sets of proceedings or to proceed wholly in the County Court on a claim for damages. To be forced to bring two sets of proceedings for two small sums of money in relation to one dismissal is wasteful of time and money. It brings the law into disrepute and is not calculated to ensure that employees recover their full legal entitlement when wrongfully dismissed."

Delaney v. Staples [1992] I.R.L.R. 191 at 195, HL.

The combined effect of ITA 1996, s.3(2) and Article 3 of the 1994 Order,[81] is to give industrial tribunals jurisdiction to hear a claim for failure to pay money due under a compromise agreement made in accordance with ERA 1996, s.203. In *Rock-It-Cargo Ltd v. Green*[82] the EAT held that Article 3(2) of the 1994 Order provides jurisdiction for the industrial tribunal if "the claim arises or is outstanding on the termination of the employee's employment." and a compromise agreement was held to be an agreement as to the terms on which the employee's employment was to be brought to an end, and "is quite plainly connected with that contract of employment".

The Industrial Tribunal has not, through the 1994 Regulations, gained exclusive jurisdiction over contractual matters since there is no compulsion to use the tribunal route, although the advantage of doing so is that the statutory maximum in respect of any one contract (regardless of the number of claims brought on it) is £25,000, which exceeds that available for a compensatory award for unfair dismissal.[83] By Article 7(a) a complaint must be presented within three months of the effective date of termination. However, unlike Industrial Tribunal proceedings, under the 1994 Regulations[84] the employer may present a counter-claim, but must do so within six weeks of receiving the employee's originating application. As with Industrial Tribunal proceedings no legal aid is available.

In *Pendragon plc v. Jackson*[85] the EAT held that ITA 1996, s.21, which re-enacted EPCA 1978, s.136, contained a drafting error in that the words "this Act" were omitted, as a result of which section 21 of the 1996 Act is defective in that it does not confer jurisdiction on the EAT to hear appeals in breach of contract cases. A statement issued by the President of the Employment Appeal Tribunal following the *Pendragon* case,[86] points out that prior to the hearing of the *Pendragon* appeal a clause had been inserted into the Employment Rights (Dispute Resolution) Bill, then proceeding through Parliament, to restore to the EAT the jurisdiction which it previously had, and making the change retrospective, the EAT making a working assumption that that jurisdiction would be restored "in about April 1998". In the meantime none of the appeals, and 10 per cent of all appeals raise a breach of contract issue, would be listed for hearing.

---

[81] Industrial Tribunals Extension of Jurisdiction Order 1994 (S.I. 1994 No. 1623).
[82] [1997] I.R.L.R. 581, EAT.
[83] Under Employment Rights (Increase of Limits) Order 1998 (S.I. 1998 No. 924), the maximum compensatory award is £12,000.
[84] reg. 8.
[85] [1998] I.R.L.R. 17, EAT.
[86] [1998] I.R.L.R. 22.

7.5.2 Pre-hearing review

The pre-hearing review procedure, which is intended to reduce the number of cases proceeding to a full hearing and to filter out those which do not on their merits justify a hearing, was introduced by TURERA 1993 as a successor to the pre-hearing assessment procedure. Governed by ITA 1996, s.9 and regulations,[87] either party may apply for a PHR before the hearing of an originating application, or a tribunal may hold one on its own motion. The PHR involves a consideration of:

"(a) the contents of the originating application and notice of appearance;

(b) any representations in writing; and

(c) any oral argument advanced by or on behalf of a party."[88]

and if the tribunal considers that a party's contentions have "no reasonable prospect of success" it may make a costs warning. In addition, it may also make an order requiring a deposit of up to £150 as a condition of continuing with the application. If a party against whom an order has been made fails to pay the amount specified within twenty-one days the tribunal has power to strike out the originating application. If the deposit is paid and the case proceeds to a hearing, but the party against whom the order was made loses and has a costs order made against them, the deposit then goes towards the settlement of costs.[89]

7.5.3 Employment Appeal Tribunal

The Employment Appeal Tribunal was constituted by the Employment Protection Act 1975 and is a superior court of record. Its jurisdiction, membership and composition of the Employment Appeal Tribunal is now governed by ITA 1996, Pt. II, and Rules,[90] which consolidates the law. Rule 30 requires the Employment Appeal Tribunal to sit in private where the industrial tribunal has been required to do so on grounds of national security under ITA 1996, s.10. In provisions which mirror those applicable to the industrial tribunal, in appeals which appear to involve allegations of the commission of a sexual offence the Registrar is required[91] to omit from documents available to the public, any "identifying matter", and in relation to appeals involving allegations of sexual misconduct a restricted reporting order may be made on a application by either party, or of its own motion.[92]

The appellate jurisdiction of the EAT, which by ITA 1996, s.21 is confined to points of law only, has repeatedly been stressed:

"The function of the Employment Appeal Tribunal is to correct errors of law where one is established and identified. I think care must be taken to avoid

[87] Industrial Tribunal (Constitution and Rules of Procedure) Regulations 1993 (S.I. 1993 No. 2687), Sched. 1, r. 7.
[88] *ibid.*, r. 7(1).
[89] *ibid.*, r. 7(8) as substituted by Industrial Tribunals (Constitution and Rules of Procedure) (Amendment) Regulations 1996, (S.I. 1996 No. 1757), reg. 10.
[90] Employment Appeal Tribunal Rules 1993 (S.I. 1993 No. 2854).
[91] *ibid.*, r. 23(2).
[92] *ibid.*, 23(3).

concluding that an experienced Industrial Tribunal by not expressly mentioning
some point or breach has overlooked it, and care must be taken to avoid, in a case
where the Employment Appeal Tribunal members would on the basis of the
merits and the oral evidence have taken a view different from that of the
Industrial Tribunal, searching around with a fine-tooth comb for some point of
law." *per* Lord Russell

Retarded Children's Aid Society v. Day [1978] I.R.L.R. 128 at 130, CA.

and in *Martin v. Glynwed Distribution Ltd*[93] Sir John Donaldson observed:

"It is very important, and sometimes difficult, to remember that where a right of
appeal is confined to questions of law, the appellate tribunal must loyally accept
the findings of fact with which it is presented and where, as can happen from time
to time, it is convinced that it would have reached a different conclusion of fact, it
must resist the strong temptation to treat what are in truth findings of fact as
holdings of law or mixed findings of fact and law. The correct approach involves a
recognition that Parliament has constituted the industrial tribunal the only
tribunal of fact and that conclusions of fact must be accepted unless it is apparent
that, on the evidence, no reasonable tribunal could have reached them. If such be
the case, and happily it is a rarity, the tribunal, which is to be assumed to be a
reasonable tribunal, must have misdirected itself in law and the Employment
Appeal Tribunal will be entitled to intervene." *per* Sir John Donaldson

Martin v. Glynwed Distribution Ltd [1983] I.C.R. 511 at 514, CA.

This was emphasised by the Court of Appeal in *Post Office v. Lewis*[94] where it was
held that the EAT could only intervene if the tribunal's decision was perverse or
contained an error or law: it could not intervene simply on its view of the weight of the
evidence. Despite this confinement of appeals to points of law only, the composition of
the EAT mirrors that of industrial tribunals insofar as the "industrial jury" aspect is
concerned[95] and in *Martin v. Glynwed Distribution Ltd* Sir John Donaldson pointed to
the advantages of this composition and the anomaly that on appeal to the Court of
Appeal this benefit is lost:

"On the face of it, there is no very obvious reason why a court which is concerned
solely with questions of law should be so composed that a majority having no
formal legal qualifications can and, as occurred in the present case, on occasion
does overrule the legally qualified member. . . . I was astonished to find that this
was the situation . . . I thought it must be a mistake. . . . (but) after I began sitting
with lay members to hear unfair dismissal and redundancy appeals I very soon
found out that my initial reaction had been wholly mistaken. The field of
industrial relations has its own very specialised 'know-how' and this is something
which, initially at least, is more familiar to Members of Parliament than to judges.
Parliament, in legislating in the field of industrial relations, does so against the
background of that 'know-how' and the words which it uses have to be interpreted
in the light of that background. Upon more than one occasion I found that the

[93] [1983] I.C.R. 511, CA.
[94] *The Times*, April 25, 1997.
[95] ITA 1996, s.29(2).

industrial relations expertise of the lay members . . . cast an entirely new light upon what must have been the intention of Parliament. . . . my regret was not that it was a mixed court of judges and industrial members, but that there was a right of appeal to the Court of Appeal which did not have similar advantages, albeit perhaps with the industrial members being in a minority." *per* Sir John Donaldson

Martin v. Glynwed Distribution Ltd [1983] I.C.R. 511 at 513–4, CA.

The number of appeals registered with the Employment Appeal Tribunal in 1995–6 was 1,358 (1,298 1994–95) with a total of 998 cases disposed of during the year (868). There was a fall in the number of preliminary hearings held by the EAT in 1995–96 to 605, of which 326 were dismissed at the hearing and 279 were allowed to proceed to a full hearing. The preliminary hearing procedure allows for *ex parte* preliminary hearings to be held in order to determine whether the notice of appeal raises a reasonably arguable point of law. With effect from October 1997 all appeals to the EAT are to be listed for a preliminary hearing/directions at which the appellant will be required to satisfy the EAT that it is reasonably arguable that the industrial tribunal made an error of law in its decision. Guidance notes regarding the new procedure, together with sample appellant's and respondent's PHD forms have been published.[96]

7.5.4 Reform

The priorities identified by Donovan in recommending the reconstituting of industrial tribunals to have jurisdiction over complaints of unfair dismissal were that they would operate in all major industrial centres, thus be easily accessible, speedy, informal and non legalistic and as a consequence, cheap. Increasing costs and delays, together with challenges to the perceived increasing legalism have led to a number of calls for change.[97]

A review of the operation of industrial tribunals, set up with the twin aims of increasing efficiency in the face of increasing caseloads and complexity while containing demands on public expenditure, led to a Green Paper which invited views on a number of issues.[98] The Paper identifies a number of changes that had to that date been made with a view to re-establishing the Donovan Commission's prescription for tribunals:

- the introduction, by the TURERA 1993, of a power for tribunal Chairmen to sit without lay members when hearing certain cases;

- an extension of the scope for the parties to individual employment rights disputes to reach binding settlements which disbar subsequent application to an industrial tribunal;

- a power for the Employment Appeal Tribunal to disqualify vexatious litigants from bringing complaints before the industrial tribunals and

- changes in the rules of procedure[99] "intended to encourage tribunals to take a more investigatory approach, to weed out cases which seemed to have no

---

[96] [1997] I.R.L.R. at 618–620.
[97] See R. Lewis and J. Clark (1993); Dickens, *et al.* (1985).
[98] *Resolving Employment Rights Disputes—Options for Reform,* Cm. 2707 (1994).
[99] Currently Industrial Tribunals (Constitution and Rules of Procedure) Regulations 1993 (S.I. 1993 No. 2687).

reasonable change of success and generally to improve the speed and accessibility of the tribunal system.

The paper proposed a review of service targets to reduce waiting times, the implementation of targets for other aspects in line with the Citizens Charter[1] and the setting up of an Executive Agency under the Next Steps Initiative.[2] The Employment Rights (Dispute Resolution) Bill, based on the proposals outlined in the Green Paper, is a Private Member's Bill introduced into the House of Lords by Lord Archer of Sandwell, but with cross-party support it is expected to pass into law.[3]

The key points of the Bill, which is divided into four parts are:

Part I

- Renames industrial tribunals as employment tribunals, and the Industrial Tribunals Act 1996 renamed Employment Tribunals Act 1996 with consequential amendments in other legislation.

- Permits new procedural rules to be introduced to streamline procedures and extends jurisdiction of tribunals; the Secretary of State will have powers to amend tribunal procedure regulations to allow tribunals to determine cases without a "full" hearing in a limited number of circumstances. These are:

  - Both parties have given their consent for the proceedings to be determined on the basis of written evidence alone;
  - Where the respondent has done nothing to defend the case or where it appears that the tribunal does not have the power to grant the relief claimed or the applicant is not entitled to the relief he is claiming or the proceedings relate only to a preliminary issue or permit a tribunal to require written answers to questions posed by the tribunal to be given by the parties.
  - Although not as extensive as proposed in the Green paper, it extends the categories of case where an employment tribunal must consist of the chairman alone (unless he exercises the discretion to sit as a tribunal of three) to a range of additional proceedings.

Part II:

- Provides for ACAS to draw up an arbitration scheme for resolution of unfair dismissal disputes (with a power for the Secretary of State to extend this to other areas of employment law) and for agreements under the arbitration scheme to oust the jurisdiction of employment tribunals.

- Amends the law relating to compromise agreements by relaxing the restrictions on who is qualified to give advice. At committee stage in the House of Lords an amendment was made that advice must be obtained by a person specified in a list, as opposed to any independent advice and the list includes qualified lawyers, union officials, advice workers (whose advice must be free to qualify as valid), and anyone specified by the Secretary of State, who can attach conditions.

[1] para. 7.42–43.
[2] para. 7.40. The Employment Tribunals Service was launched in April 1997.
[3] The original bill fell in the lead up to the 1997 General Election.

- Extends the duties of conciliation officers to claims relating to statutory redundancy payments and provides for the Secretary of State to act as guarantor for a sum due under an agreement settling a dispute about a statutory redundancy payment arrived at after conciliation or compromise agreement.

- Amends the law relating to dismissal procedures agreements by requiring such agreements to provide for arbitration or a right to arbitration on a point of law.

Part III

- Introduces measures to encourage use by employees and employers of internal appeals procedures in cases of dismissal: employment tribunals are to be able to take into account, when determining compensation, whether an employee attempted to make use of an in-house procedure provided by his employer to appeal against his dismissal with power to make a deduction of up to two weeks' pay from the employee's compensation for such a failure. If the employer provided such a procedure but prevented the employee from using it the tribunal could make a supplementary award of up to two weeks' pay. The tribunal would be required to have regard to all the circumstances of the case, including in particular the chances that an appeal under the procedure provided by the employer would have been successful.

- Makes provision to avoid double recovery in cases of unfair dismissal which involve disability discrimination.

All the changes are being made with the stated aim of reducing the number of cases to be heard before employment tribunals and the consequent costs involved. The proposal to appoint legal officers to undertake a range of preliminary and interlocutory duties, although controversial, has survived from the Green Paper and has been the subject to a pilot scheme. With little information about the qualifications to be required for legal officers, fears have been expressed that the opportunity will be taken to save money by not appointing enough tribunal chairmen or by appointing a "more lowly 'mysterious' judicial figure".[4]

In connection with the arbitration scheme, fears have been expressed that not only will such a scheme be extended to more complex areas of the law, such as discrimination cases, but that although only applicable where the parties volunteer, some employees will come under pressure to agree, and that such a scheme will sacrifice "justice" to increased throughput.[5] A point of criticism has been that details of the ACAS arbitration scheme were not available to accompany the bill in its passage through Parliament.

Entry to the scheme of arbitration, which is to be voluntary and only available where both parties agree, is to be through a settlement of the complaint under the auspices of a conciliation officer or by means of a compromise agreement, thus ensuring that any applicant opting for arbitration would have had the process explained to them by a conciliation officer or professional. The arbitration process is to be in parallel to the reformed employment tribunal system but is to be mutually exclusive: by agreeing to

---

[4] I.R.L.B. 577, September 1977, p. 2.
[5] *ibid.*

arbitration the parties would be agreeing that there are no jurisdictional matters between them, and having agreed to arbitration the case may not be referred back to a tribunal, except in limited circumstances relating to jurisdiction.

Proceedings will be in private and it is envisaged that the standard terms of reference would be to ask the question whether the decision to dismiss should be confirmed, revoked and the applicant be re-employed or whether compensation should be paid, the arbitrator having regard to the ACAS Code of Practice[6] and the ACAS handbook[7] in making the decision. There is to be no appeal on a point of law.

ACAS is to establish a panel, from which an arbitrator would be appointed, to be composed of individuals with a wide experience of the world of work and to possess analytical and social skills, but legal experience is not considered to be necessary, initial training and regular refresher training being seen as a necessary part of the process.

Any compensation awarded would be subject to the same limit as tribunal awards and be legally enforceable. Should an award of re-employment not be complied with the case would be referred to an industrial tribunal for a remedy in the same way as such an order issued by the tribunal.

7.5.5 Remedies

7.5.5.1 *Reinstatement and re-engagement*

The Donovan Commission[8] expressed a clear preference for reinstatement as the primary remedy in cases of unfair dismissal, but it was not until the Trade Union and Labour Relations Act 1974 that reinstatement was specified separately from re-engagement and in the Employment Protection Act, 1975 that tribunals were empowered to order, and not merely to recommend, re-employment.[9] Under the ERA 1996, s.112, when a tribunal finds that the grounds of the complaint for unfair dismissal are well-founded, regardless of expressions on Form IT1, it is required to explain the orders for reinstatement or re-engagement to the applicant and ask whether he wishes the tribunal to make such an order. If so, the tribunal has a discretion as to whether to do so.

By section 116 in exercising its discretion under section 113 the tribunal is first required to consider an order of reinstatement, which is an order that the employer treat the employee in all respects as if he had not been dismissed, section 114(1), and in doing so is required by section 116(1) to take into account—

(a) whether the employee wishes to be reinstated,

(b) whether it is practicable for the employer to comply with an order for reinstatement, and

(c) where the employee caused or contributed to some extent to the dismissal, whether it would be just to order his reinstatement.

and on making a reinstatement order the tribunal is required, as provided in section 114(2)(a)–(c), to specify:

---

[6] *Disciplinary Practice and Procedure in Employment.*
[7] *Discipline at Work.*
[8] Royal Commission on Trade Unions and Employers' Associations 1965–1968 Cmnd. 3623, June 1968, para. 551.
[9] Dickens *et al.* (1985).

(a) any amount payable by the employer in respect of any benefit which the employee might reasonably be expected to have had but for the dismissal (including arrears of pay) or the period between the date of termination of employment and the date of reinstatement,

(b) any rights and privileges (including seniority and pension rights) which must be restored to the employee, and

(c) the date by which the order must be complied with.

The employee is entitled to receive the benefit from any improvement in his terms and conditions that he would have received had he not been dismissed and there is no maximum limit to the sum that can be awarded for arrears of pay. However, the tribunal must reduce the employer's liability by the amount of any wages received in lieu of notice, *ex gratia* payments paid by the employer, or remuneration received for employment with another employer, and any other benefits the tribunal thinks appropriate in the circumstances. When an order is made under section 113 regulations[10] provide for employment to be continuous.

Where the tribunal does not make an order for reinstatement, by section 116(2) it is then required to consider whether to make an order for re-engagement and, if so on what terms, and in doing so to consider the factors in section 116(3)(a)–(c), which mirror those for consideration of a reinstatement order contained in section 116(1)(a)–(c). An order for re-engagement is a more flexible order and requires the employee to be taken back on by the employer, or an associated employer, not in his old job, but in comparable or other suitable employment, and the tribunal is required to specify the details of the re-engagement under the headings listed in section 115(2)(a)–(f). Although the job must be comparable, it was held in *Rank Xerox (UK) Ltd v. Stryczek*[11] that the tribunal had erred in making a re-engagement order specifying a position which would have amounted to a promotion, attracting both a substantially higher salary and a company car.

In considering whether it is "practicable" under section 116(1)(b) and (3)(b) for the employer to comply with a reinstatement or re-engagement order, it was held in *Coleman v. Magnet Joinery Ltd*[12] that "practicable" means practical in the industrial relations sense. Where an employer has appointed a permanent replacement to do the employee's job the tribunal is not, by section 116(5) permitted to take that into account in determining whether it is practicable to comply with an order for reinstatement or re-engagement.

Dickens *et al.* (1985) reported that very few successful applicants are awarded reinstatement and that the legislative changes implemented in 1976 did not halt the downward trend in the level of re-employment: in 1995–96 re-engagement orders made up only 0.6 per cent of the cases upheld.

7.5.5.2 *Compensation*

For failure to reinstate and re-engage

If an order for reinstatement or re-engagement is made and the employee is reinstated or re-engaged, but the terms are not fully complied with, or the employee is not

---

[10] Employment Protection (Continuity of Employment) Regulations 1993 (S.I. 1993 No. 2687).
[11] [1995] I.R.L.R. 568, EAT.
[12] [1974] I.R.L.R. 343, CA.

reinstated or re-engaged in accordance with the order, the tribunal must make an award of compensation. In the event of failure to fully comply the amount of the compensation, by section 117(2), is to be "such as the tribunal thinks fit having regard to the loss sustained by the employee in consequence of the failure to comply fully with the terms of the order". By ERA 1996, s.117(3) if the employee is not reinstated or re-engaged in accordance with an order made under section 113, the tribunal must make, not only an award of compensation, but also an additional award of compensation of an "appropriate amount", which is defined in section 117(5)(a) and (b) as:

- in cases of dismissal for unlawful sex discrimination contrary to SDA 1975 and unlawful race discrimination contrary to RRA 1976, a higher additional award of not less than 26 nor more than 52 weeks' pay;

- in any other case, not less than 13 nor more than 26 weeks' pay.

The tribunal has a discretion to exercise and in *Morganite Electrical Crbon Ltd v. Done*[13] it was held that a tribunal should not simply announce a maximum additional award without carrying out a reasoned exercise to determine what the figure should be. The tribunal may take into account the conduct of the employer in refusing to comply with the re-employment order, as in *A.J. George v. Beecham Group*,[14] and the extent to which the compensatory award has met the actual loss suffered by the employee. The provisions regarding an additional award do not apply where the employer satisfies the tribunal that it was not practicable to comply with the order or, by section 117(4)(b) where the reason, or principal reason, for selection for redundancy or dismissal was:

- health and safety case within section 100(1)(a)

- trustee of an occupational pension scheme within section 102(1) or

- an employee representative within section 103

An additional award is not subject to reduction because of the employee's contributory conduct, although it would be rare for a reinstatement or re-engagement order to be made in those circumstances. Any *ex gratia* payment made by the employer may be set off against the additional award.

Section 124 provides that the compensatory order is subject to a statutory maximum.[15] Intended to provide compensation for losses suffered, it is increasingly incapable of doing so because of a failure to increase, or increase sufficiently the maximum figure. However, in cases involving failure to reinstate or re-engage ERA 1996, s.124(3) and (4) provides that the statutory limit on the compensatory award may be exceeded by the extent necessary to enable the aggregate of the compensatory and additional awards fully to reflect the amount of arrears of pay and benefits specified in the original order. This amendment, made in TURERA 1993, enables an employee in whose favour an additional award has been made to be fully compensated where he is either highly paid, or a long period of time has elapsed between dismissal and the tribunal hearing and reflects the view expressed by Lord Donaldson in *O'Laoire v. Jackel International Ltd*[16] that the limit could discourage employers from complying with a reinstatement order and creates injustice to higher-paid employees.

---

[13] [1987] I.R.L.R. 363, EAT.
[14] Case No. 29759/76 [1977] I.R.L.R. 43.
[15] Employment Rights (Increase of Limits) Order 1998 (S.I. 1998 No. 924), £12,000.
[16] [1990] I.R.L.R. 70, CA.

In *Selfridges Ltd v. Malik*[17] the industrial tribunal made a reinstatement order and specified a sum of £25,000 under section 114(2)(a) to compensate for the earnings which the employee had lost during the period from dismissal to reinstatement. When the employer refused to comply with the order the tribunal made an award of compensation for unfair dismissal under section 117(3) of £43,647 made up of a basic award of £1,845, a compensatory award representing loss of earnings for a further 26 weeks after the date specified for reinstatement plus loss of pension rights and loss of statutory rights, reduced to the maximum permissible under section 124(1) and therefore amounting to £11,300; an additional award under section 117(3)(b) of £5,460; and the sum of £25,042 already calculated under section 114(2)(a) as part of the reinstatement order. The employers appealed against the quantum on the basis that it exceeded the maximum permitted under section 124(4): they argued that the award should be £26,887 made up of a basic award, the additional award and a maximum compensatory award of £19,582, and that the employee was not entitled to two sets of compensatory award, the first, made as part of the re-engagement order not being subject to the statutory maximum. The EAT held that the industrial tribunal had been wrong, in the case of an employer refusing to comply with a re-engagement order, to specify that the employee was entitled to compensation consisting of the sum specified in the re-engagement order as well as a maximum compensatory award for loss of future benefits and an additional award: the compensatory award includes any amount specified in the reinstatement order which is not a free-standing head to be awarded whether or not the order for reinstatement is complied with.

This judgment appears surprising and can mean that the employee is left under compensated when an order for reinstatement is not complied with, and the employer can benefit from non-compliance. It is submitted that this cannot surely, be right.

In a case of failure to comply with an order for reinstatement or re-engagement where the dismissal is unfair for trade union reasons under TULRCA 1992, the provisions regarding an additional award do not apply, but the provisions regarding a special award do apply.

By ERA 1996, s.112(4) if no order for reinstatement or re-engagement is made, the tribunal may make an order of compensation for unfair dismissal. Calculation is to be made in accordance with sections 118–127 and section 118 provides that compensation shall consist of a basic and a compensatory award.

Basic award

The basic award, introduced by Employment Protection Act 1975, is the main remedy for unfair dismissal and is designed to compensate the employee for the loss of job security caused by the unfair dismissal by awarding a sum almost exactly equivalent to a statutory redundancy payment, being calculated on age and length of continuous service as provided in section 119(2) as follows:

- for service below the age of 22—half a week's pay for each year of service
- for service between 22 and 41—one week's pay for each year of service
- for service over the age of 41—one and a half week's pay for each year of service

A week's pay is subject to a statutory maximum of £220[18] a week and service is limited to a maximum of twenty years. Where the employee is dismissed in the twelve months

---

[17] [1997] I.R.L.R. 577, EAT.
[18] Effective April 1, 1998.

after his 64th birthday, the award is reduced by one-twelfth for each month he works between 64 and 65, so that by 65 there is no longer an entitlement, section 119(4) and (5).

The basic award is subject to a minimum amount of £2,900, before being subject to reduction under section 122, where the reason for dismissal or selection for redundancy is one of the following:

- trade union membership or activities within TULRCA 1992, ss.152–3, s.156 and by ERA 1996, s.120(1),

- on health and safety grounds falling within ERA 1996, s.100(1)(a) and (b),

- pension fund trustee within section 102(1) or

- representative for redundancy or transfer consultation purposes within section 103.

Reduction

By ERA 1996, s.122 there are three grounds upon which the basic award may be reduced:

- where the employee has unreasonably refused an offer of reinstatement, section 122(1);

- any conduct of the employee before dismissal (or where the dismissal was with notice, before notice was given) where it was such that it would be just and equitable to reduce or further reduce the amount of the basic award (contributory negligence) section 122(2), but this does not apply to dismissals was for health and safety reason within section 100(1)(a) or (b), as a trustee of an occupational pension scheme, for performing any functions as a trustee or being an employee representative for redundancy consultation purposes, performing or proposing to perform any duties associated with that appointment;

- any redundancy payment received where the employee was made redundant, section 122(4). This will extinguish the redundancy payment, except that this is subject to the minimum basic award provisions where dismissal for redundancy is for an inadmissible reason, TULRCA 1992, s.156 and ERA 1996, s.122(3).

These categories are the only ones by which a reduction in the basic award may be made, and this is demonstrated in *Cadbury Ltd. v. Doddington*[19] where the EAT held that failure to award a basic award because the employee's long term sickness meant that he would be unable to return to work was not a ground for reducing the basic award, but only for reducing the compensatory award.

Compensatory award

The Employment Protection Act, 1975 introduced a separate basic award for compensation for loss of job security which was to be added to the existing

---

[19] [1977] I.C.R. 982, EAT.

compensatory provision for financial loss. Now governed by ERA 1996, s.123 the amount of the compensatory award is such as the tribunal considers just and equitable in all the circumstances having regard to the loss sustained, but subject to a statutory maximum which currently stands at £12,000.

In National Industrial Relations Court case of *Norton Tool Co. Ltd v. N.J. Newson*[20] Sir John Donaldson said:

> ". . . the common law rules and authorities on wrongful dismissal are irrelevant. That course is quite unaffected by the Act which has created an entirely new cause of action, namely the 'unfair industrial practice' of unfair dismissal. The measure of compensation for that statutory wrong is itself the creature of statute and is to be found in the Act and nowhere else. But we do not consider that Parliament intended the Court or tribunal to dispense compensation arbitrarily. On the other hand the amount has a discretionary element and is not to be assessed by adopting the approach of a conscientious and skilled cost accountant or actuary. Nevertheless that discretion is to be exercised judicially and upon the basis of principle." *per* Sir John Donaldson

Norton Tool Co. Ltd v. N.J. Newson [1972] I.R.L.R. 86 at 87, NIRC.

The heads of compensation suggested by Sir John Donaldson are:

- loss of earnings—between the date of dismissal and the date of the hearing;

- future loss of earnings based on an estimate of how long the employee is likely to be unemployed; in *Simrad Ltd v. Scott*[21] following dismissal the employee decided to retrain as a nurse via a three year training programme. The EAT held that in order to recover future losses there had to be a direct and natural link between the losses claimed and the dismissal, and that losses incurred as a result of retraining were not properly attributable to the conduct of her employer;

- the manner of dismissal; in *D. R. Vaughan v. Weighpack Ltd*[22] Sir Hugh Griffiths said that whilst a dismissal may be a distressing experience, that of itself is not a matter for compensation. It is only if there is cogent evidence that the manner of dismissal caused financial loss, as, for example, by making it more difficult to find future employment, that the manner of dismissal becomes relevant, and that this will be only on the very rarest of occasions. However, it was held in *Cleveland Ambulance NHS Trust v. Blane*[23] that in a claim for compensation arising from unlawful action short of dismissal the tribunal can award compensation for financial and non-financial loss. Non-financial loss may clearly include injury to feelings;

- loss of statutory employment protection rights, both unfair dismissal and redundancy; to which should be added

- expenses;

[20] [1972] I.R.L.R. 86, NIRC.
[21] [1997] I.R.L.R. 147, EAT.
[22] [1974] I.R.L.R. 105, NIRC.
[23] [1997] I.R.L.R. 332, EAT.

- loss of past and future fringe benefits, such as company car, low interest mortgage, subsidised accommodation and medical insurance;

- loss of pension rights. This head has the potential to be an important and costly element in the compensatory award, but its importance has yet to be appreciated. In order to assist in quantifying loss of pension rights, a committee of tribunal chairman in conjunction with the Government Actuary's Department has produced a report suggesting methods of quantifying loss of pension rights.[24]

As with damages at common law, damages awarded under a compensatory award are subject to mitigation, section 123(4).

Reduction

There are two separate provisions which allow the tribunal to reduce the compensatory award to reflect the employee's conduct: the general provision in section 123(1) that the amount be such as the tribunal considers just and equitable in all the circumstances and section 123(6) which provides that the tribunal must reduce the compensatory award where it considers that the dismissal was to any extent caused or contributed to by any action of the employee (contributory negligence). In *W. Davis & Sons Ltd v. Atkins*[25] Lord Dilhorne indicated that there is nothing inconsistent in finding unfairness but then in reducing compensation to nil or a merely nominal amount to reflect the employee's contribution to the dismissal. In *Tele-Trading Ltd v. Jenkins*[26] the Court of Appeal held that when considering contributory conduct under section 123(6) the tribunal may only use conduct known to the employer at the time of dismissal: subsequently discovered conduct cannot have "caused or contributed" to the dismissal and does not therefore fall under this head to justify a reduction in the award. On the other hand, section 123(1) applies where the employee's conduct is not known to the employer at the time of dismissal or notice.

In *Polkey v. A.E. Dayton Services Ltd*[27] the House of Lords held that procedural flaws associated with a dismissal are likely to make the dismissal unfair, but that a tribunal, may reduce the compensatory award under section 123(1) in order to reflect the fact that the employee would have been dismissed, notwithstanding the procedural flaws:

> "If the Industrial Tribunal thinks there is a doubt whether or not the employee would have been dismissed, this element can be reflected by reducing the normal amount of compensation by a percentage representing the chance that the employee would still have lost his employment." *per* Lord Bridge

> *Polkey v. A.E. Dayton Services Ltd* [1987] I.R.L.R. 503 at 508, HL.

In *McNee v. Charles Tennant & Co. Ltd*[28] the EAT upheld a nil award of compensation in the face of a finding of unfair dismissal because of a flawed procedure, because if the proper procedure had been carried out the employee could have been fairly dismissed for another reason. The EAT said that the criteria was "just and equitable" and it was not just and equitable to make a compensatory award if the employee could have been fairly dismissed for another reason.

---

[24] *Industrial Tribunals: Compensation of Loss of Pension Rights* (HMSO, 1991).
[25] [1977] I.R.L.R. 314, HL.
[26] [1990] I.R.L.R. 430, CA.
[27] [1987] I.R.L.R. 503, HL.
[28] [1989] I.C.R. 747, EAT.

In *Campbell v. Dunoon & Cowall Housing Association Ltd*[29] there was a finding of unfair dismissal for a failure to consult, but with a 75 per cent reduction to reflect the finding that even if consultation had taken place, the dismissals would have occurred anyway. The reduction was upheld by the Court of Session and in *James W. Cook & Co. (Wivenhoe) Ltd v. Tipper*[30] the Court of Appeal, despite upholding the finding of unfair dismissal, restricted the compensatory award to two weeks' pay to coincide with the closure of the firm.

These decisions transfer to the assessment of compensation the *BLP v. Byrne* principle of the tribunal making a "guess" at ascertaining what would have happened if what should have happened did in fact take place, which was so criticised in *Sillifant v. Powell Duffryn Timber Ltd*[31] because, as pointed out by Browne-Wilkinson J., how could one know what facts would have emerged if proper investigation/consultation had taken place and what would have been the employer's attitude in the light of those facts. Such hypothetical finding of fact as to what would have happened in a hypothetical event is, he said, pure guesswork. Given that consultation is meant to be a meaningful process which, in a potential redundancy situation, the employer under-takes at an early stage, with the intention of exploring the options available this test in this context seems to be subject to the same criticism as it was when applied to the finding of whether the dismissal was fair or unfair.

In *Rao v. Civil Aviation Authority*[32] the Court of Appeal considered whether by an application of section 123(1) and (6) it was intended that an employee could suffer a double reduction in compensation. Sir Thomas Bingham M.R. held, in a judgment of the court, that the two subsections were aimed at different events, and that it was therefore possible, in an appropriate case, for the employee to suffer two sets of deductions from the compensatory award.

Where the employee has received an *ex gratia* payment or a redundancy payment in excess of the amount calculated using the statutory formula, the tribunal is required by section 123(7) to off set the additional sum against the compensatory award. Some uncertainty has surrounded the method by which such sums are to be deduced and since the final figure can show a considerable variation depending on the method adopted, this issue has caused some controversy. In *Digital Equipment v. Clements*[33] the employee received a contractual severance payment in excess of the statutory redundancy payment. The industrial tribunal held that if the employer had followed a fair procedure there was a 50 per cent chance that the employee would have been retained, therefore not only did the contractual severance payment have to be off set against the compensatory award, but the result of that had to be reduced by 50 per cent, and then the result subjected to the statutory maximum. This produced compensation of £11,250, reduced to the statutory maximum at the time of £11,000.

On appeal to the EAT, under the Chairmanship of Mummery J., the employer's appeal was allowed,[33a] it being held that the statutory provisions, section 123(7) requires that the amount of compensatory award must be determined before the amount paid in excess redundancy payment is deduced. This calculation involved a reduction in the award to £837. Clements applied for a review of the EAT decision and this restored

---

[29] [1993] I.R.L.R. 496, CS.
[30] [1990] I.C.R. 716, CA.
[31] [1983] I.R.L.R. 91, EAT.
[32] [1994] I.R.L.R. 240, CA.
[33] [1996] I.R.L.R. 513, EAT.
[33a] *Digital Equipment Co. Ltd v. Clements* [1996] I.R.L.R. 513, EAT.

the original decision.[34] On appeal the Court of Appeal allowed the company's appeal,[35] agreeing with the reasoning of Mummery J. The Court held that the method of calculation should, in accordance with the ERA 1996, s.123(7) give the employer who pays redundancy payments on a more generous scale than the statutory code, full credit for that additional payment by deducting it after arriving at the compensatory award, reduced by the appropriate amount to reflect the chance that the employee would still have lost his employment if a fair procedure had been followed. Compensation is therefore arrived at in the following way:

— a calculation of the employee's net loss: that is the balance struck after the losses and gains flowing from the dismissal have been reckoned in accordance with section 123, this must reflect all the circumstances;

— the tribunal is entitled to reduce the amount of compensation awarded by a percentage representing the chance that the employee would still have lost his employment[36]: that, it was held, is part of the process of determining what loss has been sustained by the employee;

— if the amount of redundancy payment received exceeded the amount available by application of the statutory scheme, the excess goes to reduce the net loss, as opposed to being part of the net loss as decided by the Industrial Tribunal;

— the sum arrived at is then subject to application of the statutory maximum.

The Court of Appeal recognised that this calculation involved treating the excess redundancy payment differently from the way the Court of Appeal in *Ministry of Defence v. Wheeler*[37] treated the loss of earnings, but held that "Parliament has drawn a clear distinction in the treatment of the excess of redundancy payments which have actually been made by an employer and the other elements which go to make up the loss. . . . Parliament intended that the employer who paid compensation for redundancy on a more generous scale than the statutory scale was to be entitled to full credit for the additional payment against the amount of the loss which made up the compensatory award."

Recoupment provisions

In order to ensure that the employer pays the full sum due and that the state is repaid for any jobseeker's allowance or income support received between dismissal and the date of the hearing recoupment provisions exit which arc governed by the 1996 regulations[38] whereby the Department of Trade and Industry recovers from the employer any benefit paid to the employee during that period, before the element comprising loss of earnings is paid to the employee. The remainder is then paid by the employer to the employee.

---

[34] *Digital Equipment Co. Ltd v. Clements (No. 2)* [1997] I.R.L.R. 140, EAT.
[35] [1988] I.R.L.R. 134, CA.
[36] The *Polkey* deduction (*Polkey v. A.E. Dayton Services Ltd* [1987] I.R.L.R. 503, CA).
[37] [1998] I.R.L.R. 23, CA.
[38] Employment Protection (Recoupment of Jobseeker's Allowance and Income Support) Regulations 1996 (S.I. 1996 No. 2349).

Special award

By TULRCA 1992, s.157(1), the provisions of ERA 1996, s.117(3)(b) which provides for an additional award of compensation in a case of failure to comply with an order for reinstatement or re-engagement does not apply in a case where the dismissal is unfair for trade union reasons under TULRCA 1992, ss.152–3, being instead subject to a special award. This is available, in addition to basic and compensatory award, where the dismissal is for the following reasons, all of which are automatically unfair reasons and the employee has requested an order for reinstatement or re-engagement:

- by TULRCA 1992, s.157, where dismissal or selection for redundancy is for an inadmissible reason under TULRCA 1992, ss.152–3;

- by ERA 1996, s.118(3), where dismissal or selection for redundancy is that the employee:

  - in health and safety cases

    - ★ was a designated employee for the purposes of carrying out activities in connection with preventing or reducing risks to health and safety at work,
    - ★ was a workers representative for health and safety purposes or a member of a safety committee by virtue of arrangements under statutory provisions or merely by being acknowledged as such by the employer,

    for performing or proposing to perform any functions as such a designated employee/representative;

  - was a trustee of an occupational pension scheme for performing or proposing to perform any function as a trustee;

  - was an employee representative for redundancy consultation or transfer of undertakings purposes, or a candidate in an election for such a representative.

If a reinstatement or re-engagement order is not made, or is made but the employer satisfies the tribunal that it is not practical to comply with it, then a special award must be ordered made up of 104 weeks' pay subject to a minimum of £14,500 and a maximum of £29,000, TULRCA 1992, s.158(2) and ERA 1996, s.125(1). If such an order is made, but the employer does not comply with it and fails to satisfy the tribunal that it was not practical to comply with the order, the amount of the special award is increased to 156 weeks' pay or £21,800, subject to a minimum of £21,800, but with no maximum, (TULRCA 1992, s.158(2) and ERA 1996, s.125(2)).

A special award is reduced by one-twelfth for each completed month after age 64, to zero at age 65, TULRCA 1992, s.158(3) and ERA 1996, s.125(3). There is a discretion to make a reduction:

- where the employee's conduct before dismissal (or before notice was given if dismissal was with notice) makes it just and equitable to reduce the award, TULRCA 1992, s.158(4) and ERA 1996, s.125(4);

- if the employee has unreasonably prevented an order for reinstatement or re-engagement from being complied with, or unreasonably refused an offer by the employer which if accepted would have the effect of reinstating the employee in his employment as if he had not been dismissed, TULRCA 1992, s.158(5)(a) and (b); ERA 1996, s.125(5)(a) and (b).

Interim relief

Where dismissal is for any of those reasons for which a special award is available an applicant may apply for interim relief, TULRCA 1992, s.161(1) and ERA 1996, s.128.

In the event of dismissal for an inadmissible reason an application must be presented, along with Form "IT1", by the end of seven days following the effective date of termination and in the case of a dismissal for being or proposing to become a member of the trade union, falling within TULRCA 1992, s.152, a certificate must be presented within the same time scale, signed by an authorised trade union official stating that at the date of dismissal the employee was or proposed to become a member of the union and that there appear to be reasonable grounds for supposing that the reason (or principal reason) for the employee's dismissal was one alleged in the unfair dismissal complaint—a section 152 reason, TULRCA 1992, s.161(3). The employer must be given at least seven days' notice of the hearing, and the tribunal are not allowed to postpone a hearing of an application for interim relief unless there are special circumstances. The tribunal is required to decide whether it is likely that the employee will succeed at a full hearing of the unfair dismissal complaint and in *Taplin v. C. Shippam Ltd*[39] the EAT held that the burden of proof in an interim relief application is greater than that at a full hearing. Where the tribunal is satisfied that interim relief should be granted, they must, after explaining their powers to the parties, ask the employer whether he is willing to reinstate or re-engage the employee pending a full hearing or a settlement, TULRCA 1992, s.163(2), ERA 1996, s.129(2) and (3). If the employer is unwilling to reinstate or to re-engage in another job on terms and conditions not less favourable, the employee reasonably refuses such an offer or the employer fails to attend the interim relief hearing, the tribunal must make a continuation of contract order (CCO). By TULRCA 1992, s.164(1) and ERA 1996, s.130 the effect of a continuation of contract order is that the employee's contract continues in force for the purposes of pay and other benefits derived from the employment, including seniority and pension rights and for calculating the period of continuity, until determination or settlement of the complaint, TULRCA 1992, s.164(1) and ERA 1996, s.130(1). Any payments made under a CCO are not recoverable even if the employee loses their unfair dismissal claim at the full hearing, but the employer may apply for revocation or variation of the order pending the full hearing if the circumstances change, TULRCA 1992, s.165(1), for example, if the employee has found new employment, ERA 1996, s.131.

7.6 SUMMARY

The Employment Rights (Dispute Resolution) Bill received Royal Assent on April 8, 1998 and the various provisions will come into force over the course of the next 12 months.

Hepple (1992) notes that critics have exposed as illusory as "lofty ambitions" the promise of "job security", "job property" and a "right to work" that accompanied the

---

[39] [1978] I.R.L.R. 450, EAT.

unfair dismissal legislation. Hepple points out, however, that despite being relegated as "a failed social experiment"[40] the paradigm has "survived virtually unscathed through the onslaught of regulatory legislation in the eighties", owing its survival, he concludes, to the fact that the law "displays chameleon-like qualities both in protecting individuals against arbitrary management, and simultaneously strengthening managerial legitimacy and control". These qualities are probably best demonstrated in the application of procedural fairness as between *Polkey v. A.E. Dayton Services Ltd*[41] and *Mathewson v. R.B. Wilson Dental Laboratory.*[42]

Lightfoot (1996), in an argument of its time, puts the view that the piecemeal changes to legislation made over the last fifteen years have not been enough, and that it is necessary to remove the overarching, framework of employment protection legislation on redundancy compensation and unfair dismissal. A change of Government, incorporation of the European Convention of Human Rights via the Human Rights Bill, and a greater respect for international convention obligations than was previously displayed, has, perhaps, rendered such aspirations somewhat dated.

In any event, Hepple (1992) argues that, "For successive governments the gains from unfair dismissal legislation have been considerable", and that one of the future challenges is to reconcile conflicting objectives, the legitimate demand by employers for flexible and efficient use of labour; the demand by workers and unions for security of employment and the universalisation of security of employment legislation to accommodate the growing excluded classes of "atypical" workers, which Hepple identifies as a EC-wide problem.[43] This has been advanced in a limited way by the signing by the social partners of the framework agreement on part-time working and the subsequent Directive 97/81 incorporating that agreement. Although the Directive applies only to regular part-timers, it leaves it to Member States whether to legislate to include casuals employees. It should be remembered, however, that various drafts on atypical workers have since 1990 failed to make progress and the agreement limited to part-time workers followed a breakdown in the formal negotiations between the social partners over the types of atypical work that should be included in an atypical work agreement.

The various qualifying conditions and compensation limits that have been discussed in this chapter are summarised at p. 528 for ease of reference.

---

[40] Hepple (1992), p. 81.
[41] [1988] I.C.R. 142, HL.
[42] [1988] I.R.L.R. 512, EAT.
[43] *ibid.*, p. 95.

Chapter 8

ECONOMIC DISMISSALS

8.1 INTRODUCTION

In this chapter, the law on economic dismissals and on changes to an employee's terms and conditions, arising from redundancies, business reorganisations and insolvencies is examined. The text opens with a review of the purpose and historical development of the statutory domestic and European Union employee protection rights in the event of a redundancy situation. Employee protection rights arising from transfers of undertakings are dealt with in Chapter 9.

8.2 EMPLOYEE PROTECTION DURING ECONOMIC RESTRUCTURING

The public policy behind legislation devised for the protection of employees made redundant, originally had both social and economic aims. It was argued that one of the social aims, should be to both recognise and compensate for, the social aspects of loosing a job. Redundancy often meant not only immediate economic loss to the individual and their family, but the loss of self-esteem, position in society and social networks. The concept of the individual worker having "property rights" in his or her job, rights which also appreciated with long service, was adopted in the legislation. This was a relatively novel concept in labour law, which now held that workers had to be treated as more than just the economic assets of an employer, to be disposed of with relative ease, when commercial considerations demanded it. Indeed, unfair dismissal and redundancy rights have been described as being at the "cutting edge" of employment legislation because "They offer a perspective with which to assess the extent to which the interests of employees in job security are actually protected against what managers consider to be an essential prerogative, their right to terminate the employment relationship."[1]

> "Just as a property owner has a right in his property and when he is deprived, he is entitled to compensation, so a long-term employee is considered to have a right

---

[1] S. Anderman, *"Unfair Dismissals and Redundancy"* in R. Lewis, *Labour Law in Britain* (Blackwell, 1986), p. 415.

of property in his job, he has a right to security and his rights gain value with the years."

Wynes v. Southrepps Hall Broiler Farm Ltd (1968) 3 I.T.R. 407 at 408.

There was however, also a broad economic imperative to the legislation at the national level of policy making. Throughout the 1950s and early 1960s there was a shortage of labour in some industries and the Redundancy Payments Act 1965 was introduced partly to encourage labour to move to new industrial sectors and partly to encourage business to reorganise and equip themselves for the harsher realities of the post-Second World War world markets. Redundancies also gave rise to trade union disquiet where the reaction was often to oppose management proposals to reduce workforce levels.[2] This was a period when British industry was thought, by some, to be technically incompetent and managerially class-bound, "there existed 'a fantastic wealth of new scientific and technological knowledge, of new techniques and new processes, which if applied to industry would revolutionise Britain overnight.'"[3] The overall aim of governments in the period 1961 to 1966 was to encourage mobility of labour and increased flexibility by individual workers, employers and trade unions towards business restructuring. Such restructuring was regarded as essential to stimulate economic growth.

The Redundancy Payments Act 1965 was designed to encourage such economic restructuring by providing a statutory lump sum compensation payment to redundant employees, the size of which would be determined by the employee's length of service in the job. Employers could also claim a rebate[4] from the Redundancy Fund[5] which was financed from a surcharge on employers' national insurance contributions. The main provisions of the 1965 Act are still largely extant and were incorporated into the Employment Protection Act 1975. These provisions are now consolidated in the Employment Rights Act 1996 (ERA 1996), Part XI. Advice to employers and trade unions on handling what used to be called "manpower" reductions and redundancies, was given in *The Industrial Relations Code of Practice* (1972).[6] Paragraphs 44 to 46 of this code were concerned with the status and security of employees and became influential[7] on the redundancy case law which developed. The code was entirely repealed in 1991[8] as many of its provisions were incorporated into later ACAS codes. There is no code of practice relating to redundancy as such, although ACAS still publish advice on redundancy handling.[9] Advice on statutory redundancy consultation and notification is also published by the Department of Trade and Industry.[10]

At European level, the development of social policy up to the late 1960s has been described as one of "benign neglect" and it was only after the enlargement of the E.C. to nine Member States in 1971 that the Commission adopted its first Social Action programme in 1974.[11] Out of this programme there emerged three Directives: on

[2] C. Bourn, *Job Security* (Sweet & Maxwell, 1980), p. 2.
[3] Rees, Goronwy (1963) from A. Koestler (ed.) *Suicide of a Nation?* (Hutchinson, 1963). Cited in: B. Pimlott, *Harold Wilson* (Harper Collins, 1992), p. 300.
[4] This was abolished by Employment Act 1989, s.17.
[5] Redundancy Payments (Variation of Rebates) Order 1995 (S.I. 1985 No. 259).
[6] Enacted under the IRA 1971, ss. 2–4 and continued in force by EPA 1975, Sched. 17, para. 4.
[7] Particularly para. 46 on managing redundancy.
[8] Employment Codes of Practice (Revocation) Order 1991 (S.I. 1991 No. 1264).
[9] ACAS, Advisory Booklet *Redundancy Handling* B10, 1995.
[10] DTI, *Redundancy Consultation and Notification*, PL 833 (Rev. 4), URN 97/512.
[11] S. Deakin and G.S. Morris, *Labour Law* (Butterworths, 1995), p. 101.

collective redundancies[12]; on the acquired rights of employees in transfers of undertakings,[13] and on the protection of employee rights in the event of an insolvency.[14] These Directives are all concerned with extending rights to employees when their contracts of employment are affected by economic restructuring. This and the following Chapter reviews the domestic legislation in these three areas and its interaction with the law emanating from Europe. Consideration is now given to the provisions relating to redundancy.

8.3   REDUNDANCY

8.3.1   Definition of redundancy

The ERA 1996, s.139(1) provides that an employee is presumed to be dismissed for redundancy if the dismissal is "wholly or mainly" due to:

"(1)(a) the fact that his employer has ceased or intends to cease—

(i) to carry on the business for the purposes of which the employee was employed by him, or

(ii) to carry on that business in the place where the employee was so employed, or

(b) the fact that the requirements of that business—

(i) for employees to carry out work of a particular kind, or

(ii) for employees to carry out work of a particular kind in the place where the employer was employed by the employer,

have ceased or diminished or are expected to cease or diminish."

There are two main requirements, that the employer stops or intends to stop carrying on the business and the fact that the business no longer requires, or will no longer require the employees to "carry out work of a particular kind." The statutory wording is unchanged from EPCA 1978, s.81(2) but its interpretation has been subject to considerable judicial scrutiny. This has focused on the meaning to be attached to "work of a particular kind."

In *Nelson v. BBC*[15] a BBC producer employed in the corporation's Caribbean regional service was dismissed after the service was reduced in scale. Mr Nelson was offered alternative work but declined to accept it and claimed that he was then unfairly dismissed. The BBC contended that it was a fair dismissal for redundancy because there was an implied term in his contract that he was only employed to work on Caribbean broadcasts. This work was now diminished and the employee was no longer

---

[12] Council Directive 75/129/EEC on the approximation of the laws of the Member States relating to collective redundancies.
[13] Council Directive 77/187 on the approximation of the laws of the Member States relating to the safeguarding of employees' rights in the event of transfers of undertakings, businesses or parts of businesses.
[14] Council Directive 80/987 on the approximation of the laws of the Member States relating to the protection of employees in the event of the insolvency of their employer.
[15] [1977] I.R.L.R. 148; [1977] I.C.R. 649, CA.

required to carry out this work. The Court of Appeal dismissed the employer's arguments by reference to a formal written contract which clearly stated that the BBC had "the right to direct the employee to serve wherever he may be required." This document was also supported by another document which referred to "the liability of an employee to travel." The contract therefore did not limit the appointment to a specific place and in the light of this the Court of Appeal found: "The appellant's contract made express provision for him to serve wherever and however he might be required by the employers. It is a basic principle of contract law that if a contract makes express provision in almost unrestricted language, it is impossible to imply into that contract a restriction of the kind that the Industrial Tribunal in the present case sought to do."[16] The test for construing "work of a particular kind" was therefore to be based strictly on the terms of an employee's contract.

8.3.1.1   *The contract test*

This became the established test for redundancy. *In Cowen v. Haden Carrier Ltd*[17] it was followed by the Employment Appeal Tribunal in a case where a quantity surveyor took on a different position with the same company after having had a mild heart attack. Economic circumstances then caused the company management to reduce the number of quantity surveyors and they made Mr Cowen redundant. Mr Cowen claimed that this was not a redundancy, as statutorily defined because it could not be shown that under, what is now ERA 1996, s.139(1)(a)(i), he had been made redundant, "unless the employers have shown a diminution in the requirements of their business for employees to carry out work, not only of the kind done by a divisional contracts surveyor, but of the kind which under his contract of employment he could have been required to do."[18] His contract of employment stipulated that "He will be required to undertake, at the direction of the Company, any and all duties which reasonably fall within the scope of his capabilities." The EAT reviewed the statutory wording and concluded that "work of a particular kind" was not linked to the specific employee making the claim. "Moreover, in practice a redundancy has been accepted as having been shown where it is demonstrated that the actual job which the claimant was carrying out had ceased to exist."[19] The EAT felt bound however by the decision in *Nelson* and remitted the case to another industrial tribunal[20] for a rehearing of the case. On appeal, the Court of Appeal reversed the EAT decision but only on the facts of the case. They found that the contractual wording relating to other duties falling within his capability "was not to give the employer the right to transfer him from his job as divisional contracts surveyor to any job as a quantity surveyor in their organisation, but to require him to perform any duties reasonably within the scope of his capabilities as divisional contracts surveyor."[21] Work of that particular kind had ceased or diminished so Mr Cowen was made redundant as statutorily defined. To apply a contractual provision, it has also been pointed out that there has to be clear knowledge of what it means.[22]

---

[16] *ibid.* at para. 4.
[17] [1982] I.R.L.R. 225; [1983] I.C.R. 1, EAT.
[18] [1982] I.R.L.R. 225, at para. 10.
[19] [1982] I.R.L.R. 225, at para. 11.
[20] [1982] I.R.L.R. 225, at paras 13–20.
[21] *Haden Ltd v. Cowen* [1982] I.R.L.R. 314, CA.
[22] I.T. Smith & G.H. Thomas, *Smith & Wood's Industrial Law* (6th ed., Butterworths 1996), p. 455.

This decision was followed widely[23] and as was predicted *obiter* in the EAT, it did lead to uncertainty as to what exactly constituted a redundancy. Often, there may be no difference between what an employee actually does in practice and what, in theory, the contract directs them to do. The statutory wording however, is concerned with work *function*; the cessation or diminution of "work of a particular kind" and this is not directly linked in the statutory formulation, to the work of a particular employee at a particular time. So, if employers, in the process of reorganising work, dismiss some employees when there is still work of a particular kind to do and for which, those employees were originally employed, they could be acting unlawfully. In addition, the EAT in *Cowen* recognised *obiter*, that the contract test could make life difficult for employers who relied on "bumping" to implement their redundancy programme. This occurs when, because of a mismatch between the jobs and the individuals that the employer wants to dispense with, the employer moves employee A from a job which is ceasing, to employee B's job which is ongoing. Employee B is then made redundant. Obviously, the contract test which linked a specific job to a specific person would prevent this happening.

On the other hand, employees who find their work re-organised or their terms and conditions changed as a result of a re-organisation, cannot necessarily rely on the statutory wording to claim that they have been made redundant. In *Chapman v. Goonvean and Rastowrack China Cly Co. Ltd*[24] seven employees had their free transport to work discontinued by the employer who was making economies. They were offered continued employment with the employer but resigned and claimed redundancy compensation. It was held by the Court of Appeal that this was not a redundancy situation because work of a particular kind was not reduced.

8.3.1.2 *The function test*

In *Murphy v. Epsom College*[25] Mr Murphy was employed as one of two plumbers in a college. He was more experienced than the existing plumber, but he declined to do heating installation work without detailed supervision. The college decided to make the plumbers redundant and to re-employ one of them as a heating engineer. Mr Murphy was not selected and was dismissed. The EAT found that the industrial tribunal were correct in holding that "in circumstances where, as a consequence of a reorganisation, the requirements of the employers changed and a new job was created comprising almost all of the functions formerly performed by the appellant together with substantial wider responsibilities," this was a redundancy as statutorily defined.[26] The reasoning for this decision, approved by the EAT, and upheld in the Court of Appeal[27] was as follows:

> "In order to discover whether or not an employee is redundant, it is necessary first to identify what 'particular kind' of work the employee was doing and then to ask if there has been a diminution in the requirement for employees to do work of that kind.
>
> The 'kind of work' done by an employee is the combination of functions comprised in his job. Where an employee is dismissed in consequence of a

[23] *ibid.* pp. 74 and 454. See also *Pink v. White* [1985] I.R.L.R. 489.
[24] [1973] I.C.R. 310, CA.
[25] [1983] I.R.L.R. 395; [1983] I.C.R. 715, EAT.
[26] EPCA 1978, s.81(2)(b) now ERA 1996, s.139(1)(b).
[27] *Murphy v. Epsom College* [1984] I.R.L.R. 271; [1985] I.C.R. 80, CA.

reorganisation, the dismissal may be regarded as being on grounds of redundancy if substantial functions have been transferred from him to another employee so that, if retained, he would no longer be doing work of the same particular kind." *per* Browne-Wilkinson J. (President).

Murphy v. Epsom College [1983] I.R.L.R. 395 at 396, EAT.

As can be seen, the Court was, firstly, looking at the diminution in the work done by employees, in the plural, after which, it held, it was then permissible to look at the job functions of a particular employee. His or her dismissal then being due to redundancy, providing a substantial proportion of the job had been transferred to another employee. This test became known as the function test because it elevates the significance of the overall job functions required by an employer, over the contractual obligations arising from individual contracts of employment. In *Murphy* the plumber was therefore found to be fairly dismissed on grounds of redundancy and entitled to a redundancy payment but not to unfair dismissal compensation (see para. 8.3.2 below). Employees cannot assume however, that work reorganisation will necessarily lead to redundancy compensation entitlement if they are dismissed. In *Lesney Products Ltd v. Nolan* 36 machine setters making model toys were asked by their employer to stop working a single day shift accompanied by considerable overtime and to work instead on one of two day shifts at basic rates. Nine employees refused this offer, were dismissed and claimed redundancy compensation. The Court of Appeal judgment confirmed that although employers may reorganise for business reasons, that is, to cut costs or to accommodate new technology,[28] such a situation does not automatically give rise to redundancy payments for the individual employees affected.

> "A reorganisation of work will only give rise to a redundancy payment, according to the principle established by the Court of Appeal in *Johnson v. Nottingham Combined Police Authority*, if the change in terms and conditions is attributable to the fact that the requirements of that business for employees to carry out work of a particular kind have ceased or diminished within the meaning of s.1(2)(b) [now ERA 1996, s.139(1)(b)(i)]. In applying that principle, it is important that nothing should be done to impair the ability of employers to reorganise their work force and their times and conditions of work so as to improve efficiency. When overtime is reduced by a reorganisation of working hours, that does not give rise to a redundancy payment, so long as the work to be done is the same." *per* Denning Lord M.R.

Lesney Products Ltd v. Nolan [1977] I.R.L.R. 77 at 77, CA.

It seems that the 1960s legislative promotion of flexibility in the workplace was to be always interpreted, at least in the judicial arena, in the employer's interests. Wedderburn talks about judges, who as early as 1967 were primarily concerned about business efficiency, He maintains that "The judges now entered the phase of highly 'creative' manipulation of implied terms leading to the modern, extensive rights for the employer to demand changes in the employment contract to promote 'efficiency.'"[29] Wedderburn examines cases of employees who have been asked to adjust to a major

---

[28] *Cresswell v. Board of Inland Revenue* [1984] I.R.L.R. 190.
[29] Lord Wedderburn, *The Worker and The Law* (3rd ed. Rev., Penguin, 1986), p. 226.

change in their job function, but who when resisting the transition required, have been found, by the courts, not to have been dismissed for redundancy. He outlines the much cited and now very un-politically correct "bunny girls" case of *Vaux and Associated Breweries Ltd v. Ward*.[30] Here an "older" barmaid who was dismissed because the bar owner wanted to introduce younger staff to do "bunny girl" work, was found not to have been dismissed through redundancy, as the work she was being asked to do, was not, it was ruled, of a different kind. It is to be hoped that social attitudes generally and social awareness amongst some judges, have "progressed" in the 30 years since that case!

Smith and Thomas ask the central legal question: "how radical does a change in the job, or the reorganisation of it, have to be before it can be said that the function itself has changed?" They give examples of early cases where the courts took a very broad view of job functions thereby allowing employers to avoid payment of redundancy compensation, but it is argued that *Murphy* was useful in supplying a narrower interpretation of a particular "kind of work".[31]

Because the narrower definition of redundancy found in *Murphy* may make it easier for the courts, in a particular case, to find that there was a redundancy, Smith and Thomas suggest that employees and employers would take a tactical approach towards the payment of compensation. Employees would claim that the termination was an unfair redundancy dismissal (see paras 8.3.2, 4, 7) in the hope that they would gain a higher compensation award, whereas employers would be happy to contend that it was a fair redundancy dismissal in order to only have to fork out for the minimum statutory redundancy award.[32]

Two leading labour lawyers[33] predicted that: "In so far as it is possible to draw a clear conclusion from this confused case-law, it would be premature to conclude that the contract test will necessarily prevail" and were vindicated by a decision of the Employment Appeal Tribunal in *Safeway Stores plc v. Burrell*[34] which appeared to reject both the function and contract tests as mutually exclusive models. Here, the employer was slimming down the management level of employees, and Mr Burrell who was a petrol station manager was advised that there would be redundancies amongst such posts. He was invited to apply for the new post of petrol filling station controller which had a job description similar to his own post, but declined to do so because the salary was some £2,000 per year lower than his existing post. He resigned and agreed a redundancy compensation payment with the employer, but subsequently submitted an application for unfair dismissal on the grounds that as the new post was exactly the same as his old one he could not have been made redundant. The majority decision of the industrial tribunal found that he had been unfairly dismissed because, on application of the function test the new job was in practice covering the same work as the old job, only under a different job title. He was not redundant. The chairman of the tribunal, found in the minority, that on applying the contract test, Mr Burrell could have been called upon to carry out all the management responsibilities contained in his old contract, even if he did not in practice perform them, and now the empoyers had no need of his old post in that form he was redundant.

In a wide ranging review of the case law, the EAT rejected both approaches and determined that the correct approach to the application of the ERA 1996, s.139(1)(b) was to ask three questions:

---

[30] (1968) 3 I.T.R. 385; *(No. 2)* (1970) 5 I.T.R. 62.
[31] *op. cit.* n.22, p. 457.
[32] *ibid.* p. 458.
[33] *op. cit.* n.11, p. 452.
[34] [1997] I.R.L.R. 200; [1997] I.C.R. 523, EAT.

1. Was the employee dismissed?

2. If so, had the requirements of the employer's business for *employees* to carry out work of a particular kind stopped or diminished?

3. If so, was the dismissal due "wholly or mainly" to this work stopping or diminishing?

The Court held that the terms of an individual's contract of employment are irrelevant because it is the "diminution/cessation in the employer's requirements for *employees* (not the applicant) to carry out work of a particular kind" which should be examined. By applying the contract test, the courts had impermissibly imported words into the statute to the effect that "there must be a diminishing need for employees to do the kind of work for which the applicant was employed." The EAT also held that *Nelson v. BBC* and *Cowen v. Haden Carrier Ltd* were only authority for the proposition that in a redundancy situation, where a potentially redundant employee refuses a transfer to other work which is within his or her contract of employment, the reason for dismissal is not redundancy.

Nelson was distinguished on its facts so that usually an "applicant's terms and conditions of employment are irrelevant to the questions raised by the statute." In the instant case the tribunal majority "had failed to ask whether there was a redundancy situation, looking at the overall requirement of the employers for employees to carry out work of a particular kind, and then had to consider whether the redundancy had caused the employee's admitted redundancy." Lastly, the EAT found that the principle of "bumping" (discussed above) accorded with statute.

Even where the work of a particular kind remains at the same level, it appears that an employer can declare redundancies in a situation where a company is reorganising the work and anticipating job losses but is also recruiting temporary staff to cover existing work.[35] The EAT, following *Safeway* said that the industrial tribunal should not have concentrated on the workload of the four employees at their dismissal but should have looked at the likelihood of a diminution of work arising from the re-organisation.

It appears that, in a redundancy situation, the correct interpretation of the statutory wording, reinforces employer hegemony in the employment relationship. A gain perhaps, at the expense of individual employment protection? This decision has been described as an abandonment of "the complex case law on the definition of redundancy in favour of a common-sense interpretation of the ERA."[36] The argument being that: "It is surely correct that it is the employer's overall requirements which trigger a redundancy situation, rather than the nature of the job done by a particular employee."[37] Alternatively, it can also be seen that this decision is hardly supportive of the 1960s concept of property ownership by the individual worker in his or her job.

8.3.1.3 *"Bumping" and section 139*

The three-part test for redundancy adumbrated in *Safeway Stores* was, however, challenged within nine months by a different division of the EAT in *Church v. West Lancashire NHS Trust.*[38] It decided that an NHS employee who had been dismissed in

---

[35] *Strathclyde Buses Ltd v. Leonard and others; Ellum and others v. Strathclyde Buses Ltd* (1997), EAT 507 & 515/97, reported in IDS Brief 604, January 1998.
[36] IDS Brief 604, January 1998.
[37] IDS Brief 584, March 1997.
[38] [1998] I.R.L.R. 4, EAT.

a departmental reorganisation, but whose job had been offered to a colleague following a competitive selection process, could not be regarded as having been fairly dismissed through redundancy. It found that the ERA 1996, s.139(1)(b) did not make "bumping" lawful. Commenting that "It is, we think somewhat remarkable that the question at issue in this case has not been authoritatively resolved before now." Morison J. considered that the operation of voluntary redundancy schemes by many employers with enhanced compensation had perhaps made the practice of bumping acceptable.[39] In a close examination of the statutory wording the EAT looked at the meaning of section 139 as a whole and the case law emanating from it, and concluded that "work of a particular kind" is the "work of a particular kind which the dismissed employee was employed to do." The EAT also found that the dismissal of a bumped employee was not due "to the diminution in the requirements of a business for employees to do work of a particular kind but rather to the method by which the employers sought to manage that diminution in requirements."

The *Safeway Stores* decision was disagreed with, although the EAT's analysis of the case law was commended for it's clarity.[40] In coming to this decision the differently constituted EAT in *Church* looked at section 139 within the overall statutory context for unfair dismissal. Firstly, it said, if the dismissal does not fall within section 139, an employee may or may not win a claim for unfair dismissal, but that in the end an industrial tribunal's decision on this issue is "largely irrelevant" as "Fair and reasonable treatment of an employee will be unlikely to hinge on the label applied to the reason for the dismissal."[41] This may be so, but it could perhaps also be argued that the type of label affixed by the tribunal will determine whether, in many cases, a dismissed employee gets no compensation at all, redundancy compensation or unfair dismissal compensation. The difference in levels between the latter categories being considerable.

In looking at the general background to the redundancy provisions the EAT acknowledged that voluntary agreements often improve on the statutory compensation and can include arrangements which define redundancy in a broader way so as to include "bumping".[42] But the EAT also referred to the ERA 1996, s.163(2) which directs that if a question of redundancy is referred to an industrial tribunal, the dismissal is presumed to be by reason of redundancy unless shown otherwise.[43] Lastly, the statutory definition of redundancy dismissal given by the TULRCA 1992, s.195 is examined. This section is concerned with the statutory obligation on the employer to consult representatives over a specified number of dismissals and the EAT highlights the definition of redundancy given as "dismissal for a reason not related to the individual concerned . . ." and concludes that the "essence of a dismissal due to redundancy" is "that an employee loses his job through no personal fault of his own."[44]

The decision in *Church* however, seemed to be greatly influenced by the Court's forensic analysis of section 139. This section, it will be remembered, defines four circumstances where there can be a redundancy dismissal. This is where:

1. there is an actual or proposed cessation of the business;

---

[39] *ibid.* at 7, para. 28.
[40] *ibid.* at 6, para. 13.
[41] *ibid.* at 7, para. 20.
[42] [1998] I.R.L.R. 4 at 7, para. 22.
[43] para. 21.
[44] para. 23.

2. this occurs in the place where the employee is employed;

3. the stopping or decreasing of "work of a particular kind" carried out by employees;

4. the stopping/decreasing of this work in the place of employment.

In looking at the issue of bumping, the EAT decided that there can be no question of bumping redundancy in circumstances 1 and 2 "because the wording of the Act identifies as redundant the employee who was employed in the business or who worked at the place in question."[45] The EAT then asked itself why should a different situation apply in situations 3 and 4? In searching for binding guidance the EAT turned to *High Table Ltd v. Horst and others*.[46] Here the Court of Appeal had to decide the meaning of "where the employee was so employed" in a situation where waitresses were required by their contract to work at different locations. The employer reorganised the work so as to employ fewer waitresses working longer hours but the applicants did not apply for any of the vacant posts and were subsequently dismissed as redundant. Complaints of unfair dismissal on grounds of unfair selection for redundancy were made by the waitresses who submitted that the employers should have made stronger efforts to find them alternative work. The Court of Appeal found that the place of work was a matter of primary fact and "If an employee has worked in only one location under his contract of employment for the purposes of the employer's business, it defies common sense to widen the extent of the place where he was so employed, merely because of the existence of a mobility clause."[47] Drawing on the authority of this decision, the EAT in *Church* concluded that this pragmatic test could be applied to all parts of section 139. "The true position is neither contractual nor functional but a sensible blend of the two and, in that sense, the results in *Nelson* and *Haden* are not inconsistent with it."[48]

In coming to the final decision that "bumping" was not permitted by section 139, the EAT decided that there was no decided case by the Court of Appeal on the practice, except for a case[49] in the Divisional Court which was decided at a time "when an employee had no other statutory right than a redundancy payment following his dismissal."[50] Further, the EAT declared there was nothing in the Act which showed that Parliament intended "bumping" would be a fair redundancy dismissal.[51] In trying to speculate why "there are no words in the Act which say 'work of a particular kind which the relevant employee was employed to do'," the Court concluded, that it was possibly because Parliament took the view, that the relevant employee, must be doing the work of a particular kind, otherwise the cause of the dismissal must be for a reason other than redundancy.[52] This is the question, which at the time of writing is awaiting consideration by the Court of Appeal. Until it is finally resolved there will remain uncertainty about the statutory definition of redundancy and about the lawfulness of selection procedures which incorporate the practice of "bumping".

8.3.1.4 *Fair and unfair redundancy dismissal*

Redundancy is prima facie a fair ground for dismissal. In the light of the difficulties the courts have had in applying the statutory definition of redundancy, discussed above, it

[45] para. 30.
[46] [1997] I.R.L.R. 513, CA.
[47] *High Table Ltd v. Horst* [1997] I.R.L.R. 513, CA.
[48] [1998] I.R.L.R. 4 at 9, para. 42.
[49] *Gimber & Sons Ltd v. Spurrett* [1976] 2 I.T.R. 308.
[50] [1998] I.R.L.R. 4 at 9, para. 43.
[51] *ibid.* at para. 46.
[52] *ibid.* at para. 47.

is perhaps not too difficult to appreciate the conceptual problem which lies at the heart of the legislation. On the one hand, the dismissal is regarded as fair because the employer has no choice other than to dismiss, but at the same time, it is also unfair because the individual employee has not breached his or her contract of employment.[53]

The legislation distinguishes between a fair redundancy dismissal for which the employee is entitled to claim compensation,[54] and an unfair dismissal[55] under the unfair selection provisions[56] (see para. 8.3.2 below) or under a general test of fairness.[57] To rebut a redundancy compensation claim, the employer must establish that redundancy was not the principal reason for dismissal.[58] Alternatively, if the employee seeks to claim that there was an unfair dismissal on the prohibited grounds, the employer may establish a defence that the dismissal was fair because the employer acted reasonably.[59] Another employer defence to dismissing an employee in a redundancy situation is provided for in the ERA 1996, s.98(1)(b) which allows an employee to be fairly dismissed for "some other substantial reason" (SOSR defence—see para 8.4 below).

A review of the statute and case law on redundancy dismissals, is now undertaken before consideration is given to the SOSR defence which has emerged as the dominant paradigm for resolving the conceptual problem of a fair redundancy dismissal.

8.3.2 Automatic unfair selection for redundancy

The ERA 1996, s.105(1) provides that an employer who selects certain categories of employees for redundancy is automatically acting unfairly. Unfair selection for redundancy occurs when "it is shown that the circumstances constituting the redundancy applied equally to one or more other employees in the same undertaking who held positions similar to that held by the employee and who have not been dismissed by the employer".[60] Selection for redundancy on the grounds of pregnancy or childbirth[61]; for undertaking health and safety activities[62]; (see also Chapter 7, para. 7.4.4); for being: a protected shop-worker[63] (see also Chapter 7, para. 7.4.5), a pension scheme trustee[64] (see also Chapter 7, para. 7.4.6) or employee representative[65] (see also Chapter 7, para. 7.4.7) and for asserting a statutory right,[66] (see also Chapter 7, para. 7.4.8), are all prohibited under the ERA 1996, Part X. Also protected is selection on grounds related to union membership or activities under TULRCA 1992, ss.152(1)–153. These provisions originate from the notion of introducing rationality into the process of economic dismissals. They originate from ILO Recommendation No. 119 which recognises the need for employers to re-organise, but also puts an onus

---

[53] Smith and Thomas, *op. cit.* p. 414.
[54] ERA 1996, s.135(1).
[55] ERA 1996, s.98(2)(c).
[56] ERA 1996, s.105.
[57] ERA 1996, s.98(4).
[58] *Midland Foot Comfort Centre v. M.J. Richmond Nee Moppett and Secretary of State for Employment* [1973] I.R.L.R. 141; [1973] I.C.R. 219, NIRC.
[59] ERA 1996, s.98(4)(a).
[60] ERA 1996, s.105(1)(c).
[61] ERA 1996, s.105(2).
[62] ERA 1996, s.105(3).
[63] ERA 1996, s.105(4).
[64] ERA 1996, s.105(5).
[65] ERA 1996, s.105(6).
[66] ERA 1996, s.105(7).

on them to protect their employees from victimisation and to encourage them to utilise objective and fair criteria when selecting for redundancy. (see para. 8.3.4 below). It has been pointed out that the United Kingdom legislation does not fully apply the rationale behind the ILO's proposals to protect individual employment rights in such a situation.[67]

8.3.2.1   Burden of proof

The burden of proof for identifying an automatically unfair selection for redundancy falls on the employer. This was established in *Maund v. Penwith District Council*[68] where a local authority architect was made redundant, after his housing project was privatised. He claimed that he was unfairly selected for redundancy because of his trade union activities, but the industrial tribunal found that it was a fair dismissal for redundancy. The Court of Appeal disagreed declaring that the first tribunal had erred in putting the burden of proof on the employee and remitted the case to another tribunal for a rehearing of the original evidence (see Chapter 7, para. 7.4.1 for further discussion).

8.3.2.2   Pregnancy

In *Brown v. Stockton-on-Tees Borough Council*,[69] discussed in Chapter 7 above, in a decision which reached the House of Lords, it was held that the creation of inconvenience for the employer was no defence for employers who used a redundancy situation to weed out pregnant employees.

8.3.2.3   Trade union activities

The uncertainty of the protection afforded trade union officials under TULRCA 1992, s.153 is illustrated in *Dundon v. G.P.T. Ltd*[70] and in *O'Dea v. I.S.C. Chemicals Ltd*.[71] In *Dundon* the EAT held that it was automatically unfair to select a trade union official for redundancy because he spent too much time on trade union duties. It also reduced the industrial tribunal's assessment of blame on the official from 75 per cent to 33 per cent. In contrast, in *O'Dea*, the Court of Appeal upheld an industrial tribunal decision that a union official was not selected for redundancy for his trade union activities[72] but was unfairly dismissed under section 57(3) of the EPCA[73] and that his compensation was reduced by 80 per cent "to take account of the high probability that the applicant's employment would have come to an end regardless of the procedural defect." The procedural defect was that the employer had failed to instruct managers to ignore the official's trade union activities when he was being interviewed for alternative employment.

In both cases the trade union officials had agreements with their employers to spend a considerable amount of time on union work. In *Dundon* the union official fell foul of the employer's six criteria for selection for redundancy, one of which was "quantity of work". The EAT found that "the tribunal had been wrong to conclude that section 153

---

[67] S. Deakin & G.S. Morris (1995), p. 344.
[68] [1984] I.R.L.R. 24, CA.
[69] [1998] I.R.L.R. 263, HL.
[70] [1995] I.R.L.R. 403.
[71] [1996] I.C.R. 222, CA.
[72] EPCA 1978, s.58 is now found in TULRCA 1992, s.152.
[73] "the determination of the question whether the dismissal was fair or unfair . . . shall depend on . . . the size and administrative resources of the employer's undertaking . . . and determined in accordance with equity and the substantial merits of the case." Note: this subsection is now found in the ERA 1996, s.98(4).

of TULRCA did not apply because the company had not deliberately or maliciously selected him for redundancy on the ground of his trade union activity."[74] Comparison of the "position" of those selected for redundancy as defined in section 153(1) of the EPCA 1978 was closely examined by the EAT in *O'Dea*. Peter Gibson L.J. came to the conclusion that when looking at comparators it was "the relative positions of the applicant and the comparators as employees" which should be examined and not "what any of them did or had the contractual right to do as an official of a trade union".[75] A position which was also applied in a case where a trade union health and safety representative spent one-third of his time on these duties.[76] Here, the EAT found that a trade union official could not be "advantaged" by his union position in redundancy selection as this would amount to positive discrimination.[77] This somewhat weakens the legislative provisions which were designed to stop employers victimising union officials by selecting them for redundancy.

8.3.3 Information and consultation on redundancy proposals

Since 1975[78] employers have been obliged to consult with trade unions over impending redundancies. An obligation on employers to consult about a redundancy situation is at the heart of the European and United Kingdom legislation. Consultation has to be with the individuals affected,[79] with trade unions[80] and with worker representatives.[81] An employer has to consult representatives when he is proposing to dismiss 20 or more employees at one establishment.[82] This has to be done with at least 90 days notice if 100 or more employees are to be dismissed.[83] For dismissals of less than 100 employees, at least 30 days notice has to be given to the representatives.[84] An employer also has to notify the Secretary of State[85] of these proposals and is liable to a fine in a magistrates' court, not exceeding level 5, if these provisions are not complied with.[86] The relevant legislation is the TULRCA 1992, ss.188 to 194 and the Council Directive 75/129 on the approximation of the laws of Member States relating to collective redundancies, as amended by Directive 92/56; and TURERA 1993, s.34.

The development of redundancy law in this area has been dominated by the question: what is the purpose of consultation? Is it to intervene in the redundancy decision process itself, or is it to mitigate the effects of the redundancy decision after it has been taken by the employer? Has it a proactive or a reactive role in the redundancy process? Guidance is given by the Collective Redundancies Directive (Council Directive 75/129) (CRD):

> "Where an employer is contemplating collective redundancies, he shall begin consultations with the workers' representatives in good time with a view to reaching an agreement." Art. 2(1).

---

[74] I.R.L.B. 529, September 1995.
[75] [1996] I.C.R. 222 at 229H, CA.
[76] *Smiths Industries Aerospace and Defence Systems v. Rawlings* [1996] I.R.L.R. 656, EAT.
[77] [1996] I.R.L.R. 660, EAT, para. 39.
[78] EPA 1975, s.99 now found in TULRCA 1992, s.188.
[79] *Mugford v. Midland Bank* [1997] I.R.L.R. 208, EAT.
[80] TULRCA 1992, s.188(1B)(b).
[81] TULRCA 1992, s.188(1B)(a).
[82] TULRCA 1992, s.188(1).
[83] TULRCA 1992, s.188(1A)(a).
[84] TULRCA 1992, s.188(1A)(b).
[85] TULRCA 1992, s.193.
[86] TULRCA 1992, s.194(1).

"These consultations shall, at least, cover ways and means of avoiding collective redundancies or reducing the number of workers affected, and of mitigating the consequences by recourse to accompanying social measures aimed, inter alia, at aid for redeploying or retraining workers made redundant." Art. 2(2).

8.3.3.1 *When does consultation begin and who is it with?*

The consultation process, it is inferred, should begin when the employer is thinking about redundancies, but the domestic provisions in the TULRCA 1996, s.188(1) only refer to consultation when an employer is "proposing to dismiss". The case law has determined that "proposing to dismiss" is more than "the mere contemplation of a possible event."[87] The narrowness of the United Kingdom's legislation in this area was considered in *R. v. British Coal Corporation*.[88] Here the employer was seeking to close down coal-mines without, it was claimed by the trade union, complying with a statutory consultation process. Glidewell L.J. considered this issue in depth and concluded that the domestic legislation did not comply with the CRD. He maintained that section 188(1) is about consulting on "how to carry out any redundancy programme which management deems necessary". But, he went on to consider Article 2 of the CRD which stipulates that consultations should begin when an employer "is contemplating collective redundancies" and that these should be with a view to reaching agreement (Art. 2(1)); and further that in Article 2 the consultations should include ways of avoiding or reducing the redundancies. He concluded that section 188 "contains no words equivalent to those contained in Article 2(2)."[89]

At the same time that this case was progressing in the courts, the Government was having to introduce new legislation[90] to bring United Kingdom law into line with the CRD. The Commission had brought infringement proceedings[91] against the United Kingdom, claiming that it had failed to comply with the ARD and the CRD because the domestic legislation did not allow consultation with workers' representatives where there was no recognised trade union in the workplace. TULRCA, 1992 s.188(1) only referred to the duty of the employer to consult with trade union representatives whereas the CRD provided for consultation with worker's representatives. Since 1980[92] there had been no statutory provisions which obliged employers to recognise trade unions. They could still do so but on an entirely voluntary basis. Employers could evade the section 188 requirements by simply not recognising trade unions or indeed by derecognising them. In the ECJ, the Government argued that the Directive did not require trade union recognition as it defined workers' representatives as "representatives provided for by the laws or practices of the member states." Compulsory recognition of trade union representatives, it argued, went against the traditions and practices of the United Kingdom. The European Commission did not accept that argument it argued "that its interpretation of the Directive did not impose trade union recognition, but simply required the United Kingdom to provide an effective mechanism for the representation of workers," The ECJ agreed and found that the United Kingdom could not evade the requirement on Member States to consult with workers' representatives.

---

[87] *USDAW v. Leancut Bacon Ltd* [1981] I.R.L.R. 295, EAT.
[88] [1993] I.R.L.R. 103, HC.
[89] [1993] I.R.L.R. 103 at 116, para. 124, H.C.
[90] TURERA 1993, s.34.
[91] Case C–382/92 *Commission v. United Kingdom* [1994] I.R.L.R. 392; [1994] I.C.R. 664; Case C–383/92 [1994] I.R.L.R. 412; [1994] I.C.R. 664; ECJ.
[92] Employment Act 1980, s.19(b) repealed the recognition procedures in the EPA 1975, ss.11–16.

At the time of this decision the Government was introducing legislation[93] to amend the TULRCA 1992, s.188 to bring it into line with the 1992 Directive. It had to issue further amending Regulations[94] in 1995 to implement the ECJ requirement on worker representation. This section now obliges employers to consult either with employee representatives, or with trade union representatives, or to choose between the two.[95] Section 188 was also amended by the 1995 Regulations to bring the domestic provisions into line with Article 2 of the CRD by stipulating that the consultation shall include ways of avoiding dismissals or reducing them as well as mitigating their consequences.[96]

Some trade unions fearing that employers would put pressure on employee representatives in such a situation, were also unhappy about other aspects of the amendment regulations and in *R. v. Secretary of State for Trade and Industry ex parte Unison and others*[97] brought an action against the Government. The unions bringing the action argued that the regulations were defective and did not comply with Directives 77/187 and 75/129 in that they did not specify selection procedures for representatives and that there was not an adequate mechanism for complaint by affected employees. The relief sought was a declaration that the 1995 Regulations were unlawful or alternatively that they did not fully implement the Directives. The High Court found for the Government holding that

"The 1995 Regulations properly implement Directives 75/129 and 77/187 so far as they concern consultation with affected employees, and do not leave open the possibility that employers may impede protection unconditionally guaranteed to employees by the Directives.

The 1995 Regulations ensure that the employer is obliged to consult either a recognised trade union or elected employee representatives; that the employee representatives are elected by employees and, like trade union representatives, are protected against dismissal and detriment; that employee representatives have a right of access to the employees and to appropriate facilities, and time off in order to perform their functions; and that if an employer does not comply with the obligations imposed by the Regulations it is liable to an industrial tribunal complaint, and to pay compensation to aggrieved employees." *per* Otton, L.J.

R. v. Secretary of State for Trade and Industry ex parte Unison and others [1996] I.R.L.R. 438 at 439, DC.

The question of who has to be consulted and when, arose in *Griffin and Others v. South West Water Services Ltd*[98] when a privatised water company made a large number of staff redundant and derecognised the trade union, UNISON. The plaintiff employees argued that the Directive required that the company should negotiate with UNISON officials. Blackburne J. disagreed and seemed much swayed by the facts that the trade union appeared to have only 15 per cent membership amongst the workforce, as well as having eight out of 14 members on a staff consultation committee set up by the

---

[93] TURERA 1993, s.34.
[94] Collective Redundancies and Transfer of Undertakings (Protection of Employment) (Amendment) Regulations 1995 (S.I. 1995 No. 2587), reg. 3.
[95] TULRCA 1992, s.188(1B) as amended.
[96] TULRCA 1992, s.188(2) as amended.
[97] [1996] I.R.L.R. 438, DC.
[98] [1995] I.R.L.R. 15, HC.

employers. The judge considered that the employers had complied with the CRD and section 188. He also disagreed with the dictum from *R. v. British Coal Corp.* which stated that consultation should begin as early as possible, substituting his view, that it should only begin "when the employer's contemplation of redundancies has reached the point where he is able to identify the workers likely to be affected and can supply the information required by the Directive." It can thus be seen, that in addition to the uncertainties surrounding the statutory definition of redundancy, discussed in para. 8.3.1 above, there is also some doubt about the statutory purpose and process of redundancy consultation.

From the point of view of some trade unionists the decision in *R. v. Secretary of State for Trade and Industry ex parte UNISON and others* was unsatisfactory, given that an employer in a hurry may wittingly or unwittingly be able to choose the consultation route which it perceives will be met with the least resistance. The *Griffin* case discussed above, would also seem to confirm that consultation with trade union representatives is not a *sine quo non* of either the CRD or section 188. In addition, the trade unions themselves, no doubt considered that their members and indeed all affected employees would be best served by those union officials who had the training and experience to be able to negotiate in such a complex and fraught situation, rather than being dependent on ad hoc representatives who may be "over-influenced" by management. There is also evidence that not all employers comply with the spirit of the consultation provisions. In a survey[99] "about a quarter of the 90 respondents who had held elections had failed to provide appropriate representatives with facilities." TULRCA 1992, s.188(5A) requires the employer to give access to employees threatened with redundancy and to make available "such accommodation and other facilities as may be appropriate."

At the time of writing, the Government appears to be taking some of these concerns seriously and is proposing to strengthen the consultation requirements in both collective redundancy and in transfer situations.[1] There are two main changes relating to consultation proposed. First, that the employer will no longer be able to choose between consulting workplace representatives and union representatives. If there is a recognised union representative available, he or she will have to be the one consulted. This provision may also be strengthened when the White Paper *Fairness At Work*[2] brings back a statutory trade union recognition procedure onto the statute book. Secondly, there will be an onus on employers to ensure that non-union employee representatives are capable and independent, through the provision of appropriate training and selection procedures and secret ballots. The onus of proof will be put on to employers to show that employee consultation arrangements comply with the statutory requirements. In addition, the Government was considering removing the consultation threshold of 20 redundancies[3] which at present triggers the compulsory consultation measures. This would restore the pre-1995 position when consultation was triggered by only one redundancy.[4]

8.3.3.2 *Consultation with individuals affected*

Although statute concentrates on the obligations of employers to consult representatives of employees who are proposed for redundancy, there is a long line of case

---

[99] *Is it good to talk?* A report on U.K. worker consultation, Nabarro Nathanson-reviewed in I.R.L.B. 560, January 1997.
[1] DTI Employee Relations Directorate (February 1998), *Employees' Information And Consultation Rights On Transfers Of Undertakings And Collective Redundancies, Public Consultation*, URN 97/988.
[2] CM. 3968, *Fairness At Work*, DTI, May 21, 1998.
[3] TULRCA 1992, s.188(1) as amended by S.I. 1995 No. 2587, reg. 3.
[4] TULRCA 1992, s.188(1) unamended.

authority based on whether a redundancy dismissal can be rendered unfair[5] through lack of direct consultation with the individuals affected. The summary dismissal of a redundant van driver in *Polkey* established the importance of normally consulting with an individual facing redundancy, even if such consultation was thought to be useless because the employer had already decided to dismiss. The judicial House of Lords determined that "in the case of redundancy, the employer will normally not act reasonably unless he warns and consults any employees affected or their representative, adopts a fair basis on which to select for redundancy and takes such steps as may be reasonable to avoid or minimise redundancy by redeployment within his own organisation."[6]

In the key part of this decision, their Lordships also found that an industrial tribunal cannot ask itself the hypothetical question "would it have made any difference if the employers had consulted before the dismissal". It is what the employers did at the time of the dismissal which is the proper subject of examination by the tribunal in assessing whether or not consulting the individual employee was fair. This does not mean that an industrial tribunal cannot examine the decision of an employer who decides not to follow a full consultation process: "if the Tribunal is able to conclude that the employer himself, at the time of the dismissal, acted reasonably in taking the view that, in the exceptional circumstances of the particular case, the procedural steps normally appropriate would have been futile, could not have altered the decision to dismiss and therefore could be dispensed with. In such a case the test of reasonableness under s.57(3)[7] *may* be satisfied." It is therefore implied, that when an employer is dismissing for redundancy, some form of consultation would be the norm. This approach is now established, although the Court of Appeal qualified[8] *Polkey* in *Duffy v. Yeomans & Partners Ltd*[9] by determining that the absence of a deliberate decision by an employer not to consult because he thinks it would be useless, does not automatically lead to a finding of unfair dismissal.

In Mugford v. Midland Bank plc[10] a bank manager was selected for redundancy and claimed that he was unfairly dismissed because he had not been personally consulted. The EAT, in a reserved decision, decided that where an employer had consulted with a recognised trade union over redundancy selection criteria this did not "of itself release the employer from considering with the employee individually his being identified for redundancy". The overall process had to be examined to determine whether the employer acted reasonably.

> "Whether a reasonable employer would or would not consult with an individual employee is essentially a question of fact for the industrial jury, properly directing itself. Individual consultation with the employee before the final decision identifying him as redundant is not a prerequisite for a fair dismissal. On the other hand, the obligation to consult is not necessarily discharged if the employer consults with the union where one is recognised. *per* Clark J.
>
> *Mugford v. Midland Bank plc* [1997] I.R.L.R. 208 at 208, EAT.

In reviewing the authorities, Clark J. directed that an industrial tribunal, when considering whether an employer has complied with the statutory consultation provisions, must bear in mind three criteria:

---

[5] ERA 1996, s.98(4).
[6] *Polkey v. A.E. Dayton Services Ltd* [1987] I.R.L.R. 508 at para. 28, HL.
[7] now ERA 1996, s.98(4).
[8] Smith and Thomas, *op. cit.* p. 418.
[9] [1994] I.R.L.R. 642; [1995] I.C.R. 1, CA.
[10] [1997] I.R.L.R. 208, EAT.

1. If no consultation with either the union or the employee has taken place this would usually be an unfair dismissal unless an employer thought consultation would be "an utterly futile exercise";

2. Consultation with a trade union over selection criteria does not mean that the employer should not discuss the redundancy with the selected individual;

3. It's a question of fact and degree whether an employer consults collectively or individually. The absence of either does not necessarily render the dismissal unfair, but the employer must act reasonably in the matter of consultation.

8.3.3.3 *What information has to be given?*

The TULRCA 1992, s.188(4) directs that consultation has to be about ways of avoiding the dismissals, reducing the numbers of those to be dismissed and about mitigating the consequences of the dismissals. All this has to take place "with a view to reaching agreement". These provisions are designed to encourage a proactive approach in the representatives who are being consulted. This obviously cannot take place, if these representatives are not well informed. Section 188(4) therefore directs that information, in writing is given to appropriate representatives about the:

- reasons for the redundancy situation[11]
- numbers and types of employees affected[12]
- the total number of employees at the establishment[13]
- selection method[14]
- dismissal procedures[15]
- method of calculating redundancy pay[16]

Consultation can begin once a reasonable amount of information is supplied by the employer:

> "Whether a union has been provided with information which is adequate to permit meaningful consultation to commence is a question of facts and circumstances. There is no rule that full and specific information under each of the heads listed in s.99(5)[17] of the Employment Protection Act must be provided before the consultation period can begin. The judgment of Slynn J in *Spillers-French (Holdings) Ltd v. USDAW* makes clear that a failure to give information on one of the heads of s.99(5) may be a serious default but was not intended to lay down that a failure of that kind must be treated as a serious default, such as to make it impossible for meaningful consultation to begin." *per* Lord Coulsfield

> *M.S.F. v. G.E.C. Ferranti (Defence Systems) Ltd (No. 2)* [1994] I.R.L.R. 113 at 114, EAT.

[11] TULRCA 1992, s.188(4)(a).
[12] *ibid.*, s.188(4)(b).
[13] *ibid.*, s.188(4)(c).
[14] *ibid.*, s.188(4)(d).
[15] *ibid.*, s.188(4)(e).
[16] *ibid.*, s.188(4)(f).
[17] Now TULRCA 1992, s.188(4).

In addition to the above information, the employer is also obliged to allow the representatives access to those employees threatened with redundancy. The TULRCA 1992, s.188(7) permits an employer to mount a defence to an unfair redundancy dismissal claim, by allowing him to demonstrate that he could not comply with the overall consultation and information requirements of section 188. Such a defence is only available however, in a situation where "there are special circumstances which render it not reasonably practicable for the employer to comply" with section 188 providing that he "shall take all such steps towards compliance with that requirement as are reasonably practicable in the circumstances". It is perhaps not surprising, that there has been considerable case law development on what "reasonably practicable" means in relation to the actual carrying out of a redundancy, in particular, the selection methods used (see para. 8.3.4 below).

8.3.3.4 *Definition of establishment*

The TULRCA 1992, s.188(1) relates the requirement to consult with the number of proposed redundancies at "one establishment". (see para. 8.3.3 above). If there are less than 20 employees to be made redundant at an establishment the employers are not obliged to give 30 or 90 days' notice (but see also para. 8.3.3.1 above). There is no statutory definition of "establishment" and the case law has not, until *Rockfon* (see below) produced a comprehensive test. An early case pioneered the "common-sense" test:

> "What is an 'establishment' for the purposes of determining the minimum time limits for advance notification of redundancies under s.99(3) of the Employment Protection Act is a question for the Industrial Tribunal to decide, functioning as an industrial jury using its common sense, on the particular facts of the case. In the absence of a statutory definition, the word 'establishment' is intended to convey what it means to ordinary people." per Bristow J.

Barratt Developments (Bradford) Ltd v. Ucatt [1977] I.R.L.R. 403, EAT.

In *Barratt* the common sense approach meant that the 14 separate building sites administered from one headquarters were regarded as one headquarters.

Equation of "establishment" with "employer" was ruled out in *E. Green & Son (Castings) Ltd v. ASTMS*[18] where three subsidiaries of a holding company made different numbers of employees redundant amounting in total to over 100 employees. The trade union argued that this figure triggered the 90 day protected consultation period (see para. 8.3.3.5 below), but the employers claimed that since less than 30 employees at each establishment were made redundant, only a 30 day consultation period was required. The EAT held that "Once it is established that the contract of employment is genuinely made between an employee and a company, albeit part of a larger group, no further enquiry is necessary. The argument advanced on behalf of the respondents that in determining who the employer is, the corporate veil could be lifted could not be accepted." The EAT found that the employees were directly employed by three separate employers, each of whom were making less than 30 employees redundant. A maximum of 30 days protected notice therefore had to be given by the employer.

Other relevant factors in defining "establishment" identified from the case law include the separation of financial accounting, services and profit.[19]

[18] *E. Green & Son (Castings) Ltd v. ASTMS* [1984] I.R.L.R. 135, EAT.
[19] S. Deakin & G.S. Morris (1995), p. 687.

At European level, the definition of "establishment" in the CRD[20] was the question also referred to the ECJ by the Danish Courts in *Rockfon*.[21] It ruled that the establishment is usually "the unit to which the workers made redundant are assigned to carry out their duties" irrespective of whether the managerial power to effect these redundancies was maintained within this unit. The purpose of this decision was to stop companies evading the consultation provisions by reorganising their departments or subsidiaries, or by staging the timing of the redundancies. It has been argued that such an approach would also be useful in other contexts such as discrimination and equal pay.[22]

Two possible problems remain however. First, what is the position where parts of an organisation may have considerable autonomy, such as schools in a local education authority?[23] It is possible that the purposive decision in *Rockfon* may help here. Secondly, if the "establishment" becomes for the purpose of redundancy, the smallest unit of management this would exclude the majority of United Kingdom businesses from the consultation requirements.[24] Current Government proposals to restore the pre-1995 position of requiring consultation where *one* employee is made redundant would seem to be the best redress to this problem (see para. 8.3.3.1 above).

8.3.3.5 *Protective award for non-consultation*

The TULRCA 1996, ss.189–192 provide for a legal remedy where an employer fails to comply with any of the section 188 consultation provisions. Employee representatives,[25] trade union representatives[26] and employees[27] may apply for the statutory remedy. This takes two forms. First, a declaration, which may lead to a finding of unfair dismissal and secondly, a protective award,[28] the amount of which is related to "the seriousness of the employer's default."[29] Failure to consult collectively thus attracts an individual protective award to every employee for whom the employer is in default. The award is paid at the rate of one week's pay for each week, or part of a week of the protected period to a maximum of 90 days where 100 or more employees are made redundant and 30 days where less than 100 are involved. If an employer can show that there were "special circumstances" which prevent him from complying with section 188 and providing that he did as much as was "reasonably practicable" in the circumstances to comply he may avoid having to pay this award.[30]

The case law which has developed from these provisions has centred around the question of whether the protective award was intended to have a punitive effect on employers for not consulting, or whether it's principal purpose was to compensate individual employees for losses related to the statutory consultation periods. In *Talke Fashions Ltd v. ASTWKT*[31] the Employment Appeal Tribunal found that "because the Act links the maximum period of a protective award with the period of consultation required before redundancy dismissals, an award should be commensurate with the

---

[20] Collective Redundancies Directive 75/129.
[21] *Rockfon A/S v. Specialiarbejderforbunet i Danmark, acting for Nielsen and others* [1996] I.R.L.R. 168, ECJ.
[22] J. McMullen and J. Eady, *Labour Law Review*, September 1997, Institute of Employment Rights, p. 12.
[23] I.T. Smith and G.H. Thomas (1996), p. 57.
[24] Labour Research (1996) *Bargaining Report* 159, March 1996.
[25] TULRCA 1992, s.189(1)(a).
[26] TULRCA 1992, s.189(1)(b).
[27] TULRCA 1992, s.189(1)(c).
[28] TULRCA 1992, s.189(2).
[29] TULRCA 1992, s.189(4).
[30] TULRCA 1992, s.188(7), s.189(6),.
[31] [1977] I.R.L.R. 309 at 309, EAT.

loss suffered by an employee who has been given short shrift in a redundancy situation. This is consistent with the whole spirit of both the Redundancy Payments Act and the Trade Union and Labour Relations Act. The second factor that has to be considered is the seriousness of the employer's default. This should be looked at in its relationship to the employees, not to the trade union representative who was not consulted." In *TGWU v. Nationwide Haulage Ltd*[32] an industrial tribunal argued that it was the employer's default in not giving enough notice which should be penalised rather than giving compensation to employees for losses. First, because such losses might be difficult to calculate and secondly, because they were not deductible from other awards paid for unfair dismissal.

In *APAC v. Kirwin Ltd*[33] the EAT noted that the legislation requires "the continued payment of wages by the employer over a certain period known as the 'protected period". Subject to statutory limits the length of this period is to be such as the Tribunal consider to be just and equitable in all the circumstances. A Tribunal, however, is specifically enjoined to determine the period and so the amount of the award by paying regard to the seriousness of the employer's default. This introduces a punitive element into the jurisdiction of an Industrial Tribunal and is in contrast with e.g., the calculation of a compensatory award which is based upon what is just and equitable having regard to the loss sustained."

The award is therefore a discretionary one which the court has to apply in the light of the circumstances of each case. Guidance as to what it is reasonable for an employer to do, to comply with section 188 is given in *TGWU v. Ledbury Preserves (1928) Ltd*[34] where it was found that an employer who sent out dismissal notices to employees only half an hour after a first meeting with union representatives was not complying with requirements. The EAT held that "there must be sufficient meaningful consultation before notices of dismissal are sent out. The consultation must not be a sham exercise; there must be time for the union representatives who are consulted to consider properly the proposals that are being put to them."

In *Sovereign Distribution Services Ltd v. Transport & General Workers' Union*[35] it was held that the purpose of the legislation was to ensure "that consultation takes place even where the employer thinks that to consult will achieve nothing. The statutory duty to consult in many cases provides the only opportunity for employees, through their recognised trade unions, to be able to seek to influence the redundancy decision and to put forward other ideas and other considerations, not only as to the overall decision but also as to the individuals who should be made redundant and other material aspects."

Even having to sell an insolvent business quickly by shedding employees does not amount to special circumstances[36] which permit an employer to avoid consultation.[37] The early case of *Clarks of Hove Ltd v. Bakers Union*[38] established that insolvency may or may not constitute special circumstances depending on the facts. A gradual run-down of a company is not unusual but a sudden disaster, financial[39] or physical, may

[32] [1978] I.R.L.R. 143, IT.
[33] [1978] I.R.L.R. 318 at 319, EAT.
[34] [1985] I.R.L.R. 412 at 412.
[35] [1989] I.R.L.R. 334 at 334, EAT.
[36] TULRCA 1992, s.189(6)(a).
[37] *G.M.B. v. Messrs Rankin and Harrison (as joint administrative receivers of Lawtex plc and Lawtex Babywear Ltd)* [1992] I.R.L.R. 514, EAT.
[38] [1978] I.C.R. 1076; [1978] I.R.L.R. 366, CA.
[39] *USDAW v. Leancut Bacon Ltd (in liquidation)* [1981] I.R.L.R. 295.

be. The burden of proof is on employers to persuade an industrial tribunal that it should reduce or waive the protected award altogether due to special circumstances.[40] Employers can no longer claim a special circmustances defence on the grounds that the decision to dismiss was not taken by them, but by a parent company who would not supply information to them. The immediate employers are still liable for any failure to consult.[41]

Lastly, the protected award itself is not now subject to any deductions by the employer for any other payments made in the protected period or from any damages due for breach of contract by the employer.[42] An employee may be able to claim both a protective award and unfair dismissal compensation.

8.3.4   Redundancy selection procedures

There is now no statutory prescription on how redundancy selection procedures should be carried out. For over 20 years, there used to be a ground for unfair redundancy dismissal where the dismissal was in breach of a collectively agreed redundancy procedure[43], but this provision was repealed in 1995[44] by a Government which had systematically removed much of the legislative framework for formal bargaining.[45] The development of case law in this area has been and is still very important however, because of the availability of the remedy of unfair redundancy dismissal based on grounds of general fairness.[46] Although potentially fair,[47] a redundancy dismissal can be rendered unfair if an individual is unfairly selected for redundancy or unlawfully discriminated against in the selection process.[48] Such a dismissal can cost an employer a lot more in compensation than a protective award for redundancy non-consultation.

In essence, an employer can shed surplus staff in one of three main ways, by asking for employees to volunteer for redundancy, or for early retirement, or by implementing a compulsory redundancy programme. Implementation of an early retirement scheme may permit the employer to avoid paying redundancy compensation if the employee agrees to waive any such compensation,[49] although pressurising staff into early retirement may amount to constructive dismissal.[50] The first two alternatives are anyway likely to cost the employer more. To secure volunteers, an attractive financial package paying higher rates than the meagre statutory compensation sums will usually be necessary. Also, the cost of extra employer's pension scheme contributions to enable them to pay out pensions for retiring employees aged 50 years and over, could be considerable. Another disadvantage occurs when too many applicants apply for "voluntary severance". Employers, will, for the reasons discussed below, usually reserve the right to select which individuals from amongst the volunteers are to be released. This can lead to the lowering of workforce morale amongst those unselected. Perhaps

[40] TULRCA 1992, s.189(6).
[41] TULRCA 1992, s.193(7) as amended by TURERA 1993, s.34(4).
[42] TULRCA 1992, s.190(3) was repealed by TURERA 1993, s.34(3).
[43] EPCA 1978, s.59(1)(b).
[44] Deregulation and Contracting Out Act 1994, s.36 effective from January 3, 1995.
[45] J. Hendy, *A Law Unto Themselves. Conservative Employment Laws: A National And International Assessment*, (3rd ed., Institute of Employment Rights, 1993), p. 57.
[46] ERA 1996, s.98(4).
[47] ERA 1996, s.98(2)(c).
[48] ERA 1996, s.105(1)(b).
[49] *Birch and Humber v. University of Liverpool* [1985] I.R.L.R. 165, CA.
[50] *Pearl Assurance plc v. MSF*, EAT 1162/96, February 26, 1997.

the most important disadvantage of the purely voluntary approach for many employers, is that it can leave a residue of staff, whose match of skills and experience is not what is required for the future development of the business. It is for these reasons, that many employers contemplating redundancy will utilise both the voluntary and compulsory approaches. Sometimes resorting to the latter scheme after an initial trawl for volunteers. On other occasions, the precarious financial state of the business may dictate the immediate application of a compulsory redundancy procedure.

8.3.4.1 *Selection criteria*

In compulsory redundancy selection, the selection criteria themselves have to be objective and fair. They also have to be fairly applied. The traditional procedure, often negotiated with trade unions was selection based on "last in, first out" (LIFO). A procedure which was simple to understand and apply and was based on the principle that those employees who had given most service deserved more job security. With the increase of unemployment and part-time employment in the 1980s and 1990s, it is perhaps more difficult to defend such a potentially inequitable principle; although the Court of Sessions, has quite recently, granted an interdict prohibiting an employer from selecting an employee for redundancy except on LIFO criteria. This was because they found that this method of selection had been incorporated from a collective agreement into his contract of employment.[51]

LIFO could also lead to the same mismatch of experience and skills in the remaining workforce as in the voluntary schemes. The decline of trade union membership and influence and the rise of a more unitarist approach towards industrial relations in this period led to the development of selection schemes based purely on individual merit and on the employer's needs. Schemes based on a complex matrix of criteria applied to the individual employees, such as standard of work performance, adaptability, attendance and disciplinary records as well as skills and qualifications were recommended as suitable criteria for employers when selecting for redundancy.[52] Because employment tribunals have no jurisdiction in deciding the business need for a redundancy, the question arises as to how far they can be involved in assessing the fairness of these selection tests.

In applying these criteria, the courts in cases like *Polkey* (discussed in para. 8.3.3.2 above) have stressed the importance of consultation by the employers. This approach has been confirmed by the influential decision[53] of the EAT in *Williams v. Compair Maxam Ltd*[54] where the EAT stressed that it is not the job of the industrial tribunal to substitute it's own judgment of fairness in any redundancy situation but to ask itself did the employer act within the reasonable range of responses of other employers and did it apply the following principles:

1. Give as much warning as possible to the trade union and the employees so that alternative solutions and if necessary, other jobs could be sought?

2. Seek to agree and to apply selection criteria with the unions?

3. Seek to agree criteria which does not depend solely upon the opinion of the manager making the selection, but "can be objectively checked against such

---

[51] *Anderson v. Pringle of Scotland Ltd* [1998] I.R.L.R. 64, CS.

[52] ACAS, *Redundancy Handling*, Advisory Booklet No. 12, 1988, p. 16.

[53] I.T. Smith and G.H. Thomas (1996), pp. 416–418.

[54] *Williams and Others v. Compair Maxam Ltd* [1982] I.R.L.R. 83; [1982] I.C.R. 156, EAT.

things as attendance record, efficiency at the job, experience, or length of service"?

4. Seek to apply the selection process fairly and to consider comments from the union on it?

5. Offer alternative work if possible?

It is arguable that such principles now also apply to where the employer, in the absence of a recognised trade union is consulting with employee representatives.[55]

The general principle of consultation is now well established in statute and in the case law. What has become more problematical however, is how far employers are obliged to go to prove that selection criteria are fairly applied. In *Mugford v. Midland Bank*[56] the EAT confirmed the desirability of disclosing an employee's selection score to the individual concerned, particularly as trade unions traditionally often did not want to be involved in actually selecting their members for redundancy. Such disclosure gave the individual an opportunity to challenge the selection criteria with his or her manager. On the other hand, disclosure of the results of how *all* employees are scored in a competitive redundancy selection system may also be of interest to individuals affected so that their representatives can establish that objective criteria were applied. Such applications for disclosure of information have been both refused[57] and granted[58] by the courts.

In *Eaton Ltd v. King*[59] where a selected individual was not given the scores of others, the EAT held that "In determining whether an employer acted reasonably, it is going too far to require that the details of individual assessments should be disclosed to the employees and discussed with them."[60] This approach was again followed by the Court in *British Aerospace plc v. Green and others* which found: "discovery is limited to documents which are relevant to issues which have been raised. Documents relating to retained employees are not likely to be relevant in any but the most exceptional circumstances." [1995] I.R.L.R. 433 at 433, CA.

This view was not upheld by the EAT in *F.D.R. Ltd v. Holloway*[61] in a case where an employee with a much longer service record (four years) and who had received no complaints about his performance, was dismissed for redundancy in preference to a colleague who had only been employed for a few months. The employer refused to disclose the selection documents on those employees who had been retained and the EAT upheld the industrial tribunal's decision of unfair dismissal on the grounds that "Where there is an issue as to whether redundancy selection criteria were applied fairly and reasonably in the case of a particular employee, an industrial tribunal, of necessity, has to know the employee's markings and how they compare with other employees in the pool. The tribunal is not bound to accept the employer's assertion that the criteria were applied fairly." [1995] I.R.L.R. 400 at 400, EAT. The reasons for such inconsistent decisions can be found in the reluctance of the courts to allow "fishing expeditions" for information or to get too involved in the minutia of the selection process.[62]

---

[55] TULRCA 1992, s.188(1B)(a).
[56] [1997] I.R.L.R. 208, paras 35–36, EAT.
[57] *Eaton Ltd v. King* [1995] I.R.L.R. 75, EAT. See also *British Aerospace plc v. Green* [1995] I.C.R. 1006; [1995] I.R.L.R. 433, CA.
[58] *F.D.R. Ltd v. Holloway* [1995] I.R.L.R. 400, EAT.
[59] *Eaton Ltd v. King* [1995] I.R.L.R. 75, EAT.
[60] [1995] I.R.L.R. 75 at 75, EAT.
[61] [1995] I.R.L.R. 400, EAT.
[62] I.T. Smith and G.H. Thomas (1996) p. 419.

The latest decisions in this area would seem to indicate that the courts are recognising that, to be able to assess the fairness of a selection system and its application will sometimes involve the consideration of relevant records. In *Byrne v. Castrol (U.K.) Ltd*[63] the redundancy selection criteria were based solely on absence and disciplinary records. It was argued by the employee that this was unfair, because, the reasons for the absences were not examined by the employer. The absence record was taken over a two year period to take account of special circumstances said the employer. The EAT found this was not necessarily unfair, as it was unreasonable for an employer to have to examine the circumstances behind every employee's absence and possibly make subjective judgements about them. In *John Brown Engineering Ltd v. Brown and others*[64] the EAT later reaffirmed the importance of individuals being informed of the criteria on which they had been selected, and for there to be an opportunity be able to appeal against the score awarded.

8.3.4.2 *LIFO and discrimination*

In trying to implement fair selection criteria for redundancy, employers should also be aware of the requirement not to discriminate against employees on grounds of their gender,[65] race[66] or disability.[67] (See also para. 8.3.2 on automatic unfair selection). The practice of LIFO has been the subject of scrutiny by the courts on the basis that it may indirectly discriminate against women because they are more likely to work part-time. In *Clarke v. Eley (IMI) Kynoch Ltd*[68] a part-time women munitions worker with long but intermittent service, working a basic 25 hours a week plus overtime, was found to be unfairly selected for redundancy; whereas in *Kidd v. D.R.G. (U.K.) Ltd*[69] a married woman shift worker, working only with women, was held not to have been discriminated against when selected for redundancy because she was a part-time worker. The EAT did not accept her argument that it was more difficult for a married woman to be in full-time employment because of her child-care responsibilities. In both cases the recognised trade unions had approved the selection criteria.

In a case dealt with by the Northern Ireland jurisdiction, where there is statutory provision[70] for affirmative action to redress the religious imbalance of a workforce, the practice of LIFO was abandoned by an employer, because, it was claimed, its application would have undone the positive effects of the affirmative action programme by releasing a greater proportion of Catholic workers.[71]

Finally, the durability of LIFO, despite its origins in a very different post-1945 industrial climate is well illustrated in *Brook v. London Borough of Haringey*. In 1987, the local authority undertook a positive action programme of recruiting women employees to increase their representation in the crafts of carpentry, joinery, bricklaying, roofing and plumbing. Two years later, after a financial crisis, the employers instituted a redundancy programme. The redundancy selection criteria eventually agreed were based on attendance, sickness, conduct and length of service. "Individuals

---

[63] EAT 429/96, November 5, 1996.
[64] [1997] I.R.L.R. 90, EAT.
[65] SDA 1975, s.6(2)(b).
[66] RRA 1976, s.4(2)(c).
[67] DDA 1995, s.4(2)(d).
[68] [1982] I.R.L.R. 482; [1983] I.C.R. 165, EAT.
[69] [1985] I.R.L.R. 190; [1985] I.C.R. 405, EAT.
[70] Fair Employment (N.I.) Act 1989.
[71] M. Potter and E. Regan "The Legal Limits Of Affirmative Action In Redundancy Selection" (1997) N.L.J., May 16.

lost points for the first three categories and gained points for length of service. Since most women were recent employees, the proportion of women who could gain sufficient points for length of service to counterbalance the loss of points for illness, injury and conduct was considerably smaller than the proportion of men who could do so." In dismissing all the heads of claim for unfair dismissal on grounds of indirect discrimination, the EAT affirmed the traditional values of LIFO:

> "The Industrial Tribunal had correctly found in the alternative that the employers" use of length of service as a redundancy selection criterion was justifiable, notwithstanding its indirectly discriminatory effect on women.
>
> Employers, trade unions, ACAS and common sense all recognise that length of service is an essential ingredient in any redundancy selection, save in the most exceptional circumstances. Therefore, justification of length of service as a criterion will be a fairly simple burden for an employer to undertake." *per* Wood, J. (M.C.)

> *Brook and Others v. London Borough Of Haringey* [1992] I.R.L.R. 478 at 479, EAT.

This may be a simple burden for an employer, but the continuing influence of LIFO may, it is respectfully submitted, place a burden on the increasing proportion of the economically active workforce, who through no fault of their own, are forced into part-time and short-term employment.[72] If work itself is to become a scarce, but even more desirable economic and social "commodity", is this not, in some redundancy situations, an equitable reason for considering FIFO—first in, first out? Another important criticism of *Brook* is made by Smith and Thomas who reflect that "the case does perhaps show that if, in difficult times, employers (and unions) fall back on 'tried and tested' solutions, that may negate any advances in other contexts towards greater equal opportunities".[73]

Such considerations were perhaps not central to the issues raised in *Anderson v. Pringle of Scotland Ltd*[74] which is the first mainstream labour law decision in which an injunction was issued prohibiting a private sector employer from dismissing an employee in breach of a redundancy selection procedure. The Court of Session accepted that a LIFO selection procedure had been incorporated from a long-standing collective agreement into the employee's contract, and granted interim suspension and interdict against the employers selecting any employees for redundancy other than on LIFO principles.

8.3.5   Offer of suitable alternative employment

Article 2(2) of the CRD[75] provides that where the employer is consulting with workers' representatives about redundancies, he should consider mitigating their effect by "accompanying social measures aimed, *inter alia*, at aid for redeploying or retraining workers made redundant." Barnard comments on this provision, that it "is a pale

---

[72] In 1996, 45% of females and 8% of males were in part-time employment—*Labour Force Survey*, Spring 1996, Office for National Statistics.
[73] *op. cit.* p. 421.
[74] [1998] I.R.L.R. 64, CS.
[75] Council Directive 75/129.

reflection of the 'social plan' recognised by German law—a special form of redundancy programme drawn up by management and the works' council in a legally binding agreement designed to 'compensate or reduce economic disadvantages for employees in the event of a substantial alteration to the establishment'". She suggests that because this requirement is placed at the top of the consultation list, the Directive does not presume that redundancies will occur and that fair treatment of those remaining in employment is as important as fair dismissal procedures.[76]

It could be argued that there is little legal obligation on employers in the United Kingdom to reduce the "economic disadvantages for employees" at the claimed level of German provision. There are however, statutory rules relating to the terms upon which employers may offer alternative work in a redundancy situation.

Alternative work—summary

- There is no dismissal where the employer renews the contract or re-engages the employee before the end of a four week period after the end of the old contract.[77]

- This does not apply if the new contract or the renewed contract has different terms and conditions[78] and is terminated by the employer or employee during the trial period.[79]

- So, if the employer re-engages the employee there is a statutory presumption of a trial period of four calendar[80] weeks in the new job, beginning at the end of the previous contract[81] which may be extended for the purpose of retraining.[82]

- If the alternative work offered does contain major contractual changes[83] however, the employee is regarded as dismissed at the end of his previous contract.[84]

- A longer period of retraining may be agreed between the employer and the employee or his representatives,[85] if that agreement is put in writing and specifies the date it will end, plus the terms and conditions which will apply after the probationary period.[86]

- An employee is not entitled to a redundancy payment if the terms and conditions of the newly offered contract are the same as before[87] or if they do differ, they amount to "an offer of suitable employment" in relation to that employee[88] and he "unreasonably refuses the offer"[89] or if during the trial period, he unreasonably resigns.[90]

[76] C. Barnard, *EC Employment Law* (Wiley, Rev. ed. 1996), p. 390.
[77] ERA 1996, s.138(1).
[78] ERA 1996, s.138(2)(a).
[79] ERA 1996, s.138(3).
[80] *Benton v. Sanderson Kayser Ltd* [1989] I.R.L.R. 19, CA.
[81] ERA 1996, s.138(3)(a).
[82] ERA 1996, s.138(3)(b)(2).
[83] ERA 1996, s.138(2)(a).
[84] ERA 1996, s.138(4).
[85] ERA 1996, s.138(3)(b)(ii).
[86] ERA 1996, s.138(6).
[87] ERA 1996, s.141(3)(a).
[88] ERA 1996, s.141(3)(b).
[89] ERA 1996, s.141(2).
[90] ERA 1996, s.141(4)(d).

8.3.5.1 *Equivalent work*

To avoid liability for the payment of redundancy compensation, the employer will need to offer new employment which "is substantially equivalent to the employment which has ceased."[91] Offering work in the same type of occupation may not be sufficient if the employee feels that he has lost status. In *Cambridge & District Co-operative Society Ltd v. Ruse*[92] the Manager of a co-op butchers shop was offered alternative employment as butchery department manager in a store and refused it because "he did not have a key to the store and was no longer responsible for collecting and banking money". The EAT upheld the industrial tribunal's decision that although this was a suitable offer of alternative employment, the employee was entitled to a redundancy payment because of his "perceived loss of status". In explaining their decision the EAT seemed to be taking a sensibly broad view of what is now the ERA 1996, s.141(3)(b) by finding that "the question of the suitability of an offer of alternative employment is an objective matter, whereas the reasonableness of the employee's refusal depends on factors personal to him and is a subjective matter to be considered from the employee's point of view." [1993] I.R.L.R. 150 at 157, EAT.

In a much earlier case,[93] where a vehicle mechanic was changed from night work to day work, it was held that the decrease in responsibility of the new job now that the employee worked to a foreman, rather than acting independently as before, meant that the employee was redundant. This was because the new work was "separate and distinct" from what was done previously. Status was clearly in the court's mind in *Taylor v. Kent County Council*[94] when a former headmaster was not chosen as the new headmaster when his school amalgamated with a girl's school. He was offered another post at the new scool on the same pay but "in all other respects the nature of the job differed . . . because he is going to be put into a position where he has to go where he is told at any time for short periods, to any place, and be put under a headmaster and assigned duties by him."[95]

8.3.5.2 *Genuine redundancy*

In offering suitable alternative work to the employee under section 138 of the ERA 1996, there has to be a genuine redundancy situation. In *Nelson v. BBC (No. 2)*[96] the Court of Appeal increased the unfair dismissal compensation awarded to a BBC producer, who had been found by an industrial tribunal and the Employment Appeal Tribunal to "be 60% to blame for his dismissal because he had failed to accept a reasonable offer of alternative work . . ." The Court of Appeal in an earlier hearing, had overturned a decision that the employee had been fairly dismissed for redundancy, and substituted a finding that the employee had been unfairly dismissed and remitted the case to another industrial tribunal to consider an appropriate remedy (see para. 8.3.1). In its second appearance before the Court of Appeal, the issue in *Nelson* was whether the remedy of compensation awarded was appropriate. The Court found it was not. This was because the industrial tribunal to which the case had been remitted, had not taken into consideration the Appeal Court's earlier decision that the employee

---

[91] *Hindes v. Supersine Ltd* [1979] I.R.L.R. 343; [1979] I.C.R. 517, EAT.
[92] [1993] I.R.L.R. 156, EAT.
[93] *R. Archibald v. Rossleigh Commercials Ltd* [1975] I.R.L.R. 231, IT.
[94] [1969] I.T.R. 294, QBD.
[95] *Taylor v. Kent County Council* [1969] I.T.R. 294, at 297, QBD, cited with approval by Talbot J. in *Hindes v. Supersine Ltd* [1979] I.R.L.R. 343, EAT, para. 18.
[96] [1979] I.R.L.R. 346, CA.

"had been correct in asserting that he was not redundant because the job that he was employed to do continued to exist and that the proposal which the respondents were making to him was not in reality an offer of alternative employment, but a proposal to re-assign him to other work within the scope of his existing contract of employment which they were entitled to do irrespective of any consent on his part."[97] It was the employer who had been at fault in threatening to make ". . . Mr Nelson redundant as a means of persuading him to give his consent to a misdescribed proposal for which his consent was not in law required."[98]

8.3.5.3 *Trial period*

The four week trial period under a new contract of employment, if offered by the employer, is subject to the common law principle that if a contract is repudiated by the employer, the employee has a reasonable time in which to decide whether or not to accept the variation. It is only after this period has ended, that the statutory trial period comes into effect.[99] The length of this period will vary with the circumstances of the case. In *Air Canada v. Lee*[1] a telephonist agreed to move for a trial period, from a light airy office to a basement location without any natural light, when the employer moved premises. She worked for over two months and then resigned claiming unfair dismissal. Note: the employer had not dismissed the telephonist neither had they indicated what would be a reasonable trial period. The EAT held:

> "Where, as in the present case, the duration of the trial period is unspecified, it can only be regarded as lasting for what is a reasonable period in all the circumstances.
>
> Amongst the circumstances will be included the steps the employers take to enquire what the employee is going to do. If they make no such enquiries, the trial period carries on until either the employee has announced his decision, or a period of time has expired which is long enough for it to be said that it would be unreasonable to consider the trial period as still subsisting." *per* Phillips J.

Air Canada v. Lee [1978] I.R.L.R. 392 at 393, EAT.

In this case, the EAT found that the employee was dismissed on grounds of redundancy as she was not contractually compelled to move to the new premises and had not accepted the contractual variation by the employers. She was therefore entitled to redundancy compensation. Moving business to a new location can be a common cause of redundancy. The statutory formulation refers to the cessation of business "in the place where the employee was so employed,"[2] and a change in the employee's contractual place of work is prima facie a redundancy situation. Problems can occur however, where there is a dispute over the place of work.

8.3.5.4 *Place of work*

In *Bass Leisure Ltd v. Thomas*[3] a brewery ceased operations in its Coventry depot and moved them to Erdington some 20 miles west. Mrs Thomas was employed by the

[97] [1979] I.R.L.R. 346 at 348.
[98] [1979] I.R.L.R. 346 at 353, para. 69.
[99] *Turvey and Others v. C.W. Cheyney & Son Ltd* [1979] I.R.L.R. 105, EAT.
[1] [1978] I.R.L.R. 392, EAT.
[2] ERA 1996, s.139(1)(a)(ii).
[3] [1994] I.R.L.R. 104, EAT.

Brewery to collect the takings from fruit machines in pubs in the Coventry area and she "reluctantly agreed to give the move a try" but found that the extra travelling time and reorganised work considerably increased her time at work. She resigned and claimed redundancy compensation. The employers contested this and sought to rely on a mobility clause in her contract which stipulated "The company reserves the right to transfer any employee either temporarily or permanently to a suitable alternative place of work . . ." The EAT upheld the industrial tribunal's finding that she had been dismissed for redundancy and had not unreasonably refused an offer of suitable alternative employment. In so doing it clarified the legal definition of the place of work for redundancy purposes:

> "'The place' where an employee was employed for the purposes of s.81(2)[4] does not extend to any place where he or she could contractually be required to work. The question of what is the place of employment concerns the extent or area of a single place, not the transfer from one place to another." *per* Hicks, J.

Bass Leisure Ltd v. Thomas [1994] I.R.L.R. 104 at 104, EAT.

In *Bass* the contract also contained a written provision that "your geographic area may be altered, provided that it remains realistically accessible from your normal residence." The industrial tribunal found that this meant that the employer had to take account of domestic circumstances and whether the alternative place of work was objectively suitable. Being 20 miles away and adding considerably to the length of the working day the new place of work was not adjudged to meet these criteria. It has been pointed out[5] that there is a considerable body of case law which had arisen from the application of contractual mobility clauses which require compliance with contractual obligations but may require the giving of reasonable notice to any change of location and a sensible construction applied to contractual mobility terms where they are particularly broad as in *Bass.* In addition, the courts will not allow an employer to have it both ways when he decides to relocate. Either he invokes a mobility clause if the contract permits so that no redundancy occurs, or if he is able, he makes alternative offers of employment, which if suitable have the same effect, but which if not suitable may trigger the repayment of redundancy compensation.[6]

Any agreement or condition which seeks to exclude or limit the statutory redundancy provisions is rendered invalid by the ERA 1996, s.203(1). In *Tocher v. General Motors Scotland Ltd*[7] the Scottish Employment Appeal Tribunal found that if the effect of a "bumping" agreement with the trade union, was to deprive an employee of his or her right to a trial period or redundancy payment if the alternative employment was unsuitable and it was reasonably refused, then such action was unlawful under section 203.

Finally, a mistake by the employer in advertising alternative employment internally led to a post being advertised with higher than necessary qualifications. This meant that three employees were put off applying for them and were found to be unfairly dismissed.[8]

---

[4] Now ERA 1996. s.139(1).
[5] I.T. Smith and G.H. Thomas (1996), p. 448.
[6] *Curling and others v. Securicor Ltd* [1992] I.R.L.R. 549, EAT.
[7] [1981] I.R.L.R. 55, EAT.
[8] *Sun Valley Poultry Ltd v. Mitchell and others*, EAT 164/96 (reported in IDS Brief 604/January 1998).

8.3.6   Time off to look for alternative work

The ERA 1996, s.52 permits an employee who is under notice of dismissal for redundancy,[9] to take reasonable paid[10] time off during his or her working hours to look for work[11] or arrange for training.[12] Continuous service of two years is required for this provision to apply.[13] The appropriate hourly rate[14] should be paid, but this cannot exceed 40 per cent of a week's pay during the notice period.[15]

There is no requirement that an employee has to give details of appointments or interviews as a pre-condition of time off being granted[16] but he or she has to be genuinely looking for work.[17] Courtesy and good industrial relations will imply that reasonable notice of time off should be given.

Advice is published by the Department of Trade and Industry on the statutory provisions.[18]

8.3.7   Redundancy compensation payments

The ERA 1996, Part XI, s.135, provides that an employee has the right to a redundancy payment if he or she has been dismissed for redundancy[19] or laid off or kept on short-time.[20] The employee has to have been continuously employed for two years.[21] This payment is intended to compensate for long service and is in addition to any unemployment benefit which may be payable to the individual. The level of payment is extremely modest. It is related to years of continuous service, age, and a normal week's pay; so that from 18 to 21 years of age, an individual is entitled to one-half of a week's pay per year, from 22 to 40 the individual receives one week's pay per year and from 41 to 64 to one-and-a-half week's pay per year, up to a maximum of 20 years reckonable employment and a maximum week's pay of £210 (1996 rates). Many employers operate agreed redundancy compensation schemes which pay compensation at considerably higher levels.

A redundancy compensation claim usually has to be made within six months of the expiry of the contract of employment[22]; but this period can be extended if an industrial tribunal considers it "just and equitable" to do so.[23] No claim can be made after 12 months.[24] The employee's claim has to be in writing,[25] but in no particular format merely that "the notice or the writing relied on must be of such a character that the recipient would reasonably understand in all the circumstances of the case that it was

---

[9] s.52(1).
[10] s.53(1).
[11] s.52(1)(a).
[12] s.52(1)(b).
[13] s.52(2).
[14] s.53(1).
[15] s.53(5).
[16] *Dutton v. Hawker Siddeley Aviation Ltd* [1978] I.R.L.R. 390, EAT.
[17] *Seldon v. The Kendall Co. (U.K.) Ltd*, COIT 1669/22.
[18] DTI, *Time Off For Job Hunting Or To Arrange Training When Facing Redundancy*, PL 703 (REV 3).
[19] s.135(1)(a).
[20] s.135(1)(b). The provisions for the claiming of lay-off and short time redundancy payments are extremely complex and are to be found in the ERA 1996, ss.147–154.
[21] ERA 1996, s.155.
[22] ERA 1996, s.164.
[23] ERA 1996, s.164(3).
[24] ERA 1996, s.164(2).
[25] ERA 1996, s.164(1)(b).

the intention of the employee to seek a redundancy payment,"[26] and the employer has to issue a written statement indicating how the redundancy calculation is made up.[27] Failure to do this invites a fine up to level 3.[28]

An employee, whose contract is discharged through frustration (see Chapter 5, para. 5.5.1) may, under the provisions of the ERA 1996, s.136(5)(b) be deemed as dismissed by the employer, if "an event affecting [the] employer" causes the termination. In *Currie and Gray v. Pinnacle Meat Processors*[29] two employees of a meat processing company had their work terminated as a result of the BSE crisis in the beef industry. One worker was employed as an ox-head de-boner and the other as a driver whose job was transporting the offal. The employees lost their jobs after two statutory instruments were promulgated in 1996[30] ending this trade. An industrial tribunal found that an intervening event had radically altered the original contract and that the ERA 1996, s.139(4)(a) applied because of this frustrating condition. Section 139(4)(a) provides that where such an event occurs and providing it is the cause of the employer's business ceasing or diminishing as defined in section 139(1) an employee is deemed to be dismissed for redundancy. As 98 per cent of the employer's business concerned ox-head processing, the industrial tribunal was able to find that the two employees, although not dismissed in law, were statutorily entitled to redundancy compensation.

Finally, in the case of *Senior Heat Treatment v. Bell*[31] the EAT has found, rather surprisingly, that a situation may occur where an employee is entitled to two redundancy payments. This "double whammy" occurred in the context of a transfer (see Chapter 9, para. 9.8.3) where the transferor employer gave three options to the employees: (1) alternative employment; (2) transfer on existing conditions; or (3) a severance deal. Mr Bell along with most of his colleagues chose option (3), but immediately started with the transferee employer after his existing contract ended. Some 10 months later, the transferee employer made them redundant but refused to pay redundancy pay because it was claimed that the individuals did not have continuity of service. The EAT found that there was no statutory provision which would allow the transferee employer to offset the redundancy payment paid by the previous employer. Employers are advised to avoid this situation by avoiding signing up the transferor's employees before the transfer date. This is one of those relatively rare cases where redundant employees appear to have received more "protection" than was envisaged by statute.

8.3.7.1 *Exclusions*

There are a number of situations where redundancy compensation is *not* payable. These are:

- If there is a fixed term contract for two years or more and the employee has waived the right to a redundancy payment.[32] This is one of the few situations in which an employee is permitted to opt out of statutory protections. The original principle behind the waiver being to give employers flexibility in reorganising business. In practice it can be argued that these provisions have

---

[26] *Price v. Smithfield and Zwanenberg Group Ltd* [1978] I.R.L.R. 80, EAT.
[27] ERA 1996, s.165.
[28] ERA 1996, s.165(2), (3), (4).
[29] September 6, 1996, Southampton IT, 27788/96 & 27051/96, reported in I.R.L.B. 565, March 1997.
[30] March 20 and May 1, 1996.
[31] [1997] I.R.L.R. 614, EAT.
[32] ERA 1996, s.197(3).

been increasingly used by employers for an increasing percentage of their employee contracts to the overall detriment of worker security. If a fixed term contract is renewed this waiver is not renewed unless it is expressly agreed.[33] The renewal itself does not have to be for another two years for the waiver to apply however.[34]

- Men and women over 65 years or the normal retirement age are excluded.[35]

- Where an individual is employed by an overseas government[36] or is a domestic servant closely related to the employer.[37]

- Where an employee is entitled to an occupational pension or periodic lump sum the right to redundancy compensation is reduced or excluded.[38]

8.3.7.2 *Early leavers*

An employee who is under notice of redundancy dismissal but who wants to leave early, perhaps to go to another job, may still be regarded as being dismissed for redundancy, if before the termination of the employer's notice he or she gives written counter notice that they wish to go early.[39] The employer may however, if he has good reason, request that an employee works the notice period in full.[40] A problem which has arisen with these provisions is that the counter notice by the employee has to be given in the "obligatory" notice period,[41] that is the statutory[42] or contractual entitlement to notice, otherwise the employee is deemed to have resigned and looses the right to a redundancy payment. In *CPS Recruitment Ltd T/A Blackwood Associate v. Bowen and Secretary of State for Employment*[43] however, the EAT found on the facts, that the original notice period had been varied by agreement between the parties, in a situation where the employee had agreed with the employer to bring forward his date of leaving so that another employee, also under notice for redundancy, would cover for him. This is a consensual variation, not a section 136(3) situation where the notice *has* to be served within the obligatory period. The end result in *CPS Recruitment* was that the employee was entitled to a redundancy payment as he was deemed to have been dismissed for redundancy. To be certain of securing redundancy compensation an employee has to be under proper notice of dismissal and if he or she wants to go early and still get some compensation this counter notice must be given in the obligatory notice period and not before.[44]

8.3.7.3 *Polkey reduction*

Finally, the calculation of compensation for an unfair redundancy dismissal in relation to the statutory redundancy compensation payment which may also be due has been much scrutinised by two decisions of the EAT in *Digital Equipment Co. Ltd v. Clements*

---

[33] ERA 1996, s.197(5).
[34] *Housing Services Agency v. Cragg* [1997] I.R.L.R. 380, EAT.
[35] ERA 1996, s.156.
[36] ERA 1996, s.160.
[37] ERA 1996, s.161.
[38] ERA 1996, s.158(1).
[39] ERA 1996, s.136(3)(b).
[40] ERA 1996, s.142(2)(a).
[41] ERA 1996, s.136(3)(b).
[42] ERA 1996, s.86.
[43] [1982] I.R.L.R. 54, EAT.
[44] IT. Smith and G.H. Thomas (1996), p. 451.

[1996] I.R.L.R. 513, EAT and in *Digital Equipment Co. Ltd v. Clements (No. 2)*.[45] The issue here was the amount of compensation to be paid to an employee who had been found to be unfairly dismissed for redundancy because he had not been consulted and was not told about the selection criteria. The industrial tribunal also found that if the correct procedure had been followed by the employer there was a 50 per cent chance that the employee would have been retained. A *Polkey*[46] reduction of 50 per cent from the overall compensation was therefore due to be made to reflect the real loss of the employee which arose from the employer's actions. In other words if the correct redundancy procedure had been applied the employee stood only a 50% chance of not being made redundant. Mr Clements received a contractual severance payment of £20,685 and in addition, the industrial tribunal found his loss of earnings and benefits arising from an unfair redundancy dismissal came to £43,136 minus the 50 per cent *Polkey* deduction. The issue before the EAT was in what order was this deduction to be made:

> "In assessing Mr Clements's compensatory award, the tribunal calculated his total loss of earnings and other benefits at around £43,000. From that figure, the tribunal first deducted the payment of £20,500 and then halved the resultant sum to reflect the chances of his remaining in employment if his dismissal had not been procedurally unfair. That gave a figure of £11,250 to which the tribunal applied the statutory ceiling then in force and made an award of £11,000. The employers appealed against that decision, arguing that the tribunal should have applied the 50% reduction to the assessed loss of £43,000 before deducting the excess severance payment, thus producing a compensatory award nearer £1,000."[47]

In reviewing the whole issue of deductions from compensation the EAT held that the correct calculation was to first compute the employee's total loss and then to deduct any termination payment, in this case, the contractual severance payment, to assess the net loss, after which the *Polkey* reduction is taken. The overall sequence of deductions from the net loss being: (1) termination payment; (2) *Polkey* reduction; (3) contributory fault; and (4) excess over the statutory maximum. In the above case, this formulation benefited the employee some £10,000 and this decision followed recent case law which perhaps "now suggests that a pro-applicant approach is to be adopted, perhaps reflecting the more general view that compensation limits in this area are ripe for removal."[48] This argument was not accepted in the Court of Appeal by Beldam J. who decided that EPCA, s.74(7) meant "that the excess of the redundancy payment over the basic award is not to be taken into account in ascertaining the loss but is to go to 'reduce the amount of the compensatory award'." *Digital Equipment Co. Ltd v. Clements (No. 2)* [1998] I.R.L.R. 134 at 137, CA. The resolution of this matter now awaits consideration by the House of Lords.

8.3.7.4 *Industrial action, other misconduct and redundancy compensation*

The ERA 1996, s.140 provides that an employee who is dismissed "by reason of the employee's conduct" is not entitled to a redundancy compensation payment. The taking of industrial action, whether going on strike or otherwise, is usually a breach of contract and amounts to misconduct.

[45] *Digital Equipment Co. Ltd v. Clements (Respondent) (No.2)* [1997] I.R.L.R. 140, EAT.
[46] *Polkey v. A.E. Dayton Services Ltd (Formerly Edmund Walker Holdings Ltd)* [1987] I.R.L.R. 503, HL.
[47] *Digital Equipment Co. Ltd v. Clements (No. 2)* [1997] I.R.L.R. 140 at 140, EAT.
[48] J. McMullen and J. Eady, J. (1997), p. 11.

Section 140 has led to some confusion in its application however. This is because it stipulates that an employee taking such action will not be entitled to a redundancy payment providing the employer dismisses the employee: without notice[49] or with shorter notice than the contractual notice,[50] or with full notice which includes a statement that the employer, could, if he had wished, have dismissed summarily.[51] It has been pointed out that this subsection is, in theory, superfluous as dismissal for cause, for example misconduct, is not a redundancy dismissal.[52]

If an employee is already working under the obligatory period of redundancy notice and is dismissed for misconduct, an industrial tribunal has discretion as to whether to award some or all of a redundancy payment. In *Lignacite Products Ltd v. Krollman*[53] an employee who was under the statutory notice of redundancy was summarily dismissed for theft from his employer. The industrial tribunal, under the above provisions, reduced his redundancy compensation to 60 per cent of the original entitlement. On appeal, the employer argued that this should be reduced further to 25 per cent or 30 per cent, but such a draconian reduction was not accepted by the EAT. The Court considered that the tribunal award was just and equitable in the circumstances, given, that a redundancy award in part reflects service earned by the employee, which in the instant case amounted to 24 years. In a later case, concerning an employee dismissed for alleged theft at work whilst under redundancy notice the employer refused to pay any redundancy compensation at all. The industrial tribunal found that under, what is now the ERA 1996, s.140(1), the employer had acted lawfully, but the EAT remitted the case to another tribunal on the basis that the original tribunal had applied the wrong legal test:

> "Where there is a claim for a redundancy payment and the employer raises a defence under [s.140(1)] based on the employee's conduct, the 'contractual' approach indicated in *Western Excavating ECC Ltd v. Sharp* should be applied in determining whether the conduct in question was such as to entitle the employers to terminate the contract without notice. The burden is clearly on the employer to show that the employee was guilty of conduct which was a significant breach going to the root of the contract or which showed that the employee no longer intended to be bound by one or more of the essential terms of the contract" *per* Wood J.

Bonner v. H. Gilbert Ltd [1989] I.R.L.R. 475 at 475, EAT.

This seems to be a far more satisfactory test than the subjective *Burchell*[54] which the EAT rejected, especially if there is doubt about the facts (as there was in this case) and an individual's long service compensation is put at risk by perhaps one minor act of misconduct.

Industrial action

If an employee goes on strike whilst he or she is already under notice of dismissal for redundancy, it is still possible for redundancy compensation to be paid to the striking

---

[49] ERA 1996, s.140(1)(a).
[50] ERA 1996, s.140(1)(b).
[51] ERA 1996, s.140(1)(c).
[52] IT. Smith and G.H. Thomas (1996), p. 469.
[53] *Lignacite Products Ltd v. Krollman* [1979] I.R.L.R. 22, EAT.
[54] *British Home Stores Ltd v. Burchell* [1978] I.R.L.R. 379, EAT. (Note: in this case the famous three-part test for a fair dismissal for misconduct was adumbrated by Arnold J., this being that the employer need only entertain a "reasonable suspicion amounting to a belief in the guilt of the employee of that misconduct at that time").

individual. This is because the ERA 1996, s.143 provides that an employer in such a situation, may demand that an employee extends his or her contract of employment to a period equivalent to the days of work which the employer has lost through the strike action.[55] If an employee refuses to comply with this "notice of extension" the entitlement to a redundancy payment is forfeited.[56] Entitlement is only retained if the employee was either unable to comply with this request or it was unreasonable to do so. In this case, an industrial tribunal may direct that the employer pays all or some of the compensation due.[57]

No compensation is payable however, if an employee is made redundant whilst taking strike action. This is because the employer is entitled to summarily dismiss for a fundamental breach of the employment contract. "At common law an employer is entitled to dismiss summarily an employee who refuses to do any of the work which he was engaged to do and it makes no basic difference that the refusal occurs in the course of a strike. The refusal to work during a strike does not involve 'self-dismissal' by the striker. The contract of employment remains alive unless and until the employer exercises his right to dismiss the employee for committing a breach of contract by going out on strike".[58] ERA 1996, s.140(1) provides that an employee is not entitled to redundancy compensation where the employer can summarily dismiss the employee for misconduct.

Information about the redundancy compensation scheme is published by the Department of Trade and Industry.[59]

8.4   SOME OTHER SUBSTANTIAL REASON

As has been seen earlier in the text, the statutory remedy of unfair dismissal is subject to a general test of fairness,[60] so that although redundancy itself is prima facie a fair reason for dismissal,[61] an industrial tribunal also has to consider whether an employer acted fairly in dismissing the employee for that reason.[62] In addition to the four permitted reasons for dismissal[63] specified in the ERA 1996, s.98(2), the Act allows an employer to show that he dismissed an employee fairly for "some other substantial reason".[64] This has become known as an SOSR defence when an employer is seeking to defend an unfair dismissal application. Its significance in the context of redundancy is that if an employer can show that the individual worker was fairly dismissed for an SOSR reason, for example, because the employee resisted the terms of a business reorganisation, the employer could escape liability for the payment of redundancy compensation. Wedderburn has noted that "as early as 1972 tribunals were using the test of 'sound business practice'. Indeed, the employer's 'policy' or 'sound, good business reasons' will normally constitute SOSR."[65]

---

[55] ERA 1996, s.143(2).
[56] ERA 1996, s.143(3).
[57] ERA 1996, s.143(5).
[58] *W. Simmons v. Hoover Ltd* [1976] I.R.L.R. 266, EAT.
[59] DTI, *Redundancy Payments*, PL 808 (REV 4); *Offsetting Pensions Against Redundancy Payments*, RPL 1.
[60] ERA 1996, s.98.
[61] ERA 1996, s.98(2)(c).
[62] ERA 1996, s.98(4).
[63] *i.e.* capability, conduct, redundancy and contravention of an enactment.
[64] ERA 1996, s.98(1)(b).
[65] Lord Wedderburn (1986), p. 241.

At a time when European legislation[66] was strengthening the statutory requirements on collective consultation, including consultation on behalf of non-unionists,[67] consultation with all those individuals affected was at the centre of industrial relations law as then developing. Wedderburn has also observed however, that the courts were certainly not ahead of this trend when they ignored advice contained in the Industrial Relations Code of Practice[68] that employers should consult with individual employees over redundancies.

An early and influential decision in this area was made by Lord Denning in *Hollister v. National Farmers' Union.*[69] Here a National Farmers Union (NFU) official was dismissed for not accepting new terms and conditions which had been offered by the employer in the process of reorganising his business. The new terms were largely comparable but the pension scheme was less generous. The EAT found that because of insufficient consultation with the employee his dismissal was unfair. Lord Denning in the Court of Appeal considered that this decision was wrong because it put a gloss on the statute. The legislation "requires the Tribunal to look at all the circumstances of the case and at whether what the employer did was fair and reasonable in the circumstances prior to the dismissal. It does not say anything about 'consultation' or 'negotiation' in the statute. Therefore, there is no requirement that there must always be consultation. Consultation is only one of the factors which has to be taken into account when looking at the circumstances of the case and considering whether a dismissal is fair or unfair."

It is submitted that this decision on consultation, would be less authoritative today in the light of strengthened statutory consultation requirements[70] and developments in the case law.[71] Two other main issues arising from SOSR are still dominant however. First, is the legal oxymoron, that although an industrial tribunal has no jurisdiction to consider the commercial decisions[72] made by employers which give rise to redundancies and business re-organisations, they are empowered to examine the "sound business reasons"[73] advanced by an employer when deciding whether there has been a fair dismissal[74] for these reasons. Secondly, is the inventiveness of the courts in finding situations where, although individual employees have had their conditions of employment detrimentally changed, or their contract terminated as a result of these business reasons; the employees' reasonably anticipated remedy of a constructive dismissal,[75] or redundancy dismissal,[76] has been supplanted by a finding of fair dismissal based on an SOSR.[77] Examples of such situations are now considered.

---

[66] Council Directive 75/129.
[67] B. Bercusson, *The Employment Protection Act 1975* (Sweet & Maxwell, 1976), p. 71/99.
[68] Industrial Relations Code Of Practice 1972. Enacted under IRA 1971, ss. 2–4 and continued in force by EPA 1975, Sched. 17, para. 4. Repealed 1991: S.I. 1991 No. 1264.
[69] [1979] I.R.L.R. 238; [1979] I.C.R. 542, CA.
[70] TURERA 1993, s.34.
[71] *Mugford v. Midland Bank* [1997] I.R.L.R. 208, EAT.
[72] *James W. Cook & Co. (Wivenhoe) Ltd (In Liquidation) v. Tipper and Others* [1990] I.R.L.R. 386; [1990] I.C.R. 716, CA. See also: *J. Moon and Others v. Homeworthy Furniture (Northern) Ltd* [1976] I.R.L.R. 298; [1977] I.C.R. 117, EAT..
[73] In *Chubb Fire Security Ltd v. Harper* [1983] I.R.L.R. 311, the EAT, following the Court of Appeal in *Hollister v. NFU* [1979] I.R.L.R. 238; [1979] I.C.R. 542, found that the correct approach to a business re-organisation "is for the Industrial Tribunal to make a finding as to the advantages to the employers of the proposed re-organisation and whether it was reasonable for them to implement it by terminating existing contracts and offering employees new ones".
[74] ERA 1996, s.98(4).
[75] ERA 1996, s.95(1)(c).
[76] ERA 1996, s.98(2)(c).
[77] ERA 1996, s.98(4).

8.4.1   SOSR dismissals

SOSR dismissals in business reorganisations have been held to cover the following situations:

- The dismissal of an employee in *D.R. Ellis v. Brighton Co-Operative Society Ltd*[78] who refused to accept an increase in working hours and more onerous job duties arising from a reorganisation, although there was medical evidence that such hours were affecting his health. In this case, the EAT also formulated quite a narrow test for SOSR arising from re-organisation:

  > "Where there has been a properly consulted-upon reorganisation which, if it is not done, is going to bring the whole business to a standstill, a failure to go along with the new arrangements may constitute 'some other substantial reason'. Whether the circumstances in the present case constituted 'some other substantial reason' was a question of fact for the Industrial Tribunal with which the EAT could not interfere." *per* Phillips J.

  > *D.R. Ellis v. Brighton Co-Operative Society Ltd* [1976] I.R.L.R. 419 at 419, EAT.

- Where an employer made a rule that the employee must live within a reasonable travelling distance of his or her place of work and the individual refused to move when the employer moved the place of work.[79]

- Where the employee refused to work overtime.[80]

- Where a minority of employees refused to accept reductions in terms and conditions which included: reduced holidays, abolished overtime rates, the replacement of a generous sick-pay scheme with statutory sick pay only and a cap on pay levels.[81]

- Where an employee was given notice of dismissal before the decision on the reorganisation of his post had been taken.[82]

- Where a supervisor was deprived of her supervisory role because of possible racial discrimination against her.[83]

- Where seven employees were dismissed for not accepting greatly reduced terms and conditions, although they claimed there was no pressing business reason for the reorganisation.[84] In this case, the EAT reaffirmed the persistent broader approach to contractual variations "perpetrated" by the employer for business reasons, which had developed in the courts since the narrower decision made in *Ellis* (cited above) some 20 years ago:

  > "There is no principle of law that if the new terms of a contract of employment are much less favourable to an employee than the terms of

---

[78] [1976] I.R.L.R. 419, EAT.
[79] *D. M. Farr v. Hoveringham Gravels Ltd Nottingham* [1972] I.R.L.R. 104, EAT.
[80] *Chubb Fire Security Ltd v. Harper* [1983] I.R.L.R. 311, EAT.
[81] *St John of God (Care Services) Ltd v. Brooks and Others* [1992] I.R.L.R. 546, EAT.
[82] *Parkinson v. March Consulting Ltd* [1997] I.R.L.R. 308, CA.
[83] *Leicester University Students' Union v. Mahomed* [1995] I.R.L.R. 292, EAT.
[84] *Catamaran Cruisers Ltd v. Williams and Others* [1994] I.R.L.R. 386, EAT.

the old contract, dismissal of the employee for refusing to accept them will be unfair unless the business reasons are so pressing that it is vital for the survival of the employer's business that the new terms are accepted. Such a proposition is not supported by any of the authorities dealing with the need for business reorganisation. It is a principle of law, however, that the Tribunal must examine the employer's motives for the changes and satisfy itself that they are not sought to be imposed for arbitrary reasons. What has to be carried out is a balancing process." *per* Tudor Evans J.

> *Catamaran Cruisers Ltd v. Williams and Others* [1994] I.R.L.R. 386 at 386, EAT.

It has already been argued that the balancing process referred to in *Catamaran Cruisers* is somewhat one sided, in that although "technically, reasonableness as a statutory test can override contractual obligations" it would have been possible "to treat the contract and collective agreement as establishing minimum rights for employees to be improved upon by the statute."[85] Instead of which, employers have been able to widely use the SOSR defence to impose substantial variations to contracts of employment in the name of business reorganisation. It is perhaps small comfort to note the words of the lay members of the EAT in *Catamaran Crusiers* that "The fact that the authorities show that an employer is not restricted, when offering less attractive terms and conditions of employment, to a situation where the survival of his business is at stake, does not provide an open door to change. The lay members wish to add that the laws governing constructive dismissal still apply and that an employer must demonstrate, under section 57(3) of the Act of 1978[86] that, if he dismisses an employee for failing to accept changed terms and conditions of employment, his action falls within the bounds of reasonableness."[87] The difficulties which the courts continue to have in dealing with contractual variations arising from business reorganisation are well illustrated with redundancies arising from transfers of undertakings. These are considered in Chapter 9, para. 9.5.

8.5   EMPLOYER INSOLVENCY

8.5.1   Insolvency Act 1986

The Insolvency Act 1986 (IA 1986) is the major consolidating enactment dealing with company insolvency and winding up. The IA 1986, s.19 provides for the appointment of a court-appointed administrator whose job it is to try and keep an insolvent company trading. To do this the company will usually need to retain some of its employees. The legislation provides for their protection in such a situation. This is done by providing that the administrator can "adopt" a contract of employment[88] and, when he vacates office,[89] his assumed liability for any debts or sums payable from such

---

[85] S. Anderman, "Unfair Dismissals and Redundancy" in R. Lewis, *Labour Law in Britain* (Blackwell, 1986), p. 424.
[86] Now ERA 1996, s.98(4).
[87] *Catamaran Cruisers Ltd v. Williams and Others* [1994] I.R.L.R. 386, EAT, at para. 23.
[88] IA 1986, s.19(6).
[89] IA 1986, s.19(5).

contracts take priority over other creditor's claims on the company's property.[90] The effect of this is that such sums must be paid out of company property in priority to the administrator's remuneration and expenses. A similar provision applies to out-of-court receivers.[91] A 14-day period of grace is permitted to the administrator in deciding whether to adopt any contracts of employment.[92] The administrator is now only responsible for paying what are termed the "qualifying liabilities" of employees which are the "wages or salary or contribution to an occupational pension scheme,"[93] which arise from the service of the employee after the contract has been adopted.[94]

To avoid the payment of these liabilities, insolvency practitioners[95] adopted the practice of issuing disclaimers following the Act, by writing to employees to indicate that wages would be paid but contracts of employment would not be adopted. In *Powdrill and Atkinson v. Watson and others*[96] the judicial House of Lords reluctantly ruled that on a strict literal interpretation of the words of the statute this practice was unlawful: "on the true construction of the Insolvency Act 1986, s.19 (which relates to administrators) and s.44 (which relates to administrative receivers) gave such employees the right to be paid in full, and in priority to all other creditors, not only for services actually rendered during the administration or receivership but also other payments not referable to such services to which the employees were entitled under their contracts of employment with the company."

This decision meant that adopted employees were entitled to payments in lieu of notice and pensions contributions under the IA 1986, s.19. This can amount to a considerable sum for an administrator to pay if there are hundreds of employees, as there were in *Powdrill,* when deciding whether to sell the business as a going concern. To stem the alarm of many insolvency practitioners in a period of many insolvencies, the Government introduced the Insolvency Act 1994 which amended the 1986 Act so that the liability for payments of continuing employees only applied to services rendered by those employees after the adoption of the contract.[97]

8.5.2   Insolvency Act 1986, Sched. 6 and ERA 1996, Pt XII

Protection for employees whose contracts of employment are terminated because their employer has become insolvent through bankruptcy or liquidation, can be found in the provisions of the IA 1986, Sched. 6, which direct that certain debts are given priority; and in the ERA 1996, ss.182–189 which make provision for the Secretary of State to pay certain debts out of the National Insurance Fund.

The sums recoverable by the employee include wages or salary payable up to four months before the bankruptcy or insolvency, up to a maximum of £800 which is regarded as a preferential debt. Holiday pay, contractual sick pay and statutory sick pay outstanding are also payable. Other payments now regarded as wages and therefore also preferential debts include: guarantee payments,[98] medical suspension

---

[90] IA 1986, s.19(4).
[91] IA 1986, s.44(1)(b).
[92] IA 1986, s.19(6).
[93] IA 1986, s.19(7)(a).
[94] IA 1986, s.19(7)(b).
[95] Under the authority of an unreported decision: *Re Specialised Mouldings Ltd*, February 2, 1987, Ch.D. (I.R.L.B. April 1995).
[96] [1995] I.R.L.R. 269 at 269, HL.
[97] IA 1986, s.19(8) as inserted by the Insolvency Act 1994, ss.1, 5(2), Sched. 2.
[98] ERA 1996, s.28.

payments,[99] maternity suspension payments,[1] and payment due for time-off for: ante-natal care,[2] to look for work[3] and for the carrying out of trade union duties.[4]

If the employee, as a preferred creditor is unable to claim any of the above priority debts he or she may apply in writing to the Secretary of State to recover payment from the National Insurance Fund[5] for debts which may include: arrears of pay,[6] (up to eight weeks); pay owing in lieu of notice[7]; holiday pay[8] up to six weeks in the previous 12 months and any basic award of compensation for unfair dismissal.[9] Any such sums awarded which are based on weekly pay, are subject to a maximum current payment[10] of £210 per week. The rights of the employee who receives such payment are vested in the Secretary of State who becomes a preferential creditor.[11] Such provisions allow an employee to recover, what is for many individuals, a relatively modest proportion of what is owed them by the insolvent employer within a reasonable time period. The scheme is not to be regarded as a "honeypot" however: "The object of the legislation is to provide the liability of the Secretary of State as a last resort, and not as a quick means by which employees can obtain payment, leaving the burden on the Secretary of State to recoup from other persons who may be liable."[12]

8.6 SUMMARY

Writing 12 years ago, at a time when Government economic and social policies were dominated by a free-market ethos which abhorred unnecessary legislative inference with business or trade, Anderman draws attention to what was, even then, seen as the main weakness of the redundancy legislation.[13] The flaw being, that industrial tribunals were not allowed to apply their own test of reasonableness when assessing managerial decisions. They had to apply the test of whether any particular decision fell "within a band of reasonable managerial responses". Further, it was argued, the tribunals were being unrealistically asked to apply an administrative law standard of review, such as that expected of government bodies or of local authorities, to the private decisions of managers in the pursuit of profit, and he observes: "That managerial decisions are not always and automatically efficient". A dictum which has not lost its potency with the passing of time. It can perhaps be seen that, with the increasing globalisation of production and the consequent decrease in job security, the issue of management efficiency versus social equity is still at the centre of the problems associated with this legislation. At the beginning of this chapter, the text outlined the difficulties which the courts have had, over a long period, in merely interpreting the statutory definition of a redundancy now found in the ERA 1996, s.139. These difficulties prompt the question

---

[99] ERA 1996, s.64.
[1] ERA 1996, s.66.
[2] ERA 1996, s.55.
[3] ERA 1996, s.52.
[4] TULRCA 1992, s.168.
[5] ERA 1996, s.182.
[6] ERA 1996, s.184(1)(a).
[7] ERA 1996, s.184(1)(b).
[8] ERA 1996, s.184(1)(c).
[9] ERA 1996, s.184(1)(d).
[10] ERA 1996, s.186.
[11] ERA 1996, s.189.
[12] *Secretary of State for Trade and Industry v. Forde.* [1997] I.R.L.R. 387, EAT.
[13] S. Anderman (1986), p. 444.

of how far the redundancy legislation was designed to help the inutile employee or to promote the overall interests of the employer? This is what Wedderburn has called the judges' dilemma,[14] but it is a dilemma which, with the aid of SOSR, has been predominantly resolved in the employer's favour.

[14] Lord Wedderburn (1986), p. 242.

Chapter 9

TRANSFER OF UNDERTAKINGS

9.1 INTRODUCTION

This is an area of employment law which in the last five years or so, has become increasingly controversial and is the subject of much academic and judicial scrutiny. The key legislative provisions which place obligations on employers to protect employees in the event of a business or undertaking being transferred are:

- The Acquired Rights Directive 77/187 (ARD)

- The Transfer of Undertakings (Protection of Employment) Regulations 1981 (TUPE)

Before 1982, employees had only limited common law protection when their business or other employing organisation was taken over by new employers. Such a takeover fundamentally breaches the employment contract because the employment relationship is essentially viewed as a personal one, and the employee cannot be compelled, in law, to work for a new employer.[1] The common law protection was thus limited to claiming damages for wrongful dismissal which would usually be the recovery of compensation for any contractual notice period not given by the transferring employer.[2] "There is no implied right under a contract of employment enabling an employee to restrain a proposed transfer of the business in which he or she is employed."[3]

Not only was there little that an employee could do to prevent a transfer, there was also no way of ensuring that existing conditions and terms of employment would continue under the new employer. He or she was treated as a new employee with no statutory continuity rights. Only where a transferee took on new employees voluntarily, section 218 of the ERA 1996,[4] provided that there was continuity of employment for certain employee protection measures such as redundancy compensation.[5] This was not the situation in the jurisdiction of other European Community Countries. For over sixty years, French law has provided that all contracts of employment will transfer over

---

[1] *Nokes v. Doncaster Amalgamated Collieries Ltd* [1940] A.C. 1014, 3 All E.R. 549.
[2] *Newns v. British Airways plc* [1992] I.R.L.R. 575, CA.
[3] Scott L.J., in *Newns v. British Airways plc* [1992] I.R.L.R. 575 at 575, CA.
[4] These provisions are originally found in the EPCA 1978, Sched. 13, para. 17.
[5] ERA 1996, s.135.

to the new employer when there is a change in the "juridical situation of the employer, notably as a result of succession, sale, fusion, transformation of the funds and incorporation."[6] This situation changed dramatically with the enactment of the Acquired Rights Directive, otherwise known as Council Directive 77/187[7] on the approximation of the laws of the Member States relating to the safeguarding of employees' rights in the event of transfers of undertakings, businesses or parts of businesses.

The over-riding social purpose of the ARD was to protect individual employment rights at a time of great economic change in Europe. The Directive emerged from the 1974 Social Action Programme of the Council of Ministers, whose object was to relate Community Social policy to the economic integration being pursued.

The Directive obliged Member States of the European Union to introduce national laws which provided protection in **three** main ways:

- First, that employment contracts, including the rights and obligations of employees, be automatically transferred from one employer (the transferor) to another (the transferee) on the date of the transfer.

- Secondly, that there is protection from dismissal as a result of, or for reasons related to the transfer.

- Thirdly, that employers are obliged to inform and consult with employees' representatives before the transfer.

It can be seen that the Directive requires that Member States make provisions to protect individual employment rights within the context of a collective consultative framework. These are only minimum provisions . They do not prevent Member States from introducing stronger provisions within their own domestic laws.[8]

Much case law has arisen from the translation of the Directive's provisions into national laws. To understand how this has come about, an examination of the key provisions of the Directive is required.

9.1.1 The Acquired Rights Directive

Key provisions of the Directive[9]

> **Article 1** directs that the Directive ". . . shall apply to the transfer of an undertaking, business or part of a business to another employer as a result of a legal transfer or merger."[10] providing it ". . . is situated within the territorial scope of the Treaty."[11]
>
> **Article 2** provides specific definitions of "transferor", "transferee" and "representatives of the employees":

---

[6] C. Barnard, *EC Employment Law* (1996), p. 354.
[7] [1997] O.J. L61/26.
[8] Art. 7.
[9] For the full text see *Blackstone's Statutes on Employment Law* (1997–98), p. 418.
[10] Art. 1(1).
[11] Art. 2(2).

"Article 2

For the purposes of this Directive:

  (a) 'transferor' means any natural or legal person who, by reason of a transfer within the meaning of Article 1(1), ceases to be the employer in respect of the undertaking, business or part of the business;

  (b) 'transferee' means any natural or legal person who, by reason of a transfer within the meaning of Article 1(1), becomes the employer in respect of the undertaking, business or part of the business;

  (c) 'representatives of the employees' means the representatives of the employees provided for by the laws or practice of the Member States, with the exception of members of administrative, governing or supervisory bodies of companies who represent employees on such bodies in certain Member States."

Article 3 defines the nature of the employee rights so transferred:

Article 3(1) provides that the transferor's rights arise "from a contract of employment or from an employment relationship existing on the date of a transfer. . ."

Article 3(2) refers to the transfer of terms emanating from a collective agreement and provides that "the transferee shall continue to observe the terms and conditions agreed in any collective agreement on the same terms applicable to the transferor under that agreement, until the date of termination or expiry of the collective agreement or the entry into force or application of another collective agreement." This article also declares that: "Member States may limit the period for observing such terms and conditions, with the proviso that it shall be not be less than one year."

Article 3(3) specifically excludes "employees" rights to old-age, invalidity or survivors' benefits under supplementary company or inter-company pension schemes . . . from the rights and obligations which are protected.

Article 4 contains three key principles:

First, Article 4(1) stipulates that: "The transfer of an undertaking, business or part of a business shall not in itself constitute grounds for dismissal by the transferor or the transferee."

Secondly, Article 4(1) qualifies this principle by further declaring that: "This provision shall not stand in the way of dismissals that may take place for economic, technical or organisational reasons[12] entailing changes in the workforce."

Thirdly, Article 4(2) provides that: "If the contract of employment or the employment relationship is terminated because the transfer . . . involves a substantial change in working conditions to the detriment of the employee, the employer shall be regarded as having been responsible for termination of the contract of employment or of the employment relationship."

Articles 5 and 6 declare that Member States should make provision for employers to continue to recognise employee representatives "If the business preserves its autonomy . . ."[13] and to inform and to consult with representatives of the employees.

---

[12] ETO reasons.
[13] Art. 5(1).

The transferor must give this information "in good time before the transfer is carried out."

The transferee must also give this information "in good time" but also "in any event before his employees are directly affected by the transfer as regards their conditions of work and employment."

Article 6(2) provides that the object of such consultation is to try and reach agreement on the transfer arrangements: "If the transferor or the transferee envisages measures in relation to his employees, he shall consult his representatives of the employees in good time on such measures with a view to seeking agreement."

The bald wording of the Directive's provisions summarised above, perhaps hide the sea-change which would be required in employment law in the U.K. to accommodate the requirements of the ARD. It has been suggested that the approach of the ARD was to "recognise the interests of employees in changes of ownership or control of the enterprises employing them." These interests could be pursued in a narrow way such as maintaining an employee's existing rights on transfer, or promulgated in a much broader fashion, by giving the employee an influence in deciding whether the transfer went ahead and on what conditions.[14] Both approaches were unfamiliar to individual and collective labour law in the United Kingdom. With the individual employment relationship based largely upon principles of contract law and also "regulated" by the laissez-faire system of collective bargaining, the Directive appeared to run counter to British traditions of determining terms and conditions of work. Nevertheless, draft regulations to implement the Directive were made by a Labour Government in 1978 and the final regulations were promulgated by a Conservative Government in 1981.

The regulations were implemented reluctantly by the government as they appeared to impose restrictions on the free movement of capital and on the freedom of contract.[15] Such developments did not sit easily with the government's free-market economic policies then being pursued. These aimed at introducing more flexibility into the labour market. It has also been noted, that this United Kingdom Government were instrumental, with some other European countries, in ensuring that the Directive did not apply to takeovers and mergers arising from the transfer of share ownership. A method of transfer which is most common in the United Kingdom. In discussions to extend the coverage of the Directive, some twenty years later, a Labour Government was also opposing the inclusion of share transfers (see: section 9.9 below).

9.1.2   The Transfer of Undertakings (Protection of Employment) Regulations 1981

An overview of the TUPE Regulations is now given.[16] This is followed by consideration of the extensive case law to which it has given rise.

---

[14] P. Davies & M. Freedland *Labour Legislation and Public Policy* (1993), p. 578.

[15] *ibid.*, p. 579.

[16] A general guide to the TUPE Regulations and to the 1993 and 1995 amendments, (discussed later in the text) can be found in advice published by the DTI. *Employment Rights On The Transfer Of An Undertaking* P.L. 699 (Rev 3) August 1997.

Key to TUPE Regulations
  reg. 2 Interpretation
  reg. 3 Relevant transfer
  reg. 4 Receivers and liquidators
  reg. 5 Effect on employment contract
  reg. 6 Effect on collective agreements
  reg. 7 Exclusion of pension schemes
  reg. 8 Unfair Dismissal and ETO
  reg. 9 Effect on trade union recognition
  reg. 10 Duty to inform & consult representatives
  reg. 11 Failure to inform or consult
  reg. 12 Restriction on contracting out

Key provisions of TUPE Regulations[17]

Regulation 2(1) : defines terms used in the Regulations including: "collective agreement"; "collective bargaining"; "contract of employment" and "employee". The first two definitions have the same meaning as in TULRCA 1992, s.178(1) but the last two differ slightly from the TULRCA formulations: The regulation 2(1) definition of "contract of employment" is given as "any agreement between an employee and his employer determining the terms and conditions of his employment." This is arguably wider than the TULRCA 1992, s.295(1) definition which is given as "a contract of service or of apprenticeship."

The regulation 2(1) definition of "employee" is given as: "any individual who works for another person whether under a contract of service or apprenticeship or otherwise but does not include anyone who provides services under a contract for services." It can be argued that this definition is more precise than the corresponding TULRCA 1992, s.295(1) formulation which defines "employee" as "an individual who has entered into or works under (or, where the employment has ceased, worked under) a contract of employment. . ." The TUPE definition makes clear that it is only employees working under a contract of service, and not self-employed workers who are covered by the regulations.

Regulation 2(1): also defines an "undertaking" as including "any trade or business".

Regulation 2(2): defines transfers of "part of an undertaking" as "references to a transfer of a part which is being transferred as a business. . ."

Regulation 2(3): defines representatives of a recognised trade union as "an official or other person authorised to carry on collective bargaining with the employer by that union."

Regulation 3: defines a "relevant transfer". Regulation 3(1) provides that the regulations apply "to a transfer from one person to another of an undertaking situated immediately before the transfer in the United Kingdom or a part of one which is so situated."

Regulation 3(4): indicates that such a transfer may take place "by a series of two or more transactions" and "whether or not any property is transferred to the transferee by the transferor."

Regulation 4(1): concerns transfers by receivers and liquidators. It provides that where the receiver of a property of a company or the administrator appointed under the Insolvency Act 1986 transfers the undertaking or part of it:

---

[17] For the full text see *Blackstone's Statutes on Employment Law* (1997–98), p. 318.

"the transfer shall for the purposes of these Regulations be deemed not to have been effected until immediately before—

(a) the transferee company ceases (otherwise than by reason of its being wound up) to be a wholly owned subsidiary of the transferor company; or

(b) the relevant undertaking is transferred by the transferee company to another person;

whichever first occurs.."

Regulation 5(1): concerns the effects of a relevant transfer on contracts of employment. It provides that the transfer does not terminate the contract of employment with the transferor, but has the effect, after the transfer, of having been "originally made between the person so employed and the transferee. This has become known as the 'automatic transfer principle."

Regulation 5(2)(a): provides that "all the transferor's rights, powers, duties and liabilities under or in connection with any such contract, shall be transferred by virtue of this regulation to the transferee";

Regulation 5(2)(b): further provides that "anything done before the transfer is completed by or in relation to the transferor in respect of that contract or a person employed in that undertaking or part shall be deemed to have been done by or in relation to the transferee."

Regulation 5(3): stipulates that an employee must be employed in the undertaking or the part of it transferred "immediately" before the transfer takes place or before a series of two or more transactions which constitute the transfer.

Regulation 5(4A): Permits an employee to object to becoming employed by the transferee. If he does so, his contract does not transfer and under **regulation 5(4B)** the objection acts "so as to terminate his contract of employment with the transferor." This latter regulation also provides that such a termination is not a dismissal by the transferor.

Regulation 5(5): does, however, permit an employee to terminate his contract of employment "without notice if a substantial change is made in his working conditions to his detriment; but no such right shall arise by reason only that. . .the identity of his employer changes unless the employee shows that, in all the circumstances, the change is a significant change and is to his detriment."

Regulation 6: Provides that collective agreements made by recognised trade unions with the transferor and in existence at the time of the relevant transfer, shall have the same effect with the transferee. **Regulation 6(a)** also refers to the statutory presumption of the unenforceability of collective agreements. These provisions are now contained in TULRCA 1992, ss.179–180.

Regulation 7: operates to exclude occupational pension schemes from being transferred.

Regulation 8: deals with dismissal because of a relevant transfer and contains two key provisions. First, **regulation 8(1)** provides that if: "any employee of the transferor or transferee is dismissed, that employee shall be treated . . . as unfairly dismissed if the transfer or a reason connected with it is the reason or principal reason for his dismissal." The regulation refers to Part V of the EPCA 1978 as the statutory authority applying to this regulation. This authority now derives from Part X of the ERA 1996, s.94(1) which gives an employee the right not to be unfairly dismissed by his employer.

Secondly, **regulation 8(2)** provides that regulation 8(1) does not apply in a situation: "Where an economic, technical or organisational reason entailing changes in the workforce of either the transferor or the transferee before or after a relevant transfer is the reason or principal reason for dismissing the employee." This has become known as an ETO reason and under the provisions of ERA 1996, s.98(1)(b) constitutes a fair dismissal because it is a, "substantial reason of a kind such as to justify the dismissal of an employee" known as an SOSR dismissal.

Regulation 8(3): states that this regulation applies to employees: "employed in the undertaking or part of the undertaking transferred or to be transferred."

Regulation 8(5)(a): deems that the unfair dismissal provisions referred to in regulation 8(1) do not apply if the employees come within the statutory excluded classes of employment, for example, employees on fixed-term contracts or mariners, described in what was EPCA 1978, ss.141–149, but now found in ERA 1996, ss.196–201. This regulation determines that employees engaged in unoffical and other industrial action are also excluded from the unfair dismissal protections of regulation 8(1)(1), by virtue of TULRCA 1992, ss.237–238.

Regulation 9(1): provides for the continuance of trade union recognition after a relevant transfer where "the undertaking or part of the undertaking transferred maintains an identity distinct from the remainder of the transferee's undertaking." Providing that the transferor recognised "an independent trade union . . . to any extent" in respect of the employees so transferred, **regulation 9(2)(a)** directs that "the union shall be deemed to have been recognised by the transferee to the same extent in respect of employees of that description so employed. . . ."

Regulations 10 and 11: refer to the employers' (transferor's and transferee's) duty to inform and to consult with "appropriate representatives" of "affected employees". These regulations are particularly detailed in their requirements and include amendments made to TULRCA 1992, s.188 by the Collective Redundancies and Transfer of Undertakings (Protection of Employment) (Amendment) Regulations 1995 after the European Commission took the United Kingdom to the European Court for allegedly breaching the ARD.[18] In these infringement proceedings it was argued by the Commission that the Directive was not fully transposed into domestic law because the legislation only permitted consultation with employees' representatives where there was a recognised trade union *in situ*. The amended section 188 provisions and the amended TUPE, reg. 10 now provide for representation where trade unions are not present, although there have been legal challenges from the trade unions themselves as to the adequacy of these arrangements.[19]

The key provisions of **regulation 10**: duty to inform and consult representatives, are as follows:

Regulation 10(1): Defines "affected employees" as those employees of the transferor or transferee who may or may not be "employed in the undertaking or part of the undertaking to be transferred" but "who may be affected by the transfer or may be affected by measures taken in connection with it. . ." Thus it is not only employees who are directly affected who need to be consulted but any individuals who may be affected by the transfer.

Regulation 10(2): outlines the form and purpose of the consultation: the employer has to consult with the "appropriate representatives" of the "affected employees". He has to do this "long enough before a relevant transfer" to inform them when the transfer is to take place and the reasons for it. He also has to inform the

---

[18] Cases C–382/92 and C–383/92 *Commission v. U.K.*
[19] *R. v. Secretary of State For Trade and Industry ex p. Unison* [1996] I.R.L.R. 438, DC. See also para. 8.3.3.1 in the main text for discussion of this case.

representatives of "the legal, economic and social implications of the transfer". The measures pertaining to the contractual arrangements of the employees so affected by the transfer have also to be explained.

Regulation 10(2)(a): defines "appropriate representatives of any employees" as:

- "employee representatives elected by them;" or
- representatives of a recognised trade union, or
- where both are present, the employer may choose which representatives to consult.

Regulations 10(3); 10(4); 10(5); 10(6) and 10(6A): refer to how the information should be given to "appropriate representatives". Such information has to be given "at such a time" as will enable the transferor to give information about the measures envisaged. This information may be given directly to the representatives or posted to them or to a trade union headquarters. An employer who envisages taking measures in connection with the transfer "shall consult all persons who are appropriate representatives of the affected employees". This must be done "with a view to seeking their agreement to measures to be taken". The employer must then consider their representations, reply to them and explain why he has rejected any suggestions made. Accommodation and other facilities "as may be appropriate" have to be given to the representatives.

Regulation 10(7): provides that "if there are special circumstances" which make it "not reasonably practical" for the employer to comply with the consultation requirements of regulation 10 "he shall take all steps towards performing that duty as are reasonably practicable in the circumstances".

Regulation 10(8): refers to the employer having complied with the consultation requirements providing that he "has invited any of the affected employees to elect employee representatives, and the invitation was issued long enough under paragraph (2) above to allow them to elect representatives by that time. . ." Paragraph 10(2) stipulates that an employer has to consult with representatives about a relevant transfer "long enough before a relevant transfer" to give the information as specified in this paragraph. Under 10(8) this information has to be given "as soon as is reasonably practicable after the election of the representatives".

Regulation 11: provides remedies for failure to consult or inform. Essentially, a complaint maybe made by an employee representative, a trade union or an affected employee to an industrial tribunal that an employer has failed to comply with the requirements of regulation 10. Under regulation 11(3) it is not a defence for an employer to claim that it was not "reasonably practicable" to inform and consult because the transferee had not given him the requisite information, "unless he gives the transferee notice of his intention to show that fact; and the giving of the notice shall make the transferee a party to the proceedings." If the industrial tribunal finds the complaint well-founded, the employer can be ordered to pay "appropriate compensation" to a maximum of four week's pay.

Regulation 11(A): construes references to employee representatives for consultation purposes as either:

- employees elected for the specific purpose of receiving information about the transfer; or
- employees elected for another purpose, but for which it would also be appropriate for the employer to consult with them about the transfer.

Regulation 12: provides that any provisions in an agreement which preclude or limit the operation of regulations 5, 8, 10 or 11 are void.

9.2 WHO HAS TO BE CONSULTED?

Consideration is now given to the somewhat limited, albeit controversial, case law on transfer consultations arising from the TUPE, regs (10) & (11) which are outlined in Section 9.1.2 above. The focus is on:

- the overall purpose of consultation;
- who has to be consulted;
- when does consultation have to begin;
- what specific information has to be discussed;
- the difference between information giving and consultation;
- the remedies for non-compliance; and
- future proposals on consultation.

9.2.1 The overall purpose of consultation

Cavalier[20] maintains that the social policy reflected by ARD is clear: "A change of employer caused by a transfer or merger may be economically desirable, but the rights of employees cannot be sacrificed to economic considerations. Change must be handled in a consensual manner." He elaborates: "Management retains the ultimate decision making power, but this must be exercised in a manner which takes into account the rights of employees and the role of employee representatives." These consultation rights, have been the subject of a trade union challenge in the courts.[21] (See Chapter 8, para. 8.3.3.1. on economic dismissals). In addition, following a European Union Commission challenge in the ECJ they have also been amended by the Collective Redundancies and Transfer of Undertakings (Protection of Employment) (Amendment) Regulations 1995.[22]

9.2.2 Who has to be consulted?

The "appropriate representatives"[23] of the "affected"[24] employees of either the transferor or the transferee have to be consulted by the employer "long enough"[25] before the transfer itself. The amended TUPE, reg. 10 lays down specific criteria for the consultation of employee representatives:

- They have to be representatives of the "affected employees" who are defined as those employees of the transferor or the transferee who may be affected by the transfer.

---

[20] S. Cavalier *Transfer Rights: TUPE in Perspective, Institute of Employment Rights* (1997), p. 49.
[21] *R. v. Secretary of State For Trade and Industry, ex p. Unison* [1996] I.R.L.R. 438, DC.
[22] Cases C–82/92 and C–383/92 *Commission v. U.K.*
[23] TUPE reg. 10(2A).
[24] *ibid.*, (1).
[25] *ibid.*, (2).

- The employee representatives must be "appropriate representatives"[26] either elected by the affected employees for the specific purpose of consultation with the employer on the transfer; or appointed by a recognised trade union; or selected by the employer from either of the former categories, or from a committee of employees not set up primarily for this purpose but which may be appropriate for consultation about the transfer.

Government guidance on how elections for appropriate representatives should be conducted advises employers that they should consider: the categories of employees who may be affected, the balance between employee groups, and the giving of sufficient time to employees to nominate and elect their candidates.[27] Cavalier considers that this advice "provides considerable scope for challenging elections conducted by employers. Employers are left exposed by the legislation. They are not told how to conduct an election or what will satisfy the legal requirements. They are told what they must consider, but not how to achieve it."[28]

If the employer chooses to negotiate with those trade union representatives whom he recognises for collective bargaining purposes[29] it is irrelevant that some of the employees affected may not be union members:

> "The statutory obligation on an employer to consult a trade union relates to an employee of a description or category in respect of which the union is recognised, whether or not that employee is a member of that particular union. It is clear that in the phrase 'an employee of a description in respect of which a trade union is recognised by him', the words 'of a description' refer to a category of employee. To construe those words as referring to an employee who is a member of the trade union which is to be consulted would be to give the paragraph a meaning which it does not bear and would necessitate the inclusion of additional words. Had Parliament intended to limit the requirement to consult to a case where the employee was a member of the recognised union, it would have been simple to state that in clear terms." *per* Sir Brian Hutton L.C.J.

> *Governing body of the Northern Ireland Hotel and Catering College and North Eastern Education and Library Board v. National Association of Teachers in Further and Higher Education* [1995] I.R.L.R. 83 at 83, NICA.

9.2.3 When does consultation have to begin?

TUPE, Reg. 10(5) requires that an employer consult appropriate representatives and seek their agreement if he envisages taking measures which will affect employees. It is maintained by Cavalier[30] that such consultation must be genuine and should take place long enough before the transfer to allow the representatives to influence the outcome. His authority for this however, is not a transfer of undertaking's case but a classic redundancy case where the President of the Board of Trade and the National Coal Board were prevented from implementing colliery closures and employee redundancies by a declaration of the High Court until a contractual consultation procedure was

---

[26] *ibid.*, (2A).
[27] DTI, *Revised arrangements for consultation about redundancies and business transfers* (1995).
[28] S. Cavalier (1997), p. 58.
[29] TULRCA 1992, s.178(3).
[30] *op. cit.* 1997 s.53.

introduced which allowed the unions "a proper opportunity to comment and object."[31] But as Smith and Thomas have observed[32] the statutory provisions relating to the timing of redundancy consultation are much stronger than their TUPE equivalents. TULRCA, s.188(1) requires 30 to 90 days redundancy consultation "when the employer is proposing to dismiss". This can be compared with TUPE, reg. 10(8)(b) which stipulates only that information be given "as soon as is reasonably practical after the election of the representatives".

An application to an Industrial Tribunal that there has been a failure to inform or consult may be made before a transfer has taken place.[33] UNISON made an application, two weeks before the actual transfer of their members to an NHS Trust, that their representatives had not been properly informed or consulted. The first written notification to union shop stewards that a trust was to be created on the April 1, 1994 had occurred on February 7. Two weeks before the actual transfer date the union made a complaint under TUPE, reg, 11(8) that there had been a failure to consult. The EAT upheld the decision of the Industrial Tribunal that there had been insufficient consultation:

> "The union's application could not be regarded as premature. The ordinary and natural meaning of reg. 11(8), which provides that a tribunal shall not consider a complaint unless it is presented 'before the end of the period of three months beginning with . . . the date on which the relevant transfer is completed', is that it is a limitation provision which specifies an end date for the presentation of a complaint to the tribunal.
>
> The regulation does not specify a start date or prohibit an industrial tribunal from considering a complaint presented to the tribunal before any particular date." *per* Mummery J.

UNISON v. South Durham Health Authority [1995] I.R.L.R. 407 at 407, EAT; [1995] I.C.R. 495.

9.2.4 What specific information has to be discussed?

Information should be given to the employee representatives, either directly or indirectly,[34] long enough before the transfer itself,[35] to inform them when the transfer is to take place and the reasons for it.[36] This information has to be given as soon as is reasonably practicable after the election of the representatives.[37] The obligation to inform arises when only one employee is affected, there is no threshold of 20 employees as with redundancy consultation.[38]

9.2.5 The difference between information giving and consultation

The employer only has a statutory duty to consult with appropriate representatives about any measures he envisages taking in respect of affected employees.[39] Any change

[31] *R. v. British Coal ex p. Vardy* [1996] I.R.L.R. 438, DC.
[32] I.T. Smith & G. Thomas, (1996), p. 63.
[33] *UNISON v. South Durham Health Authority* [1995] I.R.L.R. 407, EAT.
[34] TUPE, reg. 10(4).
[35] *ibid.*, (2).
[36] *ibid.*, (a).
[37] *ibid.*, (8).
[38] TULRCA 1992, s.188(1).
[39] TUPE, reg. 10(5).

proposed to be made by the transferee in the contractual arrangements[40] affecting the employees has to be explained to the representatives by the transferor. This has to be done with a view to seeking agreement about the arrangements for the transfer.[41] The employer must consider any representations made by the representatives,[42] reply to them and if he has rejected any suggestions made by them he must also explain why he has done so.[43]

Information about the legal, economic and social implications of the transfer also has to be given to the representatives.[44]

If special circumstances[45] prevent the employer complying with these requirements he should do all that is reasonably practicable in the circumstances. This may be difficult in a situation where, for example, a local authority invites contractors to re-tender for a council service, but is in no position to give information to appropriate representatives on the type or number of jobs proposed, until the tender document has been received. If the contract is then awarded to another contractor, the outgoing contractor is dependant on securing information from another competitor.[46] In *Dines v. Initial and Pall Mall*[47] the Court of Appeal decided that where a health authority had awarded its hospital cleaning contract to another contractor there had been a transfer and for the purposes of the Regulations it: ". . . took place in two phases: (a) the handing back by the first respondents to the health authority of the cleaning services at the hospital and (b) the handing over by the health authority of the cleaning services to the second respondents on the following day." Cavalier maintains that because in this case it was found that the health authority "operated as transferee and then transferor and momentarily became the employer of the workers transferred" they were under an obligation "to inform, and potentially consult representatives of the employees concerned."[48] The consultation obligation arises where the transferor envisages that the transferee will be taking measures relating to the contract of employment.[49] The EU Commission's current proposals "would also introduce a provision preventing employers from seeking to excuse failure to inform and consult by blamimg lack of information from a controlling undertaking (as in its original proposal, and in line with provisions in the Collective Redundancies Directive) or from any natural or legal person."[50]

9.2.6 The remedies for non-compliance

The requirement to consult is not dependant on an actual transfer taking place.[51] Once a transfer is proposed there are the remedies of declaration[52] and compensation[53]

[40] *ibid.*, (2)(d).
[41] *ibid.*, (5).
[42] *ibid.*, (6)(a).
[43] *ibid.*, (b).
[44] *ibid.*, (2)(b).
[45] *ibid.*, (7).
[46] S. Cavalier (1997), p. 52.
[47] [1994] I.R.L.R. 336, CA.
[48] S. Cavalier 1997, p. 52.
[49] TUPE, reg. 10(2)(d).
[50] DTI Employment Rights Directorate, *European Acquired Rights Directive And Transfer Of Undertakings (Protection Of Employment) Regulations 1981 Public Consultation* (1997), para. 43.
[51] *BIFU v. Barclays Bank PLC* [1987] I.C.R. 495, EAT.
[52] TUPE, reg. 11(4).
[53] *ibid.*, (11).

to a maximum of four weeks' pay, available to employees who should have been consulted but were not:

> "The purpose of regulation 10(2) is to ensure that before a transfer there is information and consultation. Regulation 11(1) says that if the employer fails to inform or consult in accordance with regulation 10, a complaint may be presented. The two alternative time limits reinforce the argument that the transfer is not an essential element because it would not then be necessary to refer to regulation 11(8)(b), *i.e.*, the date of the tribunal order. The suggestion that compensation cannot be calculated until there has been a transfer is dealt with by regulation 11(4) which does not require compensation to be ordered but simply entitles a tribunal to make a declaration." *per* Popplewell J.
>
> *BIFU v. Barclays Bank PLC & others* [1987] I.C.R. 495, EAT.

This complaint may be presented to an industrial tribunal by employee representatives,[54] trade union representatives[55] or by affected employees.[56] Representatives have to be "appropriate" but there appears to be no right by an individual employee[57] to bring an action.[58]

A claim for compensation for non-compliance with the consultation requirements should be made either within three months of the transfer itself[59] or within three months of the declaration.[60] Some discretion is given to the industrial tribunal to consider a case outside these time limits "where it is satisfied that it was not reasonably practicable for the complaint to be presented before the end of the period of three months."[61]

Statutory protection against employer victimisation of employee representatives, that is "the right not to be subject to any detriment" is given by ERA 1996, s.47, but it can be argued that these provisions does not protect an employee for taking part in the election of the representatives.[62] Government concern about the adequacy of the information and consultation arrangements and in particular whether they still complied with the ARD was expressed in a public consultation document which appeared in February 1998 and is discussed below.

9.2.7 Future proposals on consultation

European Commission action against the United Kingdom on the consultation aspect of the Regulations, specifically the election of representatives independently of the employer was stayed after the May 1997 election of a Labour Government committed to reform. Before the anticipated White Paper in the Spring of 1998, the Government published a consultation document on the provision of information to and consultation with, employees' representatives on collective redundancies and transfers of undertakings.[63] The starting point for the Government was "that the provisions still do not

---

[54] TUPE, reg. 11(1)(a).
[55] *ibid.*, (b).
[56] *ibid.*, (c).
[57] S. Cavalier (1997), p. 63.
[58] *Keane v. Clerical Medical Investment Group Ltd*, IT, Bristol, June 19, 1997 (IDS Brief 595).
[59] TUPE reg. 11(8)(a).
[60] *ibid.*, reg. (8)(b).
[61] *ibid.*, reg. (8)(b).
[62] S. Cavalier (1997), p. 59.
[63] DTI Employee Relations Directorate (February 1998), *Employees' Information And Consultation Rights On Transfers Of Undertakings And Collective Redundancies, Public Consultation*, URN 97/988.

provide a clear and satisfactory framework for the necessary information and consultation."[64] The consultation document referred to the confusion and complexity illustrated by the 600 or so applications to industrial tribunals made under provisions arising from the 1995 Amending Regulations. It was further considered that TUPE still did not provide an adequate framework within European law because:

1. The employers could select with whom they would consult.
2. There was inadequate provision for the election of representatives.
3. There was criticism of the level of sanctions available.

The main changes[65] proposed by the Government included:

- A legal obligation on employers to inform and consult with representatives of any recognised trade union who were already involved in bargaining on behalf of the affected workers. Only in a situation where there were no such existing bargaining arrangements would employers be permitted to deal with appropriate representatives of the employees. This proposal would take away the existing right of the employer to choose between union representatives and elected representatives of the affected workers.[66]

- A requirement that non-union representatives be capable and independent. Their independence being established by a secret ballot of the affected workforce.

- Where employees do not take up the employer's invitation to appoint representatives, the employer will discharge his information and consultation responsibilities by giving that information he would have made available to elected representatives, directly to the affected employees instead.

- Reasonable paid time off for the training of union officials in handling information and consultation requests was to be extended to "other employee representatives involved in this activity."

- In the event that a complaint is made to an industrial tribunal that the consultation conditions have not been met it was proposed that "it shall be for the employer to prove to an industrial tribunal that, if existing employee arrangements were used, the employee representatives were both capable and independent, or if representatives were specially elected, that all the election conditions were met."

- The compensation for non-compliance with the information and consultation requirements on transfers of undertakings was to be brought in line with that for redundancy consultation and increased to a maximum of 90 days' pay per affected employee.

The most important change proposed, was the removal of the employer's right to choose with whom he would consult. Where a trade union was already recognised for

---

[64] DTI Employee Relations Directorate (February 1998), *Employees' Information And Consultation Rights On Transfers Of Undertakings And Collective Redundancies, Public Consultation*, URN 97/988, para. 1.
[65] *ibid.*, para. 6.
[66] TUPE, reg. 10(2A).

collective bargaining purposes, he would now have to consult with their representatives. In addition, where there was a complaint to an industrial tribunal about the employer's non-compliance with the information and consultation regulations, the burden of proof was now placed on the employer to demonstrate that he had met all the election conditions required for the election of capable and independent representatives. It could be argued that these proposed changes would strengthen the TUPE consultation regulations by bringing them more into line with the requirement of Article 6(2) ARD which provides that "the object of such consultation is to try and reach agreement on the transfer arrangements." Such agreement, it is submitted, is only likely to come from truly independent and capable representatives. At the time of writing the Government was still consulting about its proposals.[67]

9.3 IS THERE A TRANSFER?

9.3.1 Definition of a transfer

What is the definition of "a legal transfer or merger"? The starting point is TUPE, reg. 3 which refers to "a transfer from one person to another"[68] of an undertaking or part of an undertaking in a series of two or more transactions irrespective of whether property is transferred.[69] Judicial interpretation of this particular regulation has also been the subject of much litigation and controversy in the domestic and European courts.

A transfer of ownership is not required. Neither does there have to be a legal or contractual relationship between transferor and transferee. It is the change of employer which is crucial:

> "The objective of the Directive is to safeguard as far as possible the rights of workers in the event of a change of employer by allowing them to remain in the employment of the new employer on the same conditions as those agreed with the transferor."

> Case C–287/8 *Landsorganisation I Danmark v. NY Molle Kro* [1989] I.R.L.R. 37 at 38, ECJ.

In *Landsorganisation I Danmark v. NY Molle Kro* the employer was the leasee of a tavern whose lease was rescinded by the owner who took over the business. The ECJ ruled "that insofar as the managing lessee acquires under the lease the capacity of employer, the transfer must be considered as a transfer of an undertaking to another employer as a result of a legal transfer within the meaning of Article 1(1)."[70]

9.3.2 Retention of economic identity

Providing that the economic unit retains its identity, the transfer of a lease to a third party will also be considered a transfer of an undertaking under Article 1(1), ARD. In

---

[67] Public responses were being received by the DTI up to April 9, 1998.
[68] TUPE, reg. 3(1).
[69] *ibid.*, (4).
[70] [1989] I.R.L.R. 37 at 38, ECJ.

Foreningen Af Arbejdsledere i Danmark v. Daddys Dance Hall[71] the same catering staff were employed during the time that a lease was transferred by the owners of the property from one employer to another. The new lessee immediately re-employed the staff who had been given notice by their employer: the previous lessee, but who had not yet left their jobs. The ECJ ruled "that when the lessee who has the capacity of proprietor of the undertaking at the termination of the lease loses this capacity and a third person acquires it under a new lease concluded with the owner, the resulting operation is capable of falling within the scope of application of the Directive, as defined in Article 1(1)."[72] This principle was reaffirmed by the ECJ in *P Bork International A/S v. Foreningen of Arbejdsledere i Danmark*.[73]

In *Berg and Busschers v. Besselsen*[74] An employer who purchased a bar by instalments and was forced to return it to its former owner, before full ownership of the business was transferred, was also held to be in a contractual relationship with his former employees and liable to pay their salary arrears. This decision emphasises that it is the change of the employer in an undertaking, and not the change of ownership of the undertaking which triggers the rights and obligations arising from the Directive:

> "As the Court considered in its judgment of December 17, 1987 (case 207/86, *Ny Molle Kro* [1989] I.R.L.R. 37) Directive 77/187 applies as soon as, because of a transfer as a result of a contractual agreement or merger, a change occurs of the natural or legal person operating the undertaking who, in that capacity, has obligations vis-à-vis the employees employed in the undertaking, and that it is of no importance whether the ownership of the undertaking has been transferred."

> Case C–144/87 *Berg and Busschers v. Besselsen* [1989] I.R.L.R. 447 at 450, para. 18, ECJ.

Whether the switching of public subsidies from one legal person to another constituted a transfer was the question addressed by the ECJ in Dr Sophie Redmond Stichting v. Bartol and others.[75] Here, local authority funding for a drugs rehabilitation project was transferred from one organisation: the Dr Sophie Redmond foundation to another: the Sigma foundation. Some of the staff, clients/patients, equipment and the lease on a building were also taken on by the new employer from the Redmond foundation. Despite the fact that there was no agreement between the three parties concerned and that all aspects of the identity of the undertaking had not been retained, for example the "Sigma foundation did not target Surinamese or Antillean drug dependants or provide a recreational facility", the ECJ decided that the Directive did apply. This was because Article 1(1) applies to "the transfer of an undertaking, business or part of a business." It did not matter that this was not within the context of a commercial or business transfer or that only part of the undertaking was transferred. "The decisive criterion for establishing whether there is a transfer of an undertaking within the meaning of Directive 77/187 is whether the unit in question retains its identity."[76] No one factor was necessarily decisive in deciding whether the identity of the undertaking was retained. In *Redmond*[77] the ECJ approved criteria it had already established in

[71] Case 234/86 *Foreningen Af Arbejdsledere i Danmark v. Daddy's Dance Hall A/S* I.R.L.R. [1988] 315, ECJ.
[72] [1988] I.R.L.R. 315, ECJ.
[73] *P Bork International A/S* (in liquidation) *v. Foreningen of Arbejdsledere i Danmark* [1989] I.R.L.R. 41, ECJ.
[74] [1989] I.R.L.R. 447, ECJ.
[75] [1992] I.R.L.R. 366, ECJ.
[76] [1992] I.R.L.R. 367, ECJ.
[77] [1992] I.R.L.R. 372 para. 12, ECJ.

Spijkers International A/S v. Foreningen of Arbejdsledere i Danmark and in *Ny Molle Kro* for examining whether the identity had been retained. These criteria have become known as the "Spijkers Principles."

9.3.3 *Spijkers* Principles

"it is necessary to consider all the facts characterising the transaction in question, including the type of undertaking or business, whether or not the business's tangible assets, such as buildings and movable property are transferred, the value of its intangible assets at the time of the transfer, whether or not the majority of its employees are taken over by the employer, whether or not its customers are transferred and the degree of similarity between the activities carried on before and after the transfer and the period, if any, for which those activities were suspended. It should be noted, however, that all those circumstances are merely single factors in the overall assessment which must be made and cannot therefore be considered in isolation."

Spijkers v. Gebroeders Benedik Abbatoir CV Case 24/85 [1986] 2 C.M.L.R. 296; [1986] 3 E.C.R. 1119, ECJ at para. 13.

What was thought to be the broad scope of the Directive was confirmed by subsequent decisions of the ECJ which determined that it applied to a situation where undertakings or businesses contracted out parts of their functions or services:

"The decisions of the European Court of Justice demonstrate that the fact that another company takes over the provision of certain services as a result of competitive tendering does not mean that the first business or undertaking necessarily comes to an end. Moreover, as was pointed out in the decision in Daddy's Dance Hall and elsewhere, a transfer may take place in two phases.

In the present case, as the cleaning services were to be carried out by essentially the same labour force on the same premises and for the same health authority, there was a transfer of an undertaking for the purpose of the Regulations, which took place in two phases: (a) the handing back by the first respondents to the health authority of the cleaning services at the hospital and (b) the handing over by the health authority of the cleaning services to the second respondents on the following day." *per* Neil L.J.

Dines v. Initial Health Care Services Ltd and *Pall Mall Services Group Ltd* [1994] I.R.L.R. 336 at 337, CA; [1995] I.C.R. 11.

9.3.4 Contracting out

Competitive tendering was an issue of concern to the Conservative Government of the late 1980s which, as part of a policy of reducing public expenditure, had embarked on a programme of contracting out of services in the public sector.[78] It was argued that the introduction of a statutory prohibition on the insertion of union recognition clauses into tender invitations[79] now inhibited[80] local authorities from protecting the terms and

---

[78] Local Government Act 1988.
[79] now; TULRCA 1992, s.145.
[80] For example, trade unions not recognised by contractors would be unable to consult over new terms and conditions imposed by the new employers.

conditions of their contracted out employees. However the government reluctantly introduced the TUPE Regulations into domestic law in 1981[81] in order to comply with European Law.[82] Article 2(1) of the new Regulations limited the definition of an undertaking to "any trade or business but does not include any undertaking or part of an undertaking which is not in the nature of a commercial venture." There was no such qualification in the wording of Article 1, ARD and the ECJ decisions in *Redmond* and in *Rask*[83] confirmed that the contracting out of services, even where incidental to the main business of the undertaking, such as canteen services, were covered by the ARD.

Counsel for the defendant canteen subcontractors in *Rask and Christensen v. ISS Kantineservice A/S* sought a narrower interpretation of the Directive submitting: ". . . that too broad an interpretation of the concept of an undertaking would damage the encouragement for privatisation or for the subcontracting of certain public services desired by the Commission."[84] In this case, the defendant transferees were arguing that there was no transfer because the economic assets and control of the canteen services were not fully transferred to them as sub-contractors. The ECJ however, considered that the "identity" test was more important:

> "The decisive criterion for establishing whether there is a transfer of an undertaking within the meaning of Article 1(1) of EEC Directive 77/187 is whether the business in question retains its identity, as would be indicated, in particular, by the fact that its operation was either continued or resumed." *per* M. Zuleeg POC

> Case C–208/81 *Rask and Christensen v. ISS Kantineservice A/S* [1993] I.R.L.R. 133 at 134, ECJ.

The ECJ decision in *Rask* affirmed the submission of the European Commission that:

> ". . . the Directive is applicable wherever, in the context of contractual relations, there is a change in the legal or natural person who is responsible for carrying on the business and who incurs the obligations of an employer towards the employees of the undertaking. Thus, whether an agreement such as in the present case fell within the scope of the Directive had to be determined according to whether the undertaking has retained its "identity". That would be the case, in particular, where, as in the present case, its operation is continued or resumed with the same or similar activities. The absence of a transfer of ownership of the undertaking and, in particular, of tangible assets, was not conclusive."

> Case C–209/81 *Rask and Christensen v. ISS Kantineservice A/S* [1993] I.R.L.R. 133 at 133, ECJ.

Despite the above decisions which established that the criteria for applying the Directive were to be found in the identity of the undertaking transferred, the United Kingdom Government continued to maintain that the regulations did not apply to local authorities contracting out public services. "We are at present consulting interested parties on a draft of guidance to be issued under section 9 of the Local

---

[81] S.I. 1981 No. (1794).
[82] Directive 77/189.
[83] Case C–209/81 *Rask and Christensen v. ISS Kantineservice A/S* [1993] I.R.L.R. 133, ECJ.
[84] *ibid*. at 133.

Government Act 1992, which states our view that it would be most unusual for the Regulations to apply to a normal contract let under the compulsory competitive tendering legislation."[85] This official position was soon followed by confusion with different government departments issuing different advice.[86] The European Commission then brought infringement proceedings against the United Kingdom and sought a declaration that TUPE did not correctly transpose into United Kingdom law various provisions of Directive 77/187 including those provisions which excluded non-commercial undertakings.[87] However, before the ECJ delivered its decision in these proceedings the Government introduced TURERA 1993, s.33(2) into domestic law which amended TUPE, Reg. 2(1) by removing the reference to undertakings "not in the nature of a commercial venture." These amending provisions also acknowledged previous ECJ decisions[88] that a transfer "may take place whether or not any property is transferred to the transferee by the transferor".[89]

The section 33 amendments were not retrospective and generally all transfers which occurred before August 30, 1993 were not covered by the TUPE Regulations unless they were commercial ventures as defined in the unamended regulation 2(1). The exceptions to this were public employees who were transferred between public organisations. EU Directives are usually only directly binding against member states, but if a member state fails to implement them or imperfectly implements them, an individual may be able to enforce a Directive's provisions directly against the state, or an emanation of the state as an employer. An emanation of the state would include a body under the control of the state which provides a public service.

In *Porter and Nanayakkara*[90] which concerned the dismissal of two hospital consultants it was conceded by the defendant employers "that the TUPE Regulations did not give effect to the full ambit of the Directive and that in such circumstances the Directive was directly enforceable against a public body such as an NHS Trust." Porter concerned the reorganisation of paediatric and neonatal services by a District Health Authority who purchased these services from another hospital after the termination of contracts of two consultants employed by the Regional Health Authority. This was held to be a transfer, the High Court not accepting the argument "that there was no transfer when the District Health Authorities ceased to obtain services from one provider and obtained them instead from another because the responsibility of the Health Authorities for providing the services remained unchanged."

Citing *Daddy's Dance Hall* the Court considered that "The relevant responsibility is for actually doing the work of providing the services rather than for seeing that the services are provided." They further considered that although this work was being reorganised, the "undertaking of providing paediatric and neonatal services had retained its identity through the change of provider." This conclusion was maintained despite the fact that this was an example "of a business [being] carried on in a different way." It was argued that the "provision of medical services is a type of undertaking in which it is particularly likely that different ways of carrying on the undertaking may be

---

[85] Robin Squire, Secretary of State for the Environment. *Hansard*, October 25, 1992.

[86] Circular: October 8, 1992, Public Services Privatisation Research Unit.

[87] Case C–382/92 *Commission Of The European Communities v. United Kingdom Of Great Britain And Northern Ireland* I.R.L.R. [1994] 392, ECJ; [1994] I.C.R., 664.

[88] Case C–324/86 *Foreningen af Arbejdsledere i Danmark v. Daddy's Dance Hall A/S* [1988] I.R.L.R. 315, ECJ; Case C–287/86 *Landsorganisationen i Danmark v. Ny Molle Krø* [1989] I.R.L.R. 37, ECJ.

[89] TURERA 1993, s.33(3)(b).

[90] *Porter and Nanayakkara v. Queen's Medical Centre (Nottingham University Hospital* [1993] I.R.L.R. 486, HC.

adopted without destroying its identity. This is because, advances in medical science may change or modify patient care but it does not change 'the object of the undertaking." Similar arguments were used by the High Court in *Kenny*[91] when the provision of a prison education service was transferred from an education authority to a further education corporation:

"The prospective transfer of prison education services from a local education authority to the defendant college following competitive tendering was a transfer of an undertaking within the meaning of Article 1 of the EEC Business Transfers Directive, notwithstanding that there was no direct relationship between the authority and the college, no transfer of assets, no transfer of clients or customers, no transfer of employees pursuant to the contract, and the continuing function of providing education would be carried on in a different manner." *per* Sir Michael Ogden D.J.

Kenny v. South Manchester College [1993] I.R.L.R. 265 at 265, HC; [1993] I.C.R. 934.

9.3.5 Retrospective claims

A directive is not enforceable against a non-state body or a private individual.[92] Employees who had been employed by a private employer and who had lost their jobs or had become subject to reduced terms and conditions of work as a result of a transfer under the unamended TUPE Regulations , were, because of the so called *Francovich*[93] principles, able to claim compensation against the government. *Francovich* concerned a claim for wages following an employer's insolvency, which the employee was unable to pursue in the domestic courts because the Italian Government had failed to correctly implement Directive 80/97. The ECJ held that the employees could sue their national governments in such a situation providing that "the Directive conferred rights on individuals, that these rights were clearly defined by the Directive and provided that there is a causal link between the injury to the individual and the breach of the Directive by the State."[94]

Cavalier reports that groups of workers supported by their unions GMB, TGWU and UNISON were pursuing such claims in late 1997 but, that because of the United Kingdom's breach of the ARD, the Government had conceded that individuals were entitled to bring such claims.[95] The only remaining issue was the amount of compensation calculable for individual cases. This has been estimated at several thousand pounds each to about 1,500 public sector workers.[96]

9.3.6 Second generation contracting out

The somewhat broad interpretation of what situations can constitute a transfer of an undertaking given by the ECJ in the above cases and in particular the criteria set out in

---

[91] *Kenny v. South Manchester College* [1993] I.R.L.R. 265, HC; [1993] I.C.R. 934.
[92] E.E.C. Treaty (as amended by TEU), Art. 189(3).
[93] Cases C–6/90 and C–9/90 *Republic Bonifaci v. Italian Republic* [1992] I.R.L.R. 84, ECJ; [1991] ECRI 5357; [1993] 2 CMLR 66.
[94] Cases C–6/90 and C–9/90 *Republic Bonifaci v. Italian Republic* I.R.L.R. [1992] 84 ECJ at 85.
[95] S. Cavalier (1997), p. 10.
[96] *The Times* November 17, 1997.

Spijkers was qualified by an unexpected decision of the court in *Süzen v. Zehnacker Gebäudereinigung Gmbh Krankenhausservice.*[97] A school terminated its cleaning contract with one contractor and engaged another contractor to do the same work. A situation which has been described as second generation contracting out. Mrs Süzen and seven other cleaners were dismissed. The Labour Court of Bonn referred two questions to the ECJ. Firstly, is the Directive applicable "if an undertaking terminates a contract with an outside undertaking in order then to transfer it to another outside undertaking?" Secondly, in such a situation is there a legal transfer "even if no tangible or intangible business assets are transferred?" The ECJ decided that this did not constitute a transfer reaffirming previous case law that the decisive issue is whether "the entity in question retains its identity." In further clarification of what is meant by an "entity" however, the Court also declared that "An entity cannot be reduced to the activity entrusted to it."

> "EEC Business Transfers Directive 77/187 does not apply to a change of contractor if there is no concomitant transfer from one undertaking to the other of significant tangible or intangible assets or taking over by the new employer of a major part of the workforce, in terms of their numbers and skills, assigned by the transferor to the performance of the contract. The decisive criterion for establishing the existence of a transfer within the meaning of the Directive is whether the entity in question retains its identity. The term 'entity' refers to an organised grouping of persons and assets facilitating the exercise of an economic activity which pursues a specific objective. The mere fact that the service provided by the old and new contractor is similar does not support the conclusion that an economic entity has been transferred. An entity cannot be reduced to the activity entrusted to it. Consequently, the mere loss of a service contract to a competitor cannot by itself indicate the existence of a transfer within the meaning of the Directive. In order to determine whether the conditions for the transfer of an entity are met, it is necessary to consider all the facts characterising the transaction in question, including in particular the type of undertaking or business, whether or not its tangible assets, such as buildings and moveable property, are transferred, the value of its intangible assets at the time of the transfer, whether or not the majority of its employees are taken over by the new employer; whether or not its customers are transferred, the degree of similarity between the activities carried on before and after the transfer, and the period, if any, for which those activities were suspended.
>
> The absence of the transfer of assets does not necessarily preclude the existence of a transfer of an undertaking. Where an economic entity is able to function without any significant tangible or intangible assets, the maintenance of its identity following the transaction affecting it cannot depend on the transfer of such assets.
>
> In labour-intensive sectors, a group of workers engaged in a joint activity on a permanent basis may constitute an economic entity, and such an entity is capable of maintaining its identity after it has been transferred where the new employer does not merely pursue the activity in question but also takes over a major part, in terms of their numbers and skills, of the employees specially assigned by his predecessor to that task. In those circumstances, the new employer takes over a

---

[97] Case C–13/95 *Süzen v. Zehnacker Gebäudereinigung Gmbh Krankenhausservice* [1997] I.R.L.R. 255; [1997] I.C.R. 662, ECJ.

body of assets enabling him to carry on activities of the transferor undertaking on a regular basis." *per* G C Rodríguez Iglesias, President ECJ

Case C–13/95 *Süzen v. Zehnacker Gebäudereinigung Gmbh Krankenhausservice* [1997] I.R.L.R. 255 at 255; [1997] I.C.R. 662, ECJ.

Although *Süzen* was reported as causing uncertainty for those who had assumed that the ARD applied in most cases of contracting out[98] as well as attracting criticism for weakening employee protection[99]; it did further develop the concept of an economic entity and elaborated on the application of the so called *Spijkers* principles.

Summary of *Süzen* decision in the ECJ:

- An entity is "an organised grouping of persons and assets facilitating the exercise of an economic object which pursues a specific objective";

- The loss of a service contract is, in itself, not necessarily a transfer;

- In such a situation a multiplicity of factors has to be considered:

  — type of undertaking,
  — whether: tangible/intangible assets, majority of employees or customers are transferred,
  — activities undertaken before and after the transfer;

- The absence of assets transferred does not automatically prevent an undertaking being transferred;

- If an employer takes over the majority of skilled employees in a labour intensive area of work a "body of assets" may be taken over.

The Court criticised the imprecise definition of a transfer given in the ARD "whose standard content has not been expressly provided for but is taken for granted by the Community legislature."[1] It further went on to declare that it had tried to avoid developing strict formal criteria for the identification of transfers.[2] In reviewing its earlier case law it declined to follow *Schmidt*[3] when it had decided that: "The cleaning operations of a branch of an undertaking can be treated as a "part of a business" within the meaning of Article 1(1) of Directive 77/187, where the work was performed by a single employee before being contracted out to an outside firm." The reason given by the Court for distinguishing *Schmidt* was that it would be unfair in a competitive tendering situation for the transferee to have to take on the staff of a competitor, who had previously supplied the service, but whose bid had been unsuccessful. Also, unlike previous cases[4] it argued, there was no direct relationship between the two competing firms. By way of analogy, it illustrated this point by reference to *Redmond Stichting*

[98] IDS Brief 601/November 1997, p. 15 lists pending ECJ contracting out of cleaning services cases: Case C–121/960 *Bulut v. Deutsche Bundespost;* Case C–127/96 *F Hernandes Vidal SA v. P Gómez Pérez;* C–229/96 *Santer v. Hoechst A.G.*

[99] P. Davies, *Industrial Law Journal* (1997) Vol. 26, p. 193.

[1] [1997] I.R.L.R. 257, para. 4.

[2] [1997] I.R.L.R. 257, para. 5.

[3] *Schmidt v. Spar- Und Leihkasse Der Frühren Ämter Bordesholm, Kiel Und Cronshagen* [1994] I.R.L.R. 302, ECJ.

[4] *Daddy's Dance Hall* 324/86 [1988] 315; *Schmidt* [1994] E.C.R. 1–1311; *Merckx and Neuhuys* [1996] I.R.L.R. 467.

where competing public funded bodies, had an implied link "within the framework of their accountability to the public authority."

Spijkers is criticised as not giving precise enough guidance on when a transfer is present and the Court tries to "set precise limits to its scope." It does this in the present case, by stipulating that a transfer must "involve the *actual* transfer of tangible or intangible assets" on a voluntary basis between transferor and transferee.[5] Further it is declared that the transfer of a majority of the workforce is not the controlling test for the presence of a transfer.[6] Citing *Merckx v. Ford Motors Co.*,[7] where a car dealership was transferred, the Court also affirmed that a direct contractual link between transferor and transferee was not necessary for a transfer to be present. The decisive criteria is whether the economic entity retains its identity. This identity has to be stable and not limited to performing one specific works contract.[8] Taking into account *Spikjers* criteria and its decision that single factors cannot be taken in isolation, the fact that in the present case, a similar service was provided by the previous and present contractor is not evidence of a transfer. The "entity cannot be reduced to the activity entrusted to it."[9] This entity is further delineated as comprising elements such as the workforce, the management, work organisation, operations and resources deployed. These elements appear to add to the list of *Spijkers* criteria.

The conclusion of the review of previous court decisions on what constitutes a transfer was that the Directive will not apply to the transfer of a cleaning contract unless the major part of the workforce is transferred or significant tangible or intangible assets are transferred. The Court considered that in "certain labour-intensive sectors a group of workers engaged in a joint activity on a permanent basis may constitute an economic entity," which may be transferred."[10] In effect it can be argued that in a cleaning operation the main intangible assets are the employees plus the tangible assets of any cleaning equipment transferred. Cavalier[11] suggests that the effect of *Süzen* is to encourage some employers to avoid the requirements of the ARD by simply refusing to take on the major part of the staff but that this is not acceptable in view of the ECJ decision in *Rotsart De Hertaing v. J Benoidt*[12] which provides that where there is a transfer, the contracts of employment of the employees, transfer from the current to the potential employers on the date of the transfer irrespective of the wishes of the transferor or transferee. Cavalier also maintains that it will often be in the interests of the current employer for TUPE to apply when there is a change of contractor because the liability for redundancy or unfair dismissal costs will transfer to the new contractor. If a transfer does not apply, as in *Süzen* when the cleaning service was transferred between the first and second contractor, then it is the first contractor who will bear such costs.[13]

Süzen has also been criticised for weakening employee protection by substituting a commercial test for a labour law test. If, it is argued, that the transfer of assets or of a major part of the workforce are now the decisive criteria and for example, in a

---

[5] [1997] I.R.L.R. 257, para. 9.
[6] [1997] I.R.L.R. 258, para. 10.
[7] *Merckx and Neuhuys v. Ford Motors Co. (Belgium) SA* [1996] I.R.L.R. 467 at para. 28, ECJ.
[8] Case C–48/94 *Ledernes Hovedorganisation v. Dansk Arbejdsgiverforening* [1996] I.R.L.R. 51, ECJ; [1996] I.C.R. 333; *Rygaard* [1996] I.R.L.R. 51 at para. 20, ECJ.
[9] [1997] I.R.L.R. 259, at para. 15.
[10] [1997] I.R.L.R. 259, at para. 21.
[11] S. Cavalier (1997), p. 20.
[12] Case C–305/94 *Rotsart De Hertaing v. J Benoidt Sa (In Liquidation) and Igc Housing Service* SA [1997] I.R.L.R. 127, ECJ.
[13] S. Cavalier (1997), p. 20.

contracting out situation "workers are needed to tip the same dustbins as before the transfer but into refuse vehicles the transferee had lying around unused (perhaps from another contract the transferee has just lost), that will count against the Directive applying; whereas if the transferee has taken over the transferor's vehicles, in all probability that will bring the Directive into play."[14]

The influence of *Süzen,* has been seen in *Betts v. Brintel*[15] where the Court of Appeal decided that a contract to provide a helicopter service to oil rigs in the North Sea did not constitute a transfer when it was taken from one contractor and awarded to two others. None of the staff of the original contractor were taken on and only a few of the tangible assets, for example "such as the right to land on oil rigs and use oil rig facilities," were taken on by the new contractor. In these circumstances, the Court ruled that "a transfer of such a limited part of the undertaking could not lead to the conclusion that the undertaking itself was transferred so that it retained its identity". This decision has attracted criticism that the Court ignored the possibility that the successful contractor may have deliberately refused to take on the old staff in order to avoid the application of the TUPE regulations.[16]

9.3.7 Transfer of administrative functions

The protection of public sector employees transferred between public administrative bodies was put in question by the ECJ in *Henke v. Gemeinde Schierke*[17] when it held that the reorganisation of a public authority or the transfer of administrative functions between such authorities did not constitute a transfer. This is because "The Directive sets out to protect workers against the potentially unfavourable consequences for them of changes in the structure of undertakings resulting from economic trends at national and Community level. . . ." The transfer of local government functions from one authority to another only constituted "the exercise of public authority" and "Even if those activities had aspects of an economic nature, they could only be ancillary." It has been suggested that the EAT have distinguished *Henke* in *Governing Body of Clifton Middle School v. Askew*[18] where it held that a state-funded school, although not profit-making can be an economic entity.[19] Public employees directly involved in the provision or delivery of public services should be covered by TUPE, although it was perhaps disturbing to observe that the ECJ in *Henke* were imposing a narrow business test on the nature of a transfer, which it could be argued was similar to that included in the original, later amended TUPE regulation which stipulated that the definition of an undertaking "does not include any undertaking or part of an undertaking which is not in the nature of a commercial venture." (See paragraph 9.3.4 above)

9.4 THE EFFECTS OF A RELEVANT TRANSFER

TUPE, reg. 5 defines what has become known as the "automatic transfer principle" and the exceptions to its application. For an overview of the issues raised, the reader is referred to the summary of this regulation given earlier in the chapter.

---

[14] P. Davies (1997) *Industrial Law Journal* (1997), Vol. 26, p. 195.
[15] *Betts v. Brintel Helicopters Ltd and Klm Era Helicopters (U.K.) Ltd* [1997] I.R.L.R. 361, CA.
[16] S. Cavalier, (1997), p. 21.
[17] Case C–298/94) *Henke v. Gemeinde Schierke And Verwaltungsgemeinschaft "Brocken"*. [1996] I.R.L.R. 701, ECJ.
[18] *Governing Body of Clifton Middle School v. Askew* [1997] I.C.R. 808.
[19] I.R.L.B. 584, January 1998.

The limited nature of the protections afforded by the Directive was illustrated by the ECJ in *Daddy's Dance Hall*, which declared that:

"... the Directive is intended to achieve only partial harmonisation, essentially extending the protection guaranteed to workers independently by the laws of the individual Member States to cover the case where an undertaking is transferred. It is not intended to establish a uniform level of protection throughout the Community on the basis of common criteria. Thus the Directive can be relied on only to ensure that the employee concerned is protected in his relations with the transferee to the same extent as he was in his relations with the transferor under the legal rules of the Member State concerned."

Case C–324/86 *Daddy's Dance Hall* [1988] I.R.L.R. 315 at 317 at paras. 16–17, ECJ.

9.4.1 Automatic transfer of the contract of employment

TUPE, reg. 5(1) provides that the transfer itself does not terminate the contract of employment with the transferor, but transfers it to the transferee. This has the effect of creating a situation where the law regards the contract as having been made with the transferee. The contract automatically transfers, carrying with it all the original contractual obligations and liabilities attached to it.[20] The object of this provision is both to protect the employment rights of the individual employee, referred to in *Daddy's Dance Hall* above, and to benefit employers. Redundancy and notice costs are avoided by the old employer and the new employer receives an experienced workforce.

The transfer of the contract of employment does not need the conscious acceptance by the transferor, the transferee or the employee. It transfers even if it is contrary to the wishes of the transferor or transferee. employee. In *Rotstart* the ECJ clearly states:

"The rules of the Directive protecting workers against dismissal by reason of the transfer are mandatory, and it is not possible to derogate from them in a manner unfavourable to employees. In the event of the transfer of an undertaking, the contracts of employment of the staff employed by the undertaking transferred may not be maintained with the transferor and are automatically continued with the transferee. The transfer of the contracts of employment may not be made subject to the intention of the transferor or the transferee." *per* (G.F. Mancini—President of Chamber)

Case C–305/94 *Rotsart De Hertaing v. J Benoidt SA (In Liquidation) and Igc Housing Service SA* [1997] I.R.L.R. 127 at 127, ECJ.

The transfer also takes place even if the employee is kept unaware of the identity of the new employer for "If the employee needs to know, in advance, the identity of the transferee before his contract is transferred, unscrupulous employers would simply refuse to disclose what was happening."[21]

9.4.2 Automatic transfers in parts of undertakings

The automatic transfer principle applies to employees in the undertaking *or part of the undertaking transferred.*[22] The ECJ in *Botzen v. Rotterdamsche*[23] decided that the

---

[20] TUPE, reg. 5(2)(a).
[21] *Secretary of State for Trade & Industry v. Cook* [1997] I.R.L.R. 150 at 151, EAT. See also *MRS Environmental Services v. Dyke*, EAT 93/96, March 10, 1997.
[22] TUPE, reg. 4.
[23] Case C–186/83 *Botzen v. Rotterdamsche Droogdok Maatschappij BV* [1986] 2 C.M.L.R. 50.

Directive only applies to the employees who are assigned to the part transferred. This may raise difficulties when considering if the employee actually works in the part transferred. In *Gale v. Northern General Hospital*,[24] the Court of Appeal decided that a registered nurse could not count for continuity purposes, the service he had accumulated as a student nurse at the same hospital after it had become an NHS Trust Hospital. This was because, his contract as a student nurse was with the health authority who could assign him to any clinical area for work experience. The decision in *Gale* has been criticised[25] as unduly restrictive and the more flexible approach adopted by the Employment Appeal Tribunal in *Securicor Guarding v. Fraser* is preferred.[26] Here, it was held that security guards who had a mobility clause in their contract of employment were transferred, although it was argued by the transferee that they were not transferred because the mobility clause permitted the transferor to locate them to another site for which the transferee had not won the contract. The more flexible approach is also illustrated in *Duncan Webb v. Cooper*[27] where the Employment Appeal Tribunal decided *obiter* that.

> "In determining to which part of an employer's business the employee was assigned, a tribunal may consider matters such as the amount of time spent on one part of the business or the other; the amount of value given to each part by the employee; the terms of the contract of employment showing what the employee could be required to do; [and] how the cost to the employer of the employee's services was allocated between different parts of the business."

9.4.3 What is transferred?

All contractual liabilities, including continuity of service are transferred from the transferor to the transferee employer on the date of the transfer.[28] This means that wages rates and all other terms and conditions remain as if they were originally made with the transferor employee. Any breach of these conditions by the transferor employer, becomes a liability on the transferee employer after the transfer.[29] A particularly broad interpretation of this principle was made by the Employment Appeal Tribunal in *DJM International v. Nicholas* when it determined that a sex discrimination claim by a woman was a liability on the transferee employer. The transferor employer, had, some two months before the transfer, forced the woman to retire at 60 and had then re-employed her on a part-time basis before she transferred to the new company.

> "The crucial question is not whether what was done was in respect of a particular contract, but whether it was in respect of a particular person employed in the undertaking transferred. The wide words of the second limb of reg. 5(2)(b) reflect the reference in Article 3 of Directive 77/187 to "an employment relationship

---

[24] *Gale v. Northern General Hospital NHS Trust* [1994] I.R.L.R. 292, CA.
[25] S. Cavalier (1997), p. 27.
[26] *Securicor Guarding Ltd v. Fraser Security Services Ltd* [1996] I.R.L.R. 552, EAT.
[27] *Duncan Web Offset (Maidstone) Ltd v. Cooper* [1995] I.R.L.R. 633 at 633, EAT. See also *Buchanan-Smith v. Schleicher & Co. International Ltd* [1996] I.R.L.R. 547, EAT; *Hassard v. McGrath and Northern Ireland Housing Executive (NIHE)*, unreported, December 6, 1996, NICA.
[28] TUPE, reg. 5(2)(a).
[29] *ibid.*, (b).

existing on the date of a transfer", and should be construed as referring to the transfer of obligations other than those which arise out of the particular contract of employment. Therefore, a liability may be incurred by an employer to an employee, and a subsequent change in the contractual relationship between the employer and employee does not prevent that liability from transferring.

In the present case, the alleged act of sex discrimination was deemed, according to reg. 5(2)(b), to have been done by the transferee and the fact that it was done in respect of an earlier contract did not make it any the less something done to the respondent as a person employed in the undertaking transferred." *per* Mummery J.P., EAT

DJM International Ltd v. Nicholas [1996] I.R.L.R. 76 at 76, EAT; [1996] I.C.R. 214.

It is to be noted that the Court placed particular emphasis on those words of the Directive which stress that the contractual liabilities only pass over in the event that there is "an employment relationship existing on the date of a transfer". This approach was subsequently reaffirmed by the Employment Appeal Tribunal in *Tsangacos v. Amalgamated Chemicals*[30] when it was determined that a transferee company who took over the business of a company in liquidation was not liable for the unfair dismissal claim of an employee against the original business. Mr Tsangacos had been dismissed some eight months before the transfer and was not employed by the transferor company immediately before the transfer, so he was not in the statutorily required employment relationship.

9.5   VARIATION IN WORKING CONDITIONS

A substantial and detrimental change in the working conditions of an employee is not permitted as a result of a transfer.[31] If such a change is imposed, the employee may terminate the contract of employment without notice.[32] The burden of proof is on the employee to show that such changes are both significant and to his detriment.[33] An employer is allowed however to make changes for an "economic, technical or organisational (ETO) reason entailing changes in the workforce of either the transferor or the transferee".[34] Such changes, if founded in fact, permit an employer to fairly dismiss an employee.[35] What has become known as the employer's ETO defence is discussed further in para. 9.8.2 below. In summary, it can be argued that the TUPE Regulations operate in contradictory ways. Regulation 5(5) operates to prevent any detrimental variation to the employee's contract of employment whereas TUPE, reg. 8(1) permits employers to go as far as fairly dismissing employees for commercial reasons. It is perhaps not surprising that the case-law which has arisen reflects the dichotomy in the statutory wording. Two contrasting Employment Appeal Tribunal decisions in *Wilson v. St Helens Borough Council*[36] and *Meade and Baxendale v. British*

[30] *Tsangacos v. Amalgamated Chemicals Ltd* [1997] I.R.L.R. 4, EAT.
[31] TUPE, reg. 5(5).
[32] *ibid.*, 8(1).
[33] *ibid.*, 5(5).
[34] *ibid.*, 8(2).
[35] *ibid.*, 8(2)(b).
[36] *Wilson v. St Helens Borough Council* [1996] I.R.L.R. 320, EAT.

Fuels Ltd[37] illustrate the problems which have arisen. In *Wilson* the Employment Appeal Tribunal found that a variation was not permitted by TUPE whereas in *Meade* the Court found to the contrary.

In *Wilson*, a school for pupils with behavioural problems was transferred from Lancashire County Council to St Helens Council. It was common ground that a transfer of undertakings had occurred but seventy six staff accepted posts with the transferee employer on less favourable terms. Some employees had their wages reduced and others suffered a loss of allowances previously paid by the transferor employer. Some three to nine months after the transfer the transferred employees claimed arrears of wages under the then Wages Act, ss.1, 8(3).[38] The industrial tribunal found that there had been an effective variation of terms when the employees agreed the new contract with the transferee employer. This decision was overturned by the Employment Appeal Tribunal which, relying on *Daddy's Dance Hall3*[39] considered that the mandatory protection afforded by the Directive overrode even a consensual variation. This was because of the ECJ dictum in *Daddy's Dance Hall* that "a worker cannot waive the rights conferred upon him by the mandatory provisions of Directive 77/187, even if the disadvantages for him of such a course of action are offset by advantages so that, overall, he is not left in a worse position."

In *Meade and Baxendale* a similar situation obtained, in that both employees were made redundant from their previous company National Fuel Distributors (NFD) and signed contracts with the transferee company British Fuels Ltd (BFL) which contained revised and reduced terms. Here, the industrial tribunal also found that there had been no dismissal although Mr Meade had accepted severance and redundancy payments from the transferor employer. The tribunal further found that both contracts had transferred with agreed variations which had lawfully changed the terms, giving them a lower rate of pay and worse conditions. The Employment Appeal Tribunal upheld the industrial tribunal ruling in Meade and ruled that "the notice of dismissal by the transferor was effective in law, even if it was unfair." The dismissal was not a nullity, that is, the contract had not come to an end by operation of law, but the employee had agreed a new and varied contract with the transferee employer.

In trying to untie the Gordian knot around these two conflicting decisions the Court of Appeal considered the two cases together.[40] It decided that the Employment Appeal Tribunal had erred in both cases. In *Wilson* it found that there was a lawful ETO dismissal because both the transferor and transferee employers did not have the resources to run the school in the way it had been run. The employees were thus not protected under regulation 5 and started employment with the new employer on the newly agreed conditions. The Court of Appeal also found that the agreement to vary the contracts in *Meade* fell foul of TUPE, reg. 12. This stipulates that any agreement which purports to exclude or limit the provisions of regulation 5 (the automatic transfer principle) or regulation 8 (a dismissal arising from a transfer is unfair unless for an ETO reason) is void. In effect, the Court of Appeal decision means that if an ETO reason can be found, for example, the reorganisation of the school in *Wilson*, an agreed variation is effective, whereas if there is no ETO defence the only reason for the variation must be the transfer itself which under TUPE, reg. (5)(1) does not terminate the contract but preserves and transfers the existing terms and conditions.

---

[37] *Meade and Baxendale v. British Fuels Ltd* [1996] I.R.L.R. 541, EAT.
[38] Now ERA 1996, s.13.
[39] Case C–324/861 *Foreningen AF Arbejdsledere I Danmark v. Daddy's Dance Hall A/S* [1988] I.R.L.R. 316; [1989] 2 C.M.L.R. 517, ECJ.
[40] [1997] I.R.L.R. 505, CA.

This decision has been called opaque and lacking in guidance[41] and is likely to be the subject of appeals in the House of Lords and in the ECJ.

In *Merckx And Neuhuys v. Ford Motors*[42] the transferee employer refused to guarantee the same level of remuneration of two employees in the transfer of a car dealership. The ECJ ruled that:

"A change in the level of remuneration is a substantial change in working conditions within the meaning of Article 4(2), which provides that if the contract of employment or employment relationship is terminated because the transfer involves a substantial change in working conditions to the employee's detriment, the employer is to be regarded as responsible for the termination." *per* C. N. Kakouris—President of Chamber

Merckx And Neuhuys v. Ford Motors Co. (Belgium) [1996] I.R.L.R. 467 at 468, ECJ.

In the United Kingdom courts this would permit the employees to resign and claim constructive dismissal.[43] This is because such a unilateral variation could amount to a repudiatory breach of the contact of employment.

Finally, it is argued[44] that an employee's right not to suffer a substantial and detrimental change to their working conditions could encompass a situation where the transferee employer's past record would damage the future employability of the employee, such as in *Malik v. BCCI*,[45] where it was held that the collapse of a bank through corruption entitled two redundant managers to claim stigma damages. Other detriments it is claimed[46] could include transfer to an employer who is anti trade union (see the following paragraph) or who does not comply with health and safety regulations.

9.6 COLLECTIVE AGREEMENTS AND TRADE UNION RECOGNITION

9.6.1 Collective Agreements

Collective agreements made with a recognised trade union by the transferor employer, transfer over to the transferee employer and have the same effect as if made with the original employer.[47] This means that terms and conditions incorporated from collective agreements into individual contracts of employment cannot be changed by the transferee employer unilaterally withdrawing from the collective agreement after the transfer itself.[48] In *Whent v. T Cartledge Ltd*[49] the transferee employer withdrew

---

[41] IRLB 585, January 1998.
[42] Cases C–171/94 and C–172/94 *Merckx And Neuhuys v. Ford Motors Co. (Belgium) SA* [1996] I.R.L.R. 467; [1996] All E.R. 667; [1997] I.C.R. 352, ECJ.
[43] TUPE, reg. 5(5).
[44] S. Cavalier (1997), p. 29.
[45] *Malik v. Bank Of Credit And Commerce International SA* [1997] I.R.L.R. 462; [1997] 3 W.L.R. 95; [1997] I.C.R. 606; [1997] 3 All E.R. 1, HL.
[46] S. Cavalier (1997), p. 29.
[47] TUPE, reg. 6.
[48] *Robertson And Jackson v. British Gas Corporation* [1983] I.R.L.R. 302; [1983] I.C.R. 351, CA.
[49] *Whent v. T Cartledge Ltd* [1997] I.R.L.R. 153, EAT.

from the local authorities National Joint Council agreement ten days after taking over a street lighting contract from the London Borough of Brent. The new employers claimed that they wanted to negotiate pay and conditions directly with individual members of staff although they froze pay levels at the level fixed when they withdrew from the national agreement. The Employment Appeal Tribunal relying on *Robertson v. British Gas*[50] found that:

> "The transferee employers were still bound by the NJC agreement, so far as incorporated in individual contracts of employment, notwithstanding their withdrawal from the collective agreement. Until the transfer it was undisputed that the appellants" contracts incorporated the result of the annual round of negotiations, and there were no grounds of holding that the transfer caused any change in the meaning of the words." *per* Hicks J.
>
> *Whent v. T. Cartledge Ltd* [1997] I.R.L.R. 154 at 154, EAT.

In *Whent*[51] the Employment Appeal Tribunal disposed of the original industrial tribunal's reasoning that an employer could not be bound for ever by the terms of a collective agreement which had been negotiated by other bodies, by finding that: "The employer was not bound infinitum since it could, at any time, without breach of a contract, negotiate variations of contract with individual employees, or terminate their contracts on due notice and offer fresh ones".[52] The latter course of action, it was acknowledged could lead to an unfair dismissal claim under TUPE, reg. 5(5) if it involved a substantial and detrimental change in working conditions.[53]

Terms which are not impliedly incorporated into individual contracts of employment will usually not transfer over because of the statutory presumption of non-enforceability of collective agreements.[54] In addition, only clauses of collective agreements which are intended to be enforceable between an individual employee and an employer will be so incorporated.[55] In *Meechan v. Secretary of State for Scotland*[56] it was held that only a college lecturer's normal salary, the terms of which had been incorporated into his contract of employment from a collective agreement were transferred, but not those terms of the collective agreement which related to the structure of the institution and the right of the lecturer who performed the duties of head of department to receive a salary appropriate to the post.

Article 3(2) of the ARD allows EU signatory countries to legislate so as to require that transferee employers comply with the terms of a collective agreement for a minimum period of one year after the transfer. The statutory presumption of non-enforceability of such agreements in the United Kingdom and the fact that all elements of a collective agreement, for example procedures for settling disputes, are not usually incorporated into individual contracts of employment, means that no such requirement has been transposed into the domestic regulations.

9.6.2 Trade union recognition

Trade union recognition transfers over where an undertaking or part of an undertaking retains an identity after the transfer which is distinct from the rest of the transferee's

---

[50] *Robertson and Jackson v. British Gas Corporation* [1983] I.R.L.R. 302; [1983] I.C.R. 351, CA.
[51] See also *BET Catering Services Ltd v. Ball* 28.11.96 EAT 637/96.
[52] *Whent v. T Cartledge Ltd* [1997] I.R.L.R. 154, EAT.
[53] *ibid.*, para. 16.
[54] TULRCA 1992, s.179.
[55] *Alexander v. Standard Telephones & Cables Ltd Wall v. Standard Telephones & Cables Ltd* [1990] I.R.L.R. 55 HC; [1990] I.C.R. 291.
[56] *Meechan v. Secretary of State for Scotland* [1997] S.L.T. 936.

undertaking.[57] This only applies however to the group of employees who are actually transferred.[58] The statutory trade union recognition procedures were repealed in 1980[59] before the TUPE Regulations came into effect. Since then, employers have been under no legal compulsion to recognise unions and have been free to derecognise trade unions after a transfer. The Labour Government elected in May 1997 was committed to the reintroduction of a statutory trade union recognition procedure and a White Paper on *Fairness At Work* appeared in 1998.[60] It is likely that the position may radically change so that it will become unlawful for an employer to derecognise a trade union which maintains a certain level of membership in the workplace. (See Chapter 11, para. 11.5.3 on the background to the White Paper).

It can also be argued that the withdrawal of collective rights, as in *Whent* above, where the employer derecognised the trade union as well as withdrawing from the collective agreement on wage levels, is a breach of TUPE where it leads to individual employee rights being detrimentally changed. This could be the case if individuals are denied statutory rights for time off for union duties and activities after derecognition.[61]

9.7 PENSIONS NOT TRANSFERRED

The courts have ruled that TUPE, reg. 7,[62] specifically excludes occupational pension schemes from those contractual rights and liabilities which automatically transfer over. As public concern over pension rights has mounted in the 1980s because of the mis-selling of expensive private pensions and because of the loss of Maxwell pension funds, this aspect of TUPE protection has been described as "a gaping hole in the legislation—at European and national level." In *Adams v. Lancashire County Council* the plaintiffs were catering workers who had transferred from a local authority service to a private company which did not offer membership to its pension scheme to employees earning less than £15,000 per year. This excluded the former local authority employees, who in the Court of Appeal sought to argue that as pension rights are deferred pay, they are protected for current and future work under Article 3 of the ARD. Article 3(3) of the Directive excludes the automatic transfer of occupational pension schemes but it also requires that "Member States shall adopt the measures necessary to protect the interests of employees and of persons no longer employed in the transferor's business at the time of the transfer. . ." In the United Kingdom the Pensions Schemes Act 1993 does this by freezing the pension already earned and deferring payment of a pension based on these contributions until the normal retiring age of the employee.

In reviewing the statutory history and case law[63] on Article 3 the Court of Appeal found that this Article and TUPE, reg. 7 excludes the transfer of all pension rights. The Court considered that the Directive did not give transferred employees a right to "pension benefits proportionate and equivalent" to those they would have obtained from the transferor if the periods of service performed for the transferee had been

---

[57] TUPE reg. (9)(1).
[58] *ibid.*, (9)(2)(a).
[59] The Employment Act 1980, s.19(b) repealed ss.11 to 16 of the EPA 1975.
[60] Cm. 3968, *Fairness at Work*, DTI, May 21, 1998.
[61] S. Cavalier (1997) p. 32.
[62] *Adams v. Lancashire County Council and Bet Catering Services Ltd* [1997] I.R.L.R. 436, CA.
[63] *ibid.* 436 at paras. 13–25, CA.

performed for the transferor.[64] This was because this would involve giving a new right to the transferred employees rather than transferring an existing one. Occupational pension schemes stand alone and once an employee has left the scheme he can no longer contribute to it and neither could the transferee usually do so. Nevertheless, it has also been argued that the refusal of a transferee employer to offer an equivalent pension scheme could give rise to a constructive dismissal claim because such action would constitute a repudiatory breach of the employment contract.[65] Although it can be argued that it was never the intention of the European legislators to burden transferee employers with expensive and uncompetitive occupational pension schemes it is difficult not to describe a transferred employee's ejection from his transferor's scheme as a substantial and detrimental change to his working conditions, which would normally trigger a remedy of constructive unfair dismissal.[66]

9.8   Dismissal

TUPE, reg. 8 contains two key provisions. Firstly, that any employee of either the transferor or the transferee shall be regarded in law as unfairly dismissed "if the transfer or a reason connected with it is the reason or principal reason" for the dismissal.[67] Secondly, that this automatic legal remedy for dismissal does not apply where the transferor or transferee employer dismisses an employee for "an economical, technical or organisational reason" which entails making changes in their workforce.

It can be argued that "the two reasons for dismissal are mutually exclusive".[68] If the dismissal is not because of the transfer it must be for an ETO reason. These provisions also go to the heart of the Directive's purpose in protecting employees. At one extreme, its purpose is apparently to discourage any change, even consensual change, to the contract of employment, arising from the transfer. At the same time, the Directive appears to acknowledge that transfers often occur through commercial reorganisations which will involve legitimate changes to the contract of employment.

The text has already (see Section 9.5 above) dealt with contractual variations arising from a transfer and the finding by the Court of Appeal in *Wilson* that an ETO reason may make them lawful. Consideration is now given to the position of employees who are dismissed because of a transfer.

9.8.1   *Litster*

In *Litster v. Forth Dry Dock & Engineering*[69] the transferor employer went into receivership. On the same day and only one hour before the business assets of the company were sold to a new employer, the receiver summarily dismissed twelve employees without accrued holiday or notice pay. The new owner of the company did not re-employ any of the dismissed workers and when action was taken by the

---

[64] *ibid.*, para. 20.
[65] IRLB 585, January 1998.
[66] TUPE reg. 5(5).
[67] *ibid.*, 8(1).
[68] S. Cavalier (1997), p. 40.
[69] *Litster v. Forth Dry Dock & Engineering Co. Ltd (in receivership)* [1989] I.R.L.R. 161; [1989] 2 W.L.R. 634; [1989] I.C.R. 341; [1989] 1 All E.R. 1134, HL.

dismissed workers to join them with the original employer, to a claim for unfair dismissal, the company claimed that because the workers were not "employed immediately before the transfer" as required by the TUPE, reg. 5(3) that the transfer regulations did not apply. The industrial tribunal decided that there had been an unfair dismissal which was caused by the transfer itself, the liability for which, transferred to the new company. The Employment Appeal Tribunal subsequently overturned this decision finding the dismissal fair on the grounds that redundancy was an ETO reason permitted by TUPE, reg. 8(2). The case reached the judicial House of Lords on appeal from a Court of Sessions decision that liability for the unfair dismissal lay with the transferor. This decision was comprehensively overturned by their Lordships who adopted a purposive construction towards the Directive and determined that:

> "Where an employee has been unfairly dismissed before a transfer for a reason connected with the transfer, he is to be deemed to have been employed in the undertaking "immediately before the transfer" and the employment is statutorily continued with the transferee." *per* Lord Keith of Kinkel.

> *Litster v. Forth Dry Dock & Engineering Co. Ltd (In Receivership)* [1989] I.R.L.R. 161 at 162, HL.

The House of Lords decision was important because its effect is to prevent insolvent employers doing a deal with a new employer to sack existing employees so that the new employer can circumvent the payment of redundancy compensation to workers who are not re-engaged. If such a position was lawful, it would leave no meaningful remedy to a dismissed employee who would be faced with a worthless compensation claim against an insolvent employer and an ineffective remedy of re-engagement and reinstatement against a non-existent employer. Their Lordships declared that "It cannot have been contemplated that, where the only reason for determination of the employment is the transfer of the undertaking, the parties to the transfer would be at liberty to avoid the manifest purpose of the Directive by the simple expedient of wrongfully dismissing the workforce a few minutes before the completion of the transfer."[70]

Both *why* and *when* an employer dismisses an employee is relevant to the application of TUPE, reg. 8. In *Duratube Ltd v. Bhatti*[71] the Court of Appeal directed that industrial tribunals should ask two questions. Firstly, what was the reason or principal reason for the dismissal and secondly, was that reason connected to or represented by the transfer itself? In *Duratube* the Court said that it was wrong for the industrial tribunal to conclude that because a sale of the undertaking had been decided upon by the receiver, this action had automatically established the transfer as the reason for the dismissal. A receiver who had dismissed part of a transferor's work eleven days before a transfer was held to have fairly dismissed the employees because this "was a consequence of [his] primary decision to cease trading" and was not connected with the proposed sale to the transferee.[72] That there may be a fine line between a receiver deliberately encouraging a purchaser by agreeing to sack staff in advance, and on the other hand, seeking to comply with the automatic transfer provisions of the Directive,

---

[70] *Litster v. Forth Dry Dock & Engineering Co. Ltd (in receivership)* [1989] I.R.L.R. 161, HL.
[71] *Duratube Ltd v. Bhatti* reported in IRLB 585, January 1998, CA.
[72] *Ward and Lewarne v. Beresford & Hicks Furniture Ltd* 16.12.96 EAT 860/95—reported in IRLB 585 January 1998.

appears to be shown by the Employment Appeal Tribunal's warning that "had the receiver kept the employees on until only three or four days before the transfer, the reason for the dismissal might well have been 'the transfer or a reason connected with it'."

9.8.2 ETO dismissals

When businesses are transferred, or local authority contracts subjected to competitive tendering it is not unusual that the new business owners or service providers will want to make changes in the workforce for commercial reasons. A dismissal which is for an economic, technical or organisational reason, would assist an employer in avoiding a claim for automatic unfair dismissal. An ETO if interpreted broadly, could arguably permit almost any dismissals. In *Wheeler v. Patel*[73] the Employment Appeal Tribunal appeared however to put a narrow construction on the statutory wording:

> "An 'economic reason' for dismissal, to fall within Regulation 8(2), must be a reason which relates to the conduct of the business. A desire to obtain an enhanced price for the business or to achieve a sale is not a reason which relates to the conduct of the business and is therefore not an 'economic' reason for the purposes of Regulation 8(2). The reference to 'technical' and to 'organisational' reasons in Regulation 8(2) refers to reasons which relate to the conduct of the business and the adjective 'economic' must be construed *ejusdem generis* with the adjectives 'technical' and 'organisational'. Such an approach justifies giving a limited meaning to the adjective 'economic' in Regulation 8(2)." *per* Scott J.

> *Wheeler v. Patel and J Golding Group of Companies* [1987] I.R.L.R. 211 at 211, EAT.

The ETO changes which can be lawfully made have to "entail changes in the workforce of the transferor or transferee." This has been interpreted as meaning changes in the composition of the workforce and not just changes in their terms and conditions Lowering a transferred employee's wages in order to harmonise the working terms and conditions with the existing transferee's staff could not be regarded as an ETO said the Court of Appeal in *Delabole Slate Ltd v. Berriman*.[74] Changes in the jobs of those employees transferred may constitute an ETO such as in *Crawford v. Swinton*[75] where a typist was asked to change her job to an insurance salesperson but on reduced terms and conditions. The Employment Appeal Tribunal said that "There can be a 'change in a workforce' for the purpose of regulation 8(2) if the same people are kept on but they are given entirely different jobs to do." Note however, that an ETO has to be the "reason or principal reason" for dismissing the employee and an industrial tribunal has to find this as a matter of fact. In the instant case, the tribunal had not done this and the Employment Appeal Tribunal remitted the case to another industrial tribunal for reconsideration. There is evidence however, that there is some judicial confusion about what constitutes an ETO. In *Porter v. Queens Medical Centre* it is argued[76] that the rights of existing employees were not protected in line with the

---

[73] *Wheeler v. Patel and J Golding Group Of Companies* [1987] I.R.L.R. 211; [1987] I.C.R. 631, EAT.
[74] *Berriman v. Delabole Slate Ltd* [1985] I.C.R. 546; [1985] I.R.L.R. 305, CA.
[75] *Crawford v. Swinton Insurance Brokers Ltd* [1990] I.R.L.R. 42; [1990] I.C.R. 8, EAT.
[76] S. Cavalier (1997), p. 41.

Directive. Here, the Court considered that as medical science does not stand still, the employer had a right to reorganise medical services and then choose which clinical staff were suitable to transfer over to another employer.

Finally, to summarise, the onus is on the employer to prove that there is an ETO reason for dismissal which will be justifiable in fact, and in reasonableness,[77] before he can escape the obligations in TUPE, reg. 5(1) and 5(2) which require that the employment contract is not terminated, but transferred over with all its liabilities and obligations.

9.8.3 Employee's right to object

The Regulations follow the common law position in that employees are not forced to enter into an employment relationship with a new employer[78] and courts do not generally enforce specific performance of an employment contract. The ECJ has also confirmed this approach.[79] If employees object to being transferred, their contracts are terminated with the transferor, but this is not regarded in law as a dismissal.[80] In such a case, the employee is not automatically transferred to a new employer and is regarded as having resigned, so is unable to make a redundancy or unfair dismissal claim. It is highly likely that many employees in a transfer situation will feel uneasy about their future employment and may express dissent. In *Hay v. George Hanson*[81] the Scottish Employment Appeal Tribunal found that "The word 'object' in regulation 5(4A) means an actual refusal to consent to the transfer. That state of mind must be communicated to either the transferor or the transferee, before the transfer takes place. There is no particular method whereby that state of mind must be brought to the attention of either the transferor or the transferee. It can be by word or deed, or both." The Court further found "It should not be difficult in most cases to distinguish between withholding of consent and mere expressions of concern or unwillingness, which may still be consistent with accepting the inevitable." In effect, the Court is saying that whether an employee is to be regarded as having waived a statutory right to a fair dismissal is dependant upon the employer correctly interpreting an employee's "state of mind." This decision has been strongly criticised[82] and even the Scottish Employment Appeal Tribunal itself, in an *obiter* observation, criticised the Regulations for not including a provision that employees who intended to object should be warned of the consequences by the transferor employer. The general approach adopted in *Hay* was confirmed by the Employment Appeal Tribunal in *Senior Heat Treatment v. Bell*,[83] where it held that employees who had taken up the transferor's offer of voluntary severance (the other choices given: being redeployment or transfer on full protected conditions), but had subsequently taken up an offer of employment with the transferee company, had not genuinely objected to the transfer.

9.9 PROPOSED CHANGES TO THE TRANSFER REGULATIONS

It will be apparent from the fast developing case law in this area, both in the domestic and in the European jurisdictions, that the ARD and the TUPE Regulations have

---

[77] ERA 1996, s.98(4).
[78] TUPE, reg. 5(4)(A).
[79] *Katsikas v. Konstantinides* [1993] I.R.L.R. 179, ECJ.
[80] TUPE, reg, 5(4)(B).
[81] *Hay v. George Hanson (Building Contractors) Ltd* [1996] I.R.L.R. 427, EAT.
[82] S. Cavalier (1997), p. 28.
[83] *Senior Heat Treatment Ltd v. Bell* [1997] I.R.L.R. 614, EAT.

been the cause of prolonged and sometimes controversial analysis by the courts. Some governments have also been concerned that the legislation goes too far in protecting the rights of employees. The German Government has argued for a narrower interpretation of an undertaking as a business with "a clearly defined economic objective".[84] A new definition proposed by the European Commission in 1994 was criticised for its vagueness and discriminatory implications. The existing definition was considerably narrowed in *Ayse Süzen*[85] discussed above and it is claimed that there is now no need for legislative amendment on that score.[86]

In 1997, the European Commission, issued revised proposals[87] to amend the Directive and a Memorandum and Guidelines[88] summarising ECJ case law. The United Kingdom Government in its role as President of the Council of the EU in the first half of 1998, sought to take the lead in negotiations on amending the Directive and issued a public consultation document[89] summarising its proposals. A separate public consultation document which reviewed employee information and consultation rights in the event of a transfer was also issued in the Spring of 1998 and has been considered earlier in this chapter.[90]

The Government seemed content that the narrower definition of a transfer given by the ECJ in *Ayse Süzen* was appropriate,[91] and it was opposed to any amendments to the Directive which would further narrow its coverage.[92] Indeed, it appeared to be cautiously inclined to support further extending employee protection provisions in some areas. These proposals included the extension of full protection to employees on all sea-going vessels; the inclusion of comparable pension rights to be transferred; and the provision of sanctions which are effective, proportionate and dissuasive'. Additionally, the Government were proposing to amend TUPE to bring the consultation rights in line with those of the Collective Redundancies Directive. (See Section: 9.2.7 above). The Government was also considering whether the Directive should be extended to takeovers by share transfer. Although, the employer's legal identity or contractual relationship does not change in such a situation, employees do not have special protection if they are dismissed as a result of a takeover. Neither do they have any right of consultation. Noting that takeovers are not within the direct control of management and that takeover bids often do not follow through, the Government's consultation document inclined not to support an extension of the Directive in this area.[93]

Concern about the difficulties which the existing legislation had given employers in contracting-out and in insolvency situations was highlighted by the Government. In

[84] Case C–392/92 *Schmidt v. Spar- Und Leihkasse Der Frühren Ämter Bordesholm, Kiel Und Cronshagen* [1994] I.R.L.R. 302, ECJ at para. 5, Advocate General's Opinion.
[85] [1997] I.R.L.R. 255, ECJ.
[86] J. McMullen *People Management* (1997).
[87] *Amended Proposal For A Council Directive Amending Directive 77/187 On The Approximation Of The Laws Of The Member States Relating To The Safeguarding Of Employees' Rights In The Event Of Transfers Of Undertakings, Businesses Or Parts Of Businesses*, Brussels, COM(97) 60 final, February 24, 1997.
[88] *Memorandum From The Commission On Acquired Rights Of Workers In Case Of Transfers Of Undertakings, Brussels*, COM(97) 85 final, March 4, 1997.
[89] DTI, Employment Rights Directorate (1997) *European Acquired Rights Directive And Transfer Of Undertakings(Protection Of Employment) Regulations 1981 (The TUPE Regulations) Public Consultation*, December 1997, URN 98/513.
[90] DTI, *Employee's Information And Consultation Rights on Transfers Of Undertakings And Collective Redundancies, Public Consultation*, February 1998, URN 97/988.
[91] Public Consultation, December 1997, URN 98/513, para. 13.
[92] *ibid.*, para. 14.
[93] *ibid.*, paras 17 to 20.

referring to the case-law,[94] the consultation document specifically highlighted the inflexibility of the automatic transfer principle, which in practice prohibits any contractual variations "regardless of whether or not [the employees] consent to the variations and regardless of how long after the transfer they are made."

It was acknowledged that some commentators would like the Directive amended[95] so as to clearly protect all employment contracts which are assigned or reassigned in a contracting out situation, but the Government saw technical and political difficulties in securing an improvement on the present position. From the employer's perspective however, the Government's position was clearer. They wanted the Directive to be amended, to help prospective contractors make more realistic bids, by obliging a transferor employer to give them comprehensive and accurate information "about the size and terms of conditions of employment" of the existing workforce.[96]

The Government was also seeking more flexibility in the Directive where the receiver of an insolvent employer is trying to maintain the business as a going concern. The ECJ had already made the distinction between the winding up and continuation of a business in *Abels*[97] when it found that the Directive does not apply to formal judicial liquidation proceedings. This approach has been subsequently followed in *Jules Dethier Equipment SA v. Dassy*[98] where, the ECJ held that the Directive applied in the event of a transfer of undertaking being wound up by the court, providing that the undertaking continued to trade. This approach also seems to have been followed in the United Kingdom courts. In *Warner v. Adnet Ltd* where the receivers of a company were urgently trying to find a purchaser, the Court of Appeal found that there was a fair redundancy dismissal of an accountant, before the transfer, even though there had been no formal consultation and no objective criteria for redundancy selection established. The Court held that there had been a transfer which was the cause of the dismissal. The dismissal was for an economic reason under TUPE, reg. 8(2) and it was reasonable and fair in the circumstances. Mummery L.J. in delivering this decision, supported the reasoning of the industrial tribunal which said that the lack of consultation and objective redundancy criteria was not relevant in the circumstances "of a failing business which was a small concern and where formal consultation would not have made any difference to the decision to dismiss Mr Warner." The judge did say however, that it would be an exceptional case where employers did not consult in advance of a redundancy dismissal.[99]

In 1994, the EU Commission proposed that Member States be allowed to exclude the Directive from applying in a situation where an employer "is the subject of bankruptcy proceedings or any other analogous proceedings" with a view to the liquidation of it's assets. Their 1997 amended proposals retained this provision but required Member States to apply the Directive where there are proceedings which are directed to the continuation of the business.[1] The United Kingdom Government broadly supported this approach but argued "for the Directive to be applied in all insolvency cases whatever the outcome envisaged."[2] This is consistent with the existing

---

[94] *ibid.*, para. 30.
[95] *ibid.*, para. 15.
[96] *ibid.*, para. 49.
[97] *Abels v. Administrative Board of the Bedrijfsvereniging voor de Metaalindustrie en de Electrotechnische Industrie* 135/83 CR 469, [1987] 2 C.M.L.R. 406, ECJ.
[98] Case C–319/94 *Jules Dethier Equipment SA v. Dassy, The Times*, March 18, 1998.
[99] *Warner v. Adnet Ltd, The Times*, March 12, 1998, CA.
[1] COM(97) 60 final, February 24, 1997, Proposed New Article 1(5), p. 12.
[2] Public Consultation, December 1997, URN 98/513, para. 26.

TUPE, reg. 4(1). It also supported the Commission's proposal that the transferor's debts in respect of the employees do not pass to the transferee. In addition, it proposed that trade unions and employer representatives be allowed to agree variations to the employment contract "to ensure the preservation of the undertaking".[3]

To prevent employers engineering a false insolvency situation so as to avoid the transfer provisions, the Commission proposed that Member States should take measures to "ban the use of fraudulent insolvency proceedings intended to deprive employees of the rights laid down in the Directive".[4] This approach has been described as inadequate in preventing such abuse, because of the difficulty an employee would have in convincing a court that an insolvency practitioner was acting improperly.[5] The United Kingdom Government was also opposed to such a requirement because of problems in devising effective domestic legislation.

9.9.1   Summary

Barnard has pointed out that the protectionist thrust of the Directives on collective redundancies, transfers of undertakings and insolvency have been tempered somewhat by the desire of the ECJ "to prevent social dumping" (where multinational companies seek to relocate their businesses to countries with cheaper labour costs and less strict employment laws) so that the financial burden of restructuring an enterprise is the same in all Member States.[6] She also considers that the introduction of statutory protective rules across the EU is undermined by the discretion given to national legislatures in applying the Directives' provisions, giving as an example, the decision in *Katsikas*.[7] Here, the ECJ found that the ARD does not oblige Member States to provide that the contract of employment continues with a transferee if the employee objects (See para. 9.8.3 above) but, "It does not preclude it either." In the United Kingdom, in such a situation, the contract is terminated but there is no dismissal, the employee is regarded as having resigned.[8] The employee, has no recourse to any judicial remedy for the loss of employment. It has been suggested that a more equitable way of dealing with an employee who objects, would be to permit the employee to remain with the transferor who could then decide to make the worker redundant, but the redundant individual would have a right to a fair selection process and possible redundancy compensation.[9] Barnard maintains that if the ECJ was genuinely commited to worker protection it could have ruled that a worker should not be prejudiced when objecting to a transfer.

At European level, the policy debate focuses on reconciling flexibility for employers' needs at the same time as promoting security for workers: "An important part of this must be a new and stronger focus in social protection systems on employability and access to skills. Social protection must actively equip people to work, as well as provide basic support. And, just as important, labour law, and the collective arrangements governing future working patterns, must offer recognition to new forms of working

---

[3] *ibid.*, para. 27.
[4] COM(97) 60 final, February 24, 1997, Proposed New Article 3(5), p. 16.
[5] S. Cavalier (1997), p. 73.
[6] C. Barnard, *EC Employment Law*, (rev. ed. 1996), p. 400.
[7] *Katsikas v. Konstantinides* [1993] I.R.L.R. 179, ECJ.
[8] TUPE, regs 5(4A) and 5(4B).
[9] S. Cavalier (1997), p. 28.

conditions and contractual arrangements."[10] Whatever changes are made, it is likely that this area of labour law will probably remain vulnerable to extensive judicial interpretation. This is perhaps not surprising, when it is remembered, that the purpose of the legislation is to try and protect individual employment rights in a situation and at a time when commercial pressures will often bear most heavily.

On July 17, 1998 an amending Directive (Council Directive 98/50, June 29, 1998)[11] came into force which changes European Community law on the transfer of undertakings. The purpose of this Directive "is to amend Directive 77/187 in the light of the impact of the internal market, the legislative tendencies of the Member States with regard to the rescue of undertakings in economic difficulties, [and] the case law of the . . ." European Court. The preamble explains that it is the intention of the amending Directive to clarify the legal concept of a transfer and of an "employee" in the light of European Court (ECJ) case law. These clarifications reflect recent ECJ decisions such as those in *Ayse Süzen* and in *Henke* which are discussed earlier in this chapter, and also acknowledges criticisms from the Court itself that the concept of a transfer was only vaguely defined in the original Directive. A transfer is now clearly defined as "a transfer of an economic entity which retains its identity" (Article 1, para. 1(b)).

The Directive further permits certain derogations from the general provisions where transfers are effected in the context of insolvency proceedings. The object here being to try and ensure the survival of such undertakings by providing that transferor debts do not transfer to the transferee (Article 4a, para. 2(a)) and by permitting agreed variations "to terms and conditions of employment designed to safeguard employment opportunities by ensuring the survival of the undertaking . . ." (Article 4a, para. 2(b)). Member States of the European Union will have until July 17, 2001 at the latest to introduce legislative measures which comply with the Directive. The United Kingdom government have welcomed the new changes, many of which are in line with their recent proposals discussed above and are preparing new TUPE Regulations which are not expected to come into force before 1999.[12]

---

[10] Flynn, Padraig, European Commissioner for Employment, Industrial Relations and Social Affairs, from a Speech given on July 18, 1997 at the TUC, Congress House, London.

[11] Council Directive 98/50 of June 29, 1998 amending Directive 77/187 on the approximation of the laws of the Member States relating to the safeguarding of employees' rights in the event of transfers of undertakings, businesses or parts of businesses.

[12] DTI Briefing Note, June 30, 1998.

Chapter 10

Pregnancy and Childbirth

10.1 Introduction

Women now account for 44 per cent of the United Kingdom workforce, compared with 38 per cent in 1971. Seventy-two per cent of women of working age, as compared with 85 per cent of men, are economically active, and the economic activity rate of women with young children increased from 40 per cent in 1986 to 54 per cent in 1997. Whilst there has been a decline in fertility rates generally, there has been a rise in fertility rates amongst older women, and a decline amongst younger age groups. The proportion of first babies born to women over 30, whilst accounting for 18 per cent of births in 1985, increased to 36 per cent in 1995, whereas women in the age group 20 to 24 accounted for 28 per cent of all births in 1985, but 14 per cent in 1995.

This increase in fertility rates amongst older women has been accompanied by an increase in the number of mothers returning to work after childbirth. Recent research[1] shows that in 1996, 67 per cent of women returned to work within 11 months of having a baby, as compared with 45 per cent in 1988, and that return to the same employer is linked to good maternity benefits in terms of leave and pay, with 72 per cent of those returning being entitled to extended maternity absence.

Domestically, three rights in connection with pregnancy and childbirth were introduced by the Employment Protection Act 1975 (EPA) 1975 as follows:

- the right not to be unfairly dismissed because of pregnancy;
- the right to maternity pay; and
- the right to return to work after pregnancy.

A fourth right was introduced in the Employment Act 1980 (EA) 1980:

- the right to time off for anti-natal care.

Following a review of sick pay provision, which resulted in the introduction of statutory sick pay,[2] the area of maternity pay came under scrutiny in a similar way with the stated aim of cutting out what Government saw as wasteful administrative effort,

---

[1] C. Callender *et al.*, *Maternity rights and benefits in Britain 1996*, DSS Research Report No. 67.
[2] Under the Social Security and Housing Benefits Act 1982 (now Part XI of the Social Security Contributions and Benefits Act 1992 and Regulations (S.I. 1982 No. 894). See para. 4.3.2 above.

whereby maternity allowance was paid by the state directly to those who qualified, and those employed for two years or more who became eligible for maternity pay, were paid by the employer after deducting the state maternity allowance. The employer then recovered the amount paid as maternity allowance from a state fund. As a result of the review, the Social Security Act 1986 was introduced which, from 1987, reformed the area of maternity pay by the implementation of statutory maternity pay (SMP).

Rights associated with the whole area of pregnancy and childbirth underwent substantial change upon implementation of Council Directive 92/85.[3] The Directive was controversial and was opposed by the United Kingdom government because it was considered that the proposals went too far and would result in a reduction of employment opportunities for women because of the additional burdens which would be imposed on employers. In addition, the Directive was proposed under the Article 118A procedure, which authorises Directives on the health and safety of workers and permits the Council to act by qualified majority voting. The United Kingdom raised an objection to the use of this procedure, claiming that matters such as this were not truly health and safety issues so should not be subject to the Article 118A procedure, and therefore needed to be by unanimous agreement.

As originally drafted the Directive was far-reaching, but underwent considerable dilution during its legislative passage, with a reduction in the length of maternity leave, the omission of paternity leave and reversal of the burden of proof in all cases within the scope of the Directive, together with the dropping of the requirement that maternity leave should be paid in full, in favour of a requirement for payment at an "adequate" level. Agreement was finally reached, but with the United Kingdom and Italy abstaining: the United Kingdom because of its position on cost and the effect on business and its disagreement on the procedure adopted, Italy because the Directive was so diluted as to be worthless.

The Directive covers three separate groups of workers:

- pregnant workers;
- workers who have recently given birth; and
- workers who are breastfeeding,

and Article 1 states that the purpose is to implement measures to encourage improvements in the safety and health at work of those three categories of worker and may not have the effect of reducing the level of protection afforded to those workers as compared with the situation in each Member State at the time the Directive is adopted. The provisions of the Directive were introduced into domestic law by Schedule 3 of of the Trade Union Reform and Employment Rights Act 1993 (TURERA 1993) and Regulations, and the principal employment provisions are now contained in the Employment Rights Act 1996 (ERA 1996) and the various aspects may conveniently be divided into the following headings:

- time off for anti-natal care, ERA 1996, ss.55–57;
- dismissal or selection for redundancy on the grounds of pregnancy, sections 99 and 105 and the Sex Discrimination Act 1975, dismissal of maternity

---

[3] On the introduction of measures to encourage improvements in the safety and health of pregnant workers and workers who have recently given birth or are breastfeeding.

replacement and written statement of reasons for dismissal; ERA 1996, ss.106, 92(4)

- the right to maternity leave and to return to work, ERA 1996, Part VIII; general right to maternity leave, section 71; long maternity leave and the right to return, section 79;

- the right to pay on the occasion of pregnancy and during maternity leave; maternity allowance and statutory maternity pay; Social Security Contributions and Benefits Act 1992;

- health and safety and rights in relation to suspension from work on maternity grounds, Management of Health and Safety at Work Amendment Regulations; ERA 1996, ss.66–70 and

- parental leave, Directive 92/85.

10.2 TIME OFF WORK FOR ANTI-NATAL CARE

The ERA 1996, s.55, implementing Article 9 of Directive 92/85, provides that employees, regardless of length of service or hours worked, are entitled to time off during contractual working hours to keep an appointment for anti-natal care. There is no definition of anti-natal care, but the right applies to an employee who is pregnant and who has, on the advice of a registered medical practitioner, registered midwife or registered health visitor, made an appointment to attend at any place for the purposes of receiving anti-natal care. In this connection most women have their first anti-natal appointment somewhere between the eighth and twelfth week of pregnancy, and traditionally anti-natal care involves 14 appointments, although Government now recommends nine for a first pregnancy and six for subsequent pregnancies, and most health authorities are now following this recommendation. These "standard" visits will undoubtedly fall within the definition of "anti-natal care", but additional visits will be covered by this provision if they comply with section 55(1)(b) in that the appointment is on the advice of a registered medical practitioner, etc. In *Gregory v. Tudsbury Ltd*[4] it was held that "anti-natal care" was wide enough to cover relaxation classes, so long as the individual was acting on medical advice. By section 56, the employee is entitled to be paid contractual remuneration for the time off under section 55.

The employee is not entitled to time off for other than the first appointment unless she produces, if requested by her employer to do so, evidence of her pregnancy, by way of a certificate from a registered medical practitioner, registered midwife or registered health visitor, stating that she is pregnant and an appointment card, or some other evidence that an appointment has been made.

There is no requirement or provision for the time off to be made up or for any other arrangements to be made in order to avoid the necessity to take time off during working hours or to make appointments at a time to suit the employer. In *Sajil v. Carraro t/a Foubert's Bar*[5] the tribunal remarked that it was important not to allow unscrupulous employers any scope for requiring or persuading a pregnant woman to reorganise her working hours or to make up for lost time.

---

[4] [1982] I.R.L.R. 267, IT.
[5] COIT 1890/34.

A complaint may be made to an industrial tribunal for unreasonable refusal to permit time off, or to pay, or pay the appropriate rate, for that time. The complaint must be made within three months of the appointment concerned, with a discretion for the tribunal to extend that time if it is satisfied that it was not reasonably practicable for the complaint to be presented within three months.

Gregory v. Tudsbury Ltd[6] confirms that having granted permission for time off the employer is obliged to make payment, even if it was inconvenient for that time to be taken. However, if an employer fails to permit time off it is for the tribunal to decide whether the refusal was reasonable. When dismissal occurs on the basis of a poor attendance record, and the poor attendance arose from attendance at ante-natal classes, it was held in *Mains v. M.D. Homes*[7] that the dismissal was for a reason connected with pregnancy and as such automatically unfair under ERA 1996, s.99(1)(a).

10.3 DISMISSAL ON GROUNDS OF PREGNANCY

The right not to be unfairly dismissed because of pregnancy or childbirth was introduced in the EPA 1975. However, the right was hedged about with restrictions, being subject to the qualifying conditions associated with unfair dismissal generally. This meant that whilst the general qualifying period was two years[8] and a woman with a contract to work 16 or more hours a week came within that qualifying period, a woman with a contract for eight or more hours a week had to have five or more years service and someone with a contract for less than eight hours a week had no right, regardless of the length of service.

These qualifications were successfully challenged in *R. v. SS for Employment ex parte EOC*[9] where the House of Lords held the conditions to be contrary to Article 119 and the Equal Treatment Directive as being indirectly discriminatory in that they had a disparate impact on women because fewer women than men could comply with the conditions, because women generally have shorter periods of service. It was held that the limitations could not be justified on the social policy grounds put forward by the Government. As a result of the House of Lords' decision regulations were introduced to abolish the differential qualifying conditions not just for unfair dismissal and redundancy, but for a whole range of other employment rights.[10] This, however, left the general two year qualifying condition in place, and this was subsequently challenged in *R. v. SS for Employment ex parte Seymour-Smith*.[11] However, in so far as dismissal for reasons connected with pregnancy and childbirth are concerned, implementation of Directive 92/85 resulted in a new section 60 being inserted into the EPCA 1978,[12] the provisions of which are now contained in the ERA 1996, s.99, whereby the qualifying service provisions contained in the ERA 1996, s.108, by section 108(3)(b), do not apply.

---

[6] [1982] I.R.L.R. 267, IT.
[7] Case No. 2200316/96, noted in EOR Discrimination Case Law Digest No. 34.
[8] Unfair Dismissal (Variation of Qualifying Period) Order 1985 (S.I. 1985 No. 782).
[9] [1994] I.C.R. 317, HL.
[10] Employment Protection (Part-time Employees) Regulations 1995 (S.I. 1995 No. 31).
[11] [1997] 2 All E.R. 273, HL. The House of Lords referred the questions at 281 to the ECJ.
[12] Effective June 10, 1994.

ERA 1996, s.99 provides that a dismissal is automatically unfair if:

"(1) . . .
(a) the reason (or . . . principal reason) for the dismissal is that she is pregnant or any other reason connected with her pregnancy,
(b) her maternity leave period is ended by the dismissal and the reason (or . . . principal reason) for the dismissal is that she has given birth . . . or any other reason connected with her having given birth to a child,
(c) her contract of employment is terminated after the end of her maternity leave period and the reason (or . . . principal reason) for the dismissal is that she took, or availed herself of the benefits of, maternity leave,
(d) the reason (or . . . principal reason) for the dismissal is a relevant requirement, or a relevant recommendation, as defined by section 66(2), [the health and safety grounds] or
(e) her maternity leave period is ended by the dismissal, the reason (or . . . principal reason) for the dismissal is that she is redundant and section 77 has not been complied with [entitlement to be offered alternative employment]."

Employment Rights Act 1996, s.99(1).

Similarly the ERA 1996, s.105(2) provides that dismissal for redundancy for any of the reasons in section 99(1)(a)–(d) is automatically unfair.

Prior to amendment, the need to fulfil the two year qualifying period, and before that the hours threshold, for unfair dismissal, resulted in extensive use of the SDA 1975 to overcome these limitations. This route has a number of advantages in that following the repeal of the SDA 1975, s.65(2)[13] it is not, unlike unfair dismissal, subject to an upper limit on compensation, nor do the recoupment provisions, which provide for certain state benefits to be deducted from compensation for unfair dismissal, apply. However, the difficulties associated with this route are demonstrated through case law associated with interpretation of the SDA 1975 and the Equal Treatment Directive 76/207.

In *Turley v. Allders Department Store Ltd*[14] the EAT confirmed that pregnancy was not within the definition of discrimination because the SDA 1975, s.1 requires the court to look at men and women and see that they are not treated differently simply because they are men and women. To find out whether a woman has been less favourably treated it is necessary to compare like with like: to find a comparator, and in the case of a pregnant woman that was impossible because when she is pregnant a woman is no longer a woman, but is a woman with child, and there is no masculine equivalent. One of the lay members dissented saying:

"I do not accept the conclusion that a woman dismissed from her employment on the ground of pregnancy has no protection under the Sex Discrimination Act. Such a bald assertion seems to me to contradict both the spirit and the letter of the statutes." *per* Ms Smith.

Turley v. Allders Department Store Ltd [1980] I.R.L.R. 4 at 4, EAT.

She said that pregnancy is a medical condition, and one which applied only to women and one which would lead to a request for time off for confinement, just as a man

---

[13] By the Sex Discrimination and Equal Pay (Remedies) Regulations 1993 (S.I. 1993 No. 2798).
[14] [1980] I.R.L.R. 4, EAT.

might require time off for a hernia, and an employer must not discriminate by applying less favourable criteria: that, she said, is the like for like comparison. This reasoning was followed by the EAT in *Hayes v. Malleable Working Mens Club*[15] where the EAT found support in the SDA 1975, s.5(3) in that the comparison between the two cases must be the same or not materially different. They could, the EAT said, never be the same, but nevertheless could properly be regarded as lacking any material difference. In deciding that there was no principle of law preventing the application of the Sex Discrimination Act to cases where a woman claims to have been the victim of direct or indirect discrimination on grounds associated with the fact that she is pregnant, they preferred the dissenting view in *Turley*. The proper approach being to ask whether pregnancy (with its associated consequences) is capable of being matched by analogous circumstances (such as sickness) applying to a man, and if so whether they are closely enough matched to enable a fair comparison to be made between the favourableness of treatment accorded to a woman in the one situation and to a man in the other.

The ECJ was asked, in the case of *Dekker v. Stichting Vormingscentrum Voor Jonge Volwassen (VJV-Centrum) Plus*[16] whether an employer was directly or indirectly in breach of the principle of equal treatment referred to in Articles 2(1) and 3(1) of the Equal Treatment Directive 76/207, if he refuses to enter into a contract of employment with an applicant found suitable by him, where the refusal is on the ground of the possible adverse consequences for him arising from employing a woman who, at the time of the application, was pregnant.

The applicant applied for a post as a training instructor and at interview informed the selection committee that she was pregnant. Whilst the committee recommended her to the Board as the best qualified applicant, the Board refused to appoint her because under Government Regulations they would have been obliged to pay sickness benefit during the period she would be unable to work, but although insured, would be unable to claim reimbursement because they knew of a pending claim at the time she was taken on.

Advocate General Darmon proposed that Articles 2(1) and 3(1) of Directive 76/207 must be interpreted as meaning that a refusal by an employer to engage a female worker by reason of her pregnancy constitutes direct discrimination on grounds of sex while the ECJ, in a brief and to the point judgment, said that an employer is acting in direct contravention of Articles 2(1) and 3(1) of the Directive if he refuses to employ a suitable female applicant because of the possible adverse consequences to him arising from the fact that she is pregnant at the time of the application. Whether this results in direct discrimination on grounds of sex will depend upon whether the reason for refusal applies exclusively to one sex, and as employment can only be refused because of pregnancy in so far as a woman is concerned, such a refusal is direct discrimination on grounds of sex, regardless of whether there was a male applicant. The ECJ said that whether the refusal to recruit a woman constitutes discrimination depends on the motive for refusal: if the motive is because the woman is pregnant the decision is directly related to the applicant's sex.

So, the SDA 1975 requirement for a comparator appears to be in conflict with this interpretation of Directive 76/207. In addition, the Court held that liability under the Directive is not dependent upon evidence of fault or the absence of grounds of legal justification. The sanction, in accordance with the decision in *Von Colson and Kamann*

---

[15] [1985] I.R.L.R. 367, EAT.
[16] C–177/88 [1991] I.R.L.R. 27, ECJ.

v. Land Nordrhein-Westfalen[17] must be such as to guarantee real and effective judicial protection.

In *Handels-og Kontorfunktionaerernes Forbund i Danmark (Union of Clerical and Commercial Employees) (For Hertz) v. Dansk Arbejdsgiverforening (Danish Employers' Association) (For Aldi Marked K/S))* (the *Hertz* case),[18] a part-time cashier and saleswoman whose complicated pregnancy involved a lot of sick leave, had 24 weeks maternity leave after the birth and after resuming work was frequently absent as a result of problems arising from her pregnancy and confinement. She was subsequently dismissed as a result of the repeated sickness absences. The case was referred to the ECJ on the question of whether Directive 76/207, Art. 2(1), covers dismissals which are in consequence of absences due to an illness which has its origin in pregnancy and confinement.

The ECJ said that the dismissal of a female worker because of her pregnancy constitutes direct discrimination on grounds of sex, in the same way as does the refusal to recruit a pregnant woman. Therefore, a woman is protected from dismissal because of her absence during the maternity leave period. However, in connection with absences after the maternity leave period, the Court said there was no reason to distinguish it from any other illness, even where it has its origin in pregnancy. The only question after expiry of the maternity leave period is whether a woman is dismissed for absence on the same conditions as a man. If sickness absence would lead to the dismissal of a male worker under the same conditions, there is no discrimination on the ground of sex.

These decisions of the ECJ left the domestic decisions regarding interpretation of the SDA 1975 looking somewhat defective and this was put to the test in *Webb v. EMO Air Cargo (U.K.) Ltd*[19] when the Court of Appeal had to consider whether the dismissal of a woman acting as a maternity leave replacement, was discriminatory because she herself was pregnant. The reason for dismissal was not in dispute since the employer had written: "Since you have only now told me that you are pregnant I have no alternative other than to terminate your employment with our company".

Before the Court of Appeal Ms Webb's argument was two-pronged:

- only a woman could be pregnant: a woman who was dismissed for any reason related to her pregnancy would not have been dismissed but for her sex and was thus discriminated against on the ground of her sex, and

- since refusal of employment to a woman only because of her pregnancy had been held by the ECJ to be direct discrimination on grounds of sex, dismissal on the same ground was also direct discrimination and contrary to Council Directive 76/207.

The Court of Appeal, however, dismissed the appeal and held that dismissal of a pregnant woman for a reason arising out of, or related to, her pregnancy could, but would not necessarily, be direct discrimination under the SDA 1975, s.1(1)(a). In following earlier authority they held that whether it did amount to discrimination depended on whether a man would have been dismissed by the employer if in the same situation he would have been absent for medical reasons for the same length of time,

[17] Case C–14/83 [1984] E.C.R. 1891, ECJ.
[18] Case C–179/88 [1990] E.C.R. I–3979, ECJ.
[19] [1993] I.R.L.R. 27, CA.

since the comparison to be made for the purpose of determining whether there had been discrimination was between a pregnant woman and a man who required to be absent for the same period of time and at the same time because of a medical condition, rather than between a pregnant woman and a man. Glidewell L.J. said:

"... I accept ... that ss.1(1) and 5(3) of the 1975 Act expressly require a comparison to be made between the dismissal of the complainant, the pregnant woman, and what would have happened to a male employee in the nearest comparable situation." *per* Glidewell L.J.

Webb v. EMO Air Cargo (U.K.) Ltd [1992] 2 All E.R. 43 at 52, CA.

Distinguishing both *Dekker*[20] and the *Hertz* case[21] the Court of Appeal held that the decision of the industrial tribunal, that Ms Webb was dismissed because of "her anticipated inability to carry out the primary task for which she was recruited", did not conflict with the judgment in the *Dekker* case. Relying on Lord Templeman in *Duke v. GEC Reliance Ltd*[22] which, Glidewell L.J. said, "points to the correct approach for this court to adopt", the Court held that if there was a conflict with the Directive it could not be resolved because to interpret the 1975 Act so that discrimination on grounds of pregnancy was automatically discrimination on grounds of sex, would be to distort the meaning of the Act and enforce against an individual a Directive that was not, in these circumstances, directly effective.

"I do not accept that the European Court's decision in the *Dekker* case is to the effect that any refusal to employ a pregnant woman who is, apart from her pregnancy, otherwise suitably qualified for the job, or that any dismissal of a pregnant woman arising out of her pregnancy, is necessarily discriminatory. In my view it is open to this court to adopt the interpretation of ss.1(1) and 5(3) of the 1975 Act which, ... I believe to be correct without conflicting with the European Court in the *Dekker* case or with Directive 76/207." *per* Glidewell L.J.

Webb v. EMO Air Cargo (U.K.) Ltd [1992] 2 All E.R. 43 at 57, CA.

The Court also upheld the EAT decision that the dismissal was not indirect discrimination despite wrongly applying the test of justification of Eveleigh L.J. in *Ojutiku and Obuzoni v. Manpower Services Commission*.[23] Glidewell L.J. said the correct test was to be found in the judgment of Blacombe L.J. in *Hampson v. Department of Education and Science*,[24] namely: "... 'justifiable' requires an objective balance between the discriminatory effect of the condition and the reasonable needs of the party who applies the condition" which was based on the judgment of Stephenson L.J. in the *Ojutiku* case. Despite this misdirection, the decision of the EAT was held to be "plainly and unarguably correct".

On appeal the House of Lords held in *Webb* that to dismiss a woman because she is pregnant or to refuse to employ a woman of childbearing age because she may become

---

[20] [1990] E.C.R. I–3941, ECJ.
[21] [1990] E.C.R. I–3979, ECJ.
[22] [1988] 1 All E.R. 626, HL.
[23] [1982] I.C.R. 661 at 668, CA.
[24] [1990] 2 All E.R. 25 at 34, CA.

pregnant is unlawful direct discrimination since childbearing and the capacity for childbearing are characteristics of the female sex. To apply these characteristics as the criterion for dismissal or refusal to employ is to apply a gender-based criterion which had been held in *James v. Eastleigh Borough Council*[25] to be unlawful. However, it was held that in the current circumstances there was no place for the "but for their sex" test developed in the earlier case of *R. v. Birmingham City Council ex parte EOC*[26] because here Ms Webb had been dismissed not because she was pregnant, but because her pregnancy had the consequence that she would not be available for work at the critical period and the same treatment would have been given to a man who was not available: a legitimate comparison under the SDA 1975, s.5(3). That the reason for not being available was pregnancy, a condition that could only affect women, was not relevant because the precise reason for non-availability was not a relevant considera-tion. This argument is difficult to sustain taking into consideration that following implementation of the amendments introduced by TURERA 1993 it is no longer possible to fairly dismiss a woman on the grounds that she is incapable of performing her job due to her pregnancy.

In connection with indirect discrimination: Lord Keith confirmed that the correct test for justification was that formulated by Balcombe L.J. in *Hampson v. Department of Education and Science*[27] and agreed with the Court of Appeal that had the industrial tribunal applied the correct test they would inevitably have come to the same conclusion.

The House of Lords made a reference to the European Court, namely: whether it is discrimination on grounds of sex contrary to the Equal Treatment Directive for an employer to dismiss a female employee:

(a) whom he engaged for the specific purpose of replacing (after training) another female employee during the latter's forthcoming maternity leave;

(b) when, very shortly after appointment, the employer discovers that the appellant herself will be absent on maternity leave during the maternity leave of the other employee, and the employer dismisses her because he needs the job holder to be at work during that period;

(c) where, had the employer known of the pregnancy of the appellant at the date of appointment, she would not have been appointed; and

(d) where the employer would similarly have dismissed a male employee engaged for this purpose who required leave of absence at the relevant time for medical or other reasons.

The ECJ ruled[28] that the Directive envisaged special protection being given to women by prohibiting dismissal during the period from the beginning of their pregnancy to the end of their maternity leave and that there is to be no exception to, or derogation from, the prohibition on the dismissal of pregnant women during that period. In the light of this the ECJ said that there could be no question of comparing the situation of a woman who found herself incapable, by reason of pregnancy discovered shortly after

[25] [1989] I.R.L.R. 318, HL.
[26] [1989] I.R.L.R. 173, HL.
[27] [1990] I.R.L.R. 302, HL.
[28] Case C–32/93 [1994] 4 All E.R. 115, ECJ.

the conclusion of the employment contract, of performing the task for which she had been recruited, with that of a man similarly incapable for medical or other reasons, since pregnancy was in no way comparable with a pathological condition. The ECJ referred to its decision in the *Hertz* case,[29] which was confirmed in *Habermann-Beltermann v. Arbeiterwohlfahrt, Bezirksverband Ndb/Opf eV*,[30] that the dismissal of a female worker on account of pregnancy constitutes direct discrimination on grounds of sex.

Nor, said the ECJ, could the dismissal of a pregnant woman recruited for an indefinite period, be justified because she would be unavailable. Although availability is necessary for the fundamental performance of the contract, the protection afforded by Community law outweighed the necessity for her availability: any other interpretation, the Court held, would render ineffective the provisions of Directive 76/207. The later decision of the ECJ in *Gillespie v. Northern Health and Social Services Board*[31] that European law does not require that women continue to receive full pay during maternity leave was made on the basis of Article 119 and Directive 75/117, since the Equal Treatment Directive does not apply to pay. However, having held that women are afforded special protection during the protected period, and that in so doing there could not be a comparison between men and women, the consequence must surely be that similarly no comparison can likewise be made on pay. Having decided that the issue was one of direct discrimination, no question of justification arises, since direct discrimination cannot be justified.

On reference back to the House of Lords,[32] in accepting the decision of the ECJ Lord Keith, giving the judgment of the Court, attempted to fit the ruling of the European Court on an interpretation of the broad principles dealt with in Articles 2(1) and 5(1) of Directive 76/207 with those contained in the Sex Discrimination Act 1975, ss.1(1)(a) and 5(3): He said that:

> "It seems to me that the only way of doing so is to hold that, in a case where a woman is engaged for an indefinite period, the fact that the reason why she will be temporarily unavailable for work at a time when to her knowledge her services will be particularly required is pregnancy is a circumstance relevant to her case, being a circumstance which could not be present in the case of the hypothetical man. It does not necessarily follow that pregnancy would be a relevant circumstance in the situation where the woman is denied employment for a fixed period in the future during the whole of which her pregnancy would make her unavailable for work, nor in the situation where after engagement for such a period the discovery of her pregnancy leads to cancellation of the engagement." *per* Lord Keith.

Webb v. EMO Air Cargo (U.K.) Ltd (No. 2) [1995] 4 All E.R. 577 at 582, HL.

Since it was the indefinite duration of the contract that was of importance, and Ms Webb's contract was for an indefinite period, her dismissal, based as it was on her non-availability for work due to pregnancy, was direct discrimination under the 1975 Act.

[29] Case C–179/88) [1990] E.C.R. I–3979, ECJ.
[30] Case C–421/92 [1994] I.R.L.R. 364, ECJ.
[31] Case C–342/93 [1996] I.R.L.R. 214, ECJ.
[32] [1995] 4 All E.R. 577, HL.

The exception alluded to by Lord Keith in *Webb (No. 2)* arose in *Caruana v. Manchester Airport plc*[33] when a woman working on a series of fixed-term contracts was told that she would not be offered further work when she told her employers that she was pregnant, on the basis that she would not be available at the start of the contract as a result of maternity leave. The EAT, hearing the appeal after the ECJ decision in *Webb* and the resulting House of Lords decision in *Webb (No. 2)*, held that although the decision not to offer a new contract was because of non-availability, that non-availability was because of pregnancy, and therefore on grounds of her sex. As to the argument that the ruling of the ECJ, and that of the House of Lords in *Webb* attached importance to the fact that the employee was there employed for an "indefinite period" and that the ruling does not extend at all to fixed-term contracts: having considered the relevant parts of the judgment in *Webb*, Buxton J., in allowing the appeal and remitting the case for assessment of compensation said:

> "We cannot accept that. Such a contention is not consistent with Lord Keith"s limitation of a possible special rule for fixed-term contracts to cases where the employee would be available for no part of the term." *per* Buxton J.

Caruana v. Manchester Airport plc. [1996] I.R.L.R. 378 at 380, EAT.

In any event, Buxton J. observed, that the series of contracts under which the appellant had been employed constituted "employment" for a continuous period and what she was complaining of was a failure to extend that relationship:

> "That is very far away both in practical employment terms and in employment law from the case tentatively identified by Lord Keith, where the employee will be unable to perform any part of one contract, and one contract only, offered her by someone who, in popular language, will never be able to 'employ' her at all." *per* Buxton J.

Caruana v. Manchester Airport plc. [1996] I.R.L.R. 378 at 380, EAT.

The protection for pregnant women during what has become known as "the protected period" during which unfavourable treatment on the grounds of a pregnancy, which is unique to women and is direct sex discrimination without the need for comparison with the treatment that would have been given to men, is demonstrated in *Stephenson v. F. A. Wellworth & Co. Ltd*.[34] The Northern Ireland Court of Appeal, held that failure to allow a pregnant employee to return from sick leave prior to commencing maternity leave, urging her instead to stay on sick leave and claim statutory sick pay for the three remaining weeks before commencing maternity leave, amounted to discrimination on grounds of pregnancy, and hence of sex. It was held that it was not necessary for her to compare her treatment with that which would have been received by a male comparator since the court rejected that a distinction had to be made between pregnancy on the one hand and illness attributable to pregnancy on the other. The court declined to adopt the reasoning of the Court of Session in *Brown v. Rentokil*[35] in

---

[33] [1996] I.R.L.R. 378, EAT.
[34] IDS Brief 594/1997 p. 12.
[35] [1995] I.R.L.R. 211, CS.

which it was held that even after the European Court's decision in *Webb*, there is no sex discrimination against a pregnant woman dismissed as a result of absence due to a pregnancy-related illness before the start of maternity leave if she is treated the same way as a man absent through illness.

There is consequently some conflict as to when the protected period starts, and indeed when it finishes and whether, when the unfavourable treatment is pregnancy related it is necessary to compare the treatment received with that which would have been received by a sick man. Whilst in the *Hertz* case[36] the European Court, in applying the Equal Treatment Directive 76/207, said that the Directive extends to provide special protection to dismissals resulting from a pregnancy related absence, so that unfavourable treatment on the grounds of a pregnancy-related illness is direct discrimination, that special protection does not extend beyond the maternity leave period (MLP), even though the illness, which did not manifest itself until after the MLP, had its origins in pregnancy. The ECJ confirmed this reasoning in the subsequent case of *Handels-og Kontorfunktionaererernes Forbund I Danmark (acting for Larsson) v. Dansk Handel & Service (acting for Føtex Supermarked A/S)*[37] (the *Larsson* case) in a situation where the pregnancy related illness arose during maternity leave, by ruling that "the (Equal Treatment) Directive does not concern illness attributable to pregnancy or confinement" except that special protection is offered during maternity leave so as not to undermine the right to maternity leave. So that once the maternity leave period has come to an end the special protection also ends.

The decision in *Larsson* would seem to support the reasoning of the Court of Session in *Brown v. Rentokil Initial United Kingdom Ltd*,[38] whereas the Northern Ireland Court of Appeal in *Stephenson v. F. A. Wellworth & Co. Ltd*[39] proceeds on the basis that the protected period runs from the date of becoming pregnant, or perhaps more properly of the employer being aware of the pregnancy, in the light of the decision in *Dentons Directories Ltd. v. Hobbs*,[40] to the end of the maternity leave period. It should, however, be noted that both *Hertz* and *Larsson* were considering absence and dismissal after the end of the maternity leave period and before the implementation of the Pregnancy Directive, Directive 92/85.

In *Larsson* the ECJ indicated that following implementation of Directive 92/85 in October 1994 the protected period extends to cover the period prior to maternity leave namely:

> "It must, however, be noted that, in view of the harmful effects which the risk of dismissal may have on the physical and mental state of women who are pregnant, . . . the Community legislature subsequently provided, pursuant to Article 10 of Council Directive 92/85/EEC of 19 October 1992 on the introduction of measures to encourage improvements in the safety and health at work of pregnant workers and workers who have recently given birth or are breastfeeding . . . for special protection to be given to women, by prohibiting dismissal during the period from the beginning of their pregnancy to the end of their maternity leave, save in exceptional cases unconnected with her condition. . . . It is clear from the

---

[36] Case C–179/88 [1991] I.R.L.R. 31, ECJ.
[37] Case C–400/95 [1997] I.R.L.R. 643, ECJ.
[38] [1995] I.R.L.R. 211, CS.
[39] IDS Brief 594/1997, p. 12.
[40] EAT 821/96. IDS Brief 1997/589, p. 6.

objective of that provision that absence during the protected period, other than for reasons unconnected with the employee's condition, can no longer be taken into account as grounds for subsequent dismissal. . ."

Case C–400/95 *Handels-og Kontorfunktionaerernes Forbund I Danmark (acting for Larsson) v. Dansk Handel & Service (acting for Føtex Supermarked A/S)* [1997] I.R.L.R. 643 at 650, ECJ.

In the light of the ruling by the ECJ in *Larsson,* in so far as the extension of the protected period provided for by Directive 92/85 is concerned, it would appear that although the protected period covers pregnancy it does not extend to periods after the MLP, and that absences arising during pregnancy and as a result of maternity leave, cannot be taken into account in subsequent decisions regarding dismissal or promotion. In *Caisse nationale d'assutance vieillesse des travailleurs salaries (CNAVTS) v. Thibault*[41] a contractual term meant that promotion was dependent upon performance assessment, to be eligible for which employees had to have been present at work for the previous six months. The ECJ was asked to rule on the legality of such a rule in the light of the fact that women who had been absent on maternity leave were thereby deprived of the possibility of promotion. The Advocate General confirmed that the Equal Treatment Directive precluded a national provision of contractual origin which, whilst neutral in terms, the practical application of which constituted direct sex discrimination in that it permits absence on maternity leave to be counted as absence due to sickness.[42] This seems to be in line with the ECJ interpretation of Directive 76/207 in *Hertz* and *Larsson* that the Equal Treatment Directive provides special protection during the maternity leave period, and it would appear that following implementation of Directive 92/85, the same reasoning and protection now extends to absences during pregnancy.

In *Brown v. Rentokil Initial U.K. Ltd,*[43] dismissal occurred during pregnancy under a rule which applied equally to male and female workers, that non availability for work for a period of 26 consecutive weeks would result in dismissal, in circumstances where, because of lack of the necessary continuous employment, there was no right to maternity leave or to return to work. A reference was made by the House of Lords to the European Court, the questions for the Court being:

"1. (a) Is it contrary to Articles 2(1) and 5(1) of Directive 76/207 of the Council of the European Communities . . . to dismiss a female employee, at any time during her pregnancy, as a result of absence through illness arising from that pregnancy?

(b) Does it make any difference to the answer given to Question 1(a) that the employee was dismissed in pursuance of a contractual provision entitling the employer to dismiss employees, irrespective of gender, after a stipulated number of weeks of continued absence?

---

[41] Case C–136/95 ECJ, IDS Brief 583/February 1997.
[42] ECJ Employment Law Watch No. 5, Spring 1998. A decision upheld by ECJ [1998] I.R.L.R. 399, ECJ.
[43] Case C–394/96 ECJ, Employment Law Watch No. 5, Spring 1998.

2. (a) Is it contrary to Articles 2(1) and 5(1) of the Equal Treatment Directive to dismiss a female employee as a result of absence through illness arising from pregnancy who does not qualify for the right to absent herself from work on account of pregnancy or childbirth for the period specified by national law because she has not been employed for the period imposed by national law, where dismissal takes place during that period?

   (b) Does it make any difference to the answer given to Question 2(a) that the employee was dismissed in pursuance of a contractual provision entitling the employer to dismiss employees, irrespective of gender, after a stipulated number of weeks of continued absence?"

In his opinion[44] Advocate General Ruiz-Jarabo Colomer subjects the cases of *Dekker*,[45] *Hertz*,[46] *Habermann-Beltermann*[47] and *Webb*[48] to detailed analysis and says that:

"I believe, . . ., that there is very good reason, for the sake of legal certainty, for the Court to give a clear ruling on the principle of equal treatment for men and women in relation to dismissals of female workers occurring during pregnancy or after maternity leave, where account was taken to period of unavailability for work caused by pregnancy, before the commencement of maternity leave. . . ." *per* Advocate General Ruiz-Jarabo Colomer

(Case C–394/96) *Brown v. Rentokil Initial U.K. Ltd*, Opinion of Advocate General, delivered on February 5, 1998, para. 50.

Advocate General Ruiz-Jarabo Colomer goes on to conclude:

". . . I consider that the dismissal of a woman whilst she is pregnant, on account of unfitness for work caused by her pregnancy, by taking into consideration a situation in which only women can find themselves, constitutes direct discrimination contrary to Article 5(1) of Directive 76/207 . . . the fact that the dismissal is based on a contractual provision entitling the employer to dismiss a worker, regardless of gender, after a specific period of sick leave, has no impact on the foregoing answer." paras 66 and 69.

Whilst this opinion is based on a review of the decisions in the four cases considered by the ECJ to date, and the law in Member States, it appears to blur the boundaries between Directive 76/207 and Directive 92/85. *Brown v. Rentokil* fell to be considered under Directive 76/207 because at the time of Ms Brown's dismissal Directive 92/85 ". . . had not even been adopted", but if Directive 76/207 provides for a special protected period for pregnancy that extends from the beginning of pregnancy until the end of the MLP, one must ask why it was necessary to incorporate within Directive 92/85 via Article 10 that:

---

[44] Delivered on February 5, 1998. Subsequently upheld by ECJ [1998] I.R.L.R. 445, ECJ.
[45] Case C–177/88 [1991] I.R.L.R. 27, ECJ.
[46] Case C–179/88 [1990] ECR I–3979, ECJ.
[47] Case C–421/92 [1994] I.R.L.R. 364, ECJ.
[48] Case C–32/93 [1994] 4 All E.R. 115, ECJ.

"Member States shall take the necessary measures to prohibit the dismissal of workers, within the meaning of Article 2, during the period from the beginning of their pregnancy to the end of the maternity leave referred to in Article 8(1) save in exceptional cases not connected with their condition which are permitted under national legislation and/or practice and, where applicable, provided that the competent authority has given its consent;"

Article 10.1 of Council Directive 92/85.

As has been discussed above, Directive 92/85 was implemented by the Trade Union Reform and Employment Rights Act 1993, which amended the relevant provisions of the EPCA 1978 and are now contained in ERA 1996, Part VIII, and in so far as dismissals are concerned in sections 96 and 99: none of which applied in Ms Brown's case, the facts of which arose prior to implementation of these provisions.

10.3.1 Dismissal of maternity replacement

Where an employee is taken on to replace another employee who is absent wholly or partly because of pregnancy or childbirth, or because of suspension on maternity grounds, the replacement's subsequent dismissal to enable the original employee to resume work is, by the ERA 1996, s.106 deemed to be for "some other substantial reason" within the ERA 1996, s.98(1)(b), and therefore potentially fair, the fairness being judged by section 98(4).

In order for this section to apply the replacement employee must be told in writing on engagement that their employment will be terminated on the resumption of work of the person being replaced.

10.3.2 Written statement of reasons for dismissal

An employee dismissed at any time whilst pregnant or after childbirth in circumstances in which her maternity leave period ends by dismissal is by the ERA 1996, s.92(4) automatically entitled to receive a written statement of reasons for dismissal. Where dismissal is for any other reason a request must be made and the entitlement is subject to a qualifying period of not less than two years' service. By section 93 a complaint may be made to an industrial tribunal if the employer unreasonably fails to supply a statement or if the reasons given in the statement are inadequate or untrue. A statement supplied under this section is admissible in evidence in any proceedings.

10.4 RIGHT TO MATERNITY LEAVE AND TO RETURN TO WORK

Prior to the introduction of Directive 92/85, the EPCA 1978 provided for a right to maternity leave, conditional upon two years' continuous service, with a right to return to work up to 29 weeks after the week in which childbirth occurred. Article 8 of Directive 92/85 requires Member States to introduce a general right, without the necessity of qualifying conditions, to a continuous period of maternity leave of at least

14 weeks and by Article 1(3) the Directive may not have the effect of reducing the level of protection as compared with the situation which exists in each Member State when the Directive was adopted. When the Directive was implemented a new "short" maternity leave period of 14 weeks was introduced as a general right, not conditional upon either hours worked or length of service. This right is now contained in the ERA 1996, Pt. VIII. The pre-existing right to leave is retained and is now contained in the ERA, s.79 and is expressed as a right to return to work 29 weeks after the week in which childbirth occurs. Before the 1993 amendments the complexity of the maternity provisions was bemoaned by the courts as exemplified by Browne-Wilkinson J.:

> "The statutory provisions are of inordinate complexity exceeding the worst excesses of a taxing statute; we find that especially regrettable bearing in mind that they are regulating the everyday rights of ordinary employers and employees. We feel no confidence that, even with the assistance of detailed arguments from skilled advocates, we have now correctly understood them: it is difficult to see how an ordinary employer or employee is expected to do so. Doing the best we can with this unpromising matter, the position seems to be as follows. . . ." *per* Browne-Wilkinson J.

Lavery v. Plessey Telecommunications Ltd [1982] I.R.L.R. 180 at 182, EAT.

Following the introduction of a general right to maternity leave (MLP), the statutory interaction between the MLP and long leave, and the conditions associated with each, the complexity has not eased. In order to retain the rights that are given the courts have generally insisted upon adherence to the letter rather than the spirit of the legislative structure.

10.4.1   General right to maternity leave (MLP)

The ERA 1996, ss.71–78 provides a general right for employees, regardless of length of service or hours worked, to a period of 14 weeks' maternity leave (MLP), during which the woman is entitled to the benefit of the terms and conditions of employment which would have been applicable to her if she had not been absent, except the right to remuneration. Any absence for a pregnancy related reason after the sixth week before the expected week of childbirth (EWC) will trigger the statutory MLP, (s.72(1)(b)) and the woman will not then be eligible for statutory sick pay (SSP) resulting from that sickness absence.

10.4.1.1   *Informing the employer*

The general right to MLP is conditional upon the employee complying with the notice requirements contained in the ERA 1996, ss.74–75—she must inform her employer in writing at least 21 days before her maternity leave period begins, or as soon thereafter as is reasonably practicable, that:

- she is pregnant;
- the EWC (or if the baby has been born, the date of birth), and produce a certificate from a registered medical practitioner or registered midwife (if the employer requests) stating the expected week of childbirth.

In addition, she must give notice, not less than 21 days before (or as soon as reasonably practicable), of the date upon which she wishes her maternity leave to start. Failure to comply with these notice provisions will mean that the employee will cease to be protected by the legislation once she has left work and will not have a statutory right to return.

The statutory time limits are strict and the tribunal should approach the question of whether it was reasonably practicable for the employee to have given the relevant notice in the same way as it approaches the question of whether it was reasonably practicable for an unfair dismissal complaint to have been presented within three months: in *Nu-Swift International Ltd v. Mallinson*[49] the employee was unsure of whether she wanted to return and despite the employer's request for notice, none was forthcoming before she left. She gave notice shortly before the birth, having been told that the baby would be normal and having made arrangements for childcare, but was prevented by her employer from returning.

> "It seems to us that this right . . . is given to someone who, within the relevant time, and assuming she knows or reasonably ought to know, of the provisions of the legislation and of the procedure has decided that she intends to go back to work. It is not intended to protect the person who at the time does not intend to go back to work but who subsequently changes her mind outside the period and seeks to give a notice explaining that there were factors which have changed and which have caused her to change her mind. Nor, it seems to us, does it cover the case of an employee who really is not sure either way." *per* Slynn J.

Nu-Swift International Ltd v. Mallinson [1978] I.R.L.R. 537 at 540, EAT.

10.4.1.2 *Timing and length of maternity leave period*

The MLP commences on the date which the woman notifies her employer in the notification required under section 74(1)–(3), which can be at any stage the employee chooses, but cannot begin before the eleventh week before the EWC. The MLP is triggered automatically by the birth of the child, or, if the woman is absent from work wholly or partly because of pregnancy or childbirth at any time from the beginning of the sixth week before the EWC.

The MLP continues for 14 weeks, but may be longer where:

- there is a contractual entitlement to a longer maternity leave period, in which case she may, by section 78, not exercise the two rights separately but may take advantage of whichever is more favourable;

- the employee qualifies for longer statutory maternity leave under section 79 on which see para. 10.4.2 below;

- the woman is unable to return for medical reasons and the circumstances provided for in section 99(3) apply;

- a woman is prohibited from returning to work for health and safety reasons related to having recently given birth. In such circumstances, the maternity leave period will continue until it is safe for her to return (s.73(2));

- the baby is overdue, in which case the MLP is extended to the date of birth plus a minimum period of two weeks.

[49] [1978] I.R.L.R. 537, EAT.

As required by Article 8.2 of the Directive the Maternity (Compulsory Leave) Regulations 1994[50] provide that it is compulsory for a woman to take at least two weeks' leave beginning with the day of the birth and it is unlawful to employ a woman in a factory or workshop within four weeks of her giving birth.[51]

10.4.1.3 *Contractual rights during MLP*

During the MLP the employee is entitled to the benefit of the terms and conditions of employment which would have been applicable to her if she had not been absent (and not been pregnant or given birth to a child), section 71(1), but that does not give her an entitlement to remuneration during that period, section 71(2).

There has been some disagreement as to what exactly this means, principally because "remuneration" in section 71(2) is not defined. It appears to be implied that MLP is to be treated as a form of authorised absence, during which the contract continues. If the woman is contractually entitled to benefits, such as private medical insurance, company car for private use, etc., then these must continue to be provided during the MLP, and "benefit" includes any improvements in conditions of employment that take place during her absence, including any increase in pay. This was confirmed in *Gillespie v. Northern Health and Social Services Board*[52] when the ECJ held that:

> "The principle of non-discrimination . . . requires that a woman who is still linked to her employer by a contract of employment or by an employment relationship during maternity leave must, like any other worker, benefit from any pay rise, even if backdated, which is awarded between the beginning of the period covered by reference pay and the end of maternity leave. To deny such an increase to a woman on maternity leave would discriminate against her purely in her capacity as a worker since, had she not been pregnant, she would have received the pay rise."

(Case C–342/93) *Gillespie v. Northern Health and Social Services Board* [1996] I.R.L.R. 214 at 224, ECJ.

10.4.1.4 *Statutory maternity pay (SMP) and maternity leave*

There is no right under the ERA to be paid during the MLP (s.71(2)): SMP being governed by the Social Security Contributions and Benefits Act 1992, Part XIII, which provides for an overall payment period of 18 weeks. The MLP, at 14 weeks, is therefore four weeks shorter than the period covered by SMP. If a woman does not return to work after the 14 weeks' MLP she loses her right to return, however, the conditions governing SMP provide that the right to SMP is lost if any work is undertaken during the SMP period. This leads to the situation that it is only possible to get the full period of SMP if the woman is not going to return to work, or if she qualifies for long maternity leave. Maternity pay is discussed at para. 10.5, below.

10.4.1.5 *Failure to return for medical reasons*

The ERA 1996, s.99(3) provides that it is unfair dismissal if an employer dismisses an employee within four weeks of the end of her MLP where the reason for dismissal is that the employee has given birth to a child, or any other reason connected with her having given birth to a child if:

---

[50] S.I. 1994 No. 2479, reg. 2.
[51] Public Health Act 1936, s.205.
[52] Case C–342/93 [1996] I.R.L.R. 214, ECJ.

- she has, before the end of her MLP, provided a medical certificate stating that she would be incapable of work at the end of that period, and

- she remains incapable of work, and

- the medical certificate remains current.

This provides an additional four week protected period for a woman incapable of returning to work for a pregnancy related reason, but there is no provision for a further extension.

10.4.1.6   *The right to return and notification of early return*

Unlike long leave, there is no requirement for the employee to notify her intention to return at the end of MLP, because the leave period is fixed at 14 weeks and it is implicit that when the leave period comes to an end the employee will present herself for work again. However, if the employee intends to return before the end of the MLP, she must, by section 76(1), give seven days' notice to her employer of the date on which she intends to return. If she fails to do so her employer is entitled to postpone her return for seven days, thereby ensuring he has the required seven days' notice. The suspension cannot, however, extend beyond the end of the maternity leave period (s.76(2) and (3)). If the employee nevertheless returns, the employer is not under a contractual obligation to pay her until the date upon which she may return by the giving of proper notice or the end of her MLP.

The right to return is protected by section 99(1)(b), which provides that it is automatically unfair to dismiss a woman if her maternity leave period is ended by her dismissal and the reason for her dismissal is that she has given birth to a child or any other reason connected with her having given birth to a child. The MLP is a special protected period and it was confirmed by the ECJ in the *Larsson* case[53] that this protected period comes to an end at the end of the leave period. Therefore, if the employee fails to return at the end of the 14-week period, even where the reason for non-return is pregnancy-related, that special protection no longer applies.

Loss of the right to return

The right to MLP and the consequential right to return at the end of the 14-week MLP, are conditional upon the notice provisions contained in sections 74 to 75, although in *Gray v. Smith*[54] it was held that since he had given no guidance concerning maternity rights, the employer had waived his rights relating to compliance with the strict provisions of the maternity rights legislation.

Where an employer prevents a woman who has complied with the notice requirements from returning at the end of the MLP in circumstances where that amounts to a dismissal, that is automatically unfair if the reason falls within section 99(1)(b) or (c):

- her maternity leave period is ended by the dismissal and the reason is that she has given birth to a child or any other reason connected with her having given birth; or

- her contract of employment is terminated after the end of her maternity leave period and the reason is that she took, or availed herself of the benefits of, maternity leave.

---

[53] Case C–400/95 [1997] I.R.L.R. 643, ECJ.
[54] COIT Case No. 03216–17/95, IDS Brief 584/March 1997.

Whereas section 96 deems a failure to permit return after long leave to be a dismissal, and subject to the test of fairness under ERA 1996, s.98(4), this section does not apply where the MLP is concerned. It could, in any event be argued that as the contract continues during the MLP, to prevent a woman from resuming work, and not to pay her in accordance with her contract when she is ready and willing to work, is, on general principles constructive dismissal.

Controversy and confusion has surrounded the position where the right to return is lost through failure to comply with the relevant notice requirements, or where on the expiry of MLP, or postponed maternity leave, the employer refuses to permit a return to work. In these circumstances the question arises as to whether the contract comes to an end automatically and if so when—when the woman leaves work; at the end of the MLP; at the end of the 18 week period during which statutory maternity pay is being received. Or if the employer fails to permit the woman to return because of a failure to comply with the notice requirements, the question arises as to whether that refusal amounts to a dismissal, and if so, whether it is automatically unfair because the motivating cause is based in pregnancy and childbirth, or whether such a "dismissal" is merely potentially unfair or discriminatory, and if discriminatory whether it is discriminatory *per se* or whether the treatment in question needs to be compared with that which would have occurred to a man in the same situation.

These questions have arisen over a period of time in connection with long leave and are discussed at para. 10.4.2 below, but in *McPherson v. Drumpark House*[55] the situation arose in connection with short leave. Mrs McPherson failed to give the required notices under sections 74 to 75 and when she indicated her intention to return she was told that she was no longer employed, a view her employer repeated when she later submitted a sick note. As a result she claimed that she had been dismissed for a pregnancy related reason, and that as such, the dismissal was automatically unfair. In doing so she relied on the EAT decisions in *Hilton International Hotels (U.K.) Ltd v. Kaissi*[56] and *Crouch v. Kidsons Impey*.[57] The EAT in *McPherson*[58] rejected reliance on *Crouch v. Kidsons Impey*[59] which they said did not support the argument that the contract continued whilst the woman is in receipt of SMP, notwithstanding that the woman had not complied with the relevant notification requirements:

> "A close examination of the decision (in *Crouch v. Kidsons Impey*) reveals that all it decided was that the latest possible date for termination would be the conclusion of the period of entitlement to maternity pay: and, in that case, what was being considered was a period extending well beyond that point. It does not follow that the case determines that the contract was actually subsisting during the period of payment. More importantly, it refers to the need to judge that matter against common-law rules in respect of express or implied agreement." *per* Lord Johnston.

McPherson v. Drumpark House [1997] I.R.L.R. 277 at 279, EAT.

It was held that if *Hilton International Hotels (U.K.) Ltd v. Kaissi*[60] intended to establish that as a general rule a contract of employment will subsist during the payment of

[55] [1997] I.R.L.R. 277, EAT.
[56] [1994] I.R.L.R. 270, EAT.
[57] [1996] I.R.L.R. 79, EAT.
[58] [1997] I.R.L.R. 277, EAT.
[59] [1996] I.R.L.R. 79, EAT.
[60] [1994] I.R.L.R. 270, EAT.

maternity leave, unless terminated by express or implied agreement, it was wrong and should not be followed. The EAT also said that the recent decision in *Blair v. Inverclyde Association for Mental Health*,[61] in which it was stated that it was at least arguable that so long as maternity payments were being given and received a contract would subsist, should be considered afresh.

In referring *McPherson*[62] to be reheard by a differently constituted tribunal the EAT said that the only way to preserve the contract during the MLP was for the employee to comply with the notice provisions. Where the right to return is lost because of a failure to comply with the statutory notice requirements, the question of whether or not the contract of employment subsists during the MLP has to be determined in accordance with common law principles, which require the existence of an express or implied agreement to that effect and because this is a contractual matter, as opposed to being covered by statutory provisions, each case will turn on its own facts. As a matter of generality, it was held that receipt of SMP is no more than neutral on the question of whether or not the contract continues since SMP is a statutory entitlement and not dependent upon the continuation of the contract.

It therefore appears from *McPherson*[63] that, in the absence of a contractual term regarding continuation of the contract, there is no remedy where the employer refuses to allow an employee to return where the notice provisions have not been complied with since, without a contract, there can be no dismissal. Further case law on the relevance of SMP, and the payment of statutory sick pay, arose in *Lewis Woolf Griptight Ltd v. Corfield*[64] and *Halfpenny v. IGE Medical Systems Ltd*[65] both of which are discussed at para. 10.4.2.4, below.

In *Caledonia Bureau Investment & Property v. Caffrey*,[66] it was held by the EAT in Edinburgh that the continued payment of wages following the end of the MLP when the employee, instead of returning submitted a medical certificate for four weeks, followed by two further certificates each covering a four week period, indicated an intention on the part of the employers to maintain the contract. The employer's later letter giving four weeks' pay in lieu of notice therefore amounted to a dismissal and the EAT upheld the industrial tribunal decision that because the reason for dismissal, being absent from work with post-natal depression, amounted to a pregnancy-related reason which had its origins during the MLP, the dismissal was automatically unfair under the ERA 1996, s.99(1), and fell within paragraph (a):

> ". . . if a pregnancy-related illness arises during the relevant period, that is to say the period of maternity leave whether extended or not, which is the direct cause of dismissal in due course, . . . then s.99(1)(a) is (liable) to cover that position, even if it leaves an employer exposed for a considerable period of time to the consequences of having to keep such an employee who is ill for a pregnancy related reason on his books." *per* Lord Johnston
>
> *Caledonia Bureau Investment & Property v. Caffrey* [1998] I.R.L.R. 110 at 112, EAT.

This decision assumes the correctness of the proposition that the continuation of the contract of employment during the MLP is a matter of contract, and therefore of

---

[61] EAT/846/96.
[62] [1997] I.R.L.R. 277, EAT.
[63] *ibid.*
[64] [1997] I.R.L.R. 432, EAT.
[65] [1998] I.R.L.R. 10, EAT.
[66] [1998] I.R.L.R. 110, EAT.

agreement between the parties, and in doing so follows the line of cases culminating in *Kwik Save Stores Ltd v. Greaves*[67] and *Halfpenny v. IGN Medical Systems Ltd.*[68] However, both these cases were concerned with long leave under section 79 where the status of the contract is less certain than during the MLP where section 71 appears to set up MLP as a period of authorised absence, with the implication that the contract, along with the contractual terms, except for entitlement to remuneration, continues. The decision in *Greaves*[69] has been successfully appealed,[70] but on different grounds (and this is discussed further in relation to long leave at para. 10.4.2.2). However, reference was not made in the judgment in *Caledonia Bureau Investment & Property v. Caffrey*[71] to the ECJ decision in *Larsson*[72] where, although the facts occurred before Directive 92/85 was adopted, the ECJ said that the Directive provided special protection by prohibiting dismissal during the period from the beginning of pregnancy to the end of maternity leave. Absences after the protected period do not attract special protection, even where the reason for the absence arose as a result of, or manifested themselves during, pregnancy or childbirth. It is submitted that as a result of the decision in *Larsson*,[73] it would appear that although the facts of *Caffrey* do not bring the case within the special protection intended to be provided by section 99, the employer cannot take into account as grounds for dismissal, absences during the protected period. Therefore, whether or not the dismissal is unfair in such circumstances will depend on the treatment afforded to the woman as compared with that which would be afforded to a man absent for the same period of time in excess of the MLP (or extended MLP where the employee has complied with section 99(3)) and with a similar record of absence.

10.4.1.7 *Redundancy*

The ERA 1996, s.77 provides that where, during an employee's maternity leave period, it is not practicable, by reason of redundancy, for the employer to continue to employ the woman under her existing contract, she is entitled to be offered (before the end of her existing contract) alternative employment under a new contract with her employer, successor or an associated employer, where there is a suitable available vacancy. Section 77(2) provides that the new contract of employment must provide for work which is both suitable in relation to her and appropriate for her to do in the circumstances and the terms and conditions must not be substantially less favourable than if she had continued to be employed under the previous contract. In the event that maternity leave is ended by dismissal because of redundancy and the provisions laid down in section 77 have not been complied with, the dismissal is automatically unfair under section 99(1)(e).

10.4.2   Long maternity leave and the right to return

An employee:

- who has a right to short leave under section 71;

[67] [1997] I.R.L.R. 268, EAT.
[68] [1998] I.R.L.R. 10, EAT.
[69] [1997] I.R.L.R. 268, EAT.
[70] *Daily Telegraph*, February 28, 1998; IDS Brief 609/March 1998.
[71] [1998] I.R.L.R. 110, EAT.
[72] Case C–400/95 [1997] I.R.L.R. 643, ECJ.
[73] *ibid.*

- continues to be employed by her employer (whether or not she is at work) until immediately before eleventh week before EWC;

- at the beginning of the eleventh week before the EWC she has been continuously employed for not less than two years;

continues, by section 79, to be entitled to long extended maternity leave. This gives an entitlement to return to work at any time up to 29 weeks after the beginning of the week in which the child was born (s.79(1)). This means that providing the conditions are fulfilled there is a right to take a maximum of 40 weeks maternity leave—up to eleven weeks before the expected week of childbirth and 29 weeks after the week in which the child was born.

10.4.2.1 *Notification requirements*

The right to return from long leave is conditional upon complying with the statutory notification requirements which arise both before MLP is taken and during maternity leave. Failure to comply with one or more of the conditions means that the employee loses the right to return and ceases to be entitled to special protection. Because long leave is taken after the MLP, the notice conditions for short leave must be complied with:

- by section 74 not less than 21 days before the woman intends her period of absence to begin, she must give notice of the date on which she intends it to commence, and if that is not practicable, as soon as is reasonably practicable (s.74(1)–(3));

- by section 75(1) she must inform her employer in writing, at least 21 days before her maternity leave period commences, of her pregnancy and the expected week of childbirth, and if requested to do so by her employer, produce a certificate from a registered medical practitioner or a registered midwife, stating the expected week of childbirth (s.75(2)).

Additionally

- she is required by section 80(1) to include with the notice given under section 75(1) the additional information that she intends to exercise her right under section 79—to take long leave.

Tribunals have taken a strict approach to the necessity to include in the notice information of the intention to return. In *F.W. Woolworth plc v. Smith*[74] the EAT found that since the employee had failed to state an actual intention to return to work and had simply provided the employer with a "certificate of expected confinement", she had not satisfied the notice requirements and had, as a result, lost her statutory right to return. In *Osbourne v. Thomas Bolton & Sons Ltd*[75] the employee was diabetic and had been warned that there was a chance that the pregnancy could have complications. As a result she simply informed her employer that if she lost the child she would return to work. It was held that this was a conditional notice and as such was inadequate for these purposes.

---

[74] [1990] I.C.R. 45, EAT.
[75] Case 794/248, EAT.

In *Nu-Swift International Ltd v. Mallinson*[76] Slynn J. said of the right to return to work:

> "Is not intended to protect the person who at the time does not intend to go back to work but . . . who subsequently changes her mind outside the period and seeks to give a notice explaining that there were factors which have changed and which have caused her to change her mind. Nor, it seems to us, does it cover the case of an employee who really is not sure either way." *per* Slynn J.

Nu-Swift International Ltd v. Mallinson [1978] I.R.L.R. 537 at 540, EAT.

In a curious EAT decision it was held in *King v. The Hundred Hoo Nursery*, EAT 789/97, May 21, 1998, that notice under section 80(1) does not have to be in writing or given at the same time as notice under section 75(1). This is difficult to reconcile with both the statutory provisions and authority.

10.4.2.2 *Exercise of right to return*

By section 82(1) a woman can exercise the right to return from long leave at any time up to 29 weeks after the beginning of the week in which childbirth occurs, providing she has complied with all the statutory requirements.

Notice requirements

In addition to the notice requirements under section 74(1), and sections 75(1)–(2) and 80(1), a further notice requirement was introduced by the Employment Act 1980, and is now contained in the ERA 1996, s.80(2). If an employer makes a request for confirmation that the employee intends to exercise her right to return from long leave, she retains the right to long leave under section 79 only if she gives written confirmation within 14 days of receiving the request, or if that is not reasonably practicable, as soon as is reasonably practicable, that she intends to exercise her right to return. The employer's request may not be made earlier than 21 days before the end of the employee's MLP, must be made in writing and be accompanied by a written statement of the effect of failing to comply with the request: that the right to return after long leave is lost.

By section 82(1) the employee exercises her right to return under section 79 by giving written notice to the employer, at least 21 days before the day on which she proposes to return, of her proposal to return on that day. That day then becomes known as the notified date of return (NDR). The EAT in *F.W. Woolworths plc v. Smith*[77] confirmed that to retain the right to return the expiry of the 21 days notice served under section 82(1) must fall within the 29 week period of leave, otherwise the employee will forfeit her right to return. This is demonstrated in *Lavery v. Plessey Telecommunications Ltd*[78] where Ms Lavery had given notice of her intention to return, but was not permitted to do so because the notice expired outside the 29 week leave period. In the EAT Browne-Wilkinson J. said:

---

[76] [1978] I.R.L.R. 573, EAT.
[77] [1990] I.R.L.R. 39, EAT.
[78] [1982] I.R.L.R. 180 (confirmed on different grounds [1983] I.R.L.R. 202, CA).

"Although we sympathise with Ms Lavery, there is no escaping the fact that she has not given the statutory notice upon which her statutory right to return to work depends." *per* Browne-Wilkinson J.

Lavery v. Plessey Telecommunications Ltd [1982] I.R.L.R. 180 at 182, EAT.

In *Institute of the Motor Industry v. Harvey*[79] it was held that the obligation on an employer to permit an employee on maternity leave to return to work is brought about by the serving of written notice under section 82(1), and without that notice there is no obligation on the employer to permit the woman to return:

"The written notice is mandatory and there is no other way in which the applicant can exercise her right to return. The use of the word 'shall' in [s.82(1)] is to be noted." *per* Wood J. (President)

Institute of the Motor Industry v. Harvey [1992] I.R.L.R. 343 at 347, EAT.

It was held by the EAT in *Crees v. Royal London Insurance*[80] that the proper meaning of "shall exercise the right to return to work" in the ERA 1996, s.82(1) is that after serving notice the employee will psychically return to work. The EAT rejected the suggestion that a woman notionally returns to work when she serves notice of her intention to do so, and then if she submits a medical certificate between then and the time she should physically return, complying with section 82(2), she is to be regarded as on sick leave. In *Kwik Save Stores Ltd v. Greaves*,[81] the EAT held that:

". . . as a matter of statutory construction, and subject to any binding authority to the contrary, something more is required of an employee to complete the statutory process than simply to acquire the right to return by a valid [ss.74–75 and s.80(1)] notice and to exercise it by a valid [s.82(1)] notice." *per* Hicks J.

Kwik Save Stores Ltd. v. Greaves [1997] I.R.L.R. 268 at 272, EAT.

It was held to be necessary to physically return to work, but physically returning to work for the purposes of handing in a medical certificate before going off sick was held in *Greaves*[82] to be insufficient as being "incompatible" with exercising her right to return to work. Both *Crees* and *Greaves* have been successful on appeal to the Court of Appeal[83] where it was held an actual presence at work on the notified day of return is not necessary in order to effectively exercise the right to return. In delivering the judgment Lord Woolf M.R. said that section 82(1) sets out what is required for an employee to exercise her right to return. A failure to attend on the notified day of return did not mean that the right had not been exercised or that the right to return had been lost, because the women had already exercised their right by complying with the requirements laid down in section 82(1): exercising the right to return to work is complete before the notified date of return actually arrives. Lord Woolf said that the contrary construction contended for by the employers "produces results so absurd and

[79] [1992] I.R.L.R. 343, EAT.
[80] [1997] I.R.L.R. 85, EAT.
[81] [1997] I.R.L.R. 268, EAT.
[82] *ibid.*
[83] [1988] I.R.L.R. 245, CA.

unjust that it cannot have been a part of the scheme of protection for female employees."

The result of so holding was held to be that both women were treated as dismissed under section 95(1)(a) for the reason that the employer had failed to permit them to return to work.

Postponement of return

The employer may, by section 82(2), postpone an employee's return to work until a date no more than four weeks after the notified day of return if he notifies her before the date of return that for specified reasons he is postponing her return. The date of return will then be the date notified by the employer.

The employee may postpone her return until not more than four weeks after the notified date of return by giving the employer, before the notified date of return, a medical certificate certifying that because of disease or bodily injury or mental disablement she will be incapable of returning. If the medical certificate is given before the 21 days notice has been given under section 82(1), the medical certificate has the effect of extending the time the employee has to give the notice, so that she returns to work not more than four weeks after the end of the 29 weeks.

This right to postpone return is for a maximum of four weeks and may not be exercised again in connection with the same return to work, even if the employee is still incapable of returning to work (s.82(5)). Discussion has taken place on the decisions in both *Crees v. Royal London Insurance* and *Kwik Save Stores Ltd v. Greaves*[84] but it should be noted that *Greaves*[85] did not involve the valid serving of a notice to postpone, whilst in *Crees* the notice to postpone had expired.

In *Kelly v. Liverpool Maritime Terminal Ltd*,[86] following the initial four week period, the woman continued to send in medical certificates until her employer, who had previously not replied, terminated her employment. The Court of Appeal held that the woman lost her right to return when she failed to return from maternity leave following the four week postponement. Her subsequent medical certificates did not mean that she was on sick leave, merely that she had failed to exercise her right to return from maternity leave. In *Lewis Woolf Griptight Ltd v. Corfield*[87] the employee had a right to return under section 79 but before the notified day of return submitted a medical certificate for two weeks, exercising her right to postpone return. She subsequently served a second certificate, for a further two weeks, together delaying her return for the maximum permitted under section 82(3)–(4). Although Ms Corfield never did return, no issue was taken in the subsequent unfair dismissal and discrimination proceedings on the question of the submission of two certificates in connection with one period of maternity leave. Nevertheless, it would appear from the wording of section 82(5) that an employee intending to exercise a right of postponement should submit, before the NDR, a certificate for the maximum permitted period of four weeks, since if a certificate is submitted for a shorter period and the woman is unable to resume work on its expiry she is prohibited from submitting a further certificate, albeit that following the Court of Appeal decision in *Crees* and *Greaves*[88] failure to permit return will be deemed to be a dismissal under section 96(1).

---

[84] [1997] I.R.L.R. 268, EAT. ([1998] I.R.L.R. 245, CA).
[85] *ibid.*
[86] [1988] I.R.L.R. 310, CA.
[87] [1997] I.R.L.R. 432, EAT.
[88] [1998] I.R.L.R. 245, CA.

Where there is a contractual right to return, the employee may instead rely on the contractual scheme: in *Watson v. Marylebone Optical Co Ltd*,[89] in support of her right to return in these circumstances, the applicant pointed to the employer's statement of maternity rights in which the relevant paragraph did not state that a medical certificate to postpone return could only be submitted once. The employee was therefore entitled to enjoy the contractual provision which gave her the right to return up to the end of the 33rd week after childbirth.

Continuity

The ERA 1996, s.212(2)–(3), provides that an employee's period of absence from work wholly or partly because of pregnancy or childbirth or on maternity leave, after which she returns to work under the right contained in section 79, counts in computing the employee's period of employment. This means that providing that the employee returns from maternity leave, not only will there be continuity of employment, but the whole period of absence on maternity leave will count towards the period of continuity.

10.4.2.3 *Right to return to what?*

In connection with long leave, the position is much less clear than that applicable to short leave. The ERA 1996, s.79(2) provides a "right to return to work with the person who was her employer", or his successor, in the *job* in which the woman was employed, on terms and conditions as to remuneration not less favourable than those that would have been applicable had she not been absent from work, with her seniority, pension rights and similar rights unaffected by her absence and on terms and conditions no less favourable than those that would have been applicable had she not been absent after the end of the MLP. "Job" in section 79(2) is defined in section 235 as meaning "the nature of the work which he is employed to do in accordance with his contract and the capacity and place in which he is so employed." There is therefore no right to return to the same job when returning from long leave under section 79: the same type of work will suffice. The right to return is diluted further in that section 96(2) provides a small employer exemption: section 96(3) permits an employer to offer alternative employment where it is not reasonably practicable to permit return and section 81 makes it mandatory to offer alternative employment in the event of it not being practicable by reason of redundancy to permit return in accordance with section 79.

Just as the woman has no right to return to exactly the same job she held before her maternity leave, neither is there a right to return on different terms, for example on a job-share or part-time basis. However, failure to permit a woman to return on a different working arrangement to suit her domestic responsibilities may amount to discrimination on grounds of sex contrary to the SDA 1975, s.1(1)(b) and s.6(2)(b) in that the requirement to work full-time may be a "requirement or condition" that a considerably smaller proportion of women than men can, in practice, comply because of child care responsibilities, and which operates to the woman's detriment because she cannot comply. If the employer is unable to objectively justify the requirement irrespective of sex, then refusal will amount to indirect discrimination.

Nevertheless, there is a conflict of authorities on whether a failure to allow return on altered working arrangements amounts to unlawful indirect discrimination. In *Holmes v. Home Office*[90] a rejection by the Home Office of a request to return to work part-

---

[89] COIT 2056/212, IDS Brief 591.
[90] [1984] I.R.L.R. 299, EAT.

time on the basis that there were no part-time posts available within that grade, and in the belief that Ms Holmes only had the right to return to work under her exiting terms, was held by EAT to be unlawful discrimination. The obligation to serve full-time was held to be a "requirement or condition" within the SDA 1975, s.1(1)(b) in that it was an essential term of Ms Holmes' engagement, it was to her "detriment" within sections 1(1)(b)(iii) and 6(2)(b) because: it would, it was held, place excessive demands upon her time and energy and she could not "comply" with it without suffering, when this was added to her new parental responsibilities.

This approach was followed in *Greater Glasgow Health Board v. Carey*,[91] the EAT holding that the respondent's requirement for a health visitor to work a five-day week, either part-time or full-time, was a "requirement" with which a considerably smaller proportion of women than men could comply, taking the pool for comparison as the health visitors employed by the respondent Board. It was held that, even though only four of the 296 health visitors were male, the industrial tribunal was entitled to take account and draw an inference, in accordance with the SDA 1975, s.74(2)(b), from the failure of the appellants to answer questions from the respondent relating to the number of health visitors who either fail to return to their employment, or to continue their employment, after maternity leave because of the employer's policy of refusing to allow them to job share or work half weeks. However, a narrower interpretation was taken in *Clymo v. Wandsworth Borough Council*[92] where the EAT held that working full-time was a condition of employment, part of the job's nature, not a "requirement or condition" and that the employer's refusal to allow Ms Clymo to switch to part-time working was not seen as applying a "requirement" within the meaning of the SDA. Whether or not a job of itself required full-time work was held to be for the management to decide, provided the decision was reasonable, in that it was made upon adequate grounds, and responsible, bearing in mind the need to avoid discrimination based on sex and balancing that against other needs and responsibilities. The EAT held that if the decision in *Home Office v. Holmes* was to be read as indicating that it was for the tribunal to decide whether or not a job of itself required full-time work, it was disagreed with.

However, although only persuasive, the Northern Ireland Court of Appeal in *Briggs v. North Eastern Education and Library Board*[93] preferred the "less narrow construction" of Wood J. in *Holmes*, and that of Browne-Wilkinson J. in *Clarke v. Eley (IMI) Kynoch Ltd*.[94] Hutton L.C.J. said that a "requirement" to work full-time was to Ms Briggs' "detriment" because she could not comply with it, stating that because in practice women still bore the main responsibility for looking after children, a considerably smaller proportion of them could comply with the requirement to work full-time. No statistical evidence was considered for this assertion, the court saying instead that they were entitled to take account of their own knowledge and experience. However, applying the test set out in *Hampson v. Department of Education and Science*[95] it was necessary to balance the discriminatory effects of the requirement against the reasonable needs of the employer and since the school had demonstrated a need, in the interests of the pupils, to conduct badminton practice in the afternoon after school, they had successfully provided an objective justification of their needs within the SDA 1975, s.1(1)(b)(ii).

[91] [1987] I.R.L.R. 484, EAT.
[92] [1989] I.R.L.R. 241, EAT.
[93] [1990] I.R.L.R. 182, NICA.
[94] [1982] I.R.L.R. 482, EAT.
[95] [1989] I.R.L.R. 69, CA.

The policy of the organisation is important in seeking to justify a decision to refuse a request to alter a working arrangement. In *Putick v. Eastbourne Borough Council*[96] a request to job share, which was refused on the basis that it was inappropriate, was held not to be justifiable in that the request had been dismissed without consideration and in conflict with a discussion paper produced by the authority which stressed the need to draw up detailed job descriptions when job sharing was requested. This had not been done and the industrial tribunal found that as the requirement to work full-time had not been objectively justified a claim of indirect discrimination was upheld.

In *British Telecommunications plc v. Roberts*[97] a request to job share made by two staff returning from maternity leave, rejected on grounds of "operational needs of the job", was found by the industrial tribunal to be discriminatory within the SDA 1975, s.6 and because this "followed directly from their pregnancy and maternity leave", was held to be direct discrimination in line with the ECJ decisions in both *Dekker v. Stichting Vormingscentrum voor Jonge Volwassenen (VJV-Centrum) Plus*[98] and *Webb v. EMO Air Cargo (U.K.) Ltd.*[99] On appeal, however, the EAT found that a request to job share after maternity leave is not covered by the special protection accorded to women during pregnancy and maternity leave and that the ECJ decision in *Webb* ought not to be extended beyond its intended scope. Here the refusal to job share was held to be a gender neutral reason which had nothing to do with the applicant's pregnancy or maternity leave. Since indirect discrimination was not argued the case was referred back to the tribunal on the question of whether the refusal was indirectly discriminatory.

The ECJ in *Brown*[1] has confirmed the reasoning of the EAT in *British Telecommunications plc v. Roberts*[2] in that Directive 76/207 provides for special protection to be given to women in the period from the beginning of pregnancy to the end of maternity leave and for absences connected with pregnancy and childbirth during that period. It does not extend to cover periods outside the MLP. A refusal to reduce or otherwise rearrange working hours on return from maternity leave is not therefore directly discriminatory, but may be indirectly discriminatory. A defence of justification will be upheld if the employer can show that, after giving consideration to all the available options, and weighing the employee's proposals for a reduction in hours/job sharing, etc., against the company's perceived needs, the request is refused on real operational and business grounds, rather than as a matter of policy or because it is merely inconvenient.

Other considerations apart from a SDA challenge, may weigh with employers in response to a request for a range of working arrangements following childbirth. With women making up a growing and increasing percentage of the labour market and with an increase in the age of fertility, women returning to work may well increasingly reflect a greater part of a firm's pool of skill and expertise and a substantial investment in training. Firms may therefore be reluctant to see a waste of these resources by adhering to a "standard" full-time working week, and be more willing to introduce a range of "family friendly" working arrangements, available to men as well as women, and implementation of the parental leave directive may encourage such policies.

The following chart sets out the various rules relating the MLP and long leave.

---

[96] COIT 3106/2, IDS Brief 590/June 1997.
[97] [1996] I.R.L.R. 601, EAT.
[98] Case C–177/88 [1991] I.R.L.R. 27, ECJ.
[99] Case C–32/93 [1995] I.R.L.R. 645, HL.
[1] Case C–394/96 [1998] I.R.L.R. 445, ECJ.
[2] [1996] I.R.L.R. 601, EAT.

MATERNITY LEAVE EMPLOYMENT RIGHTS ACT 1996	
MATERNITY LEAVE PERIOD (MLP)	**LONG MATERNITY LEAVE (LML)**
Qualifications	
ERA 1996, s.71 provides for a general right to MLP for employees regardless of hours worked or length of service.	ERA 1996, s.79(1)—must have a right to MLP under s.71 and at 11th week before EWC have not less than two years' continuous employment.
Length of Leave	
ERA 1996, s.73: 14 weeks' leave from commencement or until birth of child, if later. Must take at least two weeks' leave beginning with the day of birth (Maternity (Compulsory Leave) Regs. 1994) or four weeks if a factory or shop worker (Public Health Act 1936, s.205). If wish to return before expiry of MLP, must give seven days' notice of date on which intend to return, ERA 1996, s.76. Failure means employer can postpone return for two days and does not have to pay employee during postponement.	By ERA 1996, s.79(1) has the right to return at any time during the period beginning at the end of MLP and ending 29 weeks after the beginning of the week in which childbirth occurs. This gives a maximum of 29 weeks, 11 weeks MLP before the birth and a maximum of 29 weeks after the beginning of the week in which childbirth occurs.
Notice Provisions	
ERA 1996, s.74 no right to MLP unless notifies employer not less than 21 days before the date she intends MLP under s.71 to commence. In addition not less than 21 days before MLP commences, by s.75 she informs employer in writing of: • her pregnancy • the expected week of childbirth • produces a certificate confirming EWC if requested to do so.	By s.80 employee must comply with requirements of ss.74–75 as for MLP, and include in the s.75 notice the information that she intends to exercise the right to long leave. Note additional notice requirements, s.80(2): not earlier than 21 days before the end of the MLP the employer may make a written request for confirmation that the woman intends to exercise her right to leave under s.79. Request must be accompanied by a warning that a failure to respond to the request in writing within 14 days will result in loss of the right to return.
Start of Leave	
By s.74(2) MLP cannot start until the beginning of the 11th week before the EWC, but must not be later than the date the baby is born. Leave is triggered automatically if the woman is absent for a maternity related reason after the 6th week before the EWC s.72(1).	Leave under s.79 follows on from the maternity leave period.

Contractual Rights During Leave	
By s.71 the woman is entitled to the benefit of the terms and conditions of employment which would have been applicable to her had she not been absent, except for remuneration. NB. *Adcock v. H Flude & Co. (Hinckley) Ltd.*	Position after MLP uncertain. Where woman exercises her right to return from LML continuity is, however, preserved by s.212(2) and period of absence counts towards continuity.
Right to Return	
No specific statutory right, but because contract continues and leave is for 14 weeks, the effect is to give the right to return (if notice provisions adhered to) on expiry of the 14 weeks MLP, or earlier by giving not less than 7 days' notice, s.76(1). Because the contract is continuing, the right to leave appears to give a right to return to the same job on the same terms and conditions	S.79(1)—right to return at any time from the end of MLP and 29 weeks after the beginning of the week in which childbirth occurs. By s.79(2) the right is to return to work with the person who was her employer before the end of the MLP in the "job" in which she was then employed: • on terms and conditions as to remuneration not less favourable than those which would have been applicable; • with seniority, pension rights and similar rights as they would have been if the period of employment prior to the end of her MLP were continuous with employment following return to work; • otherwise on terms and conditions not less favourable than those which would have been applicable to her had she not been absent from work after the end of her MLP, s.79(2)(a)–(c)
Additional Notice Provisions	
N/A By s.99(3) automatically unfair dismissal if before end of MLP submitted medical certificate stating incapable of work after end of MLP and contract terminated within four weeks of end of MLP where certificate remained current and reason for dismissal is connected with having given birth.	By s.82 the right to return is exercised by the giving of written notice to the employer at least 21 days before the day on which she proposes to return: this becomes the 'notified date of return' (NDR). Expiry of the 21 days' notice must fall within the 29 week period of leave - *F W Woolworths Plc v. Smith* [1990] I.C.R. 45, EAT. Section 82(3)–(4) provides that a woman who gives her employer, before NDR, a medical certificate stating that she will be incapable of work on the NDR may postpone her return by four weeks whilst retaining right to return. Postponement may only be exercised once, s.82(5).

10.4.2.4 *Failure to permit return*

The ERA 1996, s.96(1) provides that in the case of longer extended maternity leave provided for by section 79, where notice of return has been given under section 82(1) failure to permit a return to work is treated as dismissal at the notified date of return (NDR) and employment is deemed to have been continuous until that date.

There are, however, exceptions:

- There is a small firm exception in that by the ERA 1996, s.96(2) a failure to permit a return from long leave is not to be treated as dismissal if immediately before the end of her maternity leave period the number of employees, added to the number employed by any associated employer, did not exceed five and it is not reasonably practicable for the employer to permit her to return to work or for him or an associated employer to offer her suitable alternative employment. "Suitable alternative employment" is defined in section 96(4) as being of a kind which is both suitable in relation to the employee and appropriate for her to do in the circumstances and that provisions of the contract as to the capacity and place in which she is to be employed, and as to the terms and conditions of her employment, are not substantially less favourable to her than if she had returned to work under section 79.

- Section 96(3) provides that if a woman has a right to return from long leave and it is not reasonably practicable for a reason other than redundancy for her employer to permit her to return under section 79, if her employer, or an associated employer, offers her alternative employment which complies with section 96(4)(a) and (b) and either the woman accepts or unreasonably refuses, there is no deemed dismissal under section 96(1). In order to fall within this section the conditions in section 96(4)(a) and (b) are that the work to be done under the contract offered must be of a kind which is both suitable in relation to the employee and appropriate for her to do in the circum-stances, and the provisions of the contract as to the capacity and place in which she is to be employed and other terms and conditions are not substantially less favourable to her than if she had returned to work under section 79.

By section 96(5), in the event of a complaint of unfair dismissal, the burden of proof in connection with both section 96(2) and (3) falls on the employer.

By section 81 where it is not practicable by reason of redundancy to permit a woman to return from maternity leave, where there is a suitable available vacancy, the employee is entitled to be offered alternative employment with her employer or his successor, or an associated employer, under a new contract. The provisions contained in section 96(4)(a) and (b) with regard to the conditions of alternative work are the same as those attached to an offer under section 81, and (applicable on return from MLP) contained in section 81(3)(a) and (b). Where a suitable alternative vacancy is "available" and the woman is not offered it, a dismissal is deemed to have occurred and by section 99(4) is automatically unfair. In *Community Task Force v. Rimmer*[3] the EAT held that "available" in section 81 is a matter of fact and is not to be qualified by

---

[3] [1986] I.R.L.R. 203, EAT.

considerations of what is economic or reasonable. So the fact that external funding was not available if the woman filled the particular post, with the result that it was not offered to her, made the dismissal unfair under this provision.

In *Philip Hodges & Co. v. Kell*[4] it was held that the right to return to work crystallises when notice is given under the ERA 1996, ss.74–75, not when notice is served under section 82, so if after giving notice under sections 74–75 it becomes "not practicable" for the woman to return by reason of redundancy, she acquires a substitute right under section 81 to be offered alternative work, and the employer acquired a corresponding obligation to make an offer when a suitable vacancy became available after she has gone on maternity leave. In *Hodges*[5] the employer argued that the right to return did not crystallise until notice was served under section 82(1), with the result that if a vacancy arose before there is a notified date of return, there is no obligation to offer it to the woman on maternity leave whose job is redundant. This was not, however, accepted and the judgment means that the requirement in section 82(1) to give at least 21 days' notice of her intention to return is merely a vehicle for exercising the right already established by the giving of notice under section 75(1) in which is contained her intention to return as required under section 80(1).

Where an employer refuses to permit an employee to return the SDA 1975 requires the tribunal to have regard to whether the treatment complained of was on the grounds of sex. In *O'Neill v. Governors of St Thomas More RCVA Upper School*[6] it was held that the critical question is whether, on an objective consideration of all the surrounding circumstances, the dismissal or other treatment complained of is on the ground of pregnancy, or on some other ground, and that this must be determined by an objective test of casual connection. The EAT allowed an appeal by a teacher of religious education who had become pregnant through a relationship with a Roman Catholic priest, finding that she had been discriminated against because the surrounding circumstances relied upon as the reason for dismissal were all casually related to the fact that the applicant was pregnant. The paternity of the child; the publicity of that fact and the consequent untenability of the applicant's position as a religious education teacher were all held to be pregnancy related to the extent that "her pregnancy precipitated and permeated the decision to dismiss her".

Although the principal reason for dismissal may be gender-neutral, unlawful discrimination may nevertheless occur where there is a gender-specific reason for carrying out the dismissal. In *Lewis Woolf Griptight Ltd v. Corfield*[7] it was held that Ms Corfield's employment had been terminated when she failed, through ill health, to return from maternity leave at the appropriate time. Although the principal reason for the dismissal was gender neutral, in that it was found to be because of a breakdown in the relationship, it was held to be discriminatory because the employer had used a gender-specific reason to carry out the dismissal:

"We compare the case of the applicant, dismissed because of the breakdown in relations between herself and (her employer), with a man whose relationship has similarly broken down. Whereas in the applicant's case the employer used as an excuse for terminating the employment a fact which applied only to a woman, the expiry of the four-week period following maternity leave, that excuse would not

[4] [1994] I.R.L.R. 568, EAT.
[5] [1994] I.R.L.R. 568, EAT.
[6] [1996] I.R.L.R. 372, EAT.
[7] [1997] I.R.L.R. 432, EAT.

have been open to the employer in the case of the male comparator. He would not have been dismissed in similar circumstances." *per* Peter Clark J.

Lewis Woolf Griptight Ltd v. Corfield [1997] I.R.L.R. 432 at 436, EAT.

This was held to be a variation of the facts in *Rees v. Apollo Watch Repairs*,[8] where the immediate cause of dismissal was a gender-neutral reason, but the underlying reason was the employee's absence on maternity leave.

Following the Court of Appeal decision in *Crees v. Royal London Insurance* and *Greaves*[9] it now appears that when a woman is unable to return on the NDR, or following expiry of an extended period when a valid certificate is served under section 82(3), failure to permit her to do so at a later date is a deemed dismissal under section 96(1). A deemed dismissal is potentially fair and has to be tested on general principles as to fairness. However, following the ECJ decision in *Brown*[10] in deciding to dismiss for sickness absence, periods of absence on maternity leave, during pregnancy for a pregnancy related reason and during any extension under section 82(3), the protected period, cannot be taken into account.

10.4.2.5   *Contractual rights to return*

In provisions that mirror those contained in section 78 for MLP, section 85(1) provides that an employee with a right to return under section 79 and a contractual right to return to work, may not exercise the two rights separately, but may take advantage of the more favourable in any particular aspect. However, section 85(2) provides that section 79 and sections 81–84, and other subsequent sections in the ERA 1996 relating to the right to return, apply to the exercise of the "composite right" granted in section 85(1). In *Kolfor Plant Ltd. v. Wright*[11] Lord McDonald explored the meaning of "composite right" and said that section 96(1), the right to treat a failure to permit return as a dismissal, can only be relied upon if the woman has sought to exercise her right to return in accordance with section 82:

> "The provisions of these sections however may be modified . . . to give effect to any more favourable contractual terms (s.85). Thus, for example, the statutory periods for notification of intention to return and regulating the date of return could be extended by separate agreement. Where this is done, however, the employee still falls to be regarded as exercising her statutory right to return on amended terms.
>
> This we take to be the meaning of the expression 'composite right' used in [s.85(2)] and the veto upon the use of two rights separately in [s.85(1)]." *per* Slade L.J.

Kolfor Plant Ltd v. Wright [1982] I.R.L.R. 311 at 313, CA.

The Court of Appeal in *Lavery v. Plessey Telecommunications Ltd*[12] followed this decision holding that the "composite" right to return "must fall to be exercised strictly

[8] [1996] I.C.R. 466, EAT.
[9] [1998] I.R.L.R. 245, CA.
[10] *Brown v. Rentokil Ltd* (Case C–394/96) [1998] I.R.L.R. 445, ECJ.
[11] [1982] I.R.L.R. 311, EAT.
[12] [1983] I.R.L.R. 202, CA.

within the terms of the statute". This is demonstrated in *Dowuona v. John Lewis plc*[13] where, following the birth of twins, one of which died, Ms Dowuona's date of return was fixed after adding a weeks' holiday which, it was held by the Court of Appeal, she was permitted to do by her terms of employment. A new return date was fixed to reflect four weeks' postponement following submission of a medical certificate. However, when Ms Dowuona failed to return on the postponed date because she was unwell, obtaining a further medical certificate for four weeks, her employer refused to allow her to return. On her complaint for unfair dismissal the question arose as to whether she was attempting to return from maternity leave, in which case she had lost the right by failing to return at the appropriate time, or whether, having had a weeks' holiday added to the end of her maternity leave, she was attempting to return from holiday. The Court of Appeal held that the argument that Ms Dowuona was attempting to return from holiday required the tribunal "to assume that she notionally returned to work at the end of her maternity leave and immediately departed on a week's holiday, from which she did not return on the due date". This was referred to as "a wholly unrealistic approach" and it was held that the holiday arrangement fell within the interpretation of section 85 in *Kolfor Plant Ltd v. Wright*, and that since she had failed to exercise her right to return to work in accordance with section 82, "because she sought to return to work at a date later than that at which (. . .) she was entitled so to do", she had lost her right to return. Because she had failed to comply with the statutory provisions she did not have a right to complain of unfair dismissal since a deemed dismissal under section 96 depended upon a proper exercise of her right to return as provided for in section 96(1)(b).

Although the contractual agreement must be exercised within the statutory framework in so far as the notice provisions are concerned, section 85(1) provides that the statutory and contractual rights may not be exercised separately, although section 85(2) refers to "more favourable contractual terms" as opposed to the more favourable contract. The interpretation put on this can be seen from *Bovey v. Board of Governors of the Hospital for Sick Children*[14] where the EAT held, *inter alia*, that the employee cannot subdivide a contractual arrangement by taking out those parts which are to her advantage. So, when Ms Bovey claimed a statutory right to return to her original job and to combine this with a contractual right to return on a part-time basis, and a statutory right to return on terms no less favourable in order to avoid a reduction in grade associated with the contractual right to return part-time, Phillips J. referred to the arrangement as "an illegitimate progeny" and dismissed the appeal as being "misconceived" which would produce an "absurdity".

10.4.2.6 *Status of the contract during long leave*

The status of the contract during the long maternity leave period is somewhat uncertain and the ERA 1996 is silent as to the contractual position for employees who fail to return. If the employee serves the necessary notices under sections 74–75, containing the information required by section 80(1) and exercises her right to return in accordance with section 82(1), and subsequently returns, or postpones return in accordance with section 82(2)–(5) and then returns on the postponed date, no issue arises, since the contract is, by section 212(2) continuous, absent weeks counting towards the period of continuity.

---

[13] [1987] I.R.L.R. 310, CA.
[14] [1978] I.R.L.R. 241, EAT.

Although by section 96, a failure to permit an employee to return after childbirth is deemed to be a dismissal, that section, by section 96(1)(a)–(b), as demonstrated in *Lavery v. Plessey Telecommunications Ltd*,[15] only applies where the right to return has been exercised by the giving of the appropriate notices. Such a dismissal is not, however, automatically unfair, whether it is unfair depends on general principles and has to be tested under section 98. However, if the employee fails to comply with the necessary notice requirements, to return on the notified day of return or fails to return after postponed maternity leave, the question arises as to whether the employer's subsequent refusal to allow her to return to work amounts to a dismissal under section 95 and then falls to be considered on general principles. Clearly the contract of employment has come to an end, but when this occurred and the mechanism by which it occurred is less clear, but is nevertheless of importance in establishing whether a woman has any rights, not only to claim to have been unfairly dismissed, but also to claim to have been discriminated against. This is because the right not to be unfairly dismissed, contained in the ERA 1996, section 94 applies only to an "employee" and in connection with discrimination, under the SDA 1975, section 6 provides that discrimination in the employment field is only unlawful in relation to "a person employed by him". Although the definition of employee, contained in section 82 of the SDA 1975, is wider than the common law definition of "employee" for unfair dismissal purposes, and extends to cover the self-employed, the Court of Appeal in *Adekeye v. The Post Office (No. 2)*,[16] following *Nagarajan v. Agnew*,[17] held that "a person employed by him" imports a requirement that the employment must continue to subsist at the relevant time. Therefore, the woman must be an employee at the time that the refusal to allow her to return occurs. This particular interpretation of the SDA was referred to the ECJ by the EAT in *Coote v. Granada Hospitality Ltd.*[18]

The consequences of finding that the contract terminated by some mechanism other than dismissal at some time before attempting to return are demonstrated in *Halfpenny v. IGE Medical Systems Ltd*[19] in which the EAT held that there was no dismissal under section 95 because when Ms Halfpenny's employer declined to extend her maternity leave beyond the four weeks provided for by section 82(2)–(5) she was no longer employed and was not therefore "dismissed". The industrial tribunal were therefore unable to entertain a complaint for unfair dismissal, for damages for breach of contract or for discrimination since:

> "If she fails to exercise her right (to return), the contract comes to an end. . . . The simple fact is that the contract remains on foot solely for the purposes of permitting the employee to revive it when she exercises her statutory right to return. If she does not do so, it comes to an end by implied agreement, not by dismissal." *per* Peter Clark J.

Halfpenny v. IGE Medical Systems Ltd [1999] I.R.L.R. 10 at 13, EAT.

This reasoning is based on the broader decision in *Kolfor Plant Ltd v. Wright*,[20] where Lord McDonald held that an employee must bring herself within section 96, a deemed

---

[15] [1983] I.R.L.R. 202, CA.
[16] [1997] I.R.L.R. 105, CA.
[17] [1994] I.R.L.R. 61, EAT.
[18] Case C–185/97, ECJ Employment Law Watch No. 5, Spring 1998.
[19] [1997] I.R.L.R. 10, EAT.
[20] [1982] I.R.L.R. 311, EAT.

dismissal, otherwise, "even where her contact of employment subsists an ordinary claim for unfair dismissal is not open where the dismissal occurs in the course of attempting to return to work". This judgment was relied on by the Court of Appeal in *Lavery v. Plessey Telecommunications Ltd*[21]:

> "Like the Employment Appeal Tribunal, we conclude that, however Miss Lavery's case is put, her failure to give adequate notice under [s.82(1)] precludes her from having any claim for unfair dismissal whether or not her contract of employment still subsisted on [the day she attempted to serve notice to return under s.82(1)]."
> *per* Slade L.J.

> *Lavery v. Plessey Telecommunications Ltd* [1983] I.R.L.R. 202 at 206, CA.

However, in *Institute of Motor Industry v. Harvey*,[22] Wood J. held that when a woman gives notice of her intention to take maternity leave, her contract is likely to continue, albeit that there is a "suspension" of the basic obligations on each side respectively to provide and carry out work during maternity absence, unless terminated by agreement, resignation or dismissal, and that, Ms Harvey could therefore proceed by section 92. This suggests that there is a presumption that the contract of employment is likely to continue during maternity leave and in *Hilton International Hotels (U.K.) Ltd v. Kaissi*[23] the EAT held that even where failure to comply with the maternity leave procedure meant that the statutory right to return to work was lost, that did not in itself terminate the contract of employment, since that was a matter of contract. Therefore failure to allow Ms Kaissi to return, even though their was no right to return, amounted to a dismissal, which was on the facts unfair because on general principles the employer failed to make further investigation before terminating the contract.

It appears that when the right to return is lost there are several possibilities as to how and when the contract comes to an end:

- When maternity pay ends: this was a view expressed by the EAT in *Crouch v. Kidsons Impey*,[24] but in *McPherson v. Drumpark*[24] Lord Johnston said:

  > ". . . we do not consider that *Crouch* is authority for the view, in the absence of an entitlement under [s.71] because of a failure to give notice under the ensuing sections, [that] payment of maternity pay per se continues the contact. . . . as a matter of generality, maternity leave payments over the statutory period to which the employee is entitled are in themselves no more than neutral to the question of whether or not the contract of employment subsists, since it is a statutory entitlement not dependent upon the continuance of the particular contract. . . .if in a particular case the only relevant factor apparently bearing on whether the contract subsists during the relevant period is maternity payments, in our opinion that factor is certainly not conclusive of the continuance of the contract, and could properly be regarded in itself as immaterial unless supported by other factors spelling out an agreement, express or

---

[21] [1983] I.R.L.R. 202, CA.
[22] [1992] I.R.L.R. 343, EAT.
[23] [1994] I.R.L.R. 270, EAT.
[24] [1996] I.R.L.R. 79, EAT.
[25] [1997] I.R.L.R. 277, EAT.

implied, between the parties that the contract could subsist." *per* Lord Johnston.

McPherson v. Drumpark [1997] I.R.L.R. 277 at 279, EAT.

Likewise, the EAT in *Halfpenny v. IGE Medical Systems Ltd*, agreed with the attack by the respondents on the industrial tribunal reasoning based on *Crouch*.

- The contract comes to an end by operation of law at the time of failure to serve notice under section 82(1), to return on the NDR or after expiry of postponed leave or to apply for a postponement of NDR under section 82(3); this was the view expressed by the EAT in *Crees v. Royal London Insurance*,[26] Hull J. saying that when an employee has lost her right to return to work any contract of employment is "emptied of all useful content" and as a matter of common sense as well as law comes to an end, in the absence of express agreement to the contrary. This was based on the Court of Appeal decision in *Kelly v. Liverpool Maritime Terminals*[27] where Glidewell L.J. concluded that when the appellant's maternity leave entitlement came to an end and she failed to return from postponed leave, her contract also ended.

- The contract is terminated by the employer's refusal to allow the woman to return following no (or defective) notice, or because of a failure to exercise the right on the notified date of return; in *Hilton International Hotels (U.K.) Ltd v. Kaissi*[28] Mummary J. in the EAT held that where a woman gives the required notices before going on maternity leave, but fails to comply with the statutory procedure to enable her to maintain her right to return to work, the contract of employment may continue to subsist in the absence of agreement to the contrary. As no such agreement, express or implied was found to exist and defective notice meant that Ms Kaissi had lost her right to claim under section 98, the employer's letter refusing to permit her to return was a termination which amounted to a dismissal which gave a right to claim unfair dismissal on general principles, via sections 95 and 98. In addition, in *Kwik Save Stores Ltd v. Greaves*[29] Hicks J. in the EAT held that there is no universal rule that a contract of employment cannot survive a failure to return at the end of maternity leave, nor that an employee who cannot claim a deemed dismissal under section 96 is precluded from claiming to have been dismissed under section 95;

- The contract terminates when the employee goes on maternity leave, but is capable of being resurrected by the giving of proper notice under section section 82(1), and complying with a notice under section 80(2); this is the implication of the EAT decision in *Kwik Save Stores Ltd v. Greaves*[30] where it was held that it is for the woman to establish that the contract of employment is still in existence and that she was dismissed, implying a presumption against continuity of the contract.

- The contract terminates consensually on the notified date of return, or the date of failure to serve notice under section 82(1) or to reply or reply in time

---

[26] [1997] I.R.L.R. 85, EAT. Note CA decision at [1998] I.R.L.R. 245, CA.
[27] [1988] I.R.L.R. 310, CA.
[28] [1994] I.R.L.R. 270, EAT.
[29] [1997] I.R.L.R. 268, EAT.
[30] *ibid.*

to a request in accordance with section 80(2); this view was supported by the EAT in *Halfpenny v. IGE Medical Systems Ltd.*[31] When a woman goes on maternity leave with a right to return, her contract continues to subsist, but solely for the purpose of permitting the employee to revive it when she exercises her statutory right to return. If she does not do so, it comes to an end by "implied agreement", not by dismissal. To find otherwise, the EAT said would be to make the employer liable for complying strictly with the statutory provisions.

What does emerge from the development of the case law is that, not being provided for by statute, the contractual position between the parties during maternity leave is a matter, express or implied, for the contract itself. What is less clear, however, is whether, there is a presumption that the contract will end, necessitating the parties to express their intention that it continue, or whether the contract continues in the absence of express or implied agreement that it would be brought to an end in the event of a failure to comply with the statutory provisions regarding return from leave. On this point the authorities are somewhat confused.

For example, in *McPherson v. Drumpark House*[32] the EAT, *per* Lord Johnston, held that whether or not the contract of employment subsists during maternity leave has to be determined under common law principles, which require an express or implied agreement between the parties to that effect, the implication being that the contract comes to an end unless there is agreement to the contrary and in *Hilton International Hotels (U.K.) Ltd v. Kaissi*, Mummery J said:

> "The essential point is that the question whether or not the contract of employment comes to an end or continues depends on the agreement and actions of the parties, which may differ from case to case. In brief, the contract may continue if that is what the parties expressly or impliedly agree and neither takes any action to bring it to an end. If the parties agree expressly or impliedly to bring the contract to an end or either of them takes appropriate action to bring it to an end, then the contract will determine." *per* Mummery J. (President)

Hilton International Hotels (U.K.) Ltd v. Kaissi [1994] I.R.L.R. 270 at 274, EAT.

This approach, requiring some positive action to keep the contract in existence during maternity leave, does not, of course, solve the question of when, in the absence of agreement to the contrary, and by what mechanism, the contract terminates, and in *Halfpenny v. IGE Medical Systems Ltd*,[33] it was held that, in the absence of any express or implied agreement to the contrary, the contract continues to subsist during leave, but on a "mutual understanding" that it is solely for the purposes of permitting the employee to revive it when she exercises her statutory right to return. If she does not return then the contract comes to an end by "implied agreement" giving rise to a situation that the woman has no claim for dismissal in statute or contract, or under the Sex Discrimination Act. However, since agreement to keep the contract may be implied, agreement that the employee may continue to retain into the long. leave period, those contractual benefits to which she is entitled during the MLP, or which

---

[31] [1998] I.R.L.R. 10, EAT.
[32] [1997] I.R.L.R. 277, EAT.
[33] [1998] I.R.L.R. 10, EAT.

she has been permitted to retain, such as PHI, private sickness benefit, company car, reimbursement of telephone expenses, personal computer, etc., could be regarded as indications that it was intended that the contract continue. So, for example, in *Lewis Woolf Griptight Ltd v. Corfield*[34] it was held that indicating that an employee was entitled to SSP was sufficient to show an intention to continue the contract, as was the continuation of the payment of wages by the employers following the submission of medical certificates after expiry of postponed MLP—*Caledonia Bureau Investment & Property v. Caffrey*.[35]

The failure to deal with the status of the contract during maternity leave is a lacuna in an otherwise tediously detailed set of provisions, and being a matter of contract, permits employers to make consensual termination agreements reminiscent of that in *British Leyland (U.K.) Ltd v. Ashraf*,[36] and finally held by the Court of Appeal in *Igbo v. Johnson Matthey*[37] to be void as in breach of the ERA 1996, section 203(1), as an attempt to preclude a person from bringing any proceedings under the Act. In *Crees v. Royal London Insurance Ltd*[38] the EAT observed that such an agreement, in the light of it's judgment that the contract, being emptied of all useful content came to an end by the lapse of time "if it has not done so previously", did no more than state the obvious. The Court of Appeal decision in *Crees v. Royal London Insurance* and *Kwik Save Stores Ltd v. Greaves*,[39] although it clarified the position in so far as a deemed dismissal is concerned, has done nothing to clarify the issue regarding the status of the contract during long leave. It was held that having complied with the statutory notice requirements the women had the right to return to work regardless of their non-availability due to sickness "whether a contract of employment actually continued to exist during the period of their absence on extended maternity leave or whether it had actually been terminated prior to the notified date of return".

10.5 MATERNITY PAYMENTS

The Social Security Act 1986 made substantial reforms to the system of maternity pay by the introduction of statutory maternity pay (SMP), a system modelled on the earlier introduction of statutory sick pay (SSP) and which makes the employer primarily responsible for making payments to qualifying employees, with provision for payments to be reclaimed via a deduction from employer national insurance contributions (NICs). The intention behind the introduction of SMP was to cut out what the Government saw as wasteful duplication of administrative effort whereby maternity allowance (MA) was paid to employees direct by the DHSS, and subsequently deducted by the employer from maternity pay, which was payable to those with at least two years' service regardless of the intention to return to work, and the costs of which were recouped from the Maternity Pay Fund.

In August 1993 the Government published a consultation document inviting views on the options available for amending the maternity benefits schemes to comply with the requirements of Directive 92/85 under which during the MLP a woman is entitled

[34] [1997] I.R.L.R. 432, EAT.
[35] [1998] I.R.L.R. 110, EAT.
[36] [1978] I.R.L.R. 330, EAT.
[37] [1986] I.R.L.R. 215, CA.
[38] [1997] I.R.L.R. 85, EAT.
[39] *Daily Telegraph*, February 28, 1998, IDS Brief 609/March 1998.

to be paid an amount equivalent to the amount she would receive if absent from work due to sickness. As a result of these consultations further changes were made to the maternity pay scheme by equalising lower rate SMP with SSP and granting all those entitled to receive SMP the right to be paid at the higher rate for the first six weeks. These changes were brought into effect in 1994, via the TURERA 1993, with the additional cost involved being reflected in a reduction in the amount employers may recover: this was reduced to 92 per cent[40] but with a small employer relief whereby a small employer (an employer whose NICs do not exceed £20,000 for the qualifying tax year) can recover the full amount and to deduct seven per cent of the SNP paid.[41]

Under statute there are two types of maternity pay available:

10.5.1 *Maternity allowance*

Maternity allowance (MA) is paid by the Department of Social Security directly to pregnant women not eligible to receive SMP either because they are not within the category of "employee", or because as an employee they do not fulfil the necessary qualifications for SMP. In order to be eligible for maternity allowance a pregnant woman must:

- have reached (or been confined before reaching) the commencement of the eleventh week before the expected week of childbirth (EWC);

- not be entitled to SMP;

- have been engaged in employment as an employed or self-employed earner and satisfy the contribution requirements: have paid sufficient Class 1 or Class 2 non-reduced NICs for at least 26 weeks in the 66 weeks immediately preceding the fourteenth week before the EWC.

MA is a weekly benefit and is paid at a rate equal to the lower rate of SMP, in the year 1998/99 £57.50 per week.

Payment cannot be made before the beginning of the eleventh week before EWC and is payable for up to 18 weeks; this period is called the maternity allowance period (MAP). Unless the birth is premature, the MAP must always include a core period of 13 weeks, which starts six weeks before the EWC. The remaining period may be taken in any combination of before or after the core period, but cannot start more than five weeks before the core period, which means that it cannot be paid before the eleventh week before the EWC. Payment cannot start later than the beginning of the core period and cannot be taken while the employee continues working. Therefore, if the woman continues to work into the core period she will lose some of her 18 week entitlement. Maternity allowance, unlike SMP, is not liable to income tax or NICs.

10.5.2 Statutory maternity pay (SMP)

The provisions regarding SMP can now be found in Part XII of the consolidating Social Security Contributions and Benefits Act 1992. The right to receive SMP is dependent upon a number of conditions:

---

[40] Statutory Maternity Pay (Compensation of Employers) and Miscellaneous Amendment Regulations 1994 (S.I. 1994 No. 1882), reg. 4.
[41] Statutory Maternity Pay (Compensation of Employers) Amendment Regulations 1998 (S.I. 1998 No. 522).

10.5.2.1 *Eligibility*

To be eligible to receive SMP the woman must, regardless of whether she intends to return to work, have given the person who will be liable to pay SMP, notice that she is going to be absent from work wholly or partly because of pregnancy or confinement,[42] and must have done so at least 21 days before her absence from work is due to begin or, if that is not reasonably practicable, as soon as is reasonably practicable, 1992 Act, section 164(4). Additionally the woman must have:

- been continuously employed by her employer "in employed earner's employment" for a continuous period of at least 26 weeks ending with the week immediately preceding the fourteenth week before the EWC;

- stopped working for the employer who is liable to pay SMP, or any other employer wholly or partly as a result of pregnancy or confinement;

- reached, or confined before reaching the commencement of the eleventh week before the expected week of confinement;

- average weekly earnings at least equal to the lower earnings limit (LEL), in force at the time, for payment of NICs for a period of eight weeks ending with the last normal pay day before the end of the qualifying week (QW). The LEL for the year 1998/99 is £64 per week, and an employee paid less than this is not entitled to receive SMP.

---

[42] Social Security Contributions and Benefits Act 1992 uses the word "confinement", whereas the ERA 1996 uses the word "childbirth".

**SUMMARY
STATUTORY MATERNITY PAY (SMP)**

1. ELIGIBILITY CONDITIONS

- continuously employed for 26 weeks at 15th week before expected week of childbirth (EWC) - the qualifying week (QW)
- employee
- average weekly earnings at least equal to lower earnings limit (LEL) for 8 weeks ending with the QW - 1998-99 £64pw[1]
- provide medical certificate of EWC if employer requests it
- worked up to 11th week before EWC
- stopped working
- have given 21 days' notice of intention to stop working

2. DURATION OF MATERNITY PAY

18 Weeks

3. RATE

90% of average weekly earnings for first 6 weeks (higher rate)
£57.70 (lower rate) for remaining 12 weeks

4. WHO PAYS?

- employer: entitled to recover 92% from National Insurance Contributions (NICs)[2]
- employer who qualifies for Small Employers' Relief (employer who was liable to pay total gross Class 1 NICs of £20,000 or less in the qualifying tax year) entitled to recover 107%.[3]

---

[1] At April 6, 1998. Rates reviewed annually for implementation from April 6.
[2] Statutory Maternity Pay (Compensation of Employers) and Miscellaneous Amendment Regulations 1994 (S.I. 1994 No. 1882).
[3] Statutory Maternity Pay (Compensation of Employers) Amendment Regulations 1998 (S.I. 1998 No. 522).

Challenges to rules which have the result of excluding or limiting maternity benefits have met with limited success. In *Banks v. Tesco Stores*[43] Ms Banks, a former part-time employee with Tesco Stores, whose earnings were below the LEL, and who was consequently not entitled to SMP, challenged these provisions as being in breach of the Equal Pay Act 1970 and contrary to Article 119 because male employees were unconditionally entitled to three days' paid paternity leave. She also claimed that the application of a LEL, resulting in a refusal to pay her SMP, was indirectly discriminatory. The industrial tribunal upheld the complaint under Equal Pay Act, on the basis that the comparator, also a part-time checkout operator, had a right to three days' unconditional paid leave, whereas the leave arrangements for Ms Banks were conditional both on her fulfilling the service requirements for SMP and on her earnings being in excess of the LEL. The industrial tribunal therefore held that Ms Banks' contract should be modified by the insertion of an equality clause providing that she was entitled to three days' paid maternity leave (or the pro-rata equivalent), whether or not she was entitled to SMP.

In connection with the claim of discrimination, Ms Banks, utilising Article 119 and the ECJ decision in *Gillespie v. Northern Health and Social Services Board*,[44] that women taking maternity leave are in a special position requiring them to be afforded special protection and that the application of a LEL was discriminatory, without the need for a comparator. Whilst the tribunal held that SMP was "pay" for the purposes of Article 119, based on the Court of Appeal decision in *Clark v. Secretary of State for Employment*,[45] they rejected the argument that because a comparison could not be made with either a man or a woman at work there was no need for a comparator and hence any infringement of the special protection to which women are entitled in connection with pregnancy and childbirth. In *Clark* the Court of Appeal held, in connection with the exclusion of women absent on account of pregnancy and childbirth from the right to claim notice pay from the National Insurance Fund, that women taking maternity leave were in a special position and not comparable with men, and that under Community law, in the light of *Hofmann v. Barmer Ersatzkasse*[46] it was permissible to make special provision for women absent from work because of pregnancy or childbirth. Such arrangements, amounting to a special code, could not be "compared" with that of a man or with that of a woman at work, and therefore just as exclusion from claiming from the National Insurance Fund did not amount to discrimination on grounds of sex, neither did exclusion from SMP.

In *Gillespie v. Northern Health and Social Services Board*[47] the ECJ rejected the claim that Article 119 requires that women should continue to receive full pay during maternity leave, or that it lays down criteria for determining the amount of benefit payable during maternity leave. The Court did, however, hold that the amount of maternity pay must not be "so low as to undermine the purpose of maternity leave, namely the protection of women before and after giving birth". The challenge in *Banks*[48] was that not being eligible at all for pay whilst on maternity leave does not fulfil this criteria. In *Iske v. P&O European Ferries (Dover) Ltd*[49] a challenge, *inter alia*, to the level of statutory maternity pay that was received when Ms Iske was forced to

43 IDS Brief 599/October 1997, p. 12.
44 Case C–342/93 [1996] I.R.L.R. 214, ECJ.
45 [1997] I.C.R. 64, CA.
46 [1984] E.C.R. 3047, ECJ.
47 Case C–342/93 [1996] I.R.L.R. 214, ECJ.
48 IDS Brief 599/October 1997, p. 12.
49 [1997] I.R.L.R. 401, EAT.

take early maternity leave in the absence of her employer offering her suitable alternative work or suspending her, was rejected by the EAT on the basis that it was not appropriate to extend the principle of adequate pay referred to in *Gillespie* to a respondent who was not an emanation of the state or in respect of a period outside the statutory MLP. It is submitted that this decision is somewhat confused in the light of the ECJ's decision in *Gillespie* in which the ECJ said, in response to one of the questions referred to it by the Court of Appeal in Northern Ireland:

> ". . . it should be borne in mind that the benefit paid during maternity leave constitutes pay and therefore falls within the scope of Article 119 of the Treaty and Directive 75/117 [which has been held to explain and expand upon Article 119]. It cannot therefore be covered by Directive 76/207 as well. That Directive, . . ., does not apply to pay within the meaning of the above mentioned provisions."
>
> (Case C–342/93) *Gillespie v. Northern Health and Social Services Board* [1996] I.R.L.R. 214 at 224, ECJ.

It was held as long ago as 1976 in the second *SABENA* case[50] that Article 119 is directly applicable, the fact that the respondent in *Iske* was not an emanation of the state is therefore irrelevant.

10.5.3 Maternity pay period

Maternity pay is payable for 18 weeks (the MPP). It cannot commence earlier than the eleventh week before the EWC, but the employee can delay the commencement of the MPP until the week following confinement. The exception to this occurs if the woman is absent from work due to a pregnancy related illness at any time during the six weeks prior to the EWC. Under these circumstances she is deemed to be on maternity leave and entitled to maternity pay. If the employee's MPP has started and she undertakes any work she loses her entitlement to SMP during the week or weeks in which she works. Any attempt to contract out of the SMP scheme is void and if the employee is dismissed before the QW she is deemed still to be eligible for SMP.

10.5.4 Payment and administration of SMP

SMP is regarded as earnings for social security purposes and therefore subject to deduction by the employer of PAYE and National Insurance Contributions (NICs), together with any other deductions from SMP as though it were earnings. There are, however, no specific provisions detailing the timing or the manner of payment, which may continue to be paid through the normal payroll system, or may be paid as a lump sum at the start of the leave period, bearing in mind that if the employee returns to work at the end of the maternity leave period of fourteen weeks, she is no longer entitled to receive SMP.

Upon introduction of SMP the employer could recover the cost of payments, plus 4.5 per cent, by making a deduction of the appropriate amount from the payment of employer's NICs. From September 1994 this was reduced to a total recovery of 92 per

---

[50] Case C–43/75 *Defrenne v. SABENA* [1976] I.C.R. 547, ECJ.

cent of SMP,[51] except for small employers who are permitted to continue to receive full reimbursement, plus an administration charge—this was increased from 6.5 per cent to 7 per cent from April 6, 1998[52] For these purposes a small employer is one who pays £20,000 or less annually in gross NICs.[53]

10.5.5   Rate of SMP

There are two rates of payment:

- **Higher rate**—is paid for the first six weeks of absence and is paid at the rate which is equivalent to nine-tenths (90 per cent) of the employee's normal weekly earning, and

- **Lower rate**—which is payable for the remaining twelve weeks, at a rate equivalent to Statutory Sick Pay (SSP). In the year 1998/99 this is payable at £57.70 per week.

In *Gillespie v. Northern Health & Social Services Board*[54] the ECJ was asked whether Article 119, the Equal Pay Directive 75/117, or Equal Treatment Directive 76/207 requires that, while a woman is absent from work on maternity leave provided for by the relevant national legislation or by her contract of service, she be paid the full pay to which she would have been entitled if at the time she had been working normally for the employer.

The Court ruled that Article 119 and Directive 75/117 does not require that women should continue to receive full pay during maternity leave, nor lays down specific criteria for determining the amount of benefit payable during maternity leave. Although Directive 92/85 provides for an "adequate" allowance to workers on maternity leave, that was not in force at the relevant time. It was therefore for national legislation to set the amount of maternity pay, but the amount payable must not be set so low as to jeopardise the purpose of maternity leave, which is the protection of women before and after giving birth. To assess the adequacy of the amount payable, the national court must take account of other forms of social protection afforded by national law in the case of justified absence from work, as well as the length of maternity leave. The court also held that the principle of non-discrimination requires that a woman who is still employed during maternity leave must, like any other worker, benefit from any pay rise, even if backdated, which she would have received had she not been pregnant.

As a result of the ECJ decision in *Gillespie* new regulations[55] were introduced which effect the way in which the earnings are calculated for assessing both whether the employee qualifies for SMP and the level of that payment. Under the new Regulations, if an employer grants a pay rise which is back-dated and arrears are paid after the end of the period used to calculate the woman's SMP, the employer must calculate or recalculate the average weekly earnings taking into account the arrears. This may

[51] Statutory Maternity Pay (Compensation of Employers) and Miscellaneous Amendment Regulations 1994 (S.I. 1994 No. 1882), reg. 4.
[52] Statutory Maternity Pay (Compensation of Employers) Amendment Regulations 1998 (S.I. 1998 No. 522).
[53] n. 51 above, reg. 2(1).
[54] Case C–342/93 [1996] I.R.L.R. 214, ECJ.
[55] Statutory Maternity Pay (General) Amendment Regulations 1996 (S.I. 1996 No. 1335).

mean that for some women who get a back-dated rise, they will qualify for SMP for the first time because their average weekly earnings will match or exceed the LEL for the payment of NICs. Where a woman qualifies for SMP as a result of the back-dated pay rise, the employer must pay the difference between any MA received and the new SMP due. This amendment does not, however, address the problem of basing SMP on the average earnings formula which appears to be in contradiction with the decision of the ECJ in *Gillespie*.

On return, the Northern Ireland Court of Appeal in *Gillespie v. Northern Health and Social Services Board (No. 2)*[56] held that maternity pay paid under a contractual arrangement, which was greater than statutory sickness benefit was not inadequate or such as to undermine the purpose of maternity leave. The Court also decided the joined case of *Todd v. Eastern Health and Social Services Board*, an equal pay claim that was adjourned pending the ECJ's decision in *Gillespie*. The Court held that the tribunal had been wrong to hold that the applicant was entitled to the equivalent of contractual sick pay during maternity leave because this was higher than maternity pay. The Court said that it was clearly established by the ECJ in *Webb (No. 2)*,[57] that a comparison could not be made with a sick man, and therefore provided the level of maternity pay was not so low as to undermine the purpose of maternity leave there was no requirement that it should be equivalent to sick pay.

10.5.6   Contractual arrangements

An employer cannot opt-out of the liability to pay SMP to qualifying employees and any agreement to exclude, limit or otherwise modify the relevant provisions of the Social Security Contributions and Benefits Act 1992 or to require an employee or former employee to contribute towards the cost is void by section 164(6) of the 1992 Act. However, an employer may make contractual arrangements over and above the SMP requirements and such a scheme is operated by the Equal Opportunities Commission (EOC). In *Boyle v. EOC*[58] the EOC scheme, under which maternity pay in excess of the statutory scheme is available, but only to women who state that they intend to return to work, and who agree to be liable to repay any money paid under the scheme if they fail to return for a minimum of one month at the conclusion of maternity leave. This rule has been challenged and referred to the ECJ on the question of whether such a scheme infringes Article 119 and/or Directive 76/207 and/or Directive 92/95 in that such conditions are not attached to anybody else taking paid leave. In addition, a challenge is being made to the condition whereby a female employee who goes on sick leave with a pregnancy-related illness and who gives birth during her absence, can have her maternity leave backdated to the later date of either six weeks before the expected week of childbirth or when the sickness leave began. This challenge is based on the fact that a man taking sick leave does not at any time risk being placed on a less favourable form of leave.

The U.K. Government and the Republic of Ireland both argue that employers have a right to make whatever contractual arrangements they wish in excess of the statutory minimum, and that, utilising *Gillespie*,[59] there is no requirement to pay women on

[56] [1997] I.R.L.R. 410, NICA.
[57] [1995] I.R.L.R. 654, HL.
[58] Case C–411/96 Employment Law Watch No. 5, Spring 1998.
[59] Case C–342/93 [1996] I.R.L.R. 214, ECJ.

maternity leave the same as a man or a woman who is working since women taking maternity leave are in a special position and one for which there is no comparator. In addition, the U.K. Government is arguing that to permit women to complain of maternity benefits that go beyond the statutory scheme would operate as a "serious disincentive to employers to provide benefits."[60]

In *Boyle* a challenge is also being made to the rule that pensionable service during maternity leave only accrues when the woman is in receipt of contractual or statutory maternity pay, therefore excluding any period of unpaid maternity leave. In *Davies v. Girobank plc*[61] a reference has been made to the ECJ on the question, *inter alia*, of whether a rule within the firm's redundancy scheme under which unpaid maternity leave is not counted as pensionable service or for purposes of calculating redundancy payment, is contrary to Article 119. Likewise, a question as to the validity of a similar rule is incorporated within the questions referred to the ECJ in *Boyle v. EOC*.[62]

10.5.7   National rules under challenge

In *Handels- og Kontorfunktionaeenes Fobund I Danmak (acting for Pedersen and Others) v. Faellesfoeningen for Danmaks Brugsforeninger (acting for Kvickly Skive and Others*[63] national legislation in Denmark provides that, in connection with women absent from work for a pregnancy related illness, or illness aggravated by pregnancy, the employer is obliged to pay her only half her salary during the three months before and three months following the birth, whereas for incapacity for work for a non-pregnancy related reason employers are obliged to pay full remuneration. In his Opinion the Advocate General said that Article 119 precludes national legislation from providing such an arrangement. In addition, Directive 76/207 precludes national legislation under which an employer is permitted to decide at his discretion whether he continues to provide work to a pregnant employee who has not been declared incapable of work.

10.6   HEALTH AND SAFETY AND SUSPENSION FROM WORK

At common law there is a duty on employers to provide a safe system of work for all employees. Whenever an employer knows, or should know, of a risk to an employee or person, they must take reasonable steps to either remove or minimise the risk. As the duty is subjective, the burden on the employer increases when the employee is vulnerable. Under the Congenital Disabilities Civil Liabilities Act 1976 an employer, who owes a duty of care to the mother, will also owe a duty to her unborn child in connection with occurrences before its birth which result in it being born disabled. In addition to the statutory provisions contained in the ERA 1996, which provide protection against unfair dismissal for refusal to undertake work which the employee reasonably believes to be harmful or potentially harmful,[64] there are three sets of Regulations of specific relevance to new and expectant mothers that provide for employees to be suspended from work in order to safeguard their health and safety.[65]

---

[60] *People Management* January 22, 1998.
[61] Case C–197/97, EOR No. 75, September/October 1997, p. 43.
[62] Case C–411/96, ECJ, Employment Law Watch No. 5, Spring 1998.
[63] Case C–66/96 ECJ, Employment Law Watch No. 5, Spring 1998.
[64] s.100.
[65] Control of Lead at Work Regulations 1980 (S.I. 1980 No. 1248), reg. 16; Ionising Radiations Regulations 1985 (S.I. 1985 No. 1333), reg. 16; Control of Substances Hazardous to Health Regulations 1988 (S.I. 1988 No. 1657), reg. 11.

Following implementation of Directive 92/85 regulations were introduced to comply with the health and safety provisions laid down in the Directive[66] which require:

"For all activities liable to involve a specific risk of exposure to agents, processes or working conditions of which a non exhaustive list is given in Annex 1, the employer shall assess the nature, degree and duration of exposure, in the undertaking and/or establishment concerned, or workers within the meaning of Article 2, either directly or by way of the protective and preventive services referred to in Article 7 of Directive 89/391/EEC, in order to—
— assess any risks to the safety or health and any possible effect on the pregnancies to breastfeeding to worker within the meaning of Article 2,
— decide what measures should be taken."
Directive 92/85, Art. 4, para. 1.

Article 5 sets out the action to be taken if the assessment reveals a risk to the safety or health or an effect on the pregnancy or breastfeeding of a worker covered by the Directive. The employer is required to take the necessary measures to ensure that the risk is avoided by making adjustments to working conditions and/or working hours, moving the worker concerned to another job or granting leave for a period necessary to protect the woman's safety or health.

The 1994 Regulations deal with the identification of risk and are in addition to the risk assessment requirements of the general Management of Health and Safety at Work Regulations 1992,[67] under which employers are required to assess the risks to which employees and non-employees are exposed at work and to take any protective measures required by the Health and Safety at Work, etc., Act 1974 and other health and safety legislation. Under the 1994 Regulations employers must undertake a risk assessment, if the workforce includes women of child-bearing age, in order to assess the health and safety risks which might be posed to: pregnant workers; workers who have given birth within the previous six months; and workers who are breastfeeding. In this context "birth" means a child born alive or a still-born child delivered after 24 weeks of pregnancy. The necessity to carry out a risk assessment under the 1994 Regulations covers employed women, including those who are self-employed, and applies to contractors and contractors' staff, although, they should have their risks assessed primarily by their own employer and unlike employees do not have statutory rights against the employer of the site being visited, only against their own employer.

The 1992 Regulations (as amended) require that:

"Where—

(a) the persons working in an undertaking include women of child-bearing age; and

(b) the work is of a kind which could involve risk, by reason of her condition, to the health and safety of a new or expectant mother, or to that of her baby, from any processes or working conditions, or physical, biological or chemical agents, including those specified in Annexes I and II of Council Directive

---

[66] Management of Health and Safety at Work Amendment Regulations 1994 (S.I. 1994 No. 2865) amending the Management of Health and Safety at Work Regulations 1992 (S.I. 1992 No. 2051).
[67] S.I. 1992 No. 2051.

92/85/EEC . . . the assessment required by regulation 3(1) shall also include an assessment of such risk."

Management of Health and Safety at Work Regulations 1992, reg. 13A.[68]

An employer is required to take protective measures specified in any relevant health and safety legislation once it becomes apparent that there is a risk to an employee who has notified him in writing that she falls into one of the three specified categories. If the woman has not notified her employer that she falls into one of the three categories covered by the Directive, the employer still has a duty to take protective steps under the Health and Safety at Work, etc., Act 1974 and the general risk assessment procedure under the 1992 Regulations.[69] The Health and Safety Executive has issued practical guidance on the risks to pregnant women and how to avoid them[70] and advice on carrying out a risk assessment.[71]

Under the amended 1992 Regulations[72] where the woman has notified her employer in writing that she falls into one of the affected categories, and the steps set out in the relevant legislation would not avoid the risk, then he must alter her working conditions or hours of work, and by regulation 13A(3) if it is not reasonable to alter the working conditions or hours of work, or if it would not avoid the risk, the employer is required to suspend the employee from work for as long as it is necessary to avoid the risk. Such a suspension is subject to the ERA 1996, s.67 by which, if the employer has suitable alternative work available the employee has a right to be offered that work before being suspended. In order to be suitable alternative work the work offered must fall within section 67(2)(a) and (b). An employee for whom there is no suitable alternative work and who is suspended from work under regulation 13A(3) of the 1992 Regulations, is by the ERA 1996, s.68 entitled to be paid unless she unreasonably refused to perform work which was offered and which was suitable for the purposes of section 67.[73] During the period of suspension the employee continues to be employed and the period of suspension counts towards her period of continuous employment.

The 1992 Regulations (as amended) provide that where a new or expectant mother who works at night has a certificate from a doctor or mid-wife showing that it is necessary for her health and safety that she should not work at night for a period specified in the certificate, he is required to suspend her from work[74] unless, under the ERA 1996, s.67 he is able to offer her suitable alternative daytime work on terms and conditions no less favourable than her normal terms and conditions. The Health and Safety Executive point out in their guidance[75] "HSE experts are not at present aware of any risks to pregnant or breastfeedng workers or their children from working at night *per se*" and they recommend seeking advice from an occupational health specialist should this situation occur. They also caution against breaches of the Equal Pay Act 1970 and the Sex Discrimination Act 1975.

In *Iske v. P&O European Ferries (Dover) Ltd*[76] the EAT upheld a complaint of direct discrimination contrary to section 1(1)(a) and section 6(2)(a) of the SDA 1975 when a

---

[68] reg. 13A of the 1992 Regulations (as amended) inserted by the Management of Health and Safety at Work (Amendment) Regulations 1994 (S.I. 1994 No. 2865) from December 1, 1994.

[69] reg. 3.

[70] *New and expectant mothers at work: a guide for employers* (1994) HS(G)122, ISBN 0 71760826 3, Health & Safety Executive.

[71] *5 Steps to Risk Assessment*, HSE, IND(G)143(L).

[72] reg. 13A(2).

[73] ERA 1996, s.68(2)(a)–(b).

[74] reg. 13B of the Management of Health and Safety at Work Regulations 1992.

[75] See n. 70.

[76] [1997] I.R.L.R. 401, CA.

sea-going ferry stewardess, who was 28 weeks pregnant, was prohibited by statutory regulations from going to sea, but whose request for a transfer to shore based duties was refused. It was demonstrated that the reason she had not been offered alternative work was because of a company policy not to offer women seafarers shore based work after the twenty-eighth week of pregnancy. In response to the employer's argument that there was no suitable alternative vacancy because the vacancies which would have been suitable had been filled by agency staff, the EAT referred to the SDA 1975, s.50(1):

"In our view, s.50(1) is inserted for the avoidance of doubt where access to benefits, facilities or services are provided indirectly by the employer through a third party. It follows that the same principle applies to access to opportunities for promotion, transfer or training. . . .

In our judgment an employer cannot avoid the effect of s.6(2)(a) of the SDA by contracting out a job to which the employee could be transferred." *per* Peter Clark J.

Iske v. P&O European Ferries (Dover) Ltd [1997] I.R.L.R. 401 at 404, EAT.

A woman, regardless of her length of service or hours of work, has a right under the ERA 1996, s.70 to complain to an industrial tribunal if:

- she is suspended on medical grounds under the ERA 1996, s.64, and her employer fails to pay her in whole or in part remuneration to which she is entitled under section 64(1);

- she is suspended from work on maternity grounds within the ERA 1996, s.66, but is not paid in accordance with section 68;

- she is not made an offer of suitable alternative work under section 67, when such work exists.

If the employee fails to accept an offer of suitable alternative work, as described in section 67(2)(a)–(b) as work of a kind which is both suitable and appropriate for her to do in the circumstances, and on terms and conditions which are either the same or not substantially less favourable, she is not entitled to be paid if she unreasonably refuses to perform that work.

For the right to be offered suitable alternative work under the ERA 1996, s.67 it is necessary for the suspension to be on maternity grounds as defined in section 66: in consequence of any relevant requirement or relevant recommendation. A "relevant requirement" means a requirement imposed by or under a specified provision of an enactment or of an instrument made under an enactment and "relevant recommendation" means a recommendation in a specified provision of a code of practice issued or approved under the Health and Safety at Work, etc., Act 1974, s.16. In *Iske v. P&O European Ferries (Dover) Ltd*[77] it was held that the applicant exercised her right to commence maternity leave by signing the maternity leave form which constituted notice under the ERA 1996, s.72 and once that leave commenced there could be no compulsory suspension. The EAT said that the applicant was unable to rely on section 66 because the regulations under which she was prohibited from carrying out her

---

[77] [1997] I.R.L.R. 401, EAT.

normal job were not on the list of "relevant" provisions,[78] which was a breach of Directive 92/85 and steps, the EAT said were being taken to remedy that breach.[78a]

The industrial tribunal case of *Hickey v. Lucas Service U.K. Ltd*[79] demonstrates a number of the above points. After Hickey became pregnant she was transferred as part of an unconnected disciplinary action, but no risk assessment was carried out on her new job which both she and her doctor felt could be a risk to her pregnancy because of the amount of lifting. The tribunal found that the company had eventually carried out a risk assessment, but did not provide Ms Hickey with a copy, had confined the assessment to general risks and did not consider specific risks to new and expectant mothers: they were reported as not having heard of the 1994 Health and Safety Executive's 1994 guidance on risk assessment for new and expectant mothers, having given Ms Hickey advice to "take sensible precautions". The company eventually found clerical work for Hickey, who returned to work until her maternity leave. While off work she received only sick pay which was less than her usual rate of pay which meant that she did not meet the lower earnings threshold to qualify for statutory maternity pay when she went on maternity leave. On her complaint to an industrial tribunal that she should have been suspended from work on maternity ground, and therefore, under section 68 would have been entitled to her usual remuneration: the tribunal decided that she should have been suspended from the time when she first went off sick until when she returned to clerical duties and was therefore entitled to be paid at her normal rate for that period, not merely the rate for sick pay.

10.7 PARENTAL AND PATERNITY LEAVE

There is currently no provision in domestic law for parental, family or paternity leave, although research shows that voluntary arrangements, whether for different types of leave arrangements or forms of flexible working to accommodate the birth of a child are not uncommon.[80] In the twin Policy Studies Institute (PSI) reports[81] amongst those surveyed around one-quarter of employers (24 per cent) provided paternity leave, usually paid and typically limited to about four days, whereas in the survey completed by 300 members of the Institute of Personnel and Development (IPD) more than half (57 per cent) provided paternity leave of five days or less.[82]

Parental leave arrangements are more commonly confined to natural parents, and although there has been a drop in the number of adoptions, the age of the child at adoption has increased, with children aged five or more accounting for two-thirds of

---

[78] This part of the case was based on the EPCA 1978, s.66 "relevant provisions", which were contained in the Suspension from Work (on Maternity Grounds) Order 1994. Under the corresponding provision in the ERA 1996, s.66, the wording is "relevant requirement or relevant recommendation".

[78a] See now the Suspension from Work on Maternity Grounds (Merchant Shipping and Fishing Vessels) Order 1998 (S.I. 1998 No. 587), which specifies regs 8(3) and 9(2) of the Merchant Shipping and Fishing Vessels (Health and Safety at Work) Regulations 1997 (S.I. 1997 No. 2962) as relevant provisions for the purpose of ERA 1996, s.66, places women employed at sea on the same footing as those employed on land to whom Suspension from Work (on Maternity Grounds) Order 1994 (S.I. 1994 No. 2930) applies.

[79] Case No. 1400979/96, Health and Safety Bulletin 260, August 1997.

[80] A report by the think-tank Demos, *Parental leave; the price of family values?* showed only 3% of the organisations surveyed had parental leave policies.

[81] C. Callender *et al., Maternity rights and benefits in Britain 1996,* DSS Research Report, No. 67; J. Forth *et al., Family-friendly working arrangements in Britain 1996,* DfEE Research Series Report No. 16.

[82] Hammond Studdards, *Maternity rights survey 1997,* Survey for IPD, reported EOR No. 75 September/October 1997, pp. 4–5.

adoptees in 1994.[83] Research by Incomes Data Services (IDS) shows a variety of policies on this issue, ranging from treating adoption on the same basis as maternity and/or paternity leave, treating adoption leave (for mothers and fathers) on the same basis as paternity leave and using the same service requirement as for maternity leave but offering reduced leave or offering the same leave entitlement, but on an unpaid basis.[84]

Both natural and adoptive parents are covered by Directive 96/34,[85] the Parental Leave Directive, which was adopted by the Council on June 3, 1996 to give effect to the framework agreement on parental leave concluded by the social partners.[86] Implementation of the Directive by Member States is to be accomplished by June 3, 1998, or an additional period of a maximum of a year is permitted by Article 2.2 if this is necessary to take account of special difficulties or implementation by a collective agreement.

The legal basis of the Directive is the social policy Agreement annexed to the Protocol on Social Policy to the Treaty on European Union, and as such would not have been applicable to the United Kingdom. However, following agreement at the Amsterdam Intergovernmental Conference that the social policy Protocol and Agreement annexed to the Maastricht Treaty are to be brought within the main body of the Treaty and the subsequent readoption of the existing two Directives agreed under the social policy Agreement on a whole-Community basis, the Parental Leave Directive extends to the United Kingdom from December 15, 1997, and there are two years for implementation.

The Directive gives all workers (men and women who have an employment contract or employment relationship), an individual right to at least three months' unpaid leave following the birth or adoption of a child, to enable them to take care of the child, and the right to return at the end of the parental leave, to the same or an equivalent or similar job consistent with their employment contract or relationship. The right to leave may be exercised at any time before the child's eighth birthday at the latest, and it should, in principle, be granted "on a non-transferable basis". That is, where both parents work, on the basis that they take three months' parental leave each. Female workers will continue to retain rights to paid maternity leave.

Member States and/or management and workers may:

- adjust the provisions to the special circumstances of adoption;
- decide the basis upon which the leave is taken, whether piecemeal, full-time, part-time, or by a time-credit system;
- make the entitlement subject to a period of work and/or length of service qualification, which may not exceed a year; and
- establish notice periods to be given when exercising the right to leave.

Workers must be protected against dismissal on the grounds of taking, or applying for leave and any rights acquired must be maintained until the leave ends, when they have a right to return to the same, or if that is not possible, to an equivalent or similar job consistent with their employment contract or employment relationship.

[83] 1994 figures. IDS Study 630, *Maternity & Parental Leave,* July 1997, p. 9.
[84] *ibid.* pp. 9–10.
[85] On the framework agreement on parental leave concluded by the social partners.
[86] UNICE, CEEP and the ETUC.

The Directive also covers family leave in that Member States are required to take the necessary measures to entitle workers to time off work for urgent family reasons in cases of sickness or accident which makes the immediate presence of the worker indispensable. Member States have the right to lay down conditions for access and a maximum entitlement.

10.8   REFORM AND SUMMARY

The law regarding rights during pregnancy, maternity leave and maternity pay were criticised as long ago as 1982 for being too complex and since then nothing has happened to improve the situation. In particular, the law has been considerably muddied by the use of the Sex Discrimination Act, which provided an avenue for grievances for those who did not qualify to bring a claim under the employment protection provisions. Whilst implementation of Directive 92/85 has resolved the issue of eligibility for employment protection rights for those with less than two years' service, in the interim the provisions of the Sex Discrimination Act, and interpretation of the Equal Treatment Directive 76/207 have been subjected to some stretching and pulling of statutory provisions in order to fit the requirements of equal treatment for pregnant women, with issues being decided on a case by case basis. This has done nothing to help the general understanding of this already complex area of the law and although there are still cases being dealt with under the SDA, increasingly such cases will be brought under the relevant provisions of the ERA 1996.

Although the ECJ decisions in *Larsson* and *Brown v. Rentokil Ltd*[87] are to be welcomed as clarifying the position regarding the protected period as extending from pregnancy through to the end of the MLP, and that absences during the protected period cannot be taken into consideration in disciplinary or dismissal decisions, and the Court of Appeal decisions in *Crees v. Royal London Insurance* and *Kwik Save Stores Ltd v. Greaves*[88] clarify the meaning of "exercise the right" to return to work, there remain a number of areas that need clarification, not least of which is the status of the contract during extended maternity leave. However, following the decision in *Crees* this becomes less important, the issue now being whether the dismissal, as a result of failure to return, is unfair on general principles.

Eligibility for SSP in terms of the threshold of NICs is an area where cases are outstanding, although the issue as to adequacy of the level of SSP appears to be settled.

In the White Paper *Fairness at Work*[89] in the chapter on "family friendly policies[90] the Government announced its intention to implement the Parental Leave Directive and to integrate implementation with existing employment rights for pregnant women which it will review in order "to achieve a coherent package that is easier to understand and operate", with legislation to create a framework of basic rights, supported by regulations on the detail on which consultation will take place.[91]

It is proposed to:

- extend the maternity leave period from 14 to 18 weeks in order to coincide with the period of SMP;

---

[87] Case C–400/95 [1997] I.R.L.R. 643, ECJ; Case C–394/96 [1998] I.R.L.R. 445, ECJ.
[88] [1998] I.R.L.R. 245, CA.
[89] Cm. 3968 (1998).
[90] Chapter 5.
[91] para. 5.13.

- simplify the notice provisions and seek views as to how this might be achieved and what notice provisions should apply to parental leave;

- reduce the qualifying period for the extended maternity leave period from two years to one year with parental leave being subject to the same qualifying period;

- provide for the contract of employment to continue during the whole period of maternity leave unless it is expressly terminated by either party, by dismissal or resignation and for the same to apply to parental leave;

- provide for similar rights to return after parental leave as apply after maternity leave—this is taken to mean those that apply after MLP, as opposed to after return from extended leave;

- seek views as to the particular difficulties that might be faced by small employers in complying with the rights proposed in Chapter 5 and how these might be alleviated;

- provide a right to reasonable time off for family emergencies, applicable to all employees regardless of length of service; and

- provide similar protection against unfair dismissal for those exercising their right to parental leave and time off for urgent family reasons as currently apply to dismissal on grounds of pregnancy and the exercise of the right to maternity leave, which apply regardless of length of service.

The following chart summarises the main eligibility criteria for statutory maternity leave and pay.

ELIGIBILITY FOR STATUTORY MATERNITY LEAVE (SML) AND PAY (SMP)

Continuous Service	*Leave Details*	*Pay Details*
Employment Rights Act 1996 Part VIII		**Social Security Act 1975 Social Security Contributions and Benefits Act 1992 and Regulations**
Engaged in employment as employed or self-employed earner with less than 26 weeks' continuous employment.	• a general right to 14 weeks' MLP, ERA 1996 s.73; • can be taken at any time from 11th week before expected week of childbirth (EWC).	**Maternity Allowance** *Qualifications* • have reached the start of 11th week before EWC; • not entitled to SMP; • satisfied contribution requirements - have paid full-rate class 1 or 2 NICs in at least 26 weeks in the 66 weeks immediately preceeding 14th week before EWC. Paid as weekly benefit for maximum of 18 weeks at lower rate of SMP: £57.70 (1998-99).
Employees with 26 weeks' continuous employment at 15th week before expected week of childbirth.	As above.	**SMP** *Qualifications* • 26 weeks' continuous employment up to and including 15th week before expected week of childbirth: qualifying week (QW); • not paid less than lower earnings limit (1998-99 £64) a week in the eight weeks ending with the QW; • given employer medical evidence of EWC if requested to do so; • reached 11th week before the EWC, or have recently given birth; • stopped working and have given 21 days' notice of intention to do so. *Rate* 6 weeks at 90% of normal weekly earnings and up to 12 weeks at £57.70 per week (1998–99): reviewed annually for implementation from April 6.

Continuous Service	Leave Details	Pay Details
Employment Rights Act 1996 Part VIII		**Social Security Act 1975 Social Security Contributions and Benefits Act 1992 and Regulations**
Employees with 2 years' continuous service at 11th week before EWC, ERA 1996, s.79(1)	As above but entitled to return at any time after end of MLP and 29 weeks after the week in which the child was born ERA 1996, s.79(1)(b). This means a max. of 40 weeks leave: up to 11 weeks before and 29 weeks after expected week of childbirth.	As above and/or any contractual arrangement of excess statutory limits above, but exercised in accordance with statutory rules.

Chapter 11

COLLECTIVE ISSUES AND THE INDIVIDUAL EMPLOYMENT RELATIONSHIP

11.1 COLLECTIVE LABOUR LAW AND THE INDIVIDUAL EMPLOYMENT RELATIONSHIP

The text has largely concentrated on an examination of the legal relationship between the individual employee and the employer, but from time to time, the reader will have noticed references to statutory provisions[1] attaching to the role of a third party to this relationship, namely the trade union and its officials. Collective labour law, as it is known, deals specifically with the relationship of trade unions with employers and with their own individual members. The law in this area is particularly complex and sometimes controversial, especially the legislation relating to the taking of industrial action. Whether the considerable legislative regulation of trade union industrial action and activities undertaken by Conservative Governments from 1980 to 1991, was a factor which significantly contributed to a weakening of their influence in the workplace or was merely incidental to a "natural" loss of membership arising from unemployment and labour restructuring is a matter of some debate.[2] However, at the time of going to press, the Labour Government elected in 1997, although committed to not restoring the previous legal position of trade unions[3] has prepared a White Paper *Fairness at Work* which contains proposals to reintroduce a statutory trade union recognition procedure, a measure which is welcomed in principle by many trade unionists.

Such a procedure, will compel employers to negotiate and consult with trade unions if the relevant workforce achieves a statutory threshold of employee support. These proposals, when enacted, will not only impact upon the relationship between the employer and the trade union, but will also affect the rights of individual employees as trade union members and officials. The text briefly outlines the role of trade unions

---

[1] For example: Collective Redundancy Consultation TULRCA 1992, s.188 and TUPE, reg. 10 as amended.

[2] W. McCarthy *Legal Intervention in Industrial Relations: Gains and Losses* (Blackwell Business, Oxford, 1992).

[3] The Prime Minister Tony Blair in responding to Opposition criticism said in 1997: "Let me state the position clearly, so that no one is in any doubt. The essential elements of the trade union legislation of the 1980s will remain. There will be no return to secondary action, flying pickets, strikes without ballots, the closed shop and all the rest. The changes that we do propose would leave British law the most restrictive on trade unions in the western world." Speech cited in: J. Mortimer *In Defence of Trade Unionism* (Institute of Employment Rights, 1988).

and the development of collective bargaining in the United Kingdom. It then seeks to explain the complex relationship between the legal rights of individual employees as trade union members and the rights of trade unions as quasi-corporate bodies.[4] Finally, consideration is given to the objectives and difficulties associated with the implementation of the impending statutory trade union recognition procedure.

11.1.1   The development of trade unions

Statutes regulating the wages of agricultural labourers first appear in the mid-fourteenth century[5] but the development "of the modern trade union is to be found in the small craft organisations which developed during the eighteenth century as a consequence of the decay of the mediaeval system of statutory wage fixing."[6] The growth of an impoverished industrial labouring class concentrated in factories at the end of this century, combined with a fear by the ruling classes that the republican ideals triumphing in France would cross the channel, led to a savage statutory[7] and common law antipathy towards any form of collective action by the working classes. Workpeople who combined together to ask for better wages and conditions faced deportation and imprisonment whilst a servant who broke his contract of employment committed a criminal offence and could be jailed by the magistrate. Wages were set by the magistrates who were often the same factory owners, "trying their workman for offences against themselves."[8] It was only at the end of the nineteenth century that trade unions and their officials were given immunity from criminal and civil liability for industrial action.[9]

The legal rights granted to trade unions did not give individual workers a legal right to strike but merely gave immunity to the trade unions themselves from being prosecuted for committing tortious acts such as interfering with the legal rights of others in an industrial dispute.[10] The tortious acts included conspiracy and inducing a breach of contract of employment. These immunities eventually became known as the "Golden Formula". This was because individuals and trade unions were protected when taking industrial action if this action was "in contemplation or furtherance of a trade dispute" as defined in the 1845 and 1906 Acts. The modern statutory formulation of a trade dispute is contained in the Trade Union and Labour Relations (Consolidation) Act 1992 (TULRCA 1992), s.218 and it provides protection from litigation under section 219 of the same statute providing such a dispute is concerned with the terms and conditions of employees including their appointment and dismissal, the allocation of work to them, disciplinary matters, the membership or non-membership of a union and facilities for negotiations and consultation including the recognition of a trade union.[11] Most of the time, trade union members and officials are engaged with

[4] For example, they can make contracts, sue and be sued but they cannot be incorporated TULRCA 1992, s.12. See also: S. Deakin and G. Morris (1995) p. 622.
[5] 1349 Ordinance of Labourers (23 Edw. 3).
[6] N.A. Citrine, *Trade Union Law* (Stevens, London, 1960), p. 3.
[7] The 1799 & 1800 Combination Acts "though they drew an important distinction between masters and men, did on paper profess to restrain the masters from combining. In fact they were never interpreted by the masters as applying to the masters at all." J.L. Hammond and Barbara (1920) *The Town Labourer 1760–1832*, LRD & Longmans, London, 1920), p. 65.
[8] *ibid*.
[9] The Trade Union Act 1871, Conspiracy & Protection of Property Act 1875 and the Trade Disputes Act 1906, together with the Trade Union Act 1913 are the keystone statutes which established the legal basis of 20th century trade unionism. A foundation which lay largely unchanged until the 1970s.
[10] Trade Disputes Act 1906, s.4(1).
[11] TULRCA 1992, s.244.

employers in discussing such terms and conditions without the need for judicial intervention. The text now looks at how such bargaining has developed.

11.2   DEVELOPMENT OF COLLECTIVE BARGAINING IN THE UNITED KINGDOM

In the mid 1950s a distinguished labour lawyer wrote:

> "There is, perhaps, no major country in the world in which the law has played a less significant role in the shaping of [labour-management] relations than in Great Britain . . ."[12]

This statement from the leading exponent of the laissez-faire model of industrial relations was only partly true then and has become increasingly less so since the 1980s. The characteristic of this model of collective bargaining was, that by and large, government let employers and trade unions conduct their negotiations without, or at least with as little, state intervention as possible. There had always been exceptions to this, when for example, in war time the state imposed compulsory conciliation and arbitration procedures in industry to ensure continuity of production. Another development arising from the First World War was the introduction of the Whitley[13] system of bargaining. This was essentially a system of bargaining which relied upon joint consultation and negotiation between employers' representatives and trade union representatives in a specific industrial sector. The impetus was to try to reach agreements which were ultimately honoured by both sides. Such bargaining was developed first in the industrial sector and then in the public sector.

A negative system of trade union immunities which protected trade unions from civil prosecution whilst engaged in "contemplation on furtherance of a trade dispute"[14] combined with a tradition of industry-wide bargaining remained in place during the post-war period of reconstruction. The structural decline of heavy industry and growing unemployment from the late sixties combined with increasing inflation, caused governments to intervene in bargaining by encouraging and by imposing wage restraint. This latter model of industrial relations hardly fits in with the laissez-faire processes described by Kahn-Freund. Davies and Freedland[15] point out that the laissez-faire model of labour law had always been subject to exceptions in that there was some government intervention to maintain minimum employment standards. The Truck Acts, Wage Council legislation and health and safety legislation are all cited as examples of where the law rather than "free collective bargaining" was employed to establish a floor of standards.

Individual employment rights, such as the right to a statutory notice period of termination of the employment contract,[16] the right to a redundancy payment and the

---

[12] O. Kahn-Freund in A. Flanders and H.A. Clegg, *The System of Industrial Relations in Great Britain* (Oxford, 1954).
[13] Named after John H. Whitley, the Liberal M.P. and Speaker of the House of Commons, who chaired (1917–18) a Government committee on relations between employers and employees.
[14] The so called "Golden Formula" now found in ss.218 and 219 of the Trade Union and Labour Relations (Consolidation) Act 1992.
[15] Peter Davies and Mark Freedland, *Labour Legislation and Public Policy* (Clarendon Press, 1993), p. 186.
[16] s.86 of the Employment Rights Act 1996, originally found in the Contracts of Employment Act 1963.

right not to be unfairly dismissed[17] were however a quantum leap in the development of these standards in that they introduced regulatory elements into the employment relationship which were to be imposed by statute law. Such regulation derived from international standards and marked a significant departure from the hegemony of the common law in this area.

11.2.1   Donovan Report

At the same time as these developments affecting individual workers, the "freedom" of trade unions to act without fear of litigation providing they were acting "in furtherance of a trade dispute"[18] was being called into question by some commentators who were concerned at the rising levels of industrial unrest. "Wildcat strikes" and the perceived lack of control of the union bureaucracy over their local officials was seen as inimical to the economy as well as to industrial relations. A Royal Commission was established[19]: "The central issue for Donovan was how to restore order, peace and efficiency to industrial relations and yet preserve and even extend the voluntarist tradition of collective bargaining."[20]

The Commission was much concerned with difficulties caused by the two prevalent levels of bargaining, the formal multi-employer bargaining conducted at national level and the shop-steward bargaining at plant and workplace level. Essentially, the formal system was seen as imposing order through industry wide agreements which not only were clear as to content but also acted as a regulator of wages and prices in the industry. Shop-steward negotiating was much more ad hoc and broader in its scope dealing with many issues besides the application of nationally agreed basic rates.[21] Locally agreed wage rates outwith the national industry agreement were, however, seen as often leading to "anomalous and inequitable payments systems and to be a frequent cause of grievance among, and industrial action (often unofficial) by, the work groups".[22]

In its quest to inject more order into the bargaining process the Commission rejected proposals to make collective agreements legally binding but recommended the adoption of more formal procedures for plant level bargaining. Deakin and Morris remind us that "Employment protection legislation was to be an important part of this".[23] Unfair dismissal provisions first appeared in the Industrial Relations Act 1971 and still remain on the statute book, unlike the collective bargaining provisions of that statute. Formulated by a Conservative Government and modelled on American legislation, trade unions were offered positive legal rights including recognition if they registered. Most refused and were technically outside the law when taking industrial action because their liability for civil action was removed if they were unregistered. The 1906 negative immunities were restored to trade unions with the return of a Labour Government in 1974.

11.2.2   Rights to trade union membership and activity

Industrial justice not only implied things like equal pay for men and women but it was also concerned with the relationship of the worker with his or her trade union. In

[17] now s.94 of the ERA 1996, but originally introduced in the Industrial Relations Act 1971.
[18] now s.219 of the TULRCA 1992, but originally defined in s.5(3) of the Trade Disputes Act 1906.
[19] Donovan Royal Commission on Trade Unions and Employers' Associations 1965–1968, *Report.*, Cmnd. 3623 (London, HMSO, 1968).
[20] R. Lewis, *Labour Law in Britain* (Blackwell, Oxford, 1986).
[21] P. Davies and M. Freedland, *Labour Law: Text and Materials* (2nd ed., Weidenfeld, London, 1984), p. 121.
[22] *ibid.* p. 122.
[23] Deakin and Morris (1995), p. 34.

particular, *rights to* union membership and *rights arising* from union membership. The former was important in that Donovan had recommended that the closed shop[24] was not prohibited. Workers could be fairly dismissed for non-membership where there was a union membership agreement.[25] The right to disassociate from a trade union and not lose one's job was an increasingly important issue with those on the Right during this period of industrial unrest, a right which seemed eventually to be confirmed by the judgment of the European Court in *Young, James and Webster v. United Kingdom.*[26] The Court found, that because the alternative was for them to lose their jobs, the dismissal of three railway employees for refusing to join a closed shop was an interference in the freedom guaranteed under Article 11 of the European Convention on Human Rights. This was however a controversial judgment[27] and has been criticised by both Wedderburn[28] and Davies and Freedland.[29] Essentially what this complicated judgment said, was that in this particular case it was wrong to force a closed shop on employees when it was not an original condition of their employment; but a dissenting minority in the Court also found that "There is no logical link between positive and negative freedom of association . . . the former is a collective right exercised by a plurality of individuals protecting common interests and pursuing common goals; the latter aims at protecting the individual against being grouped with other individuals with whom he does not agree."

Rights arising from trade union membership were also considered important by Kahn-Freund. These he summarised as equal representation by and participation in the union.[30] Both the common law and statute law has played a part in protecting the membership rights of individual union members. The controversy, which has arisen, is how far can these be protected at the expense of collective rights? The right to take industrial action is a collective right but some would argue that this has been much undermined since 1988 by the statutory right of an individual not to have disciplinary action taken against her by her trade union for refusing to participate in industrial action.[31] On the Left, commentators like Hyman would maintain that "it is only through the power over its members which is vested in the trade union that it is able to exert power for them."[32]

11.3 LEGAL FRAMEWORK FOR COLLECTIVE BARGAINING

The legal framework for collective bargaining in any particular country depends upon:

[24] The "closed shop" was the traditional way that some unions maintained their membership levels. Entry to a job was via a union membership card. EPCA 1978, s.58(3) provided that workers could be dismissed if they refused to join a trade union without a good reason. This practice was attacked by a series of enactments which first widened the exemptions permitted for non-membership followed by the introduction of secret ballots which required 80 to 85% majorities every five years to maintain the closed shop. The Employment Act 1990, s.(1)(a) virtually ended the statutory closed shop by stipulating that it was unlawful for an employer to refuse employment to anyone on the grounds of membership or non-membership of a trade union. See: K. Ewing *The Employment Act 1990, A European Perspective*, Institute of Employment Rights, 1991.
[25] s.58 of the Employment Protection Consolidation Act 1978.
[26] [1981] I.R.L.R. 408.
[27] Lord Wedderburn, *The Worker and the Law* (3rd ed. Penguin, 1986), p. 377.
[28] *ibid.*
[29] P. Davies and M. Freedland, *Labour Law: Text and Materials* (2nd ed., Weidenfeld, 1984).
[30] P. Davies and M. Freedland (1993), p. 232.
[31] s.3 of the Employment Act 1988, now found in TULRCA 1992, s.64.
[32] R. Hyman, *Industrial Relations, A Marxist Introduction* (Macmillan, 1975), p. 65.

- The right of workers to associate in trade unions.
- Legislative policy towards collective agreements.
- The recognition of trade unions by employers for collective bargaining purposes.

It can probably safely be said that the freedom of association arguments aroused by the closed shop in the 1960s and 1970s and the key case of *Young, James and Webster v. The United Kingdom*[33] are not perceived to be as relevant to collective bargaining today. The decline of closed shops or union membership agreements (UMAs) in the United Kingdom in their traditional heartlands of heavy industry probably predated and made unnecessary their final legislative prohibition in 1990.[34]

11.3.1   The legal status of the collective agreement

Apart from the period 1971 to 1974[35] the statutory status given to collective agreements was that of legal non-enforceability. During this period all collective agreements were presumed to be legally enforceable unless the contracting parties had an express exclusion clause. The situation is now the reverse, the TULRCA 1992, s.179(1) directs that collective agreements are presumed to be not legally enforceable contracts unless there is an express provision in writing that they are.[36]

The statutory formulation of the content of a collective agreement is defined in the TULRCA 1992, s.178 as "negotiations relating to or connected with" terms and conditions, engagement or non-engagement, allocation of duties, discipline, membership or non-membership of a trade union, facilities for union officials and machinery for negotiation or consultation.[37] If an employer chooses to recognise a trade union under these provisions it will incur statutory obligations to consult with it over redundancies,[38] transfer of undertakings,[39] and health and safety,[40] as well as pension matters.[41] In addition, union members and representatives of a recognised trade union have a statutory entitlement to time off for specific union duties and activities.[42]

Under the TULRCA 1992, s.181 employers also have a statutory obligation to recognised trade unions to disclose information "without which the trade union representatives would be to a material extent impeded in carrying on collective bargaining with him"[43] and "which it would be in accordance with good industrial relations practice that he should disclose to them for the purposes of collective bargaining."[44] This would seem to provide the opportunity for trade union negotiators

---

[33] [1981] I.R.L.R. 408, ECHR.
[34] see K. Ewing (1991), p. 8.
[35] as s.34 and 35 of the now repealed Industrial Relations Act 1971.
[36] TULRCA 1992, s.179(2).
[37] TULRCA 1992, s.178(2).
[38] TULRCA 1992, s.188 as amended by the TURERA 1993, s.34.
[39] Transfer of Undertakings (Protection of Employment) Regulations 1981, S.I. 1981 No. 1794 as amended by the TUREREA 1993, s.33.
[40] Health and Safety at Work etc. Act 1974 and two approved codes of practice. See Deakin and Morris (1995) pp. 701–704.
[41] Occupational Pension Schemes (Contracting Out) Regulations 1984 (S.I. 1984 No. 380), as amended by S.I. 1984 No. 1104.
[42] TULRCA 1992, ss.168 and 170. See also ACAS Code of Practice 3 *Time Off For Trade Union Duties and Activities*, 1991 as amended.
[43] s.181(2)(a).
[44] s.181(2)(b).

to mine rich seams of information for bargaining purposes. In reality this is rarely so. The "material extent" hurdle is a difficult one for a union negotiator to cross. In addition, the code of practice[45] does not "provide even a 'checklist' of items which should be disclosed, on the basis that this will vary according to such factors as the subject-matter and level of negotiations and the size of the company and business."[46] Another considerable restriction on the general duty to disclose is found in the TULRCA 1992, s.182. Employers are, amongst other things, not obliged to disclose material "against the interests of national security,"[47] or confidential material[48] or information "the disclosure of which would cause substantial injury to his undertaking".[49]

Unlike the situation in many other European jurisdictions the collective agreement itself attracts no overall contractual status in the employment relationship. Some terms of the agreement *may be* incorporated into the individual employment contract. But this process is fraught with all sort of difficulties.[50]

11.3.2 Trade union recognition

Since the Employment Act 1980, there has been no statutory recognition procedure to assist trade unions in the securing of bargaining rights. Prior to this, the controversial Industrial Relations Act 1971 introduced a recognition procedure as part of a short lived attempt by the Conservative Government to legally regulate all aspects of industrial relations. Registration of a trade union was linked to the granting of sole bargaining agency rights.[51] An incoming Labour Government repealed this legislation and restored the largely voluntarist position through the Employment Protection Act 1975 which introduced a procedure whereby unions, refused recognition by an employer, could refer the matter to ACAS which could make enquiries[52] and conduct a ballot of the workers.[53] An employer who refused to recognise a trade union could have a reference to the Central Arbitration Committee (CAC) made against him, which if successful, could lead to the CAC inserting a variation to the employment contract of the workers so referred. The lack of an effective enforcement remedy and the failure of ACAS to agree "criteria for determining bargaining units and for choosing bargaining agents"[54] led to the repeal of the legislation in 1980.

Since the election of a new Labour Government in 1997, the change of policy towards collective organisation has been indicated by the restoration of trade union recognition rights to civil service unions[55] representing government employees at GCHQ[56] and by the much trailed manifesto commitment to the reintroduction of a

---

[45] ACAS Code of Practice 2 *Disclosure of Information to Trade Unions for Collective Bargaining Purposes*, 1977.
[46] Deakin and Morris (1995), p. 674.
[47] s.182(1)(a).
[48] s.182(1)(c).
[49] s.182 (1)(e).
[50] A.C. Neal, *The Collective Agreement as a Public Law Instrument, U.K. Law in the 1980s* Dr E. K. Banakas (Ed.) (1988), pp. 205–229.
[51] Industrial Relations Act, ss.45 and 46.
[52] EPA 1975, s.12(1).
[53] EPA 1975, s.14(1).
[54] L. Dickens and G.S. Bain, *A Duty to Bargain? Union Recognition and Information Disclosure* from R. Lewis, *Labour Law in Britain* (Blackwell, Oxford, 1986), p. 102.
[55] A legally binding collective agreement has also been signed with the PTC (Public Service, Tax and Commerce Union), *see* IRLB 578, October 1997, p. 16.
[56] IRLB June 1997, p. 16.

compulsory trade union recognition procedure for certain collective bargaining purposes. As already mentioned, the Government has prepared a White Paper on *Fairness At Work* which includes proposals on compulsory trade union recognition where a majority of the relevant work force vote to be represented by a trade union. In such a situation it is proposed that there should be a legal obligation on employers to recognise a union for collective bargaining on the issues of pay, hours and holidays and training." Note the restricted agenda[57] there appears to be no intention to impose a broad compulsion to bargain.

A timely review of the practical obstacles on the legal road to statutory union recognition procedures was made by Wood[58] who looked at the role of ACAS between 1976 and 1980 and found that only 16,000 employees "were affected by collective bargaining" as a consequence of ACAS arbitration. He also pointed out that the lack of any legal compulsion on employers to co-operate with ACAS who were charged with carrying out surveys of employee attitudes towards union membership, was another fatal weakness in the procedure, and concluded that another agency should be given responsibility for resolving such disputes, providing that positive government support and legal sanctions are also applied. The level of union density which triggers recognition, the definition of the workplace constituency chosen for any recognition ballots, the level of representation, (*i.e.* individual and collective consultation and negotiation rights) afforded by the employer, together with the nature of the "enforcing agency" are just some of the crucial questions which are addressed by the Government in the White Paper.

Hendy and Walton in an implicit criticism[59] of what appeared to be the Government's intention to introduce a United States system of recognition based on majority unionism have mounted a robust attack on what they term is "The most contagious and virulent industrial relations disease of the late twentieth century . . . union exclusion, achieved in particular by employer imposition of 'individualised' contracts of employment in substitution of collective bargaining." The authors in reviewing the international authorities on the freedom of association apply themselves to the vexed question of the nature of the right to trade union representation. This is a question which has been addressed for some time by Ewing who considers that "Trade union recognition is one of the most important issues in the reconstruction of British labour law."[60] One of his concerns is how to discourage the judiciary from undermining the statutory provisions. Judges, it is argued, are wedded to the protection of individual rights deriving from contract, rather than to the promotion of collective rights deriving from agency.[61] These concerns are reiterated in a recent comparative study published by the Institute of Employment Rights: *Need To Be Heard At Work? Recognition Laws—Lessons From Abroad.*[62] (These concerns are examined briefly in para. 11.5.1 below.)

[57] D. Antill "Trade union and labour law" [1996] 146 N.L.J. 1165–1170.
[58] S. Wood, *Statutory union recognition IPD* Issues in People Management No. 17 IPD reviewed in: *IRS Employment Trends* 630, April 1997.
[59] J. Hendy, and M. Walton "An Individual Right to Union Representation in International Law" [1997] 26 I.L.J. 205–223.
[60] K.D. Ewing "Trade Union Recognition—A Framework for Discussion" [1970] 19 I.L.J. 226.
[61] *ibid*. pp. 226–227.
[62] B. Bercusson *et al. Need to Be Heard At Work? Recognition Laws—Lessons From Abroad*, Institute Of Employment Rights, London, February 1998.

11.4 EMPLOYEES AS TRADE UNION MEMBERS AND OFFICIALS

Employees who are members of a trade union, or who act in a voluntary capacity as officials, are, as has been seen, legally entitled to time off work[63] to undertake bona fide union activities such as representing members,[64] consulting with employers and to attend training for such activities. This does not cover participation in industrial action,[65] which usually constitutes a repudiatory breach of the individual employment contract,[66] although the union itself is protected from tortious liability if it has held a ballot of its members authorising that action.[67] There is only limited protection for the individual striker against victimisation by the employer for taking part in a strike[68] and trade union members as employees may lose their entitlement to redundancy pay if they take part in industrial action.[69] To participate in industrial action, even if it is only a partial withdrawal of labour, is therefore quite a precarious activity for the individual worker who wants to be sure of retaining his or her job. It has also been shown that refusing to agree to new terms of employment, offered by an employer in return for relinquishing union membership is also a precarious activity. In the 1980s and 1990s, as part of an attack on strong unionisation in some industries such as printing, journalism and in the pre-privatised dock yards, the employers sought to rid themselves of collectively negotiated contracts and union influence by "buying-out" trade union membership. Such victimisation of employees was prohibited by statute but, in the end, did not prevent such activity by employers.

11.4.1 Personal contracts and action short of dismissal

Statutory protection against victimisation of employees on the grounds of their trade union membership or activity was originally found in the EPCA 1978, s.23(1). These provisions in turn becoming section 146 of the TULRCA 1992.

Section 23(1) provided that: ". . . every employee shall have the right not to have action (short of dismissal) taken against him as an individual for the purpose of preventing or deterring him from being or seeking to become a member of an independent trade union, or penalising him for doing so."

This right was the central issue in two similar cases where employers were intent on reducing trade union power. In *Associated Newspapers v. Wilson*[70] the employers derecognised the union and terminated the collective agreement. Wilson was a journalist and NUJ member who refused to sign an individual contract of employment in exchange for an additional pay increase. He claimed that this was prohibited action against the employee as defined in section 23(1)(a). A similar offer was made by the employers in *Associated British Ports v. Palmer*[71] when manual employees who were

---

[63] TULRCA 1992, s.168.
[64] TULRCA 1992, s.170(1)(b).
[65] TULRCA 1992, s.170(2).
[66] In order to try and reflect the reality of most strike situations where both parties eventually enter fully into the contract of employment after the dispute is over, Lord Denning in *Morgan v. Fry* [1968] 2 Q.B. 710, famously tried to insert the concept of the suspended contract of employment into English law but the transplant did not take.
[67] TULRCA 1992, s.226.
[68] TULRCA 1992, s.238.
[69] ERA 1996, s.143.
[70] [1995] I.R.L.R. 258.
[71] *ibid.*

members of the National Union of Rail, Maritime and Transport Workers were offered substantial pay rises to relinquish their right to union representation. In this case, those who did not sign their rights away, were still employed on their original contracts and the employers still negotiated with their union—but their pay rise was much less than that of their colleagues who did relinquish union membership.

In both cases the original industrial tribunals found that the employers had breached section 23(1)(a). Upon appeal to the EAT the employers succeeded in reversing this decision in similar judgments which distinguished between the right, as an individual, to be a member of a trade union and actions taken by the employer to end collective bargaining. In both cases the EAT declared that the continuation of union membership had not been threatened.

The Court of Appeal considering the cases together allowed appeals in both cases, approving *Discount Tobacco and Confectionery Ltd v. Armitage*[72] which said that there was no real distinction between membership of a union and being able to make use of its essential services. By threatening the former you lose the latter. Upon appeal to the House of Lords a new point of law was considered. This was whether an omission to confer a benefit was the same as an "action short of dismissal". The Lords, in an extensive review of the statutory construction, and with some dissenting judgments, overruled authority from the Court of Appeal in *National Coal Board v. Ridgway*[73] and ruled that: "Withholding from an employee a benefit which is conferred upon another employee cannot amount to 'action', whatever the purpose of the omission."

In the light of the ruling by the House of Lords in *Associated Newspapers v. Wilson; Associated British Ports v. Palmer*,[74] that "action" against trade union members to discourage representation did not include "omissions", Deakin and Morris[75] consider that: ". . . the courts have gone well beyond what even the government thought desirable, or at least politically expedient, in this area." In coming to their judgment, the Law Lords overruled the Court of Appeal's decision in earlier cases including *National Coal Board v. Ridgway*[76] that an omission to offer a pay rise to one group of union members but not to a group from another union was unlawful. The Lords also decided that the EAT decision in *Discount Tobacco and Confectionery Ltd v. Armitage*[77] was a one-off and did not establish that a right to trade union membership equates with a right to representation.

The TURERA 1993, s.13 considerably weakened the statutory protections afforded to employees in such a situation. It reinforced the power of employers to discriminate against trade unionists. With the effective demise of the closed shop and the progressive loss of trade union membership and influence, it could be argued that the premise upon which these changes are founded, the power of a trade union to suppress individual interests for the sake of collective power, must have a weaker factual basis than was the case at the beginning of the eighties. Writing at the end of the 1980s free-market commentators like Hanson[78] claim that because of the success of these reforms the logical development of trade unions is as providers of professional legal services to individual members "to assist them in negotiating a favourable [employment] contract"[79] but not as agents of collective power.

---

[72] [1990] I.R.L.R. 15, EAT.
[73] [1987] I.R.L.R. 80, CA.
[74] [1995] 2 All E.R. 100.
[75] (1995), p. 643.
[76] [1987] I.C.R. 641; [1987] I.R.L.R. 80.
[77] [1990] I.R.L.R. 15.
[78] C.G. Hanson, *Taming the Trade Unions—A guide to the Thatcher Government's Employment Reforms, 1980–90* (Macmillan/Adam Smith Institute, 1991).
[79] *ibid.* p. 158.

11.5.   THE 1998 WHITE PAPER AND TRADE UNION RECOGNITION

11.5.1   Fairness at Work

The appearance of a strongly argued study in the Spring of 1998, entitled *Need To be Heard At Work?*[80] shortly before the much anticipated White Paper *Fairness At Work* could be seen as part of the public debate on the role of trade unions which was triggered by the 1997 election. A debate which was getting increasingly heated: "We are talking about a clear manifesto commitment [to recognition]. If they break it, it will be war . . ."[81-85] In an attempt to learn from mistakes in our past legislation and in the hope of learning lessons from other countries, the co-authors of *Need To Be Heard At Work* compared the North American experience of recognition procedures with collective bargaining law in Europe.

This comparative study of Italy, Germany and Sweden emphasises the main structural difficulties between the European and North American models of bargaining. The study concludes that the high rates of collective bargaining structures seen in these countries "are not the direct result of legal intervention" but is more to do with individual rights to workplace representation and strong traditions of co-determination at sectoral and workplace levels.

The concept of majority unionism is central to the American system of union recognition which is based on the National Labour Relations Act of 1935. In outline: this system is based on a duty by employers and trade unions to bargain in good faith with an intention to reach an agreement once a majority vote for the union in a representation election ballot. Bargaining must then take place on a number of *mandatory* subjects such as term and conditions. Bargaining is also allowed regarding *permissive* subjects (*e.g.* scope of the bargaining unit) and "is forbidden in relation to *illegal* subjects" such as discriminatory terms.[86]

The problems arising from this system are identified as:

- delay by employers in operating the system;

- victimisation and dismissal of union members;

- the use of the constitutional guarantees of free expression by employers to intimidate workers;

- the lack of a statutory right for trade unions to enter employers' premises without agreement; and

- the lack of an effective enforcement remedy.

The lessons to be learnt from the American experience, appear to include the need to:

- Develop a framework of clear principles[87] for the definition of a bargaining unit based for example on common interests, bargaining history, the employer's structure, viability, cohesion and agreement.

[80] B. Bercusson *et al. Need to Be Heard At Work? Recognition Laws—Lessons From Abroad*, Institute of Employment Rights, London, February 1998.
[81-85] Roger Lyons, MSF General Secretary, *The Observer*, December 14, 1997.
[86] para. 6.6.
[87] para. 7.3.

- The issuing of a code of practice to give clear guidance to the Courts on complicated issues such as the definition of a bargaining unit. The authors refer to the model contained in the now repealed U.K. *Industrial Relations Code of Practice* (1972)[88] and by implication suggest that a similar such model will need to be reintroduced.

This publication strongly criticises the American Model for its "all or nothing" effect which is based on giving bargaining rights to one union following a ballot. The ability of employers to delay or evade the duty of good faith bargaining is also much criticised.

11.5.2   The CBI/TUC debate

A public and private debate between the Confederation of British Industries (CBI) representing employers and the Trades Union Congress (TUC) about trade union recognition lasted for over a year after the General Election of 1997. On December 9, 1997 the parties met the President of the Board of Trade to discuss a joint statement.[89] This statement did contain some areas of agreement with both sides wanting voluntary recognition where ever possible: "In 1996, ACAS dealt with 112 disputes over union recognition or de-recognition and in 57% of those cases some form of recognition was agreed. Given the existence of a statutory fall-back, it is likely that the success of voluntary conciliation will improve." But there were strong differences between the two sides. The CBI wanted a 30 per cent threshold of union membership before a ballot could be held to determine the issue finally, whereas the TUC wanted one ballot of members to take place. A crucial sticking point on the balloting process was that the CBI wanted a majority of the total workforce supporting recognition in a ballot, whereas the TUC wanted a majority of those individuals voting to determine the issue, as it does in parliamentary and local elections. The CBI also wanted firms with less than 50 employees to be exempt from the provisions and for the employers to decide on the make-up of the balloting constituency. The TUC considered that the latter issue, if in dispute, should be referred to an outside agency. At a meeting of its general council in April 1998, the TUC appeared to make some concessions to influence an apparently hostile Government, by accepting a minimum threshold of 30 per cent yes vote of those eligible in a workplace ballot and also by accepting that firms employing less than 10 people may be exempt.[90]

---

[88] U.K. Industrial Relations Code of Practice 1972
"Bargaining units . . .

78. Factors which should be taken into account in defining a bargaining unit include:
    (i) the nature of the work;
    (ii) the training, experience and professional or other qualifications of the employees concerned;
    (iii) the extent to which they have interests in common;
    (iv) the general wishes of the employees concerned;
    (v) the organisation and location of the work;
    (vi) hours, working arrangements and payment systems;
    (vii) the matters to be bargained about;
    (viii) the need to fit the bargaining unit into the pattern of union and management organisation;
    (ix) the need to avoid disruption of any existing bargaining arrangements which are working well;
    (x) whether separate bargaining arrangements are needed for particular categories of employees, such as supervisors or employees which represent management in negotiation."
[89] CBI/TUC, *Statutory Trade Union Recognition Joint Statement by TUC And CBI*, 1997.
[90] *The Guardian*, April 21, 1998.

When the Director General of the CBI was interviewed[91] his main concern appeared to be that the membership threshold to trigger a ballot for representation should be based on achieving a majority of the relevant workforce rather than on a majority of those voting. The TUC were opposed to this:

> "Of course we want union recognition to be resolved voluntarily wherever possible. We have no wish to erect obstacles for companies who practice partnership. But a new law has to deal with the worst and most exploitative employers and must implement the basic human right to be represented by a union where employees want it. The CBI are advocating so many barriers, exemptions and opt-outs that their version of the law would fail to meet these basic tests."[92]

11.5.3   1998 White Paper *Fairness at Work*[93]

The White Paper long awaited by the trade unions appeared a year after the 1997 General Election and its main surprise was not so much in the proposed solution to the well rehearsed arguments about the legal mechanism for the reintroduction of trade union recognition, but rather in the extended employment rights proposed for individual workers. Some of these proposals are dealt with elsewhere in this text, but in summary, they involve: reducing the qualifying period for protection against unfair dismissal to one year[94]; abolishing the maximum limit on awards for unfair dismissal,[95] and index-linking limits in statutory awards and payments.[96] The Government were also inviting views on: the use of the waiver clause in fixed-term contracts[97]; the abuse of zero hours contracts by employers[98]; and on whether employee protection measures should be extended to all those who work for another person.[99] The individualist so called "Third Way" thrust of the proposed legislation is indicated in a foreword by the Prime Minister:

> "The White Paper steers a way between the absence of minimum standards of protection at the workplace, and a return to the laws of the past. It is based on the rights of the individual, whether exercised on their own or with others, as a matter of their choice. It matches rights and responsibilities. It seeks to draw a line under the issue of industrial relations law."

Despite retaining most of the Conservative legislation which strictly regulates union activities, particularly industrial action, the changes proposed by the White Paper were described by *The Times* as "the biggest overhaul of employment law for more than a decade."[1] This view probably reflected a corporate sigh of relief by the business community that these provisions were "not as bad for the functioning of free

---

[91] *BBC Today Programme*, February 5, 1998, at 07.52 a.m. Newsroom Note: NN.9.98.
[92] John Monks, TUC General Secretary, February 5, 1998, 20:00 hrs.
[93] Cm. 3968, *Fairness At Work*, DTI, May 21, 1998.
[94] para. 3.10.
[95] para. 3.5.
[96] para. 3.8.
[97] para. 3.13.
[98] para. 3.16.
[99] para. 3.18.
[1] *The Times*, May 22, 1998.

enterprise as they could have been."[2] Given this endorsement, it was perhaps surprising to find that there were some long advocated changes in the document which may have given some comfort to some trade unionists. These are considered briefly.

11.5.3.1.   *Trade union recognition*

Acknowledging both the decline in trade union influence[3] and the fact that out of the 50 largest United Kingdom companies, 44 recognise trade unions,[4] the White Paper signalled that the closed shop remained dead and buried[5] before passing on to outline the justification for the reintroduction of a trade union recognition procedure. It emphasised that where ever possible it preferred such a process to be entirely voluntary and without any state intervention.[6] Where this was not possible, it was proposed that a procedure be introduced only after substantial support is demonstrated.[7] The essential features[8] of this process will be:

1. A legal procedure with time limits.
2. CAC rulings on issues which cannot be voluntarily agreed, such as:

   - "Whether a trade union has reasonable support" for recognition amongst the employees.
   - What is the appropriate bargaining unit? The White Paper stresses that "Employers must and will be free to organise their business in the way they choose."
   - Whether a sufficient majority of employees support recognition. In any event, a ballot must result in a majority of those voting and 40 per cent of the total eligble workforce voting in favour.
   - The procedure for negotiations between the employer and the trade union. Statutory recognition will cover negotiations over pay, hours and holidays, but the White Paper invited views over whether this should cover training.

3. There will be a similar system for de-recognition although the Government was inviting views on exactly how this should work. It proposed that once determined, new applications for recognition or de-recognition should not be considered for three years after that application.

4. Employers with less than 20 employees will be exempt.

5. Where there is already 50 per cent of the employees in membership, recognition will be automatic without a ballot.

6. Trade unions will be expected to sort out competing claims between themselves.

An Annex to the White Paper added more detail on the proposals. The employer will only have 14 days in which to respond to a written request for recognition from a trade

---

[2] *The Times*—editorial, May 22, 1998.
[3] para. 4.6.
[4] para. 4.7.
[5] para. 4.8.
[6] para. 4.10.
[7] para. 4.16.
[8] para. 4.18.

union.[9] If he agrees to this request the formal procedure is closed. If the employer only objects to an aspect of the recognition application such as the definition of the bargaining unit, and is willing to negotiate with the union, they will have at least 28 days to sought this out, with ACAS assistance if necessary and thereafter "for as long as both sides are willing".[10] The formal process proposed, comes into action if the employer rejects the application, refuses to negotiate, or does not respond within 14 days. In such a situation the trade union may make an immediate application to the CAC to determine whether the bargaining unit is appropriate and whether the workforce in it "has the support of a majority of the employees".[11]

The job of CAC appears to be to try and secure agreement on these issues and in particular on the appropriateness of the criteria,[12] some of which corresponded to those identified in the now defunct 1972 Industrial Relations Code of Practice. (See para. 11.5.1 above.) If it does not secure any such agreement it may determine the appropriate bargaining unit itself.[13] The CAC will also be given powers to order a secret ballot be carried out within 21 days of its determination of the appropriate bargaining unit and the employer will be required to "grant the union reasonable access to the employees to be balloted".[14] Employers will be obliged to give the names of employees to the balloting body and to the trade unions and not to victimise employees who take part in a recognition campaign. Where a ballot is successful the employer and the union will be obliged to agree a procedure agreement which sets out how they are going to conduct collective bargaining.[15] If they cannot agree the CAC will be empowered to impose a legally binding collective agreement, which if broken can be enforced in a court by an order for specific performance.[16] An ACAS code of practice will be introduced to advise employers and trade unions on all aspects of this procedure.[17]

These proposals if read alongside the Institute of Employment Rights critique of the USA recognition system discussed above, would seem to address some of the failures of that system. It permits more than one union to obtain recognition status, includes safeguards against victimisation of employees, requires that an employer responds within a short time limit, and theoretically has the ultimate enforcement remedy of specific performance of a collective agreement. In practice however, trade unions will have two thresholds to overcome: the requirement of 40 per cent support in an appropriate bargaining unit, the nature of which is, in the event of disagreement to be determined by the CAC, before even a ballot can be lawfully considered and then the ballot itself. The wording of the White Paper that in determining bargaining units: "Employers must and will be free to organise their business in the way they choose", may encourage some employers to play the long game and not oppose recognition outright, but to "negotiate" for as long as possible on the criteria for the "appropriate bargaining unit". Lastly, the Government did not propose any changes to the law on the incorporation of terms from a collective agreement. With the well known difficulties associated with this process, it is perhaps difficult to see how the CAC, if it

[9] Annex 1(ii).
[10] Annex 1(ii).
[11] Annex 1(iii).
[12] Annex 1(v).
[13] Annex 1(v).
[14] Annex 1(vi).
[15] Annex 1(viii).
[16] Annex 1(ix).
[17] Annex 1(vi).

is only able to impose a collective bargaining *procedure* on the parties, can also impose specific contractual terms unless it has powers similar to those which it formerly had under the Equal Pay Act 1970,[18] to unilaterally insert amendments into collective agreements which were then incorporated into individual contracts of employment.

Individual representation rights

The White Paper proposed to create "a legal right for employees to be accompanied by a fellow employee or trade union representative of their choice during grievance and disciplinary procedures".[19] This strengthens the existing provisions which have for 20 years, only been promulgated in the form of guidance contained in the ACAS *Code of Practice on Disciplinary Practice and Procedures in Employment.*[20]

Collective representation rights

The provisions for consultation with worker's representatives at company level in large multinational companies which are contained in the European Works Council Directive, are to be implemented into United Kingdom domestic law by December 1999[21]; but this principle is not to be applied to companies purely active only in the United Kingdom.[22]

Industrial action changes

The White Paper proposes extending limited protection to some employees taking industrial action. Workers taking official industrial action, that is action supported by a lawful ballot,[23] will have the right to complain of unfair dismissal to an industrial tribunal.[24] But as the White Paper itself admits "the tribunal would not get involved in looking at the merits of the dispute; its role would be to decide whether the employer had acted fairly and reasonably taking into account all the circumstances of the case". The ability of employers to convince industrial tribunals that they have acted fairly, is, as this text has tried to show, somewhat enhanced by the SOSR defence[25] available to employers, and the general requirements of tribunals to take into consideration the administrative resources and size of a business when determining such questions.[26] The new proposed right of complaint may therefore not be of much value for some workers who have been dismissed for taking part in lawful industrial action. Certainly this provision does not radically alter the law to comply with ILO standards or, as in other European countries to give workers a right to strike without being in breach of their contract of employment, let alone a right to be protected from dismissal or to be reinstated at the end of a dispute.[27]

Other perhaps less controversial proposals contained in the White Paper, included the Government's intention to streamline the lengthy and complex *Code of Practice on Industrial Action,*[28] to remove the obligation on trade unions to supply the names of

---

[18] EqPA 1970, s.3 as amended by the EPA 1975.
[19] para. 4.29.
[20] ACAS Code of Practice No. 1, originally enacted by EPA 1975.
[21] para. 4.4.
[22] para. 4.5.
[23] TULRCA 1992, s.226.
[24] para. 4.22.
[25] ERA 1996, s.98(1)(b).
[26] ERA 1996, s.98(4).
[27] K.D. Ewing, *Working Life A New Perspective on Labour Law,* Institute of Employment Rights/Lawrence & Wishart, London, 1996.
[28] para. 4.26.

their members[29] who may be taking industrial action.[30] and to abolish and transfer the duties of the CROTUM and the CPAUIA to the Certification Officer.[31]

11.5.3.2 *Protection against victimisation on grounds of union membership and activities*

Here the White Paper has arguably sought to undo the mischief wrought by the TURERA 1993, s.13 which much weakened the protection afforded trade union members who are subject to pressure from employers to relinquish their trade union membership. The Labour Government obviously agreed with the view of Lord Brownc-Wilkinson that the existing law "leaves an undesirable lacuna in the legislation protecting employees against victimisation".[32] and proposed to restore the pre-1993 position so that employees can complain to an industrial tribunal that an employer is taking action short of dismissal against them on the grounds of their trade union membership or activities.[33]

---

[29] *Blackpool and the Fylde College v. NATFHE* [1994] I.R.L.R. 227, CA.
[30] para. 4.27.
[31] para.4.31. The CROTUM (Commissioner for the rights of trade union members) and the CPAUIA (Commissioner for protection against unlawful industrial action) apart from being inelegant acronyms were statutory offices ostensibly set up by previous Conservative administrations to preserve the individual rights of trade union members, but really to undermine the taking of collective action. They never did attract much "business" from disgruntled trade unionists.
[32] *Associated Newspapers Ltd v. Wilson; Associated British Ports v. Palmer and Others* [1995] I.R.L.R. 258, HL.
[33] para. 4.25.

APPENDIX 1

1998

IDS *Brief*

Employment Law Fact Card

Compensation and time limits for key employment rights 1998–9

IDS Employment Law Service

IDS produces a number of publications which, together, provide the most comprehensive service on employment law published in the UK. The Card is merely a summary of information on compensation and time limits—the full details are to be found in the various components of the IDS Employment Law Service.

- **IDS Brief** is a twice-monthly journal which reports on all the latest case law and other developments in the field of UK and EU employment law. The Brief also considers particular subjects in depth, ranging from indirect discrimination to industrial disputes.

- **Employment Law Handbooks and Supplements** provide Brief subscribers with an unmatched library on employment law. The series of Handbooks covers all the bread-and-butter areas of law from Redundancy to Equal Pay, while Supplements analyse specific subjects from Retirement to Disability.

- **IDS Employment Law Cases** is an eleven-volume set of annotated case reports for the employment law specialist. Regularly updated, they provide key information and comment on each case, arranged in a clear and easy-to-use structure.

- **Employment Law-Link** is a CD ROM service providing all the employment law information you will ever need. Case reports, commentary and all relevant UK legislation and EU Directives are included in this exciting new product.

For full details of the IDS Employment Law Service contact the IDS Subscriptions hotline on:

Telephone – 0171 324 2599

Incomes Data Services Ltd
77 Bastwick Street, London EC1V 3TT
Tel: 0171 250 3434 Fax: 0171 608 0949
E-mail: ids@incomesdata.co.uk www.incomesdata.co.uk

Compensation limits

Employment right	Maximum award
Unfair dismissal	
Basic award	£6,600
Compensatory award	£12,000
Additional award	£2,860–£5,720 i.e. 13–26 weeks' pay
	£5,720–£11,440 i.e. 26–52 weeks' pay
Additional award for sex, race or disability discrimination dismissals	
Redundancy Pay	£6,600
Discrimination	
Race, Sex and Disability	No limit
Dismissal for union/health and safety/employee representative or pension trustee reasons	
Basic award	£6,600 (minimum £2,900)
Compensatory award	£12,000
Special award depends on whether reinstatement/re-engagement:	
• sought, but no order made	£29,000 (minimum £14,500)
• order made and complied with	No maximum—all losses from dismissal to re-employment
• order made, but not complied with	156 weeks' pay—(minimum £21,800)
• not sought	no special award
Guarantee pay	£76.75 (5 days in any period of 3 months) (£15.35 a day)
Contract claims in a tribunal	£25,000

Limit on week's pay = £220 (where applicable)

IDS

Statutory right/ complaint	Qualifying period	Time limit for IT complaint
Dismissal		
Written reasons for dismissal (a)	2 years	3 months starting with EDT*
Unfair dismissal	2 years (b)	3 months starting with EDT*
UD for trade union reason	None	3 months starting with EDT*
UD for pregnancy reason	None	3 months starting with EDT*
UD for asserting a statutory right, for health and safety reasons or for refusing to work on a Sunday	None	3 months starting with EDT*
UD for performing functions as a pension trustee or employee representative	None	3 months starting with EDT*
Redundancy/Business transfers		
Redundancy payment	2 years (c)	6 months starting with relevant date** (d)
Consultation with trade union or employee representatives over redundancies or transfer of undertaking	N/A	Either before dismissal or 3 months from the date the dismissal takes effect (redundancies) or 3 months from the date transfer completed (transfers)*
Discrimination		
Sex, race and disability discrimination	None	3 months from date of act complained of** (f)
Equal pay	None	6 months from date employment ceases (g)
Maternity		
Right to return to work up to 29 weeks after week in which childbirth occurs	2 years (e)	3 months from notified day of return when employer refuses right*
Right to 14 week's maternity leave	None	
Unions and other representatives		
Time off for union duties, for safety reps, employee reps or pension trustees	None	3 months from date of failure to give time off or to pay remuneration*
Time off for union activities	None	3 months from failure to give time off*
Interim relief pending complaint of unfair dismissal	None	7 days immediately following EDT***
Action short of dismissal	None	3 months from date of last action complained of*
Unjustifiable discipline by union	None	3 months from date of union's decision****
Refusal of employment on grounds related to union membership	N/A	3 months from date of conduct complained of*
Miscellaneous		
Guarantee pay	1 month (h)	3 months from day for which payment claimed*
Itemised pay statement	None	3 months from date employment ceased*
Written particulars of employment	1 month	3 months from date employment ceased*
Unlawful deduction from wages	None	3 months from date of (last) deduction*
Contract claim by employee	None	3 months from date of EDT*
Contract claim by employer	None	6 weeks* (i)

Notes.

(a) No qualifying period in relation to a woman dismissed during pregnancy or maternity leave.

(b) This qualifying period is presently subject to a legal challenge before the House of Lords.

(c) Starting with 18th birthday if employee started work before that date.

(d) Extended to one year if employee dies during 6 months following relevant date.

(e) At the beginning of the 11th week before the expected week of childbirth.

(f) However, an act may be treated as done at the end of a period if it is an act 'extending over' that period (S.76(6)(b) SD Act/S.68(7)(b) RR Act/Sch 3 para 3(3)(b) DD Act).

(g) According to EAT in Preston & ors v (1) Wolverhampton Healthcare NHS Trust (2) Secretary of State for Health & ors; Fletcher & ors v Midland Bank plc. 1996 IRLR 484.

(h) Unless the claimant was employed under a fixed-term contract for 3 months or less or a contract for the performance of a specific task which was not expected to last more than 3 months and he or she was not continuously employed for more than 3 months.

(i) From receipt of details of employee's contractual claim.

* IT can extend time limit where it was 'not reasonably practicable' to present the complaint in time.

** IT can extend the time limit where they consider it 'just and equitable' to do so.

*** No extension of time allowed, except possibly where there has been deliberate fraud by the employer, causing the employee to suffer real injustice in missing the time limit.

**** IT can extend time limit on 'not reasonably practicable' grounds, as above, or where delay was caused by reasonable attempts to pursue an internal appeal, etc.

BIBLIOGRAPHY

ACAS, *Discipline at Work The ACAS advisory handbook* (1987).

ACAS (1988) *Redundancy Handling,* Advisory Booklet No. 12.

ACAS (1995) *Redundancy Handling,* Advisory Booklet No. 10.

Steven Anderman, *Unfair Dismissals and Redundancy,* in Roy Lewis, *Labour Law in Britain* (Blackwell, Oxford, 1986).

Stephen Bailey, David Harris and Brian Jones, *Civil Liberties Cases and Materials* (4th ed., London, Butterworths, 1995).

Catherine Barnard, *EC Employment Law* (Rcv. ed. Wiley, Chichester, 1996).

Brenda Barrett and Richard Howells, *Cases & Materials on Occupational Health and Safety Law* (London: Cavendish Publishing Ltd, 1995).

Brian Bercusson, *et al., Need to Be Heard At Work? Recognition Laws—Lessons From Abroad*, Institute Of Employment Rights, February 1998.

Brian Bercusson, *The Employment Protection Act 1975* (Sweet & Maxwell, London, 1976).

Patrick Birkinshaw (1966) *Freedom of information, the law, the practice and the ideal,* Law in Context Series (2nd ed., London, Butterworths, 1966).

Colin Bourn, *Job Security* (Sweet & Maxwell, London 1980).

Colin Bourn and John Whitmore, *Anti-Discrimination Law in Britain* (3rd ed., London, Sweet & Maxwell, 1996).

John Bowers and Simon Honeyball, *Textbook on Labour Law* (4th ed., Blackstone Press, London, 1996).

Anthony W. Bradley and Keith D. Ewing, *Constitutional and Administrative Law* (Harlow, Essex: Addison, Wesley & Longman, 1997).

Douglas Brodie, "The heart of the matter: mutual trust and confidence" (1996) 25 *Industrial Law Journal* No. 2.

Douglas Brodie, "Specific Performance And Employment Contracts" (1998) 27 *Industrial Law Journal* No. 1, p. 37.

W.A. Brown (1972) "A consideration of 'custom & practice'", 10 *British Journal of Industrial Relations* No. 1, pp. 42–61.

Hazel Carty, (1989) "Dismissed Employees: The Search For A More Effective Range Of Remedies" (1989) 52 *The Modern Law Review* No. 4, pp. 449–498.

Stephen Cavalier, *Transfer Rights: TUPE in Perspective* (Institute of Employment Rights, London, 1997).

Andrew Charlesworth and Holley Cullen, *European Community Law* (London, Pitman Publishing 1940).

Paul Craig and Gráinne De Burca, *EC Law Text, Cases & Materials* (Oxford: Oxford University Press, 1997).

Paul Davies and Mark Freedland, *Labour Law Text and Materials* (2nd ed., London: Butterworths, 1984).

Paul Davies and Mark Freedland, *Labour Legislation and Public Policy* (Clarendon/ OUP, Oxford, 1993).

Paul Davies, "Taken to the Cleaners? Contracting Out of Services Yet Again" (1997) 26 *Industrial Law Journal* No. 2, p. 193.

Simon Deakin, and Gillian S. Morris, *Labour Law* (Butterworths, 1995).

Linda Dickens, *et al., Dismissed, A study of unfair dismissal and the industrial tribunal system* (Oxford, Blackwell, 1985).

Linda Dickens and G.S. Bain, *A Duty to Bargain? Union Recognition and Information Disclosure from R. Lewis, Labour Law in Britain* (Blackwell, Oxford, 1986, p. 102).

Donovan Report, *Royal Commission on Trade Unions and Employers" Associations* 1965–1968, Report, Cmnd 3623 (1968) London, HMSO.

Brian J. Doyle, *Disability Discrimination Law & Practice* (Bristol, Jordans 1996).

DTI (1995) *Revised arrangements for consultation about redundancies and business transfers*, October 1995.

DTI (1997) *Redundancy Consultation and Notification*, PL 833 (Rev 4), URN 97/512.

DTI (1997) *Redundancy Payments* PL 808 (REV 4); *Offsetting Pensions Against Redundancy Payments* RPL.

DTI. Employment Rights Directorate (1997) *European Acquired Rights Directive And Transfer Of Undertakings(Protection Of Employment) Regulations 1981* (The TUPE Regulations), *Public Consultation*, December 1997, URN 98/513.

DTI. *Employment Rights On The Transfer Of An Undertaking* PL 699 (Rev 3) August 1997.

DTI. *Time Off For Job Hunting Or To Arrange Training When Facing Redundancy.* PL 703 (REV 3).

DTI Employee Relations Directorate (February 1998), *Employees' Information And Consultation Rights On Transfers Of Undertakings And Collective Redundancies, Public Consultation*, URN 97/988.

European Commission (1997) *Memorandum From The Commission On Acquired Rights Of Workers In Case Of Transfers Of Undertakings*, Brussels, 04.03.1997. COM(97)85 final.

European Commission (1997) *Amended Proposal For A Council Directive Amending Directive 77/187/EEC On The Approximation Of The Laws Of The Member States Relating To The Safeguarding Of Employees' Rights In The Event Of Transfers Of Undertakings, Businesses Or Parts Of Businesses*, Brussels, 24.02.1997 COM(97)60 final.

Keith Ewing, "Trade Union Recognition—A Framework for Discussion" (1990) 19 *Industrial Law Journal* No. 4, p. 226.

Keith Ewing, *The Employment Act 1990 A European Perspective*, (Institute of Employment Rights 1991), p. 8.

Keith Ewing, "Remedies For Breach Of The Contract Of Employment" (1993) 52 *Cambridge Law Journal* No. 3, p. 405.

Keith Ewing, *Working Life A New Perspective on Labour Law* (Institute of Employment Rights/Lawrence & Wishart, London, 1996).

Keith Ewing, and Aileen McColgan (1995) *Law at Work*, (2nd ed., Unison Open College, London 1995).

Alan Felstead, Nick Jewson with John Goodwin (1996) *Homeworkers in Britain*, Research Studies, DfEE and dit, RS1P.

T.C. Hartley, *The Foundations of European Community Law* (3rd ed., Oxford: Harvey on Industrial Relations, London: Butterworths, 1994).

John Hendy and Michael Walton, "An Individual Right to Union Representation in International Law" (1997) 26 *Industrial Law Journal* No. 3, pp. 205–223.

John Hendy, *A Law Unto Themselves. Conservative Employment Laws: A National And International Assessment* (Institute Of Employment Rights, London, 3rd ed., 1993).

Bob Hepple, David Howarth, M.H. Matthews, *Tort: Cases and Materials* (London: Butterworths, 1998).

Bob Hepple, *et al., Improving equality law: the options*, Justice and the Runnymede Trust, March 1997.

Bob Hepple, *Employment Law* (London: Sweet & Maxwell 1981).

Bob Hepple, *The fall and rise of unfair dismissal in McCarthy, Industrial Intervention in Industrial Relations* (Oxford: Blackwell 1992), pp. 79–102.

Tamara Hervey and Phillip Rostant, "After Francovich; State liability and British employment law" (1996) 25 *Industrial Law Journal* No. 4, pp. 259–285.

Simon Honeyball, "Employment Law and the primacy of Contract" (1989) 18 *Industrial Law Journal* No. 2, pp. 97–108.

Ian Hunter, "Importing talent while staying within the law" (1997) *People Management* (August 28), p. 49.

Richard Hyman, "The Historical Evolution of British Industrial Relations" in P. Edwards (ed.) *Industrial Relations Theory and Practice in Britain* (Oxford: Blackwell Business, 1995).

IDS Employment Law Handbook, Series 2, No. 13, *Continuity of Employment*, August 1997.

IDS Employment Law Handbook, Series 2, No. 14, *Compensation and Remedies*.

IDS Employment Law Handbook, Series 2, No. 2, *Sex Discrimination* Journal Vol. 21, No. 1. March 1992, p. 1.

Otto Kahn-Freund, "Legal Framework" in Flanders, A. and Clegg, H.A. (eds) *The System of Industrial Relations in Great Britain* (Oxford, Blackwell, 1954).

Otto Kahn-Freund, *Labour and the Law, Hamlyn Lecture* (Sweet & Maxwell 1972).

Richard Kidner, *Blackstone's Statutes on Employment Law* (7th ed., Blackstone Press, London, 1997–8).

David Lewis, "Whistleblowers And Job Security" (1995) 58 *The Modern Law Review*, No. 2, pp. 209–221.

R. Lewis and J. Clark, *Employment rights, industrial tribunals and arbitration: the case for alternative dispute resolution* (London 1993) Institute of Employment Rights.

Warwick Lightfoot, *Unfinished business: the economic case for a more liberal labour market*, London: Politeia, Policy Series No. 1, London, 1996.

William McCarthy, *Legal Intervention in Industrial Relations: Gains and Losses* (Blackwell Business, Oxford 1992).

John McMullen, "Contracting Out and Marketing Testing—The Uncertainty Ends?" (1994) 23 *Industrial Law Journal* No. 3, p. 230.

Jeremy McMullen and Jennifer Eady, *Labour Law Review 1997* (Institute of Employment Rights, London 1997).

Jim Mortimer, *In Defence of Trade Unionism* (Institute of Employment Rights, 1998).

Brian Napier, *Computerization and Employment Rights*, Industrial Law (1992).

Alan Neal, "The Collective Agreement as a Public Law Instrument" in Dr E.K. Banakas (ed.) *UK Law in the 1980s* (Butterworths/Sweet and Maxwell), p. 205.

R. Norton Taylor, *Blacklist: the Inside Story of Political Vetting* and generally R.W. Painter, A. Holmes, S. Migdal, *Cases & materials on Employment law* (London, Blackstone Press Ltd, 1960).

Gwyneth Pitt, "Dismissal At Common Law: The Relevance In Britain Of American Developments" (1989) 52 *The Modern Law Review* 23.

M. Potter and E. Regan, "The Legal Limits Of Affirmative Action In Redundancy Selection" (1997) *New Law Journal*, May 16, 1997.

Elizabeth Rossiter, *Reregulating Sunday Trading: a study of the Sunday Trading Act 1994, Employment Protection and the Trade Union Response*, M.A. Dissertation. In Law and Employment Relations, International Centre for Management Law and Industrial Relations, University of Leicester, 1996.

Michael Rubenstein and Yvonne Frost, *Unfair Dismissal A Guide To Relevant Case Law* (15th ed., Industrial Relations Services 1997).

Stephen Sedley, "Public Law And Contractual Employment" (1994) 23 *Industrial Law Journal* No. 3, p. 20.

Norman Selwyn, *Law of Employment* (9th ed., Butterworths, London, 1996).

Ian Smith, and Gareth Thomas, *Smith & Wood's Industrial Law* (6th ed., Butterworths, London, 1996).

Steve Uglow and Venous Telford, *The Police Act 1997* (Bristol: Jordans, 1997).

Robert Upex, *The Law of Termination of Employment* (4th ed., Sweet & Maxwell, London 1994).

L. Vickers, "Whistleblowing in the public sector and the ECHR", *Public Law*, Winter, pp. 594–602.

Peter Wallington (Editor), *Butterworths Law Employment Handbook* (7th ed., Butterworths, London, 1996). (The 4th (1987), 5th (1990) and 6th (1993) editions have also been used in the preparation of the text.)

Stephen Weatherill, *Cases & Materials on EC Law* (Blackstone Press, London 1994).

Lord Wedderburn, *The Worker and The Law* (3rd ed. Rev., Penguin Books 1986).

Brian Weeks, *et al., Industrial Relations and the Limits of Law* (1975), pp. 156–161.

Robert Wintemute, *Time for a single anti-discrimination act (and commission)*? (1997) 26 *Industrial Law Journal.*

INDEX

ACAS,
codes of practice, 2.6.2
Access to Health Records Act 1990, 1.9.2
Access to Medical Reports Act 1988, 1.9.1
Acquired Rights Directive, 9.1.1
Action short of dismissal, 11.4.1
Advertisement,
discrimination, and, 1.15
Agency workers, 1.14.5
Ante-natal care,
time off work for, 10.2
Apprenticeship, contract of, 1.14.6
Article 119, E.C. Treaty, 6.1.1
Asylum and Immigration Act 1996, 1.7
race discrimination, and, 1.7

Bumping,
redundancy, and, 8.3.1.3

Case law, 2.1
Casual workers, 1.14.4
mutuality, 1.14.4
Central Arbitration Committee, 11.5.3
Childbirth, 10.1–10.8. *See also* Pregnancy
health and safety, 10.6
reform proposals, 10.8
unfair dismissal, and, 7.4.3
Children, 1.5
Closed shop, 1.10
Codes of practice, 2.6.2
ACAS, 2.6.2
Commission for Racial Equality, 2.6.2
criminal conviction certificates, 2.6.2
disability discrimination, 2.6.2
discrimination, 6.1.4
failure to observe, 2.6.2
Health and Safety Commission, 2.6.2
issue of, 2.6.2
status, 2.5.2, 2.6, 2.6.2
Collective agreements,
equal pay, 6.2.7

Collective agreements—*cont.*
legal status, 11.3.1
transfer of undertakings, and, 9.6
Collective bargaining,
development in United Kingdom, 11.2
legal framework for, 11.3
Collective bargaining agreements, 2.4
contractual intent, 2.4
contractual terms, 2.4
discontinuance, 2.4.3
enforceability, 2.4
implied incorporation, 2.4.2
burden of proof, 2.4.2
custom, 2.4.2
implied terms, 2.4
implying term into, 2.4.3
incorporation, 2.4.1
agency, 2.4.1
express, 2.4.1
implied, 2.4.1, 2.4.2
meaning, 2.4
normative terms, 2.4
objective test, 2.4
problems of incorporation, 2.4.3
purpose, 2.4
status, 2.4
subjective test, 2.4
termination, 2.4.3
Tinalea clause, 2.4
transfer of undertaking, and, 2.4.3
withdrawal of employer from association,
2.4.3
Collective issues, 11.1–11.5.3.2
Donovan Report, 11.2.1
individual employment relationship, and,
11.1–11.5.3.2
Collective labour law,
individual employment relationship, and,
11.1
Commission for Racial Equality, 6.4.1
codes of practice, 2.6.2

Compromise agreements, 7.2.6
Confidential information, 3.1.3
  content of duty, 3.1.3
  disclosure in public interest, 3.1.3.4
    press, to, 3.1.3.4
    whistleblowing, 3.1.3.4
  duty not to disclose, 3.1.3
  knowledge of confidentiality, 3.1.3.1
  matters included, 3.1.3
  mutuality of duty, 3.1.3
  notice of, 3.1.3.1
  price information, 3.1.3
  protection post-employment of information
      falling short of trade secret, 3.1.3.3
    solicitors, 3.1.3.3
  publication, 3.1.3.1
  sales information, 3.1.3
  springboard doctrine, 3.1.3.2
    duration, 3.1.3.2
    equity, 3.1.3.2
    unfair advantage, 3.1.3.2
  stages of employment relationship, 3.1.3
  "stock of knowledge", and, 3.1.3
  trade secrets, 3.1.3.1
Constructive dismissal, 3.2.1, 5.3.3, 7.2.1.5
  compensation, and, 5.3.3
  examples of breaches, 5.3.3
  meaning, 5.3.3
  repudiatory breach, 7.2.1.5
Consultation,
  redundancy, and. See Redundancy
Continuity of employment,
  unfair dismissal, and. See Unfair dismissal
Contract of employment, 1.1–1.16
  agency workers, 1.14.5
  apprenticeship, 1.14.6
  capacity, 1.4
  casual workers, 1.14.4
  common law tests, 1.16
  conditional offer, 1.2
  consideration, 1.3
  Crown, 1.4
  fixed term contracts, 1.14.2
  formation, 1.1–1.16
  homeworkers, 1.14.3
  nature of relationship, 1.14
  offer and acceptance, 1.2
  part-time workers, 1.14.1
  right to work, 1.3
  sources, 2.1–2.9
  temporary workers, 1.14.4
  termination, 5.3 et seq.
  terms, 2.1–2.9
  underlying basis of employment
      relationship, 1.1
  unequal nature of relationship, 1.1
  variation, 5.1 et seq.

Contract of service,
  multiple test, 1.14
  tests, 1.14
Contracting out,
  transfer of undertaking, and, 9.3.4
Copyright, 3.1.2.2
Course of employment,
  harassment, and, 6.3.4.1
Criminal conviction certificates, 1.8
Criminal record certificates, 1.8
Criminal records, 1.8
Crown,
  capacity, 1.4
Custom, 2.5.1
  certain, 2.5.1
  effect, 2.5.1
  meaning, 2.5.1
  notorious, 2.5.1
  reasonable, 2.5.1

Damages,
  wrongful dismissal, 5.6.1
Data protection, 1.9.3
  controllers, 1.9.3
  data, meaning, 1.9.3
  enforcement notice, 1.9.3
  processing, meaning, 1.9.3
  rights of subjects, 1.9.3
  unauthorised disclosure, 1.9.3
Death,
  equal pay, and, 6.2.8
  frustration of contract, 5.5.3
Declaration,
  wrongful dismissal, and, 5.6.4
Deductions from pay, 4.4
  consent by employee, 4.4.1
  contractual term authorising, 4.4.1
  entire performance, doctrine of, 4.4.3
  excepted, 4.4.2
  fairness, 4.4.1
  industrial action, and, 4.4.3
  industrial tribunal, and, 4.4.1
  statutory, 4.4.1
  Truck Acts, 4.4
  unauthorised, 4.4.1
  unearned commission, 4.4.1
Detriment,
  health and safety, 7.4.4
Disability discrimination, 1.15, 6.3.2
  codes of practice, 2.6.2
  meaning, 6.3.2
Discharge of contract of employment, 5.5
Disciplinary procedures,
  unfair dismissal, and, 7.3.1
Discrimination, 1.15, 6.1–6.5
  advertisement, 1.15
  aggravated damages, 6.3.8
  codes of practice, 6.1.4

Discrimination—*cont.*
  Commission for Racial Equality, 6.4.1
  compensation, 6.3.8
  complaint to industrial tribunal, 6.3.8
    time limit, 6.3.8
  detriment, 6.3.3.4
  direct, 6.3.1
  disability, 1.15, 6.3
  domestic framework, 6.1.3
  dress codes, 6.3.4.3
  employment, and, 1.15
  enforcement, 6.3.8
  Equal Opportunities Commission, 6.4.1
  equal pay principle, 6.1.1
  equal treatment, 6.1.2
  gender reassignment, 6.3.4.2
  genuine occupational qualifications, 6.3.5
  harassment 6.3.4.1. *See also* Harassment
  indirect, 6.3.3
    can comply, 6.3.3.2
    considerably smaller proportion, 6.3.3.2
    justification of requirement or condition, 6.3.3.3
  justification of requirement or condition, 6.3.3.3
    criteria, 6.3.3.3
    E.C. law, 6.3.3.3
    objective test, 6.3.3.3
    reasonable needs of employer, 6.3.3.3
    social policy, 6.3.3.3
  legislative framework, 6.1
  less favourable treatment, 6.3.1
  motives, and, 6.3.1
  National Disability Council, 6.4.2
  pensions, 6.1.3
  pregnancy, and, 10.3
  proving, 6.3.7
  race, 1.15, 6.3
  redundancy, and, 8.3.4.2
  reform proposals, 6.5
  remedies, 6.3.8
  requirement or condition, 6.3.3.1
  sex, 1.15, 6.3
  sexual orientation, 6.3.4.2
  variation of contract, and, 5.2.3.2
  victimisation, 6.3.6
Dismissal,
  constructive. *See* Constructive dismissal
  summary, 5.3.4
Dissolution,
  frustration of contract, and, 5.5.3
Donovan Report, 11.2.1
Dress codes, 6.3.4.3
Duties of parties, 3.1–3.3.6
  maintain trust and confidence of other party, 3.2.1
    constructive dismissal, 3.2.1
    fraud, 3.2.1

Duties of parties—*cont.*
  maintain trust and confidence of other party—*cont.*
    impact on obligations of employer, 3.2.1
    modern approach, 3.2.1
    references, 3.2.1
    scope, 3.2.1
    suspension, 3.2.1
    unjustified criticism, 3.2.1
    unreasonable behaviour, 3.2.1
  mutual, 3.2

Economic dismissals, 8.1–8.6
  some other substantial reason, 8.4
    business reorganisations, 8.4.1
Employee,
  agency worker, 1.14.5
  apprentice, 1.14.6
  homeworker, 1.14.3
  meaning, 1.14
  person with controlling interest in company, 1.14
Employee, duties of, 3.1
  confidential information. *See* Confidential information
  co-operation and obedience, 3.1.1
    importance, 3.1.1
    lawful orders, 3.1.1
    managerial prerogatives, and, 3.1.1
    scope, 3.1.1
  fidelity, 3.1.2. *See also* Fidelity, duty of
Employee protection during economic restructuring, 8.2
Employee representatives,
  payment, 4.3.5
  unfair dismissal, 7.4.7
Employer, duties of, 3.3
  keep employees informed, 3.3.3
    pension entitlement, 3.3.3
  provide opportunity to obtain redress of grievance, 3.3.4
    smoking, 3.3.4
  references, 3.3.2.1
  respect employees' privacy, 3.3.5
  statements, 3.3.2
  welfare and health and safety, 3.3.1
Employment Appeal Tribunal, 7.5.3
  appellate jurisdiction, 7.5.3
Employment incentives, 1.16
Enhanced criminal record certificate, 1.8
Equality clause, 6.2
Equal Opportunities Commission, 6.4.1
Equal pay, 6.1.1, 6.2
  application, 6.2.1
  Article 119, E.C. Treaty, 6.1.1
  collective agreements, 6.2.7
  comparator, need for, 6.2.2

Equal pay—*cont.*
  consequences of decision in *ex parte EOC*,
    6.2.1.3
  consequences of ECJ decision in *Barber*,
    6.2.1.1
  consequences of ECJ decision in *Vroege*
    and *Fisscher*, 6.2.1.2
  death, and, 6.2.8
  defence, 6.2.6
  domestic framework, 6.1.3
  equal value, 6.2.5
    procedural rules, 6.2.5
    reasonable grounds, 6.2.5
  equality clause, 6.2
  genuine material factor, 6.2.6
  like work, 6.2.3
  objective justification, 6.2.6
  pay, meaning, 6.1.1
  pensions, 6.1.1
  personal equation, 6.2.6
  red circling, 6.2.6.1
  reform proposals, 6.5
  retirement, 6.2.8
  statistics, 6.2.6
  temporal limitation, 6.2.1.1
  time limits for bringing actions, 6.2.1.2
  work rated as equivalent, 6.2.4
Equal treatment, 6.1.2
  Directives, 6.1.2
  occupational and social security schemes,
    6.1.2
  Recommendations, 6.1.2
ESOPS, 4.5.2
Establishment,
  meaning, 8.3.3.4
E.U. Directives, 2.7.1
European citizenship, 1.6
European law, 2.7
  Amsterdam Treaty, 7.3
  Directives, 2.7.1
    direct effect, 2.7.1
    effect, 2.7.1
    state body, 2.7.1
  effect in Member States, 2.7
  failure to implement Community
    obligations, 2.7.2
    remedies, 2.7.2
  fundamental social rights of workers, 7.3
  national law, and, 2.7
  precedence of, 2.7
  preliminary rulings, 2.7
  Social Action programme, 7.3
  social policy, 7.3
  treaties, 2.7
  Treaty of Rome, 2.7
  work of equal value, 7.3

Fidelity, duty of, 3.1.1
  copyright, 3.1.2.2
  disclosure, 3.1.2
  duty to account, 3.1.2.1
  entering into competition with employer,
    3.1.2.3
    casual work, 3.1.2.3
    preparatory actions, 3.1.2.3
    repudiatory breach, 3.1.2.3
  garden leave, 3.1.2.5
  inventions, 3.1.2.2
  limitation on contractual restrictions,
    3.1.2.4
  scope, 3.1.2
  secret profits, 3.1.2.1
Fixed term contracts, 1.14.2
  expiry date, 1.14.2
    unfair dismissal, and, 7.2.1.6
  termination, and, 5.5.2
Flexibility,
  variation of contract, and, 5.2.1.4
Free movement of workers, 1.6
  migrant workers, 1.6
  public service, 1.6
Frustration of contract, 5.5.1
  death, 5.5.3
  dismissal, and, 5.5.1.1
  dissolution, 5.5.3
  fairness, 5.5.1.1
  fixed term contracts, 5.5.2
  imprisonment, 5.5.1.2
  insolvency, 5.5.3
  legal requirements, 5.5.1.1
  sickness, 5.5.1.1
  transfer of assets, 5.5.3

Garden leave, 3.1.2.5
  benefits gained by employee, 3.1.2.5
  damages, 3.1.2.5
  enforcement, 3.1.2.5
  injunction, and, 3.1.2.5
Gender reassignment, 6.3.4.2
Genuine occupational qualifications, 6.3.5
Gross misconduct,
  summary dismissal, 5.3.4

Harassment, 6.3.4.1
  bullying, 6.3.4.1
  course of employment, 6.3.4.1
  meaning, 6.3.4.1
  Public Order Act 1986, 6.3.4.1
  racial, 6.3.4.1
  sexual, 6.3.4.1
  verbal, 6.3.4.1
Health and safety, 3.1.5, 3.3.1
  Act of 1974, 3.3.1.1
    section 2, 3.3.1.1
    section 3, 3.3.1.1

Health and safety—*cont.*
  childbirth, 10.6
  common law, 3.1.5
  Directive 89/391, 3.3.1.1
  duty of care in tort, 3.3.1.3
    breach of statutory duty, and, 3.3.1.3
    knowledge, 3.3.1.3
  duty of employer, 3.3.1
  Health and Safety (Display Screen
    Equipment) Regulations 1992, 3.3.1.1
  implied terms, 3.3.2.1
    complaints, 3.3.2.1
    dangers, 3.3.2.1
    instruction, 3.3.2.1
    passive smoking, 3.3.2.1
    psychiatric damage, 3.3.2.1
    suitable environment, 3.3.2.1
    training, 3.3.2.1
    working hours, 3.3.2.1
  Management of Health and Safety at Work
    Regulations 1992, 3.3.1.1
  Manual Handling Operations Regulations
    1992, 3.3.1.1
  occupational stress, 3.3.1.3
  Personal Protective Equipment at Work
    Regulations 1992, 3.3.1.1
  post-traumatic stress disorder, 3.3.1.3
  pregnancy, 10.6
  Provision and Use of Work Equipment
    Regulations 1992, 3.3.1.1
  psychiatric injury, 3.3.1.3
  regulations, 3.1.5
  repetitive strain injury, 3.3.1.3
  rescuers, 3.3.1.3
  Robens Committee, 3.3.1
  statute, 3.1.5
  unfair dismissal, 7.4.4
  witness to accident, 3.3.1.3
  Workplace (Health, Safety and Welfare)
    Regulations 1992, 3.3.1.1
  young persons, 3.3.1.1
Health and Safety Commission,
  codes of practice, 2.6.2
Holiday pay, 4.3.3
Holidays, 1.12
Homeworkers, 1.14.3
  employees, as, 1.14.3
  statistics, 1.14.3

Illegality,
  unfair dismissal, and, 7.2.3
Immigration, 1.6
Imprisonment,
  frustration of contract, and, 5.5.1.2
Independent contractor, 1.14
Industrial action,
  deductions from pay, and, 4.4.3

Industrial action—*cont.*
  redundancy payments, and, 8.3.7.4
  unfair dismissal, and, 7.2.5
Industrial tribunal, 7.5
  contract jurisdiction, 7.5.1
  deductions from pay, and, 4.4.1
  evidence, 7.5
  jurisdiction, 7.5.1
  pre-hearing review, 7.5.2
  procedure, 7.5
  reform, 7.5.4
  regulations, 7.5.1
  renaming, 7.5.4
Injunction,
  garden leave, and, 3.1.2.5
  restrictive covenant, and, 3.1.4
  wrongful dismissal, and, 5.6.2, 5.6.3
Insolvency, 8.5
  Act of 1986, 8.5.1
  frustration of contract, and, 5.5.3
Inventions, 3.1.2.2
Itemised pay statement,
  right to, 4.2.4

Job schemes, 1.16
Judicial review,
  public servant, and, 5.6.4
  wrongful dismissal, and, 5.6.4

Like work,
  meaning, 6.2.3
Looking for work,
  payment whilst, 4.3.4
Low Pay Commission, 4.5.4

Managerial power, 2.5.2
Maternity allowance, 10.5.1
Maternity leave, 10.4
  contractual rights during, 10.4.1.3
  Employment Rights Act, 10.4.2
  failure to permit return, 10.4.2.4
  failure to return for medical reasons,
    10.4.1.5
  length of period, 10.4.1.2
  long, 10.4.2
    continuity of employment, and, 10.4.2.2
    exercise of right to return, 10.4.2.2
    notification requirements, 10.4.2.1
    postponement of return, 10.4.2.2
    right to return to what, 10.4.2.3
    status of contract during, 10.4.2.6
  notification of early return, 10.4.1.6
  redundancy, and, 10.4.1.7
  right to, 10.4.1
  right to return, 10.4.1.6
    contractual, 10.4.2.5
    loss of, 10.4.1.6

Maternity leave—*cont.*
  statutory maternity pay, and, 10.4.1.4
  timing, 10.4.1.2
Maternity payments, 10.5
Migrant workers, 1.6
Mobility,
  variation of contract, and, 5.2.1.4
Mobility clauses, 2.3

National Disability Council, 6.4.2
National Minimum Wage, 4.5.4
  enforcement, 4.5.4
  level, 4.5.4
  penalties, 4.5.4
  rate, 4.5.4
New Deal, 1.16
Notice, 5.4
  common law, 5.4.1
  minimum period, 5.4.2
  statutory, 5.4.2
  wages in lieu, 5.4.2
    contractual notice, 5.4.2
    summary dismissal, 5.4.2
    voluntary termination, 5.4.2
    wages in advance, 5.4.2
  waiver of right, 5.4.2

Occupational pension scheme,
  trustee,
    unfair dismissal, 7.4.6
Occupational stress, 3.3.1.3

Parental leave, 10.7
Part-time workers, 1.14.1
  framework agreement, 1.14.1
  meaning, 1.14.1
  statistics, 1.14.1
Paternity leave, 10.7
Pay, 4.1–4.5.4. *See also* Wages
  calculation, 4.2.3
  contractual regulation, 4.3.1
  deductions, 4.4. *See also* Deductions from
    pay
  employee representatives, 4.3.5
  ESOPS, 4.5.2
  meaning, 4.2.1
  "no work no pay", 4.2
  performance related, 4.5.2
  profit related, 4.5.2
  public duties, 4.3.6
  regulation of rates, 4.5
  right to be paid when absent from work,
    4.3
  right to be paid whilst working, 4.2
  role in employment relationship, 4.1–4.5.4
  state regulation of rates as tool of
    economic policy, 4.5.1

Pay—*cont.*
  tips, 4.2
  whilst looking for work or retraining, 4.3.4
Payment in lieu, 4.2.2
  categories, 4.2.2
  wages, whether, 4.2.2
Pensions,
  transfer of undertakings, and, 9.7
Permanent health insurance, 4.3.1.1
  dismissal for incapacity, and, 4.3.1.1
Personal information, access to, 1.9
Policy statements, 2.5.2
Post-traumatic stress disorder, 3.3.1.3
Posted workers, 1.13
  meaning, 1.13
Precedent, 2.1
Pregnancy, 10.1–10.8. *See also* Childbirth
  Council Directive 92/85/EEC, 10.1
  discrimination, and, 10.3
  dismissal of maternity replacement, 10.3.1
  dismissal on grounds of, 10.3
  health and safety, 10.6
  parental leave, 10.7
  paternity leave, 10.7
  "protected period", 10.3
  reform proposals, 10.8
  right to maternity leave, 10.4
  statistics, 10.1
  suspension from work, 10.6
  time off work for ante-natal care, 10.2
  unavailability for work, and, 10.3
  unfair dismissal, and, 7.4.3
  written statement of reasons for dismissal,
    10.3.2
Public duties,
  payment whilst on, 4.3.6
Public servant,
  judicial review, and, 5.6.4

Race discrimination, 1.15
Red circling, 6.2.6.1
Redundancy, 8.3
  automatic unfair selection, 8.3.2
    burden of proof, 8.3.2.1
    pregnancy, 8.3.2.2
    trade union activities, 8.3.2.3
  bumping, 8.3.1.3
  compensation payments, 8.3.7
    early leavers, 8.3.7.2
    exclusions, 8.3.7.1
    industrial action, 8.3.7.4
    misconduct, 8.3.7.4
    Polkey reduction, 8.3.7.3
  consultation on proposals, 8.3.3
    establishment, meaning, 8.3.3.4
    individuals affected, 8.3.3.2
    information to be given, 8.3.3.3

Redundancy—*cont.*
  consultation on proposals—*cont.*
    protective award, 8.3.3.5
    start of, 8.3.3.1
    with whom, 8.3.3.1
  contract test, 8.3.1.1
  definition, 8.3.1
  discrimination, and, 8.3.4.2
  function test, 8.3.1.2
  information on proposals, 8.3.3
  last in first out (LIFO), 8.3.4.2
  maternity leave, and, 10.4.1.7
  offer of suitable alternative employment,
    8.3.5
    equivalent work, 8.3.5.1
    genuine redundancy, 8.3.5.2
    place of work, 8.3.5.4
    trial period, 8.3.5.3
  selection criteria, 8.3.4.1
  selection procedures, 8.3.4
  terms of contract, and, 8.3.1.2
  time off to look for alternative work, 8.3.6
  unfair dismissal, and, 7.3.2.4, 8.3.1.4
Re-engagement, 7.5.5.1
References,
  duty of employer, 3.3.2.1
Rehabilitation of offenders, 1.8
Reinstatement, 7.5.5.1
Repetitive strain injury, 3.3.1.3
Requirement or conditions,
  meaning, 6.3.3.1
Restrictive covenants, 3.1.4
  employer and employee, 3.1.4.2
  general policy of law, 3.1.4
  injunction, and, 3.1.4
  joint venture, 3.1.4.3
  legitimate interest capable of protection,
    3.1.4.3
  protection from competition, 3.1.4.3
  reasonableness, 3.1.4.2
  reasonableness of restraint, 3.1.4.4
    adequate protection, 3.1.4.4
    non-competing, 3.1.4.4
    senior employees, 3.1.4.4
    severance payments, 3.1.4.4
  severance, 3.1.4.6
    conditions, 3.1.4.6
  stable, trained workforce, 3.1.4.3
  validity in event of employer's breach of
    contract, 3.1.4.5
    dissolution of partnership, 3.1.4.5
    legal impossibility, 3.1.4.5
    reasonableness, 3.1.4.5
    repudiatory breach, 3.1.4.5
  vendors and purchasers, 3.1.4.1
Retirement,
  equal pay, and, 6.2.8

Retraining,
  payment whilst, 4.3.4
Right to work, 1.3

Secret profits, 3.1.2.1
Self-employment, 1.14
Sex discrimination, 1.15
Sexual orientation, 6.3.4.2
Shop and betting workers, 1.11
  opted-out, 1.11
  protected, 1.11
  Sunday working, 1.11
Sick pay, 4.3.1.1
  contractual, 4.3.1.1
  implied term, 4.3.1.1
  permanent health insurance, 4.3.1.1
Sickness,
  frustration of contract, and, 5.5.1.1
Specific performance, 5.6.3
  acceptance theory, 5.6.3
  authorities, 5.6.3
  contractual obligations, and, 5.6.3
  employee, and, 5.6.3
  redundancy selection procedure, and, 5.6.3
Staff handbooks, 2.5.2
State body,
  meaning, 2.7.1
Statutes, 2.6
Statutory instruments, 2.6.1
  enabling powers, 2.6.1
    Europan Communities Act 1972, 2.6.1
    Health and Safety at Work etc. Act 1974,
      2.6.1
  procedures, 2.6.1
Statutory maternity pay, 10.5.2
  administration, 10.5.4
  contractual arrangements, 10.5.6
  eligibility, 10.5.2.1
  maternity leave, and, 10.4.1.4
  national rules under challenge, 10.5.7
  payment, 10.5.4
  period, 10.5.3
  rate, 10.5.5
Statutory sick pay, 4.3.2
  ceasing of payment, 4.3.2
  claims, 4.3.2
  "employees", 4.3.2
  exclusions, 4.3.2
  level due, 4.3.2
  main points, 4.3.2
  opting-out, 4.3.2
  period of entitlement, 4.3.2
  qualifying days, 4.3.2
  rebate, 4.3.2
  specified disease or disablement, 4.3.2
Statutory statement of terms of employment,
  2.8
  changes in information contained in, 2.8.1

Statutory statement of terms of employment
—*cont.*
content, 2.8
employers, 2.8
enforcement, 2.8.3
failure to object to, 2.8.4
oral evidence, and, 2.8.4
status, 2.8.4
Sunday working, 2.8
Strike,
unfair dismissal, and, 7.2.5
Summary dismissal, 5.3.4
gross misconduct, 5.3.4
procedural fairness, 5.3.4
refusal to obey single order, 5.3.4
Sunday working, 1.11
opted-out workers, 1.11
protected workers, 1.11
unfair dismissal, and, 7.4.5

Temporary workers, 1.14.4
single contract, 1.14.4
Termination of contract of employment, 5.3
et seq.
agreement, with, 5.3.1
evidence, 5.3.1
redundancy, 5.3.1
voluntary, 5.3.1
automatic theory relevant but not
dominant, 5.3.2.4
constructive dismissal. *See* Constructive
dismissal
discharge. *See* Discharge of contract of
employment
effective date, 7.2.1.7
frustration. *See* Frustration of contract
notice. *See* Notice
repudiation, 5.3.2
acceptance by innocent party, 5.3.2.2
anticipatory, 5.3.2
automatic theory, 5.3.2.1
characteristics, 5.3.2
elective theory, 5.3.2.1
fundamental contractual breach, 5.3.2
implied, 5.3.2
remedy of innocent party, 5.3.2.2
seriousness of breach, 5.3.2.2
non-enforcement rule, 5.3.2.2
unilateral variation, 5.3.2
self-dismissal, 5.3.2.3
constructive dismissal, 5.3.2.3
date of termination, 5.3.2.3
summary dismissal, 5.3.4
Terms of contract of employment, 2.1–2.9
business efficacy test, 2.3
code of practice, 2.5.2, 2.6
collective bargaining agreements, 2.4

Terms of contract of employment—*cont.*
contractual approach, 2.2
custom, 2.5.1
disciplinary procedures, 2.2
"employed", 2.2
European law, 2.7
express, 2.2
subject to implied term, 2.2
flexibility clause, 2.2
implied, 2.3
mobility, 2.3
necessity, 2.3
reasonableness, 2.3
working hours, 2.3
managerial power, 2.5.2
"overriding", 2.3
policy statements, 2.5.2
reasonableness, 2.2
sources, 2.1–2.9
staff handbooks, 2.5.2
statute, 2.6
statutory instruments, 2.6.1
statutory provisions, 2.2
statutory statement, 2.8
Unfair Contract Terms Act 1977, 2.2
working hours, 2.2
works rules, 2.5.2
Time off work,
ante-natal care, for, 10.1
Tips,
pay, whether, 4.2
Trade secrets, 3.1.3, 3.1.3.1
discounts, 3.1.3.1
meaning, 3.1.3.1
prices, 3.1.3.1
Trade union,
action short of dismissal, 11.4.1
development, 11.1.1
fairness at work, 11.5.1, 11.5.3
members,
exployees as, 11.4
officials,
employees as, 11.4
personal contracts, 11.4.1
White Paper 1998, 11.5, 11.5.3
collective representation rights, 11.5.3.1
individual representation rights, 11.5.3.1
industrial action changes, 11.5.3.1
protection against victimisation, 11.5.3.2
trade union recognition, 11.5.3.1
Trade union activity,
rights to, 11.2.2
Trade union membership,
rights to, 11.2.2
Trade union membership and activities, 1.10
Trade union recognition, 11.3.2
CBI/TUC debate, 11.5.2

Transfer of assets,
  frustration of contract, and, 5.5.3
Transfer of undertakings, 9.1–9.8
  Acquired Rights Directive, 9.1.1
  automatic transfer of contract of
    employment, 9.4.1
  automatic transfers in parts of
    undertakings, 9.4.2
  collective agreements, 9.6
  collective bargaining agreement, and, 2.4.3
  common law, 9.1
  consultation, 9.2
    future proposals, 9.2.7
    information giving, and, 9.2.5
    overall purpose, 9.2.1
    remedies for non-compliance, 9.2.6
    specific information to be discussed, 9.2.4
    start, 9.2.3
    who has to be, 9.2.2
  definitions, 9.1.2
  dismissal, 9.8
    employee's right to object, 9.8.3
    ETO, 9.8.2
    Litster, 9.8.1
  effect, 9.4
  pensions, 9.7
  proposed changes to Regulations, 9.9
  Regulations, 9.1.2
    key to, 9.1.2
  retrospective claims, 9.3.5
  second generation contracting out, 9.3.6
  statutory regulation, 9.1
  trade union recognition, 9.6
  transfer, 9.3
    contracting out, 9.3.4
    meaning, 9.3.1
    retention of economic identity, 9.3.2
    Spijkers principles, 9.3.3
  transfer of administrative functions, 9.3.7
  unfair dismissal, 7.4.9
  variation in working conditions, 9.5
  what is transferred, 9.4.3
Treaty of Rome, 2.7
Trustee of occupational pension scheme,
  unfair dismissal, 7.4.6

Unfair Contract Terms Act 1977, 2.2
Unfair dismissal, 7.1–7.6
  ACAS Code of Practice, 7.3.1
  assertion of statutory right, 7.4.8
  automatically unfair reasons, 7.4
    burden of proof, 7.4.1
    trade union reasons, 7.4.2
  capability, 7.3.2.1
  childbirth, 7.4.3
  compensation, 7.5.5.2
    additional award, 7.5.5.2

Unfair dismissal—*cont.*
  compensation—*cont.*
    basic award, 7.5.5.2
    compensatory award, 7.5.5.2
    deductions, 7.5.5.2
    interim relief, 7.5.5.2
    Polkey deduction, 7.5.5.2
    recoupment provisions, 7.5.5.2
    reduction, 7.5.5.2
    special award, 7.5.5.2
  compromise agreements, 7.2.6
  conduct, 7.3.2.2
    criminal offences, 7.3.2.2
    dishonesty, 7.3.2.2
    fighting, 7.3.2.2
    inconsistency of treatment, 7.3.2.2
    inevitability rule, 7.3.2.2
  constructive dismissal, 7.2.1.5
  continuity of employment, 7.2.8
    change of employer, 7.3.8.3
    periods of absence, 7.2.8.1, 7.2.8.2
    re-employment after dismissal, 7.2.8.4
  contracting out, 7.2.6
  contravention of statutory duty of
    restriction, 7.3.2.3
  disciplinary procedures, 7.3.1
  dismissal, 7.2.1
    effective date of termination, 7.2.1.7
    expiry of fixed term contract, 7.2.1.6
    final contract test, 7.2.1.6
    long term absences, 7.2.1.4
    resignation, and, 7.2.1
    self-dismissal, 7.2.1.2
    voluntary early retirement, 7.2.1.3
  dismissal procedure agreements, 7.2.7
  Donovan Committee, 7.1
  economically motivated dismissals, 7.3.2.4
  employee representative, 7.4.7
  employment outside Great Britain, 7.2.4
  excluded classes of employment, 7.2.4
  exclusions, 7.2
  forum, 7.5
  health and safety, 7.4.4
    detriment, 7.4.4
  illegality, 7.2.3
    continuous employment, and, 7.2.3
  ILO Recommendation, 7.1
  industrial action, 7.2.5
  interim relief, 7.4.11
  mariners, 7.2.4
  minimum notice periods, 7.2.11
  offshore employment, 7.2.4
  police officers, 7.2.4
  potentially fair reasons, 7.3.2
  pregnancy, 7.4.3, 10.3
    redundancy, and, 7.4.3
  protected or opted-out shop or betting
    shop worker, 7.4.5

Unfair dismissal—*cont.*
  qualifications, 7.3.2.1
  qualifying conditions, 7.2
  qualifying period of employment, 7.2.8
  reasons for dismissal, 7.3
    label, 7.3
    reasonableness, and, 7.3
  redundancy, 7.3.2.4, 8.3.1.4
  re-engagement, 7.5.5.1
  reinstatement, 7.5.5.1
  remedies, 7.5
  right to written statement of reasons, 7.2.9
  share fishermen, 7.2.4
  some other substantial reason, 7.3.2.4, 8.4
  special award, 7.4.11
  spent conviction, 7.4.10
  strike, 7.2.5
  time restriction, 7.2.2
  trade union reasons, 7.4.2
    activities of independent trade union, 7.4.2
    appropriate time, 7.4.2
    complaint to tribunal, 7.4.2
    personal activities, 7.4.2
    redundancy, 7.4.2
  transfer of undertaking, 7.4.9
  trustee of occupational pension scheme, 7.4.6
  upper age limits, 7.2.10
  whether dismissal is appropriate response, 7.3.3

Variation of contract of employment, 5.1 *et seq.*
  acceptance, 5.2.3
  continuing to work, 5.2.3.1
  discriminatory variations, 5.2.3.2
  express, 5.2.2
  flexibility, 5.2.1.4
  implied, 5.2.2
  meaning, 5.2.1
  mobility, 5.2.1.4
  mutual trust and confidence, and, 5.2.1.4

Variation of contract of employment—*cont.*
  parties to contract, 5.2
  rejection, 5.2.3
  statutory statement of employment particulars, and, 5.2.4
  unilateral, 5.2.2
  wage-work bargain, and, 5.2.1
Victimisation, 6.3.6
  meaning, 6.3.6

Wages, 4.1–4.5.4. *See also* Pay
  "error of computation", 4.2.2
  essential characteristics, 4.2
  meaning, 4.2.2
  payment in lieu, 4.2.2
Wages Councils, 4.5.3
  abolition, 4.5.3
  criticisms of, 4.5.3
  history, 4.5.3
  purpose, 4.5.3
Welfare to Work, 1.16
Work permits,
  application for, 1.6
Work rated as equivalent,
  meaning, 6.2.4
Working time, 1.12
Works rules, 2.5.2
  no smoking, 2.5.2
  status, 2.5.2
Wrongful dismissal, 5.6
  damages, 5.6.1
    double recovery, 5.6.1
    loss of reputation, 5.6.1
    manner of dismissal, 5.6.1
    mitigation, 5.6.1
  declaration, and, 5.6.4
  definition, 5.6
  injunction, 5.6.2, 5.6.3
  judicial review, 5.6.4
  remedies, 5.6
  specific performance, 5.6.3

Young people, 1.5